Fodor's 99

Canada

The complete guide, thoroughly up-to-date

Packed with details that will make your trip

The must-see sights, off and on the beaten path

What to see, what to skip

Mix-and-match vacation itineraries

City strolls, countryside adventures

Smart lodging and dining options

Essential local do's and taboos

Transportation tips, distances and directions

Key contacts, savvy travel tips

When to go, what to pack

Clear, accurate, easy-to-use maps

Books to read, videos to watch

Fodor's Travel Publications, Inc.
New York • Toronto • London • Sydney • Auckland
www.fodors.com

Fodor's Canada

EDITOR: Linda Cabasin

Editorial Contributors: Rosemary Allerston, Taiya Barss, David Brown, Susan Brown, Audra Epstein, Sue Kernaghan, Ed Kirby, Helga Loverseed, Terrence Moloney, Jens Nielsen, Helayne Schiff, M. T. Schwartzman (Gold Guide editor), Tina Sebert, Don Thacker, Elizabeth Thompson, Paul Waters, Ana Watts, Sara Waxman
Editorial Production: Stacey Kulig
Maps: David Lindroth, *cartographer*; Robert Blake, *map editor*
Design: Fabrizio La Rocca, *creative director*; Guido Caroti, *associate art director*; Jolie Novak, *photo editor*
Production/Manufacturing: Rebecca Zeiler
Cover Photograph: Peter Guttman

Copyright

Special Sales

Fodor's Travel Publications are available at special discounts for bulk purchases for sales promotions or premiums. Special editions, including personalized covers, excerpts of existing guides, and corporate imprints, can be created in large quantities for special needs. For more information, contact your local bookseller or write to Special Markets, Fodor's Travel Publications, 201 East 50th Street, New York, NY 10022. Inquiries from Canada should be directed to your local Canadian bookseller or sent to Random House of Canada, Ltd., Marketing Department, 2775 Matheson Boulevard East, Mississauga, Ontario L4W 4P7. Inquiries from the United Kingdom should be sent to Fodor's Travel Publications, 20 Vauxhall Bridge Road, London SW1V 2SA, England.

PRINTED IN THE UNITED STATES OF AMERICA

10 9 8 7 6 5 4 3 2 1

CONTENTS

Maps

ON THE ROAD WITH FODOR'S

WHEN I PLAN A VACATION, the first thing I do is cast around among my friends and colleagues to find someone who's just been where I'm going. That's because there's no substitute for a recommendation from a good friend who knows your tastes, your budget, and your circumstances, someone who's just been there. Unfortunately, such friends are few and far between. So it's nice to know that there's Fodor's *Canada*.

In the first place, this book won't stay home when you hit the road. It will accompany you every step of the way, steering you away from wrong turns and wrong choices and never expecting a thing in return. It includes a wonderful, full-color map from Rand McNally, the world's largest commercial mapmaker. Most important of all, it's written and assiduously updated by the kind of people you *would* hit up for travel tips if you knew them. They're as choosy as your pickiest friend, except they've probably seen a lot more of Canada. In these pages, they don't send you chasing down every town and sight in Canada but instead have selected the best ones, the ones that are worthy of your time and money. To make it easy for you to put it all together in the time you have, they've created short, medium, and long itineraries and, in cities, neighborhood walks that you can mix and match in a snap. Just tear out the map at the perforation, and join us on the road in Canada.

About Our Writers

Our success in helping to make your trip the best of all possible vacations is a credit to the hard work of our extraordinary writers.

Editor of the magazine *Up Here, Life in Canada's North* for 10 years, **Rosemary Allerston,** who updated and expanded the Northwest Territories and Nunavut sections of the Wilderness Canada chapter, knows what's going on in the region. Painter, writer, and serious cook **Taiya Barss** added a lyrical voice and plenty of good places to the chapter on her province, Nova Scotia. She lives in Bras d'Or. Writer **Susan Brown,** based in Washington State, updated the Gold Guide material on Canada to make your travels even easier. Vancouver-born freelance writer **Sue Kernaghan,** a fourth-generation British Columbian, pestered elderly relatives for historical insights and covered a lot of dirt roads, open water, and country pubs while researching the Vancouver and British Columbia chapters. **Ed Kirby,** a Newfoundland and Labrador tourism writer who lives in St. John's, added a walking tour of the city and carefully combed through his chapter. **Helga Loverseed,** a well-traveled freelance journalist and photographer based in Magog in the Eastern Townships, shared her insights on Québec province, Prince Edward Island, and Ontario. She also writes columns for the Montréal *Gazette* and the Chicago *Sun-Times*. Writer and law student **Terrence Moloney,** who updated the Toronto chapter, has a master's degree in classics from the University of Toronto. He has also worked on Fodor's *Greece* and has spent time in Toronto during his legal studies. **Jens Nielsen,** a travel writer based in Saskatoon, Saskatchewan, updated the Prairie Provinces chapter. Award-winning writer and film scout **Tina Sebert,** updater of the Yukon section, lives in Whitehorse. She leads tours of the region and enjoys backpacking and rafting the Yukon River. **Don Thacker** is an Edmonton-based geographer and writer who particularly enjoys the rugged natural beauty of the mountains while updating the Canadian Rockies chapter. **Elizabeth Thompson,** a Québec City–based reporter, returned to the city after her family left it for Montréal nearly 150 years ago. She covers the provincial government and delights in exploring the city (her Fodor's beat) with her husband and daughter. **Paul Waters,** travel editor of the *Gazette* in Montréal, is the expert who handled the Montréal chapter and also wrote the book's introduction. Award-winning Fredericton columnist **Ana Watts** is passionate about her province, New Brunswick, and provided fresh material on new attractions and adventures. Columnist and cookbook and restaurant-guide author **Sara Waxman** shares her insider's knowledge in the Toronto dining section.

Connections

We're pleased that the American Society of Travel Agents continues to endorse Fodor's as its guidebook of choice. ASTA is the world's largest and most influential travel trade association, operating in more than 170 countries, with 27,000 members pledged to adhere to a strict code of ethics reflecting the Society's motto, "Integrity in Travel." ASTA shares Fodor's devotion to providing smart, honest travel information and advice to travelers, and we've long recommended that our readers—even those who have guidebooks and traveling friends—consult ASTA member agents for the experience and professionalism they bring to your vacation planning.

On Fodor's Web site (www.fodors.com), check out the new Resource Center, an online companion to the Gold Guide section of this book, complete with useful hot links to related sites. In our forums, you can also get lively advice from other travelers and more great tips from Fodor's experts worldwide.

How to Use This Book

Organization

Up front is the **Gold Guide,** an easy-to-use section arranged alphabetically by topic. Under each listing you'll find tips and information that will help you accomplish what you need to in Canada. You'll also find addresses and telephone numbers of organizations and companies that offer destination-related services and detailed information and publications.

The first chapter in the guide, Destination: Canada helps get you in the mood for your trip. New and Noteworthy cues you in on trends and happenings, What's Where gets you oriented, Pleasures and Pastimes describes the activities and sights that make Canada unique, Fodor's Choice showcases our top picks, and Festivals and Seasonal Events alerts you to special events you'll want to seek out.

Chapters in *Canada '99* are arranged geographically from west to east. Each city chapter begins with Exploring information, which is divided into neighborhood sections; each recommends a walking or driving tour and lists sights in alphabetical order. Each regional chapter is divided by geographical area; within each area, towns are covered in logical geographical order, and

attractive stretches of road and minor points of interest between them are indicated by the designation *En Route*. And within town sections, all restaurants and lodgings are grouped together.

To help you decide what to visit in the time you have, all chapters begin with our recommended itineraries. You can mix and match those from several chapters to create a complete vacation. The A to Z section that ends all chapters covers getting there and getting around. It also provides helpful contacts and resources.

Icons and Symbols

★   Our special recommendations
✕   Restaurant
🏠   Lodging establishment
✕🏠   Lodging establishment whose restaurant warrants a special trip
⚠   Campgrounds
🐤   Good for kids (rubber duck)
☞   Sends you to another section of the guide for more information
✉   Address
☎   Telephone number
🕐   Opening and closing times
💵   Admission prices (those we give apply to adults; substantially reduced fees are almost always available for children, students, and senior citizens)

Numbers in white and black circles ③ ❸ that appear on the maps, in the margins, and within the tours correspond to one another.

Currency

Unless otherwise stated, all prices, including dining and lodging, are given in Canadian dollars.

Dining and Lodging

The restaurants and lodgings we list are the cream of the crop in each price range. Price charts appear in the Pleasures and Pastimes section that follows each chapter introduction or, in city chapters, at the start of the dining and lodging sections.

Hotel Facilities

We always list the facilities that are available—but we don't specify whether you'll be charged extra to use them: When pricing accommodations, always ask what's included. Assume that all rooms have private baths unless noted otherwise. In addition, when you book a room, be sure to mention if you have a disability or are traveling with children, if you prefer a private bath or a certain type of bed, or if you have specific dietary needs or other concerns.

Assume that hotels operate on the **European Plan** (EP, with no meals) unless we specify that they use the **Continental Plan** (CP, with a Continental breakfast daily), **Modified American Plan** (MAP, with breakfast and dinner daily), or the **American Plan** (AP, with all meals).

Restaurant Reservations and Dress Codes

Reservations are always a good idea; we mention them only when they're essential or are not accepted. Book as far ahead as you can, and reconfirm as soon as you arrive. Unless otherwise noted, the restaurants listed are open daily for lunch and dinner. We mention dress only when men are required to wear a jacket or a jacket and tie. Look for an overview of local dining-out habits in the Pleasures and Pastimes section that follows each chapter introduction and in city chapter dining sections.

Credit Cards

The following abbreviations are used: **AE,** American Express; **D,** Discover **DC,** Diners Club; **MC,** MasterCard; and **V,** Visa.

Don't Forget to Write

You can use this book in the confidence that all prices and opening times are based on information supplied to us at press time; Fodor's cannot accept responsibility for any errors. Time inevitably brings change, so always confirm information when it matters—especially if you're making a detour to visit a specific place.

Were the restaurants we recommended as described? Did our hotel picks exceed your expectations? Did you find a museum we recommended a waste of time? Keeping a travel guide fresh and up-to-date is a big job, and we welcome your feedback, positive *and* negative. If you have complaints, we'll look into them and revise our entries when the facts warrant it. If you've discovered a special place that we haven't included, we'll pass the information along to our correspondents and have them check it out. So send us your thoughts via e-mail at editors@fodors.com (specifying the name of the book on the subject line) or on paper in care of the Canada editor at Fodor's, 201 East 50th Street, New York, NY 10022. In the meantime, have a wonderful trip!

Karen Cure
Editorial Director

Canada

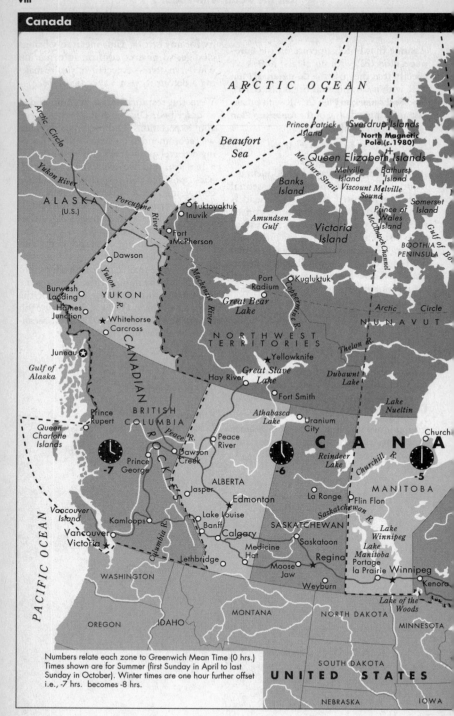

ARCTIC OCEAN

Arctic Circle

Yukon River

Beaufort Sea

Prince Patrick Island

Sverdrup Islands

North Magnetic Pole (c.1980)

ALASKA (U.S.)

Porcupine River

McClure Strait

Queen Elizabeth Islands

Melville Island

Bathurst Island

Banks Island

Viscount Melville Sound

Prince of Wales Island

Somerset Island

BOOTHIA PENINSULA

Gulf of Bo

Tuktoyaktuk

Inuvik

Amundsen Gulf

Victoria Island

McClintock Channel

Dawson

Fort McPherson

Mackenzie River

Yukon R.

Port Radium

Kugluktuk

Coppermine R.

Arctic Circle

NUNAVUT

Burwash Landing

YUKON

Great Bear Lake

Haines Junction

CANADIAN

★ Whitehorse
Carcross

NORTHWEST TERRITORIES

Thelon R.

Dubawnt Lake

Juneau ✪

Gulf of Alaska

★ Yellowknife

Great Slave Lake

Hay River

Fort Smith

Lake Nueltin

Prince Rupert

BRITISH COLUMBIA

Peace R.

Athabasca Lake

Uranium City

C A N A

Churc

Queen Charlotte Islands

Peace River

R O C K I E S

Reindeer Lake

Churchill R.

🕐 -7

Prince George

Dawson Creek

ALBERTA

La Ronge

Flin Flon

🕐 -6

Saskatchewan R.

🕐 -5

MANITOBA

PACIFIC OCEAN

Vancouver Island

Kamloops

Columbia R.

Jasper

Lake Louise

Banff

Edmonton

Calgary

SASKATCHEWAN

Saskatoon

Lake Winnipeg

Vancouver

Victoria ★

Lethbridge

Medicine Hat

Moose Jaw

Regina ★

Lake Manitoba

Portage la Prairie

Winnipeg ★

Kenora

WASHINGTON

Weyburn

Lake of the Woods

OREGON

IDAHO

MONTANA

NORTH DAKOTA

MINNESOTA

Numbers relate each zone to Greenwich Mean Time (0 hrs.)
Times shown are for Summer (first Sunday in April to last
Sunday in October). Winter times are one hour further offset
i.e., -7 hrs. becomes -8 hrs.

SOUTH DAKOTA

U N I T E D   S T A T E S

NEBRASKA

IOWA

ICELAND

GREENLAND
(Denmark)

Ellesmere Island

Devon Island

Lancaster Sound

Baffin Bay

Denmark Strait

Baffin Island

Davis Strait

Prince Charles Island

Foxe Basin

Lake Amadjuak

Iqaluit ★
Lake Harbour

Southampton Island

Hudson Strait

Cape Chidley

Labrador Sea

Coats Island

Mansel Island

Ivujivik

Ungava Bay

Nain

NEWFOUNDLAND

Hudson Bay

Battle Harbour

D   A

LABRADOR

⏱ 🕖 -2:30

Fort Severn

Belcher Islands

Schefferville

Goose Bay

⏱ 🕘 -4

Gander

Severn R.

Fort George

Q U E B E C

Labrador City

St. John's

James Bay

Lake Mistassini

Sept-Îles

Anticosti Island

⏱ 🕘 -3

Moosonee

O N T A R I O

Chicoutimi

Rimouski

River

GASPÉ PENINSULA

PRINCE EDWARD ISLAND

ST. PIERRE AND MIQUELON
(France)

Sydney

Lake Nipigon

Cochrane

Ste.-Agathe-Des-Monts

Québec City ★

Trois-Rivières

NEW BRUNSWICK

Charlottetown

Fredericton ★

NOVA SCOTIA

Timmins

Montréal

Saint John

Halifax

Thunder Bay

Lake Superior

Sudbury

North Bay

Ottawa ✪

St. Lawrence

MAINE

Bay of Fundy

ATLANTIC OCEAN

Sault Ste. Marie

Lake Huron

Toronto

Lake Ontario

VT.

N.H.

WISCONSIN

Lake Michigan

MICHIGAN

Niagara Falls

Lake Erie

NEW YORK

MASSACHUSETTS

CONN.

R.I.

N

0   400 miles

0   600 km

ILLINOIS

INDIANA

OHIO

PENNSYLVANIA

N.J.

SMART TRAVEL TIPS A TO Z

Basic Information on Traveling in Canada, Savvy Tips to Make Your Trip a Breeze, and Companies and Organizations to Contact

AIR TRAVEL

BOOKING YOUR FLIGHT

Price is just one factor to consider when booking a flight: Frequency of service and even a carrier's safety record are often just as important. Major airlines offer the greatest number of departures. Smaller airlines—including regional and no-frills airlines—usually have a limited number of flights daily. On the other hand, so-called low-cost airlines usually are cheaper, and their fares impose fewer restrictions, such as advance-purchase requirements. Safety-wise, low-cost carriers as a group have a good history—about equal to that of major carriers.

When you book, **look for nonstop flights** and **remember that "direct" flights stop at least once.** Try to **avoid connecting flights,** which require a change of plane. Two airlines may jointly operate a connecting flight, so ask if your airline operates every segment—you may find that your carrier flies you only part of the way. International flights on a country's flag carrier are almost always nonstop; U.S. airlines often fly direct.

Ask your airline if it offers electronic ticketing, which eliminates most paperwork. There's no ticket to pick up or misplace. In many airports you go directly to the gate and give the agent your confirmation number.

CARRIERS

When flying internationally, you must usually choose between a domestic carrier, the national flag carrier of the country you are visiting, and a foreign carrier from a third country. You may, for example, choose to fly Air Canada to Canada. National flag carriers have the greatest number of nonstops. Domestic carriers may have better connections to your home town and serve a greater number of gate-

way cities. Third-party carriers may have a price advantage.

Within Canada, regularly scheduled flights to every major city and to most smaller cities are available on Air Canada or Canadian Airlines International, the two major domestic carriers, or the domestic carriers associated with them. The smaller airlines can also be contacted through their parent carrier's (Air Canada or Canadian Airlines) toll-free numbers or at local numbers within each of the many cities they serve.

You should check with the regional tourist agencies for charter companies and with the District Controller of Air Services in the territorial (and provincial) capitals for the locations of air bases that allow private flights and for regulations. Private pilots should obtain information from the Canada Map Office.

➤ MAJOR AIRLINES: **Air Canada** (☎ 800/776–3000) to Montréal, Toronto, Ottawa, Halifax, Winnipeg, Calgary, and Vancouver. **American** (☎ 800/433–7300) to Montréal, Toronto, Ottawa, Calgary, Vancouver. **Canadian Airlines International** (☎ 800/426–7000) to Toronto, Calgary, Vancouver. **Continental** (☎ 800/525–0280) to Montréal, Toronto. **Delta** (☎ 800/221–1212) to Montréal, Toronto, Vancouver. **Northwest** (☎ 800/225–2525) to Montréal, Toronto, Halifax, Ottawa, Calgary, Edmonton, Vancouver. **TWA** (☎ 800/221–2000) to Toronto. **United** (☎ 800/241–6522) to Montréal, Toronto, Vancouver. **US Airways** (☎ 800/428–4322) to Montréal, Ottawa, London, Hamilton, Toronto.

➤ SMALLER AIRLINES: **Alaska Airlines** (☎ 800/426–0333) to Vancouver from many western U.S. cities. **Horizon Air** (☎ 800/547–9308) to Vancouver, Victoria, Calgary, Edmonton. ☞ *Also see* Within Canada, *below.*

➤ FROM THE U.K.: **Air Canada** (☎ 0990/247–226). **British Airways** (☎ 0345/222–111).

➤ WITHIN CANADA: **Air Canada** (☎ 800/776–3000) operates in every province. **Canadian Airlines International** (☎ 800/426–7000). **Air Alliance** (☎ 514/393–3333) and **Inter–Canadien** (☎ 514/847–2211) serve Québec; **Air Atlantic** (☎ 902/427–5500 or 800/563–8359), **Air Nova** (☎ 902/429–7111), and **Air Labrador** (☎ 709/896–3387) fly in the Atlantic region; **Air BC** (☎ 604/688–5515) and **Canadian Regional** (☎ 604/279–6611) serve British Columbia and Alberta with extended service out of Portland and Seattle. **Air Ontario** (☎ 416/925–2311) serves the Ontario region. **Canadian North** (☎ 403/873–5533), **First Air** (☎ 800/267–1247), and **NWT Air** (☎ 403/920–2500) service communities in the Yukon, Nunavut, and Northwest Territories. **Canada 3000 Airlines** (☎ 416/259–1118) flies between many major Canadian cities and may offer lower rates. **WestJet Airlines** (☎ 800/538–5696) serves destinations throughout western Canada with good rates.

➤ INFORMATION FOR PRIVATE PILOTS: The **Canada Map Office** (✉ 130 Bentley Ave., Nepean, ON K1A 0E9, ☎ 800/465–6277) has the "Canada Flight Supplement" (lists of airports with Canada Customs services) as well as aeronautical charts.

CONSOLIDATORS

Consolidators buy tickets for scheduled international flights at reduced rates from the airlines, then sell them at prices that beat the best fare available directly from the airlines, usually without restrictions. Sometimes you can even get your money back if you need to return the ticket. Carefully read the fine print detailing penalties for changes and cancellations, and **confirm your consolidator reservation with the airline.**

➤ CONSOLIDATORS: **Cheap Tickets** (☎ 800/377–1000). **Up & Away Travel** (☎ 212/889–2345). **Discount Travel Network** (☎ 800/576–1600). **Uni-travel** (☎ 800/325–2222). **World Travel Network** (☎ 800/409–6753).

CUTTING COSTS

The least-expensive airfares to Canada are priced for round-trip travel and usually must be purchased in advance. It's smart to **call a number of airlines, and when you are quoted a good price, book it on the spot**—the same fare may not be available the next day. Airlines generally allow you to change your return date for a fee. If you don't use your ticket, you can apply the cost toward the purchase of a new ticket, again for a small charge. However, most low-fare tickets are nonrefundable. To get the lowest airfare, **check different routings.** Compare prices of flights to and from different airports if your destination or home city has more than one gateway. Also price off-peak flights.

Travel agents, especially those who specialize in finding the lowest fares (☞ Discounts & Deals, *below*), can be especially helpful when booking a plane ticket. When you're quoted a price, **ask your agent if the price is likely to get any lower.** Good agents know the seasonal fluctuations of airfares and can usually anticipate a sale or fare war. However, waiting can be risky: The fare could go *up* as seats become scarce, and you may wait so long that your preferred flight sells out. A wait-and-see strategy works best if your plans are flexible.

CHECK IN & BOARDING

Airlines routinely overbook planes, assuming that not everyone with a ticket will show up, but sometimes everyone does. When that happens, airlines ask for volunteers to give up their seats. In return these volunteers usually get a certificate for a free flight and are rebooked on the next flight out. If there are not enough volunteers, the airline must choose who will be denied boarding. The first to get bumped are passengers who checked in late and those flying on discounted tickets, so **get to the gate and check in as early as possible,** especially during peak periods.

Although the trend on international flights is to drop reconfirmation requirements, many airlines still ask you to reconfirm each leg of your international itinerary. Failure to do so may result in your reservation being canceled.

Always **bring a government-issued photo ID to the airport.** You will be asked to show it before you are allowed to check in.

FLYING TIMES

Flying time to Montréal is 1½ hours from New York, 2 hours from Chicago, 6 hours from Los Angeles, 6½ hours from London. To Toronto: 1½ hours from New York and Chicago, 4½ hours from Los Angeles. To Vancouver: 6½ hours from Montréal, 4 hours from Chicago, 2½ hours from Los Angeles.

HOW TO COMPLAIN

If your baggage goes astray or your flight goes awry, complain right away. Most carriers require that you **file a claim immediately.**

➤ AIRLINE COMPLAINTS: U.S. Department of Transportation **Aviation Consumer Protection Division** (✉ C-75, Room 4107, Washington, DC 20590, ☎ 202/366–2220). **Federal Aviation Administration Consumer Hotline** (☎ 800/322–7873).

AIRPORTS

The major airports are Montréal's **Dorval International Airport,** Toronto's **Lester B. Pearson International Airport,** and **Vancouver International Airport** in Vancouver. For further information about using these airports, *see* Arriving and Departing *in* the A to Z section at the end of Chapters 2, 6, and 8; and Customs & Duties, *below.*

➤ AIRPORT INFORMATION: In Montréal, **Dorval Airport** (☎ 514/633–3105) . In Toronto, **Lester B. Pearson International Airport** (☎ 416/247–7678). In Vancouver, **Vancouver International Airport** (☎ 604/276–6101).

BOAT & FERRY TRAVEL

Car ferries provide essential transportation on both the east and west coasts of Canada. Ferries also operate between the state of Washington and British Columbia's Vancouver Island. Individual chapters in the book have additional information about these.

➤ FERRY COMPANIES: **Bay Ferries** (☎ 888/249–7245) go between Bar Harbor, Maine, and New Brunswick to Nova Scotia. On the west coast, **British Columbia (BC) Ferry Corporation** (✉ 1112 Fort St., Victoria, BC V8V 4V2, ☎ 250/386–3431) has 42 ports of call. **Marine Atlantic** (✉ Box 250, North Sydney, NS B2A 3M3, ☎ 902/794–5700 or 800/341–7981 in the U.S.) operates ferries between Nova Scotia and Newfoundland. **Scotia Prince** (☎ 800/341–7540) sails between Portland, Maine, and Nova Scotia.

BOOKS AND VIDEOS

FICTION

Mordecai Richler's *St. Urbain's Horseman* and *The Apprenticeship of Duddy Kravitz* (made into a movie starring Richard Dreyfus) are classics about growing up Jewish in Montréal. Margaret Atwood, a prolific poet and novelist, is regarded as a stateswoman of sorts in her native Canada. Her novel *Cat's Eye* is set in northern Canada and Toronto. Alice Munro writes about small-town life in Ontario in *The Progress of Love.* The mordant wit of Robertson Davies lovingly skewers Canadian academic life in works such as *The Deptford Trilogy* and *The Lyre of Orpheus.* *Northern Lights,* by Howard Norman, focuses on a child's experiences growing up in Manitoba and, later, Toronto. Howard Engel's mystery series follows the adventures of Bennie Cooperman, a Toronto-based detective; *The Suicide Murders* is especially compelling. Jack Hodgin's *Spit Delaney's Island* is peopled with loggers, construction workers, and other rural Canadians. Joy Kogawa's first novel, *Obasan,* tells about the Japanese community of Canada during World War II. *Medicine River* is a collection of short stories by Native American writer Thomas King. For an excellent view of New Brunswick, especially the famed salmon-fishing region called the Miramichi, look for the humorous books *The Americans Are Coming* and *The Last Tasmanian* by local author Herb Curtis. Thomas Raddall's *His Majesty's Yankees* (1994) is a vivid account of a local family's deeply divided loyalties during the American Revolution. E. Annie Proulx's Pulitzer Prize–winning *The Shipping News* gives a feeling for life in a Newfoundland outport today.

NONFICTION

Stuart McLean's *Welcome Home: Travels in Small-town Canada* profiles seven small towns across the country. *Canada North* is a more recent title by Farley Mowat, whose *Never Cry Wolf* is a humorous account of a naturalist who goes to a remote part of Canada to commune with wolves. Andrew Malcolm gives a cultural and historical overview of the country in *The Canadians*. Stephen Brook's *The Maple Leaf Rag* is a collection of idiosyncratic travel essays. *Why We Act Like Canadians: A Personal Exploration of Our National Character* is one of Pierre Berton's many popular nonfiction books focusing on Canada's history and culture; another is *Niagara: A History of the Falls*. *Klondike,* one of Berton's best books, recounts the sensational history of the Klondike gold rush. *Short History of Canada,* by Desmond Morton, is a recent historical account of the country. *Local Colour—Writers Discovering Canada,* edited by Carol Marin, is a series of articles about Canadian places by leading travel writers. Thomas King, Cheryl Calver, and Helen Hoy collaborated on *The Native in Literature,* about the literary treatment of Native Americans.

MOVIES

Black Robe (1991) evokes 17th-century Québec in the story of a missionary priest. *Jesus of Montréal* (1989) is a perceptive observation of French Canadian society; it focuses on the conflict between the Church and an actor chosen to play Christ in a religious performance. In the witty *Decline of the American Empire* (1986) intellectuals explore their concepts of gender, sex, and love. The wry comedy *My Uncle Antoine* (1971) focuses on Québec village life.

BUS TRAVEL

The bus is an essential form of transportation in Canada, especially if you want to visit out-of-the-way towns that do not have airports or rail lines.

➤ BUS COMPANIES: **Greyhound** (✉ 877 Greyhound Way, Calgary, AB T3C 3V8, ☎ 800/661–8747 in Canada or 800/231–2222 in the U.S.) and **Voyageur** (✉ 505 E. Boulevard Maisonneuve, Montréal, Québec H2L 1Y4, ☎ 514/842–2281) offer interprovincial service. **SMT** (☎ 506/859–5105) operates bus service throughout Atlantic Canada. In the United Kingdom, contact **Greyhound International** (✉ Sussex House, London Road, E. Grinstead, East Sussex RHI9 1LD, UK, ☎ 01342/317317).

➤ FROM THE U.S.: **Greyhound** (☎ 800/231–2222).

BUSINESS HOURS

BANKS

Most banks in Canada are open Monday–Thursday 10–3 and Friday 10–5 or 6. Some banks are open longer hours and also on Saturday morning. All banks are closed on national holidays.

SHOPS

Stores, shops, and supermarkets are usually open Monday–Saturday 9–6, although in major cities supermarkets are often open from 7:30 AM to 9 PM. Blue laws are in effect in much of Canada, but a growing number of provinces have stores with limited Sunday hours, usually noon–5 (shops in areas highly frequented by tourists are usually open on Sunday). Retail stores are generally open on Thursday and Friday evenings, most shopping malls until 9 PM. Drugstores in major cities are often open until 11 PM, and convenience stores are often open 24 hours a day, seven days a week.

CAR RENTAL

Rates in Montréal begin at $14 a day and $75 a week for an economy car with air conditioning, a manual transmission, and 100 free km (62 mi). This does not include tax on car rentals, which is 15%. Rates in Toronto begin at $14 a day and $79 a week. Rates in Vancouver begin at $23 a day and $133 a week.

➤ MAJOR AGENCIES: **Alamo** (☎ 800/327–9633, 0800/272–2000 in the U.K.). **Avis** (☎ 800/331–1212, 800/879–2847 in Canada, 008/225–533 in Australia). **Budget** (☎ 800/527–0700, 0800/181181 in the U.K.). **Dollar** (☎ 800/800–4000; 0990/565656 in the U.K., where it is known as Eurodollar). **Hertz** (☎ 800/654–3131, 800/263–0600 in Canada, 0345/555888 in the U.K., 03/9222–2523 in Australia, 03/358–6777 in New Zealand). **National InterRent** (☎ 800/227–7368; 0345/222525 in the U.K., where it is known as Europcar InterRent).

CUTTING COSTS

To get the best deal, **book through a travel agent who is willing to shop around.** When pricing cars, **ask about the location of the rental lot.** Some off-airport locations offer lower rates, and their lots are only minutes from the terminal via complimentary shuttle. You also may want to **price local car-rental companies,** whose rates may be lower still, although their service and maintenance may not be as good as those of a name-brand agency. Remember to ask about required deposits, cancellation penalties, and drop-off charges if you're planning to pick up the car in one city and leave it in another.

INSURANCE

When driving a rented car you are generally responsible for any damage to or loss of the vehicle. You also are liable for any property damage or personal injury that you may cause while driving. Before you rent, **see what coverage you already have** under your personal auto-insurance policy and credit cards.

REQUIREMENTS

In Canada your own driver's license is acceptable.

SURCHARGES

Before you pick up a car in one city and leave it in another, **ask about drop-off charges or one-way service fees,** which can be substantial. Note, too, that some rental agencies charge extra if you return the car before the time specified in your contract. To avoid a hefty refueling fee, **fill the tank just before you turn in the car,** but be aware that gas stations near the rental outlet may overcharge.

CAR TRAVEL

Canada's highway system is excellent. It includes the Trans-Canada Highway (which uses several different numbers), the longest highway in the world, which runs about 5,000 mi from Victoria, British Columbia, to St. John's, Newfoundland, using ferries to bridge coastal waters at each end. The second-longest Canadian highway, the Yellowhead Highway (Highway 16), follows a route from the Pacific Coast and over the Rockies to the prairies. North of the population centers, roads become fewer and less developed.

AUTO CLUBS

➤ IN AUSTRALIA: **Australian Automobile Association** (☎ 06/247–7311).

➤ IN CANADA: **Canadian Automobile Association** (CAA; ☎ 613/247–0117).

➤ IN NEW ZEALAND: **New Zealand Automobile Association** (☎ 09/377–4660).

➤ IN THE U.K.: **Automobile Association** (AA; ☎ 0990/500–600), **Royal Automobile Club** (RAC; ☎ 0990/722–722 for membership, 0345/121–345 for insurance).

➤ IN THE U.S.: **American Automobile Association** (☎ 800/564–6222).

FROM THE U.S.

Drivers must carry owner registration and proof of insurance coverage, which is compulsory in Canada. The Canadian Non-Resident Inter-Provincial Motor Vehicle Liability Insurance Card, available from any U.S. insurance company, is accepted as evidence of financial responsibility in Canada. The minimum liability coverage in Canada is $200,000, except in Québec, where the minimum is $50,000. If you are driving a car that is not registered in your name, carry a letter from the owner that authorizes your use of the vehicle.

The U.S. Interstate Highway System leads directly into Canada: I–95 from Maine to New Brunswick; I–91 and

I–89 from Vermont to Québec; I–87 from New York to Québec; I–81 and a spur off I–90 from New York to Ontario; I–94, I–96, and I–75 from Michigan to Ontario; I–29 from North Dakota to Manitoba; I–15 from Montana to Alberta; and I–5 from Washington State to British Columbia. Most of these connections hook up with the Trans-Canada Highway within a few miles. There are many smaller highway crossings between the two countries as well. From Alaska, take the Alaska Highway (from Fairbanks), the Klondike Highway (from Skagway), and the Top of the World Highway (to Dawson City).

GASOLINE

Gasoline costs from 44¢ to 63¢ a liter. (There are 3.8 liters in a U.S. gallon.) Distances are always shown in kilometers, and gasoline is always sold in liters.

ROAD CONDITIONS

The A to Z sections of each chapter have information about road conditions.

RULES OF THE ROAD

By law, you are required to wear seat belts (and use infant seats). Some provinces have a statutory requirement to drive with vehicle headlights on for extended periods after dawn and before sunset. In the Yukon, the law requires that you drive with your headlights on when using territory highways. Right turns are permitted on red signals in all provinces except Québec.

Speed limits vary from province to province, but they are usually within the 90–100 kph (50–60 mph) range outside the cities.

CHILDREN & TRAVEL

CHILDREN IN CANADA

Travelers crossing the border with children should **carry identification for them** similar to that required by adults (i.e., passport or birth certificate). Children traveling with one parent or other adult should **bring a letter of permission** from the other parent, parents, or legal guardian. Divorced parents with shared custody rights should **carry legal documents establishing their status.**

Most hotels in Canada allow children under a certain age to stay in their parents' room at no extra charge, but others charge them as extra adults; be sure to **ask about the cutoff age for children's discounts.**

FLYING

If your children are two or older, **ask about children's airfares.** As a general rule, infants under two not occupying a seat fly at greatly reduced fares or even for free.

When booking, **ask about carry-on allowances for those traveling with infants.** In general, for babies charged 10% of the adult fare you are allowed one carry-on bag and a collapsible stroller, which may have to be checked; you may be limited to less if the flight is full.

Experts agree that it's a good idea to use safety seats aloft for children weighing less than 40 pounds. Airlines, however, can set their own policies: U.S. carriers allow FAA-approved models but usually require that you buy a ticket, even if your child would otherwise ride free, since the seats must be strapped into regular seats. It's important to **check your airline's policy about using safety seats during takeoff and landing.** Safety seats cannot obstruct the movement of other passengers in the row, so get an appropriate seat assignment as early as possible.

When making your reservation, **request children's meals or a free-standing bassinet** if you need them; the latter are available only to those seated at the bulkhead, where there's enough legroom. Remember, however, that bulkhead seats may not have their own overhead bins, and there's no storage space in front of you—a major inconvenience.

CONSUMER PROTECTION

Whenever possible, **pay with a major credit card** so you can cancel payment or get reimbursed if there's a problem, provided that you can provide documentation. This is the best way to pay, whether you're buying travel arrangements before your trip or shopping at your destination.

If you're buying a package or tour, always **consider travel insurance** that includes default coverage (☞ Insurance, *below*).

➤ LOCAL BBBs: **Council of Better Business Bureaus** (⊠ 4200 Wilson Blvd., Suite 800, Arlington, VA 22203, ☎ 703/276–0100, FAX 703/525–8277).

CUSTOMS & DUTIES

When shopping, **keep receipts** for all of your purchases. Upon reentering the country, **be ready to show customs officials what you've bought.** If you feel a duty is incorrect, appeal the assessment. If you object to the way your clearance was handled, get the inspector's badge number. In either case, first ask to see a supervisor, then write to the appropriate authorities, beginning with the port director at your point of entry.

U.S. Customs and Immigration has preclearance services at the following international airports in Canada: Vancouver, Calgary, Edmonton, Winnipeg, Ottawa, and Montréal. This allows U.S.-bound air passengers to depart their airplane directly on arrival at their U.S. destination without further inspection and delays.

IN CANADA

American and British visitors may bring in the following items duty-free: 200 cigarettes, 50 cigars, and 14 ounces of tobacco; 1 bottle (1.1 liters or 40 imperial ounces) of liquor or wine, or 24 355-milliliter (12-ounce) bottles or cans of beer for personal consumption. Any alcohol and tobacco products in excess of these amounts is subject to duty, provincial fees, and taxes. You can also bring in gifts up to the value of $60 (Canadian) per gift. A deposit is sometimes required for trailers (refunded upon return). Cats and dogs must have a certificate issued by a licensed veterinarian that clearly identifies the animal and certifies that it has been vaccinated against rabies during the preceding 36 months. Seeing-eye dogs are allowed into Canada without restriction. Plant material must be declared and inspected. There may be restrictions on some live plants, bulbs and seeds. With certain restrictions or prohibitions on some fruits and vegetables, visitors may bring food with them for their own use, providing the quantity is consistent with the duration of the visit.

Canada's firearms laws are significantly stricter than the U.S.'s. All handguns and semiautomatic and fully automatic weapons are prohibited and cannot be brought into the country. Sporting rifles and shotguns may be imported provided they are to be used for sporting, hunting, or competition while in Canada. All firearms must be declared to Canada Customs at the first point of entry. Failure to declare firearms will result in their seizure, and criminal charges may be made.

IN AUSTRALIA

Australia residents who are 18 or older may bring back $A400 worth of souvenirs and gifts (including jewelry), 250 cigarettes or 250 grams of tobacco, and 1,125 ml of alcohol (including wine, beer, and spirits). Residents under 18 may bring back $A200 worth of goods.

➤ INFORMATION: **Australian Customs Service** (Regional Director, ⊠ Box 8, Sydney, NSW 2001, ☎ 02/9213–2000, FAX 02/9213–4000).

IN NEW ZEALAND

Homeward-bound residents with goods to declare must present themselves for inspection. If you're 17 or older, you may bring back $700 worth of souvenirs and gifts. Your duty-free allowance also includes 4.5 liters of wine or beer; one 1,125-milliliter bottle of spirits; and either 200 cigarettes, 250 grams of tobacco, 50 cigars, or a combo of all three up to 250 grams.

➤ INFORMATION: **New Zealand Customs** (⊠ Custom House, 50 Anzac Ave., Box 29, Auckland, New Zealand, ☎ 09/359–6655, ☎ 09/309–2978).

IN THE U.K.

From countries outside the EU, including Canada, you may import, duty-free, 200 cigarettes or 50 cigars; 1 liter of spirits or 2 liters of fortified or sparkling wine or liqueurs; 2 liters of still table wine; 60 milliliters of perfume; 250 milliliters of toilet water; plus £136 worth of other goods, including gifts and souvenirs.

➤ INFORMATION: **HM Customs and Excise** (✉ Dorset House, Stamford St., London SE1 9NG, ☎ 0171/202–4227).

IN THE U.S.

U.S. residents may bring home $400 worth of foreign goods duty-free if they've been out of the country for at least 48 hours (and if they haven't used the $400 allowance or any part of it in the past 30 days).

U.S. residents 21 and older may bring back 1 liter of alcohol duty-free. In addition, regardless of your age, you are allowed 200 cigarettes and 100 non-Cuban cigars. Antiques, which the U.S. Customs Service defines as objects more than 100 years old, enter duty-free, as do original works of art done entirely by hand, including paintings, drawings, and sculptures.

You may also send packages home duty-free: up to $200 worth of goods for personal use, with a limit of one parcel per addressee per day (and no alcohol or tobacco products or perfume worth more than $5); label the package PERSONAL USE, and attach a list of its contents and their retail value. Do not label the package UNSOLICITED GIFT, or your duty-free exemption will drop to $100. Mailed items do not affect your duty-free allowance on your return.

➤ INFORMATION: **U.S. Customs Service** (Inquiries, ✉ Box 7407, Washington, DC 20044, ☎ 202/927–6724; complaints, Office of Regulations and Rulings, ✉ 1301 Constitution Ave. NW, Washington, DC 20229; registration of equipment, Resource Management, ✉ 1301 Constitution Ave. NW, Washington DC 20229, ☎ 202/927–0540).

DISABILITIES & ACCESSIBILITY

ACCESS IN CANADA

➤ LOCAL RESOURCES: **Canadian Paraplegic Association National Office** (✉ 1101 Prince of Wales Dr., Ottawa, ON K2C 3W7, ☎ 613/723–1033) provides information about touring in Canada.

MAKING RESERVATIONS

When discussing accessibility with an operator or reservations agent, **ask hard questions.** Are there any stairs, inside *or* out? Are there grab bars next to the toilet *and* in the shower/tub? How wide is the doorway to the room? To the bathroom? For the most extensive facilities meeting the latest legal specifications, **opt for newer accommodations,** which are more likely to have been designed with access in mind. Be sure to **discuss your needs before booking.**

TRANSPORTATION

➤ COMPLAINTS: **Disability Rights Section** (✉ U.S. Department of Justice, Civil Rights Division, Box 66738, Washington, DC 20035–6738, ☎ 202/514–0301 or 800/514–0301, TTY 202/514–0383 or 800/514–0383, FAX 202/307–1198) for general complaints. **Aviation Consumer Protection Division** (☞ Air Travel, *above*) for airline-related problems. **Civil Rights Office** (✉ U.S. Department of Transportation, Departmental Office of Civil Rights, S-30, 400 7th St. SW, Room 10215, Washington, DC 20590, ☎ 202/366–4648, FAX 202/366–9371) for problems with surface transportation. In Canada, contact the **Canadian Disability Rights Council** (✉ 428 Portage Ave., Suite 208, Winnipeg, MN R3C 0E2, ☎ 204/943–4787). Contact the Director, **Accessible Transportation Directorate** (☎ 819/997–6828), to file a complaint about transportation obstacles at Canadian airports (including flights), railroads, or ferries.

TRAVEL AGENCIES & TOUR OPERATORS

As a whole, the travel industry has become more aware of the needs of travelers with disabilities. In the U.S., the Americans with Disabilities Act requires that travel firms serve the needs of all travelers. Note, though, that some agencies and operators specialize in making travel arrangements for people with disabilities.

➤ TRAVELERS WITH MOBILITY PROBLEMS: **Access Adventures** (✉ 206 Chestnut Ridge Rd., Rochester, NY

14624, ☎ 716/889–9096), run by a former physical-rehabilitation counselor. **Accessible Journeys** (✉ 35 W. Sellers Ave., Ridley Park, PA 19078, ☎ 610/521–0339 or 800/846–4537, FAX 610/521–6959), for escorted tours exclusively for travelers with mobility impairments. **CareVacations** (✉ 5019 49th Ave., Suite 102, Leduc, AB T9E 6T5, ☎ 403/986–6404, 800/648–1116 in Canada) has group tours and is especially helpful with cruise vacations. **Flying Wheels Travel** (✉ 143 W. Bridge St., Box 382, Owatonna, MN 55060, ☎ 507/451–5005 or 800/535–6790, FAX 507/451–1685), a travel agency specializing in customized tours and itineraries worldwide. **Hinsdale Travel Service** (✉ 201 E. Ogden Ave., Suite 100, Hinsdale, IL 60521, ☎ 630/325–1335), a travel agency that benefits from the advice of wheelchair traveler Janice Perkins. **Twin Peaks Press** (✉ Box 129, Vancouver, WA 98666, ☎ 360/694–2462 or ☎ 800/637–2256 publishes a directory listing more than 300 travel agencies specializing in helping travelers with disabilities.

➤ TRAVELERS WITH DEVELOPMENTAL DISABILITIES: **Sprout** (✉ 893 Amsterdam Ave., New York, NY 10025, ☎ 212/222–9575 or 888/222–9575, FAX 212/222–9768).

DISCOUNTS & DEALS

Be a smart shopper and **compare all your options** before making any choice. A plane ticket bought with a promotional coupon may not be cheaper than the least expensive fare from a discount ticket agency. For high-price travel purchases, such as packages or tours, keep in mind that what you get is just as important as what you save.

CREDIT-CARD BENEFITS

When you use your credit card to make travel purchases you may get free travel-accident insurance, collision-damage insurance, and medical or legal assistance, depending on the card and the bank that issued it. American Express, MasterCard, and Visa provide one or more of these services, so **get a copy of your credit card's travel-benefits policy.** If you are a member of an auto club, always **ask hotel and car-rental reservations**

agents about auto-club discounts. Some clubs offer discounts on tours, cruises, and admission to attractions.

DISCOUNT RESERVATIONS

To save money, **look into discount-reservations services** with toll-free numbers, which use their buying power to get a better price on hotels, airline tickets, even car rentals. When booking a room, always **call the hotel's local toll-free number** (if one is available) rather than the central reservations number—you'll often get a better price. Always ask about special packages or corporate rates.

When shopping for the best deal on hotels and car rentals, **look for guaranteed exchange rates,** which protect you against a falling dollar. With your rate locked in, you won't pay more, even if the price goes up in the local currency.

➤ AIRLINE TICKETS: ☎ 800/FLY–4–LESS. ☎ 800/FLY–ASAP.

➤ HOTEL ROOMS: RMC Travel (☎ 800/245–5738). Steigenberger Reservation Service (☎ 800/223–5652).

PACKAGE DEALS

Packages and guided tours can save you money, but don't confuse the two. When you buy a package, your travel remains independent, just as though you had planned and booked the trip yourself. Fly-drive packages, which combine airfare and car rental, are often a good deal.

ELECTRICITY

Canada, like the United States, uses 110-volt, 60-cycle electric power.

EMBASSIES & EMERGENCIES

All embassies are in Ottawa; there are consulates in some major cities. Emergency information is given in the A to Z section at the end of each chapter.

➤ AUSTRALIA: ✉ 50 O'Connor St., Suite 710, ☎ 613/236–0841.

➤ NEW ZEALAND: ✉ 99 Bank St., Suite 727, ☎ 613/238–5991.

➤ UNITED KINGDOM: ✉ 80 Elgin St., ☎ 613/237–1530.

➤ UNITED STATES: ✉ 85 Albert St., ☎ 613/238–5335.

GAY & LESBIAN TRAVEL

➤ GAY- AND LESBIAN-FRIENDLY TOUR OPERATORS: **R.S.V.P. Travel Productions** (✉ 2800 University Ave. SE, Minneapolis, MN 55414, ☎ 612/379–4697 or 800/328–7787, FAX 612/379–0484), for cruises and resort vacations for gays. **Toto Tours** (✉ 1326 W. Albion Ave., Suite 3W, Chicago, IL 60626, ☎ 773/274–8686 or 800/565–1241, FAX 773/274–8695), for groups.

➤ GAY- AND LESBIAN-FRIENDLY TRAVEL AGENCIES: **Corniche Travel** (✉ 8721 Sunset Blvd., Suite 200, West Hollywood, CA 90069, ☎ 310/854–6000 or 800/429–8747, FAX 310/659–7441). **Islanders Kennedy Travel** (✉ 183 W. 10th St., New York, NY 10014, ☎ 212/242–3222 or 800/988–1181, FAX 212/929–8530). **Now Voyager** (✉ 4406 18th St., San Francisco, CA 94114, ☎ 415/626–1169 or 800/255–6951, FAX 415/626–8626). **Yellowbrick Road** (✉ 1500 W. Balmoral Ave., Chicago, IL 60640, ☎ 773/561–1800 or 800/642–2488, FAX 773/561–4497). **Skylink Travel and Tour** (✉ 3577 Moorland Ave., Santa Rosa, CA 95407, ☎ 707/585–8355 or 800/225–5759, FAX 707/584–5637), serving lesbian travelers.

HEALTH

MEDICAL PLANS

No one plans to get sick while traveling, but it happens, so **consider signing up with a medical-assistance company.** Members get doctor referrals, emergency evacuation or repatriation, 24-hour telephone hot lines for medical consultation, cash for emergencies, and other personal and legal assistance. Coverage varies by plan, so **review benefits carefully.**

➤ MEDICAL-ASSISTANCE COMPANIES: **International SOS Assistance** (✉ 8 Neshaminy Interplex, Suite 207, Trevose, PA 19053, ☎ 215/245–4707 or 800/523–6586, FAX 215/244–9617; ✉ 12 Chemin Riant-bosson, 1217 Meyrin 1, Geneva, Switzerland, ☎ 4122/785–6464, FAX 4122/785–6424; ✉ 10 Anson Rd., 14-07/08 International Plaza, Singapore, 079903, ☎ 65/226–3936, FAX 65/226–3937).

HOLIDAYS

NATIONAL HOLIDAYS

Canadian national holidays for 1999 are as follows: New Year's Day, Good Friday (April 2), Easter Monday (April 5), Victoria Day (May 17), Canada Day (July 1), Labor Day (September 6), Thanksgiving (October 11), Remembrance Day (November 11), Christmas, and Boxing Day (December 26).

PROVINCIAL HOLIDAYS

Alberta: Heritage Day (August 2). British Columbia: British Columbia Day (August 2). New Brunswick: New Brunswick Day (August 2). Newfoundland: St. Patrick's Day (March 15), St. George's Day (April 19), Discovery Day (June 21), Memorial Day (July 1), Orangemen's Day (July 12). Manitoba, Northwest Territories, Ontario, Saskatchewan, and Nova Scotia: Civic Holiday (August 2). Québec: St. Jean Baptiste Day (June 24). Yukon: Discovery Day (August 16).

INSURANCE

Travel insurance is the best way to **protect yourself against financial loss.** The most useful plan is a comprehensive policy that includes coverage for trip cancellation and interruption, default, trip delay, and medical expenses (with a waiver for preexisting conditions).

Without insurance, you will lose all or most of your money if you cancel your trip, regardless of the reason. Default insurance covers you if your tour operator, airline, or cruise line goes out of business. Trip-delay covers unforeseen expenses that you may incur due to bad weather or mechanical delays. It's important to **compare the fine print regarding trip-delay coverage when comparing policies.**

For overseas travel, one of the most important components of travel insurance is its medical coverage. Supplemental health insurance will pick up the cost of your medical bills should you get sick or injured while traveling. U.S. residents should note that Medicare generally does not cover health-care costs outside the United States, nor do many privately issued policies. Residents of the United Kingdom can buy an annual travel-insurance policy valid for most vacations taken during the year in which the coverage is purchased. If you are pregnant or have a pre-existing condition, make sure you're covered. British citizens should buy extra medical coverage when traveling overseas, according to the Association of British Insurers. Australian travelers should buy travel insurance, including extra medical coverage, whenever they go abroad, according to the Insurance Council of Australia.

Always **buy travel insurance directly from the insurance company**; if you buy it from a cruise line, airline, or tour operator that goes out of business, you probably will not be covered for the agency or operator's default, a major risk. Before you make any purchase, **review your existing health and home-owner's policies** to find out whether they cover expenses incurred while traveling.

➤ TRAVEL INSURERS: In the U.S., **Access America** (✉ 6600 W. Broad St., Richmond, VA 23230, ☎ 804/285–3300 or 800/284–8300). **Travel Guard International** (✉ 1145 Clark St., Stevens Point, WI 54481, ☎ 715/345–0505 or 800/826–1300). In Canada, **Mutual of Omaha** (✉ Travel Division, 500 University Ave., Toronto, ON M5G 1V8, ☎ 416/598–4083, 800/268–8825 in Canada).

➤ INSURANCE INFORMATION: In the U.K., **Association of British Insurers** (✉ 51 Gresham St., London EC2V 7HQ, ☎ 0171/600–3333). In Australia, the **Insurance Council of Australia** (☎ 613/9614–1077, FAX 613/9614–7924).

LANGUAGE

Canada's two official languages are English and French. Though English is widely spoken, it is useful to **learn a few French phrases** if you plan to travel to the province of Québec or to the French-Canadian communities in the Maritimes (Nova Scotia, New Brunswick, and Prince Edward Island), northern Manitoba, and Ontario. Canadian French has many

distinctive words and expressions, but it's no more different from the language of France than North American English is from the language of Great Britain.

LODGING

Aside from the quaint hotels of Québec, Canada's range of accommodations more closely resembles that of the United States than of Europe. In the cities you'll have a choice of luxury hotels, moderately priced modern properties, and smaller older hotels with perhaps fewer conveniences but more charm. Options in smaller towns and in the country include large, full-service resorts; small, privately owned hotels; roadside motels; and bed-and-breakfasts. Even here you'll need to make reservations at least on the day on which you're planning to pull into town.

There is no national government rating system for hotels, but many provinces rate their accommodations. For example, in British Columbia and Alberta, a blue Approved Accommodation decal on the window or door of a hotel or motel indicates that it has met provincial hotel association standards for courtesy, comfort, and cleanliness. Ontario's voluntary rating system includes about 1,000 Ontario properties.

Expect accommodations to cost more in summer than in the off-season (except for places such as ski resorts, where winter is high season). When making reservations, **ask about special deals and packages.** Big-city hotels that cater to business travelers often offer weekend packages, and many city hotels offer rooms at up to 50% off in winter. If you're planning to visit a major city or resort area in high season, **book well in advance.** Also be aware of any special events or festivals that may coincide with your visit and fill every room for miles around. For resorts and lodges, consider the winter ski-season high as well and plan accordingly.

APARTMENT & VILLA RENTALS

If you want a home base that's roomy enough for a family and comes with cooking facilities, **consider a furnished rental.** These can save you money, especially if you're traveling with a large group. Home-exchange directories list rentals (often second homes owned by prospective house swappers), and some services search for a house or apartment for you. Up-front registration fees may apply.

➤ RENTAL AGENTS: **Property Rentals International** (✉ 1008 Mansfield Crossing Rd., Richmond, VA 23236, ☎ 804/378–6054 or 800/220–3332, FAX 804/379–2073). **Rent-a-Home International** (✉ 7200 34th Ave. NW, Seattle, WA 98117, ☎ 206/789–9377 or 800/488–7368, FAX 206/789–9379).

B&BS

Bed-and-breakfasts can be found in both the country and the cities. For assistance in booking these, **contact the appropriate provincial tourist board,** which either has a listing of B&Bs or can refer you to an association that will help you secure reservations. Room quality varies from house to house as well, so you can **ask to see a room before making a choice.**

HOME EXCHANGES

If you would like to exchange your home for someone else's, **join a home-exchange organization,** which will send you its updated listings of available exchanges for a year and will include your own listing in at least one of them. It's up to you to make specific arrangements.

➤ EXCHANGE CLUBS: **HomeLink International** (✉ Box 650, Key West, FL 33041, ☎ 305/294–7766 or 800/638–3841, FAX 305/294–1148; $83 per year).

HOSTELS

No matter what your age, you can **save on lodging costs by staying at hostels.** In some 5,000 locations in more than 70 countries around the world, Hostelling International (HI), the umbrella group for a number of national youth hostel associations, offers single-sex, dorm-style beds and, at many hostels, "couples" rooms and family accommodations. Membership in any HI national hostel association, open to travelers of all ages, allows you to stay in HI-affiliated hostels at member rates (one-year membership is about $25 for adults; hostels run

about $10–$25 per night). Members also have priority if the hostel is full; they're eligible for discounts around the world, even on rail and bus travel in some countries.

➤ HOSTEL ORGANIZATIONS: **Hostelling International—American Youth Hostels** (✉ 733 15th St. NW, Suite 840, Washington, DC 20005, ☎ 202/783–6161, FAX 202/783–6171). **Hostelling International—Canada** (✉ 400-205 Catherine St., Ottawa, ONK2P 1C3, ☎ 613/237–7884, FAX 613/237–7868). **Youth Hostel Association of England and Wales** (✉ Trevelyan House, 8 St. Stephen's Hill, St. Albans, Hertfordshire AL1 2DY, ☎ 01727/855215 or 01727/845047, FAX 01727/844126; membership in the U.S. $25, in Canada C$26.75, in the U.K. £9.30).

HOTELS

➤ HOTEL CHAINS: **Best Western International** (☎ 800/528–1234, 0181/541–0033 in the U.K.), **Canadian Pacific Hotels & Resorts** (☎ 800/441–1414, 0800/898852 in the U.K.), **Choice Hotels International** (☎ 800/424–6423, 0800/444–4444 in the U.K.), **Days Inns** (☎ 800/329–7466, 01483/440470 in the U.K.), **Delta Hotels** (☎ 800/877–1133, 0171/937–8033 in the U.K.), **Four Seasons Hotels** (☎ 800/332–3442, 0800/526648 in the U.K.), **Hilton Hotels** (☎ 800/445–8667), **Holiday Inns** (☎ 800/465–4329, 0800/897121 in the U.K.), **Hyatt Hotels** (☎ 800/223–1234, 0171/580–8197 in the U.K.), **Inter-Continental** (☎ 800/327–0200), **Marriott Hotels and Resorts** (☎ 800/228–9290, 0800/282811 in the U.K.), **Novotel Hotels** (☎ 800/668–6835), **Radisson Hotels** (☎ 800/333–3333, 0800/891999 in the U.K.), **Ramada** (☎ 800/228–2828, 0181/681–1418 in the U.K.), **Relais & Châteaux** (☎ 212/856–0115), **Sheraton** (☎ 800/325–3535, 0800/353535 in the U.K.), **Travelodge** (☎ 800/255–3050, 0345/404040 in the U.K.), and **Westin Hotels** (☎ 800/228–3000, 0171/408–0636 in the U.K.).

MAIL

In Canada you can **buy stamps at the post office or from automatic vending**

machines in most hotel lobbies, railway stations, airports, bus terminals, many retail outlets, and some newsstands. If you're sending mail to Canada, **be sure to include the postal code** (six digits and letters). Following are postal abbreviations for provinces and territories: Alberta, AB; British Columbia, BC; Saskatchewan, SK; Manitoba, MB; New Brunswick, NB; Newfoundland and Labrador, NF; Northwest Territories, NT; Nova Scotia, NS; Ontario, ON; Prince Edward Island, PE; Québec, PQ; Yukon, YT.

POSTAL RATES

Within Canada, postcards and letters up to 30 grams cost 45¢; between 31 grams and 50 grams, the cost is 71¢ and between 51 grams and 100 grams the cost is 90¢. Letters and postcards to the United States cost 52¢ for up to 30 grams, 77¢ for between 31 and 50 grams, and $1.17 for up to 100 grams. Prices include GST (Goods and Services Tax).

International mail and postcards run 90¢ for up to 20 grams, $1.37 for between 21 and 50 grams, and $2.25 for between 51 and 100 grams.

RECEIVING MAIL

Visitors may have mail sent to them c/o General Delivery in the town they are visiting, for pickup in person within 15 days, after which it will be returned to the sender.

MONEY

COSTS

The following typical prices are for Toronto (prices in other cities and regions are often lower): A soda (pop) costs $1–$1.25; a glass of beer, $3–$6; a sandwich, $3.50–$6; a taxi, as soon as the meter is turned on, $2.50, and $1 for every kilometer (½ mile); a movie, about $8.

CREDIT & DEBIT CARDS

Should you use a credit card or a debit card when traveling? Both have benefits. A credit card allows you to delay payment and gives you certain rights as a consumer (☞ Consumer Protection, *above*). A debit card, also known as a check card, deducts funds directly from your checking account and helps you stay within your budget.

Otherwise, the two types of plastic are virtually the same. Both will get you cash advances at ATMs worldwide if your card is properly programmed with your personal identification number (PIN). (For use in Canada, your PIN must be four digits long.) Both offer excellent, wholesale exchange rates. And both protect you against unauthorized use if the card is lost or stolen. Your liability is limited to $50, as long as you report the card missing.

➤ ATM LOCATIONS: **Cirrus** (☎ 800/424–7787). **Plus** (☎ 800/843–7587) for locations in the U.S. and Canada, or visit your local bank.

➤ REPORTING LOST CARDS: **American Express** (☎ 800/528–4000). **Diners Club** (☎ 800/234–6377). **Discover** (☎ 800/347–2683). **MasterCard** (☎ 800/307–7309). **Visa** (☎ 800/336–8472).

CURRENCY

American money is accepted in much of Canada (especially in communities near the border). However, to get the most favorable exchange rate, **exchange at least some of your money into Canadian funds at a bank or other financial institution.** Traveler's checks (some are available in Canadian dollars) and major U.S. credit cards are accepted in most areas.

The units of currency in Canada are the Canadian dollar (C$) and the cent, in almost the same denominations as U.S. currency ($5, $10, $20, 1¢, 5¢, 10¢, 25¢, etc.). The $1 and $2 bill are no longer used; they have been replaced by $1 and $2 coins (known as a "loonie," because of the loon that appears on the coin, and a "toonie," respectively). At press time the exchange rate was US$1 to C$1.38 and £1 to C$2.35.

EXCHANGING MONEY

For the most favorable rates, **change money through banks.** Although fees charged for ATM transactions may be higher abroad than at home, Cirrus and Plus exchange rates are excellent, because they are based on wholesale rates offered by major banks. You won't do as well at exchange booths in airports or rail and bus stations, in hotels, in restaurants, or in stores, although you may find their hours convenient. To avoid lines at airport exchange booths, **get a bit of local currency before you leave home.**

➤ EXCHANGE SERVICES: **Chase** *Currency to Go* (☎ 800/935–9935; 935–9935 in NY, NJ, and CT). **International Currency Express** (☎ 888/842–0880 on the East Coast, 888/278–6628 on the West Coast). **Thomas Cook Currency Services** (☎ 800/287–7362 for telephone orders and retail locations).

TRAVELER'S CHECKS

Do you need traveler's checks? It depends on where you're headed. If you're going to rural areas and small towns, go with cash; traveler's checks are best used in cities. Lost or stolen checks can usually be replaced within 24 hours. To ensure a speedy refund, **buy your own traveler's checks**— don't let someone else pay for them: Irregularities like this can cause delays. The person who bought the checks should make the call to request a refund.

NATIONAL PARKS

If you plan to visit several parks in a region, you may be able to **save money on park fees by buying a multi-park pass,** available to Canadians and non-Canadians. Parks Canada currently has 8 passes: Alberta Federal and Provincial Historic Sites Pass, Atlantic Regional National Park Pass, Cabot Pass, Eastern Newfoundland National Historic Sites Pass, Saskatchewan National Historic Sites Pass, Saskatchewan National Parks and National Historic Sites Pass, Western Canada Annual Pass, Western Newfoundland Pass. Parks Canada is decentralized, so it's best to contact the park you plan to visit for information. You can buy passes at the parks covered by the pass.

➤ PARK PASSES: For Parks Canada information on-line, **http:// parkscanada.pch.gc.ca. Parks Canada national office** (✉ 25 Eddy St., Hull, Québec K1A 0M5, ☎ 819/997–0055.

OUTDOOR ACTIVITIES & SPORTS

BICYCLING

Association: CANADIAN CYCLING ASSOCIATION (✉ 1600 JAMES NAISMITH DR., GLOUCESTER, ON K1B 5N4, ☎ 613/748–5629).

CANOEING AND KAYAKING

Provincial tourist offices can be of assistance, especially in locating an outfitter to suit your needs.

➤ ASSOCIATION: **Canadian Recreational Canoeing Association** (✉ 5– 1029 Hyde Park Rd., London, ON N0M 1Z0, ☎ 519/473–2109).

CLIMBING/MOUNTAINEERING

➤ ASSOCIATION: **Alpine Club of Canada** (✉ Box 2040, Canmore, AB T0L 0M0, ☎ 403/678–3200).

GOLF

➤ ASSOCIATION: **Royal Canadian Golf Association** (✉ 1333 Dorval Dr., Oakville, ON L6J 4Z3, ☎ 905/849– 9700).

SCUBA DIVING

➤ ASSOCIATION: **Canadian Amateur Diving Association** (✉ 1600 James Naismith Dr., Suite 705, Gloucester, ON K1B 5N4, ☎ 613/748–5631).

TENNIS

➤ ASSOCIATION: **Tennis Canada** (✉ 3111 Steeles Ave. W, Downsview, ON M3J 3H2, ☎ 416/665–9777).

PACKING

LUGGAGE

How many carry-on bags you can bring with you is up to the airline. Most allow two, but the limit is often reduced to one on certain flights. Gate agents will take excess baggage—including bags they deem oversize—from you as you board and add it to checked luggage. To avoid this situation, make sure that everything you carry aboard will fit under your seat. Also, get to the gate early, and request a seat at the back of the plane; you'll board first, while the overhead bins are still empty. Since big, bulky baggage attracts the attention of gate agents and flight atten-

THE GOLD GUIDE / SMART TRAVEL TIPS

dants on a busy flight, make sure your carry-on is really a carry-on.

If you are flying internationally, note that baggage allowances may be determined not by piece but by weight—generally 88 pounds (40 kilograms) in first class, 66 pounds (30 kilograms) in business class, and 44 pounds (20 kilograms) in economy.

Airline liability for baggage is limited to $1,250 per person on flights within the United States. On international flights it amounts to $9.07 per pound or $20 per kilogram for checked baggage (roughly $640 per 70-pound bag) and $400 per passenger for unchecked baggage. You can buy additional coverage at check-in for about $10 per $1,000 of coverage, but it excludes a rather extensive list of items, shown on your airline ticket.

Before departure, **itemize your bags' contents** and their worth, and label the bags with your name, address, and phone number. (If you use your home address, cover it so that potential thieves can't see it readily.) Inside each bag, **pack a copy of your itinerary.** At check-in, **make sure that each bag is correctly tagged** with the destination airport's three-letter code. If your bags arrive damaged or fail to arrive at all, file a written report with the airline before leaving the airport.

PACKING LIST

How you pack will depend on when you go and what you plan to do. In winter, **bring layers,** the best defense against Canada's cold winters; a hat, scarf, and gloves are essential. For summer travel, **select loose-fitting natural-fiber clothes;** bring a wool sweater and light jacket. If you're planning to spend time in Canada's larger cities, pack both casual clothes for day touring and more formal wear for evenings out.

If you plan on camping or hiking in the deep woods in summer, particularly in northern Canada, **always carry insect repellent,** especially in June, which is blackfly season.

In your carry-on luggage **bring an extra pair of eyeglasses or contact lenses** and **enough of any medication you take** to last the entire trip. You may also want your doctor to write a spare prescription using the drug's generic name, since brand names may vary from country to country. **Never put prescription drugs or valuables in luggage to be checked.** To avoid customs delays, carry medications in their original packaging. And don't forget to copy down and carry addresses of offices that handle refunds of lost traveler's checks.

PASSPORTS & VISAS

When traveling internationally, **carry a passport even if you don't need one** (it's always the best form of ID) and **make two photocopies of the data page** (one for someone at home and another for you, carried separately from your passport). If you lose your passport, promptly call the nearest embassy or consulate and the local police.

ENTERING CANADA

Citizens and legal residents of the United States do not need a passport or a visa to enter Canada, but proof of citizenship (a birth certificate or valid passport) and photo identification will be requested. Naturalized U.S. residents should carry their naturalization certificate. Permanent residents who are not citizens should carry their "green card." U.S. residents entering Canada from a third country must have a valid passport, naturalization certificate, or "green card."

Citizens of the United Kingdom need only a valid passport to enter Canada for stays of up to six months.

PASSPORT OFFICES

➤ AUSTRALIAN CITIZENS: **Australian Passport Office** (☎ 13/1232).

➤ NEW ZEALAND CITIZENS: **New Zealand Passport Office** (☎ 04/494–0700 for information on how to apply, 0800/727–776 for information on applications already submitted).

➤ U.K. CITIZENS: **London Passport Office** (☎ 0990/21010), for fees and documentation requirements and to request an emergency passport.

SENIOR-CITIZEN TRAVEL

To qualify for age-related discounts, **mention your senior-citizen status up**

front when booking hotel reservations and before you're seated in restaurants. Note that discounts may be limited to certain menus, days, or hours. When renting a car, **ask about promotional car-rental discounts,** which can be cheaper than senior-citizen rates.

➤ EDUCATIONAL PROGRAMS: **Elderhostel** (✉ 75 Federal St., 3rd floor, Boston, MA 02110, ☎ 617/426–8056).

STUDENT TRAVEL

Persons under 18 years of age who are not accompanied by their parents should **bring a letter from a parent or guardian** giving them permission to travel to Canada.

TRAVEL AGENCIES

To save money, **look into deals available through student-oriented travel agencies.** To qualify you'll need a bona fide student ID card. Members of international student groups are also eligible.

➤ STUDENT IDS & SERVICES: **Council on International Educational Exchange** (CIEE; ✉ 205 E. 42nd St., 14th floor, New York, NY 10017, ☎ 212/822–2600 or 888/268–6245, FAX 212/822–2699), for mail orders only, in the United States. **Travel CUTS** (✉ 187 College St., Toronto, ON M5T 1P7, ☎ 416/979–2406 or 800/667–2887) in Canada.

➤ STUDENT TOURS: **Contiki Holidays** (✉ 300 Plaza Alicante, Suite 900, Garden Grove, CA 92840, ☎ 714/740–0808 or 800/266–8454, FAX 714/740–2034).

TAXES

A goods and services tax of 7% (GST) applies on virtually every transaction in Canada except for the purchase of basic groceries.

In addition to imposing the GST, all provinces except Alberta, the Northwest Territories, and the Yukon levy a sales tax from 6% to 12% on most items purchased in shops, on restaurant meals, and sometimes on hotel rooms. In Newfoundland, Nova Scotia, and New Brunswick, the single harmonized sales tax (HST) is used.

PROVINCIAL TAX REFUNDS

Manitoba, Québec, Newfoundland, Nova Scotia, and Prince Edward Island offer a sales-tax rebate system similar to the federal one. For provincial tax refunds, **call the provincial toll-free visitor information lines for details** (☞ Visitor Information, *below*). Most provinces do not tax goods shipped directly by the vendor to the visitor's home address.

GST REFUNDS

You can **get a GST refund on purchases taken out of the country and on short-term accommodations** (but not on food, drink, tobacco, car or motorhome rentals, or transportation); rebate forms, which must be submitted within 60 days of leaving Canada, may be obtained from certain retailers, duty-free shops, customs officials, or from Revenue Canada. Instant cash rebates up to a maximum of $500 are provided by some duty-free shops when leaving Canada, and most provinces do not tax goods that are shipped directly by the vendor to the purchaser's home. Always **save your original receipts** from stores and hotels, and **be sure the name and address of the establishment is shown on the receipt.** Original receipts are not returned. The total amount of GST on each receipt must be at least $3.50 and visitors have to claim at least $14 in tax per rebate application form.

➤ INFORMATION: **Revenue Canada** (✉ Visitor Rebate Program, Summerside Tax Centre, Summerside, PE C1N 6C6, ☎ 902/432–5608 or 800/668–4748 in Canada).

TELEPHONES

COUNTRY CODES

The country code for Canada is 1.

DIRECTORY & OPERATOR INFORMATION

For operator assistance, dial "0." For directory assistance in Canada, dial the area code followed by 555–1212; dial 1 before the area code if the area code is not the same as the one you are calling from.

INTERNATIONAL CALLS

International calls can be direct-dialed from most phones. If you're dialing

Canada from the United States, dial 1 plus the area code and telephone number. If you're dialing the United States from Canada, dial 1 plus the area code and telephone number.

To call Great Britain, Australia, New Zealand, or other countries except the U.S. from Canada, dial 011 followed by the appropriate country code, city code, and number. For operator assistance, dial "0" and ask for the overseas operator. The country codes are 44 for Great Britain, 61 for Australia, and 64 for New Zealand. To dial Canada from these countries, you should be able to dial 001 followed by the area code and telephone number.

LOCAL CALLS

For local calls, simply dial the number. No area code is needed.

LONG-DISTANCE CALLS

To dial another province or an area of the same province that has a different area code, dial 1 followed by the area code and number.

Competitive long-distance carriers make calling within the United States and Canada relatively convenient and let you avoid hotel surcharges. By dialing an 800 number, you can get connected to the long-distance company of your choice.

➤ LONG-DISTANCE CARRIERS: **AT&T** (☎ 800/225–5288). **MCI** (☎ 800/888–8000). **Sprint** (☎ 800/366–2255).

PUBLIC TELEPHONES

Pay telephones take coins, and charge phones are found in many locations, including airports and some shopping malls. These phones can be used to charge a call to a telephone company card, your home, or the party you are calling.

TIPPING

Tips and service charges are not usually added to a bill in Canada. In general, tip 15% of the total bill. This goes for waiters, waitresses, barbers and hairdressers, and taxi drivers. Porters and doormen should get about $1 a bag (or more in a luxury hotel). For maid service, $1 a day is sufficient ($2 in luxury hotels).

TOUR OPERATORS

Buying a prepackaged tour or independent vacation can make your trip less expensive and more hassle-free. Because everything is prearranged, you'll spend less time planning.

Operators that handle several hundred thousand travelers per year can use their purchasing power to give you a good price. Their high volume may also indicate financial stability. But some small companies provide more personalized service; because they tend to specialize, they may be more knowledgeable about an area.

BOOKING WITH AN AGENT

Travel agents are excellent resources. In fact, large operators accept bookings made only through travel agents. But it's a good idea to **collect brochures from several agencies,** because some agents' suggestions may be influenced by relationships with tour and package firms that reward them for volume sales. If you have a special interest, **find an agent with expertise in that area;** ASTA (☞ Travel Agencies, *below*) has a database of specialists worldwide.

Make sure your travel agent knows the accommodations and other services. Ask about the hotel's location, room size, beds, and whether it has a pool, room service, or programs for children, if you care about these. Has your agent been there in person or sent others you can contact?

Do some homework on your own, too: Local tourism boards can provide information about lesser-known and small-niche operators.

BUYER BEWARE

Each year consumers are stranded or lose their money when tour operators—even very large ones with excellent reputations—go out of business. So **check out the operator.** Find out how long the company has been in business, and ask several travel agents about its reputation. If the package or tour you are considering is priced lower than in your wildest dreams, **be skeptical.** Try to **book with a company that has a consumer-protection program.** If the operator has such a program, you'll find information about it in the company's brochure. If an operator does not offer some kind of consumer protection, then ask for references from satisfied customers.

In the U.S., members of the National Tour Association and United States Tour Operators Association are required to set aside funds to cover your payments and travel arrangements in case the company defaults. It's also a good idea to choose a company that participates in the American Society of Travel Agent's Tour Operator Program (TOP). This gives you a forum if there are any disputes between you and your tour operator; ASTA will act as mediator.

➤ TOUR-OPERATOR RECOMMENDATIONS: **American Society of Travel Agents** (☞ Travel Agencies, *below*). **National Tour Association** (NTA; ✉ 546 E. Main St., Lexington, KY 40508, ☎ 606/226–4444 or 800/755–8687). **United States Tour Operators Association** (USTOA; ✉ 342 Madison Ave., Suite 1522, New York, NY 10173, ☎ 212/599–6599 or 800/468–7862, ℻ 212/599–6744).

COSTS

The more your package or tour includes, the better you can predict the ultimate cost of your vacation. Make sure you know what is covered, and **beware of hidden costs.** Are taxes, tips, and service charges included? Transfers and baggage handling? Entertainment and excursions?

Prices for packages and tours are usually quoted per person, based on two sharing a room. If traveling solo, you may be required to pay the full double-occupancy rate. Some operators eliminate this surcharge if you agree to be matched with a roommate of the same sex.

GROUP TOURS

Among companies that sell tours to Canada, the following have a proven reputation and offer plenty of options. The classifications used below represent different price categories. The key difference is usually in accommodations, which run from budget to better, and better-yet to best.

➤ DELUXE: **Globus** (✉ 5301 S. Federal Circle, Littleton, CO 80123-2980, ☎ 303/797–2800 or 800/221–0090, ℻ 303/347–2080). **Maupintour** (✉ 1515 St. Andrews Dr., Lawrence, KS 66047, ☎ 785/843–1211 or 800/255–4266, ℻ 785/843–8351). **Tauck Tours** (✉ Box 5027, 276 Post Rd. W, Westport, CT 06881-5027, ☎ 203/226–6911 or 800/468–2825, ℻ 203/221–6866).

➤ FIRST-CLASS: **Brendan Tours** (✉ 15137 Califa St., Van Nuys, CA 91411, ☎ 818/785–9696 or 800/421–8446, ℻ 818/902–9876). **Caravan Tours** (✉ 401 N. Michigan Ave., Chicago, IL 60611, ☎ 312/321–9800 or 800/227–2826, ℻ 312/321–9845). **Collette Tours** (✉ 162 Middle St., Pawtucket, RI 02860, ☎ 401/728–3805 or 800/340–5158, ℻ 401/728–4745). **Gadabout Tours** (✉ 700 E. Tahquitz Canyon Way, Palm Springs, CA 92262–6767, ☎ 619/325–5556 or 800/952–5068). **Mayflower Tours** (✉ Box 490, 1225 Warren Ave., Downers Grove, IL 60515, ☎ 708/960–3430 or 800/323–7064). **Trafalgar Tours** (✉ 11 E. 26th St., New York, NY 10010, ☎ 212/689–8977 or 800/854–0103, ℻ 800/457–6644).

➤ BUDGET: **Cosmos** (☞ Globus, *above*).

PACKAGES

Like group tours, independent vacation packages are available from major tour operators and airlines. The companies listed below offer packages in a broad price range.

➤ AIR/HOTEL: **Air Canada's Canada** (☎ 800/774–8993). **American Airlines Vacations** (☎ 800/321–2121). **Continental Vacations** (☎ 800/634–5555). **Delta Vacations** (☎ 800/872–7786). **Northwest WorldVacations** (☎ 800/754–8599). **US Airways Vacations** (☎ 800/455–0123).

➤ AIR/HOTEL/CAR: **Air Canada's Canada** (☞ Air/Hotel, *above*). **American Airlines Vacations** (☞ Air/Hotel, *above*). **Delta Vacations** (☞ Air/Hotel, *above*).

➤ FLY/DRIVE: **Delta Vacations** (☞ Air/Hotel, *above*). **Budget WorldClass Drive** (☎ 800/527–0700, 0800/181181 in the U.K.).

THE GOLD GUIDE / SMART TRAVEL TIPS

➤ FROM THE U.K.: **British Airways Holidays** (⊠ Astral Towers, Betts Way, London Rd., Crawley, West Sussex RH10 2XA, ☎ 01293/723–191).

THEME TRIPS

The companies listed below provide multiday tours in Canada. Additional local or regionally based companies that have different-length trips with these themes are listed in each chapter, either with information about the town or in the A to Z section that concludes the chapter.

➤ ADVENTURE: **American Wilderness Experience** (⊠ Box 1486, Boulder, CO 80306, ☎ 303/444–2622 or 800/444–0099, FAX 303/444–3999). **Canadian Adventure Tours** (⊠ Box 929, Whistler, BC V0N 1B0, ☎ 604/938–0727, FAX 604/938–0728). **Ecosummer Expeditions** (⊠ 1516 Duranleau St., Vancouver, BC V6H 3S4, ☎ 604/669–7741 or 800/465–8884). **Mountain Travel-Sobek** (⊠ 6420 Fairmount Ave., El Cerrito, CA 94530, ☎ 510/527–8100 or 888/687–6235, FAX 510/525–7710). **OARS** (⊠ Box 67, Angels Camp, CA 95222, ☎ 209/736–4677 or 800/346–6277, FAX 209/736–2902). **TrekAmerica** (⊠ Box 189, Rockaway, NJ 07866, ☎ 973/983–1144 or 800/221–0596, FAX 973/983–8551). **Wells Gray Park Backcountry Chalets** (⊠ Box 188, Clearwater, BC V0E 1N0, ☎ 250/587–6444 or 888/754–8735, FAX 250/587–6446).

➤ BICYCLING: **Backroads** (⊠ 801 Cedar St., Berkeley, CA 94710-1800, ☎ 510/527–1555 or 800/462–2848, FAX 510/527–1444. **Bicycle Adventures** (⊠ Box 11219, Olympia, WA 98508, ☎ 360/786–0989 or 800/443–6060, FAX 360/786–9661). **Bike Riders** (⊠ Box 254, Boston, MA 02113, ☎ 617/723–2354 or 800/473–7040, FAX 617/723–2355). **Butterfield & Robinson** (⊠ 70 Bond St., Toronto, ON M5B 1X3, ☎ 416/864–1354 or 800/678–1147, FAX 416/864–0541). **Classic Adventures** (⊠ Box 153, Hamlin, NY 14464-0153, ☎ 716/964–8488 or 800/777–8090, FAX 716/964–7297). **Easy Rider Tours** (⊠ Box 228, Newburyport, MA 01950, ☎ 508/463–6955 or 800/488–8332, FAX 508/463–6988). **Imagine Tours** (⊠ Box 123, Davis, CA 95617, ☎ 530/758–8782 or 888/592–8687, FAX 530/758–8778). **Rocky Mountain Worldwide Cycle Tours** (⊠ 333 Baker St., Nelson, BCV1L 4H6, ☎ 250/354–1241 or 800/661–2453, FAX 250/354–2058). **Timberline** (⊠ 7975 E. Harvard, No. J, Denver, CO 80231, ☎ 303/759–3804 or 800/417–2453, FAX 303/368–1651). **Vermont Bicycle Touring** (Box 711, Bristol, VT, 05443-0711, ☎ 800/245–3868 or 802/453–4811, FAX 802/453–4806).

➤ CULTURAL: **First Nations Hospitality Tours** (⊠ 226 Rideau St., Ottawa, ON K1N 5Y1, ☎ 613/562–3970).

➤ CUSTOMIZED SELF-DRIVE ITINERARIES: **Off the Beaten Path** (⊠ 27 E. Main St., Bozeman, MT 59715, ☎ 406/586–1311 or 800/445–2995, FAX 406/587–4147).

➤ DUDE RANCHES: **American Wilderness Experience** (☞ Adventure, above).

➤ FISHING: **Cutting Loose Expeditions** (⊠ Box 447, Winter Park, FL 32790-0447, ☎ 407/629–4700 or 800/533–4746, FAX 407/740–7816). **Fishing International** (⊠ Box 2132, Santa Rosa, CA 95405, ☎ 707/539–3366 or 800/950–4242, FAX 707/539–1320). **Oak Bay Marine Group** (⊠ 1327 Beach Dr., Victoria, BC V8S 2N4 , ☎ 250/598–3366 or 800/663–7090. **Rod & Reel Adventures** (⊠ 566 Thomson La., Copperopolis, CA 95228, ☎ 209/785–0444, FAX 209/785–0447).

➤ FOOD AND WINE: **Le Cordon Bleu** (⊠ 404 Airport Executive Park, Nanuet, NY 10954, ☎ 800/457–2433).

➤ GOLF: **ITC Golf Tours** (⊠ 4134 Atlantic Ave., No. 205, Long Beach, CA 90807, ☎ 310/595–6905 or 800/257–4981).

➤ HORSEBACK RIDING: **American Wilderness Experience** (☞ Adventure, *above*). **Equitour Worldwide Riding Holidays** (⊠ Box 807, Dubois, WY 82513, ☎ 307/455–3363 or 800/545–0019, FAX 307/455–2354). **Holiday on Horseback** (⊠ Box 2280, Banff, AB T0L 0C0, ☎ 403/762–4551.

➤ LEARNING: **Creeway Wilderness Experiences** (⊠ Box 347, Moose

Factory, ON P0L 1W0, ☎ FAX 705/
658–4390). **Earthwatch** (✉ 680
Mount Auburn St., Watertown, MA
02272, ☎ 617/926–8200 or 800/
776–0188, FAX 617/926–8532) for
research expeditions. **National
Audubon Society** (✉ 700 Broadway,
New York, NY 10003, ☎ 212/979–
3066, FAX 212/353–0190). **Natural
Habitat Adventures** (✉ 2945 Center
Green Ct., Boulder, CO 80301,
☎ 303/449–3711 or 800/543–8917,
FAX 303/449–3712). **Naturequest** (934
Acapulco St., Laguna Beach, CA
92651, ☎ 714/499–9561 or 800/
369–3033, FAX 714/499–0812).
Questers (✉ 381 Park Ave. S, New
York, NY 10016, ☎ 212/251–0444
or 800/468–8668, FAX 212/251–
0890). **Smithsonian Study Tours and
Seminars** (✉ 1100 Jefferson Dr. SW,
Room 3045, MRC 702, Washington,
DC 20560, ☎ 202/357–4700,
FAX 202/633–9250). **Victor Emanuel
Nature Tours** (✉ Box 33008, Austin,
TX 78764, ☎ 512/328–5221 or 800/
328–8368, FAX 512/328–2919).

➤ PHOTOGRAPHY: **Joseph Van Os
Photo Safaris** (Box 655, Vashen, WA
98070, ☎ 206/463–5383, FAX 206/
463–5484).

➤ SINGLES AND YOUNG ADULTS: **Contiki Holidays** (✉ 300 Plaza Alicante,
No. 900, Garden Grove, CA 92840,
☎ 714/740–0808 or 800/266–8454,
FAX 714/740–0818).

➤ SKIING: **Canadian Mountain Holidays** (✉ Box 1660, Banff, ABT0L
0C0, ☎ 403/762–7100 or 800/661–
0252, FAX 403/762–5879). **Selkirk
Tangiers Helicopter Skiing** (✉ Box
1409, Golden, BC V0A 1H0, ☎ 250/
344–5016 or 800/663–7080). **Skican**
(✉ 443 Mt. Pleasant Rd., Toronto,
ON M4S 2L8, ☎ 416/488–1169 or
888/475–4226. **Tyax Heli-Skiing**
(✉ Box 894, Whistler, BC V0N 1B0,
☎ 604/932–7007 or 888/435–4754,
FAX 604/932–9992).

➤ SPAS: **Spa-Finders** (✉ 91 5th Ave.,
No. 301, New York, NY 10003-
3039, ☎ 212/924–6800 or 800/
255–7727).

➤ WALKING/HIKING: **Backroads**
(☞ Bicycling, *above*). **Butterfield &
Robinson** (☞ Bicycling, *above*).
Canadian Mountain Holidays

(☞ Skiing, *above*). **Country Walkers**
(✉ Box 180, Waterbury, VT 05676-
0180, ☎ 802/244–1387 or 800/464–
9255, FAX 802/244–5661). **New
England Hiking Holidays** (Box 1648,
North Conway, NH 03860, ☎ 603/
356–9696 or 800/869–0949). **Timberline** (☞ Bicycling, *above*). **Walking
the World** (✉ Box 1186, Fort Collins,
CO 80522, ☎ 970/498–0500 or 800/
340–9255, FAX 970/498–9100) specializes in tours for ages 50 and older.

➤ YACHT CHARTERS: **Ocean Voyages**
(✉ 1709 Bridgeway, Sausalito, CA
94965, ☎ 415/332–4681, FAX 415/
332–7460).

TRAIN TRAVEL

Amtrak currently has service from
New York to Montréal, New York
and Buffalo to Toronto, Chicago to
Toronto, and Seattle to Vancouver,
providing connections between Am-
trak's U.S.-wide network and VIA
Rail's Canadian routes. Transconti-
nental rail service is provided by VIA
Rail Canada. Rocky Mountaineer
Railtours operates spectacular two-
day, all-daylight rail trips through the
Canadian Rockies to the west coast.

➤ INFORMATION: **Amtrak** (☎ 800/
872–7245). **Rocky Mountaineer
Railtours** (☎ 800/665–7245). **VIA
Rail Canada** (☎ 800/561–3949). In
the U.K., **Long-Haul Leisurail** (✉
Box 113, Peterborough, PE3 8HY
UK, ☎ 01733/335599) represents
both VIA Rail and Rocky Mountaineer Railtours.

DISCOUNT PASSES

If you're planning to travel a lot by
train, **look into the Canrailpass.** It
allows 12 days of coach-class travel
within a 30-day period; sleeping cars
are available, but they sell out very
early and must be reserved at least a
month in advance during the high
season (June 1–mid-October), when
the pass is C$569 for adults age 25–
60, C$499 for travelers under 25 or
over 60. Low-season rates (October
16–May 31) are C$369 for adults
and C$339 for youths and senior
citizens. The pass is not valid during
the Christmas period (December 15–
January 5). For more information and
reservations, contact a travel agent in

THE GOLD GUIDE / SMART TRAVEL TIPS

the U.S. or Long-Haul Leisurail in the United Kingdom (☞ *above*).

Train travelers can **check out the new 30-day North American Rail Pass** offered by Amtrak and Via Rail. It allows unlimited coach/economy travel in the U.S. and Canada. You must indicate the itinerary when purchasing the pass. The cost is $645 June 1–October 15, $450 at other times.

TRAVEL AGENCIES

A good travel agent puts your needs first. Look for an agency that has been in business at least five years, emphasizes customer service, and has someone on staff who specializes in your destination. In addition, **make sure the agency belongs to a professional trade organization,** such as ASTA in the United States. (If your travel agency is also acting as your tour operator, *see* Buyer Beware in Tour Operators, *above*).

➤ LOCAL AGENT REFERRALS: **American Society of Travel Agents** (ASTA, ☎ 800/965–2782 for 24-hr hot line, FAX 703/684–8319). **Association of Canadian Travel Agents** (✉ Suite 201, 1729 Bank St., Ottawa, ON K1V 7Z5, ☎ 613/521–0474, FAX 613/521–0805). **Association of British Travel Agents** (✉ 55–57 Newman St., London W1P 4AH, ☎ 0171/637–2444, FAX 0171/637–0713). **Australian Federation of Travel Agents** (☎ 02/9264–3299). **Travel Agents' Association of New Zealand** (☎ 04/499–0104).

VISITOR INFORMATION

TOURIST INFORMATION

➤ PROVINCES AND TERRITORIES: U.S.: In Alberta, **Travel Alberta** (✉ 10155 102nd St. NW, Edmonton, T5J 4G8, ☎ 800/661–8888); in British Columbia, **Tourism British Columbia** (✉ 802–865 Hornby St., Vancouver, V6E 2GE, ☎ 800/663–6000); in Manitoba, **Travel Manitoba** (✉ 155 Carlton St., 7th floor, Winnipeg, R3C 3H8, ☎ 800/665–0040); in New Brunswick, **Tourism New Brunswick** (✉ Box 12345, Woodstock, E0J 2B0, ☎ 800/561–0123); in Newfoundland and Labrador, **Newfoundland and Labrador Department of Tourism,**

Recreation and Culture (✉ Box 8730, St. John's, A1B 4K2, ☎ 800/563–6353); in the Northwest Territories, **Northwest Territories Tourism** (✉ Box 1320, Yellowknife, X1A 2L9, ☎ 800/661–0788); in Nova Scotia, **Nova Scotia Tourism** (✉ Box 519, Halifax, B3J 2M7, ☎ 800/565–0000); in Nunavut (eastern Arctic), **Nunavut Tourism** (✉ Box 1450, Iqaluit, X0A 0H0, ☎ 800/491–7910; in Ontario, **Ontario Tourism** (✉ 1 Concord Gate Pl., 9th floor, Don Mills, ON M36 3N6, ☎ 800/668–2746); in Prince Edward Island, **Prince Edward Island Department of Tourism, Parks and Recreation** (✉ Box 940, Charlottetown, C1A 7M5, ☎ 800/463–4734); in Québec, **Tourisme Québec** (✉ C.P. 979, Montréal, Québec H3C 2W3, ☎ 800/363–7777); in Saskatchewan, **Tourism Saskatchewan** (✉ 1900 Albert St., Suite 500, Regina S4P 4L9, ☎ 800/667–7191); in the Yukon, **Tourism Yukon** (✉ Box 2703, Whitehorse, Y1A 2C6, ☎ 867/667–5340).

➤ IN THE U.K.: **Visit Canada Center** (✉ 62–65 Trafalgar Sq., London, WC2 5DYUK, ☎ 0891/715–000). Calls to the Visit Canada Center cost 50p per minute peak rate and 45p per minute cheap rate. **Québec Tourism** (✉ 59 Pall Mall, London SW1Y 5JHUK, ☎ 0990/561–705) ☎ 0171/930–8314).

WEB SITES

Do **check out the World Wide Web** when you're planning. You'll find everything from up-to-date weather forecasts to virtual tours of famous cities. Fodor's Web site, www.fodors.com, is a great place to start. There are also many sites with information specifically on Canada, a few of which follow.

➤ CANADIAN WEB SITES: For Parks Canada, **parkscanada.pch.gc.ca**; for Alberta, **www.discoveralberta.com**; for British Columbia, **travel.bc.ca**; for Vancouver, **www.tourism-vancouver.org**; for Manitoba, **www.gov.mb.ca/travel-manitoba**; for New Brunswick, **www.gov.nb.ca/tourism**; for Newfoundland and Labrador, **www.gov.nf.ca**; for the Northwest Territories,

www.nwttravel.nt.ca; for Nova
Scotia, explore.gov.ns.ca/irtualns;
for Nunavut, www.nunato.nca;
for Ontario, www.travelirom; for
Toronto, www.tourism-nto.com;
for Prince Edward Islarww.gov.
pe.ca; for Québec, wurisme.gouv.
qc.ca; for Montréal, tourism-
montreal.org; for, hewan,
www.sasktourisr
www.touryuko

WHEN TO GO

For more information on when to visit, *see* the When to Tour section at the beginning of each chapter that deals with a province.

CLIMATE

The following are average daily maximum and minimum temperatures for some major cities.

CALGARY

		C	May	61F	16C	Sept.	63F	17C
		7		37	3		39	4
Jan.		2C	June	67F	19C	Oct.	54F	12C
		13		44	7		30	− 1
Feb.		1C	July	74F	23C	Nov.	38F	3C
		−10		49	9		17	− 8
		9C	Aug.	72F	22C	Dec.	29F	− 2C
		− 3		47	8		8	−13

	F	−10C	May	63F	17C	Sept.	62F	17C
	3	−19		41	5		41	5
	22F	− 6C	June	69F	21C	Oct.	52F	11C
	4	−16		48	9		32	0
Mar.	31F	− 1C	July	74F	23C	Nov.	32F	0C
	13	−11		53	12		17	− 8
Apr.	49F	9C	Aug.	71F	22C	Dec.	21F	− 6C
	29	− 2		50	10		5	−15

HALIFAX

Jan.	33F	1C	May	58F	14C	Sept.	67F	19C
	20	− 7		41	5		53	12
Feb.	33F	1C	June	67F	19C	Oct.	58F	14C
	19	− 7		50	10		44	7
Mar.	39F	4C	July	73F	23C	Nov.	48F	9C
	26	− 3		57	14		36	2
Apr.	48F	9C	Aug.	73F	24C	Dec.	37F	3C
	33	1		58	13		25	4

MONTRÉAL

Jan.	23F	− 5C	May	65F	18C	Sept.	68F	20C
	9	−13		48	9		53	12
Feb.	25F	− 4C	June	74F	23C	Oct.	57F	14C
	12	−11		58	14		43	6
Mar.	36F	2C	July	79F	26C	Nov.	42F	6C
	23	− 5		63	17		32	0
Apr.	52F	11C	Aug.	76F	24C	Dec.	27F	− 3C
	36	2		61	16		16	− 9

THE GOLD GUIDE / SMART TRAVEL TIPS

OTTAWA

Jan.	20F	− 7C	May	65F	18C	Sept.	68F	20C
	4	−16		44	7		49	9
Feb.	23F	− 5C	June	75F	24C	Oct.	57F	14C
	6	−14		54	12			4
Mar.	34F	1C	July	80F	27C	Nov.	41F	5C
	18	− 8		58	14		39	
Apr.	51F	11C	Aug.	77F	25C	Dec.	29	− 2
	33	1		56	13		5F	− 4C
								−11

QUÉBEC CITY

Jan.	20F	− 7C	May	62F	17C	Sept.		
	6	−14		43	6		4	
Feb.	23F	− 5C	June	72F	22C	Oct.	53F	39C
	8	−13		53	12		39	
Mar.	33F	1C	July	78F	26C	Nov.	39F	
	19	− 7		58	14		28	
Apr.	47F	8C	Aug.	75F	24C	Dec.	24F	
	32	0		56	13		12	

TORONTO

Jan.	30F	− 1C	May	64F	18C	Sept.	71F	22
	18	− 8		47	8		54	12
Feb.	32F	0C	June	76F	24C	Oct.	60F	16C
	19	− 7		57	14		45	7
Mar.	40F	4C	July	80F	27C	Nov.	46F	8C
	27	− 3		62	17		35	2
Apr.	53F	12C	Aug.	79F	26C	Dec.	34F	1C
	38	3		61	16		23	− 5

VANCOUVER

Jan.	42F	6C	May	60F	16C	Sept.	65F	8C
	33	1		47	8		52	11
Feb.	45F	7C	June	65F	18C	Oct.	56F	13C
	36	2		52	11		45	7
Mar.	48F	9C	July	70F	1C	Nov.	48F	9C
	37	3		55	13		39	4
Apr.	54F	12C	Aug.	70F	21C	Dec.	43F	6C
	41	5		55	13		35	2

➤ FORECASTS: **Weather Channel Connection** (☎ 900/932−8437), 95¢ per minute from a Touch-Tone phone.

1 Destination: Canada

A GRAND PLACE

ET'S FACE IT— Canadians have an image problem. To most people we come across as a bit, well, dull. Nice enough and certainly polite. But boring. Good at driving in snow, perhaps, and excellent at helping little old ladies across the street, but not the kind of people you're likely to run into in a soap opera or a gunfight. Not heroic or sexy and certainly not nasty. Canadians can't even curse each other without adding a faintly interrogatory "eh" at the end, as if seeking approval for the harsh words. As in "Go to hell, eh?"

We also get overlooked a lot. The *Boston Globe* runs a regular quiz in its travel section, and one week it asked which country most foreign visitors to the United States come from. The answer given was Japan. Huh? What about us? We're foreign, too, and on any given night there are more Canadians bedding down in Vermont than there are Japanese in all 50 states.

So, given all this, how do you explain hockey—12 guys on ice with steel blades on their feet and big sticks in their hands, slamming each other around in a wood and Plexiglas box? That's not the sort of thing you'd expect from a polite and diffident people. But it's our national passion—almost a religion in some places. "You don't like hockey," Stuart McLean writes in his delightful *Welcome Home*. "You believe in it." And the reputation we have is dreadful. Russians, the conventional wisdom goes, play with skill. Americans play with heart. Canadians just play dirty.

Mary Henderson sees no contradiction. She's a sweet and tiny lady who runs a day-care center in Manitoba and helps raise money for the local hospital. But every Saturday night from September through April, she watches *Hockey Night in Canada* on CBC television with blood in her eye and heat in her heart. "We're so nice everybody takes us for granted," she says. "In hockey we're allowed to be nasty. We can even break the rules. You can't take us for granted there."

Maybe she's right. It's hard to overlook Stéphane Richer or Eric Lindros on the ice,

no matter whose sweater they're wearing. Or maybe it's just that hockey is one of the few patriotic outlets Canadians allow themselves. The rest of the time we're too busy being diffident to indulge in any kind of showy display. Sometimes this goes to ridiculous extremes. My daughter goes to a French high school for girls in Montréal. One day the school took everyone to Ottawa, the nation's capital, to tour the Parliament Buildings and visit a couple of museums. On the way home, some of the girls, mostly English-speaking ones, wanted to sing "O Canada." The teachers said "non." It might offend the Québec nationalists on the bus. Even if they sang it in French.

Canada's kind of an accident, a big, disjointed puzzle spread across the top of a continent, and it's much too large for the people who inhabit it. There are only 30 million Canadians—no more than the population of New York and California combined—scattered across a land bigger than China. It's true that most Canadians live within 325 km (200 mi) of the American border, and 75% of them live in cities, but even that doesn't create much density. Cole Harris, an editor of *The Canadian Encyclopedia,* described the inhabited part of Canada as "an island archipelago spread over 4,000 east–west miles."

In a particularly unkind moment, Lucien Bouchard, the leader of the separatist Parti Québécois, angered the nation by saying Canada wasn't a real country at all— this from a man who served as the non-country's ambassador to France for several years. Still, he had something of a point. Canada's not so much a country as a work in progress, an unfinished symphony. And we can be irritatingly undecided about who we are. Take our spelling, for example. We see plays in "theatres" just like the English, but we live in "neighborhoods" just like the Americans.

Then there's our birthday. We celebrate it on July 1 because on that day in 1867, the British Parliament joined the four provinces of Québec, Ontario, Nova Scotia, and New Brunswick into a new and independent federation. Well, sort of independent. The holiday used to be called Dominion Day, because Canada was once officially a dominion, whatever that is. Then, for some reason, the name was changed to Canada Day, a lamentable choice. There's no such thing as Greece Day or France Day. And it gives the unfortunate impression that Canada popped out of nowhere in 1867, without history or feeling. And that just isn't true.

THE CONSTITUTIONAL conundrum that is Canada was actually conceived, if not born, in a flash of smoke and passion more than 100 years earlier on a warm September night in 1759 when Major-General James Wolfe scrambled up the 300-ft cliffs outside Québec City and mustered his men on the Plains of Abraham. Wolfe had about 4,500 men on the field that day and so did his French opponent, General the Marquis de Montcalm. A lot of Montcalm's soldiers, however, were militiamen, good at the cat-and-mouse tactics of Indian warfare, but lacking the stand-and-take-it discipline required to fight a pitched battle in the 18th century. Once Wolfe had lured them out of their fortified position, his hardened regulars took about an hour to drive them from the field. When it was all over, the British crown had a new French-speaking colony to govern, the "Canadiens" had new imperial masters to manipulate, and the undertakers had two dead generals to bury.

It all worked fairly well for a while. As conquerors go, the British were pretty benign, and the French kept their faith, their language, and their seigneurs. Then those pesky Americans to the south rebelled against their British masters. Tory refugees—traitors at home, Loyalists to us—fled north. Presto—biculturalism was born. And so was the struggle that consumes our poetry and our politics.

The province of Québec is the true cradle of Canada. Its population is about 85% French, and it totters on the brink of going it alone, of leaving the federation. Its most popular politicians are separatists, and its poets and singers are relentlessly nationalist. Talk of independence is everywhere.

Eric Deschênes is a merry little man who's mayor of Godbout on the North Shore of the Gulf of St. Lawrence. It's a tiny place of austere beauty, but it's Eric's hometown and he loves it dearly. He gave up an academic career to go back there to fish and hunt and to run a little inn. He's cheerfully matter-of-fact about his nationalism. Eric took my family for a boat ride on his favorite lake and then to his fishing camp on the Rivière Godbout, where we devoured a whole salmon he'd smoked himself. He tried to explain the reluctance of half the province's population to buy the nationalist dream. A lack of self-confidence, he suggested. "People here thought Godbout was finished when the American paper company pulled out," he said. "They were wrong. People have to learn to rely on themselves. And they will."

None of which washes with Malcolm Turner, a peach farmer in British Columbia's warm and lush Okanagan Valley. Quebecers like to paint themselves as oppressed, he told me as we rode a chairlift together at the Big White ski resort. "What a crock. Right now the prime minister is French, the governor general is French, the chief justice of the Supreme Court is French, and I think the next commander of the armed forces is going to be French. That's an oppressed people? Give me a break."

The odd thing about all this is the civilized way in which this passionate debate is conducted. Rancorous things get said, all right, and spokespeople for both sides can sometimes come off sounding like bigots, but all in all we seldom lose our cool. When floods wiped out thousands of homes in the notoriously nationalist Saguenay–Lac-St-Jean region of Québec in summer 1996, Canadians raised $28 million in aid and sent the area truckloads of clothing, toys, and food. Even on October 30, 1995, when a Québec referendum on independence ended in a virtual dead heat, nothing much happened. Tempers were high and patience thin, but there were no riots and no angry demonstrations, just a few scuffles outside the various campaign headquarters. Then everyone went out for a drink.

To many Canadians, of course, the endless debate and the "neverendums" are irrelevant, even plain silly. A lot of people have moved to Canada since 1867, people from Italy, Greece, China, Ukraine, Portugal, Ireland, Iceland, India, Spain, the

Caribbean, and, most recently, Latin America. They've brought their faiths and their customs, their food and their music, and sometimes even their own quarrels. And they have irrevocably changed the country: Women in veils drive Montréal buses; Edmonton has an Ethiopian restaurant; and at least one Mountie wears a turban. Toronto is now the most multicultural city on earth; French-speaking Montréal counts smoked meat and bagels among its distinctive dishes; and Vancouver has been struggling with ways to accommodate the thousands of Hong Kong Chinese who have poured into the city. Most of these people have a hard time understanding what the English and the French are fighting about.

"What this country needs is a real problem," a Guatemalan refugee told me. He smiled when he said it, but I could see the pain in his eyes. He was sitting in a church-sponsored legal clinic finding out what he had to do to become a landed immigrant. "There are people who look at Canada from afar. Canada—big, rich, and beautiful—and they just can't understand what's happening."

He, too, has a point. Our economy is shaky, the national debt is high, and our social-safety net has taken a bit of a beating. And we've had some shocks in the last few years. A madman gunned down 14 women at an engineering school in Montréal in 1989, and our well-loved peace-keeping soldiers beat a Somali teenager to death in 1992. But all those troubles must seem pretty trivial to someone from Guatemala or India or Vietnam.

FOR THIS IS STILL a rich and tolerant land. No one has to go hungry, medical care is free for anyone who needs it, and even the poorest of our poor are affluent beyond the imagining of much of the world. The cities where most of us live are safe and clean, with downtowns that are bright and full of life.

And there's always that landscape, that endless and achingly beautiful landscape. We may be an urban people now, but the wilderness is never far away. I live in Montréal, one of the country's great metropolises, but in 4 hours I can be skiing on Mont-Tremblant, in 4 I can be

hopelessly lost in the tundra of Charlevoix, and in 12 I can be on the shore of James Bay, celebrating the annual goose hunt with Cree whose lifestyle has changed little over the centuries.

Canadians make much ado about winter. They love to whine about the cold and daydream about palm trees. But the truth is, winter is part of what makes us Canadian, and many of us revel in it. "Mon pays, ce n'est pas un pays, c'est l'hiver," chansonnier Gilles Vigneault sang in his most famous song. "My country's not a country; it's winter."

I remember a night in late January walking along the shores of Lac Turgeon in the middle of northeastern Québec. The drifts were deep enough to bury me standing up and stiff enough to bear my weight. It was bitterly cold. The snow squeaked as I walked, and my sinuses crackled every time I inhaled. But the air smelled sweetly of wood smoke, and the black velvet sky sparkled with a million stars.

And all this landscape and beauty is ours. From the coves of Newfoundland to the mountains of British Columbia, from the Great Lakes to the Arctic desert. It's all ours—the wheat farms of the prairies, the beef ranches of the Rocky Mountain foothills, the Gaelic songs of Cape Breton, the great cathedrals of Québec, the vineyards of the Niagara Peninsula, the clouds of snow geese that fill our sky every spring and fall—ours to hold, ours to pass on to our children and our grandchildren, ours to share with whoever wants to join us.

One July 1, I rode into the Yukon backcountry with a Tutchone grandfather named Fred Brown. He's a lean, wiry whip of a man who owns a modern bungalow with all the conveniences but who prefers to live in the bush. We spent the morning plodding a zigzag course from a hot, dusty valley to the cool uplands of the Ruby Mountains. In the evening we camped by a lake whose water was so clean and cold we could lie on our stomachs and suck it up the way the horses did. I caught a trout and Fred fried it over an open fire. We drank tea and he told me outrageous stories about how his grandmother used to snare moose. At midnight it was still bright enough outside to play cards without a lantern. We hadn't said anything about Dominion Day or Canada Day, but just before we turned in, Fred looked at me with a smile and said, "This is a grand place, white man. Be thankful."

And so I am.

— Paul Waters

Paul Waters, a Canadian journalist, was raised and educated on the Atlantic coast and has lived in all three of Canada's major cities: Montréal, Toronto, and Vancouver. He now lives in Montréal with his family.

NEW AND NOTEWORTHY

You may be planning to visit Canada for any number of reasons—to enjoy the great outdoors in spectacular national parks, to explore the beautiful Atlantic and Pacific coasts, or to savor the pleasures of sophisticated cities. Wherever you're heading, it's good to know that your dollar will go further in Canada, even with higher Canadian taxes. Following the trend of the past few years, the exchange rate (summer 1998) is about US$1 to C$1.38, and £1 to C$2.35.

BRITISH COLUMBIA➤ Transportation into popular **Vancouver** is improving, with more direct flights and with Amtrak daily train service into Vancouver from Seattle. A new way to explore the province is the *Pacific Starlight* Dinner Train, which travels along Howe Sound, leaving from North Vancouver. A new BC Ferries route, the Discovery Coast Passage, has opened up the previously inaccessible midcoast.

NEW BRUNSWICK➤ The **Kingsbrae Gardens** opened on a historic estate in St. Andrews, incorporating mature cedar hedges, rare Acadian old-growth forest, and knot and other gardens. The new **Bay of Fundy Parkway** from St. Martins to Fundy National Park enhances a spectacular coastal drive. Footpaths and multiuse trails are also planned.

NEWFOUNDLAND AND LABRADOR➤ A major celebration in 1999 (called **Soirée '99** at press time) will coincide with the 50th anniversary of the province's joining Canada. Look for activities throughout Newfoundland.

NOVA SCOTIA➤ The movie *Titanic* has drawn visitors to **Halifax,** where more than 150 victims of the disaster are buried in three cemeteries. The Maritime Museum of the Atlantic has a permanent exhibit about the *Titanic*.

ONTARIO➤ Boom times have hit **Toronto** in the past few years: The posh Bloor Street shops near Yorkville are bustling, and College Street in Little Italy has emerged to rival Queen Street West as the center of late-night fun. The Raptors and the Maple Leafs will have a new downtown arena in 1999—the Air Canada Centre. On the political front, Toronto and five neighboring municipalities have merged into what is being called—seriously—the MegaCity.

PRAIRIE PROVINCES➤ The **Eau Claire Market** in downtown Calgary, Alberta, continues to draw locals and visitors alike to its appealing, eclectic mix of shops, restaurants, and night spots. Now developers are building housing in the area.

PRINCE EDWARD ISLAND➤ Travelers coming to the province via New Brunswick can now use the 13-km (8-mi) **Confederation Bridge,** the Island's first fixed link to the mainland. You'll be able to get to the Island in about 12 minutes instead of waiting for the ferry.

QUÉBEC➤ The transformed **Tremblant,** the Laurentians ski resort at Mont-Tremblant, has been drawing rave reviews and crowds of skiers and snowboarders. Grosse Ile, east of **Québec City,** has been turned into a national park where visitors can learn about the hardships faced by early immigrants to Canada. Many buildings erected when Grosse Ile served as a quarantine station have been restored.

WILDERNESS CANADA➤ This is the year Canada creates its new eastern Arctic territory. **Nunavut,** once part of the old Northwest Territories, will have its own government as of April 1999, and the Inuit will celebrate on Nunavut Day, July 9, with festivals and traditional contests in every community. The new capital, Iqaluit, will host its biggest party ever.

WHAT'S WHERE

The sections below correspond to regional chapters in this book; major cities that have their own chapters are indicated below in boldface type.

British Columbia

British Columbia's caffeine addicts have a choice between two major coffee shop chains—Seattle's Starbucks and Toronto's Second Cup. Local legend has it that they usually let their Pacific sympathies triumph over their Canadian ones. This clash of the coffees illustrates once again that British Columbia is clearly a world apart, a brash young province with a booming economy and a population that sees its future on the Pacific Rim. Even winter in much of British Columbia is different—soft, gentle, and very un-Canadian. Victoria, the provincial capital, has a climate like that of Devon in Great Britain, with springs that are glorious with flowers and sunshine. **Vancouver,** the province's vibrant metropolis, is rainier but just as mild. Visitors to British Columbia can visit a Haida village, catch a chinook salmon, ski and play golf in the mountains (often on the same day), and shop for native art in the boutiques of Vancouver.

Canadian Rockies

Much of what sets British Columbia apart is this broad granite spine that straddles the British Columbia–Alberta line from the U.S. border north through the Yukon. The mountains were once a block to Canada's western expansion—the first prime minister, Sir John A. Macdonald, had to promise to push a railroad through these formidable ranges to entice the British colonies on the west coast to join the fledgling Confederation—but now they are one of the country's favorite playgrounds. National and provincial parks like Banff and Jasper protect much of the land from development and attract skiers, hikers, climbers, horseback riders, and fishers.

New Brunswick

New Brunswick is where the great Canadian forest, sliced by sweeping river valleys and modern highways, meets the Atlantic. To the north and east, the gentle, warm Gulf Stream washes quiet beaches. Besides the seacoast, there are pure inland streams, pretty towns, and historic cities such as Fredericton and Saint John. The province's dual heritage (35% of its population is Acadian French) provides added cultural spice.

Newfoundland and Labrador

The youngest member of the Canadian family, the island of Newfoundland and Labrador on the mainland joined the Confederation in 1949. But the province has a long history. Norsemen settled briefly in L'Anse-aux-Meadows around 1000, and explorer John Cabot landed on the rocky coast in 1497. The land has a raw beauty, with steep cliffs, roaring salmon rivers, and fishing villages that perch precariously on naked rock. Its people are a rich mix of English, Irish, and Scots who have a colorful grasp of language and a talent for acerbic commentary. St. John's, the capital, is a classic harbor city.

Nova Scotia

This little province on the Atlantic coast, compact and distinctive, has a capital city, Halifax, the same size as Christopher Marlowe's London. The days when Nova Scotians were prosperous shipwrights and merchants trading with the world left Victorian mansions in all the salty little ports that dot the coastline and created a uniquely Nova Scotian outlook: worldly, approachable, and sturdily independent. These are also some of the country's most musical people—Scots Highlanders sing Gaelic lullabies, and the sound of the fiddle is everywhere.

Ontario

Ontario has both Canada's political capital, Ottawa, and its commercial capital, **Toronto.** It's also big (four times the size of Great Britain), rich, and growing. You can see a first-rate musical in cosmopolitan Toronto, ice-skate on a canal in Ottawa, indulge in Shakespeare in rural Startford, sail on four of the Great Lakes, or go get lost in a wilderness that stretches all the way to the shores of James Bay. And in the past 20 years or so, Ontario has shuffled off its staid, Scottish ways and learned to eat and drink well and even how to party, thanks largely to an influx of settlers from just about every country on earth.

Prairie Provinces

Fewer than 5 million people live in Alberta, Saskatchewan, and Manitoba, which together fill an area twice the size of France. This makes for a lot of wide and lonely landscapes that have produced people who combine a rugged individualism with a sense of community unrivaled anywhere in the country. The climate is harsh—

frigid in winter and hot and dry in summer—but the region is Canada's bread-basket and the source of much of its oil and natural gas. The area's major cities—Calgary, Edmonton, Saskatoon, Regina, and Winnipeg—provide a good base for exploring the area's history: dinosaurs, native sites, frontier forts, and a variety of ethnic communities. National and provincial parks preserve grasslands, badlands, waterways, and forests.

Prince Edward Island

In the Gulf of St. Lawrence north of Nova Scotia and New Brunswick, Prince Edward Island seems too good to be true, with its crisply painted farmhouses, manicured green fields rolling down to sandy beaches, warm ocean water, lobster boats in trim little harbors, and a vest-pocket capital city, Charlottetown, packed with architectural heritage. The opening of the Confederation Bridge in 1997 made the Island more easily accessible to the mainland.

Québec

Québec is probably what all North America would have been like if the French rather than the English had won the Seven Years' War. This eastern province has always been able to find an excuse for a party. Its historic capital, **Québec City**, for example, celebrates one of the world's most brutal winters with a carnival that features parades of majorettes and teams who race boats across an ice-choked river. Throughout the province, the rest of the year is full of festivals celebrating jazz, international folklore, film, classical music, fireworks, beer, and hot-air balloons. What really sets Québec apart, of course, is language. The island city of **Montréal** is the second-largest French-speaking city in the world. French in Québec is more than the language of love—it's the language of law, business, politics, and culture and of more than 80% of the people.

Wilderness Canada

Stretched across the top of Canada above the 60th parallel is the country's last frontier—Yukon, the Northwest Territories, and Nunavut. Here, tundra plains reach to the Arctic Ocean, remote ice fields dot the St. Elias Mountains, and white-water rivers snake through mountain ranges and deep canyons. In this thinly populated expanse, native cultures have survived the coming of the white man and are showing signs of new vitality. You can cross the Arctic tundra by dogsled with Inuit hunters, ride through the Ruby Mountains with a Tutchone guide, or visit native soapstone carvers, painters, printmakers, and clothesmakers.

PLEASURES AND PASTIMES

Dining

Canadian fine dining really began in Québec, where eating out in a good restaurant with a good bottle of wine has long been a traditional part of life. Eating out was slower to catch on in other parts of the country, however, and right up until the early 1970s, Toronto was notorious for its poor food and barbarous drinking laws. But immigrants from places like Italy, Greece, Portugal, Japan, China, and India changed all that. They liked to eat and found the drinking laws incomprehensible. Soon, even the stuffiest Torontonians were eschewing the traditional overdone beef and learning how to pronounce things like velouté, forestière, tagliolini, manicotti, and tzatziki. In Vancouver there's plenty of West Coast flair, a kind of modified California fusion that makes fine use of local specialties from salmon to Pacific halibut and Dungeness crab. The country, of course, is rich in the basic ingredients—native cheeses from Québec and Ontario; lobster, mussels, salmon, and sole from both oceans; fine beef from Alberta; and lots of local delicacies like fiddlehead ferns, wild rice, and game meat.

The Great Outdoors

Most Canadians live in towns and cities within 325 km (200 mi) of the American border, but the country does have a splendid backyard to play in. Even major cities like Montréal and Vancouver are just a few hours' drive from a wilderness full of rivers, lakes, and mountains. A network of more than 30 national parks, from Kluane in Yukon to Cape Breton Highlands in Nova Scotia, are backed by dozens of provincial and regional parks. All this wilderness provides abundant opportunities for bicycling, camping, canoeing, hiking, boating, horseback riding, mountain climbing, skiing, white-water sporting, and fishing. The coasts of British Columbia, the Gulf of St. Lawrence, and the Atlantic provinces are also ideal for whale-watching.

Nightlife and the Arts

Canadians rejoice in their cities, which are clean, safe, and lively. A night on the town still means just that. Dinner, a play or concert, drinks, and maybe even a late show can be squeezed into an evening. And you can walk or take public transport from one event to the next. If you prefer, you can just stroll the brightly lit, crowded streets and do some people-watching. No one will mind. They'll be watching you.

Musically, Canada has managed to hold its own against its giant neighbor to the south. Festivals celebrating everything from fiddles to fugues ornament summer schedules across the country and provide showcases for local talent. Names like Teresa Stratas, Anne Murray, k. d. lang, Joni Mitchell, Céline Dion, and Bryan Adams are already familiar south of the border. Less well-known people to look for are the Tragically Hip, perhaps the country's most popular rock band; Cape Breton's Rankin Family, who blend modern rhythms with traditional Gaelic songs; and Ashley MacIsaac, who has made Scottish fiddle music popular among the urban young. In French there are the heartbreaking lyrics of traditional chansonniers like Gilles Vigneault and Felix Leclerc and the carefully crafted pop rock of Daniel Bélanger. On the classical scene, conductor Charles Dutoît has given the Orchestre Symphonique de Montréal international luster, and Toronto's Canadian Opera Company is highly rated.

Toronto has emerged as the third most important center for English-language theater after London and New York. The city has more than four dozen venues staging original plays, musicals, classics, and touring big hits. Montréal is a center of French-language production, with 10 major companies. Shakespeare's classics are honored along with more-modern plays at the Stratford Festival in rural Ontario every summer, and the works of George Bernard Shaw anchor another major festival at Niagara-on-the-Lake, Ontario.

Shopping

Distinctively Canadian items include furs from Montréal, fashions from Montréal and Toronto, wood carvings from rural Québec, woven goods and hooked rugs from the Maritimes, quilts from the Mennonite communities of Ontario, Inuit carvings from the Northwest Territories, native art and prints from the West Coast, native handicrafts from the prairies, and antiques from Montréal, Toronto, and Victoria. Some of the most distinctive Canadian products, of course, come from the maple tree—sugar, syrup, taffy, candy, and even liqueur. Eastern Canada, in fact, produces more than three-quarters of the world's supplies of such products.

Sports to Watch

Officially, Canada's national sport is lacrosse, but the nation's dominant passion is hockey. There are only six Canadian teams in the NHL—the Vancouver Canucks, Calgary Flames, Edmonton Oilers, Toronto Maple Leafs, Ottawa Senators, and Montréal Canadiens—but American teams are well stocked with Canadian-born stars. Getting tickets to NHL games is only slightly less difficult than getting a royal audience, so try going to see a Junior A or college game instead. The play is fast, tough, and entertaining.

Canadians also excel at something called curling, a game invented in Scotland. It looks a little like bowling, except that it's played on ice with 40-pound lumps of polished granite. Millions of Canadians participate in local leagues, especially in the prairie provinces, and major competitions, called bonspiels, get national television coverage.

Other sports do have their fans. There are two major-league baseball teams—the Montréal Expos and the Toronto Blue Jays—and two National Basketball Association franchises—the Toronto Raptors and the Vancouver Grizzlies. (Oddly enough, basketball was invented by Canadian James Naismith.) As for football, Canada has its own version of the game played with three downs on a bigger field than the American version. The Canadian Football League, however, is in a constant state of financial crisis, and it's nearly impossible to tell from one year to the next how many teams it will have.

Winter

If asked, most Canadians would probably claim they hate winter. But the fact is, the country revels in winter. There are major carnivals celebrating the season in Québec City, Ottawa, Montréal, Winnipeg, and Edmonton. Every town and village has at least a few skating rinks, and everyone has a favorite toboggan hill. In January and February fishermen erect whole villages of little huts on frozen rivers and lakes, and dog teams yap through the forest as soon as the snow is deep enough. There are thousands of miles of cross-country ski trails, and first-rate downhill ski resorts in Québec, Alberta, and British Columbia. Several major ski magazines have rated the Whistler-Blackcomb ski resort, north of Vancouver, the best in the world; in the Laurentian Mountains in Québec, the revitalized Tremblant resort at Mont-Tremblant is winning new fans. One of the fastest-growing sports is snowmobiling. A network of 112,255 km (69,600 mi) of trails with its own restaurants, road signs, and maps crisscrosses much of the country, but the purists head for the backcountry to roar through untracked powder.

FODOR'S CHOICE

No two people will agree on what makes a perfect vacation, but it's fun and helpful to know what others think. We hope you'll have a chance to experience some of Fodor's Choices yourself in Canada. For detailed information about each entry, refer to the appropriate chapter.

Historic Sites

★ **Basilique Notre-Dame-de-Montréal, Montréal.** The enormous (3,800-seat) neo-Gothic church, opened in 1829, has a medieval-style interior with stained-glass windows; a star-studded, vaulted blue ceiling; and pine and walnut carving.

★ **Basilique Ste-Anne-de-Beaupré, outside Québec City.** The monumental church is an important shrine that draws hordes of pilgrims. According to local legend, St. Anne was responsible over the years for saving voyagers from shipwrecks; she is also believed to have healing powers.

★ **Vieux-Québec, Québec City.** The old town is small and dense, steeped in four centuries of history and French tradition. Immaculately preserved as the only fortified city in North America, it is a UNESCO World Heritage Site.

★ **Plains of Abraham, Québec City.** The site of the famous 1759 battle between the French and the British that decided the fate of New France is now part of a large park overlooking the St. Lawrence River.

★ **Kings Landing Historical Settlement, outside Fredericton, New Brunswick.** This reconstructed village—including homes, an inn, a forge, a store, a church, a school, working farms, and a sawmill—illustrates life in the central Saint John River valley between 1790 and 1900.

★ **Dawson City, the Yukon, Wilderness Canada.** The entire town tells the story of the fascination with the yellow metal. Century-old Klondike Gold Rush buildings stand next to the modern log homes of present-day miners.

Parks and Gardens

★ **Butchart Gardens, Victoria, British Columbia.** This world-class horticultural collection grows more than 700 varieties of flowers and has Italian, Japanese, and English rose gardens.

★ **Pacific Rim National Park, Vancouver Island, British Columbia.** The first national marine park in Canada comprises a hard-packed white-sand beach, a group of islands, and a demanding coastal hiking trail where you'll find panoramic views of the sea and the rain forest.

★ **Banff National Park, Canadian Rockies.** Canada's first national park was officially established in 1887 and includes Lake Louise and part of the Icefields Parkway. Its spectacular mountain peaks, forests, and wildlife remain relatively untouched by human development.

★ **Jardin Botanique de Montréal, Montréal.** This botanical garden, with 181 acres of gardens in summer and 10 greenhouses open all year, has one of the best bonsai collections in the West and the largest Ming-style garden outside Asia.

★ **Cape Breton Highlands National Park, Nova Scotia.** A wilderness of wooded valleys, plateau barrens, and steep cliffs, it stretches across the northern peninsula of Nova Scotia's Cape Breton Island.

⋆ **Prince Edward Island National Park, Prince Edward Island.** Along the north shore of the Island, sky and sea meet red sandstone cliffs, rolling dunes, and long stretches of sand.

⋆ **Nahanni National Park, Northwest Territories, Wilderness Canada.** Access to this mountainous park in the Northwest Territories is possible only by helicopter or plane; inside the park, canoes and rafts are the principal means of travel.

⋆ **Kluane National Park, Yukon, Wilderness Canada.** Kluane is home to the largest and most diverse wildlife population north of the 60th parallel, the highest mountains in Canada, and the largest nonpolar ice field in the world.

Views to Remember

⋆ **Chesterman Beach, Tofino, British Columbia.** The open Pacific Ocean meets old-growth forest at Canada's western edge. The dramatic beauty of winter storms has made even harsh weather an attraction.

⋆ **The view from the Jasper Tramway, Canadian Rockies.** From the steep flank of Whistlers Mountain you can see Mt. Robson (the Canadian Rockies' highest mountain), the Miette valley to the west, and Athabasca valley to the east.

⋆ **View of Niagara Falls by helicopter, Ontario.** Niagara Helicopters Ltd. takes you over the Giant Whirlpool, up the Niagara Gorge, and past the American Falls and then banks around the curve of the Horseshoe Falls.

⋆ **Peggy's Cove, Nova Scotia.** At the mouth of a bay facing the open Atlantic, the cove, with its houses huddled around the narrow slit in the boulders, has the only Canadian post office in a lighthouse.

⋆ **Signal Hill National Historic Site, St. John's, Newfoundland.** Overlooking the snug, punch-bowl harbor of St. John's and the sea, this hilltop was taken and retaken by opposing forces in the 17th and 18th centuries.

⋆ **Arctic Circle from the Dempster Highway, Yukon, Wilderness Canada.** This is an immense tundra vista, inhabited by caribou, wolves, foxes, and eagles, with the gently curving Richardson Mountains catching the midnight sun in the distance.

Restaurants

⋆ **Star Anise, Vancouver.** Pacific Rim cuisine with French flair shines in this intimate restaurant on the west side of town. $$$–$$$$

⋆ **Emerald Lake Lodge, Yoho, Canadian Rockies.** The eclectic menu of this glass-enclosed dining room at the edge of a glacier-fed lake in Yoho National Park joins traditional Canadian and American fare with nouvelle sauces. $$$$

⋆ **Toqué, Montréal.** This is the most fashionable and the most zany restaurant in Montréal. The menu depends on what the two chefs found fresh that day and on which way their ever-creative spirit moves them. $$$$

⋆ **Centro, Toronto.** French-Mediterranean style joins fine regional ingredients at a restaurant that sets city standards of excellence. $$$$

⋆ **L'Eau à la Bouche, Ste-Adèle, Québec.** At this Bavarian-style property you'll find a superb marriage of nouvelle cuisine and traditional Québec cooking in such dishes as roast veal in a cognac and Roquefort sauce. $$$$

Hotels

⋆ **English Bay Inn, Vancouver.** In this 1930s Tudor house a block from the ocean, the guest rooms have wonderful sleigh beds with matching armoires. A small, sunny Italian country garden brightens the back of the inn. $$–$$$

⋆ **Four Seasons Toronto.** The most exclusive property in town, it often tops all the "best hotel" lists. A great location, fine service, afternoon tea—what could be more civilized? $$$$

⋆ **Auberge du Vieux-Port, Montréal.** In an 1880s building in Vieux-Montréal, the inn overlooks the Vieux-Port and has tall windows and massive exposed beams. $$–$$$

⋆ **Kingsbrae Arms, St. Andrews by-the-Sea, New Brunswick.** The antique furnishings in this restored 1897 estate are eclectic and amusing. Guests are well pampered. $$$$

⋆ **West Point Lighthouse, West Point, Prince Edward Island.** A functioning lighthouse in a provincial park, this small inn sits next to the beach. $–$$

FESTIVALS AND SEASONAL EVENTS

Contact local or provincial tourist boards for more information about these and other festivals.

WINTER

DECEMBER➤ **British Columbia:** The **Carol Ships,** sailboats full of carolers and decorated with colored lights, ply Vancouver harbor.

Newfoundland and Labrador: In St. John's, **New Year's** revelers gather on the waterfront to ring in the new year.

Prince Edward Island: The Prince Edward Island Crafts Council **Annual Christmas Craft Fair** brings juried producers to Charlottetown.

JANUARY➤ **Alberta:** The **Jasper Winter Festival** in Jasper and Marmot Basin presents dogsledding, skating, and ice sculpting.

British Columbia: The **Polar Bear Swim,** on New Year's Day in Vancouver, is said to bring good luck all year. **Skiing competitions** take place at most alpine ski resorts (through February).

Ontario: The **Niagara Falls Festival of Lights** is an extravaganza of colored lights in the parks surrounding the Falls.

FEBRUARY➤ **Alberta: Calgary Winter Festival** is a 10-day celebration with winter sports and ice sculpting.

Manitoba: Festival du Voyageur, in St. Boniface, Winnipeg, celebrates the area's early fur traders.

Ontario: Ontario Winter Carnival Bon Soo animates Sault Ste. Marie. Ottawa's **Winterlude** encourages ice sculpting, snowshoe racing, and ice boating.

Québec: *La Fête des Neiges* is Winter Carnival in Montréal. Winter Carnival in Québec City is an 11-day festival of winter-sports competitions, ice-sculpture contests, and parades.

Yukon: The winter blahs are driven away by the Frostbite Music Festival, with visiting musicians from across North America. The **Yukon Sourdough Rendezvous** has leg wrestling, log-sawing, and snowshoe racing. Mushers completing the 1,620-km-long (1,000-mi-long) **Yukon Quest International Dog Sled Race** from Fairbanks, Alaska, to Whitehorse, celebrate in town.

SPRING

MARCH➤ **British Columbia:** The **Pacific Rim Whale Festival** on Vancouver Island celebrates the spring migration of gray whales with guided tours by whale experts and music and dancing.

Manitoba: The **Royal Manitoba Winter Fair** takes place in Brandon.

Northwest Territories: The **Caribou Carnival** fills three days with traditional Inuit and Dene games, ice sculpting, cultural exhibits, and races in Yellowknife. The **Canadian Championship Dog Derby** is a three-day dogsled race on frozen Great Slave Lake that attracts top mushers from the United States and Canada.

APRIL➤ **Alberta: Silver Buckle Rodeo** at Red Deer attracts cowboys from all over North America.

British Columbia: TerrifVic Jazz Party, in Victoria, has top international Dixieland bands. The Vancouver International Wine Festival is held at this time.

Northwest Territories: Inuvik's **Muskrat Jamboree** is an old-fashioned spring festival with muskrat-skinning contests, dogsled and snowmobile races, log-sawing duels, and more.

Ontario: The Maple Syrup Festival sweetens Elmira. The distinguished Shaw Festival in Niagara-on-the-Lake (through October) presents plays by George Bernard Shaw and his contemporaries.

Québec: Sugaring-off parties celebrate the maple syrup season.

MAY➤ **Alberta:** The **International Children's Festival** in Calgary and Edmonton draws musicians, mimes, jugglers, clowns, puppeteers, and singers. At the **Red Deer Annual Westerner Spring Quarter Horse Show,** horses from western Canada and the United States compete.

British Columbia: Cloverdale Rodeo in Surrey is rated sixth in the world by the Pro Rodeo Association. **Vancouver**

Children's Festival provides free open-air stage performances.

New Brunswick: Celebrations of **Loyalist Day** take place on May 18.

Nova Scotia: In the Annapolis Valley, the **Apple Blossom Festival** includes dancing, parades, and entertainment.

Ontario: The internationally known **Stratford Festival,** in Stratford, presents many of Shakespeare's plays (through early November). The **Canadian Tulip Festival,** in Ottawa, celebrates spring with 3 million tulips.

Saskatchewan: The **International Band and Choral Festival,** in Moose Jaw, attracts 7,000 musicians. **Vesna Festival,** in Saskatoon, is the world's largest Ukrainian cabaret, with traditional Ukrainian food and crafts.

SUMMER

JUNE➤ **Alberta: Jazz City International Festival** in Edmonton has 10 days of jazz concerts, workshops, and free outdoor events. **Ponoka Annual Stampede** professional rodeo attracts participants from across the continent. **Banff Festival of the Arts** (through August) showcases nearly 1,000 artists in music, dance, drama, comedy, and visual arts.

British Columbia: The **Canadian International Dragon Boat Festival,** in Vancouver, includes entertainment and the ancient "awakening the dragons" ritual of long, slender boats decorated with dragon heads.

Whistler Summer Festivals, through September, present daily street entertainment and a variety of music festivals at the ski and summer resort.

Manitoba: Winnipeg's **Red River Exhibition** features lumberjack contests, body-building shows, and an international band festival. Winnipeg **International Children's Festival** provides top national and international entertainment and activities.

Nova Scotia: The **International Blues Festival** draws music lovers to Halifax.

Ontario: Toronto's **Metro International Caravan** is an ethnic fair. **Changing of the Guard** begins at Ottawa's Parliament Buildings (through August).

Prince Edward Island: Charlottetown Festival Theatre offers concerts and musicals (through September). In Summerside the annual **Summerside Highland Gathering** kicks off a summer of concerts and "Come to the Ceilidh" evenings.

Québec: Some of the world's best drivers compete in the **Player's Grand Prix** in Montréal. Québec City hops with the **International Jazz Festival.** Beauport hosts the **International Children's Folklore Festival.**

Saskatchewan: Frontier Days Regional Fair and Rodeo, in Swift Current, is a community fair with parades, a horse show, and a rodeo. **Mosaic,** in Regina, celebrates cultures from around the world.

Yukon: The **Yukon International Festival of Storytelling,** in Whitehorse, draws storytellers from all over the North.

Northwest Territories: The **Midnight Classic Golf Tournament** in Yellowknife tees off at midnight on the first day of summer. The **Kingalik Jamboree** is a typical Inuit spring celebration, with a week of friendly contests from square dancing to duck plucking.

JULY➤ **Alberta: Ukrainian Pysanka Festival** in Vegreville celebrates with costumes and song and dance. **Calgary Exhibition and Stampede** is one of the most popular Canadian events and includes 10 days of western showmanship, hot-air balloon races, chuck-wagon races, agricultural shows, and crafts. **Edmonton's Klondike Days** celebrate the town's early frontier community with pancake breakfasts, gold panning, and raft races.

British Columbia: The **Symphony of Fire,** an international musical fireworks competition, blasts off over four evenings from a barge in English Bay in Vancouver.

Manitoba: At the **Winnipeg Folk Festival,** in Birds Hill Park, 24 km (15 mi) northeast of Winnipeg, country, bluegrass, folk, Acadian music, and jazz can be heard on 10 stages. **Manitoba Stampede and Exhibition** in Morris is an agricultural fair with rodeos and chuck-wagon races.

New Brunswick: Loyalist City Festival, in Saint John, celebrates the town's founding with parades, dancing, and sidewalk festivities. The **Shediac Lobster Festival** takes place in the town that calls itself the Lobster Capital of the World. There's an **Irish Festival** in Miramichi. The **New Brunswick Highland Games & Scottish Festival** is in Fredericton. In Edmunston the **Foire Brayonne** has music, cultural events, and sports.

Newfoundland and Labrador: The **Hangashore Folk Festival** is in Corner Brook; the **Exploits Valley Salmon Festival** in the Grand Falls area; the **Fish, Fun and Folk Festival** in Twillingate; and the **Conception Bay Folk Festival** in Carbonear. **Musicfest** in Stephenville celebrates music, from rock and roll to traditional Newfoundland. **Signal Hill Tattoo** in St. John's (through August) reenacts the final 1762 battle of the Seven Years' War between the British and the French. The **Burin Peninsula Festival of Folk Song and Dance** features traditional Newfoundland entertainment.

Nova Scotia: Antigonish Highland Games, staged annually since 1861, has Scottish music, dance, and such ancient sporting events as the caber toss. Halifax hosts the **Nova Scotia International Tattoo**. The **Atlantic Jazz Festival** is a Halifax highlight.

Ontario: Ottawa celebrates **Canada Day** (July 1) with entertainment and fireworks. The **Queen's Plate** Thoroughbred horse race takes place in Toronto. The two-week International **Freedom Festival** celebrates two nations' birthdays in Windsor and neighboring Detroit.The **Molson INDY** race roars through Toronto. **Caribana** festival celebrates Toronto's West Indian community. The **Glengarry Highland Games,** in Maxville, is North America's largest Highland gathering.

Prince Edward Island: The **Annual Outdoor Scottish Fiddle and Dance Festival** skirls through Richmond. Summerside's Lobster Carnival is a weeklong feast of lobster. Canada Day festivities abound on the first of the month.

Québec: Festival International de Jazz de Montréal draws more than 2,000 musicians from all over the world for this 11-day series. **Québec International Summer Festival** offers entertainment in the streets and parks of old Québec City. Montréal's **Juste pour Rire** (Just for Laughs) comedy festival features comics from around the world, in French and English. At **Festival Orford** international artists perform in Orford Park's music center (through August). **Matinée Ltd. International** spotlights the best male tennis players in Montréal.

Saskatchewan: *The Trial of Louis Riel*, in Regina, one of Canada's longest-running stage shows, reenacts the events surrounding the Northwest Rebellion of 1885 (late July through August). Shakespeare on the Saskatchewan Festival, in Saskatoon, has productions near the South Saskatchewan River (early July–late August).

Northwest Territories: The **Annual Great Northern Arts Festival** in Inuvik presents displays, workshops, live performances, and artist demonstrations for the region's premier cultural event. The **Midway Lake Festival** in Fort McPherson showcases musicians from across Canada's north and elsewhere in the country, who play alongside Dene drummers and folk and country artists.

AUGUST➤ **Alberta:** The **Fringe Theatre Festival,** in Edmonton, is one of the major festivals for alternative theater in North America.

British Columbia: Squamish Days Loggers Sports Festival draws loggers from around the world to compete in a series of incredible logging feats.

Manitoba: Folklorama, a large multicultural festival, sets up more than 40 pavilions throughout Winnipeg. The **National Ukrainian Festival,** in Dauphin, offers costumes, artifacts, exhibits, fiddling contests, dancing, and workshops. The **Icelandic Festival,** in Gimli, gathers the largest Icelandic community outside of Iceland. **Pioneer Days,** in Steinbach, celebrates the heritage of the Mennonites with demonstrations of threshing and baking, a parade, a horse show, and Mennonite foods.

New Brunswick: The **Miramichi Folk Song Festival** features traditional and contemporary folk songs steeped in Maritime lore. **Acadian Festival,** at Caraquet, celebrates Acadian heritage with folk singing and food. The **Chocolate**

Festival in St. Stephen includes suppers, displays, and children's events.

Newfoundland and Labrador: Gander's Festival of Flight celebrates this town as the aviation "Crossroads of the World," with dances, parades, and a folk festival. The **Folk Festival** in St. John's is an outstanding traditional music event.

Northwest Territories: The **South Slave Festival** in Fort Smith brings northerners and visitors together for a weekend of music and dancing.

Nova Scotia: Lunenburg holds the **Nova Scotia Fisheries Exhibition and Fishermen's Reunion.** The **Nova Scotia Gaelic Mod** in St. Ann's celebrates Scottish culture on the grounds of the only Gaelic college in North America. The **Halifax International Buskerfest** has daily outdoor shows by street performers and a food festival.

Ontario: Brantford's Six Nations Native Pageant celebrates Iroquois culture and history. The huge **Canadian National Exhibition** in Toronto lasts until Labor Day and has rides, displays, performances, and an air show.

Prince Edward Island: Old Home Week fills Charlottetown with nostalgia. An **International Hydroplane Regatta** brings speed to the Summerside waterfront.

Québec: Montréal hosts a **World Film Festival. St-Jean-sur-Richelieu's Hot Air Balloon Festival** is the largest gathering of hot-air balloons in Canada.

Saskatchewan: Buffalo Days Exhibition, in Regina, features rides, livestock judging, and horse racing.

AUTUMN

SEPTEMBER➤ **Alberta: Spruce Meadows Masters' Tournament,** in Calgary, is an international horse-jumping competition at one of North America's leading equestrian centers.

British Columbia: The **Vancouver International Film Festival** is a popular event.

Ontario: The **Canadian Open Golf Championship** takes place in Oakville. Toronto's **International Film Festival** salutes the world of film. St. Catharines toasts the

Niagara Grape and Wine Festival.

Prince Edward Island: Festival Acadien de la Région Evangeline is an agricultural fair with Acadian music, a parade, and lobster suppers, at Wellington Station.

Québec: Québec International Film Festival screens in Québec City. The **Gatineau Hot Air Balloon Festival** brings together hot-air balloons from across Canada, the United States, and Europe.

OCTOBER➤ **British Columbia:** The **Okanagan Wine Festival** takes place in the Okanagan-Similkameen area.

Nova Scotia: The 10-day **Celtic Colors International Festival** celebrates traditional music in 20 locations across Cape Breton.

Ontario: Kitchener–Waterloo's **Oktoberfest** attracts more than a half-million enthusiasts to its beer halls and tents.

Québec: The **Festival of Colors** celebrates foliage throughout the province.

NOVEMBER➤ **Ontario:** Toronto's **Royal Agricultural Winter Fair** draws exhibitors and contestants to the largest indoor agricultural fair and equestrian competition in the world.

2 Vancouver

The spectacular setting of cosmopolitan Vancouver, Canada's answer to San Francisco, has drawn people from around the world to settle here. The ocean and mountains form a dramatic backdrop to downtown's gleaming towers of commerce and make it easy to pursue all kinds of outdoor pleasures. You can trace the city's history in Gastown and Chinatown, savor the wilderness only blocks from the city center in Stanley Park, or dine on superb ethnic or Pacific Northwest cuisine before you sample the city's vibrant nightlife.

VANCOUVER IS A YOUNG CITY, even by North
American standards. Although 300 to 400 years
of settlement may make cities like Québec and
Halifax historically interesting, Vancouver's youthful vigor attracts people to its powerful elements that have not yet been ground down by
time. Vancouver is just over 100 years old; it was not yet a town in
1871, when British Columbia became part of the Canadian confederation. The city's history, such as it is, remains visible to the naked eye:
Eras are stacked east to west along the waterfront like some century-
old archaeological dig—from cobblestone late-Victorian Gastown to
shiny postmodern glass cathedrals of commerce.

Updated by
Sue Kernaghan

The Chinese were among the first to recognize the possibilities of Vancouver's setting. They came to British Columbia during the 1850s
seeking the gold that inspired them to name the province Gum-shan,
or Gold Mountain. As laborers they built the Canadian Pacific Railway, giving Vancouver's original townsite (the town and its surroundings) a purpose—one beyond the natural splendor that Royal Navy
captain George Vancouver admired during his lunchtime cruise around
its harbor on June 13, 1792. The transcontinental railroad, along with
the city's Great White Fleet of clipper ships, gave Vancouver a full week's
edge over the California ports in shipping tea and silk to New York at
the dawn of the 20th century.

Vancouver's natural charms are less scattered than those in many other
cities. On clear days, the mountains appear close enough to touch. Two
1,000-acre wilderness parks lie within the city limits. The salt water
of the Pacific and fresh water direct from the Rocky Mountain Trench
form the city's northern and southern boundaries.

Bring a healthy sense of reverence when you visit: Vancouver is a spiritual place. For its original inhabitants, the Coast Salish peoples, it was
the sacred spot where the mythical Thunderbird and Killer Whale
flung wind and rain all about the heavens during their epic battles—
how else to explain the coast's fits of meteorological temper? Devotees of a later religious tradition might worship in the lofty groves of
Stanley Park or in the fir and cedar interior of Christ Church Cathedral, the city's oldest church.

Today Vancouver, with a metropolitan area population of 1.8 million
people, is booming. A tremendous number of Asians have migrated
here, including many from Hong Kong. The mild climate, exquisite natural scenery, and thriving cultural scene also bring Canadians from the
East to British Columbia's business center. The number of visitors is
increasing, too, because of the city's scenic attractions and its proximity to outdoor activities. Many people get their first glimpse of Vancouver when catching an Alaskan cruise (Vancouver is the major port
of embarkation/disembarkation for these cruises), and almost all return at some point to spend more time here.

Vancouver has a level of nightlife possible only in a place where the
finer things in life have never been driven out to the suburbs and
where sidewalks have never rolled up at 5 PM. But you can find good
theater, accommodations, and dining in many places these days. Vancouver's real culture consists of its tall fir trees practically downtown
and its towering rock spires close by, the ocean at your doorstep, and
people from every corner of the earth all around you.

Pleasures and Pastimes

Dining
The gastronomical experience here is satisfyingly diverse; restaurants—from the bustling downtown area to trendy beachside neighborhoods—have enticing locales in addition to succulent cuisine. A new wave of Asian immigration and tourism has brought a proliferation of upscale Asian (Chinese, Japanese, Korean, Thai, and Vietnamese) restaurants, serving dishes that would be at home in their own leading cities. Cutting-edge restaurants currently perfecting and defining Pacific Northwest fare—including such homegrown regional favorites as salmon and oysters, accompanied by British Columbia and Washington State wines—have become some of the city's leading attractions.

The Great Outdoors
Mother Nature has truly blessed this city, surrounding it by verdant forests, towering mountains, coves, inlets, rivers, and the wide sea. Biking, hiking, skiing and snowboarding, rafting, and sailing are among the many outdoor activities available within minutes of anywhere in the city. Whether you prefer to relax on a beach by yourself or join a kayaking tour with an outfitter, Vancouver has plenty to offer.

Nightlife and the Arts
The best arts and entertainment, and the most enthusiastic audiences for music, theater, film, and comedy, are here during various festivals, most held between June and October. Live theater and dance are both healthy. Two fairly new performing arts centers (the Ford and the Chan) provide venues for large touring shows, and many smaller theaters run shows year-round. There are also symphonic, opera, and ballet companies. The city has a fair amount of live music—from jazz and blues to head-bangers' heavy metal and everything in between. Visitors may find the nightlife a bit dry, though. Byzantine liquor laws have created such a shortage of pubs and bars that many places charge admission. The situation may ease if the city council decides to allow a number of new pubs and cabarets to open.

EXPLORING VANCOUVER

Vancouver may be small when compared to New York or even San Francisco, but it still takes time to explore. You can see a lot of the city in two days, but a day or two more will give you time to explore sights in the larger Vancouver area and the surrounding countryside.

Many sights of interest are concentrated in the hemmed-in peninsula of downtown Vancouver. The heart of Vancouver—which includes the downtown area, Stanley Park, the West End high-rise residential neighborhood, and the newly refurbished Yaletown area—sits on this peninsula bordered by English Bay and the Pacific Ocean to the west; by False Creek, the inlet home to Granville Island, to the south; and by Burrard Inlet, the working port of the city, to the north, past which loom the North Shore mountains. The oldest part of the city—Gastown and Chinatown—lies at the edge of Burrard Inlet, around Main Street, which runs north–south and is roughly the dividing line between the east side and the west side. All the avenues, which are numbered, have east and west designations. One note about printed Vancouver street addresses: Suite numbers often appear *before* the street number, followed by a hyphen.

You'll find places of interest elsewhere in the city, either on the North Shore across Burrard Inlet, south of downtown in the Kitsilano area across English Bay, or in the Granville Island area across False Creek.

Then, too, there's Whistler, a renowned winter and summer resort a few hours' drive north of Vancouver.

Numbers in the text correspond to numbers in the margin and on the Vancouver, Downtown Vancouver, Stanley Park, and Granville Island maps.

Great Itineraries

IF YOU HAVE 1–2 DAYS

If you have only one day in Vancouver, start with an early morning walk, bike, or shuttle ride through Stanley Park to see the Vancouver Aquarium and other sights, such as Second Beach on English Bay. Allow at least two hours to take in the exhibits at the aquarium and another hour or two for a tour through the park. In the early afternoon, your visit to the park will conclude in the West End; head northeast on Denman Street to Robson Street to lunch and meander on foot through the trendy shops, and then walk northeast on Burrard Street to view the many buildings of architectural interest. Stops along the way at the Vancouver Art Gallery, the Canadian Craft Museum, and the Lookout at Harbour Centre will make for a full day of sightseeing.

Day 2 can follow a more leisurely paced walking tour of the shops, eateries, and cobblestone streets of Gastown, the original site of Vancouver, and Chinatown, the third-largest Chinatown in North America. Take a camera to capture the false-front buildings and the steam-powered clock in Gastown and the brightly painted buildings, Chinese gates, and the Dr. Sun Yat-Sen Gardens in Chinatown. From Chinatown it's a short walk or bus or cab ride to the trendy new warehouse district of Yaletown, where art galleries and brew pubs have set up shop along some of Vancouver's most atmospheric streets.

IF YOU HAVE 3–4 DAYS

If you have another day or two to tour Vancouver and have followed the itinerary above, head to the south side of False Creek and English Bay on Day 3 to delve into the many boutiques, dining outlets, theaters, and the public market on Granville Island. Buses and ferries provide easy transit, and there is plenty of parking if you drive; Granville Island is best toured on foot. A short walk or ferry ride to the west takes you to the beachfront neighborhood of Kitsilano. Here you'll find the Vancouver Museum (showcasing the city's history), the Pacific Space Centre (focusing on outer space), and the Vancouver Maritime Museum, all right next to one of the city's liveliest beaches.

On Day 4, a scenic waterfront drive will take you to the University of British Columbia, home to the Museum of Anthropology, which houses fantastic totem poles, canoes, jewelry, costumes, and other art of Pacific Northwest native peoples and other groups, and the Nitobe Memorial Gardens, a traditional Japanese strolling garden. Garden enthusiasts will also want to visit VanDusen Botanical Garden (55 ornamental acres displaying the abundant plant life of the Pacific Northwest), and Queen Elizabeth Park (outstanding views of downtown), both south of downtown in residential Vancouver.

Thrill-seekers might prefer to head across the Lions Gate Bridge to the North Shore mountains, where they can swing high above the Capilano River on a suspension bridge and ride the Skyride for a panoramic view of Vancouver from the top of Grouse Mountain.

IF YOU HAVE 5–7 DAYS

If you have another two days to explore and you've already seen the sights in the two itineraries above, don't miss a side trip to beautiful Whistler, in the mountains north of the city. Although it's ranked as one of the top ski destinations in the world, this growing resort has an ever-expanding array of outdoor activities and festivals that make it worth a visit any time of year. The 2½-hour drive here on the scenic Sea to Sky Highway takes you from glorious seaside vistas into the heart of lush alpine country.

Robson to the Waterfront

Museums and buildings of architectural and historical significance are the primary draw in downtown Vancouver. Plenty of fine shopping provides breaks (or distractions, depending on your perspective) along the way. Vancouver is a new city, when compared to others, but still rich in culture and diversity.

A Good Walk

If you're a shopaholic, coffee junkie, and/or people-watcher, begin your tour of Vancouver on **Robson Street** ①, also referred to as Vancouver's Rodeo Drive because of the sheer number of see-and-be-seen sidewalk cafés and high-end boutiques. Start at the cross street of Bute or Thurlow and follow Robson southeast to Hornby to reach **Robson Square** ②, a central park area that encompasses landscaped walkways, government office buildings, and the **Vancouver Art Gallery** ③. On the north side of the gallery across Hornby Street sits the **Hotel Vancouver** ④, its copper, château-style roof making it one of the city's best-known landmarks. Cathedral Place, a spectacular office tower, stands across the street on the corner of Hornby and Georgia. Three large sculptures of nurses at the corners of the building are replicas of the statues that ornamented the Art Deco Georgia Medical-Dental Building, the site's previous structure.

West of Cathedral Place, a walkway leads to a peaceful green courtyard, home to the **Canadian Craft Museum** ⑤, one of the first national cultural facilities dedicated to crafts. Farther to the left of Cathedral Place is the Gothic-style **Christ Church Cathedral** ⑥, the oldest church in Vancouver. If you walk north down Burrard Street toward the water for three blocks, on the opposite side of the street is the **Marine Building** ⑦, with terra-cotta bas-reliefs that make it one of Canada's best examples of Art Deco architecture.

Cross Burrard Street and follow Hastings Street east to the elaborate **Vancouver Club** ⑧, the private haunt of the city's top business movers and shakers. This marks the start of the old financial district, which runs southeast along Hastings, where temple-style banks, investment houses, and businesspeople's clubs survive as evidence of the city's sophisticated architectural advances prior to World War I. Until the period between 1966 and 1972, when the first of the bank towers and underground malls on West Georgia Street was developed, this was Canada's westernmost business terminus. **Sinclair Centre** ⑨, at Hastings and Howe streets, is a magnificently restored complex of government buildings that now houses offices and retail shops. Across Granville Street you'll find the former headquarters of the **Canadian Imperial Bank of Commerce (CIBC)** ⑩, now also known as the Birk's Building. The more Gothic **Royal Bank** ⑪ stands directly across the street. Across Seymour Street is **Lookout at Harbour Centre** ⑫, where you can ride 50 stories up to see a panoramic view of Vancouver.

Head northeast down Seymour Street toward Burrard Inlet and you'll find the **Waterfront Station** ⑬, a former Canadian Pacific Railway passenger terminal and now a SeaBus and SkyTrain station (☞ Getting Around *in* Vancouver A to Z, *below*). Here you can catch a 13-minute

20

Vancouver *(Boxes Refer to Detail Maps)*

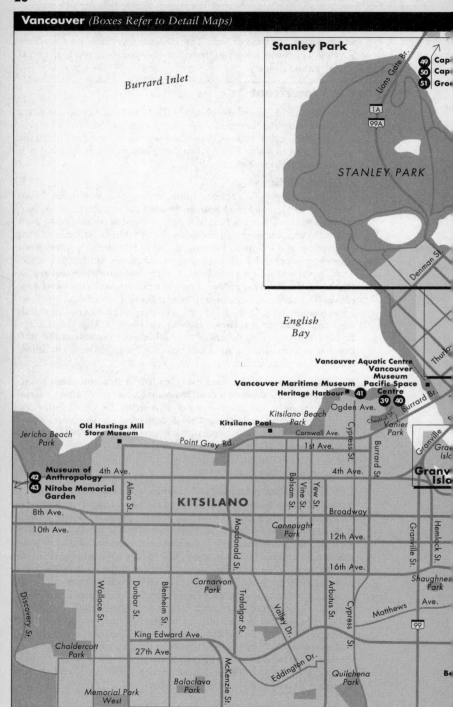

Stanley Park

49 Cap
50 Cap
51 Gro

Burrard Inlet

1A
99A

STANLEY PARK

Lions Gate Br.

Dennman St.

Thurlo

English
Bay

Vancouver Aquatic Centre
Vancouver
Museum
Vancouver Maritime Museum   Pacific Space
Heritage Harbour   41   Centre   Burrard Br.
Ogden Ave.   39   40

Kitsilano Beach   Chestnut St.   Vanier
Park   Park

Kitsilano Pool   Cornwall Ave.

Cypress St.

Granville

Gra
Isla

Old Hastings Mill   1st Ave.   Burrard St.   Granv
Store Museum   Point Grey Rd.   Isla

Jericho Beach
Park

Museum of   4th Ave.   4th Ave.
42 Anthropology
43 Nitobe Memorial   Alma St.   Balsam St.
Garden   Yew St.
Vine St.

KITSILANO   Broadway   Granville St.

Hemlock St.

8th Ave.   Connaught
10th Ave.   Park   12th Ave.

Macdonald St.   16th Ave.   Shaughnes
Park

Carnarvon   Arbutus St.   Ave.
Park

Wallace St.   Trafalgar St.   Matthews   99
Dunbar St.   Cypress St.
Blenheim St.   Valley Dr.

King Edward Ave.

Discovery St.   27th Ave.   McKenzie St.   Quilchena   Be
Park
Chaldercott   Eddington Dr.
Park

Balaclava
Memorial Park   Park
West

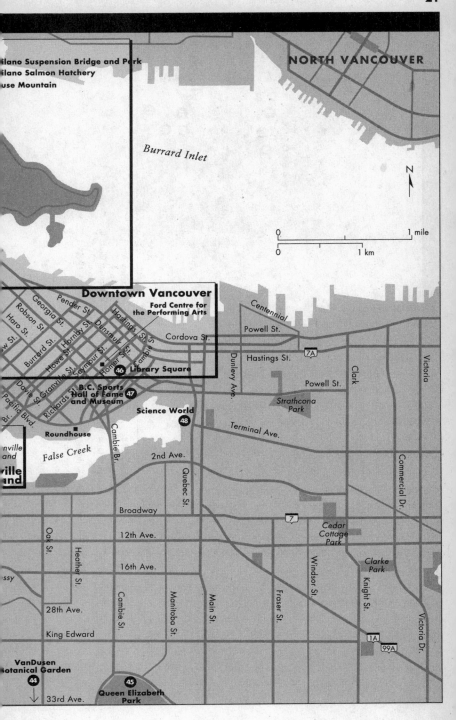

...ilano Suspension Bridge and Park
...ilano Salmon Hatchery
...use Mountain

NORTH VANCOUVER

Burrard Inlet

N

0 — 1 mile
0 — 1 km

Downtown Vancouver
**Ford Centre for
the Performing Arts**

Pender St.
Georgia St.
Robson St.
Haro St.
...w St.
Burrard St.
Hornby St.
Howe St.
Dunsmuir St.
Hastings St.
Seymour St.
Cambie
Homer St.

Cordova St.

Centennial

Powell St.

Hastings St.

7A

Clark

Victoria

Davie St.
Granville St.
Richards St.
Pacific Blvd.
...Br.

46 **Library Square**

**B.C. Sports
Hall of Fame
and Museum** **47**

Powell St.

Strathcona
Park

Science World
48

Roundhouse

Dunlevy Ave.

...nville
...and
**...ll...
...nd**

False Creek

Cambie Br.

Quebec St.

Terminal Ave.

Commercial Dr.

2nd Ave.

Broadway

Oak St.

Heather St.

Cambie St.

Manitoba St.

Main St.

12th Ave.

16th Ave.

...ssy

28th Ave.

King Edward

Fraser St.

Windsor St.

Knight St.

7

Cedar
Cottage
Park

Clarke
Park

Victoria Dr.

1A
99A

**VanDusen
Botanical Garden**

44

33rd Ave.

45

**Queen Elizabeth
Park**

22

Downtown Vancouver

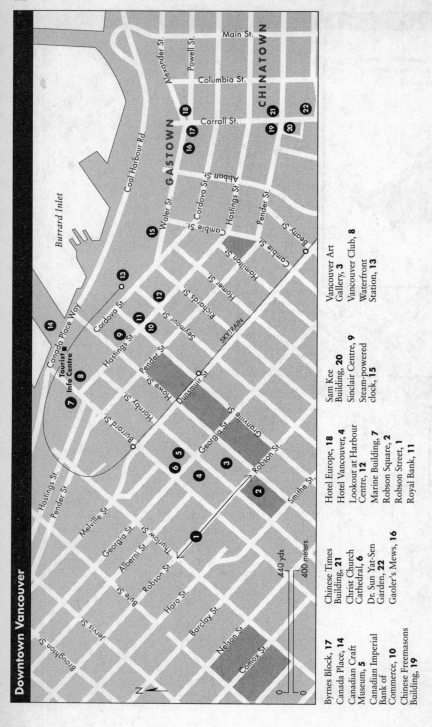

Byrnes Block, **17**
Canada Place, **14**
Canadian Craft
Museum, **5**
Canadian Imperial
Bank of
Commerce, **10**
Chinese Freemasons
Building, **19**

Chinese Times
Building, **21**
Christ Church
Cathedral, **6**
Dr. Sun Yat-Sen
Garden, **22**
Gaoler's Mews, **16**

Hotel Europe, **18**
Hotel Vancouver, **4**
Lookout at Harbour
Centre, **12**
Marine Building, **7**
Robson Square, **2**
Robson Street, **1**
Royal Bank, **11**

Sam Kee
Building, **20**
Sinclair Centre, **9**
Steam-powered
clock, **15**

Vancouver Art
Gallery, **3**
Vancouver Club, **8**
Waterfront
Station, **13**

SeaBus trip across the harbor to the waterfront public market at Lonsdale Quay (☞ Shopping, *below*).

To continue with the walking tour, leave by the station's west staircase and wander across Granville Square Plaza to the SkyTrain station at the far side. You'll face the soaring canopies of **Canada Place** ⑭, site of Vancouver's primary cruise-ship pier, the Trade and Convention Center, and the Pan Pacific Hotel, with its three-story lobby, waterfall, and totem poles. Here you can stop for a snack in one of the dining outlets on the water or catch a film at the IMAX theater. Stop off at the **Vancouver Tourist Info Centre** across the street (next door to the Waterfront Centre Hotel) to pick up brochures on other attractions and events before leaving the area.

TIMING

This walking tour, with time to soak in the intriguing architecture along the route, will take two to three hours if you're not drawn into all the shops along the way. Allow about an hour at the Canadian Craft Museum, and another two at the Vancouver Art Gallery.

Sights to See

⑭ **Canada Place.** Originally built on an old cargo pier to be the off-site Canadian pavilion in Expo '86, Canada Place was later converted into Vancouver's **Trade and Convention Center.** It is dominated at the shore end by the luxurious **Pan Pacific Hotel** (☞ Lodging, *below*), with its spectacular three-story lobby and waterfall. The fabric roof shaped like 10 sails that covers the convention space has become a landmark of Vancouver's skyline. Below is a cruise-ship facility, and at the north end are the CN IMAX theater, a restaurant, and an outdoor performance space. A promenade along the pier's west side has views of the Burrard Inlet harbor and Stanley Park. ☒ *999 Canada Pl.,* ☎ *604/775–8687, 604/682–4629 for IMAX theater.*

❺ **Canadian Craft Museum.** Opened at this location in 1992, the museum is one of the first national cultural facilities dedicated to crafts, both functional and decorative. Craft embodies the human need for artistic expression in everyday life, and examples here range from elegantly carved utensils with decorative handles to colorful hand-spun and handwoven garments. The two-level museum has exhibits, lectures, and a museum shop that specializes in Canadian crafts. The restful courtyard is a quiet place to take a break. ☒ *639 Hornby St. (also accessible from 925 W. Georgia St.),* ☎ *604/687–8266.* ☞ *$4; Thurs. evenings 5–9 by donation.* ☉ *June–Aug., Mon.–Wed. and Fri.–Sat. 10–5, Thurs. 10–9, Sun. noon–5; Sept.–May, Mon. and Wed. 10–5, Thurs. 10–9, Fri.–Sat. 10–5, Sun. noon–5.*

❿ **Canadian Imperial Bank of Commerce (CIBC).** Built between 1906 and 1908, the former headquarters of one of Vancouver's oldest and most powerful chartered banks has columns, arches, and details that reflect a typically Roman influence. It now houses Birk's, a jewelry store. The clock on the corner is a Vancouver landmark that Birk's brought along when it moved in. ☒ *698 W. Hastings St.*

❻ **Christ Church Cathedral.** This tiny church, built in 1889, is the oldest in Vancouver. Constructed in Gothic style with buttresses and pointed-arch windows, it looks like the parish church of an English village from the outside. In contrast, the interior of local Douglas fir and cedar is thoroughly Canadian. The stained glass is stunning, and the church has excellent acoustics for the choral evensong, carols, and Gregorian chants frequently sung here. ☒ *690 Burrard St.,* ☎ *604/682–3848.* ☉ *Weekdays 10–4.*

④ Hotel Vancouver. Completed in 1939, the Hotel Vancouver (☞ Lodging, *below*) is one of the last railway-built hotels (the final one was the Chateau Whistler, in 1989). It is built in the château style, with details reminiscent of a medieval French castle, that has been incorporated into hotels in almost every major Canadian city. The depression slowed construction, which began in 1937, and the hotel was finished only in time for the visit of King George VI in 1939. During the 1960s the hotel was unfortunately modernized, but a refurbishment in 1996 was more in keeping with the spirit of what is the most recognizable roof on Vancouver's skyline. The exterior of the building has carvings of malevolent-looking gargoyles at the corners, an ornate chimney, native chiefs on the Hornby Street side, and an assortment of grotesque mythological figures. ✉ *900 W. Georgia St.,* ☎ *604/684–3131.*

⑫ Lookout at Harbour Centre. Resembling a flying saucer stuck atop a highrise, the Harbour Centre and its 553-ft-high lookout have one of the best views in Vancouver. A glass elevator whizzes you up 50 stories to a circular observation deck with a 360-degree view of the city. Guides will point out the sights (on a clear day, you can see Vancouver Island) and tickets are good until closing time, so you can return after dark. A restaurant on the top floor revolves once an hour; the elevator is free for diners. ✉ *555 W. Hastings St.,* ☎ *604/689–0421.* ✈ *$8.* ☯ *May– Aug., daily 8:30 AM–10:30 PM; Sept.–Apr., daily 9–9.*

⑦ Marine Building. Constructed in 1930, this Art Deco building is ornamented with terra-cotta bas-reliefs depicting the history of transportation: airships, steamships, locomotives, and submarines. These motifs were once considered radical and modernistic adornments, because most buildings were still using classical or Gothic ornamentation. From the east, the Marine Building is reflected in bronze by 999 West Hastings, and from the southeast it is mirrored in silver by the Canadian Imperial Bank of Commerce. Step inside for a look at the Art Deco interior; then walk to the corner of Hastings and Hornby streets for the best view of the building. ✉ *355 Burrard St.*

② Robson Square. Completed in 1979 and designed by architect Arthur Erickson to be *the* gathering place of downtown Vancouver, Robson Square links a courthouse complex and the ☞ **Vancouver Art Gallery.** Government offices and law courts are woven together by landscaped walkways. An ice-skating rink (used for ballroom dancing, public chess tournaments, political protests, and the occasional concert in summer) and restaurants occupy the below-street level. ✉ *Bordered by Howe, Hornby, Robson, and Smithe Sts.*

① Robson Street. Whatever you do in Vancouver, you'll end up here at some point. Linking downtown to the West End, Robson Street is Vancouver's shopping (☞ Shopping, *below*), strolling, and cruising artery. Even to those without a gold card, the section between Jervis and Burrard streets is compelling. The shops—Gap, Marks and Spencer, and the like—may be like those elsewhere, but the café-lounging, window-shopping scene draws crowds day and night. The street is also known as Robsonstrasse because of its European flavor.

⑪ Royal Bank. Gothic in style, this building constructed between 1929 and 1931 was intended to be half of a symmetrical building that was never completed due to the Depression. Striking, though, is the magnificent hall, reminiscent of a European cathedral. The building is still a bank. ✉ *685 W. Hastings St.*

⑨ Sinclair Centre. Outstanding Vancouver architect Richard Henriquez has knitted four government office buildings (built between 1905 and 1939) into Sinclair Centre, an office-retail complex. The two Hastings

Street buildings—the 1905 **Post Office** with the elegant clock tower and the 1911 **Winch Building**—are linked with the **Post Office Extension** and **Customs Examining Warehouse** to the north. Painstaking and very costly restoration involved finding master masons—the original terrazzo suppliers in Europe—and uncovering and refurbishing the pressed-metal ceilings. ✉ *757 W. Hastings St.,* ☎ *604/666–4438.*

❸ Vancouver Art Gallery. The city's art museum has sculpture and modern art, as well as some native works, but the most notable permanent collection contains works by artist Emily Carr (1871–1945). Born in Victoria, Carr shocked middle-class Victorian society by running off to paint the wilderness around her. Her work speaks of mysticism and danger—no pretty landscapes here—and Carr did much to record the passing of the area's native cultures. Her totems are haunting. The museum was a classical-style 1911 courthouse until architect Arthur Erickson converted it to a spacious gallery in 1983. The Gallery Café has imaginative snacks and a peaceful terrace; the Gallery Shop has a great collection of prints and cards. You can visit both without buying a ticket to the gallery. ✉ *750 Hornby St.,* ☎ *604/662–4719.* ☞ *$9.50; Thurs. 5–9 by donation (minimum $3).* ☉ *Apr.–Oct., Mon.–Wed. and Fri. 10–6, Thurs. 10–9, Sat. 10–5, Sun. noon–5; Nov.–Mar., Wed. and Fri. 10–6, Thurs. 10–9, Sat. 10–5, Sun. noon–5.*

❽ Vancouver Club. Architects George Lister Thornton Sharp and Charles Joseph Thompson, the brains behind many city landmarks including the original University of British Columbia, built this elite private club between 1912 and 1914. Its architecture evokes that of private clubs in England inspired by Italian Renaissance palaces. The Vancouver Club is still the private haunt of city businesspeople. ✉ *915 W. Hastings St. Closed to the public.*

Vancouver Tourist Info Centre. Here you'll find brochures and personnel to answer questions (☞ Visitor Information *in* Vancouver A to Z, *below*). ✉ *200 Burrard St.,* ☎ *604/683–2000.*

⓭ Waterfront Station. This former Canadian Pacific Railway passenger terminal was constructed between 1912 and 1914 as the western terminus for Canada's transcontinental railway. After Canada's railways merged, the station became obsolete until a 1978 renovation turned it into an office-retail complex and SeaBus terminal. Murals in the waiting rooms (now used by SkyTrain, SeaBus, and West Coast Express passengers) show the scenery travelers once saw on journeys across Canada. ✉ *601 W. Cordova St.,* ☎ *604/521–0400 for BC Transit.*

Chinatown and Gastown

Gastown is where Vancouver originated after smooth talker "Gassy" Jack Deighton arrived at Burrard Inlet in 1867 with his native wife, some whiskey, and few amenities and managed to con local loggers and trappers into building him a saloon for a barrel of whiskey. When the transcontinental train arrived in 1887, Gastown became the transfer point for trade with the Far East and was soon crowded with hotels and warehouses. The Klondike gold rush encouraged further development until 1912, when the "Golden Years" ended. From the 1930s to the 1950s hotels were converted into rooming houses, and the warehouse district shifted elsewhere. The neglected area gradually became run down. However, both Gastown and Chinatown were declared historic districts in the late 1970s and have been revitalized. Gastown is now chockablock with boutiques, cafés, loft apartments, and souvenir shops.

The Chinese were among the first inhabitants of Vancouver, and some of the oldest buildings in the city are in Chinatown, the third-largest such area in North America. There was already a sizable Chinese community in British Columbia because of the 1858 Cariboo gold rush in central British Columbia, but the greatest influx from China came in the 1880s, during construction of the Canadian Pacific Railway, when 15,000 laborers were brought in. Even while doing the hazardous work of blasting the rail bed through the Rocky Mountains, however, the Chinese were discriminated against. The Anti-Asiatic Riots of 1907 stopped growth in Chinatown for 50 years, and immigration from China was discouraged by more and more restrictive policies, climaxing in a $500 head tax during the 1920s. In the 1960s the city council planned bulldozer urban renewal for Strathcona, the residential part of Chinatown. Fortunately, the project was halted, and today Chinatown is an expanding, vital neighborhood fueled by investment from immigrants from Hong Kong. It is best to view the buildings in Chinatown from the south side of Pender Street, where the Chinese Cultural Center stands. From here you'll see important details that adorn the upper stories. The style of architecture in Vancouver's Chinatown is patterned on that of Canton and isn't seen in any other Canadian city. At press time, the Chinese Cultural Centre Museum and Archives (⌧ 555 Columbia St., ☎ 604/687–0282), dedicated to promoting an understanding of Chinese-Canadian history and culture, had just opened.

A Good Walk

Pick up Water Street at Richards Street and head east into Gastown. At the corner of Water and Cambie streets, you can see and hear the world's first **steam-powered clock** ⑮ (it chimes on the quarter hour). From the clock, cross Water Street, continue east past Abbott Street, and watch for **Gaoler's Mews** ⑯, a street tucked behind 12 Water Street. Two buildings of historical and architectural note are the **Byrnes Block** ⑰ on the corner of Water and Carrall streets and the **Hotel Europe** ⑱ at Powell and Alexander streets. A statue of Gassy Jack stands on the west side of Maple Tree Square, at the intersection of Water, Powell, Alexander, and Carrall streets, where he built his first saloon.

From Maple Tree Square it's only three blocks south on Carrall Street to Pender Street, where Chinatown begins. However, this route passes through a rough part of town, so it's far safer to backtrack two blocks on Water Street through Gastown to Cambie Street, then head south to Pender and east to Carrall. The corner of Carrall and Pender streets, now the western boundary of Chinatown, is one of the neighborhood's most historic and photogenic spots. It's here that you'll find the **Chinese Freemasons Building** ⑲ (circa 1901) and the **Sam Kee Building** ⑳ (circa 1913), and, directly across Carrall Street, the **Chinese Times Building** ㉑ (circa 1902). Across Pender is the first living classical Chinese garden built outside China, the **Dr. Sun Yat-Sen Garden** ㉒. It's tucked behind the Chinese Cultural Center, which houses exhibition space, classrooms, and the occasional mah-jongg tournament. Finish up by poking around in the open-front markets and import shops that line several blocks of Pender running east.

TIMING

The walk itself will take about an hour depending on your pace; allow extra time for the guided tour of the garden in Chinatown. Daylight hours are best, although shops and restaurants are open into the night in both areas. There are few traffic signals for safe crossings in Gastown, so avoid commuter rush hours.

Sights to See

⑰ Byrnes Block. This building was constructed on the site of Gassy Jack Deighton's second saloon after the 1886 Great Fire. The date is just visible at the top of the building above the door where it says "Herman Block," which was its name for a short time. ⊠ *2 Water St.*

⑲ Chinese Freemasons Building. Two completely different facades distinguish a fascinating structure on the northwest corner of Pender and Carrall streets: The side facing Pender presents a fine example of Cantonese-imported recessed balconies; the Carrall Street side displays the standard Victorian style common throughout the British Empire. It was in this building that Dr. Sun Yat-Sen hid for months from the agents of the Manchu dynasty while he raised funds for its overthrow, which he accomplished in 1911. ⊠ *3 W. Pender St.*

㉑ Chinese Times Building. Police officers could hear the clicking sounds of clandestine mah-jongg games played after sunset on the building's hidden mezzanine floor. Attempts by vice squads to enforce restrictive policies against the Chinese gamblers proved fruitless, because police were unable to find the players. The building, on the north side of Pender Street just east of Carrall, dates to 1902. Meandering down Pender Street, you can still hear mah-jongg games going on behind the colorful facades of other buildings in Chinatown. ⊠ *1 E. Pender St.*

★ **㉒ Dr. Sun Yat-Sen Garden.** The garden was built in 1985 by 52 artisans from Suzhou, the Garden City of the People's Republic. It incorporates design elements and traditional materials from several of that city's centuries-old private gardens. As you walk through the garden, remember that no power tools, screws, or nails were used in the construction. Forty-five-minute guided tours are offered throughout the day; telephone for times. A free public park is next door. ⊠ *578 Carrall St.,* ☎ *604/689–7133.* ⊡ *$5.25.* ☼ *June 15–Sept. 15, daily 10–7:30; Sept. 16–Apr. 30, daily 10–4:30; May 1–June 14, daily 10–6.*

⑯ Gaoler's Mews. Once the site of the city's first civic buildings—the constable's cabin and customs house, and a two-cell log jail—today this atmospheric cobblestone street with antique lighting is home to architectural offices. ⊠ *Behind 12 Water St.*

⑱ Hotel Europe. Once billed as the best hotel in the city, this circa 1908 flatiron building was Vancouver's first reinforced concrete structure. Designed as a functional commercial building, the hotel lacks ornamentation and fine detail, making it unusually utilitarian for the time. ⊠ *43 Powell St.*

⑳ Sam Kee Building. Constructed in 1913, this 6-ft-wide building is recognized by *Ripley's Believe It or Not!* as the narrowest building in the world. Its bay windows overhang the street, and the basement burrows under the sidewalk. ⊠ *8 W. Pender St.*

⑮ Steam-powered clock. The world's first steam clock is powered by an underground steam system. Every quarter hour the whistle blows, and on the hour a huge cloud of steam spews from the clock. It was built by Ray Saunders of Landmark Clocks (⊠ 123 Cambie St., ☎ 604/669–3525). ⊠ *Water and Cambie Sts.*

Stanley Park

A 1,000-acre wilderness park just blocks from the downtown section of a major city is both a rarity and a treasure. In the 1860s, because of a threat of American invasion, the area that is now Stanley Park was designated a military reserve (though it was never needed). When the city of Vancouver was incorporated in 1886, the council's first act was to request that the land be set aside for a park. In 1888 permission was granted and the grounds were named Stanley Park after Lord Stanley, then governor general of Canada.

A morning or afternoon in Stanley Park gives you a capsule tour of Vancouver that includes beaches, the ocean, the harbor, Douglas fir and cedar forests, and a good look at the North Shore mountains. To get here, drive down Georgia Street to the park entrance, or take a BC Transit bus. From Hastings and Granville streets downtown, catch a Stanley Park Bus 35 or 135 (year-round), or a Stanley Park Bus 23 or 123 (June to September only) to the Stanley Park loop on Lost Lagoon. You can also catch North Vancouver Bus 240, 241, 242, 246, or 247 from anywhere on Georgia Street to the park entrance at Georgia and Chilco streets.

The most popular ways to get around Stanley Park—by bicycle, foot, car, or the new Stanley Park Shuttle—take different routes, but all reach the main sights. A bike, available for rent on Denman Street, near the park entrance (☞ Biking *in* Outdoor Activities and Sports, *below*), gives access to the seawall path—a 9-km (5½-mi) flat, paved shoreline route popular with walkers, cyclists, and in-line skaters—and to other car-free zones within the park. Cyclists must ride in a counterclockwise direction and stay on their side of the path. Walkers, of course, have the run of the park. Many sights, including the aquarium, are within easy walking distance of the bus loop. If you have the energy, a walk around the seawall makes a classic half-day hike.

The **Stanley Park Shuttle** (☎ 604/257–8400), operating daily 9:30–6 between mid-May and mid-September, provides frequent (15 minute intervals), free or low-cost transportation between 14 major park sites and to and from parking lots at the park entrance. An easy place to pick it up is the park entrance at the foot of Georgia Street.

A driving tour of the park is a good option between September and May, when the shuttles aren't running and there's little competition for parking. At other times, it's best to avoid driving. Stanley Park Drive goes one way, counterclockwise, but the park roads do change and can be confusing; a turnoff could land you on the bridge and across the bay. Parking is available at or near all major park sights, although there's never enough to accommodate all summertime visitors. A $5 ticket allows you to park all day and to move between lots.

For a more offbeat way to see the park, try **Stanley Park Horse Drawn Tours** (☞ Guided Tours *in* Vancouver A to Z, *below*). One-hour tours leave every 20–30 minutes from the information booth on Stanley Park Drive.

A Good Tour

If you're walking or biking, start at the foot of Alberni Street beside Lost Lagoon. Bikers should go through the underpass and veer right, following the cycle path markings, to the seawall. If you're driving, enter the park at the foot of Georgia Street, keep to your right, and go under an underpass. This will put you on Stanley Park Drive—a scenic route following the circumference of the park. Either way, the old wood structure that you pass on your right is the Vancouver Rowing Club, a private athletic club established in 1903. On your left, watch for an information booth (open March 15–October 31) and the turnoff to the **Vancouver Aquarium** ㉓ and the **Miniature Railway and Children's Farmyard** ㉔.

Continuing along Stanley Park Drive or the seawall, the next thing you'll pass is the Royal Vancouver Yacht Club. About ½ km (⅓ mi) farther

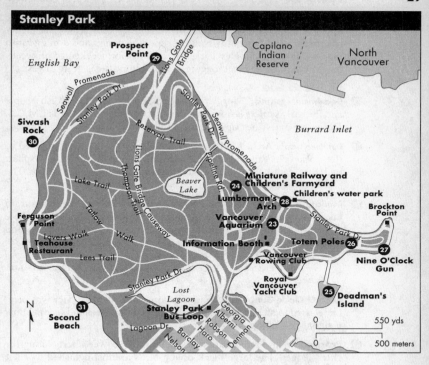

along is the causeway to **Deadman's Island** ㉕. The **totem poles** ㉖, which are a bit farther down the drive and slightly inland on your left, make a popular photo stop. Just ahead at the water's edge is the **Nine O'-Clock Gun** ㉗. To the north is Brockton Point and its small lighthouse and foghorn (cyclists and walkers will pass too close underneath to see it). At km 3 (mi 2) of the drive is **Lumberman's Arch** ㉘, a log archway. A children's water park is across the road. Cyclists and walkers can turn off here for a shortcut back to the aquarium, the Miniature Railway and Children's Farmyard, and the park entrance.

About 2 km (1 mi) farther along is the Lions Gate Bridge. Here drivers and cyclists part company. Cyclists ride under the bridge and past the cormorants' nests tucked beneath **Prospect Point** ㉙. Drivers gain elevation to pass over the bridge and reach a viewpoint and café at the top of Prospect Point. Both routes then continue around to the English Bay side of the park and its sandy beaches. The imposing rock just offshore is **Siwash Rock** ㉚, the focus of a native legend.

The next attraction along the seawall is the large heated pool at **Second Beach** ㉛. If you're walking or cycling, you can take a shortcut back to Lost Lagoon by walking along the perpendicular road behind the pool, which cuts into the park. The wood footbridge that's ahead will lead you to a path along the south side of the lagoon to your starting point at the foot of Alberni or Georgia Street. If you continue along the seawall, you will emerge into a high-rise residential neighborhood, the **West End.** You can walk back to Alberni Street along Denman Street, which has places to stop for coffee or a drink.

TIMING

If you're driving, take the time to stop and get a better look or take pictures. With that advice in mind, expect a driving tour to take about an hour. Your biking time will depend on your speed, but with stops to see the sights, allow several hours. Add at least two hours to see the aquarium, and you've filled a half- to full-day tour. There are plenty of other trails if you enjoy walking, but take a map and don't go into the woods alone. Stanley Park gets crowded on weekends; on weekday afternoons the local jogging and biking traffic is at its lowest.

Sights to See

25 **Deadman's Island.** A former burial ground for the local Salish people and the early settlers is now a small naval training base called H.M.C.S. *Discovery* and is not open to the public.

28 **Lumberman's Arch.** Made of logs, this large archway is dedicated to the workers in Vancouver's first industry. Beside the arch is an asphalt path that leads back to Lost Lagoon and the Vancouver Aquarium. The children's water park across the road is popular in summer.

24 **Miniature Railway and Children's Farmyard.** A child-size steam train takes kids and adults on a ride through the woods. Next door is a whole farmyard full of tame, pettable critters, including goats, rabbits, and guinea pigs. ⊠ *Off Pipeline Rd. in Stanley Park,* ☎ *604/257–8530.* ☞ *$2.25 for each site.* ☉ *Apr. 2–Sept., daily 11–4; Oct.–Dec. 4 and Jan. 4–Apr. 1, weekends 11–4; Dec. 5–12, daily 5–9; Dec. 13–Jan. 3, daily 2–9.*

27 **Nine O'Clock Gun.** This cannonlike apparatus by the water was originally used to alert fishermen to a curfew ending weekend fishing; now it signals 9 o'clock every night.

29 **Prospect Point.** Here cormorants build their seaweed nests along the cliff's ledges. The large black diving birds are distinguished by their long necks and beaks; when not nesting, they often perch atop floating logs or boulders. Another bird found along the park's shore is the beautiful great blue heron, which reaches up to 4 ft tall and has a wingspan of 6 ft. Herons prey on passing fish in the waters here. The oldest heron rookery in British Columbia is in the trees near the aquarium, and the birds join in when it's feeding time for the whales.

31 **Second Beach.** In summer a draw is the 50-meter pool with lifeguards and water slides. The beach also has a playground and covered picnic sites.

30 **Siwash Rock.** Legend tells of a young Native American who, about to become a father, bathed persistently to wash his sins away so that his son could be born pure. For his devotion he was blessed by the gods and immortalized in the shape of Siwash Rock, just offshore. Two small rocks, said to be his wife and child, are on the cliff above the site.

26 **Totem poles.** Totem poles were not made in the Vancouver area; these eight poles, carved of cedar by the Kwakiutl and Haida peoples late in the last century, were brought to the park from the north coast of British Columbia. The carved animals, fish, birds, and mythological creatures were like family coats-of-arms or crests.

★ **23** **Vancouver Aquarium.** Displays show the underwater life of coastal British Columbia, the Canadian Arctic, and other areas of the world. Huge tanks (populated with orca and beluga whales and playful sea otters) have large windows for underwater viewing. The humid Amazon rain-forest gallery has piranhas, giant cockroaches, alligators, tropical birds, and jungle vegetation. ☎ *604/682–1118.* ☞ *July–Labor Day $12, Labor Day–June $10.* ☉ *July–Labor Day, daily 9:30–7; Labor Day–June, daily 10–5:30.*

West End. Filling the downtown peninsula from Thurlow Street west to Stanley Park, the West End is said to be the most densely populated square mile in North America. It's a vibrant, livable, neighborhood whose residents—generally single, senior, gay, European, or some combination thereof—have a large range of incomes. The main streets of Davie, Denman, and Robson are lined with cafés, restaurants, and shops both functional and bizarre. Side streets repay exploration, hiding tiny parks and an intriguing jumble of modern high-rises, stately '30s apartment houses, and Victorian homes. Lively English Bay Beach is here, as are many of Vancouver's best-value restaurants, several Victorian guest houses, and the heart of the city's gay community.

Granville Island

Granville Island, today a place for relaxing and shopping, was just a sandbar until World War I, when the federal government dredged False Creek for access to the sawmills that lined the shore. The sludge from the creek was heaped up onto the sandbar to create the island and to house industrial- and logging-equipment plants. By the late 1960s, however, many buildings were rotted and dangerous. In 1971 the federal government bought up leases from businesses that wanted to leave and offered an imaginative plan to refurbish the island with a public market and artisans' studios. The small island has no residents except for a houseboat community. Most of the former industrial buildings and tin sheds have been retained but are painted in upbeat reds, yellows, and blues. Through a committee of community representatives, the government regulates the types of businesses on Granville Island; most involve food, crafts, marine activities, and the arts.

A Good Walk

To reach Granville Island on foot, make the 15-minute walk from downtown Vancouver to the south end of Hornby Street. Aquabuses (☎ 604/689–5858) depart here and deliver passengers across False Creek to Granville Island Public Market. Another option is False Creek Ferries (☎ 604/684–7781), which leave every five minutes from a dock behind the Vancouver Aquatic Centre. Still another way to reach the island is to take a 20-minute ride on a BC Transit bus (☎ 604/521–0400). From Waterfront Station or stops on Granville Street take a False Creek South Bus 50 to the edge of the island. Or, from Granville and Broadway, catch a Granville Island Bus 51 for direct service to Granville Island. Parking is free for one to three hours; paid parking is available in garages on the island.

The ferry will drop you off at the **Granville Island Public Market** ㉜, with its fast food-outlets and fruit and vegetable, meat, coffee, and flower stalls. At the **Granville Island Information Centre** ㉝, catercorner to the market, stop to pick up a map of the island.

Walk south on Johnston Street to begin a clockwise loop tour of the island. Ocean Cement is one of the last of the island's former industries; its lease does not expire until the year 2004. Next door is the **Emily Carr Institute of Art and Design** ㉞. Follow a walkway along the south side of the art school to Sea Village, one of the only houseboat communities in Vancouver. Take the boardwalk that starts at the houseboats and continues partway around the island.

Cut in front or walk around the Granville Island Hotel and turn right onto Cartwright Street. This end of the island is home to a mix of crafts galleries, studios, and workshops and is a fascinating place to watch artisans at work. You can see printmaking in action at New Leaf Editions (✉ No. 1370) or peak through the windows at the Alder Bay Boat Company (✉ No. 1247) and see wooden boats being built. The next two attractions will make any child's visit to Granville Island a

Granville Island

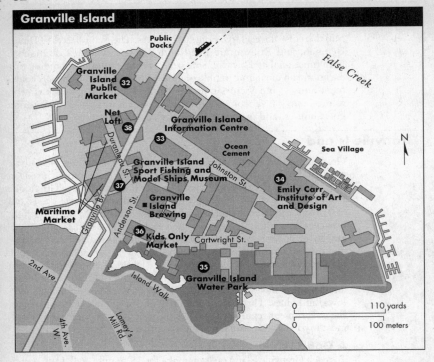

Public Docks

False Creek

Granville Island Public Market ③②

Net Loft ③⑧

Granville Island Information Centre ③③

Ocean Cement

Sea Village

Duranleau St.

Johnston St.

Granville Island Sport Fishing and Model Ships Museum ③⑦

Emily Carr Institute of Art and Design ③④

N

Maritime Market

Granville Island Brewing

Anderson St.

Granville Br.

Kids Only Market ③⑥

Cartwright St.

2nd Ave

Granville Island Water Park ③⑤

Island Walk

Lamey's Mill Rd.

4th Ave. W.

0 — 110 yards

0 — 100 meters

thrill. First, on Cartwright Street, is the **Granville Island Water Park** ㉟, with a wading pool and sprinklers. A bit farther down the street is the **Kids Only Market** ㊱, selling anything and everything a child could desire. Adults might prefer a microbrewery tour at **Granville Island Brewing.** Kids are welcome, too.

Cross Anderson Street and walk down Duranleau Street. On your left are the seafaring shops of the Maritime Market and the **Granville Island Sport Fishing and Model Ships Museum** ㊲. The last place to explore is the **Net Loft** ㊳, a collection of high-quality stores. Once you have come full circle, you can either take the ferry back to downtown Vancouver or stay for dinner and catch a play at the Arts Club (☎ 604/687–1644) or the Waterfront Theater (☎ 604/685–6217).

TIMING
If your schedule is tight, you can tour Granville Island in three to four hours; if you're a shopping fanatic, plan for a full day here.

Sights to See

㉞ **Emily Carr Institute of Art and Design.** Just inside the front door of the institute, to your right, is the **Charles H. Scott Gallery,** which hosts contemporary multimedia exhibits. ⊠ *1399 Johnston St.,* ☎ *604/844–3811.* ⊡ *Free.* ☉ *Weekdays noon–5, weekends 10–5.*

Granville Island Brewing. Tours of Canada's first microbrewery last about an hour and include a souvenir glass and a taste of four brews, some of which aren't on the market yet. Kids are welcome—they get root beer. ⊠ *1441 Cartwright St.,* ☎ *604/687–2739.* ⊡ *Tour $6.* ☉ *May–Oct., daily 9:30–7 (tours hourly); Nov.–Apr., daily 9:30–7 (call for tour times).*

㉝ **Granville Island Information Centre.** Maps are available here, and a slide show depicts the evolution of Granville Island. Ask about special-events days; perhaps there's a boat show, an outdoor concert, a dance performance, or some other happening. ⊠ *1592 Johnston St.,* ☎ *604/ 666–5784.* ⊙ *Daily 8–6.*

★ ㉜ **Granville Island Public Market.** The government allows no chain stores, so each outlet in the 50,000-square-ft building is unique, and most are of good quality. You probably won't be able to leave the market without a snack, espresso, or fixings for lunch on the wharf. Year-round you'll see mounds of raspberries, strawberries, blueberries, and more exotic fruits like persimmons. There's plenty of outdoor seating on the water side of the market. ⊠ *1669 Johnston St., under Granville Street bridge,* ☎ *604/666–6477.* ⊙ *Memorial Day–Labor Day, daily 9–6; Labor Day–Memorial Day, Tues.–Sun. 9–6.*

㊲ **Granville Island Sport Fishing and Model Ships Museum.** Opened in 1997, the Sport Fishing Museum houses one of North America's leading collections of sport-fishing artifacts. On the same site, the Model Ships Museum shows off its collection of exquisitely detailed, early 20th-century model ships. Shops in the surrounding Maritime Market are all geared to the sea. The first walkway to the left, Maritime Mews, leads to marinas and dry docks. ⊠ *1502 Duranleau St.,* ☎ *604/683– 1939.* ⊟ *$2.* ⊙ *Tues.–Sun. 10–5:30.*

🐣 ㉟ **Granville Island Water Park.** This kids' paradise has a wading pool, sprinklers, and a fire hydrant made for children to shower one another. ⊠ *1318 Cartwright St.,* ☎ *604/257–8195.* ⊟ *Free.* ⊙ *Late May–early Sept., daily 10–6.*

🐣 ㊱ **Kids Only Market.** A slice of kids' heaven on Granville Island, the Kids Only Market has two floors of small shops selling toys, arts-and-crafts materials, dolls, records and tapes, chemistry sets, and other good kid stuff. ⊠ *1496 Cartwright St.,* ☎ *604/689–8447.* ⊙ *Daily 10–6.*

㊳ **Net Loft.** This blue-and-red building houses small, high-quality stores, including a bookstore, a crafts store–gallery, a kitchenware shop, a post-card shop, a custom-made hat shop, a handmade-paper store, a British Columbian native art gallery, and a do-it-yourself jewelry store. ⊠ *1661 Johnston St., across from Public Market.* ⊙ *Daily 10–6.*

Kitsilano

The beachfront district of Kitsilano (popularly known as Kits), just south of downtown Vancouver, is among the trendiest of Canadian neighborhoods. Originally inhabited by the Squamish people, whose Chief Khahtsahlanough gave the area its name, Kitsilano began to attract daytrippers from Vancouver in the early part of this century. Some stayed and built lavish waterfront mansions; others built simpler Craftsman-style houses farther up the slope.

During the '60s, cheap rents, empty storefronts, the nearby University of British Columbia, and its great beach made Kits the ideal site for Vancouver's hippie community. Today Kits hangs on to that era with some pride, and, despite having some of Vancouver's priciest real estate, it's still the place to go for anything organic, ecological, or alternative. In the Kits of 1999, it's widely suspected (though not yet proven) that the wealthy professionals restoring the neighborhood's wood-frame Craftsman houses (and, in extreme cases, commuting to work by kayak) are the same people who squatted here in the '60s.

A day in Kitsilano is a relaxed one. It's home to three of Vancouver's best museums (clustered conveniently in Vanier Park on the waterfront), fashionable shops, and some of the city's most popular pubs and cafés. Kits has hidden treasures, too: rare boats moored at Heritage Harbour, stately mansions on forested lots, and, all along the waterfront, quiet coves and shady paths within a stone's throw of Canada's liveliest beach.

A Good Walk

Vanier Park, the grassy beachside setting for three museums and the best kite-flying venue in Vancouver, is the logical gateway to Kits. The most enjoyable way to get here is by False Creek Ferries (☎ 604/684–7781) from Granville Island, or from behind the Vancouver Aquatic Centre on Beach Avenue. The ferries dock at Heritage Harbour behind the Vancouver Maritime Museum. You can also walk or cycle about half a mile along the waterfront pathway from Granville Island (leave the island by Anderson Road and keep to your right along the waterfront). If you prefer to come by road, drive over the Burrard Street Bridge, turn right at Chestnut Street, and park in either of the museum parking lots, or take Bus 2 or 22 from downtown, get off at Cypress Street and Cornwall Avenue, and walk down to the park.

In Vanier Park you'll find the **Vancouver Museum** ㊟, which showcases the city's history in cheerful, life-size displays. It shares a building with the **Pacific Space Centre** ㊿, a high-tech museum focusing on outer space. Just to the west and toward the water is the **Vancouver Maritime Museum** ㊶, which traces the maritime history of the West Coast. Each museum has hands-on exhibits to appeal to kids.

Behind the Maritime Museum, where you'll dock if you come in by ferry, is the delightful Heritage Harbour, home to a changing variety of historically interesting boats, including *BCP 45*, the picturesque fishing boat that used to appear on Canada's five-dollar bill. In summer the big tent set up in Vanier Park is the venue for the Bard on the Beach Shakespeare series (☞ Nightlife and the Arts, *below*).

Just to the west of the Maritime Museum is a quiet, grassy beach. A wooden staircase leads from the beach up to a paved walkway. Take a moment to look at the huge Kwakiutl totem pole in front of the museum, then follow the walkway west to popular **Kitsilano Beach**. Ahead is Point Grey, across the water you can see Stanley Park, and behind you is Vancouver's downtown core. Continue past the pool, keep to the water, and you'll enter a shady pathway lined with blackberry bushes running behind the Kitsilano Yacht Club. Soon the lane opens up to a viewpoint and gives access to another quiet, sandy cove.

About ½ km (¼ mi) from the yacht club, the path ends at another wooden staircase. This leads up to a viewpoint and a park on Point Grey Road. Across the street from the top of the staircase is an Edwardian era, wood-turreted mansion (✉ 2590 Point Grey Rd.) built by a member of Kitsilano's early elite. Double back the way you came—heading east toward Kits Beach—but this time follow Point Grey Road for a look at the front of the waterfront homes you could just see from the beach path. The Logan House (✉ 2530 Point Grey Rd.), built in 1909, is an ivory-colored Edwardian dream home with a 180-degree curved balcony.

Follow Point Grey Road as it curves to the right, and cross Cornwall Avenue at the lights at Balsam Street. Turn left on First Avenue and walk two blocks to Yew Street, where in summer you'll find the biggest concentration of sidewalk pubs and cafés in Greater Vancouver. Alternatively, you can hike up the hill to 4th Avenue, once the heart of the hippie district, and explore the shops between Maple and Arbutus streets. You can catch a bus back to downtown Vancouver on Cornwall or 4th Avenue, or cut across Kits Beach Park back to Vanier Park.

TIMING

The walk alone will take about an hour and a half. Add 2½ hours to see the Pacific Space Centre and an hour for each of the other museums. With time out for shopping or swimming, a visit to Kitsilano could easily fill a whole day.

Sights to See

Kitsilano Beach. At Kits Beach (☞ Outdoor Activities and Sports, *below*) you'll find a playground, picnic sites, Vancouver's biggest outdoor pool, and some of the best people-watching anywhere. Just inland from the pool, the Kitsilano Showboat has free performances, mostly of the children's dancing variety, during summer. ☒ *Off Point Grey Rd.,* ☎ 604/257–8400.

ⓒ ④ **Pacific Space Centre.** After major expansion in 1997, this new facility has a host of interactive exhibits and high-tech learning systems, including a kinetic space-ride simulator and a theater showcasing Canada's achievements in space. During the day, catch the astronomy show at the **H. R. MacMillan Star Theatre** on site. When the sky is clear, the half-meter telescope at the **Gordon MacMillan Southam Observatory** (☎ 604/738–2855) is focused on whatever stars or planets are worth watching that night. Admission to the observatory is free; it's open evenings, weather permitting, so call for hours. ☒ *1100 Chestnut St., Vanier Park,* ☎ 604/738–7827. ☒ *$12.* ☉ *Tues.–Thurs. 10–5, Fri. 10–9, weekends 10–5.*

ⓒ ④ **Vancouver Maritime Museum.** Fully half the museum has been turned over to kids, with touchable kid-proof displays that give them a chance to drive a tug, build an underwater robot, or dress up as a seafarer. Toddlers and school-age children will appreciate the hands-on displays in Pirates' Cove and the Children's Maritime Discovery Centre. Adults may like the model boat displays. The Maritime Museum is also the last moorage for the RCMP schooner the *St. Roch,* the first ship to sail in both directions through the treacherous Northwest Passage. Restored historic boats from different cultures are moored at **Heritage Harbour** behind the museum, and a huge Kwakiutl totem pole stands out front. ☒ *1905 Ogden Ave., north end of Cypress St.,* ☎ 604/257–8300. ☒ *Museum $6, Heritage Harbour free.* ☉ *May–Aug., daily 10–5; Sept.–Apr., Tues.–Sun. 10–5.*

ⓒ ③ **Vancouver Museum.** The museum's permanent exhibits focus on the city's early history and native art and culture. Life-size replicas of an 1897 Canadian Pacific Railway passenger car, a trading post, and a Victorian parlor, as well as a real dugout canoe, are highlights. ☒ *1100 Chestnut St., Vanier Park,* ☎ 604/736–4431. ☒ *$5.* ☉ *Tues.–Thurs. 10–5, Fri. 10–9, weekends 10–5.*

Greater Vancouver

Some of Vancouver's best gardens, natural sights, and museums, including the renowned Museum of Anthropology, are found south of downtown, on the campus of the University of British Columbia and in the city's southern residential districts. Individual sights are easily reached by BC Transit buses (☎ 604/521–0400), but you'll need a car to see them all comfortably in a day.

A Good Drive

From downtown Vancouver, cross the Burrard Street Bridge and follow the marked scenic route. This will take you along Cornwall Avenue, which becomes Point Grey Road and follows the waterfront to Alma Street. The little wooden structure at the corner of Point Grey Road and Alma Street is the Hastings Mill Store, Vancouver's first store and now a museum. It was built in 1865 on Dunlevy Street near Gastown and moved to this pretty seaside spot in 1930.

The scenic route continues south on Alma Street and then west (to the right) on 4th Avenue. This flows into Northwest Marine Drive, which takes you past Jericho and Locarno beaches and up to the University of British Columbia (UBC). Here you'll find the **Museum of Anthropology** ㊷, which houses an amazing collection of totem poles and other native artifacts, and **Nitobe Memorial Garden** ㊸, a Japanese-style strolling garden. Just past the Nitobe Memorial Garden are the **University of British Columbia Botanical Gardens.**

For more gardens, follow Marine Drive through the university grounds and take the left fork onto 41st Avenue. Turn left again onto Oak Street to reach the entrance of the **VanDusen Botanical Garden** ㊹ (it will be on your left); the complex is planted with English-style mazes, water gardens, herb gardens, and more. Return to 41st Avenue, continue farther east, and then turn left on Cambie Street to reach **Queen Elizabeth Park** ㊺, which overlooks the city. To get back downtown, continue north on Cambie and over the Cambie Street Bridge.

TIMING

Outside of rush hour, it takes about 30 minutes to drive from downtown to the University of British Columbia. You should add another 30 to 45 minutes' driving time for the rest of the tour, and about two hours to visit each of the main sites.

Sights to See

★ ㊷ **Museum of Anthropology.** The MOA on the University of British Columbia campus is Vancouver's most spectacular museum, focusing on Northwest Coast First Nations art, including the works of Bill Reid, Canada's most respected Haida carver. His *Raven and the First Men,* which took five carvers more than three years to complete, is its centerpiece. Set on a cliff overlooking the Pacific, the museum is housed in an award-winning glass-and-concrete structure designed by Arthur Erickson. In the Great Hall are dramatic totem poles, ceremonial archways, and dugout canoes—all adorned with carvings of frogs, eagles, ravens, bears, and salmon. Also showcased are exquisite carvings of gold, silver, and argillite (a black stone found in the Queen Charlotte Islands), as well as masks, tools, and costumes from many other cultures. The museum contains a ceramics wing with about 600 pieces from 15th- to 19th-century Europe. To reach the museum by public transit, take a UBC Bus 4 or UBC Bus 10 from Granville Street downtown. At Alma Street you can transfer to the infrequent Chancellor Bus 42 for direct service to the museum, or stay on Bus 4 or 10 to the university loop, which is a 10-minute walk from the museum. ⊠ *6393 N.W. Marine Dr.,* ☎ *604/822–3825.* ☞ *$6; free Tues. 5–9.* ☉ *Memorial Day–Labor Day, Tues. 10–9, Mon. and Wed.–Sun. 10–5; Labor Day–Memorial Day, Tues. 11–9, Wed.–Sun. 11–5.*

㊸ **Nitobe Memorial Garden.** This 2½-acre garden is one of the most authentic Japanese gardens outside Japan. The circular path around the park symbolizes the cycle of life and provides a tranquil view from every direction. In April and May cherry blossoms are the highlight, and in June the irises are magnificent. ⊠ *1903 West Mall, University of British Columbia,* ☎ *604/822–9666.* ☞ *Mid-Mar.–mid-Oct., $2.50; mid-Oct.–mid-Mar., free.* ☉ *Mid-Mar.–mid-Oct., daily 10–6; mid-Oct.–mid-Mar., weekdays 10–2:30.*

㊺ **Queen Elizabeth Park.** Besides views of downtown, the park has lavish gardens brimming with roses and other flowers, an abundance of grassy picnicking spots, and illuminated fountains. Other park facilities include 20 tennis courts, pitch and putt, and a restaurant. In the **Bloedel Conservatory,** you can see tropical and desert plants and 60 species of free-flying tropical birds in a glass geodesic dome. To reach the park by public transportation, take a Cambie Bus 15 from Granville Street downtown to 33rd Avenue. ⊠ *Cambie St. and 33rd Ave.,* ☎ 604/ 257–8570. ⊟ *Parking free; conservatory $3.25.* ⊙ *Apr.–Sept., weekdays 9–8, weekends 10–9; Oct.–Mar., daily 10–5.*

University of British Columbia Botanical Gardens. Seventy acres of gardens display temperate plants from around the world. ⊠ *6804 S.W. Marine Dr.,* ☎ *604/822–9666.* ⊟ *Summer $4.50, winter free.* ⊙ *Mid-Mar.–mid-Oct., daily 10–6; mid-Oct.–mid-Mar., weekdays 10–2:30.*

㊹ VanDusen Botanical Garden. On what was once a 55-acre golf course grows one of the largest collections of ornamental plants in Canada. Native and exotic plant displays include an Elizabethan maze; the colorful rhododendrons bloom in May and June. For a bite to eat, stop in Sprinklers Restaurant (☎ 604/261–0011), on the grounds. An Oak Bus 17 will get you here from downtown. Queen Elizabeth Park is a 1-km (½-mi) walk away, on 37th Avenue. ⊠ *5251 Oak St., at 37th Ave.,* ☎ *604/878–9274.* ⊟ *$5.50; ½ price Oct.–Mar.* ⊙ *June–mid-Aug, daily 10–9; call for off-season hrs.*

Yaletown and False Creek

In 1985 and '86, the provincial government cleared up a derelict industrial site on the north shore of False Creek, built a World's Fair, and invited the world. Twenty million people showed up, making Vancouver's Expo '86 a huge success. Now that site has become one of the largest urban redevelopment projects in North America, creating—and, in some cases, reclaiming—a whole new downtown district that Vancouverites themselves are only beginning to discover.

Tucked in among the forest of new, green-glass high-rise condo towers is the old warehouse district of Yaletown. First settled by railroad workers who had followed the newly laid tracks down from the town of Yale in the Fraser Canyon, Yaletown was, in the 1880s and '90s, probably the most lawless place in Canada—the Royal Canadian Mounted Police complained it was too far through the forest for them to police it. It's now one of the city's chicest neighborhoods, and the Victorian brick loading docks have become terraces for cappuccino bars. The area makes the most of its waterfront location, with a seaside walk and cycle path that runs completely around the shore of False Creek.

A Good Walk

Start at **Library Square** ㊻ at Hamilton and Georgia streets, the city's multimillion-dollar central library project. Leave by the Robson Street exit, cross Robson, and continue south on Hamilton Street. On your right you'll see a row of Victorian frame houses built between 1895 and 1900, all painted in candy-box colors and looking completely out of place among the surrounding high-rises. In 1995, these historic homes were plucked from the West End and moved here to protect them from the onslaught of development.

Cross Smithe Street, veer to your left a bit, and continue down Mainland Street. You're now in the heart of Yaletown, an eight-block neighborhood of refurbished warehouses. It holds restaurants, a brew pub, and galleries that supply art and avant-garde home decor to the neighborhood's new loft and condo owners. Stop for a coffee on one of Yaletown's loading-dock cafés or take the time to poke around the shops on Hamilton and Homer streets.

From the foot of Mainland Street, turn left on Davie Street and cross Pacific Boulevard. This takes you to the **Roundhouse,** a former turnaround point for trains that is now a showcase for local arts groups. Continue to the waterfront at the foot of Davie. Here you'll find an intriguing iron and concrete sculpture, with panels displaying archive images of events around False Creek. To your right is the Yaletown dock for Aquabus Ferries (☎ 604/689–5858), where you can catch a boat to Granville Island or Science World.

Turn left and follow the waterfront walkway. After about 1 km (½ mi) you'll reach the Plaza of Nations, the heart of the old Expo site, home to pubs, cafés, and outdoor entertainment in the summer. Cross the plaza toward Pacific Boulevard and take the pedestrian overpass to B.C. Place Stadium. Walk around to Gate A, where you'll find the **B.C. Sports Hall of Fame and Museum** ㊼, devoted to British Columbia's favorite sons and daughters who made a name for themselves in sports. To your left as you leave the museum you'll see the Terry Fox Memorial. This archway at the foot of Robson Street was built in honor of Terry Fox (1958–1981), a local student whose cross-Canada run raised millions for cancer research. From here you can walk two blocks north on Beatty Street and take the SkyTrain one stop east, or retrace your steps to the waterfront and walk another 1 km (½ mi) east to **Science World** ㊽, a hands-on museum. From Science World, the SkyTrain will take you back downtown.

TIMING

It takes about 1½ hours to walk around all the sights. Allow about an hour for the B.C. Sports Hall of Fame and museum and two hours for Science World. Shoppers may not make it past Yaletown.

Sights to See

㊼ **B.C. Sports Hall of Fame and Museum.** Part of the B.C. Place Stadium complex, this museum celebrating the province's sports achievers shows video documentaries and has photographs, uniforms, sporting equipment, and a high-tech, hands-on participation gallery. ⊠ *B.C. Place, 777 Pacific Blvd. S, Gate A,* ☎ *604/687–5520.* ☜ *$6.* ☉ *Daily 10–5.*

㊻ **Library Square.** The spiraling library building, open plazas, frescoed waterfall, and shaded atriums of the new Library Square were built to evoke images of the Colosseum in Rome. This architectural stunner is a favorite backdrop for movie productions, so you may see it at the movies or on television before you visit it. A high-tech library fills the core of the structure; the outer edge of the spiral houses boutiques, coffee shops, and a fine book and gift shop. ⊠ *350 W. Georgia St.,* ☎ *604/331–3600.* ☉ *Mon.–Tues. 10–9, Wed.–Sat. 10–6, Sun. hrs vary.*

Roundhouse. Now a community arts center, the brick Roundhouse was originally built in 1888 as the turnaround point for transcontinental trains reaching the end of the line at Vancouver. A spirited local campaign helped create a home here for **Engine 374,** the engine that pulled the first passenger train into Vancouver on May 24, 1887. These days the Roundhouse is a favorite festival venue and a showcase for local arts groups. ⊠ *181 Roundhouse Mews,* ☎ *604/713–1800.* ☜ *Free; admission may be charged to some events.* ☉ *Tues.–Fri. 9 AM–10 PM, weekends 9–5.*

㊽ **Science World.** This hands-on museum, in a gigantic, shiny dome built over an Omnimax Theater for Expo '86, encourages visitors to touch and participate in the theme exhibits. The special Search Gallery is aimed at younger children, as are the fun-filled demonstrations given in Center Stage. A new 3-D laser theater appeals to older kids. ⊠ *1455 Quebec St.,* ☎ *604/268–6363.* ☜ *Science World $10.50, Omnimax $9,* *combination ticket $13.50.* ⏲ *July–Aug., daily 10–6; Sept.–June, weekdays 10–5, weekends 10–6.*

North Vancouver

All those mountains that form a stunning backdrop to Vancouver lie in the district of North Vancouver, a bridge or SeaBus ride away on the North Shore of Burrard Inlet. Although the area is part suburb, the mountainous terrain (and more recently, good sense) has kept large parts of North Vancouver forested, almost wilderness parkland. This is where Vancouverites and visitors go for easily accessible hiking, skiing, and views of the city lights. A car is handy for a tour, but public transportation works too—making Vancouver one of the few places in the world where you can take a city bus to the ski slopes.

A Good Drive

From downtown, drive west down Georgia Street to Stanley Park and across the Lions Gate Bridge to North Vancouver. Follow the signs into the mountains of the North Shore to see the **Capilano Suspension Bridge and Park** ㊾, where a cedar-plank footbridge swings high above the Capilano River. Nearby, in the Capilano Regional Park, the **Capilano Salmon Hatchery** ㊿ is another good spot to visit. Up the hill a bit farther, at the end of Nancy Greene Way, is **Grouse Mountain** (51), where a Skyride to the summit gives you great city views.

Alternatively, you can take the SeaBus from Waterfront Station to Lonsdale Quay and then catch a Grouse Mountain Bus 236. This stops at Capilano Park and near the Salmon Hatchery on its way up to the base of the Grouse Mountain Skyride.

TIMING

You'll need a half day to see the sights, a full day if you want to hike at Grouse Mountain or Capilano Park. It's important to time your visit carefully: Don't even think about driving over the Lions Gate Bridge during a weekday rush hour (about 7–9 AM and 3–6 PM).

Sights to See

㊿ **Capilano Salmon Hatchery.** The hatchery, in the Capilano Regional Park, has viewing areas and exhibits about the life cycle of the salmon. ⊠ *4500 Capilano Park Rd., North Vancouver,* ☎ *604/666–1790.* 🎟 *Free.* ⏲ *June–Aug., daily 8–8; call for off-season hrs.*

㊾ **Capilano Suspension Bridge and Park.** At Vancouver's oldest tourist attraction (the original bridge was built in 1889), you can get a taste of the mountains and test your mettle on the swaying, 450-ft cedar-plank suspension bridge that hangs 230 ft above the rushing Capilano River. The amusement park also has viewing decks, nature trails amid tall firs and cedars, a gift shop, totem poles, a totem-carving shed, and displays for the kids. Free guided tours run throughout the day. ⊠ *3735 Capilano Rd., North Vancouver,* ☎ *604/985–7474.* 🎟 *$9.25.* ⏲ *May–Oct., daily 8–dusk; Nov.–Apr., daily 9–5.*

First Nations Feast House. Opened in 1998 at ☞ Grouse Mountain, the feast house presents a traditional Coast Salish feast and entertainment in a mountaintop longhouse. Reservations are essential. ⊠ *6400 Nancy Greene Way, North Vancouver,* ☎ *604/980–9311.* 🎟 *$69 Mon.–Thurs., $79 Fri.–Sun.; includes Skyride.* ⏲ *May–Oct., daily 5:30 PM and 7:30 PM seatings.*

★ (51) **Grouse Mountain.** The Skyride to the top is a great way to take in stunning city, sea, and mountain vistas, and there's plenty to do when you arrive. A Skyride ticket includes a half-hour video presentation at the Theatre in the Sky and admission to a variety of mountaintop events, including loggers' sports shows, chairlift rides, walking tours, horse-back riding, and, in winter, ice-skating, snowshoeing, skiing, and snow-cat-drawn sleigh rides. The mountaintop, which has a café, pub, and restaurant, is a popular festival venue, with both jazz and Shakespeare performances during the summer. The new ☞ **First Nations Feast House** is an additional attraction for which reservations are needed. ✉ *6400 Nancy Greene Way, North Vancouver,* ☎ *604/984–0661.* ◱ *Skyride and theater $15.95.* ⊙ *Daily 9 AM–10 PM.*

OFF THE BEATEN PATH
LYNN CANYON PARK – Vancouver's alternative suspension bridge is free and, at 165 ft above the raging Lynn Creek, plenty scary and scenic enough for most. Hardy North Vancouverites swim in the icy river; others bask on the rocks. The park's steep canyon landscape and temperate rain forest, with nearby waterfalls, are stunning. The Ecology Centre offers guided walks, maps of area hiking trails, and information about the flora and fauna. To get here, take Lions Gate Bridge, go east on Highway 1, take the Lynn Valley Road exit, and follow signs. You can also take the SeaBus to Lonsdale Quay and Westlynn Bus 229 to the corner of Peters and Duval streets. ✉ *3663 Park Rd., North Vancouver,* ☎ *604/981-3103.* ◱ *Ecology Centre by donation; suspension bridge free.* ⊙ *Mar.–Sept., daily 10–5; Oct.–Feb., weekdays 10–5, weekends noon–4.*

DINING

Vancouver dining is usually fairly informal; casual but neat dress is appropriate everywhere except the few expensive restaurants that require jacket and tie (indicated in the text). A bylaw bans smoking in all Vancouver restaurants, though observance is uneven.

CATEGORY	COST*
$$$$	over $40
$$$	$30–$40
$$	$20–$30
$	under $20

per person, in Canadian dollars, including appetizer, entrée, and dessert and excluding drinks, service, and 7% GST

American/Casual

$$ ✕ **Griffin's.** Sunday brunch here is cheerful, energetic, and family-oriented, but the rest of the week the emphasis is on the adult crowd. This brasserie uniquely blends the charm of old Italy with sophisticated design. Squash-yellow walls, bold black and white tiles, and splashy food art keep it lively. The open kitchen prepares inspired cuisine from fresh, regional ingredients, including such buffet selections as roast cedar-plank salmon and chicken pasta al pesto. A traditional British high tea is served from 2:30 to 4:30 daily. ✉ *900 W. Georgia St.,* ☎ *604/662–1900. Reservations essential. AE, D, DC, MC, V.*

$ ✕ **The Tomahawk.** North Vancouver was mostly trees in 1926, when the Tomahawk opened. Over the years, the original hamburger stand grew and mutated into part Northwest Coast native arts-and-craft museum, part gift shop, and part restaurant. Renowned for its Yukon breakfast—five slices of back bacon, two eggs, hash browns, and toast—the Tomahawk also serves gigantic muffins, excellent French toast, and pancakes. At lunch and dinner the menu switches to oysters, trout, and burgers. ✉ *1550 Philip Ave., off Marine Dri., 7 blocks east of Lions Gate Bridge,* ☎ *604/988–2612. AE, DC, MC, V.*

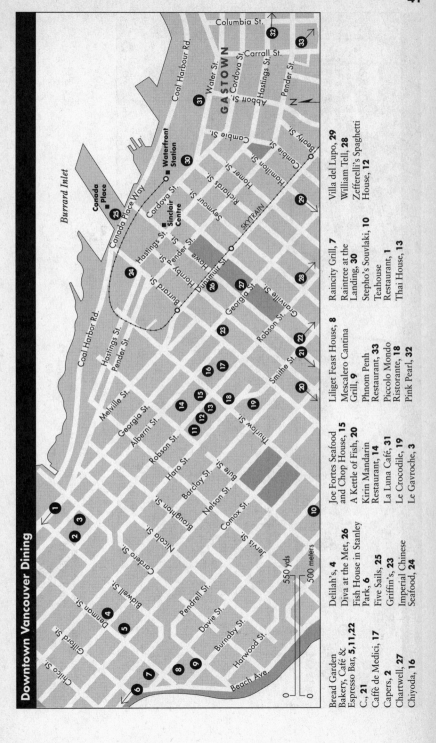

41

Downtown Vancouver Dining

Bread Garden Bakery, Café & Espresso Bar, **5,11,22**
C., **21**
Caffè de Medici, **17**
Capers, **2**
Chartwell, **27**
Chiyoda, **16**

Delilah's, **4**
Diva at the Met, **26**
Fish House in Stanley Park, **6**
Five Sails, **25**
Griffin's, **23**
Imperial Chinese Seafood, **24**

Joe Fortes Seafood and Chop House, **8**
A Kettle of Fish, **20**
Kirin Mandarin Restaurant, **14**
La Luna Café, **31**
Le Crocodile, **19**
Le Gavroche, **3**

Liliget Feast House, **8**
Mescalero Cantina Grill, **9**
Phnom Penh Restaurant, **33**
Piccolo Mondo Ristorante, **18**
Pink Pearl, **32**

Raincity Grill, **7**
Raintree at the Landing, **30**
Stepho's Souvlaki, **10**
Teahouse Restaurant, **1**
Thai House, **13**

Villa del Lupo, **29**
William Tell, **28**
Zefferelli's Spaghetti House, **12**

42

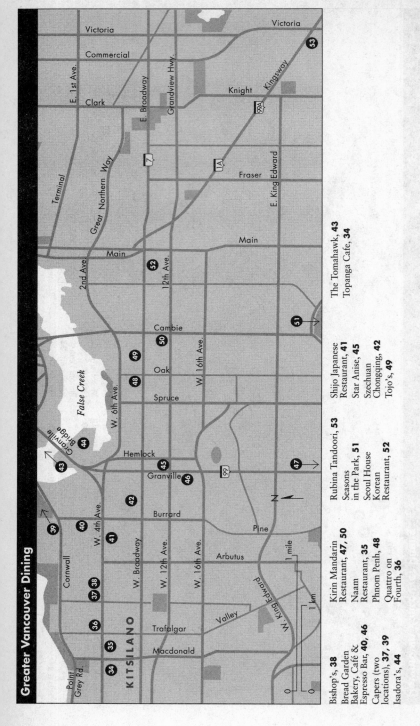

Greater Vancouver Dining

Bishop's, **38**
Bread Garden Bakery, Café & Espresso Bar, **40, 46**
Capers (two locations), **37, 39**
Isadora's, **44**

Kirin Mandarin Restaurant, **47, 50**
Naam Restaurant, **35**
Phnom Penh, **48**
Quattro on Fourth, **36**

Rubina Tandoori, **53**
Seasons in the Park, **51**
Seoul House Korean Restaurant, **52**

Shijo Japanese Restaurant, **41**
Star Anise, **45**
Szechuan Chongqing, **42**
Tojo's, **49**

The Tomahawk, **43**
Topanga Cafe, **34**

Cafés

$ ✕ **Bread Garden Bakery, Café & Espresso Bar.** Once a croissant bakery, this is now a five-location chain and late-night hangout. Salads, quiches, elaborate cakes and pies, giant muffins, and cappuccino draw a steady stream of the young and fashionable. The wait in line may be long anywhere. The Bute and Granville Street outlets are open 24 hours; the others, 6 AM to midnight. ✉ *1880 W. 1st Ave., Kitsilano,* ☎ *604/738–6684;* ✉ *2996 Granville St.,* ☎ *604/736–6465;* ✉ *812 Bute St.,* ☎ *604/688–3213;* ✉ *1040 Denman St.,* ☎ *604/685–2996;* ✉ *1109 Hamilton St.,* ☎ *604/689–9500. AE, MC, V.*

$ ✕ **Capers.** These casual cafés, tucked into Vancouver's most lavish health food stores, offer light organic and vegetarian meals, treats from the in-store bakeries, and the good strong coffees that Vancouverites have come to expect. The West Vancouver store also has a full-service restaurant. ✉ *2496 Marine Dr., West Vancouver,* ☎ *604/925–3374;* ✉ *2285 W. 4th Ave.,* ☎ *604/739–6676;* ✉ *1675 Robson St.,* ☎ *604/ 687–5288. MC, V.*

$ ✕ **La Luna Café.** This bi-level deli in the heart of Gastown serves fragrant coffees and teas and fresh soup and salad lunches, but it's the luscious sourdough cinnamon rolls that steal the show. You can have one heated and slathered with butter if you plan to eat in at one of the small tables, or get the staff to bag a roll to go. These rolls are not to be missed. ✉ *117 Water St.,* ☎ *604/687–5862. No credit cards.*

Chinese

$$–$$$$ ✕ **Imperial Chinese Seafood.** This elegant Cantonese restaurant in the
★ Art Deco Marine Building has two-story floor-to-ceiling windows with stupendous views of Stanley Park and the North Shore mountains across Coal Harbour. Any dish with lobster, crab, or shrimp from the live tanks is recommended, as is the dim sum, served from 11 to 2:30. Portions tend to be small and pricey (especially the abalone, shark's fin, and bird's-nest delicacies) but never fail to please. ✉ *355 Burrard St.,* ☎ *604/688–8191. Reservations essential. AE, DC, MC, V.*

$$–$$$ ✕ **Szechuan Chongqing.** Some good choices at this unpretentious, white-tablecloth restaurant are the Szechuan-style crunchy green beans tossed with garlic and ground pork or the Chongqing chicken. In the latter, a boneless chicken is served on a bed of spinach cooked in dry heat until crisp, giving it the texture of dried seaweed and a salty, rich, and nutty taste. ✉ *205–1668 W. Broadway,* ☎ *604/734–1668. Reservations essential. AE, DC, MC, V.*

$$ ✕ **Kirin Mandarin Restaurant.** King crab and lobsters swim in tanks set into the slate-green walls, part of the lavish decorations of this restaurant offering a smattering of northern Chinese cuisines. Dishes include Shanghai-style smoked eel, Peking duck, and Szechuan hot-and-spicy scallops. Kirin is just two blocks from most of the major downtown hotels. A second location at Cambie Street, called the Kirin Seafood Restaurant, focuses on milder Cantonese seafood creations. A new Richmond location opened in 1998. ✉ *102–1166 Alberni St.,* ☎ *604/682–8833;* ✉ *555 W. 12th Ave., 2nd floor,* ☎ *604/879–8038;* ✉ *3 West Centre, Suite 200, 7900 Westminster Hwy., Richmond,* ☎ *604/303–8833. Reservations essential. AE, DC, V.*

$$ ✕ **Pink Pearl.** This noisy, 680-seat Cantonese restaurant has tanks of live seafood—crab, shrimp, geoduck, oysters, abalone, rock cod, lobsters, and scallops. Menu highlights are clams in black-bean sauce, crab sautéed with five spices (a spicy dish sometimes translated as crab with peppery salt), and Pink Pearl's version of crisp-skinned chicken. Dim sum is served daily from 9 to 3, but arrive early on the weekend if you don't want to be caught in the lineup. ✉ *1132 E. Hastings St.,* ☎ *604/ 253–4316. Reservations essential. AE, DC, MC, V.*

Contemporary

$$$–$$$$ ✕ **Bishop's.** John Bishop established this restaurant as a favorite in 1985 by serving West Coast Continental cuisine with an emphasis on organic produce and British Columbia seafood. Medallions of venison, smoked Alaskan black cod, or roasted duck breast with dried fruit and ginger may be on the seasonal menu. The small white rooms—their only ornament some splashy expressionist paintings—are favored by Robert De Niro, Glenn Close, Richard Gere, and other stars when they're on location in Vancouver. ⊠ *2183 W. 4th Ave.,* ☎ *604/738–2025. Reservations essential. AE, DC, MC, V. Closed 1st wk in Jan. No lunch.*

$$$–$$$$ ✕ **Chartwell.** Named after Sir Winston Churchill's country home (a
  ★   painting of which hangs over the green marble fireplace), the flagship dining room at the Four Seasons hotel (☞ Lodging, *below*) has floor-to-ceiling rich wood paneling and deep leather chairs that help create a perfect setting for the city's top spot for a power lunch. The chefs cook robust, inventive Continental food with a West Coast flair as well as lighter offerings and low-calorie, low-fat entrées. Some favorites are tomato basil soup with gin, rack of lamb, and a number of salmon offerings. ⊠ *791 W. Georgia St.,* ☎ *604/689–9333. Reservations essential. Jacket required. AE, DC, MC, V. No lunch Sat.*

$$$–$$$$ ✕ **Diva at the Met.** This multitiered restaurant at the Metropolitan Hotel
  ★   (☞ Lodging, *below*) opened in 1996 and quickly scooped up a fistful of awards. Presentation of the innovative contemporary cuisine is as appealing as the art deco decor. The menu changes seasonally, but top creations from the open kitchen have included smoked Alaska black cod and porcini-crusted veal loin steak. The after-theater crowd heads here for late-evening snacks and desserts: Prawn tempura, vegetable chips, fresh sorbets, and Stilton cheesecake are available until midnight. The creative weekend brunches are also popular. ⊠ *645 Howe St.,* ☎ *604/602–7788. AE, DC, MC, V.*

$$$–$$$$ ✕ **Five Sails.** A special-occasion restaurant at the Pan Pacific Hotel (☞ Lodging, *below*), Five Sails has a stunning panoramic view of Canada Place, Lions Gate Bridge, and the lights of the North Shore across the inlet. Austrian chef Ernst Dorfler has a special flair for presentation, from the swan-shape butter served with breads early in the meal to the chocolate ice cream bonbon served at the end. The broad-reaching, seasonally changing Pacific Northwest menu showcases fresh fish and seafood and often lists caramelized swordfish, ahi in red Thai curry vinaigrette, terrine of duck, and old favorites like medallions of British Columbia salmon or lamb from Salt Spring Island. ⊠ *Pan Pacific Hotel, 300–999 Canada Pl.,* ☎ *604/891–2892 or 604/662–8111. Reservations essential. AE, DC, MC, V. No lunch.*

$$$–$$$$ ✕ **Star Anise.** Pacific Rim cuisine with French flair shines in this inti-
  ★   mate location just off Granville Street. The menu varies with the seasons, but highlights, creatively and imaginatively prepared by chef Julian Bond, have included grilled emu set on a torta woven with shiitake mushrooms and potato, seafood creations such as tandoori salmon with minted mango chutney, and a ricotta and leek tart. The presentation and attentive service are legendary. ⊠ *1485 W. 12th Ave.,* ☎ *604/737–1485. Reservations essential. AE, D, DC, MC, V. No lunch weekends.*

$$–$$$$ ✕ **Raintree at the Landing.** In a beautifully renovated historic building in busy Gastown, Vancouver's first Pacific Northwest restaurant has waterfront views, fireplaces, a local menu, and a wine list with British Columbia, Washington, and Oregon vintages. The kitchen, focusing on healthy regional cuisine, teeters between willfully eccentric and exceedingly simple; it bakes its own bread and makes luxurious soups. Main courses change daily but may include crab cakes and pan-seared halibut in pickled ginger butter sauce. ⊠ *375 Water St.,* ☎ *604/688–5570. Reservations essential. AE, DC, MC, V.*

$$–$$$ ╳ **Raincity Grill.** A West End hot spot across the street from English Bay, this is a neighborhood favorite. The setting, with candlelit tables, balloon-back chairs, cushioned banquettes, and enormous flower arrangements, is very sophisticated. All the same, it plays second fiddle to a creative, fresh weekly menu that highlights the best regional seafood, meats, and produce. Grilled romaine spears are used in the Caesar salad, giving it a delightful smokey flavor. Varying preparations of salmon and duck are usually available, as is at least one vegetarian selection. ⊠ 1193 Denman St., ☎ 604/685–7337. Reservations essential. AE, DC, MC, V.

$$ ★ ╳ **Delilah's.** Cherubs dance on the ceiling, candles flicker on the tables, and martini glasses clink in toasts at this incredibly popular restaurant. Under the direction of chef Peg Montgomery, the West Coast Continental cuisine is delicious, innovative, and beautifully presented. The menu, which changes seasonally, lets you choose two- or five-course prix-fixe dinners. Try the pancetta, pine nut, Asiago, and mozzarella fritters with sun-dried tomato aioli and the grilled swordfish with blueberry-lemon compote if they're available. Patrons have been known to line up before Delilah's opens for dinner. ⊠ 1789 Comox St., ☎ 604/687–3424. Reservations not accepted, except for parties of 6 or more. AE, DC, MC, V. No lunch.

$$ ╳ **Isadora's.** The "West Coast–fresh" menu here ranges from salmon served with bannock bread (a Native American specialty) to elaborate vegetarian pastas and some of the best burgers, both meat and veggie, in town. This child-friendly restaurant also has children's specials (the pizzas come with faces) and an inside play area packed with toys. In summer the restaurant opens onto Granville Island's water park. ⊠ 1540 Old Bridge St., Granville Island, ☎ 604/681–8816. DC, MC, V. No dinner Mon. Sept.–May.

Continental

$$$–$$$$ ╳ **William Tell.** Silver service plates, embossed linen napkins, and a silver vase on each table set the tone of Swiss luxury in this establishment in the Georgian Court Hotel. Chef Todd Konrad prepares excellent sautéed veal sweetbreads with red onion marmalade and marsala sauce and such Swiss dishes as cheese fondue, pickled herring with apples, and Zürcher Geschnetzeltes (thinly sliced veal with mushrooms in a light white wine sauce). A bar-and-bistro area caters to a more casual crowd. Reserve in advance for the all-you-can-eat Swiss Farmer's Buffet on Sunday nights. ⊠ 765 Beatty St., ☎ 604/688–3504. Reservations essential. AE, D, DC, MC, V.

$$$ ╳ **Teahouse Restaurant.** This former officers' mess in Stanley Park is perfectly poised for watching sunsets over the water, especially from a glassed-in wing that resembles a conservatory, or from the patio in summer. The West Coast Continental menu lists such specialties as cream of carrot soup, lamb with herb crust, and perfectly grilled fish. ⊠ 7501 Stanley Park Dr., Ferguson Point, Stanley Park, ☎ 604/669–3281. Reservations essential. AE, MC, V.

$$–$$$ ╳ **Seasons in the Park.** Seasons, in Queen Elizabeth Park, has a commanding view over the park gardens to the city lights and the mountains beyond. A comfortable room with lots of light wood and white tablecloths is matched with a conservative Continental menu, including such standards as herb-crusted sea bass and confit of muscovy duck. This is a very popular choice with the weekend brunch crowd. ⊠ Queen Elizabeth Park, 33rd Ave. and Cambie St., ☎ 604/874–8008. Reservations essential. AE, MC, V.

French

$$$–$$$$ ╳ **Le Crocodile.** Chef Michael Jacob serves well cooked, simple food in a roomy location on Smithe Street off Burrard. His Alsatian back-

ground shines with the caramel-sweet onion tart. Anything that involves innards is superb, and even such old standards as duck à l'orange are worth ordering. ⊠ *100–909 Burrard St.,* ☎ *604/669–4298. Reservations essential. AE, DC, MC, V. Closed Sun. No lunch Sat.*

$$$–$$$$ ✕ **Le Gavroche.** This charming, somewhat formal turn-of-the-century house, with an open fireplace and an upstairs terrace, has been a French restaurant for more than 20 years. The classic French cooking, lightened—but by no means reduced—to contemporary cuisine, includes such simple dishes as smoked salmon with potato galette and more complex offerings such as grilled pork tenderloin with calvados and Stilton sauce. The excellent 30-page wine list stresses Bordeaux. Tables by the front window promise views of mountains and water. ⊠ *1616 Alberni St.,* ☎ *604/685–3924. Reservations essential. AE, DC, MC, V. No lunch weekends.*

Greek

$ ✕ **Stepho's Souvlaki.** A line of people waiting outside a restaurant on a street full of good, inexpensive eateries has to mean something. Regulars swear by, and are quite prepared to wait in line for, Stepho's cheap and tasty roast lamb, moussaka, and souvlaki, served in a dark and bustling taverna. Lunch is less busy, and there's a takeout menu, too—handy for picnics on the beach just down the street. ⊠ *1124 Davie St.,* ☎ *604/683–2555. AE, MC, V.*

Indian

$$–$$$ ✕ **Rubina Tandoori.** For the best Indian food in the city, many people
★ go to Rubina Tandoori, 20 minutes from downtown. The large menu spans most of the subcontinent's cuisines, including tandoori, Balti, and vegetarian Gujarati specialties. The popular *chevda* (a salty snack) is shipped to fans all over North America. ⊠ *1962 Kingsway,* ☎ *604/ 874–3621. Reservations essential. AE, DC, MC, V. Closed Sun. No lunch Sat.*

Italian

$$$–$$$$ ✕ **Caffè de Medici.** This elegant restaurant has ornate molded ceilings, portraits of the Medici family, and a courtly, peaceful atmosphere. Although an enticing antipasto table sits in the center of the room, the risotto with *frutta di mare* (seafood) is also a worthwhile appetizer. You can try the rack of lamb in a mint, mustard, and vermouth sauce, and any of the pastas is a safe bet. ⊠ *109–1025 Robson St.,* ☎ *604/669– 9322. Reservations essential. AE, D, DC, MC, V. No lunch weekends.*

$$$–$$$$ ✕ **Villa del Lupo.** Ask the top chefs in town where they go for Italian,
★ and Villa del Lupo is the answer more often than not. Country-house-elegant decor sets a romantic tone, but come prepared to roll up your sleeves and mop up the sauce with a chunk of crusty bread. Rabbit braised with Pinot Grigio and braised lamb osso buco in a sauce of tomatoes, red wine, cinnamon, and lemon are favorites here. ⊠ *869 Hamilton St.,* ☎ *604/688–7436. Reservations essential. AE, DC, MC, V. No lunch.*

$$–$$$$ ✕ **Piccolo Mondo Ristorante.** Soft candlelight, elegantly set tables, bountiful flower arrangements, and fine European antiques create a fairly formal atmosphere at this intimate northern Italian restaurant on a quiet street a block off Robson. Start with a goat cheese tart with tomato, prosciutto, and basil, and follow up with the classic osso buco or the linguine tossed with smoked Alaskan cod, capers, and red onions. The award-winning wine cellar stocks more than 3,000 bottles (450 varieties). ⊠ *850 Thurlow St.,* ☎ *604/688–1633. Reservations essential. AE, DC, MC, V. Closed Sun. No lunch weekends.*

$$–$$$ ✕ **Quattro on Fourth.** This northern Italian restaurant in Kitsilano shot to stardom quickly. A mosaic floor, mustard-color walls with stark-

green-and-mauve stenciled borders, cherry-stained tables, and a wraparound covered porch for alfresco dining enhance the Mediterranean atmosphere. Mushroom lovers usually jump at the Portobello fusilli, but if you can't make up your mind, there's the *combinazione* (a plate for two with the five most popular pastas and sauces). The gelato trio is a perfect topper. ⊠ *2611 W. 4th Ave.,* ☎ *604/734–4444. Reservations essential. AE, DC, MC, V.*

$$–$$$ ✕ **Zefferelli's Spaghetti House.** As you might guess from the name, spaghetti, penne, fusilli, tortellini, and fettuccine dressed in creative but subtle sauces—from smoked salmon, wild mushrooms, feta cheese, and tomato sauce to traditional meat sauce—play first string at Zefferelli's, but the antipasto table, grilled prawns, and chicken with shiitake mushrooms are strong competitors. Done up in forest green, mustard, and persimmon, the trendy, somewhat rushed dining room has an open kitchen at one end and a wall of windows overlooking busy Robson Street at the other. ⊠ *1136 Robson St.,* ☎ *604/687–0655. Reservations essential. AE, DC, MC, V. No lunch weekends.*

Japanese

$$$ ✕ **Tojo's.** Hidekazu Tojo is a sushi-making legend here, with more than
★ 2,000 special preparations stored in his creative mind. His handsome blond-wood tatami rooms, on the second floor of a modern green-glass tower on West Broadway, provide the proper ambience for intimate dining, but Tojo's 10-seat sushi bar stands as the centerpiece. With Tojo presiding, it offers a convivial ringside seat for watching the creation of edible art. Although tempura and teriyaki dinners will satisfy, the seasonal menu is more exciting. In fall, ask for *dobin mushi,* a soup made from pine mushrooms. In spring, try salad made from scallops and pink cherry blossoms. ⊠ *202–777 W. Broadway,* ☎ *604/872–8050. Reservations essential. AE, DC, MC, V. Closed Sun. No lunch.*

$$–$$$ ✕ **Chiyoda.** The *robata* (grill) bar curves through Chiyoda's main room: On one side are the customers and an array of flat baskets full of the day's offerings; on the other side are the chefs and grills. There are 35 choices of things to grill, from squid, snapper, and oysters to eggplant, mushrooms, onions, and potatoes. You can dress your picks with sake, soy sauce, or *ponzu* (vinegar and soy sauce). ⊠ *200–1050 Alberni St.,* ☎ *604/688–5050. Reservations essential. AE, DC, MC, V. Closed Sun. No lunch Sat.*

$$ ✕ **Shijo Japanese Restaurant.** Shijo has an excellent and very large sushi bar, a smaller robata bar, tatami rooms, and a row of tables overlooking bustling 4th Avenue. The epitome of urban Japanese chic is conveyed through the jazz music, handsome lamps with a bronze finish, and lots of black wood. You can count on creatively prepared sushi in generous proportions, eggplant *dengaku* (topped with light and dark miso paste and broiled), and shiitake *yaki* (fresh shiitake mushrooms cooked in foil with lemony ponzu sauce). ⊠ *1926 W. 4th Ave.,* ☎ *604/732–4676. Reservations essential. AE, DC, MC, V. No lunch weekends.*

Korean

$ ✕ **Seoul House Korean Restaurant.** This bright, popular restaurant, decorated in Japanese style, serves a full menu of Japanese and Korean food, including sushi. The best bet is the Korean barbecue, which you cook at your table; the dinner of marinated beef, pork, chicken, or fish comes complete with a half dozen side dishes—*kimchi* (a spicy condiment), salads, stir-fried rice, and pickled vegetables—as well as soup. Service can be chaotic. ⊠ *36 E. Broadway,* ☎ *604/874–4131. Reservations essential. MC, V.*

Mexican

$$$–$$$$ ✕ **Mescalero Cantina Grill.** Here you find the look and feel of a Santa Fe cocina, from stucco walls and leather chairs inside to a charming greenery-draped patio for open-air dining. On weekends the restaurant and attached bar become party central, but weekdays are more subdued. Tapas, many with Asian Pacific influences, are the main draw—mussels with sun-dried tomato cream; chicken and chorizo chimichangas with Brie; and grilled salmon, asparagus, and goat-cheese burritos—but dinner selections such as chili-dusted halibut fillet and duck marinated in tequila are equally creative. The Bandito Brunch on Sundays draws a crowd. ⊠ *1215 Bidwell St.,* ☎ *604/669–2399. Reservations essential. AE, DC, MC, V.*

Native American

$$–$$$ ✕ **Liliget Feast House.** A downstairs "longhouse" a few blocks from
★   English Bay serves the original Northwest Coast cuisine: bannock bread, baked sweet potato with hazelnuts, alder-grilled salmon, toasted seaweed with rice, steamed fern shoots, barbecued venison, and soapberries for dessert. Try the authentic but odd dish known as oolichan grease, which is prepared from candlefish. Native music is piped in, and Northwest Coast native artworks (for sale) decorate the walls. ⊠ *1724 Davie St.,* ☎ *604/681–7044. Reservations essential. AE, DC, MC, V. No lunch.*

Pan-Asian

$–$$ ✕ **Phnom Penh Restaurant.** Part of a small cluster of Southeast Asian
★   shops on the fringes of Chinatown, this eatery has potted plants and framed views of Angkor Wat. The hospitable staff serves unusually robust Vietnamese and Cambodian fare, including crisp, peppery garlic prawns fried in the shell and a salad with sliced warm beef crusted with ground salt and pepper. The decor at the Broadway location is fancier, but the food is every bit as good at East Georgia Street. ⊠ *244 E. Georgia St.,* ☎ *604/682–5777;* ⊠ *955 W. Broadway,* ☎ *604/734–8898. AE, MC. Both locations closed Tues.*

Seafood

$$$–$$$$ ✕ **C.** Its marina-side location overlooking False Creek makes a perfect setting for this seafood restaurant. Opened in 1997 to high expectations, C appears to have met, or exceeded, most of them. Danish chef Soren Fakstorp trained in Europe and worked in Asia before coming to Canada, and his experience shows in his innovative approach to seafood, from the salmon grilled in wasabi to the monkfish tournedos with seared foie gras. A certain wit characterizes the setup here: The appetizer selection is delivered in a box, and the one meat dish on the menu is called the catch of the day. The two-tiered interior is done in cool, almost stark grays; outside, a heated seaside patio has views of Granville Island. ⊠ *2–1600 Howe St.,* ☎ *604/681–1164, Reservations essential. AE, DC, MC, V. No lunch weekends Sept.–June.*

$$–$$$$ ✕ **A Kettle of Fish.** Since opening in 1979, this family-run restaurant at the northeast end of Burrard Bridge has attracted a strong following. The gardenlike interior, with plants and fig trees, is quiet and cool. The menu varies daily according to market availability, but there are generally 15 kinds of fresh seafood that are either grilled, sautéed, poached, barbecued, or blackened Cajun-style. The British Columbia salmon and the seafood combo plate are always good choices. ⊠ *900 Pacific Blvd.,* ☎ *604/682–6661. AE, DC, MC, V. No lunch weekends.*

$$–$$$ ✕ **Fish House in Stanley Park.** Tucked between Stanley Park's tennis courts and putting green, this gracious 1930s former sports pavilion, with its conservatory, veranda, and fireplace, has a delightful Pimms-on-the-lawn feel. The cuisine, though, is a far cry from cucumber

sandwiches. Chef Karen Barnaby writes cookbooks, and the titles—*Pacific Passions* and *Screamingly Good Food*—say a lot about the food here, which is hearty, flavorful, and unpretentious. Good choices are the ahi tuna steak Dianne or the cornhusk-wrapped salmon with maple glaze. Pre-dinner, head straight for the oyster bar, or arrive between 5 and 6 to take advantage of the early-bird specials. ⊠ *8901 Stanley Park Dr., near the Beach Ave. entrance to Stanley Park,* ☎ *604/681–7275. Reservations essential. AE, DC, MC, V.*

$$–$$$ ✕ **Joe Fortes Seafood and Chop House.** Reserve a table on the second-floor balcony at this seafood hot spot to take in the view of the broad wall murals, the mounted blue marlins, and, most especially, the ever-entertaining boy-meets-girl scene at the bar downstairs. The complex takes in a piano bar, bistro, oyster bar, and rooftop patio, but the menus and the extensive wine list largely overlap. The signature tiger shrimp and diver scallops, or cedar-plank-roasted salmon smoked with vanilla tea, are tasty and filling but often overlooked in favor of the reasonably priced blue-plate special. ⊠ *777 Thurlow St.,* ☎ *604/669–1940. Reservations essential for restaurant. AE, D, DC, MC, V.*

Tex-Mex

$ ✕ **Topanga Cafe.** Arrive before 6:30 or after 8 PM to avoid waiting in line for this 40-seat Kitsilano classic. The Tex-Mex food hasn't changed much since 1978, when the Topanga started dishing up fresh salsa and homemade tortilla chips. Quantities are still huge and prices low. Kids can color blank menu covers while waiting for food; a hundred of their best efforts are framed on the walls. ⊠ *2904 W. 4th Ave.,* ☎ *604/733–3713. Reservations not accepted. MC, V. Closed Sun.*

Thai

$ ✕ **Thai House.** A sun-filled second-floor diner overlooking Robson Street offers a great lunch deal from 11 to 3: For under $8, patrons feast on a spring roll, salad, rice, and a choice of 18 typical Thai dishes for the main course. The mild, smoky flavor of *kai pad khing* (boneless chicken with ginger, mushroom, and onions) is satisfying, but the boneless chicken in coconut milk is even better. ⊠ *1116 Robson St.,* ☎ *604/683–3383. AE, DC, MC, V.*

Vegetarian

$ ✕ **Naam Restaurant.** Vancouver's oldest natural foods eatery is open 24 hours, so if you need to satisfy a late-night veggie-burger craving, rest easy. The Naam also serves wine, beer, cappuccino, fresh juices, and wicked chocolate desserts, along with vegetarian stir-fries. Wood tables, an open fireplace, and live blues, folk, and jazz help create a homey atmosphere. On warm summer evenings, you can sit in the out-door courtyard at the back of the restaurant. ⊠ *2724 W. 4th Ave.,* ☎ *604/738–7151. AE, MC, V.*

LODGING

The hotel industry has become a major business for Vancouver, which hosts large numbers of conventioneers, Asian businesspeople, and others who are used to an above-average level of service. Although by some standards pricey, properties here are highly competitive, and you can expect service to reflect this. Of the more than 16,000 rooms in greater Vancouver, just over 10,000 are in the downtown core. The chart below shows high-season prices, but from mid-October through May, rates throughout the city can drop as much as 50%.

Vancouver hotels, especially the more expensive properties downtown, are fairly comparable in facilities. Unless otherwise noted, expect to find the following amenities: minibars, in-room movies, no-smoking rooms and/or floors, room service, massage, exercise room, baby-sitting, laundry service and dry cleaning, concierge, business services, meeting rooms, and parking (there is usually an additional fee). Lodgings in the inexpensive to moderate category do not generally offer much in the way of amenities (no in-room minibar, restaurant, room service, pool, exercise room, and so on).

CATEGORY	COST*
$$$$	over $300
$$$	$200–$300
$$	$125–$200
$	under $125

*All prices are for a standard double room, excluding 10% room tax and 7% GST, in Canadian dollars.

$$$$ ⊞ **Four Seasons.** Famous for pampering guests (kids and pets in-
★ cluded), the Four Seasons sits at the geographic center of downtown Vancouver. The bustling, 28-story luxury hotel adjacent to the Vancouver Stock Exchange is attached to the Pacific Centre shopping mall. Standard rooms are average in size and comforts; roomier corner rooms are recommended. Service at the Four Seasons is top notch, and the attention to detail is outstanding. The formal dining room, Chartwell (☞ Dining, *above*), is one of the best in the city. Even pets receive red-carpet treatment—they're served Evian and pet treats in silver bowls. ⊠ *791 W. Georgia St., V6C 2T4,* ☎ *604/689–9333, 800/ 268–6282 in Canada, 800/332–3442 in the U.S.;* FAX *604/844–6744. 309 rooms, 67 suites. 2 restaurants, bar, indoor-outdoor pool, hot tub, sauna, shops, piano. AE, DC, MC, V.*

$$$$ ⊞ **Hotel Vancouver.** The copper roof of this grand château-style hotel (☞ Robson to the Waterfront *in* Exploring Vancouver, *above*) dominates Vancouver's skyline. Opened in 1939 by the Canadian National Railway, the hotel commands a regal position in the center of town. Even the standard guest rooms have an air of prestige, with mahogany furniture, attractive linens, and the original, deep bathtubs. Suites, with French doors and graceful wing chairs, take up two floors and come with extra services and amenities. ⊠ *900 W. Georgia St., V6C 2W6,* ☎ *604/684–3131 or 800/441–1414,* FAX *604/662–1937. 550 rooms, 44 suites. 2 restaurants, lobby lounge, in-room modem lines, indoor lap pool, beauty salon, hot tub, saunas, spa, health club, piano, car rental. AE, D, DC, MC, V.*

$$$$ ⊞ **Pan Pacific Hotel.** Sprawling Canada Place, on a pier right by the financial district, houses the luxurious Pan Pacific, the Vancouver Trade and Convention Centre, and a cruise-ship terminal. The three-story atrium lobby has a dramatic totem pole and waterfall, and the lounge, restaurant, and café all have huge expanses of glass with views of the harbor and mountains. Guest rooms were freshly decorated in 1998. Eighty percent of the rooms have a water view, although corner rooms overlooking the harbor are favorites. ⊠ *300–999 Canada Pl., V6C 3B5,* ☎ *604/662–8111, 800/663–1515 in Canada, 800/ 937–1515 in the U.S.;* FAX *604/685–8690. 466 rooms, 40 suites. 2 restaurants, café, coffee shop, lobby lounge, in-room modem lines, pool, barbershop, beauty salon, hot tubs, outdoor hot tub, saunas, steam rooms, aerobics, health club, indoor track, paddle tennis, racquetball, squash, convention center, travel services. AE, DC, MC, V.*

$$$$ ⊞ **Sutton Place.** The feel here is more exclusive guest house than
★ large hotel: The lobby has sumptuously thick carpets, enormous displays of flowers, and elegant European furniture. Guest rooms are furnished with rich, dark woods reminiscent of 19th-century France, and suites have modem lines and safes. Despite its size, this hotel maintains a significant level of intimacy. The Fleuri Restaurant serves Con-

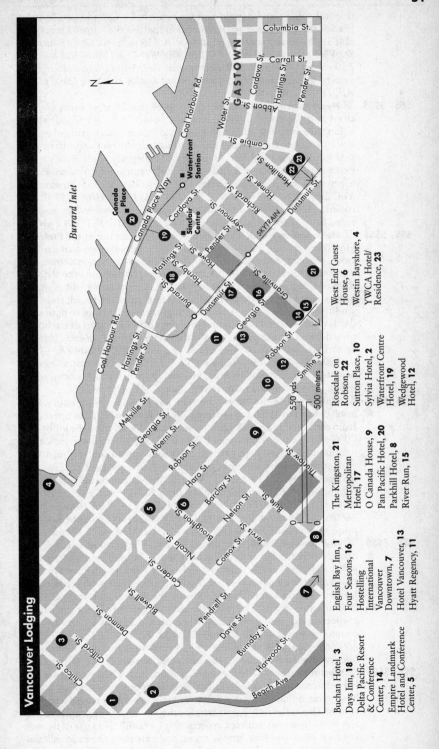

Vancouver Lodging

Buchan Hotel, **3**
Days Inn, **18**
Delta Pacific Resort & Conference Center, **14**
Empire Landmark Hotel and Conference Center, **5**

English Bay Inn, **1**
Four Seasons, **16**
Hostelling International Vancouver Downtown, **7**
Hotel Vancouver, **13**
Hyatt Regency, **11**

The Kingston, **21**
Metropolitan Hotel, **17**
O Canada House, **9**
Pan Pacific Hotel, **20**
Parkhill Hotel, **8**
River Run, **15**

Rosedale on Robson, **22**
Sutton Place, **10**
Sylvia Hotel, **2**
Waterfront Centre Hotel, **19**
Wedgewood Hotel, **12**

West End Guest House, **6**
Westin Bayshore, **4**
YWCA Hotel/Residence, **23**

tinental cuisine and a great Sunday brunch. Le Grande Residence, a luxury, fully equipped apartment hotel (part of the Sutton Place) suitable for extended stays, is next door at 855 Burrard. ⊠ *845 Burrard St., V6Z 2K6,* ☎ *604/682–5511 or 800/961–7555,* ℻ *604/682–5513. 350 rooms, 47 suites, 162 apartments. Restaurant, bar, indoor pool, beauty salon, sauna, spa, steam room, health club, bicycles, piano. AE, D, DC, MC, V.*

$$$–$$$$ ⊞ **Hyatt Regency.** The standard rooms of this 34-story hotel are spacious and decorated in deep, dramatic colors and dark wood; all are equipped with irons and ironing boards, coffeemakers, bathrobes, and voice mail. Ask for a corner room with a balcony on the north or west side for the best view. For a small fee, the Regency Club gives you the exclusivity of a floor accessed by keyed elevators, your own concierge, a private lounge, and complimentary breakfast. ⊠ *655 Burrard St., V6C 2R7,* ☎ *604/683–1234 or 800/233–1234,* ℻ *604/689–3707. 612 rooms, 34 suites. Restaurant, 2 bars, café, in-room modem lines, in-room safes, pool, sauna, shops, travel services, car rental. AE, D, DC, MC, V.*

$$$–$$$$ ⊞ **Metropolitan Hotel.** This 18-story hotel, a member of the Preferred Hotels group, has freshly renovated (1998) guest rooms that are spacious, peaceful, and well soundproofed. Business-class rooms come with in-room printers, fax machines, and cordless phones; and even the standard rooms feature a number of luxuries, including bathrobes, newspapers, valet service, down duvets, and free use of the health club. The studio suites—even bigger and only slightly more expensive than standard rooms—are a favorite, and the lobby offers glimpses of the hotel's award-winning restaurant, Diva at the Met (☞ Dining, *above*), through an etched-glass wall. ⊠ *645 Howe St., V6C 2Y9,* ☎ *604/687–1122 or 800/667–2300,* ℻ *604/643–7267. 179 rooms, 18 suites. Restaurant, bar, in-room modem lines, indoor lap pool, hot tub, sauna, steam room, exercise room, racquetball, squash. AE, DC, MC, V.*

$$$–$$$$ ⊞ **Waterfront Centre Hotel.** Dramatically elegant, this 23-story glass
     ★   hotel opened in 1991 across from Canada Place, which can be reached from the hotel by an underground walkway. Views from the lobby and 70% of the guest rooms are of Burrard Inlet; other rooms look onto a fragrant, terraced herb garden. The rooms are attractively furnished with contemporary artwork, and armoires conceal the TV. Large corner rooms have the best views. A string quartet entertains in the lobby restaurant, Herons, during Sunday brunch. ⊠ *900 Canada Pl. Way, V6C 3L5,* ☎ *604/691–1991 or 800/441–1414,* ℻ *604/691–1999. 460 rooms, 29 suites. Restaurant, lobby lounge, some in-room modems, pool, steam room, health club, shops. AE, D, DC, MC, V.*

$$$–$$$$ ⊞ **Wedgewood Hotel.** The small, elegant Wedgewood is run by an
     ★   owner who cares fervently about her guests. The lobby is decorated with polished brass, beveled glass, a fireplace, tasteful artwork, and fine antiques. All the extra touches are here, too: turndown service, afternoon ice delivery, dark-out drapes, flowers on the balcony, robes, and a morning newspaper. The Wedgewood's clients are almost exclusively corporate, except on weekends, when the place turns into a romantic couples' retreat. ⊠ *845 Hornby St., V6Z 1V1,* ☎ *604/689–7777 or 800/663–0666,* ℻ *604/608–5348. 51 rooms, 38 suites. Restaurant, bar, some in-room modems, in-room safes, sauna. AE, D, DC, MC, V.*

$$$–$$$$ ⊞ **Westin Bayshore.** The Bayshore, perched on the best part of the harbor adjacent to Stanley Park, has truly fabulous views. Many rooms have great mountain and marina views; those in the tower have balconies. This is the only resort hotel in the downtown area and the perfect place to stay in summer, especially for a family, because of its huge outdoor pool, sundeck, grassy areas, and extensive recreational facilities. There's a free downtown shuttle, too. ⊠ *1601 W. Georgia St., V6G 2V4,* ☎ *604/682–3377 or 800/228–3000,* ℻ *604/687–3102.*

484 rooms, 33 suites. Restaurant, 2 bars, cafés, in-room modem lines and safes in tower rooms, indoor pool, outdoor pool, barbershop, beauty salon, steam rooms, boating, fishing, bicycles, piano, travel services, car rental. AE, D, DC, MC, V.

$$$ ⊞ **Rosedale on Robson.** If you plan to be in town awhile and want to
★ keep expenses down by doing some of your own cooking, look into a room at the all-suite Rosedale, opened in 1995. Rooms in shades of peach and light green are generous in size and have European kitchens, bleached hemlock furniture, and garden patios or balconies over-looking the city. The rooms on upper floors on the south and east side have views of False Creek. You'll find charming gardens with strolling paths on the second and third floors of the complex. ⊠ *838 Hamilton St., V6B 6A2,* ☎ *604/689–8033 or 800/661–8870,* ℻ *604/689–4426. 275 suites. Restaurant, bar, kitchenettes, refrigerators, room service, indoor lap pool, hot tub, sauna, steam room, exercise room, coin laundry. AE, DC, MC, V.*

$$–$$$ ⊞ **Delta Pacific Resort & Conference Center.** It's the facilities that make this 14-acre site a resort: swimming pools (one indoor, with a three-story tubular water slide), tennis courts with a pro, an outdoor fitness circuit, aqua-exercise classes, outdoor volleyball nets, a play center and summer camps for children, and a playground. The hotel, near the airport and about a 30-minute drive south of downtown Vancouver, is large but casual and friendly. Guest rooms are modern, with contemporary decor and a pleasant blue-and-green color scheme. The Delta Vancouver Airport Hotel and Marina, with 415 rooms, is a few minutes' shuttle ride away and even closer to the airport. Guests here also have access to the resort facilities. ⊠ *10251 St. Edwards Dr., Richmond V6X 2M9,* ☎ *604/278–9611 or 800/268–1133,* ℻ *604/276–1121. 526 rooms, 30 suites. 2 restaurants, lobby lounge, in-room modem lines, indoor pool, 2 outdoor pools, barbershop, beauty salon, hot tub, saunas, putting green, squash, bicycles, children's programs (ages 5–12), convention center, car rental. AE, DC, MC, V.*

$$–$$$ ⊞ **Empire Landmark Hotel and Conference Center.** The former Sheraton Landmark is still, at 42 stories, one of the tallest hotels in the downtown area; it also has some of the best views and prettiest guest rooms in town. Prints of work by British Columbia's beloved Emily Carr decorate many rooms, and the bold jewel tones (emerald, sapphire, and ruby) of the paintings are repeated in the furnishings. All rooms have a fine view, but the Cloud Nine revolving restaurant on the top floor is a great place for an unobstructed view of Vancouver over an early breakfast buffet; go elsewhere for dinner. ⊠ *1400 Robson St., V6G 1B9,* ☎ *604/687–0511 or 800/830–6144,* ℻ *604/687–2801. 351 rooms, 7 suites. Restaurant, café, sports bar, saunas, convention center, travel services, car rental. AE, DC, MC, V.*

$$–$$$ ⊞ **English Bay Inn.** This renovated 1930s Tudor-style house is one block
★ from the ocean and Stanley Park. The guest rooms—each with a private bath—have wonderful sleigh beds (in all but one room) with matching armoires and Ralph Lauren linens. The common areas of the no-smoking inn are elegantly furnished with museum-quality antiques: The sophisticated but cozy parlor has wing chairs, a fireplace, a gilt Louis XV clock and candelabra, and French doors overlooking the front garden. Breakfast, included in the price, is served in a formal room with a Gothic dining-room suite, a fireplace, and a 17th-century grandfather clock. This B&B is both small and popular—summer rooms often book up by February. ⊠ *1968 Comox St., V6G1R4,* ☎ *604/683–8002,* ℻ *604/899–1501. 5 rooms. Free parking. AE, MC, V.*

$$–$$$ ⊞ **Parkhill Hotel.** Cool pastel shades echo the colors of impressionist prints decorating the surprisingly spacious rooms in this West End hotel just a few blocks from either downtown or English Bay Beach. Many

of the rooms will sleep four, and large, comfortable sitting areas, half-moon balconies with city or bay views, mini-refrigerators, hair dryers, and complimentary downtown shuttle services are part of the package. ✉ *1160 Davie St., V6E 1N1,* ☎ *604/685–1311 or 800/663–1525,* FAX *604/681–0208. 191 rooms. 2 restaurants, lounge, pool, sauna, concierge, car rental. AE, D, DC, MC, V.*

$–$$$ 🏠 **West End Guest House.** The lovely West End, built in 1906, is a true
★   Victorian "painted lady," from its gracious front parlor, cozy fireplace, and early 1900s furniture to its green-trimmed pink exterior. Most of the small but handsome rooms have high brass beds, antiques, and gorgeous linens. The inn's genial host, Evan Penner, adds small touches such as a pre-dinner glass of sherry, terry bathrobes, and turndown service. The inn is in a residential neighborhood two minutes from Robson Street. Room rates at this no-smoking establishment include a full breakfast. Book by March for a stay in the summer. ✉ *1362 Haro St., V6E 1G2,* ☎ *604/681–2889,* FAX *604/688–8812. 8 rooms. Bicycles, free parking. AE, D, DC, MC, V.*

$$ 🏠 **Days Inn.** Business travelers looking for a bargain will find this location convenient. The six-story hotel, which opened as the Abbotsford in 1920, is the only moderately priced hotel in the business core. Rooms are bright, clean, and utilitarian, but there are few amenities and no room service. In-room data ports and voice mail are available, though. ✉ *921 W. Pender St., V6C 1M2,* ☎ *604/681–4335,* FAX *604/681–7808. 85 rooms, 4 suites. Restaurant, 2 bars, in-room safes, billiards, coin laundry. AE, D, DC, MC, V.*

$$ 🏠 **O Canada House.** Beautifully restored, this 1897 Victorian in a res-
★   idential neighborhood within walking distance of downtown is the house in which the first version of "O Canada," the national anthem, was written in 1909. Winner of Vancouver's top Heritage Restoration award, it oozes with period charm. Each spacious bedroom of the B&B is appointed in late-Victorian antiques; modern comforts, like in-room TVs, VCRs, phones, and bathrobes, help make things homey. The top-floor room is enormous, with two double beds and a private sitting area. You also have the use of a guest pantry and can sit in the evening near the fireplace in the front parlor. Breakfast, served in the dining room or on the wraparound porch, is lavish. O Canada is popular—book well ahead if you plan to visit in summer. ✉ *1114 Barclay St., V6E 1H1,* ☎ *604/688–0555,* FAX *604/488–0556. 5 rooms. Free parking. MC, V.*

$–$$ 🏠 **River Run.** A unique bed-and-breakfast, River Run sits in the serene Fraser River delta in the village of Ladner, 30 minutes' drive south of downtown Vancouver, 10 minutes north of the ferries to Vancouver Island, and just off Highway 99 on the way from Seattle. You can choose among a little gem of a floating house; a net loft (complete with Japanese soaking tub on the deck and a cozy captain's bed); and one of two river's-edge cottages, each with a fireplace and deck over the water. There are also two sea kayaks and a canoe for guest use. Afternoon refreshments and breakfast are included in the tariff at this no-smoking inn. ✉ *4551 River Rd. W, Ladner V4K 1R9,* ☎ *604/946–7778,* FAX *604/940–1970. 4 suites. Kitchenettes in two suites, TV and VCR on request, bicycles, free parking. MC, V.*

$ 🏠 **Buchan Hotel.** The three-story 1930s building is set on a tree-lined residential street a block from Stanley Park. For the budget price, you rent tiny, institutional rooms with basic furnishings, ceiling fans, and color TV but no telephone or air-conditioning. There's also a lounge with a fireplace, public telephone, and storage for bikes and skis. The pension-style rooms with shared bath down the hall are perhaps the most affordable accommodations near downtown. This is a no-smoking hotel, and, though there is no elevator, the addition of wheelchair-accessible garden-level rooms was being considered at press time. ✉ *1906*

*Haro St., V6G 1H7, ☎ 604/685–5354 or 800/668–6654, FAX 604/685–
5367. 65 rooms, 30 with bath. Coin laundry. AE, DC, MC, V.*

$ 　 ⊡ **Hostelling International Vancouver Downtown.** Vancouver's newest
★ 　 hostel, in the West End downtown, is just blocks from English Bay Beach
and within walking distance of Stanley Park and a quick ferry ride to
Granville Island. The hostel itself is very tidy and secure; access to the
wings of private rooms and the men's and women's dorms requires a
card key. Amenities include a shared kitchen and dining room, a TV
room, a garden patio, a games room, bicycles, and storage for luggage
and bikes. The staff here are extremely friendly and informative, and
the prime location and inexpensive price can't be beat. ⊠ *1114 Burnaby St., V6E 1P1, ☎ 604/684–4565, FAX 604/684–4540. 23 rooms,
44 4-bed dorms. No-smoking floors, bicycles, library, coin laundry.*

$ 　 ⊡ **The Kingston.** The Kingston is a small budget hotel convenient for
shopping. It's an old-style, four-story building, with no elevator—the
type of establishment you'd find in Europe. The spartan rooms, renovated in 1995, are small and immaculate and share a bathroom down
the hall. All rooms have phones, and a few have TVs and private
baths; there's a TV lounge. Rooms on the south side are sunnier. Continental breakfast is included in the price. ⊠ *757 Richards St., V6B
3A6, ☎ 604/684–9024, FAX 604/684–9917. 56 rooms, 8 with bath.
Sauna, coin laundry. AE, MC, V.*

$ 　 ⊡ **Sylvia Hotel.** To stay here from June through August you'll need to
book six months to a year ahead. This ivy-covered older building is so
popular because of its low rates and near-perfect location: about 25 ft
from the beach on scenic English Bay, 200 ft from Stanley Park, and
a 20-minute walk from Robson Street. The unadorned rooms have worn,
plain furnishings. Some suites are huge, and all have kitchens. ⊠ *1154
Gilford St., V6G 2P6, ☎ 604/681–9321, FAX 604/682–3551. 97
rooms, 22 suites. Restaurant, café, lounge, laundry service, dry cleaning, parking (fee). AE, DC, MC, V.*

$ 　 ⊡ **YWCA Hotel/Residence.** Opened in the entertainment district in
★ 　 1995, the secured 12-story building has bright, airy, and very comfortable
rooms. All have floral bedspreads, framed floral prints, nightstands and
desk, a mini-refrigerator, a phone, and a sink. Some share a bath down
the hall, others share a bath between two rooms, and still others have
private baths. The hotel is open to men and women and offers discounts
for seniors, students, and YWCA members. Rates include use of the
YWCA pool and fitness facility at 535 Hornby Street (☞ Health and
Fitness Clubs *in* Outdoor Activities and Sports, *below*). ⊠ *733 Beatty
St., V6B 2M4, ☎ 604/895–5830, 800/663–1424 in British Columbia
and Alberta; FAX 604/681–2550. 155 rooms. 3 shared kitchens, 2
shared kitchenettes, no-smoking floors, refrigerators, 3 shared TV
lounges, 2 coin laundries, meeting rooms. MC, V.*

NIGHTLIFE AND THE ARTS

For **information on events,** pick up a free copy of *Georgia Straight* (available at cafés and bookstores around town), or look in the entertainment section of the *Vancouver Sun* (Thursday's paper has listings in
the "What's On" column). Call the **Arts Hotline** (☎ 604/684–2787)
for the latest lineups in entertainment. For tickets, book through **Ticketmaster** (☎ 604/280–3311).

The Arts

Dance

Watch for **Ballet British Columbia**'s (☎ 604/732–5003) Dance Alive!
series November–April, presenting visiting and local ballet companies

from the Kirov to Ballet British Columbia. Performances are held at the Queen Elizabeth Theatre (☞ Music, *below*). A few of the 18 professional dance companies in town are Karen Jamison, DanceArts Vancouver, and JumpStart. For information on dance in British Columbia, call the **Dance Centre** (☎ 604/606–6400). Popular dance venues include the **Firehall Arts Centre** (✉ 280 E. Cordova, ☎ 604/689–0926) and the **Vancouver East Cultural Centre** (☞ Theater, *below*).

Film

For **foreign films and original works,** try the Fifth Avenue Cinemas (✉ 2110 Burrard St., ☎ 604/734–7469), the Park Theater (✉ 3440 Cambie St., ☎ 604/876–2747), the Ridge Theatre (✉ 3131 Arbutus St., ☎ 604/738–6311), and the Varsity Theater (✉ 4375 W. 10th Ave., ☎ 604/222–2235). **Pacific Cinématèque** (✉ 1131 Howe St., ☎ 604/688–8202) shows esoteric foreign and art films. Tickets are half price on Tuesdays at all **Cineplex Odeon** theaters. The **Vancouver International Film Festival** (☎ 604/685–0260) is held during September or October.

Music

The **Vancouver Symphony Orchestra** (☎ 604/684–9100) plays at the Orpheum Theatre (✉ 601 Smithe St.). The **CBC Radio Orchestra** (☎ 604/662–6080) is one of the groups that use the Orpheum Theatre (☞ *above*). **Choral groups** like the Bach Choir (☎ 604/921–8012), the Vancouver Cantata Singers (☎ 604/921–8588), and the Vancouver Chamber Choir (☎ 604/738–6822) play a major role in Vancouver's classical music scene. The **Early Music Society** (☎ 604/732–1610) performs medieval, Renaissance, and Baroque music and hosts the Vancouver Early Music Summer Festival, one of the most important early music festivals in North America. Concerts by the **Friends of Chamber Music** (☎ 604/437–5747) are worth watching for. Programs of the **Vancouver Recital Society** (☎ 604/602–0363) are always of excellent quality.

Opened in 1997, the **Chan Centre for the Performing Arts** (✉ 6265 Crescent Rd., on the University of British Columbia campus, ☎ 604/822–2697), includes a 1,400-seat concert hall, a theater, and a movie theater. The **Queen Elizabeth Theatre** (✉ 600 Hamilton St., ☎ 604/665–3050) is a major venue for traveling musicals, opera, and other events.

The **Vancouver Folk Music Festival** (☎ 604/602–9798 or 800/883–3655)), a leading folk and world music event, takes place at Jericho Beach Park on the third weekend of July. For folk and traditional Celtic concerts year-round, call the **Rogue Folk Club** (☎ 604/736–3022).

Opera

Vancouver Opera (☎ 604/682–2871) stages five high-caliber productions a year, usually in October, November, February, March, and June, at the Queen Elizabeth Theatre (✉ 600 Hamilton St., ☎ 604/665–3050).

Theater

The **Arts Club Theatre** (✉ 1585 Johnston St., ☎ 604/687–1644) has two stages on Granville Island and theatrical performances all year. **Carousel Theatre** (☎ 604/669–3410) performs works for children and young people at the Waterfront Theatre (✉ 1411 Cartwright St., ☎ 604/685–6217) on Granville Island. The **Ford Centre for the Performing Arts** (✉ 777 Homer St., ☎ 604/602–0616) showcases major productions and top touring companies. **Touchstone** (✉ 280 E. Cordova St., ☎ 604/215–3853) is a small but lively company. The **Vancouver East Cultural Centre** (✉ 1895 Venables St., ☎ 604/254–9578) is a multipurpose performance space that always hosts high-caliber shows. The **Vancouver Playhouse** (✉ 160 W. 1st. Ave., ☎ 604/872–6622) is the best-established venue in Vancouver for mainstream theatrical shows.

Bard on the Beach (☎ 604/739–0559) is a summer series of Shakespeare plays performed under a huge tent on the beach at Vanier Park. The **Fringe** (☎ 604/257–0350), Vancouver's annual theatrical arts festival, is staged in September at churches and theater halls. **Theatre Under the Stars** (☎ 604/687–0174) performs musicals at Malkin Bowl, an outdoor amphitheater in Stanley Park, during July and August.

Nightlife

Bars and Lounges

BaBalu (⊠ 654 Nelson St., ☎ 604/605–4343) leads the local lounge revival with its house band, the Smoking Section. The **Bacchus Lounge** (⊠ 845 Hornby St., ☎ 604/689–7777) in the Wedgewood Hotel is stylish and chic, with a pianist providing soothing background music. The **Garden Terrace** (⊠ 791 W. Georgia St., ☎ 604/689–9333) in the Four Seasons (☞ Lodging, *above*) is bright and airy with African flora and a waterfall, plus big soft chairs you won't want to get out of; a pianist plays here every night. The **Gérard Lounge** (⊠ 845 Burrard St., ☎ 604/682–5511) at the Sutton Place Hotel is probably the nicest in the city because of its fireplaces, wing chairs, dark wood, and leather; it's also the major film industry hangout in town. For a pint of real Irish Guinness, with live traditional Irish music, try the **Irish Heather** (⊠ 217 Carrall St., ☎ 604/688–9779), in Gastown. The **900 West** (⊠ 900 W. Georgia St., ☎ 604/684–3131) wine bar at the Hotel Vancouver has 55 wines available by the glass.

One of the city's "hot" pool halls is the **Automotive Billiards Club** (⊠ 1095 Homer, ☎ 604/682–0040). The lively **Joe Fortes** (⊠ 777 Thurlow St., ☎ 604/669–1940) is known as the local meet market. Billiards is very popular here, and the **Soho Café and Billiards** (⊠ 1144 Homer, ☎ 604/688–1180) is the place to go to sip and shoot.

The **Backstage Lounge** (⊠ 1585 Johnston St., ☎ 604/687–1354), behind the main stage at the Arts Club Theatre on Granville Island, stocks more than 50 varieties of Scotch and is a hangout for local touring musicians and actors. On Granville Island, the after-work crowd heads to **Bridges** (☎ 604/687–4400) near the Public Market.

Brew Pubs

At **Steam Works** (⊠ 375 Water St., ☎ 604/689–2739) on the edge of bustling Gastown, they use a steam brewing process and large copper kettles (visible through glass walls in the dining room downstairs) to whip up six to nine brews; the espresso ale is interesting. The **Yaletown Brewing Company** (⊠ 1111 Mainland St., ☎ 604/681–2739), based in a huge renovated warehouse, has a glassed-in brewery turning out eight tasty microbrews; it also holds a darts and billiards pub and a restaurant with an open-grill kitchen.

Casinos

Vancouver has a few casinos; proceeds go to local charities and arts groups. No alcohol is served. The **Great Canadian Casino** (⊠ 2477 Heather St., ☎ 604/872–5543), in the Holiday Inn, is an option for gamblers downtown. The **Royal Diamond Casino** (⊠ 106B–750 Pacific Blvd. S, ☎ 604/685–2340) is in the Plaza of Nations Expo site downtown.

Comedy

Vancouver's renowned **Theatresports League** (☎ 604/738–7013), an improv troupe, performs regularly at the Arts Club New Review Stage on Granville Island. **Yuk Yuks** (⊠ 750 Pacific Blvd., ☎ 604/687–5233), in the Plaza of Nations Expo site downtown, hosts stand-up comics. The **Vancouver International Comedy Festival** (☎ 604/683–

0883), held in late July and early August on Granville Island, keeps you giggling at all kinds of silliness; much of the festival is free.

Dance Clubs

The nitrogen fog screen and automated lighting at **Mars** (✉ 1320 Richards St., ☎ 604/662–7707) get dancers into the swing of things. The **Palladium** (✉ 1250 Richards St., ☎ 604/688–2648), a luxurious-looking place with a massive dance floor, showcases progressive music and occasionally hosts live bands. Dance clubs come and go, but lines still form every weekend at **Richard's on Richards** (✉ 1036 Richards St., ☎ 604/687–6794) for live and taped dance tunes.

Music

JAZZ AND SOUL

The **Coastal Jazz and Blues Society** runs a year-round jazz and blues hot line (☎ 604/682–0706) with current information on concerts and clubs. The same dedicated bunch runs the Vancouver International Jazz Festival, which lights up 37 venues around town every June. The DJ at **Bar None** (✉ 1222 Hamilton St., ☎ 604/689–7000) in trendy Yale-town favors funk and soul and steps aside for live bands on Monday and Tuesday nights. Beatnik poetry readings would seem to fit right in at the **Chameleon Urban Lounge** (✉ 801 W. Georgia St., ☎ 604/669–0806) in the basement of the Hotel Georgia, but it's the sophisticated mix of jazz, R&B, and Latin tunes that draws the crowds. A Big Band dance sound carries into the night at **Hot Jazz** (✉ 2120 Main St., ☎ 604/873–4131). The **Jazz Cellar** (✉ 3611 W. Broadway, ☎ 604/738–1959) has everything from acid jazz to mainstream quartets, both live and recorded. **Rossini's** (✉ 1525 Yew St., ☎ 604/737–8080), a restaurant near Kits Beach, invites bands to jam on Saturday afternoons and weekend evenings.

ROCK

You'll find taped classic rock and roll, plenty of music memorabilia, and specialty salads and sandwiches dished up at Vancouver's version of the **Hard Rock Cafe** (✉ 686 W. Hastings St., ☎ 604/687–7625). The **Rage** nightclub (✉ 750 Pacific Blvd. S, ☎ 604/685–5585) plays Top 40 hits, with occasional weeknight bands.

OUTDOOR ACTIVITIES AND SPORTS

Beaches

An almost continuous string of beaches runs from Stanley Park to the University of British Columbia. The water is cool, but the beaches are sandy, edged by grass. Liquor is prohibited in parks and on beaches. For information, call the **Vancouver Board of Parks and Recreation** (☎ 604/257–8400).

Kitsilano Beach, over the Burrard Bridge from downtown, has a lifeguard and is the city's busiest—in-line skaters, volleyball games, and sleek young people are ever present. The part of the beach nearest the Vancouver Maritime Museum is the quietest. Facilities include a playground, tennis courts, a heated pool, concession stands, and nearby restaurants and cafés.

The **Point Grey beaches** give you a number of different options. Jericho, Locarno, and Spanish Banks, which begin at the end of Point Grey Road, offer a huge expanse of sand, especially in summer and at low tide. The shallow water here, warmed slightly by sun and sand, is best for swimming. Farther out, toward Spanish Banks, you'll find the beach less crowded, but the last concession stand and washrooms are at Locarno. If you keep walking along the beach just past Point Grey, you'll hit Wreck Beach, Vancouver's nude beach.

Among the **West End beaches,** Second Beach and Third Beach, along Beach Drive in Stanley Park, draw families. Second Beach has a guarded pool. Both have concession stands and washrooms. The liveliest of the West End beaches is English Bay Beach, at the foot of Denman Street. A water slide, kayak rentals, street performers, and artists keep things interesting all summer. Farther along Beach Drive, Sunset Beach is a little too close to the downtown core for reliably safe swimming.

Participant Sports

Biking

Cycling helmets are a legal requirement in safety-conscious Vancouver; they come with bike rentals, too. **Stanley Park** (☞ Stanley Park *in* Exploring Vancouver, *above*) is the most popular spot for family cycling. A good biking route is along the north or south shore of **False Creek.**

Rentals are available from a number of shops near Stanley Park, including **Bayshore Bicycles** (⊠ 745 Denman St., ☎ 604/688–2453). **Spokes Bicycle Rentals & Espresso Bar** (⊠ 1798 W. Georgia St., ☎ 604/688–5141) is near Stanley Park.

Boating

Several charter companies offer a cruise-and-learn vacation, usually to the Gulf Islands. **Blue Pacific Sailing and Power** (⊠ 1519 Foreshore Walk, Granville Island, ☎ 604/ 682–2161) is one of several boat charter companies on the island. **Cooper's Boating Centre** (⊠ 1620 Duranleau, Granville Island, ☎ 604/687–4110) has a three-hour introduction to sailing around English Bay, as well as longer cruise-and-learn trips lasting from five days to two weeks.

Fishing

You can fish for salmon all year in coastal British Columbia. **Sewell's Marina Horseshoe Bay** (⊠ 6695 Nelson St., Horseshoe Bay, ☎ 604/921–3474) organizes a daily four-hour trip on Howe Sound or has hourly rates on U-drives. **Westin Bayshore Yacht Charters** (⊠ 1601 W. Georgia St., ☎ 604/691–6936) has fishing charters.

Golf

Lower Mainland golf courses are open all year. All courses listed below are 18 holes and par 72, unless otherwise noted. For a spur of the moment game, call **Last Minute Golf** (☎ 604/878–1833). They match golfers and courses at substantial greens fee discounts. **West Coast Golf Shuttle** (⊠ 9–1040 W. 7th Ave., ☎ 604/ 878–6800) offers half-day golf packages, including greens fees, clubs, cart, and hotel pick-up.

North of Vancouver is **Furry Creek** (⊠ Lion's Bay, ☎ 604/922–9576), a challenging but forgiving 6,200-yard all-terrain public course overlooking scenic Howe Sound. **McCleery Golf Course** (⊠ 7188 McDonald St., ☎ 604/257–8191) is a par-71 public golf course and includes a driving range, club house, and pro shop. **Northview Golf and Country Club** (⊠ 6857 168th St., Surrey, ☎ 604/574–0324), a par-71 course easily accessible from Vancouver, just 15 minutes from the U.S. border, has two Arnold Palmer–designed courses and is the home of the Greater Vancouver Open, held at the end of August. One of the finest public courses in the area is **Peace Portal** (⊠ 16900 4th Ave., Surrey, ☎ 604/538–4818), near White Rock, a 45-minute drive from downtown. **Seymour Golf and Country Club** (⊠ 3723 Mt. Seymour Pkwy., North Vancouver, ☎ 604/929–5491), on the south side of Mt. Seymour on the North Shore, is a semiprivate club open to the public on Monday and Friday. **Westwood Plateau Golf and Country Club** (⊠ 3251 Plateau Blvd., Coquitlam, ☎ 604/552–0777), near Vancouver is a newer, superior course.

Health and Fitness Clubs

The **Bentall Centre Athletic Club** (⊠ 1055 Dunsmuir St., lower level, ☎ 604/689–4424) has racquetball and squash courts, weight rooms, and aerobics. The **YMCA** (⊠ 955 Burrard St., ☎ 604/681–0221) downtown has daily rates; facilities include pools, weight rooms, and racquetball, squash, and handball courts. The **YWCA** (⊠ 535 Hornby St., ☎ 604/895–5800) has daily drop-in rates; the facility has pools, weight rooms, and fitness classes.

Hiking

A number of companies lead guided walks and hikes in nearby parks and wilderness areas (☞ Ecology Tours *in* Vancouver A to Z, *below*). The **Capilano Regional Park** (☞ North Vancouver *in* Exploring Vancouver, *above*), on the North Shore, provides a scenic hike. **Pacific Spirit Park** (⊠ 4915 W. 16th Ave., ☎ 604/224–5739), more rugged than Stanley Park, has 61 km (38 mi) of trails, a few washrooms, and a couple of signboard maps. You can take a wonderful walk in evergreen woods only 20 minutes from downtown.

Jogging

The **Running Room** (⊠ 1519 Robson St., ☎ 604/684–9771) is a good source for information on fun runs in the area. The seawall around **Stanley Park** (☞ Stanley Park *in* Exploring Vancouver, *above*) is 9 km (5½ mi) long and gives an excellent minitour of the city. You can take a shorter run of 4 km (2½ mi) in the park around Lost Lagoon.

Skiing

CROSS-COUNTRY

The best cross-country skiing, with 16 km (10 mi) of groomed trails, is at **Cypress Bowl Ski Area** (⊠ Cypress Bowl Ski Area Rd., Exit 8 off Hwy. 1 westbound, ☎ 604/922–0825).

DOWNHILL

Vancouver is two hours from **Whistler/Blackcomb** (☞ Side Trip from Vancouver, *below*), a top-ranked ski destination.

There are three ski areas on the **North Shore mountains,** close to Vancouver, with night skiing. The snow is not as good as at Whistler, and the runs are generally used by novice, junior, and family skiers or those who want a quick ski after work. **Cypress Bowl** (⊠ End of Cypress Bowl Ski Area Rd., Exit 8 off Hwy. 1 westbound, North Vancouver, ☎ 604/926–5612, 604/419–7669 snow report) has a large number of runs, four chairlifts, and a vertical drop of 1,750 ft. **Grouse Mountain** (⊠ 6400 Nancy Greene Way, North Vancouver, ☎ 604/984–0661, 604/986–6262 snow report) has four chairlifts, a vertical drop of 1,300 ft, extensive night skiing, restaurants, bars, a new snowshoeing park, and the best views of the city from the runs. **Mt. Seymour** (⊠ 1700 Mt. Seymour Rd., North Vancouver, ☎ 604/986–2261, 604/879–3999 snow report) has three chairlifts and a vertical drop of 1,042 ft, beginners' lessons, and snowshoe rentals.

Tennis

There are 180 free public courts around town; contact the **Vancouver Board of Parks and Recreation** (☎ 604/257–8400) for locations. **Stanley Park** has 15 well-surfaced outdoor courts near English Bay Beach.

Water Sports

KAYAKING

Rent a kayak from **Ecomarine Ocean Kayak Center** (✉ 1668 Duranleau St., ☎ 604/689–7575) on Granville Island to explore False Creek and the shoreline of English Bay. **Ocean West Expeditions** (☎ 604/898–4979 or 800/660–0051) at English Bay Beach rents kayaks.

WINDSURFING

Sailboards and lessons are available at **Windsure Windsurfing School** (✉ Jericho Beach, ☎ 604/224–0615). The winds aren't very heavy on English Bay, making it a perfect locale for learning. You'll have to travel north to Squamish for more challenging high-wind conditions.

Spectator Sports

A number of Vancouver's teams play at **General Motors (G.M.) Place Stadium** (✉ 800 Griffiths Way). Tickets for many sports events are available from **Ticketmaster** (☎ 604/280–4400).

Baseball

The Pacific Coast League **Canadians** (☎ 604/872–5232) play at Nat Bailey Stadium (✉ 4601 Ontario St.), an old-time outdoor stadium; their season runs April–September.

Basketball

The **Vancouver Grizzlies** (☎ 604/899–4666), members of the National Basketball Association, hoop it up at G.M. Place Stadium late October–April.

Football

The **B.C. Lions** (☎ 604/583–7747) football team scrimmages at the B.C. Place Stadium downtown June–November.

Hockey

The **Vancouver Canucks** (☎ 604/899–4600) of the National Hockey League play at G.M. Place Stadium October–April.

SHOPPING

Unlike many other cities where suburban malls have taken over, Vancouver is full of individual boutiques and specialty shops. A multitude of antiques stores, ethnic markets, art galleries, high-fashion outlets, and fine department stores dot the city. Stores are usually open daily, Thursday and Friday nights, and Sunday noon to 5 PM.

Auctions

At 6 PM on the last Wednesday and Thursday of each month, antiques and collectibles auctions are held at **Love's** (✉ 1635 W. Broadway, ☎ 604/733–1157). **Maynard's** (✉ 415 W. 2nd Ave., ☎ 604/876–6787) has home furnishings auctions on Wednesdays at 7 PM.

Department Stores

Among Vancouver's top department stores is Canadian-owned **Eaton's** (✉ 701 Granville St., ☎ 604/685–7112), which carries everything: clothing, appliances, furniture, jewelry, accessories, and souvenirs. Many malls have branches, too. **Holt Renfrew** (✉ 633 Granville St., ☎ 604/681–3121) is smaller, focusing on high fashion for men and women. You'll find this Canadian store in many malls as well.

Shopping Districts and Malls

Fourth Avenue, from Burrard to Balsam Street, has an eclectic mix of stores, from sophisticated women's clothing to surfboards (☞ Kitsilano *in* Exploring Vancouver, *above*). About two dozen high-end art galleries, antiques shops and Oriental rug emporiums are packed end to end between 6th and 15th avenues on Granville Street, in an area that's come to be called **Gallery Row. Lonsdale Quay** (☎ 604/985– 6261 for general market information), a 13-minute ferry ride across the harbor from downtown in North Vancouver, has unusual toy and fashion shops set above a lavish farmer's market–style food fair. It's open daily. **Oakridge Shopping Centre** (✉ 650 W. 41st Ave., at Cambie St., ☎ 604/261–2511) has chic, expensive stores that are fun to browse through. The immense **Pacific Centre Mall** (✉ 550–700 W. Georgia St., ☎ 604/688–7236), on two levels and mostly underground, in the heart of downtown, connects Eaton's and the Bay department stores, which stand at opposite corners of Georgia and Granville streets. **Robson Street,** stretching from Burrard to Bute Streets, is chockablock with boutiques and cafés. Vancouver's liveliest street is not only for the fashion-conscious; it also provides excellent corners for an array of street performers. A commercial center has developed around **Sinclair Centre** (✉ 757 W. Hastings St., ☎ 604/666–4483), which caters to sophisticated and upscale tastes (☞ Robson to the Waterfront *in* Exploring Vancouver, *above*).

Ethnic Districts

Chinatown—centered on Pender and Main streets—is a bustling place for restaurants, exotic foods, and distinctive architecture (☞ Chinatown and Gastown *in* Exploring Vancouver, *above*). **Commercial Drive** (✉ North of E. 1st Ave.) is the heart of the Italian and Latin American communities. You can sip cappuccino in coffee bars where you may be the only one speaking English, or buy sun-dried tomatoes or an espresso machine. **Little India** is on Main Street around 50th Avenue. Curry houses, sweet shops, grocery stores, discount jewelers, and silk shops abound. A small **Japantown** on Powell Street at Dunlevy Street is made up of grocery stores, fish stores, and a few restaurants.

Specialty Stores

Antiques

Two key antiques hunting grounds are Gallery Row on Granville (☞ Shopping Districts and Malls, *above*) and the stretch of antiques stores along Main Street from 19th to 35th avenues. **Folkart Interiors** (✉ 3715 W. 10th Ave., ☎ 604/228–1011) specializes in whimsical British Columbia folk art and Western Canadian antiques. The **Vancouver Antique Center** (✉ 422 Richards St., ☎ 604/681–3248) has two floors of antiques and collectibles dealers under one roof.

Art Galleries

There are many private galleries throughout Vancouver. **Buschlen Mowatt** (✉ 1445 W. Georgia St.,, ☎ 604/682–1234), among the best in the city, is a showcase for Canadian and international artists. **Diane Farris** (✉ 1565 W. 7th Ave., ☎ 604/737–2629) often spotlights hot new artists. The **Douglas Reynolds Gallery** (✉ 2335 Granville St., ☎ 604/731–9292) has one of the city's finest collections of Northwest Coast native art. The **Inuit Gallery of Vancouver** (345 Water St., ☎ 604/ 688–7323) features an array of coastal native art. The **Marion Scott Gallery** (✉ 481 Howe St., ☎ 604/685–1934) specializes in Inuit art.

Books

Duthie Books (⊠ 710 Granville St., ☎ 604/689–1802) carries 250,000 books and CD-ROM titles and has several comfortable sitting areas, including a little café, for browsers. Duthie's nine other locations (including ⊠ 919 Robson St., ☎ 604/684–4496, and ⊠ Library Square, 205–345 Robson St., ☎ 604/602–0610) make this home-grown chain a favorite in Vancouver. **World Wide Books and Maps** (⊠ 736A Granville St., downstairs, ☎ 604/687–3320), one of several specialty bookstores in town, sells travel books and maps that cover the world.

Clothing

Fashion is big business in Vancouver, and there are clothing boutiques on almost every corner downtown. For truly unique women's clothing, try **Dorothy Grant** (⊠ 757 W. Hastings St., ☎ 604/681–0201), where traditional Haida native designs meld with modern fashion in a boutique that looks more like an art gallery. Handmade Italian suits, cashmere, and leather for men are sold at stylish **E. A. Lee** (⊠ 466 Howe St., ☎ 604/683–2457); there are also a few women's items to browse through. **Leone** (⊠ 757 W. Hastings St., ☎ 604/683–1133) is an ultrachic boutique, dividing designer collections in themed areas. Trendy men's, women's, and children's casual wear by Ralph Lauren is available at the **Polo Store** (⊠ 375 Water St., ☎ 604/682–7656). If your tastes are traditional, don't miss **Straith** (⊠ 900 W. Georgia St., ☎ 604/685–3301) in the Hotel Vancouver, offering tailored designer fashions for both sexes. At the architecturally stunning **Versus** (⊠ 1008 W. Georgia St., ☎ 604/688–8938) boutique, ladies and gents sip cappuccino as they browse through fashionable Italian designs. Buttoned-down businesswomen usually shop at **Wear Else?** (⊠ 789 W. Pender St., ☎ 604/662–7890), focusing on career women's fashions.

Gifts

Some of the best places in Vancouver for good-quality souvenirs (West Coast native art, books, music, jewelry, and so on) are the **museum and gallery gift shops,** including the Clamshell Gift Shop (⊠ Vancouver Aquarium, ☎ 604/685–5911) in Stanley Park, the Gallery Shop (⊠ 750 Hornby St., ☎ 604/662–4706) in the Vancouver Art Gallery, and the Museum of Anthropology Gift Shop (⊠ 6393 N.W. Marine Dr., ☎ 604/822–3825). Northwest native art is available in Gastown at **Hill's Indian Crafts** (⊠ 165 Water St., ☎ 604/685–4249). Near Granville Island, the **Leona Lattimer Gallery** (⊠ 1590 W. 2nd Ave., ☎ 604/732–4556), built like a longhouse, is full of native arts and crafts ranging from cheap to priceless. The **Salmon Shop** (☎ 604/669–3474) in the Granville Island Public Market will wrap smoked salmon for travel.

SIDE TRIP FROM VANCOUVER

If you think of skiing when you hear mention of Whistler, British Columbia, you're thinking on track. Whistler and Blackcomb mountains, part of Whistler Resort (☎ 800/944–7853), are the two largest ski mountains in North America and are consistently ranked the first- or second-best ski destinations on the continent. There's winter and summer glacier skiing, the longest vertical drop in North America, and one of the most advanced lift systems in the world. Whistler has also grown in popularity as a summer destination, with a range of outdoor activities and events to fill the warm, sunny months. All this action is just a couple of hours from Vancouver. Take Highway 1 west to the narrow, winding Highway 99, the Sea to Sky Highway, which takes you past Shannon Falls and the Tantalus Range glaciers to Whistler.

Adjacent to the area is the 78,000-acre Garibaldi Provincial Park (☎ 604/898–3678), with dense mountainous forests splashed with hospitable lakes and streams. Even if you don't want to roam much farther than the village, there are five lakes for canoeing, fishing, swimming, and windsurfing, and many nearby hiking and mountain-bike trails.

If you're planning a trip to Whistler, you can also consider the Coast Mountain Circle, which links Vancouver to Cariboo Country. This 702-km (435-mi) route takes in spectacular Howe Sound, the deep-water port of Squamish, Whistler Resort, and Pemberton Valley before heading back to Vancouver through scenic Fraser Canyon and Harrison Hot Springs (☞ Chapter 3). The loop makes a comfortable two- to three-day journey.

Whistler

120 km (74 mi) from Vancouver.

At the base of Whistler and Blackcomb mountains are Whistler Village, Village North, and Upper Village—a rapidly expanding, interconnected community of lodgings, restaurants, pubs, gift shops, and boutiques. With dozens of hotels and condos within a five-minute walk of the mountains, the site is frenzied with activity. Culinary options in the resort range from burgers to French, Japanese to deli cuisine; nightly entertainment runs the gamut from sophisticated piano bars to casual pubs.

Whistler Village is a pedestrian-only community. Anywhere you want to go within the resort is at most five minutes away, and parking lots are just outside the village. The bases of Whistler and Blackcomb mountains are also just at the edge; in fact, you can ski right into the lower level of the Chateau Whistler Hotel. With all of the recent expansion in Whistler, there is now space to rest 17,910 sleepy heads within 400 yards of the lifts.

In winter, the village buzzes with skiers and snowboarders taking to the slopes, but as the scenery changes from winter's snow-white to summer's lush-green landscapes, the mood of Whistler changes, too. Things seem to slow down a bit, and the resort sheds some of its competitive edge and relaxes to a slower pace. Even the local golf tournaments and the triathlon are interspersed with Mozart and bluegrass festivals.

Dining

Dining at Whistler is informal; casual dress is appropriate everywhere. At press time, record numbers of promising new restaurants were coming on the scene, so you're bound to find something worthwhile to suit virtually any craving. Japanese and Mediterranean offerings are especially strong in the village. For price categories, *see* the dining price chart *in* Dining, *above.* Many restaurants close for a week or two between late October and late November. In the winter or summer, you'll need dinner reservations in all but the fast-food joints.

$$$ ✕ **Il Caminetto di Umberto, Trattoria di Umberto.** Umberto offers home-style Italian cooking in a relaxed atmosphere; he specializes in such pasta dishes as crab-stuffed cannelloni and a four-cheese lasagna. Il Caminetto is known for its veal, osso buco, and zabaglione. The Trattoria is the more casual of the two (there are ski racks just outside) and has a new open show kitchen. ☒ *Il Caminetto, 4242 Village Stroll,* ☎ *604/932–4442.* ☒ *Trattoria, Mountainside Lodge, 4417 Sundial Pl.,* ☎ *604/932–5858. Reservations essential at both restaurants. AE, DC, MC, V. No lunch.*

$$$ ✕ **La Rúa.** One of the brightest lights on the Whistler dining scene is
★ on the ground floor of Le Chamois (☞ Lodging, *below*). Reddish flag-
stone floors and sponge-painted walls, a wine cellar behind a wrought-
iron door, modern oil paintings, and sconce lighting give the restaurant
an intimate, Mediterranean ambience. Favorites from the Continen-
tal menu include charred rare tuna, loin of deer, rack of lamb, and baked
sea bass fillet in red wine and herb sauce. ✉ *4557 Blackcomb Way,*
☎ *604/932–5011. Reservations essential. AE, DC, MC, V. No lunch.*

$$$ ✕ **Les Deux Gros.** The name means "the two fat guys," which may ex-
★ plain the restaurant's motto, "Never trust a skinny chef." Portions of
the country French cuisine are generous indeed. Alsatian onion pie, steak
tartare, juicy rack of lamb, and salmon Wellington are all superbly crafted
and presented, and service is friendly but unobtrusive. A five-minute
drive southwest of the village, this is the spot for a special romantic
dinner; request one of the prime tables by the massive stone fireplace.
✉ *1200 Alta Lake Rd.,* ☎ *604/932–4611. Reservations essential. AE,
DC, MC, V. No lunch.*

$$$ ✕ **Wildflower.** The main dining room of Chateau Whistler (☞ Lodg-
ing, *below*) is an informal, comfortable restaurant with huge windows
overlooking the ski slopes. The rustic effect of the hotel's lobby con-
tinues here—more than 100 antique wood birdhouses decorate the room,
and chairs and tables have a farmhouse look. An à la carte menu fo-
cuses on creative concoctions starring fresh British Columbia fare; the
signature dish is pan-seared, cinnamon-smoked pheasant breast served
with roasted corn, spiced squash, sheep's-milk Brie, and risotto. ✉
Chateau Whistler Resort, 4599 Chateau Blvd., ☎ *604/938–2033.
Reservations essential. AE, D, DC, MC, V.*

$$ ✕ **The Brewhouse.** Whistler's first brew pub serves up six of its own
ales and lagers, with names like Big Wolf Bitter and Dirty Miner Stout,
in a cozy setting in Village North. The restaurant is already gaining a
reputation for its wood-oven pizza, rotisserie prime rib, and spit-roast
chicken; the casual pub on the same premises has pool tables, TV screens,
and some creative pub grub. ✉ *4355 Blackcomb Way,* ☎ *604/905–
2739. AE, MC, V.*

$–$$ ✕ **Hard Rock Cafe.** You know you're in a big-time tourist destination
when you see a Hard Rock Cafe. Guitars and gold records adorn the
walls, but the incredible mural of rock icons on the ceiling of the main
dining room is the primary attraction. Steaks, sandwiches, and salads
are tasty and filling if rather uninventive at this cheerful, popular diner.
✉ *4295 Blackcomb Way,* ☎ *604/938–9922. AE, DC, MC, V.*

$ ✕ **Zeuski's.** This friendly taverna in Village North brings tasty, inex-
★ pensive Greek fare to Whistler. Wall murals of the Greek islands surround candlelit tables, helping create a Mediterranean atmosphere.
There's also a patio for alfresco dining. It's hard to pass on the spaniko-
pita, souvlaki, and other standards, but the house special, *katapoulo*
(chicken breast rolled in pistachios and roasted), is not to be missed,
nor are the tender, delicately herb-battered calamari. ✉ *4314 Main St.,*
☎ *604/932–6009. Reservations essential. AE, MC, V.*

Lodging

At press time, Whistler was undergoing a tremendous building boom,
much of it centered on new lodging complexes. Lodgings, including
hundreds of time-share condos, can be booked through the **Whistler
Resort Association** (☎ 604/932–4222, 604/664–5625 in Vancouver,
or 800/944–7853 in the U.S. and Canada). B&Bs can be booked
through **Whistler Bed and Breakfast Inns** (☎ 800/665–1892).

For price categories and facilities information, *see* the price chart *in*
Lodging, *above*. Price categories are based on January to April ski season rates; summer rates are greatly discounted. You can add moun-

tain bikes, a hot tub, skiing, and bike and ski storage to the list of facilities often found in the higher-price accommodations.

$$$$ ⊡ **Chateau Whistler.** This large and friendly-looking fortress in the Upper Village at the foot of Blackcomb Mountain was built and is run by Canadian Pacific Hotels. The marvelous lobby is filled with rustic Canadiana, handmade Mennonite rugs, enormous fireplaces, and enticing overstuffed sofas. The standard rooms are average, but the suites are fit for royalty, with specially commissioned quilts and artwork, complemented by antique furnishings. ⊠ *4599 Chateau Blvd., Box 100, V0N 1B4,* ☎ *604/938–8000 or 800/606–8244,* FAX *604/938–2055. 558 rooms, 47 suites. 2 restaurants, lobby lounge, indoor-outdoor pool, beauty salon, hot tubs, saunas, spa, steam rooms, 18-hole golf course, 3 tennis courts, mountain bikes, piano, meeting rooms, travel services. AE, D, DC, MC, V.*

$$$$ ⊡ **Le Chamois.** Enjoying the prime ski-in, ski-out location at the base
★   of the Blackcomb runs is this elegant luxury hotel. Of the spacious guest rooms with convenience kitchens, the most romantic are the executive studios with Jacuzzi tubs set in front of the living room's bay windows overlooking the slopes and lifts. Guests can also keep an eye on the action from the glass elevators and the heated outdoor pool. ⊠ *4557 Blackcomb Way, V0N 1B0,* ☎ *604/932–8700 or 800/777–0185,* FAX *604/905–2576. 47 suites, 6 studios. 2 restaurants, lounge, kitchenettes, refrigerators, room service, pool, hot tubs, coin laundry, meeting rooms. AE, DC, MC, V.*

$$$$ ⊡ **Pan Pacific Lodge.** A newer development, this eight-story resort lodge, opened in 1997, is tucked in at the base of both mountains, just steps from either the Whistler or Blackcomb gondola. The all-suite lodge has studios and one- and two-bedroom units, all with kitchens, balconies, gas fireplaces, and tall windows that make the most of the mountain views. The Mountain Adventure Centre in the lobby rents snowboards, skis, and cross-country equipment and can book most outdoor activities. ⊠ *4320 Sundial Crescent, V0N 1B4,* ☎ *604/905–2999 or 888/905–9995,* FAX *604/905–2995. 76 suites, 45 studios. Restaurant, kitchenettes, pool, outdoor hot tubs, exercise room, steam room, ski shops, coin laundry, concierge. AE, DC, MC, V.*

$$$–$$$$ ⊡ **Delta Whistler Resort.** The resort, at the base of Whistler Mountain, near the Whistler Village Gondola and across the road from the Whistler Golf Course, is a large complex, complete with shopping, dining, and fitness amenities. Rooms are very generous in size (almost every room will easily sleep four). Many rooms have fireplaces, whirlpool bathtubs, balconies, and/or kitchenettes. Delta has also recently opened Delta Whistler Village Suites, an all-suite hotel, at 4306 Main Street in Village North. ⊠ *4050 Whistler Way, Box 550, V0N 1B4,* ☎ *604/ 932–1982, 800/268–1133 in Canada,* FAX *604/932–7332. 276 rooms, 24 suites. Restaurant, sports bar, kitchenettes, pool, indoor and outdoor hot tubs, massage, steam room, 2 indoor/outdoor tennis courts, exercise room, video games, coin laundries. AE, DC, MC, V.*

$$–$$$ ⊡ **Durlacher Hof.** Custom fir woodwork and doors, exposed ceiling beams, a *kachelofen* (traditional farmhouse fireplace-oven), and antler chandeliers hung over fir benches and tables carry out the rustic European theme of this fancy Tyrolean inn. The green and maroon bedrooms contain more fine examples of custom-crafted wooden furniture. Four upgraded rooms are very spacious and have such added amenities as whirlpool tubs. The inn also has a guest refrigerator, a lounge, and a pay phone. A hearty European breakfast and afternoon tea are included in the tariff, and Sunday-night dinners are also available at this no-smoking inn. German is spoken here. ⊠ *Box 1125, 7055 Nesters Rd., V0N 1B0,* ☎ *604/932–1924,* FAX *604/938–1980. 8 rooms.*

No-smoking rooms, massage, hot tub, sauna, ski storage, airport shuttle. MC, V. May be closed part of Nov., Apr., or May; call for dates.

$$ ⌂ **Edgewater.** This intimate lodge nestles right on pretty little Green Lake. All rooms are on the lake with water and mountain views, and the interior is simple and relaxing, a true country retreat. You can do everything here from sleigh riding and singing around a campfire to canoeing, bird-watching, boating, horseback riding, and cross-country skiing. An expanded Continental breakfast (juice, granola, fruit, and breakfast breads) is included in the tariff at this no-smoking inn, and highly rated evening meals are also available. ⊠ *8841 Hwy. 99, Box 369, 3 km (2 mi) north of the village, V0N 1B0,* ☎ *604/932– 0688,* FAX *604/932–0686. 6 rooms, 6 suites. Dining room, bar, lounge, outdoor hot tub, hiking, ski storage, meeting rooms. AE, MC, V.*

$$ ⌂ **Pension Edelweiss.** The Edelweiss, one of several charming and very European bed-and-breakfasts around Whistler, is within walking distance of Whistler Village. Rooms have a crisp, spic-and-span feel, in keeping with the Bavarian chalet style of the house; some have balconies. Each morning a different breakfast (included in the room rate) is served: Scandinavian, American, French, German. A bus stop just outside provides easy access to Whistler Village. Smoking is not permitted here. ⊠ *7162 Nancy Greene Way, Box 850, V0N 1B0,* ☎ *604/ 932–3641 or 800/665–2003,* FAX *604/938–1746. 8 rooms, 1 suite. Hot tub, sauna, ski storage. AE, MC, V. No smoking.*

$ ⌂ **Hostelling International Whistler.** One of the nicest hostels in Canada is also the cheapest sleep in town. Bunks in men's or women's dorms, a shared kitchen, and a game room make up the basic accommodations of this hostel overlooking Alta Lake. Reservations are recommended. BC Rail will make a request stop at the hostel. ⊠ *5678 Alta Lake Rd., V0N 1B0,* ☎ *604/932–5492,* FAX *604/932–4687. 32 beds in 5 dorms, 1 private room (no bath). Kitchenette, ski storage. MC, V.*

Outdoor Activities and Sports

The best first stop for any Whistler outdoor activity is the **Whistler Activity and Information Center** (⊠ 4010 Whistler Way, ☎ 604/932–2394) in the village, where you can book activities and pick up hiking and biking maps.

CANOEING, KAYAKING, RAFTING, AND WINDSURFING

You'll see canoes, kayaks, and sailboards at the many lakes and rivers near Whistler. Rentals are available at **Alta Lake** at both Lakeside Park and Wayside Park. A spot that's perfect for canoeing is the **River of Golden Dreams,** from Alta Lake to Green Lake. For white-water kayaking lessons and rentals, try **Sea to Sky Kayaking** (☎ 604/898–5498). There are several rivers with mild rapids around Whistler, and **Whistler River Adventures** (☎ 604/932–3532) offers a variety of half- and full-day rafting trips priced from $50 to $150.

The breezes provide reliable windsurfing on Alpha, Alta, and Green lakes; call **Whistler Outdoor Experience** (☎ 604/932–3389) or **Whistler Sailing and Water Sports** (☎ 604/932–7245).

FISHING

All five of the lakes around Whistler are stocked with trout, but the area around Dream River Park is one of the most popular. Slightly farther afield, try Cheakamus Lake, Daisy Lake, and Callaghan Lake. **Whistler Backcountry Adventures** (⊠ 4314 Main St., No. 36, ☎ 604/ 932–3474) or **Whistler Fishing Guides** (⊠ Carlton Lodge, 4218 Mountain Sq. [base of both gondolas], ☎ 604/932–4267) will take care of anything you need—equipment, guides, and transportation.

GOLF

Chateau Whistler Golf Club (⊠ 4612 Blackcomb Way, ☎ 604/938–2092) is an excellent 18-hole, par-72 course designed by Robert Trent Jones II. The **Nicklaus North Golf Course** (⊠ 8080 Nicklaus North Blvd., Box 580, ☎ 604/938–9898, or 800/386–9898) is a challenging 18-hole, par-71 course designed by Jack Nicklaus. Arnold Palmer designed the 18-hole, par-71 championship **Whistler Golf Course** (⊠ 4010 Whistler Way, ☎ 604/932–4544).

SKIING

Cross-Country. The meandering trail around the Whistler Golf Course in the village is an ideal beginners' route. For more advanced skiing, try the 28 km (17 mi) of track-set trails that wind around scenic Lost Lake, Chateau Whistler Golf Course, and the Nicklaus North Golf Course and Green Lake. Cross-country trail maps and equipment rental information are available at the **Whistler Activity and Information Center** (⊠ 4010 Whistler Way, ☎ 604/932–2394) in the village.

Downhill Skiing and Snowboarding. The vertical drops and elevations at **Blackcomb** and **Whistler** (☎ 604/932–3434 or 800/766–0449, FAX 604/938–9174) mountains are perhaps the most impressive features to skiers here. The resort covers 6,998 acres of skiable terrain in 12 alpine bowls, on three glaciers, and more than 200 marked trails, served by the most advanced high-speed lift system on the continent. Blackcomb has a 5,280-ft vertical drop, North America's longest, while Whistler comes in second, with a 5,020-ft drop. The top elevation is 7,494 ft on Blackcomb and 7,160 on Whistler. Blackcomb and Whistler receive an average of 360 inches of snow per year; Blackcomb is open June–August for summer glacier skiing. Whistler Ski and Snowboard School and Blackcomb Ski and Snowboard School (☎ 800/766–0449 for both) provide lessons to skiers of all levels.

Heli-Skiing. In Whistler, **Mountain Heli-Sports** (☎ 604/932–2070), **Tyax Heli-Skiing** (☎ 604/932–7007 or 800/663–8126), and **Whistler Heli-Skiing** (☎ 604/932–4105) have guided day trips with up to four glacier runs, or 12,000 ft of skiing, for experienced skiers; the cost is about $400.

SPORTS CENTER

Meadow Park Sports Centre (⊠ 8107 Camino Dr., ☎ 604/938–3133), about 6 km (4 mi) north of Whistler Village, has a six-lane pool, a children's wading pool, a hockey–ice-skating rink, a hot tub, a sauna, a steam room, and two squash courts.

Whistler A to Z

Arriving and Departing

BY BUS

Maverick Coach Lines (☎ 604/255–1171 in Vancouver, 604/932–5031 in Whistler) has buses leaving every couple of hours for Whistler Village from the depot in downtown Vancouver. The fare is approximately $32 round-trip. During ski season, the last bus leaves Whistler at 7:15 PM. **Perimeter Bus Transportation** (☎ 604/266–5386 in Vancouver, 604/905–0041 in Whistler) has daily service, November–April and June–September, from Vancouver International Airport to Whistler. Prepaid reservations are necessary 24 hours in advance; the ticket booth is on Level One of the airport. The fare is around $45 one-way. **Westcoast City and Nature Sightseeing** (☎ 604/451–1600 in Vancouver) offers a sightseeing tour to Whistler that allows passengers to stay over and return on their date of choice to Vancouver. The tours run year-round; the cost is about $55.

BY CAR
Whistler is 120 km (74 mi), or 2½ hours, north of Vancouver on winding Highway 99, the Sea to Sky Highway.

BY TRAIN
BC Rail (☎ 604/984–5246 or 800/663–8238, FAX 604/984–5505)
travels north from Vancouver to Whistler along a beautiful route. One
train a day leaves the North Vancouver BC Rail Station at 7 AM and
arrives at Whistler at 9:10 AM. The return train leaves Whistler at 6:10
PM and arrives in Vancouver at 8:45 PM. The $58 round-trip fare in-
cludes a full meal each way. The Vancouver Bus Terminal and the North
Vancouver Station are connected by bus shuttle during the summer.

Getting Around
Streets in Whistler Village, Village North, and Upper Village are all pedestrian-only; pay parking is readily available on the village outskirts.
Whistler Municipality operates a **free public transit system** that loops
throughout the village, and public transit serves the whole valley; call
604/932–4020 for information and schedules.

Contacts and Resources
B&B RESERVATION AGENCIES
Whistler Bed and Breakfast Inns (☎ 800/665–1892) represents some
of the leading inns of Whistler.

CAR RENTALS
Alamo (☎ 604/623–2281 or 800/327–9633, FAX 604/688–5369).
Budget Rent-A-Car (☎ 604/932–1236, FAX 604/932–3026).

EMERGENCIES
Ambulance, poison control, police (☎ 911).

GUIDED TOURS
Alpine Adventure Tours (☎ 604/683–0209) has day tours from Vancouver to Squamish and Whistler. If four-wheel-drive and all-terrain
vehicle tours of the backcountry appeal to you, contact **Whistler Backcountry Adventures** (☎ 604/932–3474). **Whistler Nature Tours** (☎ 604/
932–4595) provides guided alpine hiking tours. It also runs a half-day
bus tour of the Whistler and Pemberton area for $39.

VISITOR INFORMATION
Contact the **Whistler Resort Association** (✉ 4010 Whistler Way, Whistler
V0N 1B4, ☎ 604/932–4222, 604/664–5625 in Vancouver, or 800/944–
7853 in the U.S. and Canada, FAX 604/938–5758). For maps and in-
formation on activities in the area, call or visit the **Whistler Activity and
Information Center** (✉ 4010 Whistler Way, Whistler VON 1B4, ☎ 604/
932–2394). There is an **information booth** (☎ 604/932–2394) in
Whistler Village at the front door of the conference center; it's open year-
round, daily 9–5. If you're traveling in the area around Whistler, contact the **Coast & Mountains Tourism Association** (✉ 204–1755 W.
Broadway, Vancouver V6J 4S5, ☎ 604/739–9011 or 800/667–3306,
FAX 604/739–0153). A provincial government **Travel Infocentre** (☎ 604/
932–5528) is on Highway 99 about 4 km (2½ mi) south of Whistler.

VANCOUVER A TO Z

Arriving and Departing

By Bus
Greyhound Lines (☎ 604/662–3222, 800/661–8747 in Canada, 800/
231–2222 in the U.S.) is the largest bus line serving Vancouver. The Pacific Central Station (✉ 1150 Station St.) is the depot. **Quick Shuttle** (☎

604/940–4428, 800/665–2122 in the U.S.) bus service runs between Vancouver and Seattle five times a day in winter and up to eight times a day in summer. The depot is at the Sandman Hotel (⊠ 180 W. Georgia St.).

By Car

From the south, I–5 from Seattle becomes **Highway 99** at the U.S.–Canada border. Vancouver is a three-hour drive (226 km, or 140 mi) from Seattle. It's best to avoid border crossings during peak times such as holidays and weekends. Highway 1, the **Trans-Canada Highway,** enters Vancouver from the east. To avoid traffic, arrive rush hours.

By Ferry

BC Ferries (☎ 250/386–3431 for information, 888/223–3779 in British Columbia; for automated reservations, 604/444–2890, 888/724–5223 in British Columbia) operates two major ferry terminals outside Vancouver. From Tsawwassen to the south (an hour's drive from downtown), ferries sail to Victoria and Nanaimo on Vancouver Island and to the Gulf Islands (the small islands between the mainland and Vancouver Island). From Horseshoe Bay (30 minutes north of downtown), ferries sail to the Sunshine Coast and a short distance across the strait and up the coast to Nanaimo on Vancouver Island. Vehicle reservations on Vancouver to Victoria routes are optional and cost $15 in addition to the fare.

By Plane

Vancouver International Airport (⊠ Grant McConachie Way, ☎ 604/276–6101) is on Sea Island, about 14 km (9 mi) south of downtown off Highway 99. An airport improvement fee is assessed on all flight departures: $5 for flights within British Columbia, $10 for flights within North America, and $15 for international flights. American Airlines, Continental Airlines, Delta, Horizon Air, and United fly into the airport. The two major domestic airlines are Air Canada and Canadian Airlines. *See* Air Travel *in* the Gold Guide for airline numbers.

Air B.C. (☎ 604/688–5515 or 800/663–3721) serves destinations around the province, including Vancouver International Airport, South Terminal, to Victoria International Airport. **Harbour Air** (☎ 604/688–1277 or 800/665–0212) and **West Coast Air** (☎ 604/688–9115 or 800/347–2222) both offer 35-minute harbor-to-harbor service (downtown Vancouver to downtown Victoria) several times a day. Planes leave from near the Pan Pacific Hotel (⊠ 300–999 Canada Pl.). **Helijet Airways** (☎ 604/273–1414) has helicopter service from downtown Vancouver to downtown Victoria, Victoria International Airport, and Seattle. The heliport is near Vancouver's Pan Pacific Hotel (⊠ 300–999 Canada Pl.).

BETWEEN THE AIRPORT AND DOWNTOWN

The drive from the airport to downtown takes 20–45 minutes, depending on the time of day. Airport hotels offer free shuttle service to and from the airport.

The **Vancouver Airporter Service** (☎ 604/946–8866) bus leaves the international and domestic arrivals levels of the terminal building approximately every half hour, stopping at major downtown hotels. It operates from 5:23 AM until midnight. The fare is $10 one-way and $18 round-trip.

Taxi stands are in front of the terminal building on domestic and international arrivals levels. Taxi fare to downtown is about $22. Area cab companies are **Yellow** (☎ 604/681–1111) and **Black Top** (☎ 604/681–2181). Limousine service from **Airlimo** (☎ 604/273–1331) costs a bit more than the taxi fare to downtown: The current rate is about $30.

By Train

The **Pacific Central Station** (⊠ 1150 Station St.), at Main Street and Terminal Avenue, near the Main Street SkyTrain station, is the hub for rail and bus service. **Amtrak** (☎ 800/872–7245) has one round-trip per day between Seattle and Vancouver. **VIA Rail** (☎ 800/561–8630) provides transcontinental service through Jasper to Toronto three times a week. Passenger trains leave the **BC Rail Station** (⊠ 1311 W. 1st. St., ☎ 604/631–3500) in North Vancouver for Whistler and the interior of British Columbia.

Getting Around

By Bus

Exact change is needed to ride **BC Transit** (☎ 604/521–0400) buses: $1.50; $2.25 for the SeaBus to the North Shore. Books of 10 tickets are sold at convenience stores and newsstands; look for a red, white, and blue FARE DEALER sign. Day passes, good for unlimited travel all day, cost $6. They are available from fare dealers and any SeaBus or SkyTrain station. Transfers are valid for 90 minutes, allow travel in both directions, and are good on buses, SkyTrain, and SeaBus. A guide called "Discover Vancouver on Transit" is available free at the Tourist Info Centre (☞ Visitor Information *in* Contacts and Resources, *below*).

By Car

Because no freeways cross Vancouver, rush-hour traffic still tends to be horrendous. The worst bottlenecks outside the city center are the North Shore bridges, the George Massey Tunnel on Highway 99 south of Vancouver, and Highway 1 through Coquitlam and Surrey. Parking downtown is both expensive and tricky to find. Right turns are allowed on most red lights after you've come to a full stop.

By Ferry

The **SeaBus** is a 400-passenger commuter ferry that crosses Burrard Inlet from the foot of Lonsdale Avenue (North Vancouver) to downtown. The ride takes 13 minutes and costs the same as the transit bus (and it's much faster). With a transfer, connection can be made with any BC Transit bus or SkyTrain. **Aquabus Ferries** (☎ 604/689–5858) and **False Creek Ferries** (☎ 604/684–7781) connect several stations on False Creek, including Science World, Granville Island, Stamp's Landing, Vanier Park, Yaletown, and the Hornby Street dock.

By Rapid Transit

A one-line, 25-km (16-mi) rapid transit system called **SkyTrain** travels underground downtown and is elevated for the rest of its route to New Westminster and Surrey. Trains leave about every five minutes. Tickets, sold at each station from machines (correct change is not necessary), must be carried as proof of payment. You may use transfers from SkyTrain to SeaBus (☞ *above*) and BC Transit buses and vice versa. The SkyTrain is convenient for transit between downtown, B.C. Place Stadium, Pacific Central Station, and Science World.

By Taxi

It is difficult to hail a cab in Vancouver; unless you're near a hotel, you'd have better luck calling a taxi service. Try **Yellow** (☎ 604/681–3311) or **Black Top** (☎ 604/683–4567).

Contacts and Resources

B&B Reservation Agencies

Best Canadian Bed and Breakfast Network (⊠ 1064 Balfour Ave., V6H 1X1, ☎ 604/738–7207, FAX 604/732–4998). **A Home away from Home** (⊠ 1441 Howard Ave., Burnaby V5B 3S2, ☎ 604/294–1760,

FAX 604/294–0799). **Town & Country Bed and Breakfast Reservation Service** (✉ 2803 W. 4th Ave., Box 74543, V6K 1K2, ☎ 604/731–5942).

Car Rentals
Avis (☎ 604/606–2847 or 800/331–1212). **Budget** (☎ 604/668–7000 or 800/527–0700). **Thrifty Car Rental** (☎ 604/606–1666 or 800/367–2277).

Consulates
United States (✉ 1095 W. Pender St., ☎ 604/685–4311). **United Kingdom** (✉ 800–1111 Melville St., ☎ 604/683–4421).

Doctors and Dentists
Doctors are on call through the emergency ward at **St. Paul's Hospital** (✉ 1081 Burrard St., ☎ 604/682–2344), a downtown facility open around the clock. **Medicentre** (✉ 1055 Dunsmuir St., lower level, ☎ 604/683–8138), a drop-in clinic in the Bentall Centre, is open weekdays. Dentists are on call at **Dentacentre** (✉ 1055 Dunsmuir St., lower level, ☎ 604/669–6700), which is open weekdays.

Emergencies
Ambulance, fire, police (☎ 911).

Guided Tours
Tour prices tend to fluctuate, so inquire about current rates when booking tours. Kids are generally charged half the adult fare.

AIR
Tour the mountains and fjords of the North Shore by helicopter for around $200 per person (minimum of three people) for 45 minutes: **Vancouver Helicopters** (☎ 604/270–1484) flies from the Harbour Heliport, near Canada Place, downtown. You can see Vancouver from the air for $72 for 30 minutes: **Harbour Air**'s (☎ 604/688–1277) seaplanes leave from beside the Pan Pacific Hotel.

BOAT
Aquabus Ferries (✉ 1617 Foreshore Walk, Granville Island, ☎ 604/689–5858) runs a 30-minute cruise of False Creek for $6. **False Creek Ferries** (✉ 1804 Boatlift La., Granville Island, ☎ 604/684–7781) has 30-minute and one-hour cruises of False Creek and English Bay, for $6 and $8, respectively.

Harbour Cruises (✉ 1 N. Denman St., ☎ 604/688–7246), at the foot of Denman Street on Coal Harbour, operates a 1¼-hour narrated tour of Burrard Inlet aboard the paddle wheeler M.P.V. *Constitution*; the tour operates April–October and costs less than $20. Sunset dinner cruises are also available. Harbour Cruises also offers sunset dinner cruises and links with the Royal Hudson Steam Train (☞ Train tours, *below*) to make a daylong boat-train excursion to Howe Sound.

Paddlewheeler River Adventures (✉ 810 Quayside Dr., New Westminster, ☎ 604/525–4465), in the Information Centre at Westminster Quay, will take you out on the Fraser River in an 1800s-style paddle wheeler. Choose from a three-hour tour of the working river—past log booms, tugs, and houseboats—for about $40; a day trip to historic Fort Langley, for about $50; or a sunset dinner cruise.

ECOLOGY
Hike B.C. (☎ 604/469–4443) has guided hikes and snowshoe trips to the North Shore mountains. Between May and October, **Lotus Land Tours** (☎ 604/684–4922 or 800/528–3531) runs an easygoing four-hour sea kayak trip that includes a salmon barbecue lunch. The trip visits Twin Island (an uninhabited provincial marine park) to explore marine life

in the intertidal zone. Experience and fitness are not required; the kayaks are easy for beginners to handle. One good operator with a number of interpretive day hikes around Vancouver is **Path of Logic Wilderness Adventures** (☎ 604/802–2082). Guided hikes through the rain forests and canyons surrounding the city are available through **Rockwood Adventures** (☎ 604/926–7705). It has many tours to choose from; prices start around $45. A unique way to see the heights of the city with an environmental focus is the Grouse Mountain downhill mountain-biking trip offered by **Velo-City Cycle Tours** (☎ 604/924–0288).

There are also a few companies with **multiday adventure trips** out of Vancouver. **Ecosummer Expeditions** (☎ 604/669–7741 or 800/465–8884) has two- to five-day introductory sea kayaking trips to the Gulf Islands. Prices start at $255. **Ocean West Expeditions** (☎ 604/898–4979 or 800/660–0051) run three- to eight-day sea kayaking trips to the Gulf Islands, Johnstone Strait, and Desolation Sound. **Wild West Adventures** (☎ 604/688–2008) offers five- to seven-day Rocky Mountain camping and hiking trips, starting at $450. The company also schedules whale-watching trips to Tofino, using Zodiac boats to explore Clayoquot Sound and seek out migrating gray whales each spring; cost is $210.

ORIENTATION

Gray Line (☎ 604/879–3363), the largest tour operator, offers the 3½-hour Grand City bus tour year-round. Departing from the Sandman Inn in winter and the Plaza of Nations in summer, the tour picks up at all major downtown hotels, includes Stanley Park, Chinatown, Gastown, English Bay, and Queen Elizabeth Park, and costs about $39. Between May and October, Gray Line also has a narrated city tour aboard double-decker buses; passengers can get on and off as they choose and are allowed to ride free the following day if they haven't had their fill. Adult fare is about $22.

Using minibuses departing from downtown hotels and transit stations, **Vance Tours** (☎ 604/941–5660) has a highlights tour (3½ hours, $33) that includes a visit to the University of British Columbia and a shorter city tour (2½ hours, $30, hotel pickup included). **Westcoast City and Nature Sightseeing** (☎ 604/451–1600) accommodates up to 31 people in minibuses that run a four-hour City Highlights tour for about $40 (pickup available from all major hotels downtown).

Stanley Park Horse Drawn Tours (☎ 604/681–5115) has a one-hour tour of Stanley Park, along the waterfront and through a cedar forest and a rose garden, for about $12 per person ($36 for a family of four); the tours leave every 20–30 minutes from the information booth on Park Drive.

The **Vancouver Trolley Company** (☎ 604/451–5581) runs turn-of-the-century–style trolleys through Vancouver mid-March–October on a two-hour narrated tour of Stanley Park, Gastown, English Bay, Granville Island, and Chinatown. A day pass allows you to complete one full circuit, getting off and on as often as you like. Start the trip at any of the sights and buy a ticket on board. Adult fare is $20.

North Shore tours usually include any or several of the following: a gondola ride up Grouse Mountain, a walk across the Capilano Suspension Bridge, a stop at a salmon hatchery, a visit to Lonsdale Quay Market, and a ride back to town on the SeaBus. Half-day tours cost anywhere from $45 to $55 and are offered by **Landsea Tours** (☎ 604/255–7272), **Gray Line** (☎ 604/879–3363), and **Pacific Coach Lines** (☎ 604/662–7575).

Early Motion Tours (☎ 604/687–5088) will pick you up at your hotel for a tour of Vancouver in a Model-A Ford convertible. For about $70–$80, up to four people can take an hour-long trip around downtown, Chinatown, and Stanley Park; longer tours can also be arranged. Individualized tours, in six European languages, are available from **VIP Tourguide Services** (☎ 604/214–4677).

On the **Pacific Starlight Dinner Train** (☎ 604/984–5500, 604/631–3500, or 800/363–3733), you sample West Coast cuisine as you travel up the coast in a vintage rail coach. The train leaves the North Vancouver BC Rail station at 6:15 PM, stops at Porteau Cove on Howe Sound, and returns to the station at 10 PM. This service runs Wednesday–Sunday, May–October. Fares, including a three-course meal, are $71 for salon seating, $86 for the dome car. Reservations are essential.

The Royal Hudson (☎ 604/984–5246 or 800/663–8238 from outside British Columbia), Canada's only functioning main-line steam train, leaves the North Vancouver BC Rail station for a trip along the mountainous coast up Howe Sound to the logging town of Squamish. After a break there, you can return by train or sail back to Vancouver on the M.V. *Britannia*. The trip runs May 30–September 20, Wednesday–Sunday. Round-trip fare by train is $46.50; by train and boat, about $75. Reservations are advised.

The **Gastown Business Improvement Society** (✉ 12 Water St., ☎ 604/683–5650) sponsors free 90-minute historical and architectural walking tours daily June–August. Meet the guide at 2 PM at the statue of "Gassy" Jack in Maple Tree Square. **Rockwood Adventure** (☎ 604/926–7705) has guided walks around Vancouver neighborhoods, including Gastown, Granville Island, and Chinatown, and a special walk for art lovers. **Love Vancouver Walks** (☎ 604/731–0968), **Walkabout Historic Vancouver** (☎ 604/808–1650), **World-in-a-City Tours** (☎ 604/738–9223), and **World Wide Walks** (☎ 604/254–7088) offer historical and cultural walking tours of Vancouver's neighborhoods.

Late-Night Pharmacy

Shopper's Drug Mart (✉ 1125 Davie St., ☎ 604/669–2424) has 24-hour service daily.

Opening and Closing Hours

Banks traditionally are open Monday–Thursday 10–3 and Friday 10–6, but many banks have extended hours and are open on Saturday, particularly outside of downtown. **Department store** hours are Monday–Wednesday and Saturday 9:30–6, Thursday–Friday 9:30–9, and Sunday noon–5. Many smaller stores are also open Sunday. **Museums** are generally open 10–5, including weekends. Most are open one evening a week as well.

Road Emergencies

BCAA (☎ 604/293–2222) has 24-hour emergency road service for members of AAA and CAA.

Travel Agencies

American Express Travel Service (✉ 666 Burrard St., ☎ 604/669–2813). **Carlson Wagonlit** (✉ 150–409 Granville St., ☎ 604/682–4272). **Mirage Holidays** (✉ 14–200 Burrard St., ☎ 604/685–4008).

Visitor Information

Vancouver Tourist Info Centre (✉ 200 Burrard St., V6C 3L6, ☎ 604/ 683–2000, FAX 604/682–6839) provides maps and information about the city and is open daily 8–6 from late May to August; for the rest of the year, hours are weekdays 8:30–5, Saturday 9–5. A visitor information booth is open in summer at the corner of Granville and Georgia streets. **Super, Natural British Columbia** (☎ 800/663–6000) is available year-round to assist with visitor information and reservations.

3 British Columbia

Lush inland valleys and rugged mountains, magnificent beaches and forested islands: This western province has an abundance of natural beauty. There are plenty of opportunities for whale- and nature-watching, as well as for skiing, golfing, fishing, and kayaking, or you can simply relax in a peaceful country inn. Your visit may take you to places as different as small coastal and island towns, the Anglophile city of Victoria, and a re-created native village.

BRITISH COLUMBIA, CANADA'S WESTERNMOST province, harbors Pacific beaches, verdant islands, year-round skiing, world-class fishing—a wealth of outdoor action and beauty. The people of the province are a similarly heterogeneous mix: descendants of the original Native American peoples and 19th-century British and European settlers and more recent immigrants from Asia and Eastern Europe.

Updated by
Sue Kernaghan

Canada's third-largest province (only Québec and Ontario are bigger), British Columbia occupies almost 10% of Canada's total surface area, stretching from the Pacific Ocean eastward to the province of Alberta, and from the U.S. border north to the Yukon and Northwest Territories. It spans more than 360,000 square mi, making it larger than every American state except Alaska.

British Columbia's appeal as a vacation destination stems from its status as the most spectacular part of the nation, with salmon-rich waters, abundant coastal scenery, and stretches of snowcapped peaks. Outdoor enthusiasts have gravitated here for sports including fishing, golfing, kayaking, rafting, and skiing. Whale-watching adventures, whether by charter boat or in a kayak, are increasingly popular.

It is the region's natural splendor that has ironically become the source of conflict. For more than a century, logging companies have depended on the abundant supply of British Columbia timber, and whole towns are still centered on the industry. Environmentalists and many residents now see the logging industry as a threat to the natural surroundings. Compromises have been achieved in recent years, but the issue is far from resolved.

The province used to be very British and predictable, reflecting its colonial heritage; but no longer. Vancouver (☞ Chapter 2) is an international city whose relaxed lifestyle is spiced by a varied cultural scene embracing large ethnic communities. Even Vancouver Island's Victoria, which clings with restrained passion to British traditions, has undergone an international metamorphosis in recent years.

No matter how modern the province may appear, evidence remains of the earliest settlers: Pacific Coast natives (Haida, Kwakiutl, Nootka, Salish, and others) who occupied the land for more than 12,000 years before the first Europeans arrived en masse in the late-19th century. Today's native residents often face social barriers that have kept them from the mainstream of the province's rich economy. Although some have gained university educations and have fashioned careers, many are just now beginning to make demands on the nonnative population. In dispute are thousands of square miles of land claimed as aboriginal territory, some of which is within such major cities as Vancouver, Prince George, and Prince Rupert. The issue of ownership remains undecided, but British Columbia's roots show throughout the province, from such native arts as wood-carved objects and etched-silver jewelry in small-town boutiques to authentic culinary delights created from traditional recipes in big-city dining establishments.

Pleasures and Pastimes

Dining

Although Vancouver has the most varied and creative restaurants, a number of fine country inns have helped define a local cuisine based on the best local fare from seafood and lamb to fine produce and herbs. Victoria has lots of seafood spots and places serving British-style dishes.

The food here overall is fresh and hearty. Prices vary from location to location, but ratings reflect the categories on the dining chart. Attire is generally casual in the region. Most Victoria restaurants ban smoking; regulations vary in other towns.

CATEGORY	COST*
$$$$	over $35
$$$	$25–$35
$$	$15–$25
$	under $15

per person, in Canadian dollars, excluding drinks, service, and 7% GST

Lodging

Accommodations range from bed-and-breakfasts and rustic cabins to deluxe chain hotels. In the cities you'll find an abundance of lodgings, but once you get off the beaten path, guest rooms are often a rare commodity and usually require advance booking. Most small inns and bed-and-breakfasts in the province ban smoking indoors.

CATEGORY	COST*
$$$$	over $250
$$$	$170–$250
$$	$90–$170
$	under $90

All prices are for a standard double room, excluding 10% provincial accommodation tax, and 7% GST, in Canadian dollars.

Outdoor Activities and Sports

CANOEING AND KAYAKING

The Inside Passage, Queen Charlotte Strait, the Strait of Georgia, and the other island-dotted straits and sounds that border the mainland provide fairly protected sea-going from Washington State to the Alaskan border, with numerous marine parks to explore along the way. BC Ferries' Discovery Coast Passage service now gives kayakers direct access to the channels and islands of the midcoast. Another favorite among paddlers is the Powell Forest Canoe Route, an 80-km (50-mi) circuit of seven lakes. The Broken Islands Group, off the west coast of Vancouver Island, draws kayakers from around the world to its protected, wildlife-rich waters.

FISHING

Miles of coastline and thousands of lakes, rivers, and streams bring more than 750,000 fishers to British Columbia each year. The waters of the province hold 74 species of fish (25 of them sport fish), including Chinook salmon and rainbow trout.

GOLF

There are more than 230 golf courses in British Columbia, and the number is growing. The province is now an Official Golf Destination of both the Canadian and American PGA tours. The topography here tends to be mountainous, and many courses have fine views as well as treacherous approaches to greens.

HIKING

Virtually all of British Columbia's provincial parks have fine hiking-trail networks. Heli-hiking is also very popular here; helicopters deliver hikers to high alpine meadows and verdant mountaintops.

RAFTING

A wide range of rafting trips are available on the many beautiful rivers lacing British Columbia, including the Adams, Chilcotin, Chilliwack, Fraser, Illecillewaet, Nahatlach, and Thompson lacing British Columbia.

SKIING

With more than half the province higher than 4,200 ft above sea level, new downhill areas are constantly opening. Currently, more than 40 major resorts in the province have downhill facilities. British Columbia also has hundreds of miles of groomed cross-country (Nordic) ski trails in the provincial parks and more than 40 cross-country resorts. Most downhill destinations have carved out cross-country routes along the valleys, and there are thousands more trails in unmanaged areas of British Columbia.

WHALE-WATCHING

Three resident and several transient pods of orcas (killer whales) travel the province's coastal waters. These, and the gray whales living along the west coast of Vancouver Island, are the primary focus of the many whale-watching boat tours leaving Victoria, Telegraph Cove, Ucluelet, Bamfield, and Tofino during the summer months. July, August, and September are the best time to see orcas; in March and April thousands of migrating gray whales pass close to the west coast of Vancouver Island on their way from Baja California to Alaska. Harbor seals, sea lions, porpoises, and marine bird sightings are a safe bet anytime.

Native Culture

Before the arrival of Europeans, the lush landscapes of the Pacific Northwest gave rise to one of the richest and most artistically prolific cultures on the continent. In recent years a resurgence of this culture has added a new perspective to a tour of the province. There have long been archaeological sights and museums (Victoria's Royal British Columbia Museum is one outstanding example), but newer sights, including the re-created villages at 'Ksan, near Hazleton, and Secwepemc, near Kamloops, are run by First Nations people themselves and offer ways to share a living culture through music, dance, and food.

Exploring British Columbia

Vancouver Island, off the province's west coast, is effectively a small offshore mountain range, its gentle, rural east coast and wild, rain-lashed west separated by a hilly, forested spine. Victoria, the provincial capital at the island's southern tip, and the rural Gulf Islands sprinkled off the mainland side have long attracted escapists of every kind. These days, though, adventurous travelers are also seeking out the deep, temperate rain forests and dramatic beaches of the island's west coast, as well as the migrating whales to be seen here. The mainland coast to the north of Vancouver Island is a roadless, fjord-cut wilderness leading to the mist-shrouded Haida Gwaii, or Queen Charlotte Islands—home to the Haida people and to old-growth forest.

Most of British Columbia's population huddles in a region known as the Lower Mainland, in and around Vancouver in the southwest corner of the province. From here, three highways and a rail line climb over the Coast Mountains to the rolling high plateau that forms the central interior. To the north are the Cariboo ranch country and, beyond that, the vast, sparsely inhabited northern half of the province. To the east are the Okanagan and Shuswap valleys, which hold the province's fruit- and wine-growing region and its lake district. Farther east are the mountainous Kootenays and the foothills of the Rockies.

The coast and islands, touched by Pacific currents, have relatively mild winters and summers (usually above 32°F in winter, below 80°F in summer), although winter brings frequent rains. The interior is drier, with greater extremes, including hot summers and reliably snowy

Southern British Columbia

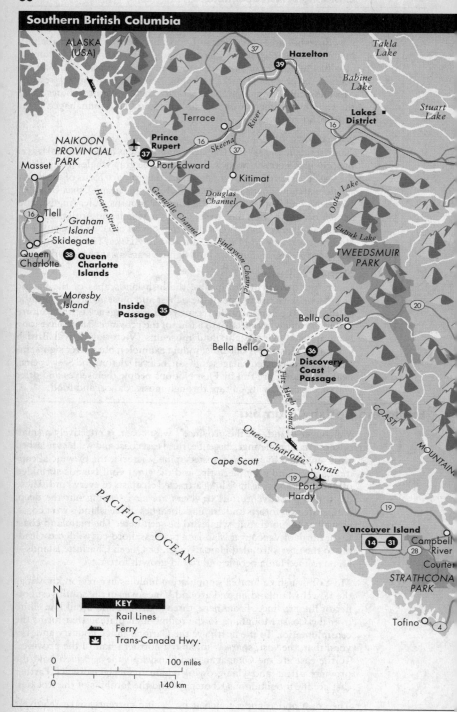

ALASKA (USA)

Takla Lake

37

Hazelton

39

Babine Lake

Terrace

River

Stuart Lake

NAIKOON PROVINCIAL PARK

Prince Rupert

37

16

Skeena

Lakes District

16

Masset

Port Edward

Kitimat

Douglas Channel

Oatsa Lake

Hecate Strait

16

Tlell

Graham Island

Skidegate

Grenville Channel

Eutsuk Lake

TWEEDSMUIR PARK

Queen Charlotte

38

Queen Charlotte Islands

Finlayson Channel

Moresby Island

Inside Passage

35

20

Bella Coola

Bella Bella

36

Discovery Coast Passage

Fitz Hugh Sound

COAST

MOUNTAIN

Queen Charlotte

Strait

Cape Scott

19

Port Hardy

19

Vancouver Island

14 — 31

Campbell River

28

PACIFIC

OCEAN

Courte

STRATHCONA PARK

N

Tofino

4

KEY

— Rail Lines

⚓ Ferry

🚗 Trans-Canada Hwy.

0 _____ 100 miles

0 _____ 140 km

ALBERTA

Grande Cache

JASPER NATIONAL PARK (40)

(43)

(16)

(27) Vanderhoof

(39)

(29)

(97)

(16) (40) **Prince George**

(93)

MT. ROBSON PARK

(16)

BOWRON LAKE PARK

Wells

(26) Quesnel

Barkerville

Valemount

COLUMBIA

Fraser

(97)

Quesnel Lake

WELLS GRAY PARK

MOUNTAINS

Kinbasket Lake

FRASER

★ Williams Lake

(20)

PLATEAU

(5)

MONASHEE MOUNTAINS

Adams Lake

Shuswap Lake

(23)

Jesmond

Clinton

Cache Creek

(97)

Lillooet

(12)

(41) **Kamloops**

(97)

Okanagan Lake

(42) **Vernon**

Oyama

(6)

Pemberton

Lytton

(1) Yale

Merritt

Kelowna

Westbank

Peachland

(43)

Whistler

(99)

GARIBALDI PARK

(1)

(5A)

Summerland

(44) **Penticton**

Powell River

Squamish

Howe Sound

Britannia Beach

Boston Bar

(5)

Harrison Hot Springs

(3)

CATHEDRAL PROV. PARK

(3)

Harrison Mills

(7)

MANNING PARK

CANADA

USA

(97)

nay

(19)

Vancouver

Nanaimo

Gulf Islands

(1)

32 — **34**

(1)

(46) **Rosedale**

(45)

542

(20)

(21)

Port Alberni

Duncan

(5)

(9)

NORTH CASCADES NATIONAL PARK

(153)

(155)

1 — **13**

Victoria ✪

(20)

530

(112)

Port Angeles

(101)

TO SEATTLE

winters. Temperatures here drop below freezing in winter and sometimes reach 90°F in summer.

When you travel by car, keep in mind that more than three-quarters
of British Columbia is mountainous terrain. Trips that appear relatively
short may take longer. Many areas, including the north coast of the
mainland and most of the west coast of Vancouver Island, have no roads
at all and are accessible only by air or sea.

*Numbers in the text correspond to numbers in the margin and on the
Southern British Columbia, Downtown Victoria, and Vancouver Island maps.*

Great Itineraries

British Columbia is about the size of Western Europe, with as much
geographical variety and substantially fewer roads. The good news is
that many great sights, stunning scenery, and even wilderness lie within
a few days' tour of Vancouver or the U.S. border.

IF YOU HAVE 1–3 DAYS

For a short trip, ⊡ **Victoria** ①–⑬ is a fine place to begin. There's
plenty to explore, from flower-fringed Inner Harbour and the museums and attractions nearby to Bastion Square and the red gates of Chinatown. World-famous Butchart Gardens is only half an hour away
by car, and you might take a full day to explore the beautiful grounds.
On Day 3, head out to ⊡ **Sooke** ⑭ or to one of the Gulf Islands—⊡
Galiano ㉜, ⊡ **Mayne** ㉝, or ⊡ **Salt Spring** ㉞—to stay at a romantic
country inn for a night.

A mainland alternative is to take the Coast Mountain Circle tour,
driving north from Vancouver to the resort town of ⊡ **Whistler** (☞
Side Trip from Vancouver *in* Chapter 2) and over the scenic Duffy Lake
Road to the gold-rush town of **Lillooet.** You can then return to Van-
couver through the steep gorges of the **Fraser Canyon,** with stops at
Hell's Gate on the Fraser River, ⊡ **Harrison Hot Springs** ㊺ and the Kilby
Historic Store and Farm, and Minter Gardens at **Rosedale** ㊻.

IF YOU HAVE 4–6 DAYS

A brief stay in ⊡ **Victoria** ①–⑬ can be followed by a leisurely tour of
Vancouver Island and perhaps a portion of the mainland coast if you
have more time. Assuming you plan to stay on Vancouver Island, Day
4 allows time to stop to see the Cowichan Native Village in **Duncan** ⑮
and the murals and restored Victorian buildings of ⊡ **Chemainus** ⑯.
On Day 5, one alternative is to trek across island to the scenic west
coast to visit ⊡ **Tofino** ㉒ and ⊡ **Ucluelet** ㉑ (pick one for your overnight)
and spend some time whale-watching or hiking around **Pacific Rim National Park** ㉓. Another choice is to continue up the east coast to do
some salmon fishing in ⊡ **Campbell River** ㉙ or to visit ⊡ **Port Hardy** ㉚
to see the resident whale pods near Telegraph Cove.

If you've gone the eastern route, Day 6 will take you by ferry from ⊡
Courtenay and Comox ㉗ across the Strait of Georgia to **Powell River** ㉘
on the Sunshine Coast, a paradise for outdoors lovers. Ferries and short
highway jaunts will carry you down the scenic coast to Vancouver. If
you've crossed to the west coast, you can spend Day 6 backtracking
to **Victoria** or making your way to **Nanaimo** ⑰ to catch the ferry to
Vancouver and the mainland.

IF YOU HAVE 7–10 DAYS

A longer trip will allow time to see Vancouver Island, as described above,
then cruise the breathtaking **Inside Passage** ㉟ from Port Hardy to ⊡
Prince Rupert ㊲, where you can catch another ferry to see the old-growth
forest and abandoned Haida villages of the ⊡ **Queen Charlotte Islands** ㊳.

From Port Hardy you could also take the equally scenic but, so far, less-traveled **Discovery Coast Passage** ㊱, served by a smaller ferry that explores the midcoast and stops at native villages, fishing lodges, and coastal ghost towns before cruising up a deep fjord to Bella Coola. You can then complete the circle back to Vancouver by air, ferry, road, or, from Prince Rupert, train.

Another option, after visiting Vancouver Island, is to tour British Columbia's mainland. Day 7 takes you into the interior, either over the mountains via ⛺ **Whistler** (☞ Side Trip from Vancouver *in* Chapter 2) and **Lillooet,** or through the **Fraser Canyon.** Days 8 through 10 are best spent making the loop through the Okanagan Valley, the fruit-growing and wine-producing region of the province. You can make stops in ⛺ **Penticton** ㊹ to see the Kettle Valley Steam Railway and Cathedral Provincial Park, ⛺ **Kelowna** ㊸ to tour the vineyards, ⛺ **Vernon** ㊷ to enjoy the O'Keefe Historic Ranch, and ⛺ **Kamloops** ㊶ to fish in one of the many lakes or visit the Secwepemc Native Heritage Museum. Any of these towns is fine for your overnights.

When to Tour British Columbia

Victoria is at its peak from late spring to early fall, but high summer is the most appealing time in a city proud of its gardens. Rooms can be hard to come by, so book well in advance if you plan to visit from June through August. Summer and fall are the best seasons to tour the islands of the province (frequent ferry service to the Gulf Islands, the Queen Charlottes, and Prince Rupert drops off in winter and spring). Vancouver Island is very busy during summer and fall; the winter resorts draw more locals than visitors, so the crowds are much smaller than on the mainland. The Cariboo, High Country, and the Okanagan Valley have year-round appeal: Winter brings snow for downhill and cross-country skiing, spring is filled with blossoms on fruit trees, and summer has warm, dry temperatures conducive to all outdoor activities. Fall harvest time is a particular favorite; pears, apples, and other produce are readily available, and harvest festivals are frequent.

VICTORIA

Originally Fort Victoria, Victoria was the first European settlement on Vancouver Island and is the oldest city on Canada's west coast. It was chosen in 1843 by James Douglas to be the Hudson's Bay Company's westernmost outpost, and it became the capital of British Columbia in 1868. This outpost of the Empire has evolved into a walkable, livable seaside town of gardens, waterfront walks, and restored 19th-century architecture. Victoria is often (some say too often) called the most British city in Canada. These days, though, except for the odd red phone box, good beer, and well-mannered drivers, this very Canadian town is working to shed its tea-cozy image, preferring to celebrate its combined native, Asian, and European heritage.

After dark, there are more than enough quasi-British pubs in which to watch a hockey game, but Victoria also has thriving dining, music, art, and theater scenes, all on an accessible scale. The stunning Butchart Gardens (☞ Side Trip from Victoria, *below*), north of the city, is a great way to enjoy the area's outdoors.

Victoria fills up in the summertime, when the flowers, trinket sellers, and tour buses are all in attendance. Many visitors prefer the slower pace and deep discounts available during Victoria's mild (and, by Canadian standards, warm) winters. The city is 71 km (44 mi), and about 3 hours by car and ferry, south of Vancouver; it's about 2½ hours by high-speed passenger ferry from Seattle.

Downtown Victoria

Great waterfront views, historic buildings, funky shopping areas, lush gardens, and fine museums are the highlights of a visit to Victoria's walkable downtown.

A Good Walk and Tour

For some wonderful views, begin your tour of Victoria on the water-front at the **Visitor Information Centre** ①. Just across the way is the **Empress** ②, a majestic railroad hotel that originally opened in 1908. A short walk around the harbor leads you to the **Royal London Wax Museum** ③, housed in a former steamship terminal, and the **Pacific Undersea Gardens.** Across Belleville Street are the **Parliament Buildings** ④, seat of the provincial government.

Follow Government Street four blocks south to **Emily Carr House** ⑤, the birthplace of one of British Columbia's best-known artists; then take Simcoe Street east to **Beacon Hill Park** ⑥, a beautiful green space near the waterfront. Follow Douglas Street north or wander through the park back up to Belleville Street and the **Royal British Columbia Museum** ⑦, one of the most impressive museums in Canada. Just behind the museum and bordering Douglas Street is Thunderbird Park, where totem poles and a ceremonial longhouse stand in one corner of the garden of **Helmcken House,** the oldest house in British Columbia. Behind Helmcken House is St. Ann's Schoolhouse, one of the province's oldest schools. Cross Douglas Street and stop off at the glass-roofed **Crystal Garden** ⑧, a former swimming pool where you can see 75 varieties of birds, hundreds of flowers, and monkeys.

From Crystal Garden, continue five blocks north on Douglas Street to View Street and turn left, walking three blocks to **Bastion Square** ⑨, with its restaurants, cobblestone streets, and small shops. While you're here, you can stop in at the **Maritime Museum of British Columbia** ⑩ and learn about an important part of the province's history. Just around the corner on Wharf Street is the **Victoria Bug Zoo,** a creepy-crawly attraction popular with kids. North of Bastion Square, west of Government Street between Johnson Street and Pandora Avenue, is **Market Square** ⑪, one of the most picturesque shopping districts in the city. Just around the corner from Market Square is Fisgard Street, the heart of **Chinatown** ⑫.

A 25-minute walk or a short drive east on Fort Street will take you to Joan Crescent and lavish **Craigdarroch Castle** ⑬ and, five minutes down the hill on Moss Street, the **Art Gallery of Greater Victoria.** From the corner of Douglas and Yates streets downtown, you can take the BC Transit Munro Bus 25 for 3 mi to **Anne Hathaway's Cottage,** a replica of the original home in England.

TIMING

Many of the sights are within easy walking distance of one another and could be covered in a day, but there's so much to see at the Royal British Columbia Museum and the other museums that you could easily fill two days. This would allow time for some shopping and a visit to Craigdarroch Castle, too.

Sights to See

OFF THE BEATEN PATH

ANNE HATHAWAY'S COTTAGE – A full-size replica of the original thatched home of Shakespeare's wife in Stratford-upon-Avon, England, is part of the English Village, a complex with re-created period buildings. The 16th-century antiques inside are typical of Shakespeare's era. The Olde England Inn here is a pleasant spot for tea or an English-style meal, and you can also stay in one of the 50 antiques-furnished rooms.

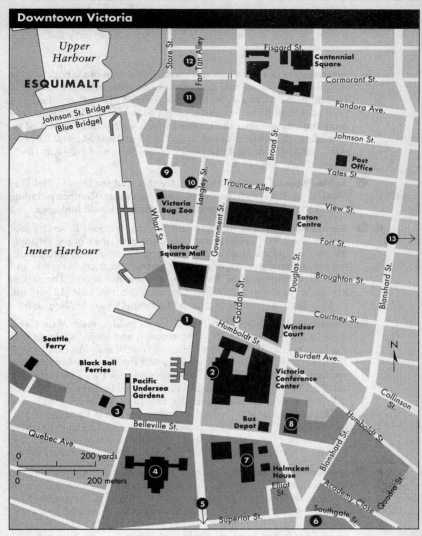

Downtown Victoria

Upper Harbour

ESQUIMALT

Johnson St. Bridge (Blue Bridge)

Inner Harbour

Store St.

Fan Tan Alley

⑫

⑪

Fisgard St.

Centennial Square

Cormorant St.

Pandora Ave.

Broad St.

Johnson St.

⑨

⑩

Langley St.

Trounce Alley

Post Office

Yates St.

Victoria Bug Zoo

View St.

Wharf St.

Harbour Square Mall

Government St.

Eaton Centre

Fort St.

Douglas St.

Broughton St.

⑬

Blanshard St.

①

Humboldt St.

Gordon St.

Courtney St.

Seattle Ferry

Windsor Court

Burdett Ave.

N

Black Ball Ferries

②

Victoria Conference Center

Collinson St.

Pacific Undersea Gardens

③

Belleville St.

Bus Depot

⑧

Humboldt St.

Blanshard St.

Quebec Ave.

0 — 200 yards

0 — 200 meters

④

⑦

Helmcken House

Elliot St.

Academy Close

Quadra St.

⑤

Superior St.

⑥

Southgate St.

Bastion Square, **9**
Beacon Hill Park, **6**
Chinatown, **12**
Craigdarroch Castle, **13**
Crystal Garden, **8**
Emily Carr House, **5**
The Empress, **2**

Maritime Museum of British Columbia, **10**
Market Square, **11**
Parliament Buildings, **4**
Royal British Columbia Museum, **7**
Royal London Wax Museum, **3**

Visitor Information Centre, **1**

Guided tours leave from the inn in winter and from the cottage in summer. The village is touristy but appeals to many people. ⊠ *429 Lampson St.,* ☎ *250/388–4353.* ⌨ *$7.50.* ⊙ *June–Sept., daily 9–8; Oct.–May, daily 10–4.*

Art Gallery of Greater Victoria. This fine museum is home both to large collections of Chinese and Japanese ceramics and other art and to the only authentic Shinto shrine in North America. The gallery also has a permanent exhibit of British Columbia native Emily Carr's work and numerous temporary exhibitions yearly. It's a few blocks west of ☞ Craigdarroch Castle, off Fort Street. ⊠ *1040 Moss St.,* ☎ *250/384–4101.* ⌨ *$5; Mon. by donation.* ⊙ *Mon.–Wed. and Fri.–Sat. 10–5, Thurs. 10–9, Sun. 1–5.*

❾ **Bastion Square.** James Douglas chose this spot for the original Fort Victoria in 1843 and the original Hudson's Bay Company trading post. Today boutiques and restaurants occupy the old buildings.

★ ❻ **Beacon Hill Park.** The southern lawns of this spacious haven for joggers, walkers, and cyclists have one of the best views of the Olympic Mountains and the Strait of Juan de Fuca. There are also lakes, walking paths, gardens, a wading pool, a petting zoo, a cricket pitch, and an outdoor amphitheater for Sunday afternoon concerts. The park is also home to the world's tallest freestanding totem pole (127 ft) and to Mile Zero of the Trans-Canada Highway. ⊠ *East of Douglas St.*

⓬ **Chinatown.** The Chinese were responsible for building much of the Canadian Pacific Railway in the 19th century, and their influences still mark the region. If you enter Chinatown (one of the oldest in Canada) from Government Street, you'll walk under the elaborate **Gate of Harmonious Interest,** made from Taiwanese ceramic tiles and decorative panels. Along the street, merchants display paper lanterns, embroidered silks, imported fruits, and vegetables. **Fan Tan Alley,** off Fisgard Street, holds claim not only to being the narrowest street in Canada but also to having been the gambling and opium center of Chinatown, where games of mah-jongg, fan-tan, and dominoes were played. Look for it between Numbers 545½ and 549½ on the south side of the street.

★ ⓭ **Craigdarroch Castle.** This haunted-looking mansion was built as the home of British Columbia's first millionaire, Robert Dunsmuir, who oversaw coal mining for the Hudson's Bay Company. He died in 1889, just a few months before the castle's completion. Converted into a museum depicting turn-of-the-century life, the castle has elaborately framed landscape paintings, stained-glass windows, hunting trophies peering from the walls, carved woodwork—precut in Chicago for Dunsmuir and sent by rail—and rooms for billiards and smoking. The fourth-floor tower has a wonderful view of downtown Victoria. ⊠ *1050 Joan Crescent,* ☎ *250/592–5323.* ⌨ *$7.50.* ⊙ *Mid-June–early Sept., daily 9–7; mid-Sept.–mid-June, daily 10–4:30.*

❽ **Crystal Garden.** Opened in 1925 as the largest saltwater swimming pool in the British Empire, this glass-roof building, owned by the provincial government, is now home to flamingos, macaws, 75 varieties of other tropical birds, monkeys, and hundreds of blooming flowers. At street level there are several boutiques and the Water Club Restaurant (☞ Dining, *below*). ⊠ *713 Douglas St.,* ☎ *250/381–1213.* ⌨ *$7.* ⊙ *Daily; call for seasonal hrs.*

❺ **Emily Carr House.** Emily Carr (1871–1945), one of Canada's most celebrated artists and a respected writer as well, was born and raised in this very proper wooden Victorian house before she abandoned her middle-class life to live in, and paint, the wilds of British Columbia. Carr's own descriptions, from her autobiography *Book of the Small,* were used to restore the house. ⊠ *207 Government St.,* ☎ *250/383–5843.* ⊟ *$4.50.* ◷ *Mid-May–mid-Oct., daily 10–5; mid-Oct.–mid-May, tours by prearrangement.*

★ ❷ **The Empress.** Originally opened in 1908, the Empress (☞ Lodging, *below*) is a symbol of both the city and the Canadian Pacific Railway. Designed by Francis Rattenbury, who also designed the Parliament Buildings, the property is another of the great châteaus built by Canadian Pacific, still the owners. The ingredients that made the 483-room hotel a tourist attraction in the past—Old World architecture and ornate decor, a commanding view of the Inner Harbour—are still here. Stop in for afternoon tea, served at hour-and-a-half intervals during the afternoon (a dress code calls for smart-casual wear). Hotel staff run tours daily in summer, and the archives, a historical photo display, are open to the public anytime. ⊠ *721 Government St.,* ☎ *250/384–8111.* ⊟ *Free; historical tours $6.*

Helmcken House. The oldest house in British Columbia, built in 1852 by pioneer doctor and statesman John Sebastian Helmcken, is a treasure trove of history, from the early Victorian furnishings to an unnerving collection of 19th-century medical tools. Audio tours last 20 minutes. Next door is **St. Ann's Schoolhouse,** one of the first schools in British Columbia. **Thunderbird Park,** with totem poles and a ceremonial longhouse constructed by Kwakiutl chief Mungo Martin, occupies one corner of the garden; it's part of the ☞ **Royal British Columbia Museum.** For further information on these and other historic attractions in Victoria (Craigflower Farm and Schoolhouse and Point Ellice House), call ☎ 250/387–4697. ⊠ *Helmcken House, 10 Elliot St.,* ☎ *250/361–0021.* ⊟ *$4.* ◷ *May–Sept., daily 10–5; call for winter hrs.*

❿ **Maritime Museum of British Columbia.** Dugout canoes, model ships, Royal Navy charts, photographs, uniforms, and ship's bells, now housed in Victoria's original courthouse, chronicle the city's seafaring history. A seldom-used 100-year-old cage lift, believed to be the oldest in North America, ascends to the third floor, where the original admiralty courtroom looks set for a court-martial. ⊠ *28 Bastion Sq.,* ☎ *250/385–4222.* ⊟ *$5.* ◷ *Daily 9:30–4:30.*

⓫ **Market Square.** During Victoria's late-19th-century heyday, this two-level square, built like an old inn courtyard, provided everything a sailor, miner, or up-country lumberjack could want. Now, beautifully restored to its original architectural, if not commercial, character, it's a traffic-free, café- and boutique-lined hangout—now, as then, a great spot for people-watching.

Ⓒ **Pacific Undersea Gardens.** Floating in the harbor next to the ☞ **Royal London Wax Museum,** the undersea gardens (basically an aquarium) display about 5,000 marine specimens in a somewhat claustrophobic underwater setting. Small children thrill to the 20-minute scuba diver and octopus show; adults can console themselves with the knowledge that part of the admission fee goes to help orphaned seal pups. ⊠ *490 Belleville St.,* ☎ *250/382–5717.* ⊟ *$7.* ◷ *Oct.–May, daily 10–5; June–Sept., daily 9–9; show every 35 min.*

★ ❹ **Parliament Buildings.** The massive stone structures, designed by Francis Rattenbury and completed in 1897, dominate the Inner Harbour and are flanked by statues of two men: Sir James Douglas, who chose the site where Victoria was built, and Sir Matthew Baille Begbie, the man in charge of law and order during the gold-rush era. Atop the central dome is a gilded statue of Capt. George Vancouver, the first European to sail around Vancouver Island. A statue of Queen Victoria stands in front of the complex; more than 3,000 lights outline the buildings at night. When the legislature is in session, you can sit in the public gallery and watch British Columbia's often polarized and acrimonious democracy at work (tradition has the opposing parties sitting two sword lengths apart). Free, informative half-hour tours are obligatory on summer weekends and optional the rest of the time. ⊠ *501 Belleville St.,* ☎ *250/387–3046.* ⊡ *Free.* ⊙ *June–Aug., daily 9–5; Sept.–May, weekdays 8:30–5; tours daily at 4.*

★ Ⓒ ❼ **Royal British Columbia Museum.** The museum, easily the best attraction in Victoria, is as much a research and educational center as a draw for the public, and its exhibits, although gripping with their sound, scent, and visual effects, are all informed by historical context. The definitive First People's exhibit includes a genuine Kwakwaka'wakw longhouse (the builders retain rights to its ceremonial use) and provides insights into the daily life, art, and mythology of both coastal and lesser-known interior peoples, before and after the arrival of Europeans. The Modern History Gallery re-creates most of a frontier town, complete with cobblestone streets, silent movies, and rumbling train sounds. The Natural History Gallery realistically reproduces the sights, sounds, and smells of many of the province's natural habitats, and the Open Ocean mimics, all too realistically, a submarine journey. A new on-site IMAX theater shows National Geographic films on a six-story-high screen. ⊠ *675 Belleville St.,* ☎ *250/387–3701 or 800/661–5411.* ⊡ *June–Sept., $7; Oct.–May, $5.35; IMAX theater, $9.* ⊙ *Museum daily 9–5; theater daily 9–8 in winter, 9–9 in summer.*

Ⓒ ❸ **Royal London Wax Museum.** This museum, in the old Canadian Pacific Railway Steamship Terminal designed by Francis Rattenbury and completed in 1924, houses some 300 wax figures, including replicas of Elvis, Marilyn Monroe, Princess Diana, and, of course, Queen Victoria. ⊠ *470 Belleville St.,* ☎ *250/388–4461.* ⊡ *$7.50.* ⊙ *May–Aug., daily 9–9; Sept.–Apr., daily 9:30–5.*

Ⓒ **Victoria Bug Zoo.** Kids love bugs, and this offbeat minizoo, opened in 1997, is drawing kids big and little to its two small rooms displaying at least 30 insects—mostly large tropical varieties such as stick insects, scorpions, and centipedes. Many bugs can be held, and staff are always on hand with scientific information. ⊠ *1107 Wharf St.,* ☎ *250/384–2847.* ⊡ *$6.* ⊙ *Daily 9–6.*

❶ **Visitor Information Centre.** A waterfront location near the harbor ferries dock adds to the center's appeal. Johnson Bridge immediately to the south gives you a grand view of the Inner Harbour. ⊠ *812 Wharf St.,* ☎ *250/953–2033.* ⊙ *July–Aug., daily 8:30–8; May–June and Sept., daily 9–7; Oct.–Apr., daily 9–5.*

Dining

$$$$ ✕ **Empress Room.** A fireside table in the elegant restaurant of the Empress hotel is one choice for a special-occasion dinner. Innovative and
★ beautifully presented Pacific Northwest cuisine vies for attention with the setting when candlelight dances on the tapestried walls. Fresh local ingredients go into imaginative seasonal dishes, such as wild mushroom and chicken terrine, veal tenderloin with wild rice–herb crust and black currant sauce, and Fraser Valley smoked marinated duck breast. The wine list is excellent, as are the six-course table d'hôte menus. The dining room is no-smoking. ⊠ *The Empress, 721 Government St.,* ☎ *250/384–8111 or 800/664–6611. Reservations essential. AE, D, DC, MC, V. Closed Sun.–Mon. Oct.–May. No lunch.*

$$$-$$$$ ✕ **Chez Daniel.** This small, cozy Oak Bay restaurant, about a 12-minute drive from the city center, is widely considered one of Victoria's finest. The menu, with a selection of rabbit, salmon, duck, and steak dishes, is traditional French with some nouvelle influences. The award-winning wine list ranks among the best in the country. ✉ *2524 Estevan Ave.,* ☎ *250/592–7424. Reservations essential. AE, DC, MC, V. Closed Sun.–Mon. No lunch.*

$$$-$$$$ ✕ **Il Terrazzo.** A charming redbrick terrace edged by potted greenery
★   and warmed by fireplaces and overhead heaters makes Il Terrazzo—tucked away off Waddington Alley near Market Square and not visible from the street—the locals' choice for romantic alfresco dining. Scallops dipped in roasted pistachios and garnished with arugula, Belgian endive, and mango salsa; grilled lamb chops on angel-hair pasta with tomatoes, garlic, mint, and black pepper; and other hearty northern Italian dishes come piping hot from the restaurant's wood oven. ✉ *555 Johnson St., off Waddington Alley (call for directions),* ☎ *250/361–0028. Reservations essential. AE, MC, V. No lunch Sun.*

$$$-$$$$ ✕ **Marina Restaurant.** This lovely, round restaurant with a 180 degree
★   view over Oak Bay Marina is very popular with locals and visitors alike. While seasonings and presentation often change, the extensive menu usually lists creative appetizers like warm salmon and spinach salad or mussels in black bean broth, pastas, grills, and seafood entrées (try the bouillabaisse). There's a choice of more than 500 wines. If you don't have reservations and the dining room and sushi bar are full, head downstairs to the Café Deli for Mediterranean picnic foods prepared by the chefs upstairs; go early for the best selection. The Marina is also a prime spot for Sunday brunch. ✉ *1327 Beach Dr.,* ☎ *250/598–8555. Reservations essential. AE, D, DC, MC, V.*

$$-$$$$ ✕ **Siam Thai.** The Thai chefs here work wonders with both hot and mild Thai dishes. The *phad Thai goong* (fried rice noodles with prawns, tofu, peanuts, eggs, bean sprouts, and green onions), *bami goreng* (a noodle-based dish with shreds of shrimp, pork, vegetables, and an Indonesian blend of herbs and spices), and *satay* (grilled, marinated cubes of meat served with a spicy peanut sauce) are particularly good options. Siam Thai is spacious and conveniently near the Inner Harbour. Its well-stocked bar has a variety of beers. ✉ *512 Fort St.,* ☎ *250/383–9911. Reservations essential. AE, MC, V. No lunch Sun.*

$$$ ✕ **Camille's.** Quiet and intimate, Camille's is tucked away off Bastion Square. The menu concentrates on fresh local products, and such regional exotica as ostrich, quail, and emu often appear, too. These, and favorites like roast venison with wild mushroom polenta and grainy Dijon-and-mint-crusted lamb, are served in generous portions. ✉ *45 Bastion Sq.,* ☎ *250/381–3433. AE, MC, V. No lunch.*

$$$ ✕ **Pescatore's Fish House.** Conveniently situated across from the Inner Harbour, upbeat Pescatore's specializes in fresh seafood. Its oyster bar stocks East and West Coast varieties, hot and on the half shell, or you can choose a crab and lobster straight from the tank. Lunch specials, usually fresh fish, are a good value and popular with the business crowd. Come evening, there's live dinner music on the grand piano. ✉ *614 Humboldt St.,* ☎ *250/385–4512. AE, DC, MC, V. No lunch Sun.*

$$-$$$ ✕ **Don Mee's.** A large neon sign invites you inside this traditional Chinese restaurant, with its long staircase that leads to an expansive, comfortable dining room. Some of the Szechuan and Cantonese entrées are sweet-and-sour chicken, Peking duck, and bean curd with broccoli. Dim sum is served daily during lunch hours. ✉ *538 Fisgard St.,* ☎ *250/383–1032. AE, DC, MC, V.*

$$-$$$ ✕ **Herald Street Caffe.** An established favorite, this jazz- and art-
★   filled bistro in Victoria's warehouse district has been open since 1982. Inventive taste combinations and intriguing Asian touches are notable

on a menu that changes seasonally but always lists fresh local cuisine, daily fish grills, and great pastas. Try, if available, the calamari in tomato-dill ratatouille with crumbled feta or roasted chicken breast in a cashew crust. The wine list is excellent, and the staff knowledgeable. ⊠ *546 Herald St.,* ☎ *250/381–1441. Reservations essential. AE, DC, MC, V. No lunch Mon.–Tues.*

$$–$$$ ✕ **Le Petit Saigon.** An intimate café-style restaurant offers quiet dining with beautifully presented meals and fare that is Vietnamese, with a touch of French. The crab, asparagus, and egg swirl soup is a specialty, and combination meals are a good value and tasty. ⊠ *1010 Langley St.,* ☎ *250/386–1412. AE, MC, V. Closed Sun.*

$$–$$$ ✕ **Pagliacci's.** This fine Italian bistro is a must: Dozens of pasta dishes, quiches, veal, and chicken in marsala sauce with fettuccine are standard, and the pastas are freshly made in-house. Save room for the divine cheesecake. Photos of Hollywood movie stars cover the orange walls. ⊠ *1011 Broad St.,* ☎ *250/386–1662. Reservations not accepted. AE, MC, V.*

$$–$$$ ✕ **Tomoe.** A sushi bar, several tatami rooms, and tables set comfortably apart are the elements of this low-key Japanese restaurant. Satisfying seafood dishes (watch for the occasional exotic offering flown in from Japan) share the menu with standards such as tempura and teriyaki. The set meals, with soup, salad, rice, and dessert for under $20, are a good value. ⊠ *726 Johnson St.,* ☎ *250/381–0223. AE, DC, MC, V. No lunch weekends.*

$$–$$$ ✕ **Water Club.** Set in an expansive 180-seat room in the Crystal Garden building, the Water Club, run by the same folks as the Herald Street Caffe (☞ *above*), defies the notion that eateries on the tourist trail have to be disappointing. Co-owner Helen Bell calls the cuisine sensible avantgarde, meaning inventive, local, often organic—but recognizable. Among the seasonal creations are entrées like Vancouver Island rainbow trout stuffed with snow crab mousse, starters like warm smoked duck salad with blue goat cheese, and some inventive pizzas, pastas, and risottos. This casual restaurant has a lounge with a fireplace in winter and two patios. Soft jazz, low-key blue and cream decor, and 53 wines available by the glass keep things relaxed. ⊠ *703 Douglas St.,* ☎ *250/388–4200 or 250/388–7202. AE, DC, MC, V.*

$$ ✕ **Cafe Mexico.** Hearty portions of Mexican food, such as *pollo chipotle* (grilled chicken with melted cheddar and spicy sauce on a bed of rice) are served at a spacious, funky, upbeat cantina just off the waterfront. The lively atmosphere is great for big groups and families, and you can order half portions of anything on the dinner menu. ⊠ *1425 Store St.,* ☎ *250/386–1425. AE, DC, MC, V.*

$$ ✕ **Six-Mile-House Pub.** Although it's a 10-km (6-mi) drive from downtown (on the way to Sooke), this 1855 carriage house is a Victoria landmark and the oldest pub in British Columbia. The brass, carved oak moldings, and stained glass set a festive mood. The menu constantly changes but always has seafood selections and burgers. Try the cider or one of the many international beers. ⊠ *494 Island Hwy.,* ☎ *250/ 478–3121. AE, DC, MC, V.*

$ ✕ **Barb's Place.** This funky, blue-painted take-out shack is on Fisherman's Wharf, on the south side of Victoria Harbour west of the Inner Harbour just off Marine Drive, where fishing boats come in. It has become an institution in Victoria, and locals consider the authentic fish-and-chips (halibut) to be the best. You can catch a ferry to Fisherman's Wharf from the Inner Harbour, pick up an order, and take another ferry to Songhees Point for a picnic. ⊠ *310 Lawrence St.,* ☎ *250/384–6515. No credit cards. Closed Nov.–Mar.*

Lodging

$$$$
★ 🏨 **Coast Victoria Harbourside.** On the more residential section of the harborfront next to Fisherman's Wharf (west of the Inner Harbour), the Coast Victoria has water views but is removed from the traffic on Government Street. Serene relaxation in modern comfort is a theme, from the mahogany-paneled lobby and the soothing shades of blue-gray and pale pink in average-size guest rooms to an extensive health club. Fishing and whale-watching charters and the harbor ferries stop at the hotel's marina. The hotel's downtown shuttle is free. ⊠ *146 Kingston St., V8V 1V4,* ☎ *250/360–1211 or 800/663–1144,* FAX *250/ 360–1418. 126 rooms, 6 suites. Restaurant, lounge, no-smoking rooms, room service, indoor-outdoor pool, hot tub, sauna, health club, business services, meeting rooms, free parking. AE, DC, MC, V.*

$$$$
★ 🏨 **The Empress.** For titled ladies, empire builders, movie stars, and a great many others, the exquisitely comfortable Empress (☞ *Exploring, above*) is the only place to stay in Victoria. Opened in 1908, this Canadian Pacific château has aged gracefully, with sympathetically restored Edwardian decor, discreet modern amenities, and service standards that date back to a more gracious age. Nonguests can stop by the Empress for a traditional afternoon tea (reservations essential), meet for a curry tiffin under the tiger skin in the Bengal Room, or sample superb regional cuisine in the Empress Room (☞ *Dining, above*). ⊠ *721 Government St., V8W 1W5,* ☎ *250/384–8111 or 800/441– 1414,* FAX *250/381–4334. 474 rooms, 36 suites. 2 restaurants, 2 lounges, fans, minibars, no-smoking rooms, room service, indoor pool, hot tub, sauna, exercise room, laundry service and dry cleaning, concierge, concierge floor, business services, convention center, parking (fee). AE, D, DC, MC, V.*

$$$–$$$$
★ 🏨 **The Aerie.** The million-dollar view of Finlayson Arm and the Gulf Islands persuaded Leo and Maria Schuster to build their small, luxury resort here, 30 km (19 mi) north of Victoria. Ten acres of parkland surround the Mediterranean-style villa, in which some plush rooms have a patio; others have fireplaces and whirlpool tubs tucked into window nooks. Three large suites in a 1997 addition have leather sleigh beds, gas fireplaces, soaker tubs, steam showers, and large balconies. The dining room is open to the public from 6 PM for stunning dinner views and outstanding cuisine. The herb-crusted pheasant breast and the chanterelle, potato, and rosemary bisque are worth the drive from Victoria. A full breakfast is included in the tariff. ⊠ *600 Ebedora La., Box 108, Malahat V0R 2L0,* ☎ *250/743–7115,* FAX *250/743–4766. 11 rooms, 12 suites. Restaurant, lounge, fans, no-smoking rooms, indoor pool, indoor and outdoor hot tubs, sauna, spa, tennis court, exercise room, hiking, library, meeting room, helipad. AE, DC, MC, V.*

$$$–$$$$
🏨 **Beaconsfield Inn.** Built in 1905 and restored in 1984, the Beaconsfield has retained its Old World charm. Dark mahogany wood appears throughout the house; down comforters and canopy beds adorn some of the rooms, reinforcing its Edwardian style. Some of the rooms in this no-smoking inn have fireplaces and whirlpool bathtubs. Added pluses are the guest library and the conservatory-sunroom. Full breakfast and afternoon tea are included in the room rates. The inn is on a quiet residential street nine blocks from the Inner Harbour. The owners also operate a newer one-bedroom beach cottage about 10 minutes away. ⊠ *998 Humboldt St., V8V 2Z8,* ☎ *250/384–4044,* FAX *250/384–4052. 5 rooms, 4 suites. Breakfast room, library. MC, V.*

$$$–$$$$
🏨 **Clarion Hotel Grand Pacific.** One of Victoria's finest modern hotels the Clarion has mahogany furniture and an elegant ambience. Overlooking the harbor, adjacent to the legislative buildings, the hotel accommodates business travelers and vacationers looking for comfort,

convenience, and great scenery; all rooms have balconies and most have views of either the harbor or the Olympic Mountains. The elaborate health club is one of the best in the city, and the downtown shuttle is free. ✉ *450 Quebec St., V8V 1W5,* ☎ *250/386–0450 or 800/663–7550,* FAX *250/386–8779. 130 rooms, 15 suites. Restaurant, lounge, air-conditioning, in-room modem lines, in-room safes, minibars, no-smoking rooms, room service, indoor pool, massage, sauna, aerobics, exercise room, racquetball, squash, laundry service and dry cleaning, business services, meeting rooms, free parking. AE, D, DC, MC, V.*

$$$–$$$$ 🏨 **Ocean Pointe Resort Hotel and Spa.** Across the "blue bridge" (John-
★   son Street Bridge) from downtown Victoria, the Ocean Pointe occupies the site of an old shingle mill in an area once claimed by the Songhees natives. From here you have the best possible view of the lights of the Parliament Buildings across the Inner Harbour. Public rooms and half of the guest rooms offer romantic evening views of downtown Victoria. Amenities include a full European aesthetics spa with beauty treatments. ✉ *45 Songhees Rd., V9A 6T3,* ☎ *250/360–2999 or 800/667–4677,* FAX *250/360–5856. 213 rooms, 37 suites. 2 restaurants, lounge, kitchenettes, no-smoking floors, indoor pool, sauna, spa, 2 tennis courts, exercise room, racquetball, squash, laundry service and dry cleaning, business services, meeting rooms, parking (fee). AE, DC, MC, V.*

$$$–$$$$ 🏨 **Prior House Bed & Breakfast Inn.** This beautifully restored 1912 manor home, on a quiet residential street near Craigdarroch Castle, has a pretty garden, a guest library and sitting room, antique furniture, leaded-glass windows, and oak paneling throughout. Originally the home of the king's representative in British Columbia, the no-smoking inn is now one of the city's more stately places to stay. Rooms, all with fireplaces and some with whirlpool tubs and private balconies, vary from cozy to spacious and opulent. The Garden Suite, with a private entrance, two bedrooms, and a full kitchen, is an especially good value. A lavish breakfast and complete afternoon (high) tea are included. ✉ *620 St. Charles St., V8S 3N7,* ☎ *250/592–8847,* FAX *250/592–8223. 5 rooms, 1 suite. Breakfast room, refrigerators, library. MC, V.*

$$–$$$$ 🏨 **Abigail's Hotel.** A Tudor-style country inn with gardens and crys-
★   tal chandeliers, Abigail's is both lovely and convenient—it's within walking distance of the shops and restaurants of downtown. The guest rooms are prettily detailed in soothing pastel colors. Down comforters, together with whirlpool tubs and fireplaces in some, add to the pampering atmosphere. The elegant informality in this no-smoking hotel is especially noticeable in the guest library and sitting room, where hors d'oeuvres are served each evening. Breakfast is included in the rate. ✉ *906 McClure St., V8V 3E7,* ☎ *250/388–5363 or 800/561–6565,* FAX *250/388–7787. 16 rooms, 6 suites. Breakfast room, library, concierge, free parking. MC, V.*

$$$ 🏨 **Haterleigh Heritage Inn.** The Haterleigh, a 6,000-square-ft 1901 mansion just two blocks from the Inner Harbour, was opened as a bed-and-breakfast after arduous restoration. Leaded- and stained-glass windows and ornate plasterwork on 11-ft ceilings transport you to a more gracious time. Mounds of pillows and plump down comforters dress the beds, and several rooms have whirlpool tubs. A full breakfast and afternoon sherry in the guest sitting room are included in the rates. ✉ *243 Kingston St., V8V 1V5,* ☎ *250/384–9995,* FAX *250/384–1935. 5 double rooms, 1 2-bedroom suite. Free parking. MC, V.*

$$$ 🏨 **Laurel Point Inn.** Set on a parklike 6-acre peninsula in the Inner Harbour, a few minutes' walk from the Victoria Clipper dock and the town center, this modern resort and convention hotel has water views from every room. The decor, especially in the newer Arthur Erickson–designed suites, is modern, light, and airy, with a strong Asian influence. Historic Chinese art decorates many public areas, and the Terrace

Room lounge looks out over a Japanese garden. Most rooms are wheelchair accessible; all have balconies, hair dryers, and coffeemakers. ⊠ *680 Montreal St., V8V 1Z8,* ☎ *250/386–8721 or 800/663–7667,* FAX *250/386–9547. 120 rooms, 80 suites. Café, 2 lounges, air-conditioning, no-smoking floors, room service, indoor pool, sauna, hot tub, exercise room, laundry service and dry cleaning, concierge, business services, meeting rooms, free parking. AE, DC, MC, V.*

$$–$$$ 🛏 **Bedford Regency.** This European-style hotel in the heart of downtown is reminiscent of San Francisco's small hotels, with personalized service and careful attention to details. Rooms are in earth colors, and many have goose-down comforters, fireplaces, and whirlpool bathtubs. Four rooms on the west side have views of the harbor and are much quieter than those facing the traffic on Government Street. ⊠ *1140 Government St., V8W 1Y2,* ☎ *250/384–6835 or 800/665–6500,* FAX *250/386–8930. 40 rooms. Pub, no-smoking rooms, laundry service and dry cleaning, business services, meeting rooms, parking (fee). AE, DC, MC, V.*

$$–$$$ 🛏 **Holland House Inn.** A picket fence surrounds this no-smoking hotel decorated with antiques and English country florals. Some of the individually designed rooms have four-poster beds; others have soaker tubs and fireplaces. All but two have their own balconies. A lavish breakfast, served in the conservatory, is included in room rates. The inn is two blocks from the Inner Harbour and the Victoria Clipper terminal. ⊠ *595 Michigan St., V8V 1S7,* ☎ *250/384–6644 or 800/335–3466,* FAX *250/384–6117. 14 rooms. No-smoking rooms. AE, MC, V.*

$$–$$$ 🛏 **Mulberry Manor.** The last building designed by Victoria architect Samuel McClure has been restored and decorated to magazine-cover perfection with antiques, sumptuous linens, and tile baths. The Tudor-style mansion sits behind a high stone wall on an acre of carefully manicured grounds. Charming hosts Susan and Tony Temple serve sumptuous breakfasts with homemade jams, and sherry in the sitting room in the early evening. The inn is a five-minute drive from the Inner Harbour, among the mansions of the Rockland neighborhood. ⊠ *611 Foul Bay Rd., V8S 1H2,* ☎ *250/370–1918,* FAX *250/370–1968. 3 rooms, 1 suite. Breakfast room, no-smoking rooms. MC, V.*

$$–$$$ 🛏 **Swans.** When English-born shepherd Michael Williams bought supplies for his kennel at the Buckerfield Company Feed Store during the 1950s, he never dreamed he would one day own the building and turn it into a waterfront hotel. Extensive renovations have given the 1913 brick warehouse a new look: There's a brewery, bistro, and pub on the first floor and a jazz bar in the cellar; large, apartment-like suites, decorated with Pacific Northwest art, fill the upper floors. Swans is a good choice for families. ⊠ *506 Pandora Ave., V8W 1N6,* ☎ *250/361–3310 or 800/668–7926,* FAX *250/361–3491. 29 suites. Restaurant, pub, kitchenettes, no-smoking floor, no-smoking rooms, room service, nightclub, coin laundry. AE, DC, MC, V.*

$$ 🛏 **Admiral Motel.** On Victoria harbor along the tourist strip, this small, modern motel is in the center of things, although it is relatively quiet in the evening. If you're looking for basic, clean lodging, the Admiral is just that. The amiable owners take good care of the rooms, and small pets are permitted. Kids under 12 stay free in their parents' room. ⊠ *257 Belleville St., V8V 1X1,* ☎ FAX *250/388–6267. 22 rooms, 10 suites. Kitchenettes, no-smoking rooms, coin laundry, free parking. AE, D, MC, V.*

$$ 🛏 **Carberry Gardens.** A 1907 gambrel-roof, board-and-shingle home in the historic Rocklands neighborhood, Carberry Gardens is just blocks from Craigdarroch Castle. The original fir floors, moldings, and staircase, as well as the fine collection of antiques, are eye-catching. In the spacious second-floor rooms, the sun filters through lace cur-

tains onto fluffy down comforters on antique bedsteads. One bedroom has a detached bathroom, but that bathroom is fun, with French doors that open to a little balcony. The inn, entirely no-smoking, has a pantry and a parlor with a fireplace and TV. A hot, hearty breakfast is included. ⊠ *1008 Carberry Gardens, V8S 3R7,* ☎ *250/595–8906,* FAX *250/595–8185. 3 rooms. Refrigerator. MC, V.*

$$ 🖥 **Chateau Victoria.** Wonderful views from the upper-floor rooms and rooftop restaurant are a plus at this centrally located 19-story hotel. All suites have balconies and sitting areas; some have kitchenettes. The rooms are modern, comfortable, and fairly standard in size. ⊠ *740 Burdett Ave., V8W 1B2,* ☎ *250/382–4221 or 800/663–5891,* FAX *250/380–1950. 60 rooms, 118 suites. 2 restaurants, lounge, no-smoking floors, room service, indoor pool, hot tub, exercise room, laundry service and dry cleaning, concierge, business services, meeting rooms, free parking. AE, DC, MC, V.*

$ 🖥 **Cat's Meow.** If you're on a tight budget, you may appreciate this small hostel operated by bubbly Daphne Cuthill. The hostel has a six-bed dorm room and two private rooms (with bunks and a shared bath), as well as a guest lounge. It's only a 15-minute walk east of downtown in the quiet Fernwood neighborhood, not far from Craigdarroch Castle. Dorm space costs $17.50 per night, a private room $43 for two people; the rates include breakfast. Daphne can arrange whale-watching trips at a substantial discount. ⊠ *1316 Grant St., V8R 1M3,* ☎ FAX *250/595–8878. 1 dorm with 6 beds shares bath, 2 private rooms share bath. Coin laundry. No credit cards.*

Nightlife and the Arts

The Arts

MUSIC

The **Pacific Opera Victoria** performs three productions a year in the 900-seat McPherson Playhouse (⊠ 3 Centennial Sq., ☎ 250/386–6121), adjoining the Victoria City Hall. The **Victoria Symphony** has a winter schedule and a summer season, playing in the recently refurbished Royal Theatre (⊠ 805 Broughton St., ☎ 250/386–6121) and at the University Centre Auditorium (⊠ Finnerty Rd., ☎ 250/721–8480).

Thursdays to Saturdays, the **Millennium Jazz Club** (⊠ Under Swan's Hotel at 1601 Store St., ☎ 250/360–9098) has live music from big band to funk, bebop to rumba. The **TerriVic Jazz Party** (☎ 250/953–2011) showcases internationally acclaimed musicians every April. The **Victoria Jazz Society** (☎ 250/388–4423) organizes an annual JazzFest International in late June.

THEATER

Live productions can be seen at the **Belfry Theatre** (⊠ 1291 Gladstone Ave., ☎ 250/385–6815), **Langham Court Theatre** (⊠ 805 Langham Ct., ☎ 250/384–2142), **McPherson Playhouse** (⊠ 3 Centennial Sq., ☎ 250/386–6121), and the **Phoenix Theatre** (⊠ Finnerty Rd., ☎ 250/721–8000) at the University of Victoria.

Nightlife

Planet Harpo's (⊠ 15 Bastion Sq., ☎ 250/385–2626) has live rock, blues, and jazz, with visits from internationally recognized bands. In addition to live music, darts, and brewery tours, **Spinnakers Brew Pub** (⊠ 308 Catherine St., ☎ 250/386–2739), a short ferry ride across the harbor, pours plenty of British Columbian microbrewery beer. **Steamers Public House** (⊠ 570 Yates St., ☎ 250/381–4340) has four pool tables and live music six nights a week. The **Strathcona Hotel** (⊠ 919 Douglas St., ☎ 250/383–7137) is something of an entertainment complex, with the Sticky Wicket Pub on the main floor and Legends nightclub in the basement. Its biggest draw, though, is the beach volleyball played on the roof in summer. **Swan's Pub** (⊠ 1601 Store St., ☎ 250/ 361–3310) is a popular brew pub and café with live folk and jazz five nights a week. For dancing, head to **Sweetwater's** (⊠ 27-560 Johnson St., in Market Sq., ☎ 250/383–7844). **Uforia** (⊠ 1208 Wharf St., ☎ 250/381–2331) is a waterfront spot for dancing.

Outdoor Activities and Sports

Golf

Golf Central provides a transportation and booking service for golfers all over southern Vancouver Island (☎ 250/380–4653). The **Cordova Bay Golf Course** (⊠ 5333 Cordova Bay Rd., ☎ 250/658–4075), Victoria's newest public course, is an 18-hole, par-72 course set on the shoreline. The 18-hole, par-72 **Olympic View Golf Club** (⊠ 643 Latoria Rd., ☎ 250/474–3673), 20 minutes from downtown, offers both challenging and forgiving tees and stunning views. Although the 18-hole, par-70 **Victoria Golf Club** (⊠ 1110 Beach Dr., ☎ 250/598–4321) is private, it's open to other private-club members; the windy course is the oldest (1893) in British Columbia and has spectacular views.

Hiking

The **Galloping Goose Regional Trail** (☎ 250/478–3344), an old railroad line reclaimed for walkers, cyclists, and equestrians, runs 56 scenic km (35 mi) from Victoria to just east of Sooke. **Goldstream Provincial Park** (☎ 250/478–9414), 19 km (12 mi) northwest of Victoria on Highway 1 at Finlayson Arm Road, has an extensive trail system, old-growth forest, waterfalls, a salt marsh, and a river. Park staff lead walks and interpretive programs.

Swan Lake Christmas Hill Nature Sanctuary, a few miles from downtown, has a 23-acre lake set in 110 acres of fields and wetlands. From the 2½-km (1½-mi) chip trail and floating boardwalk, birders can spot a variety of waterfowl even in winter, as well as nesting birds in the tall grass. ⊠ *3873 Swan Lake Rd. (Bus 70 or 75),* ☎ *250/479–0211.* ☞ *Free.* ☉ *Nature House weekdays 8:30–4, weekends noon–4.*

Whale-Watching

To see the pods of orcas (killer whales) that travel in the waters around Vancouver Island, you can take **charter boat tours** from Victoria from May through October. Half-day tours in Zodiacs (motor-powered inflatable boats) and covered speed boats cost about $75–$80 per person. **Great Pacific Adventures** (☎ 250/386–2277), **Ocean Explorations** (☎ 250/383–6722), and **Seacoast Expeditions** (☎ 250/383–2254) are among the many operators in town. To book just about any kind of marine activity, including whale-watching, seaplane touring, fishing, and diving, contact the **Victoria Marine Adventure Centre** (⊠ 950 Wharf St., V8W 1T3, ☎ 250/995–2211). It's open May–September, daily 7 AM–10 PM; October–April, daily 9–5.

Shopping

Shopping Centers

For a wide selection, head to the larger shopping centers downtown, such as **Eaton Centre** (⊠ 1 Victoria Eaton Centre, at Government and Fort Sts., ☎ 250/382–7141), a department store and mall with about 100 boutiques and restaurants. **Market Square** (⊠ 560 Johnson St., ☎ 250/386–2441) has two stories of specialty shops and offbeat stores; there's everything from fudge, music, and comic books to jewelry, local arts, and New Age accoutrements.

Specialty Stores

Shopping in Victoria is easy: Virtually everything can be found in the downtown area on or near Government Street stretching north from the Empress Hotel. The **Cowichan Trading Co., Ltd.** (⊠ 1328 Government St., ☎ 250/383–0321) sells native jewelry, art, moccasins, and Cowichan Indian sweaters. **Hill's Indian Crafts** (⊠ 1008 Government St., ☎ 250/385–3911) has a mixture; you'll have to plow through some schlocky souvenirs to find the good-quality West Coast native art. As the name would suggest, **Irish Linen Stores** (⊠ 1019 Government St., ☎ 250/383–6812) stocks fine linen and lace items—hankies, napkins, tablecloths, and place mats. The high ceiling, elaborate moldings, and murals at **Munro's Books** (⊠ 1108 Government St., ☎ 250/382–2464) are worth a peek. If the British spirit of Victoria has you searching for fine teas, head to **Murchie's** (⊠ 1110 Government St., ☎ 250/383–3112) for a choice of 40 varieties, plus blended coffees, tarts, and cakes.

ANTIQUES

At last count, Victoria had 60-plus antiques shops specializing in coins, stamps, estate jewelry, rare books, crystal, china, furniture, or paintings and other works of art. A short walk on Fort Street going away from the harbor will take you to Antique Row between Blanshard and Cook streets. You will also find antiques on the west side of Government Street near the Old Town.

ART GALLERIES

The **Fran Willis Gallery** (⊠ 1619 Store St., ☎ 250/381–3422) shows contemporary paintings and sculpture by local artists. Original art and fine Canadian crafts are the focus at the **Northern Passage Gallery** (⊠ 1020 Government St., ☎ 250/381–3380).

Side Trip from Victoria

Butchart Gardens

★ *21 km (13 mi) north of downtown Victoria.*

Originally a private estate and still family-run, this stunning 50-acre garden has been drawing visitors since it was planted in a limestone quarry in 1904. The site's Japanese, Italian, rose, and sunken gardens now grow 700 varieties of flowers in a setting that looks beautiful year-round. Butchart is a display rather than a horticultural garden, but the knowledgeable staff can handle most gardening queries. From mid-June to mid-September many of the exhibits are illuminated at night, and musicians and other entertainers perform in the afternoons and evenings. In July and August, fireworks light the sky over the gardens every Saturday night; picnickers are welcome. Also on the premises are a conservatory, teahouse, seed and gift shop, and restaurants. A million people visit every year, most on summer mornings. Come in the afternoon if you can. ⊠ *800 Benvenuto Ave., Brentwood Bay,* ☎ *250/652–5256 or 250/652–4422; 250/652–8222 for dining reservations.* ☜ *$15.50; discounts in winter.* ☼ *June 15–Sept. 15, 9 AM– 10:30 PM; Sept. 16– June 14, daily 9 AM–dusk.*

Victoria A to Z

Arriving and Departing

BY BOAT

BC Ferries (☎ 250/386–3431 in Victoria or outside B.C.; 888/223–3779 from elsewhere in B.C.) provides frequent year-round passenger and vehicle service between Vancouver and Vancouver Island. The Vancouver terminal is in Tsawwassen (about one hour's drive from Vancouver), 38 km (24 mi) southwest of downtown at the end of Highway

17. In Victoria, ferries arrive at and depart from Swartz Bay Terminal (30 minutes' drive from Victoria) at the end of Pat Bay Highway, 32 km (20 mi) north of downtown. Sailing time is 1 hour, 35 minutes. Fares vary by day and season but run about $40, one-way, for a car and driver ($9 for foot passenger). Vehicle reservations on Vancouver-to-Victoria routes are optional and cost $15 in addition to the fares; the automated reservation line is 888/724–5223 in British Columbia, 604/444–2890 from outside the province.

Year-round passenger-only service between Victoria and Seattle on jet catamarans is operated by **Clipper Navigation** (☎ 250/382–8100 in Victoria; 206/448–5000 in Seattle; 800/888–2535 elsewhere). Between mid-May and mid-September Clipper Navigation also provides direct passenger and vehicle service between Seattle and Victoria on the *Princess Marguerite III*. Reservations are advised if you're traveling with a vehicle.

Black Ball Transport (☎ 250/386–2202; 360/457–4491 in the U.S.) operates between Victoria and Port Angeles, Washington. **Washington State Ferries** (☎ 250/381–1551; 206/464–6400 in the U.S.) cross daily, year-round, between Sidney, just north of Victoria, and Anacortes, Washington.

BY BUS
Pacific Coach Lines (☎ 250/385–4411 in Victoria; 604/662–8074 in Vancouver; 800/661–1725 elsewhere) operates daily service between downtown Vancouver and downtown Victoria on BC Ferries.

BY CAR
Highway 17 connects Swartz Bay ferry terminal on the Saanich Peninsula with downtown Victoria. **Island Highway** (Highway 1, also known as the Trans-Canada Highway) runs south from Nanaimo to Victoria. **Highway 14** connects Sooke to Port Renfrew, on the west coast of Vancouver Island, with Victoria.

BY HELICOPTER
Helijet Airways (☎ 604/273–1414, 250/382–6222, or 800/665–4354) helicopter service is available from downtown Vancouver and downtown Seattle to downtown Victoria.

BY PLANE
Among the airlines serving **Victoria International Airport** (✉ Willingdon Rd. off Hwy. 17, Sidney, ☎ 250/953–7500), Air B.C., Canadian Airlines, and Horizon Air (☞ Air Travel *in* the Gold Guide for telephone numbers) provide service between Vancouver, Seattle, and Victoria airports. The **Airporter** service (☎ 250/386–2525) leaves from the Empress hotel and meets all flights at Victoria International Airport.

West Coast Air (☎ 604/688–9115 or 800/347–2222) and **Harbour Air** (☎ 604/688–1277 or 800/665–0212) both offer 35-minute harbor-to-harbor service (downtown Vancouver to downtown Victoria) several times a day. **Kenmore Air** (☎ 425/486–1257 or 800/543–9595) offers direct daily floatplane service from Seattle to Victoria's Inner Harbour.

Getting Around
BY BUS
The **BC Transit System** (☎ 250/382–6161) runs a fairly extensive service in Victoria and the surrounding areas, with an all-day pass that costs $5.50 for adults, $4 for students and senior citizens.

BY FERRY

Victoria Harbour Ferries (☎ 250/480–0971) makes eight stops around the Inner Harbour, including the Empress hotel, Point Ellis Historic House, Spinnaker's Brew Pub, Ocean Pointe Resort, and Fisherman's Wharf. The fee is $3 each time you get on; harbor tours are $12. There's service every 12–20 minutes daily, March 15–October 31.

BY TAXI

Taxis are available from **Empress Taxi** (☎ 250/381–2222) and **Victoria Taxi** (☎ 250/383–7111).

Contacts and Resources

CAR RENTALS

Avis (☎ 250/386–8468). **Budget** (☎ 250/953–5300). **Enterprise** (☎ 250/475–6900). **Island Autos** (☎ 250/384–4881). **National Tilden** (☎ 250/386–1213). **Rent-a-Wreck** (☎ 250/413–4638).

EMERGENCIES

Dial **911.**

GUIDED TOURS

Gray Line (☎ 250/388–5248) offers city tours on double-decker buses that visit the city center, Chinatown, Antique Row, Oak Bay, and Beacon Hill Park; a combination tour stops at Butchart Gardens as well. It's possible to tour downtown Victoria by pedicab; contact **Kabuki Kabs** (☎ 250/385–4243). Between March and October, **Tally-Ho Horsedrawn Tours** (☎ 250/383–5067) offers a get-acquainted session with downtown Victoria that includes Beacon Hill Park. **Victoria Carriage Tours** (☎ 250/383–2207) has horse-drawn tours of the city. The best way to see the sights of the Inner Harbour is by **Victoria Harbour Ferry** (☎ 250/480–0971).

A growing number of companies provide ways to get acquainted with Victoria's outdoors. **Go Green Eco Adventures Tours** (☎ 250/336–8786 or 888/324–7336) has multiday hiking, caving, whale-watching, biking, and kayaking trips. **Island Outings** (☎ 250/642–4469 or 888/345–4469) has hikes, cross-country skiing, river tours, and whale-watching. **Nature Calls Eco-Tours** (☎ 250/361–4453) leads half- and full-day guided hikes in wilderness areas near Victoria. Prices include lunch, hotel pickup, and transportation. The **Royal British Columbia Museum** (☎ 250/387–5745) schedules hands-on, adult-oriented, educational, ecological day-trips around southern Vancouver Island.

HOSPITAL

Victoria General Hospital (✉ 35 Helmcken Rd., ☎ 250/727–4212).

LATE-NIGHT PHARMACY

London Drugs (✉ 911 Yates St., ☎ 250/381–1113) is open daily until 10 PM.

LODGING RESERVATION SERVICE

Super, Natural British Columbia (☎ 800/663–6000) and **Tourism Victoria** (☎ 800/663–3883) can assist with reservations year-round. **Garden City B&B Reservation Service** (✉ 660 Jones Terr., V8Z 2L7, ☎ 250/479–1986, FAX 250/479–9999) can book bed-and-breakfast accommodations throughout Vancouver Island.

VISITOR INFORMATION

Tourism Victoria (✉ 812 Wharf St., V8W 1T3, ☎ 250/953–2033, FAX 250/382–6539).

VANCOUVER ISLAND

The largest island on Canada's west coast, Vancouver Island stretches 564 km (350 mi) from Victoria in the south to Cape Scott in the north. Some 97% of the island's population of 684,000 live between Victoria and Campbell River (halfway up the island); 50% live in Victoria itself. A ridge of mountains crowns the island's center, providing opportunities for skiing, climbing, and hiking. Thick conifer forests blanket it down to soft, sandy beaches on the eastern shoreline and rocky, wave-pounded grottoes and inlets along the western shore.

The western side is wild, often inhospitable, with just a handful of small settlements. Nevertheless, the west coast is invaded every summer by fishers, kayakers, scuba divers, and hikers. The west-coast towns of Ucluelet and Tofino are the whale-watching capitals of Canada, if not of the whole west coast of North America. Virtually all of the island's permanent human habitation is on the eastern coast, where the weather is gentler and the topography is low-lying.

The cultural heritage of the island is from the Kwakiutl, Nootka, and Coastal Salish native groups. Native art and cultural centers flourish throughout the region.

Mining, logging, and tourism are the important island industries. Environmental issues, such as the logging practices of British Columbia's lumber companies, are becoming important to islanders—both native and nonnative.

Sooke

⑭ *42 km (26 mi) west of Victoria on Hwy. 14.*

Sooke is a logging, fishing, and farming community. **East Sooke Park,** on the east side of the harbor, has 350 acres of beaches, hiking trails, and wildflower-dotted meadows. The **Sooke Region Museum and Travel Infocentre** displays Salish and Nootka crafts and artifacts from 19th-century Sooke. ⊠ *2070 Phillips Rd., Box 774, V0S 1N0,* ☎ *250/642–6351,* FAX *250/642–7089.* ☞ *Donations accepted.* ☼ *July–Aug., daily 9–6; Sept.–June, Tues.–Sun. 9–5.*

Dining and Lodging

$$–$$$ ✕ **Seventeen Mile House.** Originally built as a hotel, this 1894 house is a study in turn-of-the-century island architecture. This is a good place for pub fare, a beer, or fresh local seafood on the road between Sooke and Victoria. ⊠ *5126 Sooke Rd.,* ☎ *250/642–5942. MC, V.*

$$$–$$$$ ✕🏨 **Sooke Harbour House.** This oceanfront 1931 clapboard farmhouse
★ turned country inn has three suites, a 10-room addition, and a dining room—all of which exude elegance. The restaurant, open to the public for dinner, is one of the finest in British Columbia: The menu changes daily, the seafood is just-caught fresh, and the herbs are grown on the property. In the romantic guest rooms, natural wood and white finishes add to each unit's unique theme. Rooms range from the Herb Garden Room—decorated in shades of mint—to the Longhouse Room, complete with native furnishings. All rooms and suites are no-smoking and have hot tubs and fireplaces. Breakfast and lunch are included in room rates, and the inn offers massage and other spa treatments. ⊠ *1528 Whiffen Spit Rd., R.R. 4, V0S 1N0,* ☎ *250/642–3421,* FAX *250/642–6988. 9 rooms, 17 suites. Restaurant, no-smoking rooms, massage, beach, meeting room. AE, DC, MC, V.*

$$–$$$ 🏨 **Ocean Wilderness Inn and Spa Retreat.** A large 1940s log cabin sits on 5 forested, beachfront acres, 13 km (8 mi) west of Sooke. Auction-buff owner Marion Rolston built a rough cedar addition in 1990 and

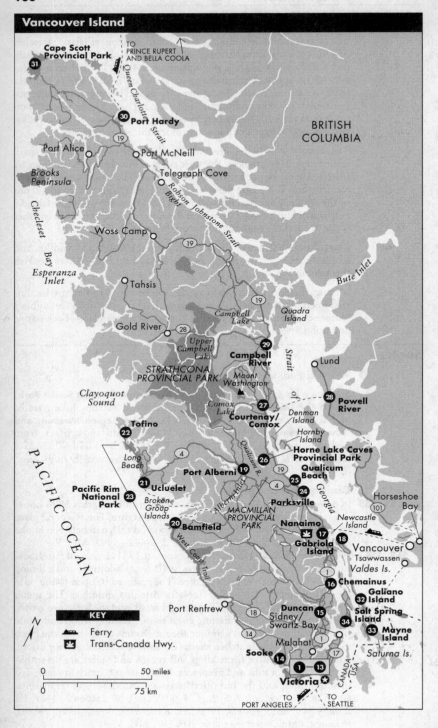

Vancouver Island

BRITISH COLUMBIA

TO PRINCE RUPERT AND BELLA COOLA

31 Cape Scott Provincial Park

Queen Charlotte Strait

30 Port Hardy

19

Port Alice

Port McNeill

Brooks Peninsula

Telegraph Cove

Robson Johnstone Strait

Checleset Bay

Woss Camp

19

Esperanza Inlet

Tahsis

Campbell Lake

Quadra Island

Bute Inlet

Gold River

28

Upper Campbell Lake

29 Campbell River

Lund

STRATHCONA PROVINCIAL PARK

Mount Washington ▲

Strait

28 Powell River

Clayoquot Sound

Comox Lake

27 Courtenay/Comox

Denman Island

Hornby Island

22 Tofino

Long Beach

4

Qualicum R.

26

Horne Lake Caves Provincial Park

Qualicum Beach

21 Ucluelet

23 Pacific Rim National Park

Broken Group Islands

19 Port Alberni

19

25

Georgia

Horseshoe Bay

101

PACIFIC OCEAN

Alberni Inlet

4

24 Parksville

MACMILLAN PROVINCIAL PARK

Newcastle Island

20 Bamfield

West Coast Trail

Nanaimo

17 Gabriola Island

18

Vancouver

Tsawwassen

Valdes Is.

1

16 Chemainus

Galiano Island

Port Renfrew

18

Duncan 15

Sidney/Swartz Bay

32

34

Salt Spring Island

33 Mayne Island

14

Malahat

1

Saturna Is.

14 Sooke

1 13

17

CANADA USA

Victoria ☆

TO PORT ANGELES   TO SEATTLE

KEY

🛳 Ferry

🍁 Trans-Canada Hwy.

N

0   50 miles

0   75 km

has furnished her home with Victorian antiques. Canopies and ruffled linens on high beds dominate the spacious guest rooms, which have views of either the Strait of Juan de Fuca or the pretty gardens in the back. Some rooms have soaker tubs, and most have sitting areas as well as private decks or patios. The guest-only dining-room fare is innovative West Coast treatments of fresh local fish and meats. Pets are welcome at this family-oriented inn. ⊠ *109 W. Coast Rd., V0S 1N0,* ☎ *250/646–2116 or 800/323–2116,* ℻ *250/646–2317. 9 rooms. Dining room, no-smoking rooms, outdoor hot tub, massage, hiking, fishing, boating. MC, V.*

Shopping

At the **Blue Raven Gallery** (⊠ 1971 Kaltasin Rd., ☎ 250/881–0528), Victor and Carey Newman, a father-and-son team of Kwagulth and Salish artists, display beautiful traditional and modern prints, masks, and jewelry. Watercolor artist and author **Sue Coleman** (☎ 250/478–0380) in Metchosin, 35 minutes west of Victoria on the road to Sooke, invites visitors to tour her studio by appointment.

Duncan

🔟 *60 km (37 mi) north of Victoria on the Trans-Canada Hwy. (Hwy. 1).*

Duncan is nicknamed City of Totems for the many totem poles that dot the small community. The two carvings behind the City Hall are worth a short trip off the main road. The **Cowichan Native Village,** covering 13 acres on the banks of the Cowichan River, includes native longhouses, a theater, traditional theatrical and dance performances, an arts-and-crafts gallery with a stunning red cedar carving of a Nootka whaling scene, and a bookstore. The Bighouse Restaurant serves native feasts (reservations essential). ⊠ *200 Cowichan Way,* ☎ *250/746–8119,* ℻ *250/746–4143.* 🎟 *$8.* ☼ *Daily 9–5.*

The **British Columbia Forest Museum,** more a park than a museum, spans some 100 acres, combining indoor and outdoor exhibits that focus on the history of forestry in the province. In the summer you can ride an original steam locomotive around the property. The exhibits show logging and milling equipment. ⊠ *2892 Drinkwater Rd. (Trans-Canada Hwy.),* ☎ *250/715–1113,* ℻ *250/715–1170.* 🎟 *$8.* ☼ *Apr.– Oct., daily 9:30–6; Nov.–Mar., call for seasonal hrs.*

Shopping

Duncan is the home of Cowichan wool sweaters, hand-knit by the Cowichan people. A large selection of sweaters is available from **Hill's Indian Crafts** (☎ 250/746–6731) on the main highway, about 1½ km (1 mi) south of Duncan. **Modeste Indian Sweaters** (⊠ 2615 Modeste Rd., ☎ 250/748–8983), about 1 km (½ mi) off the highway, carries a selection of handmade knitwear.

Chemainus

★ 🔟 *85 km (53 mi) north of Victoria, 27 km (17 mi) south of Nanaimo.*

Chemainus is known for the bold epic murals that decorate its townscape, as well as its beautifully restored Victorian homes. Once dependent on the lumber industry, the small community began to revitalize itself in the early 1980s when its mill closed down. Since then, the town has brought in international artists to paint more than 30 murals depicting local historical events around town. Footprints on the sidewalk lead you on a self-guided tour of the murals. Restaurants, shops, tearooms, coffee bars, art galleries, a mini-train line, several B&Bs, and antiques dealers have helped create one of the prettiest little towns on Vancouver Island. The **Chemainus Dinner Theatre** (✉ 9796 Willow St., ☎ 250/246–9820 or 800/565–7738) has added to the town's growth.

Lodging

$$ 🏠 **Bird Song Cottage.** A whimsical white and lavender Victorian cottage has been playfully decorated with antiques and collectibles, including a grand piano, a Celtic harp, and an assortment of Victorian hats. A gourmet breakfast (often with piano accompaniment) is served on the sunporch. The Nightingale room has a private garden and a claw-foot tub; the other two have baths with showers. All rooms have pure cotton sheets and window seats. This fun, no-smoking inn is an easy walk from the beach and town. ✉ 9909 Maple St., Box 1432, V0R 1K0, ☎ 250/246–9910, ℻ 250/246–2909. 3 rooms. AE, MC, V.

Nanaimo

⑰ 110 km (68 mi) northwest of Victoria, 115 km (71 mi) southeast of Courtenay, 155 km (96 mi) southeast of Campbell River, 23 km (14 mi) on land plus 38 nautical mi west of Vancouver.

Nanaimo is the primary commercial and transport link for the mid-island, with direct ferry service to the mainland. The **Nanaimo District Museum** (✉ 100 Cameron Rd., ☎ 250/753–1821) has information about the petroglyphs (rock carvings) representing humans, birds, wolves, lizards, sea monsters, and supernatural creatures that have been found in the area. At **Petroglyph Provincial Park** (✉ Hwy. 1 south of Nanaimo, ☎ 250/387–5002), 8 km (5 mi) south of town, marked trails begin at the parking lot and lead to designs carved thousands of years ago.

From Nanaimo, you can take a 10-minute ferry ride (☎ 250/753–5141) to **Newcastle Island,** where you can picnic, ride your bicycle, walk on trails leading past old mines and quarries, and catch glimpses of deer, rabbits, and eagles.

Dining and Lodging

$$–$$$$ ✕ **The Grotto.** This Nanaimo institution specializing in a variety of
★ seafood has a casual waterfront setting. Try the sushi, spareribs, garlic prawn pasta, or the seafood platter, which is big enough for two. The Kitchen Sink, a heaping bowl of clams, shrimp, and salmon steamed in white wine, herbs, and butter, is a favorite. ✉ 1511 Stewart Ave., ☎ 250/753–3303. AE, MC, V. Closed Mon. in winter. No lunch.

$$–$$$ ✕ **Mahle House.** The casually elegant Mahle House serves innovative
★ Northwest cuisine, such as braised rabbit with Dijon mustard and red wine sauce. Among the items on the regular menu are a succulent carrot and ginger soup and a catch of the day. Attention to detail, an intimate setting, and three country-style rooms make this one of the finest dining experiences in the region. ✉ Cedar and Heemer Rds., about 10 min south of Nanaimo on Cedar Rd., ☎ 250/722–3621. AE, MC, V. Closed Mon.–Tues. No lunch.

$$–$$$ 🏠 **Best Western Dorchester Hotel.** Beautifully restored, this 1889 hotel in the city center was once the Nanaimo Opera House. Rooms are comfortably furnished with antiques and modern comforts like TVs and coffeemakers, and there's air-conditioning in many. Most have views of the harbor, as does the rooftop patio. ✉ 70 Church St., V9R 5H4, ☎ 250/754–6835 or 800/661–2449, ℻ 250/754–2638. 56 rooms, 9 suites. Restaurant, lounge, no-smoking floors, exercise room, library, laundry service and dry cleaning, meeting rooms. AE, D, DC, MC, V.

$$ 🏠 **Coast Bastion Inn Nanaimo.** This convenient hotel is downtown near the ferry terminal and train and bus stations. Rooms with balconies and modern furnishings have views of the old Hudson's Bay fort and the ocean. There's an Irish deli-pub. ✉ 11 Bastion St., V9R 2Z9, ☎

250/753–6601, 800/663–1144, FAX 250/753–4155. 179 rooms. Restaurant, lounge, pub, air-conditioning, no-smoking floor, room service, hot tub, sauna, exercise room, laundry service and dry cleaning, meeting rooms. AE, D, DC, MC, V.

$$ ⊡ **Yellow Point Lodge.** Yellow Point is a very popular resort area on
★ a spit of land 24 km (15 mi) south of Nanaimo, 13 km (8 mi) northeast of Ladysmith. Rebuilt in 1986 after a fire, the lodge lost almost nothing of its homey, summer-camp ambience. Nine large lodge rooms and a range of cabins have private baths (rooms in some cabins share baths); most are available year-round. Perched on a rocky knoll overlooking the Stuart Channel are beach cabins, field cabins, and beach barracks for the hardy; these are closed mid-October to mid-April, have no running water, and share a central bathhouse. You can stroll the lodge's 178 acres, and there are canoes and kayaks. Three full meals are included in the rate. ✉ *3700 Yellow Point Rd., R.R. 3, Ladysmith V0R 2E0, ☎ 250/245–7422, FAX 250/245–7411. 9 lodge rooms, 16 cabins. Dining room (guests only), outdoor saltwater pool, hot tub, sauna, 2 tennis courts, badminton, jogging, volleyball, boating, mountain bikes. AP. AE, MC, V.*

Outdoor Activities and Sports

CANOEING AND KAYAKING

One- to six-day guided sea-kayak expeditions are offered by **Wild Heart Adventures** (✉ 2774 Barnes Rd., Site H2, C-7, R.R. 2, V9R 5K2, ☎ 250/722–3683, FAX 250/722–2175).

GOLF

Fairwinds Golf and Country Club (✉ 3730 Fairwinds Dr., Nanoose Bay, ☎ 250/468–7666 or 800/663–7060) is an 18-hole, par-71 course open year-round.

Gabriola Island

⑱ *3½ nautical mi (20-min ferry ride) east of Nanaimo.*

BC Ferries (☎ 250/386–3431 in Victoria or outside B.C.; 888/223–3779 from elsewhere in B.C.) can take you to rustic, rural Gabriola Island, which has lodging.

Port Alberni

⑲ *80 km (50 mi) northwest of Nanaimo, 195 km (121 mi) northwest of Victoria.*

Port Alberni is a former pulp- and sawmill town and a stopover on the way to Ucluelet and Tofino on the west coast. The salmon-rich waters attract fishers. The **Port Alberni Tourist Infocentre** (✉ Port Alberni Hwy. and Johnston, St., ☎ 250/724–6535) has information about the area.

From here, you can take a breathtaking trip to towns along the Alberni Inlet and Barkley Sound aboard the **Lady Rose**, a Scottish ship built in 1937, or the newer **M.V. Francis Barkley**. ✉ *Argyle Pier, 5425 Argyle St., ☎ 250/723–8313; 800/663–7192 for reservations Apr.–Sept.* ⊡ *Bamfield $40, Broken Group Islands $40, Ucluelet $44.* ☉ *Sailings daily 8 AM.*

Bamfield

⑳ *100 km (62 mi) southwest of Port Alberni.*

In Bamfield, a remote village of about 200, the seaside boardwalk affords an uninterrupted view of ships heading up the inlet to Port Alberni. The town is well equipped to handle overnight visitors. Bamfield is also a good base for boating trips to the Broken Group Islands and hikes along the West Coast Trail (☞ Pacific Rim National Park, *below*).

Dining and Lodging

$$$ ✕🏨 **Eagle Nook Ocean Wilderness Resort.** This wilderness country inn, ★   accessible only by sea or air, sits on a narrow strip of land in Barkley Sound. For all its blissful isolation, Eagle Nook offers some highly civilized comforts. Every spacious room has a water view, and the lounge has leather chairs and a stone fireplace. The dining room serves fine Pacific Northwest cuisine, which you can enjoy inside or alfresco. Hiking trails lace the woods, and many activities, including fishing, kayaking, and whale-watching, can be prebooked. Getting here, by floatplane, by water taxi from China Creek near Port Alberni, or by prearrangement on the *Lady Rose* ferry (☞ Port Alberni, *above*), is a scenic adventure in its own right. There's a two-night minimum stay; prices are per person and include meals and nonguided activities. ⊠ *Box 575, Port Alberni V9Y 7M9,* ☎ *250/723–1000 or 800/760–2777,* 𝔽𝔸𝕏 *250/ 723–9842. 23 rooms. Restaurant, lounge, outdoor hot tub, exercise room, hiking, dock, boating, fishing, laundry services, meeting room, helipad. AP. AE, MC, V. Closed Oct.–Apr.*

Ucluelet

㉑   *100 km (62 mi) west of Port Alberni, 295 km (183 mi) northwest of Victoria.*

Ucluelet, which in the native language means "people with a safe landing place," is, along with Bamfield and Tofino, one of the towns serving Pacific Rim National Park (☞ *below*). A little town strung out along the highway, Ucluelet is both smaller and less visitor-oriented than Tofino. This may change, though: at press time plans were in place for a new 300-room resort here.

A variety of charter companies (☞ Outdoor Activities and Sports, *below, and* Contacts and Resources *in* British Columbia A to Z, *below*) take boats to greet the 20,000 gray whales that pass close to Ucluelet on their migration to the Bering Sea every March and April. Sometimes the whales can even be seen from the Ucluelet shore. Increasingly, visitors are coming in the off-season to watch the dramatic winter storms that pound the coast here. **Amphitrite Point Lighthouse** has a panoramic view of the beach and open ocean, and there's a boardwalk trail through the rain forest at **Hetinkus Park.**

Dining and Lodging

$–$$ ✕ **Matterson House.** In a tiny 1931 cottage with just seven tables, husband-and-wife team Sandy and Jennifer Clark serve up generous portions of seafood, burgers, pasta, and filling standards like prime rib and roast beef. It's simple food, prepared well with fresh local ingredients; everything, including soups, desserts, and the wonderful bread, is homemade. The wine list has local island wines unavailable elsewhere and worth trying. ⊠ *1682 Peninsula Rd.,* ☎ *250/726–2200. MC, V.*

$$–$$$ 🏨 **A Snug Harbour Inn.** Set on a cliff above the Pacific, this new, very couples-oriented B&B offers some of the most dramatic views anywhere. The rooms, all with fireplaces, private balconies or decks, jet tubs, and ocean views, are decorated in a highly individual style. The Sawadee room reflects hosts Skip and Denise Rowland's time in Thailand, and the Atlantis is done in ultramodern yellow and black. Eagles nest nearby, and trails through the woods lead to the seaside. Skip can organize helicopter trips from here. ⊠ *460 Marine Dr., Box 367, V0R 3A0,* ☎ *250/726–2686 or 888/936–5222,* 𝔽𝔸𝕏 *250/726–2685. 4 rooms. Breakfast room, outdoor hot tub, hiking, helipad. MC, V.*

$–$$$ 🏨 **Canadian Princess Fishing Resort.** If vintage ships are to your liking, book a cabin on this converted, 230-ft, steam-powered survey ship, which has 30 comfortable but hardly opulent staterooms. Each has one to four berths, and all share washrooms. Larger than the ship cabins, the resort's 46 deluxe shoreside rooms have more contemporary furnishings; a few have fireplaces. This unique resort appeals to nature enthusiasts and fishers, and whale-watching can be arranged. The Stewart Room Restaurant is open to nonguests; the specialty is (no surprise here) seafood. ⊠ *Boat Basin, 1943 Peninsula Rd., Box 939, V0R 3A0,* ☎ *250/726–7771 or 800/663–7090,* 𝔽𝔸𝕏 *250/726–7121. 46 shoreside and 30 shipboard sleeping units. Restaurant, 2 bars, boating, fishing. AE, DC, MC, V. Closed Sept. 25–Mar. 7.*

Outdoor Activities and Sports

Most Ucluelet operators offer a variety of whale-watching, fishing, or cruising options. The **Canadian Princess Fishing Resort** (☎ 250/726–7771 or 800/663–7090) will take you out in a 50-ft cabin cruiser. **Subtidal Adventures** (☎ 250/726–7336) specializes in whale-watching and nature tours; there's a choice of an inflatable Zodiac or a 36-ft former coast guard rescue boat. Some local operators include **Island West Fishing Resort** (☎ 250/726–7515), **Quest Charters** (☎ 250/726–7532), and **Viking Charters** (☎ 250/726–4410).

Tofino

★ ㉒   *42 km (26 mi) northwest of Ucluelet, 337 km (209 mi) northwest of Victoria, 130 km (81 mi) west of Port Alberni.*

The end of the road makes a great stage—and Tofino is certainly that. On a narrow peninsula just beyond the north end of the Pacific Rim National Park (☞ *below*), this is as far west as you can go on Vancouver Island by paved road. One look at the pounding Pacific surf and the old-growth forest along the shoreline convinces many people that they've reached not just the end of the road but the end of the earth.

Tofino's tiny number of year-round residents know what they like and have made what could have been a tourist trap into a funky little town with nine art galleries, an excellent bookstore, several sociable cafés, and plenty of opportunity to get out to the surrounding wilds—to see the forests of Meares Island, the natural hot springs at Hot Springs Cove, the long stretches of beach, and, of course, the whales.

Dining and Lodging

$$$$ ✕🏨 **The Wickaninnish Inn.** Opened in 1996, the Wickaninnish is already
★   the best-known luxury inn on this coast. Set on a rocky promontory above Chesterman Beach, with open ocean on three sides and old-growth forest as a backdrop, the three-story weathered cedar building is a very comfortable place to enjoy the area's dramatic wilderness scenery, summer or winter. The whole inn is no-smoking, and every spacious room has a sitting area, an ocean view, and its own balcony, fireplace, and soaker tub. The staff takes very good care of guests; spa services, planned for 1999 at press time, will add to the pampering. Chef Rodney Butters of the Pointe Restaurant selects his catch personally at the Tofino docks. The menu has featured scallops in Rainforest Ale broth, venison and hazelnut paté, and steamed Long Beach Dungeness crabs. If you can, try the chef's special seven-course dinner, available with 12 hours' notice. ⊠ *Osprey La. at Chesterman Beach, Box 250, 5 km (3 mi) south of Tofino, V0R 2Z0,* ☎ *250/725–3100 or 800/333–4604,* 𝔽𝔸𝕏 *250/725–3110. 46 rooms. Restaurant, lounge, in-room modem lines, minibars, refrigerators, massage, spa, steam room, exercise room, hiking, beach, fishing, laundry services, meeting room, helipad. AE, D, DC, MC, V.*

$$$ ⊞ **Clayoquot Wilderness Resort.** Floating on a barge in Quait Bay, 20 to 30 minutes by water taxi from Tofino, this new (1998) resort is moored next to 127 acres of wilderness park. The property, part of the pristine wilderness of Clayoquot Sound, includes two lakes, hiking trails, and acres of old-growth forest. Host Randy Goddard, who describes the informal, family-oriented resort as an "adult kids' camp," offers fresh- and saltwater fishing, whale-watching, heli-hiking, and nature cruises. The comfortable rooms all have water or forest views (but no phones or TVs) and open onto a wraparound veranda. Room rates include water taxi pickup from Tofino; meals are $85 additional per person per day. ⊠ *Box 728, V0R 2Z0,* ☎ *250/725–2688 or 888/ 333–5405,* FAX *250/725–2689. 15 rooms. Restaurant, bar, fans, exercise room, outdoor hot tub, sauna, 2 lakes, fishing, dock, boating, hiking, meeting rooms, helipad. MC, V.*

$$–$$$ ⊞ **Chesterman Beach Bed and Breakfast.** The front yard of this small,
★   rustic, West Coast cedar bed-and-breakfast on the beach is the rolling ocean surf. The self-contained two-bedroom suite in the main house (complete with sauna, woodstove, and kitchen) and the Lookout room with its gas fireplace and private balcony are both romantic and cozy. The self-sufficient one-bedroom Garden Cottage has a secluded garden and a large deck; it's a good option for families. ⊠ *1345 Chesterman Beach Rd., Box 72, V0R 2Z0,* ☎ *250/725–3726,* FAX *250/ 725–3706. 1 room, 2 suites. Kitchenettes, no-smoking rooms, refrigerators, beach. MC, V.*

$$–$$$ ⊞ **Pacific Sands Beach Resort.** Just 2 km (1 mi) north of Pacific Rim National Park, this beachside resort has suites with private entrances and individual two-bedroom cottages, each with a beautiful bay view. The motel rooms have modern furnishings, and fireplaces make them cozy. Some specialty suites in the three-story addition have hot tubs outside on the deck. Dangerous currents and riptides off the beach in front of the resort make it unsuitable for swimming. ⊠ *1421 Pacific Rim Hwy., Box 237, V0R 2Z0,* ☎ *250/725–3322 or 800/565–2322,* FAX *250/725–3155. 54 rooms, 10 cottages. Kitchenettes, no-smoking rooms, beach, coin laundry. AE, MC, V.*

$$ ⊞ **Red Crow Guest House.** On the sheltered side of the Tofino peninsula, this Cape Cod–style house sits amid 17 acres of cedar and hemlock, about 2 km (1 mi) from the village. Two large rooms underneath the main part of the house open onto a covered veranda and directly onto a private pebble beach. Decorated with family heirlooms and native art, the comfortable rooms have sitting areas and stunning views of tidal waters. A smaller room on the top floor is available in summer only, and a rustic cedar cottage in the woods has a full kitchen and sleeps six. ⊠ *1084 Pacific Rim Hwy., Box 37, V0R 2Z0,* ☎ FAX *250/725–2275. 3 rooms, 1 cottage. Refrigerators, hiking, beach, boating. V. Closed Dec.–Feb.*

Outdoor Activities and Sports

CANOEING AND KAYAKING

Remote Passages Sea Kayaking (⊠ 71 Wharf St., ☎ 250/725–3330, 800/666–9833) has guided day and evening paddles; no experience is necessary. **Tofino Sea-Kayaking Company** (⊠ 320 Main St., ☎ 250/ 725–4222 or 800/863–4664) rents kayaks and runs guided wilderness trips.

FISHING

Local charter companies include **Bruce's Smiley Seas Charters** (☎ 250/725–2557) and **Weigh West Marine Resort** (☎ 250/725–3277 or 800/665–8922).

GOLF

Long Beach Golf Course (⊠ Hwy. 4, ☎ 250/725–3332) is a 9-hole, par-36 course.

WHALE-WATCHING

Whale-watching is what Tofino is about, and there are plenty of operators. Most also have trips to Meares Island and Hot Springs Cove. **Jamie's Whaling Station** (⊠ 606 Campbell St., ☎ 250/725–3919; 800/667–9913 in Canada) is one of the most established operators on the coast and has both Zodiacs and more comfortable 65-ft tour boats. The **Whale Centre** (⊠ 411 Campbell St., ☎ 250/725–2132) has a museum with a 40-ft whale skeleton you can admire while waiting for your boat. **Chinook Charters** (☎ 250/725–3431 or 800/665–3646), **Remote Passages Whale Watching** (☎ 250/725–3330 or 800/666–9833), and **Sea Trek Tours and Expeditions** (☎ 250/725–4412 or 800/811–9155) have trips in the area.

Shopping

The magnificent **Eagle Aerie Gallery** (⊠ 350 Campbell St., ☎ 250/725–3235) houses a collection of prints, paintings, and carvings by the renowned native artist Roy Henry Vickers. **House of Himwista** (⊠ 300 Main St., ☎ 250/725–2017) sells native crafts, jewelry, and clothing. The complex has a seafood restaurant and lodge rooms, too. **Island-folk Gallery** (⊠ 120 4th St., ☎ 250/725–3130) stocks crafts, glass, jewelry, and prints by local artisans. **Wildside Booksellers** (⊠ 320 Main St., ☎ 250/725–4222) is one of the island's best small bookshops.

Pacific Rim National Park

★ ㉓ *85 km (53 mi) west of Port Alberni.*

The first national marine park in Canada, Pacific Rim National Park (⊠ Box 280, Ucluelet V0R 3A0, ☎ 250/726–7721, FAX 250/726–4720) has some of Canada's most stunning coastal and rain-forest scenery, abundant wildlife, and a unique marine environment. It comprises three separate areas—Long Beach, the Broken Group Islands, and the West Coast Trail—for a combined area of 20,243 acres, including 130 km (81 mi) of shoreline. The **Park Information Centre** (⊠ 2 km, or 1 mi, north of the Tofino-Ucluelet junction on Hwy. 4, ☎ 250/726–4212) has maps and informative staff. It's open mid-March to Mid-October, daily 9:30–5. Park use fees apply in all sections of the park. In the Long Beach section, an $8 Daily Group Pass, available from dispensers in the parking lots, admits up to 10 people in one vehicle for a day and includes admission to the Wickaninnish Centre (☞ *below*).

The **Long Beach** unit gets its name from an 18-km (11-mi) strip of hard-packed white sand strewn with driftwood, shells, and the occasional Japanese glass fishing float (there is, after all, nothing between here and Japan). Long Beach is the most accessible part of the park and roads can get busy in summer. People come in the off-season to watch waves in the winter storms and to see migrating whales in early spring.

A first stop for many visitors, the **Wickaninnish Centre** is the park's visitor and interpretive center, right on the ocean edge about 16 km (10 mi) north of Ucluelet. It's a great place to learn about the wilderness; theater programs and exhibits provide information about the park's marine ecology and rain-forest environment. It's also a good lunch stop—the center was originally an inn and its **restaurant** still serves up hearty seafood lunches and dinners. ⊠ *Hwy. 4,* ☎ *250/726–4701 for center, 250/726–7706 for restaurant.* ☺ *Free with park use fee.* ☺ *Mid-Mar.–mid-Oct., daily 10:30–6.*

The 100 **Broken Group Islands** can be reached only by boat. Many commercial charter tours are available from Ucluelet, at the southern end of Long Beach, and from Bamfield and Port Alberni. The islands and their waters are alive with sea lions, seals, and whales. The inner waters near Gibraltar, Jacques, and Hand islands offer protection and good boating conditions, but go with a guide if it's your first trip.

The third element of the park, the **West Coast Trail,** stretches along the coast from Bamfield to Port Renfrew. On the trail you'll encounter steep slopes and gullies, cliffs (with ladders), slippery boardwalks, and insects. The rewards are the panoramic views of the sea, the dense rain forest, sandstone cliffs with waterfalls, offshore rock formations, and wildlife that includes gray whales, sea lions, and seals. This extremely rugged 77-km (48-mi) trail is for experienced hikers. It can be traveled only on foot, takes an average of six days to complete, and is open from May to the end of September. A permit (costing $115 with the registration and ferry fees) is necessary, and a quota system is in place. Advance reservations are recommended and can be made with **Super, Natural British Columbia** (☎ 800/663–6000) between March and September.

En Route Heading back to the east coast from Port Alberni, stop off at **Cathedral Grove** in MacMillan Provincial Park on Highway 4. Walking trails lead past Douglas fir trees and western red cedars, some as much as 800 years old. Their remarkable height creates a spiritual effect, as though you were gazing at a cathedral ceiling.

Parksville

㉔ *38 km (24 mi) northwest of Nanaimo, 47 km (29 mi) east of Port Alberni, 72 km (45 mi) southeast of Courtenay, 154 km (95 mi) north of Victoria.*

Parksville is one of the primary resort areas on the eastern side of the island; lodges and waterfront motels cater to families, campers, and boaters. In **Rathtrevor Beach Provincial Park** (⊠ Off Hwy. 19, ☎ 250/248–9449), 1½ km (about 1 mi) south of Parksville, high tide brings ashore the warmest ocean water in British Columbia. It's a good place for a swim.

The **North Island Wildlife Recovery Association's Museum of Nature** showcases the wildlife and environment typical of Vancouver Island. The recovery center houses injured, ill, or orphaned wildlife, including bears, owls, hawks, and eagles, and the largest flight cage in Canada (bald eagles are readied for release here). Errington is a short drive west of Parksville. ⊠ *1240 Leffler Rd., Errington,* ☎ *250/248–8534.* ☜ *$2.* ⊙ *May–Sept., daily 10–4.*

Outdoor Activities and Sports

Morningstar Golf Course (⊠ 525 Lowery Rd., ☎ 250/752–9744) is an 18-hole, par-72 course.

Qualicum Beach

㉕ *10 km (6 mi) north of Parksville.*

Qualicum Beach is known largely for its salmon fishing and opportunities for beachcombing. The nonprofit **Old School House Gallery and Art Centre** (⊠ 122 Fern Rd. W, ☎ 250/752–6133), with seven working studios, shows and sells the work of local artists and artisans.

Horne Lake Caves Provincial Park

26 *25 km (16 mi) north of Parksville, then 15 km (9 mi) west off Hwy. 19.*

Three of the six caves in this park near Horne Lake are open at all times. If you decide to venture in, bring along a flashlight, warm clothes, and a hard hat and be prepared to bend and crawl. Riverbend Cave, 1,260 ft long, requires ladders and ropes in some parts and can be explored only with a guided tour. Spelunking lessons and tours are offered for all levels; reservations are needed for tours. ⊠ *Off Hwy. 19,* ☎ *250/ 248–7829.* ☜ *Tour fee varies depending on participants' ability.*

En Route Between the Horne Lake turnoff and the twin cities of Courtenay and Comox is tiny Buckley Bay, where ferries (☎ 250/386–3431 or 888/ 223–3779) leave for **Denman Island,** with connecting service to **Hornby Island.** Denman offers forests and long sandy beaches, while Hornby's spectacular beaches have earned it the nickname the Undiscovered Hawaii. Many artists have settled on the islands, establishing studios for pottery, jewelry, and sculpture.

Courtenay and Comox

27 *220 km (136 mi) northwest of Victoria, 17 nautical mi west of Powell River, 46 km (29 mi) southeast of Campbell River; Comox is 6 km (4 mi) east of Courtenay.*

Courtenay and Comox are commercial towns that also provide a base for Mt. Washington and Forbidden Plateau skiers; Courtenay is the larger of the two. You can also hike along the beach north of here. A ferry from Comox goes to Powell River (☎ 888/223–3779); in Courtenay you can catch the E&N small-gauge railway to Nanaimo, Victoria, and other South Island stops (☞ Getting Around *in* British Columbia A to Z, *below*).

Dining and Lodging

$$–$$$ ✕ **Old House Restaurant.** This riverside restaurant set among gardens
★ provides casual dining in a restored 1938 house with cedar beams, four stone fireplaces, and a patio for dining. People flock here for the West Coast homestyle cuisine—pastas, salads, and sandwiches, along with fancier, more innovative dishes (seafood stir-fry, panfried flounder, California cioppino)—on the fresh-daily sheet. ⊠ *1760 Riverside La., Courtenay,* ☎ *250/338–5406. AE, DC, MC, V.*

$$ 🏨 **Quality Inn and Suites—Kingfisher.** Ten minutes south of Courtenay, this Quality Inn hotel stands among trees and overlooks the Strait of Georgia. Solid furnishings, white stucco walls, and rooms with mountain and ocean views make it special. ⊠ *4330 S. Island Hwy., Site 672, R.R. 6, Courtenay V9N 8H9,* ☎ *800/663–7929 or 250/338– 1323,* 𝔽𝔸𝕏 *250/338–0058. 28 rooms, 33 suites. Restaurant, lounge, pool, hot tubs, spa, tennis court. AE, D, DC, MC, V.*

$ 🏨 **Greystone Manor.** A no-smoking bed-and-breakfast, set in a 1918 house with period furnishings, looks out on Comox Bay, where a colony of seals is often visible. The antiques, woodstove, and wood paneling add to the hospitable, cozy feel. Breakfast, which includes fresh fruit, muffins, and fruit pancakes, can keep you filled most of the day. You can walk in the 1½-acre English garden and on trails nearby. ⊠ *4014 Haas Rd., Site 684–C2, R.R. 6, Courtenay V9N 8H9,* ☎ *250/ 338–1422. 3 rooms. Breakfast room, hiking. MC, V.*

Outdoor Activities and Sports

Forbidden Plateau (⊠ Box 3268, Courtenay V9N 5N4, ☎ 250/334– 4744), near Mt. Washington and about 20 minutes from Courtenay, has 23 runs, one chairlift, night skiing, and a vertical drop of 1,050 ft.

Mt. Washington Ski Resort Ltd. (✉ Box 3069, Courtenay V9N 5N3, ☎ 250/338–1386), with nearly 42 downhill runs, a 1,657-ft vertical drop, five chairlifts, and an elevation of 5,200 ft, is the island's largest ski area, and the third-largest in terms of visitors in the province. The resort also has 29 km (18 mi) of double track–set cross-country trails.

Powell River

㉘ *17 nautical mi (75-min ferry ride) east across Strait of Georgia from Comox, 121 km (75 mi) plus 12½ nautical mi northwest of Vancouver.*

Powell River was established around a pulp-and-paper mill in 1912. The forestry industry continues to have a strong presence in this area. Renowned as a year-round salmon-fishing destination, this mainland Sunshine Coast town has 30 regional lakes with exceptional trout fishing. The town has several bed-and-breakfasts and restaurants, as well as a park with oceanfront camping and RV hookups. An 80-km (50-mi) canoeing circuit, the **Powell Forest Canoe Route**, can be accessed here. For information, contact the **Powell River Visitor Information Centre** (✉ 4690 Marine Ave., ☎ 604/485–4701).

Campbell River

㉙ *155 km (96 mi) northwest of Nanaimo, 270 km (167 mi) northwest of Victoria.*

Campbell River draws people who want to fish; some of the biggest salmon ever caught on a line have been landed just off the coast here. You can try for membership in the Tyee Club, which would allow you to fish in a specific area and possibly land a giant chinook. Requirements include registering and landing a tyee (a spring salmon weighing 30 pounds or more). Coho salmon and cutthroat trout are also plentiful in the river.

The primary access to Strathcona Provincial Park (☞ *below*) is on Highway 28 west from town. Other recreational activities include diving in Discovery Passage, where a battleship has been sunk; kayaking; or taking a summer whale-watching tour. For information, contact **Campbell River Visitor Information Centre** (✉ 1235 Shoppers Row, Box 400, V9W 5B6, ☎ 250/287–4636, ℻ 250/286–6490).

Dining and Lodging

$–$$ ✗ **Royal Coachman Neighbourhood Pub.** Informal, blackboard-menu
★   restaurants like this one dot the landscape of the island. The menu, which changes daily, is surprisingly daring for what is essentially a high-end pub, and the inn draws crowds nightly, especially on Tuesday and Saturday (prime rib nights). Come early for both lunch and dinner to avoid a wait. ✉ *84 Dogwood St.,* ☎ *250/286–0231. AE, MC, V.*

$$$ ✗🏨 **April Point Lodge and Fishing Resort.** This popular 1944 cedar lodge
★   is surrounded by refurbished fishermen's cabins and guest houses that spread across a point of Quadra Island, a 10-minute car ferry ride from Campbell River. Most of the comfortable accommodations have kitchen facilities, fireplaces, and sundecks. Kwakiutl and Haida art adorns the lounge and dining room, which serves fine regional cuisine using produce from April Point's own organic farm. ✉ *1000 April Point Rd., Box 1, Quathiaski Cove V0P 1N0,* ☎ *250/285–2222 or 888/334–3474,* ℻ *250/285–2411. 39 units. Restaurant, 2 bars, breakfast room, coffee shop, lobby lounge, picnic area, sushi bar, no-smoking rooms, saltwater pool, exercise room, hiking, scuba diving, dock, snorkeling, marina, fishing, bicycles, piano, baby-sitting, coin laundry, laundry service, business services, meeting rooms, airport shuttle, helipad. AE, D, DC, MC, V. Restaurant closed Nov.–Mar.*

$$ ✕▦ **Tsa-Kwa-Luten Lodge.** Authentic Pacific Coast native food and cultural activities are highlights of this resort operated by members of the Kwakiutl tribe. It stands on a high bluff amid 1,100 acres of forest on Quadra Island, a 10-minute ferry ride from Campbell River. Each room in the main lodge has a sea view; many have a fireplace and loft. Four beachfront cabins have fireplaces, whirlpool tubs, kitchen facilities, verandas, and two to four bedrooms. You can take part in traditional dances in the lounge, which resembles a longhouse, and visit nearby petroglyphs. Nonguests must make dinner reservations. ✉ *Lighthouse Rd., Box 460, Quathiaski Cove V0P 1N0,* ☎ *250/285–2042 or 800/665–7745,* ℻ *250/285–2532. 36 units. Restaurant, lounge, no-smoking rooms, hot tub, sauna, exercise room, fishing, mountain bikes, laundry service, business services, meeting rooms. AE, D, DC, MC, V.*

Outdoor Activities and Sports

CANOEING AND KAYAKING

Island Sauvage (✉ R.R. 1, Sayward V0P 1R0, ☎ 250/282–3644 or 800/667–4354, ℻ 250/287–8840) specializes in guided sea kayaking but does have canoes and kayaks for rent.

GOLF

Storey Creek Golf Club (✉ McGimpsey Rd., ☎ 250/923–3673) is an 18-hole, par-72 course 20 minutes south of Campbell River.

Strathcona Provincial Park

40 km (25 mi) west of Campbell River.

Strathcona Provincial Park (☎ 250/387–5002), the largest provincial park on Vancouver Island, encompasses **Mt. Golden Hinde,** at 7,220 ft the island's highest mountain, and **Della Falls,** Canada's highest waterfall, reaching 1,440 ft. This wilderness park's lakes and 161 campsites attract summer canoeists, hikers, fishermen, and campers. The main access is by Highway 28 from Campbell River; Mt. Washington and Forbidden Plateau can be reached by roads out of Courtenay.

The **Strathcona Park Lodge and Outdoor Education Center,** well known for its wilderness-skills programs, also has a variety of accommodations. ✉ *Hwy. 28, Upper Campbell Lake, about 45 km (28 mi) west of Hwy. 19, Box 2160, Campbell River V9W 5C9,* ☎ *250/286–3122.* ☺ *Call for hrs.*

Johnstone Strait

East side of Vancouver Island, roughly between Campbell River and Telegraph Cove.

Pods of resident orcas (killer whales) live year-round in the Inside Passage and around Vancouver Island; in **Robson Bight** they like rubbing against the beaches. Whales are most often seen during the salmon runs of July, August, and September. Because of their presence, Robson Bight has been made into an ecological preserve: whales there must not be disturbed by human observers. Some of the island's best whale-watching tours, however, are conducted nearby, out of **Telegraph Cove,** a village built on pilings over water.

Outdoor Activities and Sports

CANOEING AND KAYAKING

In Telegraph Cove, **North Island Boat, Canoe, and Kayak** (☎ 250/949–7707) rents canoes and kayaks. In Sayward, try **Island Sauvage** (☞ *below*).

Canadian Outback Adventure Company (✉ 100−657 Marine Dr., West Vancouver V7T 1A4, ☎ 604/921−7250 or 800/565−8735), **Eco-summer Expeditions** (✉ 1516 Duranleau St., Vancouver V6H 3S4, ☎ 604/669−7741 or 800/465−8884), and **Island Sauvage** (✉ R.R. 1, Sayward V0P 1R0, ☎ 250/282−3644 or 800/667−4354, FAX 250/287−8840) run multiday sea-kayaking trips among the orcas in the strait.

WHALE-WATCHING

Most trips run between June and October. Half and full-day whale-watching expeditions are available through **Island Sauvage** (☎ 250/282−3644 or 800/667−4354, FAX 250/287−8840) in Sayward, **Seasmoke Tours** (☎ 250/974−5225) in Alert Bay, and **Stubbs Island Whale Watching** (☎ 250/928−3185 or 800/665−3066) in Telegraph Cove.

Port Hardy

➂⓪ *238 km (148 mi) northwest of Campbell River, 499 km (309 mi) northwest of Victoria, 274 nautical mi southeast of Prince Rupert.*

Port Hardy is the departure and arrival point for BC Ferries (☞ Getting Around *in* British Columbia A to Z, *below*) going through the scenic Inside Passage to and from Prince Rupert, the coastal port serving the Queen Charlotte Islands. BC Ferries has also added a Discovery Coast Passage route out of Port Hardy that travels to Bella Coola and other small communities along the scenic midcoast. (For more information about these areas, ☞ North Coast, *below*.) In summer the town can be crowded, so book your accommodations early. Ferry reservations for the trip between Port Hardy and Prince Rupert and Port Hardy and Bella Coola should also be made well in advance.

Lodging

$−$$ 🏨 **Glen Lyon Inn.** The rooms have a full ocean view of Hardy Bay and, like most other area motels, have clean, modern amenities. Eagles can often be spotted eyeing the water for fish to prey on. The inn is a short ride from the ferry terminal. Fishing charters can be arranged here. ✉ *6435 Hardy Bay Rd., Box 103, V0N 2P0,* ☎ *250/949−7115,* FAX *250/949−7415. 29 rooms, 1 suite. Restaurant, lounge, no-smoking rooms. AE, DC, MC, V.*

Cape Scott

60 km (37 mi) northwest of Port Hardy on logging roads.

➂① The northernmost part of Vancouver Island is Cape Scott. **Cape Scott Provincial Park** (☎ 250/387−5002), a wilderness camping region, is designed for well-equipped and experienced hikers. At Sand Neck, a strip of land that joins the cape to the mainland of the island, you can see both the eastern and the western shores at once.

THE GULF ISLANDS

Traveling up the northeastern coastline of Vancouver Island in the late 1790s, Capt. George Vancouver dubbed the expansive body of water on which he sailed the Gulf of Georgia, thinking that it led to open sea. While the name of the waterway was later changed to the Strait of Georgia when further exploration revealed that the British Columbia mainland lay to the east, the islands dotting the strait continue to be known as the Gulf Islands.

Of the hundreds of islands in this strait, the most popular are Galiano, Mayne, North and South Pender, Saturna, and Salt Spring. A temperate climate (warmer, with half the rainfall of Vancouver), scenic beaches, towering promontories, rolling pasturelands, and virgin forests are common to all, but each has its unique flavor. Marine birds are numerous, and there is unusual vegetation such as arbutus trees (also known as madrones, a leafy evergreen with red peeling bark) and Garry oaks. Writers, artists, craftspeople, weekend cottagers, and retirees take full advantage of the undeveloped islands.

For a first visit to the Gulf Islands, make a stopover on Salt Spring Island, the most commercialized of the southern islands, or on more subdued, pastoral Mayne Island. Outdoors enthusiasts will appreciate Galiano, which is far less developed than other Gulf Islands. Their proximity to Vancouver by ferry makes each of these islands feasible for a one- or two-day trip (☞ Getting Around *in* British Columbia A to Z, *below*). Free maps are available on the ferry or in island stores.

Galiano Island

㉜ *20 nautical mi (almost 2 hrs by ferry due to interisland stops) from Swartz Bay (32 km, or 20 mi, north of Victoria), 13 nautical mi (a 50-min ferry ride) from Tsawwassen (39 km, or 24 mi, south of Vancouver).*

The activities on Galiano Island are almost exclusively of the outdoor type. The long, unbroken eastern shoreline is perfect for leisurely beach walks, while the numerous coves and inlets along the western coast make it a prime area for kayaking. Miles of trails through Douglas-fir forest beg for exploration by foot or bike. Hikers can climb to the top of **Mt. Galiano** for a view of the Olympic Mountains in Washington or trek the length of **Bodega Ridge.** The best spots to view Active Pass and the surrounding islands are Bluffs Park, Bellhouse Park, and Centennial Park; these are also good for picnicking and bird-watching.

Biological studies show that the straits between Vancouver Island and the mainland of British Columbia are home to the largest variety of marine life in North American. The frigid waters offer superb visibility, especially in winter. Acala Point, **Porlier Pass,** and Active Pass are top locations for scuba diving. Fishermen head to the point at **Bellhouse Park** to spin cast for salmon from shore, or head by boat to Porlier Pass and **Trincomali Channel.**

Lodging

$$–$$$ 🏠 **Woodstone Country Inn.** This serene, no-smoking inn sits on the edge of a forest overlooking a meadow that's fantastic for bird-watching. Stenciled walls and tall windows bring the pastoral setting into spacious bedrooms. Most of the rooms have fireplaces and patios, and a few have oversize soaker tubs. A hearty gourmet breakfast and afternoon tea are included in the cost. Guests and nonguests can have four-course dinners here by advance reservation. ⊠ *Georgeson Bay Rd., R.R. 1, V0N 1P0,* ☎ *250/539–2022 or 888/339–2022,* 𝔽𝔸𝕏 *250/539–5198. 13 rooms. Dining room, meeting room. AE, MC, V.*

$–$$ 🏠 **Sutil Lodge.** Family photos from the 1920s and heavy Art Deco furnishings re-create a sense of lodge life in an earlier era at this 1927 bungalow set on 20 wooded acres on picturesque Montague Bay. The simple guest rooms have throw rugs on dark hardwood floors and beds tucked into window nooks. Nature-watching and picnic cruises by kayak and sailboat can be arranged. The kayak center on the property attracts folks from around the world (rentals and guided trips are available); catamaran cruises can also be arranged. A full breakfast is included in the rate. ⊠ *637 Southwind Rd., Montague Harbour V0N 1P0,* ☎ *250/539–2930 or 888/539–2930,* 𝔽𝔸𝕏 *250/539–5390. 7 rooms share 3 baths. Dining room, hiking. MC, V.*

Outdoor Activities and Sports

BIKING

There are miles of trails to explore, and biking is a fun way to do it. Bike rentals are available from **Galiano Bicycle** (⊠ 36 Burrill Rd., ☎ 250/539–9906), within walking distance of the Sturdies Bay ferry terminal.

DIVING

For **dive charters** on Galiano, contact Martin Karakas (☎ 250/539–5186) or George Parson (☎ 250/539–3109).

FISHING

Bert's Charters (☎ 250/539–3181) runs fishing charters. **Mel-n-i Fishing Charters** (☎ 250/539–3171) is one of the primary fishing operators on the island.

GOLF

The **Galiano Golf Course** (⊠ 24 St. Andrew St., ☎ 250/539–5533) is a 9-hole, par-32 course in a forest clearing. It's moderate in difficulty.

KAYAKING

Galiano Island Seakayaking (☎ 250/539–2930 or 888/539–2930) has rentals and tours. **Gulf Islands Kayaking** (☎ 250/539–2442) has equipment rentals and guided kayak tours.

Mayne Island

③③ *28 nautical mi from Swartz Bay (32 km, or 20 mi, north of Victoria), 22 nautical mi from Tsawwassen (39 km, or 24 mi, south of Vancouver).*

Middens of clam and oyster shells give evidence that tiny Mayne Island—only 21 square km (8 square mi)—was inhabited as early as 5,000 years ago. It later became the stopover point for miners headed from Victoria to the gold fields of Fraser River and Barkerville and by the mid-1800s had developed into the communal center of the inhabited Gulf Islands, with the first school, post office, police lockup, church, and hotel. Farm tracts and orchards established in the 1930s and 1940s and worked by Japanese farmers until their internment during World War II continue to thrive today, and a farmers' market is open each Saturday during harvest season. There are few stores, restaurants, or historic sites here, but Mayne's manageable size and slower pace make it very popular. The mild hills and wonderful scenery make it great territory for a vigorous bike ride; bikes can be rented at the Miners Bay gas station.

Mount Parke was declared a wilderness park in 1989. A 45-minute hike leads to the highest point on the island and a stunning, almost 360-degree view of Vancouver, Active Pass, and Vancouver Island.

The small town of **Miners Bay,** is home to Plumbers Pass Lockup (closed September–June), built in 1896 as a jail but now a minuscule museum chronicling the island's history. From Miners Bay head east on Georgia Point Road to **St. Mary Magdalene Church,** a pretty stone chapel built in 1898 that now doubles as an Anglican and United church. The graveyard beyond is also interesting; generations of islanders—the Bennets, Georgesons, Maudes, and Deacons (whose names are all over the Mayne Island map)—are buried here. Across the road, a stairway leads down to the beach.

Active Pass Lighthouse, at the end of Georgia Point Road, was built in 1855 and still signals ships into the busy waterway. The grassy grounds are great for picnicking. There's a pebble beach for beachcombing at shallow (and therefore warmer) **Campbell Bay.** A fencepost near a pullout on Campbell Bay Road marks the entrance to the path leading to the beach. Campbell Bay Road ends at Fernhill Road; turn right here and you'll end up back in Miners Bay.

Dining and Lodging

$$–$$$$ ✕▥ **Oceanwood Country Inn.** This Tudor-style house on 10 quiet,
★ forested acres overlooking Navy Channel has English country decor throughout. Fireplaces, ocean-view balconies, and whirlpool or soaking tubs make several rooms deluxe; all are inviting, with cozy down comforters on the beds, cheerful wall stenciling, and cushioned chairs in brightly lit reading areas. For dinner, the waterfront dining room, which is open to the public, serves outstanding regional cuisine. You may find grilled salmon, tomato and Dungeness crab soup, or wild mushroom and goat cheese ravioli on the prix-fixe, fresh-daily menu. Afternoon tea and breakfast are included in the room rates. ⊠ *630 Dinner Bay Rd., V0N 2J0,* ☎ *250/539–5074,* ℻ *250/539–3002. 12 rooms. Restaurant, no-smoking rooms, hot tub, sauna, hiking, jogging, beach, bicycles, library, meeting room. MC, V. Closed Dec.–Feb.*

$$ ✕▥ **Fernhill Lodge.** This 1983 West Coast cedar contemporary has fantastical theme rooms—Moroccan, East Indian, and Old English. Two of them have outdoor hot tubs. On the 5-acre grounds are an Elizabethan herb garden and a rustic gazebo with a meditation loft. Hosts Mary and Brian Crumblehulme offer, on request, historical four-course dinners (Rome, Chaucer, and Cleopatra, to name a few themes) for guests and nonguests. Breakfasts, included in the room rate, are rather less exotic. This is a no-smoking inn, and pets are not allowed. ⊠ *Fernhill Rd., R.R. 1, C-4, V0N 2J0,* ☎ ℻ *250/539–2544. 3 rooms. Dining room, sauna, library. MC, V.*

Salt Spring Island

❸❹ *28 nautical mi from Swartz Bay (32 km, or 20 mi, north of Victoria), 22 nautical mi from Tsawwassen (39 km, or 24 mi, south of Vancouver).*

Named for the saltwater springs at its north end, Salt Spring is the largest and most developed of the Gulf Islands. Among its first nonnative settlers were black Americans who came here to escape slavery in the 1850s. The agrarian tradition they and other immigrants established remains strong (a Fall Fair has been held every year since 1896), but tourism and art now support the local economy. A government wharf, three marinas, and a waterfront shopping complex at Ganges serve a community of more than 10,000 residents.

Ganges, a pedestrian-oriented seaside village and the island's cultural and commercial center, has dozens of smart boutiques, galleries, and restaurants. Mouat's Trading Company (Fulford–Ganges Road), built in 1912, was the original village general store. It's now a hardware store but still houses a display of historical photographs.

Ganges is also the site of **ArtCraft,** a summer-long arts-and-craft sale featuring the work of more than 200 artisans, and of the **Salt Spring Festival of the Arts**, a festival of international music, theater, and dance held in July. Dozens of working **artists' studios** are open to the public here; pick up a studio tour map at the Visitor Information Centre (⊠ 121 Lower Ganges Rd., ☎ 250/537–5252). From Ganges, you can circle the northern tip of the island by bike or car (on Vesuvius Bay Road, Sunset Road, North End and North Beach Roads, Walker Hook Road, and Robinson Road) past fields and peek-a-boo marine views.

St. Mary Lake, on North End Road, and **Cusheon Lake,** south of Ganges, are the best bets for warm-water swimming.

Near the center of Salt Spring, the summit of **Mt. Maxwell Provincial Park** (⊠ Mt. Maxwell Rd., off Fulford–Ganges Rd.) affords spectacular views of south Salt Spring, Vancouver Island, and other Gulf Islands. It's also a great picnic spot. The last portion of the drive is steep, winding, and unpaved.

Ruckle Provincial Park (⊠ Beaver Point Rd., ☎ 250/653–4115) is the site of an 1872 heritage homestead and extensive fields still being farmed by the Ruckle family. The park also has camping and picnic spots, 11 km (7 mi) of coastline, and trails leading to rocky headlands.

Dining and Lodging

The **Visitor Information Centre** (☞ *above*) can book you into any of Salt Spring's 120 B&Bs. There are also a number of provincial campsites and a youth hostel (☎ 250/537–4149) on the island.

$$$–$$$$ ✕ **House Piccolo.** Blue-and-white tablecloths and framed pastel prints on whitewashed walls give this cozy restaurant a casual feel. Broiled sea scallop brochette, roasted British Columbia venison with juniper berries, and the salmon du jour are good choices from the dinner menu, but save room for homemade ice cream or the signature chocolate terrine. ⊠ *108 Hereford Ave., Ganges,* ☎ *250/537–1844. Reservations essential. AE, DC, MC, V. Closed Tues. in winter. No lunch.*

$$$$ ✕🏠 **Hastings House.** Guests are nicely pampered at Hastings House.
★   The centerpiece of this luxurious 25-acre seaside farm estate is a Tudor-style manor built in 1939. Guest quarters are in the manor or the farmhouse, in garden cottages, and in lovely suites in the reconstructed barn. All are furnished with fine antiques in an English country theme. Elegant dinners in the manor house are open to the public (reservations essential): The five-course prix-fixe menu may include grilled eggplant with goat cheese, peppered sea bass on wilted spinach with nasturtium butter, and Salt Spring lamb loin with rosemary. Dinner guests can choose the formal dining room (jacket required) or the more casual lower-floor dining area, or they can eat in the kitchen and watch chef Marcel Kauer at work. ⊠ *160 Upper Ganges Rd., Box 1110, Ganges, V0S 1E0,* ☎ *250/537–2362 or 800/661–9255,* 𝐅𝐀𝐗 *250/537–5333. 3 rooms, 7 suites. Restaurant, minibars, massage, croquet, mountain bikes. AE, MC, V. Closed Jan.–early Mar.*

$$$ 🏠 **Beach House on Sunset.** The sunsets over Stuart Channel and Vancouver Island are stunning from this Mediterranean-style house set on a waterfront slope 5 km (3 mi) north of the Vesuvius ferry terminal. Three upstairs rooms in the bed-and-breakfast have private entrances and balconies; one has French doors framing lovely sea views, a fireplace, a claw-foot tub, and a private deck with an outdoor shower. A one-bedroom cedar cottage with wraparound porch sits over the boathouse at water's edge. Extras include down comforters, terry robes, slippers, fruit platters, decanters of sherry, and a bountiful breakfast. You can also arrange boat charters and kayak tours. ⊠ *930 Sunset Dr., V8K 1E6,* ☎ *250/537–2879,* 𝐅𝐀𝐗 *250/537–4747. 3 rooms, 1 cottage. Breakfast room, boating. MC, V. Closed Dec.–Feb.*

$$–$$$ 🏠 **Anne's Oceanfront Hideaway.** Perched on a steep slope above the sea, 6 km (4 mi) north of the Vesuvius ferry terminal, this modern, no-smoking waterfront home has panoramic ocean views, a cozy library, a sitting room, and two covered verandas. A lavish hot breakfast is included in the price, and one room is wheelchair accessible. Every room has a hydromassage tub and water view; three have private balconies. The Douglas Fir and Garry Oak rooms have the best views. Luxurious details, like morning coffee in the rooms, robes, and a welcoming bottle of wine, make this a comfortable place to unwind. ⊠ *168 Simson Rd., V8K 1E2,* ☎ *250/537–0851 or 888/474–2663,* 𝐅𝐀𝐗 *250/*

537–0861. 4 rooms. Air-conditioning, breakfast room, outdoor hot tub, exercise room, boating, bicycles, library. MC, V.

$$–$$$ ⊞ **Salty Springs Spa Resort.** The only property to take advantage of the island's natural mineral springs is perched on a 50-ft bluff on the northern shore of Salt Spring. The one- and two-bedroom chalet-style pine cabins have Gothic-arch ceilings, fireplaces, kitchenettes, hot mineral-springs baths for two, and private decks with gas barbecues. Most have unobstructed ocean views; two chalets tucked away in the woods are more private. At press time, a full-service spa with 11 treatment rooms offering herbal wraps, massage, facials, mineral baths, steam cabinets, hydrotherapy, and reflexology for guests and nonguests was set to open in 1999. ⊠ *1460 N. Beach Rd., V8K 1J4,* ☎ *250/537–4111 or 800/665–0039,* FAX *250/537–2939. 12 cabins. Kitchenettes, refrigerators, massage, sauna, spa, boating, bicycles, recreation room, coin laundry, meeting room. AE, MC, V.*

$$ ⊞ **Old Farmhouse Bed and Breakfast.** Gerti and Karl Fuss operate this delightful bed-and-breakfast near St. Mary Lake. Their gray-and-white saltbox farmhouse sits in a quiet 3-acre meadow. The style of the main house, a registered historic property built in 1894, is echoed in the four-room guest wing added in 1989, which has country-comfortable guest rooms furnished with pine bedsteads, down comforters, lace curtains, and wicker chairs. Each has a private balcony or patio. Gerti is a European-trained chef, and her breakfasts of fresh baked goods and hot entrées like smoked salmon soufflé are legendary. ⊠ *1077 Northend Rd., V8K 1L9,* ☎ *250/537–4113,* FAX *250/537–4969. 4 rooms. Breakfast room, no-smoking rooms, boating. MC, V.*

Outdoor Activities and Sports

Operators tend to double up on their activities here. For guided day paddles, kayak lessons, and kayak and bike rentals, try **Salt Spring Kayaking** (⊠ 2923 Fulford-Ganges Rd., Ganges, ☎ 250/653–4222). **Salt Spring Marine Rentals** (⊠ at the head of Ganges Harbour, ☎ 250/537–9100) has fishing charters, nature cruises, and boat and scooter rentals. A source for kayak rentals, tours, and lessons is **Sea Otter Kayaking** (⊠ 1186 North End Rd., Ganges, ☎ 250/537–5678). **Island Escapades** (⊠ 118 Natalie La., near Cusheon Lake, ☎ 250/537–2537 or 888/529–2567) offers kayaking, sailing, hiking, and climbing tours.

BIKING

At 100 km (62 mi) on a circular route, Salt Spring Island offers a challenge. Some bed-and-breakfasts have bicycles; ask that they be set aside for you when you make your reservations. For rentals on Salt Spring, try **Salt Spring Kayaking** (☎ 250/537–4664) or **Salt Spring Marine Rentals** (⊠ 250/537–9100), both at the head of the harbor on Lower Ganges Road.

GOLF

Blackburn Meadows Golf Course (☎ 250/537–1707) and **Salt Spring Island Golf and Country Club** (☎ 250/537–2121) are both pleasant 9-hole courses.

Shopping

There are bargains galore at Ganges' **Market in the Park,** held in Centennial Park every Saturday from April through October. Fresh produce, seafood, crafts, clothing, candles, toys, home-canned items, and more are on offer. The **Sophisticated Cow Gallery** (⊠ 133 Hereford Ave., Ganges, ☎ 250/537–0070) uses every room of a funky Victorian house to display the work of more than 100 island artisans.

NORTH COAST

Gateway to Alaska and the Yukon, this vast, rugged region is marked by soaring, snowcapped mountain ranges; scenic fjords; primordial islands; and towering rain forests. Once the center of a vast trading network, the mid- and north coasts are home to First Nations (native) people who have lived here for 10,000 years and more recent immigrants drawn by the natural resources of fur, fish, and forest. The region is thin on roads, but you can travel by ferry, sailboat, cruise ship, plane, or kayak to explore the ancient native villages of the coast and the Queen Charlotte Islands (☞ Getting Around *in* British Columbia A to Z, *below*).

Inside Passage

★ ㉟ *507 km (314 mi), or 274 nautical mi, between Port Hardy on northern Vancouver Island and Prince Rupert.*

The Inside Passage, a sheltered marine highway, follows a series of natural channels behind protective islands along the green-and-blue shaded British Columbia coast. The undisturbed landscape of rising mountains and humpbacked islands has a striking, prehistoric look. You can take a ferry cruise along the Inside Passage or see it on one of the more expensive luxury liners that sail along the British Columbia coast from Vancouver to Alaska.

The comfortable ferry **Queen of the North,** carrying up to 800 passengers and 157 vehicles, takes 15 hours (almost all in daylight during summer sailings) to make the trip from Port Hardy to Prince Rupert. Reservations are required for the cruise and advised for hotel accommodations at ports of call. ⊠ *BC Ferries, 1112 Fort St., Victoria V8V 4V2,* ☎ *250/386–3431 in Victoria or outside B.C.; 888/223–3779 elsewhere in B.C.* ⌨ *One-way summer passage for car and driver $318; $104 for each adult passenger.* ☉ *Sailings Oct.–Apr., once weekly; May, twice weekly; June–Sept., daily, departing on alternate days from Port Hardy and Prince Rupert; departure time 7:30 AM, arrival time 10:30 PM; call to verify schedule.*

Discovery Coast Passage

★ ㊱ *258 km (161 mi), or 138 nautical mi, between Port Hardy on northern Vancouver Island and Bella Coola.*

Until 1996, British Columbia's central coast was almost inaccessible to anyone without access to a floatplane or ocean-going canoe. That year, BC Ferries introduced a new route—part low-budget cruise ship, part public transportation for midcoast communities—that travels up the Inside Passage to the native community of Bella Bella and then takes a sharp right up Dean Channel to the mainland town of Bella Coola. The scenery is stunning, and the route allows passengers to visit communities along the way, including Namu, Shearwater, Klemtu, and Ocean Falls. It also provides an alternative route into the Cariboo region, via Highway 20 from Bella Coola to Williams Lake. Accommodation at ports of call varies from luxury fishing lodges to rough camping, but it's limited and must be booked in advance. BC Ferries can arrange travel, activity, and accommodation packages.

The **Queen of Chilliwack,** carrying up to 375 passengers and 115 vehicles, takes from 17 to 33 hours (depending on the number of stops) to make the trip from Port Hardy on Vancouver Island to Bella Coola. Reservations are required for vehicles and advised for foot passengers. ⊠ *BC Ferries, 1112 Fort St., Victoria V8V 4V2,* ☎ *250/386–3431 in Victoria or outside B.C.; 888/223–3779 elsewhere in B.C.* ⌨ *One-*

way fares between Port Hardy and Bella Coola are approximately $112 for a passenger, $225 for a vehicle. ☉ *Late-May–late Sept., 1 sailing daily, on 1 of 6 different itineraries.*

Prince Rupert

㊲ *1,502 km (931 mi) by highway and 750 km (465 mi) by air northwest of Vancouver; 15 hrs by ferry northwest of Port Hardy on Vancouver Island.*

Prince Rupert, the final stop on the BC Ferries route through the Inside Passage, has a mild but wet climate; it's a good idea to take rain gear. The town lives off fishing, fish processing, logging, saw- and pulp-mill operations, deep-sea shipping, and tourism. The **Museum of Northern British Columbia** has one of the province's finest collections of coastal native art, some artifacts dating back 10,000 years. Native artisans work on totem poles in the carving shed, and in summer, the museum runs a 2½-hour boat tour of the harbor and Metlakatla native village. ✉ *100 1st Ave. W,* ☎ *250/624–3207.* 🎫 *$5.* ☉ *Sept.–May, Mon.–Sat. 9–5; June–Aug., Mon.–Sat. 9–8, Sun. 9–5.*

The **North Pacific Cannery Village Museum** in Port Edward, 20 km (12 mi) south of Prince Rupert, is the oldest salmon cannery on the West Coast. You tour the cannery buildings, mess hall, and managers' houses, where interpretive displays about the canning process and village life are set up. ✉ *Off Hwy. 16, Box 1104, Port Edward,* ☎ *250/628–3538,* 🖷 *250/628–3540.* 🎫 *$6.* ☉ *May–Sept., daily 9–6.*

Dining and Lodging

$$ ✕🏨 **Crest Hotel.** Warm and modern, the Crest is a block from the two
★ shopping centers but stands on a bluff overlooking the harbor. Some rooms have minibars and whirlpool tubs. The restaurant, pleasantly decorated with brass rails and beam ceilings, has a waterfront view and specializes in seafood; particularly outstanding are the salmon dishes. ✉ *222 1st Ave. W, V8J 3P6,* ☎ *250/624–6771 or 800/663–8150,* 🖷 *250/627–7666. 97 rooms, 5 suites. Restaurant, coffee shop, lounge, in-room modem lines, no-smoking floor, room service, outdoor hot tub, steam room, exercise room, fishing, baby-sitting, dry cleaning, business services, meeting rooms. AE, D, DC, MC, V.*

$–$$ 🏨 **Highliner Inn.** This modern high-rise near the waterfront is conveniently situated and relatively well priced. It's in the downtown shopping district only one block from the airline terminal building. Ask for a room with a balcony and view of the harbor. ✉ *815 1st Ave. W, V8J 1B3,* ☎ *250/624–9060 or 800/668–3115,* 🖷 *250/627–7759. 94 rooms. Restaurant, lounge, beauty salon, coin laundry. AE, D, DC, MC, V.*

Shopping

Native art and other local crafts are for sale at **Studio 9** (✉ 516 3rd Ave. W, ☎ 250/624–2366).

Queen Charlotte Islands

★ ㊳ *93 nautical mi southwest of Prince Rupert, 367 nautical mi northwest of Port Hardy.*

The Queen Charlotte Islands, or Haida Gwaii ("Islands of the People"), have been called the Canadian Galápagos. Their long isolation off the province's north coast has given rise to subspecies of wildlife found nowhere else in the world. The islands are also the preserve of the Haida people, who make up half the population. Their vibrant culture is undergoing a renaissance, evident throughout the islands.

In the Queen Charlottes, 150 km (93 mi) of paved road, most of it on Graham Island (the northernmost and largest of the group of 150), connect the town of Queen Charlotte in the south to Masset in the north. Some of the other islands are laced with gravel roads. The rugged, rocky west coast of the archipelago faces the ocean; the east coast has many broad sandy beaches. The incredible scenery makes the islands an artisans' delight, and kayaking enthusiasts from around the world are drawn to waterways here. Throughout, the mountains and shores are often shrouded in fog and rain-laden clouds.

Three **Visitor Information Centres,** in Queen Charlotte (⊠ Wharf St., ☎ 250/559–8316), Sandspit (⊠ 1 Airport Rd., ☎ 250/637–5362), and Masset (⊠ Main St., ☎ 250/626–3982), are open during the summer.

Naikoon Provincial Park (☎ 250/557–4390), in the northeast corner of Graham, preserves a large section of unique wilderness with low-lying swamps, pine and cedar forests, lakes, beaches, trails, and wildlife. The 5-km (3-mi) walk leads from the Tlell Picnic Site to the beach and on to the bow section of the old wooden shipwreck of the *Pezuta*, a 1928 log-hauling vessel. At the north end of the park, a climb up the 400-ft Tow Hill gives the best views of McIntyre Bay.

On the southern end of Graham Island, the **Haida Gwaii Museum** has an impressive display of Haida totem poles, masks, and carvings of both silver and argillite (hard black slate). A gift shop sells Haida art, and a natural history exhibit gives interesting background on the wildlife of the islands. ⊠ *Box 1373, Skidegate V0T 1S1*, ☎ *250/559–4643*. ☜ *$2.50.* ☉ *Apr.–Oct., weekdays 9–5, weekends 1–5; Nov.–Mar., weekdays 10–5, Sat. 1–5.*

South of Graham, the 3,400-square-km (1,313-square-mi) **Gwaii Haanas National Park Reserve,** administered jointly by the government of Canada and the Council of the Haida Nation, protects a vast tract of wilderness, unique species of flora and fauna, and many important Haida sites, including the village of **Ninstints,** a UNESCO World Heritage Site that contains some of the finest First Nations totems anywhere. The reserve, accessible only by air or sea, is both ecologically and culture fragile. Access is by permit only, and solo travel is not recommended. The best (and pretty much only) way to visit is with a sailing or kayaking outfitter (☞ Outdoor Activities and Sports, *below*). ⊠ *Parks Canada, Box 37, Queen Charlotte V0T 1S0*, ☎ *250/559–8818*, ℻ *250/559–8366.*

Dining and Lodging

Accommodation is available in Sandspit, Queen Charlotte, Tlell, Port Clements, and Masset. Reservations are recommended. **Super, Natural British Columbia** (☎ 800/663–6000) can be of assistance.

$ ⊞ **Alaska View Lodge.** On a clear day, you can see the mountains of Alaska from the large front deck of this bed-and-breakfast, 13 km (8 mi) east of Masset. A sandy beach borders the lodge on one side and woods on the other. Eagles are a familiar sight, and in winter you can often catch glimpses of the northern lights. A full breakfast is included in the rates; with advance notice, the owner can provide evening meals. Book early in summer. ⊠ *Tow Hill Rd., Box 227, Masset V0T 1M0*, ☎ *250/626–3333 or 800/661–0019 in Canada*, ℻ *250/626–3303. 4 rooms. Dining room, no-smoking rooms, hiking. MC, V.*

$ ⊞ **Spruce Point Lodge.** This cedar-sided building, encircled by a balcony, is right on the beach and, like many other Queen Charlotte accommodations, has pine furnishings and a rustic, down-home feel. A Continental breakfast, delivered to your room, is included in the price. ⊠ *609 6th Ave., Box 735, Queen Charlotte V0T 1S0*, ☎ ℻ *250/559–8234. 7 rooms. Boating, fishing. MC, V.*

Outdoor Activities and Sports

ECOLOGICAL TOURS

Bluewater Adventures (☎ 604/980–3800, ⓕ 604/980–1800) has eight- and nine-day sailboat tours around the Charlottes; trips start and end in Sandspit. **Ecosummer Expeditions** (☎ 604/669–7741 or 800/465–8884, ⓕ 604/669–3244) and **Inside Passage Cruises Inc.** (☎ 604/683–2174 or 888/357–7111, ⓕ 604/688–6972) visit Gwaii Haanas National Park and other sites in a 70-passenger cruise ship. **Moresby Explorers** (☎ 250/637–2215 or 800/806–7633) offers one- to four-day Zodiac boat tours to the Gwaii Haanas National Park Reserve, with accommodation on a floating cabin. **Queen Charlotte Adventures** (☎ 250/559–8990 or 800/668–4288, ⓕ 250/559–8983) leads multiday guided tours around the islands.

KAYAKING

Moresby Explorers (✉ 469 Alliford Bay Rd., Sandspit, ☎ 250/637–2215 or 800/806–7633, ⓕ 250/637–2215) is a source for kayak rentals.

Shopping

The Haida carve valuable figurines from argillite, a variety of hard, black slate. Other island specialties are silk-screen prints and silver jewelry. A number of shops in Queen Charlotte City are on **3rd Avenue.** The **Haida Gwaii Museum** (☞ *above*) has an excellent gift shop. Some shops around the islands are **Haida Arts and Jewellery** (✉ 387 Eagle Rd., Old Masset, ☎ 250/626–5560) and the **Long House Gift Shop** (✉ 107A Front St., Skidegate, ☎ 250/559–8013).

En Route   From Prince Rupert, Highway 16 heads east to interior British Columbia. It passes through or near such communities as **Terrace,** with a hot-springs complex at the Mt. Layton Resort, skiing at Shames Mountain, and excellent fishing in the Skeena River. **Kitimat** (Highway 37, south of Terrace), at the head of the Douglas Channel, has superb fishing.

THE CARIBOO AND THE NORTH

This is British Columbia's wild west, a vast, thinly populated plateau stretching from the dense spruce and fir forests of the north to the ranching country of the south. The Cariboo covers an area roughly bordered by Bella Coola on the west, Lillooet in the south, Wells Gray Park on the east, and Prince George in the north. Distances here are hard to grasp: Driving times are measured in days, not hours; many parks are larger than some countries; and some private ranches are larger than many states in the United States. In the last century, thousands made the trip, looking for—and finding—gold. Those times are remembered throughout the region, most vividly at the re-created gold-rush town of Barkerville. You can still pan for gold here, but these days visitors are more likely come to enjoy ranch holidays, horseback riding, fly-fishing, mountain biking, and cross-country skiing.

Hazelton

③⑨ *293 km (182 mi) northeast of Prince Rupert, 439 km (272 mi) northwest of Prince George, 1,217 km (755 mi) northwest of Vancouver.*

Hazelton is rich in the culture of the Gitksan and Wet'suwet'en peoples. ★ **'Ksan Historical Village and Museum,** just outside town, is a re-created Gitksan village. The elaborately painted community of seven longhouses is a replica of the one that stood on the site when the first European explorers arrived in the 19th century. The carving shed, often used by 'Ksan artists, is open to the public, and three other longhouses can be visited: One displays contemporary masks and robes, another has song-and-dance dramas in the summer, and the third exhibits pre-European tools of bone, sinew, stone, and wood. The museum displays works and artifacts from the region as well as modern-day regalia. ✉ *Box 326, V0J 1Y0,* ☎ *250/842–5544.* ☜ *$2; $7 with tour.* ☉ *Apr. 15–Sept. daily 9–6, with site tours on the ½ hr; Oct.–Apr. 14, museum and gift shop only, weekdays 9–5.*

Prince George

⓵ *721 km (447 mi) east of Prince Rupert, 786 km (487 mi) north of Vancouver.*

At the crossroads of two railways and two highways, Prince George has grown to become the capital of northern British Columbia and the third-largest city in the province. Nestled on the edge of a vast forested plateau, it has an economy fueled by forest industries, from tree farms to logging to lumber and paper processing.

In Ft. George Park, you can visit the **Fraser–Ft. George Regional Museum** to see the fine collection of artifacts illustrating local history. ✉ *333 Gorse St.,* ☎ *250/562–1612.* ☜ *$4.25.* ☉ *May–Sept., daily 9–5; Oct.–Apr., Tues.–Sun. noon–5.*

A collection of photos, rail cars, and logging and sawmilling equipment at the **Central BC Railway and Forest Industry Museum** traces the history of the town and the region, from the arrival of the railroad. ✉ *850 River Rd., next to Cottonwood Park,* ☎ *250/563–7351.* ☜ *$4.* ☉ *Call for seasonal hrs.*

The **Prince George Native Art Gallery** sells traditional and contemporary works (carvings, sculpture, jewelry, literature). ✉ *1600 3rd Ave.,* ☎ *250/614–7726.* ☜ *Free.* ☉ *Tues.–Fri. 9–5, weekends 10–4.*

Gold Rush Trail

Begins at Prince George and ends at Lillooet, 170 km (105 mi) west of Kamloops, 131 km (81 mi) northeast of Whistler.

From Prince George, Highway 97 heads south toward Kamloops and the Okanagan Valley, following the 640-km (397-mi) Gold Rush Trail, along which frontiersmen traveled in search of gold in the 19th and early 20th centuries. The trail goes through Quesnel, Williams Lake, Wells, and Barkerville, and along the Fraser Canyon and Cache Creek. Many towns and communities through which the trail passes have re-created villages, history museums, or historic sites that help tell the story of the gold-rush era. The **Cariboo Tourism Association** (✉ 266 Oliver St., Williams Lake V2G 1M1, ☎ 250/392–2226 or 800/663–5885, ℻ 250/392–2838) has information about the trail.

★ The most vivid re-creation of the gold rush is at **Barkerville Historic Town,** 90 km (56 mi) east of Quesnel on Highway 26. Once the biggest town west of Chicago and north of San Francisco, today it's a provincial historic site where actors in period costume, merchants vending 19th-century goods, stagecoach rides, and live musical revues capture the town's heyday. Many of the 125 buildings are original structures, and as a museum the town stakes more claim to historical accuracy than the average theme park. The town is open year-round, but most of the theatrical fun happens in the summer. There are B&Bs in Barkerville and a campground nearby. ✉ *Box 19, Barkerville V0K 1B0,* ☎ *250/994–3302,* ℻ *250/994–3435.* ☜ *Mid-May–mid-Sept., $5.50 for a 2-day pass; free in winter.* ☉ *Daily dawn–dusk.*

Lodging

$$$$ ☷ **Echo Valley Ranch Resort.** At the base of Mt. Bowman, 50 km (31 mi) northwest of Clinton, this new, adult-oriented ranch makes the most of its scenic setting. Included in the rates are a range of activities and three hearty country meals using the ranch's own organic produce. Guests can indulge in spa and beauty treatments or hike, bike, fish, or ride. Tennessee Walker horses and experienced Cariboo cowboys take riders on day and overnight trips. White-water rafting, flight-seeing, and staying at a First Nations tepee village can be arranged, too. ✉ *Box 16, Jesmond V0K 1K0,* ☎ *250/459–2386 or 800/253–8831,* ℻ *250/459–0086. 20 rooms, 3 cabins. Dining room, indoor pool, lake, outdoor hot tub, sauna, massage, hiking, horseback riding, fishing and ice fishing, bicycles, cross-country skiing, sleigh rides, snowshoeing, recreation room, business services, meeting rooms. AP. V.*

$–$$ ☷ **Wells Hotel.** This no-smoking, faithfully refurbished 1930s hotel makes a good base for visiting Barkerville and the Bowron Lakes canoeing area. The sitting room has a fireplace and period artifacts. Rooms are simple, comfortable, and newly decorated. Wells is 81 km (50 mi) east of Quesnel on Highway 26; the hotel can arrange pickups from Quesnel. ✉ *2341 Pooley St., Box 39, Wells V0K 2R0,* ☎ *250/994–3427 or 800/860–2299,* ℻ *250/994–3494. 17 rooms, 7 with bath. Restaurant, pub, outdoor hot tub, meeting rooms. AE, MC, V.*

THE HIGH COUNTRY
AND THE OKANAGAN VALLEY

This roughly triangular territory, stretching from Valemount in the north just past Revelstoke in the southeast to Merritt, farther south and west, presents a spectacular diversity of scenery, from deep canyons carved by the Thompson and Fraser rivers to the towering ranges of the Monashees and Selkirks. Skiing, white-water rafting, heli-skiing, and other challenging outdoor activities can be a focus of any High Country tour. If you were driving here from Prince George, you could continue on Highway 16 to Highway 5 for a spectacular drive through the High Country to Kamloops.

The Okanagan Valley region, five hours east of Vancouver by car, or one hour by air, is part of a highland plateau between the Cascade range of mountains on the west and the lower Monashees on the east. Though small in size (only 3% of the province's total land mass), the area contains the interior's largest concentration of people. Dominating the valley is Okanagan Lake, a magnet for visitors from both the west coast and Alberta. In summer, rooms can be scarce here. The largest towns along the lake, bordered by Highway 97, are Vernon at the north end, Kelowna in the middle, and Penticton to the south. Between these towns, and along the lake, are the recreational and resort communities of Summerland, Peachland, Westbank, and Oyama, which have camping facilities, motels, and cabins. The valley is the fruit-growing capital of Canada, producing apricots, pears, cherries, plums, apples, grapes, and peaches, plus clouds of fragrant blossoms from mid-April through early June. The Okanagan is also Canada's main wine-producing area, and most wineries have tours and tastings.

Kamloops

④ *355 km (220 mi) northeast of Vancouver, 163 km (101 mi) northwest of Kelowna.*

Kamloops is a convenient passageway into the Okanagan Valley from the Fraser Canyon and the Thompson Valley. It's a stop on both the

Canadian National and Canadian Pacific railroads and a major cross-roads with plenty of accommodations. The town is surrounded by 500 lakes, which provide an abundance of trout, Dolly Varden, and koka-nee. In late September and October, attention turns to the sockeye salmon, when thousands of these fish, intent on breeding, return home to the waters where they were spawned, in the Adams River (80 km, or 50 mi, east of Kamloops off the Trans-Canada Highway).

Once every four years—the next time will be 2002—the sockeye run reaches a massive scale as more than a million salmon pack the waters. In 1999, a secondary run will bring 300,000 fish to the river. The **Roderick Haig-Brown Provincial Park,** which protects the 11-km (7-mi) stretch of Adams River, is the best vantage point; call the BC Parks district office (☎ 250/851–3000) for information.

Kamloops Wildlife Park houses 70 species in fairly natural habitats on 55 acres and is a breeding center for a number of endangered species, including Siberian tigers. Hiking trails, a miniature railroad, and adjacent water slides are other attractions. ⊠ *East of Hwy. 1,* ☎ *250/573–3262.* ⊡ *$6.50.* ☉ *July–Aug., daily 8–6; Sept.–June, daily 8–4:30.*

The **Secwepemc Museum and Native Heritage Park,** a reconstructed village set on a traditional gathering site, interprets and celebrates the culture and lifestyle of the Secwepemc people, who have lived in this area for thousands of years. Displays include winter houses, summer lodges, and, in summer, scheduled music and dance performances. The on-site museum houses recorded oral history and photographs, as well as artifacts and artwork. ⊠ *355 Yellowhead Hwy.,* ☎ *250/828–9801 or 250/828–9781.* ⊡ *$5.* ☉ *Daily; call for seasonal hrs.*

Lodging

$$ ⊡ **Corbett Lake Country Inn.** The inn's single (with extra beds) and du-
★   plex cabins are comfortable and basic, as are rooms in the main lodge. Every night the restaurant presents a different fixed menu; favorites include rack of lamb and chateaubriand, whipped up by owner-chef Peter McVey. Fly-fishing for rainbow trout on the private lake is a big attraction. Room rates are per person and include breakfast and dinner. Small pets are allowed. The inn is 19 km (12 mi) southeast of Merritt on the road to Kelowna, and 97 km (60 mi) southwest of Kamloops. ⊠ *Off Hwy. 5A, Box 327, Merritt V1K 1B8,* ☎ *250/378–4334. 3 rooms, 10 cabins. Restaurant, hiking, boating, fishing, cross-country skiing. MAP. V. Closed mid-Jan.–Apr. and Nov.–Dec. 23.*

$$ ⊡ **Lac le Jeune Resort and Conference Centre.** With miles of hiking trails, a lake stocked with trout, and a restaurant that serves robust helpings, this resort encourages enjoyment of the outdoors. The rustic, self-sufficient cabins have ample space and amenities for families, and pets are permitted. In the large, comfortable rooms in the main lodge, no phones or televisions distract from the beauty of the setting. ⊠ *Lac le Jeune Rd., off Coquihalla Hwy., 29 km (18 mi) southwest of Kamloops, V2C 6B8,* ☎ *250/372–2722 or 800/561–5253,* ℻ *250/372–8755. 28 rooms, 4-plex chalet, 6 cabins. Restaurant, lounge, boating, fishing, theater, meeting room. AE, D, DC, MC, V. Closed Oct. 31–Apr. 7.*

Outdoor Activities and Sports

GOLF

Rivershore Golf Links (⊠ Off Old Shuswap Rd., ☎ 250/573–4211), an 18-hole, par-72 Robert Trent Jones–designed course, is one of British Columbia's longest, at 7,007 yards. At press time, 9 of 18 holes at the **Sun Peaks Resort Golf Course** (⊠ 1280 Alpine Rd., Sun Peaks, ☎ 250/578–5431) were open; the other 9 were well under way.

SKIING

With a 2,953-ft vertical drop, **Sun Peaks Resort** (⊠ 1280 Alpine Rd., Sun Peaks, ☎ 250/578–7222 or 800/807–3257, FAX 250/578–7223) has 61 runs and five chairlifts. A source for Sno-cat skiing is **Cat Powder Skiing** (⊠ Box 1479, Revelstoke V0E 2S0, ☎ 250/837–5151 or 800/991–4455).

Vernon

㊷ *117 km (73 mi) southeast of Kamloops.*

The main businesses in Vernon are forestry and agriculture. The town borders on two other lakes besides Okanagan, the more enticing of which is Kalamalka Lake. Vernon is also the town closest to the ski area and all-season gaslight era–theme village resort atop Silver Star Mountain.

Kalamalka Lake Provincial Park (☎ 250/387–5002) has warm-water beaches and some of the most scenic viewpoints and hiking trails in the region.

★ North of Vernon, the **O'Keefe Historic Ranch** provides a window on cattle-ranch life at the turn of the century. The late-19th-century Victorian mansion is opulently furnished with original antiques. On the 50 acres are a Chinese cooks' house, St. Anne's Church, a blacksmith shop, a reconstructed general store, a display of the old Shuswap and Okanagan Railroad, and a modern restaurant and gift shop. ⊠ *9380 Hwy. 97, 12 km (7 mi) north of Vernon,* ☎ *250/542–7868.* ☞ *$5.50.* ⊙ *May 12–Oct. 15, daily 9–5.*

Dining and Lodging

$$–$$$$ ✕ **Craigellachie Dining Room.** The home-cooked meals in the dining room of the Putnam Station Hotel are filling rather than fancy. Soups and sandwiches are on the lunch menu, while old favorites like barbecue ribs, lasagna, pork chops, steaks, and pastas are offered in the evenings. The daily special is generally a good deal. ⊠ *Silver Star Mountain Resort, 22 km (14 mi) east of Vernon,* ☎ *250/542–2459. Reservations essential. AE, MC, V.*

$$ 🏨 **Delta Silver Star Club Resort.** Looking more like the set of a spaghetti
★ western than a modern hotel, the former Vance Creek Hotel has a prime location in the heart of the resort. Now owned by the Delta chain, it has expanded, adding a more luxurious, all-suite building. The rooms in the main hotel are simple, the suites a good deal fancier. ⊠ *Box 3003, Silver Star Mountain V1B 3M1,* ☎ *250/549–5191 or 800/ 610–0805,* FAX *250/549–5177. 84 rooms, 69 suites. Restaurant, bar, lobby lounge, kitchenettes, no-smoking rooms, refrigerators, hot tubs, bicycles, cross-country and downhill skiing, ski storage, coin laundry, meeting rooms. AE, D, MC, V. Closed mid-Apr.–mid-May.*

$$ 🏨 **Swiss Hotel Silver Lode Inn.** Owners Isidore and Heidi Borgeaud serve hearty helpings of real raclette or fondue in their cheerful Silver Lode Restaurant. The inn's no-frills rooms offering the basic comforts are the most reasonably priced in the village; some rooms have kitchenettes, fireplaces, and whirlpool baths. Packages including breakfast and dinner are also available. ⊠ *Box 3005, Silver Star Mountain V1B 3M1,* ☎ *250/549–5105 or 800/554–4881,* FAX *250/549–2163. 32 rooms. Restaurant, lobby lounge, hot tub, bicycles, ski storage, meeting room. AE, DC, MC, V.*

Outdoor Activities and Sports

GOLF

Predator Ridge Golf Resort (⊠ 360 Commonage Rd., ☎ 250/542–3436) is an 18-hole, par-73 course with lovely mountain scenery.

SKIING

Silver Star Mountain Resort (✉ Box 3003, Silver Star Mountain V1B 3M1, ☎ 250/542–0224 or 800/663–4431, FAX 250/542–1236), near Vernon, has eight lifts, a vertical drop of 2,500 ft, more than 80 runs, and well-lighted night downhill skiing. The resort also has 35 km (22 mi) of groomed, track-set cross-country trails, 4 km (2½ mi) of which are lighted for night skiing.

Kelowna

43 *46 km (29 mi) south of Vernon, 68 km (42 mi) north of Penticton.*

Kelowna is the largest town in the Okanagan Valley and the geographic center of the valley's wine industry. For information about winery tours, call the **B.C. Wine Information Centre** in Penticton (☎ 250/490–2006). **Calona Wines Ltd.** (✉ 1125 Richter St., ☎ 250/762–9144 or 800/663–5086) is British Columbia's oldest and largest wine maker. **Cedar Creek Estate Winery** (✉ 5445 Lakeshore Rd., off Hwy. 97, ☎ 250/764–8866 or 800/730–9463) is 12 km (7 mi) south of Kelowna; it's a smaller area winery. One of the area's more intimate wineries is **Gray Monk Estate Winery** (✉ 1055 Camp Rd., Okanagan Centre, ☎ 250/766–3168 or 800/663–4205), 6 km (4 mi) west of Winfield, off Highway 97.

Dining and Lodging

$$–$$$ ✕ **Agapi's Greek Taverna.** This contemporary-looking restaurant has a Greek menu that lists seafood, lamb, and, of course, standards such as spanakopita, dolma, hummus, and kebabs. The wine list includes a wide selection of imported and local wines. ✉ *375 Leon Ave.,* ☎ *250/763–0997. AE, DC, MC, V.*

$$$ 🏨 **Grand Okanagan.** On the shore of Okanagan Lake, this resort is a five-minute stroll from the shops, theaters, and restaurants of downtown Kelowna. The guest rooms in the high-rise tower have peach decor and views of the lake and surrounding mountains. Waterfront condo units have fully equipped kitchens. ✉ *1310 Water St., V1Y 9P3,* ☎ *250/763–4500 or 800/465–4651,* FAX *250/763–4565. 150 rooms, 55 suites. Restaurant, lounge, indoor-outdoor pool, exercise room, laundry service and dry cleaning, business services, convention center, meeting rooms. AE, DC, MC, V.*

$$–$$$ 🏨 **Lake Okanagan Resort.** The rooms of this self-contained resort on
   ★   the west side of Okanagan Lake have either kitchens or kitchenettes and range in size from one-room suites in the main hotel to spacious three-room chalets spread around the 300 acres. Large rooms, functional furnishings, wood-burning fireplaces, perfect views of the lake, and all the resort activities make this a good choice. ✉ *2751 Westside Rd., V1Z 3T1,* ☎ *250/769–3511 or 800/663–3273,* FAX *250/769–6665. 150 suites. Restaurant, café, no-smoking rooms, refrigerators, pool, hot tub, sauna, 9-hole golf course, 7 tennis courts, exercise room, beach, dock, bicycles, video games, children's programs (ages 6–12), playground, coin laundry, laundry service and dry cleaning, meeting rooms, helipad. AE, DC, MC, V.*

$$ 🏨 **Hotel Eldorado.** Rebuilt in the style of the 1926-vintage Eldorado Arms, which burned down in the early 1990s, the new Eldorado has much of the original's charm. Rooms tend to be small and cozy, with light carpets and floral patterns; many have balconies with views of Okanagan Lake. The dining room serves rack of lamb and seafood dishes. ✉ *500 Cook Rd., V1W 3G9,* ☎ *250/763–7500,* FAX *250/861–4779. 20 rooms. Restaurant, lounge, boating. AE, DC, MC, V.*

Outdoor Activities and Sports

CANOEING

For guided trips on some of the numerous waterways in the region, try **Okanagan Canoe Holidays** (✉ 2910 N. Glenmore Rd., V1V 2B6, ☎ FAX 250/762–8156).

GOLF

Gallaghers Canyon Golf and Country Club (✉ 4320 Gallaghers Rd. W, ☎ 250/861–4240) is an 18-hole, par-72 course. **Harvest Golf Club** (✉ 2725 KLO Rd., East Kelowna, ☎ 250/862–3103) has 18 holes and is a par-72 course.

HIKING

Hikers can try the rail bed of the **Kettle Valley Railway** network along Lake Okanagan between Penticton and Kelowna. The Visitors Bureau for Kelowna (☎ 250/861–1515) can provide maps and information.

SKIING

Cross-Country. Postill Lake Lodge (✉ Postill Lake Rd., Box 854, V1Y 7P5, ☎ 250/860–1655) has 50 km (31 mi) of excellent trails northeast of Kelowna.

Downhill. Big White Ski Resort (✉ Box 2039, Station R, V1X 4K5, ☎ 250/765–3101 or 800/663–2772, FAX 250/765–8200) has nine lifts and more than 100 runs on about 2,075 acres of skiable terrain and is expanding rapidly. Night skiing is available five nights a week.

Shopping

At **Geert Maas Sculpture Gardens, Gallery, and Studio** (✉ 250 Reynolds Rd., ☎ 250/860–7012), in the hills above Kelowna, world-class sculptor Geert Maas exhibits his distinctive bronze, stainless steel, stoneware, and mixed-media semi-abstract figures. The **Okanagan Pottery Studio** (☎ 250/767–2010), on Highway 97 in Peachland, south of Kelowna, sells handcrafted ceramics.

Penticton

44 *395 km (245 mi) east of Vancouver.*

Although Penticton's winter population is about 25,000, its summer population nears 130,000. Sixteen kilometers (10 mi) north of town, you can ride the historic **Kettle Valley Steam Railway** (✉ 10112 S. Victoria Rd., Summerland, ☎ 250/494–8422), which passes through 10 km (6 mi) of orchards, vineyards, and mountain terrain along the 1915 line that opened up the interior of British Columbia by connecting Vancouver with the Kootenays. There are no rides in December or January.

West of Penticton is British Columbia's **Kootenay Country,** named for one of the mountain ranges that fill it. Nelson is an attractive mountain town with arts and crafts shops and bed-and-breakfasts.

Dining and Lodging

$$$–$$$$ ✕ **Granny Bogner's.** The theme is determinedly homey—flowing lace
★ curtains, Oriental rugs, wood chairs, cloth-covered tables, and waitresses in long skirts—and the food at this mostly Continental restaurant is excellent. The poached halibut and roasted duck have contributed to the widely held belief that this is the best restaurant in the Okanagan. ✉ *302 Eckhardt Ave. W, ☎ 250/493–2711. Reservations essential. AE, MC, V. Closed Sun.–Mon. and Jan. No lunch.*

$$–$$$ ⊞ **Penticton Lakeside Resort and Conference Center.** On the shore of Okanagan Lake, this resort is a peaceful retreat, although it's right in the center of the action. Vancouver businesspeople love this place for its comfort and conference facilities. The rooms are bright and airy,

and half of them have lake views; some have whirlpool baths. ✉ *21 Lakeshore Dr. W, V2A 7M5,* ☎ *250/493–8221 or 800/663–9400,* FAX *250/493–0607. 204 rooms. Restaurant, bar, outdoor café, in-room modem lines, no-smoking floor, room service, indoor pool, beauty salon, hot tub, massage, sauna, 2 tennis courts, aerobics, health club, volleyball, beach, dock, bicycles, recreation room, baby-sitting, children's programs (ages 5–12), dry cleaning, concierge, business services, convention center, meeting rooms. AE, D, DC, MC, V.*

$ ▦ **Riordan House.** John and Donna Ortiz didn't expect to give guided tours of their newly spiffed-up 1921 house. But people seemed to like the place, built by a Prohibition rum-runner and furnished now with family antiques, so the Ortizes opened it as a bed-and-breakfast. One bedroom has a fireplace and one a sitting area; all are no-smoking and look out on the surrounding hills. The Continental breakfast stars home-baked croissants, scones, muffins, and a selection of seasonal fruit; box lunches are packed on request. ✉ *689 Winnipeg St., V2A 5N1,* ☎ FAX *250/493–5997. 3 rooms share 3 baths. Breakfast room, in-room VCRs, bicycles, airport shuttle. AE, DC, MC, V.*

Outdoor Activities and Sports

For downhill skiing, **Apex Resort** (✉ Fairview Rd., Box 1060, V2A 7N7, ☎ 250/492–2880 or 800/387–2739, FAX 250/292–8622) has 56 trails, two chairlifts, a vertical drop of 2,000 ft, and a peak elevation of 7,187 ft.

Red Mountain Resorts (✉ Box 670, Rossland V0G 1Y0, ☎ 250/362–7384 or 800/663–0105), which spans two mountains and three mountain faces in Kootenay Country, has 83 marked runs, five lifts, and a vertical drop of 2,900 ft. In Kootenay Country, **Whitewater** (✉ Box 60, Nelson V1L 5P7, ☎ 800/666–9420, or 250/354–4944), has 38 runs, three lifts, a 1,300-ft drop, and plenty of powder skiing.

Cathedral Provincial Park

75 km (47 mi) southwest of Penticton, 356 km (221 mi) east of Vancouver.

Off Highway 3 along the U.S. border, Cathedral Provincial Park (☎ 250/494–6500) preserves 82,000 acres of lakes and rolling meadows, teeming with mule deer, mountain goats, and bighorn sheep. To reach the main part of the park, visitors either take the steep eight-hour hike or arrange (and pay in advance) for **Cathedral Lakes Lodge** (☎ 250/226–7560 or 888/255–4453) to transport them by four-wheel-drive vehicle. There are a number of rough, hike-in camping spaces in the park. Dogs are not permitted in the park, which is open mid-June–early October.

COAST MOUNTAIN CIRCLE

Some of British Columbia's most dramatic scenery is within a day's drive of Vancouver, on Highways 1 and 99. Truckers and anyone else in a hurry usually take Highway 5, the Coquihalla toll highway, to the High Country, leaving the back roads through the Coast Mountains for those with time to explore. A stunning sampler of mainland British Columbia, a drive into the Coast Mountains follows the Sea to Sky Highway (Highway 99) past fjordlike Howe Sound and the international resort of Whistler and then continues on a quiet back road to the gold-rush town of Lillooet. From Lillooet, it's possible to continue into the High Country or return to Vancouver through the gorges of the Fraser Canyon, stopping for a soak at the spa town of Harrison Hot Springs on the way. This is a scenic two- to three-day drive; the roads are good but are best avoided in snow past Whistler. A BC Rail line also cuts a dramatic swath through the mountains from North Vancouver to Lillooet, on its way north to Prince George.

Sea to Sky Highway

120 km (74 mi) between Vancouver and Whistler.

Most people driving north from Vancouver on the Sea to Sky Highway (Highway 99) are eager to reach the resort town of Whistler (☞ Side Trip from Vancouver *in* Chapter 2), two hours north of Vancouver. A number of sights are worth a stop, though. Past Whistler, Highway 99 is much less traveled as it makes its way way past lakes and glaciers, through the Mount Currie native reserve, and over the mountains to Lillooet. On the way to Whistler is **Porteau Cove Marine Provincial Park** (✉ Hwy. 99, ☎ 250/387–5002), where sunken wrecks attract scuba divers.

At the **B.C. Museum of Mining,** once the largest copper mine in the British Empire and now a national historic site, knowledgeable staff offer guided tours of old mine workings, including a chance to pan for gold. ✉ *Hwy. 99, about 1 hr north of Vancouver, Britannia Beach,* ☎ *604/896–2233 or 604/ 688–8735 (toll free from Vancouver).* ✍ *$9.50.* ☉ *May–Oct., daily from 10; tours on the ½ hr; last tour at 4:30. Nov. and Feb.–Apr., prebooked group tours only.*

Just south of the town of Squamish is **Shannon Falls,** which at 1,105 ft is Canada's third-highest waterfall. It's well marked on the highway. Between Squamish and Whistler is the 231-ft-high **Brandywine Falls,** well signposted and reached from the highway.

Lillooet

131 km (81 mi) northeast of Whistler.

The arid gullies and Wild West landscape around Lillooet may come as a surprise after the greenery of the coast and mountains. During the 1850s and 1860s this was Mile Zero of the Cariboo Wagon Road, which took prospectors to the gold fields. From here, travelers can return to Vancouver through the Fraser Canyon (☞ *below*) via Highways 12 and 1, or continue on the 99 to the High Country. There are several motels in Lillooet and a BC Rail station. The **Lillooet Museum** (☎ 250/ 256–4308) presents native and gold-rush history.

Fraser Canyon

Highway 1, the Trans-Canada Highway, follows the Fraser River as it cuts its way from the High Country through the Coast Mountains to Vancouver. The deepest, and most dramatic, cut is the 38-km (24-mi) gorge between Yale and Boston Bar, where the road and rail line cling to the hillside high above the water.

At **Hell's Gate,** about 40 km (23 mi) south of Lytton, a glimpse through the mists above the roiling Fraser River hints at how the region got its name. An airtram (cable car) carries passengers across the foaming canyon above the fishways, where millions of sockeye salmon fight their way upriver to spawning grounds four times a year—April, July, August, and October. The lower airtram terminal has displays on the life cycle of the salmon, a fudge factory, a gift shop, and a restaurant. This site is about 2½ hours east of Vancouver. ✉ *Hell's Gate Airtram, Exit 170 off Hwy. 1, Hope,* ☎ *604/867–9277.* ✍ *$9.50.* ☉ *Mid-Apr.–mid-Oct., daily 9 AM; closing time between 4 and 6, depending on season.*

Harrison Hot Springs

⑤ *128 km (79 mi) northeast of Vancouver.*

The small resort community of Harrison Hot Springs lies at the southern tip of picturesque Harrison Lake, off Highway 7 in the Fraser Valley. Ever since fur traders and gold miners discovered the soothing hot springs in the late 1800s, Harrison has been a favored stopover spot. Mountains surround the 64-km-long (40-mi-long) lake, which is ringed by pretty beaches. The lake provides a broad range of outdoor activities in addition to the hot springs.

The **Harrison Hot Springs Hotel** (☞ Dining and Lodging, *below*), across from the beach, has a spring-fed public pool. ⊠ *100 Esplanade,* ☎ *604/796–2244.* ⊠ *$7.50.* ☉ *Sun.–Thurs. 8 AM–9 PM, Fri.–Sat. 8 AM–10 PM.*

★ ☾ A tour of **Kilby Historic Store and Farm,** a fine slice of living history in nearby Harrison Mills, is a visit back in time to the British Columbia of the 1920s. You can tour the general store and farm buildings of T. Kilby and other pioneers of the area; chat with the shopkeeper; and tramp through the orchards, stockroom, fueling station, barn, and dairy house on the grounds. There is 1920s-style home cooking in the **Harrison River Tearoom**. ⊠ *215 Kilby Rd. (1½ km, or 1 mi, off Hwy. 7 on north shore of Fraser River; follow signs), Harrison Mills,* ☎ *604/796–9576.* ⊠ *$5.* ☉ *Daily 10–5.*

Dining and Lodging

$$$ ✕ **Black Forest.** Ask the locals where to dine and they'll send you here, to a charming Bavarian dining room on Harrison Village Esplanade, overlooking the lake. It comes as no surprise that the specialties are German standards, from schnitzels to Black Forest cake, with a few Continental dishes (mainly steaks and seafood) for good measure. Hearty German beer and an array of wines round out the selection. ⊠ *180 Esplanade,* ☎ *604/796–9343. AE, MC, V. No lunch Oct.–Apr.*

$$–$$$ ⊞ **Harrison Hot Springs Hotel.** Built beside the lake in the 1920s, the hotel has grown over the decades. The most reasonably priced rooms, in the original building and the west tower, have an old English look, with Edwardian furnishings; those in the east tower are more modern and plush. Amenities include hot spring–fed pools. ⊠ *100 Esplanade, V0M 1K0,* ☎ *604/796–2244 or 800/663–2266,* ℻ *604/796–3682. 290 rooms, 16 cottages. 2 restaurants, lounge, no-smoking floors, room service, 3 outdoor and 1 indoor pools, 9-hole golf course, 2 tennis courts, exercise room, massage, hiking, bicycles, playground, laundry service, business services, meeting rooms. AE, MC, V.*

Rosedale

⑥ *8 km (5 mi) southwest of Harrison Hot Springs, 120 km (74 mi) east of Vancouver.*

The attractions in Rosedale are a beautiful garden and a water park. The well-signed **Minter Gardens** is a 27-acre compound with 11 beautifully presented theme gardens—Chinese, rose, English, fern, fragrance, and more—along with aviaries and ponds. There are playgrounds and a giant evergreen maze. ⊠ *Exit 135 off Hwy. 1, 52892 Bunker Rd.,* ☎ *604/794–7191; 888/646–8377 in Canada.* ⊠ *$9.50.* ☉ *Apr.–Oct., daily 9–dusk.*

BRITISH COLUMBIA A TO Z

Arriving and Departing

By Boat
For information, *see* Victoria A to Z, *above.*

By Bus
Greyhound (☎ 604/482–8747; 800/661–8747 in Canada; 800/231–2222 in the U.S.) connects destinations throughout British Columbia with cities and towns all along the Pacific North Coast.

By Car
Driving time from Seattle to Vancouver is about three hours by I–5 and Highway 99. From other Canadian regions, three main routes lead into British Columbia: through Sparwood, in the south, Highway 3; from Jasper and Banff, in the central region, Highways 1 and 5; and through Dawson Creek, in the north, Highways 2 and 97.

By Plane
British Columbia is served by Victoria International Airport (☞ Victoria A to Z, *above*) and Vancouver International Airport (☞ Vancouver A to Z *in* Chapter 2). There are domestic airports in most cities. **Air Canada** and **Canadian Airlines International** (☞ Air Travel *in* the Gold Guide) are the two dominant carriers. **Kenmore Air** (☎ 425/486–1257 or 800/543–9595) offers direct daily flights from Seattle to Victoria, Nanaimo, Campbell River, Port Hardy, and other northeast Vancouver Island stops.

Getting Around

By Bus
MAINLAND
Greyhound Lines of Canada (☎ 604/482–8747; 800/661–8747 in Canada) serves most towns on the mainland. **Maverick Coach Lines** (☎ 604/662–8051) serves Whistler from Vancouver.

VICTORIA AND VANCOUVER ISLAND
Island Coach Lines (☎ 250/385–4411) serves most towns on Vancouver Island. **Maverick Coach Lines** (☎ 604/662–8051) serves Nanaimo from Vancouver. **Pacific Coach Lines** (☎ 250/385–4411 in Victoria; 604/662–8074 in Vancouver; 800/661–1725 elsewhere) operates daily connecting service between Victoria and Vancouver on BC Ferries.

By Car
Major roads in British Columbia, and most secondary roads, are paved and well engineered, though snow tires and chains are needed for winter travel. B.C Highways (☎ 604/660–9770) has 24-hour highway reports. There are no roads on the mainland coast once you leave the populated areas of the southwest corner near Vancouver.

GULF ISLANDS
The roads on the islands are narrow and winding. Exercise extreme caution around the many cyclists, especially in summer.

MAINLAND
Highway 99, also known as the Sea to Sky Highway, connects Vancouver to Whistler and continues to Lillooet in the interior. The **Trans-Canada Highway** (Highway 1) connects Vancouver with Kamloops and points east via the Fraser Canyon. The **Coquihalla Highway** (Highway 5), a toll road ($10 for cars and vans), linking Hope and Kamloops, is the fastest route to the interior.

Highway 14 connects Sooke to Port Renfrew, on the west coast of Vancouver Island, with Victoria. **Highway 19** extends from Nanaimo to Port Hardy at the island's northern tip. **Highway 17** connects the Swartz Bay ferry terminal on the Saanich Peninsula with downtown Victoria. The **Trans-Canada Highway** (Highway 1) runs south from Nanaimo to Victoria.

By Ferry

BC Ferries (☎ 250/386–3431 in Victoria or outside B.C.; 888/223–3779 from elsewhere in B.C.) provides frequent, year-round passenger and vehicle service between Vancouver and Vancouver Island: from Tsawwassen (about an hour south of Vancouver) to Swartz Bay (30 minutes by car north of Victoria); Tsawwassen to Duke Point, south of Nanaimo; and Horseshoe Bay (a 30-minute drive north of Vancouver) to Departure Bay, near Nanaimo. Vehicle reservations (☎ 604/444–2890 from outside B.C.; 888/724–5223 in B.C.) can be made on any of these routes for an extra $15. BC Ferries also connects Courtenay, north of Nanaimo, to Powell River on the mainland, with boarding on a first-come, first-served basis.

GULF ISLANDS

BC Ferries provides service to Galiano, Mayne, Pender, Saturna, and Salt Spring Islands from Tsawwassen (reservations required; ☎ 888/223–3779) and from Swartz Bay (reservations not accepted). Northern Gulf Islands, including Gabriola, Hornby, and Quadra, can be reached from Nanaimo, Comox, and Campbell River, respectively.

THE INSIDE PASSAGE

BC Ferries sails along the Inside Passage from Port Hardy to Prince Rupert and from Port Hardy to Bella Coola (summer only). Vehicle reservations (☎ 888/223–3779) are required.

QUEEN CHARLOTTE ISLANDS

The *Queen of Prince Rupert* (☎ 250/386–3431 in Victoria; 888/223–3779 elsewhere in B.C.), a BC Ferries ship, sails six times a week between late May and September (three times a week the rest of the year) and can easily accommodate recreational vehicles. The crossing from Prince Rupert to Skidegate, near Queen Charlotte on Graham Island, takes about eight hours. Schedules vary and reservations are required. The **M.V.** *Kwuna,* another BC Ferries ship, connects Skidegate Landing to Alliford Bay on Moresby Island. Access to smaller islands is by boat or air; plans should be made in advance through a travel agent.

By Plane

Air B.C. and Canadian Airlines serve towns around the province (☞ Air Travel *in* the Gold Guide for phone numbers). **North Vancouver Air** (☎ 604/278–1608 or 800/228–6608) serves Nanaimo, Tofino, Victoria, Port Alberni, Nelson, and Creston.

GULF ISLANDS

Harbour Air Ltd. (☎ 604/688–1277 in Vancouver; 250/385–2230 in Victoria; 800/665–0212 from elsewhere) provides regular service from Victoria, Nanaimo, and Vancouver to Salt Spring, Thetis, Mayne, Saturna, and South Pender islands. **Pacific Spirit Air** (☎ FAX 250/537–9359; ☎ 800/665–2359 in British Columbia) provides several regularly scheduled 20- to 30-minute daily floatplane flights from Coal Harbour in downtown Vancouver and the Vancouver Airport to Ganges on Salt Spring Island.

QUEEN CHARLOTTE ISLANDS

Harbour Air Ltd. (☎ 250/627–1341) runs scheduled floatplanes between Sandspit, Masset, Queen Charlotte City, and Prince Rupert daily except December 25–26 and January 1.

By Train

MAINLAND

BC Rail (☎ 604/984–5500 or 800/663–8238) travels from Vancouver to Prince George, a route of 747 km (463 mi), and offers daily service to Whistler. **Via Rail** (☎ 800/561–8630 in Canada; 800/561–3949 in the U.S.) provides service between Prince Rupert and Prince George; between Vancouver and Jasper; and between Prince Rupert and Jasper.

VANCOUVER ISLAND

Esquimalt & Nanaimo Rail Liner (✉ 450 Pandora Ave., Victoria V8W 3L5, ☎ 800/561–8630 in Canada; 800/561–3949 in the U.S.), operated by Via Rail, runs a small-gauge rail line from Victoria's Pandora Street Station to Courtenay, with stops that include Duncan, Chemainus, and Nanaimo. Schedules vary seasonally.

Contacts and Resources

B&B and Lodging Reservation Agencies

Reservations for lodging anywhere in the province can be made through **Super, Natural British Columbia**'s reservation service (☎ 800/663–6000). Between March and October, the provincial government runs a toll-free **Campground Reservation Line** (☎ 800/689–9025).

Garden City B&B Reservation Service (✉ 660 Jones Terr., Victoria V8Z 2L7, ☎ 250/479–1986, FAX 250/479–9999) can book bed-and-breakfast accommodations throughout Vancouver Island. The **Gourmet Trail** books packages at five of the province's finest inns (☞ Guided Tours, *below*). **Gulf Islands B&B Reservation Service** (☎ 888/539–2930) can book about 100 Gulf Island B&Bs.

Car Rentals

Most major agencies, including Avis, Budget, Enterprise, and Hertz, serve cities throughout the province (☞ Car Rentals *in* the Gold Guide). Car rentals are available on Salt Spring Island through **Heritage Rentals** (☎ 250/537–4225, FAX 250/537–4226).

Emergencies

Ambulance, fire, poison control, police (☎ 911). A few outlying areas do not have 911 service. If you don't get immediate response, dial **0**.

Guided Tours

Town listings also have information about cruises, outfitters, and tour operators, including whale-watching tours.

CRUISES

Bluewater Adventures (☎ 604/980–3800, FAX 604/980–1800) has multiday natural history sailboat cruises to the Queen Charlotte Islands, Vancouver Island, and Desolation Sound. **Inside Passage Cruises Inc.** (☎ 604/683–2174 or 888/357–7111, FAX 604/688–6972) runs three- and four-day natural history–oriented Inside Passage, Queen Charlotte, and Gulf Island cruises aboard the 70-passenger *Pacific Aurora*.

ECOLOGICAL

The **Canadian Outback Adventure Company** (✉ 100–657 Marine Dr., West Vancouver V7T 1A4, ☎ 604/921–7250 or 800/565–8735) and **Ecosummer Expeditions** (✉ 1516 Duranleau St., Vancouver V6H 3S4, ☎ 604/669–7741 or 800/465–8884, FAX 604/669–3244) run ecological tours of Johnstone Strait and of the Queen Charlotte and Gulf Islands.

FIRST NATIONS

The history and culture of the First Nations (native) people of the region are the focus of summer tours run by **Lheidl T'enneh Nation El-**

ders **Salmon Camp Tours** (✉ Lheidl T'enneh Native Heritage Society, R.R. 1, Site 27, Compartment 60, Prince George V2N 2H8, ☎ 250/963–8451, FAX 250/963–6954). At **High Bar Tepee Village** (☎ 800/253–8831), guests can stay at a tepee camp overlooking the Fraser Canyon and try traditional meals.

The **Canadian Outback Adventure Company** (☞ Ecological Tours, *above*) and **Queen Charlotte Adventures** (✉ Box 196, Queen Charlotte V0T 1S0, ☎ 250/559–8990 or 800/668–4288, FAX 250/559–8983) have unique summer tours of the abandoned Haida villages of the Queen Charlotte Islands.

FOOD AND WINE

The **Gourmet Trail** (✉ 304–1913 Sooke Rd., Victoria V9B 1V9, ☎ 800/970–7722) offers self-drive and all-inclusive escorted tours linking five places famous for their cuisine (the Empress in Victoria; the Aerie, Sooke Harbour House, and the Wickaninnish Inn on Vancouver Island; and Hastings House on Salt Spring Island), with visits to wineries, farms, and artisans' studios along the way.

ORIENTATION

Classic Holidays Tour & Travel (✉ 102–75 W. Broadway, Vancouver V5Y 1P1, ☎ 604/875–6377) has tours around the province. **Gray Line of Vancouver** (✉ 255 East 1st Ave., Vancouver V5T 1A7, ☎ 604/879–3363 or 800/667–0882) has tours from Vancouver to Victoria, to Whistler, and to Banff in the Rockies.

Hospitals

British Columbia has hospitals in many towns: **Kelowna General Hospital** (✉ 2268 Pandosy St., ☎ 250/862–4000); on the Gulf Islands, **Lady Minto Hospital** (☎ 250/537–5545) in Ganges on Salt Spring Island; **Prince George Regional Hospital** (✉ 2000 15th Ave., ☎ 250/565–2000; 250/565–2444 emergencies); in Kamloops, **Royal Inland Hospital** (✉ 311 Columbia St., ☎ 250/374–5111).

Outdoor Activities and Sports

For whale-watching operators, *see* the listings under individual towns.

CANOEING

Mt. Robson Adventure Holidays (✉ Box 687, Valemount V0E 2Z0, ☎ 250/566–4386 or 800/882–9921, FAX 250/566–4351) arranges canoe trips at the northern end of the High Country near Mt. Robson Provincial Park.

FISHING

A saltwater-fishing license for one day costs $3.75 for both Canadian residents and non-Canadians and is available at virtually every fishing lodge and sporting-goods outlet along the coast. Annual licenses are about $11 for non–British Columbia Canadians and $38 for non-Canadians. For updated fishing information and regulations, contact the **B.C. Fish Branch** (✉ Ministry of Environment, Parliament Buildings, Victoria V8V 1X4, ☎ 250/387–9688). For a guide to saltwater fishing, contact the **Department of Fisheries and Oceans** (✉ Recreational Fisheries Division, 555 W. Hastings St., Vancouver V6B 5G3, ☎ 604/666–3545).

GOLF

Greens fees are about $25–$50 in the province.

HIKING

B.C. Parks (✉ 800 Johnson St., 2nd floor, Victoria V8V 1X4, ☎ 250/387–5002) offers detailed information. For heli-hiking, **Highland Helicopter** (✉ 1685 Tranmer, Agassiz V0M 1K0, ☎ 604/796–9610), **Mt.**

Robson Adventure Holidays (☞ Canoeing, *above*), and **Peak Experiences** (✉ 29 Oersted St., Kitimat V8C 1J6, ☎ 250/632–7512, ⅀ 250/632–2248) can provide further information.

KAYAKING

Ecosummer Expeditions (☞ Guided Tours, *above*), **Gabriola Cycle and Kayak Tours** (☎ 250/247–8277), and **Wild Heart Adventure Tours** (☎ 250/722–3683, ⅀ 250/722–2175) run multiday paddles among the province's inlets and islands.

MULTIACTIVITY

Fresh Tracks (✉ 1823 West 4th Ave., Vancouver V6J 1M4, ☎ 604/737–8743 or 800/667–4744) has 55 different outdoor adventure trips, including hiking, kayaking, river rafting, and sailing adventures, all over the province and Canada. **Wild West Adventures** (☎ 604/688–2008, ⅀ 604/688–8030) offers camping trips in the Rocky Mountains.

RAFTING

The following companies provide options from lazy half-day floats to exhilarating white-water journeys of up to a week: **Alpine Rafting Company** (✉ Box 1272, Golden V0A 1H0, ☎ 250/344–6778 or 888/599–5299, ⅀ 250/344–7102), **Canadian Outback Adventure Company** (☞ Guided Tours, *above*), **Canadian River Expeditions** (✉ Box 1023, Whistler V0N 1B0, ☎ 604/938–6651; 800/898–7238 in Canada), **Fraser River Raft Expeditions Ltd.** (✉ Box 10, Yale V0K 2S0, ☎ 604/863–2336 or 800/363–7238, ⅀ 604/863–2355), **Hyak Wilderness Adventures** (✉ 204B–1975, Maple St., Vancouver V6J 3S9, ☎ 604/734–8622 or 800/663–7238, ⅀ 604/734–5718), and **Suskwa Adventure Outfitters** (✉ Box 3262, Smithers V0J 2N0, ☎ ⅀ 250/847–2885).

SKIING

The **Canada West Ski Areas Association** (✉ 810 Waddington Dr., Suite 102, Vernon V1T 8T3, ☎ 250/542–9020, ⅀ 250/542–5070) has information about the top heli- and Sno-cat ski operators in British Columbia.

Visitor Information

For information concerning the province, contact **Tourism B.C.** (✉ 802–865 Hornby St., Vancouver V6Z 2G3, ☎ 604/660–2861 or 800/663–6000). More than 140 communities have **Travel Infocentres.**

The principal regional tourist offices are: **Cariboo Tourism Association** (✉ 266 Oliver St., Williams Lake V2G 1M1, ☎ 250/392–2226 or 800/663–5885, ⅀ 250/392–2838); **Northern British Columbia Tourism Association** (✉ 3167 Tatlow Rd., Box 1030, Smithers V0J 2N0, ☎ 250/847–5227 or 800/663–8843, ⅀ 250/847–4321), for information on the Queen Charlotte Islands and northern British Columbia; **Peace River Alaska Highway Tourist Association** (✉ 10631 100th St., Box 6850, Fort St. John V1J 4J3, ☎ 250/785–2544, ⅀ 250/785–4424); **Thompson Okanagan Tourism Association** (✉ 1332 Water St., Kelowna V1Y 9P4, ☎ 250/860–5999 or 800/567–2275, ⅀ 250/860–9993); **Tourism Rockies** (✉ 1905 Warren Ave., Box 10, Kimberley V1A 2Y5, ☎ 250/427–4838, ⅀ 250/427–3344); **Tourism Vancouver Island** (✉ 302–45 Bastion Sq., Victoria V8W 1J1, ☎ 250/382–3551, ⅀ 250/382–3523), for information on Vancouver Island, the Gulf Islands, and the midcoast; and **Vancouver, Coast and Mountains Tourism Association** (✉ 204–1755 W. Broadway, Vancouver V6J 4S5, ☎ 604/739–9011 or 800/667–3306, ⅀ 604/739–0153).

Galiano Island Visitor Information Centre (✉ Box 73, Galiano V0N 1P0, ☎ ⅀ 250/539–2233), **Mayne Island Chamber of Commerce** (✉ General Delivery, Mayne Island V0N 2J0, ☎ no phone), and **Salt**

Spring Island Visitor Information Centre (✉ 121 Lower Ganges Rd., Ganges V8K 2T1, ☎ 250/537–5252, FAX 250/537–4276) provide information on the Gulf Islands. The **Prince Rupert Convention and Visitors Bureau** (✉ 100 1st Ave. W, Box 669, Prince Rupert V8J 3S1, ☎ 250/624–5637 or 800/667–1994, FAX 250/627–8009) has information about that town. For information on the Queen Charlotte Islands, contact the **Queen Charlotte Visitor Information Centre** (✉ Box 819, Queen Charlotte V0T 1S0, ☎ 250/559–8316) in Queen Charlotte. For information and accommodation reservations for towns serving Pacific Rim National Park, contact the **Tofino Chamber of Commerce** (✉ Box 249, V0R 2Z0, ☎ 250/725–3414) or the **Ucluelet Chamber of Commerce** (✉ 227 Main St., Box 428, V0R 3A0, ☎ 250/726–4641). For information about Prince George, contact **Tourism Prince George** (✉ 1198 Victoria St. V2L 2L2, ☎ 250/562–3700 or 800/668–7646, FAX 250/563–3584).

4 The Canadian Rockies

The ranges that form the rugged
Canadian Rockies arch north-northwest
for more than 1,000 mi from the U.S.
border in the south to the Yukon in the
north. The majestic beauty of the
Rockies has been preserved in provincial
and national parks that hold some of
the most spectacular drives in the
world. In these mountains you can
also fish, ski, hike, climb, boat, ride,
and stay at some of the best resort
facilities anywhere.

Updated by
Don Thacker

COMPARING MOUNTAINS IS A SUBJECT and imprecise business. Yet few would argue that the 640-km (400-mi) stretch of the Canadian Rockies that marks part of the Alberta–British Columbia border easily ranks as one of the most extravagantly beautiful ranges on earth. Approaching the mountains from the east, you are struck by the wall of rock on the western horizon, made more dramatic by the white snowfields that cling to the upper slopes until well into the summer. First visible from about 100 km (about 60 mi) away, the mountains become progressively more imposing with each passing mile. Near the south end of the range (Waterton Lakes National Park), the view is particularly dramatic as gently rolling prairie butts up abruptly against the edge of the mountains. Farther north, in Banff and Jasper national parks, tree-covered foothills roll out of the mountains.

It is obvious how the Rockies got their name. Wildly folded sedimentary and metamorphic rocks have been thrust up to form ragged peaks and high cliffs; you can't help but be awed by the forces of nature that operated here. Add glaciers and snowfields to the high peaks, carpet the valleys with forests, mix in a generous helping of large mammals, wildflowers, rivers, and lakes, and you've got the recipe for the Canadian Rockies.

The peaks of the Rockies are aligned in long, closely spaced ranges that run in approximately a north–south direction. From east to west these can be grouped into the foothills, front ranges, main ranges, and a small area of west ranges. Apart from forming distinct sets of mountains, these groupings differ somewhat in geology and age—which increases from 40 to 50 million years in the foothills to 110 to 120 million years in the western ranges. The main ranges have the highest peaks.

The Columbia Mountains, a series of parallel ranges just west of the Rockies, are often grouped with the Rockies. Many recreational activities that are prohibited in the national parks of the Rockies (notably helicopter-assisted skiing and heli-hiking) are allowed in the Columbias. The Columbias were formed about 180 million years ago and consist of four subranges: the Cariboos to the north and, farther south, the Purcells, Selkirks, and Monashees (from east to west).

Recognizing early the region's exceptional natural beauty, the Canadian government began shielding the area from human development and resource exploitation in the 1880s. In 1885, the government created a park preserve around the Cave and Basin Hot Springs in Banff. Two years later, Canada's first national park, Rocky Mountain Park (later Banff National Park), was officially established. Lands that would later become Yoho National Park and Glacier National Park in the Columbias were set aside in 1886.

Today, about 25,000 square km (roughly 10,000 square mi)—an area larger than the state of New Hampshire—are protected in seven national parks in the Rockies and the Columbias. The parks of the Rockies—Waterton Lakes, Banff, Kootenay, Yoho, and Jasper—have large areas that remain untouched by human development. The only significant clusters of human settlement are in the town centers of Banff, Jasper, and Waterton Park, and the area around Lake Louise. Several thousand more square miles are also protected as wilderness areas and provincial parks, most notably Mt. Robson and Mt. Assiniboine provincial parks and Kananaskis Country.

Most of the facilities and roads of the Rockies are concentrated in the valleys, where the elevations are 3,000 to 4,500 ft, only about 1,000 ft higher than in the major prairie cities to the east. Consequently, temperatures in the mountain towns are rather similar to those in Calgary and Edmonton. The mountains themselves rise to elevations above 10,000 ft, and the alpine areas (above tree line) may be whitened by snowfalls even in midsummer. The Icefields Parkway runs down the heart of the Rockies for 230 km (143 mi) from Jasper to Lake Louise. While all roads in the Rockies offer stunning scenery, the Icefields Parkway, with more than 100 glaciers along the way, is without doubt the most impressive. Even if you're on a tight schedule, make a point of driving at least part of it.

Pleasures and Pastimes

Dining

Eating out is, for the most part, a casual affair. Given the mix of travelers to the region—families, active outdoorspeople, nature lovers, and sightseers—the emphasis is on good food served in large quantities, at slightly inflated prices. This is not the place for the traveler who expects haute service and cuisine, although the region has a number of top-caliber restaurants. People who like fresh game and fish will not be disappointed—trout, venison, elk, moose, quail, and other game appear on the menus of even modest establishments. Although Continental and American-style cuisine dominate, ethnic restaurants are becoming more popular. Japanese restaurants are the latest trend.

CATEGORY	COST*
$$$$	over $35
$$$	$25–$35
$$	$15–$25
$	under $15

*per person, in Canadian dollars, excluding drinks, service, and sales tax (7% in Alberta, 14% in British Columbia)

Lodging

The hotels, inns, and lodges of the Canadian Rockies compose an eclectic list, ranging from rustic, backcountry lodges without electricity or running water to numerous standard roadside motels to hotels of supreme luxury. With just a few exceptions (ski resorts being the main one) they share one common trait—room rates that are considerably higher in summer than during the rest of the year. The week between Christmas and New Year's often commands a higher rate as well. For this reason, flexibility in travel planning can mean considerable savings—a room that goes for $150 a night in summer may well drop to $75 from mid-October through May.

Lodgings are categorized according to their peak-season rates. Low-season discounts are noted within each listing, where applicable. High-season rates generally run from mid-June to late September. Several weeks before and after these dates are considered the shoulder season, with rates a bit lower than in peak season. Check in advance for off-season rates—the period considered peak season has been getting longer.

Bed-and-breakfast accommodations are plentiful around the parks, but most are simply ordinary rooms in small, ordinary homes. The main attractions are price and the fact that you can often find a B&B with a room available if you arrive in town without a reservation.

Most cabin-style accommodations are not insulated (though they have gas heat) and are open almost exclusively in peak season, along with perhaps a brief shoulder season of a few weeks at each end of peak season.

Backcountry lodges have been an integral part of Canadian Rockies travel since the '20s. They vary considerably in terms of accommodations and accessibility. At the luxurious end are lodges with private rooms, private baths, full electricity, telephones, and restaurant-style dining; at the rugged extreme are lodges with bunk beds, kerosene lamps for evening light, and outhouses. A few are accessible by car in summer; some can be reached only by hiking or skiing or by helicopter. Note that most backcountry lodges are priced on a per-person basis (the price generally includes meals) rather than the double-room rate used for more standard accommodations. Rating classes for these are based on a single-person rate.

Guest ranches, mainly in the ranching area just east of Kananaskis Country, are another alternative accommodation. These provide comfortable lodging with a definite ranching theme; horseback riding and pack trips are standard visitor activities.

Of the more than 40 public campgrounds within the national parks (not including backcountry sites for backpackers and climbers), most operate on a first-come, first-served basis, though some allow reservations. The season generally runs from mid-May through October, although some campgrounds remain open year-round. Hookups are available at most of the 40 national park campgrounds and at 4 of the 30 Kananaskis Country campgrounds. Prices for a one-night stay are $18–$22 at hookup sites, $13–$16 at sites without hookups, and $10 at sites with pit toilets only. Numerous privately run campgrounds, which usually take reservations, can be found outside park boundaries.

CATEGORY	COST*
$$$$	over $200
$$$	$150–$200
$$	$100–$150
$	under $100

All prices are for a standard double room (or an equivalent, where not applicable), excluding 7% GST and a 5% room tax in Alberta, 8% room tax in British Columbia, in Canadian dollars.

Outdoor Activities and Sports
See individual towns or Contacts and Resources *in* Canadian Rockies A to Z, *below,* for addresses and telephone numbers.

BIKING
Biking is a popular pastime in the Rockies, whether for a short spin around town or on a multiday guided tour. Around Banff, the Vermilion Lakes loop and the more strenuous loop over Tunnel Mountain are popular half-day bike tours. For a longer ride, Highway 1A between Banff and Lake Louise is a good choice. For a rugged workout you can test lungs and legs on the steep switchbacks leading up to Mt. Norquay ski area. Highway 93 is a long and strenuous route for cycling but is becoming increasingly popular because of the wide paved shoulders along most of the way and the beautiful scenery. The Overlander Bike Trail in Jasper National Park takes you through four different scenic zones: marshland, river, meadow, and mountain.

Mountain biking has become increasingly popular in recent years, leading to controversy. Park officials have reported problems resulting from breakdowns (flat tires, broken frames) in remote areas, occasionally requiring rescue. Problems have also been reported with mountain bikers unwittingly breaking scent lines between mother bears and cubs. As a result, mountain bikes are restricted to relatively few trails, primarily fire roads in the parks. Check with the nearest park warden or bike store before heading off-road. Mountain bikers may find Kananaskis Country, with its more lenient restrictions, preferable.

CLIMBING

Except for Waterton Lakes, where the rock is generally crumbly, the Canadian Rockies is one of the world's great climbing regions. Among the classic ascents are Mt. Assiniboine, the "Matterhorn of the Rockies"; glacier-cloaked Mt. Athabasca; Mt. Sir Donald, in Glacier National Park; the daunting Mt. Robson; and, in the Purcells, the spires of the Bugaboos. Climbing and mountaineering are year-round activities, although October and November—after the summer and before icefalls are solid enough for winter climbing—are the least desirable months.

FISHING

The principal game fish in the Canadian Rockies is trout—cutthroat and rainbow are the most common varieties. The best fishing tends to be in streams, rivers, and lakes in the valleys rather than in alpine lakes and rivers. Fishing is generally better outside the national parks because fish-stocking programs are more common. The Bow River, the lakes of British Columbia, and the streams of Crowsnest Pass are prime fishing spots outside the national parks.

GOLF

The golf season is short, running from about mid-May through mid-October. Golf courses are generally in excellent playing condition, with lush grasses and well-kept greens. If hole lengths seem long, keep in mind that at the elevation of Canadian Rockies courses (about 4,000 ft), a golf ball tends to travel 10% farther than at sea level. The area between Golden and Kimberley in British Columbia is growing as a golfing hotbed: Golfers here can now choose from ten 18-hole courses and two 9-hole courses.

HIKING

The four contiguous parks (Banff, Jasper, Kootenay, and Yoho) have 2,900 km (1,800 mi) of hiking trails. In Waterton Lakes there are 183 km (113 mi) of trails, with further access to more than 1,200 km (744 mi) of trails in adjacent Glacier National Park in the United States. Kananaskis Country has numerous hiking and backpacking opportunities (water can be in short supply, especially in late summer and fall), while Revelstoke and Glacier parks in British Columbia are generally best for shorter day hikes.

The snow-free hiking season usually runs from early April to early November for trails in the valleys and mid-June to mid- or late September for trails that extend into alpine areas. Though most trails are restricted to foot traffic, horses and mountain bikes are permitted in some areas; check with the park warden.

HORSEBACK RIDING

A unique way to explore the Canadian Rockies is on horseback. Horses are prohibited on many trails within the national parks, but there are still some opportunities; among the most attractive areas for pack trips within the parks is Tonquin Valley in Jasper. More options are available in Kananaskis Country, the provincial parks, and the British Columbia Rockies region.

RAFTING

Rafting opportunities range from gentle floats along the Bow River near Banff to rollicking white-water rides on the Kicking Horse River near Golden. Most trips are half- or full-day. The season runs from May through October; if you want white water at its frothiest, June is usually the best month, when rivers are still swollen with the snowmelt, but not dangerously so.

SKIING

There are 11 lift-service ski areas in the region, 5 of which are within an hour's drive of Banff; daily lift tickets cost between $30 and $50. Cross-country opportunities are also plentiful, and many backcountry lodges are winterized and offer guide services for backcountry touring. Numerous tour operators have ski packages designed to fit a variety of interests (including heli-skiing), abilities, and budgets.

WATER SPORTS

Swimmers generally avoid the icy, glacier-fed waters of the Rockies. However, several lakes near Jasper can become comfortable during spells of warm summer weather. Motorized boats are not allowed on most lakes in the parks, but rowboat and canoe rentals are available at Lake Minnewanka, Lake Louise, and Moraine Lake in Banff National Park; at Emerald Lake and Lake O'Hara in Yoho; and at Lac Beauvert, Pyramid Lake and Patricia Lake in Jasper National Park.

Spray Lakes Reservoir and Kananaskis Lake are the main sites of boating activity in Kananaskis Country—where motorized boating is allowed. Lake Windermere, in British Columbia, is popular among sailors, board sailors, and water-skiers and is pleasant for swimming. To the north, the long, dam-controlled Kinbasket and Revelstoke lakes give boaters, canoeists, and fishermen more of a wilderness experience. There are several boat ramps on the lakes but few services.

For sailors and board sailors who like strong winds, Waterton Lakes, with winds often exceeding 50 km (31 mi) per hour, is the place to be. The water is numbingly cold, though, so be sure to wear a wet suit. The Athabasca, Bow, Kicking Horse, and Maligne rivers provide various levels of river-running challenges for canoeists and kayakers—from relatively still water to roaring white water.

Exploring the Canadian Rockies

The Canadian Rockies can be divided into four broad regions. The Banff and Lake Louise area is the main hub of tourism and makes a convenient reference point for the other regions. North and west of Banff lie the spectacular Icefields Parkway and Jasper National Park (north), and the smaller Kootenay, Yoho, and Glacier national parks (west). Jasper National Park includes the townsite (meaning the town and surrounding cabins and campgrounds) of Jasper—a smaller and more relaxed version of Banff. Kootenay, Yoho, and Glacier parks have comparatively few visitor facilities but make good destinations to escape the crowds of Banff and Jasper parks.

The region south of Banff includes Kananaskis Country and Waterton Lakes National Park. Kananaskis Country, adjacent to Banff National Park but outside the national park system, allows many activities—for example, snowmobiling and hunting—that are prohibited in the national parks. Waterton, a small park along the United States border contiguous with Glacier National Park in Montana, has smaller mountains but a very unhurried atmosphere in contrast to the main parks of the Canadian Rockies.

The British Columbia Rockies region, west of the main Rocky Mountains, consists of a series of parallel, somewhat more weathered mountain ranges. The parks here are smaller and more scattered, interspersed with mostly functional rather than visitor-oriented towns.

The national parks system in Canada has a somewhat complex **fee structure** based on which combination of parks will be visited and whether the traveler is an individual or in a group (☞ Visitor Information *in* Canadian Rockies A to Z, *below*).

Numbers in the text correspond to numbers in the margin and on the Canadian Rockies and Banff maps.

Great Itineraries

The Canadian Rockies region is a sizable chunk of real estate, about twice the area of New York State. You could easily spend a month and still just skim the surface. The heart of the Canadian Rockies—the adjoining national parks of Banff, Jasper, Kootenay, and Yoho—puts the major attractions relatively close together. Ten days would allow for a leisurely tour of the main parks, with time left over for hiking or exploring some outlying regions. Five days would be sufficient for a visit to the major attractions in both Banff and Jasper parks, but there wouldn't be much time spent sitting about. A weekend would be time enough to get a flavor for Banff and Lake Louise, the hub of the region.

IF YOU HAVE 2 DAYS

The best option is to visit the Banff–Lake Louise region. One day could be spent in and around 🖽 **Banff** ①–⑩—exploring, shopping, or just relaxing, perhaps with visits to one or two of the attractions on the outskirts of town—the **Upper Hot Springs** ④, the **Sulphur Mountain Gondola** ⑤, the **Cave and Basin National Historic Site** ⑥, or one of the short drives near town. The second day would allow a visit to the **Lake Louise** ⑪ area, including scenic Moraine Lake, where you can hike, rent a boat, or just sightsee.

Alternatively, you could choose to make 🖽 **Jasper** ⑭ your destination and spend one day in and around the town (shopping, taking the **Jasper Tramway** ⑮, exploring **Pyramid and Patricia lakes** ⑯). The second day could be filled with a visit to one or two of the scenic attractions within an hour's drive of Jasper—**Mt. Edith Cavell** ⑰, **Athabasca Falls** ⑱, **Maligne Lake** ⑲, **Miette Hot Springs** ⑳, or **Mt. Robson** ㉑.

IF YOU HAVE 5 DAYS

A few more days allow you to explore a bit further. If you are feeling energetic, an ideal option would be a two-day visit to the 🖽 **Banff** ①–⑩ and **Lake Louise** ⑪ area, a day spent exploring the **Icefields Parkway** between Lake Louise and Jasper, and a two-day visit to the 🖽 **Jasper** ⑭ area.

IF YOU HAVE 10 DAYS

This is enough time to do some serious exploring. You could spend five days touring the 🖽 **Banff** ①–⑩ and **Lake Louise** ⑪ area, the **Icefields Parkway,** and 🖽 **Jasper** ⑭ and environs. You can spend the additional five days just relaxing, or you can focus on a specific activity such as hiking (which could easily fill up the remaining time).

If you aren't one to sit around in the same spot for too long, spend the extra five days visiting and overnighting in the out-of-the-way regions—🖽 **Yoho National Park** (perhaps visiting the famous **Burgess Shale** ㉕ fossil beds), 🖽 **Glacier National Park** ㉝, **Mt. Revelstoke National Park** ㉞ (overnight in 🖽 **Revelstoke** ㉟), or the **British Columbia Rockies.** Possible stops in the Rockies are 🖽 **Golden** ㉛, 🖽 **Radium Hot Springs** ㊲, or 🖽 **Kimberley** ㊵.

When to Tour the Canadian Rockies

The main places of interest in the Rockies attract crowds in the peak summer season, so try to reach them early in the day if you want to avoid the midday crush. If hiking is your passion, remember that high-

The Canadian Rockies

altitude trails may be snow covered until well into June. Animals are more common before the July crowds arrive, although midsummer visitors are still certain to see plenty. Wildflowers, especially in the alpine meadows, reach their peak from early July to mid-August.

Although the weather is best during the mid-June to mid-September period, you can avoid crowds and make substantial savings on lodgings by scheduling your visit outside this period. Check on rates, though, as many hotel operators are now aware that they can keep rates high to early October and still fill their rooms.

BANFF AND LAKE LOUISE

Most people who come to the Canadian Rockies make the Banff and Lake Louise area their first destination, perhaps their only destination; both towns are within Banff National Park. Banff, just an hour's drive west of Calgary, is the largest townsite in the parks and a logical first stop in the mountains. Most people also make a point of visiting smaller but majestic Lake Louise, a half hour's drive north of Banff. From Banff, the most popular excursions are the spectacular drive north along the Icefields Parkway (Highway 93) to Jasper, 280 km (174 mi) away, and the short trip immediately south into Kananaskis Country. Excursions into the less-frequented Yoho and Kootenay parks offer the same magnificent scenery without the crowds.

Banff National Park

Eastern boundary of park: 113 km (70 mi) west of Calgary, Alberta.

★ With an area of 6,641 square km (2,564 square mi), **Banff National Park** is the second largest of Canada's mountain parks, filled with areas of majestic beauty. Bordered by Jasper National Park to the north, Kootenay and Yoho national parks to the west, the Bighorn Wildland Recreation Area to the east, and Kananaskis Country and Peter Lougheed Provincial Park to the south, Banff is at the center of a huge block of protected wilderness.

You can soak up the rugged alpine scenery, hike on more than 1,600 km (1,000 mi) of trails, tour the region by automobile or tour bus, watch wildlife, soak in hot springs, visit historic sites, and enjoy fine dining, lodging, and shopping in the town of Banff. The Banff–Lake Louise hub (☞ Banff *and* Lake Louise, *below*) is not only the geographic center of the park but also the cultural, dining, lodging, and activity center. Expect crowds here but pristine wilderness in the rest of the park; a day pass is $5 or $10 for a group of 2–10 people.

Parks Canada information is available at the **Parks Information Centre** (✉ 224 Banff Ave., Box 900, Banff, Alberta T0L 0C0, ☎ 403/762–1550). For local information, contact the **Banff–Lake Louise Tourism Bureau** (✉ 224 Banff Ave., Banff, Alberta T0L 0C0). For free information and bookings for summertime outdoor activities and sightseeing, try **Summertime Activities & Excursions** (✉ 225 Banff Ave., Banff, Alberta T0L 0C0, ☎ 403/762–0745 or 888/228–4889).

Outdoor Activities and Sports

The hiking trails of Banff National Park tend to get a lot of traffic during the summer peak season. The most interesting hikes are north of the townsite of Banff. The most popular day-hiking areas, both accessible and scenic, are around **Lake Louise** and **Moraine Lake.** The short (2½-km, or 1½-mi), steep **Parker Ridge Trail** at the northern end of the park along the Icefields Parkway is one of the easiest hikes in the national parks to bring you into the alpine world above tree line. There's an excellent view of the Saskatchewan Glacier, where the river of the same name begins. Snowbanks can persist into early summer, but sunshine lays intricate carpets of wildflowers across the trail in late July and August. Trail information is available from any Parks Canada office (☞ Visitor Information *in* Canadian Rockies A to Z, *below*).

Banff

128 km (79 mi) west of Calgary.

Unlikely contrasts are the rule in Banff, a town that has been serving visitors to the Rockies for more than 100 years: Amid the bustle of commercialism, elk regularly wander into town to graze the lush grass on the town common; tour-bus sightseers carrying souvenir-stuffed bags mix on Banff Avenue (the main drag) with rugged outdoorspeople. For almost all who come to the Canadian Rockies, Banff is the central depot in their travel.

Banff straddles a thin line between mountain resort town and tourist trap. The town was governed by Parks Canada until January 1990, when the residents voted to become an autonomous municipality (a move rejected by the residents of Jasper to the north). This allowed Banff to reduce the strict and vigilant zoning laws the park authorities had in place. An expansion of both commercial and residential properties has followed. Thus Banff is certainly no quaint little western outpost; except for the oft-photographed Banff Springs Hotel, its architecture is mostly modern, simple, and undistinguished. But the park authorities placed limits on the acreage of the town, and so, instead of expanding, Banff has compressed itself. The result is a hub of hyperactivity, especially during summer.

❶ An amazing number of shops and restaurants have been crammed together on the short stretch of **Banff Avenue** that composes the core of downtown. Clustered together in about a half dozen indoor malls and several blocks of street-front stores with modern-alpine architecture are clothing stores, art galleries, sports stores, gift shops, photo shops, bookstores, and fudge and cookie shops. Items sold in the galleries range from trinkets to kitsch to genuine art; price does not necessarily indicate real value.

The Victorian **Banff Park Museum** houses a taxidermy collection of animals indigenous to Banff National Park as well as wildlife art and a library on natural history. This is western Canada's oldest natural history museum, and the rustic building is a National Historic Site. ⊠ *92 Banff Ave.,* ☎ *403/762–1558.* 🎫 *$2.25.* ⊙ *June–Labor Day, daily 10–6; Sept.–May, daily 1–5.*

The **Whyte Museum** displays art, photography, historical artifacts, and exhibits about life in the Canadian Rockies. The museum hosts special events for families in summer. ⊠ *111 Bear St.,* ☎ *403/762–2291.* 🎫 *$3.* ⊙ *July–Aug., daily 10–9; mid-May–June and Sept.–mid-Oct., daily 10–6; off-season hrs vary.*

The **Natural History Museum** reveals the geological and biological evolution of the Rockies with dioramas and collections of fossils, rocks, and gemstones. ⊠ *Clock Tower Mall, 112 Banff Ave., upstairs,* ☎ *403/762–4747.* 🎫 *Free.* ⊙ *July–Aug., daily 10–9; mid-May–June and Sept.–mid-Oct., daily 10–8; limited hrs in off-season.*

❷ For a pleasant after-dinner walk, stroll to the **Parks Administration Building** (⊠ 1 Cave Ave.), with its splendid summertime flower gardens at the rear. It stands at the south end of Banff Avenue, across a stone bridge over the Bow River. For park information, such as maps, park regu-

Banff

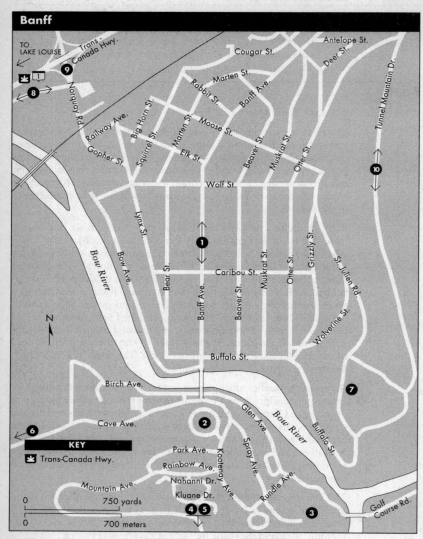

TO LAKE LOUISE

Trans-Canada Hwy.

Antelope St.
Cougar St.
Deer St.
Tunnel Mountain Dr.
Marten St.
Banff Ave.
Rabbit St.
Norquay Rd.
Railway Ave.
Big Horn St.
Moose St.
Gopher St.
Squirrel St.
Marten St.
Elk St.
Beaver St.
Muskrat St.
Otter St.
Wolf St.
Lynx St.
Bow River
Bow Ave.
Caribou St.
Bear St.
Banff Ave.
Beaver St.
Muskrat St.
Otter St.
Grizzly St.
St. Julien Rd.
Wolverine St.
Buffalo St.
N
Birch Ave.
Bow River
Buffalo St.
Cave Ave.
Glen Ave.
KEY
Trans-Canada Hwy.
Park Ave.
Spray Ave.
Golf Course Rd.
Rainbow Ave.
Kootenay Ave.
Nahanni Dr.
Rundle Ave.
Mountain Ave.
Kluane Dr.
0   750 yards
0   700 meters

lations, and so on, the **Information Centre** can provide a wealth of help. ⊠ *224 Banff Ave.,* ☎ *403/762–1550.* ⊙ *June–Sept., daily 8–8; Oct.–May, daily 9–5.*

★ ❸ The **Banff Springs Hotel** (☞ Dining and Lodging, *below*) is the architectural highlight of Banff and can at times resemble a year-round three-ring circus. Built in 1888, the hotel is easily recognized by its castlelike exterior; inside, you can expect to get lost in the crazy-quilt network of restaurants, shops, salons, and ballrooms. ⊠ *Spray Ave., 2 km (1 mi) south of downtown Banff.*

❹ The **Upper Hot Springs** is a sulphur pool that can be soothing, invigorating, or both. The hot-spring water is especially inviting on a dull, cold day. Lockers, bathing suits (period or modern), and towels can be rented, and spa services are available. ⊠ *Mountain Ave., 3 km (2 mi) south of downtown Banff; or via 20-min hike up steep trail from Banff Springs Hotel parking area,* ☎ *403/762–1515; 403/760–2500 for spa bookings.* ☜ *$5–$7; spa services begin at $30.* ⊙ *Mid-May–mid-Sept., daily 9 AM–11 PM; mid-Sept.–mid-May, daily 10–10.*

❺ For great vistas, ride the **Sulphur Mountain Gondola.** Views during the steep eight-minute ride to and from the 7,500-ft summit are spectacular, but they are hardly private. The observation decks and short trails are well visited, especially in summer. From the main deck you can hike the short distance to the summit of Samson Peak and frolic among the lazy Rocky Mountain bighorn sheep that graze there, or visit the gift shop or the reasonably priced restaurant. ⊠ *Mountain Ave., 3 km (2 mi) south of downtown Banff, lower terminal next to Upper Hot Springs,* ☎ *403/762–5438 or 403/762–2523.* ☜ *$14.* ⊙ *Daily 8–8.*

❻ The **Cave and Basin National Historic Site** became the birthplace of the Canadian Rockies park system when the region was given national park protection in 1885. Two interpretive trails provide good insight into geology and plant life here, with half-hour and one-hour ranger-guided tours available. Cave and Basin also has hands-on interpretive displays on the wildlife and history of the national park. The **Cave and Basin Centre Pool** is no longer open for swimming, but you can take a guided tour. A boardwalk leads to a marsh where the warm spring water supports a variety of tropical fish that were illegally dumped into the waters. ⊠ *Cave Ave., 2 km (1 mi) west of downtown Banff,* ☎ *403/762–1557.* ☜ *$2.25.* ⊙ *June–early Sept., daily 9–6; early Sept.–May, daily 9:30–5.*

❼ The **Banff Centre,** a 50-year-old, highly renowned training center for musicians, artists, and writers, is *the* place in town and in the parks for performances ranging from poetry readings to rock concerts. The Banff Festival of the Arts (☞ Nightlife and the Arts, *below*) is held here every summer. Within the center, the **Walter Philips Gallery** focuses on contemporary works by Canadian and international artists. ⊠ *St. Julien Rd.,* ☎ *403/762–6300, 403/762–6281 gallery.* ☜ *Free.* ⊙ *Tues.–Sun. noon–5.*

❽ One pleasant, short ride near town is the **Vermilion Lakes Drive,** just off the west Banff exit from Highway 1. Wildlife sightings are excellent: elk, bighorn sheep, muskrat, and the occasional moose. Dawn and dusk are the best times.

❾ The short drive up the steep **Norquay Road** leads to a parking lot with a prize view of Banff townsite and the Bow River valley. Just below, bighorn sheep, deer, goats, elk, and Columbian ground squirrels negotiate their pastoral existence on some extremely treacherous slopes.

⑩ Tunnel Mountain Drive (east side of Banff) makes a scenic 5-km (3-mi) loop. It's closed in winter, but just off the drive, the **Hoodoos**—fingerlike, eroded rock formations—are accessible year-round.

Dining and Lodging

$$$$ ✕ **Le Beaujolais.** Elegantly decorated in neoclassical style, this restaurant is strikingly out of place in casual Banff. Tapestries on the wall lend a hint of baronial splendor, and the rich food is a suitable match. Traditional French preparations of beef, veal, and lamb are menu highlights. Fish and seafood specialties include arctic char, salmon, sea bass, and lobster. For dessert, spoil yourself with the Raspberry Balloon—a mixture of fresh raspberries, raspberry-flavored ice cream, and raspberry liqueur, all smothered in whipped cream. The wine cellar is lavishly and imaginatively stocked. ⊠ *212 Buffalo St., at Banff Ave.,* ☎ *403/762–2712. Reservations essential. MC, V. No lunch.*

$$$–$$$$ ✕ **The Keg and The Keg–Downtown.** The only difference between the Keg's downtown (117 Banff Avenue) and uptown Caribou Lodge (521 Banff Avenue) location is that breakfast, including a hearty buffet, is available only uptown. Dark wood tables and chairs balance the huge wooden beams and stone fireplace, creating a warm, rustic atmosphere. Historical prints detail the early settlement of the region. Steak is the specialty here, seasoned with the Keg's secret blend of spices and grilled over high heat. Some seafood, pasta, rib, and chicken dishes are also available. ⊠ *117 Banff Ave.,* ☎ *403/760–3030;* ⊠ *521 Banff Ave.,* ☎ *403/762–4442. AE, D, DC, MC, V.*

$$$–$$$$ ✕ **Ristorante Classico.** The restaurant at the Rimrock hotel (☞ *below*) juxtaposes northern Italian cuisine with a backdrop of the Bow Valley. The dining room—complete with abstract paintings and intricate moldings on the high ceiling—is divided into three cozy sections. You can try such dishes as *roulade di salmone picante* (seared peppered salmon roulade with gazpacho), *cotoletta di vitello ai ferri al rosmarino* (grilled veal chop with rosemary), and rack of lamb baked in an aromatic crust. Fresh fruit desserts and an extensive wine list will complete your evening. ⊠ *Rimrock Resort Hotel, Mountain Ave.,* ☎ *403/762–3356. Reservations essential. AE, D, DC, MC, V. No lunch.*

$$–$$$$ ✕ **Balkan Restaurant.** The bright blue-and-white decor, with tile trim, cane-back chairs, and plants, evokes the Mediterranean. You can choose between classic Greek dishes, such as moussaka and souvlaki, or creative ethnic mixes, such as Greek stir-fry (rice and veggies with feta cheese). ⊠ *120 Banff Ave.,* ☎ *403/762–3454. AE, MC, V.*

$$–$$$$ ✕ **Banff Springs Hotel.** Restaurants, bars, and lounges of varying formality and cuisine—from coffeehouses to a grand dining room—create a small culinary universe in this hotel in the heart of the Rockies. Samurai, a Japanese restaurant, may have the best food—the standard of its sushi and *shabu-shabu* (thin strips of beef, chicken, or fish cooked in a copper bowl full of boiling water) must be high enough to satisfy the hotel's large Japanese clientele. The best overall dining experience may be at the Waldhaus (closed mid-November–mid-December), where a Bavarian-style meal—they specialize in fondues—is followed by a raucous, popular, Bavarian-style sing-along. The Grapes Wine Bar, which serves a light-fare menu with adventurous salads, pâtés, and a choice selection of cheeses, is tucked away on the mezzanine level. Big windows provide nice views here. A summer highlight is the barbecue lunch on the Red Terrace. The savory barbecued entrées—steaks, salmon, or chicken breast on salad—seem greatly enhanced by the view of Rundle Mountain and the Bow River. One of Banff's best-kept secrets is the Golf Clubhouse Restaurant, with unparalleled mountain views on all sides. The Continental menu lists such delights as wild mushroom terrine with a light chive dressing for an appetizer, and pepper-glazed pork tenderloin as an entrée. The clubhouse is open for breakfast, lunch, and dinner in summer and welcomes nongolfers. ⊠ *Spray Ave.,* ☎ *403/762–2211. Reservations essential. AE, D, DC, MC, V.*

$$–$$$$ ✕ **Buffalo Mountain Lodge.** An exposed, rough-hewn post-and-beam interior gives the dining room a comfortable likeness to a converted barn. This is a woodcrafter's showcase, highlighted by the large polished wine cabinet that separates the dining and bar areas. On the menu is Rocky Mountain cuisine—fish, meat, and numerous game dishes with sweet nouvelle sauces, supplemented by hearty soups, fresh-baked breads, and a superbly extensive and frequently updated wine list. ⊠ *Tunnel Mountain Rd.,* ☎ *403/762–2400. AE, DC, MC, V.*

$$–$$$$ ✕ **Caboose.** In the railway depot, the Caboose recalls the bygone train era. Old train-engine, rail-car, and train-depot paraphernalia fills the dining room; dim lighting adds to the spirit of nostalgia, with a karaoke lounge adding a modern twist. Continental dishes, served with salad, are good but basic: slow-roasted prime rib and steaks, plus crab legs, salmon, lobster, prawns, and trout. ⊠ *Elk and Lynx Sts.,* ☎ *403/762– 3622. AE, DC, MC, V. No lunch.*

$$–$$$$ ✕ **Giorgio's Trattoria.** This split-level eatery serves high-quality Italian food that is immensely popular with the locals, so you might have to wait a bit during busy hours. Philippine mahogany tables and bar, Tuscany-style sponged walls, a beamed ceiling, and detailed wrought-iron work on the stairway create an elegant look. The menu consists mainly of pizzas cooked in a wood-burning oven—try the exotic pizza *mare* with tiger shrimp, mussels, cilantro, sun-dried tomatoes, and roast garlic topping—and such pasta dishes as the ricotta ravioli *con gamberetti* (ravioli tossed with baby shrimps in oregano butter and virgin olive oil). ⊠ *219 Banff Ave.,* ☎ *403/762–5114. MC, V. No lunch.*

$$–$$$$ ✕ **Miki Japanese Restaurant.** Several Japanese restaurants have sprung up in Banff in the past few years; this is one of the best. The dining room is bright and cozy, and its second-floor location provides one of the better views along Banff Avenue. Sushi and Japanese seafood dishes hold center stage: *sunomona* (cold noodles with vegetables and seafood), *yakizakana* (broiled fish), sushi, and sashimi for appetizers; and hot pots, *shabu-shabu* (meat or vegetables cooked in broth and served with a choice of sauces), tempura, and seafood for entrées. ⊠ *Inns of Banff, 600 Banff Ave.,* ☎ *403/762–0600. AE, MC, V. No lunch.*

$$–$$$$ ✕ **Ticino.** This stucco-and-wood-beam dining room serves Swiss-Italian fare, from numerous standard pasta and meat dishes to more adventurous alpine cuisine. Fondue is a house specialty; the *mar-e-mont* (Italian for "ocean and mountain") is a beef-and-shrimp fondue you cook yourself in hot broth. Baked salmon, beef medallions, and pan-fried veal are among the other entrées. Ticino is open for breakfast, too. ⊠ *High Country Inn, 415 Banff Ave.,* ☎ *403/762–3848. AE, DC, MC, V. No lunch.*

$–$$$ ✕ **Earls Restaurant.** At this popular chain eatery, giant imitation parrots, rhino masks resembling native spirit masks, and stylized chickens in karate attire are all part of the fun, campy atmosphere. The dining area is large and open, and service is prompt and attentive without being overbearing. Popular international dishes on the menu include California shrimp rolls, Hunan chicken, and pizzas and Forno roast hunter chicken cooked in a wood-burning oven. This popular local haunt has lines at the usual busy times. ⊠ *229 Banff Ave.,* ☎ *403/762–4414. Reservations not accepted. AE, MC, V.*

$$$$ 🏨 **Banff Rocky Mountain Resort.** Numerous outdoor facilities are a draw at this resort 5 km (3 mi) east of Banff. Inside the chalet-style building, rooms are bright, with white walls, wall-to-wall carpeting, and lots of blond-wood trim. Many rooms have fireplaces and kitchenettes with microwave ovens. Rates decrease by 40% off-season. ⊠ *Banff Ave.*

and Tunnel Mountain Rd., Box 100, T0L 0C0, ☎ 403/762–5531 or 800/661–9563, FAX *403/762–5166. 171 suites. Indoor pool, 2 tennis courts, exercise room, squash. AE, D, DC, MC, V.*

$$$$ ⊞ **Banff Springs Hotel.** Built in 1888 by the Canadian Pacific Railway,
★ this massive, castlelike hotel marked the beginning of Banff's tourism boom. The dozens of different styles of guest rooms are linked by their blue, burgundy, and green color schemes and such old-hotel characteristics as high ceilings, antique furniture, and marble sinks. The hotel is well aware of its importance in Banff's heritage, and the paintings and other artwork here are mostly turn-of-the-century Rocky Mountain historical art. A world-class spa is an oasis of pampering and luxury. Prior to 1996, individual travelers were only allotted rooms that tour groups failed to fill. By 1998, 200 rooms per night were reserved for individual travelers on all-inclusive packages (including use of full hotel facilities, all meals, and gratuities). If the hotel is the focus of your visit to Banff, these packages represent good value. Rates decrease by about 25% off-season. ⊠ *Spray Ave., Box 960, T0L 0C0,* ☎ *403/762–2211 or 800/441–1414,* FAX *403/762–5755. 804 rooms, 80 suites. 12 restaurants, 3 bars, indoor pool, spa, 27-hole golf course, 5 tennis courts, bowling, health club, horseback riding, nightclub, convention center. AE, D, DC, MC, V.*

$$$$ ⊞ **Rimrock Resort Hotel.** Perched on the slope of Sulphur Mountain,
★ with a gondola and hot pools nearby, this hotel looks deceptively like a two- or three-story motel from the front. But the mountain-modern–style structure, clad in broken-face Tyndall stone and built into the steep mountain, is actually 11 stories high. The huge lobby has a 25-ft ceiling, giant windows facing the Rockies, and an oversize marble fireplace. Nearly all rooms have views of the Bow Valley, though the views from the lower floors are compromised by trees. Each room is decorated individually, but all have dark color schemes of burgundy, brown, and blue and plush leather and velvet furnishings. Rates decrease by one-third off-season. ⊠ *Mountain Ave., Box 1110, T0L 0C0,* ☎ *403/762–3356 or 800/661–1587,* FAX *403/762–4132. 310 rooms, 41 suites. 2 restaurants, lobby lounge, indoor pool, sauna, exercise room, squash. AE, D, DC, MC, V.*

$$$ ⊞ **Banff Park Lodge.** The high, slanted ceiling and dark cedar paneling, in addition to the modern and unembellished style, exude a Scandinavian feeling. On a quiet street downtown, the lodge is within walking distance of shops and restaurants. Rooms are bright, with lots of beige and ecru. You should ask for a room that doesn't face busy Lynx Street. Rates are cut in half off-season. ⊠ *222 Lynx St., Box 2200, T0L 0C0,* ☎ *403/762–4433 or 800/661–9266,* FAX *403/762–3553. 211 rooms. 2 restaurants, indoor pool, sauna, steam room. AE, DC, MC, V.*

$$$ ⊞ **Castle Mountain Village.** Six different chalet styles can satisfy a variety of needs. The smallest have kitchens, bathrooms, and sleeping areas with fireplaces. Although cramped and on the dark side, they are clean and quiet. Larger and newer pine-log chalets, which make up the vast majority of the units, have two bedrooms, Jacuzzis, and sleep up to six. For four people, the large chalets are a comfortable, economical choice. Five one-bedroom cabins (one wheelchair accessible) are another choice. Request a room with a view of Castle Mountain. Rates decrease by 35% off-season; pets are $20 extra each. ⊠ *Hwy. 1A, halfway between Banff and Lake Louise, Box 1655, Banff T0L 0C0,* ☎ *403/762–3868,* FAX *403/762–8629. 24 chalets. Grocery, steam room, exercise room, coin laundry. MC, V.*

$$–$$$ ⊞ **Buffalo Mountain Lodge.** Part of the Canadian Rocky Mountain Re-
★ sorts group, along with Emerald Lake Lodge (☞ Yoho National Park *in* North and West of Banff, *below*) and Deer Lodge in Lake Louise, this complex shares their ambience and style. Polished pine, rough-hewn

beams, and a stone hearth set the tone in the lobby. There is a hotel-condo cluster as well as 42 renovated rooms that reopened in 1997. Rooms are dressed in pastel shades and have fireplaces, willow chairs, and pine cabinetry. Rates decrease by 35% off-season. ⊠ *Tunnel Mountain Rd., Box 1326, T0L 0C0,* ☎ *403/762–2400 or 800/661–1367,* FAX *403/762–4495. 82 rooms, 20 studios. 2 restaurants, lobby lounge, hot tub, steam room. AE, MC, V.*

$$ 🏨 **High Country Inn.** There is nothing fancy here—just clean, simple, comfortable motel rooms. The units are of standard size, cedar-covered walls give some rooms a touch of regional character, and many rooms have a balcony. You should ask for a room in the back, away from the Banff Avenue traffic. Rates decrease by one-half off-season. ⊠ *419 Banff Ave., Box 700, T0L 0C0,* ☎ *403/762–2236, 800/661–1244 in Canada,* FAX *403/762–5084. 70 rooms. Restaurant, indoor pool, hot tub. AE, MC, V.*

$$ 🏨 **Red Carpet Inn.** Under the same management as the High Country Inn next door, the no-frills Red Carpet is one of the few good budget hotel options in downtown Banff. Small motel-style rooms are decorated in pastel shades, right down to the pastel-painted wooden furnishings. Front rooms, on Banff Avenue, can be noisy. Rates decrease by 50% off-season. ⊠ *425 Banff Ave., Box 1800, T0L 0C0,* ☎ *403/762–4184, 800/563–4609 in Canada,* FAX *403/762–4894. 52 rooms. Hot tub. AE, MC, V.*

$$ 🏨 **Storm Mountain Lodge.** This is one of the original Canadian Pacific
★ Railway backcountry lodges, built in 1922. Not nearly as backcountry today, it is on Highway 93, just east of Vermilion Pass. The sitting area of the main, log cabin–style lodge is dominated by a large fireplace crowned by the head of a bighorn sheep. The dining area embodies simple elegance: straight-back wood chairs and white tablecloths on an enclosed porch with big glass windows overlooking the pass. Cabins, tucked in the woods, are smallish but cozy, made so by fireplaces, old lamps, and down comforters. ⊠ *Hwy. 93, 5 km (3 mi) west of Hwy. 1, Box 670, T0L 0C0,* ☎ FAX *403/762–4155. 12 cabins. Restaurant, lounge, hiking. AE, MC, V. Closed late Sept.–late May.*

Nightlife and the Arts

THE ARTS

Most of the cultural activity in the Canadian Rockies is in and around Banff, and the hub of it is the **Banff Centre** (⊠ St. Julien Rd., ☎ 403/762–6300, 800/413–8368 in Alberta and British Columbia). Presenting a performing-arts grab bag throughout the year, with pop and classical music, theater, and dance, the center peaks in summer with the three-month **Banff Festival of the Arts.**

The **Lux Cinema** (⊠ Wolf and Bear Mall, ☎ 403/762–8595) plays major releases daily in a four-screen theater.

NIGHTLIFE

For enjoying cocktails and socializing, the **Banff Springs Hotel** (☞ Dining and Lodging, *above*) has lounges and dining rooms with entertainment and dancing. **Barbary Coast** (⊠ 119 Banff Ave., ☎ 403/762–4616) has late-night blues and good food. If you prefer rock and roll with your drink, try **Outa Bounds** (⊠ 137 Banff Ave., ☎ 403/762–8434). **Wild Bill's** (⊠ Banff Ave. and Caribou St., ☎ 403/762–0333) is a cowboy bar with live music where two-steppers can strut their stuff.

Outdoor Activities and Sports

BIKING

Mountain bikes can be rented from **Backtrax Bike Rentals** (⊠ 337 Banff Ave., ☎ 403/762–8177), **Clock Tower Sports** (⊠ 110 Banff Ave., ☎ 403/762–3525), **Park and Pedal Bike Shop** (⊠ 229 Wolf St., ☎ 403/

762–3190), **Peak Experience** (✉ 209 Bear St., ☎ 403/762–0581), **Performance Ski and Sports** (✉ 208 Bear St., ☎ 403/762–8222), and **Unlimited** (✉ 111 Banff Ave., ☎ 403/762–3725).

Backtrax (☞ *above*) offers one- to four-hour guided interpretive tours on local Banff trails, suitable for any age or physical ability. **Rocky Mountain Cycle Tours** (☞ Guided Tours *in* Canadian Rockies A to Z, *below*) has weeklong tours in the Banff area and in British Columbia.

BOATING

Lake Minnewanka Boat Tours (✉ Box 2189, T0L 0C0, ☎ 403/762–3473) provides 1½-hour tours in summer on Lake Minnewanka, near town. The cost is $22.

GOLF

The **Banff Springs Hotel** (✉ Spray Ave., ☎ 403/762–6801) has a highly rated 18-hole, par-71 golf course, as well as an additional 9-hole, par-36 course (advance bookings required). The season runs from early May to mid-October.

HORSEBACK RIDING

Arrangements for hourly or daily rides, as well as lessons, can be made through the concierge at the **Banff Springs Hotel** (☎ 403/762–6801). **Sundance Stables** (☎ 403/762–2832) and **Brewster's Kananaskis Guest Ranch** (☎ 403/673–3737), on the Bow River 30 minutes east of Banff, have horses to hire. **Holiday on Horseback** (✉ 132 Banff Ave., Box 2280, T0L 0C0, ☎ 403/762–4551) offers rides in the mountains and foothills, from one hour to six days in length.

RAFTING

Rocky Mountain Raft Tours (✉ Box 1771, T0L 0C0, ☎ 403/762–3632) has one- to three-hour trips on the Bow River and also offers canoe rentals.

SKIING

Cross-country. Banff Alpine Guides (✉ Box 1025, T0L 0C0, ☎ 403/678–6091) leads ski tours into Banff's backcountry. **Michele's Cross Country Ski Tours** (✉ 1725 11th Ave., Canmore, Alberta T1W 1X9, ☎ 403/678–2067) leads day tours and weekend getaways to backcountry lodges around Banff, Lake Louise, and Kananaskis Country and provides lessons for beginners. **White Mountain Adventures** (✉ 5 Larch Close, Canmore, Alberta T1W 1S3, ☎ 403/678–4099) conducts ski tours and lessons throughout the Bow Valley for beginner and intermediate skiers.

Downhill. Mt. Norquay (✉ Mt. Norquay Rd., Box 219, Suite 7000, T0L 0C0, ☎ 403/762–4421) runs are generally short and steep with a growing range of expert terrain. The vertical drop is 1,650 ft; there are 25 runs and 5 lifts. At **Sunshine Village** (✉ Box 1510, T0L 0C0, ☎ 403/762–6500 or 800/661–1363) the terrain is mostly intermediate and above the tree line. The vertical drop is 3,510 ft, and there are 89 trails and 12 lifts. These resorts and **Lake Louise** (☞ *below*) have dining options, ski schools, day-care facilities, and licensed day lodges. A good bargain is the $150 three-day pass from **Ski Banff/Lake Louise** (✉ Box 1805, T0L 0C0, ☎ 403/762–4561), which allows you to ski at three areas and includes free shuttle service to the slopes.

Heli-skiing. Mike Wiegele Helicopter Skiing (✉ Box 249, T0L 0C0, ☎ 403/762–5548 or 800/661–9170) serves the Banff region. *See also* Skiing *in* Canadian Rockies A to Z, *below.*

Ski Rentals. Skis and the increasingly popular snowboards can be rented from **Abominable Ski & Sportswear** (✉ 229 Banff Ave., ☎ 403/

762–2905; ✉ 120 Banff Ave., ☎ 403/762–4888), **Clock Tower Sports** (✉ 110 Banff Ave., ☎ 403/762–4206), **Performance Ski & Sports** (✉ 208 Bear St., ☎ 403/762–8222), **Rude Boy's Snowboard Shop** (✉ 215 Banff Ave., ☎ 403/762–8480), and **Unlimited** (✉ 111 Banff Ave., ☎ 403/762–3725).

SPORTING GEAR

Monod's (✉ 111 Banff Ave., ☎ 403/762–3725; ✉ 129 Banff Ave., ☎ 403/762–4571) sells a wide array of sports equipment and clothing. **Mountain Magic** (✉ 224 Bear St., ☎ 403/762–2591) has three floors of hiking, climbing, skiing, running, and biking equipment and a 30-ft indoor climbing wall for testing gear.

Shopping

When shopping in the Rockies, you'll find the best selection in Banff, but you may pay a resort premium for souvenirs as well as native crafts, sporting gear, landscape paintings, woolens, and outdoor wear.

Banff Book & Art Den (✉ 110 Banff Ave., ☎ 403/762–3919) has an extensive selection of books on the Rocky Mountains. The **Banff Indian Trading Post** (✉ Birch and Cave Aves., ☎ 403/762–2456) has a good selection of crafts. For arts and crafts, including handmade jewelry and watercolor paintings, check out **Canada House Gallery** (✉ 201 Bear St., ☎ 403/762–3757). Of the numerous shops along Banff Avenue, perhaps the best for crafts and other art items, principally by Canadian craftspeople, is **Quest for Handcrafts** (✉ 105 Banff Ave., ☎ 403/762–2722). **Rock & Gems Canada** (✉ 137 Banff Ave., ☎ 403/762–4331) has an excellent selection of fossils, semiprecious and precious stones, jewelry, and rock and gemstone carvings. Often considered the epitome of tackiness by locals, and cherished Canadiana by tourists, every imaginable Royal Canadian Mounted Police (Mountie) gift can be found under one roof at **Sergeant Preston's Outpost** (✉ 208 Caribou St., ☎ 403/762–5335). **Welch's Chocolate Shop** (✉ 126 Banff Ave., near Wolf St., ☎ 403/762–3737) carries an excellent selection of homemade candies, including chocolate and sugar sculptures of local wildlife.

Lake Louise

★ ⑪ *56 km (35 mi) north of Banff, 184 km (114 mi) west of Calgary.*

Ask people what pops to mind when they think of the Canadian Rockies and they are as likely to say Lake Louise as Banff. What they are really thinking of is the lake itself, with the impressive Victoria Glacier flowing off the mountain at the lake's end, and the hotel at the lakeshore—the classy Chateau Lake Louise. The scenery here is among the most spectacular in all of Banff National Park, and the Chateau Lake Louise is comparable in quality to the Banff Springs Hotel in Banff—both are owned and operated by the Canadian Pacific chain of luxury hotels. The town of Lake Louise, though, is another story; blink and you'll miss it on your way through. That's not to say there aren't hotels, restaurants, shopping, and other services here—there are, and some very good ones at that.

Most people traveling from Banff to Lake Louise take Highway 1 for about 56 km (35 mi) north along the Bow River. But if you aren't in a hurry, the two-lane Highway 1A, running approximately parallel to Highway 1, is the more scenic option.

For local information, contact the **Banff–Lake Louise Tourism Bureau** (✉ 224 Banff Ave., Banff, Alberta T0L 0C0, ☎ 403/762–8421) or the **Lake Louise Visitor Centre** (✉ Village Rd. beside Samson Mall, Box 213, Lake Louise, Alberta T0L 1E0, ☎ 403/522–3833).

In summer you can ride the **Lake Louise Summer Sightseeing Lift** to the summit of Mt. Whitehorn for a stunning view that includes more than a dozen glaciers. In good weather, the sundeck of the Whitehorn Tea House (open June 1–September 15 for breakfast and lunch; June 15–August 31 for dinner), at the top of the lift, is a good place to break for lunch. The ski area here is generally regarded as one of Canada's best and is frequent home to World Cup downhill races. There are free 30- to 90-minute naturalist-led hikes at the top of the mountain; check with the operator, as schedules vary. ⊠ *Lake Louise exit, Hwy. 1,* ☎ *403/522–3555.* ⊠ *$10.* ☉ *June–mid-Sept., daily.*

Chateau Lake Louise (☞ Dining and Lodging, *below*), opened in 1890, overlooks blue-green Lake Louise and the Victoria Glacier at the far end of the lake. The hotel's setting is as scenic as it is popular. Canoe rentals are available at the boathouse. The chateau is also a departure point for several short, moderately strenuous, well-traveled hiking routes. The most popular hike (about 3½ km, or 2¼ mi) is to Lake Agnes. The tiny lake hangs on a mountain-surrounded shelf that opens to the east with a distant view of the Bow River valley. ⊠ *Lake Louise Dr., 6 km (4 mi) south of Hwys. 93 and 1, 6 km (4 mi) northwest of Hwy. 1 and Bow Valley Pkwy.; follow signs.*

Moraine Lake, 11 km (7 mi) south of Lake Louise, is a photographic highlight in Banff National Park. Set in the Valley of the Ten Peaks, the lake reflects the snow-clad peaks of sedimentary rock that rise abruptly around it. As beautiful as it is, don't expect Moraine Lake necessarily to offer an escape from the Lake Louise crowd; it is a major stop for tour buses as well as a popular departure point for hikers. However, a hiking path that runs along the lakeshore will quickly take you away from the crowds. If you are seeking real solitude, several moderate hiking trails lead from Moraine Lake into some spectacular country. A popular day hike is the trek over Sentinel Pass and through Paradise Valley to Lake Louise. For great views, the short (3-km, or 2-mi) but steep hike from Moraine Lake to Larch Valley is well worth the effort. From June through September, another option is to rent a canoe from the office of **Moraine Lake Lodge** (☎ 403/522–3733). ⊠ *Moraine Lake Rd. off Great Divide Hwy.*

Dining and Lodging

$$$$ ✕ **Post Hotel.** Here is one of the true epicurean experiences in the Cana-
★   dian Rockies. A low, exposed-beam ceiling and a stone, wood-burning hearth in the corner lend a warm, in-from-the-cold atmosphere; white tablecloths and fanned napkins provide an elegant touch. Daring European cuisine is reflected in the combination of modern and classic dishes. The house specialty is Alberta rack of lamb; veal and venison are also good choices. Alternatively, try the free-range duck sausage served with gnocchi and mango-lime salsa, or salmon with one of the house specialty sauces, which change twice a year. Homemade pastries and desserts cap off the meal. ⊠ *200 Pipestone Rd.,* ☎ *403/ 522–3989. Reservations essential. AE, MC, V.*

$$–$$$$ ✕ **Chateau Lake Louise.** The many choices at the Chateau range from light snacking in the Poppy Room to night-on-the-town elegance in the Edelweiss Dining Room (jacket required for dinner). Wherever you eat, dining inevitably defers to the view through the 10-ft-high windows. The size of the Victoria Dining Room (jacket for dinner), with seating for more than 300, is nicely tempered by plush carpeting, wood paneling with hand-painted motifs, and the original 1913 wood-burning fireplaces. The food and ambience are European hotel–style—croissants and jam for breakfast, Continental fare for lunch and dinner—with white cotton tablecloths and polished silver. For something

different, try Walliser Stube, a Swiss wine bar with warm, cherry-wood decor and a good selection of fondues. From early June to early September, afternoon tea in the Lakeview Lounge is a highlight that usually includes fresh scones, pastries, or croissants—along with coffee and tea—served on silver. In summer you can sample Continental cuisine with a Russian flair at the Tom Wilson's dining room. Dinner reservations are necessary in summer for most of the restaurants. ⊠ *Lake Louise Dr.,* ☎ *403/522–3511, ext. 1818. AE, D, DC, MC, V.*

$$–$$$ ✕ **The Station.** Housed in a lovingly restored railway station and two
★ early 20th-century burgundy Canadian Pacific rail cars, this restaurant stands on the site of the original railway station in Lake Louise. The centerpiece of the station is a huge three-sided fireplace that faces out onto each of three small dining rooms. The fresh fare on the menu is expertly prepared but quite predictable, with Alberta beef, chicken, and fish dishes dominating. ⊠ *200 Sentinel Rd.,* ☎ *403/522–2600. Reservations essential. MC, V.*

$–$$ ✕ **Laggan's Mountain Bakery and Deli.** This six-table coffee shop in the Samson Mall is where the local work crews, mountain guides, and park wardens come for an early morning muffin and a cup of coffee. Laggan's has excellent baked goods, especially the sweet poppy-seed breads. You can pick up a sandwich here if you're driving north on the Icefields Parkway. ⊠ *Samson Mall, off Hwy. 1,* ☎ *403/522–2017. Reservations not accepted. No credit cards.*

$$$$ 🏨 **Chateau Lake Louise.** There's a good chance that no hotel—anywhere—has a more dramatic view out its back door. Terraces and lawns reach to the famous aquamarine lake, backed up by the Victoria Glacier. Inside, off-white walls, polished wood and brass, and burgundy carpeting blend well with the lake view, seen through large, horseshoe-shape windows. Guest rooms have neocolonial furnishings; some have terraces. The stone-facade hotel was opened in 1890. Reader feedback suggests that tour groups receive preferential service; some individual travelers have felt neglected. There's a minimal off-season rate decrease. ⊠ *Lake Louise Dr., T0L 1E0,* ☎ *403/522–3511 or 800/441–1414,* 𝔽𝔸𝕏 *403/522–3834. 511 rooms, 60 suites. 6 restaurants, 2 lounges, indoor pool, hot tub, steam room, exercise room, horseback riding, boating. AE, D, DC, MC, V.*

$$$$ 🏨 **Post Hotel.** The log-beam architecture and bright red roof evoke the
★ mood of a grand chalet. All rooms are furnished in solid Canadian pine and come in 15 different configurations, from standard doubles to units with sleeping lofts, balconies, fireplaces, and whirlpool tubs. Two streamside log cabins create a feeling of old-fashioned, in-the-mountains romance. Seven deluxe, two-level suites come with a king-size bed and a large living room with a river-stone fireplace. The restaurant (☞ *above*) is regularly rated as one of the best in the Canadian Rockies. Rates decrease by about 40% off-season. ⊠ *Box 69, T0L 1E0,* ☎ *403/522–3989 or 800/661–1586,* 𝔽𝔸𝕏 *403/522–3966. 91 rooms, 7 suites. Restaurant, lounge, pub, indoor pool, steam room. AE, MC, V. Closed late Oct.–early Dec.*

$$$$ 🏨 **Skoki Lodge.** An 11-km (7-mi) hike or ski jaunt from the Lake Louise ski area, Skoki is the kind of backcountry lodge you must work to get to. The high-alpine scenery of Skoki Valley makes the trek well worthwhile, as does the small lodge itself, built in 1930. The log walls and big stone fireplace epitomize backcountry coziness, but don't expect such luxuries as private baths, running water, or electricity. Meals are included in the rate, which is $110 per person. An afternoon tea, with freshly baked bread and sweets, is also served to lodge guests and day-trippers. Reserve far in advance. ⊠ *Box 5, T0L 1E0,* ☎ *403/522–3555,* 𝔽𝔸𝕏 *403/522–2095. 4 rooms, 3 cabins. Dining room. AE, MC, V. Closed late Sept.–Dec. 21 and Easter–late June.*

$$$ 🏨 **Lake Louise Inn.** Five buildings hold a variety of accommodations from small motel-style rooms to two-bedroom condo units, some with a balcony, fireplace, and kitchenette. Fifty-five units are equipped with fireplaces and kitchenettes. In winter there's a shuttle to the mountain, and multiday ski packages. Rates decrease by 50% off-season. ✉ *210 Village Rd., Box 209, T0L 1E0,* ☎ *403/522–3791 or 800/661–9237,* FAX *403/522–2018. 222 rooms. Restaurant, pizzeria, pub, indoor pool, hot tub, sauna, ice-skating. AE, DC, MC, V.*

$$–$$$ 🏨 **Paradise Lodge and Bungalows.** Only 2 km (1 mi) down the access road from Lake Louise, this lodge has one- and two-bedroom suites with wood furnishings and oak paneling in the two main log buildings. One-bedroom units come with a full kitchen and a fireplace, while the two-bedroom option includes a balcony. The bungalows, or log-sided cabins (some with kitchenettes), are more rustic from the outside than on the inside. Set in a spruce and pine grove, they can be somewhat dark and feel cramped, but they are well maintained. ✉ *105 Lake Louise Dr., Box 7, T0L 1E0,* ☎ *403/522–3595,* FAX *403/522–3987. 24 suites, 21 bungalows. Playground, coin laundry. MC, V. Closed mid-Oct.–mid-May.*

Nightlife and the Arts

If you don't want to spend the evening outdoors, **Chateau Lake Louise** (☞ Dining and Lodging, *above*) has lounges and dining rooms with entertainment and dancing.

Outdoor Activities and Sports

HORSEBACK RIDING

The concierge at **Chateau Lake Louise** (☞ Dining and Lodging, *above*) can arrange for trail rides and lessons.

SKIING

At **Lake Louise Ski Area** (✉ Box 5, T0L 1E0, ☎ 403/522–3555) the downhill terrain is large and varied, with a fairly even spread of novice, intermediate, and expert runs (☞ Skiing *in* Banff, *above*). The vertical drop is 3,257 ft, and there are 77 trails and 11 lifts.

SPORTING GEAR

Monod's (✉ Chateau Lake Louise, ☎ 403/522–3837) has a wide selection of gear and clothing.

NORTH AND WEST OF BANFF

Just north of Lake Louise, Highways 1 and 93 diverge. Highway 93, the spectacularly scenic Icefields Parkway, continues northward for 230 km (143 mi) to Jasper National Park and the town of Jasper. Highway 1 bears west over Kicking Horse Pass—named, according to local lore, after an unpleasant encounter between a pack animal and a member of an exploratory expedition in the mid-1800s—into Yoho National Park and British Columbia (if you're continuing in this direction, ☞ the British Columbia Rockies, *below*).

The Icefields Parkway

230 km (143 mi), running from Lake Louise to Jasper.

★   Powerfully rugged mountain scenery, glaciers, waterfalls and icefalls, and big-game animals: The **Icefields Parkway** has all these and more as it snakes its way between Lake Louise and Jasper. The original highway was built in the Great Depression to provide badly needed jobs but has since been reconstructed. The parkway is now a modern two-lane road, with wide paved shoulders along most of the route. It needs to be: Some 4 million people drive the parkway each year.

More than 100 glaciers show off their blue ice along this drive; at the Columbia Icefields, the Athabasca Glacier reaches almost to the roadway (a short walk takes you right up to the ice). Large animals such as elk, moose, deer, and bighorn sheep are fairly common along this route; occasionally you can see bears and mountain goats. Two high passes, the Bow Pass in the south and the Sunwapta Pass about halfway along the route, rise almost to tree line, offering a chance to see carpets of alpine wildflowers in summer.

For the best views, try to choose a clear day for your trip. There aren't many facilities, so be sure to check the gas gauge and maybe pack some sandwiches. Although you could drive this winding road in three to four hours if you were in a hurry, it's more likely to be a full-day trip when you add in some stops. The road rises to near tree line at several points, and the weather can be chilly and unsettled at these high elevations even in midsummer—bring some warmer clothing along.

The most dramatic scenery is in the north end of Banff National Park and the south end of Jasper National Park, where ice fields and glaciers become common on the high mountains surrounding the route (ice fields are massive reservoirs of ice; glaciers are the slow-moving rivers of ice that flow from the ice fields). Scenic overlooks and hiking trails of varying lengths abound along the route.

⑫ **Bow Summit,** at 6,787 ft the highest drivable pass in the national parks of the Canadian Rockies, may be covered with snow as late as May and as early as September. On the south side of the pass is Bow Lake, source of the Bow River, which flows through Banff. Above Bow Lake hangs the edge of Crowfoot Glacier, and beyond this is the beginning of the Waputik Icefield. Around the lake are stubby trees and underbrush—this is where the trees end and high-alpine country begins. On the north side of the pass is **Peyto Lake**; its startlingly deep aqua-blue color comes from the minerals in glacier runoff. ☒ *41 km (25 mi) north of Lake Louise, 190 km (118 mi) south of Jasper.*

Sunwapta Pass marks the juncture of Banff and Jasper national parks. Wildlife abounds here and is most visible in spring and autumn after a snowfall, when herds of bighorn sheep come to the road to lick up the salt used to melt snow and ice. At 6,675 ft, Sunwapta is the second-highest drivable pass in the national parks of the Canadian Rockies. Regardless of whether you approach it from the north or south, be prepared for a series of hairpin turns as you switchback your way up to the pass summit. ☒ *122 km (76 mi) north of Lake Louise, 108 km (67 mi) south of Jasper.*

The **Athabasca Glacier** is a 7-km (4½-mi) tongue of ice flowing from the immense Columbia Icefield almost to the highway. Several other glaciers are visible from here; they all originate from the Columbia Icefield—a giant alpine lake of ice covering 325 square km (130 square mi), whose edge is visible from the highway. You can take a trip onto the Athabasca Glacier on buses (called snow-coaches) modified to drive on ice (tickets available at the Icefield Centre). Hikers can also walk onto the tongue of the glacier, but venturing very far without a trained guide is dangerous due to hidden crevasses and slippery, sharp ice. ☒ *127 km (79 mi) north of Lake Louise, 103 km (64 mi) south of Jasper. Bus tour, Brewster Tours,* ☎ *403/762–6700.* ☒ *$21.50.* ☼ *May–mid-Oct. Guided ½-day walking tour, Athabasca Glacier Ice Walks,* ☎ *403/347–1828 in-season, 403/852–3803 off-season.* ☒ *3-hr walk $28, 5- to 6-hr walk $32. Reserve through Jasper Adventure Centre,* ☎ *403/852–5595 or 800/565–7547; tickets also available at Icefield Centre (☞ below).*

⓭ The **Icefield Centre,** the interpretive center for the Athabasca Glacier and Columbia Icefield, houses interpretive exhibits, a gift shop, and two dining facilities (one cafeteria style, one buffet style). There are even 32 hotel rooms, available from early May to mid-October (book through Brewster's Transport in Banff, ☎ 403/762–6735). Keep in mind that the summer midday rush between 11 and 3 can be intense. ✉ *Opposite Athabasca Glacier on Hwy. 93, 127 km (79 mi) north of Lake Louise, 103 km (64 mi) south of Jasper,* ☎ *403/852–7030 summer, 403/852–6176 winter.* ☉ *Late May–mid-June and Sept., daily 10–5; mid-June–Aug., daily 10–7.*

Jasper

⓮ *287 km (178 mi) north of Banff, 362 km (224 mi) west of Edmonton.*

The town of Jasper, a less-hectic version of Banff and about one-half the size of its larger cousin, is a convenient central location for exploring the sights in Jasper National Park. The shopping and dining scene is even more casual than Banff's, and the center of town has space for adults to hang out and for kids to play. Jasper has grown considerably in recent years, with prices to match. Still, it remains a relaxed and somewhat less commercialized place to stay in the parks.

Jasper is set in one of the preeminent backpacking areas in North America. Multiday loops of more than 160 km (100 mi) are possible on well-maintained trails. Backpacking and horse-packing trips in the northern half of the park offer legitimate wilderness seclusion, if not the dramatic glacial scenery of the park's southern half. However, day trips are much more common, especially around Mt. Edith Cavell, Tonquin Valley, Miette Hot Springs, and Maligne Lake for hiking, and Pyramid Lake and Jasper Park Lodge for horseback riding. For local information, contact the **Jasper Information Centre** (✉ 500 Connaught Dr., ☎ 403/852–6176) or **Jasper Tourism and Commerce** (✉ Box 98, 632 Connaught Dr., Jasper, Alberta T0E 1E0, ☎ 403/852–3858).

The main drag in Jasper is **Connaught Drive;** railroad tracks border one side of the road, and a dense collection of shops, restaurants, and motels line the other.

★ ⓯ The **Jasper Tramway** whisks riders 3,191 vertical ft up the steep flank of Whistlers Mountain to an impressive overlook of the town of Jasper. You can see the summit of Mt. Robson (when that mountain isn't shrouded in clouds), the Miette Valley to the west, and the Athabasca Valley to the east. The seven-minute ride takes you to the upper station, above the tree line (be sure to bring warm clothes). From there, a 30-to-45-minute scramble will take you to the summit, at 8,085 ft above sea level. Several unmarked trails lead through the alpine meadows beyond. ✉ *Whistlers Mountain Rd., 3 km (2 mi) south of Jasper off Hwy. 93,* ☎ *403/852–3093.* ⌁ *$14.* ☉ *Mid-May–Aug., daily 8:30 AM–10 PM; Sept., daily 9:30–9; Apr.–mid-May and Oct., daily 9–4:30.*

The **Jasper-Yellowhead Museum** has historical exhibits showing what life in the area was like when prospectors, surveyors, settlers, and others arrived more than a century ago. ✉ *400 Pyramid Lake Rd.,* ☎ *403/852–3013.* ⌁ *Donations accepted.* ☉ *Mid-May–early Sept., daily 10–9; early Sept.–mid-May, call for hrs.*

☙ **Jasper Aquatic Center** pleases children with an indoor water slide, a kids' pool, and a huge regular pool. ✉ *Pyramid Lake Rd.,* ☎ *403/852–3663.* ⌁ *$4.* ☉ *Public swim Mon.–Thurs. 6 PM–8:30 PM, Fri. 4–9:30, weekends 2–9:30; call for other hrs.*

⑯ **Pyramid** and **Patricia lakes** are on the outskirts of Jasper. Motorboats, sailboats, rowboats, canoes, kayaks, catamarans, and four-seater pedal boats can be rented from Pyramid Lake Resort. Pyramid Lake is one of only two lakes in Jasper National Park where boat motors are allowed (the other is a section of Maligne Lake). There are picnic tables and a sandy beach at Pyramid Lake, but you're likely to find the water too cold for swimming. At Patricia Lake Bungalows, you can rent from a small selection of canoes and rowboats. ⊠ *Pyramid Lake Resort, Pyramid Lake Rd., 6 km (4 mi) north of Jasper,* ☎ *403/852–4900.* 🖃 *Boat rentals start at $10 per hr per boat.* ☉ *May–Oct., approximately 8 AM–10 PM.* ⊠ *Patricia Lake Bungalows, Pyramid Lake Rd., 5 km (3 mi) north of Jasper,* ☎ *403/852–3560.* 🖃 *Boat rentals $6 per hr.*

Dining and Lodging

$$$–$$$$ ✕ **Jasper Park Lodge.** For fancy dining around Jasper, Moose's Nook and the Edith Cavell Dining Room are the places to go. Moose's Nook has intimate dining with a range of Canadian dishes—pasta, Alberta prime rib of beef, and buffalo with wild mushrooms—as well as a popular salad and dessert bar. The Edith Cavell Dining Room overlooks the impressive mountain of the same name and has tall wooden pillars, wall tapestries, and live classical piano music. The menu is very French, with a few local nuances. The chowder of wild mushrooms and mixed grains and the hearts of romaine lettuce with roast garlic in anchovy dressing are each meals in themselves. The Beauvert Room, a huge dining room with stone pillars and hard angles, has a big-hotel-style ambience. Menu favorites include the warm artichoke pâté with water biscuits and garden crudités, and the slow-roasted loin of Alberta pork, honey-glazed and served with apricot chutney. For a taste of the Far East, try the Sushi Bar, a small eatery with a good selection of sushi served at a counter. The Beauvert Room and Moose's Nook are open only in summer; the Edith Cavell Dining Room, the Beauvert Room and the Sushi Bar are open for dinner only. ⊠ *Off Hwy. 16, 4 km (2½ mi) northeast of Jasper,* ☎ *403/852–3301 or 800/441–1414. Reservations essential. AE, D, DC, MC, V.*

$$$–$$$$ ✕ **Le Beauvallon.** This is often the restaurant of choice for Jasperites ★ going out for a special meal. Upholstered chairs, blue tablecloths, and wood-trimmed walls give the dining room an air of elegance that is enhanced by the strains of a world-class harpist playing in the nearby lounge. The menu has some seafood items, but meat and game dishes are the highlight, including beef, caribou, elk, lamb, ostrich, and venison. The giant Sunday-brunch buffet is an epic feast. Le Beauvallon is open for breakfast, too. ⊠ *Chateau Jasper, 96 Giekie St.,* ☎ *403/852–5644. Reservations essential in summer. AE, D, DC, MC, V.*

$$$–$$$$ ✕ **Tokyo Tom's.** Japanese restaurants are the latest trend in the Rockies, and this is a good place to sample their fare. The dining area is filled with small wooden tables and straight-back chairs—choose one of the partly enclosed booths for more privacy. Sushi and sashimi highlight the authentic Japanese food. Hot pots, sukiyaki, shabu-shabu, tempura, and stir-fries are also available. ⊠ *410 Connaught Dr.,* ☎ *403/852–3780. AE, MC, V.*

$$–$$$$ ✕ **Fiddle River Seafood Company.** Here you'll find a taste of the sea ★ in high-and-dry Jasper. Oil lamps at every table, dried flower arrangements on the walls and over the small bar, and plenty of wood highlight the cozy, second-floor dining room. Tables facing Connaught Drive have an excellent view of Mt. Tekarra. Seafood is the star, from the relatively simple beer-battered cod with lemon-pepper fries to more exotic choices such as sesame-crusted salmon. Chicken, T-bones, lamb, and pasta dishes are also available. ⊠ *620 Connaught Dr.,* ☎ *403/ 852–3032,* 🖶 *403/852–5058. AE, MC, V. No lunch.*

$–$$$ ✕ **Earls Restaurant.** Part of a popular chain that has recently expanded
into the mountains, Earls has good food, a campy atmosphere (chick-
ens in karate attire), and efficient service. This is not haute cuisine—
dining is fun and draws a young crowd. The menu lists international
favorites with spices tempered somewhat to appeal to a North Amer-
ican clientele. California shrimp rolls recall sushi, Hunan chicken is
Earls's version of stir-fry, and Forno roast hunter chicken has an Ital-
ian flavor. There are lines at the usual busy hours. ⊠ *600 Patricia St.,*
☎ *403/852–2393. Reservations not accepted. AE, MC, V.*

$ ✕ **Mountain Foods & Cafe.** Here's a good place to pick up a morning
cup of coffee or sandwiches for a picnic. The café serves breakfast, lunch,
and light dinner items, to eat in or take out. Packed trail lunches are
a specialty. Although you can dine on bacon and eggs for breakfast
and meat sandwiches or meat pies for lunch or dinner, the emphasis
is on healthier alternatives such as soup and focaccia, pizza melts, tor-
tilla wraps, and falafel for lunch or dinner. Local beer is on tap. ⊠ *606
Connaught Dr.,* ☎ *403/852–4050. MC, V.*

$$$$ ⊞ **Chateau Jasper.** Large wood beams cantilevered over the front
door of this two-story inn suggest a Scandinavian interior, but rooms
are of the American motel style, with a colonial motif that's most no-
table in the headboards. Burgundy carpets and low ceilings add cozi-
ness to largish rooms. The hotel's restaurant, Le Beauvallon (☞ *above*),
is excellent. Rates drop by almost half October–May. ⊠ *96 Giekie St.,
T0E 1E0,* ☎ *403/852–5644,* 𝖥𝖠𝖷 *403/852–4860. 119 rooms. Restau-
rant, indoor pool, hot tub. AE, DC, MC, V.*

$$$$ ⊞ **Jasper Park Lodge.** This lakeside resort northeast of town hums with
★   on-site recreational amenities and is a notable mountain destination
in itself, whether or not you stay here. Rooms vary: Most are arranged
in four-unit chalets; specialty cabins with three, five, six, or eight bed-
rooms are also options. Besides bright down comforters and a porch,
patio, or balcony, many units also include a fireplace. There's year-round
outdoor swimming in a pool (you swim to it from the warm indoors)
heated to 30°C (86°F) in winter—a major draw for winter guests. Some
readers have complained in recent years that tour groups receive pref-
erential treatment, and overbooking for individual travelers can be a
problem in peak season. Improved booking procedures have reduced
the problem, but it hasn't entirely been resolved. Rates drop by almost
one-half October–May. ⊠ *Off Hwy. 16, 4 km (2½ mi) northeast of
Jasper, Box 40, T0E 1E0,* ☎ *403/852–3301 or 800/441–1414,* 𝖥𝖠𝖷 *403/
852–5107. 442 rooms. 4 restaurants, bar, coffee shop, deli, 3 lounges,
pool, 18-hole golf course, 4 tennis courts, horseback riding, boating,
bicycles, ice-skating, rollerblading, sleigh rides. AE, D, DC, MC, V.*

$$$–$$$$ ⊞ **Jasper Inn.** A modern interpretation of chalet-style architecture, this
inn has oblique angles and hard edges, with sleek, low-slung furniture
to match. The angular coolness is warmed by slanted cedar ceilings and
brick fireplaces. Accommodations vary, but living areas in condo-style
units are particularly spacious. Most units have kitchenettes and fire-
places. The rooms facing Bonhomme Street have the best views. Rates
drop by more than half October–May. ⊠ *Giekie St. and Bonhomme
Ave., Box 879, T0E 1E0,* ☎ *403/852–4461,* 𝖥𝖠𝖷 *403/852–5916. 129
rooms, 14 suites. Restaurant, lobby lounge, indoor pool, sauna, steam
bath. AE, D, DC, MC, V.*

$$–$$$ ⊞ **Alpine Village.** One of Jasper's bargains is just south of town. Logs
★   in many cabins are left exposed on interior walls, adding to the warm,
rustic feeling of this family-run operation. Rooms have pine furnish-
ings, fireplaces, and beamed ceilings. Most units have sundecks; two-
bedroom cabins have full kitchens. Mt. Edith Cavell rises in the
distance, and the Athabasca River runs out front, though you must cross
a small road to reach it. Rates decrease by one-third off-season. ⊠ *Hwy.*

93A, 1 km (½ mi) south of Jasper, Box 610, T0E 1E0, ☎ 403/852–3285. 42 units. Outdoor hot tub. MC, V. Closed mid-Oct.–Apr.

$–$$ 🏠 **Patricia Lake Bungalows.** Just a short drive from Jasper, this great place for peace and quiet is on the shores of Patricia Lake. The clean, bright, roomy cabins have basic furnishings—queen-size beds, dressers and tables, kitchen facilities, and TV. Shower stalls are the rule here, not bathtubs. This is one of the few remaining bargain accommodations in Jasper. The motel-style rooms have recently been remodeled into large family units, but the cabins remain the most popular choice for most visitors. Rates decrease by 20% off-season. ✉ *Pyramid Lake Rd., 5 km (3 mi) from Jasper, Box 657, Jasper, T0E 1E0, ☎ 403/852–3560,* FAX *403/852–4060. 6 rooms, 29 cabins. Boating, bicycles, coin laundry. AE, MC, V. Closed mid-Oct.–Apr.*

Nightlife and the Arts

THE ARTS

The **Chaba Movie Theatre** (✉ Connaught Dr., ☎ 403/852–4749) plays major releases daily. The **Jasper Activity Centre** (✉ 303 Pyramid Ave., ☎ 403/852–3381) hosts local theater, music, and dance troupes throughout the year. The **Jasper Folk Festival** (☎ 403/852–3858), on the first weekend in August, presents Canadian folk music in the town center and at other venues.

NIGHTLIFE

The **Astoria Hotel's Dead Dog Bar & Grill** (✉ 404 Connaught Dr., ☎ 403/852–3351) is a popular spot that can become crowded and raucous. The **Athabasca Hotel**'s nightclub (✉ 510 Patricia St., ☎ 403/852–3386) has dancing to Top 40 music and live bands. **Pete's on Patricia** (✉ 614 Patricia St., 2nd floor, ☎ 403/852–6262) is a crowded spot that showcases live bands weekly. For cocktails and socializing, the **Jasper Park Lodge** (✉ Off Hwy. 16, ☎ 403/852–3301) has lounges and dining rooms with entertainment and dancing. The **Whistle Stop** (✉ Whistlers Inn, Connaught Dr., ☎ 403/852–3361) is a local haunt with the ambience of a British pub.

Outdoor Activities and Sports

BIKING

Bikes can be rented from **Freewheel Cycle** (✉ 611 Patricia St., ☎ 403/852–3898). The **Jasper Park Lodge** (✉ Off Hwy. 16, ☎ 403/852–3301) has bikes for rent.

CLIMBING

The **Jasper Climbing School and Mountaineering Service** (✉ Box 452, T0E 1E0, ☎ 403/852–3964) offers daylong guided trips as well as climbing instruction.

GOLF

Jasper Park Lodge (☎ 403/852–6090) has an 18-hole, par-75 course that has been rated one of the world's top 10 by *Golf Magazine*.

GUIDED TOURS

Currie's Guiding (✉ Box 105, 414 Connaught Dr., T0E 1E0, ☎ 403/852–5650) offers four- to six-hour driving tours of scenic highlights in the area, as well as a "wildlife search" tour. Prices begin around $39. **Edge Control Outdoors** (✉ Box 52, 614D Connaught Dr., T0E 1E0, ☎ 403/852–4945) has a Walks and Talks Jasper program, with two- to four-hour guided walking programs to Maligne Canyon, Mt. Edith Cavell, and a bird and wildlife viewing tour, as well as customized walking tours. Prices begin at $25. The **Jasper Adventure Centre** (✉ Box 1064, T0E 1E0, ☎ FAX 403/852–5595) provides guided tours of popular sights in Jasper National Park as well as birding trips, ice walks, and snowshoeing tours. Rates are about $24–$32 per adult, with most tours lasting about three hours. The center rents skis, snow-boards, and snowshoes. It also handles bookings for a number of other adventure companies (canoeing, rafting, and other sports).

HIKING

For information on Skyline and Tonquin Valley trail quotas, contact **Jasper National Park Information Centre** (✉ 500 Connaught Dr., T0E 1E0, ☎ 403/852–6177). **Rocky Mountain Hiking** (✉ Box 2623, T0E 1E0, ☎ 403/852–5015) has trained backcountry guides to take visitors on customized multiday hikes and also offers interpretive programs, day hikes, and some caving.

HORSEBACK RIDING

For trail rides or lessons contact the concierge at **Jasper Park Lodge** (☎ 403/852–3301) or **Skyline Trail Rides** (✉ Box 207, T0E 1E0, ☎ 403/852–4215 or 403/852–3301, ext. 6189).

RAFTING

Jasper Raft Tours (✉ Box 398, T0E 1E0, ☎ 403/852–3613) runs half-day float trips on the Athabasca. **Maligne River Adventures** (✉ Box 280, 616 Connaught Dr., T0E 1E0, ☎ 403/852–3370) runs half-day white-water trips on the Maligne. Prices begin at $50.

SCUBA DIVING

For scuba divers **Patricia Lake,** near Jasper, is a popular spot to explore the remains of the *Habakkuk*. This was a ship made of ice: a military prototype, secretly designed during World War II to take advantage of the fact that the plastic nature of ice (maintained by a cooling system) could absorb an impact without major structural damage to the vessel. What remains is mostly a skeleton of cooling pipes.

SKIING

Cross-Country. Jasper National Park has excellent groomed trails at Pyramid and Patricia lakes and on the Icefields Parkway near town. Maligne Lake has a range of moderate to challenging lakeside and forest cross-country ski trails. Reservations for backcountry huts in Tonquin Valley can be made through **Tonquin Valley Pack and Ski Trips** (✉ Box 550, 712 Connaught Dr., T0E 1E0, ☎ 403/852–3909).

Downhill. Marmot Basin (✉ Box 1300, Jasper T0E 1E0, ☎ 403/852–3816), near Jasper, has a wide mix of terrain, and slopes are a little less crowded than those around Banff. This area has 53 runs and 8 lifts; vertical drop is 2,944 ft.

SPORTING GEAR

Totem Ski Shop (✉ 408 Connaught Dr., ☎ 403/852–3078 or 800/363–3078) is the major sporting goods outlet.

SWIMMING

Pyramid Lake has a large beach, although it would be unusual for the water to warm above 20°C (68°F). Lake Annette and Lake Edith, near Jasper Park Lodge, also have beaches and somewhat warmer water that reaches the low 20s°C (low 70s°F) during warm spells. These waters are among the clearest anywhere.

Shopping

In Jasper the main **shopping streets** are Patricia Street and Connaught Drive; expect to pay a resort premium for most goods. **Christmas in the Rockies** (✉ Beauvert Promenade, Jasper Park Lodge, ☎ 403/852–4779) carries quality Christmas ornaments and decorations year-round. You'll find a large selection of native arts and crafts at **E&A Studio** (✉ 105 Miette Ave., ☎ 403/852–3606). **Jasper Originals** (✉ Beauvert Promenade, Jasper Park Lodge, ☎ 403/852–5378) has a good selection of regional arts and crafts. The **Maligne Canyon Gift Shop** (⊠ Maligne Canyon, Maligne Lake Rd., ☎ 403/852–3583) has an extensive selection of stone sculptures and native arts and crafts. Every conceivable Royal Canadian Mounted Police (Mountie) gift is under one roof at **Sergeant Preston's Outpost** (⊠ 614 Patricia St., ☎ 403/852–2182). **Timber Wolf** (⊠ 609b Patricia St., ☎ 403/852–4082) has a good choice of native arts and crafts.

Jasper National Park

South border of park: 178 km (110 mi) north of Banff townsite, 152 km (94 mi) south of Jasper townsite. East border of park: 323 km (200 mi) west of Edmonton, 50 km (31 mi) east of Jasper townsite.

Apart from the innumerable scenic vistas and hiking trails, a number of special attractions in Jasper National Park make for easy half-day trips south, east, north, or west from the Jasper townsite. Don't expect much in the way of accommodations, though; apart from a single motel at Miette Hot Springs, and two cabin-type facilities near the east gate, all the lodging in this huge park—almost as large as the entire state of Connecticut—is clustered in the town. A day pass is $5 per person or $10 for a group of 2–10 people. For park information, contact **Jasper National Park Information Centre** (⊠ 500 Connaught Dr., T0E 1E0, ☎ 403/852–6176).

⑰ **Mt. Edith Cavell,** the highest mountain in the vicinity of the town of Jasper, towers above the surroundings at 11,033 ft and shows off its permanently snow-clad north face to the town. It was named after a heroic nurse who was shot by the Germans during the First World War. From Highway 93A, a narrow, winding 14½-km (9-mi) road (often closed until the beginning of June) leads to the base of the mountain. Because the route has become very busy, traffic is now one-way, with the direction reversed every 1½ hours. Check at the Jasper Information Centre (☎ 403/852–6176) for specific timing. Trailers are not permitted on this road, but they can be dropped off at a parking lot near the junction with 93A. Several pullouts offer spectacular views, as well as access to trails leading up the **Tonquin Valley,** one of the premier hiking (and horse-packing and backcountry skiing) areas in the park.

The mountain itself is arguably the most spectacular site in Jasper National Park reachable by automobile. From the parking lot—which can become quite congested—a short trail leads to the base of an imposing mile-high, almost vertical cliff. The Angel Glacier drips out of a valley partway up the slope, highlighting the scene. If you feel ambitious, a steep 3-km (2-mi) trail climbs up the valley opposite the mountain, opening into an alpine meadow—**Cavell Meadows.** Wildflowers carpet the meadows from mid-July to mid- or late August, and there's an excellent view of the Angel Glacier on the opposite slope. ⊠ *27 km (17 mi) south of Jasper off Hwy. 93A.*

⑱ At **Athabasca Falls,** the Athabasca River is compressed through a narrow gorge, producing a violent torrent of water. The falls are especially dramatic in early summer, when the river is swollen by snowmelt. Trails and overlooks provide places to view the falls. ⊠ *31 km (19 mi) south of Jasper at Icefields Pkwy. and Hwy. 93A.*

Maligne Canyon, along the way to Maligne Lake, is where the Maligne River cuts a narrow 165-ft-deep gorge through limestone bedrock. An interpretive trail winds its way along the river, switching from side to side over six bridges as the canyon progressively deepens. It is an impressive sight, but the 4-km (2½-mi) trail along the canyon can be crowded, especially near the start of the trail. Just off the path, you'll find a restaurant and one of the better native craft stores in the Jasper area at the Maligne Canyon Chalet. ⊠ *Maligne Lake Rd., 11 km (7 mi) south of Jasper.*

Medicine Lake has a complex, underground drainage system that causes the lake to empty almost completely at times. This led the early natives to suspect that spirits were responsible for the dramatic fluctuations in the level of the placid waters. ⊠ *Maligne Lake Rd., 26 km (16 mi) south of Jasper.*

★ ⓳ The remarkably blue, 22-km-long (14-mi-long) **Maligne Lake** is one of the largest glacier-fed lakes in the world. You can explore it on a 1½-hour guided cruise or in a rented boat. A couple of day hikes (approximately four hours round-trip), with some steep sections, lead to alpine meadows that have panoramic views of the lake and the surrounding mountain ranges. You can also take horseback riding and fishing trips, and there's an excellent cafeteria here. ⊠ *Maligne Lake Rd., 44 km (27 mi) southeast of Jasper. Tour reservations,* ⊠ *Maligne Lake Scenic Cruises, 626 Connaught Dr.,* ☎ *403/852–3370.* 🎫 *Boat tour $31.* ☉ *Mid-May–Oct., daily 10–5, every hr on the hr.*

⓴ **Miette Hot Springs** is a relaxing spot, especially when the weather turns inclement. You can soak in naturally heated mineral waters originating from three springs that reach 54°C (129°F) and have to be cooled to 40°C (104°F) to allow bathing. There are two hot pools and one cool pool (27°C, or 80°F). A short walk leads to the remnants of the original hot-spring facility, where several springs still pour heated sulphurous water into the adjacent creek. Day passes and bathing suit (period or modern), locker, and towel rentals are available. ⊠ *Miette Hot Springs Rd. off Hwy. 16, 58 km (36 mi) northeast of Jasper,* ☎ *403/ 866–3939.* 🎫 *$5.* ☉ *Late May–mid-June and early Sept.–early Oct., daily 10:30–9, late-June–early Sept., daily 8:30 AM–10:30 PM.*

Outdoor Activities and Sports

Jasper National Park, with nearly 1,000 km (620 mi) of hiking trails, is popular with hikers who want to go deep into the wilderness for several days at a time. In an effort to minimize environmental impact, park officials in Jasper have set quotas for some of the park's most popular backpacking routes. In the height of the summer season, be prepared to encounter filled quotas for such areas as the Skyline Trail and Tonquin Valley. About a third of each trail's quota is prebooked by reservations, which can be made up to three weeks in advance by contacting the Jasper National Park Information Centre (☞ Outdoor Activities and Sports *in* Jasper, *above*).

Tonquin Valley, near Mt. Edith Cavell, is one of Canada's classic backpacking areas. Its high mountain lakes, bounded by a series of steep, rocky peaks known as the Ramparts, attract many visitors in the height of summer. The **Skyline Trail** wanders for 44 km (27 mi), at or above the tree line, past some of the park's most spectacular scenery. Good **day-hiking areas** in Jasper are around Maligne Lake, Mt. Edith Cavell, and Miette Hot Springs.

Mt. Robson Provincial Park

80 km (50 mi) west of Jasper.

This provincial park, contiguous with Jasper National Park, makes a pleasant hour-long drive from Jasper townsite on Highway 16. The terrain and scenery are similar to Jasper's, although the vegetation is more lush because of higher rainfall. The park has a number of hiking trails, plus some campgrounds. Another draw is the Fraser River. The park is free, and the **Mt. Robson Visitor Centre** (⊠ Hwy. 16, ☎ 250/566–4325), open mid-May to early October, has a fine view of Mt. Robson and a small restaurant. For general information, contact **BC Parks** (⊠ 4051 18th Ave., Box 2045, Prince George, British Columbia V2N 2J6, ☎ 250/563–6340).

㉑ At 12,972 ft, towering **Mt. Robson** is the highest mountain in the Canadian Rockies was not successfully scaled until 1913. Certain routes on Robson are still considered by experienced mountaineers to be among the world's most challenging. Mt. Robson's weather is notoriously bad even when the weather elsewhere is perfectly fine; it is a rare day that the summit is not encircled by clouds. A favorite backpacking trip on the mountain is the strenuous 18-km (11-mi) hike to **Berg Lake,** through the wonderfully named Valley of a Thousand Falls. Berg Lake is no tranquil body of water; the grunt and splash as Robson's glaciers calve chunks of ice into the lake are regular sounds in summer. The 5-km (3-mi) mostly level hike to **Kinney Lake,** along the Berg Lake trail, is a good option for day hikers.

Kootenay National Park

34 km (21 mi) west of Banff townsite, 162 km (100 mi) west of Calgary.

When the tourist population of Banff swells during the busy summer months, Kootenay park remains surprisingly quiet, although not for lack of natural beauty; the scenery certainly matches that of Banff and Jasper parks. Named for the Kootenai people who settled in the area, Kootenay National Park is just over the Alberta border in British Columbia, touching the west side of Banff National Park and the south end of Yoho National Park. Facilities are few here, so most people see the park only as they drive through on Highway 93, which traverses the length of the park, while on their way to points in British Columbia. A day pass is $5 per person or $10 for 2–10 people.

For local information, contact the **Kootenay National Park Visitor Centre** (⊠ Aquacourt at Radium Hot Springs pools, Box 220, Radium Hot Springs, V0E 1M0, ☎ 250/347–9505 in summer; 403/292–4401 or 250/347–9551 in winter). The center is open only from late May to early October.

㉒ At 5,416 ft, **Vermilion Pass** is not one of the highest passes in the Canadian Rockies, but it marks the boundary between Alberta and British Columbia and the Continental Divide—rivers east of here flow to the Atlantic Ocean; rivers to the west flow to the Pacific Ocean. The pass is at the juncture of Banff and Kootenay national parks, on Highway 93.

Just beyond the Vermilion Pass summit is the head of the **Stanley Glacier trail,** one of the fine choices for a day hike in the park. The trail climbs easily for 4 km (2½ mi) through fire remnants and new growth, across rock debris and glacial moraine, ending in the giant amphitheater of the Stanley Glacier basin. ⊠ *3 km (2 mi) from east gate of Kootenay National Park.*

㉓ **Floe Lake,** at the base of a 3,300-ft-high cliff called the Rockwall, is one of the most popular hiking destinations in Kootenay National Park. The 10-km (6-mi) trail from the highway passes through characteristic Kootenay backcountry terrain. Plan a full day for this one. ⊠ *Trailhead, 22 km (14 mi) from east gate of Kootenay park.*

Outdoor Activities and Sports

The trail that best characterizes the hiking in Kootenay is the strenuous **Rockwall Trail,** which runs along the series of steep rock facades that are the predominant feature of the park. Floe Lake, sitting at the base of a sheer 3,300-ft wall, is a trail highlight. Several long day-hike spurs connect the trail with Highway 93.

En Route   Along the stretch of Highway 93 that leads through Kootenay National Park from Banff National Park to Radium Hot Springs, 63 km (39 mi) to the south, the only service area is at **Vermilion Crossing,** the approximate halfway point. Here you'll find fuel and basic groceries (summer only). Between Vermilion Crossing and Radium, the mountains open up gradually, their flanks covered by thick stands of Douglas fir, as the Vermilion River joins with the wider Kootenay River. The highway then heads west, winding through the narrow limestone canyon cut by the Sinclair River.

Yoho National Park

57 km (35 mi) northwest of town of Banff, 185 km (115 mi) west of Calgary.

The name "Yoho" is a native word that translates, approximately, to "awe inspiring." Indeed, Yoho National Park contains some of the most outstanding scenery in the Canadian Rockies and a well-known fossil site. The park adjoins Banff National Park to the east and Kootenay National Park to the south, but it is quieter than its eastern neighbor. Highway 1 divides Yoho into the northern half, which includes Takakkaw Falls, the Yoho River valley, and Emerald Lake, and the southern half, of which Lake O'Hara is the physical and spiritual epicenter. A day pass is $5 per person or $10 for 2–10 people. For park and local information, contact the **Yoho National Park Visitor Centre** (✉ Hwy 1, at the intersection for Field, Box 99, Field, British Columbia V0A 1G0, ☎ 250/343–6783).

❷❹ **Takakkaw Falls,** in the northern half of Yoho park, is 833 ft high, making it the highest waterfall in Canada. The falls are spectacular in early summer, when melting snow and ice provide ample runoff. (The flow of the falls can also increase during summer hot spells, which speed the melt of glacial ice.) But the falls are just a taste of what lies ahead for day hikers and backpackers who choose to explore the region's trail network through the Yoho River valley with its ice fields and high cliffs. ✉ *Access from 13-km (8-mi) Yoho Valley Rd., off Hwy. 1, 13 km (8 mi) west of Banff National Park.*

❷❺ The **Burgess Shale site,** halfway between the Takakkaw Falls road and the Emerald Lake Lodge road, contains the fossilized remains of 120 marine species dating back 515 million years. It was designated a World Heritage Site in 1981. Guided hikes are the only way to see the actual fossil sites, and they're popular, so make reservations. The hikes are conducted July through mid-September, and the going is fairly strenuous; the round-trip distance is 20 km (12 mi). A shorter, steeper hike leads to the Mt. Stevens trilobite fossil beds. Guided hikes are also offered to extensions of the Burgess Shale fossils in Kootenay and Banff national parks. Allow a full day for any of the hikes. ✉ *Trailhead, 16 km (10 mi) west of Banff National Park on Hwy. 1. Reservations for guided hikes,* ✉ *Canadian Wilderness Tours, 1010 Larch Pl., Canmore, Alberta T1W 1S7,* ☎ *403/678–3795; or* ✉ *Yoho-Burgess Shale Research Foundation, Box 148, Field, British Columbia V0A 1G0,* ☎ *800/343–3006.* 🎫 *Guided hike $35–$45.*

❷❻ At **Emerald Lake,** a vivid turquoise shimmer at the base of the President Range, you can rent a canoe, have a cup of tea at the teahouse by Emerald Lake Lodge (☞ Dining and Lodging, *below*), or take a stroll around the lake. The lake also is a trailhead for hikers, as well as a haunt of cross-country and backcountry skiers. ⊠ *Access from 8-km (5-mi) road off Hwy. 1, 19 km (12 mi) west of Banff National Park.*

㉗ Lake O'Hara, in Yoho's southern half, is widely regarded as one of *the* ultimate destinations for outdoor enthusiasts in the Canadian Rockies. For summer, Lake O'Hara Lodge (☞ Dining and Lodging, *below*) is booked months in advance. Although the forest-lined fire road between Highway 1 and the lake can be hiked, it makes more sense to ride the lodge-run bus. (Call the lodge for times and space availability.) Save your legs for hiking any of several moderately strenuous trails that radiate from the lodge into a high-alpine world of small lakes surrounded by escarpments of rock and patches of year-round snow. Keep in mind, however, that the bus makes the Lake O'Hara area accessible to many other people. If you're looking for a true wilderness experience, other places (notably Kootenay National Park) are better choices. ⊠ *Access from 11-km (7-mi) Lake O'Hara Fire Rd. off Lake Louis–Great Divide Dr., 3 km (2 mi) west of Banff National Park.*

Dining and Lodging

$$$$ ✕⌂ **Emerald Lake Lodge.** This enchanted place at the edge of a secluded,
★ glacier-fed lake is only a 20-minute drive from Lake Louise and an hour from Banff. You can get light meals in a comfortable sitting area by the large stone hearth in the log-cabin main lodge. Guest rooms have fireplaces and balconies. The main dining room is a glass-enclosed terrace, with views of the lake through tall stands of evergreens. The menu mixes traditional Canadian and American fare—steaks, game, and fish—with such nouvelle sauces as ginger-tangerine glaze. Cilantro-on-the-Lake serves café-style light meals (summer only). Room rates are reduced by half in off-season. ⊠ *Yoho National Park, 9½ km (6 mi) north of Field, Box 10, Field, British Columbia V0A 1G0,* ☎ *250/343–6321 or 800/663–6336,* ℻ *250/343–6724. 85 units in 2- and 4-room cottages. 2 restaurants, bar, tea shop, sauna, outdoor hot tub, exercise room, horseback riding, boating. AE, DC, MC, V.*

$$$$ ⌂ **Lake O'Hara Lodge.** In summer guests are ferried by a lodge-operated bus along an 11-km (7-mi) fire road between Highway 1 and the grounds. In winter guests must ski the distance. The lodge and lakeside cabins offer fairly luxurious backcountry living; the rooms have baths, and a dining room serves three meals a day (included in the room rates). Reservations for the high summer season (mid-June–September) should be booked several months in advance. Rates are based on double-occupancy rooms; there are no off-season rates. ⊠ *Off Hwy. 1, Yoho National Park, Box 55, Lake Louise, Alberta T0L 1E0,* ☎ *250/343–6418 or 403/678–4110. 23 rooms. Dining room, hiking, cross-country skiing, boating. No credit cards. Closed mid-Apr.–mid-June and Oct.–mid-Feb.*

Outdoor Activities and Sports

HIKING

Yoho is divided into two parts: the popular hiking area around Lake O'Hara, dotted with high-alpine lakes, and the less-traveled Yoho River valley, terminating at the Yoho Glacier. Access to the Lake O'Hara region is somewhat restricted by the long, rather uneventful fire road from Highway 1. Most hikers and climbers take the Lake O'Hara Lodge shuttle bus. Entry into the Yoho River valley is more immediate, either from Takakkaw Falls or from Emerald Lake.

HORSEBACK RIDING

The concierge at **Emerald Lake Lodge** (☎ 250/343–6321) can arrange for horseback riding expeditions and lessons.

SOUTH OF BANFF

The region immediately southeast of Banff—the town of Canmore and, south of it, the group of provincial parks and recreation areas jointly known as Kananaskis Country—attracted mostly locals until the 1988 Olympics brought new facilities—ski jumps, cross-country trails, and other sports installations, as well as hotels and restaurants—to the region. Farther south, Waterton Lakes National Park marks the meeting of the prairie and the mountains. With Glacier Park in Montana, it forms Waterton-Glacier International Peace Park.

Canmore

㉘ *24 km (15 mi) southeast of Banff townsite, 106 km (66 mi) west of Calgary.*

A modern boomtown, Canmore attracts a mix of high-end tourism developments, residents who crave a mountain lifestyle at an affordable price, and commuters from Calgary who feel the hour-long drive to the city is a fair trade-off for living in the mountains. The boutique-lined Main Street and several good restaurants are indications that Canmore is no longer a locals-only town, although much of its character and small-town charm remain. Canmore is also home to many outdoor activities and numerous outfitters—climbing, hiking, and mountain biking in summer, cross-country and downhill skiing in winter.

Canmore makes a good base for exploring both Kananaskis Country and Banff National Park, without the crowds or cost of Banff. But if shopping and dining options, a resort town atmosphere, or the hustle and bustle of a major tourist destination are important to you, then spend the extra dollars and make Banff your destination. If you want a quieter location with fewer amenities and the remnants of a small-town atmosphere, consider Canmore.

Dining and Lodging

$$–$$$$ ✕ **Pepper Mill.** The small dining room is simply decorated with off-
★ white walls, green tablecloths, and hanging lamps. This European-Swiss restaurant is known for its pepper steak but also serves well-prepared pasta dishes, fish, pork, chicken, and seafood. ⊠ *726 9th St.,* ☎ *403/ 678–2292. AE, MC, V. No lunch.*

$$–$$$ ✕ **Sinclair's.** This restaurant looks remarkably like someone's grand-
★ mother's house, complete with white clapboards and a white picket fence. The cozy dining room contains a fireplace (used during the cool season only), and colorful framed prints of flowers and historical sketches adorn the walls. Although the restaurant takes pride in serving an array of vegetarian dishes, it is definitely not a vegetarian outpost. Steak, chicken, buffalo burgers, salmon, lamb, and grilled turkey are available, along with the more adventuresome Louisiana hot pot (seafood, veggies, and rice) or Bombay chicken hot pot (chicken, cashews, veggies, curry, and rice). The exotic pastas and pizzas are menu highlights. ⊠ *637 Main St.,* ☎ *403/678–5370. MC, V.*

$$ ✕ **Musashi Japanese Restaurant.** There's not much in the way of atmosphere at this small, strip mall–style restaurant, but if you want Japanese food in Canmore, this is the best place to find it. You can choose from a range of tempura, teriyaki, udon noodles, fried seafood, and sushi. ⊠ *1306 Bow Valley Trail,* ☎ *403/678–9360. MC, V.*

$$$$ 🏨 **Mt. Assiniboine Lodge.** Built in 1928, this lodge appears to have changed little over the years. The backcountry setting is classically alpine—at the edge of 2-km-long (1 mi-long) Lake Magog, with the rocky pyramid of Mt. Assiniboine in full view. Guests can hike in (20–30 km, or 12–19 mi) or fly in by helicopter from Canmore. Hearty meals are served family-style. There are cabins that sleep two to four people, as well as lodge rooms. The lodge has some electricity and running water, but guests should be prepared to use outhouses. Room rates are $135–$175 per person and include all meals and hiking (or skiing) guide service. Rates decrease by about 15% off-season. ⊠ *Box 8128, T1W 2T8,* ☎ *403/678–2883,* FAX *403/678–4877. 6 rooms without bath, 6 cabins without bath. Dining room. MC, V. Closed Oct.– mid-Feb. and mid-Apr.–late June.*

$$ 🏨 **Rocky Mountain Ski Lodge.** Several motels in Canmore provide lower-price alternatives to Banff. Of these, Rocky Mountain Ski Lodge is a notch above the rest. It's really three separate motel properties rolled into one. Slanting, exposed wood-and-beam ceilings give a chaletlike feel to otherwise simple motel rooms. Rooms in the older section have kitchenettes, but the decor is more '60s American than Swiss-chalet. Rates drop by 40% off-season. ⊠ *Hwy. 1A, Box 8070, T1W 2T8,* ☎ *403/678–5445, 800/665–6111 in Canada,* FAX *403/678–6484. 82 rooms. Sauna, hot tub, playground. AE, DC, MC, V.*

$ 🏨 **Bow Valley Motel.** This two-story, few-frills motel in the center of Canmore is within easy walking distance of dining and shopping. Rooms are clean and simply furnished with a bed, a dresser, a small refrigerator, and a TV. Five rooms have kitchens. Rates drop by 40%– 50% off-season. ⊠ *610 8th St., T1W 2B5,* ☎ *403/678–5085,* FAX *403/ 678–6560. 25 rooms. Outdoor hot tub, coin laundry. AE, D, MC, V.*

Nightlife and the Arts

Join Canmore's locals and kick back at **Sherwood House** (⊠ 738 8th St., ☎ 403/678–5211), which occasionally has live bands on weekends.

Outdoor Activities and Sports

Many **outfitters and operators** who run tours in Banff National Park are based in Canmore. These operators provide a wide range of activities and often have tours in the Canmore region also, primarily in Kananaskis Country (☞ Banff *and* Lake Louise, *above*).

CROSS-COUNTRY SKIING

Canmore Nordic Centre (⊠ 1988 Olympic Way, Suite 100, T0L 0M0, ☎ 403/678–2400) has an extensive trail network (☞ Kananaskis Country, *below*). The **Canadian School of Mountaineering** (⊠ 629 10th St., T1W 2E5, ☎ 403/678–4134) leads backcountry tours.

GOLF

Canmore Golf Course (⊠ Off Hwy. 1, ☎ 403/678–4784) has 18 holes; par is 71.

Shopping

Altitude Sports (⊠ 801 Main St., ☎ 403/678–6272) has equipment for mountain biking, skiing, and snowboarding. The **Fudgery** (⊠ 721 8th St., ☎ 403/678–2898) is the place to satisfy a sweet tooth. **Mountain Avens Gallery** (⊠ Main St., ☎ 403/678–4471) displays local arts and crafts, with a focus on paintings. **Stonecrop Studios & Gallery** (⊠ 8th Ave. and Main St., ☎ 403/678–4151) showcases the works of local artists in media such as bronze, ceramics, pottery, and silver.

Kananaskis Country

㉙ *North entrance: 26 km (16 mi) southeast of Canmore, 80 km (50 mi) west of Calgary.*

Three provincial parks make up the 4,200-square-km (1,600-square-mi) recreational region known as Kananaskis Country, which includes inspiring mountain scenery, though perhaps not quite as spectacular as that in the adjacent national parks. Kananaskis has a multitude of outdoor activities, some of which are prohibited or discouraged in the national parks. Camping, hiking, bicycling, fishing, golfing, boating, canoeing, horseback riding, and exploring in all-terrain vehicles predominate in spring, summer, and fall. Downhill skiing, cross-country skiing, snowshoeing, ice-skating, snowmobiling, dogsledding, ice fishing, and camping are popular winter activities.

The main highway through Kananaskis Country is Highway 40, also known as the **Kananaskis Trail.** It runs north–south through the impressive scenery of the front ranges of the Rockies. Only the northern 40 km (25 mi) of the road remain open from December 1 to June 15, in part because of the extreme conditions of the **Highwood Pass** (at 7,280 ft, the highest drivable pass in Canada), and in part to protect winter wildlife habitat in **Peter Lougheed Provincial Park** and southward. Highway 40 continues south to join Highway 541, west of Longview. Access to East Kananaskis Country, a popular area for horseback trips, is on Highway 66, which heads west from Priddis.

For local information, contact **Kananaskis Country** (⊠ 3115 12th St. NE, Calgary, Alberta T2E 7J2, ☎ 403/297–3362).

The **Canmore Nordic Centre,** built for the 1988 Olympic Nordic skiing events, has 70 km (43 mi) of groomed cross-country trails. This state-of-the-art facility is in the northwest corner of Kananaskis Country, just south of Canmore. Some trails are lighted for night skiing, and a 1½-km (1-mi) paved trail is open in summer for roller skiing and in-line skating. Lessons and rentals are available. ⊠ *1988 Olympic Way, Canmore,* ☎ *403/678–2400.* ◻ *Trail use free.* ☉ *Lodge daily 9–5:30, some trails until 9.*

Kananaskis Village (☞ Dining and Lodging, *below*), a full-service resort built for the 1988 Olympics, brings first-class lodging, dining, and golfing to Kananaskis Country. A lodge, a hotel, and an inn cluster next to an attractively landscaped artificial pond on a small plateau between the Nakiska ski area and two 18-hole golf courses. Many visitors to the region stay at one of the several campgrounds, most of which can accommodate recreational vehicles.

The **William Watson Lodge** is unique in the Canadian Rockies in that it is designed exclusively for senior citizens and people who have disabilities. Access points have been built along Mt. Lorette Ponds north of Kananaskis Village to accommodate anglers using wheelchairs, and many hiking trails near the village have been cut wide and gentle enough for wheelchair travel. Overnight and day-use facilities, including cabins, are available to people with disabilities and Alberta senior citizens. Albertans get preference; people with disabilities from out of the province must book 60 days in advance. ⊠ *30 km (19 mi) south of Kananaskis Village on Hwy. 40, Box 130, Kananaskis T0L 2H0,* ☎ *403/591–7227.* ☉ *Office weekdays 8 AM–9 PM.*

Dining and Lodging

$$$$ ✕ **L'Escapade.** The signature dining room of the Hotel at Kananaskis
★   (☞ *below*) has an intimate atmosphere and attentive service. On the menu are innovative Canadian dishes such as Brome Lake duck, arctic musk ox, Yukon char, and desserts flambéed at the table. Soft, live music plays nightly for dancing. ⊠ *Hotel at Kananaskis, Hwy. 40, Kananaskis Village,* ☎ *403/591–7711 or 800/441–1414. Reservations essential. AE, D, DC, MC, V.*

$$$$ ✕◻ **Hotel and Lodge at Kananaskis.** The Hotel and Lodge are part of Canadian Pacific's chain of luxury hotels, and many of the hotel's large, lavish rooms have fireplaces, hot tubs, and large sitting areas. Several restaurants, skewed toward high-end elegance, serve food from

Spanish tapas to haute cuisine. For casual dining, try the Peaks Dining Room in the lodge, with family favorites, including burgers for lunch or dinner and a buffet-style breakfast, plus nightly family entertainment. Room rates drop by up to 50% off-season. ⊠ *Hwy. 40, 28 km (17 mi) south of Hwy. 1, Kananaskis Village T0L 2H0*, ☎ *403/591–7711 or 800/441–1414*, ℻ *403/591–7770. 243 rooms, 78 suites. 3 restaurants, 2 lounges, indoor pool, sauna, steam room, 2 18-hole golf courses, health club. AE, D, DC, MC, V.*

$$$$ 🏨 **Homeplace Ranch.** Just east of the Kananaskis Country foothills, this guest ranch is what its name suggests: homey. The principal activity is horseback riding over the rolling land near the ranch. Multiday pack trips are available, but there's no riding mid-October–spring. The small living-dining area is cluttered with books and magazines that provide good reading, the main evening activity. Meals, included in the guest rate, are served family-style. A "south ranch," 1½ hours away (30 km, or 19 mi, south of Longview), opened in 1995. It is similar to the main ranch, but accommodation is in six bunkhouses (no electricity). Rates are $125–$150 per person and decrease by one-third off-season. There's a minimum three-night stay during summer. ⊠ *Main ranch, off Hwy. 2, 10 km (6 mi) west of Priddis, R.R. 1, Box 6, Priddis T0L 1W0*, ☎ ℻ *403/931–3245. Main ranch, 7 rooms; south ranch, 6 bunkhouses. Dining room. No credit cards.*

$$$–$$$$ 🏨 **Kananaskis Guest Ranch.** Cabins and larger "chalets" surround the main lodge of this ranch near the Bow River, at the edge of Kananaskis Country. Cedar walls and, in some units, cedar-beam ceilings give a rustic flavor to otherwise plain, double-bed bedrooms. The Donut Tent—a log-and-wood-roof "tent" with a large hole in the middle, where bonfires are built for family-style barbecues—is the ranch's claim to fame. In addition to the obligatory horseback riding, the ranch also has jet-boat trips on the Bow River. The $90–$110 per-person price includes all meals. ⊠ *Ranch Rd., from Seebe-Exshaw exit on Hwy. 1 east of Canmore, General Delivery, Seebe T0L 1X0*, ☎ *403/673–3737 or 800/691–5085*, ℻ *403/673–2100. 33 units in cabins and chalets. Dining room, lounge, hot tub, boating, horseback riding. AE, MC, V. Closed mid-Oct.–Apr.*

$$$–$$$$ 🏨 **Mt. Engadine Lodge.** Hiking and cross-country skiing trails lead out
★   the back door of this backcountry lodge to the mountains and lakes of Kananaskis Country. Rooms (shared as well as private) have a scrubbed simplicity, as do the common areas. Meals, served family-style, are included in the $75–$120 per-person rate. There is a small decrease in off-season rates. The lodge operators are also backcountry guides; hiking packages are available. ⊠ *At Mt. Shark, turn onto Spray Trail, 38 km (24 mi) south of Canmore, Box 8239, Canmore T1W 2T9*, ☎ *403/678–4080*, ℻ *403/678–2109. 10 rooms and 2 cabins, with shared baths. Restaurant, outdoor hot tub, sauna, hiking. MC, V. Closed May–mid-June, Oct.–Dec. 25, and weekdays Jan.–Apr.*

$$–$$$ 🏨 **Kananaskis Inn Best Western.** Part of the complex built for the 1988 Olympics, and overlooking the resort's pond, the inn has log pillars and an inviting redwood exterior. Some of the motel-style rooms have private balconies, kitchenettes, or fireplaces. Rates drop by one-third off-season. ⊠ *Hwy. 40, 28 km (17 mi) south of Hwy. 1, Box 10, Kananaskis Village T0L 2H0*, ☎ *403/591–7500*, ℻ *403/591–7633. 94 rooms. Restaurant, bar, indoor pool, hot tub, steam room, coin laundry. AE, D, DC, MC, V.*

Nightlife and the Arts

Nightlife in Kananaskis is mostly of the do-it-yourself variety, but the **Hotel and Lodge at Kananaskis** (☞ Dining and Lodging, *above*) has lounges and dining rooms with entertainment and dancing.

Outdoor Activities and Sports

GOLF

Kananaskis Country Golf Course (⊠ Off Hwy. 40, ☎ 403/591–7272 in-season, 403/591–7070) has two 18-hole, par-72 links.

HORSEBACK RIDING

Boundary Ranch (⊠ Off Hwy. 40, Kananaskis Village, ☎ 403/591–7171) has horses to rent for trail rides.

SKIING

Nakiska (⊠ Off Hwy. 40, Kananaskis Village, ☎ 403/591–7777), 45 minutes southeast of Banff, was the site of the 1988 Olympic alpine events and has wide-trail intermediate skiing and not always reliable snow. The vertical drop is 2,493 ft, and there are 28 trails and four lifts.

Waterton Lakes National Park

30 *354 km (219 mi) south of Banff, 267 km (166 mi) south of Calgary.*

The mountains at Waterton Lakes National Park, near the southern end of the Canadian Rockies, seem a bit friendlier—not quite so high, not quite so rugged. This is a small park compared to Jasper or Banff, and you can cover its highlights in a day or two and still have time to relax. Several hundred miles of highway separate Waterton from the other six mountain parks. As a result, the park is a rare side trip from Banff—it's generally a destination in itself or combined with a vacation in the much larger Glacier National Park across the U.S. border in Montana.

Waterton is the meeting of two worlds—the flatlands of the prairie and the abrupt upthrust of the mountains. In this juncture of worlds, the park squeezes into a relatively small area (525 square km, or 200 square mi) an unusual mix of wildlife, flora, and climate zones.

Politically, too, Waterton represents a meeting of worlds. Although the park was officially established in 1895, it was joined in 1932 with Glacier National Park in Montana to form **Waterton/Glacier International Peace Park**—a symbol of friendship and peaceful coexistence between Canada and the United States. In fact, some services in the park, including the Prince of Wales Hotel—perhaps the park's most recognizable landmark—are under Glacier Park management in the United States. In 1995 this park was designated a World Heritage Site by UNESCO.

Whether it is a pervading spirit of international peace or the park's isolation, Waterton is decidedly low-key. The townsite of Waterton Park is a small, quiet community, in roughly the geographical center of the park. In winter it essentially closes down; in summer several hundred residents call the park home. Hiking, horseback riding, and boating are the main activities. The park contains numerous short hikes for day-trippers and some longer treks for backpackers. Boats (nonmotorized) can be rented at Upper Waterton Lake and Cameron Lake. For windsurfing enthusiasts, the winds that rake across Upper Waterton Lake create an exciting ride. Bring a wet suit, though—the water remains numbingly cold throughout the summer.

Because of Waterton's proximity to the U.S. border and its bond with Glacier National Park, many visitors arrive from the south. A day pass is $4 per person or $8 for a group of 2–10 people. You can fly into Great Falls or Kalispell, Montana, and drive to Waterton. If you drive from Calgary (via Highways 2, 3, and 6), you can take an interesting side trip to Crowsnest Pass (☞ Off the Beaten Path, *below*). For local information, contact **Waterton Lakes National Park** (⊠ Superintendent, Waterton Park, Alberta T0K 2M0, ☎ 403/859–2224) or **Waterton Park**

Chamber of Commerce (✉ Box 55, Waterton Park, Alberta T0K 2M0, ☎ 403/859–2203).

Red Rock Canyon is one of the more popular natural attractions in Waterton park. "Canyon" is stretching the term, as it is little more than a gully carved into the rock by a mountain stream. But "red rock" is appropriate; the exposed rock throughout the canyon displays a remarkably red hue. This is a popular spot for a picnic and a stroll along the paths that line the canyon. ✉ *Red Rock Pkwy., off park access road, 10 km (6 mi) north of Waterton Park; watch for signs.*

Cameron Lake, the jewel of Waterton, sits in a land of high basins and glacially carved cirques. In summer the area is filled with hundreds of varieties of alpine wildflowers, including 22 varieties of wild orchids. You also can rent canoes and paddleboats to explore Cameron Lake. ✉ *Akima Pkwy., 13 km (8 mi) southwest of town of Waterton Park.*

One of the park's most popular activities is the two-hour cruise on Upper Waterton Lake from the townsite of Waterton Park south to **Goat Haunt,** Montana. From here several short, easy hikes are possible before you return to Waterton; properly equipped overnighters can also camp out at Goat Haunt. (Because Goat Haunt is in the United States, travelers must clear Customs. Stops are included only from mid-June to mid-September, as the Customs office is closed at other times.) ✉ *Waterton International Shoreline Cruise Company, Box 126, Waterton Park T0K 2M0,* ☎ *403/859–2362.* 🎫 *$18.* ☼ *Mid-May–Sept.*

Lodging

$$$–$$$$ ★ 🏨 **Prince of Wales Hotel.** Perched between two lakes, the hotel has both a mountain backdrop and a lake-and-prairie setting. A high steeple crowns the building, which is fantastically ornamented with eaves, balconies, and turrets. The baronial, dark-paneled interior evokes the feeling of a royal Scottish hunting lodge. Expect creaks and rattles at night—the old hotel (built in the 1920s) is exposed to rough winds. Rates decrease by about 25% off-season. ✉ *Off Hwy. 5, General Delivery, Prince of Wales Hotel, Waterton Lakes National Park, Waterton Park T0K 2M0; off-season:* ✉ *Waterton Park, Reservations, Station 0928, Phoenix, AZ 85077,* ☎ *403/859–2231 or 403/236–3400. 89 rooms. Restaurant. D, MC, V. Closed late-Sept.–mid-May.*

$$ 🏨 **Bayshore Inn.** As the name suggests, this two-story inn is on the lakeside, and rooms with balconies take full advantage of the setting. Otherwise, the inn's common areas and motel-style rooms are rather ordinary. The lakeside patio is a great spot for light meals and drinks. Rates decrease by 25% off-season. ✉ *Main St., Box 38, Waterton Park T0K 2M0,* ☎ *403/859–2211, 403/238–4847 off-season,* ℻ *403/ 859–2291. 62 rooms, 8 suites. Restaurant, bar, coffee shop, lobby lounge, pizzeria. AE, D, MC, V. Closed mid-Oct.–Mar.*

$ ★ 🏨 **Kilmorey Lodge.** This 60-year-old inn with a log-cabin facade sits at the edge of Waterton Park. Rooms are steeped in country-cottage atmosphere, with pine walls, eiderdown comforters, sloped floors, and homespun antique furnishings. Some rooms have additional sleeping or sitting areas. ✉ *117 Evergreen Ave., Box 100, Waterton Park T0K 2M0,* ☎ *403/859–2334,* ℻ *403/859–2342. 23 rooms. Restaurant, lounge. AE, D, DC, MC, V.*

Outdoor Activities and Sports

Waterton Golf Course (✉ Off Hwy. 5, 2 km, or 1 mi, east of Waterton Park, ☎ 403/859–2383) is an 18-hole, par-71 course.

OFF THE
BEATEN PATH

CROWSNEST PASS – Between Calgary or Banff and Waterton, you can visit the site of Frank, a turn-of-the-century coal-mining settlement now under an immense pile of rocks. From the outset, the industry here was ill-fated. In April 1903, some 90 million tons of rock from Turtle Mountain screamed down the mountainside and buried a portion of the town, killing 70 residents. Then in 1914, a massive mine explosion killed 189 people, and a few years later the coal-mining industry all but collapsed. The story of the slide and the history of coal mining in the region are well recorded at the **Frank Slide Interpretive Centre.** ✉ *Hwy. 3, 35 km (22 mi) west of Hwy. 6,* ☎ *403/562–7388.* 🎫 *$4.* ☉ *Daily 9–5.*

THE BRITISH COLUMBIA ROCKIES

The national and provincial parks of the British Columbia Rockies match the grandeur found in Alberta's parks to the east. But the parks in British Columbia are smaller, and most of the British Columbia Rockies are not protected within park boundaries. This means that enthusiasts of activities such as motorboating, heli-skiing, or heli-hiking will find more opportunities here than elsewhere in the region.

"British Columbia Rockies" is in part a misnomer. The term is often used to refer to the Columbia Mountains of southeastern British Columbia, which flank the western slope of the Rockies but geologically are not a part of the Rockies. If differentiating the Columbias from the Rockies seems confusing, at least their separation is made obvious by the broad, low valley of the Columbia River, known colloquially as the Columbia River trench. Four separate ranges form the Columbias themselves: To the north are the Cariboos, west of Jasper and Mt. Robson parks; reaching south like three long talons from the Cariboos are (west to east) the Monashees, the Selkirks, and the Purcells. Finally, there are the Bugaboos—a few dramatic peaks in the Purcells that are often thought of as encompassing the entire region.

The British Columbia Rockies are a bit older than the true Rockies. Numerous peaks exceed 10,000 ft in height, the upper slopes have extensive areas of alpine meadows above tree line, evergreen forests cover the valleys and lower slopes, and glaciers and snowfields are not uncommon (especially in Glacier National Park, not to be confused with the U.S. Glacier National Park, in Montana).

As the first ranges to capture storms moving from the west across the plains of interior British Columbia, the Columbias get much more rain and snow than do the Rockies. Annual precipitation in many areas exceeds 60 inches, and in the Monashees, the most westerly of the subranges, annual snowfalls can exceed 65 ft. This precipitation has helped create the large, deep glaciers that add to the high-alpine beauty of the Columbias. Lower down, the moist climate creates much more lush forests than those in the Rockies to the east. In winter, the deep snows make the Columbias a magnet for deep-powder and helicopter skiers.

Because only a relatively small portion of the British Columbia Rockies is protected from development, human encroachment from residential and commercial development, farming, mining, and lumbering is rather common in the accessible portions of these ranges. The towns reflect this difference—tourism is a secondary pursuit; their primary function is to serve the local residents and industries. The advantage for visitors is that prices, for the most part, are substantially less than in the Alberta Rockies.

From Banff, there are two main routes to the British Columbia Rockies. The first follows the Trans-Canada Highway (Highway 1), northwest from Banff to Lake Louise, then west through Golden, Glacier National Park, Mt. Revelstoke National Park, and finally the town of

Revelstoke. The second route follows the Trans-Canada from Banff halfway to Lake Louise, then cuts south on Highway 93 through the southern British Columbia Rockies and Kootenay National Park (☞ North and West of Banff, *above*), then through Radium Hot Springs, Invermere, Fairmont Hot Springs, Fort Steele, Cranbrook, Kimberley (a small side trip), and finally through Fernie on a return swing to southern Alberta through the Crowsnest Pass.

Golden

③1 *80 km (50 mi) west of Lake Louise, 105 km (65 mi) north of Radium Hot Springs.*

For the most part, the towns of the Columbia River trench are not beautiful, nor do they aspire to be. Golden—a town best described as a service center—is the epitome of this unassuming character. Primarily a stopping-off point for anyone journeying elsewhere, Golden is a base for several river runners, outfitters, and guide services.

Lodging

$ ▦ **Swiss Village.** A combination motel and campground, this complex has a little more modern polish than some of its Golden neighbors. There is nothing special here, just basic motel rooms—bed, bathroom, TV— at a fair price. The RV sites have electrical hookups and water. Rates drop 40% off-season. ⊠ *Off Hwy. 1, west end of Golden, Box 765, V0A 1H0,* ☎ *250/344–2276,* ℻ *250/344–5259. 40 rooms, 10 RV sites. Sauna. AE, MC, V.*

Outdoor Activities and Sports

Alpine Rafting Company (⊠ Box 2446, V0A 1H0, ☎ 250/344–5016 or 888/666–9494) runs a variety of white-water trips on the Kicking Horse River, including multiday trips.

En Route The 105 km (65 mi) south from Golden to Radium Hot Springs, where Highway 93 joins Highway 95, is a pleasant drive, rambling along the rolling **flood plain of the Columbia River.** To the right are the river and the Purcell Mountains; more immediately to the left are the Rockies, although the major peaks are hidden by the ranges in the foreground. Resorts catering to RVs abound here.

Bugaboo Provincial Park

③2 *Access on unpaved roads off Hwy. 95 out of Spillimacheen and Brisco, between 65 and 77 km (40 and 48 mi) south of Golden.*

Climbers and hikers in search of solitude can find it in the Bugaboo Provincial Park. The Bugaboos are especially popular among experienced rock climbers. Rock spires that rise from glaciers like giant rocket cones are both dramatic to look at and challenging to climb. This is wild country: Except for the Bugaboo Lodge (owned by Canadian Mountain Holidays; ☞ Outdoor Activities and Sports *in* Canadian Rockies A to Z, *below*)—reserved mainly for heli-hiking and heli-skiing guests—and remote alpine huts, there are no facilities in this area. For information, contact the regional **BC Parks** office (⊠ Wasa Lake Dr., Box 118, Wasa V0B 2K0, ☎ 250/422–4200).

Glacier National Park

③3 *58 km (36 mi) west of Golden, 45 km (28 mi) east of Revelstoke.*

Relatively small Glacier National Park is marked by rugged mountains and, not surprisingly, an abundance of glaciers (more than 400). The glaciers result not because of the exceptionally high elevation—although some peaks here do exceed 10,000 ft—but because of the high winter snowfalls in the park. Many of the glaciers can be seen from the highway, but to appreciate Glacier National Park fully, you must take to the trail (☞ Outdoor Activities and Sports, *below*). A day pass is $4 per person or $8 for 2–10 people. For local information, contact **Mt. Revelstoke and Glacier National Parks Visitor Centre** (⊠ Box 350, Revelstoke V0E 2S0, ☎ 250/837–7500).

At **Rogers Pass,** near the center of Glacier National Park along Highway 1, the heavy winter snowfalls made rail and road construction particularly difficult. Avalanches claimed the lives of hundreds of railway-construction workers in the early 1900s and continued to be a threat during highway construction in the 1950s.

Today, the Rogers Pass war against avalanches is both active and passive. Heavy artillery—105mm howitzers—is used to shoot down snow buildups before they become so severe as to threaten a major avalanche. (If you're traveling in the backcountry, even in summer, be alert to unexploded howitzer shells that pose a potential hazard.) On the passive side, train tunnels and long snow sheds along the highway shield travelers from major slide paths.

Glacier National Park's history is well documented at the **Rogers Pass Centre**—worth a visit whether you're staying in Glacier or just passing through. Open year-round, the center displays geology and wildlife and screens 30-minute movies on subjects from avalanches to bears. ⊠ *Hwy. 1,* ☎ *250/837–6274.* ☞ *Free with park pass.* ☉ *May–June 15 and Sept. 15–Oct., daily 9–5; June 16–Sept. 14, daily 7 AM–9 PM; Nov.–Apr., daily 7–5.*

Lodging

$$ 🏨 **Glacier Park Lodge.** This modern, two-story Best Western at the top of Rogers Pass—the only lodging within Glacier National Park—offers ambience in the chain's familiar format: wood-veneer tables and chairs, and pink wall-to-wall carpeting. The steep-sloping A-frame roof is a design concession to the heavy winter snows. The lodge accommodates long-distance travelers with its 24-hour service station, 24-hour coffee shop, and gift shop. Rates drop 40% off-season. ⊠ *The Summit, Rogers Pass, Hwy. 1, Glacier National Park V0E 2S0,* ☎ *250/ 837–2126 or 800/528–1234,* 🖷 *250/837–2126. 51 rooms. Restaurant, coffee shop, indoor pool, outdoor hot tub. AE, D, DC, MC, V.*

Outdoor Activities and Sports

From the Ilecillewaet Campground, a few miles west of the park's Rogers Pass Centre, several **hiking** trails lead to good overlooks and glacier tongues, offering day-hiking opportunities. One of the best, although fairly strenuous, is the Asulkan Valley trail. This 13-km (8-mi) loop passes waterfalls and yields views of the Asulkan Glacier and three massifs—the Ramparts, the Dome, and Mt. Jupiter. A much easier hike is the 1½-km (1-mi) loop Brook trail (6 km, or 4 mi, west of the Rogers Pass Centre), with views of the glaciers of Mt. Bonney.

Mt. Revelstoke National Park

34 *20 km (12 mi) west of Glacier National Park on eastern border; western edge is by town of Revelstoke.*

On the western flanks of the Selkirk mountains, this park has smaller mountains than those in the Rocky Mountains to the east, and lusher vegetation, thanks to the additional rain and snow on the west-facing slopes. Conceived primarily as a day-use park, Mt. Revelstoke National Park covers just 260 square km (100 square mi). The park's principal attraction is the 26-km (16-mi) **Summit Road** to the top of the mountain, at 6,395 ft. The gravel road begins from Highway 1, 1½ km (1 mi) before the turnoff to the town of Revelstoke, and its last couple of miles may be closed off by melting snows until July. Several easy hikes from the summit parking lot meander past small lakes and have views of the Selkirk and Monashee ranges as well as mountain meadows full of wildflowers. A day pass is $4 per person or $8 for 2–10 people. For information, contact **Mt. Revelstoke and Glacier National Parks Visitor Centre** (✉ Box 350, Revelstoke V0E 2S0, ☎ 250/837–7500).

Revelstoke

③⑤ *148 km (92 mi) west of Golden, on western edge of Mt. Revelstoke National Park.*

The town of Revelstoke is a skiers' headquarters in winter. The downtown district, an attractive, authentic turn-of-the-century renovation, today houses modern shops, restaurants, and businesses.

③⑥ The two pools at **Canyon Hot Springs,** tucked between Mt. Revelstoke and Glacier national parks about 35 km (22 mi) east of Revelstoke, take advantage of the hot springs and make a good rest stop. A 15,000-gallon hot pool is naturally heated to 40°C (104°F), and a 60,000-gallon cooler pool is mixed with cool water to maintain a temperature of 27°C (80°F). The Albert Canyon ghost town, site of the original hot-spring facility built by railroad workers at the turn of the century, is a short distance south of the present facility. ✉ *Off Hwy. 1, Box 2400, Revelstoke,* ☎ *205/837–2420.* 💲 *$4.50.* ☉ *May, June, and Sept., daily 9–9; July–Aug., daily 9 AM–10 PM.*

Dining and Lodging

$$–$$$$ ✕ **One-Twelve.** In the Regent Inn (☞ *below*), this restaurant has low
★ cedar ceilings and an abundance of historic photos that lend warmth to the atmosphere. Continental dishes such as chicken Cordon Bleu and beef brochette are the basic fare, but the blue ribbon of the menu is the lamb broiled with rosemary and red wine. ✉ *112 1st St. E,* ☎ *250/837–2107. Reservations essential. AE, DC, MC, V.*

$$ 🏨 **Regent Inn.** The inn mixes many styles: colonial, with its brick-arcade facade; true Canadian, in its pine-trimmed lobby area and restaurant; and Scandinavian, in the angular, low-slung wood furnishings of the guest rooms. Rooms are on the large side but have no spectacular views. Continental breakfast is complimentary. There are no off-season rate reductions. ✉ *112 1st St. E, Box 450, V0E 2S0,* ☎ *250/837–2107,* 🖷 *250/837–9669. 43 rooms. Restaurant, pub, outdoor hot tub, sauna. AE, D, DC, MC, V.*

Outdoor Activities and Sports

BIKING
Spoketacular (✉ 11 Mackenzie Ave., ☎ 250/837–2220) has bikes for rent.

SKIING
Cat Powder Skiing (✉ Box 1479, 1601 W. 3rd St., Revelstoke V0E 2S0, ☎ 250/837–5151) organizes two-, three-, and five-day all-inclusive packages that run into the Selkirks and on the upper slopes of Mt. MacKenzie in Revelstoke. **Selkirk Tangiers Helicopter Skiing** (✉ Box 1409, Golden V0A 1H0, ☎ 250/344–5016 or 800/663–7080) runs three-, five-, and seven-day all-inclusive packages in the Selkirk and Monashee mountains from its base in Revelstoke.

Radium Hot Springs

③⑦ *127 km (79 mi) southwest of Banff, 103 km (64 mi) south of Golden, at junction of Hwys. 93 and 95.*

Radium Hot Springs is little more than a service town for the busy highway traffic passing through it, but the town makes a convenient access point for Kootenay National Park (☞ North and West of Banff, *above*) and has lower prices than the national parks.

Radium Hot Springs, the springs that give the town its name, are the town's longest-standing attraction and the summer lifeblood for the numerous motels in the area. Two outdoor pools are tucked beneath the walls of Sinclair Canyon. The hot pool is maintained at 41°C (106°F); in a cooler pool the hot mineral water is diluted to 28°C (82°F). Lockers, towels, and suits (period and modern) are available to rent. ⊠ *Hwy. 93, 2 km (1 mi) northeast of Hwy. 95,* ☎ *250/347–9485 or 800/767–1611.* 🎫 *$5; day passes available.* ☉ *Hot pool summer, daily 9 AM–10:30 PM; mid-Oct.–Apr., daily noon–9; cooler pool schedule varies with weather.*

Lodging

$$ 🏨 **Radium Hot Springs Resort.** Recreational facilities and activities bring this resort to life. Accommodations are in hotel rooms or one-, two-, or three-bedroom condo units. Rooms are modern, with hardwood furnishings and sponge-painted walls, and each has a sundeck, a wet bar, and a view overlooking the golf fairways. Condos have full kitchens. Golf packages are available. There's a small rate reduction off-season. ⊠ *8100 Golf Course Rd., Hwy. 93/95, Box 310, V0A 1M0,* ☎ *250/347–9311 or 800/665–3585,* 📠 *250/347–6299. 90 rooms, 30 condo units. Dining room, indoor pool, hot tub, sauna, 18-hole golf course, 2 tennis courts, exercise room, racquetball, squash, mountain bikes, cross-country skiing. AE, D, DC, MC, V. Closed Nov.–Feb.*

$–$$ 🏨 **The Chalet.** The hotel sits on a crest above town; all rooms have expansive views of the Columbia River valley. The decor is nothing special—lots of browns, navy blue, and wood veneer—but each room comes with a sitting area and minikitchen (microwave, refrigerator, sink), and all have balconies. Rates drop one-third off-season. ⊠ *Madsen Rd., Box 456, V0A 1M0,* ☎ *250/347–9305,* 📠 *250/347–9306. 17 suites. Sauna, hot tub. AE, D, DC, MC, V.*

Outdoor Activities and Sports

GOLF

Radium Hot Springs Resort (☎ 250/347–9652 or 800/665–3585) has one 18-hole, par-69 course on site and another 18-hole, par-72 course in town (☞ Lodging, *above*).

RAFTING

Kootenay River Runners (☎ 250/347–9210 in Radium Hot Springs, 403/762–5385 in Banff, or 800/599–4399) provides Class II and III whitewater rafting on the Kicking Horse and Kootenay rivers. Trips are half-day, full-day, or overnight, with prices starting at $49.

Invermere

18 km (11 mi) south of Radium Hot Springs.

Invermere, another of the many highway-service towns in the British Columbia Rockies, is the central access point for Windermere Lake, Panorama Resort, and the Purcell Wilderness area.

For summer water sports, **Windermere Lake**—actually an extrawide stretch of the Columbia River—is popular among swimmers, boaters, and board sailors. Invermere has a good beach on the lake.

One of the best area museums is the **Windermere Valley Pioneer Museum,** which depicts the life of 19th-century settlers through artifacts and other memorabilia. ✉ *622 3rd St.,* ☎ *250/342–9769.* ⌨ *$2.* ☉ *June, Tues.–Sat. 1–4; July–Labor Day, Tues.–Sat. 9:30–5:30.*

Panorama Resort (☞ Dining and Lodging *and* Outdoor Activities and Sports, *below*) is a year-round accommodation known best for skiing in winter. For summer visitors it has tennis courts, an outdoor pool, and hiking and biking trails. The resort is on the edge of the **Purcell Wilderness**—a large section of the southern British Columbia Rockies devoted to backcountry hiking, camping, and fishing, with relatively few facilities.

Dining and Lodging

$$–$$$$ ✕ **Toby Creek Dining Lounge.** The restaurant, part of a 1960s-era ski lodge, has cedar walls, a slanted ceiling, and—in winter—a big roaring fire in the central fireplace. In summer an outside deck offers fresh air, though not much of a view. The varied menu includes salads, steaks, stir-fries, and chicken dishes, as well as breakfast in summer. ✉ *Panorama Resort, Panorama Resort Rd., 18 km (11 mi) west of Invermere,* ☎ *250/342–6941. Reservations essential. AE, D, MC, V.*

$$ 🏨 **Panorama Resort.** At this resort near the edge of the Purcell Wilderness, the lodge at the base of the ski lift conveys a college-dorm atmosphere; other accommodations are in condo villas that look to be part of a mountainside suburb. Many have fireplaces, patios, or balconies. Skiing, hiking, biking, an outdoor pool, and tennis courts are available, depending on the season. The restaurants are open only during winter. Peak season is Christmas week, February break, and late June–early September; rates decrease by 25% off-season. ✉ *Panorama Resort Rd., 18 km (11 mi) west of Invermere, V0A 1T0,* ☎ *250/342–6941 or 800/663–2929,* ⨳ *250/342–3395. 105 lodge rooms, 250 condo units. 3 restaurants, 3 bars, cafeteria, pool, sauna, 8 tennis courts, downhill skiing, nightclub. AE, D, MC, V.*

$ 🏨 **Delphine Lodge.** Originally built in 1899, the hotel has been restored
★ and now feels like a cozy bed-and-breakfast. Big, lace-curtained windows shed lots of light on a living-dining area distinguished by its polished wide-board floors, huge stone hearth, and antique straight-back chairs and wicker rockers. Handcrafted pine furnishings and down comforters fill the smallish, pastel-shade bedrooms. All rooms are no-smoking. Full breakfast is served every morning. ✉ *Main St., 5 km (3 mi) west of town, Box 2797, V0A 1K0,* ☎ *250/342–6851. 6 rooms, 1 with private bath, 5 sharing 2 baths. V.*

Outdoor Activities and Sports

DOWNHILL SKIING

Panorama Resort (☞ Dining and Lodging, *above*), in the Purcells, has the second-highest lift-served vertical drop (4,300 ft) in North America; there are 80 runs and eight lifts.

HELI-SKIING

R.K. Heli-Ski (✉ Box 695, V0A 1K0, ☎ 250/342–3889 or 800/661–6060), based at the Panorama ski area, has daily tours.

Fairmont Hot Springs

❸ *20 km (12 mi) south of Invermere, 94 km (58 mi) north of Fort Steele.*

Fairmont Hot Springs is named for the hot springs and the resort that has sprouted around it. The "town" is little more than a service strip along the highway, but turn in to the resort and things become more impressive. The town is also close to Columbia Lake, popular with boaters and board sailors. Golf is a growing attraction at several fine courses in the area.

Lodging

$$–$$$ 🏨 **Fairmont Hot Springs Resort.** With a wide selection of activities from golf to heli-hiking, vacationing at this resort is like being at camp. In addition to the recreational facilities, Fairmont also has hot springs, a spa, and an airport. Inside the attractive, low-slung bungalow-style structure, rooms are contemporary, many with wood paneling; some are equipped with kitchens and have balconies or patios. Other options are the RV sites. Golf, ski, and spa packages are available. Rates decrease by 40% off-season. ✉ *Hwy. 93/95, Box 10, V0B 1L0,* ☎ *250/345–6311, 800/663–4979 in Canada,* FAX *250/345–6616. 140 rooms, 294 RV sites. 7 restaurants, lobby lounge, snack bar, 4 pools, hot springs, spa, 2 18-hole golf courses, 2 tennis courts, private airstrip. AE, D, DC, MC, V.*

Outdoor Activities and Sports

Arrangements for golfing can be made through **Fairmont Hot Springs Resort** (☎ 250/345–6514 or 800/663–4979), with two 18-hole courses: a par-72 course at the resort, and a par-71 course along the river in town.

Fort Steele

㊴ *94 km (58 mi) south of Fairmont Hot Springs.*

Fort Steele and nearby Kimberley were home to many German and Swiss immigrants who arrived in the late 19th century to work as miners and loggers. Southeastern British Columbia was not unlike the Tyrol region they had left, so it was comfortable to settle here. Later, a demand for experienced alpinists to guide and teach hikers, climbers, and skiers brought more settlers from the Alpine countries, and a Tyrolean influence is evident throughout southeastern British Columbia. Schnitzels and fondues appear on menus as often as burgers and fries.

★   **Fort Steele Heritage Town,** a reconstructed 19th-century mining outpost consisting of more than 60 buildings, is a step back to silver- and lead-mining days. Its theater, millinery, barbershop, and dry-goods store breathe authenticity, helping to preserve the 1890s flavor. There's enough here to hold the interest of children and adults alike for a half-day or more. ✉ *3 km (2 mi) south of Fort Steele on Hwy. 93/95,* ☎ *250/426–7352.* 🎟 *$5.50; grounds free Sept.–mid-June, weather permitting.* ☉ *Concessions and museum mid-June–early Sept., daily 9:30–8; grounds daily 9:30–dusk.*

Nightlife and the Arts

The **Wild Horse Theater** (✉ Fort Steele Heritage Town, Hwy. 93/95, ☎ 250/426–6923) has college presentations from late June to mid-September.

Cranbrook

16 km (10 mi) southwest of Fort Steele, 27 km (17 mi) southeast of Kimberley.

Cranbrook is primarily a service center for motorists and the surrounding mining and logging industries. As one of the largest towns in the region, it has more choice in the way of moderately priced basic motels and restaurants.

Dining

$$–$$$ ✕ **City Cafe.** If you find yourself stuck for lunch in the fast-food world of Cranbrook, City Cafe will be a breath of fresh air. The low ceilings and pine banquettes give the small dining room a French country-bistro air. Sandwiches served on fresh, crusty French bread are tasty and very reasonably priced. A German side to the menu lists schnitzel, a popular choice. ⊠ *1015 Baker St.,* ☎ *250/489–5413. DC, MC, V.*

Kimberley

⑩ *40 km (25 mi) west of Fort Steele, 98 km (61 mi) south of Fairmont Hot Springs.*

A cross between quaint and kitschy, Kimberley is rich with Tyrolean character. The Platzl ("small plaza," in German), a walking mall of shops and restaurants styled after a Bavarian village, is crowned by what is reputed to be the world's largest cuckoo clock. Chalet-style buildings are as common here as log cabins are in the national parks. In summer Kimberley plays its alpine theme to the hilt: Merchants dress up in lederhosen and dirndls, and promotional gimmicks abound.

Dining and Lodging

$$–$$$ ✕ **Chef Bernard's Kitchen.** Dining in this small, homey storefront
★ restaurant on the Kimberley pedestrian mall is like dining in someone's pantry. Goat horns, cowbells, and photos fill the walls and set an alpine mood. The menu is international, ranging from German to Thai to Cajun. Homemade desserts are always a favorite. Breakfast is served in summer. ⊠ *170 Spokane St.,* ☎ *250/427–4820. Reservations essential. AE, D, DC, MC, V.*

$ ☷ **Inn of the Rockies.** In keeping with downtown Kimberley's Bavarian theme, the hotel's exterior is exposed-wood beams and stucco. Large rooms have a small sitting area and are plainly furnished with dark brown wood–veneer furniture, including a bed, bureau, and TV. The restaurant serves good, reasonably priced food. Just a block from the Platzl, this is *the* hotel in Kimberley. There is a minimal rate decrease during the off-season. ⊠ *300 Wallinger Ave., V1A 1Z4,* ☎ *250/427–2266 or 800/661–7559,* 𝗙𝗔𝗫 *250/427–7621. 43 rooms. Restaurant, lounge, hot tubs, exercise room, coin laundry. AE, DC, MC, V.*

Nightlife and the Arts

In summer Bavarian bands in Kimberley strike up with oompah music on the Platzl, especially when festivals are in swing. The **Old Time Accordion Championships,** in early July, is a Kimberley highlight.

Outdoor Activities and Sports

Kimberley Ski Resort (⊠ Kimberly Ski Area Rd., Box 40, V1A 2Y5, ☎ 250/427–4881 or 800/667–0871) has a vertical drop of 2,300 ft, 47 runs, six lifts, and on-mountain facilities.

Fernie

96 km (60 mi) east of Fort Steele, 331 km (205 mi) southwest of Calgary.

Fernie is primarily a winter destination, serving skiers at the Fernie Alpine Resort ski area. One of the largest towns between Cranbrook and Calgary, it has a wider selection of motels and restaurants than the other centers along this route.

Outdoor Activities and Sports

Fernie Alpine Resort (⊠ Ski Area Rd., V0A 1M1, ☎ 250/423–4655) has a vertical drop of 2,400 ft, 89 runs, seven lifts, and on-mountain facilities for skiers.

CANADIAN ROCKIES A TO Z

Arriving and Departing

By Bus

Brewster Transportation and Tours (☎ 800/661–1152) offers service between the Calgary International Airport and Banff, Jasper, and Lake Louise. **Greyhound Lines** (☎ 800/321–222 in the U.S., ☎ 800/661–8747) provides regular service to Calgary, Edmonton, and Vancouver, with connecting service to Jasper and Banff. **Laidlaw Transportation** (☎ 403/762–9102) also operates between Calgary Airport and the Banff–Lake Louise area.

By Car

Highway 1, the Trans-Canada Highway, is the principal east–west route into the region. Banff is 128 km (79 mi) west of Calgary on Highway 1 and 858 km (532 mi) east of Vancouver on Highway 1. The other major east–west routes are Highway 16 to the north, the main highway between Edmonton and Jasper, and Highway 3 to the south. The main routes from the south are U.S. 89 (Highway 2 in Canada), which enters Canada east of Alberta's Waterton Lakes National Park from Montana, and U.S. 93, also from Montana, which provides access to the British Columbia Rockies.

By Plane

Calgary is the most common gateway for travelers arriving by plane. If you plan to visit only Jasper and northern park regions, you may prefer to use Edmonton as a gateway city. Both cities have international airports served by several major carriers; the Calgary flight schedule is somewhat more extensive. (For airline information, ☞ Calgary A to Z *and* Edmonton A to Z *in* Chapter 5.)

Air Canada and **Canadian Airlines** (☞ Air Travel *in* the Gold Guide) have daily flights to and from many points in southern British Columbia; most of these flights connect with flights through the international airports in Vancouver, Calgary, and Edmonton.

By Train

VIA Rail (☎ 800/561–8630) trains stop in Jasper, with connecting overnight runs to and from Toronto, Edmonton, and Vancouver. A specialty train-tour service, **Rocky Mountaineer RailTours** (✉ 1150 Station St., Suite 130, Vancouver, British Columbia V6A 2X7, ☎ 604/606–7200 or 800/665–7245, FAX 604/606–7201) connects Vancouver, Kamloops, Banff, Jasper, and Calgary. Dome cars allow panoramic mountain views, and food and service are excellent. A luxury bi-level dome coach has two spiral staircases, a private dining area, an open-air observation platform, and on-board hosts.

Getting Around

By Car

Automobile is the way to travel in the Canadian Rockies, though some guided tour operators have good sightseeing trips by bus and train. Unless you plan to go off the beaten path (in Kananaskis Country or in the British Columbia Rockies only; vehicles aren't permitted off major roadways in the national parks), a four-wheel-drive vehicle is not necessary. Major roadways are well maintained. Keep in mind, however, that snow arrives in early fall and remains until late spring. When traveling between October and April, stay informed of local road conditions, especially if you're traveling over mountain passes or along the

Icefields Parkway (Highway 93). A few roads, such as Highway 40 over Highwood Pass in Kananaskis Country, are closed in winter.

Car-rental outlets are at the Calgary and Edmonton airports, as well as in Banff and Jasper, Alberta, and Cranbrook, British Columbia. Daily rentals for sightseeing are available but should be reserved well ahead of time, especially in summer.

Contacts and Resources

B&B Reservation Agencies
In Alberta, **Gem B&B Reservation Agency** (☎ 403/434–6098) represents licensed B&Bs and charges a booking fee. The **Bed-and-Breakfast Agency of Alberta** (☎ 403/277–8486 or 800/425–8160) handles about 50 B&Bs and inspects each property. For bed-and-breakfasts in the British Columbia Rockies, contact the **British Columbia Bed-and-Breakfast Association** (☎ 604/276–8616).

Camping
Campground information is available from **Parks Canada** (✉ Canadian Heritage—Parks Canada, Information Services, Room 552, 220 4th Ave. SE, Calgary, Alberta T2G 4X3, ☎ 403/292–4401 or 800/651–7959, ℻ 403/292–6004) and from **Kananaskis Country** (✉ 3115 12th St. NE, Calgary, Alberta T2E 7J2, ☎ 403/297–3362, ℻ 403/297–2180). Contact **Discover British Columbia** or **Travel Alberta** (☞ Visitor Information, *below*) for special camping publications.

Emergencies
Ambulance, police (☎ 911).

Guided Tours
AIRPLANE
Alpenglow Aviation (✉ Box 241, 210 Fisher Rd., Golden, British Columbia V0A 1H0, ☎ 250/344–7117 or 888/244–7177) runs one-to four-hour tours, mostly of the British Columbia Rockies, with one tour east to the Columbia Icefields. Prices begin at $100 per person; there's a minimum of two people per flight.

BIKING
Several operators offer guided on-road and off-road bicycle tours: **Rocky Mountain Cycle Tours** (✉ 333 Baker St., Nelson, British Columbia V1L 4H6, ☎ 250/354–1241 or 800/661–2453, ℻ 250/354–2058) runs seven-day tours in the Banff area and in British Columbia. Prices begin at U.S. $795.

BUS
Brewster Transportation and Tours (✉ 100 Gopher St., Box 1140, Banff, Alberta T0L 0C0, ☎ 403/762–6700 in Banff; 403/852–3332 in Jasper; 403/221–8242 in Calgary; or 800/661–1152; ℻ 403/762–2090) offers half-, full-, and multiday sightseeing tours of the parks. Prices start at about $33 per person. **Tauck Tours** (✉ 276 Post Rd. W, Box 5027, Westport, CT 06880, US, ☎ 800/468–2825) conducts multiday bus tours through the region.

DRIVING
Audiocassette tapes for self-guided auto tours of the parks are produced by **Auto Tape Tours** (☎ 201/236–1666). **Canadian Wilderness Videos** (✉ 1010 Larch Pl., Canmore, Alberta T1W 1S7, ☎ 403/678–3795) produces a series of videotapes illustrating highlights along specific routes. Tapes can be rented or purchased at news or gift shops in Banff, Lake Louise, and Jasper.

HELICOPTER

Alpine Helicopters (✉ 91 Bow Valley Trail/Hwy. 1A, Canmore, Alberta T1W 1N8, ☎ 403/678–4802) is 20 minutes southeast of Banff and provides year-round, guided "flightseeing" tours (25–45 minutes) above the Banff and Kananaskis valleys. It also offers half- and full-day heli-hiking tours. Prices begin at $110.

SEASONAL

Challenge Enterprises (✉ Box 8127, Canmore, Alberta T1W 2T8, ☎ 403/678–2628) specializes in half-day to multiday guided snowmobile tours. Prices start at $120 per person. **Kingmik Expeditions** (✉ Box 227, Lake Louise, Alberta T0L 1E0, ☎ 250/344–5298) specializes in dogsledding tours through the mountains. Tours range from 35 minutes to five-day outings. Each sled can carry two adults and one small child. **Mountain Fly Fishers** (✉ 909 Railway Ave., Canmore, Alberta T1W 1P3, ☎ 403/678–9522 in-season, 403/678–2915 off-season) offers fly-fishing instruction, guide services, float-fishing tours, and equipment rentals. "Hike and wade" programs start at $110 per person, two people per guide.

Outdoor Activities and Sports

BACKPACKING AND HIKING

Backpackers need to register with the nearest park warden for permits. This is principally for safety reasons—so that you can be tracked down in case of emergency—as well as for trail-usage records. The fee is $6 per person per night (to a maximum of $30 per person per trip or $42 annually) for the use of backcountry campsites. You can make reservations up to three weeks in advance ($10 reservation fee) by contacting the park office. The office can also supply trail and topographical maps and information on current trail conditions.

If you're interested in hiking or backpacking, several good books describe various routes and route combinations. One of the best, *The Canadian Rockies Trail Guide,* by Brian Patton and Bart Robinson (Summerthought Ltd., $14.95), is available in most bookstores in Banff, Lake Louise, and Jasper.

CLIMBING

Climbing permits are required within the parks and can be obtained at park warden offices. Except for very experienced mountaineers, guide and instruction services are essential here. Climbing gear can be rented at outdoor stores in Banff. **Banff Alpine Guides** (✉ Box 1025, Banff, Alberta T0L 0C0, ☎ 403/678–6091), the **Canadian School of Mountaineering** (✉ 629 10th St., Canmore, Alberta T1W 2E5, ☎ 403/678–4134), and **Yamnuska Mountain Adventures** (✉ 1316 Railway Ave., Canmore, Alberta T1W 1P6, ☎ 403/678–4164, FAX 403/678–4450) lead trips throughout the parks, catering to all ability levels.

Climbers or backpackers interested in extended stays of more than three or four days might consider membership in the **Alpine Club of Canada** (✉ Box 8040, Indian Flats Rd., Canmore, Alberta T1W 2T8, ☎ 403/678–3200). The club maintains several mountain huts in the parks.

FISHING

You need a fishing license, which you can buy at visitor information centers, sports shops, and many gas stations in the region. A British Columbia license is good only in British Columbia; an Alberta license is good only in Alberta. If you are fishing in the national parks, you need a national parks license (but not provincial licenses).

In Alberta the fee for an annual license for nonresident Canadians is $18 and for non-Canadians $36. Non-Canadians can purchase a five-day license for $24. In British Columbia, the fees for one-day, eight-day, and annual licenses for nonresident Canadians are $10, $20, and $28, respectively; for non-Canadians the fees are $10, $25, and $40. A seven-day national park license is $6; an annual license is $13.

GOLF

In Alberta parks, peak-season greens fees range from $35 to $70 and cart rentals cost from $20 to $35. All courses have full pro-shop services, including cart rentals, which are mandatory at some courses. Most courses enforce a standard dress code, requiring shirts with collars and Bermuda-length shorts or long pants.

HORSEBACK RIDING

Travel Alberta and **Tourism British Columbia** (☞ Visitor Information, *below*) can provide listings of pack-trip outfitters. They also have information about guest ranches; riding is generally a major part of a stay. In British Columbia, information is available from the **Guide-Outfitters Association** (✉ Box 94675, Richmond, British Columbia V64 4A4, ☎ 250/278–2688).

SKIING

Cross-Country. Groomed trails (and rental equipment) can be found near the Banff Springs Hotel, Chateau Lake Louise, Jasper Park Lodge, Fairmont Hot Springs Resort, and Mt. Engadine Lodge. Lake O'Hara Lodge, Mt. Assiniboine Lodge, and Skoki Lodge offer guided back-country ski touring. For information, *see* the individual towns in this chapter.

Downhill. For information, *see* individual towns in this chapter.

Heli-Skiing. The largest, heli-skiing operator in the region is **Canadian Mountain Holidays** (✉ Box 1660, Banff, Alberta T0L 0C0, ☎ 403/762–7100 or 800/661–0252, FAX 403/762–5879). It has heli-skiing (and in summer, heli-hiking) packages in the Cariboo and Purcell Ranges in the British Columbia Rockies, with accommodation at remote lodges. Reserve several months in advance.

Safety

Visitors to the backcountry must register with the nearest park warden's office. Very few of the natural hazards in the Rockies are marked with warning signs. Be wary of slippery rocks and vegetation near rivers and canyons, snow-covered crevasses on glaciers, avalanche conditions in winter, and potentially aggressive animals. Each year there are several fatalities from natural hazards in the Rockies.

Visitor Information

In terms of **national park fees,** a pass for Banff, Jasper, Kootenay, or Yoho is $5 per adult per day (or $10 per day for a group of 2–10 people). A pass for any one of these parks is valid for all four. A pass for Mt. Revelstoke or Glacier is $4 per adult per day (or $8 per day for a group of 2–10 people) and is valid for both parks. A pass for Waterton Lakes National Park is $4 per person per day ($8 per day for a group). The Great Western Annual Pass is $35 per person or $70 for a group of 2–10 people; it covers all these parks for 365 days from the date of issue. There may be additional charges for National Historic Sites in the parks. The parks are open daily, 24 hours a day.

The major sources of visitor information (☞ Individual parks for additional information) are **Travel Alberta** (✉ 10155 102nd St. NW, Edmonton T5J 4G8, ☎ 800/661–8888), **Tourism British Columbia** (⌧ 802–865 Hornby St., Vancouver V6Z 2G3, ☎ 800/663–6000), **Parks Canada** (⌧ Canadian Heritage-Parks Canada, 220 4th St. SE, Room 552, Calgary, Alberta T2G 4X3, ☎ 403/292–4401 or 800/651–7959, FAX 403/292–6004), and, in British Columbia, the **Rocky Mountain Visitors Association** (⌧ Box 10, Kimberley, British Columbia V1A 2Y5, ☎ 250/427–4838).

5 The Prairie Provinces

Alberta, Saskatchewan, Manitoba

Between the eastern slopes of the Rockies and the wilds of western Ontario lie Canada's three prairie provinces: Alberta, Saskatchewan, and Manitoba. Their northern sections are sparsely populated expanses of lakes, rivers, and forests. The fertile southern plains support farms and ranches— interspersed with river valleys, lakes, badlands, dry hills of sand, and oil wells—and five busy cities: Calgary, Edmonton, Saskatoon, Regina, and Winnipeg. Here you'll also find stunning national parks, dinosaur sites, and attractions that preserve the area's native and frontier heritage.

Updated by
Jens Nielsen

ALBERTA, SASKATCHEWAN, AND MANITOBA contain Canada's heartland, the principal source of such solid commodities as wheat, oil, and beef. These provinces are also home to a rich stew of ethnic communities that make the area unexpectedly colorful and cosmopolitan. You will find exceptional outdoor recreational facilities and a spectrum of historical attractions that focus on Mounties, Métis, dinosaurs, and railroads; excellent accommodations and cuisine at reasonable (but not low) prices; and quiet, crowdless expanses of extraordinarily wide-open spaces.

The term "prairie provinces" is a bit of a misnomer, as most of this region (the northern half of Alberta and Saskatchewan, and the northern two-thirds of Manitoba) consists of sparsely populated expanses of lakes, rivers, and forests. Most of northern Saskatchewan and Manitoba belongs to the Canadian Shield, the bedrock core of North America, with a foundation of Precambrian rock that is some of the oldest in the world. On the fertile plains of the south, wheat is still king, but other crops, as well as livestock, help boost the economy. The landscape is quite diverse, with farms and ranches interspersed with wide river valleys, lakes, rolling hills, badlands, and even dry hills of sand.

Early milestones in the history of this region include the period 75 million years ago when dinosaurs roamed what was then semitropical swampland, and the epoch when the first human settlers crossed the Bering Strait from Asia 12,000 years ago. Later, Plains Indians of the Athabascan, Algonquian, and Siouan language groups developed a culture and hunted buffalo here. In the 17th century European fur traders began to arrive, and in 1670 the British Crown granted the Hudson's Bay Company administrative and trading rights to "Rupert's Land," a vast territory whose waters drained into Hudson Bay. A hundred years later, the North West Company went into direct competition by building outposts throughout the area. From this fur-trading tradition arose the Métis—mostly French-speaking offspring of native women and European traders who followed the Roman Catholic religion but adhered to a traditional native lifestyle.

By 1873 the North West Mounted Police was established in Manitoba, just six years after the formation of the Canadian federation. In 1874, the Mounties began their march west: Their first chores included resolving conflicts between the native peoples and American whiskey traders and overseeing the orderly distribution of the free homesteads granted by the Dominion Lands Act of 1872. The Mounties played a role in the Northwest Rebellion—a revolt by Métis, who feared that the encroachment of western settlement would threaten their traditions and freedom. Although the Métis eventually succumbed and their leader, Louis Riel, was hanged in 1885, Riel is now hailed as a martyr of the Métis and a statue of him stands on the grounds of Manitoba's Legislature Building.

Railroads arrived in the 1880s, and with them came a torrent of immigrants seeking free government land. An influx of farmers from the British Isles, Scandinavia, Holland, Germany, Eastern Europe, Russia, and especially Ukraine, plus persecuted religious groups such as the Mennonites, Hutterites, Mormons, and Jews, made the prairies into a rich wheat-growing breadbasket and cultural mosaic that is still in evidence today. In 1947, a big oil strike transformed Edmonton and Calgary into gleaming metropolises full of western oil barons.

The people of the prairie provinces are relaxed, reserved, and irascibly independent. They maintain equal suspicion toward "Ottawa" (big government) and "Toronto" (big media and big business). To visitors, the people of this region convey western openness and Canadian-style courtesy: no fawning, but no rudeness. It's an appealing combination.

Pleasures and Pastimes

Dining

Although places specializing in generous helpings of Canadian beef still dominate the scene, restaurants throughout the prairie provinces now tastily reflect the region's ethnic makeup and offer a wide variety of cuisine to fit every price range. Dress in the prairie cities tends to formality in expensive restaurants and is casual in moderate and inexpensive restaurants.

CATEGORY	COST*
$$$$	over $35
$$$	$25–$35
$$	$15–$25
$	under $15

per person, in Canadian dollars, for a three-course meal, excluding drinks, service, and 7% tax

Lodging

Although finding lodging has never been a problem in the major cities, there's been a welcome improvement at many lakes and parks in recent years. Prince Albert National Park in Saskatchewan, for instance, once essentially a summer getaway, has added several excellent properties and become a legitimate four-season resort. Perhaps inevitably, prices in the larger metropolitan areas have increased dramatically of late, although prices at luxury properties are in line with those in other parts of the country. Smaller centers still offer good value. It's always a good idea to ask about special weekend rates and packages.

CATEGORY	COST*
$$$$	over $180
$$$	$110–$180
$$	$70–$110
$	under $70

All prices are for a standard double room, excluding tax (14% in Manitoba and Saskatchewan, 12% in Alberta), in Canadian dollars.

National and Provincial Parks

Throughout this vast region, some special places have preserved unique landscapes, from Riding Mountain National Park in the rolling hills of Manitoba to the vast wilderness and waterways of Prince Albert National Park in Saskatchewan. You can explore grasslands, badlands, lakes, or forests and participate in a number of activities, including fishing, in the provincial parks.

Regional History

The larger history of these provinces encompasses a number of special elements, from the dinosaurs that roamed here to the native peoples and the fur traders and frontier settlers who came from around the world. Each province has highlights, whether it's the dinosaur sites around Drumheller, Alberta; the Wanuskewin Heritage Park in Saskatoon, which interprets native culture; the Mennonite Heritage Village in Steinbach, Manitoba; the Ukrainian Cultural Heritage Village near Vegreville, Alberta; or the Western Development Museum in North Battleford, Saskatchewan, a re-created 1920s farming village. Together, these distinctly different places present an accurate microcosm of how the region was settled.

Exploring the Prairie Provinces

As you leave the Rockies, the landscape becomes dramatically flatter. From the foothills of Alberta to the Great Lakes, you can explore the prairies from west to east, with visits to the region's five major cities, Calgary, Edmonton, Regina, Saskatoon, and Winnipeg.

Numbers in the text correspond to numbers in the margin and on the Alberta, Downtown Calgary, Greater Calgary, Downtown Edmonton, Saskatchewan, Regina, Saskatoon, Manitoba, and Downtown Winnipeg maps.

Great Itineraries

Enormous distances separate many of the region's major attractions. If you're ambitious and want to include all three prairie provinces, you will need considerable time. For a shorter visit, pick a major city and the surrounding area to explore.

IF YOU HAVE 2 DAYS

If you're interested in the rich history of the Plains Indians, take the time to delve into the area around Saskatoon known as the Heart of the Old Northwest. Start in **Saskatoon** ㊸–㊾ and use it as the base for day trips. On the first day, you can go to nearby **Wanuskewin Heritage Park** ㊿, a wonderfully cerebral onetime buffalo hunting ground. Less than an hour's drive away are **Batoche** (51) and Batoche National Historic Site, where Louis Riel fought his last battle against the North West Mounted Police. In **Duck Lake** (52), 30 minutes north of Batoche along Highway 11, a series of colorful murals on town buildings depict the 1885 Northwest Rebellion. Fort Carlton Provincial Park, another 15 minutes west, is a reconstructed stockade from the fur-trade days. On the second day, go to **North Battleford** (54), 138 km (86 mi) northwest of Saskatoon, for the Fort Battleford National Historic Site, which interprets the role of the North West Mounted Police.

IF YOU HAVE 4 DAYS

If you're particularly interested in dinosaurs and fossil hunting, travel from **Calgary** ①–⑯, Alberta, to **Regina** ㉘–㉞, Saskatchewan, by way of Drumheller, Alberta, and Eastend, Saskatchewan. In **Drumheller** ⑰, just over an hour east of Calgary on the Trans-Canada Highway, you can spend an entire day at the world-class Royal Tyrell Museum of Paleontology. East on the Trans-Canada Highway en route to **Dinosaur Provincial Park,** you pass through unique badlands areas, where rivers flowed more than 70 million years ago. South along the Trans-Canada, the thriving oil-rich city of **Medicine Hat** ⑱ is a good choice for an overnight stop. Farther east, south of the Trans-Canada, you come to the small community of **Eastend** ㊴, where you can view a recently discovered, fully preserved Tyrannosaurus rex skeleton in a working lab—the Eastend Fossil Research Station.

IF YOU HAVE 12 DAYS

You can choose between two major routes westward from **Winnipeg** (56)–(68)—north on the Yellowhead (Highway 16) to **Edmonton** ㉑–㉕ via **Saskatoon** ㊸–㊾, or south on the Trans-Canada to **Calgary** ①–⑯ via **Regina** ㉘–㉞. Either is approximately 1,370 km (850 mi). On the Yellowhead route, you can stop for one or two nights in **Riding Mountain National Park,** a half hour north of Highway 16 on Highway 10, near **Wasagaming** (77). Here you'll find forested landscape and sparkling clear lakes, as well as comfortable amenities. Langenburg, just inside the Saskatchewan border, has a provincial tourism information center. Less than four hours to the northwest you come to Saskatoon, Saskatchewan's largest city. Plan on staying at least two nights. Ninety minutes farther west is the historic community of ⊡ **North Battleford** ⑤, where the Western Development Museum and Fort Battleford National Historic Site rate as the two must-see attractions. From here it is approximately four hours to Edmonton.

If you take the more southerly Trans-Canada route, you'll stop in such major centers as **Brandon** ⑦, ⊡ **Regina** ㉘–㉞, ⊡ **Swift Current** ㊱, and ⊡ **Medicine Hat** ⑱ en route to Calgary. All offer interesting diversions and adequate facilities for dining and lodging.

When to Tour the Prairie Provinces

From June through August you're likely to encounter more festivals and the greatest number of open lodgings (some close seasonally). However, the spring and fall months offer a more tranquil experience for travelers; September can be particularly rewarding, with a combination of warm weather and some autumn foliage. Unless you enjoy bone-chilling cold temperatures, it's best to skip winter.

CALGARY

With the eastern face of the Rockies as its backdrop, the crisp concrete-and-steel skyline of Calgary, Alberta, seems to rise from the plains as if by sheer force of will. In fact, all the elements in the great saga of the Canadian West—Mounties, native peoples, railroads, cowboys, oil—have converged to create a city with a brand-new face and a surprisingly traditional soul.

Calgary, believed to be derived from the Gaelic phrase meaning "bay farm," was founded in 1875 at the junction of the Bow and Elbow rivers as a North West Mounted Police post. The Canadian Pacific Railway arrived in 1883, and ranchers established major spreads on the plains surrounding the town. Incorporated as a city in 1894, Calgary grew quickly, and by 1911 its population had reached 43,000.

The major growth came with the oil boom in the 1960s and 1970s, when most Canadian oil companies established their head offices in the city. Today, Calgary is a city of nearly 800,000 mostly easygoing and downright neighborly people. It is Canada's second-largest center for corporate head offices. Downtown is still evolving, but Calgary's planners have made life during winter more pleasant by connecting most of the buildings with the Plus 15, a network of enclosed walkways 15 ft above street level. Among the major cities on the prairies, Calgary usually has the most reasonable winter, thanks to the annual series of warm chinook winds that blow in from the nearby Rockies.

Calgary supports professional football and hockey teams, and in July the rodeo events of the Calgary Stampede attract visitors from around the world. The city is also the perfect starting point for one of the preeminent dinosaur-exploration sites in the world (☞ Drumheller *in* Elsewhere in Southern Alberta, *below*). The Glenbow Museum is one of the top museums in Canada, and the Calgary Centre for the Performing Arts is a showcase for the arts. Calaway Park, on the western edge of Calgary, is a playground for children of all ages.

Downtown Calgary

A walk downtown takes you past some handsome buildings—old and new—and notable cultural venues, besides a number of interesting places to shop. In the Calgary grid pattern, numbered streets run north–south in both directions from Centre Street, and numbered avenues run east–west in both directions from Centre Avenue.

A Good Walk

Start at **Calgary Tower** ① for a bird's-eye view of the city. Take the Plus 15 walkway over 9th Avenue Southeast to the **Glenbow Museum** ②, a major showcase of art and history. Next use the Plus 15 walkway above 1st Street Southeast to join a walking tour of the **Calgary Centre for the Performing Arts** ③ theater complex. You can step outside on **Olympic Plaza** ④, where Olympic medals were presented in 1988. Nearby, you'll see the **Municipal Building** ⑤, whose mirror-glass walls reflect other city landmarks. Hop on the C-Train, Calgary's light rail system, for a free ride (along 7th Avenue downtown only) to the center of the downtown shopping district. Here, the top attraction is **Devonian Gardens** ⑥, an enclosed roof garden above Toronto Dominion Square. On 8th Avenue, between Macleod Trail and 4th Street Southwest, you'll find **Stephen Avenue Mall** ⑦, which has shopping in the ground floors of Calgary's oldest structures. Head north on 1st Street Southwest to the ornate **Calgary Chinese Cultural Centre** ⑧ to take in the architecture and the museum. A block north of the center, turn left on 1st Avenue Southwest; a two-block walk leads you to the shops and restaurants of trendy **Eau Claire Market**.

TIMING

Allow the better part of a day for this tour, for time in the museums and a bit of shopping.

Sights to See

★ ③ **Calgary Centre for the Performing Arts.** A complex of three theater spaces, a concert hall, and a shopping area, the center was pieced together with the historic **Calgary Public Building** (1930) and the **Burns Building** (1913). Come at night for a performance, or take a one-hour walking tour at noon most weekdays. ⊠ *205 8th Ave. SE,* ☎ *403/294–7455.*

⑧ **Calgary Chinese Cultural Centre.** The focal point of this ornate building in the heart of Chinatown is the Hall of Prayers of the **Temple of Heaven**; the column details and paintings include 561 dragons and 40 phoenixes. It is modeled after the Temple of Heaven in Beijing. The center also houses a cultural museum, a crafts store, an herbal medicine store, and a 330-seat Chinese restaurant. ⊠ *197 1st St. SW,* ☎ *403/262–5071.* ☞ *Center free, museum $2.* ☉ *Daily 9:30–9.*

① **Calgary Tower.** The 626-ft, scepter-shape edifice affords great views of the city's layout, the surrounding plains, and the face of the Rockies rising 80 km (50 mi) to the west. A flame on top is lit for special occasions; the revolving **Panorama Dining Room** provides refreshment. ⊠ *9th Ave. and Centre St. S,* ☎ *403/266–7171.* ☞ *$5.90.* ☉ *Weekdays and Sat. 7:30 AM–11 PM, Sun. 8 AM–10 PM.*

⑥ **Devonian Gardens.** Above Toronto Dominion Square atop Toronto Dominion Centre shopping center, a 2½-acre enclosed roof garden holds 20,000 mostly tropical plants, nearly a mile of lush walkways, a sculpture court, and a playground. Reached by a glass-enclosed elevator just inside the 8th Avenue door, Devonian Gardens has a reflecting pool that turns into a skating rink in winter and a small stage for musical performances year-round. ⊠ *Between 2nd and 3rd Sts. and 7th and 8th Aves. SW,* ☎ *403/268–3830.* ☞ *Free.* ☉ *Daily 9–9.*

Eau Claire Market. On Barclay Parade next to the entrance to Prince's Island Park, this once-neglected area has blossomed into arguably the trendiest, liveliest of all districts. The 240,000-square-ft area is crammed with a dozen restaurants and the popular **Cinescape**, an interactive entertainment center and arcade that has a 300-seat IMAX theater. Several unique boutiques in the market sell a variety of fresh foods. ⊠ *3rd St. and 1st Ave. SW,* ☎ *403/264–6450 or 403/264–6460.*

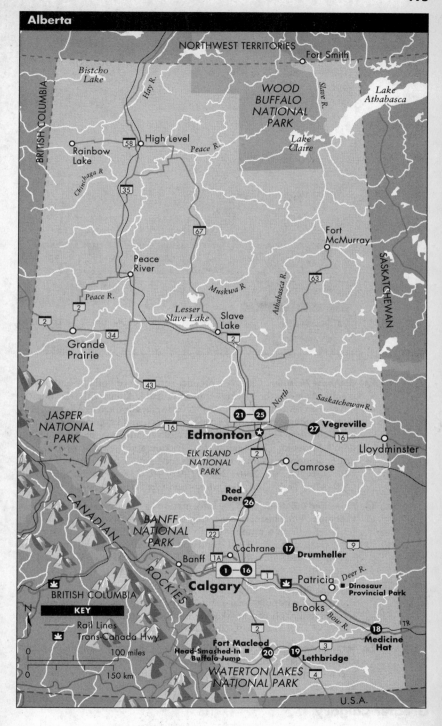

Alberta

NORTHWEST TERRITORIES

Fort Smith

Bistcho Lake

WOOD BUFFALO NATIONAL PARK

Slave R.

Lake Athabasca

BRITISH COLUMBIA

Hay R.

58 High Level

Peace R.

Rainbow Lake

Lake Claire

Chinchaga R.

35

67

Fort McMurray

Peace River

Muskwa R.

Athabasca R.

63

SASKATCHEWAN

2 *Peace R.*

Lesser Slave Lake Slave Lake

2

34

2

Grande Prairie

43

North *Saskatchewan R.*

JASPER NATIONAL PARK

16

21 — 25

Edmonton ✪

27 **Vegreville**

16

Lloydminster

ELK ISLAND NATIONAL PARK

2

Camrose

CANADIAN

Red Deer

26

BANFF NATIONAL PARK

22

9

Cochrane 17 **Drumheller**

Banff 1A

1 — 16

1

Calgary

Patricia

Deer R.

■ Dinosaur Provincial Park

ROCKIES

BRITISH COLUMBIA

Brooks

Bow R.

TR

18

Medicine Hat

N

KEY

— Rail Lines
⬇ Trans-Canada Hwy.

0   100 miles

0   1
        150 km

Fort Macleod
Head-Smashed-In ■
Buffalo Jump

2

20

19 **Lethbridge**

3

4

WATERTON LAKES NATIONAL PARK

U.S.A.

Calgary Centre for the Performing Arts, **3**

Calgary Chinese Cultural Centre, **8**

Calgary Tower, **1**

Devonian Gardens, **6**

Glenbow Museum, **2**

Municipal Building, **5**

Olympic Plaza, **4**

Stephen Avenue Mall, **7**

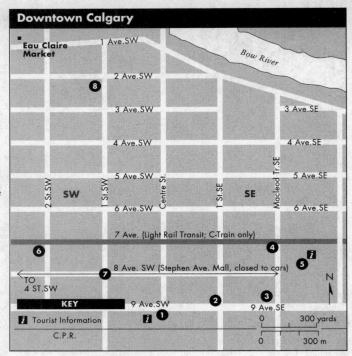

★ ❷ **Glenbow Museum.** Calgary's premier showcase of both art and history is ranked among the top museums in Canada. Along with traveling exhibits, the Glenbow has comprehensive displays devoted to Alberta's First Nations inhabitants, early European settlers, and latter-day pioneers. A highlight of the museum's extensive redevelopment is the **Alberta Children's Museum.** The mineralogy collection and the cache of arms and armor are superb. A food service area serves quick fresh meals or snacks. ⊠ *130 9th Ave. SE,* ☎ *403/268–4100 or 403/237–8988.* ☞ *$7.* ⊙ *Mid-Oct.–May, Tues.–Sun. 9–5; June–mid-Oct., daily 9–5.*

❺ **Municipal Building.** The City Information Centre on the main floor has brochures with historical walking tours. This angular, mirror-walled building reflects a number of city landmarks, including the stunning City Hall, a stately 1911 sandstone building that still houses the mayor's office and some city offices. ⊠ *8th Ave. SE and Macleod Trail SE,* ☎ *403/268–4656.*

❹ **Olympic Plaza.** The site of the Olympic medals presentation in 1988, the plaza is a popular year-round venue for city festivals, arts, and entertainment. You can go skating here in winter. ⊠ *7th Ave. SE and Macleod Trail SE,* ☎ *403/268–2300.*

❼ **Stephen Avenue Mall.** In this pedestrian-only shopping area, shops, nightclubs, and restaurants occupy the ground floors of Calgary's oldest structures, mostly sandstone buildings erected after an 1886 fire destroyed almost everything older.

Greater Calgary

With a car you can easily visit a number of top Calgary sights, from Heritage Park to the Stampede Park and Canada Olympic Park. Kid favorites such as the Calgary Zoo are here, too.

A Good Drive

From downtown, drive east on 9th Avenue about 1 km (½ mi) to **Fort Calgary Interpretive Centre** ⑨, at the confluence of the Bow and Elbow rivers, to learn the history of the region. Directly across the 9th Avenue Bridge is the **Deane House** ⑩, dating from 1906. Continue east on 9th Avenue, turn north on 12th Street and cross the bridge to St. George's Island and the **Calgary Zoo, Botanical Gardens, and Prehistoric Park** ⑪. Next head southwest to Olympic Way and **Stampede Park** ⑫ for tours of the grounds and a visit to the Grain Academy museum. Follow Macleod Trail south and go west on Heritage Drive to **Heritage Park** ⑬, where you can see historic structures from all over western Canada. East across Glenmore Reservoir, turn north on Crowchild Trail to reach the **Museum of the Regiments** ⑭ and the **Naval Museum of Alberta.** Continuing north on Crowchild Trail, turn east on 9th Avenue Southwest and then north again on 11th Street Southwest to the **Calgary Science Centre** ⑮ and multimedia theater for hands-on exhibits and a star show.

Another drive from downtown takes you west on 6th Avenue, following signs to Crowchild Trail, which you take north to 16th Avenue Northwest (Highway 1). Head west on Highway 1 about 8 km (5 mi) to **Canada Olympic Park** ⑯, site of the 1988 Winter Olympics, where you can visit ski jumps and try the bobsled and luge rides. A 20-minute drive beyond the Olympic Park is **Calaway Park,** western Canada's largest amusement park.

TIMING

Because of the distances and the size of the sights, you'd need more than a day to do everything on this tour. Pick sights based on your interests or location. If you have kids, allow a day with the zoo as the main component in the morning, leaving Calaway Park for the afternoon and evening.

Sights to See

Calaway Park. Western Canada's largest outdoor amusement park also has live entertainment, miniature golf, a driving range, a maze, a petting farm, food outlets, and shops. ⊠ *Hwy. 1, Springbank Rd. exit, 10 km (6 mi) west of Calgary,* ☏ *403/240–3822.* ☞ *$17.50 (includes all rides, shows); $8 general admission.* ☉ *May–Sept., hrs vary.*

⑮ **Calgary Science Centre.** The center has more than 35 hands-on exhibits of scientific marvels, including holograms, frozen shadows, and laser beams; demonstrations add to the fun. The Discovery Dome shows the latest in computer graphics, with motion picture images that fill an entire dome; the sound system is state-of-the-art. ⊠ *701 11th St. SW,* ☏ *403/221–3700.* ☞ *$8 (varies with program).* ☉ *Tues.–Sun. 10–5.*

★ ⑪ **Calgary Zoo, Botanical Gardens, and Prehistoric Park.** On St. George's Island in the middle of the Bow River, Canada's second-largest zoo houses more than 1,400 animals in natural settings. The Canadian Wilds section replicates endangered Canadian ecosystems. The Prehistoric Park displays 22 dinosaur replicas in a re-creation of their bygone natural habitat. ⊠ *1300 Zoo Rd. NE,* ☏ *403/232–9372.* ☞ *$9.50 May–Sept.; $8 Oct.–Apr.* ☉ *Apr.–June, weekdays 9–4, weekends 9–6; July–Sept., daily 9–6; Oct.–Mar., daily 9–4.*

⑯ **Canada Olympic Park.** The site of the 1988 Winter Olympics is today a year-round attraction. A one-hour bus tour goes over, under, around, and through the 70- and 90-meter ski jumps and the bobsled and luge tracks (in summer you have the option of walking down the slopes). In winter the slopes are open to the public (lessons available). You can try Olympic-size thrills on the scarifying one-minute bobsled simula-

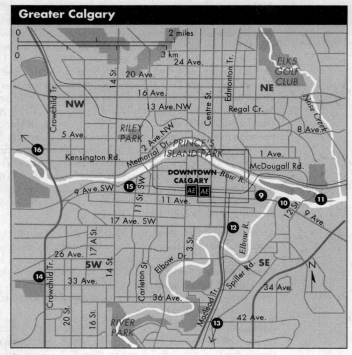

tor—the Bobsled Bullet ($39)—and the slightly briefer Tourist Luge
Ride ($12); safety equipment is provided. On the premises are a day
lodge with a cafeteria and the **Olympic Hall of Fame,** housing Olympic
memorabilia and video displays. ✉ *88 Olympic Rd. SW,* ☎ *403/286–
2632.* 🎟 *Bus or self-guided tour $6; tour and Hall of Fame $10; general admission $3.* ⏱ *Daily 8–5; Hall of Fame, daily 10–5.*

⑩ Deane House. Part of Fort Calgary, this is the restored 1906 post commander's house; it has tours and a restaurant. The **Hunt House,** just
behind the Deane House, is believed to be Calgary's oldest building,
with its likely origins traced to 1876. ✉ *806 9th Ave. SE,* ☎ *403/ 290–
1875.* 🎟 *Tours $3.*

⑨ Fort Calgary Interpretive Centre. At the confluence of the Bow and Elbow
rivers, the fort was established in 1875 by the North West Mounted
Police to subdue Montana whiskey traders, who were raising havoc
among the native peoples. The original fort is being rebuilt by a group
of volunteers. An interpretive center traces the history of area native
peoples, Mounties, and European settlers. ✉ *750 9th Ave. SE,* ☎
403/290–1875. 🎟 *$3.* ⏱ *May–Oct., daily 9–5.*

㉝ ⑬ Heritage Park. More than 100 authentic structures have been collected from all over western Canada and relocated here beside Glenmore Reservoir. The "neighborhoods," inhabited by costumed staff,
range from an 1850s fur-trading post to a 1910-era town. Steam trains,
horse-drawn buses, and paddle-wheel steamers provide transportation,
and North America's only antique amusement park re-creates bygone
thrills. Theme snacks—sarsaparilla, beef jerky, fresh apple pie—abound.
✉ *1900 Heritage Dr. SW,* ☎ *403/259–1900.* 🎟 *$10 for grounds; $17
with rides.* ⏱ *Late May–June, weekdays 10–4, weekends 10–6; July–
Sept. 2, daily 10–6; Sept. 3–early Oct., weekends 10–5.*

⓮ Museum of the Regiments. Western Canada's largest military museum has a collection of military memorabilia that depicts the history of Calgary-based regiments dating back to 1900. ✉ *4520 Crowchild Trail SW,* ☎ *403/974–2850.* ☞ *Free.* ☉ *July–Labor Day, daily 10–6; Labor Day–June, daily 10–4.*

Naval Museum of Alberta. Canada's second-largest naval museum focuses on the unlikely role of the prairie provinces in the navy. ✉ *1820 24th St. SW,* ☎ *403/242–0002.* ☞ *Free.* ☉ *July–Labor Day, daily 10–6; Labor Day–June, daily 10–4.*

⓬ Stampede Park. International attention focuses here each July for the rodeo events of the Calgary Stampede (☞ Outdoor Activities and Sports, *below*). Throughout the year, the Roundup Centre, Big Four Building, and Agriculture Building host trade shows; the **Canadian Airlines Saddledome** has concerts and Calgary Flames hockey games; and the Grandstand holds Thoroughbred and harness racing (☞ Outdoor Activities and Sports, *below*). You can wander the grounds, take free one-hour tours of the Saddledome, and visit the free **Grain Academy** in Roundup Centre, an interesting little museum that proclaims itself "Canada's only grain interpretive center." A model-train display depicts the movement of grain from the prairies through the Rockies to Vancouver. There's also a working model of a grain elevator. ✉ *17th Ave. and 2nd St. SE,* ☎ *403/261–0101, 403/ 777–4646 for Saddledome, 403/263–4594 for Grain Academy.* ☞ *Free.* ☉ *Weekdays 10–4, Sat. noon–4.*

Dining

$$$–$$$$ ✕ **Owl's Nest Dining Room.** Plush armchairs and dark-wood booths
★ are the signature of this venerable restaurant, where French cuisine reigns. Tableside preparations are a specialty, as are exclusive and rare vintage wines offered by the glass. ✉ *Westin Hotel, 320 4th Ave. SW,* ☎ *403/266–1611. Reservations essential. AE, DC, MC, V.*

$$–$$$$ ✕ **Billy MacIntyre's Cattle Company.** This western restaurant chain serves up authentic Alberta-style home cooking, following the recipes used by Alberta ranchers in the early 1900s. Try the baby-back ribs. Soups and breads are made here daily. ✉ *No. 500, 3630 Brentwood Rd. NW,* ☎ *403/282–6614;* ✉ *7104 Macleod Tail S,* ☎ *403/252–2260. Reservations not accepted on Tues. AE, DC, MC, V.*

$$–$$$$ ✕ **Mescalero.** The casual dining at this popular spot is influenced by the *cucina rustica* of the American Southwest and Latin America. There's an apple-wood grill, and tasty tapas (small dishes) are the star. The daily menu is fresh and creative. In the restaurant's Crazy Horse Bar you can sip margaritas and order from a café menu. ✉ *1315 1st St. SW,* ☎ *403/266–3339. Reservations essential. AE, MC, V.*

$$$ ✕ **Hy's Steak House.** This is where Calgary (and Edmonton, Winnipeg, Toronto, and more) goes for immense portions of charcoal-broiled steaks, fresh seafood, chicken, and a huge selection of wines. Wood paneling and plush carpeting help create a sedate Victorian ambience. ✉ *316 4th Ave. SW,* ☎ *403/263–2222. Reservations essential. AE, DC, MC, V. Closed Sun.*

$$–$$$ ✕ **Buzzards Café.** This lively European-style downtown café serves 70
★ wines by the bottle or glass and the exclusive home brew, Buzzard Breath Ale. Wine-theme prints and posters adorn the walls. Food selections include 8-ounce Alberta beef Buzzard Burgers and low-priced entrées, such as teriyaki chicken and fettuccine Alfredo. The adventurous might try buffalo chili with whiskey sausage. In summer, you can dine out on the patio. Adjoining the café is Bottlescrew Bill's Old English Pub. ✉ *140 10th Ave. SW,* ☎ *403/264–6959. AE, DC, MC, V.*

$–$$$ ✕ **Grand Isle Seafood Restaurant.** A riverfront view and appealing modern decor are added attractions at this large second-floor Chinese restaurant. Dim sum is featured, but it's also well known for seafood. ⊠ *128 2nd Ave. SE,* ☎ *403/269–7783. AE, D, DC, MC, V.*

$$ ✕ **Barley Mill Eatery and Pub.** With its stone fireplace and imported 100-year-old Scottish bar, the Barley Mill exudes comfort and coziness. It's one of the many pleasant eateries to open up in the Eau Claire Market. The extensive menu lists primarily pastas, but there's also a tapas bar. Twenty-four beers are on tap, and you can choose from 20 single-malt scotches. ⊠ *201 Barclay Parade,* ☎ *403/290–1500. AE, DC, MC, V*

$$ ✕ **Kaos Café.** A popular jazz club, this relaxed New York–style café specializes in a jazzy selection of entrées, coffees, and desserts. The patio is a pleasant choice in summer, and the Saturday and Sunday brunches are popular. There's live music most evenings. ⊠ *718 17 Ave. SW,* ☎ *403/228–9997. Reservations essential. AE, DC, MC, V.*

$$ ✕ **Osteria de Medici Restaurant.** An authentic, family-run Italian eatery serves up a wide variety of homemade pastas, seafood, and veal, along with such extras as bruschetta and rich desserts. If you're enamored enough, you can purchase the restaurant's cookbook here. ⊠ *201 10th St. NW,* ☎ *403/283–5553. AE, DC, MC, V.*

Lodging

$$$$ ⊞ **Delta Bow Valley.** The bright, 24-story high-rise occupies a relatively quiet street on the southern edge of downtown. Decent-size contemporary rooms with rose-and-green furnishings have good views from upper floors. For the brightest and most colorful units, request a room with a northern exposure. The sunny lobby—decorated in pink tones and with lush foliage—is an uplifting addition to an already lively setting. ⊠ *209 4th Ave. SE, T2G 0C6,* ☎ *403/266–1980 or 800/268–1133,* FAX *403/266–0007. 388 rooms, 10 suites. 2 restaurants, bar, no-smoking floors, indoor pool, sauna, exercise room. AE, DC, MC, V.*

$$$$ ⊞ **The Palliser.** The downtown area of every major Canadian city has
★   a grand old railroad hotel, and the Palliser is Calgary's. This landmark, built in 1914, was restored in the early 1990s. Guest rooms are tastefully appointed with traditional furnishings and have ornate moldings and high ceilings. ⊠ *133 9th Ave. SW, T2P 2M3,* ☎ *403/262–1234 or 800/268–9411,* FAX *403/260–1260. 385 rooms, 20 suites. Restaurant, bar, no-smoking floor, exercise room. AE, DC, MC, V.*

$$$$ ⊞ **Sheraton Cavalier.** The lobby of the Sheraton in northeast Calgary is decorated with pale colors, a multitude of plants, and a large marble water fountain. Barlow's Lounge hosts live entertainment from Thursday through Saturday. Henry's Pub, the hotel's sports bar, has large TV screens. Oasis River Country, on the second floor of the hotel, has two 200-ft water slides and a recreation and exercise area. ⊠ *2620 32nd Ave. NE, T1Y 6B8,* ☎ *403/291–0107 or 800/325–3535,* FAX *403/ 291–2834. 285 rooms, 21 suites. Restaurant, bar, lounge, no-smoking rooms, indoor pool. AE, DC, MC, V.*

$$$ ⊞ **Calgary Marriott.** This business-class hotel in the heart of downtown is connected to the Calgary Convention Centre. Nearby are the Glenbow Museum and the Calgary Centre for Performing Arts. The warm, inviting lobby sets the tone; rooms are done in pastels and maroons. ⊠ *110 9th Ave., T2G 5A6,* ☎ *403/266–7331 or 800/661–7776,* FAX *403/262–8442. 370 rooms, 11 suites. 2 restaurants, 2 bars, no-smoking floors, indoor pool, sauna, health club. AE, DC, MC, V.*

$$$ ⊞ **Coast Plaza Hotel.** One of the more recent additions to the Calgary hotel scene is in the northeast part of the city near the Trans-Canada Highway, with good access to the airport. Guest rooms are comfort-

able, with modern decor throughout. You have a choice of fine dining or family fare in the two restaurants. ⊠ *1316 33rd St. NE, T2A 6B6,* ☎ *403/248–888 or 800/661–1464,* FAX *403/248–0749. 148 rooms, 7 suites. 2 restaurants, sauna. AE, MC, V.*

$$$ ⊡ **Prince Royal Inn.** The inn has a great deal going for it within its 28 floors: a convenient downtown location, all-suite (studio, one-, and two-bedroom) accommodations with fully equipped kitchens, free parking, free Continental breakfast, and a health club. It's a great deal for families. ⊠ *618 5th Ave. SW, T2P 0M7,* ☎ *403/263–0520, 800/661–1592 in Canada,* FAX *403/262–9991. 300 suites. Restaurant, bar, no-smoking floors, sauna, exercise room. AE, DC, MC, V.*

$$$ ⊡ **Westin Hotel.** Calgary's Plus 15 pedway (walkway) system connects
★ this luxury high-rise in the midst of downtown to most other important nearby structures. Rooms are large and decorated with tasteful contemporary furniture and pastel and neutral tones. The rooftop pool is one of this lodging's unique attractions. The Owl's Nest (☞ Dining, *above*) is one of the better dining spots in town. For lighter meals stop in at the Lobby Court, which has Fitness Buffet breakfasts. ⊠ *320 4th Ave. SW, T2P 2S6,* ☎ *403/266–1611 or 800/228–3000,* FAX *403/265–7908. 469 rooms, 56 suites. 2 restaurants, 2 bars, no-smoking rooms, indoor pool, sauna, health club. AE, DC, MC, V.*

$$ ⊡ **Carriage House.** Fish tanks, caged songbirds, and a waterfall decorate the lobby of this unique, locally owned property, almost 10 km (6 mi) south of downtown. Room decor is comfortably mismatched. Nighttime entertainment options include a disco and rock club, a country and rock saloon, and an English pub. Guests receive discounts at the nearby Family Leisure Centre (☞ Outdoor Activities and Sports, *below*). ⊠ *9030 Macleod Trail S, T2H 0M4,* ☎ *403/253–1101 (call collect from the U.S.); 800/661–9566 in Canada;* FAX *403/259–2414. 147 rooms, 6 suites. 2 restaurants, 3 bars, no-smoking rooms, pool, sauna. AE, DC, MC, V.*

$$ ⊡ **Holiday Inn Airport.** Convenient and comfortable, this chain property is on the northeast side of town a few minutes from Calgary International Airport. The large, bright rooms are tastefully decorated with a rose-and-mauve scheme. ⊠ *1250 McKinnon Dr. NE, T2E 7T7,* ☎ *403/ 230–1999 or 800/661–5095,* FAX *403/277–2623. 170 rooms. Restaurant, bar, no-smoking rooms, indoor pool, sauna. AE, DC, MC, V.*

Nightlife and the Arts

Tickets for events at the Calgary Centre for the Performing Arts, Jubilee Auditorium, and the Saddledome are available at **Ticketmaster** outlets at the Calgary Centre box office or can be charged over the phone (☎ 403/270–6700 or 403/266–8888).

The Arts

MUSIC AND DANCE

Calgary Philharmonic Orchestra (☎ 403/294–7420) concerts, chamber groups, and a broad spectrum of other music and dance shows are presented in the 1,755-seat Jack Singer Concert Hall in the **Calgary Centre for the Performing Arts** (⊠ 205 8th Ave. SE, ☎ 403/294–7455). The **Jubilee Auditorium** (⊠ 1415 14th Ave. NW, ☎ 403/297–8000) hosts the Alberta Ballet Company and a variety of classical music, opera, dance, pop, and rock concerts. Concerts are performed at the **University of Calgary Theatre** (⊠ 2500 University Dr. NW, ☎ 403/220–4900).

THEATER

Calgary's premier theater facility is the **Calgary Centre for the Performing Arts** (⊠ 205 8th Ave. SE, ☎ 403/294–7455), with three modern auditoriums in two contiguous historic buildings. Productions by resident Alberta Theatre Projects (ATP) of works by principally Canadian playwrights are highly recommended. **Loose Moose** (⊠ 2003 McKnight Blvd. NE, ☎ 403/291–5682) features competitive "Theatresports" and all sorts of improvisational fun and games. More than 20 local companies use the stage of the **Pumphouse Theatre** (⊠ 2140 9th Ave. SW, ☎ 403/263–0079). The **University of Calgary Theatre** (⊠ Reeve Theatre, 2500 University Dr. NW, ☎ 403/220–4900) stages classic and contemporary works.

Nightlife and the Arts

BARS AND CLUBS

Gargoyle's (⊠ 1213 1st St. SW, ☎ 403/263–4810) caters to an older, upscale crowd. The club atmosphere at **Republik** (⊠ 219 17th Ave. SW, ☎ 403/244–1884) attracts a young crowd for alternative rock. The Mexican accent at **Señor Frog's** (⊠ 739 2nd Ave. SW, ☎ 403/264–5100) is popular with all ages.

COMEDY

Jester's (⊠ 239 10th Ave. SE, ☎ 403/269–6669) has comedians and Wednesday-night open mikes. **Yuk Yuk's** (⊠ Blackfoot Inn, 5940 Blackfoot Trail, ☎ 403/258–2028), part of the Canadian comedy chain, has name performers from Canada and the United States.

MUSIC

The latest country hot spot is **Cowboys** (⊠ 826 5th St. W, ☎ 403/265–0699). The **Longhorn Dance Hall** (⊠ 9631 Macleod Trail S, ☎ 403/258–0528) is one of Calgary's western hangouts. For western sights and sounds, head for **Ranchman's** (⊠ 9615 Macleod Trail S, ☎ 403/253–1100).

Outdoor Activities and Sports

Participant Sports

BIKING AND JOGGING

Calgary has about 300 km (186 mi) of bicycling and jogging paths, most of which wind along rivers and through city parks. Maps are available at visitor centers and bike shops. You can rent bikes at **Sports Rent** (⊠ 4424 16th Ave. NW, Calgary, ☎ 403/292–0077) and from **Budget Rent-A-Car** (⊠ 140 6th Ave. SE, ☎ 403/264–5212).

HEALTH AND FITNESS CLUBS

Three **Leisure Centre** water parks in Calgary have wave pools and water slides, plus gymnasiums and training facilities; Southland and Family have racquetball and squash courts. ⊠ *Village Square Leisure Centre, 2623 56th St. NE,* ☎ *403/280–9714;* ⊠ *Family Leisure Centre, 11150 Bonaventure Dr. SE,* ☎ *403/278–7542;* ⊠ *Southland Leisure Centre, 2000 Southland Dr. SW,* ☎ *403/251–3505.*

Just south of downtown, the striking white-dome **Lindsay Park Sports Centre** (⊠ 2225 Macleod Trail SW, ☎ 403/233–8393) encompasses a 50-meter natatorium, a 200-meter track, racquetball and squash courts, and a weight room.

Spectator Sports

FOOTBALL

The **Calgary Stampeders** of the Canadian Football League play home games in McMahon Stadium (⊠ 1817 Crowchild Trail NW, ☎ 403/289–0205) from July through November.

HOCKEY

The **Calgary Flames** play National Hockey League matches October–April at the Canadian Airlines Saddledome (⊠ 17th Ave. and 2nd St. SE, ☎ 403/261–0475) in Stampede Park.

HORSE RACING

There's racing year-round (except March) in **Stampede Park** (⊠ 17th Ave. and 2nd St. SE, ☎ 403/261–0101). Thoroughbreds race April–May and September–November; trotters, May–September and December–February. **Spruce Meadows** (⊠ 18011 14th St. SW, ☎ 403/974–4200) is one of the world's finest show-jumping facilities, with major competitions held June–September.

RODEO

For 10 days each July, rodeo events draw the world's top cowboys and plenty of greenhorns to one of Canada's most popular events, the **Calgary Stampede** (☎ 800/661–1260), held in Stampede Park. Besides rodeo events, there are livestock shows, concerts, and high-spirited western-style entertainment. You should make room and ticket reservations well in advance if you plan to attend.

Shopping

Calgary's best shopping is in the center of the downtown district, where you can wander through various shopping centers connected by indoor walkways. **Bankers Hall** (⊠ 315 8th Ave. SW) has exclusive specialty shops, restaurants, and cinemas. The **Eaton Centre** (⊠ Stephen Ave. Mall and 4th St. SW) has more than 500 stores. **Penny Lane Mall** (⊠ 8th Ave. between 4th and 5th Sts. SW) is in renovated, early 20th-century buildings. **Scotia Centre** (⊠ 7th Ave. and 2nd St. SW) has fashion, accessory, and other retail outlets. For outdoor shopping, the six-block stretch of 8th Avenue Southwest between 3rd Street Southwest and Macleod Trail Southeast has been turned into the traffic-free **Stephen Avenue Mall** (although traffic is allowed during the evenings). **Toronto Dominion Centre** (⊠ 7th Ave. and 2nd St. SW) is home to the indoor park—Devonian Gardens—as well as more than 100 stores.

Kensington and **Uptown 17** are trendy shopping districts northwest of the city center on Kensington Road and 10th Street, respectively; here you'll find crafts shops, antiques stores, boutiques, galleries, cafés, and coffee shops. **Eau Claire Market,** adjacent to the Bow River and Prince's Island Park, has quickly gained favor among locals and visitors. The market has a tantalizing variety of fresh produce outlets and a number of restaurants and one-of-a-kind specialty shops. A new Sheraton hotel, opening at press time, is part of the mix.

Side Trip from Calgary

Cochrane
25 km (16 mi) west of Calgary.

Cochrane, a popular center for trail rides and canoe trips on the Bow River, has western-style buildings that hold some thriving crafts shops. The **Western Heritage Centre** is an interactive interpretive center dedicated to the history of ranching, farming, and rodeos; the people who operated the first ranches in Alberta; and the men and women who still perform those same chores today. ⊠ *Near junction of Hwys. 22 and 1A,* ☎ *403/932–3514.* ◻ *$7.50.* ⊙ *Late May–Labor Day, daily 9–8; Labor Day–late May, daily 9–5.*

Calgary A to Z

Arriving and Departing
BY CAR

The Trans-Canada Highway (Highway 1) runs west to southeast across Alberta, through Calgary. Highway 2 passes through Calgary on its way from the U.S. border to Edmonton and points north. Calgary is

690 km (428 mi) northwest of Helena, Montana; it's 670 km (415 mi) northeast of Seattle, via the Trans-Canada Highway.

BY PLANE

Calgary International Airport (✉ 2000 Airport Rd. NE, ☎ 403/735–1372) is 20 minutes northeast of the city center. Airlines serving Calgary include Air Canada, Canadian Airlines International, Air BC, American, Delta, United, and Horizon (☞ Airline Travel *in* the Gold Guide for telephone numbers). Taxis make the trip between the airport and downtown for about $18.

Getting Around

BY BUS AND LRT

Calgary Transit (✉ 206 7th Ave. SW, ☎ 403/276–7801) operates a comprehensive bus system and light rail transit system (the C-Train or LRT) throughout the area. Fares on both are $1.60. Books of 10 tickets are $12. A Calgary Transit (CT) Day Pass good for unlimited rides costs $4. The C-Train has lines running northwest (Brentwood), northeast (Whitehorn), and south (Anderson) from downtown. The C-Train is free within the downtown core.

BY CAR

Although many sights are in the downtown area and can be reached on foot, a car is useful for visiting outlying attractions.

BY TAXI

Taxis are fairly expensive, at $2.05 to start and about $1 for each additional mile. Major taxi services are **Checker** (☎ 403/299–9999), **Yellow Cab** (☎ 403/974–1111), **Red Top** (☎ 403/974–4444), **Associated Cabs** (☎ 403/299–1111), and **Co-op** (☎ 403/531–8294).

Contacts and Resources

EMERGENCIES

Emergencies (☎ 911). **Police** (☎ 403/266–1234). **Poison center** (☎ 403/670–1414).

GUIDED TOURS

Several companies offer tours of Calgary and environs, although none operate on regular schedules. Call the **Calgary Convention and Visitors Bureau** (☎ 403/263–8510 or 800/661–1678) for information.

HOSPITALS

Emergency rooms are at **Alberta Children's Hospital** (✉ 1820 Richmond Rd. SW, ☎ 403/229–7211), **Foothills Hospital** (✉ 1403 29th Ave. NW, ☎ 403/670–1110), **Peter Lougheed Hospital** (✉ 3500 26th Ave. NE, ☎ 403/291–8555), and **Rocky View Hospital** (✉ 7007 14th St. SW, ☎ 403/541–3000).

LATE-NIGHT PHARMACY

The **Super Drug Mart** (✉ 504 Elbow Dr. SW, ☎ 403/228–3338) is open daily until midnight.

VISITOR INFORMATION

The main **Calgary Convention and Visitors Bureau** (✉ 237 8th Ave. SE, T2G 0K8, ☎ 403/263–8510 or 800/661–1678) office is open daily 8–5. There are also walk-in visitor centers at the base of the Calgary Tower and at Calgary International Airport.

ELSEWHERE IN SOUTHERN ALBERTA

A number of cities and varied sights in the southern part of the province provide a look at key elements of Alberta's history. You can study the world of the dinosaurs in Drumheller; learn about the role of native peoples, settlers, and the North West Mounted Police in Fort Macleod; and explore prosperous, modern Medicine Hat.

Drumheller

🔞 *20 km (12 mi) east of Calgary on Trans-Canada Hwy. (Hwy. 1), then 120 km (75 mi) north on Rte. 9.*

The road to Drumheller takes you through the vast Canadian prairie of seemingly endless expanses of flat country in every direction. Once a coal-mining center, the town lies in the rugged valley of the Red Deer River, where millions of years of wind and water erosion exposed the "strike" that produced what amounts to present-day Drumheller's major industry: dinosaurs. Besides the excellent Royal Tyrell Museum, a number of dinosaur-related businesses capitalize on the area's rich paleontological past.

★ The **Royal Tyrrell Museum of Paleontology** explores the geological and paleontological history of Alberta. The barren lunar terrain of stark badlands and eerie rock cylinders (called hoodoos) may seem an ideal setting for the dinosaurs that stalked the countryside 75 million years ago, but in fact, when the dinosaurs were here, the area had a semitropical climate and marshlands not unlike those of the Florida Everglades. You can participate in hands-on exhibits and meet the local hero, *Albertosaurus*, a smaller, fiercer version of Tyrannosaurus rex, the first dinosaur discovered around here. ✉ *Rte. 838, 6 km (4 mi) west of Drumheller,* ☎ *403/823–7707 or 403/294–1992.* 💷 *$6.50.* ☉ *Mid-May–early Sept., daily 9–9; mid-Sept.–mid-May, Tues.–Sun. 10–5.*

Reptile World (✉ Rte. 9, ☎ 403/823–8623) has a crowd-pleasing collection of poisonous snakes. The **Homestead Antique Museum** (✉ Rte. 838, ☎ 403/823–2600) packs 4,000 native artifacts, medical instruments, pieces of period clothing, and other items of Canadiana into a roadside Quonset hut. **Prehistoric Park** (✉ Off Rte. 575, ☎ 403/823–7625) depicts life-size dinosaurs in a badlands setting and sells a vast selection of fossils, bones, rocks, and petrified wood. No visit to Drumheller is complete without a family portrait beside the comic-book Tyrannosaurus rex guarding the Route 9 bridge over the Red Deer River.

Lodging

$$ 🏨 **Best Western Jurassic Inn.** Popcorn is provided nightly at this newer, family-oriented lodging. Rooms have queen-size beds, refrigerators, and microwaves. ✉ *1103 Hwy. 9 S, T0J 0Y0,* ☎ *403/823–7700,* ℻ *403/823–5002. 46 rooms, 3 suites. Pool, hot tub, exercise room. CP. AE, D, MC, V.*

$$ 🏨 **Drumheller Inn.** This local staple for two decades stands on a hillside overlooking the town and surrounding badlands. It has basic but fairly fresh rooms. ✉ *100 S. Railway Ave., T0J 0Y0,* ☎ *403/823–8400,* ℻ *403/823–5020. 99 rooms, 1 suite. Restaurant, pool, hot tub. AE, D, MC, V.*

Dinosaur Provincial Park

142 km (88 mi) south of Drumheller, 190 km (118 mi) southeast of Calgary.

Dinosaur Provincial Park encompasses 73 square km (28 square mi) of Canada's greatest badlands, as well as prairie and riverside habitats. A United Nations World Heritage Site, the park contains some of the world's richest fossil beds, including many kinds of dinosaurs. Much of the area is a nature preserve with restricted public access. Self-guided trails explore different habitats, and a public loop road leads to two outdoor fossil displays. The Royal Tyrrell Museum Field Station has ongoing fossil excavations. Interpretive programs run daily from mid-May to early September and on weekends until mid-October, but many require tickets; call for reservations. You should allow at least 1½ days for an in-depth experience. The campground has a food service center. To get here from Drumheller, take Route 56 to the Trans-Canada Highway (Highway 1) east, go north at Brooks on Route 873 and then east on Route 544, and follow signs. ⊠ *Rte. 544, Patricia,* ☎ *403/378–4342 for information, 403/378–4344 for reservations for bus tour or interpretive hikes (mid-May–Aug.), 403/378–3700 for campground reservations (May–Aug.).* ☑ *Free, bus tour $4.50.* ☉ *Daily 24 hrs; Tyrrell Museum Field Station mid-May–Aug., daily 8:15 AM–9 PM; Sept.–mid-Oct., weekdays 8:15–4:30, weekends 9–5; mid-Oct.–mid-May, weekdays 8:15–4:30.*

Medicine Hat

⑱ *95 km (59 mi) southeast of Patricia, 293 km (182 mi) southeast of Calgary on Trans-Canada Hwy.*

Medicine Hat is a prosperous, scenic city built on high banks overlooking the South Saskatchewan River. Much local lore concerns the origin of its name, but one legend tells of a battle between Cree and Blackfoot peoples: The Cree fought bravely until their medicine man deserted, losing his headdress in the South Saskatchewan River. The site's name, *Saamis,* meaning "medicine man's hat," was later translated by white settlers into Medicine Hat. Roadside views on the way to Medicine Hat consist of small well pumps and storage tanks amid endless expanses of "prairie wool," spear and blue grama grass.

Alberta's fifth-largest city's wealth derives from vast deposits of natural gas below, some of which is piped up to fuel quaint gas lamps in the turn-of-the-century downtown area. Prosperity is embodied in the striking, glass-sided **Medicine Hat City Hall,** which won the Canadian Architectural Award in 1986. Guided group and self-guided tours are available. ⊠ *1st St. SE and 6th Ave. SE,* ☎ *403/529–8100.* ☉ *Weekdays 8:30–4:30.*

Medicine Hat's greatest achievement was turning the land alongside the South Saskatchewan River and Seven Persons Creek into **parkland and environmental preserves** interconnected by 15 km (9½ mi) of walking, biking, and cross-country ski trails. Detailed trail maps are available at the **Tourist Information Centre** (⊠ 8 Gehring Rd. SW, ☎ 403/527–6422). There is 1 km (½ m) of falling water at **Riverside Amusement Park** (⊠ Hwy. 1 and Power House Rd., ☎ 403/529–6218), with water slides, go-carts, and inner tubing. **Echo Dale Regional Park** (⊠ Holsom Rd. off Rte. 3, ☎ 403/529–6225) provides a riverside setting for swimming, boating, and fishing; it also has a 1900s farm and a historic coal mine.

Lodging

$$ **🏨 Medicine Hat Lodge.** This hotel, on the edge of town adjacent to a shopping mall, has several rooms with inward views of the indoor pool and the huge, curving water slide. The Atrium Dining Room serves fine Continental meals. J. D.'s is a hotel country-and-western club with live music. ⊠ *1051 Ross Glen Dr. SE, T1B 3T8,* ☎ *403/529–2222 or 800/661–8095. 185 rooms, 4 suites. 2 restaurants, 2 bars, no-smoking rooms, indoor pool, steam room. AE, DC, MC, V.*

Lethbridge

⓳ *164 km (102 mi) west of Medicine Hat on Crowsnest Hwy. (Rte. 3),
217 km (135 mi) south of Calgary via Hwy. 2 and Rte. 3.*

Alberta's third-largest city, with a population of 60,000, Lethbridge is
an 1870s coal boomtown that is now a center of agriculture, oil, and
gas. The main attraction, **Fort Whoop-Up,** part of the **Indian Battle
Park,** is a reconstruction of a southern Alberta whiskey fort. Along with
weapons, relics, and a 15-minute audiovisual historical presentation,
Fort Whoop-Up has wagon-train tours of the river valley and other
points of local historical interest. ✉ *Whoop-Up Dr. and Oldman River,*
☎ *403/329–0444.* ✇ *Fort $2.50.* ☉ *Late May–Labor Day, Mon.–
Sat. 10–6, Sun. 2–8; off-season, call for hrs.*

Henderson Lake Park, 3 km (2 mi) east of downtown Lethbridge, is
filled with lush trees, a golf course, a baseball stadium, tennis courts,
a swimming pool, and a 60-acre man-made lake. Alongside the lake,
Nikka Yuko Japanese Gardens is a tranquil setting for manicured trees
and shrubs, miniature pools and waterfalls, a teahouse, and pebble designs originally constructed in Japan and reassembled alongside Henderson Lake. ✉ *Mayor Magrath Dr. and S. Parkside Dr.,* ☎ *403/
320–3020, 403/328–3511 gardens.* ✇ *$3.* ☉ *Mid-May–mid-June, daily
9–5; mid-June–Aug., daily 9–8; Sept.–early Oct., daily 9–5.*

Dining and Lodging

$$–$$$ ✕ **Players Lounge.** This spot in the El Rancho Motor Hotel special-
izes in aged steaks and chateaubriand made with tender Alberta beef.
For something lighter in a more informal setting, try the El Rancho
coffee shop on the same property. There's live music and dancing most
nights. ✉ *526 Mayor Magrath Dr.,* ☎ *403/327–5701. Reservations
essential. AE, DC, MC, V.*

$$–$$$ ✕ **Sven Eriksen's Family Restaurant.** Tasty versions of Canadian prairie
standards, including chicken and an especially good prime rib, are cooked
up at this homey, colonial-style eatery. "Family Restaurant" label
notwithstanding, there's a full bar. ✉ *1715 Mayor Magrath Dr.,* ☎
403/328–7756. Reservations essential. AE, MC, V.

$$ ▥ **Lethbridge Lodge Hotel.** Besides great Oldman River views, this mod-
ern lodge has a pleasant, tropical indoor courtyard filled with exotic
plants, a swimming pool, a whirlpool, a waterfall, and chairs. There
are two restaurants: At the more formal Anton's, the waiters wear tuxe-
dos, and reservations are needed. ✉ *320 Scenic Dr., T1J 4B4,* ☎ *403/
328–1123 or 800/661–1232. 155 rooms, 36 suites. 2 restaurants, bar,
no-smoking rooms, indoor pool, hot tub. AE, MC, V.*

$ ▥ **Parkside Inn.** A good bargain, this comfortable hotel is conve-
niently situated across the street from a golf course and within walk-
ing distance of Henderson Lake Park (☞ *above*) and the Japanese
gardens. The lobby is done in muted burgundies and blues, while
rooms are styled in grays and rusts. The hotel's tavern has live coun-
try-and-western music on weekends, and the lounge has video lottery
machines. ✉ *1009 Mayor Magrath Dr., T1K 2P7,* ☎ *403/328–2366.
62 rooms, 2 suites. Restaurant, bar, no-smoking rooms. AE, MC, V.*

Fort Macleod

⓴ *50 km (31 mi) west of Lethbridge on Rte. 3, 167 km (104 mi) south
of Calgary on Hwy. 2.*

The pre-1900 wood-frame buildings and the more recent sandstone-and-
brick buildings have established Fort Macleod, southern Alberta's old-
est town, as the province's first historic area. It was founded by the
Mounties in 1874 to maintain order among the farmers, native peo-

ples, whiskey vendors, and ranchers beginning to settle here. For information about guided and self-guided tours, visit the information booth (☎ 403/553–2500) beside the Fort Macleod Museum. An authentic reconstruction of the 1874 fort, the **Fort Macleod Museum** grants almost equal exhibitory weight to settlers, native peoples, old North West Mounted Police, and today's Royal Canadian Mounted Police. ⊠ *25th St. and 3rd Ave., ☎ 403/553–4703. ☎ $4. ⊙ May–mid-June and early Sept.–mid-Oct., daily 9–5; mid-June–early Sept., daily 9–8:30.*

A World Heritage Site, **Head-Smashed-In Buffalo Jump** has a large, seven-level interpretive center, built into the side of a cliff, that explains how Plains Indians herded buffalo over the edge to their death in order to harvest meat and fur from the carcasses. Museum displays describe the tradition and offer insight into the life and customs of the Plains Indians, especially the Blackfoot. Guided walks and audiovisual exhibits are offered. The site is about 18 km (11 mi) northwest of Fort Macleod. ⊠ *Rte. 785 off Hwy. 2, ☎ 403/553–2731. ☎ $6.50. ⊙ May 16–Labor Day, daily 9–8; Labor Day–May 15, daily 9–5.*

EDMONTON

Lucky Edmonton is a boomtown that never seems to go bust. The first boom arrived in 1795, when the North West Company and Hudson's Bay Company both established fur-trading posts in the area. Boom II came in 1897, when Edmonton became principal outfitter on the overland "All Canadian Route" to the Yukon goldfields; as a result, Edmonton was named capital when the province of Alberta was formed in 1905. The latest boom began on February 13, 1947, when oil was discovered in Leduc, 40 km (25 mi) to the southwest. More than 10,000 wells were eventually drilled within 100 km (62 mi) of the city, and with them came fields of refineries and supply depots. By 1965 Edmonton had solidified its role as the "oil capital of Canada."

More interesting is how wisely Edmonton has spread the wealth to create a beautiful and livable city. Shunning the uncontrolled development of some other oil boomtowns, Edmonton turned its great natural resource, the North Saskatchewan River valley, into a 27-km (17-mi) greenbelt of parks and recreational facilities. With a population approaching 900,000, Edmonton is the fifth-largest city in Canada and also Canada's second-largest city in land area—270 square mi. As the seat of the provincial government and home to the University of Alberta, the city has an unusually sophisticated atmosphere that has generated many fine restaurants and a thriving arts community. Another of its attractions, the West Edmonton Mall, is a year-round drawing card for shoppers and families, complete with facilities ranging from an amusement park and a hotel to a cinema complex and a water park. The city also has professional football and hockey teams, as well as Triple A baseball.

Downtown Edmonton

The city's striking physical feature, where most recreational facilities are located, is the broad green valley of the North Saskatchewan River, running diagonally northeast to southwest through the city center. The downtown area lies just north of the river, between 95th and 109th streets.

The Edmonton street system is a grid with numbered streets running north–south (numbers decrease as you go east) and numbered avenues running east–west (numbers decrease as you go south). Edmontonians often use the last digit or two of large numbers as shorthand for the complete number: The Inn on 7th is on 107th Street; the 9th Street Bistro can be found on 109th Street. Edmonton's main drag is Jasper Avenue, which runs east–west through the center of downtown.

A Good Walk and Ride

Start at the **Shaw Conference Centre** ㉑, an architecturally inventive space built into a hillside with terraced levels accessed by glass-enclosed escalators. Head west along Jasper Avenue and turn north on 99th Street to **Sir Winston Churchill Square** ㉒ and the Arts District, where you'll find many of the city's major cultural institutions. Across 99th Street is the **Edmonton Art Gallery** ㉓. Directly west of Churchill Square begins a maze of multilevel shopping malls, department stores, cinemas, and office buildings—all climatically controlled and interconnected by a network of tunnels and second-floor pedways (☞ Shopping, *below*). Enter the LRT station on Jasper Avenue at 103rd or 104th Street for the ride to Grandin Station and the **Alberta Government Centre** ㉔, where you can tour the **Alberta Legislature Building** ㉕.

TIMING

You can do this tour in a few hours any day of the week, although you may choose to linger to explore the cultural institutions or to shop.

Sights to See

㉔ **Alberta Government Centre.** The seat of Alberta's government, this complex encompasses several acres of carefully manicured gardens and fountains. The gardens are open for strolling. ⊠ *109th St. and 97th Ave.*

㉕ **Alberta Legislature Building.** The stately 1912 Edwardian structure overlooks the river on the site of an early trading post. Frequent free tours of the building and an interpretive center help explain the intricacies of the Albertan and Canadian systems of government. ⊠ *109th St. and 97th Ave.,* ☎ *403/427–7362.* ☜ *Tour free.* ☉ *Daily; call for hrs.*

㉓ **Edmonton Art Gallery.** More than 30 annual exhibitions of classical and contemporary art from Canada and the rest of the world are mounted here. ⊠ *2 Sir Winston Churchill Sq.,* ☎ *403/422–6223.* ☜ *$3; free Thurs. after 4.* ☉ *Mon.–Wed. 10:30–5, Thurs. and Fri. 10:30–8, weekends 11–5.*

㉑ **Shaw Conference Centre.** This most unconventional building is filled with surprises. The center has been built onto a slope, and the terraced levels are reached by glass-enclosed escalators with great views of the North Saskatchewan River valley. On the Pedway (walkway) Level check out the **Canadian Country Music Hall of Honor,** actually a wall filled with plaques memorializing such good old boys as Hank Snow, Wilf Carter, and Orval "the Canadian Plowboy" Prophet. ⊠ *9797 Jasper Ave.,* ☎ *403/421–9797.*

㉒ **Sir Winston Churchill Square** is the focus of the Arts District, a six-block area that incorporates many of Edmonton's major institutions. The newest addition is the **Francis Winspear Centre for Music,** with a 1,900-seat concert hall that is home to the Edmonton Symphony Orchestra. Also here is the largest theater complex in Canada, the **Citadel Theatre,** with five different venues (plus workshops and classrooms) and an indoor garden with a waterfall. The Edmonton Public Library's **Stanley Milner Library** (⊠ 7 Sir Winston Churchill Sq., ☎ 403/423–2331) augments books and art exhibits with a lively round of activities in the Children's Department. The **Chinatown Gate** is a symbol of friendship between Edmonton and its sister city, Harbin, China; it spans the portal to Edmonton's meager Chinatown. Nearby, the **City Hall** (⊠ 1 Sir Winston Churchill Sq., ☎ 403/496–8200) is more than a place for civic government. This architectural showcase contains a

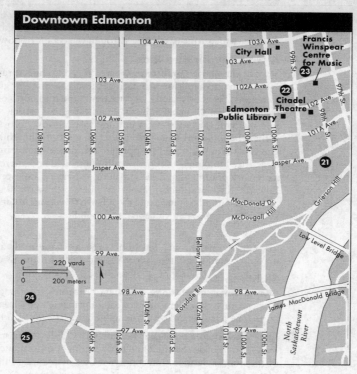

Downtown Edmonton

grand stairway, a large art exhibition space, and a 200-ft tower with an enormous 23-bell carillon.

Greater Edmonton

You'll find everything from historical sights and museums to water parks and the world's largest mall outside downtown Edmonton.

A Good Drive

To make a circuit, start northwest of city center at the **Edmonton Space and Science Centre,** where you can play with high-tech equipment in hands-on displays. On the western edge of the city is the **Wild Waters Waterslide Park,** a great place to cool off the kids. Moving toward the center again, you can visit the **West Edmonton Mall,** the world's largest. On the south side of the North Saskatchewan River, just off White-mud Drive, is **Fort Edmonton Park,** where costumed interpreters take you back in time. Still on the south side of the river, but around a few bends just off Groat Road, is **William Hawrelak Park,** a perfect place for kids to fish. After fishing, you can visit the **Valley Zoo,** just across the river. A few blocks north is the **Provincial Museum of Alberta,** which focuses on natural and human history. Across the river again, via the 109th Street High Level Bridge, you'll come to the **Old Strathcona Historic Area.** To the northeast, still on the south side of the river, lies **Muttart Conservatory,** an important botanical facility.

TIMING

You can spend several days taking in these places of interest outside downtown, depending on how much time you want to devote to shopping or playing in the amusement parks. If you have only a day, choose based on your interests.

Sights to See

🔄 **Edmonton Space and Science Centre.** You can explore the heavens using a stunning variety of high-tech techniques. Permanent exhibits and a fascinating science shop are always of interest, but the star attractions include laser-light concerts and IMAX films. ⊠ *11211 142nd St.,* ☎ *403/493–9000.* 🎟 *$12.* ☉ *Mid-June–early Sept., daily 10–10; early Sept.–mid-June, Tues.–Sun. 10–10.*

★ **Fort Edmonton Park.** Canada's largest historical park (158 acres) is home to an authentic re-creation of several periods in Edmonton history. There is a fur press (an apparatus for bundling pelts for shipping) in the 1846 Hudson's Bay Company fort; a blacksmith shop, a saloon, and a jail along 1885 Street; photo studios and a firehouse on 1905 Street; and relatively modern conveniences on 1920 Street. Horse-wagon, streetcar, stagecoach, and pony rides are available, as well as a short trip on a steam-powered train. ⊠ *Whitemud and Fox Drs.,* ☎ *403/496– 8787.* 🎟 *$6.75.* ☉ *Mid-May–June, daily 10–4; July–early Sept., daily 10–6; Sept., Mon.–Sat. 11–2, Sun. 10–6.*

Muttart Conservatory. At one of North America's most important botanical facilities, separate greenhouses each contain flora of a different climate: arid, tropical, and temperate. A show pavilion has special seasonal floral displays. ⊠ *9626 96A St.,* ☎ *403/496–8755.* 🎟 *$4.25.* ☉ *Sun.–Wed. 11–9, Thurs.–Sat. 11–6.*

Old Strathcona Historic Area. The area surrounding 104th Street and Whyte (82nd) Avenue on the south side of the river is a district of restored houses and shops built mainly when Strathcona Town amalgamated with Edmonton, in 1912. The low buildings and wide streets have a decidedly Old West air, and Old Strathcona is a good place to get out and wander. There's a farmer's market, theaters, museums, and 75 restaurants and coffee houses, which add to the ambience of the area. Call the Old Strathcona Foundation (☎ 403/433–5866) for information.

Provincial Museum of Alberta. At the province's foremost natural and human history museum, four main galleries depict Alberta's heritage. The Aboriginal Peoples Gallery has a collection of native artifacts that is among North America's finest, and the Natural History Gallery presents specimens of animals and plants from the past and present. The museum has an outdoor sculpture park. ⊠ *12845 102nd Ave.,* ☎ *403/453–9100.* 🎟 *$5.* ☉ *May–Sept., daily 9–5; Oct.–Apr., Tues.–Sun. 9–5.*

🔄 **Valley Zoo.** This small but imaginative zoo in riverside Laurier Park places exotic species in well-known storybook settings. ⊠ *134th St. and Buena Vista Rd.,* ☎ *403/496–6911.* 🎟 *Summer $4.95, winter $3.35.*

West Edmonton Mall. Listed in the *Guinness Book of Records* as the world's largest mall, this is Edmonton's preeminent shopping attraction. Its sheer magnitude and variety transform it from a mere shopping center to an indoor city with high-rent districts, blue-collar strips, and hidden byways. There are 800 stores and services, including four major department stores, more than 20 movie theaters, and 90 places to eat; the mall also contains an amusement park, an ice-skating rink, a replica of Columbus's ship the *Santa Maria,* an 18-hole miniature-golf course, the Deep Sea Adventure submarine ride and dolphin show, the 5-acre World Waterpark water amusement park, Fantasyland Hotel (☞ Lodging, *below*), a playhouse, a chapel, a bingo parlor, and a casino. If you don't feel like walking the mall, rent an electric scooter or hitch a ride on a rickshaw. ⊠ *8770 170th St.,* ☎ *403/444–5300.* 🎟 *Amusement park day pass $29.95, individual-ride tickets $1 (rides* cost 1–7 tickets), World Waterpark day pass $29.95, Deep Sea Adventure $13. ☉ Weekdays 10–9, Sat. 10–6, Sun. noon–5.

ⓒ **Wild Waters Waterslide Park.** There's plenty of wet fun at this facility. ⊠ 21515 103rd Ave., ☎ 403/447–4476.

ⓒ **William Hawrelak Park.** Children only—or adults in their company—may fish in this rainbow trout–stocked pond. The park includes paddleboats and an adventure playground. ⊠ Off Groat Rd. south of North Saskatchewan River, ☎ 403/496–7275.

Dining

$$$–$$$$ ✕ **Unheardof Dining Lounge.** Hardly "unheard-of" any longer, this is
★ a popular restaurant in an antiques-filled old house. The five-course prix-fixe dinner ($41) changes weekly but is likely to include game in autumn and poultry or beef the rest of the year. Dinners begin with a light pâté and are punctuated by surprising salads and refreshing sorbets. Desserts, especially the Danish cream-cheese cheesecake, are light and delicious. There's a choice of as many as five different red and white wines served by the glass. ⊠ 9602 82nd Ave., ☎ 403/432–0480. Reservations essential. AE, MC, V. No lunch Tues.–Sat.

$$–$$$$ ✕ **La Boheme.** On the historic east-side Gibbard Block, this fittingly splendid restaurant presents classic French cuisine, prepared with invention and served with solicitous care. Edwardian pressed-tin ceilings and a French provincial fireplace enhance the setting. Specialties include lamb sausages and fresh fish. The restaurant is part of a bed-and-breakfast that has four-poster beds and antique bathtubs. ⊠ 6427 112th Ave., ☎ 403/474–5693. Reservations essential. AE, MC, V.

$$–$$$ ✕ **Bistro Praha.** Table lamps and paintings of Prague street scenes make this European-style café feel as homey as Grandma's living room. The background music is classical, the clientele mainly urban young professional. The menu includes such Eastern European favorites as cabbage soup and Wiener schnitzel. A rich selection of desserts and a wide choice of teas make this a perfect stop for snacks. ⊠ 10168 100A St., at Jasper Ave., ☎ 403/424–4218. AE, DC, MC, V.

$$–$$$ ✕ **La Spiga.** Admirable northern Italian cuisine is served in a flower-filled 1913 house that feels more like Montréal than the western plains. Menu highlights are rack of lamb with grappa, breast of chicken with fresh tomato, and various renditions of veal. Portions are large and accompanied by fettuccine; the wine list is long. ⊠ 10133 125th St., at 102nd Ave., ☎ 403/482–3100. Reservations essential. AE, MC, V. Closed Sun. No lunch.

$–$$$ ✕ **Frank's Place.** This restaurant satisfies landlocked Edmonton's appetite for fresh seafood with daily fly-ins. Order oysters Rockefeller and whiskey shrimp as appetizers, and anything charbroiled over mesquite turns out fine. Deck flooring, corrugated walls, and nets dangling overhead set the mood. ⊠ 10020 101A Ave., ☎ 403/422–0282. Reservations essential. AE, MC, V.

$$ ✕ **Bourbon Street.** This is actually an assemblage of moderately priced restaurants around a cul-de-sac on the main floor of West Edmonton Mall. New Orleans street lamps and wrought-iron balconies are part of the "exterior" decor. Café Orleans serves such Cajun-Creole dishes as jambalaya and oysters. Albert's has deli fare including the Montréal favorite, smoked meat. Other spots are Planet Hollywood and the Hard Rock Cafe. One of the newest additions, the visually stunning Modern Art Cafe, serves an assortment of designer pizzas. ⊠ West Edmonton Mall, 8770 170th St., Entrance 6, ☎ 403/444–1752 for Albert's, 403/444–2202 for Café Orleans, 403/444–1905 for Hard

Rock Cafe, 403/444–2233 for Modern Art Cafe, 403/444–4999 for Planet Hollywood. AE, MC, V.

$$ ✕ **Chianti Café.** This extremely popular spot occupies part of the main
★ floor of Strathcona Square, a converted post office in lively Old Strathcona. A mostly young crowd gathers for square meals with tasty shellfish appetizers, more than 20 varieties of pasta, a couple dozen veal dishes, and a discriminating selection of desserts. Be prepared to wait for seating on weekend evenings. ✉ *10501 82nd Ave.,* ☎ *403/439–9829. AE, DC, MC, V.*

$$ ✕ **Vi's.** In summer, this old house has outdoor seating on a deck overlooking the river; in winter, patrons are warmed by a blazing fire. The menu emphasizes the basics: hearty soups, salads, pastas, and extravagant sandwiches, and desserts such as chocolate pecan pie. Try Vi's for Sunday brunch. ✉ *9712 111th St.,* ☎ *403/482–6402. AE, MC, V.*

Lodging

$$$$ 🏨 **Hotel Macdonald.** The city's landmark 1915 hotel underwent a massive but sensitive restoration in the late 1980s and maintains first-class modern facilities in both the traditionally furnished guest rooms and the ornate public areas. The royal suite, in the former attic, is spectacular. There's fine dining in the elegantly restored Harvest Room and Sunday brunch in the Empire Ballroom or the Wedgwood Room. The hotel offers a sweeping view of the riverbank. ✉ *10061 100th St., T5J ON6,* ☎ *403/424–5181,* FAX *403/424–8017. 181 rooms, 16 suites. Restaurant, bar, pool, massage, steam room, health club. AE, MC, V.*

$$$$ 🏨 **Sheraton Grande.** This financial-district luxury high-rise connects by second-level passageways to five office buildings and two shopping centers. Rooms—with bay windows and blue-and-gray color schemes—are decorated with sophistication and include marble tabletops, walnut furniture, and brass accents. The Rose and Crown is an English-style pub. ✉ *10235 101st St., T5J 3E9,* ☎ *403/428–7111 or 800/268–9275,* FAX *403/441–3098. 302 rooms, 11 suites. 3 restaurants, 2 bars, no-smoking floors, indoor pool, sauna. AE, DC, MC, V.*

$$$ 🏨 **Fantasyland Hotel.** A component of the massive West Edmonton Mall (☞ Greater Edmonton, *above*), the Fantasyland has standard and theme rooms; the latter include Victorian coach rooms, where guests sleep in open carriages; Roman rooms, with classic round beds; truck rooms, where the bed is the back of a pickup; and Polynesian rooms, with catamaran beds and waterfalls. All theme rooms have whirlpool baths, and nontheme quarters are comfortable and tidy. ✉ *17700 87th Ave., T5T 4V4,* ☎ *403/444–3000 or 800/661–6454,* FAX *403/ 444–3294. 350 rooms. 2 restaurants, bar. AE, DC, MC, V.*

$$$ 🏨 **Westin Hotel.** This brown block structure in the heart of downtown has an atrium lobby with a decorative mobile, trees, and plants that convey comfort and luxury. The large, comfortable beige-and-pastel rooms are tastefully decorated with attractive artwork. The experienced staff speaks a total of 29 languages. Some of the finest food in the downtown area can be found in the Pradera restaurant. ✉ *10135 100th St., T5J 0Z1,* ☎ *403/426–3636 or 800/228–3000,* FAX *403/428–6060. 413 rooms, 20 suites. Restaurant, bar, no-smoking floors, indoor pool, sauna. AE, DC, MC, V.*

$$ 🏨 **Edmonton House.** The building's cylindrical design creates oddly
★ shaped but large and comfortable one- and two-bedroom and executive suites. All units have balconies with views of the skyline or the river valley, and kitchens are fully equipped (down to a toaster). A small mezzanine-level convenience store supplies basics. Weekend and long-term rates are available. ✉ *10205 100th Ave., T5J 4B5,* ☎ *403/424–5555*

or 800/661–6562, FAX 403/425–5485. *298 suites. Restaurant, bar, no-smoking floors, indoor pool, sauna, exercise room. AE, DC, MC, V.*

$ ⌷ **Inn on 7th.** Edmonton shorthand provides the name for this cheerful property on 107th Street. In the foliage-filled lobby stand Paul Bunyan–size easy chairs. Run by the Courtyard Inn chain, this hotel caters to visitors and government employees. Rooms are comfortably modern, and the location is convenient. ⊠ *10001 107th St., T5J 1J1,* ☎ *403/429–2861 or 800/661–7327,* FAX *403/426–7225. 173 rooms. Restaurant, bar, deli, no-smoking floors. AE, DC, MC, V.*

$ ⌷ **Travelodge.** The budget chain operates two clean and functional motels in Edmonton: Travelodge West is on the edge of town, not far from West Edmonton Mall, while Travelodge South is on the road to the airport. ⊠ *Travelodge West, 18320 Stony Plain Rd., T5S 1A7,* ☎ *403/483–6031 or 800/661–9563,* FAX *403/484–2358. 227 rooms.* ⊠ *Travelodge South, 10320 45th Ave. S, T6H 5K3,* ☎ *403/436–9770. 212 rooms, 10 suites in West; 216 rooms in South. Restaurant, bar, no-smoking rooms, indoor pool. AE, DC, MC, V.*

$ ⌷ **West Harvest Inn.** The clean, modern, three-story West Harvest caters to families; it's on the western edge of town, only five minutes from the West Edmonton Mall. Rooms in the new wing are slightly larger and more expensive than those in the older wing, but all are comfortable. Grainfield's family restaurant is on the premises. ⊠ *17803 Stony Plain Rd. (Rte. 16), T5S 1B4,* ☎ *403/484–8000 or 800/661–6993,* FAX *403/486–6060. 161 rooms, 12 suites. Restaurant, bar. AE, MC, V.*

$ ⌷ **YMCA of Edmonton.** The Y has an outstanding location: in the heart of downtown adjacent to Edmonton Centre shopping mall. Rooms are small and spare but carpeted and cheerfully furnished. Singles and couples stay for $27 a night; families are accommodated as well. All the Y's facilities are available to overnight guests. ⊠ *10030 102A Ave., T5J 0G5,* ☎ *403/421–9622,* FAX *403/428–9469. 113 rooms, 30 with bath. Cafeteria, indoor pool, health club, jogging, racquetball. MC, V.*

Nightlife and the Arts

Tickets for events in Edmonton are available from **Ticketmaster** (☎ 403/451–8000) at various locations, as well as at Champions in West Edmonton Mall and at Sears stores.

One huge event that encompasses music, shows, and special events is the 10-day **Klondike Days** (☎ 403/479–3500), held late in July. The festivities celebrate the prosperity that the Yukon gold rush brought the city, which served as a supply route and stopping point for miners.

The Arts

FILM
The **Edmonton Film Society** screens an ambitious program at a theater in the Provincial Museum of Alberta (⊠ 12845 102nd Ave., ☎ 403/453–9100). **Metro Cinema** (⊠ NFB Theatre, Canada Place, 9700 Jasper Ave., ☎ 403/425–9212) presents classics, imports, and new films on weekend nights. The **Princess Theatre** (⊠ 10337 Whyte Ave., ☎ 403/433–5785), an old-time movie house in the Old Strathcona district, presents revivals, experiments, and foreign films.

MUSIC AND DANCE
The Edmonton Opera (☎ 403/424–4040) and Alberta Ballet Company (☎ 403/428–6839) perform in the **Northern Alberta Jubilee Auditorium** (⊠ 87th Ave. and 114th St., ☎ 403/427–9622) at the University of Alberta. The **Edmonton Symphony Orchestra** (☎ 403/428–1414) performs in the Francis Winspear Centre for Music.

THEATER

Edmonton has 13 professional theater companies. The paramount facility is the glass-clad downtown **Citadel Theatre** complex (⊠ 99th St. and 101A Ave., ☎ 403/425–1820), where four theaters present a mix of esoteric works and classics. **Northern Light Theatre** (⊠ Kaasa Theatre, Jubilee Auditorium, 87th Ave. and 114th St., ☎ 403/471–1586) stages avant-garde productions that usually succeed.

Nightlife

BARS AND CLUBS

Elephant & Castle Pubs are pleasant watering holes in downtown Edmonton's Eaton Centre (☎ 403/424–4555) and the West Edmonton Mall (☎ 403/444–3555). The **Rose & Crown** English-style pub in the Sheraton Grande (⊠ 10235 101st St., ☎ 403/428–7111) is a popular downtown spot with dart boards and a huge selection of beers.

CASINOS

The newest casino in town is the **Baccarat Casino** (⊠ 101st St. and 104th Ave., ☎ 403/413–3178). Roulette, blackjack, and wheel-of- fortune action usually takes place in Edmonton between noon and midnight daily at the **Casino ABS Downtown** (⊠ 10549 102 St., ☎ 403/424–9461). The **Palace Casino** at the West Edmonton Mall (☎ 403/444–2112) offers shoppers another way to part with their money.

COMEDY

Edmonton has a branch of **Yuk Yuk's,** Canada's comedy chain, at West Edmonton Mall (☎ 403/481–9857).

MUSIC

Club Malibu (⊠ 10310 85th Ave., ☎ 403/432–7300) blasts out Top 40 hits in a converted armory. **Cook County Saloon** (⊠ 8010 103rd St., ☎ 403/432–2665) has a mellow honky-tonk ambience and country-and-western music. The **Sidetrack Cafe** (⊠ 10333 112th St., ☎ 403/421–1326) has top-name entertainers, big-screen telecasts of sports events, Variety Night on Sunday, and the Monday-Night Comedy Bowl. **Thunderdome** (⊠ 9920 63rd Ave., ☎ 403/433–3661) has classic rock. **Yardbird Suite** (⊠ 10203 86th Ave., ☎ 403/432–0428) is Edmonton's premier jazz showcase.

Outdoor Activities and Sports

Participant Sports

BICYCLING AND JOGGING

The North Saskatchewan River valley is the longest stretch of urban parkland in Canada. For information about jogging and cycling trails call the **River Valley Centre** (⊠ 10125 97th Ave., ☎ 403/496–7275).

HEALTH AND FITNESS CLUBS

The **Kinsmen Sports Centre** (⊠ 9100 Walterdale Rd., ☎ 403/496–7300) and **Mill Woods Recreation Centre** (⊠ 7207 28th Ave., ☎ 403/496–2929) have swimming pools and facilities for the entire family.

Spectator Sports

AUTO RACING

Capital Raceway (⊠ Rte. 19, 2 km/1 mi west of Hwy. 2S, on the way to Devon, ☎ 403/462–8901), a multiuse motor-sport complex, has events most weekends from May through October.

BASEBALL

The **Edmonton Trappers** play in the Pacific Coast League (AAA) at Telus Field (⊠ 10233 96th Ave., ☎ 403/429–2934) from April to early September.

FOOTBALL

The **Edmonton Eskimos** play in the Canadian Football League June through November at Commonwealth Stadium (⊠ 9022 111th Ave., ☎ 403/448–3757 or 403/448–1525).

HOCKEY

The **Edmonton Oilers** play National Hockey League hockey October through April at the Edmonton Coliseum (⊠ 118th Ave. and 74th St., ☎ 403/471–2191 or 403/451–8000).

HORSE RACING

Northlands Park (⊠ 112th Ave. and 74th St., ☎ 403/471–7379) hosts harness racing from early March to mid-May and from mid-September through December. Thoroughbred racing occupies the summer months, from mid-May through early September.

Shopping

The heart of downtown, between 100th and 103rd streets, holds a complex of shopping centers—**Eaton Centre** (⊠ 102nd Ave.), **ManuLife Place** (⊠ 102nd Ave.), and **Edmonton Centre** (⊠ 100th St.)—and department stores (the Bay, Eaton's) connected by tunnels or second-level pedways. **High Street/124th Street** (⊠ Along 124th and 125th Sts. between 102nd and 109th Aves.) is an outdoor shopping area full of boutiques, bistros, bookstores, and galleries. **Old Strathcona Historic Area** (⊠ Whyte, or 82nd, Ave. and 104th St.) has restaurants and enticing boutiques. **West Edmonton Mall** (⊠ 87th Ave. and 170th St.) has 800 stores and services, including such department stores as Sears, the Bay, Eaton's, and Zeller's (☞ Greater Edmonton, *above*).

Side Trips from Edmonton

Sights relating to Alberta's Ukrainian heritage and some beautiful natural areas make good day trips from the city.

Red Deer
㉖ *149 km (92 mi) south of Edmonton, 145 km (90 mi) north of Calgary.*

Red Deer, midway between Calgary and Edmonton on Highway 2, is on the Red Deer River. Along the riverbank winds **Waskasoo Park,** with nearly 30 mi of pedestrian and bike paths, equestrian trails, and canoeing and fishing. At the **Red Deer and District Museum,** you can see a pioneer home and other historic items. ⊠ 4525 47A Ave., ☎ 403/343–6844. ☜ *Donation accepted.* ⊙ *Weekdays noon–5 and 7–9, weekends 1–5.*

Elk Island National Park
48 km (30 mi) east of Edmonton on Hwy. 16.

Probably Canada's least-known national park, but very popular with locals, Elk Island was established in 1906 as the country's first federal wildlife sanctuary for large mammals. It covers 194 square km (75 square mi) and is dedicated to protecting the environment. A herd of 850 plains and 350 wood bison roam the park, as well as elk, moose, white-tail deer, and more than 240 species of birds, including herons. There are hiking trails, 80 campsites, an interpretive center, a 9-hole golf course, and several lakes. ⊠ *Hwy. 16,* ☎ *403/992–2950.* ☜ *$4.* ⊙ *Daily, 24 hrs.*

Ukrainian Cultural Heritage Village
3 km (2 mi) east of Elk Island National Park, 51 km (32 mi) from Edmonton.

The village consists of 34 historic buildings from around the province that have been assembled to typify the lifestyle of a pre-1930s village of Ukrainian settlers. Guides in period dress interpret the displays. It's good background for a visit to Vegreville (☞ *below*). ✉ *Hwy. 16,* ☎ *403/662–3640.* ✆ *$6.50.* ☼ *Mid-May–Labor Day, daily 10–6; Sept.– mid-Oct., daily 10–4.*

Vegreville

㉗ *50 km (31 mi) east of Ukrainian Cultural Heritage Village, 101 km (63 mi) east of Edmonton.*

Vegreville is the center of eastern Alberta's Ukrainian culture and home of the "world's largest Easter egg" (*pysanka*), measuring 30 ft high, at the east end of the town's main street. Colorfully decorated, the egg consists of more than 3,500 pieces of aluminum. The **Ukrainian Pysanka Festival** (☎ 403/632–2771 for information) takes place here annually the first weekend in July. ✉ *Hwy. 16.*

Edmonton A to Z

Arriving and Departing
BY CAR
Edmonton is situated on the Yellowhead Highway (Highway 16), which runs from Winnipeg through the central parts of Saskatchewan and Alberta. This highway is four lanes and divided through most of Alberta; it intersects with the four-lane divided Highway 2, which runs south to Calgary.

BY PLANE
All flights use **Edmonton International Airport** (✉ Hwy. 2, 20 km, or 14 mi, south of downtown, ☎ 403/890–8900). Along with the major Canadian airlines (Air Canada, Canadian Airlines International, Air BC, NWT Air), Edmonton is served by Delta, Horizon, and Northwest (☞ Air Travel *in* the Gold Guide). An airport improvement fee of $5 is assessed on all flight departures within Alberta, $10 for departures outside Alberta.

Taxi rides from Edmonton International cost approximately $29 to the city center. The **Sky Shuttle** (☎ 403/463–7520) provides frequent service between the airport and major downtown hotels; fare is $11 one-way, $18 round-trip.

Getting Around
BY BUS AND LRT
Edmonton Transit (☎ 403/496–1611) operates a comprehensive system of buses throughout the area and a light rail transit (LRT) line from downtown to the northeast side of the city. The fare is $1.65; transfers are free. Buses operate 5:30 AM–2 AM. The LRT is free in the downtown area (between Churchill and Grandin stations) weekdays 9–3 and Saturday 9–6. The **Downtown Information Centre** above Central LRT Station (✉ 100A St. and Jasper Ave.) provides free information weekdays 9–5.

BY TAXI
Taxis tend to be costly: $2 for the first 105 meters, and 10¢ for each additional 105 meters. Cabs may be hailed on the street, but phoning is recommended. Call **Alberta Co-op Taxi** (☎ 403/425–8310), **Checker** (☎ 403/455–2211), or **Yellow** (☎ 403/462–3456).

Contacts and Resources
DENTISTS
For 24-hour dental care, contact **Denta Care** (✉ 472 Southgate Shopping Centre, 111th St. and 51st Ave., ☎ 403/434–9566).

EMERGENCIES
Ambulance, fire, poison center, police (☎ 911).

GUIDED TOURS
From early May to early October three **Royal Tours** (☎ 403/488–9090) itineraries hit the high points of Edmonton. Customized tours can be scheduled year-round. **Klondike Jet Boats** (☎ 403/486–0896) ply the North Saskatchewan River, May–October.

HOSPITALS
Emergency rooms are at the **Royal Alexandra Hospital** (✉ 10240 Kingsway Ave., ☎ 403/477–4111) and **University of Alberta Hospitals** (✉ 8440 112th St., ☎ 403/492–8822).

LATE-NIGHT PHARMACY
Shopper's Drug Mart (✉ 11408 Jasper Ave., ☎ 403/482–1171; ✉ 8210 109 St., ☎ 403/433–3121) is open 24 hours.

VISITOR INFORMATION
Edmonton Tourism Information Centres are at Gateway Park (✉ Hwy. 2, south of downtown, ☎ 403/496–8400 or 800/463–4667) and City Hall. Other offices are open around Edmonton; for locations call the above number.

REGINA

Regina, Saskatchewan, was originally dubbed Pile O'Bones, in reference to the remnants left by years of buffalo hunting by native peoples and later European hunters. The city was renamed after the Latin title of Queen Victoria, the reigning monarch in 1883. It was at this time that the railroad arrived and the city became the capital of the Northwest Territories. The Mounties made it their headquarters. When the province of Saskatchewan was formed in 1905, Regina was chosen as its capital. At the beginning of the 20th century, immigrants from the British Isles, Eastern Europe, and East Asia rushed in to claim parcels of river-fed prairie land for $1 per lot. Oil and potash were discovered in the 1950s and 1960s, and Regina became a major agricultural and industrial distribution center as well as the head office of the world's largest grain-handling cooperative.

The centerpiece of this city of 185,000 is Wascana Centre, created by expanding meager Wascana Creek into the broad Wascana Lake and surrounding it with 2,000 acres of parkland. This unique multipurpose site contains the city's major museums, the Saskatchewan provincial legislature, the University of Regina campus, and all the amenities of a big-city park and natural-habitat waterfowl sanctuary.

Exploring Regina

Museums, government buildings, cultural sites, and a park are highlights of a city tour. Streets in Regina run north–south; avenues, east–west. The most important north–south artery is Albert Street (Route 6); Victoria Avenue is the main east–west thoroughfare. The Trans-Canada Highway (Highway 1) bypasses the city to the south and east.

A Good Drive

Begin at the northwest corner of Wascana Centre, at the **Royal Saskatchewan Museum** ㉘, and check out the Earth Sciences Gallery and the First Nations Gallery. Continue south on Albert Street past Speakers Corner, where, as in London's Hyde Park, free speech is volubly expressed. Turn left onto Legislature Drive to the **Legislative Building** ㉙ for a tour of its marble interior. Take Saskatchewan Road (west of Leg-

islative Building) south to the **MacKenzie Art Gallery** ㉚, which displays
European and Canadian art. Continuing along Saskatchewan Road,
turn north onto Avenue G and then east onto Lakeshore Drive to the
Wascana Waterfowl Park Display Ponds ㉛ to see the many breeds of
migratory birds that stop here. Return to Broad Street (Wascana Parkway), cross the bridge to Wascana Drive, and turn east on Wascana
Drive toward Powerhouse Drive and the **Saskatchewan Science Centre** ㉜ for hands-on exhibits demonstrating various scientific phenomena. Next, take a car or bike to Broad Street and follow it north to
Dewdney Avenue, then head west to **Government House Historic Property** ㉝, once the residence of Saskatchewan's lieutenant governors. Continue west on Dewdney Avenue to the **Royal Canadian Mounted Police
Depot Division** ㉞, the Mounties' national training center.

TIMING
The tour will take most of the day, but plan your visit to catch the Royal
Canadian Mounted Police training academy's daily drill parade at
about 1. Call to check the time for this.

Sights to See

㉝ **Government House Historic Property.** Between 1891 and 1945 this was
the lavish home of Saskatchewan's lieutenant governors. It has been
restored with period furnishings and mementos of the governors and
their families. ✉ *4607 Dewdney Ave.,* ☎ *306/787–5726.* 🎫 *Free.* ☉
*Oct.–Mar. and July–Aug., Tues.–Fri. 1–4, Sun. 1–5; Apr.–June and
Sept., Tues.–Sat. 1–4, Sun. 1–5.*

㉙ **Legislative Building.** Dominating the skyline in the provincial capital
is the dome of this quasi-Versailles–style structure. "The Ledge" was
built from 1908 to 1912, with Tyndall stone from Manitoba on the
exterior and 34 types of marble from all over the world in the interior.
As you tour the Legislative Assembly Chamber, note the huge picture
of Queen Elizabeth—a reminder that Canada retains a technical allegiance to the British monarchy. Free tours leave on the half hour. ✉
Legislature Dr., ☎ *306/787–5357.* 🎫 *Free.* ☉ *Mid-May–Labor Day,
daily 8–9; Labor Day–mid-May, daily 8–5.*

㉚ **MacKenzie Art Gallery.** The museum displays 19th- and 20th-century
European art and Canadian historical and contemporary works, with
a special emphasis on western Canadian art. The popular Prairie Artists
Series allows emerging Saskatchewan artists to display recent work.
For three nights a week in August, a stage becomes the courtroom setting for the production of *The Trial of Louis Riel.* Riel led rebellions
of the Métis against the new Canadian government in the 1870s and
1880s and was tried in Regina (and ultimately hanged) for treason. ✉
3475 Albert St., ☎ *306/522–4242.* 🎫 *Free; extra charge for play.* ☉
Fri.–Tues. 11–6, Wed.–Thurs. 11–10.

★ ㉞ **Royal Canadian Mounted Police Depot Division.** This is the Mounties'
only training center. You can tour the grounds and the nondenominational RCMP Chapel, a converted cookhouse originally built in 1883
and considered Regina's oldest building. In July and August, the spectacular Sunset Retreat Ceremony takes place Tuesday evening; try to
arrive by 6:30. On the grounds is the **Centennial Museum**, which has
exhibits and mementos of the Mounties (originally the North West
Mounted Police). The order's proud history is revealed in weaponry,
uniforms, photos, and oddities such as Sitting Bull's rifle case and tobacco pouch. ✉ *11th Ave. W,* ☎ *306/780–5838.* 🎫 *Free.* ☉ *June–
mid-Sept., daily 8–6:45; mid-Sept.–May, daily 10–4:45.*

㉘ **Royal Saskatchewan Museum.** Here a time line traces local history from
before the dinosaur era to today. The Earth Sciences Gallery depicts 2

Saskatchewan

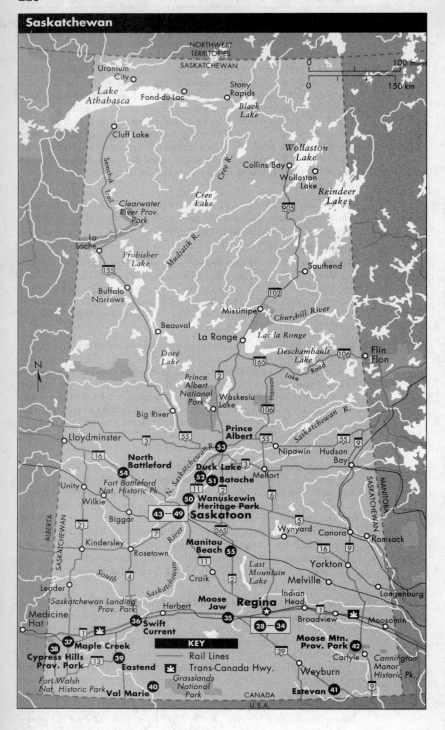

NORTHWEST
TERRITORIES
SASKATCHEWAN

0   100 miles

0   150 km

Uranium
City

Lake
Athabasca

Fond-du-Lac

Stony
Rapids

Black
Lake

Cluff Lake

Wollaston
Lake

Collins Bay

Wollaston
Lake

Reindeer
Lake

Semchuk Trail

Cree R.

905

Clearwater
River Prov.
Park

Cree
Lake

La
Loche

Mudjatik R.

Frobisher
Lake

155

Southend

102

Buffalo
Narrows

Beauval

Missinipe

Churchill River

Doré
Lake

La Ronge

Lac la Ronge

Deschambault
Lake

106

Flin
Flon

165

Hanson Lake Road

N

Prince
Albert
National
Park

2

Waskesiu
Lake

106

Big River

Saskatchewan R.

Lloydminster

3

55

Prince
Albert

55

Nipawin

Hudson
Bay

55

9

16

North
Battleford

54

N. Saskatchewan R.

53

Duck Lake

52

51

Batoche

Melfort

MANITOBA
SASKATCHEWAN

Fort Battleford
Nat. Historic Pk.

Unity

50

2

6

Wilkie

Wanuskewin
Heritage Park

43

49

Saskatoon

5

Biggar

River

Wynyard

Canora

Kamsack

ALBERTA
SASKATCHEWAN

21

7

Kindersley

Rosetown

365

Manitou
Beach

55

16

9

Yorkton

4

South

Saskatchewan River

Craik

11

2

Last
Mountain
Lake

Melville

Langenburg

Leader

Saskatchewan Landing
Prov. Park

Herbert

Moose
Jaw

Regina

Indian
Head

1

Medicine
Hat

36

Swift
Current

35

28 — 34

Broadview

Moosomin

37

1

Maple Creek

KEY

39

Moose Mtn.
Prov. Park

42

38

Cypress Hills
Prov. Park

13

39

Eastend

Rail Lines

Trans-Canada Hwy.

Carlyle

Cannington
Manor
Historic Pk.

Fort Walsh
Nat. Historic Park

Val Marie

40

Grasslands
National
Park

Weyburn

Estevan

41

9

CANADA
U.S.A.

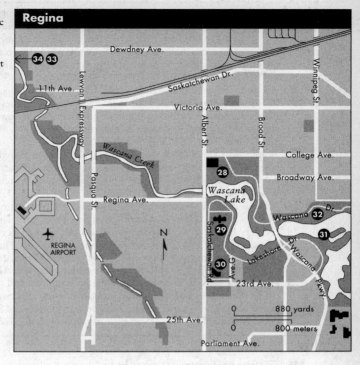

billion years of Saskatchewan geological history, while the First Nations Gallery highlights aspects of Saskatchewan aboriginal life and history. ⊠ *College Ave. and Albert St.,* ☎ *306/787–2815.* ☞ *Free.* ☉ *May–Sept. 2, daily 9–8:30; Sept. 3–Apr., daily 9–4:30.*

☞ ㉜ **Saskatchewan Science Centre.** Housed in the refurbished City of Regina powerhouse, the museum has more than 80 hands-on exhibits that encourage visitors to build bubbles and hot-air balloons, make voice prints, and take apart models of human bodies. Demonstrations of biological, geological, and astronomical phenomena begin on the hour. The Kramer IMAX Theatre shows breathtaking films several times daily on a five-story screen. ⊠ *Winnipeg St. and Wascana Dr.,* ☎ *306/352–5811, 306/522–4629 IMAX.* ☞ *$5.50.* ☉ *May–June, Mon.–Thurs. 9–6, Fri. 9–8, Sat. 10–8, Sun. 10–6; July–Aug., daily 10–8; Sept.–Apr., Tues.–Fri. 9–4, Sat. noon–8, Sun. noon–6.*

㉛ **Wascana Waterfowl Park Display Ponds.** At this serene, beautiful park, a boardwalk constructed over a marsh has display panels that help identify the more than 60 breeds of migrating waterfowl found here. ⊠ *Lakeshore Dr.,* ☎ *306/522–3661.* ☞ *Free.* ☉ *Daily 9–9; guided tour (if there is a group) June–Sept., daily at 3.*

Dining

$$$–$$$$ ✕ **The Diplomat.** One of Regina's most elegant restaurants is an upscale, traditional steak house in an old brick building downtown. The decor suggests the Victorian era, with paintings of Canada's prime ministers on the walls and dusty-rose cloths and candles on the tables. It offers an extensive selection of seafood and steaks and an outstanding rack of lamb, as well as a high-quality wine list. ⊠ *2302 Broad St.,* ☎ *306/359–3366. Reservations essential. AE, D, MC, V.*

$$–$$$ ✕ **Bartleby's.** This good-time downtown "dining emporium and gathering place" is a veritable museum of western memorabilia, musical instruments, and old-time carnival games. Victorian lamp shades and heavy leather armchairs further convey the whimsical tone. Karaoke music at night adds a bit of fun. The menu runs to big sandwiches and western beef, especially prime rib. ⊠ *1920 Broad St.,* ☎ *306/565–0040. Reservations essential. AE, DC, MC, V.*

$$–$$$ ✕ **Harvest Eating House.** There's no shortage of antiques in this family restaurant with an old-time prairie theme. Among the hearty specialties are tasty prime rib and an assortment of seafood. ⊠ *379 Albert St.,* ☎ *306/545–3777. AE, D, MC, V.*

$–$$ ✕ **Alfredo's Fresh Pasta and Grill.** The skillfully prepared Italian cuisine includes fresh pastas and vegetarian, chicken, and seafood dishes. A wine bar serves microbrewery beers, single-malt scotches, and fine wines. ⊠ *1801 Scarth St.,* ☎ *306/522–3366. AE, MC, V. Closed Sun.*

$–$$ ✕ **Brewsters.** The copper kettle and shiny fermentation tanks are proudly prominent in Saskatchewan's first brew pub. This full-mash brewery has 11 in-house concoctions on tap, as well as a large selection of imports and domestic beers, wine, and spirits. The menu consists of pub snacks and full meals. ⊠ *Victoria East Plaza, 1832 Victoria Ave. E,* ☎ *306/761–1500. Reservations not accepted. AE, MC, V.*

$ ✕ **Simply Delicious.** Everything is homemade in this small country-style café. Offerings include cinnamon buns, fresh pies, chicken noodle and vegetable soups, several salads, and specialty coffees. ⊠ *826 Victoria Ave.,* ☎ *306/352–4929. Reservations not accepted. No credit cards.*

Lodging

$$$ 🏨 **Delta Regina Hotel.** The tallest building in Saskatchewan, Regina's newest and most luxurious hotel rises 25 stories over the city and is attached to the Saskatchewan Trade and Convention Centre. Rooms are done in subtle pastels and have modern amenities. The pool has a three-story water slide. ⊠ *1919 Saskatchewan Dr., S4P 4H2,* ☎ *306/525–5255 or 800/268–1133,* 𝖥𝖠𝖷 *306/781–7188. 248 rooms, 7 suites. 2 restaurants, bar, no-smoking rooms, indoor pool. AE, DC, MC, V.*

$$$ 🏨 **Hotel Saskatchewan Radisson Plaza.** This former railway hotel built in 1927 has old-time charm and up-to-date facilities. High-ceiling rooms are decorated in an early 1930s style, with lots of wood and lace curtains. The Victoria Room serves high tea each afternoon, and there's fine dining in the Cortlandt Hall Dining Room. For a light lunch or evening cocktails visit the cozy and casually elegant Monarch Lounge. ⊠ *2125 Victoria Ave., S4P 0S3,* ☎ *306/522–7691 or 800/333–3333,* 𝖥𝖠𝖷 *306/757–5521. 191 rooms, 26 suites. 2 restaurants, bar, no-smoking rooms, health club. AE, DC, MC, V.*

$$$ 🏨 **Regina Inn Hotel.** A plant-filled lobby welcomes you into this modern downtown hotel, where all the guest rooms—decorated in blues, grays, and browns—have balconies overlooking Broad or Victoria Street. On the ground floor is Lauderdale's, a local hot spot. Applause Feast & Folly, a dinner theater, is downstairs in the Catalina Theatre. ⊠ *1975 Broad St., at Victoria Ave., S4P 1Y2,* ☎ *306/525–6767 or 800/667–8162,* 𝖥𝖠𝖷 *306/352–1858. 230 rooms, 5 suites. 2 restaurants, bar, 2 outdoor hot tubs, exercise room, nightclub. AE, DC, MC, V.*

$$ 🏨 **Chelton Suites Hotel.** An older hotel in the heart of downtown is one of Regina's bargains. Its modernized rooms are downright huge and have microwaves and 30-inch TVs. Contemporary, light-wood furnishings match the earth tones used in the draperies and upholstery. Service is particularly friendly. ⊠ *1907 11th Ave., S4P 0J2,* ☎ *306/569–4600 or 800/667–9922,* 𝖥𝖠𝖷 *306/569–3531. 53 rooms. Restaurant, bar, coffee shop. AE, DC, MC, V.*

$$ ☷ **Regina Travelodge Hotel.** The hotel's convenient location, on Regina's main thoroughfare and close to downtown, is the biggest draw for its guests. Another draw is the well-known water-slide complex on the property. In the evenings, the Blarney Stone pub is a cheerful place to grab a beer or soda. ⊠ *4177 Albert St., S4S 3R6,* ☎ *306/586–3443 or 800/ 578–7878,* FAX *306/586–9311. 193 rooms, 7 suites. Restaurant, pub, indoor pool, hot tub. AE, DC, MC, V.*

$$ ☷ **Sands Hotel and Resort.** This modern downtown property has a dra-
★ matic multilevel, sun-filled lobby enhanced by abundant foliage and a charming waterfall. A second-floor oasis is the perfect setting for a sooth-ing soak in the whirlpool or a dip in the kids' or standard pool. The modern rooms are airy and furnished in light colors and dusty-rose tones. ⊠ *1818 Victoria Ave., S4P 0R1,* ☎ *306/569–1666 or 800/ 667–6500,* FAX *306/525–3550. 237 rooms, 14 suites. 2 restaurants, bar, pub, 2 in-door pools, sauna. AE, DC, MC, V.*

$ ☷ **West Harvest Inn.** Rebuilt and refurbished in 1995, this five-story, brick 1960s-vintage hotel is dependable. The average-size rooms have low-key beige-patterned drapes and spreads and modern, dark-cherry furniture. ⊠ *4025 Albert St. (Rte. 6), S4S 3R6,* ☎ *306/586–6755 or 800/ 853–1181,* FAX *306/584–1345. 103 rooms, 2 suites. Restaurant, bar, 2 hot tubs, sauna, exercise room. AE, DC, MC, V.*

Nightlife and the Arts

The Arts

MUSIC AND DANCE

The **Saskatchewan Centre of the Arts** (⊠ Wascana Centre, 200 Lakeshore Dr., ☎ 306/565–0404) is the venue for the Regina Sym-phony Orchestra (Canada's longest-running symphony orchestra), pop concerts, dance performances, and Broadway musicals and plays.

THEATER

On a theater-in-the-round stage inside the old City Hall, the **Globe The-atre** (⊠ 1801 Scarth St., ☎ 306/525–9553) offers classic and con-temporary works from October through April. **Regina Little Theatre** (⊠ Regina Performing Arts Centre, 1077 Angus St., ☎ 306/352–5535 or 306/543–7292) presents lighthearted original productions.

Nightlife

BAR

Caper's, in the Delta Regina Hotel (⊠ 1919 Saskatchewan Dr., ☎ 306/525–5255), is where local movers and shakers mingle with visitors from the convention center next door.

CASINO

The posh **Casino Regina** (⊠ 1880 Saskatchewan Dr., ☎ 800/555–3189), in the former Union Station railroad passenger terminal, has slot ma-chines and table games such as blackjack, roulette, and baccarat.

MUSIC

Delbert's (⊠ 1433 Hamilton St., ☎ 306/757–7625) is known for high-energy rock and roll. **Longbranch Saloon** (⊠ 1400 McIntyre St., ☎ 306/525–8336) specializes in country-and-western music. The **Pump** (⊠ 641 Victoria Ave. E, ☎ 306/522–0977) presents Canadian and American country-and-western bands.

Outdoor Activities and Sports

Participant Sports

BIKING AND JOGGING

Wascana Place (⊠ 2900 Wascana Dr., ☎ 306/522–3661) provides maps of the many jogging, biking, and hiking trails in Wascana Centre. The

Devonian Pathway—8 km (about 5 mi) of paved trails that follow Wascana Creek and pass through six city parks—is a favorite.

HEALTH AND FITNESS CLUBS

The **Regina Sportplex & Lawson Aquatic Centre** (⊠ 1717 Elphinstone
St., ☎ 306/777–7156 or 306/777–7323) comprises a pool and diving well, a 200-meter track, tennis and badminton courts, weight
rooms, a sauna, and drop-in aerobic and aqua exercise sessions.

Spectator Sports

CURLING

Check out this popular local sport played on ice at the **Caledonian Curling Club** (⊠ 2225 Empress Rd., near airport, ☎ 306/525–8171).

FOOTBALL

The **Saskatchewan Roughriders** (☎ 306/525–2181) of the Canadian
Football League play at Taylor Field June through November.

HOCKEY

The **Regina Pats** play other Western Hockey League teams in the
Agridome (⊠ Exhibition Park, Lewvan Expressway and 11th Ave., ☎
306/522–5604) from September through April.

HORSE RACING

Queensbury Downs (⊠ Exhibition Park, Lewvan Dr. and 11th Ave.,
Regina, ☎ 306/781–9310) hosts Standardbred racing in summer and
televised racing year-round.

Shopping

Art and Antiques

The **Antique Mall** (⊠ 1175 Rose St., ☎ 306/525–9688) encompasses
28 antiques, art, and collectibles sellers. The **Strathdee Shoppes** (⊠
Dewdney Ave. and Cornwall St.) have arts, crafts, antiques, and specialty stores—plus a food court.

Affinity's Antiques (⊠ 1178 Albert St., ☎ 306/757–4265) sells vintage collectibles. **Patchworks** (⊠ 3026 13th Ave., ☎ 306/522–0664)
carries arts and crafts. **Sarah's Corner** (⊠ 1853 Hamilton St., ☎ 306/
565–2200) has crafts and artwork.

Malls

Cornwall Centre (⊠ 11th Ave. and Saskatchewan Dr.), downtown, is
an indoor mall with more than 100 shops, including Eaton's and Sears.
Passages connect Cornwall Centre mall to the **Galleria** (⊠ 11th Ave.
and Saskatchewan Dr.), an indoor mall with more than 50 stores.

Side Trips from Regina

In and around the modern city of Moose Jaw are attractions that will
give you a feeling for the area's past and present.

Moose Jaw

35 *71 km (44 mi) west of Regina.*

Saskatchewan's fourth-largest city, Moose Jaw is a prosperous railroad
and industrial center, renowned as a wide-open Roaring '20s haven for
American gangsters. It is said that Al Capone visited here from Chicago.
Nineteen murals on buildings in the downtown business district bring
the town's rich history to life. Today, Moose Jaw's most prominent citizen stands right on the Trans-Canada Highway: Mac the Moose, an
immense sculpture that greets travelers from beside the **visitor information center** (⊠ Hwy. 1, east of Hwy. 2, ☎ 306/692–6414).

The **Western Development Museum,** which focuses on air, land, water, and rail transportation, houses the Snowbirds Gallery, filled with memorabilia (including vintage airplanes) of Canada's air demonstration team, the Snowbirds, who are stationed at the nearby Armed Forces base. ⊠ *50 Diefenbaker Dr.,* ☎ *306/693–6556.* ⌨ *$4.50; $5.50 with Cinema 180 Theatre.* ⊙ *Apr.–Sept., daily 9–6; Oct.–Mar., Tues.–Sun. 9–6*

The Moose Jaw Art Museum (⊠ Crescent Park, Athabasca St. and Langdon Crescent, ☎ 306/692–4471) displays native art and small farm implements. While you're here, pick up *A Walking Tour of Downtown Moose Jaw* ($1.50), a guide to notable and notorious landmarks. A quirky attraction that chronicles aspects of the city's history is the **Tunnels of Little Chicago** (☎ 306/693–5251). You can view these tunnels, rumored to have been built by the Chinese in the late 1800s and later supposedly used by Al Capone to smuggle liquor during the Prohibition era. Tours start at the old Canadian Pacific Railroad station.

The **Temple Gardens Mineral Spa** (⊠ 108 Main St. N, ☎ 306/694–5055) in the heart of downtown has naturally heated indoor and outdoor pools (40°C) supplied by an artesian well, 4,500 ft below the earth's surface. The four-story geothermal spa complex adjoins a 69-room hotel. Costs for treatments and massages range from about $16 to $70.

Pioneer Village and Museum

13 km (8 mi) south of Moose Jaw, 84 km (52 mi) southwest of Regina.

At the offbeat Pioneer Village and Museum, in addition to a series of old buildings and cars, you can see the *Sukanen,* a large, unfinished ship made by a Finnish settler between 1928 and 1941 and patterned after a 17th-century Finnish fishing vessel. ⊠ *Hwy. 2,* ☎ *306/693–7315.* ⌨ *$2.50.* ⊙ *June–Sept., daily 9–5.*

Regina A to Z

Arriving and Departing
BY CAR
Regina stands at the crossroads of the Trans-Canada Highway (Highway 1) and Highway 11, which goes north to Saskatoon.

BY PLANE
Regina Airport (⊠ 1–520 Regina Ave., ☎ 306/780–5750), 8 km (5 mi) southwest of downtown, is served by Air Canada, Canadian Airlines International, Northwest Airlines, and several Canadian commuter airlines (☞ Air Travel *in* the Gold Guide for telephone numbers). Cabs charge about $7 for the 10- to 15-minute ride downtown.

Getting Around
BY BUS
Regina Transit's (☎ 306/777–7433) 19 bus routes serve the metropolitan area every day except Sunday. The fare is $1.10.

BY TAXI
Taxis are easy to find outside major hotels, or they can be summoned by phone. Call **Regina Cabs** (☎ 306/543–3333), **Capital Cab** (☎ 306/781–7777), or **Co-op Taxis** (☎ 306/586–6555).

Contacts and Resources
EMERGENCIES
Ambulance, fire, police (☎ 911).

GUIDED TOURS
Classic Carriage Service (☎ 306/543–9155) offers horse-drawn carriage rides around the city in summer and horse-drawn sleigh and

hayrides around Wascana Centre in winter. Both tours accommodate 15 to 20 people and cost $60 to $75 per hour.

HOSPITALS

Emergency rooms are located at **Pasqua Hospital** (✉ 4101 Dewdney Ave., ☎ 306/766–2222), **Plains Health Centre** (✉ 4500 Wascana Pkwy., ☎ 306/766–6211), and **Regina General Hospital** (✉ 1140 14th Ave., ☎ 306/766–4444).

LATE-NIGHT PHARMACY

Shopper's Drug Marts (✉ Northgate Mall, ☎ 306/777–8010; ✉ Broad St. and 14th Ave., ☎ 306/757–8100; ✉ Gordon Rd. and Albert St., ☎ 306/777–8040) are open daily until midnight.

VISITOR INFORMATION

Tourism Regina (✉ Box 3355, S4P 3H1, ☎ 306/789–5099) has an information center on the Trans-Canada Highway (Highway 1) on the eastern approach to the city and is open Victoria Day (late May)–Labor Day, daily 8–6; Labor Day–Victoria Day, weekdays 8:30–4:30. The **Tourism Saskatchewan information center** (✉ 500–1900 Albert St., ☎ 306/787–2300) is open weekdays 8–5.

ELSEWHERE IN SOUTHERN SASKATCHEWAN

Spread across the southern part of the province are varied attractions, including a fossil research station in Eastend, sites that interpret pioneer and native life, and unique natural areas such as Grasslands National Park in Val Marie.

Swift Current

36 *174 km (108 mi) west of Regina on the Trans-Canada Hwy.*

West of Regina, the square townships and straight roads of the grain-belt prairie farms gradually give way to the arid rolling hills of the upland plains ranches. The Trans-Canada Highway skirts the edge of the Missouri Coteau—glacial hills that divide the prairie from the dry western plain—on its way west to Swift Current (population 16,000). The town cultivates its western image during Frontier Days Regional Fair and Rodeo in June. The **Swift Current Museum** displays pioneer and native artifacts and exhibits of local natural history. ✉ *105 Chaplin St.,* ☎ *306/778–2775.* ⊡ *Free.* ☉ *May–Aug., weekdays 1:30–4:30 and 7–9, weekends 1:30–4:30; Sept.–Apr., weekdays 1:30–4:30.*

Dining and Lodging

$–$$ ✕ **Wong's Kitchen.** This longtime Swift Current favorite serves fine Canadian food and an even better Asian menu: Dry garlic ribs are the star attraction. Count on live entertainment nightly. ✉ *Hwy. 1, S. Service Rd.,* ☎ *306/773–6244. Reservations essential. AE, MC, V.*

$ ▦ **Horseshoe Lodge.** It's conveniently situated along the Trans-Canada Highway service road, yet the rooms still have fine views of the surrounding countryside. The cocktail lounge is a popular meeting spot, and the restaurant offers solid Canadian cooking. ✉ *Mobile Rte. 35, S9H 3X6,* ☎ *306/773–4643,* 𝖥𝖠𝖷 *306/773–0309. 21 rooms, 2 suites. 2 restaurants, bar, pool. AE, DC, MC, V.*

OFF THE
BEATEN PATH

A 50-km (31-mi) drive north from Swift Current on Highway 4 will bring you to **Saskatchewan Landing Provincial Park,** a 54-square-km (21-square-mi) natural preserve that lies at the point where Indians and pioneers forded the South Saskatchewan River en route to northern

Saskatchewan. It has campsites, picnic facilities, and an interpretive center. ⊠ *Hwy. 4,* ☎ *306/375–2434.* ☒ *$6 per day per car; camping mid-Sept.–mid-May $8; camping mid-May–mid-Sept. $14.* ☉ *Daily.*

Maple Creek

❸❼ *128 km (79 mi) west of Swift Current, 302 km (187 mi) west of Regina.*

The Trans-Canada Highway skirts the southern edge of the Great Sand Hills. These desertlike remnants of a huge glacial lake abound with such native wildlife as pronghorn, mule deer, coyotes, jackrabbits, and kangaroo rats. Maple Creek, a self-styled "old cow town" just south of the Trans-Canada Highway on Route 21, has a number of preserved Old West storefronts. Saskatchewan's oldest museum, the **Old Timer's Museum,** displays pictures and artifacts of Mounties, early ranchers, and natives. ⊠ *218 Jasper St.,* ☎ *306/662–2474.* ☒ *$2.* ☉ *June–Sept., daily 9–5; Apr.–May and Oct., weekdays 1–4.*

Cypress Hills Provincial Park

❸❽ *27 km (17 mi) south of Maple Creek, 330 km (205 mi) west of Regina.*

Cypress Hills Provincial Park consists of two sections, a Centre Block and a West Block, which are about 25 km (16 mi) apart and separated by nonpark land. The larger West Block abuts the border with Alberta and is connected to Alberta's Cypress Hills Provincial Park. Within the Centre Block, the Cypress Hills plateau, rising more than 4,000 ft above sea level, is covered with spruce, aspen, and lodgepole pines erroneously identified as cypress by early European explorers. From Lookout Point you have an 80-km (50-mi) view of Maple Creek and the hills beyond. Maps are available at the Administrative Building near the park entrance. ⊠ *Cypress Hills Provincial Park, Rte. 21,* ☎ *306/662–4411.* ☒ *$6 per day per car.* ☉ *Daily, 24 hrs.*

In the West Block, you'll find **Fort Walsh National Historic Park.** The original fort was built by the Mounties in 1875 to establish order between the "wolfers" (whiskey traders) and the Assiniboine. Fort Walsh remained the center of local commerce until its abandonment in 1883. Today, bus service links the Visitor Reception Centre and the reconstructed fort itself, Farwell's Trading Post, and a picnic area. No private vehicles are permitted beyond the parking area. A rough gravel road connects the Cypress Hills Centre Block plateau with the West Block plateau. During wet weather, take Route 21 north to Maple Creek and Route 271 southwest to the West Block. ⊠ *Rte. 271, 55 km (34 mi) southwest of Maple Creek,* ☎ *306/662–2645.* ☒ *$6 (includes bus trip and tour).* ☉ *Mid-May–mid-Oct., daily 9–5.*

Lodging

$–$$ 🏨 **Cypress Four Seasons Resort.** This resort in the Centre Block of Cypress Hills Provincial Park is set in the middle of a lodgepole-pine forest. Comfortable contemporary rooms are done in pastels or earth tones. The woodsy restaurant has picture windows that overlook the forest. Standard Canadian fare is more successful than the Chinese dishes. Note that this resort is not part of the Four Seasons chain. ⊠ *Box 1480, Maple Creek, S0N 1N0,* ☎ *306/662–4477,* ℻ *306/662–3238. 31 rooms, 15 cabins, 10 condos. Restaurant, bar, indoor pool. MC, V.*

Eastend

39 *120 km (74 mi) east of Cypress Hills on Rte. 13, 360 km (223 mi) south-west of Regina.*

In 1994, in the tiny Frenchman River valley town of Eastend, paleon-tologists found 1 of only 12 Tyrannosaurus rex fossils unearthed thus far anywhere in the world. The T-rex, believed to be 65 million years old, is one of a number of fossils that have been discovered in the area. You can visit a fully operational laboratory in Eastend (with a view-ing area), the **Eastend Fossil Research Station** (⌧ 118 Maple Ave. S, ☎ 306/295–4009), where paleontologists are working on the T-rex fossil. For trips on which you can dig for fossils yourself, contact the **Eastend Tourism Authority** (☎ 306/295–4144).

Val Marie

40 *152 km (94 mi) south of Swift Current, 37 km (23 mi) north of U.S. border, 375 km (232 mi) southwest of Regina.*

Val Marie is home to the information center for a special national park. **Grasslands National Park,** between Val Marie and Killdeer in south-western Saskatchewan, preserves a unique landscape. The Frenchman River valley, part of which is within the Grasslands, was the first por-tion of mixed-grass prairie in North America to be set aside as a park and is marked by strange land formations and badlands. Colonies of black-tailed prairie dogs are the most numerous of the animals here. Interpretive and visitor services are limited. Tent camping is permit-ted, and electrical hookups are provided; all sites cost $10 per night. ⌧ *Off Hwys. 4 and 18, Box 150, S0N 2T0,* ☎ *306/298–2257.* ⊙ *Park office June–Aug., daily 8–6, and Sept.–May, weekdays 8–4:30; in-formation center in Val Marie, late May–early Sept., daily 8–6.*

Estevan

41 *205 km (127 mi) southeast of Regina on Rte. 39.*

Estevan, within 16 km (10 mi) of the U.S. border, has a rich history dating back to Prohibition days in the United States, when rum-run-ning was popular here. In summer, the town hosts popular stage plays in an outdoor tent setting. You can also tour nearby megaprojects like the Rafferty and Boundary dams. An ideal place to picnic is the Este-van Brick Wildlife Display, a 70-acre compound on the south edge of the city where bison, deer, and antelope roam freely. For information call **Estevan Tourism** (☎ 306/634–6044).

Moose Mountain Provincial Park

42 *220 km (136 mi) southeast of Regina via Hwy. 1 and Rte. 9.*

Moose Mountain Provincial Park is 401 square km (155 square mi) of rolling poplar and birch forest that forms a natural refuge for moose and elk and a wide variety of birds. A 24-km (15-mi) gravel road leads in to moose and elk grazing areas (best times are early morning and early evening). You can vary the wildlife experiences with beaches, golf, tennis, and horseback riding. Of the 330 campsites, one-third have elec-tric hookups. The Kenosee Inn (⌧ Kenosee Village, Saskatchewan S0C 2S0, ☎ 306/577–2099) is a 30-room accommodation on the park grounds. ⌧ *Rte. 9,* ☎ *306/577–2131, 306/577–2144 camping reser-vations.* ▣ *$6 per day per car; camping $14 per night with electric-ity, $12 without electricity.* ⊙ *Daily, 24 hrs.*

OFF THE
BEATEN PATH

CANNINGTON MANOR HISTORIC PARK – A site southeast of Moose Mountain Provincial Park preserves the 1880s lifestyle of an experimental Victorian settlement that attempted to re-create upper-class life in England. It was abandoned after only 15 years when the railway bypassed the town. What remain are the original manor house, a church, shops, and a museum in the original schoolhouse. ⊠ *Rte. 603, 16 km (10 mi) northeast of Manor on gravel roads,* ☎ *306/787–9573.* ⊠ *Donations accepted.* ⊙ *Late May–early Sept., daily 10–6.*

SASKATOON

Saskatchewan's largest city is Saskatoon (population 219,000), nicknamed City of Bridges because it has seven spans across the South Saskatchewan River, which cuts the city in half diagonally. It is considered one of the most beautiful of Canada's midsize cities, in part because a zealous protectionist campaign has allowed the riverbanks to flourish largely in their natural state.

Saskatoon was founded in 1882 when a group of Ontario Methodists was granted 200,000 acres to form a temperance colony. Teetotaling Methodists controlled only half the land, however, and eventually the influence of those who controlled the other half turned the town wet. The coming of the railroad in 1890 made it the major regional transportation hub, but during the 20th century it became known for its three major resources: potash, oil, and wheat. Saskatoon today is the high-tech hub of Saskatchewan's agricultural industry and is also home to the University of Saskatchewan—a major presence in all aspects of local life. Many visitors are impressed by the richness of the city's cultural life, particularly the thriving theater scene.

Exploring Saskatoon

Reasonably compact for a western city, Saskatoon proper is easily accessible to drivers and cyclists. Idylwyld Drive divides the city into east and west; 22nd Street divides the city into north and south. The downtown area and Spadina Crescent are on the west side of the South Saskatchewan River.

A Good Drive

Begin exploring at **Meewasin Valley Centre** ㊣, which traces Saskatoon history back to temperance-colony days. Follow Spadina Crescent north along the river to the **Ukrainian Museum of Canada** ㊹. Just north of the museum is **Kinsmen Park** ㊺, with riverside amusements. From Spadina Crescent, head east over the river on the University Bridge to the picturesque **University of Saskatchewan** ㊻ campus. You can detour into the northeastern part of the city to the **Saskatoon Zoo Forestry Farm Park** ㊼ to see animals and hike. Return to the university campus, head west on College Drive, and then pick up University Drive, lined with grand old houses. University Drive eventually joins Broadway Avenue, the city's oldest business district. Follow Broadway Avenue south to 8th Street; head west to Lorne Avenue and then south to the **Western Development Museum** ㊽, on the **Saskatoon Prairieland Exhibition Grounds** ㊾, to see a re-creation of a 1910 boomtown. To return to downtown Saskatoon, take the scenic route: Head north on Lorne Avenue, then west on Ruth Street to the river. Follow St. Henry Avenue, Taylor Street, Herman Avenue, and Saskatchewan Crescent past the fine old homes that overlook one of the prettier stretches of the South Saskatchewan River. Cross over the 19th Street Bridge.

TIMING

By car this tour can easily be done without stops in a morning or afternoon. If you want to explore museums or hike, leave more time.

Sights to See

45 Kinsmen Park. This riverside amusement park includes a children's play village. ⊠ *Spadina Crescent and 25th St.,* ☎ *306/975–3300.* ☉ *Late May–Labor Day.*

43 Meewasin Valley Centre. This small museum traces Saskatoon history back to when it was a Methodist temperance colony. Meewasin is Cree for "beautiful valley," and this is a fitting place to embark upon the **Meewasin Valley Trail,** a 19-km (12-mi) biking and hiking trail along both banks of the South Saskatchewan River. ⊠ *402 3rd Ave. S,* ☎ *306/665–6888.* ▣ *Free.* ☉ *Weekdays 9–5, weekends 10:30–5.*

49 Saskatoon Prairieland Exhibition Grounds. This vast plot encompasses space for agricultural shows, rodeos, and horse races, and the Western Development Museum (☞ *below*). ⊠ *Ruth St. and Lorne Ave.,* ☎ *306/931–7149.*

47 Saskatoon Zoo Forestry Farm Park. More than 300 animals live in the zoo, which spotlights species native to Saskatchewan, such as deer, wolf, bear, coyote, and fox. The park offers barbecue areas, nature displays, cross-country ski trails, fishing, and sports fields. It also has train rides. ⊠ *1903 Forest Rd., off Attridge Dr.,* ☎ *306/975–3382.* ▣ *May– Labor Day $3.50, Labor Day–Apr. free, vehicle charge $2.* ☉ *May– Labor Day, daily 9–9; Labor Day–Apr., daily 10–4.*

44 Ukrainian Museum of Canada. This collection celebrates—through photos, costumes, textiles, and of course the famous *pysanky* (Easter eggs)—the rich history of the Ukrainian people who make up 10% of Saskatchewan's population. ⊠ *910 Spadina Crescent E,* ☎ *306/244–*

*3800. ⌦ $2. ⊘ Sept.–June, Tues.–Sat. 10–5, Sun. 1–5; July–Aug.,
Mon.–Sat. 10–5, Sun. 1–5.*

㊻ University of Saskatchewan. The parklike riverside campus, among the
most picturesque in Canada, occupies a 2,550-acre site on the east bank
of the river. The university grounds contain several museums and galleries, including the **Natural Sciences Museum,** the **Little Stone School
House,** the **Museum of Antiquities,** the **Biology Museum,** and the
Gordon Snelgrove Gallery. A highlight is the **Diefenbaker Canada
Centre,** a museum, art gallery, and research center in Canadian studies commemorating Canada's 13th prime minister. The center explores
John Diefenbaker's life and times. Two replica rooms represent the Privy
Council Chamber and the prime minister's Ottawa office, where he
served in the late 1950s and early 1960s. ⊠ *Diefenbaker Canada Cen-
tre, 101 Diefenbaker Point,* ☎ *306/966–8384. ⊘ Mon., Fri. 9:30–
4:30; Tues.–Thurs. 9:30–8; weekends 12:30–5.*

㊽ Western Development Museum. One of four such museums in
Saskatchewan, the Saskatoon branch is called 1910 Boomtown and
re-creates early 20th-century life in western Canada. ⊠ *2610 Lorne
Ave. S,* ☎ *306/931–1910. ⌦ $4.50. ⊘ Daily 9–5.*

Dining

$$–$$$$ ✕ **R. J. Willoughby's.** Stands of bamboo and other foliage enhance the
lush, tropical, pink-and-green color scheme of the Ramada Hotel's main
dining room. Menu highlights are Continental entrées plus themed
evenings with specialty buffets (prime rib on Wednesday, pasta on Fri-
day, seafood on Sunday). The very popular Sunday brunch has an im-
pressive array of selections, including custom-made omelets and
flambéed fruit. ⊠ *Ramada Hotel, 90 22nd St. E,* ☎ *306/665–7576.
Reservations essential. AE, DC, MC, V.*

$$ ✕ **Saskatoon Station Place.** The station is newly built, but the vintage
railroad cars and decorative antiques are fascinatingly authentic. The
newspaper-style menu headlines Canadian prime rib and steaks, seafood,
and Greek specialties, such as Greek ribs and souvlaki. ⊠ *221 Idylwyld Dr. N,* ☎ *306/244–7777. Reservations essential. AE, MC, V.*

$–$$ ✕ **Lydia's.** This Broadway Avenue–neighborhood pub presents a wide
selection of international beers and has a full menu, including beef and
chicken kebabs as well as Cajun chicken, Caesar salad, and a variety
of pasta dishes. There's live music every weekend. ⊠ *650 Broadway
Ave.,* ☎ *306/652–8595. DC, MC, V.*

$ ✕ **Genesis Family Restaurant.** You can have vegetable and fruit juices
freshly squeezed to order at this eatery with a strong emphasis on health
foods. Macrobiotic and vegetarian dishes are available, as well as authentic Chinese food that includes a popular dim sum lunch. ⊠ *901
2nd St. W,* ☎ *306/244–5516. AE, MC, V.*

$ ✕ **St. Tropez Bistro.** This sophisticated spot a short stroll from down-
town hotels offers intimate French bistro decor, with blue-and-pink flo-
rals, and candlelit tables. The imaginative preparations change daily,
but veal, fish, pastas, quiches, and outstanding homemade bread are
often on the menu. A tasty specialty is the blackened chicken. For dessert,
try the chocolate fondue. ⊠ *243 3rd Ave. S,* ☎ *306/652–1250. Reservations essential. AE, MC, V. Closed Sun.*

$ ✕ **Taunte Maria's.** Hearty soups, huge farmer's sausages, potato salad,
homemade bread, and noodles steeped in gravy are served up at this
Mennonite restaurant. The decor, too, reflects the Mennonite tradition:
simple, functional, and comfortable. Try to save room for Ho-Ho
Cake (chocolate cake with cream filling and chocolate icing) or bread

pudding with ice cream. ⊠ *212–2750 Faithful Ave., at 51st St.,* ☎ *306/ 931–3212. Reservations not accepted. MC, V. Closed Sun.*

Lodging

$$$ 🏨 **Delta Bessborough.** Saskatoon's majestic old landmark, opened in
★   1935, looks like a castle and dominates the skyline from its riverfront setting. The hotel has been upgraded with modern amenities, but it still retains its grand details. Rooms differ in size; all have traditional furniture. ⊠ *601 Spadina Crescent E, S7K 3G8,* ☎ *306/244–5521 or 800/ 268–1133,* ℻ *306/653–2458. 225 rooms, 10 suites. 2 restaurants, 2 bars, no-smoking rooms, indoor pool, sauna. AE, DC, MC, V.*

$$$ 🏨 **Radisson Hotel Saskatoon.** One of Saskatoon's newer luxury properties has a prime riverfront location downtown and 19 floors of classically styled rooms. Units are large, and the peach, gray, and pastel colors make them bright and airy; for still more atmosphere, request a river view. The elaborate Waterworks Recreation Complex has an indoor pool, a whirlpool, a sauna, and two three-story water slides. ⊠ *405 20th St. E, S7K 6X6,* ☎ *306/665–3322 or 800/ 333–3333,* ℻ *306/665–5531. 183 rooms, 8 suites. Restaurant, bar, no-smoking rooms, indoor pool, sauna. AE, DC, MC, V.*

$$$ 🏨 **Ramada Hotel Saskatoon.** Ideally located right across from Midtown Plaza shopping and Centennial Auditorium, the 15-story Ramada offers some splendid views of the city. Standard rooms are quite spacious. ⊠ *90 22nd St. E, S7K 3X6,* ☎ *306/244–2311,* ℻ *306/664– 2234. 185 rooms, 3 suites. 2 restaurants. AE, MC.*

$$$ 🏨 **Sheraton Cavalier.** Downtown, opposite Kiwanis Park, this eight-story property has unusually large rooms that face either the city or the river, and an elaborate water-sports complex. Benedict's Dining Room is the place for elegant dining, while Windows Café is more informal and has a view of the river from every table. A cigar lounge is a new addition. ⊠ *612 Spadina Crescent E, S7K 3G9,* ☎ *306/652–6770 or 800/325–3535,* ℻ *306/244–1739. 237 rooms, 12 suites. 2 restaurants, pub, no-smoking rooms, 2 indoor pools, sauna. AE, DC, MC, V.*

$$ 🏨 **Travelodge.** A sprawling property near the airport has two flora-filled indoor pool complexes; there's a water slide, too. Rooms come in a variety of sizes and shapes; many have balconies overlooking the pool. The Gardens Terrace Restaurant has informal poolside dining. ⊠ *106 Circle Dr. W, S7L 4L6,* ☎ *306/242–8881 or 800/578–7878,* ℻ *306/665–7378. 204 rooms, 16 suites. 2 restaurants, 2 bars, no-smoking rooms, 2 indoor pools, sauna, water slide. AE, DC, MC, V.*

$ 🏨 **Colonial Square Motel.** This pink-stucco, two-story motel is east of the river, along a fast-food strip. Rooms are furnished in pastel colors and have two queen-size beds or a double bed plus a pullout sofa. Across the parking lot is the Venice Pizza House and Lounge. ⊠ *1301 8th St. E, S7H 0S7,* ☎ *306/343–1676 or 800/667–3939,* ℻ *306/956–1313. 62 rooms, 17 suites. Restaurant, bar, no-smoking rooms. AE, MC, V.*

$ 🏨 **Patricia Hotel.** Conveniently located in the center of downtown, this older hotel is appealing if you're looking for a bargain. Five rooms are also available as a youth hostel. The Karz Kafe and a lounge are on the premises. ⊠ *345 2nd Ave. N,* ☎ *306/242–8861,* ℻ *306/242–8861. 42 rooms. Restaurant, bar. MC, V.*

Nightlife and the Arts

The Arts

MUSIC AND DANCE

The **Mendel Art Gallery** (⊠ 950 Spadina Crescent E, ☎ 306/975–7610) has a regular concert program. When the city symphony isn't in concert, the 2,003-seat **Saskatoon Centennial Auditorium** (⊠ 35 22nd St.

E, ☎ 306/975–7777) hosts ballet, rock and pop concerts, comedians, musical comedies, and opera. The **Saskatoon Jazz Society** performs in its permanent space, the Bassment (✉ 245 3rd Ave. S, ☎ 306/683–2277). Each summer Saskatoon is home to the popular **Saskatchewan Jazz Festival** (☎ 306/652–1421), when jazz musicians from around the world play more than 125 performances throughout the city. The **Saskatoon Symphony** (☎ 306/665–6414) performs an October–April season at the Saskatoon Centennial Auditorium (☞ *above*).

THEATER

Gateway Players (✉ 709 Cumberland St., ☎ 306/653–1200) presents five productions from October through April. **Persephone Theatre** (✉ 2802 Rusholme Rd., ☎ 306/384–7727) presents six plays and musicals a year. A summer tradition, **Shakespeare on the Saskatchewan** (☎ 306/653–2300) is staged in a riverside tent during July and August. **Saskatoon Soaps** presents weekly midnight improvisational comedy at the Broadway Theatre (✉ 715 Broadway Ave., ☎ 306/652–6556). Saskatoon's oldest professional theater, **25th Street Theatre Centre** (✉ 616 10th St. E, ☎ 306/664–2239) produces mostly works by Saskatchewan playwrights, as well as the Fringe Festival every summer.

Nightlife

BARS AND CLUBS

Amigos (✉ 632 10th St. E, ☎ 306/652–4912) is a rock hangout. The **Artful Dodger** (✉ 100–107 4th Ave. S, ☎ 306/653–2577) pub has live entertainment. Top rock groups perform at **Bud's on Broadway** (✉ 817 Broadway Ave., ☎ 306/244–4155). Saskatoon's businesspeople mingle with traveling executives at **Caper's Lounge** (✉ 405 20th St. E, ☎ 306/665–3322) in the Radisson Hotel Saskatoon. **Martini's** (✉ 410 22nd St. E, ☎ 306/244–7770) is a civilized rooftop place with river views.

Outdoor Activities and Sports

Participant Sports

BIKING AND JOGGING

The **Meewasin Valley Trail** (☎ 306/665–6888) is a gorgeous 19-km (12-mi) biking and jogging trail along both banks of the South Saskatchewan River in Saskatoon.

HEALTH AND FITNESS CLUBS

The **Riverraquet Athletic Club** (✉ 322 Saguenay Dr., ☎ 306/242–0010) has racquetball and squash courts, a weight room, aerobics classes, miniature golf, and beach volleyball in summer. The **Saskatoon Field House** (✉ University of Saskatchewan, 2020 College Dr., ☎ 306/975–3354) has tennis courts, a weight room, a gymnastics area, an indoor track, a fitness dance area, and drop-in fitness classes.

Spectator Sports

HOCKEY

The Western Hockey League's **Saskatoon Blades** play major junior hockey at Saskatchewan Place (✉ 3515 Thatcher Ave., ☎ 306/938–7800) from September through March.

HORSE RACING

Marquis Downs Racetrack (✉ Prairieland Exhibition Centre, enter on Ruth St., ☎ 306/242–6100) has Thoroughbred racing from early May through mid-October.

Shopping

Malls and Shopping Districts

If you enjoy funkier, smaller boutiques and restaurants, head to **Broadway Avenue** (✉ Between 8th and 12th Sts. east of river), the city's oldest business district and location of more than 150 shops and restaurants as well as a cinema. **Midtown Plaza** (✉ 22nd St. and 1st Ave., ☎ 306/652–9366) and **Scotia Centre Mall** (✉ 123 2nd Ave., ☎ 306/665–6120) are enclosed malls downtown. Two interesting suburban choices are the recently linked **Centre at Circle and 8th** and the **Market Mall** (✉ Louise and Preston Aves.), with its indoor miniature golf.

Specialty Stores

Local crafts are available at **Handmade House** (✉ 710 Broadway Ave., ☎ 306/665–5542). The **Homespun Craft Emporium** (✉ 250A 2nd Ave. S, ☎ 306/652–3585) has a variety of crafts. The **Trading Post** (✉ 226 2nd Ave. S, ☎ 306/653–1769) carries First Nations crafts and Canadian foodstuffs—including Saskatoon berry products.

Side Trips from Saskatoon

Day trips to a number of sights outside the city can provide an understanding of native and frontier life, including the heritage of the Métis. Prince Albert National Park may be a bit far for a day trip but is well worth an overnight stay.

Wanuskewin Heritage Park

★ ⑤ *5 km (3 mi) north of Saskatoon just off Hwy. 11.*

Wanuskewin Heritage Park portrays 6,000 years of Northern Plains native culture. The Interpretive Centre has an archaeological laboratory, displays, films, and hands-on activities. Outside, walking trails take you to archaeological sites, including a medicine wheel, tepee rings, bison kills and pounds, habitation sites, and stone cairns. ✉ *R.R. 4, Saskatoon,* ☎ *306/931–6767.* ☎ *$6.* ☉ *June–Labor Day, daily 9–9; Labor Day–May, daily 9–5. Closed Mon.–Tues. in winter.*

Batoche

⑤ *100 km (62 mi) northeast of Saskatoon.*

This small town is most notable for being near a significant historic
★ site. **Batoche National Historic Park** is a center of the Métis' heritage. It was here that the Métis under Louis Riel fought and lost their last battle against the Canadian militia in 1885. The large historical park includes a visitor center, displays, a historic church and rectory, and walking trails that take you by many of the battle sites. ✉ *Off Hwy. 11 (follow signs),* ☎ *306/423–6227.* ☎ *$4.* ☉ *July–Aug., daily 10–6; May–June and Sept.–Oct., daily 9–5.*

Duck Lake

⑤ *20 km (12 mi) north of Batoche, 120 km (74 mi) north of Saskatoon.*

Duck Lake, which lies along Highway 11 between the North and South Saskatchewan rivers, has a number of buildings decorated with life-size murals depicting the area's history, including the 1885 Northwest Rebellion. The **Regional Interpretive Centre** has more than 2,000 artifacts from the period of the Métis' last rebellion. ✉ *Hwy. 11,* ☎ *306/467–2057.* ☎ *$4.* ☉ *Mid-May–Labor Day, daily 10–5:30.*

OFF THE   **FORT CARLTON PROVINCIAL HISTORIC PARK** – This site, 24 km (15 mi)
BEATEN PATH   west of Duck Lake, has a reconstructed stockade and buildings from the mid-1800s fur-trade days. ✉ *Rte. 212,* ☎ *306/467–4512.* ☎ *$4.* ☉ *Mid-May–Labor Day, daily 10–5:30.*

Prince Albert

🔟 *141 km (87 mi) north of Saskatoon on Hwy. 11 and Rte. 2.*

Prince Albert is Saskatchewan's third-largest city (population 34,000), the center of the lumber industry, and the self-proclaimed "Gateway to the North." The prosperous modern city straddles the North Saskatchewan River; its most interesting attractions are downtown. The **Prince Albert Historical Museum,** in the old Fire Hall, also has a walking-tour pamphlet. ⊠ *River St. and Central Ave.,* ☎ *306/764–1394.* 🎟 *$1.* ☉ *Mid-May–Aug., Mon.–Sat. 10–6, Sun. 10–9.*

DINING

$$$–$$$$ ✕ **Amy's on Second Restaurant.** The favorite for locals when they want a special evening out, this small, contemporary establishment serves a limited but always interesting menu of pastas and veal, chicken, or steak dishes. Desserts and specialty coffees are tantalizing. ⊠ *2990 2nd Ave. W,* ☎ *306/763–1515. AE, DC, MC, V. Closed Sun.*

Prince Albert National Park

80 km (50 mi) north of Prince Albert, 221 km (137 mi) north of Saskatoon.

★ **Prince Albert National Park** encompasses nearly a million acres of wilderness and waterways, divided into three landscapes: wide-open fescue grassland, wooded parkland, and dense boreal forest. Besides hiking trails, the park has three major campgrounds, with more than 500 sites, plus rustic campgrounds and primitive sites in the backcountry. You can pick up maps and information at the **Waskesiu Lake Visitor Centre** in Waskesiu, a town with restaurants, motels, and stores, and a golf course within the park. The **Nature Centre,** inside the visitor center, orients you to the plant and animal life of the area. Hiking along the marked trails, you have a good chance of spotting moose, deer, bear, elk, and red fox. Canoes, rowboats, and powerboats can be rented from Waskesiu Lake Marina. Lodging in Waskesiu includes **Chateau Park Chalets** (☎ 306/663–5556), the **Hawood Inn** (☎ 306/663–5911), and **Waskesiu Lake Lodge** (☎ 306/663–6161); all offer year-round accommodation. ⊠ *Prince Albert National Park, off Rte. 2,* ☎ *306/663– 5322;* ⊠ *Waskesiu Lake Visitor Centre, Rtes. 263 and 264,* ☎ *306/ 663–5322.* 🎟 *Park entry $3.50 per day.* ☉ *Park daily; visitor center May–Sept., daily 8 AM–10 PM, and Oct.–Apr., weekdays 8–4:30.*

North Battleford

🔟 *138 km (86 mi) northwest of Saskatoon on Hwy. 16.*

The attractions in this town represent different aspects of the area's history. The **Western Development Museum** presents a re-created 1920s farming village, complete with homes, offices, churches, and a Mountie post. The museum also exhibits vintage farming tools and provides demonstrations of agricultural skills. ⊠ *Hwy. 16 and Rte. 40,* ☎ *306/ 445–8033.* 🎟 *$4.50.* ☉ *Call for hrs.*

While you're in town, visit the **Allen Sapp Gallery,** which displays the paintings of Cree artist Allen Sapp. ⊠ *1091 100th St.,* ☎ *306/445– 1760.* 🎟 *Free.* ☉ *May–Sept., daily 1–5; Oct.–Apr., Wed.–Sun. 1–5.*

Fort Battleford National Historic Site pays tribute to the role of mounted police in the development of the Canadian west. The fort was established in 1876 as the North West Mounted Police headquarters for the District of Saskatchewan. Costumed guides explain day-to-day life at the post, and an interpretive center has exhibits relating to the history of the Mounted Police and ways of life of natives and settlers. ⊠ *Central Ave.,* ☎ *306/937–2621.* 🎟 *$3.* ☉ *July–Aug., daily 9–6; May– June and Sept.–Oct., daily 9–5.*

Manitou Beach

⑤ *124 km (77 mi) southeast of Saskatoon via Hwy. 16 and Rte. 365.*

Fifty years ago the town of Manitou Beach was a world-famous spa nicknamed the Carlsbad of Canada. The mineral water in Little Manitou Lake is said to be three times saltier than the ocean and dense enough to make anyone float. Today **Manitou Springs Mineral Spa** (⊠ Rte. 365, ☎ 306/946–2233) attracts vacationers as well as sufferers from arthritis, rheumatism, and skin disorders to the spa resort (☞ *below*).

DINING AND LODGING

$$ ✕☷ **Manitou Springs Resort.** This lakeshore resort has rooms and suites with balconies and good views. The rooms are comfortable, with cushy fabrics in muted pastels; the spa is lined with cedar. Continental cuisine, including a small selection of seafood, and prairie fare such as steaks and roasts are served in a light and airy dining room overlooking the lake. ⊠ *Box 610, Watrous, SOK 4TO,* ☎ *306/946–2233; 800/667–7672 in Canada. 56 rooms, 4 suites. Dining room, massage, mineral baths, exercise room, bicycles, meeting rooms. MC, V.*

Saskatoon A to Z

Arriving and Departing

BY CAR

The two-lane Yellowhead Highway (Highway 16) passes through Saskatoon on its journey from Winnipeg through to Edmonton and west. There is also access to Saskatoon along Highway 11 from Regina.

BY PLANE

Saskatoon Airport (⊠ 2625 Airport Dr., ☎ 306/975–4274), 7 km (4½ mi) northwest of downtown, is served by Canadian Airlines International, Air Canada, Northwest Airlines, Westjet and Canadian commuter carriers (☞ Airline Travel *in* the Gold Guide). Taxis to the downtown area cost about $10–$12.

Getting Around

BY BUS

Saskatoon Transit (☎ 306/975–3100) buses offer convenient service to points around the city. Tickets cost $1.50.

BY TAXI

Taxis are plentiful, especially outside downtown hotels, but they are fairly expensive. For service, call **United Yellow Cab** (☎ 306/652–2222), **Blueline Taxi** (☎ 306/653–3333), or **Saskatoon Radio Cab** (☎ 306/242–1221).

Contacts and Resources

EMERGENCIES

Ambulance, fire, poison center, police (☎ 911).

GUIDED TOURS

W.W. Northcote River Cruises depart on the hour for 11-km (7-mi) tours of the South Saskatchewan River. Cruises run June–August, daily 10–8. *The Delta Lady* (☎ 306/934–7642) offers one-hour river cruises May–October, daily 9:30–9. Departures are directly behind the Delta Bessborough Hotel.

HOSPITALS

City Hospital (⊠ Queen St. and 6th Ave. N, ☎ 306/655–8230). **Royal University Hospital** (⊠ University Grounds, ☎ 306/655–1362). **St. Paul's Hospital** (⊠ 1702 20th St. W, ☎ 306/665–5113).

LATE-NIGHT PHARMACY
Shopper's Drug Mart (⊠ 610 Taylor St. E, at Broadway Ave., ☎ 306/343–1608) is open daily till midnight; another branch (⊠ 2410 22nd St. W, ☎ 306/382–5005) is open 24 hours.

VISITOR INFORMATION
Tourism Saskatoon (⊠ 6–305 Idylwyld Dr. N, S7L OZ1, ☎ 306/242–1206 or 800/567–2444) is open weekdays 8:30–5 most of the year and 8:30–7 mid-May–early September. In summer, visitor information centers open at various points along Highway 16.

WINNIPEG

Though geographically isolated, Manitoba's provincial capital has become a center for both commerce and culture, home to a symphony orchestra, ballet and opera companies, a lively theater scene, and a thriving community of local and native artists. The first stop on the great Canadian land rush of the late 19th century, Winnipeg still counts among its citizens descendants of the original French and British settlers, and it has distinct neighborhoods of Ukrainians, Jews, Italians, Mennonites, Hungarians, Portuguese, Poles, and Chinese.

Unlike the boom-and-bust towns farther west, Winnipeg has enjoyed steady growth, with a diversified economy based on manufacturing, banking, transportation, and agriculture. With a population of more than 650,000, it ranks as Canada's seventh-largest city and the largest population center between Toronto and Calgary. Winnipeg looks like the cosmopolitan centers of midwestern America—Minneapolis, Milwaukee, Chicago—with a downtown area filled with cast-iron buildings and established neighborhoods of older homes along curving, tree-lined streets.

Originally, buffalo-hunting Plains Indians were the only inhabitants of the area, which was franchised by the British Crown to the Hudson's Bay Company. That was until 1738, when Pierre Gaultier de Varennes established a North West Company fur-trading post at the junction of the Red and Assiniboine rivers. Lord Selkirk, a Scot, brought a permanent agricultural settlement in 1812; Winnipeg was incorporated as a city in 1873; and soon after, in 1886, the Canadian Pacific Railroad arrived, bringing a rush of European immigrants. Winnipeg boomed as a railroad hub, a center of the livestock and grain industries, and a principal market city of western Canada.

Exploring Winnipeg

You can explore a number of areas on foot, but a car is useful for traveling to spread-out sights. It can be somewhat difficult to get your bearings in Winnipeg. The downtown area lies just north of the junction of the Red and Assiniboine rivers, and its streets interconnect at skewed angles with the curving rivers, creating diagonal streets in all directions. Much of downtown is linked by a network of enclosed pedestrian overpasses and underground concourses. The intersection of Portage Avenue and Main Street is the focal point of the city, with Portage Avenue (Highway 1) the principal artery heading west and Main Street (Route 52) heading north. South of Winnipeg, the main drag is Pembina Highway (Route 42). Streets in St. Boniface, east of the Red River, are labeled in French—evidence of the community's ethnic heritage.

A Good Walk and Drive

Begin in downtown Winnipeg at the visitor information center, housed in the **Legislative Building** ⑤⑥. Walk east on Broadway and south on Carlton Street to tour the **Dalnavert Museum** ⑤⑦, the 1895 house built for Manitoba's premier. Back at the Legislature, head north on Osborne Street past the stately store called the Bay (the legacy of the Hudson's Bay Company) to the **Winnipeg Art Gallery** ⑤⑧ to view Inuit sculpture and art. Turn east at the north end of the Winnipeg Art Gallery to Portage Avenue for a look at the shopping district (☞ Shopping, *below*). Continue east on Portage Avenue to Main Street and what's reputed to be the windiest intersection in the world. Five floors above the breeze, visit the **Winnipeg Commodity Exchange** ⑤⑨, the oldest and largest futures exchange in Canada. Below ground is Winnipeg Square, a concourse with shops and fast-food stores. Emerge to street level on the north side of Portage Avenue and into the **Exchange District** ⑥⓪—a concentration of renovated warehouses, banks, and insurance companies now thriving as a nightlife center and Sunday open-air market. Continue north on Main Street to Rupert Avenue and **Centennial Centre** ⑥①, site of a concert hall, a natural history museum, and a planetarium.

The suburb of St. Boniface, about 2½ km (1½ mi) away, can be reached by crossing the Provencher Bridge east over the Red River and turning right onto avenue Taché. Here you can visit the **St. Boniface Cathedral** ⑥②, in whose churchyard Louis Riel is buried, and the **St. Boniface Museum** ⑥③, which focuses on French and Métis history and culture in Manitoba. Follow avenue Taché south to Goulet Street, turn right, and follow it onto Norwood Bridge, which takes you to the **Forks National Historic Site** ⑥④ and the Forks complex, at the junction of the Assiniboine and Red rivers. A longer drive—left on River Avenue, left on Donald Street, and right on Corydon Avenue—will bring you to **Assiniboine Park** ⑥⑤, where the zoo and several lovely gardens are. South of the park, you can follow Shaftsbury Boulevard past Assiniboine Forest across Wilkes Avenue to McCreary Road, where the **Fort Whyte Center for Environmental Education** ⑥⑥ re-creates natural habitats of Manitoba in a former cement quarry. To see where Canadian money is made, drive 6½ km (4 mi) southeast of downtown off Highway 1 or take Bus 50 (available on the east side of Fort Street between Portage and Graham avenues on weekdays) to the **Royal Canadian Mint** ⑥⑦. Also southeast of the center off Highway 1 is **Fun Mountain Waterslide Park** ⑥⑧.

TIMING

This makes for a busy day's tour; you might want to save a few sights for a second day of visiting.

Sights to See

☺ ⑥⑤ **Assiniboine Park.** West of town along the river of the same name, this park encompasses 376 acres of cycling paths, picnic areas, playgrounds, a miniature railway, formal English and French gardens, a conservatory, and a cricket pitch. The **Leo Mol Sculpture Garden** has more than 30 bronze sculptures, including Winnie the Bear. **Assiniboine Zoo**, also on the grounds, houses more than 1,200 species in reasonably natural settings. ✉ *Park Blvd. and Wellington Crescent,* ☎ *204/986–6921 or 204/986–3130.* 🎟 *Zoo $3 ($1 Nov.–Feb.).* ☉ *Zoo Oct.–Mar., daily 10–4; Apr.–May and Sept., daily 10–7; June–July, daily 10–9; Aug., daily 10–8. Park daily 7–10.*

⑥① **Centennial Centre.** A concert hall, the **Manitoba Museum of Man and Nature,** and the dazzling **Manitoba Planetarium** are the highlights of this complex. Exhibits at the museum focus on prehistoric Manitoba, local wildlife, the native peoples of the region, and the exploration of Hudson Bay. Downstairs, the planetarium presents a variety of cosmic adventures in the multimedia Star Theater; 60 interactive multisensory exhibits in Touch the Universe explain laws of nature. ✉ *190 Rupert Ave.,* ☎ *204/943–3139 or 204/943–3142.* 🎟 *Museum $4, plan-*

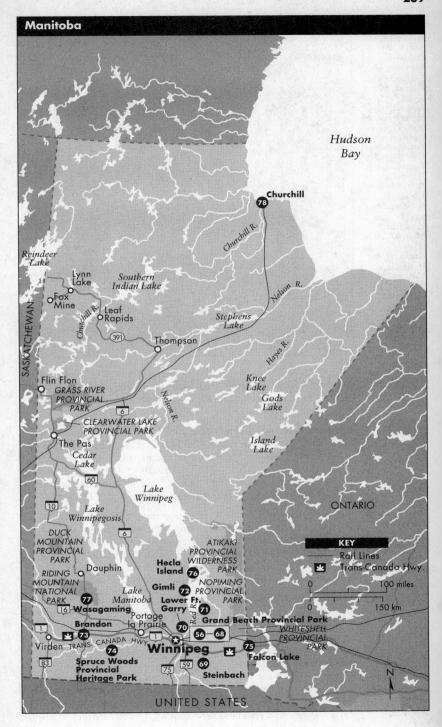

Manitoba

Hudson Bay

Churchill 78

Reindeer Lake

Lynn Lake
Fox Mine
Southern Indian Lake
Leaf Rapids
391
Thompson

SASKATCHEWAN

Churchill R.
Churchill R.
Nelson R.

Stephens Lake
Hayes R.

Knee Lake
Gods Lake

Flin Flon
GRASS RIVER PROVINCIAL PARK
6
Nelson R.
CLEARWATER LAKE PROVINCIAL PARK
The Pas
Cedar Lake
60
Island Lake

10
Lake Winnipegosis
6
Lake Winnipeg

DUCK MOUNTAIN PROVINCIAL PARK

ONTARIO

RIDING MOUNTAIN NATIONAL PARK
Dauphin
77
16
Wasagaming
Lake Manitoba

ATIKAKI PROVINCIAL WILDERNESS PARK

Hecla Island 76
Gimli 72
Lower Ft. Garry 71

NOPIMING PROVINCIAL PARK

KEY
Rail Lines
Trans-Canada Hwy.
0   100 miles
0   150 km

Brandon
1
73
Portage la Prairie
1
70
Red R.
56 68
Grand Beach Provincial Park
WHITESHELL PROVINCIAL PARK

Virden
TRANS-
CANADA HWY
Winnipeg
74
75
Falcon Lake

83
Spruce Woods Provincial Heritage Park
75
59
69
Steinbach

N

UNITED STATES

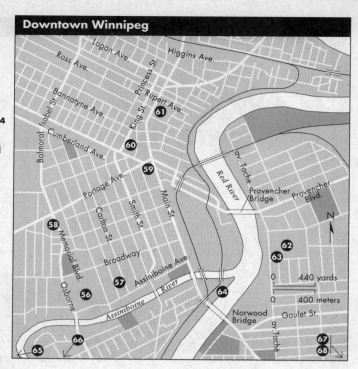

Downtown Winnipeg

etarium $3.50, science gallery $3.50, 3-day all-inclusive Omni pass $9. ☉ *Mid-May–early Sept., daily 10–6; early Sept.–mid-May, Tues.–Thurs. 10–6, weekends noon–6.*

57 **Dalnavert Museum.** This finely detailed Queen Anne Revival–style house was built in 1895 for Sir Hugh John Macdonald, who became premier of Manitoba. Costumed guides escort visitors around the premises. ⊠ *61 Carlton St.,* ☎ *204/943–2835.* ⌨ *$3.20.* ☉ *Jan.–Feb., weekends noon–4; Mar.–May and Sept.–Dec., Tues.–Thurs. and weekends noon–4:30; June–Aug., Tues.–Thurs. and weekends 10–5:30..*

60 **Exchange District.** A concentration of renovated warehouses, banks, and insurance companies built during Winnipeg's turn-of-the-century boom period now stands as a thriving nightlife spot. On Sunday, from May through October, attention focuses on **Old Market Square Park** (⊠ King St. and Bannatyne Ave.), a marketplace bursting with fresh produce, fish, and crafts. ⊠ *Between Portage Ave. and Main St.*

★ **64** **Forks National Historic Site.** Winnipeg began here, at the junction of the Red and Assiniboine rivers, with native settlements that date back 6,000 years. On 10 landscaped acres, you can learn about the region's history through interpretive displays as you stroll paths or rest on benches overlooking the river. There's also a playground and an amphitheater. Interpretive programs are presented as well; check at the Forks information center at the back of the Manitoba Children's Museum (☞ *below*). Next to the historic site and sharing the 3 km (2-mi) riverside promenade with it is the **Forks,** a 56-acre complex of renovated railway buildings and parkland now hosting a public market in former stables; a playground; a small boat dock; Johnston terminal, with shops and restaurants; and the **Manitoba Children's Museum.** In five galleries, kids can climb aboard a 1952-vintage steam engine and passenger car, try out a fully functioning TV studio, and more. The **Ex-**

plore **Manitoba Information Centre** contains a theme pavilion with more than 8,000 square ft of displays and exhibits depicting Manitoba's history and its people. ⊠ *Forks Market Rd. off Main St.,* ☎ *204/983–2007 Forks National Historic Site, 204/943–7752 the Forks, 204/956–1888 Children's Museum, 800/665–0040 Explore Manitoba.* ▣ *Museum $4.* ⊙ *Museum, Victoria Day–Labor Day, daily 9:30–5; Labor Day–Victoria Day, weekdays 8–4:30.*

🐦 **66** **Fort Whyte Center for Environmental Education.** This center, on 200 acres of land in the city's southwest corner, re-creates the natural habitats of Manitoba's lakes and rivers in and around several former cement quarries. It is home to white-tailed deer, muskrats, foxes, and numerous species of waterfowl. Self-guided nature trails and an interpretive center explain it all. ⊠ *1961 McCreary Rd.,* ☎ *204/989–8355.* ▣ *$3.50.* ⊙ *Weekdays 9–5, weekends 10–5.*

🐦 **68** **Fun Mountain Water Slide Park.** Bumper boats, a mammoth hot tub, rides, and a playground are all part of the fun at the water park 13 km (8 mi) east of downtown. ⊠ *Hwy. 1, east at Murdock Rd.,* ☎ *204/255–3910.* ▣ *$11.* ⊙ *June–Aug., daily 10–8.*

56 **Legislative Building.** The classic Greek-style structure made of local Tyndall stone contains the offices of Manitoba's premier and members of the cabinet, as well as the chamber where the legislature meets. A 240-ft dome supports Manitoba's symbol, Golden Boy—a gold-sheathed statue with a sheaf of wheat under his left arm and the torch of progress in his right hand. In the grounds fronting the river stand statues that celebrate Manitoba's ethnic diversity, including Scotland's Robert Burns, Iceland's Jon Sigurdson, Ukrainian poet Taras Ahevchenko, and Métis leader and "Father of Manitoba" Louis Riel. ⊠ *450 Broadway, at Osborne St.,* ☎ *204/945–5813.* ⊙ *Guided tour July–Labor Day, weekdays 9–6:30; Labor Day–June by appointment.*

67 **Royal Canadian Mint.** You can see Canadian coins rolling off the presses. ⊠ *520 Lagimodière Blvd., at Trans-Canada Hwy.,* ☎ *204/257–3359.* ▣ *$2.* ⊙ *Tour May–Aug., weekdays 9–5, Sat. noon–5.*

62 **St. Boniface Cathedral.** The largest French community in western Canada was founded as Fort Rouge in 1783 and became an important fur-trading outpost for the North West Company. Upon the arrival of Roman Catholic priests, the settlement was renamed St. Boniface. Remnants of a 1908 basilica that survived a 1968 fire can be seen outside the perimeter of the present cathedral, built in 1972. The grave of Louis Riel, the St. Boniface native son who led the Métis rebellion, is in the churchyard. ⊠ *Av. de la Cathédrale and av. Taché,* ☎ *204/233–7304.*

63 **St. Boniface Museum.** Housed in the oldest (1846) structure in Winnipeg and the largest oak log building in North America, the museum tells the French and Métis side of Manitoba history. Artifacts include an altar crafted from papier-mâché, the first church bell in western Canada, and a host of innovative household gadgets. ⊠ *494 av. Taché,* ☎ *204/237–4500.* ▣ *$2.15.* ⊙ *Mid-May–mid-June and Sept., weekdays 9–5, weekends 10–5; mid-June–Aug., Mon.–Thurs. 9–8, Fri.–Sat. 9–5, Sun. 10–8; Oct.–mid-May, weekdays 9–5.*

★ **58** **Winnipeg Art Gallery.** The gallery has the world's largest collection of Inuit sculpture and art; it also houses contemporary Canadian art and sculpture. ⊠ *300 Memorial Blvd.,* ☎ *204/786–6641.* ▣ *$3; free Wed.* ⊙ *Thurs.–Tues. 11–5, Wed. 11–9; times may vary with season.*

59 **Winnipeg Commodity Exchange.** At the oldest and largest futures exchange in Canada, you can observe the controlled chaos of wild men (and a few women) involved in the buying and selling of grains, cooking oils, gold, and silver. Below the exchange is **Winnipeg Square,** with shops and fast-food stores. ⊠ *360 Main St.,* ☎ *204/949–0495.* ⊙ *Weekdays 9:30–1:20.*

Dining

$$$$ ✕ **Amici.** The sophisticated and posh downtown *ristorante* is the local avatar of *cucina nuova,* the Italian version of nouvelle cuisine. Clever pastas and such dishes as roast quail on radicchio, chicken stuffed with goat cheese, and elegantly prepared Dover sole are served in a second-floor dining room divided by partitions of frosted glass. Downstairs, the Bombolini Wine Bar serves many simpler dishes, but also some of the same pastas, at lower prices. ⊠ *326 Broadway,* ☎ *204/943–4997. Reservations essential. AE, DC, MC, V. Closed Sun.*

$$$$ ✕ **Le Beaujolais.** This sophisticated, bright spot in the French St. Boni-
★   face district presents waiters in black tie; a softly lit ambience with French blue, coral, and burgundy decor; fresh-cut flowers; and a menu that combines classic French with lighter nouvelle cuisine. Fresh salmon with herb vinaigrette is the recommended seafood; bouillabaisse, tournedos with green peppercorns, veal with Roquefort and leeks, and rack of lamb are other entrées. Save room for dessert. ⊠ *131 Provencher Blvd.,* ☎ *204/237–6306. Reservations essential. AE, DC, MC, V.*

$$$–$$$$ ✕ **Restaurant Dubrovnik.** The setting is a romantic Victorian town house, with seating on an enclosed veranda overlooking the Assiniboine River. An extensive menu blends Continental specialties, such as rack of lamb, breast of duck, and pheasant, with southern Yugoslavian dishes. Two good choices are *gibanica* (feta cheese in phyllo pastry) and *muckalica* (pork, lamb, chicken, and sausage casserole). The wine list is lengthy. ⊠ *390 Assiniboine Ave.,* ☎ *204/944–0594. Reservations essential. Jacket required. AE, MC, V. Closed Sun.*

$$$ ✕ **Picasso's.** It may be named for a Spanish painter, but this is a Portuguese restaurant that serves outstanding seafood. On the street level it's a bustling café; upstairs, white tablecloths, candlelight, and soft music reinforce a subdued atmosphere. Try the salmon or Arctic char; Portuguese favorites are paella and octopus stew. ⊠ *615 Sargent Ave.,* ☎ *204/775–2469. Reservations essential. AE, DC, MC, V.*

$$–$$$ ✕ **d'8 Schtove.** The name is Mennonite for "the eating room," and,
★   true to its name, the menu has heavyweight servings of soup, salads, and Mennonite concoctions, usually involving meat, potatoes, onions, and vegetables. Try the *klopz* (ground-beef-and-pork meatballs) or *wrenikje* (cottage-cheese pierogi). The south-side location is bright and immaculately clean, and the restaurant looks spacious, although you may still have to wait for a table. ⊠ *1842 Pembina Hwy.,* ☎ *204/275–2294. Reservations not accepted. AE, DC, MC, V.*

$$–$$$ ✕ **Victor's.** In the Ramada Marlborough (☞ Lodging, *below*), with its rich wood paneling and chandeliers, Victor's serves Continental cuisine in a stylish, upscale atmosphere. Poppy-seed cake is a must for dessert. ⊠ *331 Smith St.,* ☎ *204/947–2751. Reservations essential. AE, DC, MC, V. Closed Sun.*

$$ ✕ **Bistro Dansk.** Wood tables, bright red chairs, and strains of classi-
★   cal music convey a cozy European air. Dinner entrée selections mingle Danish specialties like *frikadeller* (meat patties) and crab-topped salmon with such dishes as roast chicken. A less expensive lunch menu has a vast variety of open-face sandwiches. ⊠ *63 Sherbrook St.,* ☎ *204/775–5662. Reservations essential. DC, V. Closed Sun.*

$$ ✕ **Homer's.** This good-time downtown place with a definite Mediterranean atmosphere has been one of the city's favorite Greek restaurants for more than 15 years. Greek specialties include roast leg of lamb

and moussaka, but Homer's is also famous for ribs, steak, seafood, pasta, and fresh hot bread. In summer you can eat outdoors. ✉ *520 Ellice Ave.,* ☎ *204/788–4858. Reservations essential. AE, DC, MC, V.*

$ ✕ **Kelekis.** This north-end shrine has purveyed legendary burgers, hot dogs, and fries for more than 60 years. A photo montage of family history and autographed photos of celebrities set the tone. Breakfast, lunch, and dinner are served daily. ✉ *1100 Main St.,* ☎ *204/582–1786. Reservations not accepted. No credit cards.*

$ ✕ **Mandarin.** The Sargent Avenue Mandarin is a crowded, 12-table, west-side place with unique and reasonably exotic northern Chinese dishes. Complete Gourmet Delight dinners include soup, dumplings, entrées, and dessert. The River Mandarin, a spin-off, has a slightly different menu and a calmer pace. ✉ *Mandarin, 613 Sargent Ave.,* ☎ *204/ 775–7819; River Mandarin,* ✉ *252 River Ave.,* ☎ *204/284–8963. Reservations essential. AE, MC, V.*

Lodging

$$$ 🏨 **Crowne Plaza Winnipeg Downtown.** Winnipeg's largest hotel, this Holiday Inn is 17 stories high and connects to the convention center. Rooms are decorated in pastels and have pleasant modern furnishings— some rooms overlook the skylighted pool. Ticker's lobby bar is a lively spot for a rendezvous. ✉ *350 St. Mary Ave., R3C 3J2,* ☎ *204/942– 0551 or 800/465–4329,* FAX *204/943–8702. 389 rooms, 18 suites. 3 restaurants, bar, no-smoking rooms, indoor pool, outdoor pool, sauna, exercise room, cabaret. AE, DC, MC, V.*

$$$ 🏨 **Delta Winnipeg.** Well located in the heart of downtown, this member of the Delta chain offers a full range of luxury services, including in-room movies. The hotel is adjacent to the covered walking system that connects Eaton Place and Portage Place. The 12th-floor Signature Restaurant has fine views. ✉ *288 Portage Ave., R3C OB8,* ☎ *204/ 956–0410 or 800/268–1133,* FAX *204/947–1129. 261 rooms, 11 suites. 2 restaurants, health club. AE, DC, MC, V.*

$$$ 🏨 **Holiday Inn Airport/West.** This bright and sumptuous modern prop-
★ erty stands next to the Trans-Canada Highway's western approach to Winnipeg, near the airport, the racetrack, and shopping areas. Rooms are large, with earth-tone furnishings. Executive suites, decorated in blue and green, are a bit fancier. The atrium is a lush setting for the pool and poolside lounge. ✉ *2520 Portage Ave., R3J 3T6,* ☎ *204/885–4478 or 800/465–4329,* FAX *204/831–5734. 210 rooms, 16 suites. 2 restaurants, indoor pool, sauna, exercise room. AE, DC, MC, V.*

$$$ 🏨 **The Lombard.** The top luxury hotel in town is near Winnipeg's
★ hub—Portage and Main streets—and is connected by skywalk to office buildings and Portage Place mall. The 21st-floor rooftop indoor pool makes a dramatic setting for a swim. Chimes has a contemporary atmosphere and light meals; other restaurants are the elegant Velvet Glove Dining Room and Café Express for quick meals. The hotel is owned by a local family and managed by Canadian Pacific Hotels. ✉ *2 Lombard Pl., R3B 0Y3,* ☎ *204/957–1350 or 800/228–3000,* FAX *204/956–1791. 334 rooms, 16 suites. 3 restaurants, no-smoking rooms, indoor pool, sauna, exercise room. AE, DC, MC, V.*

$$$ 🏨 **Place Louis Riel.** This luxury-class alternative is a converted apart-
★ ment building that has contemporary suites with living rooms, dining areas, and fully equipped kitchens. Though all rooms are up-to-date, the suites on the upper floors facing west are preferred because of their view of the Legislative Building. The excellent downtown location— adjacent to Eaton Place mall—is only one of the hotel's advantages. ✉ *190 Smith St., R3C 1J8,* ☎ *204/947–6961; 800/665–0569 in*

Canada; FAX *204/947–3029. 280 suites. Restaurant, lounge, no-smoking rooms, free parking. AE, DC, MC, V.*

$$ 🏨 **Hotel Fort Garry.** Built in 1913 and known far and wide as the Grand Castle, the old railroad hotel is one of Winnipeg's gathering places. On the south edge of downtown, near Union Station, the hotel and its hushed, spacious lobby are furnished with inviting armchairs and original marble, brass, and crystal accents. Large guest rooms still have classic dark-wood furnishings and floral wallpapers. ✉ *222 Broadway, R3C 0R3,* ☎ *204/942–8251 or 800/665–8088,* FAX *204/956–2351. 235 rooms, 11 suites. 2 restaurants, cabaret, casino. AE, DC, MC, V.*

$$ 🏨 **Travelodge Hotel Downtown Winnipeg.** Canada's oldest budget chain placed this high-rise in a desirable location, next to the bus depot and adjacent to the Bay department store and the Winnipeg Art Gallery. Rooms on the south side look out on the Legislative Building, and north-side rooms overlook the city. Guest rooms have subdued modern furnishings in neutral or pastel colors. ✉ *360 Colony St., R3B 2P3,* ☎ *204/786–7011 or 800/661–9563,* FAX *204/772–1443. 156 rooms. Restaurant, no-smoking rooms, indoor pool. AE, DC, MC, V.*

$ 🏨 **Charter House.** Half the rooms in this five-story low rise on the south
★ side of downtown have balconies. Furnishings are contemporary motel style, and the atmosphere is friendly. The Rib Room is popular and moderately priced. ✉ *330 York Ave., R3C 0N9,* ☎ *204/942–0101; 800/782–0175 in Manitoba;* FAX *204/956–0665. 87 rooms. 2 restaurants, no-smoking rooms, pool. AE, DC, MC, V.*

$ 🏨 **Ramada Marlborough.** This ornate, 1914 Gothic structure in the financial district has vaulted ceilings and a stained-glass window and is home to Joanna's Café, a casual dining spot that's good for before- or after-dinner drinks, and the more formal Victor's (☞ Dining, *above*). The public areas and guest rooms are freshly decorated. Soft sofas provide comfortable seating in a spacious lobby that has marble floors, high ceilings, and wood paneling. ✉ *331 Smith St., R3B 2G9,* ☎ *204/ 942–6411, 204/942–2017, or 800/667–7666;* FAX *204/942–2017. 111 rooms, 39 suites. 2 restaurants. AE, DC, MC, V.*

Nightlife and the Arts

The Arts

FILM

In Winnipeg, a good place to find imports, art films, oldies, and midnight cult classics is **Cinémathèque** (✉ 100 Arthur St., ☎ 204/942–6795). **Cinema 3** (✉ 585 Ellice Ave., ☎ 204/783–1097) plays art films and classics. The **Winnipeg Art Gallery** (✉ 300 Memorial Blvd., ☎ 204/786–6641) has a cinema series.

MUSIC AND DANCE

Winnipeg's principal venue for serious music, dance, and pop concerts is the 2,263-seat Centennial Concert Hall in the **Manitoba Centennial Centre** (✉ 555 Main St., ☎ 204/956–1360). The **Manitoba Opera** (☎ 204/942–7479) presents three operas a year—in November, February, and May—in Centennial Concert Hall. The acclaimed **Royal Winnipeg Ballet** (☎ 204/956–2792 or 800/667–4792) performs in Centennial Concert Hall in October, December, March, and May; it's a must for dance fans. From September to mid-May Centennial Centre is the home of the **Winnipeg Symphony Orchestra** (☎ 204/949–3999).

For contemporary dance and new music, check out **Le Rendez-Vous** (✉ 768 av. Taché, ☎ 204/233–9214 or 204/237–7692) in St. Boniface. The **Pantages Playhouse Theatre** (✉ 180 Market Ave. E, ☎ 204/ 986–3003) mounts various productions and concerts. The **Winnipeg Art Gallery** (✉ 300 Memorial Blvd., ☎ 204/786–6641) hosts jazz, blues, chamber music, and contemporary groups. The **Winnipeg Convention Centre** (⊠ 375 York Ave., ☎ 204/956–1720) has popular and orchestral concerts.

THEATER

One of Canada's most acclaimed regional theaters, the **Manitoba Theatre Centre** produces serious plays from many sources at the 785-seat Mainstage (⊠ 174 Market Ave., ☎ 204/942–6537) and more experimental work in the MTC Warehouse Theatre (⊠ 140 Rupert Ave., ☎ 204/942–6537).The **Prairie Theatre Exchange** focuses on local playwrights in an attractive facility in the Portage Place mall (⊠ Portage Ave. and Carlton St., ☎ 204/942–5483).

Nightlife

BARS AND CLUBS

Hy's Steak Loft (⊠ 216 Kennedy St., ☎ 204/942–1000) is convenient for cocktails and has a late-evening piano bar. A most convincingly British pub in the Exchange District is the **King's Head** (⊠ 120 King St., ☎ 204/957–1479).

CASINOS

You can try your luck at **Club Regent** (⊠ 1425 Regent Ave., ☎ 204/957–2700). Blackjack, baccarat, la boule, and roulette are options at the **Crystal Casino** (⊠ Hotel Fort Garry, 7th floor, 222 Broadway Ave., ☎ 204/957–2600). There's state-of-the-art gaming at **McPhillips Street Station** (⊠ 484 McPhillips St., ☎ 204/957–3900).

MUSIC

Rhythm-and-blues fans can check out **Mustang Sally's** (⊠ 114 Market Ave., ☎ 204/957–2700). The **Palomino Club** (⊠ 1133 Portage Ave., ☎ 204/772–0454) is a country-and-western hangout. A somewhat sedate dance floor comes alive after 9 PM in **Windows Lounge** in the Sheraton Winnipeg (⊠ 161 Donald St., ☎ 204/942–5300).

Outdoor Activities and Sports

Participant Sports

BIKING AND JOGGING

Most public parks in Manitoba have marked biking and jogging paths.For information on routes, pick up maps from **Travel Manitoba** (☞ Visitor Information *in* The Prairie Provinces A to Z, *below*).

HEALTH AND FITNESS CLUBS

A full slate of classes and equipment are available at **Body Options** (⊠ 1604 St. Mary's Rd., ☎ 204/255–6600). **Bodyworks** (⊠ 2 Donald St., ☎ 204/477–1691) has equipment and daily rates.

Spectator Sports

BASEBALL

The **Winnipeg Goldeyes** (☎ 204/982–2273) play AA baseball in the Northern League, with games at Winnipeg Stadium.

BASKETBALL

The International Basketball League's **Winnipeg Cyclones** (☎ 204/944–8932) play at the Winnipeg Convention Centre.

FOOTBALL

The **Winnipeg Blue Bombers** (☎ 204/784–2583) of the Canadian Football League play home games at the Winnipeg Arena.

HOCKEY

The **Manitoba Moose** (☎ 204/987–7825) of the International Hockey League play home games at the Winnipeg Arena.

HORSE RACING

Assiniboia Downs (⊠ 3975 Portage Ave., at Perimeter Hwy. W, ☎ 204/885–3330) hosts Thoroughbred racing May–October.

Shopping

Art and Crafts

The **Crafts Guild of Manitoba** (⊠ 183 Kennedy St., ☎ 204/943–1190) displays works by Manitoba carvers, weavers, and jewelers. Check out the **Great Canadian Print Company** (⊠ 75 Albert St., ☎ 204/942–1002) for native art. **Northern Images** (⊠ 216 Portage Place mall, 393 Portage Ave., ☎ 204/942–5501; ⊠ Airport Executive Centre, 1790 Wellington Ave., ☎ 204/788–4806) markets the work of the Inuit and Déné members of the North Territories Co-operative, which owns the stores. The **Upstairs Gallery** (⊠ 266 Edmonton St., ☎ 204/943–2734) has prints, drawings, wall hangings, and sculpture.

Malls and Shopping Districts

Downtown shopping is dominated by **Portage Place** (⊠ Portage Ave. between Balmoral and Carlton Sts.) and **Eaton Place** (⊠ Bounded by Graham Ave., Hargrave St., St. Mary Ave., and Donald St.), two malls with numerous stores, fast-food joints, and movie theaters. Across the Assiniboine River, the **Osborne Village** area (⊠ Osborne St. between River and Corydon Aves.) has 150 trendy boutiques and specialty shops, cafés, restaurants, and crafts shops.

Side Trips from Winnipeg

Day trips outside the city include a lovely beach and sights that reveal the area's fur-trading, Mennonite, and Icelandic heritage.

Steinbach

69 *48 km (30 mi) southeast of Winnipeg.*

The town of Steinbach is populated with nearly 10,000 descendants of Mennonites who fled religious persecution in late-19th-century Europe. Note all the automobile dealerships: Manitoban car buyers flock here because of the Mennonite reputation for making square deals.

In the **Mennonite Heritage Village,** a 40-acre open-air museum with buildings re-creating a village of the late 1800s, guides demonstrate blacksmithing, wheat grinding, and old-time housekeeping. The guides occasionally converse in the Mennonite German dialect. During the Pioneer Days festival in early August, everyone wears costumes and demonstrates homespun crafts. An authentic and extremely low-priced restaurant serves Mennonite specialties, such as borscht, pierogi, and *ukrenky* (cheese or potato torte). ⊠ *Rte. 12, 2 km (1 mi) north of Steinbach,* ☎ 204/326–9661. ☞ *$4.* ☉ *May and Sept., Mon.–Sat. 10–5, Sun. noon–5; June–Aug., Mon.–Sat. 10–7, Sun. noon–7; Oct. and Apr., weekdays 10–4.*

Selkirk

32 km (20 mi) north of Winnipeg.

This town is notable for a structure that recalls Canada's early days. **70** **Lower Fort Garry,** built in 1830, is the oldest stone fort remaining from the Hudson's Bay Company fur-trading days. Nowadays, costumed employees describe daily tasks and recount thrilling journeys by York boat, the "boat that won the West." Beaver, raccoon, fox, and wolf pelts hang in the fur loft as a reminder of the bygone days. ⊠ *Rte. 9,* ☎ 204/785–6050. ☞ *$5.* ☉ *Grounds daily dawn–dusk; buildings mid-May–Sept. 2, daily 10–6.*

Grand Beach Provincial Park

71 *87 km (54 mi) northeast of Winnipeg.*

This lovely park is on the eastern shore of Lake Winnipeg, the seventh-largest lake in North America. On summer weekends, crowds flock here from Winnipeg for the white-powder sand, the grass-crowned 30-ft dunes, and a lagoon that makes bird-watchers' dreams come true. Grand Marais, at the southern portal of the park, has a few services such as a gas station and restaurant. ⊠ *Rte. 12,* ☎ *204/754–2212.* ⊙ *May–Sept., daily.*

Gimli

72 *76 km (47 mi) north of Winnipeg.*

Gimli, the largest Icelandic community outside the homeland, was once the center of the independent state of New Iceland. It still has an impressive harbor and marina on Lake Winnipeg. A giant Viking statue proclaims allegiance to the far-off island. By far the best choice for a stay here is the Country Resort by Carlson (☎ 204/642–8565), right on the waterfront.

The **Gimli Historical Museum,** on the Gimli harbor waterfront, preserves the ethnic heritage of early Ukrainian and Icelandic settlers and records the history of the Lake Winnipeg commercial fishing industry. ⊠ *Rte. 9,* ☎ *204/642–5317.* ⊠ *$2.* ⊙ *Mid-May–June, Wed.–Sun. 10–5; July–Aug., daily 10–6.*

Winnipeg A to Z

Arriving and Departing

BY CAR

Two main east–west highways link Winnipeg with the prairie provinces. The Trans-Canada Highway (Highway 1) runs through Winnipeg, Regina, and Calgary. West of Winnipeg the Yellowhead Highway (Highway 16) branches off the Trans-Canada and heads northwest toward Saskatoon and Edmonton.

Travelers from the United States can reach the Manitoba capital from Minneapolis along I–94 and I–29, connecting to Route 75 at the Canadian border. The driving distance between Minneapolis and Winnipeg is 691 km (428 mi).

BY PLANE

Winnipeg International Airport (⊠ 2000 Wellington Ave., ☎ 204/987–9400), 8 km (5 mi) from the city, is served by Northwest, Air Canada, Canadian Airlines International, and several commuter airlines (☞ Air Travel *in* the Gold Guide). Taxi fare downtown runs about $10–$15. Some airport-area hotels have free airport shuttles.

Getting Around

BY BUS

The **City of Winnipeg Transit System** (☎ 204/986–5700) operates an extensive network of buses throughout the city and metropolitan area. Adult fare is $1.45, 90¢ for senior citizens and children over four; exact change is required and transfers are free.

BY TAXI

Taxis—relatively expensive by U.S. standards—can be found outside downtown hotels or summoned by phone. Car services are **Unicity** (☎ 204/947–6611) and **Duffy's Taxi** (☎ 204/775–0101).

Contacts and Resources

EMERGENCIES

Ambulance, fire, poison center, police (☎ 911).

Several lines ply the Red and Assiniboine rivers between May and mid-October. The **Paddlewheel River Rouge** (☎ 204/942–4500) has a variety of cruises (dining, dinner-dance, evening), combining sailings with double-decker bus tours.

From June through August, **walking tours** of the turn-of-the-century Exchange District begin at the Pantages Playhouse Theater (✉ 180 Market Ave. E, ☎ 204/986–6927).

HOSPITALS
Emergency rooms are located at the **Health Sciences Centre** (✉ 700 William Ave., ☎ 204/787–3167 or 204/787–2306), **Misericordia General Hospital** (✉ 99 Cornish Ave., ☎ 204/788–8188), and **Riverview Health Centre** (✉ 1 Morley Ave., ☎ 204/452–3411).

LATE-NIGHT PHARMACY
Shopper's Drug Mart (✉ 471 River Ave., ☎ 204/958–7000) is open 24 hours daily.

VISITOR INFORMATION
The **Explore Manitoba Idea Centre** is open weekdays at the Forks (✉ 21 Forks Market Rd., ☎ 204/945–3777 or 800/665–0040). The **Government Tourist Reception Office** (✉ Broadway and Osborne St., ☎ 204/945–3777 or 800/665–0040), in the Manitoba Legislative Building, is open May–Labor Day, daily 8:30 AM–9 PM; Labor Day–April, weekdays 8:30–4:30. **Tourism Winnipeg** (✉ 320–25 Forks Market Rd., ☎ 204/943–1970) is open weekdays 8:30–4:30; an airport location (☎ 800/665–0204) is open 8 AM–9:45 PM.

ELSEWHERE IN MANITOBA

A clutch of sites from the city of Brandon to superb parks and the Hudson Bay polar-bear mecca of Churchill are some highlights of the province.

Brandon

73 *197 km (122 mi) west of Winnipeg.*

Brandon, Manitoba's second-largest city (population 40,000), is west of Winnipeg, along the Trans-Canada Highway. The **Commonwealth Air Training Plan Museum** contains pre–World War II aircraft from the time when the Royal Canadian Air Force had a major training school here. ✉ *Hangar 1, Brandon Airport,* ☎ *204/727–2444.* ⊡ *$3.* ☉ *May–Oct., daily 10–4; Nov.–Apr., daily 1–4.*

Spruce Woods Provincial Heritage Park

74 *180 km (112 mi) west of Winnipeg.*

In this park, among rolling hills covered with spruce and basswood, lies the desertlike **Spirit Sands,** a 16-square-km (7-square-mi) tract of cactus-filled sand dunes. Walk the self-guided trail through the dunes, but keep your eyes peeled for lizards and snakes. Your final destination will be **Devil's Punch Bowl,** a dramatic pit dug out by an underground stream. You can also tour the park in a horse-drawn covered wagon. The nearest town is Carberry, north of the park. ✉ *Rte. 5,* ☎ *204/827–2543.* ☉ *May–Sept., daily.*

Falcon Lake

Ⓟ *143 km (89 mi) east of Winnipeg.*

The Falcon Lake development, within a lovely provincial park, has a shopping center, a golf course, tennis courts, a very good beach, a sailing club, and top-grade accommodations in the 34-room **Falcon Lake Resort & Club** (☏ 204/349–8400). **Whiteshell Provincial Park,** a 2,590-square-km (984-square-mi) tract on the edge of the Canadian Shield, has 200 lakes with superb northern-pike, perch, walleye, and lake-trout fishing. **Beaver Creek** trail is a short walk to such wilderness denizens as beaver and deer. Farther on, **West Hawk Lake** (or Crater Lake)—formed a few thousand years ago by a falling meteor—is 365 ft deep and full of feisty smallmouth bass. Scuba divers love it. ⊞ *Hwy. 1E,* ☏ *204/369–5232.* ☉ *Daily 8 AM–11 PM.*

Hecla Island

Ⓠ *175 km (109 mi) north of Winnipeg.*

Hecla Provincial Park, about a 2½-hour drive from Winnipeg, is a densely wooded archipelago named for the Icelandic volcano that drove the area's original settlers to Canada. The park is on the central North American flyway, and 50,000 waterfowl summer here. **Moose Tower** is a good spot in the early morning and evening to view moose and other wildlife. The original 1880s **Hecla Icelandic Fishing Village** is restored near Gull Harbour, the tourist center of the park and site of the luxurious **Gull Harbour Resort** (☏ 204/475–2354), complete with a marina, hiking trails, and a devilishly difficult golf course. ⊞ *Rte. 8,* ☏ *204/378–2945.* ☉ *Daily, 24 hrs.*

Wasagaming

Ⓡ *304 km (188 mi) northwest of Winnipeg via Hwys. 1 and 10.*

★ The town of Wasagming serves Manitoba's only national park. **Riding Mountain National Park** lies among rolling hills south of Dauphin in the western part of the province. It covers 3,026 square km (1,150 square mi) and comprises forests and grasslands that support a herd of bison. Wasagaming is on Clear Lake, which is ideal for fishing and boating and offers supervised swimming. There is also a highly acclaimed 18-hole golf course. The **Elkhorn Ranch and Resort** (⊞ Box 40, Rte. 10, Dauphin, R0J 2H0, ☏ 204/848–2802) has a 9-hole golf course, tennis, and trail rides. Camping, as well as other hotels and cabins, are nearby. ⊞ *Hwy. 10, Wasagaming R0J 2HO,* ☏ *204/848–2811.*

Churchill

★ Ⓢ *1,600 km (992 mi) north of Winnipeg.*

Churchill, on the shore of Hudson Bay, is Canada's northernmost seaport and a mecca for international travelers wanting to see polar bears up close. It's also a large grain-exporting center. **Tundra Buggy Tours** (☏ 204/675–2121 or 800/544–5049) has specially designed vehicles that go out on the tundra for better viewing. Half-day tours, offered July–September, cost $74; full-day tours, offered in October and early November, cost $162. You can ride a Tundra Buggy to the Tundra Buggy Lodge. The lodge, similar to a train, has viewing balconies, berths, and a dining car, and is stationed in the Churchill wilderness wherever wildlife viewing is best.

THE PRAIRIE PROVINCES A TO Z

Arriving and Departing

By Bus

Greyhound Lines (☎ 800/231–2222 in the U.S., 800/661–8747 in Canada) and local bus companies provide service from the United States, other parts of Canada, and throughout the prairie provinces.

By Car

From the United States, interstate highways cross the Canadian border, and two-lane highways continue on to major cities of the prairie provinces. From Minneapolis, I–94 and then I–29 connect to Route 75 at the Manitoba border south of Winnipeg. A main route to Alberta is I–15 north of Helena, Montana, which connects to Highway 2 and Routes 3 and 4 to Calgary.

By Plane

Air Canada and **Canadian Airlines International** have direct or connecting service from Boston, New York, Chicago, San Francisco, and Los Angeles to Winnipeg, Regina, Saskatoon, Calgary, and Edmonton. Commuter affiliates serve other U.S. and Canadian destinations. **U.S. airlines** serving the prairie provinces include Northwest to Winnipeg; and American, Delta, and United to Calgary; American, Delta, and Northwest to Edmonton (☞ Air Travel *in* the Gold Guide).

By Train

There is no direct rail service between the United States and the prairie provinces. **VIA Rail** trains (☎ 800/361–3677 from New York and Connecticut; 800/561–3949 from the Atlantic seaboard; 800/387–1144 from the Midwest; 800/665–0200 from the western United States) connect eastern Canada and the West Coast through Winnipeg–Saskatoon–Edmonton.

Getting Around

By Car

Two main east–west highways link the major cities of the prairie provinces. The Trans-Canada Highway (Highway 1), mostly a four-lane divided freeway, runs through Winnipeg, Regina, and Calgary on its nationwide course. The two-lane Yellowhead Highway (Highway 16) branches off the Trans-Canada Highway west of Winnipeg and heads northwest toward Saskatoon, Saskatchewan, and Edmonton, Alberta. Traveling north–south, four-lane divided freeways connect Saskatoon–Regina (Highway 11) and Edmonton–Calgary (Highway 2).

By Plane

Canadian Airlines International (☎ 204/632–1250 or 800/426–7000) offers flights to cities and towns throughout the prairie provinces.

By Train

VIA Rail (☎ 800/561–8630) operates train service between major cities and towns on two east–west routes through the prairie provinces.

Contacts and Resources

Visitor Information

Travel Alberta (✉ 10155 102nd St. NW, Edmonton T5J 4G8, ☎ 403/427–4321; 800/222–6501 in Alberta; 800/661–8888 in the U.S. and Canada) distributes comprehensive and useful promotional literature. **Travel Manitoba** (✉ 155 Carlton St., 7th floor, Winnipeg R3C 3H8, ☎ 204/945–3777 or 800/665–0040) distributes a free road map and several helpful brochures. **Manitoba Travel Idea Centre** (⊠ 21 Forks Market Rd., Winnipeg R3C 4T7, ☎ 204/945–3777) is intended primarily for walk-in traffic and is open weekdays. **Manitoba Travel Information Centres,** just inside the Manitoba border along major routes, are open mid-May through early September. **Tourism Saskatchewan** (⊠ 1900 Albert St., Suite 500, Regina S4P 4L9, ☎ 800/667–7191) can provide you with brochures and maps of attractions, accommodations, and parks. **Information centers** in cities throughout Saskatchewan also open in summer along major highways leading into the province.

6 Toronto

Founded by Scots who set up banks and built churches, Toronto now thrives on a mix of cultures. You'll experience these in attractions that range from the staid architecture of its abundant bank buildings to the sensual overload of ethnic markets and eateries. This cosmopolitan city on Lake Ontario has high-tone temples of art and culture, a vibrant theater scene, and plenty of action, whether you want to shop in tony Yorkville or funky Queen Street West or explore the scene along the city's revived waterfront.

Updated by
Terrence
Moloney

MUCH OF TORONTO'S EXCITEMENT is explained by its ethnic diversity. Nearly two-thirds of the 3.2 million people who now live in the metropolitan area were born and raised somewhere else. A half million Italians live here, as do the largest Chinese community in eastern Canada and the biggest Portuguese population in North America. What this has meant to Toronto is the rather rapid creation of a mix of cultures—but without the slums, crowding, and tensions found in many other large cities around the world.

Still, to give to its developing ethnic population all, or even most, of the credit for Toronto's becoming a cosmopolitan, world-class city in just a few decades would not be totally correct. Much of the thanks must be given to the so-called dour Scots who set up the banks, built the churches, and created a solid base for a community that would come to such a healthy fruition in the four decades following World War II. Toronto, Canada's largest city, is clearly this country's center of culture, commerce, and communications—"New York run by the Swiss," according to Peter Ustinov.

Toronto has gained the nickname Hollywood North, because many major films have been made in this city, especially over the past 15 years, from Norman Jewison's *Moonstruck* to David Cronenberg's controversial *Crash* and Tim Allen's *The Santa Clause* to such popular TV series as *Road to Avonlea*. Indeed, it is hard to walk about the city nowadays without tripping over a movie crew and a number of celebrities. The city's literary community, too, is abuzz with interest from Hollywood ever since the blockbuster success of Toronto writer Michael Ondatjee's *The English Patient*.

Toronto's roots go back to 1615, when a French explorer named Etienne Brûlé was led by Hurons to the land between the Humber and Don rivers, which was known to the Indians as Toronto ("a place of meetings"). Over the following two centuries it became a busy native village named Teiaiagon, a French trading post, and a British town named York. Finally, on March 6, 1834, the city was officially named Toronto again. In 1998, Toronto and the surrounding municipalities of North York, York, East York, Scarborough, and Etobicoke merged into one "MegaCity" in the interest of reducing government and providing efficient social services.

Pleasures and Pastimes

Dining
The Toronto restaurant scene is in a state of perpetual motion, fueled by the surging economy and a savvy dining-out public. Even formal haute cuisine establishments are experiencing a renaissance, joining the ever-swelling ranks of bistros, cantinas, tavernas, trattorias, tapas bars, noodle bars, wine bars, and smart cafés. Red meat is making a comeback, and along with steak houses come cigar and martini lounges. Meanwhile, the cuisines of the world have appeared on Toronto's doorstep. Little Italy, a half dozen individual Chinatowns, and Little India have fine restaurants. The cooking of Southeast Asia—in a tidal wave of Korean, Vietnamese, Laotian, Thai, and Malaysian restaurants—is taking taste buds by storm with its assertive, clean flavors: chili, ginger, lemongrass, coconut, lime, and tamarind. Toronto's brilliant young chefs recognize that when most customers start requesting "sauce on the side," the public's collective taste is changing; those with vision are looking over their shoulders toward California and Asia for a more creative marriage of fresh-market ingredients.

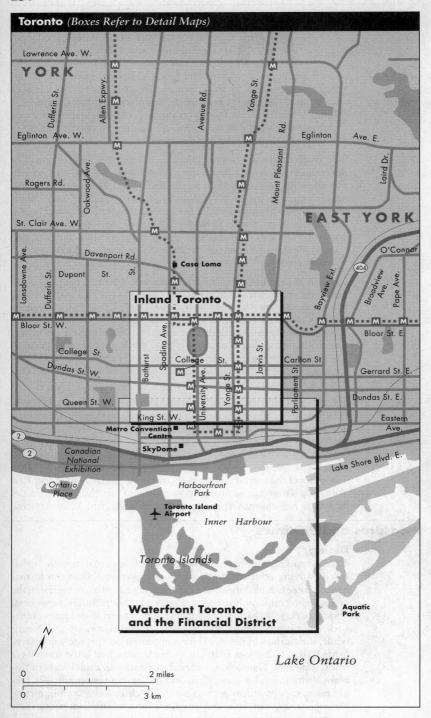

Toronto *(Boxes Refer to Detail Maps)*

YORK

Lawrence Ave. W.

Dufferin St.

Allen Expwy.

Avenue Rd.

Yonge St.

Eglinton Ave. W.

Oakwood Ave.

Mount Pleasant Rd.

Eglinton Ave. E.

Laird Dr.

Rogers Rd.

EAST YORK

St. Clair Ave. W.

Lansdowne Ave.

Dufferin St.

Davenport Rd.

Dupont St.

St.

O'Connor

Bayview Ext.

Broadview Ave.

Pape Ave.

Casa Loma

Inland Toronto

Bloor St. W.

Spadina Ave.

Bloor St. E.

College St.

Bathurst

College St.

University Ave.

Yonge St.

Jarvis St.

Carlton St.

Gerrard St. E.

Dundas St. W.

Queen St. W.

Parliament St.

Dundas St. E.

King St. W.

Eastern Ave.

Metro Convention Centre

SkyDome

Lake Shore Blvd. E.

Canadian National Exhibition

Ontario Place

Harbourfront Park

Toronto Island Airport

Inner Harbour

Toronto Islands

Waterfront Toronto and the Financial District

Aquatic Park

Lake Ontario

N

0   2 miles
0   3 km

Museums

This metropolis by the lake possesses miles of museums. The Royal Ontario Museum, affectionately known as the ROM, is a sprawling giant that presents a brilliant and wildly diverse collection from mummies and Chinese art to totem poles and musical instruments. For art lovers, Toronto is the place to explore Canadian art, which is definitely overlooked by most American and European curators. The Art Gallery of Ontario is one place to start, and the McMichael Canadian Art Collection in Kleinburg has a superb collection set in lovely woodland. Another outstanding institution is the Ontario Science Centre. Then, too, the city has offbeat museums devoted to the study of hockey, design, history, and even shoes.

Outdoor Activities and Sports

Sports are more of a religion than a pastime here. The big professional baseball, basketball, football, and hockey teams are considered civic treasures. When the Toronto Blue Jays won the World Series in 1992 and 1993, the province-wide celebration was felt across Canada. In 1996 the Toronto Argonauts football team won the 84th annual national contest for the coveted Grey Cup. When Toronto residents aren't watching sports, many pursue fitness. In the warmer months, the streets and lakefront brim with bikers, runners, in-line skaters, and walkers. When winter comes, outdoor ice-skating is very popular, especially at Harbourfront and at Nathan Phillips Square.

Performing Arts

Canada's capital of the lively arts, Toronto has also become the third most important theater city in the English-speaking world, after New York and London. Productions range from the finest in classic and contemporary drama to West End and Broadway productions. True, Winnipeg has a very fine ballet, and Montréal's orchestra is superb. But no other city in Canada, and few in North America, can compete with the variety of music, opera, dance, and theater found here.

Shopping

Toronto prides itself on having some of the finest shopping in North America; indeed, most of the world's name boutiques can be found here. There's also a large artistic and crafts community, with many art galleries, custom jewelers, clothing designers, and artisans selling everything from sophisticated glass sculpture to native art, traditional crafts, antiques, quilts, wood carvings, and pine furniture. Local food items include wild rice, available in bulk or in gift packages, and maple syrup in jars or cans.

EXPLORING TORONTO

Imagine the downtown area of Toronto as a large rectangle. The southern boundary is Lake Ontario. The western edge, shooting north to Bloor Street (the northern edge) and beyond, is Spadina Avenue, near the foot of which stand the CN (Canadian National) Tower, Harbourfront, and the spectacular SkyDome Stadium. Just west of the rectangle along the waterfront are the Canadian National Exhibition (CNE) grounds, site of the enormous annual fair (☞ Festivals and Seasonal Events *in* Chapter 1), and Ontario Place, an upscale amusement park built on man-made islands. Toward the east side of downtown, running from the lakefront north, is Yonge Street, which divides the city in half. University Avenue, a major road that parallels Yonge Street, changes its name to Avenue Road at the corner of Bloor Street, next to the Royal Ontario Museum. A further note: College Street, legitimately named, as many of the University of Toronto's buildings run along it, becomes Carlton Street where it intersects Yonge Street, then heads east.

Numbers in the text correspond to numbers in the margin and on the Waterfront Toronto and the Financial District and Inland Toronto maps.

Great Itineraries

A week's visit to Canada's largest city would give you time to explore the city's major sights and intriguing neighborhoods, as well as visit outstanding attractions outside the center. In three days, however, you can take in the cultural and architectural highlights downtown and near the waterfront and get a taste of Toronto's cultural life, whether you see a play or attend a concert. A few more days would provide time to visit the Toronto Islands, explore some city markets and shop in a number of neighborhoods, and check out some museums; you'd also be able to savor the city's varied dining scene more fully.

IF YOU HAVE 3 DAYS

Start an exploration of downtown Toronto at the grandiose Union Station; glance upward at the famed Royal York Hotel, which has defined Toronto's cityscape since 1928. Head north on Yonge, surveying the towering edifices of pride and progress in the financial district, before arriving at Eaton Centre with its more than 300 shops, services, and restaurants. Exit on Queen Street West and behold the magnificent New City Hall. Cold weather permitting, rent skates and glide across Nathan Phillips Square. On Day 2, ride the subway to Bloor and Yonge. Walk west along Bloor Street—an upscale shopping thoroughfare—to Avenue Road, where the Royal Ontario Museum awaits; plan on spending two to four hours at the museum. Exit the ROM on University Avenue, walking south to Queen's Park, home of Ontario's Romanesque-inspired Provincial Parliament Building. On Day 3, visit the Art Gallery of Ontario, which contains the largest collection in the world of Henry Moore sculptures. After that, you can stroll along the waterfront, stopping at the Queen's Quay Terminal at Harbourfront and passing by the SkyDome. On a clear day, ride to the peak of the CN Tower.

IF YOU HAVE 5 DAYS

Extra time offers the opportunity to experience the city as locals live it. Besides the attractions mentioned in the three-day tour, you might try these: On a Saturday, conquer either the Kensington or St. Lawrence Market (☞ Shopping, *below*). Both are vibrant ventures, although the St. Lawrence at Front and Jarvis streets is larger and indoors. In summer, buy fresh ingredients for a picnic lunch before cruising across Lake Ontario on a ferry boat to the Toronto Islands. Plan either to walk or bike on the islands—no automobiles are permitted. In the late afternoon, you can explore Queen Street West—an exotic mix of the avant-garde. On Day 5, return to the Yorkville district, the epicenter of wealthy Toronto. Beyond the designer boutiques and elegant restaurants, check out the Bata Shoe Museum and, farther north, Casa Loma, a 20th-century medieval-style castle.

IF YOU HAVE 7 DAYS

Follow the three- and five-day itineraries above; then, on Day Six, rent a car (or use subways and buses) and choose among some easy, first-rate excursions (☞ Side Trips from Downtown Toronto, *below*). North of downtown, the Black Creek Pioneer Village re-creates a rural community of the 1880s; it's open May–December. Farther north and west, you can visit the stunning McMichael Canadian Art Collection, on more than 100 acres of meadows. Its collection champions Canada's landscape artists known as the Group of Seven and is augmented by native and contemporary artworks. Northeast of downtown are the Ontario Science Centre and the Metro Toronto Zoo. These are great for kids; either could occupy a day. Day 7 would be a good time for exploring overlooked neighborhoods and sights, such as the Design Exchange and the Hockey Hall of Fame.

The Toronto Islands

The islands form a pleasant park with numerous attractions, including a stunning view of the Toronto skyline. The four main thin, curved, tree-lined islands—Centre, Ward's, Algonquin, and Olympic—have been attracting visitors since 1833, four years before Victoria became queen and just a year before the town of York changed its name to Toronto.

A Good Walk

Just behind the giant Westin Harbour Castle is the debarkation point for ferries to the **Toronto Islands** ①. It takes only eight minutes for the quaint little ferries to chug across the tiny bay to different landings. On these islands, all transportation comes to you compliments of your feet: No cars are allowed. Your nostrils will appreciate the lack of exhaust fumes, while your feet will wonder why you insist on walking all the way along the boardwalk from Centre to Ward's Island (2½ km, or 1½ mi). You'll be wise to rent a bike (on Centre Island, a five-minute walk from the ferry) for an hour or more and work your way across the interconnected islands, perhaps with a stop at one of the island's **beaches.** If you are traveling with children, Centre Island is certainly the one to check out first. A few hundred yards from the ferry docks lies **Centreville,** an amusement park that's supposed to be a turn-of-the-century children's village. Perhaps most enjoyable for children is **Far Enough Farm,** which is near enough to walk to. Ward's Island has **Gibraltar Lighthouse.**

TIMING
The islands are at their most appealing from spring through fall. Take the earliest possible ferry and return at your leisure. Plan on at least staying for a picnic lunch. Families may want to stay longer. If you love the outdoors and the weather is good, plan for the entire day.

Sights to See

Beaches. The islands have great swimming areas at Hanlan's Point, Manitou Beach, and Ward's Island. The beaches on Ward's tend to be the least crowded and also the cleanest; Lake Ontario's water has had problems with the cleanliness over the past decade. There are free changing rooms near each area but no facilities for checking your clothes. Swimming in the various lagoons and channels is prohibited. Except for the hottest days in August, the Great Lake tends to be uncomfortably chilly, so bring appropriate clothing.

☙ **Centreville.** The concept works wondrously well: True, the pizza, fries, and hot dogs are barely edible—pack a lunch!—but the little Main Street has charming shops, a town hall, a little railroad station, and more than a dozen rides, including a restored 1890s merry-go-round with more than four dozen hand-carved animals. There's no entrance fee to the modest, 14-acre amusement park, although you'll have to pay for each ride or buy an all-day pass. ⊠ *Centre Island,* ☎ *416/234–2345 in winter; 416/203–1113 in summer.* ⌨ *Day pass $18.* ☼ *Mid-May–Labor Day, weekdays 10:30–6, weekends 10:30–8; Labor Day–Oct., weekends 10:30–6, weather permitting.*

☙ **Far Enough Farm.** This petting zoo has all kinds of animals to pet and feed, ranging from piglets to geese, cows to birds. It's a great treat for youngsters, especially the smaller ones. ⊠ *Centre Island,* ☎ *416/393–8195.* ⌨ *Free.* ☼ *Daily, dawn–dusk.*

Waterfront Toronto and the Financial District

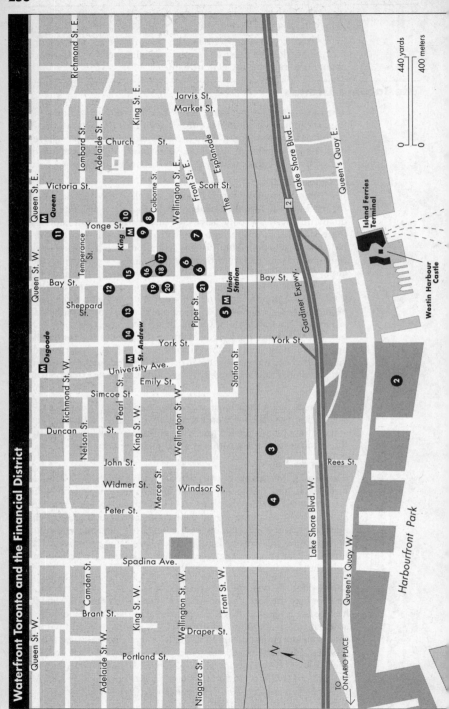

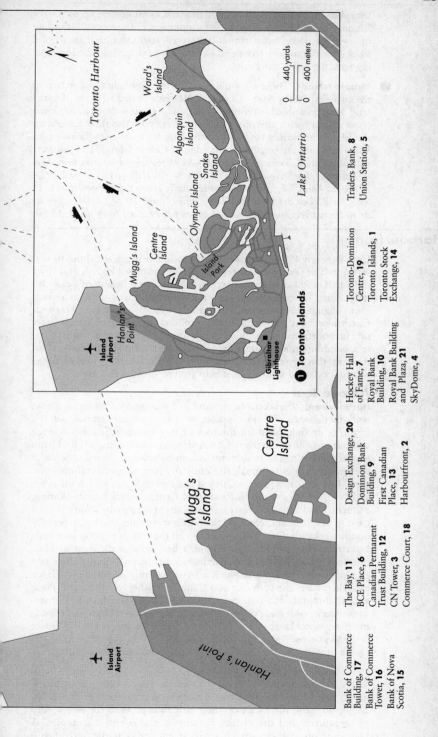

1 Toronto Islands

Bank of Commerce
Building, **17**
Bank of Commerce
Tower, **16**
Bank of Nova
Scotia, **15**

The Bay, **11**
BCE Place, **6**
Canadian Permanent
Trust Building, **12**
CN Tower, **3**
Commerce Court, **18**

Design Exchange, **20**
Dominion Bank
Building, **9**
First Canadian
Place, **13**
Harbourfront, **2**

Hockey Hall
of Fame, **7**
Royal Bank
Building, **10**
Royal Bank Building
and Plaza, **21**
SkyDome, **4**

Toronto-Dominion
Centre, **19**
Toronto Islands, **1**
Toronto Stock
Exchange, **14**

Traders Bank, **8**
Union Station, **5**

Gibraltar Lighthouse. Built in 1808 near the southwestern tip of Ward's Island, this lighthouse is the oldest monument in the city still standing on its original site, but it cannot be entered. Right next to it are a pond stocked with rainbow trout and a concession for buying bait and renting rods. ⊠ *Gibraltar Point.*

❶ Toronto Islands. These are surely among the highlights of any trip to the city—especially May–October. The more than 550 acres of parkland are irresistible for renting a bike, hiking, snowshoeing, or skiing cross-country with downtown Toronto over your shoulder. Encircling the islands are sandy ☞ **beaches**; the best are on the southeast tip of Ward's Island, the southernmost edge of Centre Island, and the west side of Hanlan's Point. ☎ *416/392–8195 for island information. Ferries, foot of Bay St. and Queen's Quay,* ☎ *416/392–8193 or 416/392–8186.* 🚢 *Ferry $4.* ☉ *Ferries winter, daily every ½ hr or so from 6:35 AM (Ward's) or 8:15 AM (Hanlan's Point) until 10 or 11 AM, every hr or so thereafter; summer, daily 3 times per hr. Last ferry at 11:45 PM.*

Harbourfront

Until the early 1980s, Toronto was notoriously negligent about its waterfront. The Gardiner Expressway, Lake Shore Boulevard, and rusty rail yards stood as hideous barriers to the natural beauty of Lake Ontario. Some 15 years ago the various levels of government began a struggle to change this situation. First came the handsome Westin Harbour Castle Hotel and a tower of condominiums at the foot of Yonge Street on Harbourfront. Today these buildings are just part of a group of hotels, condominiums, shopping malls, and recreational and cultural attractions that stretch for almost a mile along the lakefront west of Yonge Street. Taxis and a transit line help you get around this area.

A Good Tour

Harbourfront ②, a lakefront cultural and recreational center, is within walking distance of Union Station (☞ The Financial District, *below*). If you're driving, head for the foot of Bay Street or Spadina Avenue and park in one of the many lots. A streetcar also swings around from Union Station to Harbourfront and on to Spadina Avenue. Begin at the Queen's Quay Terminal, an eight-story shopping and cultural complex. Just west of Queen's Quay is the Power Plant, which hosts art shows. Next door is the Harbourfront Centre, which has ice-skating, canoeing, and concerts. You can rent boats at the nearby Nautical Centre. On Maple Leaf Quay, visit the outdoor antiques market, especially on the weekends. Otherwise, you can visit the very popular indoor Harbourfront Antique Market. About a half-hour walk west of Harbourfront (you can use the transit line along Queen's Quay to take you part of the way) is **Ontario Place,** a 96-acre family-oriented experience that showcases the province and Canada. Visible from Ontario Place and a 10-minute cab ride away is the **CN Tower** ③, which has observation decks with great views of the area; it's on Front Street, near Spadina Avenue, not far from the waterfront. In the shadow of the CN Tower is the **SkyDome** ④ stadium. SkyDome and the CN Tower are linked to Union Station by a covered walkway lined with fast-food outlets.

TIMING

While Harbourfront buzzes throughout the year, it is especially pleasant to visit May–October, when Lake Ontario's breezes aren't so bitterly cold. Still, the locals do their best to cope with the below-zero temperatures, and the district remains a year-round destination. A Harbourfront visit can stretch across an entire day, particularly if children are along. Be sure to check the local papers and magazines for special activities and events. Set aside at least one to two hours for the CN Tower, a required stop for first-time visitors.

Sights to See

☁ ❸ **CN Tower.**The tallest freestanding structure in the world, fully 1,815 ft, 5 inches high, is worth a visit despite the steep fee, if the weather is clear. Four elevators zoom up the outside of the tower. The ride takes but a minute, going at 20 ft a second, a rate of ascent similar to that of a jet-plane takeoff. But each elevator has only one floor-to-ceiling glass wall, preventing vertigo. The CN Tower resembles a self-contained amusement park: The **Skypod,** about two-thirds of the way up the tower, is seven stories high and has two observation decks, a nightclub, and a restaurant (☞ Dining, *below*) that revolves 360°. The tower was originally constructed to house microwave communication equipment for the Canadian National Railway, but unfortunately for techno buffs this is not open to the public. Level 2 of the Skypod is the **outdoor observation deck,** with an enclosed promenade and an outdoor balcony with a breathtaking **Glass Floor**—solid glass that is five times heavier than demanded for standard construction, through which you can look 1,122 ft straight down to the ground. Level 3, the **indoor observation deck,** has not only conventional telescopes but also high-powered periscopes that almost simulate flight. A unique Tour Wand System provides an audio tour of the city of Toronto. A minitheater shows a presentation on the CN Tower. Here you can also visit the **EcoDek,** multimedia environmental displays that explore air, water, land, and urban issues. The **Space Deck,** 33 stories higher, at an elevation of 1,465 ft, is the world's highest public observation gallery. Even from the Skypod below, you can often see Lake Simcoe to the north and the mist rising from Niagara Falls to the south. All the decks provide spectacular panoramic views of Toronto, Lake Ontario, and the Toronto Islands. Peak visiting hours are 11–4, particularly on weekends; you may wish to work around them. At the base of the CN Tower are several high-tech action rides and games as well as a food court. ⊠ *301 Front St. W,* ☎ *416/868–6937 or 416/362–5411 (restaurant).* ⌖ *Observation deck and Glass Floor $15; $3 additional for Space Deck; action attractions $6.* ☉ *Summer, Sun.–Thurs. 9 AM–10 PM, Fri.–Sat. 9 AM–11 PM; fall–spring times vary by up to an hr, so call ahead.*

★ ❷ **Harbourfront.** This 100-acre waterfront culture and recreation center, which draws more than 3 million visitors each year, stretches along Queen's Quay from York Street for nearly a mile to Bathurst Street. The trip is well worth planning for: Check *Now* magazine, *Eye Weekly* magazine, the Thursday edition of the *Toronto Star,* and Saturday's *Globe and Mail* to see what concerts, dances, art shows, and festivals are taking place, and build your visit around them. More than 100 dealers crowd the **Harbourfront Antique Market** (⊠ 390 Queen's Quay W, ☎ 416/260–2626) in a sprawling warehouse, peddling everything from Victorian candlesticks to 18th-century furniture, modern collectibles to vintage jewelry. At **Harbourfront Centre** (⊠ 235 Queen's Quay W, ☎ 416/973–3000) craftspeople—working in glass, metal, ceramics, and textiles—create in full view of the public. There are also concerts, live theater, and readings here. The center's York Quay Gallery presents crafts as well as fine arts, while the Bounty gift shop showcases contemporary crafts. A shallow pond at the south end is used for canoe lessons in warmer months and as the largest artificial ice-skating rink in Ontario in more wintry times. There are concerts at **Molson Place,** a band shell beside the water. The **Nautical Centre** (⊠ 283 Queen's Quay W, ☎ 416/973–4094) has many private firms renting vessels and offering sailing and canoeing lessons. On **Maple Leaf Quay,** an outdoor antiques market of 70 or so dealers doubles in size on Sun-

day. The **Queen's Quay Terminal** (✉ 207 Queen's Quay W, ☎ 416/
203–0510) is a 57-year-old food warehouse transformed into a magnificent eight-story structure with delightful (though pricey) specialty
shops, eateries, and the handsome 450-seat Premiere Dance Theatre.
The **Power Plant** (✉ 231 Queen's Quay W, ☎ 416/973–4949), in a
1927 building with a tall red smokestack, hosts exhibitions of contemporary arts, with a focus on Canadian art—painting, sculpture, architecture, video, photography, design, installation, and performance
art. Besides exhibition space, the Power Plant holds the DuMaurier Theatre (☎ 416/973–3000), which mounts a variety of live performances.
The newest attraction at Harbourfront is **The Pier** (✉ 245 Queen's Quay
West, ☎ 416/392–1990), dedicated to exploring the city's waterfront
heritage. It's open daily; admission is $7.

🐾 **Ontario Place.** From mid-May through September, this waterfront entertainment complex on three man-made islands brims with people and
concerts. Its architectural centerpiece is the **Cinesphere,** an homage to
Buckminster Fuller's acclaimed geodesic dome at Expo '67. Inside the
dome a six-story movie screen shows IMAX and 70mm films. You can
explore the *Haida,* a World War II destroyer. Nightly concerts take place
at the outdoor **Molson Canadian Amphitheatre. Children's Village** has
water games, slides, puppet shows, clowns, magicians, and a children's theater. ✉ *South of Lake Shore Blvd.,* ☎ *416/314–9900.* ✉
Free; charge for some individual attractions. ⊙ *Mid-May–mid-Sept.,
daily 10 AM–midnight.*

🐾 ❹ **SkyDome.** One of Toronto's newest and most famous landmarks, the
home of baseball's Blue Jays was the world's first stadium with a fully
retractable roof. Toronto has lost no opportunity to honor its World
Series–winning team—the official address of SkyDome is 1 Blue Jays
Way. One way to see the huge 52,000-seat stadium is to buy tickets
for a Blue Jays game or one of the many other events that take place
here. These may include cricket matches, Wrestlemania, monster truck
races, family ice shows, rock concerts, or even the opera *Aïda.* You can
also take a one-hour guided walking tour (including a 15-minute film).
The tours are not available, however, when daytime events are scheduled. ✉ *Tour entrance: Front and John Sts., between Gates 1 and 2,
northeast corner of SkyDome,* ☎ *416/341–2770 for tours, 416/341–
3663 for events and shows, 416/341–1000 for Blue Jays games.* ✉
Tour $9.50. ⊙ *Tours daily; call ahead for specific times.*

The Financial District

In this epicenter of Canada's commercial life, the nation's leading
banks have erected towering skyscrapers, handsome and modern monuments to their achievements. Many banks have more than one building named for them, reflecting the new ethic of recycling and reusing
old buildings even if corporate pride requires the building of a fancier,
more up-to-date headquarters. Many of the 20th century's best and
brightest architects have contributed to Toronto's skyline, including I.
M. Pei, Edward Durrell Stone, Mies van der Rohe, and Santiago Calatrava, among others. Running below all of this design splendor is the
Underground City, a dazzling maze of tunnels that links the Financial
District and keeps businesspeople warm during the long cold season.

A Good Walk

On the south side of Front Street, between York and Bay streets across
from the handsome Royal York Hotel, stands the monumental **Union
Station** ⑤. On Bay Street just north of Front Street, a number of historic buildings have been incorporated into the striking **BCE Place** ⑥,
with its huge, sophisticated galleria. A block east, at the northwest cor-

ner of Front Street and Yonge Street, is the **Hockey Hall of Fame** ⑦, in a former branch of the Bank of Montréal now incorporated into BCE Place. Continue north on Yonge Street until you reach the northeast corner of Yonge and Colborne, where you will see the 1905–06 **Traders Bank** ⑧, the first skyscraper in the city. The next building to the north, built in 1913, is owned by Canadian Pacific, the famous company whose transcontinental railroad literally helped build a country. At the southwest corner of King and Yonge streets is the **Dominion Bank Building** ⑨, erected in 1913. Diagonally across the intersection is the first **Royal Bank Building** ⑩.

Farther north along Yonge Street, at Richmond Street West, is the original Simpsons department store, now **The Bay** ⑪. Outside, continue a few steps west to Bay Street, a name synonymous with finance and power in Canada, as Wall Street is in the United States. Head south (left), back toward the lakefront. Just south of Adelaide Street, on the west side of Bay Street, is the **Canadian Permanent Trust Building** ⑫. Turn right (west) along King Street, and on your right stands the first of the towering bank buildings that have defined Toronto's skyline over the past two decades. Here is **First Canadian Place** ⑬, built in the early 1970s. Farther along you come to the second phase of the project, opened in 1983, which houses the ultramodern **Toronto Stock Exchange** ⑭.

Returning to Bay Street, on the northeast corner of King and Bay streets, you see the **Bank of Nova Scotia** ⑮, built between 1949 and 1951 and partially replaced by the modern Scotia Tower just to the east. On the southeast corner of King and Bay streets is the "old" **Bank of Commerce Tower** ⑯, which for a third of a century was the tallest building in the British Commonwealth. Tucked behind this tower is the **Bank of Commerce Building** ⑰, built between 1929 and 1931 and one of Toronto's premiere bank buildings. The company's 57-story glass and stainless steel **Commerce Court** ⑱ is just south of the "old tower." Due west, across Bay Street, also on the south side of King Street, are the five black towers of the **Toronto-Dominion Centre** ⑲, the first international-style skyscrapers built in Toronto, which houses the bank's Gallery of Inuit Art, one of the finest of its kind in Canada. Immediately to the south of the Toronto-Dominion Centre towers is the fabulous **Design Exchange** ⑳, an exposition complex housed in the former Toronto Stock Exchange Building of 1937. Walk south another block to the northwest corner of Bay and Front streets: Here, in all its golden glory, is the **Royal Bank Plaza** ㉑. Running beneath the financial district is Toronto's **Underground City,** a sprawling maze of convenience shops, lobbies, and even trees.

TIMING

Plan on spending at least half a day in the Financial District, more if you stop at the various museums and shops along the way. Since many of these acclaimed buildings are closed on Saturday and Sunday, schedule this walk during a weekday. Be aware that during the cold season these edifices create chilling wind tunnels; dress appropriately and use the walkways of the Underground City if you need to.

Sights to See

⑰ **Bank of Commerce Building.** Nearly 70 years after its completion in 1931, this ranks as the most stunning office tower in the financial district, combining monumentality and grace in a 34-story structure. The Romanesque exterior is awe-inspiring, as is the equally compelling interior of marble floors, limestone walls, and bronze vestibule doors decorated with masks, owls, and animals. In the alcoves on each side of the entrance, murals trace the history of transportation. The bronze elevator doors are richly decorated; the vaulted banking hall is illuminated by period chandeliers. It's so beautiful that visitors are inclined to snap a photo, but bank officials forbid it. ⊠ *25 King St. W.*

⑯ Bank of Commerce Tower. For 30 years the tallest building in the British Commonwealth, this tower has a set-back top; huge, carved human heads adorn all four sides. The base has bas-relief carvings, and there is marvelous animal and floral ornamentation around the vaulted entrance. ⊠ *King and Bay Sts.*

⑮ Bank of Nova Scotia. This 25-story 1949 building by architect John Lyle has successfully been joined to a 68-story 1989 postmodern tower, **Scotia Tower.** The original building is in neoclassical style. Above the large exterior windows are sculptural panels inspired by Greek mythology. In the lobby, reliefs symbolizing four regions of Canada fill the walls below a brightly colored, gilded plaster ceiling. The north-wall relief depicts some of the industries and enterprises financed by the bank. The original stainless-steel-and-glass stairway decorated with marine motifs leads up to the marble counters and floors. All this opens graciously into the recent Scotia Plaza building. ⊠ *30–44 King St. W.*

⑪ The Bay. One of the city's first buildings with a steel-frame construction was built in 1895 as Simpson's department store. Later bought by the Bay, the store no longer possesses the allure of Simpson's, but the top floor's **Thompson Gallery** (☎ 416/861–4571), a private collection of 398 paintings, all by Canadian artists, is worth a visit and the $2.75 admission fee. It holds the largest collection of Canadian impressionist paintings in the world, including more than 300 works by the Group of Seven and their peers. Ken Thompson recently sold his shares in the Bay, but gallery operators expect the collection to remain at the flagship store. The Bay's mélange of buildings blankets an entire block. The most stunning is the six-story 1907 structure at Queen and Yonge streets, with attractive terra-cotta decorations. The Bay is owned by Hudson's Bay Company, North America's oldest company, which received a fur-trading charter from King Charles II in 1670. ⊠ *160–184 Yonge St.,* ☎ *416/861–9111.* ☺ *Mon.–Sat. 11–5.*

⑥ BCE Place. Completed in 1990, this granite-and-glass mixed-use structure presents a dramatic contrast of old and new and represents the last hurrah of Toronto's 1980s building boom. What a triumph! Two towers—51 and 44 stories—incorporate 12 historic buildings, including the original Bank of Montréal building, plus a magnificent six-story galleria atrium designed by Santiago Calatrava. ⊠ *161 Bay St.*

⑫ Canadian Permanent Trust Building. This stout skyscraper in the New York wedding-cake style was built in 1929. Ornate stone carvings decorate both the lower stories and the top, where carved, stylized faces peer down to the street below. The imposing vaulted entrance has polished brass doors, and even the elevator doors in the foyer are embossed brass. The spacious banking hall has a vaulted ceiling, marble walls and pillars, and a marble floor with mosaic borders. ⊠ *320 Bay St.*

⑱ Commerce Court. The ☞ Bank of Commerce's sister structure is a 57-story stainless-steel-and-glass tower built in 1968. ⊠ *243 Bay St.*

⑳ Design Exchange. Since its opening in 1994, the DX has emerged as North America's most innovative design exposition and promotion center, encompassing architecture, decorative arts, graphics, and interiors. All this glory stands in a stunning Art Deco structure of polished pink granite and smooth buff limestone that once housed the Toronto Stock Exchange. The Toronto-based architectural firm of KPMB Associates gracefully blended the past with the present here, preserving Charles Comfort's famed murals above the historic trading floor. Exhibits rotate, so check the local paper to see what's on. ✉ *234 Bay St.,* ☎ *416/216–2160.* 🎫 *$5.* ☉ *Tues.–Fri. 10–6, weekends noon–5.*

❾ Dominion Bank Building. Erected in 1913, this classic Chicago-style skyscraper has a marble and bronze stairway leading to the second floor. Upstairs, the opulent banking hall has a marble floor and marble walls. On the ornate plaster ceiling are reproduced the coats of arms of the nine Canadian provinces in existence at the time it was built. ✉ *King and Yonge Sts., southwest corner.*

⓭ First Canadian Place. This 72-story office tower is difficult to miss. Designed in the early 1970s by Edward Durrell Stone for the Bank of Montréal, the edifice is covered in Italian white marble. He deliberately faced it with white to contrast with the black of the Toronto-Dominion Centre, to the south, and with the silver of the Commerce Court tower, diagonally opposite. The marble theme continues inside the glamorous lobby. ✉ *50 King St. W.*

☙ ❼ Hockey Hall of Fame. Writer John Robert Columbo observed that the two distinctly Canadian institutions are the United Church of Canada and the National Hockey League. So, it is appropriate that in this world-hockey capital sits a first-rate tribute to the fast and furious winter sport. In addition to showcasing the coveted Stanley Cup trophy, the Hall of Fame contains 13 areas, including one where you can take shots at a computer-generated target; another is a precise replica (right down to the trainer's whirlpool) of the Montréal Canadiens' dressing room. A gift store carries an array of hockey jerseys, skates, and other apparel, as well as souvenirs. Even non-hockey fans can appreciate this multimedia exhibition, which is inventively based in a historic branch of the Bank of Montréal dating from 1893. An archive and resource library is also available by appointment. ✉ *BCE Place, Concourse Level, northwest corner of Yonge and Front Sts.,* ☎ *416/360–7765.* 🎫 *$10.* ☉ *Weekdays 10–5, Sat. 9:30–6, Sun. 10:30–5.*

❿ Royal Bank Building. Built in 1913 for the Royal Bank, it has a distinctive cornice, an overhanging roof, a decorative pattern of sculpted ox skulls above the ground-floor windows, and classically detailed leaves at the top of the Corinthian columns. ✉ *King and Yonge Sts., northeast corner.*

㉑ Royal Bank Building and Plaza. This 1976 building is already a classic of its kind. In this case, all that glitters *is* gold: the exterior is coated with 2,500 ounces of the precious ore in order to keep the heat in and the cold out (or vice versa, depending on the season). The surface creates gorgeous reflections of sky, clouds, and other buildings; it's the jewel in the crown of the Toronto skyline. Be sure to go into the 120-ft-high banking hall and admire the lovely hanging sculpture by Jesús Raphaél Soto. The building, dramatic in almost any light, is stunning in a full-force sunset. ✉ *Bay and Front Sts., northwest corner.*

⓳ Toronto-Dominion Centre. Mies van der Rohe, a master of modern architecture, designed this austere five-building masterwork, even though he died in 1969 before it was fully realized. As with his acclaimed Seagram Building in New York, Mies stripped these buildings to their skin and bones of bronze-color glass and black metal I-beams. The tallest tower reaches 56 stories. The only decoration consists of geometric repetition, and the only extravagance is the use of rich materials, such as marble counters and leather-covered furniture. Inside the low-rise square banking pavilion at King and Bay streets is a virtually intact Mies interior. Here you can visit the **Gallery of Inuit Art,** one of the few galleries in North America devoted to Inuit art. The Toronto-Dominion Bank's incredible collection equals that of the Smithsonian Institution. The gallery focuses attention on Canada's huge and unexplored northern frontier. ✉ *Center: 55 King St. W. Gallery: 79 Wellington St.,* ☎ *416/982–8473.* 🎫 *Free.* ⊙ *Weekdays 8–6, weekends 10–4.*

🐾 ⑭ **Toronto Stock Exchange.** At press time many renovations were under way at North America's third-most-active stock exchange, and new seminars and tours were being planned. The new Stock Market Place is an interactive media and learning center on the main floor of the exchange. The renovations will also include a new 400-seat auditorium, a real-time stock-quotation terminal, and avant-garde artworks by General Idea and Robert Longo. ✉ *Exchange Tower, 2 First Canadian Pl.,* ☎ *416/947–4670.* 🎫 *Free.* ⊙ *Call in advance; hrs not set at press time.*

❽ **Traders Bank.** Built in 1905–06, the first "skyscraper" in the city, 15 stories high, came complete with an observation deck, now closed. The building has been dwarfed by 50-story giants. ✉ *67 Yonge St.*

🐾 **Underground City.** The origins of what is known as the largest pedestrian walkway in the world go back over a generation. One can walk—and shop, eat, and browse—without ever seeing the light of day, from beneath Union Station to the Royal York Hotel, Toronto-Dominion Centre, First Canadian Place, Sheraton Centre, Eaton Centre, and Atrium-on-Bay. Altogether, it extends through nearly 5 km (3 mi) of tunnels and seven subway stops. If you become disoriented, head for a subway station: Maps of the underground area are posted near the turnstiles. Enter the subterranean community from anywhere between Dundas Street on the north and Union Station on the south, and you'll encounter art exhibitions, buskers, fountains, and trees growing as much as two stories high, as well as crowds of businesspeople on breaks from their offices in the towers above.

❺ **Union Station.** Designed in 1907, when trains were still as exciting as space shuttles are today, the station was opened in 1927 by the Prince of Wales. If any building in Toronto can be called monumental, this is it. More than 750 ft long and set well back along its Front Street block, this landmark borrows from classical architecture to create a magnificently powerful yet simple structure. Walk along the lengthy concourse; bask in the light flooding through the high, arched windows at each end of the mammoth hall. Try to imagine the awe of the immigrants who poured into Toronto between the wars by the tens of thousands, staring up at the towering ceiling of Italian tile or leaning against one of the 22 pillars, each 40 ft tall and weighing 75 tons. ✉ *65–75 Front St. W.*

Central Toronto

This walk highlights Toronto's commercial and cultural diversity. It begins at Eaton Centre on Yonge Street and extends west to Spadina Avenue, the city's bustling discount thoroughfare. In between lie the New City Hall and the Art Gallery of Ontario. A walk through Chinatown provides a sense of the city's ethnic diversity.

A Good Walk

Start at **Eaton Centre** ㉒, a 3-million-square-ft shopping complex extending along the west side of Yonge Street all the way from Queen Street up to Dundas Street (with subway stops at each end) that has become the city's number-one tourist draw. Exit Eaton Centre at Queen Street and walk just one long block west to Toronto's city halls. The **Old City Hall** ㉓ is the very beautiful building at the northeast corner of Queen and Bay streets, sweetly coexisting with the futuristic **New City Hall** ㉔, just across the street, on the west side. West of University

Avenue on Queen Street stands **Campbell House** ㉕, a house museum. Walk up University Avenue; just west of University Avenue begins Toronto's main **Chinatown.** Huge Chinese characters hang over the **52nd Division Police Station** ㉖ on the west side of Simcoe Street, just south of Dundas Street. Turn left off Dundas Street onto McCaul Street to enter the **Ontario College of Art and Design Gallery** ㉗. Directly across the street is **Village by the Grange** ㉘, an apartment and shopping complex. Return to Dundas Street and head west to the **Art Gallery of Ontario** ㉙. The stretch of **Spadina Avenue** from Queen Street to College Street has never been fashionable, but on it you'll find a treasure trove of offbeat stores. **Kensington Market** ㉚ is a delightful side tour off Spadina Avenue, where you'll find bargains of the more edible kind. Afterward, you can rest in **Bellevue Square.**

TIMING

Set aside at least a half day for this tour. It is an excellent weekend adventure, although the New City Hall is not open then. One of the best times to explore Chinatown is on a Sunday, when business booms; Kensington Market is closed that day, however. You can plan an entire sojourn around Eaton Centre. A visit to the Art Gallery of Ontario can easily extend from two to four hours; note that the gallery is closed Monday and Tuesday.

Sights to See

★ ㉙ **Art Gallery of Ontario.** From extremely modest beginnings in 1900, the AGO (as it's known) is now in the big leagues in terms of exhibitions and support. A 1992 renovation won international acclaim and put it among North America's top 10 art museums. The **Henry Moore Sculpture Centre** has the largest public collection of Moore's sculpture in the world. The **Canadian Wing** includes major works by such northern lights as Emily Carr, Cornelius Krieghoff, David Milne, and Homer Watson. The AGO also has a growing collection of works by Rembrandt, Hals, Van Dyck, Hogarth, Reynolds, Chardin, Renoir, de Kooning, Rothko, Oldenburg, Picasso, Rodin, Degas, Matisse, and many others. Visitors of any age can drop by the **Anne Tannenbaum Gallery School** on Sunday and explore painting, printmaking, and sculpting in Toronto's most spectacular studio space. The museum arranges numerous other workshops and special activities. The **Grange,** a historic house just behind the AGO, is a perfect place to browse, either before or after a visit to the gallery. ⊠ *317 Dundas St. W,* ☎ *416/979–6648.* ☞ *$5 suggested donation.* ☉ *Wed.–Fri. noon–9, weekends 10–5:30.*

☾ **Bellevue Square.** This little park with shady trees, benches, and a wading pool and playground is a good place to rest after a visit to ☞ **Kensington Market.** ⊠ *Denison Sq. and Augusta Pl.*

㉕ **Campbell House.** Built in 1822 and tastefully restored with elegant 18th- and early 19th-century furniture, Campbell House is one of Toronto's most charming house museums. It was the home of Sir William Campbell, the sixth Chief Justice of Upper Canada, and was originally located 2 km (1 mi) to the west of its current location. Costumed hostesses discuss the social life of the upper class of the period. Guided tours are available. ⊠ *160 Queen St. W,* ☎ *416/597–0227.* ☞ *$3.50.* ☉ *Oct.–mid-May, weekdays 9:30–4:30; mid-May–Oct., weekdays 9:30–4:30, weekends noon–4:30.*

Chinatown. Diverse, exciting, and lively, this is the largest Chinatown in eastern Canada and one of the largest in North America. You'll pass shops selling reasonably priced silk blouses and antique porcelain, silk kimonos for less than half the price elsewhere, lovely sake sets, and women's silk suits. More than 100,000 Chinese live in the city; just

Central Toronto
Art Gallery of
Ontario, **29**
Campbell House, **25**
Eaton Centre, **22**
52nd Division
Police Station, **26**
Kensington
Market, **30**
New City
Hall, **24**
Old City Hall, **23**
Ontario College
of Art and Design
Gallery, **27**
Village by the
Grange, **28**

**North-Central
Toronto**
Bata Shoe Museum
Collection, **38**
Casa Loma, **39**
George R. Gardiner
Museum of Ceramic
Art, **35**
Metropolitan Toronto
Reference Library, **37**
Provincial Parliament
Buildings, **32**
Queen's Park, **33**
Royal Ontario
Museum, **34**
University of
Toronto, **31**
Yorkville, **36**

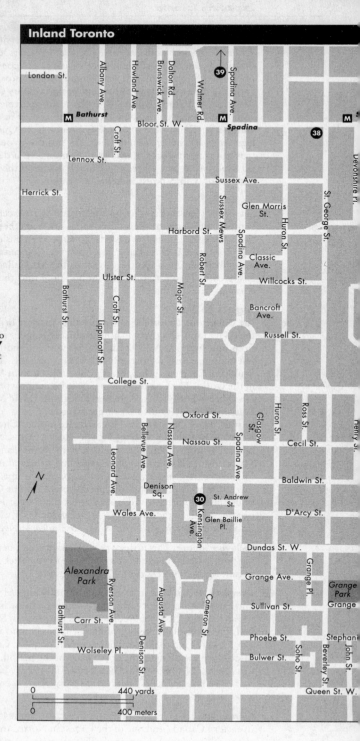

Inland Toronto

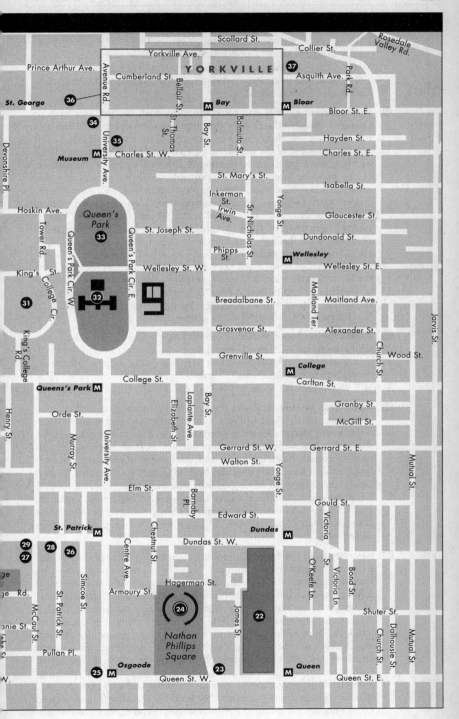

over a century ago there was only one—Sam Ching, who ran a hand laundry on Adelaide Street. Today, Chinatown covers much of the area bounded by Queen Street, Spadina Avenue, Dundas Street, and Bay Street. On Sunday, up and down Spadina Avenue and along Dundas Street, Chinese music blasts from storefronts, cash registers ring, abacuses clack, and bakeries, markets, herbalists, and restaurants do their best business of the week.

㉒ Eaton Centre. Even if you rank shopping with the flu, you may be charmed, possibly dazzled, by this impressive environment, Toronto's top tourist attraction. From its graceful glass roof, arching 127 ft above the lowest of the mall levels, to Michael Snow's exquisite flock of fiberglass Canada geese floating in the open space of the galleria, to the glass-enclosed elevators, porthole windows, and nearly two dozen graceful escalators, there are plenty of good reasons for visiting Eaton Centre. Galleria Level 1 contains two food courts; popularly priced fashions; photo, electronics, and record stores; and much "convenience" merchandise. Level 2 is directed to the middle-income shopper; Level 3 has the highest fashion and prices. **Eaton's,** one of Canada's classic department-store chains, has a nine-floor branch here. At the southern end of Level 3 is a skywalk over Queen Street that connects the Eaton Centre with the **Bay,** a seven-floor department store. Dozens of restaurants can be found here. A 17-theater cinema complex is at the Dundas Street entrance. ✉ *220 Yonge St.,* ☎ *416/598–2322.* ☉ *Weekdays 10–9, Sat. 9:30–6, Sun. noon–5.*

㉖ 52nd Division Police Station. Even the large police-station building in Chinatown has a Chinese flavor. Large Chinese characters identify it, demonstrating the Asian community's strong influence here. Otherwise, the postmodern building of 1977 recalls the Art Deco craze of the 1930s. ✉ *255 Dundas St. W,* ☎ *416/808–2222.*

㉚ Kensington Market. This old, steamy, smelly, raucous, colorful, European-style marketplace titillates all the senses. Go and explore, especially during warmer weather, when the goods pour out into the narrow streets: Russian rye breads, barrels of dill pickles, fresh fish on ice, mountains of cheese, bushels of ripe fruit, and crates of chickens and rabbits that will have your children both giggling and horrified. Jewish and Eastern European stores sit side by side with Portuguese, Caribbean, Latin American, and East Indian shops—with Vietnamese, Japanese, and Chinese establishments sprinkled throughout. ✉ *Northwest of Dundas St. and Spadina Ave.* ☉ *Daily 6–6; hrs vary. Many stores closed Sun.*

㉔ New City Hall. The futuristic-looking complex was the result of a massive international competition in 1958. The winning presentation, by Finnish architect Viljo Revell, was very controversial: two towers of differing height, and curved! But there is a logic to it all: An aerial view of the New City Hall shows a circular council chamber sitting like an eye between the two tower "eyelids." Within months of its opening in 1965, the New City Hall became a symbol of a thriving city. Annual events here include the Spring Flower Show in late March; the Toronto Outdoor Art Exhibition early each July, and the yearly Cavalcade of Lights late November–Christmas, when more than 100,000 sparkling lights are illuminated across both city halls (☞ Old City Hall, *below*). Whether the building becomes City Hall for the new mega-city (the 1998 merging of Toronto and five surrounding communities) is the subject of much political debate; upgrading the building will cost millions. The underground garage holds 2,400 cars. ✉ *100 Queen St. W,* ☎ *416/ 392–9111, TDD 416/392–7354.* ☉ *Weekdays 8:30–4:30.*

㉓ **Old City Hall.** Considered one of North America's most impressive municipal halls in its heyday, the building was designed by E. J. Lennox; it opened in 1899. When the New City Hall debuted in 1965, the Friends of Old City Hall organized to ensure its preservation, while also heightening Toronto's awareness of its architectural heritage. Since the opening of its younger sister, Old City Hall has been the site for the provincial courts, county offices, and thousands of low-cost marriages. The fabulous gargoyles above the front steps were apparently the architect's witty way of mocking certain turn-of-the-century politicians. There is a great stained-glass window as you enter. The handsome old structure stands in delightful contrast to its daring and unique sibling. ⊠ *60 Queen St. W,* ☎ *416/327–5675.* ☉ *Weekdays 8:30–4:45.*

㉗ **Ontario College of Art and Design Gallery.** Across the street from the Art Gallery of Ontario (AGO), the college's third-floor gallery shows works by students, faculty, and alumni. It is one of Canada's major art institutions and an important exhibition space for emerging artists and designers. ⊠ *291 Dundas St. W. (enter on McCaul St.),* ☎ *416/977–6000, ext. 262.* ☞ *Free.* ☉ *Wed.–Sat. noon–6.*

Spadina Avenue. Toronto's widest street has been pronounced "Spa-*dye*-nah" for a century and a half. For decades it has contained a collection of inexpensive stores, factories that sell wholesale if you have connections, ethnic food and fruit stores, and eateries, including some often first-class, if modest-looking, Chinese restaurants sprinkled throughout the area. Each new wave of immigrants—Jewish, Chinese, Portuguese, East and West Indian, South American—has added its own flavor to the mix, but Spadina-Kensington's basic bill of fare is still bargains galore. Here you'll find gourmet cheeses at gourmet prices, fresh (no, not fresh-frozen) ocean fish, fine European kitchenware at half the prices of stores in the Yorkville area, yards of remnants piled high in bins, designer clothes minus the labels, and the occasional rock-and-roll night spot and interesting greasy spoon. A new streetcar line bustles down the wide avenue to Front Street. ⊠ *Spadina Ave., between College and Queen Sts.*

㉘ **Village by the Grange.** This apartment and shopping complex has more than 100 shops selling everything from ethnic fast food to serious art. It's a perfect example of wise, careful blending of the commercial and the residential. ⊠ *122 St. Patrick St.,* ☎ *416/598–1414.*

North-Central Toronto

The competing interests of academia, culture, and commerce all converge at the corner of University Avenue and Bloor Street. In the area around this landmark intersection—where the Royal Ontario Museum stands—the major forces of Toronto metropolitan life unfold: government, industry, and the University of Toronto. Even though all these sites lie in the middle of a busy city, the area is surprisingly tranquil, particularly on weekends.

A Good Tour

University Avenue runs from downtown Toronto at Front Street to Bloor, where it becomes Avenue Road and runs to the city's northern fringes. West of the avenue, north of College Street, lies the **University of Toronto** ㉛. Follow King's College Road north from College Street to King's College Circle. At the top of the circle is Hart House, the Gothic-style student center. Continue around the circle to the Romanesque University College. Next is Knox College, whose Scottish origins are evident in the bagpipe music that escapes from the building at odd hours. On the west side of the circle, the Medical Sciences Building is a giant assemblage of Brutalist architecture. Return to College Avenue and walk west to St. George, where you can proceed north to the Forestry Building and Sidney Smith Hall. At the crossroads of Hardord and Hoskin Avenue, turn right onto Hoskin and walk past Massey College.

From Massey, follow Queen's Park Circle south. The **Provincial Parliament Buildings** ㉜ sit in the middle of **Queen's Park** ㉝. East of the park is the Ontario Legislative Building. Just to the north of Queen's Park is the revered **Royal Ontario Museum** ㉞ (ROM), which could occupy you for most of a day. Across University Avenue stands the **George R. Gardiner Museum of Ceramic Art** ㉟, home to a rarefied $25 million collection of European ceramics. Next, you can visit the upscale shopping area of **Yorkville** ㊱, just to the north. A block north of Bloor and Yonge streets, east of Yorkville, stands the magnificent **Metropolitan Toronto Reference Library** ㊲. Four blocks west, across the street from the St. George subway station near Bloor Street, is the **Bata Shoe Museum Collection** ㊳. A subway ride will take you to the final stop, **Casa Loma** ㊴, a spectacular castlelike mansion north of the center just off Spadina Avenue.

TIMING

Schedule your tour between Tuesday and Saturday, when the museums and shops are open. Give yourself a full day: Even a highly abbreviated visit to the ROM takes a minimum of two hours, and shoppers will want to allow time to browse in Yorkville.

Sights to See

㊳ **Bata Shoe Museum Collection.** The unusual collection contains more than 10,000 items of footwear from nearly every country in the world, some dating back more than 4,000 years. Items such as pressurized skydiving boots, iron-spiked shoes used for crushing chestnuts, and smugglers' clogs are just a few of the pieces on display. ⊠ *327 Bloor St. W,* ☎ *416/979–7799.* ⊡ *$6; free 1st Tues. of month.* ☉ *Tues.–Wed. and Fri.–Sat. 10–5, Thurs. 10–8, Sun. noon–5.*

㊴ **Casa Loma.** Architect E. J. Lennox, who also designed Toronto's Old City Hall and the King Edward Hotel, created a 20th-century castle here, with 98 rooms, two towers, secret panels, long and creepy passageways, and some superb views of Toronto. The medieval-style castle cost more than $3 million to build shortly before World War I. You tour it at your own speed, guided by a tape recording. Wear sensible shoes: You'll have walked a good mile by the time you're done. ⊠ *1 Austin Terr., Spadina Ave. south of St. Clair Ave., near Dupont subway stop,* ☎ *416/923–1171.* ⊡ *$8.* ☉ *Daily 9:30–4.*

㉟ **George R. Gardiner Museum of Ceramic Art.** The collection focuses on 17th-century English delftware and 18th-century yellow European porcelain but also has pre-Columbian works from Olmec and Maya times. There's also a display of Italian commedia dell'arte figures, especially Harlequin. Don't miss the museum's gift shop, which stocks many unusual items. ⊠ *111 Queen's Park, across University Ave. from ROM,* ☎ *416/586–8080.* ⊡ *Free.* ☉ *Mon. and Wed.–Sat. 10–5, Tues. 10–8, Sun. 11–5.*

㊲ **Metropolitan Toronto Reference Library.** This impressive library was designed by one of Canada's most admired architects, Raymond Moriyama, who also created the Ontario Science Centre. Arranged around an interior atrium, the library gives a delightful sense of open space. Fully one-third of the more than 1.3 million books—spread across 17 km (28 mi) of shelves—are available to the public. In the headphone-equipped audio carrels, you may listen to any one of more than 10,000 albums. Open on Saturday from 2 to 4 and by appointment, the **Arthur**

Conan Doyle Room houses the finest public collection of Holmesiana anywhere, with records, films, photos, books, manuscripts, and letters. ⊠ *789 Yonge St., north of Bloor St.,* ☎ *416/393–7000.* ⊡ *Free.* ☉ *Mon.–Thurs. 10–8, Fri. and Sat. 10–5, Sun. 1:30–5.*

㉜ Provincial Parliament Buildings. You can get a taste of Ontario's history and government inside these pink 1889 buildings, which have a heavy, almost Romanesque quality. Their huge, lovely halls, hung with hundreds of oils by Canadian artists, echo a half millennium of English architecture. If you take one of the frequent (and free) tours, you will see the chamber where the 130 elected representatives from across Ontario, called MPPs (Members of Provincial Parliament), meet on a regular basis. There are two rooms—one each for the parliamentary histories of Great Britain and Ontario—filled with old newspapers, periodicals, and pictures. The lobby holds a fine collection of minerals and rocks of the province. On the lawn in front of the Parliament Buildings, facing College Street, stand many statues, including one of Queen Victoria and one of Canada's first prime minister, Sir John A. Macdonald. These buildings are often referred to simply as Queen's Park, after the park surrounding them. ⊠ *1 Queen's Park,* ☎ *416/325–7500.* ⊡ *Free.* ☉ *Guided tour mid-May–Labor Day, daily on the hr 9–4, weekends every ½ hr 9–11:30 and 1:30–4; frequent tours rest of the yr; also at 6:45* PM *when evening sessions are held.*

㉝ Queen's Park. Many visitors consider this to be the soul of Toronto. Surrounding the large oval-shape patch of land are medical facilities to the south, the University of Toronto to the west and east, and the Royal Ontario Museum to the north. To most locals, Queen's Park is chiefly synonymous with politics, as the ☞ **Provincial Parliament Buildings** sit in the middle of this charming urban oasis. ⊠ *Queen's Park Circle, between College St. and Bloor St. W.*

★ ☾ **㉞ Royal Ontario Museum** (ROM). Ongoing renovations have restored the ROM to its status as—in the words of the Canada Council— "Canada's single greatest cultural asset." Since its inception in 1912, Canada's largest museum has continued to collect—always with brilliance—reaching more than 6 million items altogether. What makes the ROM unique is that science, art, and archaeology exhibits are all appealingly presented under one roof. The **Dinosaur Collection** absorbs children and adults alike. The **Evolution Gallery** has an ongoing audiovisual program on Darwin's theories of evolution. The **Sigmund Samuel Canadiana Collection,** a worthy assemblage of 18th- and 19th-century Canadian furnishings, glassware, silver, and period rooms, is part of the Canadian Heritage gallery. A particular strength of the ROM is the **T. T. Tsui Galleries of Chinese Art,** with stunning sculptures, paintings, and many other artifacts. The **Roman Gallery** has the most extensive collection of Roman artifacts in Canada. The brilliant **Ancient Egypt Gallery** is connected with the newer **Nubia Gallery;** both exhibit artifacts that illuminate the ancient cultures. And the **European Musical Instruments Gallery** has a revolutionary audio system and more than 1,200 instruments dating back to the late 16th century. The **Discovery Centre** allows children (over age six) to handle objects from the collections and study them, using microscopes, ultraviolet light, and magnifying glasses. There's even a **Bat Cave,** which contains 4,000 freeze-dried and artificial bats in a lifelike presentation; piped-in narration directs visitors on a 15-minute walk through a dimly lit replica of an 8-ft-high limestone tunnel in Jamaica, filled with sounds of dripping water and bat squeaks. ⊠ *100 Queen's Park,* ☎ *416/586–8000.* ⊡ *$10; by donation Tues. after 4:30.* ☉ *Mon. and Wed.–Sat. 10–6, Tues. 10–8, Sun. 11–6; Discovery Centre hrs vary, so call ahead.*

③ **University of Toronto.** One of Canada's largest and most revered institutions of higher learning began in 1827, when King George IV signed a charter for a "King's College in the Town of York, Capital of Upper Canada." The Church of England had control then, but by 1850 the college was proclaimed nondenominational, renamed the University of Toronto, and put under the control of the province. Then, in a spirit of Christian competition, the Anglicans started Trinity College, the Methodists began Victoria, and the Roman Catholics begat St. Michael's; by the time the Presbyterians founded Knox College, the whole thing was almost out of hand. The 17 schools and faculties are now united, and they welcome anyone who can meet the admission standards and afford the tuition. Like that of most large universities built over several decades, the quality of the institution's architecture catalog is mixed. There is much to see and do around the main campus. One highlight is **Hart House** (⊠ 7 Hart House Circle), the Gothic-style student center built in the 1920s; the dining hall has stained-glass windows and cheap and rather good food. The ravishing **Rosebrugh Building** (⊠ 4 Taddle Creek Rd.) of 1921 features an eye-catching display of energetic brickwork, making it one of the university's most delightful structures. Romanesque **University College** (⊠ 15 King's College Circle) was built in 1859. **Knox College** (⊠ 59 St. George St.) has been training ministers since 1844, although the building was erected in 1915. At St. Michael's College, stop by **Sullivan House** (⊠ St. Joseph St. across from the college library)), where a small plaque commemorates Marshall McLuhan, who taught at St. Mike's for many years. On the site of the **Medical Sciences Building** (⊠ 1 King's College Circle), Drs. Banting, Best, and others discovered the insulin that has saved the lives of tens of millions of diabetics around the world. The handsome redbrick **Forestry Building** (⊠ 45 St. George St.) and the modern and massive **Sidney Smith Hall** (⊠ 100 St. George St.), with its two wings, are also worth a look. **Massey College** (⊠ 4 Devonshire Pl.), of 1963, blends medieval ideas and forms into a modern architectural idiom. ⊠ *Visitors Centre, 25 King's College Circle,* ☎ *416/978–4426; call about summer walking tours.*

③⑥ **Yorkville.** One of the most dynamic and expensive areas of the city is known to some as Toronto's Rodeo Drive; other people call it Toronto's Fifth Avenue. One thing is certain: These blocks are packed with restaurants, galleries, specialty shops, and high-price stores specializing in designer clothes, furs, and jewels. ⊠ *Bordered by Avenue Rd., Yonge and Bloor Sts., and Yorkville Ave.*

DINING

By Sara
Waxman

Smoking is prohibited in most Toronto restaurants. If this is important to you, call to check. Servers expect a 15% tip on the pre-tax bill. An easy formula is that the GST (7%) plus the provinical sales tax (8%) equals the tip. There's no need to tip on the after-tax bill.

Unless noted in the reviews, dress in Toronto is casual but neat. In the more elegant and/or expensive restaurants, men are likely to feel more comfortable wearing a jacket.

CATEGORY	COST*
$$$$	over $40
$$$	$30–$40
$$	$20–$30
$	under $20

*per person, in Canadian dollars, without 7% GST, 8% provincial sales tax, tip, or drinks

American/Casual

$–$$ ✕ **Marché.** A self-service restaurant has created the atmosphere of an Old World market square. Herbs grow in pots; fresh fruits and vegetables are piled high; an enormous snowbank holds bright-eyed fish and fresh seafood; fresh pasta spews from pasta makers, ready to be cooked to order. A rotisserie roasts lacquer-crisp game birds and European sausages. Bread and croissants are baked before your eyes, and pizza is prepared to order. This high-concept, low-price dining adventure is open Wednesday–Saturday 7:30 AM–2 AM and Sunday–Tuesday 7:30 AM–1 AM; there are smaller versions all over town. ⊠ *42 Yonge St.,* ☎ *416/366–8986. Reservations not accepted. AE, DC, MC, V.*

$–$$ ✕ **Masquerade Caffè Bar.** An eclectic array of primary-color furnishings, stoves, and Murano glass mosaics fills this Fellini-esque environment. The daily-changing Italian menu lists a variety of risottos, ravioli, salads, and Italian sandwiches on homemade breads with scrumptious meat, cheese, and veggie fillings. Zabaglione, whipped to a thick, frothy cream and poured over fresh berries, is a knockout dessert. ⊠ *BCE Place, Front and Yonge Sts.,* ☎ *416/363–8971. Reservations not accepted. AE, MC, V. Closed Sun.*

Cafés

$ ✕ **The Coffee Mill.** For more than 30 years, Marta Heczy has been dispensing her special coffees, open-face sandwiches, and daily Hungarian specialties. On Saturday the city's literary and arts aficionados congregate for goulash, cappuccino or latte, and a satisfying slice of apple strudel in the off-street courtyard. ⊠ *99 Yorkville Ave.,* ☎ *416/ 920–2108. Reservations not accepted. AE, DC, MC, V.*

$ ✕ **Future Bakery & Café.** Students love this place for its generous portions of beef borscht, buckwheat cabbage rolls, and potato-cheese *varenycky* slathered with thick sour cream. It's also adored by homesick Europeans hungry for goulash and knishes, by the cheesecake-and-coffee crowd, by health-conscious foodies, and by people-watchers looking for people worth watching from 7 AM to 2 AM. ⊠ *438 Bloor St. W,* ☎ *416/922–5875;* ⊠ *2199 Bloor St. W,* ☎ *416/769–5020;* ⊠ *739 Queen St. W,* ☎ *416/504–4235;* ⊠ *St. Lawrence Market, 95 Front St. E,* ☎ *416/366–7259. Reservations not accepted. MC, V.*

Canadian

$$$$ ✕ **Canoe.** A delicious homage to regional foods is sifted through the world's finest cuisines. There's a breathtaking view of the Toronto Islands and Lake Ontario from the huge windows on the 54th floor of the Toronto Dominion Bank Tower. Some inspirational dishes are lobster baked in potato skin, glazed with old cheddar, and Québec foie gras with roasted potatoes, grilled duck livers, late-harvest Riesling dressing, and quince jam. Canadiana courses through the menu with entrées like herb-stuffed breast of Ontario pheasant on spaetzle with roasted apples. Meat eaters might enjoy roast hind of Yukon caribou with wild-mushroom celeriac and corn bread cobbler. Vegetarian and spa dishes are available. ⊠ *66 Wellington St. W, 54th floor,* ☎ *416/364–0054. Reservations essential. AE, DC, MC, V. Closed weekends.*

$$$$ ✕ **360 Revolving Restaurant.** A glassed-in bridge and a glass elevator carry you to the top of the tallest freestanding structure in the world. In the distance are New York State and the twinkling lights of Niagara Falls. The curved leather booths and windowside tables circle the core, which holds the kitchen and the award-winning Wine Cellar in the Sky. The menu is unabashedly Canadian. The kitchen blackens quails and sautées them with preserved kumquats for an intense orange glaze.

Atlas, **7**
Bellini, **29**
Boba, **33**
Canoe, **13**
Centro, **38**
Chiado, **1**
The Coffee Mill, **27**
Future Bakery
& Café, **23**
Grano, **39**
House of Chan, **30**
Il Fornello, **10**
Il Posto Nuovo, **28**
Joso's, **35**
KitKat Bar & Grill, **4**
Lai Wah Heen, **20**
Marché, **14**
Masquerade
Caffè Bar, **15**
Mercer Street Grill, **2**
Mistura, **31**
Moishes. **12**
Monsoon, **9**
Mövenpick, **11**
Nami, **16**
North 44, **40**
Pangaea, **25**
Pastis, **41**
Prego de la Piazza, **24**
Rodney's Oyster Bar, **18**
Rosewater
Supper Club, **17**
Sarkis, **19**
Scaramouche, **36**
Sotto Sotto, **34**
Splendido, **22**
Thai Magic, **37**
Tiger Lily's Noodle
House, **8**
360 Revolving
Restaurant, **3**
Truffles, **26**
Vanipha Lanna, **32**
Verona, **5**
Wah Sing, **21**
Xango, **6**

Toronto Dining

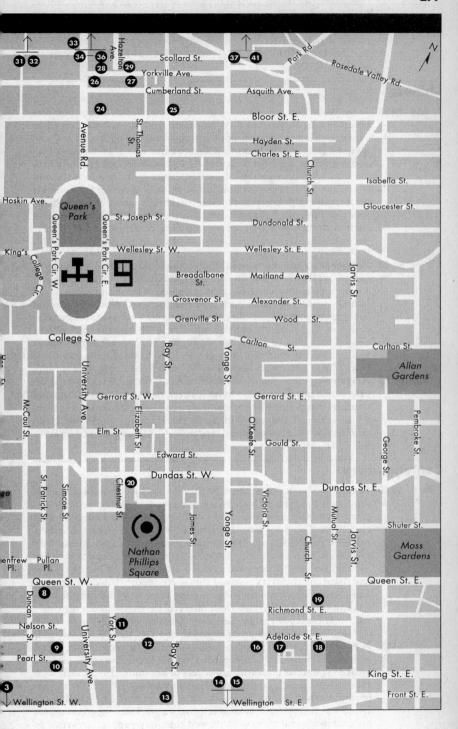

Scallops in the shell are steamed in a roasted garlic and white wine bath. Rack of lamb is crusted with fresh herbs, garlic, and peppers and paired with wild rice. You can even try locally farmed ostrich steaks. ⊠ *CN Tower, 301 Front St. W,* ☎ *416/362–5411. Reservations essential. AE, DC, MC, V.*

Chinese

$$$–$$$$ ╳ **Lai Wah Heen.** For Cantonese culinary fireworks, phone and pre-order "Lustrous Peacock." When it arrives, an explosion of white vapor reveals an arrangement of melon, barbecued duck, chicken, and honeyed walnuts. The hundred-dish menu lists wok-fried shredded beef and vegetables in a crisp potato nest, and barbecue duck in a thick taro blanket, braised in a casserole with coconut milk. At lunch the dim sum is divine: Translucent pouches burst with juicy fillings of shark's fin sprinkled with bright red lobster roe; shrimp dumplings have green tops that look like baby bok choy. The service is French in an elegant room with a sculptured ceiling, etched-glass turntables, and silver serving dishes. ⊠ *Metropolitan Hotel, 118 Chestnut St., 2nd floor,* ☎ *416/ 977–9899. AE, DC, MC, V.*

$–$$ ╳ **Tiger Lily's Noodle House.** Many come to this bright hand-painted
★ café for real egg rolls and shrimp- and spinach-dumpling-like pot stickers in a light lemony sauce. But most people come for the noodles, cooked in many ways: Hawaiian duck long-rice soup, redolent with coconut lemongrass, plump with chicken and seafood, is one option. Soups include noodles, wontons, meat or vegetable broth, and garnishes of barbecued pork, Shanghai chicken, or veggies. If you want your Chinese food steeped in tradition, not grease, you'll find double happiness here. ⊠ *257 Queen St. W,* ☎ *416/977–5499. AE, MC, V.*

$–$$ ╳ **Wah Sing.** Just one of a jumble of Asian restaurants clustered together on a tiny Kensington Market street, this meticulously clean and spacious restaurant has two-for-the-price-of-one lobsters (in season, which is almost always). With black bean sauce or ginger and green onion, they're scrumptious and tender. ⊠ *47 Baldwin St.,* ☎ *416/599– 8822. AE, MC, V.*

Contemporary

╳ **$$$$** ╳ **Centro.** Massive columns, a bright blue ceiling, salmon-color walls
★ lined with comfortable banquettes, and creative lighting turn this vast eatery into intimate spaces. Owners Tony Longo and award-winning chef Marc Thuet set city standards of excellence. French-Mediterranean style filters through fine regional ingredients into a menu with specialties such as terrine of Québec foie gras marinated with Inniskillin ice wine; a duo of fruitwood-smoked Bay of Fundy salmon and Asian cured gravlax is served with sherry-marinated Vidalia onions and arctic char caviar dressing. Among the entrées are pan-charred Chilean sea bass and grilled Delft Blue veal chop. Ask about the chef's daily *plat classique* special. Service is flawless. ⊠ *2472 Yonge St.,* ☎ *416/483–2211. Reservations essential. AE, DC, MC, V. Closed Sun.*

$$$$ ╳ **North 44.** Mirrored sconces hold exotic floral arrangements; a steel
★ compass is embedded in a gorgeous marble floor. This is the place to awaken your taste buds with appetizers of hot smoked arctic char with mustardseed crust and potato parfait or panfried oysters with cornmeal nut crust. Just try to choose from owner-chef Marc McEwen's creative alchemy, found in his seven-page menu. Exciting main courses are center-cut veal chop with toasted rosemary peppercorn crust, or oven-roasted striped sea bass with black bean sauce and shrimp dumplings. Pasta and pizzas are other options. Fifty wines sold by the glass complement every dish. A delightful private dining room seats

12–15. ✉ *2537 Yonge St.,* ☎ *416/487–4897. AE, DC, MC, V. Closed Sun. No lunch.*

$$$–$$$$ ✕ **Boba.** Barbara Gordon and Bob Bermann are a sophisticated culinary couple who cook in a charming brick house personalized with robust and gorgeous color. The dishes they've dreamed up are original and delicious: Rice paper–wrapped chicken breast on Thai black rice and big-eye tuna grilled rare with coconut noodles, mango and avocado salsa, and black bean sauce are favorites, or try the traditional grilled bone-in rib steak with Yukon Gold frites. Vegetable dinners are spontaneously created. ✉ *90 Avenue Rd.,* ☎ *416/961–2622. AE, MC, V. No lunch weekdays.*

$$$–$$$$ ✕ **Pangaea.** Partners Peter Geary and chef Martin Kouprie use unprocessed, seasonal ingredients and the bounty of produce the world has to offer. Soups are celestial, cream-free compositions; salads are creative constructions. Grilled jumbo quail is paired with Portobello mushrooms and honey lemon vinaigrette; grilled calamari sings and dances with vivacious flavors. Vegetarians will find bliss in this caring kitchen. And, on the other side of the food chain, rack of lamb gets dolled up with sunflower crust, sweet-potato mash, and apple chips. The tranquil room has an aura of restrained sophistication. ✉ *1221 Bay St.,* ☎ *416/920–2323. AE, DC, MC, V.*

$$$–$$$$ ✕ **Rosewater Supper Club.** A historic landmark building with 22-ft-high ceilings, hardwood and marble floors, and thronelike blue velvet banquettes for two is a place to go when you're in the party mood. The scintillating appetizers and beautifully presented entrées include saffron risotto with leeks, lobster and caviar, and Asian-spiced chicken supreme with sweet chili sauce. Not ready to commit to dinner? A lounge with a baby grand and a slinky torch singer can hold your attention. Or you can play a game of billiards, nibble from a tapas menu, and relax in luxe comfort in the downstairs lounge. ✉ *19 Toronto St.,* ☎ *416/214–5888. AE, DC, MC, V. Closed Sun. No lunch Sat.*

$$$–$$$$ ✕ **Scaramouche.** Consistently beautiful dishes are served in a stylish, comfortable room with a view of the city's southern skyline. Fresh lobster and scallop sausage with grilled vegetables in a rich lobster broth with roasted pepper mayonnaise is a popular appetizer or light supper. Grilled filet mignon with truffle mashed potatoes is polished with a red wine glaze. For dessert, the height of elegance is coconut cream pie with white chocolate shavings and dark chocolate sauce. The adjacent Pasta Bar, alas, takes no reservations. ✉ *1 Benvenuto Pl.,* ☎ *416/961–8011. Reservations essential. Jacket required. AE, DC, MC, V. Closed Sun. No lunch.*

Eclectic

$$$$ ✕ **Sarkis.** Meticulous, modern opulence reigns in a cozy 32-seat domain. Innovative chef Greg Couillard was cooking fusion cuisine before there was a name for it. Today his plump Thai baked crab cakes with shrimp, crispy outside with sesame seed and mild peppercorn crust; spiked with green onion, ginger, and cilantro; and enhanced with salsas, are not to be missed. Globetrotting for flavors, he grills a center-cut organic steak, flames it with bourbon, and sets it on a ragout of peppers and Portobello mushrooms. Coconut tiger prawns hellfire are inspired. These dishes hit all the notes: sweet, spicy, hot, cool, crispy, crunchy, soft, and mellow. ✉ *67 Richmond St. E,* ☎ *416/214–1337. AE, DC, MC, V. No lunch weekends.*

$$$–$$$$ ✕ **Mercer Street Grill.** Sensory thrills abound in this casual, sophisticated room where the city's trendsetters erase menu monotony with Pacific Rim–Pan-Asian delights. Appetizers include tempura of black tiger shrimp with kumquat dipping sauce, and hot nori (Japanese sea-

weed) roll of grilled jumbo quail with snow peas and sweet-pepper rose-mary relish. Among the breathtaking main courses is grilled yellowfin tuna with lemongrass shrimp satay and steamed coconut rice in hot-and-sour broth. Dine-alones love sitting at the open kitchen's eating counter, watching culinary theater in motion. Hand-rolled Belgian chocolate sushi is a dessert fantasy. There's lovely summer dining on the Japanese-style patio. ☒ *36 Mercer St.,* ☎ *416/599–3399. AE, DC, MC, V. No lunch weekends or Nov.–Apr.*

$$–$$$$ ✕ **Monsoon.** A fragrant, eclectic consort of Pan-Asian–inspired cuisine is served in a dining-and-lounge environment with a black-brown color scheme that evokes a serene yet dynamic atmosphere. Among the smaller dishes are sweet yam fries with *sambal* (a hot soy-chili dipping sauce) and tandoori salmon in rice paper. Larger dishes include Cambodian venison hot pot, char-grilled Burmese prawns in ginger plum sauce with black rice, and unique choices for vegetarians like curried vegetable hot pot with green papaya and sticky rice. Monsoon is pure, open-minded, organic, sophisticated. ☒ *100 Simcoe St.,* ☎ *416/979–7172. AE, DC, MC, V. Closed Sun. No lunch Sat.*

$$ ✕ **Atlas.** This restaurant–bar–jazz club combines California cool and New York glitz. The main-floor bar, with its high grazing tables and divine tapas menu, opens in summer to a vast streetside patio. You can watch it all from a balcony table in the dining room. There is an intensity to the lobster-vegetable spring rolls with mango chutney. Hong Kong barbecue beef burger with watercress and noodle salad fulfills a craving—as does Tennessee mountain barbecue half-chicken with grilled corn. The Satellite Lounge on the top floor is for smoking and dancing. ☒ *129 Peter St.,* ☎ *416/977–7544. AE, MC, V. Closed Mon. No lunch weekends.*

French

$$$$ ✕ **Truffles.** Through the impressive wrought-iron gates of Truffles,
★ pale wood walls glow in the reflected soft light of handcrafted candelabra. This restaurant has won the hearts of discerning gastronomes with dishes like date and goat cheese wrapped in *brique* (crisp leaves of pastry), spaghettini with Périgord black truffles, a splendid sautéed lobster flambéed with vodka, and triumphant poached and braised veal tournedos. Leave room for esoteric desserts. Patrick Lin is the new chef at one of the finest restaurants in Canada. ☒ *Four Seasons Hotel, 21 Avenue Rd.,* ☎ *416/928–7331. Reservations essential. AE, DC, MC, V. Closed Sun. No lunch.*

$$$–$$$$ ✕ **Pastis.** Diners may well feel they're in the South of France as they sit
★ within lush raspberry and violet walls, munching on fresh radishes and slices of baguette and butter, spooning up traditional fish soup with rouille, croutons, and grated cheese. Simply roasted grain-fed chicken is glazed with an intense natural *jus* (juice) and garlic cloves. Cut into four neat sections, it perches on a crisp potato pancake and gives a totally satisfying variety of taste and texture. The adventurous palate will rhapsodize over sweetbreads sautéed with shallots, white wine, and veal jus, paired with a ragout of vegetables. This place could run on the Gallic charm of owners Georges Gurnon and Claude Bouillet alone. ☒ *1158 Yonge St.,* ☎ *416/928–2212. AE, DC, MC, V. Closed Sun.–Mon. No lunch.*

Italian

$$$–$$$$ ✕ **Prego de la Piazza.** This chic Italian eatery is filled with the who's who of the city's highly visible film and TV industry. The glitterati nibble on carpaccio della casa and arugula with strawberries and indulge in butterfly trout with capers and burnt butter or crisp roast baby chicken with pepperonata. Daily fresh fish is a treat. Next door at Enoteca della

Piazza, a design award–winning wine bar, the hip and cheerful sip wine and nibble on pizza and antipasti. A third separate room is called Black and Blue, a tribute to fine steaks and wines. Upstairs, the lounge is a luxe cigar smoke-easy. ⊠ *150 Bloor St. W, ☎ 416/920–9900. AE, DC, MC, V. Closed Sun.*

$$$–$$$$ ✕ **Splendido.** Everyone loves the ambience and respects chef-owner Arpi Magyar's sparkling contemporary menu. Ricotta and potato are coaxed into plump gnocchi and served splashed with lemon butter, Parmesan, cracked pepper, and sage. Veal is the chef's masterpiece: Oven-baked rack set on garlic mashed potatoes comes with fresh horseradish, pesto sauce, sautéed kale, and sun-dried tomato mayonnaise. Casual, sophisticated good taste meets the eye at every turn. The bar is popular for nightcaps. ⊠ *88 Harbord St., ☎ 416/929–7788. AE, DC, MC, V.*

$$–$$$$ ✕ **Bellini.** From the street, it's a few steps down to this comfortable, flower-filled, romantic spot. The beef carpaccio and the warm, herb-crusted goat cheese and grilled eggplant are excellent. Try the Provimi veal osso buco with garlic mushroom risotto, or the special Bellini chicken with roasted artichokes, wild mushrooms, and baked polenta. Service pampers, and a friendly host greets you at the door. ⊠ *101 Yorkville Ave., ☎ 416/929–9111. AE, DC, MC, V. No lunch.*

$$–$$$$ ✕ **Il Posto Nuovo.** The Establishment recognizes the sophistication of this restaurant tucked into the hip of Hazelton Lanes. Excellent traditional northern Italian dishes prevail. An iced trolley of fresh fish and seafood is wheeled over for your choosing, or you may want the perfectly grilled veal chop or angel-hair pasta with a whole lobster. Signature desserts are peeled whole oranges marinated in Grand Marnier and Italian cake topped with fluffy meringue. At press time new owners were preparing to change the menu but keep the cuisine Italian. ⊠ *148 Yorkville Ave., ☎ 416/968–0469. AE, DC, MC, V. Closed Sun.*

$$–$$$$ ✕ **KitKat Bar & Grill.** This eclectic and eccentric southern Italian eatery is built around a massive tree. A theater-district locale means pre- and post-theater hours are really busy. Choose from window tables in the front, perch at the long bar, enjoy the privacy of an old-fashioned wooden booth, or sit at a picnic table in the rear. Portions are enormous. An antipasto platter for two is a meal; pastas, seafood, roast chicken, and grilled steak are all delectable. Owner Al Carbone welcomes everyone like long-lost family. ⊠ *297 King St. W, ☎ 416/977–4461. AE, DC, MC, V. Closed Sun. No lunch Sat.*

$$–$$$$ ✕ **Mistura.** This place has the buzz that's made it one of the hottest new, modern Italian restaurants in town. Two hip hospitality professionals have come up with an innovative menu in a space that combines comfort with casual luxury. Start with a mix and match of four out of six bruschetta: some choices are grilled radicchio, Gorgonzola, and roasted onion as well as mushroom, eggplant, and roasted garlic. Crispy roast chicken with garlic mashed potatoes and rosemary sauce delights; grilled turkey breast paillard is a triumph for calorie counters. Vegetarians will find true happiness here, too. ⊠ *265 Davenport Rd., ☎ 416/515–0009. AE, DC, MC, V. Closed Sun. No lunch.*

$$–$$$$ ✕ **Sotto Sotto.** A coal cellar in a turn-of-the-century home was dug out, its stone walls and floor polished, and a restaurant created that has become a dining oasis for locals and jet-setters alike. The menu gives a tantalizing tug to the taste buds. Of the 14 pasta dishes, appetizer or main-course size, *orecchiette* (tiny, disk-shape pasta) with a toss of prosciutto, mushrooms, black olives, and fresh tomatoes is a symphony of textures. Gnocchi are made daily. Cornish hen is marinated, pressed, and grilled to juicy brownness; swordfish and fresh fish of the day are beautifully done on the grill. Lots of nooks and corners and flickering candles cast uneven shadows in these charming, cavelike rooms. ⊠ *116 Avenue Rd., ☎ 416/962–0011. AE, DC, MC, V. No lunch.*

$$-$$$ ✕ **Grano.** At this joyful collage of the Martella family's Italy, there's
  ★   a small espresso bar to perch at while you wait for a table or takeout.
      Choose, if you can, from 40 delectable vegetarian dishes and numer-
      ous meat and fish antipasti. Lucia's homemade gnocchi and ravioli are
      divine, as are the tiramisu and the white chocolate and raspberry pie.
      ✉ *2035 Yonge St.,* ☎ *416/440–1986. AE, DC, MC, V. Closed Sun.*

$$ ✕ **Verona.** The kitchen sends over homemade savories as soon as
      you're seated: diced marinated vegetables in olive oil, lush olive spread,
      and a basket of fresh breads. You might start with opulent pan-seared
      sea scallops on truffled asparagus spears with champagne cream, or
      goat cheese wrapped in prosciutto with marinated eggplant. The
      kitchen blesses angel-hair pasta with tiger shrimp, scallops, and wood-
      land mushrooms. A specialty is hazelnut-crumbed pork tenderloin. Up-
      stairs, a comfortable lounge served by the same kitchen offers cigars,
      fine wines, and live music on weekends. ✉ *335 King St. W,* ☎ *416/
      593–7771. AE, DC, MC, V. Closed Sun. No lunch Sat.*

Japanese

$$–$$$$ ✕ **Nami.** In this large, attractive restaurant, diners can choose to eat
      at the sushi bar, in tatami rooms with nontraditional wells under the
      tables, or at the *robatayaki* (a cooking grill surrounded by an eating
      counter). The chef douses soft-shell crabs with a special sauce and puts
      them on the grill. Scallops, shrimp, Atlantic salmon, mackerel, and ocean
      perch sizzle on skewers. Special dinner combos at a table or booth in-
      clude soup, salad, tempura, yakitori (skewers of chicken) or a beef or
      salmon teriyaki dish, rice, and dessert. ✉ *55 Adelaide St. E,* ☎ *416/
      362–7373. AE, DC, MC, V. Closed Sun. No lunch Sat.*

Latin

$$$–$$$$ ✕ **Xango.** The beautiful people know that the discreet, red capital X
      on a black tile is where the action is. A three-tiered rack of appetizers
      can include "Honduran Fire and Ice" (fresh tuna-loin seviche with co-
      conut chilies and ginger) and fried oysters with sweet plantain, bacon,
      and spinach. Salvadorean chicken perched on saffron mashed potatoes
      and sea bass baked on a cedar plank with calamari rice and Cuban
      mojo have blasts of flavor. Coco Cabana, a coconut custard, and flan
      Borracho are dazzling desserts. Upstairs is for tango and tapas fans.
      ✉ *106 John St.,* ☎ *416/593–4407. AE, MC, V. Closed Sun. No lunch.*

Pizza

$–$$$ ✕ **Il Fornello.** Pizza aficionados especially love this thin-crust pie,
  ★   baked in a wood-burning oven. Orchestrate your own medley from
      more than 100 traditional and exotic toppings that include braised onion,
      capicolla (spicy Italian sausage), pancetta, provolone, and calamari.
      Pastas, veal dishes, and salads are available, too. Wheat-free pizza crust
      and dairy-free cappuccino are now on the menu—your taste buds
      won't know the difference. ✉ *55 Eglinton Ave. E,* ☎ *416/486–2130;*
      ✉ *86 Bloor St. W,* ☎ *416/588–5658;* ✉ *214 King St. W,* ☎ *416/977–
      2855;* ✉ *1560 Yonge St.,* ☎ *416/920–8291;* ✉ *486 Bloor St. W,* ☎
      416/588–9358; ✉ *1968 Queen St. E,* ☎ *416/691–8377;* ✉ *1218 St.
      Clair Ave. W,* ☎ *416/658–8511;* ✉ *35 Elm St.,* ☎ *416/598–1766;* ✉
      576 Danforth Ave., ☎ *416/466–2931. AE, MC, V.*

Seafood

$$$–$$$$ ✕ **Chiado.** Service is bilingual (Portuguese and English), and the fish
      are flown in from the Azores and Madeira. French doors lead to pol-
      ished wood floors, tables set with starched white napery, and plum vel-

vet armchairs. Most days you'll find bluefin tuna, piexe aspado, sword-fish, and boca negra, along with monkfish, sardines, squid, and salmon. Traditional Portuguese dishes like *asorda* of seafood, a kind of souf-flé, are served from a silver tureen. There's much for meat eaters to enjoy: beef tenderloin blessed with a wild-mushroom tawny port sauce, and roasted rack of lamb that sparkles with Duoro wine sauce. ⊠ *864 College St. W, ☎ 416/538–1910. Reservations essential. AE, DC, MC, V. Closed Sun.*

$$$–$$$$
★ ✕ **Joso's.** Joso Spralja has filled his two-story midtown restaurant with his sensual paintings of nudes and the sea, stylized busts of women, and intriguing wall hangings. Dishes from the Dalmatian coast include utterly fresh fish and unique risottos. *Risotto carajoi* is Joso's own creation of rice and sea snails simmered in an aggressively seasoned tomato sauce. Try porgy from Boston, salmon trout from north-ern Ontario, or baby clams from New Zealand. Grilled prawns, their charred tails pointing skyward, is a dish often carried aloft by speed-walking servers. ⊠ *202 Davenport Rd., ☎ 416/925–1903. Reserva-tions essential. AE, DC, MC, V. Closed Sun. No lunch Sat.*

$$–$$$$ ✕ **Rodney's Oyster Bar.** Dine-alones and showbiz and agency types fre-quent this hotbed of bivalve variety. Among the offerings are salty Lewis Islands from Cape Breton, perfect Malpeques from Rodney Clark's own oyster beds in Prince Edward Island, New York Pine Islands, and more. State-of-the-art equipment turns out soft-shell steamers, quahogs, "Oyster Slapjack Chowder," and an array of other oceanic delights. Shared meals and half-orders are okay with Rodney. Be sure to ask for the daily white-plate specials. ⊠ *209 Adelaide St. E, ☎ 416/363–8105. AE, DC, MC, V. Closed Sun.*

Steak

$$$–$$$$ ✕ **House of Chan.** Some people actually come here for the Chinese food. But it's the U.S. prime beef and the huge lobsters filling the tank that are considered by those in the know to be the best in town. Slide into a red leather booth and order a T-bone, New York strip steak, or fil-let in the size you can handle—ditto for the lobster. Go-withs are sliced fresh vegetables, crunchy batter-fried onions, and home fries. While you're waiting, have an egg roll. ⊠ *876 Eglinton Ave. W, ☎ 416/781–5575. AE, DC, MC, V. Reservations not accepted. No lunch.*

$$$–$$$$ ✕ **Moishes.** This Montréal landmark has crossed the border to take up spiffy new quarters. Courtesy reigns supreme, from complimentary valet parking after 6 PM to bar and smoking lounge service, and is car-ried through to the posh upstairs dining room. Steak, any way you like it, is king. The chopped liver appetizer piled high with fried onions is a must, but don't ignore the variety of fresh fish, chicken, and vegetables. Potato Monte Carlo, stuffed and baked, or French fries come with the main courses. Wonderful coleslaw, pickles, and a bread basket are brought with the menu. ⊠ *First Canadian Place, 77 Adelaide St. W, ☎ 416/363–3509. AE, DC, MC, V.*

Swiss

$–$$$ ✕ **Mövenpick.** Swiss hospitality makes these downtown restaurants all things to all people. Among the dinner specialties are *Zürcher G'Schnat-zlets,* the famous Swiss dish of thinly sliced veal and mushrooms in a creamy white wine sauce served with *rösti* (panfried) potatoes; *Kas-seler,* a juicy smoked, grilled pork chop served with braised savoy cab-bage; and red wine herring from Iceland marinated in wine and spices. The Swiss Farmers Sunday Brunch (York Street location only) is a vast buffet of food stations. The Yorkville location is renowned for superb fresh fish and seafood, as well as a vast selection of ice creams and desserts. ✉ *165 York St.,* ☎ *416/366–5234;* ✉ *133 Yorkville Ave.,* ☎ *416/926–9545. AE, DC, MC, V.*

Thai

$$ ✕ **Thai Magic.** Bamboo trellises, cascading vines, fish and animal carvings, and a shrine to a mermaid goddess make a magical setting for coolly saronged waiters and hot-and-spicy Thai food. "Hurricane Kettle" is a dramatic presentation of fiery seafood soup. Whole coriander lobster sparkles with flavor; chicken with cashews and whole dried chilies is for the adventurous. ✉ *1118 Yonge St.,* ☎ *416/968–7366. Reservations essential. AE, MC, V. Closed Sun. No lunch Sat.*

$–$$ ✕ **Vanipha Lanna.** People can't get enough of the clean and bright fla-
★   vors, grease-free cooking, and lovingly garnished Lao-Thai presentations at this tidy, colorful restaurant. The bamboo steamer of dumplings with minced chicken and seafood, sticky rice in a raffia cylinder, and chicken and green beans stir-fried in lime sauce are exceptional. Rice is served from a huge silver tureen. ✉ *471 Eglinton Ave. W,* ☎ *416/ 484–0895. AE, MC, V. Closed Sun.*

LODGING

Places to stay in this cosmopolitan city range from luxurious hotels to budget motels to bed-and-breakfasts. Prices are cut over weekends and during quiet times of the year (many hotels drop their rates a full 50% in January and February). Wherever you stay in Toronto, ask about a lower-than-standard rate. You can request corporate prices or inquire about special deals.

CATEGORY	COST*
$$$$	over $250
$$$	$170–$250
$$	$90–$170
$	under $90

*All prices are for a standard double room, excluding 7% GST, 5% room tax, and optional service charge, in Canadian dollars.

$$$$ 🏨 **Four Seasons Toronto.** It's hard to imagine a hotel more exclusive
★   than the elegant Four Seasons. The location is ideal: in Yorkville, a few yards from the Royal Ontario Museum. Rooms are tastefully appointed and come with comfortable bathrobes and oversize towels; maids come twice a day. Even special rates will not drop the cost much below $200 a night, but the hotel does offer some inventive packages. Its restaurants include Truffles (☞ Dining, *above*) for delectable formal dining, the Studio Cafe for all-day dining, and La Serre and the Lobby Bar for cocktails and afternoon tea. ✉ *21 Avenue Rd., 1 block north of Bloor St., M5R 2G1,* ☎ *416/964–0411,* ℻ *416/964–2301. 380 rooms. Restaurant, 2 bars, café, indoor-outdoor pool, sauna, health club, business services, meeting rooms. AE, DC, MC, V.*

$$$$ 🏨 **Grand Bay Hotel Toronto.** Formerly the Park Plaza, the freshly ren-
★   ovated Grand Bay has one of the best locations in the city, near the Royal Ontario Museum, Queen's Park, and the affluent Yorkville shopping district. Renovations in 1998 have added a pool and health club, and rooms have been enlarged. If you request a south-facing room in the older tower, you'll have stunning cityscape views—with glimpses of Lake Ontario. The Roof Restaurant, with an adjoining bar, was once described by novelist Mordecai Richler as "the only civilized place in Toronto." ✉ *4 Avenue Rd., at Bloor St. W, M5R 2E8,* ☎ *416/924– 5471 or 800/977–4197,* ℻ *416/924–4933. 348 rooms. 3 restaurants, bar, lounge, pool, health club, business services. AE, DC, MC, V.*

$$$$ ⊞ **Inter-Continental.** This handsome postmodern high-rise, part of a respected international chain, is just a half block west of the major intersection of Bloor Street, Avenue Road, and University Avenue, making it a two-minute walk to the Royal Ontario Museum and the Yorkville shopping area. Edwardian and art-deco touches enhance the public areas and the spacious, well-appointed guest rooms. The lobby lounge is especially nice for tea after a hard morning of shopping. Service here is top-notch. ⊠ *220 Bloor St. W, M5S 1T8,* ☎ *416/960–5200 or 800/267–0010,* FAX *416/324–5920. 209 rooms, 12 suites. Restaurant, lobby lounge, outdoor café, in-room modem lines, indoor lap pool, massage, sauna, exercise room. AE, DC, MC, V.*

$$$$ ⊞ **Sheraton Centre.** This busy conventioneer's favorite is across from the New City Hall, just a block from Eaton Centre, which is accessible through an underground passage. The below-ground level is part of Toronto's labyrinth of shop-lined corridors, the Underground City. The Long Bar, overlooking Nathan Phillips Square, has an unimpeded view of Ontario's highest court of law across the street; it's a favorite of lawyers, especially after winning a case. ⊠ *123 Queen St. W, M5H 2M9,* ☎ *416/361–1000,* FAX *416/947–4874. 1,314 rooms, 70 suites. 3 restaurants, bar, coffee shop, no-smoking floors, indoor-outdoor pool, hot tub, sauna, exercise room, summertime children's program (ages 18 months–12 years). AE, DC, MC, V.*

$$$$ ⊞ **Sutton Place Hotel.** The luxurious, 33-story Sutton Place draws many visiting film and stage stars because of the combination of attentive service and privacy it affords them. The spacious rooms have comfortable, traditional-style furnishings; Oriental rugs, tapestries, flowers, and plush chairs fill the public areas. The hotel is also a favorite of lobbyists, who like the proximity of the Ontario legislature and its bureaucrats. Leisure travelers appreciate the location near the Royal Ontario Museum and Yorkville. ⊠ *955 Bay St., M5S 2A2,* ☎ *416/924–9221 or 800/268–3790,* FAX *416/924–3084. 230 rooms, 60 suites. Restaurant, in-room modem lines, pool, beauty salon, health club, business services. AE, DC, MC, V.*

$$$$ ⊞ **Westin Harbour Castle.** The Westin, just steps from Harbourfront and the Toronto Islands ferry, offers the best views of Lake Ontario of any hotel in the city. A free shuttle bus and the Harbourfront LRT (light rail transit) provide links to Union Station, the subway, and downtown business and shopping. It's a favorite with conventioneers because of its enclosed bridge to the large convention center across the street. Rooms are modern in style, and frequent family and weekend rates help bring the regular price down by as much as a third. The revolving Lighthouse restaurant, atop the 37th floor, has a spectacular view. ⊠ *1 Harbour Sq., M5J 1A6,* ☎ *416/869–1600 or 800/228–3000,* FAX *416/869–3682. 980 rooms. 2 restaurants, lobby lounge, pool, health club, tennis court, playground. AE, DC, MC, V.*

$$$–$$$$ ⊞ **Delta Chelsea Inn.** Toronto's largest hotel has also become known as its theater hotel because it is within walking distance of the Pantages, Elgin, and Winter Garden theaters, and guests can book tickets with their rooms. This friendly spot has long been popular with tour groups and with business travelers on a budget. It also has more rooms than any other hotel in the British Commonwealth, so be prepared for a bustle of activity. A creative, supervised day-care service for children ages three to eight runs from 9:30 AM to 10 PM. The Delta Chelsea is a couple of short blocks north of Eaton Centre, and the College subway station is across the street in the basement of College Park shopping center. ⊠ *33 Gerrard St. W, M5G 1Z4,* ☎ *416/595–1975 or 800/ 243–5732,* FAX *416/585–4375. 1,576 rooms, 18 suites. 2 restaurants, 4 lounges, 2 pools, hot tub, sauna, exercise room, business services, children's program (ages 3–8). AE, DC, MC, V.*

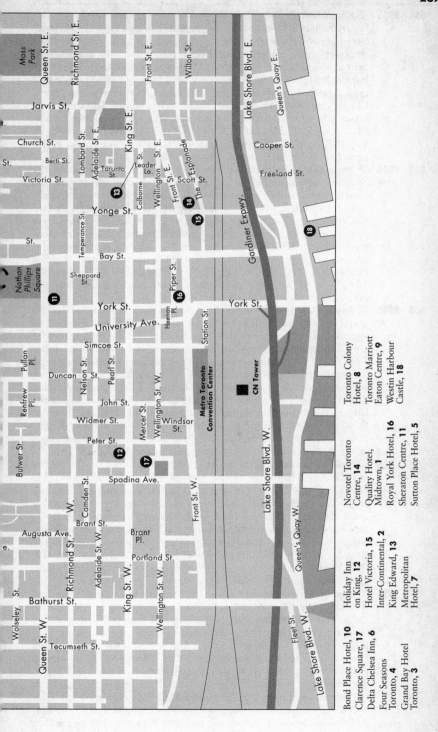

Bond Place Hotel, **10**
Clarence Square, **17**
Delta Chelsea Inn, **6**
Four Seasons
Toronto, **4**
Grand Bay Hotel
Toronto, **3**

Holiday Inn
on King, **12**
Hotel Victoria, **15**
Inter-Continental, **2**
King Edward, **13**
Metropolitan
Hotel, **7**

Novotel Toronto
Centre, **14**
Quality Hotel,
Midtown, **1**
Royal York Hotel, **16**
Sheraton Centre, **11**
Sutton Place Hotel, **5**

Toronto Colony
Hotel, **8**
Toronto Marriott
Eaton Centre, **9**
Westin Harbour
Castle, **18**

$$$-$$$$ ⊡ **King Edward.** The grande dame of downtown Toronto hotels, this beauty built in 1903 attracts a well-heeled clientele. The "King Eddie," a member of the worldwide Forte chain, still has an air of understated elegance, with its vaulted ceiling, marble pillars, and palm trees. A highlight here is the Chef's Table: for $110 per person, executive chef John Higgins will prepare an eight-course meal for up to eight people, at a table right next to the stoves in his kitchen. The hotel's restaurants, Chiaro's and the Café Victoria, are favorites among Toronto power brokers. For a genteel afternoon pastime, take tea in the lobby lounge. ⊠ *37 King St. E, M5C 1E9,* ☎ *416/863–9700 or 800/225–5843,* FAX *416/367–5515. 298 rooms. 2 restaurants, lobby lounge, spa, health club, business services, meeting rooms. AE, DC, MC, V.*

$$$-$$$$ ⊡ **Metropolitan Hotel.** This contemporary 26-story hotel could hardly
★   be more convenient: behind City Hall, a few short blocks from Eaton Centre, and near the theater district. The guest rooms, which include eight for travelers with disabilities, are decorated with finely crafted modern furniture; some have king-size beds, and executive rooms have a work center with printer and fax. Restaurants include Lai Wah Heen (☞ Dining, *above*), Hemispheres, and Mezzanine Café. The hotel is adjacent to the Museum of Textiles. ⊠ *108 Chestnut St., north of Nathan Phillips Sq., M5G 1R3,* ☎ *416/977–5000,* FAX *416/977–9513 or 800/ 323–7500. 481 rooms. 3 restaurants, 2 bars, indoor pool, sauna, hot tub, health club, business services. AE, DC, MC, V.*

$$$-$$$$ ⊡ **Royal York Hotel.** One of Canada's famous railway hotels, this
★   grand hostelry was built by the Canadian Pacific Railway for the convenience of passengers using the nearby train station. An award-winning refurbishment of the hotel has returned the lobby to its classic 1929 decor. Business floors and a work center cater to travelers' needs; the health club has picturesque views of the city. You can have full afternoon tea at the Royal Tea Room or sample wine from the Acadian Room's extensive wine list. The hotel's links to Union Station and the Underground City make it very handy in cold weather. ⊠ *100 Front St. W, M5J 1E3,* ☎ *416/368–2511 or 800/663–7229,* FAX *416/368– 9040. 1,408 rooms. 6 restaurants, 4 bars, indoor lap pool, massage, sauna, health club, business services, travel services. AE, DC, MC, V.*

$$$ ⊡ **Holiday Inn on King.** In the heart of the entertainment district, the Holiday Inn is just three blocks north of the convention center, Sky-Dome, and CN Tower; also nearby is Queen Street and its lively club scene. The hotel occupies floors 9–20 of a 20-story tower; you can request views of the lake, skyline, or SkyDome. The swimming pool is tiny, but the exercise room is appealing. All in all, this chain offering (which is at the lower end of its price category) is a good value. ⊠ *370 King St. W, M5V 1J9,* ☎ *416/599–4000 or 800/263–6364,* FAX *416/ 599–7394. 426 rooms. 2 restaurants, refrigerators, pool, massage, sauna, exercise room. AE, DC, MC, V.*

$$$ ⊡ **Toronto Marriott Eaton Centre.** The Marriott has a terrific location: It's part of Eaton Centre and within easy walking distance of SkyDome, the convention center, and the theater and financial districts. The hotel's pretty guest rooms, decorated in dusty rose and gray, have larger bedrooms than most you'll find in Toronto; irons, ironing boards, and hair dryers are standard. The indoor rooftop swimming pool provides a fabulous view of the city. At the airy Parkside Café on the main floor, you can sip your coffee while basking in the light from the enormous windows, which overlook the Church of the Holy Trinity. ⊠ *525 Bay St., M5G 2L2,* ☎ *416/597–9200,* FAX *416/597–9211. 435 rooms, 24 suites. 2 restaurants, lobby lounge, sports bar, indoor pool, health club, business services. AE, DC, MC, V.*

$$-$$$ ⊡ **Novotel Toronto Centre.** The moderately priced Novotel—part of a popular French chain—has comfortable modern rooms that are a good

value. All rooms have a hair dryer, voice mail, and video checkout, and there are a good number of fitness facilities. This nine-floor hotel is just behind the Hummingbird Centre for the Performing Arts and within walking distance of the St. Lawrence market. ✉ *45 The Esplanade, M5E 1W2,* ☎ *416/367–8900,* 𝔽𝔸𝕏 *416/860–5166. 266 rooms. Restaurant, minibars, no-smoking floors, indoor pool, hot tub, sauna, exercise room. AE, DC, MC, V.*

\$\$–\$\$\$ 🏨 **Toronto Colony Hotel.** The Colony offers somewhat less expensive accommodations than many of the large hotels in the downtown core. It has an ideal location, close to the subway, the theater district, and Eaton Centre. The lobby is drab but functional, while the rooms are simple but pleasant; some have spectacular, unimpeded views of downtown Toronto. ✉ *89 Chestnut St., M5G 1R1,* ☎ *416/977–0707,* 𝔽𝔸𝕏 *416/585–3164. 721 rooms, 15 suites. Restaurant, sports bar, in-room modem lines, minibars, indoor pool, outdoor pool, business services. AE, DC, MC, V.*

\$\$ 🏨 **Bond Place Hotel.** If you're on a limited budget but want a central location, this hotel just two blocks from Eaton Centre is a good choice. It has clean, spacious rooms with color TVs and phones but few other frills. Although the Garden Café serves breakfast, lunch, and dinner, you'll find a wider variety of food at Eaton Centre. The Bond Place is also a few minutes' walk from the Elgin, Pantages, and Winter Garden theaters. ✉ *65 Dundas St. E, M5B 2G8,* ☎ *416/362–6061 or 800/ 268–9390 in Canada and northeastern U.S.,* 𝔽𝔸𝕏 *416/362–9372. 286 rooms. Restaurant, no-smoking floors. AE, DC, MC, V.*

\$\$ 🏨 **Clarence Square.** On the edge of the entertainment and financial districts, this newly opened bed-and-breakfast has elegant accommodations in a beautiful Victorian town house that overlooks a small park. A marble fireplace, French doors, and a 12-ft ceiling enhance the delightful main salon, and all guest rooms come with whirlpool tubs and TV. Host and owner Susan Walker assiduously cares for the well-being of her guests. This property is at the lower end of the price category. ✉ *13 Clarence Sq., M5V 1H1,* ☎ *416/598–0616,* 𝔽𝔸𝕏 *416/ 598–4200. 3 rooms. AE, DC, MC, V.*

\$\$ 🏨 **Hotel Victoria.** Travelers on budgets will appreciate the personal
★ service and quiet atmosphere of this Victorian-era hotel on Yonge Street hotel a block east of Union Station. Clean and cozy, it's a good choice for those who want to be near everything downtown without paying dearly (the Victoria is at the low end of its price category). ✉ *56 Yonge St., M5E 1G5,* ☎ *416/363–1666, 800/363–8228 in Canada and N.Y.,* 𝔽𝔸𝕏 *416/363–7327. 48 rooms. Restaurant, bar. AE, DC, MC, V.*

\$\$ 🏨 **Quality Hotel, Midtown.** The Choice Hotel chain has four downtown locations plus four hotels near the airport. This one is close to the University of Toronto, the Royal Ontario Museum, and the Yorkville shopping district. Rooms are comfortable but not luxurious. The St. George subway stop is steps away, and underground parking is available. It's hard to beat the combination of convenience and price here. ✉ *280 Bloor St. W, M5S 1V8,* ☎ *416/968–0010. 210 rooms. Restaurant, coffee shop. AE, D, MC, V.*

NIGHTLIFE AND THE ARTS

Toronto's performing arts scene has flourished in recent years, aided by the introduction of some dazzling new venues and the refurbishment of some magnificent old ones. The influence of the burgeoning film industry has made nightlife in this once staid town a lot more glamorous, too.

The Arts

The best places to get information on cultural happenings are in the Thursday editions of the *Toronto Star,* the Saturday *Globe and Mail,* the free weeklies *Now* and *Eye Weekly,* and *Toronto Life* magazine. For half-price tickets on the day of a performance, try the **Five Star Tickets booth** (☎ 416/536–6468), outside Eaton Centre at Yonge and Dundas streets. The booth is open Monday–Saturday noon–7:30 and Sunday 11–3. Tickets are sold for cash only, all sales are final, and a service charge is added to the price of each ticket. The booth also gives out brochures on the city. Tickets for almost any event in the city can be obtained through **Ticketmaster** (☎ 416/870–8000). Tickets can be picked up at the door on the night of the event or at any Ticketmaster location; note that a service charge applies to all orders.

Classical Concerts

The **Toronto Symphony** has achieved world acclaim, with conductors the quality of Seiji Ozawa, Walter Susskind, Sir Thomas Beecham, and Andrew Davis. Maestro Jukka-Pekka Sarasti has reinvigorated the repertory with 20th-century pieces to complement older masterworks. When the orchestra is home, it presents about three concerts weekly from September through May in Roy Thomson Hall (☞ Concert Halls and Theaters, *below*).

The **Toronto Mendelssohn Choir** (☎ 416/598–0422) often performs with the Toronto Symphony. This 180-singer group, going since 1894, has been applauded worldwide, and its *Messiah* is handled well every Christmas. For tickets call 416/598–0422 or Roy Thomson Hall (☞ Concert Halls and Theaters, *below*).

Concert Halls and Theaters

The **Hummingbird Centre for the Performing Arts** is the home of the Canadian Opera Company and the National Ballet of Canada. It also hosts visiting comedians, pre-Broadway musicals, rock stars, and almost anyone else who can fill its 3,167 seats. Avoid the extreme front rows (lettered AA, BB, and so on). ✉ *1 Front St. E, 1 block east of Union Station,* ☎ *416/872–2262.* 🎟 *Tickets $20–$50.*

Massey Hall is cramped and dingy, but its near-perfect acoustics and its handsome, U-shape tiers sloping down to the stage have made it a happy place to hear music for almost a century. The best seats are in Rows G–M center and Rows 32–50 in the balcony. ✉ *Entrance on Shuter St., off Victoria St. or Yonge St., east of Eaton Centre,* ☎ *416/593–4828.* 🎟 *Tickets $20–$60.*

The **Roy Thomson Hall** has become the most important concert hall in Toronto. It is the home of the Toronto Symphony and the Toronto Mendelssohn Choir. It also hosts orchestras from around the world and popular entertainers, as well as Toronto Film Festival Gala Presentations. The best seats are in the center mezzanine. Rush seats are sold two hours before curtain. Tours highlight the acoustic and architectural features of the striking round structure. ✉ *60 Simcoe St., at King St. W, 1 block west of University Ave.,* ☎ *416/872–4255 or 416/593–4828.* 🎟 *Tickets $20–$90, theater tour $3.* 🕐 *Theater tour times vary; phone ahead.*

The **Royal Alexandra,** which opened in 1907, has plush red seats, gold brocade, and baroque swirls and curlicues that make theater-going a refined experience here. The best seats are in Rows C–L center; avoid Rows A and B; for musicals try the first rows of the first balcony. ✉ *260 King St. W,* ☎ *416/872–3333 or 416/872–1212.* 🎟 *Tickets $35–$75 (more for major musicals).*

Since 1970 the **St. Lawrence Centre for the Arts** has been presenting everything from live theater to string quartets and forums on city issues. The main hall, the luxuriously appointed Bluma Appel Theatre, hosts the often brilliant productions of the Canadian Stage Company and Theatre Plus. The best seats are Rows E–N, Seats 1–10. ⊠ *Front St. and Scott St.,* ☎ *416/366–7723.* 🎟 *Tickets $20–$45.*

Dance

Since its debut in 1951, the **National Ballet of Canada** has done some extraordinary things, with such principal dancers as Karen Kain, Rex Harrington, Kimberly Glasco, and Jeremy Ramson all wowing audiences. ⊠ *Hummingbird Centre for the Performing Arts, 1 Front St. E,* ☎ *416/345–9686.* 🎟 *Tickets $15–$55.* ☉ *Performances Nov.–Dec., Feb., and May.*

Toronto Dance Theatre, which has roots in the Martha Graham tradition, tours Canada and has played major festivals in England, Europe, and the United States. ⊠ *Premiere Dance Theatre, Harbourfront, 235 Queen's Quay W,* ☎ *416/973–4000.* 🎟 *Tickets $20–$32.*

Film

Toronto has a devoted film audience. The result is an embarrassment of riches: commercial first- and second-run showings, festivals, lecture series for every taste. In September the world-class **Toronto International Film Festival** (☎ 416/967–7371 or 416/968–3456) presents new work from around the world as well as retrospectives of the films of major directors and tributes to particular actors.

Carlton Cinemas (⊠ 20 Carlton St., east of College St. subway, ☎ 416/598–2309) shows rare, important films from Canada and around the world in nearly a dozen screening rooms. **Festival Cinema's Royal Cinema** (⊠ 606 College St., ☎ 416/516–4845) is a brand-new repertory cinema on a hip street in Little Italy. It plays some popular and some obscure films and will be the new flagship theater for the Toronto International Film Festival.

Opera

Since its founding in 1950, the **Canadian Opera Company** (☎ 416/363–8231) has grown into the largest producer of opera in Canada. Each year, at the Hummingbird Centre for the Performing Arts (☞ Concert Halls and Theaters, *above*), more than 150,000 people attend the season of seven operas and hear world-class performers. The COC also performs free outdoor concerts during the summer at Harbourfront.

Theater

Toronto, after London and New York, is the largest center for English-speaking theater in the world. The more than four dozen performing spaces here present everything from the finest in classic and contemporary drama to well-produced Broadway and West End fare. Full-price tickets can range from about $20 to $100.

The **Elgin** and **Winter Garden Theatres** (⊠ 189 Yonge St., north of Queen St. W, ☎ 416/872–5555 for tickets, 416/314–2901 for tours) are two renovated vaudeville palaces, stacked upon one another. The Elgin, downstairs, has about 1,500 seats; the Winter Garden is some 500 seats smaller; both are stunningly attractive. These landmark theaters from 1913 showcase traveling as well as locally based productions of all kinds. Tours are Thursday at 5 and Saturday at 11; cost is $4.

The **Ford Centre for the Performing Arts** (⊠ 5040 Yonge St., ☎ 416/872–2222 or 416/733–9388), less than a half-hour drive north of the waterfront, close to the North York subway stop, often hosts mega-musicals and classical music concerts. The stunning **Pantages Theatre**

(✉ 263 Yonge St., ☎ 416/872–2222), a restored 1920 vaudeville palace, has been home to *The Phantom of the Opera* for more than eight years. The **Princess of Wales Theatre** (✉ 300 King St. W, ☎ 416/872–1212) hosts productions such as the musical *Chicago*.

The **Factory Theatre** (✉ 125 Bathurst St., ☎ 416/504–9971) is an alternative theater devoted to original and experimental work. The **Tarragon Theatre** (✉ 30 Bridgman Ave., ☎ 416/531–1827), in an old warehouse and railroad district, is the natural habitat for excellent indigenous Canadian theater. **Théâtre Passe Muraille** (✉ 16 Ryerson Ave., ☎ 416/504–7529), in the unfashionable area of Bathurst and Queen streets, has long been the home of fine Canadian collaborative theater.

The **Young People's Theatre** (✉ 165 Front St. E, near Sherbourne, ☎ 416/862–2222), the only theater center in the country devoted solely to children, does not compromise its dramatic integrity.

Nightlife

The area bounded by Front, Adelaide, Peter, and John streets has become the center of Toronto's club and bar scene in recent years.

Bars

The **Loose Moose Tap & Grill** (✉ 220 Adelaide St. W, ☎ 416/971–5252) is a popular bar. Hockey superstar Wayne Gretzky owns, appropriately, **Wayne Gretzky's** (✉ 99 Blue Jays Way, ☎ 416/979–7825), a sports bar and restaurant.

Comedy Clubs

Second City (✉ 56 Blue Jays Way, near the SkyDome, ☎ 416/343–0011 or 800/263–4485), in brand-new quarters in the entertainment district, continues to provide some of the best comedy in North America. Among those who have cut their teeth here are Dan Aykroyd, Martin Short, Andrea Martin, Catherine O'Hara, and the late John Candy. Visitors can test their knowledge of Canadian comics by trying to identify the celebrities in the large photographs that decorate the lobby. There are shows every night at 8, with an additional late-night show Friday and Saturday at 10:30; admission is $10–$16.

Yuk-Yuk's Komedy Kabaret (✉ 2335 Yonge St., north of Eglinton Ave.; ✉ 5165 Dixie St., Mississauga; ☎ 416/967–6425 for tickets for both locations) has always been a major place for comedy. This is where Howie Mandel and Jim Carrey got their starts and where such comic luminaries as George Carlin, Rodney Dangerfield, Robin Williams, and Mort Sahl have presented their best routines. The Mississauga location is open Thursday–Sunday; the Toronto Kabaret is open daily.

Dancing

At **Big Bop** (✉ 651 Queen St. W, ☎ 416/504–6699), DJs play '60s music downstairs and '90s music upstairs in a four-story, century-old fun house. At **Fluid** (✉ 217 Richmond St. W, ☎ 416/593–6116), which caters to a Yorkville-ish older (25–35) crowd, the decor is metallic and modular, with custom-made furnishings. The **Government** (✉ 132 Queen's Quay, ☎ 416/869–1462), near Harbourfront, draws lovers of dance, rock, and alternative music, while professional dancers perform above the crowd.

Entertainment Center

Down by the lake, the new and enormous **Docks** (✉ 11 Polson St., ☎ 416/469–5655) provides complete entertainment for party goers: video games, two basketball courts, a swimming pool, 22 outdoor billiard tables, indoor and outdoor dance floors, and even a bungee-jumping platform. There are plenty of places to drink at night. The

Docks also has spectacular views of Toronto's skyline from its outdoor terrace.

Gay and Lesbian Clubs

Fab and *X-Extra* chronicle the gay and lesbian scene. These free publications can be readily found in the Church and Wellesley district. Near or along Church Street are several nightlife options. The Sunday-night window drag show at **Bar 501** (⊠ 501 Church St., ☎ 416/944–3272) is an institution. For the aspiring Versace-model crowd, **Boots** (⊠ 592 Sherbourne, ☎ 416/921–0665) rocks in a fabulous warehouse space. **Crews** (⊠ 508 Church St., ☎ 416/972–1662) is youthful. **Woody's** (⊠ 467 Church St., ☎ 416/972–0887) is fashionable yet neighborly.

Jazz Clubs

Chick 'n Deli (⊠ 744 Mt. Pleasant Rd., near Eglinton Ave., ☎ 416/489–3363 or 416/489–7931), long one of the great jazz places in Toronto, now has jazz only on Saturday; there's a dance floor, and dark wood everywhere gives it a casual, neighborhood-pub feel. **Top O' The Senator** (⊠ 249 Victoria St., ☎ 416/364–7517), this city's first club exclusively for jazz and cabaret, has the atmosphere of a 1930s lounge. It's closed on Monday.

Lounges

In the classy Four Seasons Hotel, **La Serre** (⊠ Avenue Rd. and Yorkville Ave., ☎ 416/964–0411), which looks like a library in a mansion, has a stand-up piano bar and a pianist worth standing for. Up on the 51st floor of the ManuLife Centre, the **Panorama** (⊠ 55 Bloor St. W, at Bay St., ☎ 416/967–5225) features Latin American music. The gorgeous and tasteful **Roof Lounge** (⊠ Avenue Rd. and Bloor St., ☎ 416/924–5471) at the Grand Bay Hotel Toronto has been used as a setting in the writings of such Canadian literary luminaries as Margaret Atwood and Mordecai Richler.

Rock and Popular Music

Most major international recording companies have offices in Toronto, so the city is a regular stop for top musical performers of today. Tickets ($15–$100) can usually be booked through **Ticketmaster** (☎ 416/870–8000). Major venues include the **SkyDome** (⊠ 1 Blue Jays Way, Front St. W and Peter St., ☎ 416/341–3663), **Maple Leaf Gardens** (⊠ 60 Carlton St., ☎ 416/977–1641), and the **Hummingbird Centre for the Performing Arts** (⊠ 1 Front St. E, ☎ 416/872–2262).

Kingswood Music Theatre (⊠ Paramount Canada's Wonderland at Hwy. 400, 10 min north of Hwy. 401, ☎ 905/832–8131 or 905/832–7000) has important rock and pop concerts during the warmer months. **Ontario Place** (⊠ Lake Shore Blvd. W between Dufferin and Bathurst Sts., ☎ 416/314–9900) has pop, rock, and jazz concerts all summer at very reasonable prices. You may pay around $10 to see or hear a fabulous singer or group (or orchestra or ballet corps) that would cost you $25–$50 elsewhere. This is one of the loveliest and least expensive places for concerts in the city. The **Phoenix Concert Theatre** (⊠ 410 Sherbourne St., ☎ 416/323–1251) has a wide variety of music, with DJs from local radio stations broadcasting live on Saturday (alternative music) and with sporadic live cut-ins on Monday (classic rock). A major showcase for more daring acts has long been the **Rivoli** (⊠ 332 Queen St. W, west of University Ave., ☎ 416/597–0794), where the backroom functions as a club, with theater happenings, progressive rock and jazz, and comedy troupes with very funny improvisations.

OUTDOOR ACTIVITIES AND SPORTS

Participant Sports

The **Ministry of Tourism and Recreation** (⊠ Queen's Park, M7A 2R2) has pamphlets on various activities. For information on sports in the province, call **TraveLinx Ontario** (☎ 416/314–0944 or 800/668–2746 in the continental United States and Canada, except the Northwest Territories and the Yukon).

The **Toronto and Region Conservation Authority** (☎ 416/661–6600) has information about the fine conservation areas that circle metropolitan Toronto. Most have large areas for swimming, sledding, and cross-country skiing, as well as skating, fishing, and boating.

Biking

More than 29 km (18 mi) of street bike routes cut across the city, and dozens more follow safer paths through Toronto's many parks. Maps are available at most local bike shops. Bikes can be rented on the Toronto Islands. The 19-km (12-mi) **Martin Goodman Trail** runs along the waterfront from the Balmy Beach Club in the east end past the western beaches southwest of High Park.

Toronto Parks and Recreation (⊠ 55 John St., ☎ 416/392–8186) has maps that show biking (and jogging) routes that run through Toronto parkland. **Ontario Cycling** (⊠ 1185 Eglinton Ave. E, ☎ 416/426–7242) has maps, booklets, and information.

Boating

You can rent canoes, punts, and/or sailboats at Grenadier Pond in High Park, at Centre Island, at Ontario Place, at Harbourfront, and at most of the conservation areas surrounding metro Toronto.

Fitness Facilities

Nearly every major hotel has a decent indoor swimming pool; some even have indoor-outdoor pools. Many also have health clubs; call ahead to inquire about availability and fees, particularly if you're not a guest.

Golf

The season lasts only from April to late October. For information about courses, contact **Toronto Parks and Recreation** (☎ 416/392–8186) or **TraveLinx Ontario** (☎ 416/314–0944). The top course is **Glen Abbey** (⊠ 1333 Dorval Dr., Oakville, ☎ 905/844–1800), where the Canadian Open Championship is held in late summer; cart and greens fees will cost up to $75 on weekends, but this par-73, 18-hole course is a real beauty.

Horseback Riding

Sunnybrook Stables (⊠ Leslie St. and Eglinton Ave., ☎ 416/444–4044), in Sunnybrook Park, has an indoor arena, an outdoor ring, and about 19 km (nearly 12 mi) of bridle trails through the Don valley.

Ice-Skating

Toronto operates some 30 outdoor artificial rinks and 100 natural-ice rinks—and all are free. Among the most popular are those in Nathan Phillips Square, in front of the New City Hall at Queen and Bay streets; down at Harbourfront, which has Canada's largest outdoor artificial ice rink; College Park, at Yonge and College streets; Grenadier Pond, within High Park, at Bloor and Keele streets; and inside Hazelton Lanes, the classy shopping mall on the edge of Yorkville, on Avenue Road, just above Bloor Street. Bring your own skates to most outdoor rinks; one exception is Nathan Phillips Square, which has rentals. For details on any city rink, call **Toronto City Parks** (☎ 416/392–1111).

Jogging

The **Martin Goodman Trail** (☞ Bicycling, *above*) is ideal. Also try the boardwalk of the Beaches in the east end, High Park in the west end, the Toronto Islands, or any of Toronto's parks. Some hotels will provide maps of popular jogging routes.

Sailing

This can be a breeze, especially between April and October. Contact the **Ontario Sailing Association** (✉ 65 Guise St. E., Hamilton L8L 8B4, ☎ 416/425–7245). The **Royal Canadian Yacht Club** (✉ 141 St. George St., ☎ 416/967–7245) has its summer headquarters in a beautiful Victorian mansion on Centre Island.

Skiing

CROSS-COUNTRY

Try Toronto's parks and ravines; High Park; the lakefront along the southern edge of the city; Tommy Thompson Park; Toronto Islands; and Centennial Park, in the western borough of Etobicoke, only a 20-minute drive from downtown.

DOWNHILL

The best alpine hills are a good 45–60 minutes north of the city (☞ Barrie, Collingwood, and Huntsville *in* Chapter 7).

Tennis

The city provides dozens of free courts, many of them floodlighted. Parks with courts open from 7 AM to 11 PM, in season, include High Park, off Bloor Street at Keele Street, in the west end; Stanley Park, on King Street West, three blocks west of Bathurst Street; and Eglinton Park, on Eglinton Avenue West, just east of Avenue Road. A number of indoor courts are open throughout winter. Call the **Ontario Tennis Association** (☎ 416/426–7135).

Spectator Sports

Auto Racing

For the past several years, the **Molson Indy** has been roaring around the Canadian National Exhibition grounds for three days in mid-July. You'll pay more than $85 for a three-day "red" reserved seat, but general admission can be as cheap as $10–$20, depending upon the day. For tickets and information call Ticketmaster (☎ 416/872–4639). Less than a half-hour drive away is the **Cayuga International Speedway** (☎ 705/743–6671), where international stock-car races are held May–September.

Baseball

The **Toronto Blue Jays** (☎ 416/341–1111) play at SkyDome April–September. Tickets range from $4 (for seats near heaven) to $25. Games usually sell out, so plan way ahead of your visit.

Basketball

The **Toronto Raptors** (☎ 416/366–3865) have played at SkyDome, but during 1999 the team plans to move to the new Air Canada Centre (✉ 40 Bay St.), right behind Union Station. The season runs late October–April.

Canoeing and Rowing

Canoe Ontario (☎ 416/426–7170) has information about one of the world's largest canoeing and rowing regattas, held every July 1 on Toronto Island's Long Pond.

Football

The Canadian Football League has teetered near extinction in recent years, but it continues to draw fans. The **Toronto Argonauts** (☎ 416/341–5151), which are partly owned by hockey superstar Wayne Gretzky, have been as erratic as the league itself. The Argos play their home games from June to November at the SkyDome.

Golf

The site of the **Canadian Open Golf Championship** is Glen Abbey (☞ Participant Sports, *above*), a course designed by Jack Nicklaus. This tournament is one of golf's Big Five and is played in late summer.

Hockey

The **Toronto Maple Leafs** (✉ 60 Carlton St., ☎ 416/977–1641) play 40 home games each season (October–April), usually on Wednesday and Saturday nights, in Maple Leaf Gardens. There are always tickets available at each game—at least from scalpers (scalping is illegal, but they're there) in front of the stadium on Carlton Street, a half block east of the corner of Yonge and College streets. You can also show up at the box office at 9 AM sharp on the day of the game for rush seats. During the 1999 season, the team plans to move to the new Air Canada Centre (✉ 40 Bay St.), right behind Union Station.

Horse Racing

HARNESS AND THOROUGHBRED RACING

The **Ontario Jockey Club** (☎ 416/675–7223 or 888/675–7223) operates two major racetracks, Woodbine and Mohawk. **Woodbine Race Track** (✉ Hwy. 427 and Rexdale Blvd., 30 min northwest of downtown Toronto, near the airport, ☎ 416/675–7223 or 888/675–7223) is the showplace of Thoroughbred and harness racing in Canada. Horses run late April–late October. **Mohawk** (✉ Hwy. 401, 30 min west of Toronto, Campbellville, ☎ 416/675–7223 or 888/675–7223), in the heart of Ontario's Standardbred breeding country, has a glass-enclosed, climate-controlled grandstand. Nordic Gaming operates **Fort Erie** (✉ 230 Catherine St., Queen Elizabeth Way/Bertie St. exit, Fort Erie, ☎ 905/871–3200), one of the loveliest tracks in the world, with willows, manicured hedges, and flower-bordered infield lakes.

ROYAL HORSE SHOW

This highlight of Canada's equestrian season, part of the **Royal Winter Fair** each November, is held at the CNE grounds (✉ Dufferin St., at waterfront, ☎ 416/393–6400).

Soccer

Although Toronto keeps getting and losing and getting a professional soccer team, you can catch this exciting sport, as well as collegiate football, at **Varsity Arena and Stadium** (✉ Bloor St. W at Bedford, 1 block west of Royal Ontario Museum and University Ave., ☎ 416/978–7388).

SHOPPING

Toronto, the shopping capital of Canada, has a fine selection of British Isles imports and Canadiana, as well as everything from books and antiques to clothing. The biggest sale day of the year is Boxing Day, the first business day after Christmas, when nearly everything in the city is half price. As winter fades, clothing prices tend to drop even further. Summer sales start in late June and continue through August.

Shoppers can haggle at flea markets, including the Harbourfront Antiques Market, and perhaps in the Chinatown and Kensington Market–Spadina Avenue areas. In some small boutiques, where the owner is in attendance, you may be able to negotiate for a better price than what you see on the ticket.

Most shops are open Monday–Wednesday and Saturday 10–6, Thursday– Friday until 8, and Sunday noon to 5. Many stores are closed on major holidays, including Good Friday, Easter Monday, and Victoria Day (third Monday in May).

Shopping Districts and Malls

On **Bloor Street** you'll find such wonderful stores as Zoe, with haute couture designs; the Bay, a department store with clothes for men and women; Holt Renfrew, possibly the most stunning store in Toronto, with marble, chrome, glass, and glittering fashions for both sexes; Harry Rosen for men; and such shoe shops as Boutique Quinto and David's. In the Colonnade, on the south side of Bloor Street, a few doors east of University Avenue, is another upscale cluster of stores. Perhaps the most stunning recent addition to the Bloor shopping strip is the flagship Club Monaco store at the corner of Avenue Road, which occupies a fully restored 1912 neoclassical University of Toronto building. Even with the invasion of such American chains as the Gap and Banana Republic, the tone is très expensive, and très good.

The **Eaton Centre** (⊠ 220 Yonge St., ☎ 416/598–2322; ☞ Central Toronto *in* Exploring, *above*) is a large galleria-style shopping center downtown, on Yonge Street between Queen and Dundas streets. With scores of stores and restaurants, all sheltered from the weather, it's a major tourist attraction. Generally, the lower levels are lower priced, and the higher levels are more expensive. Hours are Monday–Saturday 10–9, Sunday noon–5.

Harbourfront includes an antiques market (⊠ 390 Queen's Quay W, ☎ 416/260–2626) that is Canada's biggest on Sunday, when it draws about 200 dealers. The market is open Tuesday–Friday 11–5, weekends 10–6. The **Queen's Quay Terminal** (⊠ 207 Queen's Quay W, ☎ 416/203–0501) is a renovated warehouse that houses a collection of unique boutiques, crafts stalls, patisseries, and so on; it's a great place to buy gifts. There's frequent streetcar service from Union Station, but it's a fairly easy walk. Parking is expensive.

Queen Street West, starting just west of University Avenue and continuing past Spadina Avenue, creeping ever westward past Bathurst Street, is a trendy area near the Ontario College of Art and Design. Here, you'll find young, hip designers; new- and used-book bookstores; vintage clothes; two comic-book stores, including the biggest in North America (Silver Snail, No. 367; also check out the Dragon Lady Comic Shop at No. 200); and the more progressive private galleries.

Spadina Avenue (☞ Central Toronto *in* Exploring Toronto, *above*), from Wellington Street north to College Street, has plenty of low-price clothing for the family, as well as fur and leather factory outlets. Winner's, south of King Street, is a good discount outlet for women and children. This area can be very crowded on weekends.

The **Underground City** is a vast maze of shopping warrens that burrow between and underneath the office towers downtown. The tenants are mostly chain and convenience stores, and the shopping is rather dull. The network runs roughly from the Royal York Hotel near Union Station north to Eaton Centre.

Yorkville is where you'll find the big fashion names, fine leather goods, important jewelers, some of the top private art galleries, upscale shoe stores, and discount china and glassware. Streets to explore include

Yorkville Avenue, Cumberland Street, and Scollard Street, all running parallel to Bloor Street, and Hazelton Avenue, running north from Yorkville Avenue near Avenue Road. Hazelton Lanes, between Hazelton Avenue and Avenue Road, and the adjacent York Square are among the most chichi shopping areas in Canada, and they are headquarters for café society during the brief annual spell of warm weather.

Department Stores

The major department stores have branches around the city and flagship stores downtown. Service tends to be very slow and uninformed compared with that of boutiques. The **Bay** is on Yonge Street between Queen and Richmond streets (☎ 416/861–9111) and at Yonge and Bloor streets (☎ 416/972–3333). Another big name is **Eaton's**, in Eaton Centre (☞ *above*). The exclusive **Holt Renfrew** (⌧ 50 Bloor St. W, ☎ 416/922–2333) sings with élan and quality.

Specialty Shops

Antiques

Yorkville is the headquarters of establishment antiques dealers. There are several other pockets around town, including a strip along Queen Street East, roughly between Sherbourne and George streets. The antiques market at Harbourfront (☞ Shopping Districts and Malls, *above*) is another choice.

The **Allery** (⌧ 145 Front St. E, ☎ 416/869–9393) specializes in antique prints and maps. **Art Metropole** (⌧ 788 King St. W, ☎ 416/703–4400) specializes in limited-edition, small-press, or self-published artists' books from around the world. **Quasi Modo Modern Furniture** (⌧ 789 Queen St. W, ☎ 416/703–8300) has a quirky collection of 20th-century furniture and design; you never know what will be on display: vintage bicycles, Noguchi lamps, or a corrugated cardboard table by Frank Gehry. The **20th Century Gallery** (⌧ 23 Beverley St., north of Queen St., ☎ 416/598–2172) is for serious collectors of 20th-century design, particularly furniture, lamps, jewelry, and decorative arts.

Art Galleries

Toronto is a cosmopolitan art center with more than 300 commercial galleries offering every kind of art for viewing and sale, from representational to abstract, from Inuit to other native art. You can stroll from gallery to gallery in two major districts—the Yorkville area and Queen Street west of University Avenue. Many galleries are closed Sunday and Monday, but call to check.

For avant-garde works, look in **Cold City** (⌧ 686 Richmond St. W, ☎ 416/504–6681). **Feheley Fine Arts** (⌧ 14 Hazelton Ave. in Hazelton Lanes, ☎ 416/323–1373) deals exclusively in Canadian Inuit art with a special emphasis on the contemporary period. The **Isaacs/Inuit Gallery** (⌧ 9 Prince Arthur Ave., ☎ 416/921–9985), owned by Av Isaacs, specializes in Inuit art from prehistoric times to the present day, and in early North American Indian art, including fine arts and crafts produced in the Canadian Arctic. **Jane Corkin Gallery** (⌧ 179 John St., north of Queen St., ☎ 416/979–1980) specializes in photography. **Maslak McLeod** (⌧ 25 Prince Arthur Ave., ☎ 416/944–2577) offers an assortment of Canadian native and Inuit art. **Mercer Union** (⌧ 439 King St. W, ☎ 416/977–1412) is in the forefront of contemporary visual arts. **Prime Gallery** (⌧ 52 McCaul St., ☎ 416/593–5750) has an ever-changing array of ceramics, textiles, and some paintings, with an emphasis on the contemporary. **YYZ Artist's Outlet** (⌧ 401 Richmond

St. W, ☎ 416/410–8851) has a good collection of contemporary pieces.

Bookstores

Toronto is rich in specialty bookstores selling new books, used books, best-sellers, and remainders. If you just need a current magazine or a paperback for the plane, there are good chain stores, including Chapters and W. H. Smith.

Albert Britnell Book Shop (✉ 765 Yonge St., north of Bloor St., ☎ 416/924–3321) has been a Toronto legend since 1893, with a marvelous British ambience and great browsing. **Ballenford Architectural Books** (✉ 600 Markham St., ☎ 416/588–0800) has Canada's largest selection of architectural titles and a gallery with usually interesting exhibits of architectural drawings and related work. **Bob Miller Book Room** (✉ 180 Bloor St. W, ☎ 416/922–3557) has the best literature and philosophy section in the city and a fine staff. **Chapter** (✉ 110 Bloor St. W., ☎ 416/920–9299) is the chain's flagship store, with three floors of books, magazines, and CD-ROMs, plus Internet connections and a café. **Glad Day Books** (✉ 598A Yonge St, ☎ 416/961–4161), one block north of the Church and Wellesley gay mecca, is the city's leading gay and lesbian bookstore. **Pages Books and Magazines** (✉ 256 Queen St. W, ☎ 416/598–1447) has a wide selection of international and small-press literature; fashion and design books and magazines; and books on film, art, and literary criticism. **Theatrebooks** (✉ 11 St. Thomas St., ☎ 416/922–7175) has an astounding collection of performing arts books: theater, film, opera, jazz, television, and media studies. **This Ain't the Rosedale Library** (✉ 483 Church St., south of Wellesley Ave., ☎ 416/929–9912) stocks the largest selection of baseball books in Canada, as well as fiction, poetry, photography, design, rock, and jazz books. The **World's Biggest Book Store** (✉ 20 Edward St., 1 block north of Eaton Centre, ☎ 416/977–7009) is Canada's largest book shop. It's particularly strong in business, computer, travel, and Canadian books. **Writers & Co.** (✉ 2005 Yonge St., near Davisville, a few blocks south of Eglinton, ☎ 416/481–8432) is arguably Canada's finest literary bookstore, with hard-to-find poets, essayists, and world novelists.

Clothing

Queen Street West is well known for its stores catering to the young, hip, and zany. Among the shops are Boomer (✉ No. 309, ☎ 416/598–0013), Due West (✉ No. 431, ☎ 416/593–6267), No. 6 Clothing Company (✉ No. 290A, ☎ 416/593–2745), and Rag Tag (✉ No. 359, ☎ 416/979–3939). **Yonge Street** is a popular area for clothes shopping; try Soul Underground (✉ No. 673, ☎ 416/924–4119).

Brown's (✉ 1975 Avenue Rd., south of Hwy. 401, ☎ 416/489–1975) provides classic clothing for short men and women. There's a **Brown's** store for men only (✉ 545 Queen St. W, ☎ 416/504–5937). **Club Monaco** (✉ 157 Bloor St. W., ☎ 416/591–8837), a Canadian fashion success story, sells mid-price business clothes and sportswear for men and women in its large flagship store. **Fetoun** (✉ Four Seasons Hotel, 162 Cumberland St., ☎ 416/923–3434) sells high-fashion gowns and evening clothes. **Linda Lundstrom** (✉ 2507 Yonge St., ☎ 416/480–1602; ✉ 136 Cumberland St., ☎ 416/927–9009) is an award-winning designer of high-fashion winter clothing. This is the place to buy an eye-catching parka. **Muskat & Brown** (✉ 2528 Yonge St., ☎ 416/489–4005) is for petite women. **Venni** (✉ 274 Queen St. W, ☎ 416/597–9360; ✉ 2638 Yonge St., ☎ 416/489–9561; ✉ Bayview Village Shopping Centre, ☎ 416/223–4304) highlights trendy Canadian-designed clothing.

Food Markets

Kensington Market (✉ Northwest of Dundas St. and Spadina Ave.) is an outdoor market open every day (although many stores are closed Sunday), with a vibrant ethnic mix. Saturday is the best day to go, preferably by public transit, because parking is difficult. **St. Lawrence Market** (✉ Front and Jarvis Sts., ☎ 416/392–7219) is best early on Saturday, when, in addition to the permanent indoor market on the south side of Front Street, there's a farmer's market in the building on the north side. The historic south market was once Toronto's city hall, and it fronted the lake before extensive landfill projects were undertaken.

Gifts

Arts-on-King (✉ 169 King St. E, ☎ 416/777–9617) is a bright and spacious store with a varied selection of glass, ceramic, wood, and other creations. **Filigree** (✉ 1156 Yonge St., ☎ 416/961–5223) has a good assortment of linens, as well as drawer liners, silver frames, and other Victorian pleasures. The **Guild Shop** (✉ 118 Cumberland St., ☎ 416/921–1721) is an outlet for a wide variety of Canadian artists. Soapstone carvings from Inuit communities in the Arctic, aboriginal paintings from British Columbia and Ontario, and even woolen ties from Nova Scotia are among the items for sale. It's worth a visit for an appreciation of indigenous Canadian arts and crafts.

Robin Kay Home and Style (✉ 276 Queen St. W, ☎ 416/585–7731; ✉ 348 Danforth Ave., ☎ 416/466–1211; ✉ 394 Spadina Rd., ☎ 416/932–2833; ✉ 2599 Yonge St., ☎ 416/485–5097), this country's answer to Martha Stewart, carries lovely Canadian products to enliven any interior, from bibelots to linens.

Jewelry

Secrett Jewel Salon (✉ 150 Bloor St. W, ☎ 416/967–7500) is a reputable source of unusual gemstones and fine new and estate jewelry; local gemologists consider it the best in town.

SIDE TRIPS FROM DOWNTOWN TORONTO

Some of the city's most popular attractions are less than an hour from downtown; each could occupy half a day or more. North of downtown is the Black Creek Pioneer Village living history site. The excellent McMichael Canadian Art Collection is farther north and west, in Kleinburg. East of downtown, the technical marvels at the Ontario Science Centre draw many visitors. The sprawling Metro Toronto Zoo is farther north and east of downtown Toronto in Scarborough.

Black Creek Pioneer Village

⏱ *20 km (12 mi) north of downtown.*

This living history site is a fine reproduction of a rural Victorian community in the 1860s. Roblin's Mill, powered by a big wooden waterwheel, grinds wheat as it was done 130 years ago. At the weaver's shop, a costumed interpreter explains the magic of the loom. At other artisans' shops around the village, blacksmiths, clock makers, tinsmiths, coopers, and broom makers demonstrate their trades. Seasonal festivals are celebrated in grand style. You can drive or take a subway and bus here. ✉ *1000 Murray Ross Pkwy., corner of Jane St. and Steeles Ave., North York,* ☎ *416/736–1733.* 💲 *$9, parking $4.* ☉ *May–Dec., daily 10–4.*

McMichael Canadian Art Collection

25 km (15½ mi) north of downtown.

★ The landscape paintings of Canada's Group of Seven artists, including Tom Thomson, and extensive holdings of Inuit and native art are only part of the charm of the superb **McMichael Canadian Art Collection.** The gallery is set in 100 acres of woodland, with strategically placed windows so that visitors can appreciate the scenery as they admire art that took its inspiration from the vast outdoors. The museum is a 45-minute drive north of downtown. ⊠ *10365 Islington Ave., west of Hwy. 400 and north of Major Mackenzie Dr., Kleinburg,* ☎ *905/893–1121.* ☞ *$7.* ☉ *Mid-Oct.–mid-May, Tues.–Sat. 10–4, Sun. 10–5; mid-May–mid-Oct., daily 10–5.*

Ontario Science Centre

11 km (7 mi) northeast of downtown.

★ ☾ The **Ontario Science Centre,** a stunningly successful blend of education and entertainment, has thrilling space, communications, laser, nutrition, and electricity exhibits. Live demonstrations—lasers, glassblowing, papermaking, and more—take place throughout the day; check the schedule when you arrive. There's an Omnimax Theatre (extra charge for movies) and a fine permanent exhibition called "The Sport Show." A two-hour visit will just scratch the surface; you can spend an entire day here. ⊠ *770 Don Mills Rd.; Yonge St. subway from downtown to Eglinton station and Eglinton East bus to Don Mills Rd. stop, North York,* ☎ *416/696–3127 or 416/429–4100.* ☞ *$8, parking $5.* ☉ *Sat.–Tues. and Thurs. 10–5, Wed. 10–8, Fri. 10–9.*

Metro Toronto Zoo

35 km (22 mi) northeast of downtown.

☾ The 710 acres of the **Metro Toronto Zoo** were developed for animals, not people. In the varied terrain of the Rouge Valley, from river valley to dense forest, mammals, birds, reptiles, and fish have been grouped according to where they live in the wild. In most regions, enclosed, climate-controlled pavilions hold botanical exhibits. Don't miss the 3-ton banyan tree in the **Indo-Malayan Pavilion,** the fan-shape traveler's palm from Madagascar in the **African Pavilion,** or the perfumed flowers of the jasmine vines in the **Eurasian Pavilion.** The "round-the-world tour" takes about three hours and is suitable in any weather, because most of the time is spent inside pavilions. It's been estimated that it would take four full days to see everything, so study the map you'll get at the zoo entrance and decide what you wish to see most. For younger children, the delightful **Littlefootland** allows contact with tame animals, such as rabbits and sheep. In winter cross-country skiers follow groomed trails that skirt the animal exhibits; lessons and rentals are available. An electrically powered train moves silently among the animals. It can accommodate wheelchairs (available free inside the main gate), and all pavilions have ramp access. If you're on a very tight budget, the zoo is free if you show up the last hour of the day, enough time for a taste of this world-class institution. ⊠ *Meadowvale Rd. north of Hwy. 401, 30-min drive from downtown, or take Bus 86A from Kennedy subway station, Scarborough,* ☎ *416/392–5900.* ☞ *$12; parking Nov.–Feb. free, parking Mar.–Oct. $4.* ☉ *Daily 9:30–4:30 (call for extended summer hrs).*

TORONTO A TO Z

Arriving and Departing

By Bus

The **bus terminal** (✉ 610 Bay St., north of Dundas St., ☎ 416/393–7911) serves a number of lines, including Greyhound, Trentway-Wagar, Ontario Northland, Penetang-Midland Coach Lines (PMCL), and Can-AR. **Greyhound** (☎ 416/367–8747 or 800/231–2222 in the U.S.) has regular bus service into Toronto from the United States and Canada. From Detroit the trip takes 5 hours, from Buffalo 2–3 hours, and from Chicago and New York City 11 hours.

By Car

Detroit–Windsor and Buffalo–Fort Erie crossings can be slow, especially on weekends and holidays. The wide Highway 401—reaching up to 16 lanes as it slashes across metro Toronto from the airport on the west almost as far as the zoo on the east—is the major link between Windsor, Ontario (and Detroit), and Montréal. It's also known as the Macdonald-Cartier Freeway but is generally called simply the 401. There are no tolls, but be warned: In weekday rush hours the 401 can become dreadfully crowded, even stop-and-go.

From Buffalo or Niagara Falls, take the Queen Elizabeth Way (known as the QEW), which curves up along the western shore of Lake Ontario, eventually turns into the Gardiner Expressway, and flows right into the downtown core.

Yonge Street, which begins at the lakefront, is called Highway 11 once you get north of Toronto and continues all the way to the Ontario–Minnesota border, at Rainy River. At 1,896 km (1,175 mi), it is the longest street in the world.

By Plane

Flights into Toronto land at the **Lester B. Pearson International Airport** (✉ Airport Rd., ☎ 416/247–7678), commonly called the Toronto airport, 32 km (18 mi) northwest of downtown. Toronto is served by American, Delta, Northwest, United, US Airways, Air Canada, and Canadian Airlines International (☞ Air Travel *in* the Gold Guide for telephone numbers), as well as more than a dozen European and Asian carriers with easy connections to many U.S. cities. **Air Ontario,** affiliated with Air Canada (☎ 416/925–2311), flies from the small, downtown Island Airport to and from Ottawa, Montréal, and London (Ontario). It is a convenient alternative to Pearson International if you're staying downtown and making trips to these cities.

BETWEEN THE AIRPORT AND CENTER CITY

Although Pearson International Airport is not far from downtown, the drive can take well over an hour during weekday rush hours. Taxis and limos to a hotel or attraction near the lake typically cost $35 or more. Airport cabs have fixed rates to different parts of the city. You must pay the full fare from the airport, but it is often possible to negotiate a lower fare from downtown, where airport cabs compete with regular city cabs. It is illegal for city cabs to pick up passengers at the airport, unless they are called—a time-consuming process, but sometimes worth the wait. Some airport and downtown hotels offer free shuttle bus service from the airport.

If you rent a car at the airport, ask for a street map of the city. Highway 427 runs south some 6 km (4 mi) to the lakeshore. Here you pick up the Queen Elizabeth Way east to the Gardiner Expressway, which runs east into the heart of downtown. If you take the QEW west, you'll find yourself swinging around Lake Ontario, toward Hamilton, Niagara-on-the-Lake, and Niagara Falls.

Pacific Western (☎ 905/564–6333) offers express coach service linking the airport to three subway stops in the southwest and north-central areas of the city. Buses depart several times each hour from 8 AM to 11:30 PM. Fares average $6–$9. The service to and from several downtown hotels operates every 20 minutes from 6:25 AM to at least 10:45 PM daily and costs approximately $12.50.

By Train

Amtrak (☎ 800/872–7245) runs a daily train to Toronto from Chicago (a 12-hour trip) and another from New York City (12 hours). **Via Rail** (☎ 416/366–8411) runs trains to most major cities in Canada, and travel along the Windsor–Quebec City corridor is particularly well served. Substantial discounts are available on Via Rail if you book at least five days in advance. Amtrak and Via Rail operate from **Union Station** (✉ 65–75 Front St., between Bay and York Sts.). You can walk underground to many hotels—a real boon in inclement weather. There is a cab stand outside the main entrance of the station.

Getting Around

Much of Toronto is laid out on a grid. Yonge Street (pronounced young) is the main north–south artery. Most major cross streets are numbered east and west of Yonge Street. If you are looking for 180 St. Clair Avenue West, you want a building a few blocks *west* of Yonge Street; 75 Queen Street East is a block or so *east* of Yonge Street.

At press time the fare for buses, streetcars, and trolleys was $2 in exact change, but 10 tickets/tokens cost $16. Two-fare tickets are available for $3.50 for adults. The subways stop running at 2 AM, but the Toronto Transit Commission (TTC) has bus service from 1 AM to 5:30 AM on many major streets, including Queen, College, Bloor, Yonge, part of Dufferin, and as far north as Finch and Eglinton. The **Day Pass** costs $6.50 and is good for unlimited travel for one person, weekdays after 9:30 AM, and all day Saturday. On Sunday and holidays, it's good for up to six persons (maximum two adults) for unlimited travel. If you plan to stay in Toronto for more than a month, consider the **Metropass**, a photo-identity card that currently costs $83 for adults plus $3 extra for the photo. You can call the **TTC** (☎ 416/393–4636 or 416/393–8663) from 7 AM to 11:30 PM for information on how to take public transit to any street or attraction in the city. The TTC publishes a very useful **Ride Guide** that shows nearly every major place of interest and how to reach it by public transit. These guides are available in most subways and many other places around the city.

By Bus

All buses and streetcars accept exact change, tickets, or tokens. Paper transfers are free; pick one up from the driver when you pay your fare.

By Car

Pedestrian crosswalks are sprinkled throughout the city; they are marked clearly by yellow overhead signs and very large painted Xs. All a pedestrian has to do is stick out a hand, and cars (you hope!) screech to a halt in both directions. Right turns on red lights are nearly always permitted, except where otherwise posted. You must come to a complete stop before making the turn.

By Streetcar

The main streetcar lines running east–west are College, Queen, King, and Dundas, following those streets. The new Spadina line runs north–

south. All of them, especially the King line, are interesting rides with frequent service. Riding the city's streetcars is a great way to capture the flavor of the city, since you pass through many neighborhoods.

By Subway

The Toronto Transit Commission runs one of the safest, cleanest, most trustworthy systems of its kind anywhere. There are two subway lines, with 60 stations along the way: the Bloor/Danforth line, which crosses Toronto about 5 km (3 mi) north of the lakefront, from east to west, and the Yonge/University line, which loops north and south, like a giant "U," with the bottom of the "U" at Union Station. A light rapid transit (LRT) line extends service to Harbourfront along Queen's Quay. Tokens and tickets are sold in subway stations and at hundreds of convenience stores along the many routes of the TTC. Get your transfers just after you pay your fare and enter the subway; you'll find them in machines on your way down to the trains.

By Taxi

The meter begins at $2.50 and includes the first .2 km (roughly .1 mi). Each additional .235 km (.145 mi) is 25¢—as is each passenger in excess of four. The waiting time "while under engagement" is 25¢ for every 33 seconds—and in a traffic jam, this could add up. Still, it's possible to take a cab across downtown Toronto for $8–$9. The largest companies are **Beck** (☎ 416/751–5555), **Co-op** (☎ 416/504–2667), **Diamond** (☎ 416/366–6868), **Metro** (☎ 416/504–8294), and **Royal** (☎ 416/785–3322). For more information, call the **Metro Licensing Commission** (☎ 416/392–3000).

Contacts and Resources

B&B Reservation Services

Some 15–20 homes in various parts of the city have signed up with **Bed and Breakfast Homes of Toronto** (✉ Box 46093, College Park Postal Station, M5B 2L8, ☎ 416/363–6362); write for a brochure detailing individual homes. **Metropolitan Bed & Breakfast** (✉ 650 Dupont St., Suite 113, M6G 1Z2, ☎ 416/964–2566, FAX 416/960–9529) registry service has about 30 city and suburban homes on its books. More than two dozen private homes are affiliated with **Toronto Bed & Breakfast** (✉ 253 College St., Box 269, M5T 1R5, ☎ 416/588–8800, FAX 416/927–0838), most of them scattered around metro Toronto. Rooms cost as little as $50 a night and include breakfast.

Consulates

Consulate General of the United States (✉ 360 University Ave., north of Queen St., M56 1S4, ☎ 416/595–1700). **British Consulate General** (✉ 777 Bay St., at College St., M56 2G2, ☎ 416/593–1267).

Doctors and Dentists

Ask at your hotel desk about doctors. The **Dental Emergency Service** (☎ 416/967–5649) can help you get assistance.

Emergencies

Ambulance, police (☎ 911).

Guided Tours

ORIENTATION

Gray Line Sightseeing Bus Tours (☎ 416/594–3310) has tours April–November. The 2½-hour tours start at the bus terminal (✉ 610 Bay St., north of Dundas St.) and include Eaton Centre, the Old and New City Halls, Queen's Park, the University of Toronto, Yorkville, Ontario Place, and Casa Loma. The fare is $18.

Olde Town Toronto Tours (☎ 416/798–2424) has hop-on, hop-off tours on London double-decker buses and turn-of-the-century trolleys. Both take you around the city on a two-hour loop and cost $25; your ticket is good for 24 hours, so you can get on and off. Tours leave every 15 minutes in summer, every two hours in winter. The company also has tours to Niagara Falls.

You can take tours of the Toronto harbor and islands on comfortably equipped **Toronto Tours** (☎ 416/869–1372) boats for about $15. The hourly tour passes the Toronto Islands, with lovely city views. Boats leave from the Pier Six Building next to Queen's Quay Terminal early May–mid-October, daily 10–6. Tours leave as late as 7:15 PM in summer. Other boats depart from the Westin Harbour Castle hotel at the foot of Yonge Street.

SPECIAL-INTEREST

The **Bruce Trail Association** (☎ 416/690–4453 or 800/665–4453) arranges day and overnight hikes around Toronto and its environs.

Mosaic Environ Excursion Toronto (☎ 416/778–9686) offers a five-hour tour that visits some of the ethnic neighborhoods and green spaces that give Toronto its special character. This tour, which starts at Union Station, goes beyond the downtown area to include Cabbagetown, Little Italy, and the picturesque area around the Humber River. The cost is $34.95 and includes a picnic lunch.

Late-Night Pharmacies
Pharma Plus Drugmart (✉ Church St. and Wellesley Ave., ☎ 416/924–7760) is open daily from 8 AM to midnight.

Some locations of the **Shoppers Drug Mart** (✉ 700 Bay St., ☎ 416/979–2424; ✉ 2500 Hurontario St., Mississauga, ☎ 905/896–2500) are open 24 hours.

Road Emergencies
The **Canadian Automobile Association** (☎ 416/222–5222) has 24-hour road service; membership benefits are extended to U.S. AAA members.

Visitor Information
The **Metropolitan Toronto Convention & Visitors Association** (✉ 207 Queen's Quay W, Suite 509, M5J 1A7, ☎ 416/203–2500 or 800/363–1990) has its office at Queen's Quay Terminal. Booths providing brochures about the city and its attractions, as well as accommodations, are set up in summer outside Eaton Centre, on Yonge Street just below Dundas Street, and outside the Royal Ontario Museum.

Traveller's Aid Society (✉ Union Station, arrivals level and basement level, Room B23, ☎ 416/366–7788; ✉ Pearson Airport, Terminal I, arrivals level, past Customs, near Area B, ☎ 905/676–2868; ✉ Pearson Airport, Terminal 2, between international and domestic arrivals, ☎ 905/676–2869; ✉ Pearson Airport, Terminal 3, arrivals level, near international side, ☎ 905/612–5890) recommends restaurants and hotels and distributes subway maps and Ontario sales-tax rebate forms.

7 Province of Ontario

Ottawa, Algonquin Park, Windsor, Niagara, London

With shorelines on four of the five Great Lakes, Ontario is Canada's second-largest and most urbanized province, but only 10 million people live in this vast area, and 90% of them are within a narrow strip just north of the U.S. border. A bit north of the strip, Ottawa, Canada's capital, gathers government workers and parliamentarians.

O**NTARIO IS AN IROQUOIAN WORD** variously interpreted as beautiful lake, beautiful water, or rocks standing high beside the water (the last an apparent reference to Niagara Falls). The province contains 156,670 square km (68,490 square mi) of fresh water—one-quarter of all there is in the world.

Updated by
Helga
Loverseed

Ontario is Canada's most urban province; half of its population lives in four cities whose boundaries have spread to such an extent that they almost adjoin. Toronto (☞ Chapter 6) has more than 2.3 million people. To the east, Oshawa has 175,000 people and heavily populated suburbs. South and west of Toronto are Hamilton, with 550,000 people, and St. Catharines, with 290,000. Half of Ontario's population is of British stock, but successive waves of immigrants over the past century have turned the province into a mini–United Nations. Thunder Bay contains the largest settlement of Finns outside Finland. Toronto has a half-million Italians, the largest Chinese community in Canada, and the most Portuguese in North America. More recent arrivals include thousands of West Indians, Vietnamese, Somalis, South Africans, and Eastern Europeans, giving Ontario—Toronto in particular—a cosmopolitan flavor rivaling New York's or Chicago's.

The towns and cities of northern Ontario are strung along the railway lines that brought them into being. The discovery of deposits of gold, silver, uranium, and other minerals by railroad construction gangs sparked mining booms that established such communities as Sudbury, Cobalt, and Timmins, which owe their existence to mining.

Ontario has the most varied landscape of any Canadian province. The most conspicuous topographical feature is the Niagara Escarpment, which runs from Niagara to Tobermory at the tip of the Bruce Peninsula in Lake Huron. The northern 90% of Ontario is covered by the Canadian Shield, worn-down mountain ranges of the world's oldest rock, reaching only 2,183 ft above sea level at their highest point.

East of Hamilton toward Niagara Falls is a narrow strip along the south shore of Lake Ontario in a partial rain shadow of the Niagara Escarpment. The climate, moderated in winter by Lakes Ontario and Erie, allows the growing of tender fruits and grapes, making it Canada's largest wine-producing area.

Pleasures and Pastimes

The Arts

By combining public and private resources, Ontario has fostered one of North America's most supportive environments for the arts. Each year thousands flock to see great Shakespeare at the Stratford Festival in Stratford and top-notch plays at the Shaw Festival in Niagara-on-the-Lake. Toronto (☞ Chapter 6) is the third-largest center for English-language theater, but smaller cities have their artistic treasures, too, including fine music festivals. Hamilton has Ontario's third-largest art gallery, and Ottawa's National Arts Centre is the biggest performing arts complex in the country.

Dining

The cuisine of this vast province runs the gamut from fresh-caught fish in Cottage Country to French-influenced dishes in Ottawa and great home-style Canadian fare such as maple-syrup pie in southern Ontario. Given the enormous British influence here, there's plenty of roast beef, shepherd's pie, and rice pudding, especially in the English-dominated enclaves of London, Stratford, and Hamilton. Ontarians crave Tim Horton's doughnuts, found at franchise shops in virtually every city.

CATEGORY	COST*
$$$$	over $50
$$$	$35–$50
$$	$15–$35
$	under $15

*per person, in Canadian dollars, excluding drinks, service, 7% GST, and 8% provincial food tax

Lodging

Reservations are strongly recommended anywhere in Ontario during summer months. Generally, you get what you pay for at Ontario hotels and motels. Taxes are seldom included in quoted prices, but rates sometimes include food, especially in areas such as Muskoka and Haliburton, where many resorts offer meal plans. For information about camping, see Outdoor Activities and Sports, below.

Most major cities have bed-and-breakfast associations. Prices vary according to the location and facilities but are comparable to those found south of the border. All types of accommodations tend to be more expensive in tourist venues. In Niagara Falls, for example, hotel and motel rates are determined by the proximity to the famous waterfall.

CATEGORY	COST*
$$$$	over $200
$$$	$150–$200
$$	$100–$150
$	under $100

*All prices are for a standard double room, excluding 7% GST and 5% room tax, in Canadian dollars.

Museums

The museums of Canada's most populous province document Ontario's evolution from a pioneer outpost to a lively urban society. Living history museums, such as such as Upper Canada Village, Fort Henry, and Old Fort William, chronicle the early years. The story of the country's development can also be traced through paintings, carvings, and artifacts—the legacy of European, Canadian, and native artists—that are on display at the National Gallery of Canada in Ottawa and at regional museums like the McMichael Canadian Art Collection in Kleinburg, near Toronto (☞ Exploring Toronto in Chapter 6). Numerous institutions document the War of 1812.

Outdoor Activities and Sports

CAMPING

Most provincial parks offer a variety of services for campers, from electrical outlets and sturdy, covered picnic shelters to laundry facilities and camp stores for provisions. Some also have cottages for rent. Additionally, many sponsor educational programs that teach children about wilderness survival techniques and nature.

In southern Ontario most provincial parks operate from mid-May until Labor Day weekend; in northern Ontario provincial parks open from early June until Labor Day weekend. Even when "closed," however, the parks never completely shut down, and visitors are welcome in the off-season, though few facilities are maintained. Some parks may be gated to prevent vehicular entry, but all are accessible to pedestrians from sunrise to sunset. Vault privies will be open, fireplace grates should be available, and fees usually will be collected through self-serve registration. Winter camping is allowed in some provincial parks, though most are unsupervised and facilities are limited. During fall and winter months reservations are not required at most parks.

FISHING

Ontario has about 250,000 lakes and 150,000 rivers, which contain myriad species of fish. The favorite trophies are salmon and trout, but others lust after pike or muskie and still others swear that battling a black bass on light tackle is life's ultimate piscatorial challenge.

SKIING

This province is rich with cross-country and downhill ski trails. Nordic ski trails exist just about anywhere in the province where you find snow and accommodations for skiers. Ontario has hundreds of alpine slopes, although most have vertical drops of less than 660 ft. All major Ontario ski centers have high-tech snowmaking equipment, which has guaranteed good skiing from late November through early April.

Shopping

Visitors from the United States often relish Ontario's handsome inventory of things British, scooping up everything from china teacups and cashmere clothing to crumpet tins. Others marvel at the province's rich handicraft tradition. Ottawa, Sault Ste. Marie, Midland, and Thunder Bay have museum shops and galleries that specialize in native and Inuit crafts. Antiques stores abound. Some of the best antiques can be found at small shops in Cobourg, Peterborough, and St. Jacobs.

Exploring Ontario

You could spend several months exploring this enormous province and still not see it all. But by using three cities—Ottawa, Sault Ste. Marie, and Toronto—as bases for one- and two-day excursions, you can visit all the major sights and some special little corners that even many Ontarians don't know about. These itineraries concentrate on eastern Ontario.

Numbers in the text correspond to numbers in the margin and on the Lower Ontario Province, Downtown Ottawa, Greater Ottawa and Hull, Niagara Falls, and Upper Ontario maps.

Great Itineraries

IF YOU HAVE 3 DAYS

Spend two days in 🏛 **Ottawa** ①–⑲, beginning at the Parliament Buildings, where a variety of indoor sights and outdoor events could keep you occupied for an afternoon. Ottawa's colorful downtown and excursions to neighboring Hull are full of activities based on history and culture. On Day 3, drive to **Upper Canada Village** ⑳, which captures the spirit of the United Empire Loyalists' struggle to sustain Canadian independence during the War of 1812. Afterward, explore the Heritage Highways, stopping at historic 🏛 **Kingston** ㉒, the country's capital from 1841 to 1844. Besides the massive Fort Henry, Kingston is home to the International Hockey Hall of Fame. Consider taking a jaunt to **Prince Edward County** ㉓, a Loyalist enclave with strong ties to Sir John A. Macdonald, Canada's first prime minister. If you're ambitious, you can try to make it to 🏛 **Peterborough** ㉖ by nightfall, rather than stopping in Kingston.

IF YOU HAVE 5 DAYS

After spending three days in 🏛 **Ottawa** ①–⑲, **Kingston** ㉒, and **Prince Edward County** ㉓, you can use 🏛 **Peterborough** ㉖ as a springboard from which to explore Ontario's "cottage country." Native rock carvings can be found at the **Petroglyphs Provincial Park** ㉗, northeast of Peterborough on Highway 26. To the west via Highways 12 and 93,

Lower Ontario Province

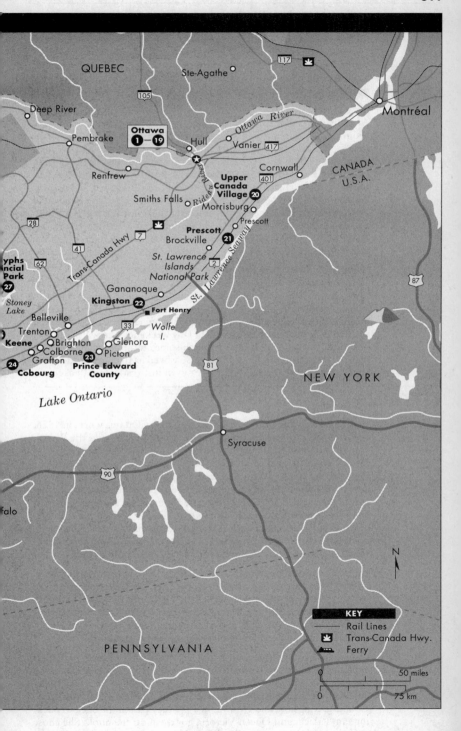

QUEBEC

Ste-Agathe

117

Montréal

Deep River

Pembroke

Ottawa River

Ottawa
1 — 19

Hull

Vanier

417

Cornwall

CANADA
U.S.A.

Renfrew

Upper
Canada
Village
20

401

Smiths Falls

Rideau River

Morrisburg

Prescott

28

Trans-Canada Hwy

7

Prescott

Brockville

21

St. Lawrence Seaway

87

41

St. Lawrence
Islands
National Park

2

62

yphs
ncial
Park
27

Gananoque

St. Lawrence Seaway

Stoney
Lake

Kingston **22**

■ **Fort Henry**

Belleville

33

Wolfe
I.

Trenton

81

NEW YORK

Keene
24

Brighton
Colborne
Grafton

23

Glenora
Picton

Cobourg

**Prince Edward
County**

Lake Ontario

Syracuse

90

falo

N

PENNSYLVANIA

KEY
—— Rail Lines
Trans-Canada Hwy.
Ferry

0 ————————— 50 miles

0 ————————— 75 km

dash to the towns of **Penetanguishene** and **Midland** ㉙, on the shores of Georgian Bay. To experience the bay's beauty, take a cruise from either town. Drive south to ⊡ **St. Jacobs** ㉖, in the heart of Mennonite and Hutterite country. On Day 5, travel to **Kitchener/Waterloo** ㉖. If you're there on a Saturday, don't miss the Kitchener Market. Head south to **Stratford** ㉗, home to the acclaimed Stratford Festival, a centerpiece of Canada's rich artistic landscape.

IF YOU HAVE 7 DAYS

After five days of visiting ⊡ **Ottawa** ①–⑲, ⊡ **Kingston** ㉒, the towns around Georgian Bay ㉙–㉜, **Kitchener/Waterloo** ㉖, and ⊡ **Stratford** ㉗, head for **London** ㉑, city of trees, via Highways 7 and 4. Next, drive along Highway 3 through United Empire Loyalist territory—the villages of **Port Stanley** ㊸, **St. Thomas** ㊷, **Port Dover** ㊶, and **Port Colborne** ㊴. By nightfall on Day 6, you will have reached ⊡ **Niagara Falls** ㊿–㊽, a good base from which to explore the Niagara Peninsula. Drive through the wine region, stopping for a few tastings, to ⊡ **Niagara-on-the-Lake** ㊺ (another choice for your overnight), with its beautifully kept Victorian homes. Devote the last day to taking in the falls and its environs, where high- and low-brow attractions flourish.

When to Tour the Province of Ontario

In winter Ontario's weather veers toward the severe, making road travel difficult away from major highways, and many museums and attractions are closed or have limited hours. It's best to visit between April and October, when most sights are open longer hours. Try to avoid touring over the busy July 1 Canada Day weekend. The warm months also offer travelers the chance to catch some cultural highlights, especially the Stratford and Shaw festivals, as well as to enjoy outdoor action, such as boating and hiking—or even just resting on a beach.

OTTAWA

Only a few scattered settlers lived in what is now Ottawa when, in 1826, Colonel John By and his Royal Engineers arrived to build the Rideau Canal, which links the Ottawa River to Lake Ontario. This new waterway was intended to protect a supply route from Montréal to the Great Lakes in the event of a repeat of the War of 1812 against the Americans. Once By's headquarters had been established, the settlement, then called Bytown, grew rapidly and fast became a rowdy, rough-and-tumble backwoods town as hordes arrived seeking employment on the largest construction project on the continent. The canal, completed in 1832, was hacked through 200 km (124 mi) of swamp, rock, and lakes whose different levels were overcome by locks.

By 1837, when its population had reached 2,400, Bytown was declared a town by the attorney general of Upper Canada. Government moved slowly even then, and it was not legally incorporated until 1850. Five years later, when the population had reached 10,000, Bytown became a city and was farsightedly given the name Ottawa, a word of Native American origin meaning "a place for buying and selling."

Canadians are taught in school that it was Queen Victoria's fault their capital is inconveniently situated off the main east–west corridor along the U.S. border. From 1841 to 1857, politicians dithered, trying to decide among five possible sites, including Québec City, Montréal, Cobourg, Kingston, and Ottawa. In 1857 they passed the buck to Buckingham Palace, and Queen Victoria got them off the hook. She chose Ottawa for five reasons, all valid at the time: The site was politically acceptable to both Canada east and Canada west. It was also centrally located, reassuringly remote from the hostile United States, and industrially prosperous. And it had a naturally beautiful setting at the confluence of the Ottawa and Rideau rivers.

In 1859 construction began on the Parliament Buildings. The buildings are magnificent, but their location in the mid-1850s earned Ottawa the nickname Westminster in the Wilderness. Today, neo-Gothic towers and spires are undergoing major renovation, with parts of the building to be shrouded in scaffolding until the year 2000.

As early as 1899, federal politicians were concerned with more than just the grounds around the Parliament Buildings, known as the Hill. A variety of commissions and committees and plans have become today's National Capital Commission (NCC). The NCC works with all municipalities within the 2,903-square-km (1,800-square-mi) National Capital Region, which includes neighboring Hull and a big chunk of Québec, to coordinate development in the best interests of the region. The result is a profusion of festivals, beautiful parks, bicycle paths, jogging trails, and the world's longest skating rink, on an 8-km (5-mi) stretch of the Rideau Canal in use from January to March.

Downtown Ottawa

Given Ottawa's architectural beauty and the fact that parking is at a premium here, one of the best ways to see many of the gems in this metropolis of 720,000 is on foot.

A Good Walk

Begin your walk at the **Parliament Buildings** ①. The Centre Block and the Peace Tower are surrounded by 29 acres of lawn interspersed by statues of celebrated Canadians. Turn right onto Wellington Street and walk past Bank Street to the Bank of Canada. On Sparks Street, a block south of Wellington, you can enter the **Bank of Canada Currency Museum** ②, where seven galleries chronicle the evolution of notes and coins within the context of Canadian history. North of Wellington, on Kent Street, is the **Supreme Court** ③, housed in a stunning Art Deco edifice. At the western end of Wellington Street is the **Garden of the Provinces** ④. Across from the park are the **National Archives of Canada** and the **National Library of Canada** ⑤, two centers of Canadian history.

Head back toward Parliament Hill via the friendly **Sparks Street Pedestrian Mall** ⑥. At the end of the street, you'll face **Confederation Square** ⑦, where homage is paid to those Canadians who didn't survive World War I. Adjacent to the square stands the **National Arts Centre** ⑧, a huge complex home to a fine orchestra plus English and French theater and dance performances. The Rideau Canal is close to the center, and you can walk north along it to Ottawa's older buildings: The **Bytown Museum** ⑨ houses a collection of 3,500 artifacts that once belonged to Colonel By. Next door are the **Rideau Locks** ⑩. Farther down the canal, back toward Wellington Street, is the **Canadian Museum of Contemporary Photography** ⑪. Several blocks east, between George and York streets, is the **Byward Market** ⑫, with food shops that date back a century. From the market, walk west on York Street for a block and turn right on Sussex Drive. It's a five-minute walk to the **National Gallery of Canada** ⑬, which reflects the Parliament Buildings in its modern mirror-and-granite facade. The **Canadian Museum of Nature** ⑭ is a brisk 20-minute walk or short car ride south of the Parliament Buildings, on Metcalfe Street at McLeod Street. The museum has a fabulous dinosaur display.

TIMING

You'll need at least a day to visit the sights downtown; allow more time if you wish to tour the museums. Most museums are closed Monday,

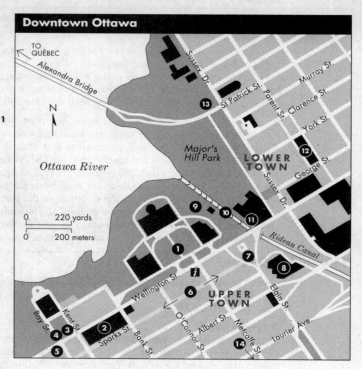

Downtown Ottawa

but the staff at the Capital Infocentre (☞ Visitor Information *in* Ottawa A to Z, *below*) will help you locate those open if that happens to be your only day in town.

Sights to See

② **Bank of Canada Currency Museum.** The ancestors of the credit card are all here: bracelets made from elephant hair, cowrie shells, whales' teeth, and what is believed to be the world's largest coin. Here, too, of course, is the country's most complete collection of Canadian notes and coins. ⊠ *245 Sparks St.,* ☎ *613/782–8914.* ☑ *$2; free Tues.* ☉ *Tues.–Sat. 10:30–5, Sun. 1–5; also open Mon. May–Labor Day.*

⑨ **Bytown Museum.** In the former commissariat used by the Royal Engineers and Colonel John By during the building of the Rideau Canal— the oldest stone masonry building in the city—you'll find exhibits that record the life and times of Bytown and Ottawa. ⊠ *Wellington St. at bottom of Ottawa Locks, behind Chateau Laurier Hotel,* ☎ *613/234– 4570.* ☑ *$2.25.* ☉ *May–mid-Oct., Mon.–Sat. 10–5, Sun. 1–5; mid- Oct.–late Nov., weekdays 10–4; Nov. 30–Apr. 1 by appointment only.*

⑫ **Byward Market.** Excellent fresh produce and maple products have been attracting shoppers to this farmer's market since 1840. Surrounding the market stalls are permanent specialty food shops, some well over 100 years old, as well as cafés and boutiques. ⊠ *Between George and York Sts.* ☉ *Sun.–Wed. 8–6, Thurs.–Sat. 8 AM–9 PM.*

⑪ **Canadian Museum of Contemporary Photography.** Opened in 1992, this museum holds more than 158,000 images, spotlighted in changing exhibitions. There is also a 50-seat theater and a boutique. ⊠ *1 Rideau Canal,* ☎ *613/990–8257.* ☑ *Donation requested.* ☉ *May– Aug., Mon.–Wed. and Fri.–Sun. 11–5, Thurs. 11–8; Sept.–Apr., Wed.–Fri.–Sun. 11–5, Thurs. 11–8.*

🐾 ⑭ **Canadian Museum of Nature.** In a castlelike building, the museum and its exhibits explore the evolution of the earth, plus the birds, mammals, and plants of Canada. The dinosaur collection is outstanding. The Viola MacMillan Mineral Gallery displays a world-class collection of mineral specimens. ✉ *McLeod St. at Metcalfe St.,* ☎ *613/566–4700.* 💲 *$4; ½ price Thurs. until 5, free 5–8.* ☉ *Fri.–Wed. 10–5, Thurs. 10–8.*

❼ **Confederation Square.** In the center of this triangular junction in the heart of the city stands the **National War Memorial,** honoring the 66,651 Canadian dead of World War I. ✉ *Wellington, Sparks, and Elgin Sts.*

❹ **Garden of the Provinces.** Two fountains and the arms and floral emblems of Canada's 10 provinces and two territories commemorate Confederation in this park. ✉ *Southwest corner of Bay and Wellington Sts.*

❺ **National Archives of Canada** and **National Library of Canada.** The archives contain more than 60 million manuscripts and government records, 1 million maps, and about 11 million photographs. The National Library collects, preserves, and promotes the published heritage of Canada and exhibits books, paintings, maps, and photographs. Both institutions mount exhibitions regularly. ✉ *395 Wellington St. at Bay St.,* ☎ *613/995–5138 archives, 613/995–9481 library.* 💲 *Free.* ☉ *Daily 9–9.*

❽ **National Arts Centre.** This complex includes an opera hall, a theater, a studio theater, and a salon for readings and concerts. The grounds are populated with sculptures by Canadian artists. The popular canalside **Le Café** spills outside in warm weather; in winter it's a cozy vantage spot from which to watch skaters on the canal. ✉ *53 Elgin St.,* ☎ *613/996–5051 center, 613/594–5127 café.*

⑬ **National Gallery of Canada.** A magnificent, glass-towered structure engineered by Canadian architect Moshe Safdie holds one of the premier collections of Canadian art in the world. Inside is the recontructed **Rideau Convent Chapel,** a classic example of French Canadian 19th-century architecture with the only neo-Gothic fan-vaulted ceiling on the continent. The building has three restaurants and a large bookstore with publications on the arts. ✉ *380 Sussex Dr.,* ☎ *613/990–1985.* 💲 *Free, except special exhibits.* ☉ *Daily 10–6 (Thurs. until 8). Closed Mon.–Tues. in winter.*

🐾 ❶ **Parliament Buildings.** Three beloved Gothic-style buildings with copper roofs dominate the nation's capital from Parliament Hill on a promontory overlooking the Ottawa River. Originally built in 1867, they were destroyed by fire and rebuilt in 1916. Currently, they are undergoing extensive restoration, slated for completion in 2000. The **Centre Block** is where the Senate and House of Commons, the two houses of Parliament, work to shape the laws of the land. The wonderfully detailed stone frieze in the foyer, which depicts Canadian history, and the masterfully carved stone pillars and provincial emblems in stained glass in the House of Commons, are all works of the nationally renowned artist Eleanor Milne.

The central **Peace Tower** houses a Memorial Chamber with an Altar of Sacrifice, which bears the names of 66,651 Canadians killed during service in World War I and the 44,895 Canadians who died in World War II. Also in the Tower is the 53-bell carillon; concerts are performed daily in summer by the Dominion Carillonneur. Outside on the lawn, there's plenty of room to observe the colorful **Changing of the Guard ceremony,** which takes place daily, late June to late August, weather permitting. The Ceremonial Guard brings together two of Canada's most historic regiments, the Canadian Grenadier Guards and the Governor General's Foot Guards.

North of the Centre Block and reached via its corridors is the **Library of Parliament**. A statue of a young Queen Victoria is the centerpiece of the octagonal-shape chamber. The walls are ornately carved pine galleries lined with books, many of them priceless.

In front of, and to either side of, the Centre Block are the **East Block** and the **West Block**. The East Block has four historic rooms open to the public: the original Governor General's office restored to the period of Lord Dufferin, 1872–1878; the offices of Sir John A. Macdonald and Sir Georges Étienne Cartier, Fathers of the Confederation in 1867; and the Privy Council Chamber. The West Block, originally designed to house the civil service, has been converted to offices for parliamentarians and is not open to the public.

Against the backdrop of the imposing Parliament Buildings, a free half-hour laser **Sound and Light Show** highlights Canada's history. ⊠ *Parliament Hill,* ☎ *613/992–4793 or 613/996–0896.* 🎟 *Free.* ☉ *Mid-May–Labor Day, daily 9–8:30; Labor Day–mid-May, daily 9–4:30; 20-min tours in English or French every ½ hr; same-day reservations for tours available at white Infotent east of Centre Block; sound-and-light shows late May–Labor Day, twice nightly (1 in English, 1 in French).*

🔟 **Rideau Locks.** On the Rideau Canal, which runs southward through the city from the Ottawa River, the locks are a downtown landmark. ⊠ *Junction of Rideau Canal and Wellington St., where Wellington becomes Rideau St.*

⑥ **Sparks Street Pedestrian Mall.** Here, the automobile has been banished, and shoppers and browsers can wander carefree in warm weather among fountains, rock gardens, sculptures, and outdoor cafés. ⊠ *1 block south of Wellington St., between Confederation Square and Kent St.*

③ **Supreme Court.** Established in 1875, this body became the ultimate court of appeal in the land in 1949. The nine judges sit in their stately Art Deco building for three sessions each year. ⊠ *Kent and Wellington Sts.,* ☎ *613/995–4330.* 🎟 *Free.* ☉ *Tours May–Aug., daily 9–5; Sept.–Apr., by appointment.*

Greater Ottawa and Hull

A car, taxi, or bus is needed to visit some other major attractions and outstanding museums in the area.

A Good Drive

Sussex Drive is Ottawa's embassy row. Take a glimpse at the entrance to 24 Sussex Drive—the **Residence of the Prime Minister** ⑮—before finding the **Rideau Hall** ⑯, the governor-general's home, at 1 Sussex Drive. Continue on Sussex Drive to the Rockcliffe Driveway, and watch for the signs that mark the 4 km (2½ mi) to the **National Aviation Museum** ⑰. It's worth the 10-minute drive from downtown to the **National Museum of Science and Technology** ⑱, where children, in particular, will enjoy the institution's hands-on exhibits. Across the Ottawa River in Hull, Québec, the **Canadian Museum of Civilization** ⑲ has an IMAX/Omnimax theater and stunning collections documenting the country's history in a fresh, interactive way.

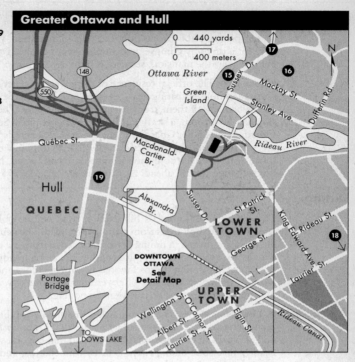

Greater Ottawa and Hull

TIMING

You'll need a full day to see the sights and museums on this drive; plan your time according to your interests. Note that many museums are closed Monday.

Sights to See

19 Canadian Museum of Civilization. Across the Ottawa River in Hull, Québec, is one of the area's most architecturally stunning museums, with striking, curved lines. Exhibits trace Canada's history from pre-historic times to the present. In the Grand Hall are six Canadian West Coast longhouses, towering totem poles, and life-size reconstructions of an archaeological dig. Kids can enjoy hands-on activities in the Children's Museum. The Cineplus holds the larger-than-life IMAX and Omnimax. ⊠ *100 Laurier St., Hull,* ☎ *819/776–7000 or 800/555–5621, 819/776–7010 Cineplus.* ☜ *Museum $5 (free Sun. 9–noon), Cineplus $7 (varies with show).* ☉ *Tues.–Sun. 9–5, Thurs. 9–9.*

17 National Aviation Museum. Among more than 100 aircraft are a replica of the model that made the first powered flight in Canada. Engines, propellers, and aeronautical antiques complete the collection. ⊠ *Rockcliffe and Aviation Pkwys.,* ☎ *613/993–2010 or 800/463–2038.* ☜ *$5; free Thurs. 5–9.* ☉ *Sept.–Apr., Tues.–Sun. 10–5, Thurs. 10–10; May–Aug., Fri.–Wed. 9–5, Thurs. 9–9.*

18 National Museum of Science and Technology. Canada's largest museum has permanent displays of printing presses, antique cars, steam locomotives, and agricultural machinery, as well as ever-changing exhibits, many of which are hands-on, or "minds-on." The evening "Discover the Universe" program uses the largest refracting telescope in Canada to stargaze into the world of astronomy. ⊠ *1867 St. Laurent Blvd.,* ☎ *613/991–3044.* ☜ *$6.* ☉ *Labor Day–Apr., daily 9–5; May–Labor Day, Sat.–Thurs. 9–6, Fri. 9–9.*

⑮ **Residence of the Prime Minister.** It has been home to men named Laurier, Massey, and Trudeau, among others. Unlike the White House, it is not open for public inspection. Lacking an invitation, you can hope only for a drive-by glimpse of a couple of roof gables. Don't even try parking near the mansion; security is tight. ✉ *24 Sussex Dr.*

⑯ **Rideau Hall.** The official residence of the governor-general of Canada since 1865 houses visiting heads of state, royalty, and the British monarch when any of them are here on official business. The 1830 mansion has a ballroom, a skating rink, and a cricket pitch. Sentries of the Canadian Grenadier Guards and the Governor General's Foot Guards are posted outside the main gate of Rideau Hall in summer. Free guided tours of the public rooms and grounds are conducted, but days and times change, so call ahead. ✉ *1 Sussex Dr.,* ☎ *613/998–7113.*

Dining

The residents of Canada's bilingual capital include politicians, bureaucrats, and diplomats from around the world. The demand for ethnic food is reflected in dining places that range from the eclectic cafés and bistros around lively Byward Market and along trendy Elgin Street to the elegant dining rooms favored by ambassadors and those who work in the upper echelons of government. In this city, as elsewhere in Canada, Italian cuisine is extremely popular.

$$–$$$ ✕ **Chez Jean Pierre.** The accomplished chef-owner of this restaurant, Jean Pierre Muller, was a cuisinier at the U.S. Embassy for 17 years, and his years serving diplomats have stood him in good stead. The elegantly furnished dining room is lit by candelabras, and patrons are treated to fine linen, silver cutlery, and freshly cut flowers. Jean Pierre prepares traditional French cuisine—escargots flavored with garlic, tournedos Rossini (fillet of beef with foie gras and truffles), veal kidneys sautéed in Madeira, and the like. ✉ *210 Somerset St. W,* ☎ *613/235–9711. AE, DC, MC, V.*

$$ ✕ **Courtyard Restaurant.** Fine French cuisine is served in this lovely, historic limestone building on a quiet cul-de-sac near Byward Market, a five-minute stroll from the Parliament Buildings. The forerunner of today's elegant dining establishment was a log tavern built in 1827. The humble tavern was replaced by the limestone Ottawa Hotel a decade later. Extensive renovations created the Courtyard Restaurant, and its cuisine and ambience have attracted a dedicated following. ✉ *21 George St.,* ☎ *613/241–1516. Reservations essential. AE, MC, V.*

$$ ✕ **Fresco.** This cozy Italian restaurant's dominant feature is the mural of mountains in Tuscany on the back wall, although the dizzying number of food options is impressive, too. You can choose from 10 sauces to accompany such house specialties as pasta, rack of lamb, and veal. ✉ *354 Elgin St.,* ☎ *613/235–7541. AE, DC, MC, V.*

$$ ✕ **Icho Restaurant.** Fans of Japanese food claim that Icho serves the best sushi east of Vancouver. This restaurant in the Byward Market area also offers the usual choices of tempura, chicken teriyaki, and katsudon (breaded, deep-fried pork tenderloin), as well as more exotic fare, such as octopus, squid, and eel cooked in sake. ✉ *87 George St.,* ☎ *613/241–2440. AE, MC, DC, V.*

$$ ✕ **The Ritz.** Don't be fooled by the fancy name. This is a small but hugely popular Italian bistro. The pasta, made on the premises, is teamed with flavorful sauces and interesting blends of vegetables, fish, and seafood. Spinach linguine with smoked salmon, rye whiskey, capers, plum tomatoes, and cream is a typical creation. The Ritz also serves veal and chicken dishes. ✉ *274 Elgin St.,* ☎ *613/235–7027. Reservations essential. AE, DC, MC, V.*

Lodging

$$$$ ⚏ **Westin Hotel.** Attached to the Rideau Centre shopping mall and convention hall, this 24-story hotel is in the heart of the city. The modern rooms are done in pastel hues. Floor-to-ceiling windows provide one of the best views in Ottawa ($20 extra for rooms facing the Rideau Canal and the Parliament Buildings). ⊠ *11 Colonel By Dr., K1N 9H4,* ☎ *613/560–7000,* ℻ *613/234–5396. 484 rooms. Restaurant, lounge, indoor pool, 2 saunas, hot tub, exercise room, squash, night club. AE, DC, MC, V.*

$$$–$$$$ ⚏ **Château Laurier Hotel.** Ottawa has posh new hotels with great ser-
★ vice and food, but this grand Canadian Pacific hotel is an institution. It's one of Canada's greatest railroad hotels, built in 1912 and named for Sir Wilfrid Laurier, who served as prime minister from 1896 to 1911. Rooms that were formerly on the small side have been combined into suites. Zoe's, the conservatory lounge, serves afternoon tea and coffee and Sunday brunch. The Château, as it's known, is truly part of the Ottawa experience. ⊠ *1 Rideau St., K1N 8S7,* ☎ *613/241–1414 or 800/441–1414,* ℻ *613/562–7030. 425 rooms. Restaurant, bar, lounge, indoor pool, health club. AE, DC, MC, V.*

$$$ ⚏ **Novotel Ottawa.** This already modern hotel, a member of the French-based chain, was renovated in 1997. The rooms are freshly decorated, and works by local artists hang in the spruced-up lobby. (The paintings are for sale.) Next door to the Rideau Centre, the main downtown shopping mall, the Novotel is a couple of minutes' walk from Parliament Hill, the National Gallery of Canada, and the Rideau Canal. ⊠ *33 Nicholas St., K1N 9M7,* ☎ *613/230–3033 or 800/668–6835,* ℻ *613/230–7865. 282 rooms. Restaurant, bar, indoor pool, sauna, steam room, exercise room. AE, DC, MC, V.*

$$–$$$ ⚏ **Albert at Bay.** One- and two-bedroom suites make up this 12-story hotel close to the Sparks Street Mall, with fully equipped kitchens and laundry facilities. ⊠ *435 Albert St. (corner Bay and Albert),* ☎ *613/ 238–8858 or 800/267–6644,* ℻ *613/238–1433. Restaurant, kitchenettes, hot tub, sauna, exercise room, grocery. AE, DC, MC, V.*

$$–$$$ ⚏ **Carmichael Inn & Spa.** Open since 1996, this hostelry in a renovated
★ turn-of-the-century brick mansion has already built up a loyal clientele. It's particularly popular with single women (including politicians), who come to get back on track at the spa. Treatments include Swedish massage, herbal body wraps, and reflexology. A full breakfast is included in the rate, and the inn is near the restaurants and cafés along fashionable Elgin Street. ⊠ *46 Cartier St., K2P 1J3,* ☎ *613/236–4667,* ℻ *613/563–7529. 10 rooms. Spa. AE, DC, MC, V.*

Nightlife and the Arts

The Arts

More than 900 performances are showcased annually at the **National Arts Centre** (⊠ 53 Elgin St., ☎ 613/996–5051), and it is the home of the National Arts Centre Orchestra. In summer the center is one of the hosts of the Ottawa International Jazz Festival Canada and Festival Canada (opera, choral works, cabaret).

Nightlife

Barrymore's (⊠ 323 Bank St., ☎ 613/233–0307) has transformed the Imperial Theatre of 1914 into one of the city's most energetic nightclubs. It draws a twenty-to-thirty-something crowd. Live musicians take center stage from Wednesday through Saturday until midnight, after which dance music thumps through the three-tiered hall until 2 AM.

Outdoor Activities and Sports

Biking

Ottawa has 150 km (93 mi) of bicycle paths. On Sunday Queen Elizabeth Drive and Colonel By Drive are closed to traffic until noon for cyclists. Rent A Bike, in the Château Laurier Hotel (☞ Lodging, *above*), rents bicycles for all ages, including tandems.

Hiking

The **Rideau Trail** runs 406 km (252 mi) along the Rideau Canal from Kingston to Ottawa. Access points from the highway are marked with orange triangles. For information, contact the Rideau Trail Association (✉ Box 15, Kingston K7L 4V6).

Ice-Skating

In winter the **Rideau Canal** becomes the longest skating rink in the world, stretching from the National Arts Centre to Dows Lake. Skates can be rented and sharpened across from the National Arts Centre, and wooden sleds for towing children can also be rented. Along the route are a few warm-up-changing shelters and food concessions. Call the NCC (☎ 613/239–5234) for daily skating conditions.

Shopping

Antiques

John Coles at the Astrolabe Gallery (✉ 112 Sparks St., ☎ 613/234–2348) is a good source for 19th-century prints of Ottawa scenes or antique maps of North America.

Shopping Center

Rideau Centre (✉ Rideau St. and Colonel By Dr.) has more than 200 stores, including the Bay and Eaton department stores.

Ottawa A to Z

Arriving and Departing

BY BUS

Voyageur Colonial Bus Lines (✉ 265 Catherine St., ☎ 613/238–5900) offers frequent service from Montréal and Toronto to Ottawa, including some express buses.

BY CAR

Highway 417 links Ottawa to Québec from the east; Highway 16 connects Ottawa with the Trans-Canada Highway (Highway 17) to the south.

BY PLANE

Ottawa International Airport (✉ 50 Airport Rd., Gloucester, ☎ 613/248–2125), 18 km (11 mi) from downtown, is served by Air Canada, First Air, Canadian Airlines International, Delta Airlines, and US Airways (☞ Air Travel *in* the Gold Guide for telephone numbers).

BY TRAIN

Trans-Canada **VIA Rail** serves the Ottawa rail station (✉ 200 Tremblay Rd., ☎ 613/244–8289) at the southeastern end of town. It's a $12 taxi ride to downtown.

Getting Around

BY BUS

OC Transpo (☎ 613/741–4390) serves the Ottawa–Carleton region on the Ontario side of the Ottawa River. It operates buses on city streets and on the Transitway, a system of bus-only roads. All bus routes in downtown Ottawa meet at the Rideau Centre (✉ Rideau St. between Nicholas and Sussex and the Mackenzie King Bridge).

BONUS MILES MAKE GREAT SOUVENIRS.

MCI
Calling Card
123 456 7891 2345
J.D. SMITH
WORLDPHONE

Earn Miles With Your MCI Card.

Take the MCI Card along on this trip and start earning miles for the next one. You'll earn frequent flyer miles on all your calls and save with the low rates you've come to expect from MCI. Before you know it, you'll be on your way to some other international destination.

Sign up for MCI by calling
1-800-FLY-FREE

Is this a great time, or what? :-)

Earn Frequent Flyer Miles.

AmericanAirlines
AAdvantage

Continental Airlines
OnePass

Delta Air Lines
SkyMiles

HAWAIIAN AIRLINES

MIDWEST EXPRESS AIRLINES

NORTHWEST AIRLINES
WORLDPERKS

Rapid Rewards
SOUTHWEST AIRLINES

MILEAGE PLUS.
United Airlines

US AIRWAYS
DIVIDEND MILES

You've read the book. Now book the trip.

For all the best deals on flights, hotels, rental cars, and vacation packages, book them online at www.previewtravel.com. Then click on our Destination Guides featuring content from Fodor's and more. You'll find hotels, restaurants, attractions, and things to do around the globe. There are even interactive maps, videos, and weather forecasts. You'll have everything you need to make your vacation exactly what you want it to be. All it takes is a trip online.

Travel on Your Terms™
www.previewtravel.com
aol keyword: previewtravel

preview travel℠

BY TAXI

Blue Line (☎ 613/238–1111). **Capital** (☎ 613/746–2233).

Contacts and Resources

EMBASSIES

See Embassies and Emergencies *in* the Gold Guide.

EMERGENCIES

Emergency assistance (☎ 911). The main hospitals in Ottawa are **Ottawa General Hospital** (✉ 501 Smyth Rd., ☎ 613/737–7777) and **Ottawa Civic Hospital** (✉ 1053 Carling Ave., ☎ 613/761–4000). **Shoppers Drug Mart** (✉ 1460 Merivale Rd., ☎ 613/224–7270) is a 24-hour pharmacy.

GUIDED TOURS

Paul's Boat Lines Limited (☎ 613/225–6781) offers seven 75-minute cruises daily on the Rideau Canal and four 90-minute cruises daily on the Ottawa River from mid-May to mid-October. Canal boats dock across from the National Arts Centre; river cruise boats dock at the Bytown Museum at the foot of the Ottawa Locks on the Rideau Canal. **Ottawa Riverboat Company** (☎ 613/562–4888) operates two-hour sightseeing boat tours on the Ottawa River May–October.

Gray Line (☎ 613/725–1441 or 800/297–6422) operates two-hour, 50-km (31-mi) orientation bus tours mid-May–October; the fee is $20.

From April through November, **Capital Double-Decker and Trolley Tours** (☎ 613/749–3666 or 800/823–6147) has a regular schedule of two-hour tours for $20 in double-decker London buses to Ottawa's major sights.

VISITOR INFORMATION

Just across from the Parliament Buildings is the **Capital Infocentre** (✉ 90 Wellington St., ☎ 613/239–5000 or 800/465–1867).

THE HERITAGE HIGHWAYS

Most of Ontario's first French, English, and Loyalist settlers entered the province from the southeast. You can retrace some of their routes on southern Ontario's Heritage Highways. Highway 2, parallel to Highway 401, is smaller than the cross-Ontario freeway and more picturesque. It's the original 19th-century route that linked Québec and Kingston to "Muddy York" (Toronto) in the west. With appropriate detours it provides a good glimpse into this area's attractions.

Upper Canada Village

★ ⓴ *86 km (53 mi) southeast of Ottawa on Hwy. 2.*

Eight villages disappeared under rising waters when the St. Lawrence Seaway opened in 1959, but their best historic buildings were moved to a new site, called Upper Canada Village, a re-creation of an Ontario community from the 1800s. The village occupies 66 acres of the 2,000-acre Crysler's Farm Battlefield Memorial Park, which figured in the War of 1812. Radios and tape players are banned in this throwback to the days of the United Empire Loyalists. The village has 3 mills, 2 farms, 2 churches, 2 hotels, and 25 other buildings. A tour takes 3–4 hours. More than 150 staff people are on site, all in early 1800s costume, to answer questions. The Village Store sells Canadian crafts and village-made bread, cheese, and flour. Willard's Hotel serves lunches, full-course meals, and teas. ✉ *Hwy. 2E, Morrisburg,* ☎ *613/543–3704.* 🖭 *$12.50.* ☉ *Mid-May–mid-Oct., daily 9:30–5; group tours may be arranged year-round.*

Prescott

★ ㉑ *40 km (25 mi) west of Morrisburg on Hwy. 2.*

Both Prescott's Fort Wellington and the Old Lighthouse saw action in the War of 1812, and both have been restored and are open to the public. **Fort Wellington** was built by the British in 1813 to protect goods and troops moving between Montréal and Upper Canada after the outbreak of the War of 1812. No harm ever came to the fort, which was completed when the war ended. The Ottawa–Kingston Rideau Canal eliminated the need for the fort, and it was abandoned. In 1837 rebellion broke out in Upper and Lower Canada, and the British built a new and stronger Fort Wellington on the same site. The buildings are furnished in 1846 period style. ✉ *370 Vankoughnet St.,* ☎ *613/925–2896.* ⌨ *$3.* ☉ *Mid-May–Aug., daily 10–6; Sept.–mid-Oct., daily 10–5; mid-Oct.–mid-May, by reservation only.*

Ontario's oldest barracks building, **Stockade Barracks and Hospital Museum,** is one block west of Fort Wellington and open in summer as a museum. Lunches and dinners here feature historic menus. By prior arrangement, groups of 15–40 can have five- or six-course meals of 1812-style dishes served by mess waiters in military uniforms. ✉ *356 East St.,* ☎ *613/925–4894.* ⌨ *$2.* ☉ *June–Sept., weekends 10–5.*

Kingston

㉒ *100 km (62 mi) southwest of Prescott on Hwy. 401.*

Kingston's imposing architecture has been impressing visitors since 1673, when La Salle chose the location as the site for a meeting between Governor Frontenac and the Iroquois. Before the meeting, Frontenac built a stockaded fort to impress the Native Americans and thus tap into the fur trade. The city occupied a strategic site at the junction of the St. Lawrence River and the Rideau Canal system, making it a major military site in Upper Canada. Four Martello towers still guard the harbor. Thanks to misguided American strategy, Kingston survived the War of 1812 almost totally unscathed; many of its beautiful limestone buildings remain in mint condition today. The city's waterfront is appealing, too. Filled with sailing boats, the harbor is also the jumping-off point for cruises around the scenic Thousand Islands.

From 1841 to 1844, Kingston was the national capital; today the gorgeous, cut-limestone **City Hall** (✉ 216 Ontario St., ☎ 613/546–4291) dominates the downtown core, facing a riverfront park. Tours are given weekdays in summer, but you can visit the lobby anytime.

Point Frederick, a small peninsula at the junction of the Cataraqui River and St. Lawrence River, is connected to downtown Kingston by a bridge. The site of the Royal Navy Dockyard until 1850, Point Frederick became home to the **Royal Military College of Canada** in 1876. You can explore the relics of the dockyard on the college grounds. Of particular note is the **Royal Military College Museum,** housed in the largest of the four Martello towers that guarded the Kingston harborfront. The museum contains the internationally renowned Douglas Arms Collection, which includes the small arms owned by General Porfirio Díaz, president of Mexico from 1886 to 1912. ✉ *Off Hwy. 2, east of Kingston,* ☎ *613/541–6000, ext. 6652.* ⌨ *Free.* ☉ *Last weekend in June–Labor Day, daily 10–5.*

★ The massive **Fort Henry** was built during the War of 1812 to repel a possible American invasion, which never came. Staff in period military costume guide visitors, hold parades, and re-create an era past.

who died in Huronia; in 1930 five of the priests were canonized by the Roman Catholic Church. The grounds include a theater, a souvenir shop, a cafeteria, and a picnic area. ⊠ *Off Hwy. 12,* ☎ *705/526–3788.* ☉ *Mid-May–mid-Oct., daily 9–9.*

The best artifacts from several hundred archaeological digs in the area are displayed at **Huronia Museum and Gallery of Historic Huronia** in Little Lake Park, Midland. Behind the museum and gallery building is **Huron Indian Village,** a full-scale replica of a 16th-century Huron settlement. ⊠ *Little Lake Park,* ☎ *705/526–2844.* ☒ *Museum and village $5.* ☉ *Daily 9–5; call for exceptions.*

Cruises leave from the town docks of both Midland and Penetang to explore the 30,000 Islands region of Georgian Bay from May to Thanksgiving (the second Monday in October). The 300-passenger MS *Miss Midland* (☎ 705/526–0161, 800/461–1767 in Ontario), which leaves from the Midland town dock, offers 2½-hour sightseeing cruises daily. From the Penetang town dock, the 200-passenger MS *Georgian Queen* (☎ 705/549–7795) takes passengers on three-hour tours of the islands, from late May through mid-October. The cruises leave once daily at 2 PM; call ahead.

Parry Sound

30 *110 km (68 mi) north of Penetang or Midland on Hwys. 12 and 69.*

Parry Sound is home to Canada's largest sightseeing cruise ship. The **Island Queen** offers an extensive three-hour cruise of Georgian Bay once or twice daily, depending on season. There's free parking at the town dock. ⊠ *9 Bay St.,* ☎ *705/746–2311.* ☒ *$16.* ☉ *June–Thanksgiving (mid-Oct.).*

From mid-July to mid-August, the **Festival of the Sound** (☎ 705/746–2410) fills the auditorium of Parry Sound High School and the decks of the *Island Queen* with jazz, popular music, and classical piano.

Lodging

$$ ▥ **Highland Inn.** An enormous atrium anchors this completely self-contained hotel-motel-resort. Honeymoon suites have heart-shape tubs or sunken Jacuzzis. Sunday brunches by the pool in the Garden Cafe are popular; there are three other dining areas (reserve ahead) as well. ⊠ *924 King St. and Hwy. 12, L4R 4L3,* ☎ *705/526–9307 or 800/461–4265,* ℻ *705/526–0099. 113 rooms, 17 suites. 2 restaurants, indoor pool, sauna, exercise room. AE, DC, MC, V.*

Orillia

31 *35 km (22 mi) northeast of Barrie on Hwy. 11.*

Orillia will be recognized by readers of Canada's great humorist Stephen Leacock as Mariposa, the "little town" he described in *Sunshine Sketches of a Little Town.* Leacock's former summer home is now a museum, the **Stephen Leacock Memorial Home.** In the Mariposa Room, characters from the book are matched with the Orillia residents who inspired them. ⊠ *Off Hwy. 12B in the east end of Orillia,* ☎ *705/329–1908.* ☒ *$7.50.* ☉ *Daily 9–5.*

Gravenhurst

32 *39 km (24 mi) northeast of Barrie on Hwy. 11.*

North along Highway 11, rolling farmland suddenly changes to lakes and pine trees amid granite outcrops of the Canadian Shield. This region, called Muskoka, is a favorite playground of people who live in the highly urbanized areas around Toronto. Gravenhurst is a town of approximately 6,000 and the birthplace of a Canadian hero. The **Bethune Memorial House,** an 1880-vintage frame structure, honors the heroic efforts of field surgeon and medical educator Norman Bethune, who worked in China during the 1930s. It has become a shrine of sorts to Chinese diplomats visiting North America. ⊠ *235 John St. N, ☎ 705/687–4261. ☜ $2.25. ☉ Late May–mid-Oct., daily 10–5; mid-Oct.–late May, weekdays 10–noon and 1–5.*

The **RMS *Segwun*** (the initials stand for Royal Mail Ship) is the sole survivor of a fleet of steamships that once provided transportation through the Muskoka Lakes. The 128-ft boat carries 99 passengers on cruises from mid-June to mid-October. Cruises range from 90 minutes to two days in length (passengers dine aboard but sleep in one of Muskoka's grand resorts). ⊠ *Muskoka Lakes Navigation and Hotel Company Limited, 820 Bay St., Sagamo Park, P1P 1G7, ☎ 705/687–6667.*

Lodging

$$$$ ▦ **Bayview-Wildwood Resort.** A 15-minute drive south of Gravenhurst, this complex is surrounded by trees and is set on scenic Sparrow Lake. The Stanton family has run the hotel for several generations, and in 1998 the resort celebrated its centenary. It is particularly geared to outdoor types and families; there are children's programs during the summer. Canoeing and kayaking are popular; floatplane excursions and golf can be arranged. Some rooms have fireplaces, whirlpool baths, and views over the lake. Bayview-Wildwood offers only all-inclusive two-, five-, and seven-day packages; the minimum stay is two days. ⊠ *1500 Port Stanton Parkway, R.R. 1, Severn Bridge P0E 1N0, ☎ 705/689–2338 or 800/461–0243, ℻ 705/689–8042. 78 rooms, 14 cottages. Boating, fishing, mountain bikes, cross-country skiing, snowmobiling. AP. AE, DC, MC, V.*

$$$–$$$$ ▦ **Muskoka Sands.** In business since 1926, the venerable Muskoka Sands has gone through many changes, but its most recent reincarnation is as an upscale hotel and conference center. Surrounded by a magnificent landscape of rocky outcrops and windswept trees that is typical of the Muskoka region, this year-round resort (many hotels in this area are open only in summer) has all kinds of diversions, from squash to ice-skating. Gourmet food is served in the Winewood Room restaurant. ⊠ *Muskoka Beach Rd., P1P 1R1, ☎ 705/687–2233 or 800/461–0236, ℻ 705/687–7474. 75 rooms. 2 restaurants, pool, exercise room, 5 tennis courts, hiking, squash, mountain bikes, ice-skating, cross-country skiing, playground. AE, DC, MC, V.*

Haliburton

③③ *60 km (37 mi) northeast of Gravenhurst via Hwy. 11 and Hwy. 118, 250 km (155 mi) northeast of Toronto.*

Close to huge Algonquin Provincial Park, Haliburton is a cross-country skiing and winter sports base. In summer the self-guided trails of **Leslie Frost Natural Resources Center** (⊠ Hwy. 35 at St. Nora's Lake, ☎ 705/766–2451) offer a great primer in Ontario's wildlife.

Lodging

$$ **Pinestone Resort & Conference Center.** Lots of blond wood and stone are part of the resort's rustic chic style. The hotel has an 18-hole, par-71 golf course and many other outdoor activities, and it's surrounded by 235 acres of rolling, wooded countryside. Pinestone is close to Sir Sam's Ski Area and to the Haliburton Wolf Center, where you can observe captive wolves (part of a breeding program) feeding and playing from the safety of a lookout point. ⊠ *Hwy. 121, 7 km (4 mi) west of Halibur-*

ton, Box 809, K0M 1S0, ☎ *705/457–1800 or 800/461–0357,* FAX *705/ 754–1783. 92 rooms, 16 villas, 6 cottages. Restaurant, indoor-outdoor pool, sauna, tennis court, 18-hole golf course, hiking, boating, fishing, mountain bikes, ice-skating, cross-country skiing. AE, DC, MC, V.*

Outdoor Activities and Sports

SKIING LODGE-TO-LODGE

Three- and four-night guided lodge-to-lodge cross-country ski packages are available along the Haliburton Nordic Trail system. There are groups for skiers of all levels, and the trips cover 8–25 km (5–16 mi) per day, depending on the group's abilities. Six lodges participate in the program, and skiers stay and dine at a different lodge each night. Packages include all meals, trail passes, and a guide.For information about ski packages, contact Brian Dean, General Manager, or John Teljeur of the **Haliburton Nordic Trail Association** (⊠ Box 147, Minden K0M 2K0, ☎ 800/461–7677).

SNOWMOBILING

C Mac Snow Tours (⊠ R.R. 3, Walton N0K 1Z0, ☎ 519/887–6686 or 800/225–4258) has three- and five-night all-inclusive excursions in Haliburton Highlands/Algonquin Park.

Bracebridge

㉞ *11 km (8 mi) north of Gravenhurst on Hwy. 11.*

Holiday cheer brightens Bracebridge in summer with Christmas-oriented amusements. The Bracebridge Falls on the Muskoka River are a good option for those who prefer a more peaceful excursion. After letting Santa know what they'd like to find under the Christmas tree, youngsters can ride the Kris Kringle Riverboat, the Candy Cane Express Train, minibikes, bumper boats, paddleboats, ponies, and more at **Santa's Village.** ⊠ *Santa's Village Rd. (west of Bracebridge),* ☎ *705/645–2512.* ⊡ *$14.95.* ⊙ *Mid-June–Labor Day, daily 10–6.*

Funland, for children 12 and older, offers go-carts, batting cages, inline skating, 18-hole mini-putt, laser tag, and an indoor activity center with video games. A separate ticket is required for each amusement. ⊠ *Santa's Village Rd. (west of Bracebridge),* ☎ *705/645–2512.* ⊡ *$2 per ticket.* ⊙ *Mid-May–mid-June, weekends 10–10; mid-June–Labor Day, daily 10–10.*

Dining and Lodging

$$–$$$$ ★ ╳⊞ **Inn at the Falls.** This Victorian inn and its annex of motel-style rooms command a magnificent view of the pretty Bracebridge Falls. Accommodations include rooms, a cottage, and suites; six of the units have fireplaces. The outdoor pool is heated. The main dining room (reserve ahead) and pub-lounge offer food and live entertainment; there's an outdoor patio as well. Try the steak-and-kidney pie. ⊠ *1 Dominion St., Box 1139, P1L 1V3,* ☎ *705/645–2245,* FAX *705/645–5093. 24 rooms, 12 suites, 1 cottage. Restaurant, pub, pool. AE, D, MC, V.*

Dorset

㉟ *48 km (30 mi) northeast of Bracebridge via Hwys. 11 and 117.*

Dorset is a pretty village on a narrows between two bays of the Lake of Bays. The village is home to **Robinson's General Store** (☎ 705/766–2415), which, with the exception of the World War II years, has been continuously owned and operated by a Robinson since its 1921 opening. You'll find everything here from moose-fur hats to stoves and pine furniture. You can circle back to Toronto on scenic Highway 35 or make Dorset a stop on a circle tour from Huntsville (☞ *below*) around the Lake of Bays.

Huntsville

36 *34 km (21 mi) north of Bracebridge on Hwy. 11, 215 km (133 mi) north of Toronto on Hwys. 400 and 11.*

The Huntsville region is filled with lakes and streams, stands of virgin birch and pine, and deer and smaller forest dwellers that browse along the trails. Because the area is part of Toronto's summer playground, there is no shortage of year-round resorts.

Dining and Lodging

$$$ ✕🏠 **Deerhurst Resort.** This spectacular, ultra-deluxe resort is a self-contained community on 800 acres. The flavor is largely modern, although the main lodge, complete with dining room and Cypress Lounge, dates from 1886 and is appointed with a rustic flair. The menu offers Ontario game—buffalo and caribou—as well as Mediterranean dishes. ✉ *1235 Deerhurst Dr., P1P 2E8,* ☎ *705/789–6411. 400 rooms. Indoor pool, 2 golf courses, tennis court, exercise room, racquetball, squash, cross-country skiing, snowmobiling. AE, DC MC, V.*

$$$–$$$$ 🏠 **Grandview Inn.** A five-minute drive east of Huntsville, this modern resort on a lake has just added a health spa where guests can relax with facials, massages, and other spa treatments. The resort offers numerous outdoor activities, some of which are led by a resident naturalist who takes small groups into nearby Algonquin Park. You can try bird-watching excursions and explore forested hiking and biking trails. There are a variety of water sports here, too. ✉ *939 Hwy. 60, P1H 1Z4,* ☎ *705/789–4417 or 800/461–4454 in Canada,* 🖷 *705/789–8334. 98 rooms, 74 suites. 2 restaurants, spa, 9-hole golf course, windsurfing, waterskiing, cross-country skiing. AE, DC, MC, V.*

$–$$ 🏠 **Walker Lake Resort.** In winter the rustic cottages here overlook deer feeding stations on either side of the frozen lake. The Norseman restaurant serves dinner only (Continental menu), but guests can cook for themselves in their cottages. Rentals are by the week only. ✉ *1040 Walker Lake Dr., R.R. 4, P1H 2J6,* ☎ *705/635–2473. 7 cottages. Restaurant, kitchenettes, cross-country skiing. AE, MC, V.*

Outdoor Activities and Sports

In southern Ontario the Huntsville area is usually the cross-country skier's best bet for an abundance of natural snow. Deerhurst, Walker Lake, and Grandview resorts (☞ Dining and Lodging, *above*) have trails.

Algonquin Park

37 *50 km (31 mi) northeast of Huntsville on Hwy. 60.*

Algonquin Provincial Park stretches across 7,600 square km (3,040 square mi) of lakes, forests, rivers, and cliffs. It is a hiker's, canoeist's, and camper's paradise. But don't be put off if you're not the athletic or rough-outdoors sort. About a third of all visitors to Algonquin come for the day to visit a museum, walk one of the 14 interpretive trails, or enjoy a swim or a picnic. Swimming is especially good at the Lake of Two Rivers, about halfway between the west and east gates along Highway 60. A morning drive through the park in May or June is often rewarded by a sighting of moose, which are attracted to the highway by the slightly salty water in roadside ditches. Wolf-howling expeditions, led by a park naturalist, take place in August. Two attractions near the east side of the park are the **visitor center,** which includes a bookstore, a restaurant, and a viewing deck, and the **Algonquin Logging Museum,** which depicts life at an early Canadian logging camp. ✉ *Box 219, Whitney K0J 2M0,* ☎ *705/633–5572.* 🎫 *$8 per vehicle.* ☉ *Park daily 8 AM–10 PM. Museum mid-June–Labor Day, daily 10–6; Labor Day–Oct., weekends 10–5.*

Outdoor Activities and Sports

Radcliffe Hills ski area (☎ 613/756–2931 or 800/668–8249, FAX 613/756–2931), near Barry's Bay, south of the park on Highway 60, has a vertical drop of 400 ft and a tubing run with a tube lift.

FORT ERIE AND WEST TO WINDSOR

Fort Erie

㊳ *155 km (96 mi) south of Toronto via the Queen Elizabeth Way.*

Fort Erie, at the extreme southeast tip of the Niagara Peninsula, is a drab, boom-or-bust town of fast-food chains, taverns, and gas stations whose profits rise or fall with the exchange rate between Canadian and U.S. dollars. Situated opposite Buffalo, New York, the city is the gateway to the scenic Niagara Parkway. This road along the Niagara River is lined with picnic tables and bicycle paths. The Peace Bridge, which links Fort Erie to its southern neighbor, is one of the busiest crossings along the Canada–U.S. border.

Historic Fort Erie, at the south end of Fort Erie, has been reconstructed to look as it did before it was destroyed at the end of the War of 1812. The fort's colorful and bloody history reveals that thousands of soldiers lost their lives within sight of the earthworks, drawbridges, and palisades. The fort itself was destroyed in 1779 and again in 1803 by spectacular storms that drove masses of ice ashore at the foot of Lake Erie. Visitors are conducted through the display rooms by guards in period British army uniforms. In summer the guards stand sentry duty, fire the cannon, and demonstrate drill and musket practice. ⊠ *350 Lakeshore Rd.,* ☎ *905/871–0540.* ☜ *$5.* ⊙ *May, weekdays 10–4, weekends 9:30–6; June–early Oct., daily 9:30–6.*

Though it dates back to 1897, **Fort Erie Race Track** is one of the most modern—and picturesque—tracks in North America. Glass-enclosed dining lounges overlook a 2-km (1-mi) dirt track and a seven-furlong turf course. Also in view are gardens, ponds, and waterways. ⊠ *Bertie St. and Queen Elizabeth Way,* ☎ *905/871–3200.* ⊙ *May–Sept., Fri.–Mon., races at 12:45; Oct., Fri.–Sun., races at 12:45.*

Port Colborne

㊴ *30 km (19 mi) west of Fort Erie on Hwy. 3.*

Port Colborne, a shipping center on Lake Erie, is at the southern end of the 44-km-long (27-mi-long) Welland Canal, which connects Lake Ontario to Lake Erie, bypassing Niagara Falls. You can view **Lock 8** from a platform. The town (population 18,800) remains an enclave for descendants of United Empire Loyalist stock.Chronicling the town's rich history and development is the **Port Colborne Historical and Marine Museum,** a six-building complex. ⊠ *280 King St.,* ☎ *905/834–7604.* ☜ *Free.* ⊙ *May–Dec., daily noon–5.*

Welland

㊵ *10 km (6 mi) north of Port Colborne on Hwy. 58 or 140.*

In 1988 Welland staged a Festival of Arts Murals to attract some of the 14–16 million tourists who were bypassing the town on their way to Niagara Falls. Today 30 giant murals decorate downtown buildings; the longest is 130 ft, and the tallest is three stories high. You can pick up a free mural tour map from **Welland Tourism** (⊠ 32 E. Main St., ☎ 905/735–8696) or from brochure racks at City Hall and in local restaurants and hotels. Welland is also the home of the annual **Niagara Food Festival.** Held in the downtown Market Square around the end of September or early October, this festival brings together an array of local farmers, wineries, and restaurants to provide the region's food.

OFF THE BEATEN PATH | **WELLAND CANAL** – At St. Catharines, about 25 km (15 mi) north of Welland, you may see a ship pass through Lock 3 of the Welland Canal, which joins Lake Erie and Lake Ontario. Also on the site, the **St. Catharines Museum** (☎ 905/984–8880) has historical exhibits and displays about the construction of the canal, part of the St. Lawrence Seaway; admission is $3. To get here from Welland, take Highway 406 north to the Queen Elizabeth Way and head west to St. Catharines; Lock 3 is on Government Road, near the QEW.

Port Dover

㊶ *107 km (66 mi) west of Welland via Hwys. 58, 23, 3, and 6.*

Port Dover is the home of the world's largest fleet of freshwater fishing boats. It's a pretty beach resort town where freshwater fish is served up steamy and golden at a number of restaurants.

St. Thomas

㊷ *75 km (47 mi) west of Port Dover on Hwy. 3 and 28 km (17 mi) east of London on Hwy. 3.*

St. Thomas's first buildings went up in 1810, over a decade and a half ahead of the first building in London, Ontario (☞ Hamilton and Festival Country, *below*). However, while St. Thomas's population has leveled at 30,000, London's has hit 320,000. The town has a **statue of Jumbo** (✉ 555 Talbot St.), the Barnum and Bailey circus elephant, killed here in a freak railway accident in 1885. The monument is a 10%-larger-than-life-size statue of the largest elephant ever in captivity. The **St. Thomas–Elgin Chamber of Commerce** (✉ 555 Talbot St., ☎ 519/631–1981), open May through Labor Day, is adjacent to the Jumbo monument and a railway caboose.

Port Stanley

㊸ *15 km (9 mi) south of St. Thomas on Hwy. 4.*

The fishing village of Port Stanley has the largest natural harbor on the north shore of Lake Erie. Its fine brown-sand beach, boutiques, snack bars, and kitsch stands make for a lively summer destination.

☯ The **Port Stanley Terminal Railroad,** built in 1856, was intended to be a main trade link between Canada and the United States. The trade didn't materialize, but the railroad survived on excursion traffic until 1957. Railroad buffs later restored some passenger cars and repaired the line as far as Union, in 1992 extending it to St. Thomas. You can take a 45-minute excursion to Union on Sunday afternoons year-round, on Saturdays from May through November, and daily in July and August. ✉ *Port Stanley Railway Station,* ☎ *519/782–3730.* 🖃 *Round-trip fare to Union $9, to St. Thomas $11.* ☉ *Call ahead.*

Dining and Lodging

$$–$$$ ★ | ✕🏠 **Kettle Creek Inn.** All the rooms and suites in this small, elegant country inn and its modern annex have views of a landscaped courtyard and gazebo. Some rooms have whirlpool baths and gas fireplaces. There are other nice touches, such as old-fashioned pedestal sinks and interesting local artwork. The three rooms (reserve ahead) in the restau-

rant in the original inn offer daily specials, including fresh Lake Erie fish and farm-raised rhea, a type of ostrich. ✉ *216 Joseph St., N5L 1C4,* ☎ *519/782–3388,* 🖷 *519/782–4747. 10 rooms, 5 suites. Restaurant. CP. AE, D, DC, MC, V.*

Point Pelee National Park

★ **㊹** *150 km (93 mi) west of Port Stanley/St. Thomas on Hwy. 401 or Hwy. 3, near Leamington on Hwy. 33.*

The southernmost tip of mainland Canada, Point Pelee National Park has the smallest dry land area of any Canadian national park, yet it draws more than a half-million visitors every year. At the park's visitor center you'll find exhibits, slide shows, and a knowledgeable staff ready to answer questions. Some 700 kinds of plants and 347 species of birds have been recorded here, including a number of endangered species. A tram operates seasonally to "the tip." September is the best time to see monarch butterflies resting in Pelee before they head to Mexico's Sierra Madres. The park is also renowned for bird-watching, especially during spring and fall migrations. This is a day-use park only. ✉ *R.R.1, Leamington N8H 3V4,* ☎ *519/322–2365.* 🖾 *$3.25 Apr.–Labor Day; $2.25 Labor Day–Mar.* ◷ *Daily 6 AM–10 PM.*

Pelee Island

㊺ *25 km (16 mi) and 90 min by ferry from Point Pelee via Hwy. 33 and Leamington ferry.*

Pelee is a small, flat island, roughly 13 by 6 km (8 by 4 mi), at the west end of Lake Erie, served spring through fall by a ferry (for which reservations are necessary) that links it with Essex County on the Canadian mainland and Sandusky in Ohio. In winter there are scheduled flights from Windsor. The island's permanent population is under 300, but in summer that quadruples as vacationers cram into private cottages. Still, Pelee maintains its island pace. You can enjoy the beaches, cycle around the island, tour the Wine Pavilion, or visit the ruins of Vin Villa winery, dating back to the mid-1800s. Pelee Island is Canada's southernmost inhabited point, on the same latitude as northern California and northern Spain.

Kingsville

㊻ *10 km (7 mi) west of Leamington on Hwy. 18.*

Kingsville, one of the southernmost towns in Ontario, is best known for its bird sanctuary. **Jack Miner's Bird Sanctuary** was started by Jack Miner, an avid hunter who realized no species could survive both its natural enemies *and* man. In 1904 he dug ponds, planted trees, and introduced four Canada geese with clipped wings to the ponds. That number grew to the 50,000 that now winter here. From 1910 to 1940 Miner lectured kings and presidents on the importance of conservation. His former home is now open year-round. No admission is charged and nothing is sold on the grounds. A museum (closed Sunday) in the former stables has a wealth of Miner memorabilia, and at a pond beside the house you can feed for free far-from-shy geese and ducks. At 4 PM daily, the birds are flushed for "air shows" and circle overhead. The best times to view migrations are late March, October, and November. ✉ *Essex County Rd. 29, 5 km (3 mi) north of Kingsville,* ☎ *519/733–4034.* 🖾 *Free.* ◷ *Mid-Mar.–Dec., Mon.–Sat. 9–5.*

The **John R. Park Homestead and Conservation Area,** 8 km (5 mi) west of Kingsville, is a pioneer village anchored by one of Ontario's few examples of American Greek Revival architecture, an 1842 home. The village's 10 buildings include the house of John R. Park, a shed built without nails, a smokehouse, an icehouse, an outhouse, a sawmill, and a stable. ⊠ *County Rd. 50 at Iler Rd.,* ☎ *519/738–2029.* 🎫 *$3.* ⊙ *July–Labor Day, daily 11–5; Labor Day–June, Sun.–Fri. 11–4.*

Southwestern Ontario Heritage Village

47 *About 10 km (6 mi) north of Kingsville on Hwy. 23.*

The turn-of-the-century Southwestern Ontario Heritage Village has 20 historic buildings spread across 54 wooded acres. Volunteers in period dress show visitors how pioneers baked, operated looms, and dipped candles. The **Transportation Museum** of the Historic Vehicle Society of Ontario, Windsor Branch, also on the grounds, displays a fine collection of travel artifacts, from snowshoes to buggies to vintage automobiles. ⊠ *County Rd. 23,* ☎ *519/776–6909.* 🎫 *$3.* ⊙ *Village and museum Apr.–Nov., Wed.–Sun. 11–5; July–Aug., daily 11–5.*

Amherstburg

48 *25 km (16 mi) west of Kingsville on Hwy. 18.*

The riverside parks in the quiet town of Amherstburg are great places to watch the procession of Great Lakes shipping. **Navy Yard Park,** with flower beds ringed by old anchor chains, has benches overlooking Bois Blanc Island and the narrow main shipping channel.

Fort Malden was the British base in the War of 1812 from which Detroit was captured, though the site dates back to 1727, when a Jesuit mission began occupying lands in the area. Now the fort is an 11-acre National Historic Park, with original earthworks, restored barracks, a military pensioner's cottage, two exhibit buildings, and picnic facilities. ⊠ *100 Laird Ave.,* ☎ *519/736–5416.* 🎫 *$2.* ⊙ *Jan.–Apr., weekdays 1–5, weekends 10–5; May–Dec., daily 10–5.*

The **North American Black Historical Museum** commemorates the U.S. slaves and the Underground Railroad system many used to flee to Canada. It is one of several sites related to this history in the area. Between 1800 and 1860, an estimated 30,000 to 50,000 U.S. slaves made the journey to Canada, and many crossed the Detroit River at Amherstburg because it was the narrowest point. An 1848-vintage church and log cabin contain artifacts and biographies. ⊠ *277 King St.,* ☎ *519/736–5433.* 🎫 *$4.50.* ⊙ *Wed.–Fri. 10–5, weekends 1–5.*

Windsor

49 *30 km (19 mi) north of Amherstburg on Hwy. 18, 150 km (93 mi) west of London on Hwy. 401.*

Long an unattractive industrial city that hosted Ford, General Motors, and Chrysler manufacturing plants, Windsor has become a pleasant place to visit. The riverfront has pretty parks, some with fountains and statues, all overlooking the spectacular Detroit skyline. The cities are linked by the Ambassador Bridge and the Windsor–Detroit Tunnel. At press time Windsor was planning to open a new casino. If you're traveling by car, start your Windsor visit at the **Convention & Visitors Bureau** (⊠ 333 Riverside Dr. W, Suite 103, ☎ 800/265–3633).

The **Art Gallery of Windsor** mounts changing displays of contemporary and historic Canadian and other art. ⊠ *Devonshire Mall, 3100 Howard Ave.,* ☎ *519/969–4494.* 🎫 *Free.* ⊙ *Tues.–Fri. 10–7, Sat. 10–5, Sun. noon–5.*

The **Windsor Community Museum** houses a collection of area artifacts in the 1812 house where the Battle of Windsor, the final incident in the Upper Canada Rebellion, was fought in 1838. ⊠ *254 Pitt St. W,* ☏ *519/253–1812.* ⊠ *Free.* ☉ *Tues.–Sat. 10–5, Sun. 2–5.*

Willistead Manor is the former home of Edward Chandler Walker, second son of Hiram, who founded Walker's Distillery in 1858. The 15-acre estate is now a city park. ⊠ *Niagara St. and Kildare Rd.,* ☏ *519/ 253–2365.* ⊠ *Manor $3.50.* ☉ *House tours Sept.–June, 1st and 3rd Sun. of each month 1–4; July and Aug., Sun. and Wed., 1–4; call to check hrs.*

Since 1959, Windsor and Detroit have combined their national birthday parties (Canada Day, July 1; and Independence Day, July 4) into a massive bash called **International Freedom Festival** (☏ 519/252–7264). The two-week party includes nonstop entertainment with more than 100 special events on both sides of the river and a spectacular fireworks display, billed as the largest in North America.

Dining and Lodging

$$–$$$ ✕ **Old Fish Market.** A wonderful ambience is created here with hanging plants, brass railings, and lovely woodwork. The menu, predictably, is heavy on seafood. The restaurant has a deserved reputation of excellence. ⊠ *156 Chatham St. W,* ☏ *519/253–7417. Reservations essential. AE, DC, MC, V.*

$–$$ ✕ **Brigantino's.** This popular establishment serves traditional home-style Italian cooking with original twists, such as veal with cognac and Portobello mushrooms, and pasta stuffed with ricotta cheese and spinach and smothered in your choice of pesto, hot red, or cream sauce. Nightly entertainment adds festivity to the atmosphere, especially when accordion players are scheduled. ⊠ *851 Erie St. E,* ☏ *519/ 254–7041. Reservations essential. AE, D, DC, MC, V.*

$$–$$$ ⊞ **Hilton International Windsor.** Each of the guest rooms in this downtown riverbank hotel has a view of Detroit's skyline and the shipping activity on the world's busiest inland waterway. The Park Terrace Restaurant and Lounge offers a wide menu and a spectacular river view. There's music and dancing in the River Runner Bar and Grill. ⊠ *277 Riverside Dr. W, N9A 5K4,* ☏ *519/973–5555 or 800/463–6655,* ᴲᴬˣ *519/973–1600. 303 rooms. 2 restaurants, bar, room service, indoor pool, hot tub, sauna, meeting rooms. AE, DC, MC, V.*

THE NIAGARA PENINSULA

The two most-visited towns on the Niagara peninsula have very different flavors. Home to a wildly popular natural attraction, Niagara Falls can have a certain tacky quality, while Niagara-on-the-Lake, which draws theatergoers to its annual Shaw festival, epitomizes ye olde British tastefulness. Still, Niagara Falls has something for everyone, from water slides and wax museums to honeymoon certificates. Because the towns are in such close proximity to each other, however, there's no need to choose; you can base your decision on the day's mood. This is also one of the three best regions for wine production in Canada—Point Pelee (☞ Fort Erie and West to Windsor, *above*) and British Columbia are the others. More than 20 small, quality vineyards produce fine wines, and most of them offer tastings and tours.

Niagara Falls

130 km (81 mi) south of Toronto via the Queen Elizabeth Way.

The town of Niagara Falls has attractions of all kinds, from the high-minded (a botanical garden) to the frankly commercial (the "museums" on Clifton Hill); the falls themselves are a one-of-a-kind reason to come here, though, in spite of the distractions. Cynics have had a field day

★ with **Niagara Falls,** calling it everything from "water on the rocks" to "the second major disappointment of American married life" (Oscar Wilde). Others have been far more glowing. Missionary and explorer Louis Hennepin, whose books were widely read across Europe, first described the falls in 1678 as "an incredible Cataract or Waterfall which has no equal." Nearly two centuries later, Charles Dickens wrote, "I seemed to be lifted from the earth and to be looking into Heaven." Henry James recorded in 1883 how one stands there "gazing your fill at the most beautiful object in the world."

Understandably, all these rave reviews began to bring out professional daredevils, as well as self-destructive amateurs. In 1859 the French tightrope walker Blondin walked across the Niagara Gorge, from the American to the Canadian side, on a 3-inch-thick rope, while some 100,000 spectators watched from both shores. "Thank God it is over!" exclaimed the future King Edward VII of England, after completion of the walk. "Please never attempt it again." But sadly, others did. From the early 18th century, dozens went over in boats and barrels. Not a single one survived, until 1901, when schoolteacher Annie Taylor made the attempt. Emerging from her barrel, she asked, "Did I go over the falls yet?" The endless stunts were finally outlawed in 1912, but not before the province of Ontario created the first provincial park in all of Canada—Queen Victoria Park—in 1887.

It all started more than 10,000 years ago, when a group of glaciers receded, diverting the waters of Lake Erie northward into Lake Ontario. The force and volume of the water as it flowed over the Niagara Escarpment caused the phenomenon we know as the falls. The area's human history is fairly interesting, too. The War of 1812 had settlers on both sides of the river killing one another, with the greatest battle taking place in Niagara Falls itself, at Lundy's Lane. Soon after, at the Treaty of Ghent, two modest cities of the same name arose on each side of the river—one in the United States, the other in Canada.

The Niagara Parks Commission (NPC) was formed in 1885 to preserve the area around the falls. Beginning with a small block of land, the NPC has gradually acquired most of the land fronting on the Canadian side of the Niagara River, from Niagara-on-the-Lake to Fort Erie. The Niagara Parkway, a 56-km (35-mi) riverside drive, is a 3,000-acre ribbon of parkland lined with parking overlooks, picnic tables, and barbecue pits; the public is welcome to use the facilities at no charge.

Winter shouldn't discourage you from coming: The **Winter Festival of Lights** is a real stunner. Seventy trees are illuminated with 34,000 lights in the parklands near the Rainbow Bridge; there is also "The Enchantment of Disney," lighted displays based on cartoon characters and movies. The Falls are illuminated nightly from 5 to 10 PM, late November–mid-January.

50 The **Niagara Parks Botanical Gardens and School of Horticulture** has been graduating professional gardeners since 1936. The art of horticulture is celebrated by its students with 80 acres of immaculately maintained gardens. Within the Botanical Gardens is the **Niagara Parks Butterfly Conservatory** (☎ 905/356–8119), home to one of North America's largest collections of free-flying butterflies—at least 2,000 are protected in a lush rain forest setting by a glass-enclosed conservatory. The climate-controlled conservatory operates year-round and contains 50 species from around the world, each with its own colorful markings. In 1997, an outdoor butterfly garden was added with 120 domestic species. ⊠ *2565 N. Niagara Pkwy.,* ☎ *905/356–8554.* ☞ *Botanical Gardens free, Butterfly Conservatory $7.* ☉ *Botanical Gardens, daily dawn–dusk; Butterfly Conservatory, daily 9–9.*

51 A short distance (downriver) from the Botanical Gardens and School of Horticulture (☞ *above*) on the Niagara Parkway is a **floral clock,** one of the world's largest; its 40-ft "living" face is designed by the NPC and planted in a different design twice every season.

52 You'll find trails maintained by the NPC in the **Niagara Glen.** A bicycle trail that parallels the Niagara Parkway from Fort Erie to Niagara-on-the-Lake winds between beautiful homes on one side and the river, with its abundant bird life, on the other.

53 The **Niagara Spanish Aero Car,** in operation since 1916, is a cable car that crosses the Whirlpool Basin in the Niagara Gorge. This trip is not for the fainthearted; when you're high above the roiling whirlpool, those cables seem awfully thin. ⊠ *Niagara Pkwy., 4½ km (3 mi) north of the falls,* ☎ *905/354–5711.* ☞ *$5.* ☉ *Mid-May–Labor Day, daily 9–9; Labor Day–mid-Oct., shorter hrs, weather permitting.*

54 The **Great Gorge Adventure** involves taking an elevator to the bottom of the Niagara Gorge, where you can walk a boardwalk beside the torrent of the Niagara River. There the gorge is rimmed by sheer cliffs as it enters the giant whirlpool. ⊠ *Niagara Pkwy., 3 km (2 mi) north of falls,* ☎ *905/354–5711.* ☞ *$4.75.* ☉ *Mid-May–Labor Day, daily 9–9; Labor Day–mid-Oct., shorter hrs, weather permitting.*

55 The **Niagara Falls Museum,** founded in 1827, claims to be North America's oldest museum. It contains everything from stuffed birds and Egyptian mummies to the **Daredevil Hall of Fame,** where the barrels and other contraptions in which people have gone over the falls pay tribute to two centuries of Niagara Falls rebels. There are 26 galleries on four floors and 700,000 exhibits, so gauge your time accordingly—this museum is well worth two hours of browsing. ⊠ *5651 River Rd.,* ☎ *905/356–2151.* ☞ *$6.75.* ☉ *June–early Oct., daily 8:30 AM–11 PM; mid-Oct.–May, daily 10–5.*

56 **Ride Niagara** is divided into three portions: a theater presentation, an elevator ride down to the tunnel, and the shuttle that simulates plunging over the falls and down the rapids in a barrel. The entire event takes about 20–25 minutes. Children under three are not admitted. ⊠ *5755 River Rd.,* ☎ *905/374–7433.* ☞ *$7.95.* ☉ *Daily 11:45–6.*

57 *Maid of the Mist* boats have been operating since 1846, when they were wooden-hulled, coal-fired steamboats. Today, boats tow fun-loving passengers on 30-minute journeys to the foot of the falls, where the spray is so heavy that raincoats must be distributed. ⊠ *Boats leave from foot of Clifton Hill,* ☎ *905/358–5781.* ☞ *$10.10.* ☉ *Apr. and Sept.–Oct. weekdays 10–5, weekends 10–6; May–Aug. hrs vary, sometimes opening as early as 9:15 AM, closing as late as 8 PM.*

58 At **Journey Behind the Falls** your admission ticket includes use of rubber boots and a hooded rain slicker. An elevator will take you to an observation deck, which allows a fish's-eye view of the Canadian Horseshoe Falls and the Niagara River. From there a walk through three tunnels cut into the rock takes you behind the wall of crashing water. ⊠ *Tours begin at Table Rock House, Queen Victoria Park,* ☎ *905/*

Niagara Falls

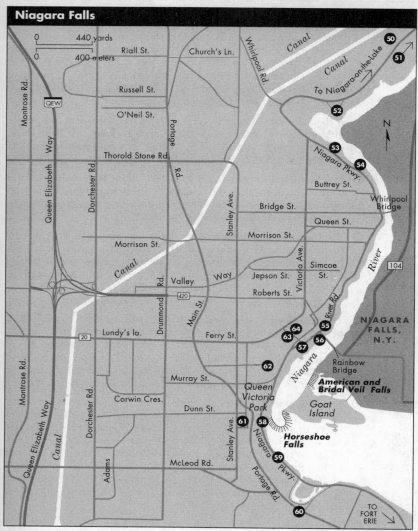

Casino Niagara, **64**
Clifton Hill, **63**
Floral Clock, **51**
Great Gorge
Adventure, **54**
Greenhouse and Plant
Conservatory, **59**

Journey Behind the
Falls, **58**
Maid of the Mist
boats, **57**
Marineland, **60**
Minolta Tower, **61**
Niagara Falls
Museum, **55**

Niagara Glen, **52**
Niagara Parks
Botanical Gardens
and School of
Horticulture, **50**
Niagara Spanish
Aero Car, **53**

Ride Niagara, **56**
Skylon Tower, **62**

354–1551. ☎ *$5.75.* ⊙ *Mid-Nov.–mid-Apr., daily 9–5:30; mid-Apr.–mid-Nov., daily 9–sunset.*

⁵⁹ The NPC's enormous **Greenhouse and Plant Conservatory,** just south of Horseshoe Falls, is open daily. Here you can see myriad plants and flowers year-round. ✉ *Niagara Pkwy.,* ☎ *905/356–4699.* ☎ *Free; parking $3 per hr.* ⊙ *Sun.–Thurs. 9:30–6; Fri.–Sat. 9:30–8.*

⁶⁰ **Marineland,** a theme park with a marine show, wildlife displays, and rides, is 1½ km (1 mi) south of the falls. The daily marine show includes performing killer whales, dolphins, harbor seals, and sea lions. Children can pet and feed members of a herd of 500 deer and get nose-to-nose with North American freshwater fish. Among the many rides is Dragon Mountain, the world's largest steel roller coaster. Marineland is signposted from Niagara Parkway or reached from the Queen Elizabeth Way by exiting at McLeod Road (Exit 27). ✉ *7657 Portage Rd.,* ☎ *905/356–8250 or 905/356–9565.* ☎ *$21.95.* ⊙ *Apr.–June and Sept., daily 10–5; July–Aug., daily 9–6.*

Niagara Falls IMAX Theatre/The Daredevil Adventure Gallery. You can see the wonder of the falls up close and travel back in time for a glimpse of its 12,000-year-old history with *Niagara: Miracles, Myths and Magic.* The movie screen, Canada's largest, is more than six stories high. The Daredevil Adventure Gallery chronicles the brave expeditions of those who have tackled the falls. ✉ *6170 Buchanan Ave.,* ☎ *905/358–3611.* ☎ *$7.50.* ⊙ *Sept.–Oct. and late Apr.–June, daily 11–8; Oct.–late Apr., weekdays and Sun. 11–4, Sat. 11–7; movies run every hr on the hr.*

⁶¹ **Minolta Tower,** 525 ft above the base of the falls, affords panoramic views of Horseshoe Falls and the area. Also in the tower are high-tech games: Cybermind Virtual Reality, offering precisely what its name suggests; Galaxian Adventure, a laser action game played from seated consoles; and Thrill Ride Simulator, a simulated roller coaster ride through a volcano mine. ✉ *6732 Oakes Dr.,* ☎ *905/356–1501 or 800/461–2492.* ☎ *Tower $5.95, Cybermind Virtual Reality $5.95, Galaxian Space Adventure $3.95, Thrill Ride Simulator $5.95.* ⊙ *9 AM until lights go off at the falls (as late as midnight in summer).*

⁶² Rising 775 ft above the falls, **Skylon Tower** offers the best view of both the great Niagara and the entire city. An indoor-outdoor observation deck facilitates the view. Amusements for children plus a revolving dining room (☞ Dining and Lodging, *below*) are other reasons to visit. ✉ *5200 Robinson St.,* ☎ *905/356–2651.* ☎ *$7.50.* ⊙ *Mid-June–Labor Day, daily 8 AM–1 AM; Labor Day–early June, daily 10–9.*

⁶³ **Clifton Hill,** almost directly opposite the American falls, is probably the most crassly commercial district of Niagara Falls. Sometimes referred to as "Museum Alley," this area encompasses the Guinness World of Records Museum, Ripley's Believe It or Not Museum, Louis Tussaud's Waxworks Museum, the Haunted House, the Funhouse, the House of Frankenstein, Castle Dracula, and Super Star Recording (where you can record the musical number of your choice), Movieland Wax Museum, Criminals Hall of Fame Wax Museum, the Elvis Presley Museum, and the That's Incredible Museum. Admission for most attractions usually runs about $6 or $7.

⁶⁴ **Casino Niagara,** set in an architectural design reminiscent of the 1920s, has a total of 3,000 slot machines and 123 gambling tables, such as blackjack, roulette, baccarat, Caribbean stud poker, Let It Ride, Pai Gow poker, and Big Six. Within the casino are several restaurants and lounges. ✉ *5705 Falls Ave.,* ☎ *888/946–3255 or 905/374–5964.* ⊙ *Daily 24 hrs.*

Dining and Lodging

$$-$$$ ✕ **Casa Mia.** This off-the-tourist-track restaurant, in a pink stucco villa
★ about 10 minutes from the center of town, is airy and modern with a
comfortable piano lounge (there's live music Friday and Saturday). All
the pasta is kitchen-made. If you've ever wondered what real cannel-
loni was like, these light pasta pancakes, filled with coarse-ground veal
and spinach, will tell you. The veal chop, grilled with lemon and caper
juice, is a thing of beauty. ✉ *3518 Portage Rd., about 10 km (6 mi)
from Niagara-on-the-Lake,* ☎ *905/356–5410. AE, MC, V.*

$$-$$$ ✕ **Skylon Tower.** Don't come here for surprises—this tower is owned
by the same people who own the local Holiday Inn—but for the view
from the Revolving Dining Room, which rotates at one revolution per
hour. Traditionally prepared rack of lamb, baked salmon, steak, and
chicken make up the list of entrées. It's an eclectic crowd, with cock-
tail wear and casual clothes seated side-by-side. Even with a reservation there may be a short wait in summer. ✉ *5200 Robin St.,* ☎ *905/
356–2651, ext. 259. AE, MC, V.*

$$ ✕ **Capri.** This award-winning restaurant is not only family-owned, but
★ has had the same chef for 43 years. Chef Carmen continues to prepare
huge, Italian-style platters such as linguine with chicken cacciatore. The
three dining rooms, decorated in dark wood paneling, draw traditional
Italian families daily. ✉ *5348 Ferry St. (Hwy. 20), about 1 km (½ mi)
from falls,* ☎ *905/354–7519. AE, DC, MC, V.*

$$ ✕ **Casa d'Oro.** You'll think you've stepped into a Disney version of a
★ Venetian castle, but huge faux-marble and bronze sculptures are some-
how not out of place in Niagara Falls. The Roberto family has been
serving steak, seafood, and Italian specialties here for more than 30
years. Folks come not only for the prime rib, T-bones, and fillets but
also for the experience. After dinner, you can cross a painted bridge
that spans a water-filled moat to the Rialto nightclub's dance floor. ✉
5875 Victoria Ave., ☎ *905/356–5646. AE, DC, MC, V.*

$-$$ ✕ **Simon's Newsstand and Restaurant.** This large, bustling room, run
by the Simon family, has Formica tables with red vinyl-and-chrome
chairs. You can take out such staples as bread, milk, and soda or sit
down at the long counter and enjoy a hearty all-day breakfast. Simon's
makes super grilled cheese sandwiches, BLTs, and tuna salads, and the
meat loaf dinner has die-hard fans. ✉ *4116 Bridge St.,* ☎ *905/356–
5310. Reservations not accepted. No credit cards.*

$-$$ ✕ **Table Rock.** Run by Niagara Parks, Table Rock serves inoffensive
U.S.-Canadian fare in an amazing setting: As it loves to advertise, "If
you were any closer, you'd go over the Falls." The dining room, in the
rear of a two-story souvenir shop, offers tourist comfort food like Caesar salads, baked salmon, veal and chicken fettuccine, beef and chicken
burritos, and shaved roast beef hoagies. ✉ *Niagara Pkwy., just above
the Scenic Tunnels,* ☎ *905/354–3631. AE, MC, V.*

$$$$ ✕▥ **Sheraton Fallsview Hotel and Conference Centre.** Overlooking the
spectacular Canadian and American falls, this modern high-rise hotel
has oversize guest rooms and suites, most with breathtaking views of
the falls and upper rapids. Business facilities are excellent; the hotel
provides high-quality teleconferencing. The fine dining room has
snagged the best view in town. In the evening, candlelight adds romance,
and the kitchen does its part with a French Continental menu that might
include tournedos with a three-peppercorn sauce. There's a two-night
minimum stay on weekends. ✉ *6755 Oakes Dr.,* ☎ *905/374–1077
or 800/267–8439, ℻ 905/374–6224. 295 rooms. 2 restaurants, lobby
lounge, pool, hot tub, sauna, spa, convention center, meeting rooms.
AE, DC, MC, V.*

$$$-$$$$ ▥ **Renaissance Fallsview Hotel.** Many rooms overlook the falls at this
luxuriously appointed hotel, about ½ km (¼ mi) from the mighty

cataracts. There are lots of recreational facilities on the premises and golf and fishing nearby. Free morning coffee is available for guests, and in summer a light breakfast is also included in the room rate. ⊠ *6455 Buchanan Ave.,* ☏ *905/357–5200,* FAX *905/357–3422. 262 rooms. 2 restaurants, indoor pool, hot tub, sauna, exercise room, racquetball, squash, business services, meeting rooms. AE, D, DC, MC, V.*

Nightlife and the Arts

There are free band concerts on summer Sundays at Queenston Heights Park, Queen Victoria Park, and Historic Fort Erie (☞ Fort Erie and West to Windsor, *above*), as well as Rainbow Bridge Carillon recitals.

Guided Tours

BY BUS

Double Deck Tours (☏ 905/374–7423) operates 4½- to 5-hour tours in double-decker English buses. The tours operate daily from mid-May through October and include most of the major sights of Niagara Falls. The $33 fare includes admissions to Journey Behind the Falls, *Maid of the Mist,* and a trip in the Niagara Spanish Aero Car.

From late April to mid-October, the NPC operates a **People Mover System** in which air-conditioned buses travel on a loop route between its public parking lot above the falls at Rapids View Terminal (well marked) and the Niagara Spanish Aero Car parking lot about 8 km (5 mi) downriver. With a day's pass (available at any booth on the system for $4.75) you can get on and off as many times as you wish at the well-marked stops along the route.

BY HELICOPTER

Niagara Helicopters Ltd. takes you on a nine-minute flight over the Giant Whirlpool, up the Niagara Gorge, and past the Canadian falls and then banks around the curve of the Horseshoe Falls for a thrill. ⊠ *3731 Victoria Ave.,* ☏ *905/357–5672.* ⊡ *$80 per person.* ☉ *Daily 9* AM– *½ hr after sunset.*

Outdoor Activities and Sports

The NPC (☏ 905/356–2241) maintains 55 km (34 mi) of **bicycle trails** along the Niagara River between Fort Erie and Niagara-on-the-Lake.

Wine Region

Some of the Niagara Peninsula's 30 wineries are on the Niagara Parkway between Niagara Falls and Niagara-on-the-Lake, or on Highway 55 from the Queen Elizabeth Way. As the quality of Ontario wines has improved in recent years, wine makers have stepped up their marketing and promotional activities. Several wineries offer wine tasting and tours; for exact times, call ahead.

For a map of the wine region, including locations of individual wineries and details of summer events, write to **Wine Council of Ontario** (⊠ 110 Hanover Dr., Suite B205, St. Catharines L2W 1A4, ☏ 905/684– 8070). The best-known wineries include **Château des Charmes Wines Ltd.** (☏ 905/262–5202), **Hillebrand Estates Winery** (☏ 905/468– 7123), **Iniskillin Wines** (☏ 905/468–3554), **Konzelmann Winery** (☏ 905/935–2866), and **Reif Winery** (☏ 905/468–7738).

Niagara-on-the-Lake

⑥⑤ *15 km (9 mi) north of (downriver from) Niagara Falls.*

Since 1962, Niagara-on-the-Lake has been considered the southern outpost of fine summer theater in Ontario because of its acclaimed Shaw Festival. But it offers more than Stratford (☞ Hamilton and Festival

Country, *below*), its older theatrical sister to the north: Stately homes sit back from tree-shaded streets; most are at least a century old, and their owners maintain their original charm by keeping rose trellises freshly painted and brass door knockers gleaming. Any proposed new business is screened by the village council to ensure that neither chrome, glass, nor neon-girdled atrocity will mar the Victorian character. Though the town of 14,000 is worth a visit any time of the year, it's most attractive from April through October, when both the Shaw Festival and the flowers are in full bloom. **Antours** (☎ 416/424–4403) provides several tours of Niagara-on-the-Lake, which include lunch and major performances at the Shaw Festival.

The **Niagara Apothecary Museum** was built in 1866 and restored in 1971. Note the exquisite walnut and butternut fixtures, crystal pieces, and a rare collection of apothecary glasses. ⊠ *5 Queen St.,* ☎ *905/468–3845.* 🎟 *Free.* 𝕆 *Mid-May–Labor Day, daily noon–6.*

The **Niagara Historical Society Museum,** built in 1906, houses a collection of artifacts from prehistory through the arrival of the Loyalists and the War of 1812. ⊠ *43 Castlereagh St.,* ☎ *905/468–3912.* 🎟 *$3.* 𝕆 *May–Oct., daily 10–5; Jan.–Feb., weekends 1–5; Mar.–Apr. and Nov.–Dec., daily 1–5.*

Originally, **Fort George** was built by the British in the late 1700s to protect the trafficking of supplies on the Niagara River. In the War of 1812, the fort was lost to the Americans, and by the time the British regained it, it had fallen into ruins. Fort George was reconstructed in the 1940s. Today, soldiers in period dress perform drills and musical programs on the parade square. ⊠ *Queens Parade, Niagara Pkwy.,* ☎ *905/468–4257.* 🎟 *$6.* 𝕆 *Apr.–June, daily 9:30–4:30; July–Labor Day, daily 10–5; Labor Day–Nov., daily 9:30–4:30.*

Dining and Lodging

$$–$$$ ✕ **On the Twenty.** A sophisticated country restaurant, named for its picturesque view of 20 Mile Creek, is part of Leonard Pennachetti's Cave Spring Cellars winery in the village of Jordan, some 10 minutes from Niagara-on-the-Lake. Dine on quail grilled with shiitake mushrooms, trout baked in parchment with Riesling and leeks, or Ontario rack of lamb with mashed potatoes, all from the fertile Niagara region. ⊠ *3836 Main St., Jordan,* ☎ *905/562–7313. AE, MC, V.*

$$–$$$ ✕ **Ristorante Giardino.** Italian marble combines with stainless steel and rich colors to create a contemporary Italian ambience on 19th-century Queen Street. Chefs recruited from Italy produce antipasti such as beef carpaccio with black olive paste and slivers of Parmesan as well as thinly sliced marinated salmon dotted with caviar. There is always a mixed seafood grill—say, salmon, swordfish, and shrimp—and the ravioli are plump with spinach and ricotta cheese. ⊠ *Gate House Hotel, 142 Queen St.,* ☎ *905/468–3263. AE, DC, MC, V.*

$$ ✕ **Fans Court.** The Chu family prepares delicate Cantonese cuisine in this lovely antiques-filled restaurant, set in a courtyard between an art gallery and a greenhouse. In summer, you can sit outdoors and sample such favorites as fried rice served in a pineapple, lemon chicken, and black-pepper-and-garlic beef. ⊠ *135 Queen St.,* ☎ *905/468–4511. AE, MC, V.*

$$$–$$$$ ✕🏨 **Oban Inn.** This elegant, historic country inn has a view of Lake Ontario. Each room is distinct, embellished with antiques in an Old World English tone; some have fireplaces. While away the day on broad verandas and beautifully manicured gardens. The popular dining room spotlights Canadian beef favorites with a fresh twist of vegetables and fruits (reserve ahead for Sunday brunch). ⊠ *160 Front St., L0S 1J0,* ☎ *905/468–2165,* 𝖥𝖠𝖷 *905/468–4165. 22 rooms. Restaurant, lounge. AE, DC, MC, V.*

$$$–$$$$ ╳⊡ **Prince of Wales.** A visit from the Prince of Wales at the turn of
★ the century prompted the name of this hotel, built in 1864. It's in the
heart of town and has been tastefully restored. The Prince of Wales
Court, adjacent to the main hotel, has many larger, newer rooms at
higher prices; some housekeeping units are available. The suede-wall
dining room has a tree-filled patio that looks out to the street. Entrées
might include veal tenderloin with shiitake mushrooms, Osaka mus-
tard, and a balsamic glaze; the dessert menu is exquisite. The more ca-
sual Queens's Royal Lounge offers soups and sandwiches daily, plus
lunch and dinner buffets, all for under $10. ⊠ *6 Picton St.,* ☎ *905/
468–3246 or 800/263–2452,* ℻ *905/468–1310. 90 rooms, 11 suites.
3 restaurants, indoor pool, hot tub, sauna, health club. AE, MC, V.*

$$$ ╳⊡ **Pillar and Post Inn, Spa and Conference Center.** This hotel, six long
blocks from the heart of town, has been a cannery, barracks, and bas-
ket factory. Most rooms have handcrafted Early American pine furniture and patchwork quilts along with such modern amenities as hair
dryers. The 100 Fountain Spa has a variety of soothing body treatments.
The casual Vintages Wine Bar and Lounge serves regional cuisine and
wines. The dining-room menu is also inspired by what the market has
to offer: four-peppercorn liver country paté with fig and onion mar-
malade, perhaps, or stuffed chicken breast with herbed goat cheese on
roasted eggplant. ⊠ *48 John St.,* ☎ *905/468–2123,* ℻ *905/468–3551.
12 rooms. 2 restaurants, lobby lounge, 3 pools, sauna, spa, health club,
business services. AE, MC, V.*

$$$ ⊡ **Queen's Landing.** The views are a knockout, since Queen's Land-
★ ing is just across from the historic Fort Niagara, at the mouth of the
Niagara River. Rooms are nicely decorated with antiques, including
canopy beds; many have working fireplaces and modern whirlpool baths.
The full range of fitness facilities makes this a most appealing new-old
inn. ⊠ *Melville and Bryon Sts., Box 1180, L0S 1J0,* ☎ *905/468–2195
or 800/361–6645,* ℻ *905/468–2227. 137 rooms. Dining room,
lounge, indoor pool, lap pool, hot tub, sauna, exercise room, baby-
sitting. AE, DC, MC, V.*

Nightlife and the Arts

The **Shaw Festival** began modestly back in the early 1960s with a sin-
gle play and a premise: to perform the plays of George Bernard Shaw
and his contemporaries, who include Noel Coward, Bertholt Brecht,
J. M. Barrie, and J. M. Synge. The season now runs from the begin-
ning of April through mid-October, staging close to a dozen plays. The
festival operates in three buildings, within a few blocks of one another.
The handsome **Festival Theatre,** the largest of the three, stands on
Queen's Parade near Wellington Street and houses the box office. The
Court House, on Queen Street between King and Regent streets, served
as the town's municipal offices until 1969. At the corner of Queen and
Victoria streets is the slightly smaller **Royal George Theater,** the most
intimate of the festival's theaters. Tickets range from $22 to $65. ⊠
Shaw Festival Box Office, Box 774, Niagara-on-the-Lake L0S 1J0, ☎
905/468–2153 or 800/511–7429.

En Route   The Niagara Peninsula is Ontario's fruit basket. From mid-summer to
late fall, fruit and vegetable stands proliferate along the highways and
byways, and there are several farmer's markets along the Queen Eliz-
abeth Way between Niagara Falls and Hamilton. Some of the best dis-
plays of fruits and vegetables are on Highway 55, between
Niagara-on-the-Lake and the Queen Elizabeth Way.

Harvest Barn Market (⊠ Hwy. 55, Niagara-on-the-Lake, ☎ 905/468–
3224), marked by a red-and-white-striped awning, not only sells re-
gional fruits and vegetables but also tempts with a bakery offering sausage

rolls, tiny loaves of bread, and fruit pies. You can test the market's wares at the picnic tables, where knowledgeable locals have lunch.

HAMILTON AND FESTIVAL COUNTRY

A combination of rural pleasures and sophisticated theater draw visitors to this region. Stratford, a small industrial city, made a name for itself with its Shakespeare festival, while Kitchener and Waterloo attract thousands with an annual Oktoberfest. Once you're in these areas, you'll also enjoy the less famous lures—parks, gardens, and country trails. Hamilton, known for its exceptionally productive iron and steel mills, maintains acre upon acre of lush gardens, and London has handsome riverside parks.

Hamilton

66 *75 km (47 mi) west of Niagara Falls on the Queen Elizabeth Way.*

Hamilton is Canada's steel capital—the Dofasco and Stelco mills produce 60% of the country's iron and steel. This isn't the sort of city where you'd expect to find 2,700 acres of gardens and exotic plants, a symphony orchestra, a modern and active theater, 45 parks, and a developed waterfront. But they're all here in Hamilton, Ontario's second-largest city and Canada's third-busiest port. The city's downtown is on a plain between the harbor and the base of "the mountain," a 250-ft-high section of the Niagara Escarpment. Downtown Hamilton is a potpourri of glass-walled high-rises, century-old mansions, a convention center, a coliseum, and a shopping complex.

With 176 stalls spread over more than 20,000 square ft, **Hamilton Farmers' Market** is Canada's largest such market. It's been around since 1837. ⊠ *Adjoining Jackson Square and Eaton Centre,* ☎ *905/546–2096.* ⊙ *Tues. and Thurs. 7–6, Fri. 9–6, Sat. 6–6.*

The **Art Gallery of Hamilton** houses 8,000 works of art, both Canadian and international, in an acclaimed three-level modern structure in the central business district. ⊠ *123 King St. W,* ☎ *905/527–6610.* 🎫 *$4.* ⊙ *Wed. and Fri.–Sat. 10–5, Thurs. 10–9, Sun. 1–5.*

The **Royal Botanical Gardens,** opened in 1932, encompass five major gardens and 48 km (30 mi) of trails that wind across marshes and ravines, past the world's largest collection of lilacs, 2 acres of roses, and all manner of shrubs, trees, plants, hedges, and flowers. Two teahouses are open May 1 to Thanksgiving (mid-October). ⊠ *Plains Rd. (Hwy. 2), Burlington, accessible from Queen Elizabeth Way and Hwys. 6 and 403,* ☎ *905/527–1158.* 🎫 *Mid-May–Labor Day $7; Labor Day–mid-May, grounds free, greenhouse $2.* ⊙ *Main building daily 9–5, outdoor garden daily 9:30–6.*

Gage Park, with 70 acres of botanical greens, is a beautiful oasis in the center of the city. Its rose garden, with more than 30 varieties, is especially stunning. ⊠ *Main St. E and Gage Ave., east of downtown.*

Sir Allan Napier MacNab, a War of 1812 hero and Upper Canada's pre-Confederation prime minister, built a 35-room mansion called ★ **Dundurn Castle** from 1832 to 1835. It has been furnished to reflect the opulence in which MacNab lived at the height of his political career. ⊠ *Dundurn Park and York Blvd.,* ☎ *905/546–2872.* 🎫 *$6.* ⊙ *June–Labor Day, daily 11–4; Labor Day–May, Tues.–Sun. 1–4.*

Flamboro Downs harness-racing track, just west of Hamilton, has matinee and evening races year-round, though not on a daily basis. The clubhouse has two dining areas that overlook the track. ⊠ *Hwy. 5.,* ☎ *905/627–3561.*

🖱 At **African Lion Safari,** lions, tigers, cheetahs, elephants, and zebras abound. You can drive your own car or take an air-conditioned tram over a 9-km (6-mi) safari trail through the wildlife park. ⊠ *Safari Rd., off Hwy. 8 south of Cambridge, Rockton,* ☎ *519/623–2620 or 800/ 461–9453.* 🖙 *$16.25.* ☉ *Grounds early Apr.–Oct., daily 9–6:30; tour weekdays 9–4, weekends 9–5.*

Dining and Lodging

$$–$$$ ✕ **Ancaster Old Mill.** Just outside Hamilton, this historic mill is worth
★ the trip if only to sample the bread, baked daily with flour ground on millstones installed in 1863. The dining rooms are light and bright with hanging plants. Try to get a table overlooking the mill stream and a waterfall. ⊠ *548 Old Dundas Rd., Ancaster,* ☎ *905/648–1827. Reservations essential. AE, DC, MC, V.*

$$ ✕🖼 **Howard Johnson Royal Connaught Plaza Hotel.** This venerable 1914 hotel in the heart of downtown Hamilton is a grand old place complete with a ballroom. The indoor swimming pool has one of Canada's longest water slides. Fran's is the hotel's very popular dining room (reserve ahead). Meat is broiled over an open mesquite fire. There's a marble floor and, after you've eaten—or while you're waiting for your entrée to be flamed—you can dance in the gazebo. ⊠ *112 King St. E, L8N 1A8,* ☎ *905/546–8111,* 🅵🅰🆇 *905/546–8144. 206 rooms, 21 suites. Restaurant, lounge, indoor pool, hot tub, sauna, cabaret, comedy club. AE, D, DC, MC, V.*

Nightlife and the Arts

Hamilton Place's (⊠ 10 MacNab St., ☎ 905/546–3050) Great Hall can accommodate 1,193 on the orchestra level, 560 in the first balcony, and 428 in the second balcony. Opera Hamilton holds performances here from September through April. Its repertoire embraces works from *Aida* to *Nixon in China.*

Outdoor Activities and Sports

The 680-km (422-mi) **Bruce Trail** stretches northwest along the Niagara Escarpment from the orchards of the Niagara Peninsula to the cliffs and bluffs at Tobermory, at the end of the Bruce Peninsula. You can access the Bruce Trail at just about any point along the route, so your hike can be any length you wish. Contact the Bruce Trail Association (⊠ Box 857, Hamilton L8N 3N9, ☎ 905/592–6821).

Brantford

➏➐ *40 km (25 mi) west of Hamilton on Hwy. 403.*

Brantford is named for Joseph Brant, the Loyalist Mohawk chief who brought members of the Six Nations Confederacy into Canada after the American Revolution. King George III showed gratitude to Chief Brant by building the **Mohawk Church.** In 1904, by royal assent, it was given the name His Majesty's Chapel of the Mohawks (now changed to Her Majesty's). This simple, white-painted frame building with eight stained-glass windows depicting the colorful history of the Six Nations people is the oldest Protestant church in Ontario and the only Indian Royal Chapel in existence. A guide is available. ⊠ *292 Mohawk St.,* ☎ *519/758–5444.* 🖙 *$1.* ☉ *Daily 1–5.*

Woodland Indian Cultural Educational Centre is a museum of sorts that aims to preserve and promote the culture and heritage of the native people of the First Nation. The modern building contains displays and exhibits showing early Woodland Indian culture. ⊠ *184 Mohawk St.,* *near Mohawk Chapel,* ☎ *519/759–2650.* 🎫 *$4.* ☉ *Weekdays 8:30–4, weekends 10–5.*

Though Brantford is the hometown of hockey star Wayne Gretzky, it is better known as the Telephone City because Alexander Graham Bell invented the device here and made the first long-distance call from his parents' home to nearby Paris, Ontario, in 1874. The **Bell Homestead,** where Bell spent his early years before moving to the United States, is now a National Historic Site. Next door (and part of the site) is the house of the Reverend Thomas Henderson, a Baptist minister who left the church when he recognized the profit potential in telephones. His home served as the first telephone office and now is a museum of telephone artifacts and displays. Guided tours can be arranged. ✉ *94 Tutela Heights Rd.,* ☎ *519/756–6220.* 🎫 *$2.50.* ☉ *Mid-Mar.–Thanksgiving, Tues.–Sun. 9:30–4:30.*

Outdoor Activities and Sports

BIKING

Brantford is protected by a flood-control dam, on top of which is a bicycle trail that passes many attractions.

HIKING

The **Grand Valley Trail** runs 128 km (79 mi) between Elora and Brantford. Contact the Grand Valley Trail Association (✉ Box 1233, Kitchener N2G 4G8) for more information.

Kitchener and Waterloo

68 *Approximately 27 km (17 mi) north of Brantford on Hwy. 24.*

Kitchener and Waterloo, which merge into one another, are usually referred to as K–W. Settled around 1800 by Swiss-German Mennonites from Pennsylvania, the region's German origins remain obvious: There's a huge glockenspiel downtown by Speakers' Corner, and each October since 1967 the city has hosted Oktoberfest. The event now draws more than 700,000 people, who swarm to more than a dozen festival halls where they dance, gorge on German-style food, listen to oompah bands, and drink with a fervor that seems driven by an irrational fear that all Canadian breweries are about to go on strike.

The **Kitchener Market** isn't the oldest or the largest farmer's market in Ontario, but it's been around since 1869 and since 1986 has been housed in spacious quarters at Market Square. The block-long complex is wrapped in green-tinted glass and contains 70 shops and snack bars, as well as an Eaton's department store. ✉ *Frederick and Duke Sts.,* ☎ *519/741–2287.* ☉ *Sat. 6–2.*

William Lyon Mackenzie King, who was prime minister of Canada for almost 22 of the years between 1921 and 1948, spent his teenage years in a rented 10-room house called Woodside, now **Woodside National Historic Sites.** There's no particular imprint here of the bachelor prime minister whose diaries reveal his belief in mysticism, portents, and communications with the dead, but the house has been furnished to reflect the Victorian period of the King family's occupancy. ✉ *528 Wellington St., Kitchener,* ☎ *519/571–5684.* 🎫 *$2.50.* ☉ *May–Dec., daily 10–5; Jan.–Apr., by appointment only.*

Doon Heritage Crossroads is a complete living history site including a restored 1914 village with two farms. The village recalls the tranquillity of rural lifestyles in the early 1900s. You can cross a covered bridge and wander tree-shaded roads to visit with costumed staff who perform authentic period trades and activities. ✉ *North of Hwy. 401,* *exit Homer Watson Blvd. N,* ☎ *519/748–1914.* 🎫 *$2.50.* ☉ *May–Labor Day, daily 10–4:30; Labor Day–Dec., weekdays 10–4:30.*

Dining and Lodging

$$$$ ✕🏨 **Langdon Hall Country House Hotel.** This magnificent Colonial Re-
★ vival–style mansion on 50 landscaped acres has grand public rooms
and huge fireplaces. It was built in 1898 as a summer home for a great-
granddaughter of John Jacob Astor and has been sensitively converted
to a grand country hotel (it's a member of Relais & Château) with 13
guest rooms in the original building and 30 in a modern annex. The
house has a billiard room, a conservatory, and a drawing room. The
restaurant (reserve ahead) specializes in regional cuisine such as Wa-
terloo County pork tenderloin and Woolwich goat cheese in phyllo pas-
try. Call for directions. ✉ *R.R. 33, Cambridge N3H 4R8,* ☎ *519/
740–2100 or 800/268–1898,* 📠 *519/740–8161. 43 rooms. Restau-
rant, room service, pool, hot tub, sauna, spa, tennis court, croquet, ex-
ercise room, boating, billiards, meeting rooms. AE, DC, MC, V.*

$$ 🏨 **Four Points Sheraton.** This modern hotel has a major sports complex in its basement and is connected by a glassed-in skywalk to the
Market Square shopping mall and Farmers' Market. Shatz's, the main,
more formal restaurant (reserve ahead), is candlelit and decorated in
earth tones. Continental fare dominates the menu. A smaller café is
fine for casual meals. ✉ *105 King St. E, N2G 2K8,* ☎ *519/744–4141,*
📠 *519/578–6889. 201 rooms. Restaurant, café, lounge, indoor pool,
hot tub, sauna, miniature golf, bowling. AE, DC, MC, V.*

St. Jacobs

★ ㊉ *10 km (6 mi) north of Kitchener and Waterloo on Hwy. 8.*

The villages of St. Jacobs and Elmira (10 km, or 6 mi, north of St. Jacobs via Route 86 and County Road 21) are in the heart of Mennonite and Hutterite country. The Meetingplace interpretation center in
St. Jacobs (seasonal hours) offers visitors a chance to learn more about
the Old Order Mennonite community in the area. St. Jacobs is also a
unique shopping destination with more than 100 shops that run the
gamut from antiques to fashion wear. The St. Jacobs Farmers' Market and Flea Market has more than 350 vendors selling fresh produce
and crafts on Thursday and Saturday from 7 AM to 3:30 PM year-round
and on Tuesday 8 AM–3 PM June–August.

Dining and Lodging

$$$–$$$$ ✕🏨 **Elora Mill.** One of Canada's few remaining five-story gristmills has
★ been converted to luxury accommodations and a superb restaurant.
There are 16 guest rooms in the 1859 mill building and 16 more in
four other historic stone buildings in the immediate vicinity of the mill.
The inn is in the heart of Elora, a village about 15 km (9 mi) north of
Elmira full of stone buildings that could have been lifted from England's
Cotswolds or southern France. The restaurant ($$$$) serves a mix of
imaginative Canadian and European dishes (reserve ahead). ✉ *77
Mill St. W, Elora N0B 1S0,* ☎ *519/846–5356,* 📠 *519/846–9180. 32
rooms. Restaurant. AE, DC, MC, V.*

$$–$$$$ ✕🏨 **Millcroft Inn.** This 19th-century stone knitting mill has been con-
★ verted to an exquisite full-service country inn beside the millpond. About
40 km (25 mi) northeast of Elmira (80 km, or 50 mi, northwest of
Toronto) in Alton, it is one of Canada's finest hostelries. Some larger
rooms have fireplaces. Rooms are available in both the older inn and
a more modern annex, where they tend to be more spacious. A spa
was added in 1997. The dining room ($$$$) offers a relatively limited
choice of traditional Continental dishes, but quality more than makes
up for the lack of variety (reserve ahead). ✉ *55 John St., Alton L0N*

1A0, ☎ 519/941–8111, FAX 519/941–0192. 52 rooms. Restaurant, pool, hot tub, 2 saunas, spa, 2 tennis courts, exercise room, recreation room. CP. AE, DC, MC, V.

$$ ✕🛏 **Benjamins.** This is a lovely re-creation of the original 1852 Farmer's Inn. Nine guest rooms on the second floor are furnished in antiques, and every bed is covered with a locally made Mennonite quilt. The120-seat restaurant (reserve ahead) has pine ceiling beams, an open-hearth fireplace, lots of greenery, and imaginative French cuisine. ✉ *17 King St., N0B 2N0, ☎ 519/664–3731, FAX 519/664–2218. 9 rooms. Restaurant. CP. AE, DC, MC, V.*

Outdoor Activities and Sports

BIKING

Two popular **bike routes** can be reached from Fergus, 18 km (11 mi) northwest of Elmira: One is a 32-km (20-mi) tour around Lake Belwood, the other a 40-km (25-mi) loop around Eramosa Township. There is little traffic on these scenic routes, and restaurants are few and far between, so take a picnic lunch.

HIKING

The 5-km (3-mi) **pathway** along the Elora Gorge between Fergus and Elora, 15 km (9 mi) north of Elmira, is a great minihike. You'll pass a whirlpool at Templin Gardens, a restored English garden, and cross a bridge at Mirror Basin.

Stratford

🕖 *46 km (29 mi) west of Kitchener on Hwys. 7 and 8.*

The city of Stratford was named by homesick English settlers; all that the town had in common with England's Stratford was a river called Avon meandering through rolling countryside—and not even particularly similar countryside. Nowadays the village is famous for hosting the annual Stratford Festival, which welcomes more than 500,000 people to its acclaimed performances of music, opera, and drama.

Dining and Lodging

$$$–$$$$ ✕ **Church Restaurant and Belfry.**It was constructed in 1873 as a Congregational church, but today white cloths gleam in the light that pours through the stained-glass windows. The meals here are production numbers: Tea-smoked salmon comes with sea scallops and shrimps; the warm salad of spiced veal sweetbreads is lively with a cherry tomato compote. Roast Ontario lamb with garlic custard and eggplant flan is outstanding. ✉ *70 Brunswick St., ☎ 519/273–3424. Reservations essential. AE, DC, MC, V.*

$$$–$$$$ ✕ **The Old Prune.** A converted Victorian house holds a number of charming dining rooms and a glass-enclosed conservatory surrounded by a tidy, sunken garden. The kitchen coaxes fresh local ingredients into innovative dishes: smoked rainbow trout with apple radish and curry oil; vegetable lasagna with roasted tomato sauce; or, with a nod to the East, chicken seasoned with coriander and cumin. ✉ *151 Albert St., ☎ 519/271–5052. AE, MC, V.*

$$ ✕ **Down the Street Bar and Café.** Funky and informal, this bistro with live jazz and food by Stratford Chefs' School graduates is the hottest place in town. Thrilling grills of chicken, salmon, and rib eye, as well as grilled stacked tomato salad and herb-crusted pizza, make for delicious dining. A late-night menu includes everything from spicy spring rolls and steamed Prince Edward Island mussels to a classic cheeseburger. ✉ *30 Ontario St., ☎ 519/273–5886. AE, MC, V.*

$–$$ ✕ **Bentley's Inn.** At this long, narrow, British-style pub, there's an unspoken tradition: The actors have claimed one side, and the locals the other. Darts are taken seriously here. The menu consists of pub fare such as good fish-and-chips, grilled steak and fries, and steak-and-mushroom pie. The ultimate club sandwich on multigrain bread hits the spot for lunch or dinner. The regulars say they come for the good selection of beers. ⊠ *99 Ontario St.,* ☎ *519/271–1121. AE, MC, V.*

$$ ✕▥ **Queen's Inn at Stratford.** This country-style inn dating from 1850 is in the heart of Stratford. The restaurant, Soltar, serves flavorful Santa Fe cuisine at reasonable prices. The Boar's Head is a popular pub-lounge with light snacks and a great variety of brews. ⊠ *161 Ontario St., N5A 3H3,* ☎ *519/271–1400,* FAX *519/271–7373. 30 rooms. Restaurant, lounge. AE, MC, V.*

$$–$$$ ▥ **Woods Villa Bed and Breakfast.** This elegant 1875 home once belonged to a wealthy magistrate; it has since been restored to its 19th-century grandeur. The public rooms hold an astonishing collection of restored vintage jukeboxes, music boxes, and player pianos. Start the day on the right foot with a grand breakfast accompanied by full table service. Five of the six rooms have fireplaces. Woods Villa does not accept children or pets; the latter might ruffle the feathers of the owner's five tropical birds. Note that while the credit cards listed below are accepted, cash is preferred. ⊠ *62 John St. N, N5A 6K7,* ☎ *519/271–4576. 6 rooms. Pool. MC, V.*

Nightlife and the Arts

★ The **Stratford Festival** hosts music, opera, and drama annually. It all started in 1953, in a massive tent, with Sir Alec Guinness playing Richard III. The next year musical programs were added to supplement Shakespeare's plays. The venture was a huge success, and the 1957 season opened in a permanent home with 2,262 seats, none of which are more than 65 ft from the stage. The 1901-vintage, 1,107-seat Avon Theatre became a partner in the festival in 1967, and the Tom Patterson Theatre, seating 496, opened in 1971. The Stratford Festival now starts around the beginning of May and runs until late October. Tickets prices range from about $50 to $70. ⊠ *55 Queens St.,* ☎ *519/273–1600 or 800/567–1600.*

London

71 *75 km (47 mi) southwest of Stratford on Hwys. 7 and 4.*

Nicknamed Forest City, London has more than 50,000 trees on city property and 1,500 acres of parks, including 1,000 acres along the Thames River. It's a quiet, provincial city where old money rules the arts and development projects, but it has also become famous for its hospitals, which specialize in organ-transplant operations. London has been called a microcosm of Canadian life; it is so "typically Canadian" that the city is often used as a test market for new products—if something will sell in London, it will probably sell anywhere in Canada.

From mid-May through October you can get another view of London by cruising on the Thames River in a 60-passenger boat: **Afternoon cruises** (⊠ Springbank Park, ☎ 519/473–0363) depart every hour from Storybook Gardens. The easiest way to get an overview of the town is to take a **bus tour** on a big, red double-decker—what else?—London bus. They operate from City Hall, July 1–Labor Day (at 10 and 2).

Because **Storybook Gardens** is owned and operated by the city's Public Utility Commission, this is one of the least-expensive children's theme parks in the country. It's on the Thames River in the 281-acre Springbank Park. You'll see a castle, storybook characters, and a zoo. Children can slide down Jack and Jill's hill and the throat of Willie the Whale. ⊠ *929 Springbank Dr.,* ☎ *519/661–5770.* ⊡ *$5.25.* ☉ *May–Labor*

*Day, daily 10–8; Labor Day–Thanksgiving (mid-Oct.), weekdays
10–5, weekends 10–6.*

London Regional Art and Historical Museum is as interesting from the
outside as its exhibits are on the inside. The gallery is contained in six
joined, glass-covered structures whose ends are the shape of croquet
hoops. An impressive collection of fine art and artifacts plus regularly
changing exhibitions are complemented by films, lectures, music, and
live performances. ⊠ *Forks of the Thames,* ☎ *519/672–4580.* ⊠ *Donation requested.* ⊙ *Tues.–Sun. noon–5.*

The **London Museum of Archaeology** maintains more than 40,000 native artifacts plus a gallery of artists' conceptions of the lives of the At-
tawandaron natives who lived on the Lawson site, a nearby
archaeological dig, some 500 years ago. Within proximity is a reconstructed multifamily longhouse on its original site. ⊠ *1600 Attawan-
daron Rd., south of Hwy. 22,* ☎ *519/473–1360.* ⊠ *$3.50.* ⊙
*May–Labor Day, daily 10–5; Labor Day–Oct., Tues.–Sun. 10–5; Jan.–
Apr., Wed.–Sun. 1–4.*

London's oldest building is also one of its most impressive. The
wrecker's ball came awfully close to the **Old Courthouse Building,** and
it got one wall of the former Middlesex County Gaol. But a citizens'
group prevailed, and the Old Courthouse, modeled after Malahide Castle in England, reopened as the home of the Middlesex County council. ⊠ *399 Ridout St. N,* ☎ *519/434–7321.* ⊠ *Free.* ⊙ *June–Aug.,
weekdays 8:30–noon and 1–4:30.*

Dining and Lodging

$$ ✕ **Marienbad and Chaucer's Pub.** The reasonably priced Czech fare
includes popular favorites like goulash, schnitzels, chicken paprika, and
Carlsbad roulade (rolled beef stuffed with ham and egg). Forget the
diet: Most dishes come with rib-sticking dumplings. ⊠ *122 Carling
St.,* ☎ *519/679–9940. AE, MC, V.*

$$ ✕ **Michael's on the Thames.** This popular lunch and dinner spot overlooks the Thames River. The Canadian and Continental cuisine includes
flambéed dishes, fresh seafood, chateaubriand, and flaming desserts
and coffees. ⊠ *1 York St., at Thames River,* ☎ *519/672–0111,* FAX *519/
672–2892. Reservations essential. AE, DC, MC, V.*

$$$ ▥ **Delta London Armouries.** This 20-story, silver-mirrored tower rises
from the center of the 1905 London Armoury. The lobby is a green-
house of vines, trees, plants, and fountains, wrapped in marble and ac-
cented by rich woods and old yellow brick. The architects left as much
of the original armory intact as possible. A set of steps through man-
icured jungle takes you to the indoor swimming pool, sauna, and
whirlpool. Guest rooms are spacious and decorated in pastel shades.
Suites vary in size and grandeur—the Middlesex Suite has a grand piano.
⊠ *325 Dundas St., N6B 1T9,* ☎ *519/679–6111 or 800/668–9999,*
FAX *519/679–3957. 242 rooms, 8 suites. Restaurant, lounge, indoor pool,
sauna, miniature golf, racquetball, squash. AE, DC, MC, V.*

$$–$$$ ▥ **Idlewylde Inn.** Though an elevator was installed in this converted
1878 mansion, the architects succeeded in preserving the house's orig-
inal details. Complimentary breakfast, snacks, and parking are in-
cluded in your room rate. ⊠ *36 Grand Ave., N6C 1K8,* ☎ FAX *519/
433–2891. 27 rooms. AE, DC, MC, V.*

SAULT STE. MARIE
AND WEST TO THUNDER BAY

Sault Ste. Marie

72 *700 km (434 mi) northwest of Toronto.*

Sault Ste. Marie has always been a natural meeting place and cultural melting pot. Long before Etienne Brulé "discovered" the rapids in 1622, Ojibwa tribes gathered here. Whitefish, their staple food, could easily be caught year-round, and the rapids in the St. Mary's River linking Lakes Huron and Superior were often the only sources of open water for miles during the winter. When Father Jacques Marquette opened a mission in 1668, he named it Sainte Marie de Sault. *Sault* is French for "rapids," which help generate hydroelectric power for the city. Today locals call the city simply "the Sault," pronounced "the Soo."

Hiawathaland Tours (☎ 705/759–6200) operates three city tours by double-decker bus and a wilderness tour by minivan to Aubrey Falls from June 15 to October 15. There's also a 75-minute evening tour.

The elegant **Ermatinger Stone House** was built by Montréal fur trader Charles Oakes Ermatinger in 1814 and is the oldest building in Canada west of Toronto. Ermatinger married a daughter of the influential Indian chief Katawebeda, a move that didn't hurt his business. Costumed interpreters guide visitors through the house. ✉ *831 Queen St. E,* ☎ *705/759–5443.* ✇ *Donation requested.* ☉ *Apr.–May, weekdays 10–5; June–Sept., daily 10–5; Oct.–Nov., weekdays 1–5.*

Lock Tours Canada runs two-hour excursions through the 21-ft-high **Soo Locks,** the 16th and final lift for ships bound for Lake Superior from the St. Lawrence River. Tours aboard the 200-passenger MV *Chief Shingwauk* leave from the Roberta Bondar Dock next door to the Holiday Inn, May 15 through October 15, and up to eight times daily July 1 through Labor Day. ✉ *Roberta Bondar Dock off Foster Dr.,* ☎ *705/ 253–9850.* ✇ *$17.*

★ The Algoma Central Railway not only operates a main line track between the Sault and iron mines at Hearst and Michipicoten Harbor, but it also runs the **Agawa Canyon Train Tours,** a lucrative sideline of tour trains that provide day trips to and from scenic Agawa Canyon, a deep valley 19 km (12 mi) long with 800-ft-high cliff walls through which the Agawa River flows. In summer the Agawa Canyon Train makes a two-hour stopover in the canyon during which passengers can lunch in a park, hike to their choice of three waterfalls, or climb to a lookout 250 ft above the train. In colder months, the Snow Train makes the same trip, minus the Agawa Canyon layover. ✉ *129 Bay St.,* ☎ *705/946–7300 or 800/242–9287.* ✇ *Agawa Canyon Train $52, Snow Train $55.* ☉ *Agawa Canyon Train June–mid-Sept. daily; Snow Train Jan.–mid-Mar. weekends; trains depart 8 AM and return at 5 PM in warmer seasons and 4 PM in cooler weather.*

Dining and Lodging

$$–$$$ 🍴 **Quality Inn Bayfront.** If you're planning to take an Agawa Canyon Train Tour (☞ *above*), book a room at this popular hotel. The rooms and suites are clean and modern with many comforts, including a sauna and in-house movies. Most important—because the train leaves at 8 AM and you should be at the station by 7:30 AM at the latest—the hotel is across the street from the Algoma Central Railroad station. When you return at night, the hotel's swimming pool and dining room await you. The hotel's Gran Sesta Ristorante, bright and airy with lots

Upper Ontario

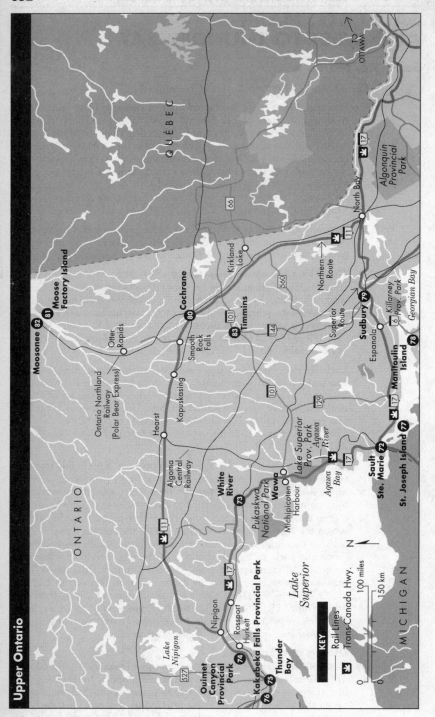

QUÉBEC

ONTARIO

Moosonee 82

81

Moose Factory Island

Otter Rapids

Ontario Northland Railway (Polar Bear Express)

Cochrane 80

Smooth Rock Falls

Kapuskasing

Hearst

Kirkland Lake

66

560

Timmins

83

101

144

Northern Route

Superior Route

North Bay

111

TO OTTAWA

117

Algonquin Provincial Park

79 Sudbury

Espanola

Killarney Prov. Park

Georgian Bay

Manitoulin Island

78

Algoma Central Railway

101

129

Lake Superior Prov. Park

Agawa River

117

77

White River 73

Wawa

Pukaskwa National Park

Michipicoten Harbour

Agawa Bay

17

Sault Ste. Marie 72

St. Joseph Island

111

Lake Superior

17

Nipigon

Rossport

Hurkett

74

Kakabeka Falls Provincial Park

Ouimet Canyon Provincial Park

527

75 Thunder Bay

76

MICHIGAN

N

KEY

— Rail Lines
Trans-Canada Hwy.

0   100 miles
0   50 km

In case you want to
be welcomed there.

We're here to see that you're always welcomed at establishments everywhere. That's why millions of people carry the
American Express® Card – for peace of mind, confidence,
and security, around the world or just
around the corner.

do more ®

Cards

In case you're running low.

We're here to help with more than 118,000 Express Cash locations around the world. In order to enroll, just call American Express before you start your vacation.

do more

Express Cash

And just in case.

We're here with American Express® Travelers Cheques and Cheques *for Two*.® They're the safest way to carry money on your vacation and the surest way to get a refund, practically anywhere, anytime.
Another way we help you...

do more

Travelers
Cheques

of brass and greenery, serves southern Italian dishes garnished with edible flowers. ⊠ *180 Bay St., P6A 6S2,* ☎ *705/945–9264 or 800/228–5151,* FAX *705/945–9766. 109 rooms, 13 suites. Restaurant, indoor pool, hot tub, sauna, exercise room, meeting rooms. AE, DC, MC, V.*

En Route **Wawa,** 225 km (140 mi) north of Sault Ste. Marie on Trans-Canada Highway 17, is the first town north of the Lake Superior Provincial Park. Its name is derived from an Ojibwa word meaning "wild goose," and the 3,700 residents of Wawa have erected a massive goose monument at the entrance to town from Highway 17. Next door is the town's new log-cabin tourist information office.

White River

🐸 *90 km (56 mi) north of Wawa on the Trans-Canada Hwy. 17.*

This town is marked by a huge thermometer indicating 72°F below zero and a sign that advises: "White River—coldest place in Canada." White River is hard to miss. The town has another claim to fame: It was the original home of the bear cub immortalized as Winnie-the-Pooh in the children's stories by British author A. A. Milne. A 25-ft-high statue honoring Winnie was put up in 1992, and each August the town holds a three-day Winnie's Homecoming Festival, with parades, street dances, and a community barbecue.

Dining and Lodging

$ ✕🖫 **Rossport Inn.** The hamlet of Rossport, about 200 km (124 mi) west of White River, on a harbor off Lake Superior, is about as close as you can get to an unspoiled outpost on the Great Lakes. The inn was built in 1884 as a railroad hotel and now it has six small guest rooms. One of the nicest country inns in the province, the Rossport is cozy and down-home—the nightlife consists of swapping lies with the innkeepers and other guests about the fish that got away. Breakfast is included in the room rate. The dining room's ($$) home-style cooking of locally caught fish, as well as of steak, chicken, pork chops, and lobster, is irresistible. ⊠ *Rossport Loop, ½ mi from Trans-Canada Hwy., Bowman St., P0T 2R0,* ☎ *807/824–3213. 6 rooms share 2 baths, 2 cabins. Restaurant. MC, V. Closed Nov.–May.*

Ouimet Canyon Provincial Park

★ 🐸 *300 km (186 mi) west of White River on Trans-Canada Hwy. 17.*

This park holds a spectacular geological anomaly; botanists have discovered Arctic plants native to the tundra growing in areas where the sun never shines. A walking path stops short at the edge of the canyon, where viewing platforms allow you to look straight down 350 ft. The far wall is only 492 ft away, and the chasm is 2½ km (1½ mi) long. Geologists believe the canyon could be a gigantic fault in the earth's surface or the result of glacial action. (Note: Access to the canyon floor is restricted due its fragile nature.) To get here, watch for signs to Ouimet Canyon, just past the town of Hurkett, west of Nipigon. ⊠ *11 km (7 mi) off Trans-Canada Hwy., 10 km (6 mi) west of Hurkett,* ☎ *807/977–2526.* 🎫 *Free.* ☉ *Mid-May–Thanksgiving (mid-Oct.), daily 9–5.*

En Route Ontario's gemstone is an imperfect quartz tinted violet or purple. There are five amethyst mines between Sleeping Giant Provincial Park and Ouimet Canyon, a distance of 50 km (31 mi) along Highways 11 and 17 east of Thunder Bay. All are signposted from the highway, and each offers the opportunity to hand-pick some samples (paid for by the pound). **Amethyst Mine Panorama** is closest to Thunder Bay (☞ *below*). Tours of the mine run four times daily at 11, 12:30, 3, and 5.

To get here, follow Loon Lake Road from Highways 11 and 17, east of Thunder Bay. ⊠ *E. Loon Rd.,* ☎ *807/622–6908.* 🖼 *$3.* ⊘ *Mid-May–mid-Oct., daily 10–5; July–Aug., daily 10–7.*

Thunder Bay

⑦⑤   *67 km (42 mi) southwest of Ouimet Canyon on Trans-Canada Hwy. 17.*

This city is one of the world's largest grain-handling centers. It has an extraordinary ethnic mix, with 42 nationalities and the largest Finnish population outside Finland. Although two towns amalgamated into one city in 1970, there are still Port Arthur and Fort Williams sections of Thunder Bay. The area has Ontario's best alpine and cross-country skiing with the longest ski season, superb fishing and hunting, great camping and hiking, unlimited canoe and boating routes, and even ice climbing. Several amethyst mines have shops in the city. There are also dozens of good restaurants, a growing number of bed-and-breakfasts, an art gallery, and nine shopping malls.

At **Old Fort William,** interpreters bring to life a reconstructed fur-trading fort with 42 historic buildings on a 125-acre site. ⊠ *Broadway Ave.,* ☎ *807/577–8461.* 🖼 *$10.* ⊘ *Mid-May–mid-Oct., daily 10–5.*

Dining and Lodging

$$–$$$ ✕🍴 **Valhalla Inn.** The warm lobby is based on old Scandinavian design and has plenty of wood and brass. Guest rooms are large, with queen-size beds and local art. The Nordic dining room offers signature Scandinavian dishes, including smoked salmon and Swedish fish chowder. ⊠ *1 Valhalla Inn Rd., P7E 6J1,* ☎ *807/577–1121 or 800/268–2500,* FAX *807/475–4723. 267 rooms. Restaurant, indoor pool, hot tub, sauna, exercise room. AE, D, DC, MC, V.*

Outdoor Activities and Sports

North of Superior Climbing Company (⊠ Box 2204, P7B 5E8, ☎ 807/344–9636) offers ice-climbing lessons, professionally led climbs, and two-day packages. Accommodations in rustic cabins or motels are provided, but meals are not included.

Kakabeka Falls Provincial Park

⑦⑥   *40 km (25 mi) northwest of Thunder Bay off Hwys. 11 and 17.*

In this park, Kakabeka Falls on the Kaministikwia River drops 154 ft over a limestone ledge. Paths lead around the falls, and there are large, free parking lots.

EAST ALONG GEORGIAN BAY AND SOUTH TO MANITOULIN ISLAND

On a half-day journey by car from Sault Ste. Marie you can see the stunning beauty of Georgian Bay and the stark landscape of industrial Sudbury. Highlights include the wild flowers of St. Joseph Island, the rugged simplicity of Manitoulin Island, and the Big Nickel Mine Tour in Sudbury.

St. Joseph Island

⑦⑦   *40 km (25 mi) southeast of Sault Ste. Marie on Hwy. 17.*

St. Joseph Island is a sparsely settled bit of land about 24 by 30 km (16 by 20 mi) in the mouth of the St. Mary's River, connected by causeway and bridge to the mainland. In spring the island is a scented riot of wild lilac, and you're likely to see moose and deer along the quiet side roads.

In fur-trading days, **Fort St. Joseph,** established by the British at the southeast tip of the island, guarded the trade route from Montréal to the upper Great Lakes. Today you can wander the national historic park on the peninsula on which the fort and commercial buildings once stood and see the outlines and few above-ground stone ruins of the 42 building sites that have been identified. Free walking tours and a booklet are available at the visitor center, about 30 minutes by car southeast of the Gilbertson Bridge. Call ahead for directions. ☎ 705/246–2664. ☻ *Late May–Thanksgiving (mid-Oct.), daily 10–5.*

Manitoulin Island

78 *149 km (92 mi) east of St. Joseph Island and south of Espanola via Trans-Canada Hwy. 17 and Hwy. 6.*

Manitoulin Island, the world's largest freshwater island, sits at the top of Lake Huron plugging the mouth of Georgian Bay. It is 160 km (99 mi) long and varies in width from 3 to 64 km (2 to 40 mi). The island is pretty and rugged, with granite outcrops, forests, meadows, rivers, and rolling countryside. Only 20% of the land is arable, and much of the rest is used for grazing sheep and cattle. Yachters rate these waters among the best in the world, and fishers have taken advantage of the island's riches for generations. Hikes and exploration could easily turn this "side trip" into a weeklong stay. For the most part the island has not been ravaged by time and human incursions. Archaeological digs have unearthed traces of human habitation that are more than 30,000 years old. There is no interim record of people living here until explorer Samuel de Champlain met some island residents in 1650. Island towns such as Little Current (closest to the mainland), Sheguiandah, and Wikwemikong are simple and picturesque.

The **MS Chi-Cheemaun** connects the picturesque town of Tobermory, at the northern tip of the Bruce Peninsula, with South Baymouth on the island. This is a convenient alternative to driving if you are heading to the island from southern Ontario (rather than from Sault Ste. Marie). The trip takes 1 hour and 45 minutes each way. There are four sailings in each direction daily between mid-June and Labor Day, and three during spring and fall. Reservations are advised. ✉ *Ontario Northland Marine Services, 343 8th St. E, Owen Sound N4K 1L3,* ☎ *519/596–2510 or 800/265–3163.* ⛴ *One-way $11, plus $24 per car.*

Little Current–Howland Centennial Museum, in the village of Sheguiandah about 11 km (7 mi) south of Little Current, displays local native and pioneer artifacts. ✉ *Hwy. 6,* ☎ *705/368–2367.* ⛴ *$3.* ☻ *Mid-May–mid-Oct., daily 10–4:30.*

Wikwemikong Unceded Indian Reserve encompasses the entire southeastern peninsula of Manitoulin Island. One of Manitoulin's most colorful events is the Wikwemikong Pow Wow, held on Civic Holiday (the first weekend in August). Dancers accompanied by drummers and singers compete while performing the steps of their ancestors.

Sudbury

79 *60 km (37 mi) east of Espanola on Trans-Canada Hwy. 17.*

The mining town of Sudbury used to bear the brunt of frequent unkind jokes. After all, didn't the U.S. astronauts go there to train in the type of terrain they were likely to encounter on the moon? Today, the greening of Sudbury, an ongoing community-wide land-reclamation project, has revived much of the landscape that suffered from years of logging, smelter emissions, and soil erosion. What you see today is typical of Canadian Shield country, with beautiful lakes, rocky outcroppings, and trees. In addition, the town has outdoor concerts, art centers, museums, and cruises on Ramsey Lake, the largest freshwater lake inside city limits in North America.

Science North is northern Ontario's largest tourist attraction, encompassing a science museum, a giant-screen IMAX theater, an underground mine tour, and the Virtual Voyages Motion Theatre. The museum explores science in the everyday world; you can touch live animals, gaze at the stars, test your senses, play with technology, watch a 3-D film, and more. Friendly staff scientists are available to share their knowledge. ⊠ *100 Ramsey Lake Rd.,* ☎ *705/522–3700.* ☞ *Museum $9.95, IMAX theater $8.* ☼ *Daily 9–5.*

The **Big Nickel,** a 30-ft replica of the 1951 Canadian commemorative coin, has been synonymous with Sudbury for almost three decades. It stands on a barren hillside on the west side of the city, overlooking Inco's smokestacks. In summer, Science North (☞ *above*) offers tours of the **Big Nickel Mine,** which at 73 ft is one of the shallowest mines in the area. Visitors are given hard hats, coats, and boots and are lowered into the mine shaft in a "cage" elevator. In the 437-yard-long drifts, or tunnels, miners demonstrate mining techniques. ⊠ *Trans-Canada Hwy. 17 and Big Nickel Mine Rd.,* ☎ *705/522–3700.* ☞ *$9.95.* ☼ *Tour May–Nov., daily 9–5.*

FROM COCHRANE TO MOOSE FACTORY ISLAND AND MOOSONEE

For many people these northern outposts are simply fly-over land, but you can find undiscovered Canada here. The terrain is densely packed with pines; moose and bear are common. Nearby lies the expansive, awe-inspiring James Bay.

Cochrane

㊿ *400 km (248 mi) north of Sudbury via Trans-Canada Hwys. 17 east and 11 north.*

Cochrane is Ontario's gateway to the Arctic, Moose Factory, and Moosonee, at the southern end of James Bay, but don't expect a road to the far north; you need to take a train or fly to those areas. There's train service to Cochrane from Toronto and North Bay. You can fly to Moosonee from Timmins (☞ *below*) via Air Creebec, but a popular option is Ontario Northland's (⊠ 65 Front St. W, Toronto M5J 1E6,
★   ☎ 416/314–3750) *Polar Bear Express* train. Every day except Friday from late June to Labor Day, the *Polar Bear* leaves Cochrane at 8:30 AM and arrives at Moosonee just before 1 PM and departs Moosonee at 5:15 PM and returns to Cochrane by 9:20 PM. Meals, light lunches, and snacks are available in the snack car. It's a 20-minute boat ride from Moosonee aboard the *Polar Princess* to Moose Factory Island.

Dining and Lodging

If you plan to take the *Polar Bear Express* train, you'll probably need to overnight in Cochrane. There are seven motels in and around the town. Not all have restaurant facilities, but they are geared to early wake-up calls for guests taking the train and late check-ins for those returning from the excursion. The three largest (all $) are ☒ **Westway Motor Motel** (⊠ 21 1st St., Cochrane P0L 1C0, ☎ 705/272–4285, FAX 705/272–4429), ☒ **Cochrane Station Inn** (⊠ 200 Railway St.,

Cochrane POL 1CO, ☎ 705/272–3500, FAX 705/272–5713), and ⊞ **Chimo Motel** (✉ Box 190, Cochrane POL 1CO, ☎ 705/272–6555, FAX 705/272–5666).

Moose Factory Island

❸❶ *300 km (186 mi) north of Cochrane by train and boat.*

One of a number of islands in the delta of the Moose River, Moose Factory Island is 8 km (5 mi) long and just over 1 km (½ mi) wide. The island was the site of the second Hudson's Bay Company trading post, established in 1672 on what was then called Hayes Island, 24 km (15 mi) up the Moose River from James Bay. It was captured by the French in 1686 and renamed Fort St. Louis. For information about getting to the island by train and boat, *see* Cochrane, *above.*

Contrary to popular myth, the holes in the floor of **St. Thomas Anglican Church** (✉ Front Rd., ☎ 705/658–4800) are to let floodwater *out* and to ventilate the foundation. When the church was being built in 1864, the foundation floated a short distance in a spring flood, but the church itself has never floated anywhere. The altar cloths and lectern hangings are of moose hide decorated with beads.

The Hudson's Bay post—now known as the North West Company after the group of fur traders who competed against the Bay in the 19th century—is a modern building, but beside it is the 1850 **Hudson's Bay Staff House** in which animal pelts, carvings, snowshoes, gloves, slippers, and beadwork are sold.

The **Blacksmith's Shop** in Centennial Park isn't the oldest wooden building in Ontario, but the stone forge inside it may be the oldest "structure" in the province. The original shop was built in the late 1600s but moved back from the riverbank in 1820. The forge stones had to be transported a long distance and were dissembled and rebuilt at the present location. In summer an apprentice smith runs the forge.

Moosonee

❽❷ *2 km (1 mi) from Moose Factory, 24 km (15 mi) from James Bay.*

Summer tides average 5 ft in Moosonee, Ontario's only tidal port. The community came into existence only in 1903, when the Revillon Frères Trading Company of France established a post to compete with the Hudson's Bay Company. It wasn't until the Ontario Northland Railway arrived in 1932 that the region's population began to catch up to that of Moose Factory. During tourist season, locals open stalls on Revillon Road to sell handicrafts ranging from moccasins and buckskin vests to jewelry, beadwork, and wood and stone carvings. For information about getting here by air or train, *see* Cochrane, *above.*

The **Moosonee visitor center** (✉ Ferguson Rd. at 1st St., ☎ 705/336–2238, FAX 705/336–3899) is in a small, one-story office building. The modern **Ministry of Natural Resources Interpretive Centre** (✉ Revillon Rd., ☎ 705/336–2489) has exhibits of regional wildlife and of the area's geological and geographical history.

Dining and Lodging

$ ✕⊞ **Polar Bear Lodge, Moosonee Lodge.** Both face the Moose River. Their rates may be high for the caliber of accommodation offered, but these are the only choices. Both hotels serve meals, but alcohol is available only to those having dinner at the hotel. ✉ *Polar Bear Lodge, 65 Enterprise Rd., Rexdale M9W 1C4,* ☎ *705/336–2345,* FAX *705/336–2185;* ✉ *Moosonee Lodge, Revillon St., Moosonee POL 1Y0,* ☎ *705/*

336–2351, 𝔽𝔸𝕏 *705/336–2773. Polar Bear Lodge, 28 rooms; Moosonee Lodge, 21 rooms. Restaurant. MC, V.*

Timmins

83   *96 km (60 mi) southwest of Cochrane on Hwys. 11 and 101.*

The mining center of Timmins prides itself on being the largest city in Canada (geographically, that is). Despite its vastness, there's not much to see in Timmins, except for one of Canada's few underground mine tours. You can fly to Moosonee (☞ *above*) via **Air Creebec** (✉ Timmins Airport, R.R.2, Timmins P4N 7C3, ☎ 705/264–9521 or 800/567–6567), which provides service from Timmins.

At **Timmins Underground Gold Mine Tour,** visitors dress in full mining attire for the 2½-hour tour of the old Hollinger gold workings. Surface attractions include a headframe, a prospector's trail with a view of mineral outcrops and ore samples, and a refurbished miner's house. The road to the tour site, near downtown Timmins, is well marked. ✉ *Park Rd. off Hwy. 101,* ☎ *705/267–6222 or 800/387–8466.* ✉ *$17.* ☉ *Tours mid-May–late June and Sept.–late Oct., Wed.–Sun. at 10:30 and 1:30; July–Aug., daily at 9:30, 10:30, noon, 1:30, and 3.*

ONTARIO A TO Z

Arriving and Departing

By Car

The **Macdonald–Cartier Freeway,** known as Highway 401, is Ontario's major highway link. It runs from Windsor in the southwest through Toronto, along the north shore of Lake Ontario, and along the north shore of the St. Lawrence River to the Québec border west of Montréal. The **Trans-Canada Highway** follows the west bank of the Ottawa River from Montréal to Ottawa and on to North Bay. From North Bay to Nipigon at the northern tip of Lake Superior, there are two branches of the Trans-Canada (Highways 11 and 17), and from just west of Thunder Bay to Kenora, near the Manitoba border, another two (Highways 11 and 17). For 24-hour **road-condition information** anywhere in Ontario, call 416/235–1110.

By Plane

Toronto (☞ Chapter 6), the province's largest city, is served by most major international airlines.

By Train

Ontario is served by cross-Canada **VIA Rail** (☎ 416/366–8411, 800/361–1235 outside Toronto, Kingston, London, Windsor, Hamilton; within those cities check local listings). VIA Rail connects with **Amtrak** (☎ 800/872–7245) service at Windsor (Detroit) and Fort Erie (Buffalo).

Getting Around

For information on Toronto travel options, *see* Chapter 6.

By Car

Ontario is a no-fault province, and minimum liability insurance is $200,000. If you're driving across the Ontario border, either bring the policy or the vehicle registration forms and a free Canadian Non-Resident Insurance Card from your insurance agent. If you're driving a borrowed car, also bring a letter of permission signed by the owner. Driving motorized vehicles while impaired by alcohol is taken seriously in Ontario and results in heavy fines, imprisonment, or both. You can be convicted for refusing to take a Breathalyzer test. Radar warning devices are not permitted in Ontario even if they are turned off. Police can seize them on the spot, and heavy fines may be imposed.

Studded tires and window coatings that do not allow a clear view of the vehicle interior are forbidden in Ontario. Right turns on red lights are permitted unless otherwise noted. Pedestrians crossing at designated crosswalks have the right of way.

By Taxi
Cabs are plentiful in Ontario's major cities.

Contacts and Resources

B&B Listing
Some cities and towns have local associations of bed-and-breakfasts. You can ask regional and municipal visitor information offices for more information. A comprehensive bed-and-breakfast guide listing about 200 establishments is published by the **Federation of Ontario Bed and Breakfast Accommodations** (⊠ Box 437, 253 College St., Toronto M5T 1R5, ☎ 416/964–2566).

Emergencies
Ambulance, fire, police (☎ 911).

Outdoor Activities and Sports

CAMPING

Peak season in Ontario's parks is June through August, and it is advised that you reserve a campsite if reservations are accepted; sites can be guaranteed by phone, by mail, or in person by using a Visa or MasterCard. All provincial parks have some sites available on a first-come, first-served basis. In an effort to avoid overcrowding on canoe routes and hiking or backpacking trails, daily quotas have been established governing the number of people permitted in the parks. Permits can be reserved ahead of time. For more detailed information on parks and campgrounds in Ontario, contact **TraveLinx Ontario** (☞ Visitor Information, *below*) for a free camping guide.

DOGSLEDDING

Burton Penner (⊠ Box 303, Vermilion Bay P0V 2V0, ☎ 807/227–5593 or 888/240–3739) of Vermilion Bay, 91 km (56 mi) east of Kenora (490 km, or 304 mi, west of Thunder Bay), offers guided dogsled tours into the wilderness, overnighting in an outpost cabin or heated wall tent.

FISHING

Licenses are required for fishing in Ontario and may be purchased from the Ministry of Natural Resources district offices and from most sporting goods stores, outfitters, and resorts. Seasons and catch limits change annually, and some districts infringe closed seasons. Restrictions are published in *Summary of the Fishing Regulations,* free from the **Ministry of Natural Resources** (⊠ Public Information Centre, Macdonald Block, Room M1-73, 900 Bay St., Toronto M7A 1W3, ☎ 416/314–2000).

There are about 500 fishing resorts and lodges listed in the current catalogue of fishing packages available free from **Ontario Tourism** (☞ Visitor Information, *below*). The establishments are not hotels located near bodies of water that contain fish but businesses designed to make sport fishing available to their guests. Each offers all the accoutrements, including boats, motors, guides, floatplanes, and freezers. Rates at these lodges are hefty.

Hike Ontario (☎ 416/462–7362) has information about hiking in the province.

Call of the Wild (✉ 23 Edward St., Markham L3P 2N9, ☎ 416/200–9453) offers guided trips of different lengths—dogsledding and cross-country skiing in winter, canoeing and hiking in summer—in Algonquin Park and other areas in southern Ontario. Prices include transportation from Toronto.

A growing number of companies in eastern Ontario offer packages ranging from half-day to weeklong trips between May and September. **Esprit Rafting Adventures** (✉ Box 463, Pembroke K8A 6X7, ☎ 819/683–3241) offers trips such as rafting on the Ottawa River, canoeing in Algonquin Park, or mountain biking in the Upper Ottawa Valley. **Owl Rafting** (✉ Box 29, Forester's Falls K0J 1V0, ☎ 613/646–2263, 613/238–7238 or 800/461–7238) offers half-day excursions on the nearby Ottawa and Madawaska rivers. **RiverRun** (✉ Box 179, Beachburg K0J 1C0, ☎ 800/267–8504), a 90-minute drive west of Ottawa, has a one-day tour on the Ottawa River.

For a recorded **snow report,** call 416/314–0998.

Overnight guided excursions are available in Haliburton Highlands/Algonquin Park (☞ Haliburton, *above*) and out of Kenora. At Kenora, **Halley's Camps** (✉ Box 608, Kenora P9N 3X6, ☎ 807/224–6531, 800/465–3325 in Ontario and Manitoba) has guided excursions on wilderness trails to outpost camps for three to six nights.

Visitor Information
Ontario has a wealth of excellent and free tourist information. The best source is **Ontario Tourism** (✉ 1 Concord Gate Pl., 9th floor, Don Mills M36 3N6, ☎ 800/668–2746 in Canada and the U.S., except the Yukon, Northwest Territories, and Alaska).

Ontario's principal regional and municipal tourist offices are as follows: **Greater Hamilton, Visitor and Convention Services** (✉ 1 James St., 3rd Floor, Hamilton L8P 4R5, ☎ 905/546–4222 or 800/263–8590, FAX 905/546–4107), **Kingston Tourist Information Office** (✉ 209 Ontario St., Kingston K7L 2Z1, ☎ 613/548–4415 or 800/367–3278, FAX 613/548–4549), **Kitchener and Waterloo Visitor and Convention Bureau** (✉ 2848 King St. E, Kitchener N2A 1A5, ☎ 519/748–0800 or 800/265–6959, FAX 519/748–6411), **Midland Chamber of Commerce** (✉ 208 King St., Box 158, Midland L4R 4K8, ☎ 705/526–7884, FAX 705/526–1744), **Niagara Falls, Canada Visitor and Convention Bureau** (✉ 5433 Victoria Ave., Niagara Falls L2G 3L1, ☎ 905/356–6061 or 800/563–2557, FAX 905/356–5567), **Peterborough–Kawartha Tourism & Convention Bureau** (✉ 175 George St. N, Peterborough K9J 3G6, ☎ 705/748–2201 or 800/461–6424, FAX 705/742–2494), **Sault Ste. Marie Chamber of Commerce** (✉ 360 Great Northern Rd., Sault Ste. Marie P6A 2A3, ☎ 705/949–7152 or 800/263–2546, FAX 705/759–8166), **Tourism Thunder Bay** (✉ 500 E. Donald St., Thunder Bay P7E 5V3, ☎ 807/625–2149 or 800/667–8386), **Convention and Visitors Bureau of Windsor, Essex County, and Pelee Island** (✉ 333 Riverside Dr. W, Suite 103, Windsor N9A 5K4, ☎ 519/255–6530 or 800/265–3633, FAX 519/255–6192).

8 Montréal

Traces of this island city's long history are found everywhere, from the 17th-century buildings in Vieux-Montréal to grand churches and verdant parks such as Mont-Royal. But Montréal, with its atmosphere of romantic elegance, is also full of very modern pleasures: fine dining, whether you want French cuisine or any kind of ethnic fare; good shopping for everything from antiques to high fashion; and nightlife, arts events, and festivals that provide diversions year-round.

By Paul and
Julie Waters

MONTRÉAL IS CANADA'S most romantic metropolis, an island city that seems to favor grace and elegance over order and even prosperity; a city full of music, art, and joie de vivre. It is rather like the European capital Vienna—past its peak of power and glory, perhaps, but still a vibrant and beautiful place full of memories, dreams, and festivals.

That's not to say Montréal is ready to fade away. It may not be so young anymore—it celebrated its 350th birthday in 1992—but it remains Québec's largest city and an important port and financial center. Its office towers are full of young Québécois entrepreneurs, members of a new breed who are ready and eager to take on the world.

Montréal is the only French-speaking metropolis in North America and the second-largest French-speaking city in the world, but it's a tolerant place that over the years has made room for millions of immigrants who speak dozens of languages. Today about 15% of the 3.1 million people who live in the metropolitan area claim English as their mother tongue, and another 15% claim a language that's neither English nor French. The city's gentle tolerance has won recognition: Several times it has been voted one of the world's most livable cities.

The city's grace, however, has been sorely tested. Since 1976, Montréal has twice weathered the election of a separatist provincial government, a law banning all languages but French on virtually all public signs and billboards, and four referendums on the future of Québec and Canada. The latest chapter in this long constitutional drama was the cliffhanger referendum on Québec independence on October 30, 1995. In that showdown Québécois voters chose to remain part of Canada but by the thinnest of possible margins. More than 98% of eligible voters participated, and the final province-wide result was 49.42% in favor of independence and 50.58% against. In fact 60% of the province's Francophones voted in favor of establishing an independent Québec. But Montréal, where most of the province's Anglophones and immigrants live, bucked the separatist trend and voted nearly 70% against independence. The drama has since cooled. The separatist Parti-Québécois controls the provincial government, but it has switched its focus to the flagging economy, and its leader, Lucien Bouchard, has tried to steer clear of arguments about language.

In spite of uncertainty about the future, most Montrealers still delight in their city, which has weathered all these storms with aplomb. It is, after all, a city that's used to turmoil. It was founded by the French, conquered by the British, and occupied by the Americans. It has a long history of reconciling contradictions and even today is a city of contrasts. The glass office tower of La Maison des Coopérants, for example, soars above a Gothic-style Anglican cathedral that squats gracefully in its shadow. The neo-Gothic facade of the Basilique Notre-Dame-de-Montréal glares across Place d'Armes at the pagan temple that is the head office of the Bank of Montréal. And while pilgrims still climb the steps to the Oratoire St-Joseph on their knees on one side of the mountain, thousands of their fellow Catholics line up to get into the very chic Casino de Montréal on the other side—certainly not what the earnest French settlers who founded Montréal envisioned when they landed on the island in May 1642.

Those 54 pious men and women under the leadership of Paul de Chomedey, Sieur de Maisonneuve, hoped to do nothing less than create a new Christian society. They named their settlement Ville-Marie in honor of the mother of Christ and set out to convert the natives.

Those early years were marked by the heroism of two women—Jeanne Mance, a French noblewoman who arrived with de Maisonneuve, and Marguerite Bourgeoys, who came 11 years later. Jeanne Mance, working alone, established the Hôpital Hôtel-Dieu de St-Joseph, still one of the city's major hospitals. In 1659 she invited members of a French order of nuns to help her in her efforts. That order, the Religieuses Hospitalières de St-Joseph, now has its motherhouse in Montréal and is the oldest nursing group in the Americas. Marguerite Bourgeoys, with Jeanne Mance's help, established the colony's first school and taught both French and native children how to read and write. Bourgeoys founded the Congrégation de Notre Dame, a teaching order that still has schools in Montréal, across Canada, and around the world. She was canonized a saint by the Roman Catholic Church in 1982.

Piety wasn't the settlement's only raison d'être, however. Ville-Marie was ideally located to be a commercial success as well. It was at the confluence of two major transportation routes—the St. Lawrence and Ottawa rivers—and fur trappers used the town as a staging point for their expeditions. But the city's religious roots were never forgotten. Until 1854, long after the French lost possession of the city, the island of Montréal remained the property of the Sulpicians, an aristocratic order of French priests. The Sulpicians were responsible for administering the colony and for recruiting colonists. They still run the Basilique Notre-Dame-de-Montréal and are still responsible for training priests for the Roman Catholic archdiocese.

The French regime in Canada ended with the Seven Years' War—what Americans call the French and Indian Wars. British troops took Québec City in 1759, and Montréal fell less than a year later. The Treaty of Paris ceded all New France to Britain in 1763, and soon English and Scottish settlers poured into Montréal to take advantage of the city's geography and economic potential. By 1832 Montréal was a leading colonial capital of business, finance, and transportation and had grown far beyond the walls of the old settlement. Much of that business and financial leadership has since moved to Toronto, the upstream rival Montrealers love to hate.

Pleasures and Pastimes

Dining
Montrealers are passionate about food. They love to dine on classic dishes in restaurants like Les Halles and the Beaver Club, or swoon over culinary innovations in places like Toqué and Mediterraneo, but they can get equally passionate about humbler fare. They'll argue with some heat about where to get the juiciest smoked meat (the city's beloved version of corned beef), the crispiest barbecued chicken, and the soggiest *stimés* (steamed hot dogs). You'll find great French food here but also cuisines from around the world; the city's restaurants represent more than 75 ethnic groups.

Faith and History
Reminders of the city's long history are found everywhere, including in its churches. Some buildings in Vieux-Montréal date to the 17th century. Other parts of the city are full of wonderful examples of Victorian architecture. Museums like the Musée McCord de l'Histoire Canadienne, the Musée d'Archéologie de la Pointe-à-Callière, and the Stewart Museum in the Old Fort on Ile Ste-Hélène attest to the city's fascination with its past.

Montréal's two most popular attractions are monuments dedicated to a Jewish couple who lived 2,000 years ago—the oratory dedicated to

Montréal

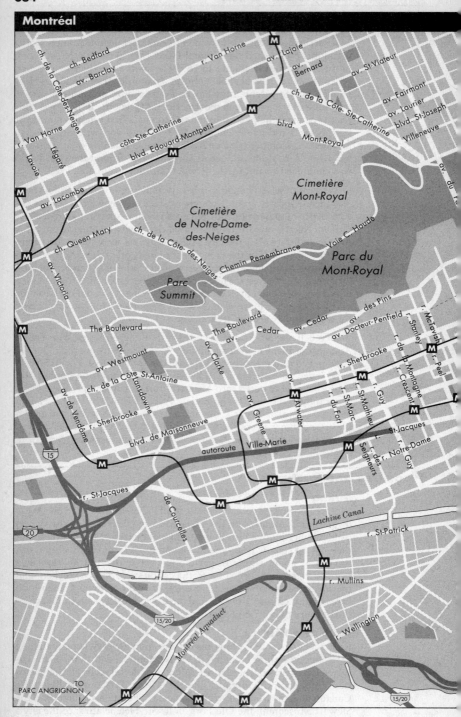

ch. de la Côte-des-Neiges
ch. Bedford
ch. Barclay
r. Van Horne
av. Lajoie
av. Bernard
av. St-Viateur
av. Fairmont
av. Laurier
blvd. St-Joseph
Villeneuve
r. Van Horne
Légaré
côte-Ste-Catherine
blvd. Édouard-Montpetit
ch. de la Côte-Ste-Catherine
blvd. Mont-Royal
av. de la ...
Lavoie
av. Lacombe
ch. Queen Mary
ch. de la Côte-des-Neiges
Chemin Remembrance
Voie C. Houde
Cimetière Mont-Royal
av. Victoria
Cimetière de Notre-Dame-des-Neiges
Parc du Mont-Royal
Parc Summit
The Boulevard
The Boulevard
av.
Cedar
av. Cedar
av. des Pins
av. Docteur-Penfield
r. McTavish
r. Peel
r. Stanley
av. Westmount
av. Clarke
r. Sherbrooke
r. Guy
r. de la Montagne
r. Crescent
ch. de la Côte St-Antoine
av. de la Côte Lansdowne
av. Greene
av. Atwater
r. St-Mathieu
r. St-Marc
r. du Fort
St-Jacques
av. de Vendôme
r. Sherbrooke
blvd. de Maisonneuve
autoroute Ville-Marie
r. des Seigneurs
r. Notre-Dame
r. Guy
I-15
r. St-Jacques
de Courcelles
Lachine Canal
r. St-Patrick
I-20
r. Mullins
15/20
Montréal Aqueduct
r. Wellington
TO PARC ANGRIGNON
15/20

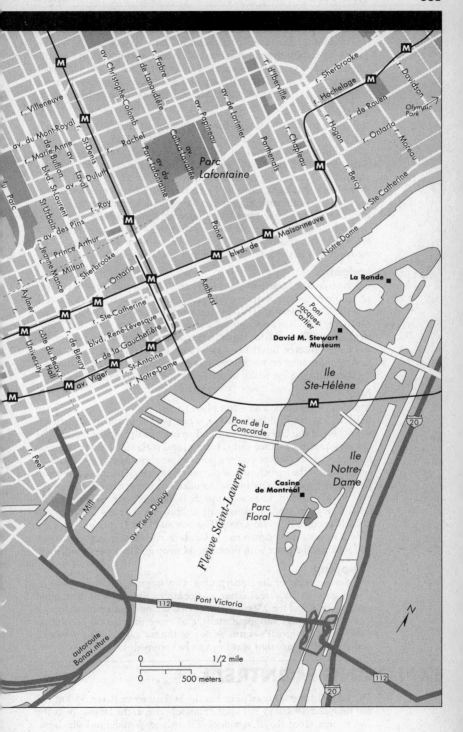

St. Joseph on the north side of Mont-Royal and the Basilique Notre-Dame-de-Montréal dedicated to his wife in the old city. These are just two of dozens of beautiful churches built in the days when the Québécois were among the most devout adherents to the Roman Catholic Church. Other gems of ecclesiastical architecture are St. Patrick's Basilica and the Chapelle Notre-Dame-de-Lourdes. Even parish churches in working-class neighborhoods are as grand as some cathedrals.

Festivals

Summer and fall are just one long succession of festivals that begin in late June with a 10-day Festival International de Jazz, when as many as a million fans descend on the city to hear more than 1,000 musicians, including giants like guitarist John Scofield and tenor saxophonist Joe Lovano. In August there's the World Film Festival and the lively Just for Laughs Comedy Festival in the Vieux-Port area. Other festivals celebrate beer, alternative films, French-language music and song from around the world, and international cuisine. Every Saturday in June and every Sunday in July the skies over the city waterfront erupt in color and flame as fireworks teams from around the world vie for prizes in the International Fireworks Competition.

Lodging

On the island of Montréal alone there are rooms available in every type of accommodation, from world-class luxury hotels to youth hostels, from student dormitories to budget executive motels. The Ritz-Carlton Kempinski has been setting standards of luxury since 1912, and the nearby Westin Mont-Royal is one of the best modern luxury hotels in the country. But the city also offers more intimate charm, at the Château Versailles on rue Sherbrooke, for example, or the tiny Auberge les Passants du Sans Soucy in the heart of Vieux-Montréal.

Nightlife

Montréal's reputation as a fun place to visit for a night on the town dates at least to Prohibition days, when hordes of thirsty Americans would flood the city every weekend to eat, drink, and be merry. The city has dozens of dance clubs, bistros, and jazz clubs, not to mention hundreds of bars where you can go to argue about sports, politics, and religion until the early hours of the morning. Much of the action takes place along rue St-Denis and adjacent streets in the eastern part of the city or rues Bishop, Crescent, and de la Montagne in the downtown area. The night scene is constantly shifting—last year's hot spot can quickly become this year's dive. The best and easiest way to figure out what's in is to stroll down rue St-Denis or rue Bishop at about 10:30 and look for the place with the longest lineup and the rudest doorman.

Shopping

The development of the Underground City has made shopping a year-round sport in Montréal. That vast complex linked by underground passageways and the Métro includes two major department stores, at least a dozen huge shopping malls, and more than 1,000 boutiques. Add to this Montréal's status as one of the fur capitals of the world, and you have a city that was born to be shopped.

EXPLORING MONTRÉAL

The Ile de Montréal is an island in the St. Lawrence River, 51 km (32 mi) long and 14 km (9 mi) wide. The only rise in the landscape is the 764-ft-high Mont-Royal, which gave the island its name and which residents call simply "the mountain." The city of Montréal is the oldest and by far the largest of the 24 municipalities on the island, which together make up the Communauté Urbaine de Montréal (the Montréal Urban Community), the regional government that runs, among other things, the police department and the transit system. There is a belt of off-island suburbs on the South Shore of the St. Lawrence, and just to the north across the narrow Rivière-des Prairies, on an island of its own, is Laval, a suburb that has grown to be the second-largest city in the province. But the countryside is never far away. The pastoral Eastern Townships, first settled by Loyalists fleeing the American Revolution, are less than an hour's drive away, and the Laurentians, an all-season playground full of lakes and ski hills, are even closer.

For a good overview of the city, head for the lookout at the Chalet du Mont-Royal. You can drive most of the way, park, and walk ½ km (¼ mi) or hike all the way up from chemin de la Côte-des-Neiges or avenue des Pins. If you look directly out—southeast—from the belvedere, at the foot of the hill will be the McGill University campus and, surrounding it, the skyscrapers of downtown Montréal. Just beyond, along the banks of the river, are the stone houses of Vieux-Montréal. Hugging the South Shore on the other side of the river are the Iles Ste-Hélène and Notre-Dame, sites of La Ronde amusement park, the Biosphere, the Casino de Montréal, acres of parkland, and the Lac de l'Ile Notre-Dame public beach—all popular excursions. To the east are rue St-Denis and the Quartier Latin, with its rows of French and ethnic restaurants, bistros, chess hangouts, designer boutiques, antiques shops, and art galleries. Even farther east you can see the flying-saucer-shape Olympic Stadium with its leaning tower.

Montréal is easy to explore. Streets, subways, and bus lines are clearly marked. The city is divided by a grid of streets roughly aligned east–west and north–south. (This grid is tilted about 40 degrees off—to the left of—true north, so west is actually southwest and so on.) North–south street numbers begin at the St. Lawrence River and increase as you head north. East–west street numbers begin at boulevard St-Laurent, which divides Montréal into east and west halves. The city is not so large that seasoned walkers can't see all the districts around the base of Mont-Royal on foot. Nearly everything else is easily accessible by the city's quiet, clean, and very safe bus and Métro (subway) system. If you're planning to visit a number of museums, look into the city's museum pass (☞ Contacts and Resources *in* Montréal A to Z, *below*).

Numbers in the text correspond to numbers in the margin and on the Vieux-Montréal, Downtown Montréal (Centre-Ville) and Golden Square Mile, Quartier Latin and Parc du Mont-Royal, and Olympic Park and Botanical Garden maps.

Great Itineraries

Getting any real feel for this bilingual, multicultural city takes some time. An ideal stay would be seven days, but you should spend at least three days walking and soaking up the atmosphere. That's enough time to visit Mont-Royal, explore Vieux-Montréal, do some shopping, and perhaps visit the Parc Olympique. It also includes enough nights for an evening of bar-hopping on rue St-Denis or rue Crescent and another for a long, luxurious dinner at one of the city's excellent restaurants.

IF YOU HAVE 3 DAYS
Any visit to Montréal should start with Mont-Royal, Montréal's most enduring symbol. Afterward wander down to avenue des Pins and then through McGill University to downtown. Make an effort to stop at the Musée des Beaux-Arts and St. Patrick's Basilica. Day 2 should be spent exploring Vieux-Montréal, with special emphasis on the Basilique Notre-Dame-de-Montréal and the Musée d'Archéologie Pointe-à-Cal-

lière. On Day 3 you can either visit the Parc Olympique (recommended for children) or stroll through the Quartier Latin.

IF YOU HAVE 5 DAYS

Once again start with a visit to Parc du Mont-Royal, but instead of going downtown after you've viewed the city from the Chalet du Mont-Royal, visit the Oratoire St-Joseph. You should still have enough time to visit the Musée des Beaux-Arts before dinner. That will leave time on Day 2 to get in more shopping as you explore downtown, with perhaps a visit to the Centre Canadien d'Architecture. Spend all of Day 3 in Vieux-Montréal, and on Day 4 stroll through the Quartier Latin. On Day 5, visit the Parc Olympique and then do one of three things: visit the islands, take a ride on the Lachine Rapids, or revisit some of the sights you missed in Vieux-Montréal or downtown.

IF YOU HAVE 7 DAYS

A week will give you enough time to do the five-day itinerary, expanding your Vieux-Montréal explorations to two days and adding a shopping spree on rue Chabanel and a visit to the Casino de Montréal.

Vieux-Montréal

When Montréal's first European settlers arrived by river in 1642 they stopped to build their houses just below the treacherous Lachine Rapids that blocked the way upstream. They picked a site near an old Iroquois settlement on the bank of the river nearest Mont-Royal. In the mid-17th century Montréal consisted of a handful of wood houses clustered around a pair of stone buildings, all flimsily fortified by a wood stockade. For almost three centuries this district—bounded by rues Berri and McGill on the east and west, rue St-Jacques on the north, and the river to the south—was the financial and political heart of the city. Government buildings, the largest church, the stock exchange, the main market, and the port were here. The narrow but relatively straight streets were cobblestone and lined with solid, occasionally elegant houses, office buildings, and warehouses—also made of stone. A thick stone wall with four gates protected the city against native people and marauding European powers. Montréal quickly grew past the bounds of its fortifications, however, and by World War I the center of the city had moved toward Mont-Royal. The new heart of Montréal became Dominion Square (now Square Dorchester). For the next two decades Vieux-Montréal (Old Montréal), as it became known, was gradually abandoned, the warehouses and offices emptied. In 1962 the city began studying ways to revitalize Vieux-Montréal, and a decade of renovations and restorations began.

Today Vieux-Montréal is a center of cultural life and municipal government. Most of the summer activities revolve around Place Jacques-Cartier, which becomes a pedestrian mall with street performers and outdoor cafés, and the Vieux-Port, one of the city's most popular recreation grounds. The Orchestre Symphonique de Montréal performs summer concerts at Basilique Notre-Dame-de-Montréal, which has one of the finest organs in North America, and English-language plays are staged in the Centaur Theatre in the old stock-exchange building. This district has six museums devoted to history, religion, and the arts.

A Good Walk

Take the Métro to the Square-Victoria Station and follow the signs to the **Centre de Commerce Mondial de Montréal** ①, one of the city's more appealing enclosed spaces, with a fountain and frequent art exhibits. Exit on the east side of the complex and turn right on rue St-Pierre, walk south to **rue St-Jacques,** and turn left. Walking east, you'll see the Victorian office buildings of the country's former financial center. This area can seem tomblike on weekends when the business and legal offices close down, but things get livelier closer to the waterfront.

Stop at **Place d'Armes** ②, a square that was the site of battles with the Iroquois in the 1600s and later became the center of Montréal's Haute-Ville, or Upper Town. There are calèches at the south end of the square; the north side is dominated by the **Bank of Montréal** ③, an impressive building with Corinthian columns. The **Basilique Notre-Dame-de-Montréal** ④, one of the most beautiful churches in North America, dominates the south end of Place d'Armes. The low, more retiring stone building behind a wall to the west of the basilica is the **Vieux Séminaire** ⑤, Montréal's oldest building. Unlike the basilica, it is closed to the public. To the east of the basilica is **rue St-Sulpice,** one of the first streets in Montréal, and catercorner from it is the Art Deco Aldred Building. Next to that is Montréal's first skyscraper, a nine-story red-stone tower built by the now defunct Québec Bank in 1888. One block farther east on rue Notre-Dame, just past boulevard St-Laurent, on the left, rises the black-glass-sheathed **Palais de Justice** (1971), or courthouse. The large domed building at 155 rue Notre-Dame Est is the **Vieux Palais de Justice** ⑥ (1857). Across the street, at 160 rue Notre-Dame Est, is the Maison de la Sauvegarde, one of the city's oldest houses. The Old Courthouse abuts the small **Place Vauquelin** ⑦, named after an 18th-century naval hero. North of this square is Champs-de-Mars, a former military parade ground and now a public park crisscrossed by archaeologists' trenches. The ornate building on the east side of Place Vauquelin is the Second Empire–style **Hôtel de Ville** ⑧, or City Hall, built in 1878.

You are in a perfect spot to explore **Place Jacques-Cartier** ⑨, the square that is the heart of Vieux-Montréal. At the western corner of rue Notre-Dame is the **Office des Congrès et du Tourisme du Grand Montréal** ⑩. Both sides of the square are lined with two- and three-story stone buildings that were originally homes or hotels. In summer the one-block **rue St-Amable** ⑪ near the bottom of the square becomes a marketplace.

Retrace your steps to the north end of Place Jacques-Cartier and continue east on rue Notre-Dame. On the right, at the corner of rue St-Claude, is **Château Ramezay** ⑫, built as the residence of the 11th governor of Montréal, Claude de Ramezay, and now a museum. Continue east to rue Berri. On the corner are two houses from the mid-19th century that have been transformed into the **Musée Georges-Étienne Cartier** ⑬, a museum honoring one of the leading figures in founding the Canadian federation in 1867.

When you come out of the museum, walk south on rue Berri to rue St-Paul and then start walking west again toward the center of the city. The first street on your right is rue Bonsecours, one of the oldest in the city. On the corner is the charming Maison du Calvet, now a restaurant and small bed-and-breakfast. Opposite it is the small but beautiful **Chapelle Notre-Dame-de-Bonsecours** ⑭, built by St. Marguerite Bourgeoys, Montréal's first schoolteacher. The long, domed building to the west of the chapel is the **Marché Bonsecours** ⑮, a public market transformed into a cultural center with exhibits on Montréal.

The fashionable 20 blocks of **rue St-Paul** are lined with restaurants, shops, and nightclubs. In an old stone building on rue St-Paul Ouest is an exhibit that focuses on the very new: **Cité des Arts et des Nouvelles Technologies** ⑯ is devoted to exploring cyberspace. Eight blocks

Vieux-Montréal

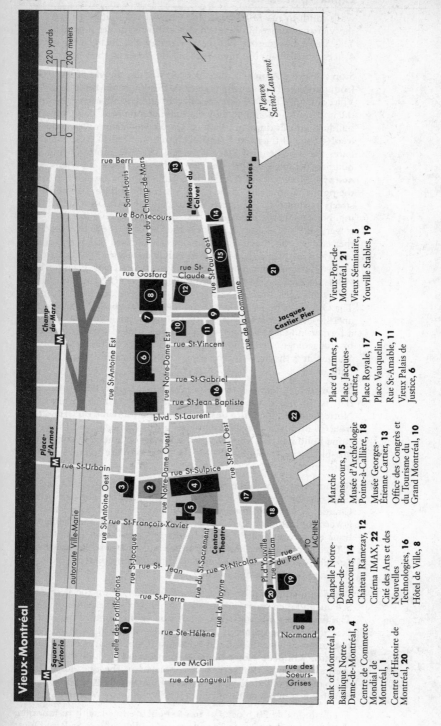

Fleuve Saint-Laurent

Harbour Cruises

Maison du Calvet

Jacques Castier Pier

Champ-de-Mars

Place-d'Armes

Square-Victoria

rue Berri
Saint-Louis
rue du Champ-de-Mars
rue Bonsecours
rue St-Paul Oest
rue St-Claude
rue Gosford
rue de la Commune
rue St-Antoine Est
rue Notre-Dame Est
rue St-Vincent
rue St-Gabriel
rue St-Jean Baptiste
blvd. St-Laurent
rue St-Urbain
rue Notre-Dame Ouest
rue St-Sulpice
rue St-Paul Oest
autoroute Ville-Marie
rue St-Antoine Oest
rue St-François-Xavier
Centaur Theatre
rue du St-Sacrement
rue St-Nicolas
rue St-Jacques
rue St- Jean
rue St-Pierre
rue Le Moyne
ruelle des Fortifications
Pl. d'Youville
rue William
rue du Port
TO LACHINE
rue Ste-Hélène
rue Normand
rue McGill
rue de Longueuil
rue des Soeurs-Grises

220 yards
200 meters

Bank of Montréal, **3**
Basilique Notre-Dame-de-Montréal, **4**
Centre de Commerce Mondial de Montréal, **1**
Centre d'Histoire de Montréal, **20**
Chapelle Notre-Dame-de-Bonsecours, **14**
Château Ramezay, **12**
Cinéma IMAX, **22**
Cité des Arts et des Nouvelles Technologies, **16**
Hôtel de Ville, **8**

Marché Bonsecours, **15**
Musée d'Archéologie Pointe-à-Callière, **18**
Musée Georges-Étienne Cartier, **13**
Office des Congrès et du Tourisme du Grand Montréal, **10**

Place d'Armes, **2**
Place Jacques-Cartier, **9**
Place Royale, **17**
Place Vauquelin, **7**
Rue St-Amable, **11**
Vieux Palais de Justice, **6**

Vieux-Port-de-Montréal, **21**
Vieux Séminaire, **5**
Youville Stables, **19**

west of Place Jacques-Cartier, rue St-Paul leads to **Place Royale** ⑰, the oldest public square in Montréal. Behind the Old Customs House on the square is **Pointe-à-Callière,** a small park that commemorates the settlers' first landing, and the **Musée d'Archéologie Pointe-à-Callière** ⑱, Montréal's dazzling museum of history and archaeology. A 1½-block walk down rue William takes you to the **Youville Stables** ⑲ on the left. These low stone buildings enclosing a garden now house offices, shops, and a restaurant.

Across rue William from the stables is the old fire station that houses the **Centre d'Histoire de Montréal** ⑳, a museum that chronicles the day-to-day life of Montrealers throughout the years. Now walk back east on rue William and turn right down rue du Port to rue de la Commune. Across the street is the **Vieux-Port-de-Montréal** ㉑, a pleasant and popular waterfront park that makes a fitting close to any walk in Vieux-Montréal. If you have time, you can arrange for a harbor excursion or a daring ride on the Lachine Rapids. The Vieux-Port is also home to the **Cinéma IMAX** ㉒, which shows films on a seven-story screen. The impact can be more terrifying than the rapids.

TIMING

If you walk briskly and don't stop, you could get through this route in under an hour. A more realistic and leisurely pace would take about 90 minutes—still without stopping—longer in winter when the streets are icy. Comfortable shoes are a must for the cobblestone streets. The Basilique Notre-Dame is one of Montréal's most famous landmarks and deserves at least a 45-minute visit; Château Ramezay deserves the same. Pointe-à-Callière could keep an enthusiastic history buff occupied for a whole day, but give it at least two hours. If you're visiting any museums, check ahead for seasonal hours.

Sights to See

❸ **Bank of Montréal.** The head office of Canada's oldest chartered bank is a neoclassical building with Corinthian columns, built in 1847 and remodeled by the renowned architectural firm McKim, Mead & White in 1905. It has a one-room museum that recounts the early history of banking in Canada. ⊠ *119 rue St-Jacques Ouest.* ☜ *Museum free.* ☉ *Weekdays 10–4.*

★ ❹ **Basilique Notre-Dame-de-Montréal** (Notre-Dame Basilica). The first church called Notre-Dame was a bark-covered structure built in 1642. Three times it was torn down and rebuilt, each time larger and more ornate. The present church is an enormous (3,800-seat) neo-Gothic structure that opened in 1829. Its architect was an American Protestant named James O'Donnell, who converted to Catholicism during construction and is buried in the church crypt. The twin towers are 228 ft high, and the western one holds one of North America's largest bells. The interior is neo-Gothic, with stained-glass windows, pine and walnut carvings, and a vaulted blue ceiling studded with thousands of 24-carat gold stars. With more than 7,000 pipes, the pipe organ is one of the largest on the continent. If you just want to hear the organ roar, drop in for the 11 AM solemn Mass on Sunday and pay special attention to the recessional. Behind the main altar is the **Sacré-Coeur Chapel,** destroyed by fire in 1978 and rebuilt in five different styles. The chapel is often called the Wedding Chapel because of the hundreds of Montrealers who get married in it every year. When pop star Céline Dion married her manager in 1994, however, the lavish and elaborate ceremony was in the main church. Also in the back of the church is a small museum of religious paintings and historical objects. Please note: Notre-Dame is an active house of worship and visitors should dress accordingly. Also, it is advisable to plan your visit around the daily 12:15 PM Mass in the chapel and the 5 PM Mass in the main church. ⊠ *116 rue Notre-Dame Ouest,* ☎ *514/849–1070 basilica, 514/842–2925 museum.* 🕮 *Basilica donation requested, tour free, museum $1.* ⊘ *Basilica Labor Day–June 24, daily 8:30–6, and June 25–Labor Day, daily 8:30–8. Guided tour (except Sun. morning) May–June 24, daily 9–4; June 25–Labor Day, daily 8:30–4:30. Museum weekends 9:30–4:30.*

❶ Centre de Commerce Mondial de Montréal (Montréal World Trade Center). This is one of the nicest enclosed spaces in Montréal, with a fountain, frequent art exhibits, and Montréal's own chunk of the Berlin Wall, complete with colorful graffiti. The center covers a block of the rundown ruelle des Fortifications, a narrow lane that marks the place where the city walls stood. Developers glassed it in and sandblasted and restored 11 of the 19th-century buildings that lined it. It's home to the Hôtel Inter-Continental Montréal (☞ Lodging, *below*) and some boutiques and restaurants. ⊠ *747 Sq. Victoria. Métro: Square-Victoria Station and follow signs.*

❷⓪ Centre d'Histoire de Montréal. Video games, soundtracks, and more than 300 artifacts re-create the day-to-day life of the ordinary men and women who have lived in Montréal, from precolonial to modern times. Some of the most touching exhibits depict family life in Montréal's working-class tenements in the 20th century. ⊠ *335 Pl. d'Youville,* ☎ *514/872–3207.* 🕮 *$4.50.* ⊘ *Tues.–Sun. 10–5.*

❹⓮ Chapelle Notre-Dame-de-Bonsecours. St. Marguerite Bourgeoys dedicated this chapel to the Virgin Mary in 1657. It became known as a sailor's church, and small wood models of sailing ships hang from the ceiling. It reopened in 1998 after a major renovation project that, among other things, revealed several priceless murals that had been hidden behind glued-on paintings. The attached Musée Marguerite Bourgeoys explores the life of the saint and the history of Montréal, with an emphasis on education. You can climb to the rather precarious bell tower (beware of the slippery metal steps in winter) for a fine view of the Vieux-Port. ⊠ *400 rue St-Paul Est,* ☎ *514/282–8670.* 🕮 *Museum $5.* ⊘ *Tues.–Sun., May 1–Oct. 31, 10–4:30; Nov. 1–mid-Jan. and mid-Mar.–Apr. 30, 11–3. Chapel open May 1–Oct. 31, daily 10–6, Nov. 1–mid-Jan. and mid-Mar.–Apr. 30, daily 11–6. The museum is closed mid-Jan.–mid-Mar. and the chapel opens only from 4:30 PM to 6 PM.*

❷⓬ Château Ramezay. This elegant colonial building was the residence of the 11th governor of Montréal, Claude de Ramezay. In 1775–76 it served as headquarters for American troops seeking to conquer Canada; Benjamin Franklin stayed here during that winter occupation. The château became a museum of city and provincial history in 1895, and it has been restored to the style of Governor de Ramezay's day. Château Ramezay is built on the lines of a Norman castle, with squat stone turrets and graceful, wood-paneled rooms. Of particular interest is the Salon Nantes, with its 18th-century carved paneling by French architect Germain Boffrand. ⊠ *280 rue Notre-Dame Est,* ☎ *514/861–3708.* 🕮 *$5.* ⊘ *June–Sept., daily 10–6; Oct.–May, Tues.–Sun. 10–4:30.*

NEED A BREAK?   In summer few places are lovelier and livelier than **Place Jacques-Cartier.** You could stop at a *terasse* (sidewalk café) for a beer or a coffee or just sit on a bench amid the flower vendors and listen to the street musicians or watch a juggler. If you're peckish, there are several snack bars and ice-cream stands. If you're really daring, you could try *poutine,* Québec's contribution to junk-food culture. It consists of french fries covered with cheese curds and smothered in gravy—an acquired taste.

☺ ㉒   **Cinéma IMAX.** Nausea and vertigo are some of the more negative things people experience the first time they see an IMAX film roar at them from a seven-story screen. Wonder and excitement are among the more positive. The films—most under an hour long—are decidedly educational. It's best to reserve ahead. ⊠ *Vieux-Port, Shed No. 7,* ☎ *514/ 790–1245.* 🎟 *$11.75.* ☉ *Tues.–Sun. from 9:45 AM.*

⑯   **Cité des Arts et des Nouvelles Technologies.** The center, dedicated to art and modern technology, has revolving exhibits that explore virtual reality, interactive art, computer animation, and other wonders of the cyber universe. In the electronic café you can have coffee and a sandwich and plug into the Internet on one of 40 computers. ⊠ *85 rue St-Paul Ouest,* ☎ *514/849–1612.* 🎟 *$11.75.* ☉ *Sun.–Thurs. 10–6, Fri.–Sat. 10–9; call for show times.*

❽   **Hôtel de Ville.** Montréal's ornate City Hall was built in 1878 in the Second Empire style. On July 24, 1967, President Charles de Gaulle of France stood on the central balcony here and made his famous *"Vive le Québec libre"* speech. There are no tours, but the main hall is used for occasional exhibitions. ⊠ *275 rue Notre-Dame Est.*

⑮   **Marché Bonsecours.** Built in 1845, this domed building was for years Montréal's main produce, meat, and fish market. It now houses municipal offices and a cultural center with exhibits on Montréal. ⊠ *350 rue St-Paul Est.*

★ ⑱   **Musée d'Archéologie Pointe-à-Callière.** Here you can get to the very foundations of New France. This museum in the ☞ **Pointe-à-Callière** park was built around the excavated remains of structures dating to Montréal's beginnings, including the city's first Catholic cemetery. It's a labyrinth of stone walls and corridors, illuminated by spotlights and holograms of figures from the past. An audiovisual show gives a historical overview of the area. It also has an excellent gift shop, full of interesting books on Montréal's history, as well as pictures and reproductions of old maps, engravings, and other artifacts. ⊠ *350 Pl. Royale,* ☎ *514/872–9150.* 🎟 *$8.* ☉ *June 24–Labor Day, Tues.–Sun. 10–8; Sept. 6–June 23, Tues.–Fri. 10–5, Sun. 11–5.*

⑬   **Musée George-Étienne Cartier.** This museum, which honors one of the architects of the 1867 Canadian federation, comprises two houses. The west house was the Cartiers' home in 1862 and has been meticulously restored to the style of that period, with plush Victorian furniture. The house on the east focuses on the political career of one of the most important French-Canadian statesmen of his day. Costumed guides act out the roles of the Cartiers' friends and servants. From mid-November to mid-December the Cartiers' home is festooned with Victorian decorations. ⊠ *458 rue Notre-Dame Est,* ☎ *514/283–2282.* 🎟 *$3.25.* ☉ *Late May–Labor Day, daily 10–6; Labor Day–mid-May, Wed.–Sun. 10–noon and 1–5.*

⑩   **Office des Congrès et du Tourisme du Grand Montréal.** This small building (1811) was the site of the old Silver Dollar Saloon, so named because there were 350 silver dollars nailed to the floor. Today it's one of two visitor information offices operated by Info-Touriste; the other is at 1001 square Dorchester. The staff can answer travel questions, and guides to the city and brochures on attractions and hotels are available. ⊠ *174 rue Notre-Dame Est,* ☎ *514/873–2015.*

  Palais de Justice. Built in 1971, this black glass building is the main courthouse for the judicial district of Montréal. Criminal law in Canada falls under federal jurisdiction and is based on British common law, but civil law is a provincial matter and Québec's is based on France's

Napoleonic Code, which governs all the minutiae of private life—from setting up a company and negotiating a mortgage to drawing up a marriage contract and registering the names of children. Lawyers and judges in Québec courts wear the same elaborate gowns as their British counterparts, but not the wigs. This building is not open for tours. ⊠ *1 rue Notre-Dame Est.*

② **Place d'Armes.** Montréal's founder, Paul de Chomedy, slew an Iroquois chief in a battle here in 1644 and was wounded in return. His statue stands in a fountain in the middle of the square. Tunnels beneath the square protected the colonists from the winter weather and provided an escape route; unfortunately they are too small and dangerous to visit. ⊠ *Bordered by rues Notre-Dame Ouest and St-Jacques.*

★ ⑨ **Place Jacques-Cartier.** This two-block-long square, at the heart of Vieux-Montréal, opened in 1804 as a municipal market, and every summer it is transformed into a flower market. The 1809 monument at the top of the square celebrates Lord Nelson's victory over Napoléon Bonaparte's French navy at Trafalgar. It was built not by patriotic British residents of Montréal but by the Sulpician priests, who didn't have much love for the Corsican emperor either. ⊠ *Bordered by rues Notre-Dame Est and de la Commune.*

⑰ **Place Royale.** The oldest public square in Montréal served as a public market during the French regime and later became a Victorian garden. The severely beautiful neoclassical Vielle Douane (Old Customs House) on its south side serves as the gift shop for the ☞ **Musée d'Archéologie Pointe-à-Callière.**

⑦ **Place Vauquelin.** The statue in this little square is of Admiral Jacques Vauquelin, a naval hero of the French regime.

Pointe-à-Callière. This small park commemorates the settlers' first landing. A small stream used to flow into the St. Lawrence here, and it was on the point of land between the two waters that the colonists landed their four boats on May 17, 1642. The settlement was almost washed away the next Christmas by a flood. When it was spared, Paul de Chomedey, Sieur de Maisonneuve, placed a cross on top of Mont-Royal as thanks to God. ⊠ *Bordered by rues de la Commune and William.*

⑪ **Rue St-Amable.** A one-block lane near Place Jacques-Cartier is a summer marketplace for local jewelers, artists, and craftspeople.

Rue St-Jacques. This was once the financial heart, not just of Montréal but of Canada. As you walk here, note the fine decorative stone flourishes—grapevines, nymphs, angels, and goddesses—on the Victorian office buildings.

Rue St-Paul. The most fashionable street in Vieux-Montréal, rue St-Paul is lined with restaurants, shops filled with Québécois handicrafts, and nightclubs for almost 20 blocks.

Rue St-Sulpice. This is one of the oldest streets in Montréal. A plaque on the eastern side marks the spot where Jeanne Mance built Hôpital Hôtel-Dieu, the city's first hospital, in 1644.

⑥ **Vieux Palais de Justice.** The old courthouse, a domed building in the Classical Revival style, was built in 1857. It once housed the civil courts but is now a warren of city offices. ⊠ *155 rue Notre-Dame Est.*

㉑ **Vieux-Port-de-Montréal.** Today the port is a recreational area rather than the heart and soul of the city's commercial life. Its docks are too small and its channels too shallow for modern megaships, and only a few freighters and cruise ships use it. However, the area is a popular waterfront park with a promenade, snack bars, and the ☞ **Cinéma IMAX.** In summer, you can rent bicycles and in-line skates, and in winter you can skate on a giant outdoor rink. A new science center is planned to open in January 2000. The port also marks the start of one of the city's most popular bicycle paths. Every weekend hundreds of Montrealers follow the route of the old Lachine Canal (built in 1825 to bypass the Lachine Rapids and rendered obsolete by the St. Lawrence Seaway) to Parc René-Lévesque in Lachine, a narrow spit of land jutting into Lac St-Louis.

⑤ Vieux Séminaire. Montréal's oldest building is considered the finest, most elegant example of 17th-century Québec architecture. It was built in 1685 as a headquarters for the Sulpician priests who owned the island of Montréal until 1854, and it is still a residence for the Sulpicians who administer the basilica. The clock on the roof over the main doorway is the oldest (pre-1701) public timepiece in North America. Behind the seminary building is a garden, which is unfortunately closed to the public, as is the seminary itself. ✉ *116 rue Notre-Dame Ouest, behind wall west of Basilique Notre-Dame-de-Montréal.*

⑲ Youville Stables. These low stone buildings enclosing a garden were originally built as warehouses in 1825 (they never were stables). They now house offices, shops, and Gibby's restaurant (☞ Dining, *below*). ✉ *298 Pl. d'Youville.*

Downtown

On the surface Montréal's downtown, or *centre-ville,* is much like the downtown core of many other major cities—full of life and noisy traffic, its streets lined with department stores, boutiques, bars, restaurants, strip clubs, amusement arcades, and bookstores. But, in fact, much of the area's activity goes on beneath the surface, in Montréal's Cité Souterrain (Underground City). Development of this unique endeavor began in 1966 when the Métro opened. Now it includes (at last count) seven hotels, 1,500 offices, 30 movie theaters, more than 1,600 boutiques, 200 restaurants, three universities, two colleges, two train stations, a skating rink, 40 banks, a bus terminal, an art museum, a complex of concert halls, the home ice of the Montréal Canadiens, and a church. All this is linked by Métro lines and more than 30 km (19 mi) of well-lit, boutique-lined passages that protect shoppers and workers from the hardships of winter and the heat of summer. A traveler arriving by train could book into a fine hotel and spend a week shopping, dining, and going to a long list of movies, plays, concerts, sports events, and discos, without once stepping outside.

A Good Walk

The start of this walk is designed for moles—it's all underground—but it will give you an idea of the extent of the Underground City. Start at the McGill Métro station, one of the central points in the Underground City. It's linked to a half dozen office towers and two of the "Big Three" department stores, Eaton (the city's biggest) and La Baie (the other is Ogilvy). Passages also link the station to such major shopping malls as Le Centre Eaton, Les Promenades de la Cathédrale, and Place Montreal Trust.

Follow the signs from the station through Eaton's bargain basement to Le Centre Eaton and then descend yet another floor to the tunnel that leads to **Place Ville-Marie** ㉓. The mall complex underneath this cruciform skyscraper was the first link in the Underground City. From here head south via the passageways toward **Le Reine Elizabeth** ㉔, or

Downtown Montréal (Centre-Ville) and Golden Square Mile

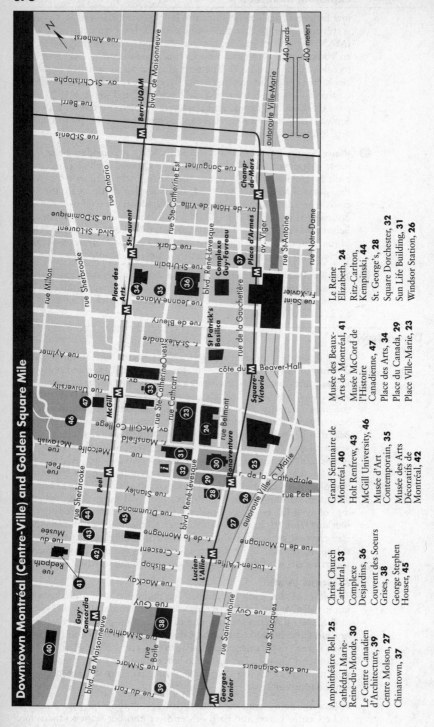

440 yards
400 meters

Amphithéâtre Bell, **25**
Cathédral Marie-
Reine-du-Monde, **30**
Le Centre Canadien
d'Architecture, **39**
Centre Molson, **27**
Chinatown

Christ Church
Cathédral, **33**
Complexe
Desjardins, **36**
Couvent des Soeurs
Grises, **38**
George Stephen
Houser, **45**

Grand Séminaire de
Montréal, **40**
Holt Renfrew, **43**
McGill University, **46**
Musée d'Art
Contemporain, **35**
Musée des Arts
Décoratifs de
Montréal, **42**

Musée des Beaux-
Arts de Montréal, **41**
Musée McCord de
l'Histoire
Canadienne, **47**
Place des Arts, **34**
Place du Canada, **29**
Place Ville-Marie, **23**

Le Reine
Elizabeth, **24**
Ritz-Carlton,
Kempinski, **44**
St. George's, **28**
Square Dorchester, **32**
Sun Life Building, **31**
Windsor Station, **26**

Queen Elizabeth, hotel, which straddles the entrance to the Gare Centrale (Central Station). Walk through the station and follow the signs marked MÉTRO/PLACE BONAVENTURE until you see a sign for Le 1000 rue de la Gauchetière, a skyscraper that's home to the **Amphithéâtre Bell** ㉕, an indoor ice rink. Return to the tunnels and follow signs to the Bonaventure Métro station and then to the Canadian Pacific Railway Company's **Windsor Station** ㉖, with its massive stone exterior and steel-and-glass roof. The rail station and the Place Bonaventure Métro station below it are all linked to **Centre Molson** ㉗, the home of the Montréal Canadiens.

By now you'll be ready for some fresh air. You'll have covered 10 city blocks and visited two train stations, a couple of malls, a major hotel, an office tower, and the city's most important sports shrine without once emerging from cover. Exit the Underground City at the north end of Windsor Station and cross rue de la Gauchetière to **St. George's** ㉘, the prettiest Anglican church in the city. Just to the east across rue Peel is **Place du Canada** ㉙, a park with a statue of Sir John A. Macdonald, Canada's first prime minister. Cross the park and rue de la Cathédrale to **Cathédrale Marie-Reine-du-Monde** ㉚, which is modeled after St. Peter's Basilica in Rome. People sometimes call the gray granite building across boulevard René-Lévesque from the cathedral the Wedding Cake, because it rises in tiers of decreasing size and has lots of columns, but its real name is the **Sun Life Building** ㉛. The park that faces the Sun Life Building just north of boulevard René-Lévesque is **Square Dorchester** ㉜, for many years the heart of Montréal. Backtrack across the park to rue Peel and walk north to rue Ste-Catherine. This intersection is regarded by many as the heart of downtown.

Turn right and walk east along rue Ste-Catherine, pausing briefly to admire the view at the corner of avenue McGill College. Look north up this broad boulevard and you can see the Victorian-era buildings of the McGill University campus with Mont-Royal looming in the background. The grim-looking gray castle high on the slopes to the right is the Royal Victoria Hospital. One block more brings you to the Eaton department store, where this whole adventure started, and next to that is **Christ Church Cathedral** ㉝ (1859), the main church of the Anglican diocese of Montréal.

You can end your stroll here or continue six blocks farther east on rue Ste-Catherine to **Place des Arts** ㉞, Montréal's main theater complex. The **Musée d'Art Contemporain** ㉟, the city's modern art museum, is also part of the complex. While still in Place des Arts, follow the signs to the **Complexe Desjardins** ㊱, an office building, hotel, and mall along the lines of Place Ville-Marie (☞ *above*). The next development south is the Complexe Guy-Favreau, a huge federal office building named after the Canadian minister of justice in the early '60s. If you continue in a straight line, you will hit the Palais de Congrès, Montréal's convention centre, above the Place d'Armes Métro stop. But if you take a left out of Guy-Favreau onto rue de la Gauchetière, you will be in **Chinatown** ㊲, a relief after all that enclosed retail space.

TIMING

Just to walk this route briskly will take a minimum of an hour, even on a fine day. The Musée d'Art Contemporain is worthy of at least two hours by itself, so plan on a half-day.

Sights to See

㉕ **Amphithéâtre Bell.** Skating is a passion in Montréal, and you can do it year-round in this indoor ice rink on the ground floor of a skyscraper. The rink is bathed in natural light and surrounded by cafés, a food court, and a winter garden. It's open to skaters of all levels of experience; skate rentals and lockers are available. There are also skating lessons, Saturday- and Sunday-night disco skating, and scheduled ice shows. To find the rink once you're inside the building, remember the French word for skating rink is *patinoire.* ⊠ *1000 rue de la Gauchetière,* ☎ *514/ 395–0555.* 🎫 *$5, skate rental $4.* ⊙ *Sun.–Thurs. 11:30 AM–9PM, Fri. 11:30 AM–10 PM, Sat. 11:30–7 for all ages; Sat. 7 PM–10 PM for those 16 and older, Sat. 10–11 for those under 12.*

30 **Cathédrale Marie-Reine-du-Monde** (Mary Queen of the World Cathedral). Seat of the Roman Catholic archbishop of Montréal, this church (1894) is modeled after St. Peter's Basilica in Rome. Victor Bourgeau, the same architect who did the interior of Notre-Dame in Vieux-Montréal, thought the idea of the cathedral's design terrible but completed it after the original architect proved incompetent. Inside there is even a canopy over the altar that is a miniature copy of Bernini's baldachin in St. Peter's. ⊠ *1085 rue de la Cathédral; through main doors on blvd. René-Lévesque.*

27 **Centre Molson.** This arena is the new (1996) home of the Montréal Canadiens, the hockey team hometown fans call simply *les Glorieux.* The brown-brick building replaces the old Forum that had been the Canadiens' home since 1917. The name refers to the Molson family, who established Montréal's first brewery in the 18th century and whose company, Molson-O'Keefe, owns the hockey team. ⊠ *1260 rue de la Gauchetière Ouest,* ☎ *514/932–2582, 514/925–5656 for tours.* 🎫 *Tour $7.* ⊙ *Tour in English at 11 and 2, in French at 10:30 and 1:30.*

37 **Chinatown.** The Chinese first came to Montréal in large numbers after 1880, following the construction of the transcontinental railroad. They settled in an 18-block area between boulevard René-Lévesque and avenue Viger to the north and south, and near rues Hôtel de Ville and Bleury on the west and east, an area now full of restaurants, food stores, and gift shops. If you have enough energy, stroll south on rue St-Urbain for a block to rue St-Antoine. A half block east is **Steve's Music Store** (⊠ 51 rue St-Antoine Ouest, ☎ 514/878–2216), a shabby warren of five storefronts jammed with just about everything you need to be a rock star except talent. Sooner or later every musician and wannabe musician in the city wanders through it.

NEED A BREAK? **Pho Bang New York** (⊠ 970 blvd. St-Laurent, ☎ 514/954–2032) is a small Vietnamese restaurant on the edge of Chinatown that specializes in traditional noodle soups served in bowls big enough to bathe a small dog. And it's cheap, too—for less than $5, you get soup, a plate of crispy vegetables, and a small pot of tea. The restaurant does not accept credit cards.

33 **Christ Church Cathedral.** This is the main church (1859) of the Anglican diocese of Montréal. In early 1988 the diocese leased the land and air rights to a consortium of developers. The consortium then built **La Maison des Coopérants**, a 34-story office tower behind the cathedral, and a huge retail complex, **Les Promenades de la Cathédrale**, under it. The church has a quiet graceful interior and frequent organ recitals and concerts. ⊠ *535 rue Ste-Catherine Ouest.* ⊙ *Daily 8–6.*

36 **Complexe Desjardins.** The large galleria space in this boutique-rich mall is the scene of all types of performances, from lectures on Japanese massage techniques to pop music. ⊠ *Bordered by rues Ste-Catherine, Jeanne-Mance, and St-Urbain and blvd. René-Lévesque.*

☺ ㉟ **Musée d'Art Contemporain.** The museum's large permanent collection of modern art represents works by Québécois, Canadian, and international artists in every medium. Its more than 5,000 works reflect all the major movements, but it focuses on the works of Québec artists. It has, for example, 72 paintings, 32 works on paper, and a sculpture by Paul-Émile Borduas, one of Canada's most important artists. The museum often has weekend programs, with many child-oriented activities, and almost all are free. The hours for guided tours vary. ⊠ *175 rue Ste-Catherine Ouest,* ☎ *514/847–6226.* ☜ *$6; Wed. evening free.* ☺ *Tues. and Thurs.–Sun. 11–6, Wed. 11–9.*

㉞ **Place des Arts.** The Place des Arts theater is a government-subsidized complex of five very modern theaters. Guided tours of the halls and backstage are available for groups of at least 15. ⊠ *175 rue Ste-Catherine Ouest,* ☎ *514/842–2112 for tickets, 514/285–4270 for information, 514/285–4275 for guided tours.*

㉙ **Place du Canada.** This park has a statue of Sir John A. Macdonald, Canada's first prime minister. In October 1995 the park was the site of a huge rally for Canadian unity that drew more than 300,000 participants from across the country. That patriotic demonstration was at least partly responsible for preserving a slim victory for the pro-unity forces in the subsequent referendum on independence for Québec. At the south end of Place du Canada is **Le Marriott Château Champlain** (☞ Lodging, *below*), known as the Cheese Grater because of its rows and rows of half-moon-shape windows. ⊠ *Bordered by blvd. René-Lévesque and rue de la Gauchetière.*

㉓ **Place Ville-Marie.** This cross-shape 1962 office tower was Montréal's first modern skyscraper; the mall complex underneath it was the first link in the Underground City. ⊠ *Bordered by blvd. René-Lévesque and rues Mansfield, Cathcart, and University.*

NEED A BREAK? The once grim passageways at the back of Central Station just below the escalators leading to Place Ville-Marie now house a trendy food court, **Les Halles de la Gare.** The food includes some of the city's best bread and pastries, salads, and sandwiches made with fresh terrines and pâtés. If it's nice out, you can take your snack up the escalator to the mall under Place Ville-Marie and then up the stairs in the middle of its food court to the terrace, a wide area with a fine view.

㉔ **Le Reine Elizabeth.** One of the city's major hotels (☞ Lodging, *below*) straddles the **Gare Centrale** (Central Station), where most trains from the United States and the rest of Canada arrive. ⊠ *900 blvd. René-Lévesque,* ☎ *514/861–3511.*

㉘ **St. George's.** A jewel of neo-Gothic architecture, the prettiest Anglican church in the city was built in 1872. St. George's dimly reverent interior has a beamed wooden ceiling, a richly carved choir screen, and some fine stained-glass windows. ⊠ *1101 rue Stanley.*

OFF THE BEATEN PATH **ST. PATRICK'S BASILICA –** A gem of church architecture rarely visited by tourists, this 1847 church is one of the purest examples of the Gothic Revival style in Canada. It is to Montréal's English-speaking Catholics what the Basilique Notre-Dame is to the city's French-speaking Catholics. The church's colors are soft, and the vaulted ceiling over the sanctuary glows with green and gold mosaics. The old pulpit has panels depicting the Apostles, and a huge lamp decorated with six 6-ft-high angels hangs over the main altar. The church is just three blocks west of Place Ville-Marie. ⊠ *460 blvd. René-Lévesque Ouest,* ☎ *514/866–7379.* ☺ *Daily 8:30–6.*

③ **Square Dorchester.** Until 1870 a Catholic burial ground occupied this downtown park, and there are still bodies buried beneath the grass. The statuary includes a monument to the Boer War and statues of Scottish poet Robert Burns and Sir Wilfrid Laurier, Canada's first French-speaking prime minister. ✉ *Bordered by rues Peel, Metcalfe, and McTavish.*

③ **Sun Life Building.** At one time this was the largest building in the British Commonwealth. During World War II much of England's financial reserves and national treasures were stored in Sun Life's vaults. ✉ *1155 rue Metcalfe.*

㉖ **Windsor Station.** This magnificent building with its massive stone exterior and steel-and-glass roof was once the eastern passenger terminus for the Canadian Pacific Railway, Canada's first transcontinental link. Alas, today it is a trainless shell. ✉ *1100 rue de la Gauchetière.*

Golden Square Mile

As Montréal grew in confidence and economic might in the 19th century, the city's prosperous merchant class moved north, building lavish stone homes on the slopes of Mont-Royal. In fact, at the turn of the century, the people who lived here—mostly of Scottish descent—controlled 70% of the country's wealth. Their baronial homes and handsome churches—Protestant, of course—covered the mountain north of rue Sherbrooke roughly between avenue Côte-des-Neiges and rue University.

Humbler residents south of rue Sherbrooke referred to the area simply as the Square Mile, a name immortalized in novelist Hugh MacLennan's *Two Solitudes*. The Square Mile was eventually gilded by newspaper columnist Al Palmer in the 1950s, long after its golden age had passed. Real Square Milers like actor Christopher Plummer still bridle at the extra adjective. Many of the area's palatial homes have been leveled to make way for high-rises and office towers, but it is still studded with architectural gems, and rue Sherbrooke is still the city's most elegant street.

This walk takes in much of the Square Mile along with an area named Shaughnessy Village to the southwest, bounded roughly by rues Atwater and Guy to the west and east and rue Sherbrooke and boulevard René-Lévesque to the north and south. The village takes its name from the very lush Shaughnessy Mansion on boulevard René-Lévesque, a house that would fit in quite comfortably up the hill in the Square Mile. But while most of the Shaughnessy family's 19th-century neighbors were well-off businesspeople and professionals who lived in elegantly comfortable homes, they certainly weren't wealthy enough to make it into the Square Mile.

A Good Walk

This walk starts at the Guy–Concordia Métro station at the rue Guy exit. The statue just north of the station on the little triangular slice of land in the middle of boulevard de Maisonneuve portrays Norman Bethune, a McGill University–trained doctor from Gravenhurst, Ontario, who served with the Loyalists in the Spanish civil war and died in China in 1939 while serving with Mao's Red Army. Walk south to rue Ste-Catherine and turn right. The long building on the south side of the street used to be a car dealership and bowling alley until it was transformed into the Faubourg Ste-Catherine, an enclosed market selling specialty foods, pastries, bagels, and ethnic lunches.

At rue St-Mathieu, turn left and head south. The huge gray building on the left side of the street is **Couvent des Soeurs Grises** ㊳, the motherhouse of an order of nuns founded by St. Marguerite d'Youville, Canada's first native-born saint. Across from the convent, turn right down rue Baile and into the heart of Shaugnessy Village, named for a family mansion that now forms part of **Le Centre Canadien d'Architecture** ㊴. Many of the area's town houses and mansions were torn down during the philistine '60s to make way for boxy high-rises, but a few remain. Note, for example, the fine row of stone town houses just across rue Baile from Le Centre Canadien d'Architecture.

Turn right on rue Fort and walk north four blocks to rue Sherbrooke. On the north side of the street you will see a complex of fine neoclassical buildings in a shady garden. This is the **Grand Séminaire de Montréal** ㊵, which trains priests for Montréal's Roman Catholic parishes. The two stone towers on the property are among the oldest buildings on the island. In 1928, the anticlerical Freemasons built their windowless and grandly Greek Masonic Temple right across the street at Number 1859.

Walk east along stately rue Sherbrooke past rows of exclusive shops and galleries housed in old town houses to the **Musée des Beaux-Arts de Montréal** ㊶ at the corner of rues Sherbrooke and du Musée. This houses the city's main art collection, which includes works from around the world. Right behind it is the **Musée des Arts Décoratifs de Montréal** ㊷, with its fine collection of furniture, hangings, and decorations. Farther east on rue Sherbrooke is the small and exclusive **Holt Renfrew** ㊸ department store, perhaps the city's fanciest, at the corner of rue de la Montagne. **Rue de la Montagne** and **rues Crescent and Bishop,** the two streets just west of it, are filled with trendy restaurants, shops, and bars. One block farther east on the south side of rue Sherbrooke at rue Drummond stands the **Ritz-Carlton Kempinski** ㊹, the grande dame of Montréal hotels. Right across from the Ritz is Le Château (1926), a huge, copper-roofed apartment building that looks somewhat like a cross between a French Renaissance château and a Scots castle. It is one of the few samples of gracious living left west of rue Atwater. Others worth looking at are the Corby House (✉ 1201 rue Sherbrooke Ouest) and the Maison Louis-Joseph Forget next door (✉ 1195 rue Sherbrooke Ouest). One of the area's most magnificent homes, however, is on rue Drummond just south of Sherbrooke. The **George Stephen House** ㊺ was built for the founder of the Canadian Pacifice Railway and is now the Mount Stephen Club, a private gathering place for Montréal business leaders.

The campus of **McGill University** ㊻ is on the north side of rue Sherbrooke just three blocks east of the Ritz-Carlton. Opposite its main gates is the Banque Commerciale Italienne (✉ 888 rue Sherbrooke Ouest), housed in a beautiful neo-Elizabethan house built in 1906 for Dr. William Alexander Molson, a scion of Montréal's most famous brewing family. A block farther east is the **Musée McCord de l'Histoire Canadienne** ㊼, one of the best history museums in Canada.

TIMING

To walk this route briskly will take a minimum of 90 minutes, but the area is rich in places—the Musée des Beaux-Arts, the Musée des Art Décoratifs, the Musée McCord de l'Histoire Canadienne, the Musée d'Art Contemporain, the Couvent des Soeurs Grises—that all deserve longer visits. It's easy to spend a day or more here.

Sights to See

㊴ **Le Centre Canadien d'Architecture** (Canadian Center for Architecture). The center's rotating exhibits on the history and philosophy of architecture are displayed in an ultramodern building and tend to be a bit academic. The attached Shaughnessy Mansion, with its paneled conservatory and vast reception rooms, is worth a look; so is the amusing sculpture garden across the street. ✉ *1920 rue Baile,* ☎ *514/939–7000.* 🎟 *$5.* ⊘ *Wed. and Fri. 11–6, Thurs. 11–8, weekends 11–5.*

㊳ Couvent des Soeurs Grises. *Soeurs grises* translates as "gray nuns," but the name has nothing to do with the color of the good sisters' habits. Their founder, St. Marguerite d'Youville (1701–71), started looking after the city's down-and-outs after her unhappy marriage to a whiskey trader ended in widowhood. Her late husband's profession and the condition of many of her clients earned her and her colleagues the sobriquet "soeurs grises," which is slang for tipsy nuns. The order ran a public hospital, opened the city's first nursing schools, and operated shelters for abandoned children. They still administer hospitals, shelters for battered women, halfway houses, and nursing homes. The order moved to this vast, graystone convent in 1874. Highlights are the beautiful Romanesque Revival chapel that was restored in 1996, the church crypt where many of the pioneer members are buried, and a small museum containing mementos of the saint's life—her books, the knife and fork she used at boarding school, a re-creation of her simple room—as well as artifacts of the order's history. ✉ *1185 rue St-Mathieu,* ☎ *514/937–9501.* 🎟 *Free.* ⊘ *Wed.–Sun. 1:30–4:30.*

㊺ George Stephen House. Scottish-born George Stephen, founder of the Canadian Pacific Railway, spent $600,000 to build this impressive home in 1883—an almost unimaginable sum at the time. He imported artisans from all over the world to panel its ceilings with Cuban mahogany, Indian lemon tree, and English oak and to decorate its walls with marble, onyx, and gold. The house is a private club now, but most Sundays, visitors can drop in for a guided tour or, if they reserve ahead, a sumptuous brunch ($25) of braised duck or roast beef served to the accompaniment of live music. ✉ *1440 rue Drummond,* ☎ *514/849–7338 for information on guided tours and brunches. Closed to public mid-July–Aug. and over Christmas.*

㊵ Grand Séminaire de Montréal. The Montréal Roman Catholic archdiocese trains its priests here in buildings that date to 1860. Two squat towers in the gardens date to the 17th century, and it was in one of these that St. Marguerite Bourgeoys set up her first school for native girls. The towers, among the oldest buildings on the island, are visible from the street; a little area just by the gates has three plaques that explain the towers and their history in French. The seminary is private, but you can go to Mass at 10:30 on Sunday morning from September through June in the lovely neoclassical chapel. ✉ *2065 rue Sherbrooke Ouest.*

㊸ Holt Renfrew. This is perhaps the city's fanciest department store (☞ Shopping, *below*). ✉ *1300 rue Sherbrooke Ouest,* ☎ *514/842–5111.*

㊻ McGill University. James McGill, a wealthy Scottish fur trader, bequeathed the money and the land for this institution, which opened in 1828 and is perhaps the finest English-language university in the nation. The student body numbers 15,000, and the university is best known for its medical and engineering schools. Most of the campus buildings are fine examples of Victorian architecture. ✉ *845 rue Sherbrooke Ouest.*

NEED A BREAK?   The **McGill University campus** is an island of green in a sea of traffic and skyscrapers. On a fine day you can sit on the grass in the shade of a 100-year-old tree and just let the world drift by.

㊷ Musée des Arts Décoratifs de Montréal. Homey things like coffeepots and chairs—some of them wildly stylish—are displayed in an ultramodern setting. The museum is attached to the ☞ **Musée des Beaux-Arts** by a glass atrium. ✉ *2200 rue Crescent,* ☎ *514/284–1242.* 🖱 *$4.* ⏱ *Tues. and Thurs.–Sun. 11–6, Wed. 11–9.*

🟠 **Musée des Beaux-Arts de Montréal** (Museum of Fine Arts). The oldest museum in the country was founded by a group of English-speaking Montrealers in 1860. The art collection is housed in two buildings—the older Benaiah-Gibb Pavilion on the north side of rue Sherbrooke and the glittering glass-fronted Pavilion Jean-Noël-Desmarais right across the street. The two buildings are connected by underground tunnels and hold a large collection of European and North American fine and decorative art; ancient treasures from Europe, the Near East, Asia, Africa, and America; art from Québec and Canada; and Native American and Eskimo artifacts. The museum is particularly strong in 19th-century works and has one of the finest collections of Canadian paintings, prints, and drawings. It also has a gift shop, an art-book store, a restaurant, a cafeteria, and a gallery from which you can buy or rent paintings by local artists. ✉ *1380 rue Sherbrooke Ouest,* ☎ *514/ 285–1600.* 🖱 *Permanent collection free, special exhibitions $10.* ⏱ *Tues. and Thurs.–Sun. 11–6, Wed. 11–9.*

🐾 🟠 **Musée McCord de l'Histoire Canadienne.** A grand, eclectic attic of a museum, the McCord documents the life of ordinary Canadians, using costumes and textiles, decorative arts, paintings, prints and drawings, and the 450,000-print-and-negative Notman Photographic Archives, which highlights 19th-century life in Montréal. The McCord is the only museum in Canada with a permanent costume gallery. There are guided tours (call for times), a reading room and documentation center, a gift shop and bookstore, and a café. ✉ *690 rue Sherbrooke Ouest,* ☎ *514/ 398–7100.* 🖱 *$7.* ⏱ *Tues.– Wed. and Fri. 10–6, Thurs. 10–9, weekends 10–5. Closed Mon. except statutory holidays.*

🟠 **Ritz-Carlton Kempinski.** The grande dame of Montréal hotels (☞ Lodging, *below*) has been in business since 1912. ✉ *1228 rue Sherbrooke Ouest,* ☎ *514/842–4212.*

Rues de la Montagne, Crescent, and **Bishop.** Today dozens of trendy bars, restaurants, and bistros are ensconced in the old row houses that line these streets between boulevard René-Lévesque and rue Sherbrooke. This area once formed the playing fields of the Montréal Lacrosse and Cricket Grounds. Later it became an exclusive suburb lined with millionaires' row houses.

Quartier Latin

Early in this century, rue St-Denis cut through a bourgeois neighborhood of large, comfortable residences. The Université de Montréal was established here in 1893, and the students and academics who moved into the area dubbed it the Quartier Latin, or Latin Quarter. The university eventually moved to a larger campus on the north side of Mont-Royal, and the area went into decline. It revived in the early 1970s, largely as a result of the 1969 opening of the Université du Québec à Montréal and the launch of the International Jazz Festival in the summer of 1980. Plateau Mont-Royal, the trendy neighborhood just north of the Quartier Latin, shared in this revival. Residents are now a mix of immigrants, working-class Francophones, and young professionals eager to find a home they can renovate close to the city center. The Quartier Latin and Plateau Mont-Royal are home to rows of French and ethnic restaurants, charming bistros, coffee shops, designer boutiques, antiques shops, and art galleries. When night falls, these streets are always full of omnilingual hordes—young and not so young, rich and poor, established and still studying.

Many of the older residences in this area have graceful wrought-iron balconies and twisting staircases that are typical of Montréal. They were built that way for practical reasons. The buildings are what Montrealers call duplexes or triplexes, that is, two or three residences stacked on top of each other. To save interior space, the stairs to reach the upper floors were put outside. The stairs and balconies are treacherous in winter, but in summer they are often full of families and couples, gossiping, picnicking, and partying. If Montrealers tell you they spend the summer in Balconville, they mean they don't have the money or the time to leave town and won't get any farther than their balcony.

A Good Walk

Begin at the Berri-UQAM Métro stop. The "UQAM" in the subway name is pronounced "oo-kam" by local Francophones and "you-kwam" by local Anglophones. It refers to the **Université du Québec à Montréal** ㊽, whose drab brick campus fills up much of three city blocks between rues Sanguinet and Berri. A few splendid fragments of the old Église St-Jacques poke up amid this modern dreck. A more substantial religious monument that has survived intact right in UQAM's resolutely secularist heart is the ornate **Chapelle Notre-Dame-de-Lourdes** ㊾, on rue Ste-Catherine.

Just west of rue St-Denis you find the **Cinémathèque Québécoise** ㊿, which houses one of the largest cinematic reference libraries in the world. Around the corner and a half block north on rue St-Denis stands the 2,500-seat **Théâtre St-Denis** (51), the city's second-largest auditorium. On the next block north is the **Bibliothèque Nationale du Québec,** which houses Québec's official archives.

Turn left on Sherbrooke and left again on boulevard St-Laurent for the **Musée Juste pour Rire** (52), the world's first museum of humor. Backtrack east on rue Sherbrooke, turn left on rue St-Denis, and walk north to **Square St-Louis** (53), a lovely green space.

The stretch of **rue Prince Arthur** (54), beginning at the western end of Square St-Louis and continuing several blocks west, is a center of youth culture. When you reach **boulevard St-Laurent** (55), take a right and stroll north through Montréal's ethnic diversity. This area was still partly rural in the mid-19th century, with lots of fresh air, which made it healthier than overcrowded Vieux-Montréal. So in 1861 the Hôpital Hôtel-Dieu, the hospital Jeanne Mance founded in the 17th century, moved into a new building at what is now the corner of avenue des Pins and rue St-Urbain, just a block west of boulevard St-Laurent. Hôtel-Dieu, one of the city's major hospitals, is still there, and right next to it is the **Musée des Hospitalières de l'Hôtel-Dieu** (56), which gives a remarkable picture of the early days of colonization.

Merchants are attempting to re-create rue Prince Arthur on **rue Duluth** (57). Turn right and walk four blocks east to rue St-Denis, where you will find Greek and Vietnamese restaurants and boutiques and art galleries. Walk east another nine blocks and you come to **Parc Lafontaine,** the smallest of Montréal's three major parks.

After exploring the park's 100 acres, walk south to rue Sherbrooke Est and then turn right and walk west on rues Sherbrooke and Cherrier to the Sherbrooke Métro station to complete the walk. Or head west to explore Parc du Mont-Royal (☞ *below*).

Quartier Latin and Parc du Mont-Royal

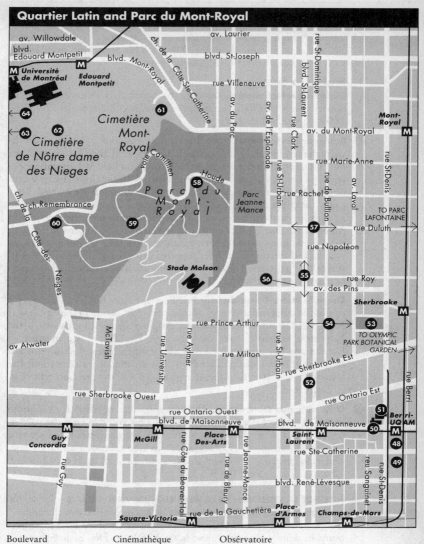

Boulevard
St-Laurent, **55**
Chalet du
Mont-Royal, **59**
Chapelle Notre-
Dame-de-Lourdes, **49**
Cimetière
Mont-Royal, **61**
Cimetière Notre-
Dame-des-Neiges, **62**

Cinémathèque
Québécoise, **50**
Collège Notre
Dame, **64**
Lac aux Castors, **60**
Musée des
Hospitalières de
l'Hôtel-Dieu, **56**
Musée Juste
pour Rire, **52**

Obsérvatoire
de l'Est, **58**
Oratoire St-Joseph, **63**
Rue Duluth, **57**
Rue Prince Arthur, **54**
Square St-Louis, **53**
Théâtre St-Denis, **51**
Université du
Québec à
Montréal, **48**

TIMING

This is a comfortable afternoon walk, lasting perhaps two hours, longer if you linger for an hour or so in the Musée des Hospitalières and spend some time shopping. There's a bit of a climb from boulevard de Maisonneuve to rue Sherbrooke.

Sights to See

Bibliothèque Nationale du Québec. This Beaux-Arts library built in 1915 houses Québec's official archives. ⊠ *1700 rue St-Denis,* ☎ *514/873–1100.* ⊙ *Tues.–Sat. 9–5.*

⑤ **Boulevard St-Laurent.** Depending on how you look at it, this street divides the city into east and west or it's where East and West meet. After the first electric tramway was installed on boulevard St-Laurent, working-class families began to move in. In the 1880s the first of many waves of Jewish immigrants escaping pogroms in eastern Europe arrived. They called the street the Main, as in "Main Street." The Jews were followed by Greeks, Eastern Europeans, Portuguese, and, most recently, Latin Americans. The 10 blocks north of rue Sherbrooke are filled with delis, junk stores, restaurants, luncheonettes, and clothing stores, as well as fashionable boutiques, bistros, cafés, bars, nightclubs, bookstores, and galleries. The block between rues Roy and Napoléon is particularly rich in delights.

㊾ **Chapelle Notre-Dame-de-Lourdes.** This tiny Roman Catholic chapel is one of the most ornate pieces of religious architecture in the city. It was built in 1876 and decorated with brightly colored murals by artist Napoléon Bourassa, who lived nearby. The chapel is a mixture of Roman and Byzantine styles, and the beautifully restored interior is a must-see, despite the panhandlers that cluster at its doors and the somewhat eccentric devotees it attracts. ⊠ *430 rue Ste-Catherine Est.* ⊙ *Daily 8–5.*

㊿ **Cinémathèque Québécoise.** This museum and repertory movie house is one of Montréal's great bargains. For $4 you can visit the permanent exhibition on the history of filmmaking equipment and see two movies. Expansion in 1997 added two exhibition rooms and a TV documentary center. ⊠ *335 blvd. de Maisonneuve Est,* ☎ *514/842–9763.* 🎫 *$3.* ⊙ *Tues.–Sun. 11–9.*

OFF THE
BEATEN PATH

ÉGLISE DE LA VISITATION DE LA BIENHEUREUSE VIERGE MARIE – Far to the north on the banks of Rivière des Prairies is the oldest extant church on the island of Montréal, the Church of the Visitation of the Blessed Virgin Mary. Its stone walls were raised in the 1750s, and the beautifully proportioned Palladian front was added in 1850. The task of decorating lasted from 1764 until 1837, with simply stunning results. The altar and the pulpit are as ornate as wedding cakes and as delicate as starlight. Mid-afternoon is the best time to visit, when the light in the church is soft and subtle. The church's most notable treasure is a rendering of the Visitation attributed to Pierre Mignard, a painter in the 17th-century court of Louis XIV. The church is a 15-minute walk from the Henri Bourassa Métro station, but the trek is worth it. Parkland surrounds the church, and the nearby Iles de la Visitation (reachable by footbridge) make a delightful walk. ⊠ *1847 blvd. Gouin Est,* ☎ *514/388–4050.* ⊙ *Daily 10–6.*

㊺ **Musée des Hospitalières de l'Hôtel-Dieu.** More than just a fascinating and sometimes chilling exhibit on the history of medicine and nursing, this museum captures the spirit of an age. France in the 17th century was consumed with religious fervor, and aristocratic men and women often built hospitals, schools, and churches in distant lands. The nuns of the Religieuses Hospitalières de St-Joseph who came to Montréal in the mid-17th century to help Jeanne Mance run the Hôpital Hôtel-Dieu were good examples of this fervor, and much of their spirit is evident in the letters, books, and religious artifacts displayed here. Pay special attention to the beautiful wooden stairway in the museum's entrance hall. ⊠ *201 av. des Pins Ouest,* ☎ *514/849–2919.* ⊠ *$5.* ⊙ *Mid-June–mid-Oct., Tues.–Fri. 10–5, weekends 1–5; mid-Oct.–mid-June, Wed.–Sun. 1–5.*

NEED A BREAK?	**Café Santropol** (⊠ 3990 rue St-Urbain, ☎ 514/842–3110) serves hearty soups, cake, salads, and unusual high-rise sandwiches garnished with fruit (the Jeanne Mance mixes pineapples and chives in cream cheese). The atmosphere is homey, with a molded tin ceiling and a little *terasse* out back. One percent of the profits go to charity, and the staff runs a meals-on-wheels program. Credit cards are not accepted.

52 **Musée Juste pour Rire** (Just for Laughs Museum). This is the first museum in the world to be dedicated to laughter. Its multimedia exhibits explore and celebrate humor by drawing visitors into their plots. Some of the visiting exhibits have a serious side, too. There is a large collection of humor videos, a cabaret where budding comics can test their material, and a restaurant where you can watch old tapes while you eat. ⊠ *2111 blvd. St-Laurent,* ☎ *514/845–2322.* ⊠ *$9.95.* ⊙ *Tues.–Sun. 1–8.*

Parc Lafontaine. Montréal's two main cultures are reflected in the layout of this very popular park: The eastern half is pure French, with paths, gardens, and lawns laid out in geometric shapes; the western half is very English, with meandering paths and irregularly shaped ponds that follow the natural contours of the land. In summer there are two artificial lakes where you can enjoy paddleboats, bowling greens, tennis courts, and an open-air theater with free arts events. In winter the two artificial lakes form a large skating rink. ⊠ *3933 av. Parc Lafontaine,* ☎ *514/872–6211.* ⊙ *Daily 9 AM–10 PM.*

57 **Rue Duluth.** Modest little ethnic restaurants with outdoor terraces have sprouted along the street, along with crafts boutiques and a few shops selling collectibles such as cookie jars and bottles.

54 **Rue Prince Arthur.** In the 1960s the young people who moved to the neighborhood transformed this street into a small hippie bazaar of clothing, leather, and smoke shops. It remains a center of youth culture, although it's now much tamer and more commercial. The city turned the blocks between avenue Laval and boulevard St-Laurent into a pedestrian mall. Hippie shops have metamorphosed into inexpensive Greek, Vietnamese, Italian, Polish, and Chinese restaurants and little neighborhood bars. ⊠ *Beginning at western end of Sq. St-Louis and stretching a few blocks west.*

53 **Square St-Louis.** This graceful square has a fountain, benches, and trees and is surrounded by 19th-century homes built in the large, comfortable style of the Second Empire. Originally a reservoir, these blocks became a park in 1879 and attracted upper-middle-class families and artists. French-Canadian poets were among the most famous creative people to occupy the houses back then, and the neighborhood is now home to painters, filmmakers, musicians, and writers. On the wall of 336 Square St-Louis you can see—and read, if your French is good—a long poem by Michel Bujold. ⊠ *Bordered by av. Laval and rue St-Denis.*

51 **Théâtre St-Denis.** This is the second-largest auditorium in Montréal (after Salle Wilfrid Pelletier in Place des Arts). Sarah Bernhardt and many

other famous actors have graced its stage. ✉ *1594 rue St-Denis,* ☎
514/849–4211.

48 **Université du Québec à Montréal.** Part of a network of provincial
campuses set up by the provincial government in 1969, UQAM is housed
in a series of massive, modern brick buildings that clog much of the
three city blocks bordered by rues Sanguinet and Berri and boulevards
de Maisonneuve and René-Lévesque. The splendid fragments of Gothic
grandeur sprouting up among the modern brick hulks like flowers in
a swamp are all that's left of Église St-Jacques.

Parc du Mont-Royal

Parc du Mont-Royal is 494 acres of forest and paths in the heart of
the city. Frederick Law Olmsted, the architect of New York's Central
Park, designed this park. He believed that communion with nature could
cure body and soul, and the park follows the natural topography and
accentuates its features, in the English style. You can jog, cycle, stroll
the miles of paths, or just scan the horizon from one of two lookouts.
Horse-drawn transport is popular year-round: sleigh rides in winter
and calèche rides in summer. On the eastern side of the hill stands the
100-ft steel cross that is the symbol of the city. Not far away from the
park and perched on a neighboring crest of the same mountain is the
Oratoire St-Joseph, a shrine that draws millions of visitors and pilgrims
every year.

A Good Walk

Begin by taking the Métro's Orange Line to the Mont-Royal station
and transfer to Bus 11 (be sure to get a transfer—*correspondance* in
French—from a machine before you get on the Métro). The No. 11
drives right through the park on the Voie Camillien Houde. Get off at
the **Obsérvatoire de l'Est** ⑤⑧, a lookout. Climb the stone staircase at the
end of the parking lot and follow the trails to the **Chalet du Mont-Royal** ⑤⑨,
a baronial building with a terrace that overlooks downtown Montréal.
The next stop is **Lac aux Castors** ⑥⓪, and there are at least three ways
to get to this lake. You can take the long way and walk down the steep
flight of stairs at the east end of the terrace and then turn right to follow the gravel road that circles the mountain. The shortest way is to
leave the terrace at the west end and follow the crowds along the road.
The middle way is to leave at the east end, but then to turn off the main
road and follow one of the shaded paths that lead through the woods
and along the southern ridge of the mountain.

Across chemin Remembrance from Lac aux Castors is what looks like
one vast cemetery. It is in fact two cemeteries—one Protestant and the
other Catholic. The **Cimetière Mont-Royal** ⑥① is toward the east in a little valley that cuts off the noise of the city; it is the final resting place
of Anna Leonowens, the real-life heroine of *The King and I*. The yel-
low-brick buildings and tower on the north side of the mountain beyond the cemetery belong to the Université de Montréal, the
second-largest French-language university in the world, with nearly
60,000 students. If you're now humming "Getting to Know You," you'll
probably change your tune to Canada's national anthem when you enter
the **Cimetière Notre-Dame-des-Neiges** ⑥②, as the song's composer, Calixa Lavallée, is buried here.

Wander northwest through the two cemeteries, and you will eventually emerge on chemin Queen Mary on the edge of a decidedly lively
area of street vendors, ethnic restaurants, and boutiques. Walk west
on Queen Mary across chemin Côte-des-Neiges, and you come to
Montréal's most grandiose religious monument, the **Oratoire St-**

Joseph ㉓. Across the street is the ivy-covered **Collège Notre Dame** ㉔, where the oratory's founder, Brother André, worked as a porter. After visiting the church, retrace your steps to chemin Côte-des-Neiges and walk to the Côte-des-Neiges station to catch the Métro.

TIMING
Allot the better part of a day for this tour, longer if you plan on catching some rays or ice-skating in the park.

Sights to See

★ ㉙ **Chalet du Mont-Royal.** The view here overlooks downtown Montréal. In the distance you can see Mont-Royal's sister mountains—Mont St-Bruno, Mont St-Hilaire, and Mont St-Grégoire. These isolated peaks—called the Montérégies, or Mountains of the King—rise quite dramatically from flat surrounding countryside. Be sure to take a look inside the chalet, especially at the murals that depict scenes from Canadian history. There's a snack bar in the back. ⊘ *Daily 9–5.*

㉑ **Cimetière Mont-Royal.** This cemetery was established in 1852 by the Anglican, Presbyterian, Unitarian, and Baptist churches and was laid out like a landscaped garden with monuments that are genuine works of art. The cemetery's most famous permanent guest is Anna Leonowens, who was governess to the children of the King of Siam and the real-life model for the heroine of the musical *The King and I.* There are no tours of the cemetery. ⊠ *1297 chemin de la Forêt,* ☎ *514/279–7375.*

㉒ **Cimetière Notre-Dame-des-Neiges.** The largest Catholic graveyard in the city is the final resting place of hundreds of prominent artists, poets, intellectuals, politicians, and clerics. Among them is Calixa Lavallée, who wrote "O Canada." Many of the monuments and mausoleums—scattered along 55 km (34 mi) of paths and roadways—are the work of leading artists. There are no tours of the cemetery, but a book at the reception gates lists graves and their location. ⊠ *4601 chemin Côte-des-Neiges,* ☎ *514/735–1361.*

㉔ **Collège Notre Dame.** Brother André, founder of the Oratoire St-Joseph, worked as a porter here. It's still an important private school and one of the few in the city that still accept boarders. Its students these days, however, include girls, a situation that would have shocked Brother André. ⊠ *3791 chemin Queen Mary.*

㉚ **Lac aux Castors.** Beaver Lake was reclaimed from boggy ground and so violates Olmsted's purist vision of a natural environment. But children like to float boats on it in summer, and it makes a fine skating rink in winter. ⊠ *Off chemin Remembrance.*

㉘ **Obsérvatoire de l'Est.** This lookout gives a spectacular view of the east end of the city and the St. Lawrence River.

㉓ **Oratoire St-Joseph.** St. Joseph's Oratory, a huge domed church perched high on a ridge of Mont-Royal, is the largest shrine in the world dedicated to the earthly father of Jesus. It is the result of the persistence of a remarkable little man named Brother André, who was a porter in the school that his religious order ran. He dreamed of building a shrine dedicated to St. Joseph—Canada's patron saint—and began in 1904 by building a little chapel. Miraculous cures were reported and attributed to St. Joseph's intercession, and Brother André's project caught the imagination of Montréal. The result is one of the most important shrines in North America. The oratory dome is one of the biggest in the world, and the church has a magnificent setting. It's also home to Les Petits Chanteurs de Mont-Royal, the city's finest boys' choir. But alas, the interior is oppressive and drab. There's a more modest and quite undistinguished crypt church at the bottom of the structure, and right behind it is a room that glitters with hundreds of votive candles lit in honor of St. Joseph. The walls are festooned with crutches discarded by the cured. Right behind that is the simple tomb of Brother André, who was beatified in 1982. Brother André's heart is displayed in a glass case upstairs in a small museum depicting events in his life. From early December through February the oratory has a display of crèches (nativity scenes) from all over the world. High on the mountain beside the main church is a beautiful garden, commemorating the Passion of Christ with life-size representations of the 14 traditional Stations of the Cross. Carillon, choral, and organ concerts are held weekly at the oratory during the summer. To visit the church you can either climb the more than 300 steps to the front door (many pilgrims do so on their knees, pausing to pray at each step) or you can take the shuttle bus that runs from the front gate. ⊠ *3800 chemin Queen Mary, near Côte-des-Neiges Métro station,* ☎ *514/733–8211.* ☉ *Sept.–May, daily 6 AM–9:30 PM; June–Aug., daily 6 AM–10:30 PM.*

Olympic Park and Botanical Garden

The Parc Olympique (Olympic Park) and the Jardin Botanique (Botanical Garden) are in the east end of the city. You can reach them via the Pie-IX or Viau Métro station (the latter is nearer the stadium entrance). The giant, mollusk-shape Stade Olympique and the leaning tower that supports the stadium's roof dominate the skyline of the eastern end of the city. But the area has more to recommend it than just the stadium complex; there's the city's world-class botanical garden, the world's largest museum dedicated to bugs, and Parc Maisonneuve. For guided tours of the Olympic complex, *see* Tour Olympique, *below*.

A Good Walk

Start with a ride on the Métro's Green Line and get off at the Viau station, which is only a few steps from the main entrance to the 70,000-seat **Stade Olympique** ㉖, a stadium built for the 1976 summer games. A trip to the top of the **Tour Olympique** ㉖, the world's tallest tilting structure, can give you a view up to 80 km (50 mi) on a clear day. The six pools of the **Centre Aquatique** ㉖ are under the tower.

Right next to the tower is the **Biodôme** ㉖, where you can explore both a rain forest and an arctic landscape. Continuing your back-to-nature experience, cross rue Sherbrooke to the north of the park (or take the free shuttle bus) to reach the **Jardin Botanique** ㉖, a botanical garden that is the second-largest attraction of its kind in the world. It includes the **Insectarium** ㉀ and the 5-acre **Montréal-Shanghai Lac de Rêve** ㉑, an elegant Ming-style garden.

After you've looked at the flowers, return to boulevard Pie-IX, which runs along the western border of the gardens. The name of this traffic artery (and the adjoining Métro station) puzzles thousands of visitors every year. The street is named for the 19th-century pope Pius IX, or Pie IX in French. It's pronounced Pee-neuf, however, which isn't at all how it looks from an English-speaker's standpoint.

TIMING

To see all the sights at a leisurely pace, you'll need a full day.

Sights to See

㉖ **Biodôme.** Not everyone thought it was a great idea to change an Olympic bicycle-racing stadium into a natural-history exhibit, but the result is one of the city's most popular attractions. It combines four ecosystems—the boreal forest, tropical forest, polar world, and St. Lawrence River—under one climate-controlled dome. You follow protected pathways through each environment, observing flora and fauna

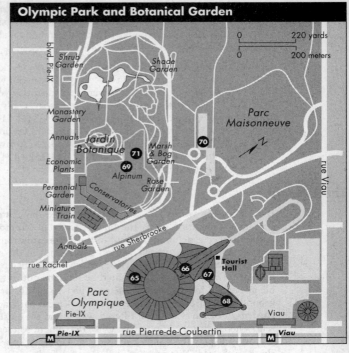

of each ecosystem. A word of warning: The tropical forest really is tropical. If you want to stay comfortable, dress in layers. ⊠ *4777 av.
Pierre-de-Coubertin,* ☎ *514/868–3000.* ⊡ *$9.50.* ⊙ *Daily 9–5.*

67 Centre Aquatique. Olympic swimmers competed here in 1976, but anyone can use the six swimming pools now. ⊠ *4141 av. Pierre-de-Coubertin,* ☎ *514/252–4622.* ⊡ *$3.30.* ⊙ *Opens weekdays at 6 AM;
closes at 10 PM Mon., 7 PM Tues. and Thurs., 9 PM Wed., 5 PM Fri.;
weekends 1–4.*

70 Insectarium. A bug-shape building in the ☞ **Jardin Botanique** houses
more than 250,000 insect specimens. Most are mounted, but the rainbow flies free in the butterfly room, and there are ant and bee exhibits,
too. In February you can taste such delicacies as deep-fried bumblebees.

★ **69 Jardin Botanique.** This botanical garden, with 181 acres of gardens in
summer and 10 exhibition greenhouses open all year, is the second-
largest attraction of its kind in the world (after England's Kew Gardens). The garden was founded in 1931 and has more than 26,000 species
of plants. The poisonous-plant garden is a favorite. Traditional tea ceremonies are held in the Japanese Garden, which also has one of the
best bonsai collections in the West. Other highlights are the ☞ **Insectarium** and the ☞ **Montréal-Shanghai Lac de Rêve.** ⊠ *4101 rue Sherbrooke Est,* ☎ *514/872–1400.* ⊡ *May–Oct. $8.75, Nov.–Apr. $6.50,
combined ticket for Biodôme and Jardin Botanique $14.75.* ⊙ *Week-
days 9–4, weekends 9–8 (Insectarium closes at 5). Metro: Pie-IX.*

71 Montréal-Shanghai Lac de Rêve. These 5 acres in the ☞ **Jardin Botanique**
are the largest Ming-style Chinese garden outside Asia, with seven elegant pavilions and a 30-ft rockery built around a reflecting pool.

65 Stade Olympique. The stadium, built for the 1976 summer games, is
beautiful to look at but not very practical. It's hard to heat, and the

retractable fabric roof, supported by the tower, has never worked properly. Nevertheless, it's home to the Expos of baseball's National League and is used for events like Montréal's annual car show. ✉ *4141 av. Pierre-de-Coubertin,* ☎ *514/252–8687.*

66 **Tour Olympique.** A trip to the top of this tower, the world's tallest tilting structure, is very popular; a two-level cable car can whisk 90 people up the exterior of the 890-ft tower. On a clear day you can see up to 80 km (50 mi) from the tower-top observatory. Daily guided tours of the Olympic complex leave from the **Tourist Hall** (☎ 514/252–8687) in the base of the tower. Tours at 12:40 and 3:40 are in English and the ones at 11 and 2 are in French; cost is $5.25. A tower ride costs $9, a tour plus tower ride is $12; call ☎ 514/252–4141, ext. 5246, to arrange the tour plus tower ride.

The Islands

Expo '67—the world fair staged to celebrate the centennial of the Canadian federation—was the biggest party in Montréal's history, and it marked a defining moment in the city's evolution as a modern metropolis. That party was held on two islands in the middle of the St. Lawrence River—Ile Ste-Hélène, which was formed by nature, and Ile Notre-Dame, which was created by humans out of the stone rubble excavated for Montréal's Métro. The two islands are still a playground—the Parc des Iles has a major amusement park, acres of flower gardens, a beach with clean filtered water, and the Casino de Montréal. There's history, too, at the Old Fort, where soldiers in colonial uniforms display the military skills of ancient wars. In winter you can skate on the old Olympic rowing basin or slide down iced trails on an inner tube. Call for more information on activities and attractions at Parc des Iles (☎ 514/872–6222).

A Good Walk

Start at the Ile Ste-Hélène station on the Métro's Yellow Line. The first thing you'll see when you emerge will be the huge geodesic dome that houses **Biosphere,** an environmental exhibition center. From the Biosphere walk to the northern shore and then east through the Parc des Iles to the **Old Fort,** now a museum of colonial life and a parade ground. Just east of the Old Fort past the Pont Jacques-Cartier (Jacques Cartier Bridge) is **La Ronde,** an amusement park.

Now cross over to the island's southern shore and walk back along the waterfront to the Cosmos Footbridge, which leads to Ile Notre-Dame. On the way you'll pass the Hélène de Champlain restaurant (☞ Dining, *below*), which probably has the prettiest setting of any restaurant in Montréal, and the military cemetery of the British garrison stationed on Ile Ste-Hélène from 1828 to 1870.

Ile Notre-Dame is laced by a network of canals and ponds, and the grounds are brilliant with flower gardens left from the 1980 Floralies Internationales flower show. Most of the Expo '67 buildings are gone, the victims of time and weather. One that has remained, however, is the fanciful French Pavilion. It and the neighboring Québec Pavilion have been turned into the **Casino de Montréal.** A five-minute walk west of the casino is the Lac de l'Ile Notre-Dame, site of **Plage de l'Ile Notre-Dame,** Montréal's only beach. In mid-June Ile Notre-Dame is the site of the Player's Grand Prix du Canada, a top Formula 1 international auto race at the **Circuit Gilles Villeneuve.**

After your walk you can either return to the Métro or walk back to the city via the Pont de la Concorde and the Parc de la Cité du Havre to Vieux-Montréal. If you walk, you'll see **Habitat '67,** an irregular pile of prefabricated concrete blocks that was built as an experiment in housing for Expo.

TIMING

This is a comfortable two-hour stroll, but the Biosphere and the Old Fort (try to time your visit to coincide with a drill display by the colonial troops of the Fraser Highlanders and the Compagnie Franche de la Marine, ☞ *below*) deserve at least an hour each, and you should leave another half hour to admire the flowers. Children will want to spend a whole day at La Ronde, but in summer the best time to go is in the evening when it's cooler. Try to visit the casino during a weekday when the crowds are at their thinnest.

Sights to See

Biosphere. An environmental center in the huge geodesic dome designed by Buckminster Fuller as the American Pavilion at Expo '67 successfully brings fun to an earnest project—heightening awareness of the St. Lawrence River system and its problems. ⊠ *Ile St-Hélène,* ☎ *514/ 496–8300.* 🎟 *$6.50.* ☉ *June–Sept., daily 10–5; Oct.–May, Tues.– Sun. 10–5.*

★ **Casino de Montréal.** This spectacular building was built as the French Pavilion for Expo '67, Montréal's world fair. It's now one of the biggest gambling palaces in the world (☞ Nightlife and the Arts, *below*). ⊠ *Ile Notre-Dame.*

Circuit Gilles Villeneuve. All the big names in motor sports gather at this track every summer for the Player's Grand Prix, one of the racing season's most important Formula 1 events. One of the hottest stars these days is Québécois driver Jacques Villeneuve, who won the world championship in 1997. The track is named for his father, Gilles, who was killed in a racing crash in Belgium in 1982. ⊠ *Ile Notre-Dame.*

Habitat '67. This private apartment complex, a pile of concrete blocks that resembles an updated version of a Hopi cliff dwelling, was designed by Moshe Safdie and built as an experiment in housing for Expo. ⊠ *Av. Pierre-Dupuy.*

☺ **Old Fort.** In summer the grassy parade square of this fine stone fort comes alive with the crackle of colonial musket fire. The French are represented by the Compagnie Franche de la Marine and the British by the kilted 78th Fraser Highlanders, one of the regiments that participated in the conquest of Québec in 1759. The fort itself, built to protect Montréal from American invasion, is now the David M. Stewart Museum at the Fort, which tells the story of colonial life in Montréal through displays of old firearms, maps, and uniforms. The two companies of colonial soldiers raise the flag every day at 11, practice their maneuvers at 1, put on a combined display of precision drilling and musket fire at 2:30, and lower the flag at 5. Children can participate. ⊠ *Ile Ste-Hélène,* ☎ *514/861–6701.* 🎟 *$5.* ☉ *Summer, Wed.– Mon. 10–6; winter, Wed.–Mon. 10–5.*

Plage de l'Ile Notre-Dame. This strip of sand is often filled to capacity in summer. The swimming beach is an oasis, with clear, filtered lake water and an inviting stretch of lawn and trees. Lifeguards are on duty, a shop rents swimming and boating paraphernalia, and there are picnic areas and a restaurant. 🎟 *$3.* ☉ *Daily.*

☺ **La Ronde.** A world-class amusement park has Ferris wheels, boat rides, simulator-style rides, and the second-highest roller coaster in the world. It is also the site of the popular Benson & Hedges International Fireworks Competition, which takes place every weekend in June and July. ⊠ *Ile Ste-Hélène,* ☎ *514/872–6222.* 🎟 *$24.75; grounds only (no*

rides) $13. ⊙ *May, weekends 10–9; June 1–20, daily 10–9; June 21–
Sept. 2, daily 11–11; fireworks June–July, weekends, 10 PM–midnight.*

DINING

Montréal has more than 4,500 restaurants of every price range, representing dozens of ethnic groups. When you dine out, you can, of course, order à la carte, choosing each course yourself. But be sure to look for the table d'hôte, a two- to four-course package deal. It's usually cheaper, often offers interesting special dishes, and may also take less time to prepare. If you want to splurge with your time and money, indulge yourself with the *menu de dégustation*, a five- to seven-course dinner executed by the chef. It generally includes soup, salad, fish, sherbet (to refresh the taste buds), a meat dish, dessert, and coffee or tea. At the city's finest restaurants, such a meal for two, along with a good bottle of wine, can cost more than $200 and last four hours; it's worth every cent and every second.

A word about language: Menus in many restaurants are bilingual, but some are in French only. If you don't understand what a dish is, don't be shy about asking; a good server will be delighted to explain. If you feel brave enough to order in French, remember that in French an entrée is an appetizer and what English-speakers call an entrée is a *plat principal*, or main dish.

CATEGORY	COST*
$$$$	over $40
$$$	$30–$40
$$	$20–$30
$	under $20

per person, in Canadian dollars, excluding tax (combined GST of 7% and provincial tax of 7.5% on all meals), service, and drinks

Canadian

$ ✕ **Chez Clo.** Deep in east-end Montréal, where seldom is heard an English word, lies that rarest of the city's culinary finds—authentic Québécois food. A meal could start with a bowl of the best pea soup in the city, followed by a slab of *tourtière* (meat pie), mounds of mashed potatoes, carrots and turnips, and a bowl of gravy on the side. Desserts include bread pudding and several flavors of *renversées* (upside-down cakes). But the specialty is *pudding au chomeur* (literally, pudding for the unemployed), a kind of shortcake smothered in a thick brown-sugar sauce. The service is noisy and friendly and the clientele mostly local. ⊠ *3199 rue Ontario Est,* ☎ *514/522–5348. No credit cards.*

Chinese

$$–$$$$ ✕ **Piment Rouge.** High ceilings, crystal chandeliers, and floor-to-ceiling windows serve as an elegant Edwardian backdrop for excellent Szechuan and northern Chinese food. Starters include beef and banana rolls and sliced kidneys in hot sauce. Crispy shrimp with honeyed walnuts, shredded lamb in spiced sauce, and steamed fish in ginger are among the main dishes. Servings are generous, and prices are high. ⊠ *Le Windsor, 1170 rue Peel,* ☎ *514/866–7816. AE, D, DC, MC, V.*

$$–$$$ ✕ **Zen.** This very fine modern restaurant specializes in "Zen fusion": Asian dishes combining styles from China, Thailand, Indonesia, and Malaysia are all presented with artistic flair. For $27 try the "Zen Experience," picking as many items as you want from a menu of more than 40 magnificently prepared Szechuan items. ⊠ *Le Westin Mont-*

Royal, *1050 rue Sherbrooke Ouest,* ☎ *514/499–0801. Reservations essential. AE, DC, MC, V.*

$–$$ ✗ **Bon Blé Riz.** The food in this little restaurant is flamboyantly Chinese, but the prices are as modest as its unpretentious decor. Shrimp sizzled with onion, green pepper, and carrot, and finely chopped lamb served with celery and bamboo shoots in a peppery anise-flavored sauce are some of the intriguing dishes. The Beijing-style dumplings are good starters. ✉ *1437 rue St-Laurent,* ☎ *514/844–1447. AE, MC, V.*

$–$$ ✗ **Maison Kam Fung.** This bright, airy restaurant serves the most reliable dim sum lunch in Chinatown. Every day from 10 to 3, waiters push a parade of trolleys through the restaurant, carting treats like firm dumplings stuffed with pork and chicken, stir-fried squid, and delicate pastry envelopes filled with shrimp. ✉ *1008 rue Clark,* ☎ *514/878–2888. Reservations not accepted for dim sum. AE, MC, V.*

Continental

$$–$$$$ ✗ **Nuances.** The main restaurant at the Casino de Montréal (☞ The
★ Islands *in* Exploring Montréal, *above*) on Ile Notre-Dame is simply stunning. Diners sit amid rosewood paneling and have a magnificent view of the city. You might start with sautéed duck foie gras with exotic fruits and progress to lightly grilled red tuna with vegetables marinated in balsamic vinegar and olive oil. Even dishes that have been approved by the Québec Heart and Stroke Foundation sound exciting, like the saddle of rabbit pot-au-feu served with mushrooms. ✉ *1 av. de Casino,* ☎ *514/392–2708. Reservations essential. AE, DC, MC, V. No lunch.*

$ ✗ **Chez Better.** Fieldstone walls and casement windows create a classy ambience for this branch of a popular European sausage house. Although the decor is upscale, the limited menu keeps prices down, to only $3.95 in the case of the "Better Special," a satisfying sandwich of a sausage on freshly baked bread. It's a convenient refueling stop if you're touring Vieux-Montréal. The Notre-Dame restaurant is more elegant. ✉ *160 rue Notre-Dame Est,* ☎ *514/861–2617;* ✉ *5400 chemin Côte-des-Neiges,* ☎ *514/344–3971. AE, MC, V.*

Delicatessens

$ ✗ **Bens.** This big, brassy deli serves up cheesecake smothered in chocolate sauce, drinks the color of electric cherry juice, and a "Big Ben Sandwich"—two slices of rye bread enclosing a pink pile of juicy smoked meat (Montréal's version of corned beef). The decor is strictly '50s, with yellow and green walls and institutional furniture. The waiters are often wisecracking characters but incredibly efficient. Beer, wine, and cocktails are served. ✉ *990 blvd. de Maisonneuve Ouest,* ☎ *514/844–1000. Reservations not accepted. MC, V.*

$ ✗ **Schwartz's Delicatessen.** Its proper name is the Montreal Hebrew Delicatessen, but everyone calls it Schwartz's. The sandwiches are huge; the steaks are tender and come with grilled liver appetizers. To drink you'll find nothing stronger than a Coke. The furniture looks like it was rescued from a Salvation Army depot, and the waiters are briskly efficient. Don't ask for a menu (there isn't one) and avoid the lunch hour unless you don't mind long lines. ✉ *3895 blvd. St-Laurent,* ☎ *514/842–4813. Reservations not accepted. No credit cards.*

$ ✗ **Wilensky's Light Lunch.** Since 1932 the Wilensky family has served up its special: salami and bologna on a "Jewish" (kaiser) roll, generously slathered with mustard. You can also get a chopped-egg sandwich, which comes with a pickle and a cherry or pineapple cola from the fountain (there's no liquor license). This neighborhood haunt was a setting for the film *The Apprenticeship of Duddy Kravitz,* from the

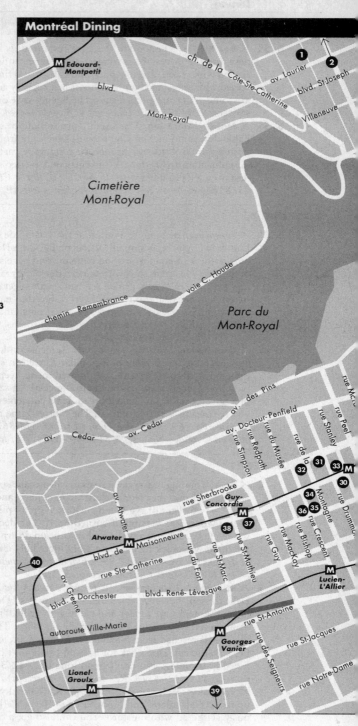

Montréal Dining

0   1/2 mile

0   500 meters

rue Villeneuve

av. du Mont-Royal

Mont-Royal **M**

rue Marie-Anne

rue St-Denis

av. Laval

blvd St-Laurent

de Bullion

St-Urbain

av. du Parc

rue Rachel

av. du Parc-Lafontaine

Parc Lafontaine

av. Calixa-Lavallée

av. de Lorimier

av. Papineau

rue Sherbrooke

av. Duluth

rue Berri

6 **7**

4
5

rue Roy

Cherrier

10

av. des Pins

Sherbrooke **M**

rue Prince Arthur

rue Jeanne-Mance

8

St-Christophe

Robin

Amherst

Panet

Beaudry **M**

9 rue Milton

rue Sherbrooke

rue Ontario

de Maisonneuve

Berri-UQAM **M**

rue Ste-Catherine

11

rue Aylmer

blvd.

St-Hubert

McTavish

av. du President Kennedy

St-Laurent **M**
12

29
av. Victoria

Place des Arts **M**

av. Union

City Councillors
côte du Beaver-Hall

rue de Bleury

blvd. René-Lévesque

rue de la Gauchetière

Champ-de-Mars **M**

McGill **M**
28

27 McGill Col.

26 Peel

25 Mercalfe

Mansfield

24

r. Cathcart

rue University

23

Belmont

13

Place-d'Armes **M**

av. Viger

rue St-Antoine

rue Notre-Dame

14

Bonaventure **M**

Square-Victoria **M**

16 rue St-Xavier

17

15

rue de la Commune

rue de la Montagne

rue Peel

rue McGill

18

19

rue Ottawa

autoroute Bonaventure

rue Murray

20

Fleuve Saint-Laurent

21

22

novel by Mordecai Richler. ✉ *34 rue Fairmount Ouest,* ☎ *514/271–0247. Reservations not accepted. No credit cards. Closed weekends.*

Eclectic

$$$–$$$$ ✕ **Mediterraneo.** Sandstone floors, a space-age ceiling, and huge win-
★   dows that wrap around two walls set off some of the trendiest food in
           Montréal. Dinner could start with tuna sashimi or spring rolls stuffed
           with chicken, spinach, and ricotta, and then move on to duck with sweet
           potatoes, dried cranberries, and a marmalade of pears and exotic
           fruits. ✉ *3500 blvd. St-Laurent,* ☎ *514/844–0027. Reservations es-
           sential. AE, MC, V.*

$$–$$$ ✕ **Bazou.** The name means "jalopy," and a car theme appears in the
★   decor and menu of this charming little eatery. To start, for example,
           you can have Crevettes Thais Suzuki (shrimp cooked with peanut but-
           ter, coriander, chili, and fried spinach), and one main dish is rabbit cooked
           in a "Mustang sauce" of cream, white wine, and mushrooms. This is
           one of the best of Montréal's many "bring-your-own-bottle" restau-
           rants, so you can keep the bill low by buying your plonk at a grocery
           store or an outlet of the government-run Société des Alcools du Québec.
           ✉ *1271 rue Amherst,* ☎ *514/526–4940. AE, MC, V.*

French

$$$$ ✕ **Toqué.** The name means "a bit crazy." Its young and innovative chef-
★   owner, Normand Laprise, and partner Christin LaMarche are among
           the best and most eccentric chefs in the city. They whip market-fresh
           ingredients into dazzling combinations and colors. The menu often fea-
           tures salmon tournedos, smoked salmon, and warm foie gras, all fla-
           vored with fresh ingredients like red peppers, thinly shredded leeks,
           celery roots, and Québec goat cheese. The portions don't look big but
           are surprisingly filling. ✉ *3842 rue St-Denis,* ☎ *514/499–2084. Reser-
           vations essential. AE, DC, MC, V.*

$$$$ ✕ **Les Trois Tilleuls.** About an hour southeast of town, you can lunch
           or dine on delectable food next to the Rivière Richelieu. This small,
           romantic inn, one of the prestigious Relais et Châteaux chain, has a
           terrace and a large, airy dining room with beautiful sunset views. The
           chef specializes in cream of onion soup, sweetbreads, and game dishes.
           ✉ *290 rue Richelieu, St-Marc sur Richelieu,* ☎ *450/584–2231. Reser-
           vations essential. AE, DC, MC, V.*

$$$–$$$$ ✕ **Allumette.** The chef focuses on ingredients from Québec—lamb
★   from the salt marshes of Ile Verte grilled with crushed garlic flowers,
           or caribou cutlets from the tundra served with sweet-potato gnocchi.
           Good dessert choices are the chestnut soufflé and the crème brûlée with
           white chocolate. This small, elegant restaurant with red walls and
           plain white tables is just south of Carré St-Louis. ✉ *3434 rue St-
           Denis,* ☎ *514/284–4239. AE, D, DC, MC, V. No lunch weekends.*

$$$–$$$$ ✕ **Beaver Club.** This fine French restaurant was a social club for the
           city's elite in the 19th century, and it still has the atmosphere of an ex-
           clusive men's club, even if it's open to anyone with a reservation. The
           menu lists such classics as roast prime rib of beef au jus, but more ad-
           venturous offerings include appetizers like cold lobster carpaccio—paper-
           thin slices of raw lobster tail served with wasabi-based sauce—and main
           dishes like panfried salmon fillets sandwiching a layer of grilled egg-
           plant and tomato. There's dancing on Saturday. Service is excellent,
           and the bar serves the best martini in the city. ✉ *Le Reine Elizabeth
           hotel, 900 blvd. René-Lévesque Ouest,* ☎ *514/861–3511. Jacket and
           tie. AE, D, DC, MC, V. Closed Sun. and July. No dinner Mon.*

$$$–$$$$ ✕ **Bonaparte.** Piped-in Mozart serenades diners surrounded by exposed
★   brick walls in a wonderful little restaurant in the heart of Vieux-Mont-

réal. The traditional French dishes here have a light touch. You could start with a wild mushroom ravioli seasoned with fresh sage and move on to a lobster stew flavored with vanilla and served with a spinach fondue, or a roast rack of lamb in a port wine sauce. Lunch is a good value. At press time the restaurant planned to open a little auberge upstairs. ⊠ *443 rue St-François-Xavier,* ☎ *514/844–4368. AE, D, DC, MC, V. No lunch weekends.*

$$$–$$$$ ✕ **Le Café de Paris.** Patrons sit at large, well-spaced tables in a room ablaze with flowers and with light streaming through the French windows. The Ritz garden, with its picturesque duck pond, is open for summer dining alfresco. You can choose from such classics as *escalope de veau Viennoise* or steak tartare. At meal's end the waiter will trundle over the dessert cart; the *royale chocolat* and the *îles flottant* (puffs of soft meringue in custard) are favorites. ⊠ *Ritz-Carlton Kempinski, 1228 rue Sherbrooke Ouest,* ☎ *514/842–4212. Reservations essential. Jacket required. AE, D, DC, MC, V.*

$$$–$$$$ ✕ **Champs Elysées.** Unobtrusive elegance lets the food do the talking in this dining room in the Golden Square Mile. You could start with snails with Parma ham or a simple goat-cheese salad before moving on to quail with grapes or sea bass with fennel. Peach crumble or a crème brûlée lightly flavored with jasmine completes the experience. ⊠ *1800 rue Sherbrooke Ouest,* ☎ *514/499–2084. AE, DC, MC, V.*

$$$–$$$$ ✕ **Les Halles.** Main dishes like Grapefruit Marie-Louise with scallops and lobster or roasted duck with pears sit comfortably beside the chef's ventures into nouvelle cuisine, such as his lobster with herbs and butter. The desserts are classic—the Paris-Brest, a puff pastry with praline cream inside, is one of the best in town. Mirrors, murals, and light colors are part of the Paris-market decor. ⊠ *1450 rue Crescent,* ☎ *514/ 844–2328. Reservations essential. AE, DC, MC, V. Closed Sun. No lunch Mon. or Sat.*

$$$–$$$$ ✕ **Hélène de Champlain.** The food here is good if unadventurous (rack of lamb, fillet of sole amandine, veal marsala, filet mignon with roasted peppers), but people come for the setting. The restaurant is in the middle of the park on Ile Ste-Hélène, with views over the river and the city. The large dining room with its two fireplaces and antique furnishings is delightful. ⊠ *Ile Ste-Hélène near Métro station,* ☎ *514/395–2424. Reservations essential. AE, DC, MC, V.*

$$$–$$$$ ✕ **Le Passe-Partout.** New York–born James MacGuire might make the
★ best bread in Montréal—moist but airy with a tight, crispy crust. He and his wife, Suzanne Baron-Lafrenière, sell this delicacy, along with homemade pâtés and terrines, in a bakery next door to their restaurant. The handwritten menu is short and changes according to mood and availability. You might start with smoked salmon, a potage of curried sweet potatoes, or perhaps a venison terrine. Entrées include swordfish steak served with a puree of red cabbage or loin of veal with poached cucumbers and noodles. ⊠ *3857 blvd. Décarie (5-min walk south from Villa Maria Métro),* ☎ *514/487–7750. Reservations essential. AE, DC, MC, V. No lunch Sat.–Mon., no dinner Sun.–Wed.*

$$$–$$$$ ✕ **Les Remparts.** A stone-walled cellar under the Auberge du Vieux-Port showcases innovative French cooking in an atmosphere redolent of Nouvelle France. Wild mushroom soup with walnut croutons and quail with squash and sage gnocchi are some of the enticing appetizers, fitting preparation for main courses such as venison steak with parsley, salsify root and juniper berries and Atlantic salmon cooked with endives, shallots, and red wine. ⊠ *97 rue de la Commune Est,* ☎ *514/ 392–1649. AE, DC, MC, V.*

$$–$$$$ ✕ **L'Express.** This Paris-style bistro has mirrored walls, a smoky atmosphere, and noise levels that are close to painful on weekends. But the food's good, the service fast, and the prices reasonable. The steak

tartare with french fries, the salmon with sorrel, and the calves' liver with tarragon are marvelous. Jars of gherkins, fresh baguettes, and cheeses aged to perfection make the pleasure last longer. L'Express has one of the best and most original wine cellars in town. ✉ *3927 rue St-Denis,* ☎ *514/845–5333. Reservations essential. AE, DC, MC, V.*

$$–$$$$ ✗ **Guy and Dodo Morali.** Pale yellow walls and lots of art decorate this comfortable restaurant in the very exclusive Cours Mont-Royal shopping plaza. In summer, dining spills out onto a little terrace on rue Metcalfe. Guy's cooking is classic French with a splash of modern flair; his menu is 70% seafood. His daily table d'hôte menu is the best bet, with openers such as excellent lobster bisque followed by *agneau en croûte* (lamb in a pastry) with thyme sauce (a house specialty), or fillet of halibut with leeks. For dessert try the *tatan,* apples and caramel with crème anglaise. ✉ *Les Cours Mont-Royal, 1444 rue Metcalfe,* ☎ *514/842–3636. Reservations essential. AE, D, DC, MC, V.*

$$–$$$ ✗ **Le Caveau.** Lost among the glass-and-steel towers of downtown is
★ an eccentric Victorian house where buttery sauces, creamy desserts, and fairly reasonable prices have survived the onslaughts of inflation and nouvelle cuisine. Appetizers include sautéed brains with a caper mousseline and snails cooked in meat glaze, butter, and Danish blue cheese. A main course might be rabbit cooked with sweet wine, spices, and raisins, or rack of lamb crusted with bread crumbs, mustard, garlic, and herbs. A children's menu—rare in restaurants as fine as Le Caveau—is available. ✉ *2063 av. Victoria,* ☎ *514/844–1624. AE, DC, MC, V.*

Greek

$$$$ ✗ **Milos.** Nets, ropes, and floats hang from Milos's walls and ceilings. The real display, however, is in the refrigerated cases and on the beds of ice in the back by the kitchen—octopus, squid, shrimp, crabs, oysters, and sea urchins. The main dish at Milos is usually fish grilled over charcoal and seasoned with parsley, capers, and lemon juice. It's done to a turn and is achingly delicious. The fish are priced by the pound, and you can order one large fish to serve two or more. You'll also find lamb and veal chops, cheeses, and olives. Milos is a healthy walk from Métro Laurier. ✉ *5357 av. du Parc,* ☎ *514/272–3522. Reservations essential. AE, D, DC, MC, V. No lunch Sat.*

Indian

$$ ✗ **Le Taj.** The cuisine of the north of India, less spicy and more refined than that of the south, is showcased here. The tandoori ovens seal in the flavors of the grilled meat and fish. Vegetarian dishes include the *taj-thali,* made of lentils; basmati rice; and *saag panir*—spicy white cheese with spinach. A nine-course lunch buffet is under $10, and at night there's an "Indian feast" for $20. The desserts—pistachio ice cream or mangoes—are often decorated with pure silver leaves. ✉ *2077 rue Stanley,* ☎ *514/845–9015. AE, MC, V.*

Italian

$$$–$$$$ ✗ **Bocca d'Oro.** This restaurant next to Métro Guy has a huge menu. One pasta specialty is *tritico di pasta:* one helping each of spinach ravioli with salmon and caviar, shellfish marinara, and spaghetti primavera. Also recommended is the *pasta mistariosa*—no cream, no butter, no tomatoes, but delicious nonetheless. With dessert and coffee, the waiters bring out a bowl of walnuts for you to crack at your table. The two-floor dining area is inexplicably decorated with a huge display of golf pictures, and Italian pop songs play in the background. The staff is extremely friendly and professional; if you're in a hurry, they'll serve your meal in record time. ⊠ *1448 rue St-Mathieu,* ☏ *514/933–8414. Reservations essential. AE, DC, MC, V. Closed Sun.*

$ ✕ **Pizzaiole.** Pizzaiole brought the first wood-fired pizza ovens to Montréal, and it's still the best in the field. Whether you choose a simple tomato-cheese or a ratatouille on a whole-wheat crust—there are about 30 possible combinations—all the pizzas are made to order and brought to your table piping hot. The calzone is worth the trip. ⊠ *1446A rue Crescent,* ☏ *514/845–4158;* ⊠ *5100 rue Hutchison,* ☏ *514/274–9349. AE, DC, MC, V.*

Japanese

$$–$$$ ✕ **Katsura.** The sushi chefs in this elegant Japanese restaurant create an assortment of raw seafood delicacies, as well as their own delicious invention, the cone-shaped Canada roll (smoked salmon and salmon caviar). Service is excellent, but if you sample all the sushi, the tab can be exorbitant. ⊠ *2170 rue de la Montagne,* ☏ *514/849–1172. Reservations essential. AE, DC, MC, V. No lunch weekends.*

Polish

$–$$ ✕ **Café Stash.** On chilly nights many Montrealers turn to Café Stash in Vieux-Montréal for sustenance—for pork chops or duck, hot borscht, pierogi, or cabbage and sausage—in short, for all the hearty specialties of a Polish kitchen. Diners sit on pews from an old chapel at refectory tables from an old convent. ⊠ *200 rue St-Paul Ouest,* ☏ *514/845–6611. AE, MC, V.*

Seafood

$$–$$$$ ✕ **Chez Delmo.** The long, shiny wooden bar at Chez Delmo is crammed at lunchtime with lawyers and businesspeople gobbling oysters and fish. In the back is a more relaxed and cheerful dining room. The poached salmon with hollandaise is a nice slab of perfectly cooked fish served with potatoes and broccoli. Also excellent are the arctic char and the Dover sole. ⊠ *211–215 rue Notre-Dame Ouest,* ☏ *514/849–4061. Reservations essential. AE, DC, MC, V. Closed Sun., 3 wks in midsummer, and 3 wks at Christmas.*

$$–$$$ ✕ **Bleu Marin.** Fish here comes with an Italian touch. Antipasto Bleu Marin, for example, includes little plates of baby clams, mussels, and oysters with a light gratinée of crumbs and cheese. All fish are baked or steamed; a main course could be fillets of sea bass, baked in their own juices with olive oil, lemon juice, white wine, and capers. ⊠ *1437A rue Crescent,* ☏ *514/847–1123. AE, D, DC, MC, V.*

Steak

$$$–$$$$ ★ ✕ **Gibby's.** While the extensive menu is rich in items like broiled lobster, Dover sole meunière, and Cajun-blackened grouper, it was Gibby's first-class steaks—some say the best in the city—that made this restaurant famous. Gibby's also boasts its own on-site bakery and makes its own ice cream. The thick gray stone walls here date to 1825, and the attention to service and detail also seems to belong to another age. ⊠ *298 Pl. d'Youville,* ☏ *514/282–1837. AE, D, DC, MC, V.*

$$$–$$$$ ✕ **Moishe's.** The steaks here are big and marbled, and the Lighter brothers still age them in their own cold rooms for 21 days before charcoal grilling them, just the way their father did when he opened Moishe's more than 50 years ago. There are other things on the menu, such as lamb and grilled arctic char—but people come for the beef. The selection of single-malt Scotches is exquisite. ⊠ *3961 blvd. St-Laurent,* ☏ *514/845–3509. AE, DC, MC, V. No lunch.*

$–$$ ✕ **Magnan.** The atmosphere in this tavern in working-class Pointe St-Charles is decidedly and defiantly masculine. The decor is upscale warehouse, and the half dozen television sets are noisily stuck on professional sports. You can't beat the roast beef, though, and the industrial-strength steaks that range from 6 to 22 ounces. Everyone eats here—from dock workers to corporate executives. In summer the tavern adds Québec lobster to its menu and turns its parking lot into an outdoor dining room. It also has excellent beer from several local microbreweries on tap. ✉ *2602 rue St-Patrick,* ☎ *514/935–9647. AE, DC, MC, V.*

$ ✕ **Entrecôte St-Jean.** The shortest menu in the city can be found in this restaurant in the heart of downtown. The choices are a walnut salad followed by french fries and a steak cooked in a special sauce, or the same meal bracketed by the soup du jour and chocolate profiteroles. Lots of brass and polished wood give the place the air of a Paris bistro. ✉ *2002 rue Peel,* ☎ *514/281–6492. AE, DC, MC, V.*

Thai

$ ✕ **Salsa Thai.** It began as a tiny hole in the wall in Chinatown, but Salsa Thai's popularity enabled the owners to move into plusher digs on Square Dorchester. Prices are still reasonable, though, and portions are generous. Some appealing choices are hot-and-sour seafood soup with coconut milk; squid salad with onion, hot chilies, and mint leaves; and deep-fried whole pomfret (butterfish) flavored with garlic and hot green peppers, onions, basil, and Thai seasonings. Frogs' legs are fried with pepper, garlic, and sesame seeds; beef with satay sauce comes on a sizzling hot plate. ✉ *1237 rue Metcalfe,* ☎ *514/874–9047. MC, V.*

LODGING

Keep in mind that during peak season (May–August) it may be difficult to find a bed without reserving, and most, but not all, hotels raise their prices. Rates often drop from mid-November to early April. Throughout the year a number of the better hotels have two-night, three-day double-occupancy packages that offer substantial discounts.

CATEGORY	COST*
$$$$	over $160
$$$	$120–$160
$$	$85–$120
$	under $85

All prices are for a standard double room, excluding 14.5% tax, in Canadian dollars.

$$$$ 🏨 **Le Centre Sheraton.** This huge 37-story complex is well placed between the downtown business district and the restaurant-lined streets of Crescent and Bishop. It offers services to both the business and tourist crowds. Rooms have coffeemakers, irons, and ironing boards. The 10-story Club section is geared toward business travelers, and there are lots of meeting rooms for conventions. The bar in the busy lobby is in a pleasant forest of potted trees, some of them 30 ft tall. ✉ *1201 blvd. René-Lévesque Ouest, H3B 2L7,* ☎ *514/878–2000 or 800/325–3535,* 𝖥𝖠𝖷 *514/878–3958. 784 rooms, 25 suites. Restaurant, 2 bars, indoor pool, beauty salon, health club, baby-sitting, business services. AE, D, DC, MC, V.*

$$$$ 🏨 **Delta Montréal.** The Delta has the city's most complete exercise and pool facility and an extensive business center. The hotel's public areas spread over two stories and are decorated to look a bit like a French château, with a huge baronial chandelier and gold patterned carpets.

Rooms are big, with plush broadloom, pastel walls, mahogany-veneer furniture, and windows that overlook the mountain or downtown. The Cordial Music bar serves lunch on weekdays. ✉ *475 av. President-Kennedy, H3A 1J7,* ☎ *514/286–1986 or 800/268–1133,* FAX *514/284–4306. 453 rooms, 10 suites. 2 restaurants, bar, indoor and outdoor pools, hot tub, sauna, aerobics, health club, squash, recreation room, video games, baby-sitting, business services. AE, D, DC, MC, V.*

$$$$ 🏨 **Hotel Inter-Continental Montréal.** On the edge of Vieux-Montréal, this luxury hotel is part of the Montréal World Trade Center, a block-long retail and office development. Rooms are in a modern 26-story brick tower with fanciful turrets and pointed roofs. They're large, with lush carpets, pastel walls, heavy drapes, and big windows over-looking downtown or Vieux-Montréal and the waterfront. The main lobby is home to Le Continent, which serves fine international cuisine. ✉ *360 rue St-Antoine Ouest, H2Y 3X4,* ☎ *514/987–9900 or 800/327–0200, 800/361–3600 in the U.S. and Canada,* FAX *514/847–8550. 335 rooms, 22 suites. 2 restaurants, room service, indoor pool, sauna, health club, concierge, meeting rooms. AE, D, DC, MC, V.*

$$$$ 🏨 **Loews Hôtel Vogue.** Tall windows and a facade of polished rose gran-
★ ite grace this chic hotel in the heart of downtown, right across the street from Ogilvy department store. The lobby's focal point, L'Opéra Bar, has an expansive bay window overlooking the trendy rue de la Mon-tagne. Room furnishings are upholstered with striped silk, and the beds are draped with lacy duvets. The bathrooms have whirlpool baths, tele-visions, and phones. ✉ *1425 rue de la Montagne, H3G 1Z3,* ☎ *514/285–5555 or 800/465–6654,* FAX *514/849–8903. 126 rooms, 16 suites. Restaurant, bar, exercise room. AE, D, DC, MC, V.*

$$$$ 🏨 **Ritz-Carlton Kempinski.** This is the closest Montréal comes to a grand
★ hotel. Power meals are the rule at Le Café de Paris (☞ Dining, *above*). Guest rooms are a successful blend of Edwardian style—some suites have working fireplaces—with such modern accessories as electronic safes. Careful and personal attention are hallmarks of the Ritz-Carl-ton's service: Your shoes get shined, there's fresh fruit in your room, and everyone calls you by name. It was good enough for Elizabeth Tay-lor and Richard Burton, who celebrated one of their weddings here. ✉ *1228 rue Sherbrooke Ouest, H3G 1H6,* ☎ *514/842–4212 or 800/223–6800,* FAX *514/842–3383. 201 rooms, 39 suites. Restaurant, bar, piano bar, room service, barbershop. AE, DC, MC, V.*

$$$$ 🏨 **Le Westin Mont-Royal.** Service and hospitality make the Westin
★ stand out among Montréal's best hotels. Its concierge desk can orga-nize anything. The clientele here is primarily corporate, and the large rooms are decorated to serve that market: floral chintzes, plush car-peting, and traditional English furnishings. One of the city's best Chi-nese restaurants is the Zen (☞ Dining, *above*), downstairs. The revamped ground floor holds Opus II, a contemporary French restau-rant with a glassed-in atrium. ✉ *1050 rue Sherbrooke Ouest, H3A 2R6,* ☎ *514/284–1110 or 800/228–3000,* FAX *514/845–3025. 300 rooms, 28 suites. 2 restaurants, lobby lounge, minibars, room service, pool, hot tub, 2 saunas, health club. AE, D, DC, MC, V.*

$$$–$$$$ 🏨 **Bonaventure Hilton International.** The large Hilton occupies the top
★ three floors of the Place Bonaventure exhibition center. From the out-side the massive building is uninviting, but you step off the elevator into an attractive reception area flanked by an outdoor swimming pool (heated year-round) and 2½ acres of gardens—all refurbished with new lighting and a marble floor in the lobby. All rooms have sleek modern furniture, pastel walls, plug-ins for computers, and irons and ironing boards. The Bonaventure has excellent access to the Métro and the Un-derground City. ✉ *1 Pl. Bonaventure, H5A 1E4,* ☎ *514/878–2332 or*

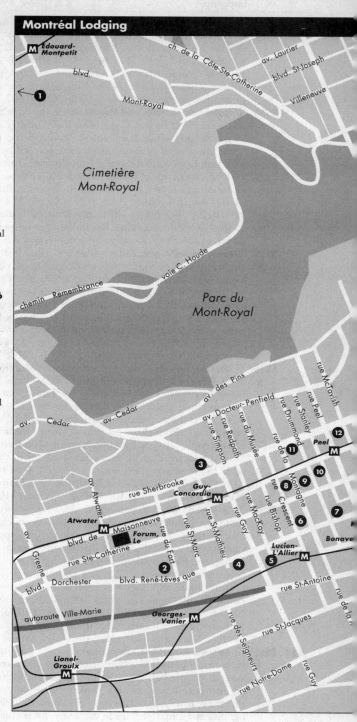

Montréal Lodging

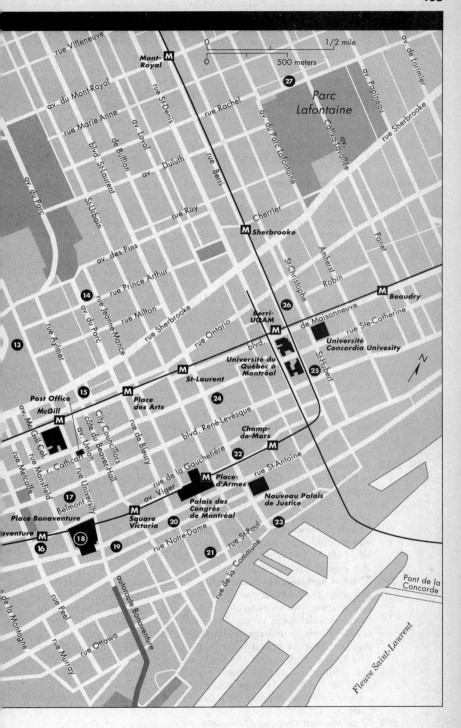

800/267–2575, FAX 514/028–1442. *395 rooms. 3 restaurants, minibars, room service, pool, shops, business services. AE, D, DC, MC, V.*

$$$-$$$$ 🔲 **Hôtel de la Montagne.** Upon entering the reception area you'll be
★ greeted by a naked, butterfly-winged nymph who rises out of a fountain; an enormous crystal chandelier hangs from the ceiling. The decor resembles Versailles rebuilt with a dash of art nouveau, although management prefers to describe it as a mix of Early American and rococo. The rooms are tamer, large and comfortable. There's a piano bar and a rooftop terrace, and a tunnel connects the hotel to Thursdays/Les Beaux Jeudis, a popular singles bar, restaurant, and dance club. ⊠ *1430 rue de la Montagne, H3G 1Z5,* ☎ *514/288–5656 or 800/361–6262,* FAX *514/288–9658. 135 rooms. 2 restaurants, bar, pool, concierge. AE, D, DC, MC, V.*

$$$-$$$$ 🔲 **Le Reine Elizabeth.** In the center of the city, this Canadian Pacific hotel sits on top of the Gare Centrale train station. The lobby is a bit too much like a railroad station—hordes march this way and that—but upstairs the rooms are modern, spacious, and spotless, with lush pale carpets, striped Regency wallpapers, and chintz bedspreads. The Penthouse floors—20 and 21—have business services, and the Gold Floor is a hotel within a hotel with its own elevator, check-in, and concierge. The hotel is home to the Beaver Club (☞ Dining, *above*). Conventions are a specialty here. ⊠ *900 blvd. René-Lévesque Ouest, H3B 4A5,* ☎ *514/861–3511 or 800/441–1414,* FAX *514/954–2256. 1,020 rooms. 2 restaurants, 3 bars, indoor pool, beauty salon, health club, baby-sitting. AE, D, DC, MC, V.*

$$-$$$$ 🔲 **Holiday Inn Select.** This Chinatown hotel is full of surprises, from
★ the two pagodas on the roof to the Chinese garden in the lobby. Its restaurant, Chez Chine, is excellent. An executive floor has all the usual business facilities. The hotel has a pool and a small exercise room, but guests also have access to a plush private health and leisure club downstairs with a whirlpool, saunas, a billiard room, and a bar. The hotel is catercorner to the Palais des Congrès and a five-minute walk from the World Trade Center. ⊠ *99 av. Viger Ouest, H2Z 1E9,* ☎ *514/878–9888 or 888/878–9888,* FAX *514/878–6341. 235 rooms. Restaurant, bar, pool, exercise room, business services. AE, D, DC, MC, V.*

$$-$$$$ 🔲 **Hôtel du Fort.** All rooms here have good views of the city, the river, or the mountain. The hotel is in the west end of downtown in a residential neighborhood known as Shaughnessy Village, close to shopping at the Faubourg Ste-Catherine and Square Westmount, and just around the corner from the Canadian Center for Architecture. Rates include Continental breakfast served in the charming Louis XV Lounge, which doubles as a bar in the evening. ⊠ *1390 rue du Fort, H3H 2R7,* ☎ *514/938–8333 or 800/565–6333,* FAX *514/938–2078. 127 rooms. Bar, exercise room. AE, DC, MC, V.*

$$$ 🔲 **Hôtel Radisson des Gouverneurs de Montréal.** Abutting the stock exchange, the Radisson rises above a three-story atrium-reception area and is attractive to convention crowds. It's near Place Bonaventure, the western fringe of Vieux-Montréal, and the Square Victoria Métro (accessible via an underground passage). There's an exclusive floor for higher-paying guests and a shopping arcade on the underground level. The Tour de Ville on the top floor is the city's only revolving restaurant, and its bar has live music nightly. ⊠ *777 rue University, H3C 3Z7,* ☎ *514/879–1370 or 800/333–3333,* FAX *514/879–1831. 550 rooms, 25 suites. 2 restaurants, bar, indoor pool, steam room, health club. AE, DC, MC, V.*

$$$ 🔲 **Le Marriott Château Champlain.** At the southern end of Place du Canada is this 36-floor skyscraper with distinctive half-moon-shape windows that give the rooms a Moorish feel. The furniture is elegantly French and the bedspreads are brightly patterned. Underground

passageways connect the Champlain with the Bonaventure Métro station and Place Ville-Marie. ⊠ *1050 rue de la Gauchetière Ouest, H3B 4C9,* ☎ *514/878–9000 or 800/200–5909,* FAX *514/878–6761. 611 rooms, 33 suites. Restaurant, bar, no-smoking rooms, indoor pool, sauna, health club. AE, DC, MC, V.*

$$–$$$ ⊞ **Auberge de la Fontaine.** The decor of this small hotel in the heart ★ of the trendy Plateau Mont-Royal district sounds wild—contrasting purple and bare-brick walls, a red molding separating yellow walls from a green ceiling—but the hotel is delightful. Its 21 rooms are scattered over three floors in two turn-of-the-century residences. Some of them have whirlpool baths and a few have private balconies. Guests can use the little ground-floor kitchen and take whatever they like from its fridge full of snacks. The hotel is right on one of the city's bicycle paths and just across the street from Parc Lafontaine. ⊠ *1301 rue Rachel Est, H2J 2K1,* ☎ *514/597–0166 or 800/597–0597,* FAX *514/597–0496. 21 rooms. Meeting room. AE, DC, MC, V.*

$$–$$$ ⊞ **Auberge du Vieux-Port.** A splendid little hotel—27 rooms over five ★ floors—backs onto fashionable rue St-Paul and overlooks the Vieux-Port. The Vieux-Montréal building dates to the 1880s. Rooms have stone or brick walls, tall casement windows, brass beds, and massive exposed beams; many have whirlpool tubs. In summer guests can watch the fireworks competitions from a rooftop terrace. Rates include a full breakfast in Les Remparts, the hotel's French restaurant (☞ Dining, *above*). ⊠ *97 rue de la Commune Est, H2Y 1J1,* ☎ *514/876–0081,* FAX *514/ 876–8923. 27 rooms. Restaurant, coffee shop. AE, DC, MC, V.*

$$–$$$ ⊞ **Auberge les Passants du Sans Soucy.** A little gem on rue St-Paul, ★ the inn is a former fur warehouse dating to 1836—the foundations date to 1684. The lobby is also an art gallery that opens onto the street. Behind it are a living room and a breakfast room separated by a fireplace that crackles with burning hardwood in winter. This is one of the most romantic city hostelries you'll find anywhere, with brass beds, bare stone walls, exposed beams, soft lighting, whirlpool baths, and lots of fresh-cut flowers. A full breakfast is included in the rates. ⊠ *171 rue St-Paul Ouest, H2Y 1Z5,* ☎ *514/842–2634,* FAX *514/842–2912. 8 rooms, 1 suite. Breakfast room. AE, DC, MC, V.*

$$–$$$ ⊞ **Hôtel du Parc.** This L-shape brick tower overlooks Parc du Mont-Royal; the McGill University campus is a five-minute walk to the west. The hotel is a briskly efficient operation, the rooms are large, and the decor is modern with blond wood and pastel shades. A large, comfortable bar dominates the lobby. ⊠ *3625 av. du Parc, H2X 3P8,* ☎ *514/288– 6666 or 800/363–0735,* FAX *514/288–2469. 429 rooms, 20 suites. Restaurant, bar, café, no-smoking floors. AE, D, DC, MC, V.*

$$–$$$ ⊞ **Le Nouvel Hôtel.** This hotel has brightly colored and functional studios and 2½-room apartments. It is near the restaurants and bars on rues Crescent, de la Montagne, and Bishop and is two blocks from the Guy-Concordia Métro station. It is also home to the Comedy Nest Cabaret (☞ Nightlife and the Arts, *below*). ⊠ *1740 blvd. René-Lévesque Ouest, H3H 1R3,* ☎ *514/931–8841 or 800/363–6063,* FAX *514/931–3233. 126 rooms. Restaurant, bar, pool, comedy club. AE, DC, MC, V.*

$$ ⊞ **Château Versailles.** This charming hotel occupies a row of four con- ★ verted mansions on rue Sherbrooke Ouest near Métro Guy-Concordia. The public areas are decorated with antique paintings and tapestries. Some guest rooms have ornate moldings and plaster decorations, and most are generously sized, with comfortable but functional furnishings. Half the rooms have king-size beds. Across the street, at 1808 rue Sherbrooke Ouest, is the 107-room Tour Versailles, a converted apartment hotel that serves as an annex to the original town houses. There is a fine French restaurant, the Champs-Elysées (☞ Dining, *above*), in La

Tour, and a breakfast room in the Château. The staff is extremely helpful and friendly. ⌂ *1659 rue Sherbrooke Ouest, H3H 1E3,* ☎ *514/933–3611 or 800/361–3664, 800/361–7199 in Canada,* ℻ *514/933–7102. 70 rooms in Château; 105 rooms, 2 suites in La Tour. Restaurant, breakfast room. AE, DC, MC, V.*

$–$$ ⌂ **Hôtel Lord Berri.** Rooms in this hotel near the restaurants and nightlife of rue St-Denis have brightly colored bedspreads, modern furniture, and in-room movies. The restaurant, Il Cavaliere, serves Italian food and is popular with locals. ⌂ *1199 rue Berri, H2L 4C6,* ☎ *514/845–9236 or 888/363–0363,* ℻ *514/849–9855. 154 rooms. Restaurant, no-smoking floors, meeting rooms. AE, DC, MC, V.*

$ ⌂ **Hostelling International.** This hostel in the heart of downtown has same-sex dorms that sleep 4, 6, or 10 people. Members pay $17.50 for a bed and nonmembers $22. Some rooms are available for couples and families. There are kitchen facilities and lockers for valuables. Reserve early during summer. ⌂ *1030 rue Mackay, H3G 2H1,* ☎ *514/843–3317,* ℻ *514/934–3251. 263 beds. Coin laundry. DC, MC, V.*

$ ⌂ **Hôtel l'Abri du Voyageur.** Price and location are this little hotel's main selling points, but it manages to squeeze in some unassuming charm as well, with high ceilings, bare brick walls, original pine and maple floors, and paintings by local artists (including a few by owner Guy Bisson). The hotel's three floors are over a restaurant in a pre–World War I commercial building. Bathrooms are shared, but each room has a TV and a sink. ⌂ *9 rue Ste-Catherine Ouest, H2X 1Z7,* ☎ *514/849–2922,* ℻ *514/499–0151. 30 rooms without bath. MC, V.*

$ ⌂ **Hôtel Thrift Lodge.** The Thrift Lodge is adjacent to the Terminus Voyageur bus station (buses park directly beneath one wing of the hotel), and some of the bus-station aura has rubbed off on the place: It's a little dingy. But if you're stumbling after a long bus ride and want somewhere to stay *now,* the rooms are large and clean, the service is friendly, and the price is right. It's also handy to the Berri-UQAM Métro station. ⌂ *1600 rue St-Hubert, H2L 3Z3,* ☎ *514/849–3214,* ℻ *514/849–9812. 147 rooms. Restaurant. AE, MC, V.*

$ ⌂ **McGill Student Apartments.** From mid-May to mid-August, when McGill is on summer recess, you can stay in its dorms on the grassy, quiet campus in the heart of the city. Nightly rates are $32 for students, $38 for nonstudents (single rooms only); some more expensive rooms include a kitchenette. As a visitor, you may use the campus swimming pool and gym facilities for a fee. The university cafeteria is also open during the week, serving breakfast and lunch. Be sure to book early. ⌂ *3935 rue University, H3A 2B4,* ☎ *514/398–6367,* ℻ *514/398–6770. 1,000 rooms without baths. MC, V.*

$ ⌂ **Université de Montréal Residence.** The university's student housing accepts visitors from early May to late August. It's on the other side of Mont-Royal from downtown and Vieux-Montréal but is right next to the Edouard-Monpetit Métro station. The rooms have phones for local calls; common lounges have microwaves and TVs. For a fee you may use the campus sports facilities. Rates are $23 per night or $141 per week. ⌂ *2350 blvd. Edouard-Montpetit, H3T 1J4,* ☎ *514/343–6531,* ℻ *514/343–2353. 750 rooms without baths. MC, V.*

$ ⌂ **YMCA.** This clean Y is downtown, next to Peel Métro station. Men should book at least two days in advance; women should book seven days ahead, because there are fewer rooms with showers for them. Anyone staying summer weekends must book at least a week ahead. There is a full gym facility and a typical Y cafeteria. ⌂ *1450 rue Stanley, H3A 2W6,* ☎ *514/849–8393,* ℻ *514/849–8017. 353 rooms, 3 with bath. Cafeteria, health club. AE, MC, V.*

$ ⌂ **YWCA.** Very close to dozens of restaurants, the Y is right downtown, one block from rue Ste-Catherine. Although men can eat at the café, the overnight facilities and health club are for women only. If you want a room with any amenities, you must book in advance; not all the rooms come with a sink and bath. There are single, double, and triple rooms. ⊠ *1355 blvd. René-Lévesque, H3G 1P3,* ☎ *514/866–9941,* FAX *514/ 861–1603. 63 rooms. Café, pool, sauna, aerobics, exercise room, shops. MC, V.*

NIGHTLIFE AND THE ARTS

The Friday Preview section of the *Gazette,* the English-language daily paper, has an especially good list of all events at the city's concert halls, theaters, clubs, dance spaces, and movie houses. Other publications listing what's on include the *Mirror, Hour, Scope,* and *Voir* (in French), distributed free at restaurants and other public places. You can also phone **Info-Arts (Bell)** (☎ 514/790–2787) for events information.

For **tickets** to major pop and rock concerts, shows, festivals, and hockey and baseball games, go to the individual box offices or call Admission (☎ 514/790–1245 or 800/361–4595). Call **Ticketmaster** (☎ 514/790–1111) for tickets to Théâtre St-Denis. **Place des Arts** tickets may be purchased at its box office underneath the Salle Wilfrid-Pelletier, next to the Métro station.

The Arts

Dance

Traditional and contemporary dance companies thrive in Montréal, though many take to the road or are on hiatus in the summer. **Ballets Classiques de Montréal** (☎ 514/866–1771) performs mostly classical programs. **Les Ballets Jazz de Montréal** (☎ 514/982–6771) experiments with new musical forms. **Les Grands Ballets Canadiens** is the leading Québec company (☎ 514/849–8681 or 514/849–0269). **LaLaLa Human Steps** (☎ 514/277–9090) is an avant-garde, exciting powerhouse of a company. **Margie Gillis Fondation de Danse** (☎ 514/845–3115) gives young dancers and choreographers opportunities to develop their art. **Montréal Danse** (☎ 514/845–2031) is a postmodern dance repertory company. **Ouest Vertigo Danse** (☎ 514/251–9177) stages innovative, postmodern performances. **Tangente** (☎ 514/525–1860) is a nucleus for many of the more avant-garde dance troupes.

Montréal's dancers have a downtown performance and rehearsal space, the **Agora Dance Theatre** (⊠ 840 rue Chérrier Est, ☎ 514/525–1500), affiliated with the Université de Montréal dance faculty. When not on tour, many dancers can be seen at Place des Arts or at any of the **Maisons de la Culture** (☎ 514/872–6211) performance spaces around town. Every other September (that is, in the odd-numbered years, such as 1999), the **Festival International de Nouvelle Danse** (☎ 514/287–1423 or 514/521–1212 for tickets) brings "new" dance to various venues around town. Tickets for this event always sell quickly.

Music

The city is home to one of the best chamber orchestras in Canada, **I Musici de Montréal** (☎ 514/982–6037). McGill University's Pollack Concert Hall (☎ 514/398–4547) is the site of concerts, notably by the **McGill Chamber Orchestra.** The **Orchestre Métropolitain de Montréal** (☎ 514/598–0870) stars at Place des Arts most weeks during the October–April season. The **Orchestre Symphonique de Montréal** (☎ 514/842–9951) has gained world renown under the baton of Charles Dutoit. When the group is not on tour, its regular venue is the Salle Wilfrid-Pelletier at the Place des Arts. The orchestra also gives Christmas and summer concerts in Notre-Dame Basilica and pop concerts at the

Arena Maurice Richard in Olympic Park. Also check the *Gazette* listings for its free summertime concerts in Montréal's city parks.

The **Spectrum** (✉ 318 rue Ste-Catherine Ouest, ☎ 514/861–5851) is an intimate concert hall. **Stade Olympique** (✉ Olympic Park, ☎ 514/252–8687) hosts rock and pop concerts. The 2,500-seat **Théâtre St-Denis** (✉ 1594 rue St-Denis, ☎ 514/849–4211) is the second-largest auditorium in Montréal (after Salle Wilfrid-Pelletier in Place des Arts).

Opera
L'Opéra de Montréal (☎ 514/985–2258) stages four productions a year at Place des Arts.

Theater
French-speaking theater lovers will find a wealth of dramatic productions. There are at least 10 major companies in town, some that have an international reputation. Anglophones have less to choose from. **Théâtre de Quat'Sous** (✉ 100 av. des Pins Est, ☎ 514/845–7277) performs modern, experimental, and cerebral plays. **Théâtre du Nouveau Monde** (✉ 84 rue Ste-Catherine Ouest, ☎ 514/866–8667) is the North American temple of French classics. **Théâtre du Rideau Vert** (✉ 4664 rue St-Denis, ☎ 514/844–1793) specializes in modern French repertoire.

The **Centaur Theatre** (✉ 453 rue St-François-Xavier, ☎ 514/288–3161), the best-known English theatrical company, stages Beaux Arts–style productions in the former stock exchange building in Vieux-Montréal. English-language plays can also be seen at the **Saidye Bronfman Centre** (✉ 5170 chemin de la Côte Ste-Catherine, ☎ 514/739–2301 or 514/739–7944), a multidisciplinary institution that is a focus of cultural activity for Montréal as a whole and for the Jewish community in particular. Many of its activities, such as gallery exhibits, lectures on public and Jewish affairs, performances, and concerts, are free. The center is home to the Yiddish Theatre Group, one of the few Yiddish companies performing today in North America. Touring companies of Broadway productions can often be seen at the **Théâtre St-Denis** (✉ 1594 rue St-Denis, ☎ 514/849–4211), as well as at Place des Arts (☎ 514/842–2112)—especially during summer.

Festivals

Montréal loves a party, and every summer festivals celebrate everything from beer to Yiddish theatre; here are some of the largest.

At the **Concours d'Art International Pyrotechnique** (International Fireworks Competition, ☎ 514/935–5161 or 800/678–5440, 800/361–4595 in Canada), held every Saturday and Sunday in June and July, teams from around the world compete to see who can best light up the sky. Their launch site is La Ronde on Ile Ste-Hélène, and you can buy a ticket, which includes an amusement park pass, to watch from a reserved seat. But thousands of Montrealers take their lawn chairs and blankets down to the Vieux-Port or across the river to the park along the South Shore and watch the show for nothing.

The **Festival International de Jazz de Montréal,** the world's biggest jazz festival, brings together more than 2,000 musicians for more than 400 concerts over a period of 11 days, from the end of June to the beginning of July. About 75% of concerts are presented free on outdoor stages. You can also hear blues, Latin rhythms, gospel, Cajun, and world music. Bell Info-Jazz (☎ 514/871–1881 or 888/515–0515) answers all queries about the festival and about travel packages. You can charge tickets over the phone (☎ 514/790–1245 or 800/678–5440, 800/361–4595 in Canada).

At the **Festival International des Films du Monde** (World Film Festival, ☎ 514/848–3883) at the end of August and the beginning of September, international stars and directors show off their best.

The **Festival Juste pour Rire** (Just for Laughs Comedy Festival, ☎ 514/790–4242) begins in early July; the comics show up for a 12-day festival that attracts about 650 performers and 350,000 spectators. Highlight acts have included Bobby Slayton and illusionists Penn and Teller.

Nightlife

Casino
The **Casino de Montréal** (✉ 1 av. du Casino, ☎ 514/392–2746 or 800/665–2274), on Ile Notre-Dame in the St. Lawrence River, is one of the world's 10 biggest, with 1,835 slot machines and 88 tables for baccarat, blackjack, and roulette. The government has tried to capture the elegance of Monte Carlo: The building glitters with glass and murals and offers stunning city views. There's a strict dress code, and croupiers are trained in politeness as well as math. The casino has five restaurants, including Nuances (☞ Dining, *above*), and a delightfully bilingual cabaret theater. There are some oddities for those used to Vegas—no drinking on the floor, no crap games (dice games are illegal in Canada), and no tipping the croupiers. The casino is a $10 cab ride from downtown, or you can take the Métro to the Ile Ste-Hélène station and transfer to Bus 167. Driving here is a hassle. It's open daily 9 AM–5 AM.

Comedy
The **Comedy Nest** (✉ 1740 blvd. René-Lévesque Ouest, ☎ 514/932–6378) has shows by name performers and up-and-comers.

Dance Clubs
Club 737 (✉ 1 Place Ville-Marie, ☎ 514/397–0737), on top of Place Ville-Marie, does the disco number every Thursday, Friday, and Saturday night. This has become very popular with the upscale, mid-20s to mid-30s crowd. The view is magnificent and there's an open-air rooftop bar. **Hard Rock Cafe** (✉ 1458 rue Crescent, ☎ 514/987–1420) is Montréal's version of this establishment. **Kokino** (✉ 3556 blvd. St-Laurent, ☎ 514/848–6398) is *the* place for the beautiful people, with jazz, Brazilian, and house music. **Thursdays/Les Beaux Jeudis** (✉ 1449 rue Crescent, ☎ 514/288–5656) is a popular dance club.

Folk Music
An enthusiastic crowd sings along with Québécois performers at the **Deux Pierrots Boîte aux Chansons** (✉ 104 rue St-Paul Est, ☎ 514/861–1270). **Hurley's Irish Pub** (✉ 1225 rue Crescent, ☎ 514/861–4111) attracts some of the city's best Celtic musicians and dancers.

Jazz
The best-known jazz club is Vieux-Montréal's **L'Air du Temps** (✉ 191 rue St-Paul Ouest, ☎ 514/842–2003). This small, smoky club presents 90% local talent and 10% international acts from 5 PM on into the night. Downtown, duck into **Biddle's** (✉ 2060 rue Aylmer, ☎ 514/842–8656), where bassist Charles Biddle holds forth most evenings. Biddle's serves pretty good ribs and chicken. You might try the **Quai des Brumes Dancing** (✉ 4481 rue St-Denis, ☎ 514/499–0467).

Rock
Rock clubs seem to spring up, flourish, then fizzle out overnight. **Club Soda** (✉ 5240 av. du Parc, ☎ 514/270–7848), the granddaddy of them all, sports a neon martini glass complete with neon effervescence outside. Inside it's a small hall with a stage, three bars, and room for about 400 people. International rock acts play here, as does local talent. It's

also a venue for the comedy and jazz festivals. The club is open only
for shows. Phone the box office to find out what's on. **Déjà Vu** (✉ 1224
rue Bishop, ☎ 514/866–0512), a rock club with a nostalgia theme, is
popular with young English-speakers. **L'Ours Qui Fume** (✉ 2019 rue
St-Denis, ☎ 514/845–6998), or the Smoking Bear, is loud, raucous,
and very Francophone.

OUTDOOR ACTIVITIES AND SPORTS

Most Montrealers would probably claim they hate winter, but the city
is rich in cold-weather activities—skating rinks, cross-country ski trails,
toboggan runs, and even a downhill ski run. In summer there are tennis courts, miles of bicycle trails, golf courses, and two lakes for boating and swimming.

Participant Sports

Biking

The island of Montréal—except for Mont-Royal itself—is quite flat,
and there are more than 20 cycling paths in the metropolitan area. Bikes
are welcome on the first and last cars of Métro trains during non–rush
hours. Ferries at the Vieux-Port will take you to Ile Ste-Hélène and the
South Shore of the St. Lawrence River. You can rent bicycles at **Vélo
Aventure** on the grounds of the Vieux-Port (☎ 514/847–0666).

One interesting path starts at the Vieux-Port and follows the **Lachine
Canal** (1825) from Vieux-Montréal to the shores of Lac St-Louis in suburban Lachine. Along the way you can stop at the bustling Atwater
Farmer's Market (✉ 110 av. Atwater) to buy the makings of a picnic
or take a break at Magnan (☞ Dining, *above*) in summer for a steak
or a cheap lobster. In Lachine you can visit the Fur Trade at Lachine
Historic Site (✉ 1255 blvd. St-Joseph, Lachine, ☎ 514/637–7433).
Parks Canada (☎ 514/283–6054 or 514/637–7433) conducts guided
cycling tours along the Lachine Canal every summer weekend.

Boating

In Montréal you can get in a boat at a downtown wharf and be crashing through Class V white water minutes later. Jack Kowalski of **Lachine Rapids Tours Ltd.** (✉ 105 rue de la Commune, or Quai de
l'Horloge, or Clock Tower Pier, ☎ 514/284–9607) takes thrill seek-
ers on a 45-minute voyage through the rapids in big, sturdy aluminum
jet boats. He supplies heavy-water gear. You can also choose a half-
hour trip around the islands in 10-passenger boats that can go about
100 kph (60 mph). Reservations are required; trips are narrated in French
and English. There are five trips daily through the rapids from May
through September; cost is $48. Rafting trips are also available.

Golf

For a complete listing of the many golf courses in the Montréal area,
call **Tourisme-Québec** (☎ 514/873–2015 or 800/363–7777).

Ice-Skating

The city has at least 195 outdoor and 21 indoor rinks. There are huge
ones on Ile Ste-Hèléne and at the Vieux-Port. Call the **Parks and Recreation Department** (☎ 514/872–6211) for information. You can skate
year-round in the **Amphithéatre Bell** (☎ 514/395–0555, ext. 237) in
Le 1000 rue de la Gauchetière.

Jogging

There are paths in most city parks, but for running with a panoramic
view, head to the dirt track in **Parc du Mont-Royal** (take rue Peel, then
the steps up to the track).

Skiing

CROSS-COUNTRY

Trails crisscross most city parks, including Parc des Iles, Maisonneuve, and Mont-Royal, but the best are probably the 46 km (28 mi) in the 900-acre **Cap St-Jacques Regional Park** (⊠ Off blvd. Gouin, ☎ 514/280–6871) in Pierrefonds on the west end of Montréal Island.

DOWNHILL

For the big slopes you'll have to go northwest to the Laurentians (☞ Chapter 10) or south to the Eastern Townships (☞ Chapter 10), an hour or two away by car. There is a small slope in Parc du Mont-Royal. A "Ski-Québec" brochure is available from **Tourisme-Québec** offices (☎ 514/873–2015 or 800/363–7777).

Squash

Court time should be reserved three days ahead at **Nautilus Centre St-Laurent Côte-de-Liesse Racquet Club** (⊠ 8305 chemin Côte-de-Liesse, ☎ 514/739–3654).

Swimming

There is a large indoor pool at the Olympic Park's **Centre Aquatique** (⊠ 4141 av. Pierre-de-Coubertin, ☎ 514/252–4622). **Centre Sportif et des Loisirs Claude-Robillard** (⊠ 1000 av. Emile Journault, ☎ 514/872–6900) has a big indoor pool. The outdoor pool on **Ile Ste-Hélène** is a popular (and crowded) gathering place, open June–Labor Day. The city-run beach, **Plage de l'Ile Notre-Dame** (☎ 514/872–6211), on Ile Notre-Dame is the only natural swimming hole in Montréal.

Tennis

There are public courts in the Jeanne-Mance, Kent, Lafontaine, and Somerled parks. For details call the **Parks and Recreation department** (☎ 514/872–6211).

Windsurfing and Sailing

Sailboards and small sailboats can be rented at **L'Ecole de Voile de Lachine** (⊠ 2105 blvd. St-Joseph, Lachine, ☎ 514/634–4326) and the **Société du Parc des Iles** (⊠ 12 Pl. de la Concorde, ☎ 514/872–4537).

Spectator Sports

Baseball

The National League's **Montréal Expos** (☎ 514/253–3434 or 800/463–9767) play at Olympic Stadium April–September.

Football

The venerable **Montréal Alouettes** (☎ 514/254–2400 for information, 514/254–1818 for tickets) of the Canadian Football League play the Canadian version of the game—bigger field, just three downs, and a far more wide-open style—on real grass under open skies at McGill University's Molson Stadium June–October. It's one of the best sporting deals in town.

Grand Prix

The annual **Player's Grand Prix du Canada** (☎ 514/392–0000 or 514/350–4731), which draws top Formula 1 racers from around the world, takes place every June at Circuit Gilles Villeneuve on Ile Notre-Dame.

Hockey

The **Montréal Canadiens,** winners of 23 Stanley Cups, meet National Hockey League rivals at the Centre Molson (⊠ 1250 rue de la Gauchetière Ouest, ☎ 514/932–2582) October–April. Buy tickets in advance.

SHOPPING

Montrealers *magasinent* (go shopping) with a vengeance, so it's no surprise that the city has 160 multifaceted retail areas encompassing some 7,000 stores. The law allows shops to stay open weekdays 9–9 and weekends 9–5. However, many merchants close Monday–Wednesday evenings and on Sunday. Many specialty service shops are closed on Monday, too. Just about all stores, with the exception of some bargain outlets and a few selective art and antiques galleries, accept major credit cards. Most purchases are subject to a federal goods and services tax (GST) of 7% as well as a provincial tax of 8%.

If you think you might be buying fur, it is wise to check with your country's customs officials before leaving to find out which animals are considered endangered and cannot be imported. Do the same if you think you might be buying Inuit carvings, many of which are made of whalebone and ivory and cannot be brought into the United States.

Montréal Specialties

Many visitors usually reserve at least one day to hunt for either exclusive fashions along rue Sherbrooke. But there are specific items that you should seek out in Montréal.

Antiques and Secondhand Books

The fashionable place for antiquing is a once run-down five-block strip of rue Notre-Dame Ouest between rue Guy and avenue Atwater (a five-minute walk south from the Lionel-Groulx Métro station). **Antiquités Landry** (⊠ 1726 rue Notre-Dame Ouest, ☎ 514/937–7040) has solid pine furniture. **Deuxièmement** (⊠ 1880 rue Notre-Dame Ouest, ☎ 514/933–8560) sells a fascinating jumble of objects from every age. **Héritage Antique Métropolitain** (⊠ 1645 rue Notre-Dame Ouest, ☎ 514/931–5517) has elegant English and French furniture. A Sunday tour might begin with brunch at **Salon de Thé Ambiance** (⊠ 1874 rue Notre-Dame Ouest, ☎ 514/939–2609), a charming restaurant that also sells antiques. **Viva Gallery** (⊠ 1970 rue Notre-Dame Ouest, ☎ 514/932–3200) specializes in Asian antiques.

Antiques stores are beginning to pop up along **rue Amherst** between rues Ste-Catherine and Ontario (a five-minute walk west of the Beaudry Métro station). The area is shabbier than rue Notre-Dame but a lot cheaper. **L'Antiquaire Joyal** (⊠ 1475 rue Amherst, ☎ 514/524–0057) includes rosaries, crucifixes, and religious art among its two floors of Victorian and earlier furniture. **Antiquités Curiosités** (⊠ 1769 rue Amherst, ☎ 514/525–8772) has a wide selection of well-priced wooden toys and Victorian-era tables and tallboys. **Cité Déco** (⊠ 1761 rue Amherst, ☎ 514/528–0659) specializes in the chrome and plastic furnishings of the '50s.

Biblomania (⊠ 1841A rue Ste-Catherine Ouest, ☎ 514/933–8156) has some gems among its extensive shelves of secondhand books. **Ex Libris** (⊠ 1628B rue Sherbrooke Ouest, ☎ 514/932–1689) houses a fine collection of secondhand books in an elegant graystone on rue Sherbrooke. One of the most fascinating bookstores in Montréal is **Russell Books** (⊠ 275 rue St-Antoine Ouest, ☎ 514/866–0564), a huge, dusty place full of remainders, secondhand paperbacks, children's books, and shelves of old volumes on every subject from algebra to zoology. The back rooms are full of treasures that have never been catalogued. Lovers of old books can browse through the shelves at **S.W. Welch** (⊠ 3878 blvd. St-Laurent, ☎ 514/848–9358).

Fur

Montréal is one of the fur capitals of the world. Close to 85% of Canada's fur manufacturers are based in the city, as are many of their retail outlets. Many of them are clustered along rue Mayor and boulevard de Maisonneuve between rue de Bleury and rue Aylmer. **Alexandor** (✉ 2055 rue Peel, ☎ 514/288–1119) is nine blocks west of the main fur trade area, and its storefront showroom caters to the downtown trade. **Birger Christensen at Holt Renfrew** (✉ 1300 rue Sherbrooke Ouest, ☎ 514/842–5111) is perhaps the most exclusive showroom of the lot, with prices to match. **Grosvenor** (✉ 400 blvd. de Maisonneuve Ouest, ☎ 514/288–1255) caters more to the wholesale trade but has several showrooms where customers can view its decidedly European styles. **McComber** (✉ 402 blvd. de Maisonneuve Ouest, ☎ 514/845–1167) has been in business for 100 years; its present owner has a flair for mink designs.

Downtown

Downtown is Montréal's largest retail district. It takes in rue Sherbrooke, boulevard de Maisonneuve, rue Ste-Catherine, and the side streets between them. Because of the proximity and variety of shops, it's the best shopping bet if you're in town overnight or over a weekend. The area bounded by rues Sherbrooke and Ste-Catherine, and rues de la Montagne and Crescent has antiques and art galleries in addition to designer salons. Rue Sherbrooke is lined with fashion boutiques and art and antiques galleries. Rue Crescent is a tempting blend of antiques, fashions, and jewelry displayed beneath colorful awnings.

Brisson et Brisson (✉ 1472 rue Sherbrooke Ouest, ☎ 514/937–7456) is perhaps the most exclusive men's store in the city. **Casa del Habano** (✉ 1434 rue Sherbrooke Ouest, ☎ 514/849–0037) stocks the finest cigars Cuba produces. (Warning: U.S. law forbids its citizens to buy Cuban products.) **Galerie Tansu** (✉ 1622 rue Sherbrooke Ouest, ☎ 514/864–1039) has Chinese and Japanese antiques. The craftspeople at **Kaufmann de Suisse** (✉ 2195 rue Crescent, ☎ 514/848–0595) make finely wrought jewelry.

Complexe Desjardins

Complexe Desjardins (✉ blvd. René-Lévesque and rue Jeanne Mance) is filled with splashing fountains and exotic plants. To get here, take the Métro to the Place des Arts and follow the tunnels to Desjardins' multitiered atrium mall. The roughly 80 stores include budget outlets like Le Château for clothing as well as the exclusive Jonathan Roche Monsieur for men's fashions.

Les Cours Mont-Royal

Les Cours Mont-Royal (✉ 1550 rue Metcalfe) is *très élégant*. This mall is linked to both the Peel and McGill Métro stations and caters to expensive tastes, but even bargain hunters find it an intriguing spot for window shopping. Beware: The interior layout can be disorienting.

Department Stores

La Baie (✉ 585 rue Ste-Catherine Ouest, ☎ 514/281–4422)—the Bay in English—has been a department store since 1891. It's known for its duffel coats and Hudson Bay red-, green-, and white-striped blankets. La Baie also sells the typical department store fare.

Eaton (✉ 677 rue Ste-Catherine Ouest, ☎ 514/284–8411) is the city's leading department store and part of Canada's largest chain. Founded in Toronto by Timothy Eaton, the first Montréal outlet appeared in 1925. It now sells everything—from fashions and furniture to meals in the Art Deco top-floor restaurant and zucchini loaves in the basement bakery. Everything, that is, except tobacco. Timothy was a good Methodist, and his descendants honor his principles.

Exclusive **Holt Renfrew** (⊠ 1300 rue Sherbrooke Ouest, ☏ 514/842–5111) is known for furs and fashions. It has supplied coats to four generations of British royalty, and when Queen Elizabeth II got married in 1947, Holt's gave her a priceless Labrador mink. Holt carries the pricey line of furs by Denmark's Birger Christensen, as well as the haute couture and prêt-à-porter collections of Yves Saint Laurent.

A kilted piper regales shoppers at **Ogilvy** (⊠ 1307 rue Ste-Catherine Ouest, ☏ 514/842–7711) every day at noon. Founded in 1865, the department store still stocks traditional apparel by retailers like Aquascutum and Jaeger. The store has been divided into individual designer boutiques selling pricier lines than La Baie or Eaton. It used to be Ogilvy's (just as Eaton used to be Eaton's) before Québec's French-only sign laws made apostrophes illegal.

Faubourg Ste-Catherine
The Faubourg Ste-Catherine (⊠ 1616 rue Ste-Catherine Ouest, at rue Guy) is a vast bazaar abutting the Gray Nuns' convent grounds. There are clothing and crafts boutiques, but the main product is food—fresh bagels, pastries, fruits and vegetables, and gourmet meats. A dozen or so very reasonably priced lunch counters sell ethnic foods.

Place Bonaventure
Place Bonaventure (⊠ Rues de la Gauchetière and University) is one of Canada's largest commercial exhibition centers. It's directly above the Bonaventure Métro station and has a mall with some 120 stores, including the trendy Au Coton and Bikini Village and the practical Bata Shoes. There are also a number of fun shops: Ici-Bas for outrageous hose, Le Rouet for handicrafts, and Miniatures Plus for exquisite dolls' furniture and tiny gifts.

Place Montréal Trust
Place Montréal Trust (⊠ 1600 rue McGill College, at rue Ste-Catherine Ouest) is the lively entrance to an imposing glass office tower. Shoppers, fooled by the aqua and pastel decor, may think they have stumbled into a California mall. Prices at the 110 outlets range from hundreds (for designs by Alfred Sung, haute couture at Gigi, or men's fashions at Rodier) to only a few dollars (for T-shirts or steak-and-kidney pies at the outpost of famed British department store Marks & Spencer). This shopping center is linked to the McGill Métro station.

Place Ville-Marie
Weatherproof shopping began in 1962 beneath the 42-story cruciform towers of Place Ville-Marie (⊠ Blvd. René-Lévesque and rue University). Stylish men and women head to Place Ville-Marie's 100-plus retail outlets for the clothes—Tristan & Iseut, Cactus, and Aquascutum at the upper end and Dalmys and Reitmans for more affordable fashions. For shoes try Mayfair, Brown's, François Villon, and French.

Les Promenades de la Cathédrale
The Promenades de la Cathédrale (⊠ 625 rue Ste-Catherine Ouest) are directly beneath Christ Church Cathedral, the seat of Montréal's Anglican (Episcopal) bishop. Les Promenades, which is connected to the McGill Métro station, has Canada's largest Linen Chest outlet, with hundreds of bedspreads and duvets draped over revolving racks plus aisles of china, crystal, linen, and silver. It's also home to the Anglican Church's Diocesan Book Room, which sells an unusually good and ecumenical selection of books as well as religious objects.

Rue Chabanel

In the north end of the city, rue Chabanel is the soul of Montréal's extensive garment industry. Every Saturday, from about 8:30 to 1, many of the manufacturers and importers in the area open their doors to the general public. At least they do if they feel like it. What results is part bazaar, part circus, and often all chaos—but friendly chaos. When Montrealers say "Chabanel," they mean the eight-block stretch just west of boulevard St-Laurent. The factories and shops there are tiny—dozens of them are crammed into each building. The goods seem to get more stylish and more expensive the farther west you go. For really cheap leather goods, sportswear, children's clothes, and linens, try the shops at 99 rue Chabanel. For more deluxe options drop into 555 rue Chabanel. The manufacturers and importers here have their work areas on the upper floors and have transformed the mezzanine into a glitzy mall with bargains in men's suits, winter coats, knitted goods, and stylish leather jackets. A few places on Chabanel accept credit cards, but bring cash anyway. It's easier to bargain if you can flash bills, and if you pay cash, the price will often "include the tax."

Square Westmount and Avenue Greene

Square Westmount (⊠ Rue Ste-Catherine Ouest and av. Greene) has some of the city's finest shops, which is hardly surprising—it serves the mountainside suburb of Westmount, home to executives and former prime ministers. Humbler types can get there easily by taking the Métro to the Atwater station and following the tunnel to Square Westmount. **Collange** (☎ 514/933–4634) sells lacy lingerie. **Hugo Nicholson** (☎ 514/937–1937) carries exclusive fashions for men and women. **Ma Maison** (☎ 514/933–0045) stocks quality housewares. The very elegant **Marché de Westmount** has an array of gourmet boutiques that sell pastries, cheeses, pâtés, fruits, cakes, and chocolates. You can assemble your own picnic and eat it at one of the little tables scattered among the stalls. If shopping tires you out, you can stop in at the **Spa de Westmount** (☎ 514/933–9966) for a massage.

Square Westmount opens onto **avenue Greene,** two flower-lined blocks of restored redbrick row houses full of boutiques, restaurants, and shops. The **Coach House** (⊠ 1325 av. Greene, ☎ 514/937–6191) is a source for antique silverware. **Double Hook** (⊠ 1235A av. Greene, ☎ 514/932–5093) sells only Canadian books.

Upper Boulevard St-Laurent and Avenue Laurier Ouest

Upper boulevard St-Laurent—which runs roughly from avenue du Mont-Royal north to rue St-Viateur and climbs the mountain to rue Bernard—has blossomed into one of Montréal's most chic *quartiers*. It's not entirely surprising, given that much of this area lies within or adjacent to Outremont, an enclave of wealthy Francophone Montrealers, with restaurants, boutiques, nightclubs, and bistros catering to the upscale visitor. **J. Schrecter** (⊠ 4350 blvd. St-Laurent, ☎ 514/845–4231) had been supplying work duds for blue-collar workers for decades when the grunge look suddenly made the store trendy. **Scandale** (⊠ 3639 blvd. St-Laurent, ☎ 514/842–4707) has designs for the very hip as well as great lingerie and a secondhand-clothes store.

Shoppers flock to the two blocks of **avenue Mont-Royal** just east of boulevard St-Laurent for a series of shops that sell secondhand clothes and recycled clothes (things like housecoats chopped into sassy miniskirts). **Eva B** (⊠ 2013 blvd. St-Laurent, ☎ 514/849–8246) sells new clothes as well as used. **Hatfield & McCoy** (⊠ 156 av. Mont-Royal

Est, ☎ 514/982–0088) recycles elegant lounge clothes from the 1930s to the 1970s. **Scarlett O'Hara** (✉ 254 av. Mont-Royal Est, ☎ 514/844–9435) started the whole secondhand trend.

Avenue Laurier Ouest, from boulevard St-Laurent to chemin de la Côte-Ste-Catherine, is roughly an eight-block stretch; you'll crisscross it many times as you explore its fashionable and trendy shops, which carry everything from crafts and clothing to books and paintings. Asian and African crafts are sold at **Artefact** (✉ 102 av. Laurier Ouest, ☎ 514/278–6575). **Boutique Gabriel Filion** (✉ 1127 av. Laurier Ouest, ☎ 514/274–0697) sells interesting imported toys and marvelous dolls, dolls' clothes, stuffed animals, and music boxes. **Tilley Endurables** (✉ 1050 av. Laurier Ouest, ☎ 514/272–7791) sells the famous Canadian-designed Tilley hat and other easy-care travel wear.

Vieux-Montréal

Despite Vieux-Montréal's abundance of garish souvenir shops, a shopping spree there can be worthwhile. Both rues Notre-Dame and St-Jacques, from rue McGill to Place Jacques-Cartier, are lined with low to moderately priced fashion boutiques and shoe stores. **Desmarais et Robitaille** (✉ 60 rue Notre-Dame Ouest, ☎ 514/845–3194), a store that supplies churches with vestments and liturgical aids, has Québécois carvings and handicrafts as well as tasteful religious articles.

Rue St-Paul has some interesting shops and art galleries. At the **Cerf Volanterie** (✉ 224 rue St-Paul Ouest, ☎ 514/845–7613), Claude Thibaudeau makes sturdy, gloriously colored kites that he signs and guarantees for three years. **Drags** (✉ 367 rue St-Paul Est, ☎ 514/866–0631) is crammed with fragments of military uniforms and loads of clothes, shoes, hats, and accessories from the '30s and '40s. **L'Empreinte Coopérative** (✉ 272 rue St-Paul Est, ☎ 514/861–4427) has a fine collection of Québec handicrafts. The **Galerie Art & Culture** (✉ 227 rue St-Paul Ouest, ☎ 514/843–5980) specializes in Canadian landscapes. **Galerie des Arts Relais des Époques** (✉ 234 rue St-Paul Ouest, ☎ 514/844–2133) sells some fascinating work by contemporary Montréal painters. **La Guilde Graphique** (✉ 9 rue St-Paul Ouest, ☎ 514/844–3438) has an exceptional selection of original prints, engravings, and etchings. **Rita R. Giroux** (✉ 206 rue St-Paul Ouest, ☎ 514/844–4714) makes flamboyant creations with fresh, dried, and silk flowers.

MONTRÉAL A TO Z

Arriving and Departing

By Bus

For information about bus companies, contact the city's downtown bus terminal, **Terminus Voyageur** (✉ 505 blvd. de Maisonneuve Est, ☎ 514/842–2281), which connects with the Berri-UQAM Métro station. **Greyhound** (☎ 800/231–2222) has coast-to-coast service and serves Montréal with buses arriving from and departing for various cities in North America. **Vermont Transit** (☎ 800/231–2222), a Greyhound subsidiary, serves Montréal via Boston, New York, and other points in the Northeast. **Voyageur** and Voyageur-Colonial service destinations primarily within Québec and Ontario.

By Car

Montréal is accessible from the rest of Canada via the Trans-Canada Highway (Highway 1), which enters the city from the east and west via Routes 20 and 40. The New York State Thruway (I–87) becomes Route 15 at the Canadian border, and then it's 47 km (29 mi) to the outskirts of Montréal. U.S. I–89 becomes two-lane Route 133, which eventually joins Route 10, at the border. From I–91 from Massachusetts, you must take Routes 55 and 10 to reach Montréal. At the border you must clear Canadian Customs, so be prepared with proof of citizenship and your vehicle's ownership papers. On holidays and during the peak summer season, expect waits of a half hour or more at the major crossings.

Once you're in Québec, the road signs will be in French, but they're designed to be understandable to everyone. The speed limit is posted in kilometers; on highways the limit is 100 kph (about 62 mph). There are heavy penalties for driving while intoxicated, and drivers and front-seat passengers must wear over-the-shoulder seat belts. Gasoline is sold in liters (3¾ liters equal 1 U.S. gallon), and lead-free is called *sans plomb*. New York, Maine, and Ontario residents should drive with extra care in Québec: Traffic violations in the province are entered on their driving records back home (and vice versa).

By Plane
Flying time from New York is 1½ hours; from Chicago, two hours; from Los Angeles, 6½ hours (with a connection). **Dorval International** (✉ 975 blvd. René-Vachon, ☎ 514/633–3105), 22½ km (14 mi) west of the city, handles all scheduled flights foreign and domestic and some charter operations. **Mirabel International** (✉ 12600 rue Aérogare, ☎ 514/476–3010), 54½ km (34 mi) northwest of the city, serves most charter traffic. Major **airlines** serving Montréal are Air Canada, American Airlines, Canadian Airlines International, Delta, and US Airways (☞ Air Travel *in* the Gold Guide). A $10 airport tax (for capital improvements) is charged when you leave. You can pay cash or with a credit card.

A **taxi** from Dorval to downtown will cost $25; from Mirabel, about $56. All taxi companies in Montréal must charge the same rates by law. **Autobus Connaisseur** (☎ 514/934–1222) is a much cheaper alternative to taxis into town from Mirabel and Dorval. Shuttle service from Mirabel to the terminal next to the Gare Centrale (✉ 777 rue de la Gauchetière) is frequent and costs only $7.25. The shuttle from Dorval runs about every half hour and stops at Le Centre Sheraton, Le Château Champlain, Le Reine Elizabeth, and the Voyageur terminal. It costs $9. If you plan to use the bus to go back to either airport, you can save by buying a round-trip ticket.

By Train
The Gare Centrale, on rue de la Gauchetière between rues University and Mansfield (behind Le Reine Elizabeth), is the rail terminus for all trains from the United States and from other Canadian provinces. It is connected underground to the Bonaventure Métro station.

Amtrak's (☎ 800/872–7245) *Adirondack* leaves New York's Penn Station every morning for the 10½-hour trip through scenic upstate New York to Montréal. Amtrak also has bus connections with the *Vermonter* in St. Albans, Vermont.

VIA Rail (☎ 514/989–2626 or 800/561–3949, 800/361–5390 in Québec Province) connects Montréal with all the major cities of Canada, including Québec City, Halifax, Ottawa, Toronto, Winnipeg, Edmonton, and Vancouver.

Getting Around

By Bus and Métro
Public transportation is easily the best and cheapest way to get around. The **Métro** (subway) is clean, quiet (it runs on rubber wheels), and safe,

and it's heated in winter and cooled in summer. Métro hours on the Orange, Green, and Yellow lines are weekdays 5:30 AM–12:58 AM, Saturday 5:30 AM–1:28 AM, and Sunday 5:30 AM–1:58 AM. The Blue Line runs daily from 5:30 AM to 11 PM. Trains run as often as every three minutes on the most crowded lines—Orange and Green at rush hours. The Métro is also connected to the 29 km (18 mi) of the Underground City. Each of the 65 Métro stops has been individually designed and decorated; Berri-UQAM has stained glass, and at Place d'Armes a small collection of archaeological artifacts is exhibited. The stations between Snowdon and Jean-Talon on the Blue Line are worth a visit, particularly Outremont, with its glass-block design. Each station connects with one or more bus routes, which cover the rest of the island. The STCUM (Société de Transport de la Communauté Urbaine de Montréal) administers both the Métro and the buses, so the same tickets and transfers (free) are valid on either service. You should be able to get within a few blocks of anywhere in the city on one fare. At press time rates were: single ticket $1.85, six tickets $7.75, monthly pass $44.50. Visitors can buy a day pass for $5 or a three-day pass for $12. They're available at some major hotels, at Berri-UQAM and some other downtown stations, and at Info-Touriste (☞ Visitor Information *in* Contacts and Resources, *below*) at place Jacques-Cartier.

Free maps may be obtained at Métro ticket booths. Try to get the *Carte Réseau* (system map); it's the most complete. Transfers from Métro to buses are available from the dispenser just beyond the ticket booth inside the station. Bus-to-bus and bus-to-Métro transfers may be obtained from the bus driver. For more information on reaching your destination call the **Société de Transport de la Communauté de Montréal** (☎ 514/288–6287).

By Car

Finding your way around Montréal by car is not difficult. The streets are laid out in a fairly straightforward grid, and one-way streets are clearly marked. But parking is difficult and the narrow cobbled streets of Vieux-Montréal can be a trial. It's much easier to park near a Métro station and walk and use public transit.

Montréal police have a diligent tow-away and fine system for cars double-parked or stopped in no-stopping zones in downtown Montréal during rush hours and business hours. A parking ticket will cost between $35 and $40. All Montréal parking signs are in French, so brush up on your *gauche* (left), *droit* (right), *ouest* (west), and *est* (east). If your car is towed away while illegally parked, it will cost an additional $35 to retrieve it. Be especially alert in winter: Montréal's snow-clearing crews are the best in the world and a joy to watch in action after a blizzard—but they're ruthless in dealing with any parked cars in their way. If they don't tow them, they'll bury them.

In winter, remember that your car may not start on extra cold mornings unless it has been kept in a heated garage. And if you drive in the city, remember two things: Québec law forbids you to turn right on a red light, and Montrealers are notorious jaywalkers.

By Taxi

Taxis in Montréal all run on the same rate: $2.25 minimum and $1 per kilometer (½ mi). They're usually reliable, although they may be hard to find on rainy nights after the Métro has closed. Each carries on its roof a white or orange plastic sign that is lit when available and off when occupied.

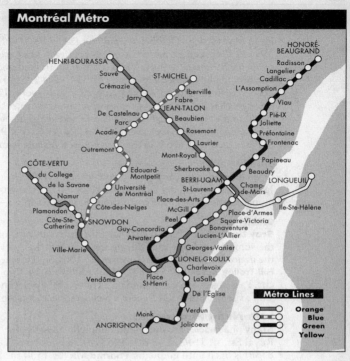

Montréal Métro

HONORÉ-BEAUGRAND

HENRI-BOURASSA

Sauvé
ST-MICHEL
Radisson
Langelier
Cadillac
L'Assomption

Crémazie
Iberville
Fabre
JEAN-TALON
Viau

Jarry
De Castelnau
Beaubien
Pié-IX
Joliette
Préfontaine
Frontenac

Parc
Acadie
Rosemont

Outremont
Laurier

Mont-Royal
Papineau

CÔTE-VERTU
du College
de la Savane

Edouard-Montpetit
Sherbrooke
Beaudry
LONGUEUIL

Université
de Montréal
BERRI-UQAM
St-Laurent
Champ-de-Mars

Namur
St-Laurent
Place-des-Arts
Ile-Ste-Hélène

Plamondon
Côte-des-Neiges
McGill
Place-d'Armes

Côte-Ste-Catherine
SNOWDON
Peel
Square-Victoria
Bonaventure
Lucien-L'Allier

Guy-Concordia
Atwater

Ville-Marie
Georges-Vanier

LIONEL-GROULX
Charlevoix

Vendôme
Place
St-Henri
LaSalle

De l'Eglise

Monk
Verdun

ANGRIGNON
Jolicoeur

Métro Lines
- Orange
- Blue
- Green
- Yellow

Contacts and Resources

Car Rentals
Avis (☎ 514/866–7906 or 800/879–2847). **Budget** (☎ 514/938–1000 or 800/268–8900). **Discount** (☎ 514/286–1554 or 800/357–0123). **Enterprise** (☎ 514/931–3722 or 800/736–8222). **Hertz** (☎ 514/842–8537 or 800/263–0600). **National/Tilden** (☎ 514/878–2771 or 800/387–4747). **Via Route** (☎ 514/521–5221).

Consulates
United States (✉ 1155 rue St-Alexandre, ☎ 514/398–9695) is open weekdays 8:30–4:30. **United Kingdom** (✉ 1000 rue de la Gauchetière Ouest, ☎ 514/866–5863) is open weekdays 9–5.

Doctors and Dentists
The **U.S. Consulate** cannot recommend specific doctors and dentists but does provide a list of various specialists in the Montréal area. Call in advance (☎ 514/398–9695) to make sure the consulate is open.

Dental clinic (☎ 514/342–4444) is open 24 hours; Sunday appointments are for emergencies only. **Montréal General Hospital** (☎ 514/937–6011). **Québec Poison Control Centre** (☎ 800/463–5060). **Touring Club de Montréal–AAA, CAA, RAC** (☎ 514/861–7111).

Emergencies
Ambulance, fire, police (☎ 911).

English-Language Bookstores
Chapters (✉ 1171 rue Ste-Catherine Ouest, ☎ 514/849–8825), a branch of the Canadian chain, has books, magazines, and a coffee shop. **Double Hook** (✉ 1235A av. Greene, ☎ 514/932–5093) sells only Canadian books. **Paragraphe** (✉ 2065 rue Mansfield, ☎ 514/845–5811) has a café.

Guided Tours

BOAT

From May through October, **Amphi Tour** (℡ 514/849–5181 or ℡ 514/386–1298 for cell phone in season only) offers a unique one-hour tour of Vieux-Montréal and the Vieux-Port on both land and water in an amphibious bus. **Bateau-Mouche** (℡ 514/849–9952) runs four harbor excursions and an evening supper cruise every day from May through October. The boats are reminiscent of the ones that cruise the canals of the Netherlands—wide-beamed and low-slung, with a glassed-in passenger deck. Boats leave from the Jacques Cartier Pier at the foot of Place Jacques-Cartier in the Vieux-Port (Métro Champs-de-Mars).

CALÈCHE RIDES

Open **horse-drawn carriages**—fleece-lined in winter—leave from Place Jacques-Cartier, Square Dorchester, Place d'Armes, and rue de la Commune. An hour-long ride costs about $50 (℡ 514/653–0751).

ORIENTATION

Gray Line (℡ 514/934–1222) has nine different tours of Montréal in the summer and one tour during the winter. It has pickup service at the major hotels or at Info-Touriste (⌗ 1001 Sq. Dorchester). **Murray Hill Trolley Buses** (℡ 514/871–4733) follow a 14-stop circuit of the city. Passengers can get off and on as often as they like and stay at each stop as long as they like. There's pickup service at major hotels.

Late-Night Pharmacies

Many pharmacies are open until midnight. **Jean Coutu** (⌗ 501 Mont-Royal Est, ℡ 514/521–3481; ⌗ 5510 Côte-des-Neiges, ℡ 514/344–8338) is open until midnight. **Pharmaprix** (⌗ 1500 rue Ste-Catherine Ouest, ℡ 514/933–4744; ⌗ 5157 rue Sherbrooke Ouest, ℡ 514/484–3531) stays open until midnight. **Pharmaprix** (⌗ Promenades du Musée; ⌗ 5122 Côte-des-Neiges, ℡ 514/738–8464; ⌗ 901 rue Ste-Catherine Est, ℡ 514/842–4915) is open 24 hours.

Lodging Reservations

Bed and Breakfast à Montréal (⌗ Marian Kahn, Box 575, Snowdon Station, H3X 3T8, ℡ 514/738–9410 or 800/738–4338, FAX 514/735–7493) represents more than 50 homes in downtown and in the elegant neighborhoods of Westmount and Outremont. Singles run $45–$55, doubles $60–$95.

Downtown B&B Network (⌗ Bob Finkelstein, 3458 av. Laval, H2X 3C8, ℡ 514/289–9749 or 800/267–5180) represents 75 homes and apartments, mostly around the downtown core and along rue Sherbrooke, that have one or more rooms available for visitors. Singles are $30–$40, doubles $40–$65.

There is a room reservation service at **Info-Touriste** (℡ 800/665–1528), which can find you a room in one of 80 hotels, motels, and bed-and-breakfasts.

Museum Pass

The Montréal **museum pass** allows access to 19 major museums. A day pass costs $15, a three-day pass $28; family passes are $30 for one day and $60 for three days. They are available at museums or Centre Info-Touriste (⌗ 1001 Sq. Dorchester).

Travel Agencies

American Express (⌗ 1141 blvd. de Maisonneuve Ouest, ℡ 514/284–3300). **Canadian Automobile Club** (⌗ 1180 rue Drummond, ℡ 514/861–5111). **Vacances Tourbec** (⌗ 595 blvd. de Maisonneuve Ouest, ℡ 514/842–1400). **Voyages Campus** (⌗ McGill University, 3480 rue McTavish, ℡ 514/398–0647).

Visitor Information

Centre Info-Touriste (✉ 1001 Sq. Dorchester, ☎ 514/873–2015 or 800/363–7777) on Square Dorchester is open June 10–Labor Day, daily 8:30–7:30, and Labor Day–June 9, daily 9–6. A second branch (✉ 174 rue Notre-Dame Est, at Pl. Jacques-Cartier, ☎ 514/873–2015) is open Labor Day–mid-May, daily 9–1 and 2–5, and mid-May–Labor Day, daily 9–7.

9 Québec City

Whether you're strolling along the Plains of Abraham or exploring the Vieux-Port, Québec City will give you a feeling for centuries of history and French civilization. The city, which has one of the most spectacular settings in North America, is perched on a cliff above a narrow point in the St. Lawrence River. It is the capital of, as well as the oldest municipality in, Québec province.

NO EXCURSION TO FRENCH-SPEAKING Canada is complete without a visit to exuberant, romantic Québec City, which can claim one of the most beautiful natural settings in North America. The well-preserved Vieux-Québec (Old Québec) is small and dense, steeped in four centuries of history and French tradition. Here are 17th- and 18th-century buildings, the ramparts that once protected the city, and numerous parks and monuments. The Québec government has completely restored many of the centuries-old buildings of Place Royale, one of the oldest districts on the continent. Because of its immaculate preservation as the only fortified city remaining in North America, UNESCO has designated Vieux-Québec a World Heritage Site.

Updated by
Elizabeth
Thompson

Perched on a cliff above a narrow point in the St. Lawrence River, Québec City is the oldest municipality in Québec province. In the 17th century the first French explorers, fur trappers, and missionaries came here to establish the colony of New France. Today it still resembles a French provincial town in many ways; its family-oriented residents have strong ties to their past. An estimated 96% of the Québec City region's population of more than 650,000 are French-speaking.

In 1535 French explorer Jacques Cartier first came upon what the Algonquin people called "Kebec," meaning "where the river narrows." New France, however, was not actually founded in the vicinity of what is now Québec City until 1608, when another French explorer, Samuel de Champlain, recognized the military advantages of the location and set up a fort. On the banks of the St. Lawrence, on the spot now called Place Royale, this fort developed into an economic center for fur trade and shipbuilding. Twelve years later, Champlain realized the French colony's vulnerability to attacks from above and expanded its boundaries to the top of the cliff, where he built the fort Château St-Louis on the site of the present-day Château Frontenac.

During the early days of New France, the French and British fought for control of the region. In 1690, when an expedition led by Admiral Sir William Phipps arrived from England, Comte de Frontenac, New France's most illustrious governor, defied him with the statement, "Tell your lord that I will reply with the mouth of my cannons."

The French, preoccupied with scandals at the courts of Louis XV and Louis XVI, gave only grudging help to their possessions in the New World. The French colonists built walls and other military structures and had the strong defensive position on top of the cliff, but they still had to contend with Britain's naval supremacy. On September 13, 1759, the British army, led by General James Wolfe, scaled the colony's cliff and took the French troops led by General Louis-Joseph Montcalm by surprise. The British defeated the French in a 20-minute battle on the Plains of Abraham, and New France came under British rule.

The British brought their mastery of trade to the region. During the 18th century, Québec City's economy prospered because of the success of the fishing, fur-trading, shipbuilding, and timber industries. Wary of new invasions, the British continued to expand upon the fortifications left by the French. They built a wall encircling the city and a star-shape citadel, both of which mark the city's urban landscape today. The constitution of 1791 established Québec City as the capital of Lower Canada until the 1840 Act of Union united Upper and Lower Canada and made Montréal the capital. The city remained under British rule until 1867, when the Act of Confederation united several Canadian

Metropolitan Québec City

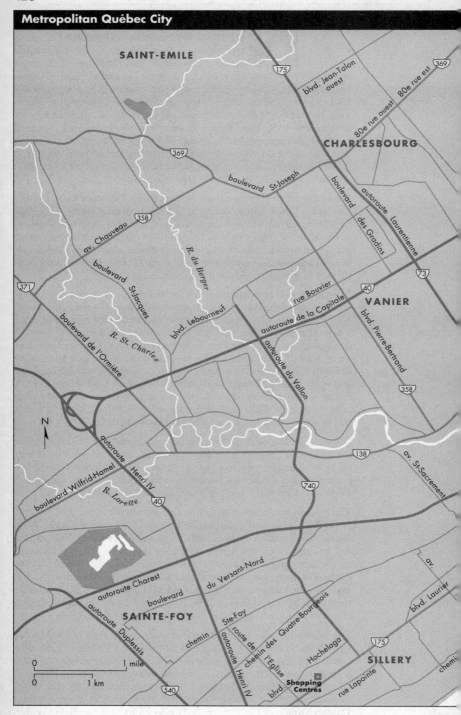

SAINT-EMILE

175

blvd. Jean-Talon ouest

80e rue ouest

80e rue est

369

CHARLESBOURG

369

boulevard St-Joseph

358

av. Chauveau

boulevard St-Jacques

R. du Berger

boulevard des Gradins

autoroute Laurentienne

73

371

blvd. Lebourneuf

rue Bouvier

40

VANIER

R. St. Charles

autoroute de la Capitale

blvd. Pierre-Bertrand

boulevard de l'Ormière

autoroute du Vallon

358

N

138

av. St-Sacrement

autoroute Henri IV

boulevard Wilfrid-Hamel

740

R. Lorette

40

du Versant-Nord

av.

blvd. Laurier

autoroute Charest

boulevard Ste-Foy

chemin des Quatre-Bourgeois

autoroute Duplessis

SAINTE-FOY

chemin Ste-Foy

route de l'Église

Hochelaga

175

SILLERY

chemi

0   1 mile

0   1 km

540

autoroute Henri IV

blvd.

rue Lapointe

chemi

Shopping
Centres

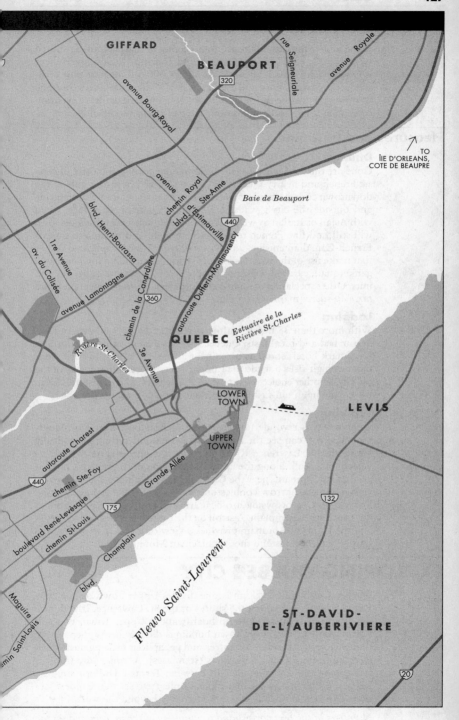

GIFFARD

BEAUPORT

rue Seigneuriale

avenue Royale

avenue Bourg-Royal

320

avenue Royal

chemin Royal

blvd. d' Ste-Anne

blvd. d' Estimauville

Baie de Beauport

TO
ÎLE D'ORLEANS,
CÔTE DE BEAUPRÉ

blvd. Henri-Bourassa

1re Avenue

av. du Colisée

avenue Lamontagne

chemin de la Canardière

440

autoroute Dufferin-Montmorency

360

QUEBEC

Estuaire de la
Rivière St-Charles

Rivière St-Charles

3e Avenue

LOWER
TOWN

LEVIS

UPPER
TOWN

autoroute Charest

chemin Ste-Foy

440

boulevard René-Lévesque

175

chemin St-Louis

Grande Allée

132

blvd. Champlain

Maguire

min Saint-Louis

Fleuve Saint-Laurent

ST-DAVID-
DE-L'AUBERIVIERE

20

provinces (Québec, Ontario, New Brunswick, and Nova Scotia) and established Québec City as capital of the province of Québec.

In the mid-19th century, the economic center of eastern Canada shifted west from Québec City to Montréal and Toronto. Today, government is Québec City's main business: About 27,000 full- or part-time civil-service employees work and live in the area. Office complexes continue to spring up outside the older part of town; modern malls, convention centers, and imposing hotels now cater to a business clientele.

Pleasures and Pastimes

Dining

Gone are the days when Québec City dining consisted mostly of classic French and hearty Québécois cuisine, served in restaurants in the downtown core. Nowadays the city's finest eateries, found both inside and outside the city's walls, offer lighter contemporary fare, often with Asian or Italian as well as French and Québécois influences. You will still find fine French restaurants, though, and be able to sample French-Canadian cuisine, composed of robust, uncomplicated dishes that make use of the region's bounty of foods, including fowl and wild game (quail, caribou, venison), maple syrup, and various berries and nuts. Other specialties include *cretons* (pâtés), *tourtière* (meat pie), and *tarte au sucre* (maple-syrup pie).

Lodging

With more than 35 hotels within its walls and an abundance of family-run bed-and-breakfasts, Québec City has a range of lodging options. Landmark hotels stand as prominent as the city's most historic sites; modern high-rises outside the ramparts have spectacular views of the old city. Another choice is to immerse yourself in the city's historic charm by staying in an old-fashioned inn where no two rooms are alike.

Walking

Québec City is a wonderful place to wander on foot. From Parc Montmorency, you can see the Laurentian Mountains jutting majestically above the St. Lawrence River. Even more impressive vistas are revealed on a walk along the city walls or a climb to the city's highest point, Cap Diamant, near the Citadelle. It's possible to spend days investigating the narrow cobblestone streets of Vieux-Québec, visiting historic sites, or browsing for local arts and crafts in the boutiques of quartier Petit-Champlain. A stroll on the Promenade des Gouverneurs and the Plains of Abraham provides a view of the river as well as the Laurentian foothills and the Appalachian Mountains.

EXPLORING QUÉBEC CITY

Québec City's split-level landscape divides Upper Town on the cape from Lower Town, along the shores of the St. Lawrence. If you look out from the Terrasse Dufferin boardwalk in Upper Town, you will see the rooftops of Lower Town buildings directly below. Separating these two sections of the city is steep and precipitous rock, against which were built more than 25 *escaliers* (staircases). A *funiculaire* (funicular) climbs and descends the cliff between Terrasse Dufferin and the Maison Jolliet in Lower Town. There's plenty to see in the oldest sections of town, as well as in the modern city beyond the walls.

Numbers in the text correspond to numbers in the margin and on the Upper and Lower Towns (Haute-Ville, Basse-Ville), Outside the City Walls, and Ile d'Orléans maps.

Great Itineraries

Whether you take a weekend or almost a week, there's enough history, scenery, and entertainment for even the most seasoned traveler. On a weekend or four-day trip, you can take in the historic sites of Vieux-Québec, walking along ancient streets and the boardwalk by the river before dining at some of the city's fine restaurants. A longer stay allows you to wander beyond the city proper.

IF YOU HAVE 2 DAYS

With only a couple of days, you should devote one day to Lower Town, where you will find the earliest site of French civilization in North America, and the second day to Upper Town, where more of the later British influence can be seen. On Day 1, stroll through the narrow streets of the Petit-Champlain, visiting the Maison Chevalier and browsing through the many handicraft boutiques. Moving on to Place Royale, you'll find the Église Notre-Dame-des-Victoires; in summer there's a wide variety of entertainment in the square. On Day 2, take the time to view the St. Lawrence River from Terrasse Dufferin and visit the impressive buildings of Upper Town, where 17th- and 18th-century religious and educational institutions predominate.

IF YOU HAVE 4 DAYS

A four-day trip allows you to wander farther afield, outside the walls of the Old Town. On Day 3, watch the pomp and ceremony of the changing of the guard at the Citadelle; roam the Plains of Abraham, site of the battle that decided the fate of New France; and tour the National Assembly, where the battles for power are still being waged. On Day 4, you can take a more in-depth look at the Musée du Québec or the Musé de la Civilisation. See the city from a different vantage point—aboard a horse-drawn calèche or from a walk atop the ramparts. In summer, do what the locals do—grab a seat on an outdoor *terrasse*, sip a cool drink, and watch the world go by.

IF YOU HAVE 6 DAYS

A trip this length gives you time to experience some of Quebec's scenic countryside. Follow the itinerary above for a four-day trip. On Day 5, you could spend more time exploring the Old Town. Or you could take historic avenue Royale (Route 360) east to the Basilica of Ste-Anne-de-Beaupré and Montmorency Falls, higher than Niagara. Afterward, you can cross the bridge to explore the farms and woodlands of Ile d'Orléans. On Day 6, do something you've never done before. In summer, you can take a boat cruise along the St. Lawrence or raft down the Jacques Cartier River. In winter, strap on skis and head to Mont Ste-Anne. Try ice canoeing on the St. Lawrence, dogsledding, or even ice climbing at the Montmorency Falls.

Upper Town

The most prominent buildings of Québec City's earliest European inhabitants, who set up political, educational, and religious institutions, stand here. Haute-Ville, or Upper Town, became the political capital of the colony of New France and, later, of British North America. Historic buildings with thick stone walls, large wood doors, glimmering copper roofs, and majestic steeples fill the heart of the city.

A Good Walk

Begin your walk where rue St-Louis meets rue du Fort at **Place d'Armes** ①, a large plaza bordered by government buildings. To your right is the colony's former treasury building, **Maison Maillou**, interesting for its 18th-century architecture. A little farther along, at 25 rue St-Louis, is Maison Kent, where the terms of the surrender of Québec to the British were signed in 1759. South of Place d'Armes stands Québec City's most celebrated landmark, **Château Frontenac** ②, an impressive green-turreted hotel on the site of what was once the administrative and military headquarters of New France. As you head to the board-walk behind the Frontenac, notice the glorious bronze statue of Samuel de Champlain, standing where he built his residence.

Walk south along the boardwalk called the **Terrasse Dufferin** ③ for a panoramic view of the city and its surroundings. As you pass to the southern side of the Frontenac, you will come to a small park called **Jardin des Gouverneurs** ④. From the north side of the park, follow rue Haldimand and turn left on rue St-Louis; then make a right and fol-low rue du Parloir until it intersects with tiny rue Donnacona. Here you'll find the **Couvent des Ursulines** ⑤, a private school that houses a museum and has a lovely chapel next door.

On the nearby rue des Jardins, you'll see the **Holy Trinity Anglican Cathe-dral** ⑥, a dignified church with precious objects on display. Next come two buildings interesting for their Art Deco details: the **Hôtel Claren-don** ⑦, just east of the cathedral, on the corner of rue des Jardins and rue Ste-Anne, and, next door, the **Edifice Price** ⑧. Continue along rue Ste-Anne up to rue St-Stanislas and **Morrin College** ⑨, a building that started out as a prison and now houses the Literary and Historical So-ciety library. Walk along rue St-Stanislas and turn left up rue Dauphine to the **Chapelle des Jésuites** ⑩ at the corner of rues Dauphine and d'Au-teuil. Turn right on rue d'Auteuil and head down the hill to rue St-Jean and the entrance to the **Parc de l'Artillerie** ⑪, a complex of 20 mili-tary, industrial, and civilian buildings.

On your way out of Artillery Park, turn left, away from the walls, and walk along rue St-Jean, one of Québec City's most colorful thor-oughfares; turn left on rue Collins. The cluster of stone buildings at the end of the street is the **Monastère des Augustines de l'Hôtel-Dieu de Québec** ⑫, which can be toured. Turn right along rue Charlevoix, then left on rue Hamel to rue des Remparts. To the right, on rue des Remparts between rues Hamel and St-Flavien, is the **Maison Montcalm** ⑬, the former home of General Montcalm.

Continue along rue des Remparts and then turn right on rue Ste-Famille. When you reach côte de la Fabrique, you will find the iron entrance gates of the **Séminaire du Québec** ⑭. Head north across the courtyard to the **Musée de l'Amérique Française** ⑮. Next, you can visit the seminary's Chapelle Extérieure, at the seminary's west entrance.

Nearby, at the corner of rue Ste-Famille and rue Buade you'll see the historic **Basilique Notre-Dame-de-Québec** ⑯, which has an ornate in-terior. Turn left on rue Buade; then cross the street halfway down the block and wander through the outdoor art gallery of **rue du Trésor** ⑰. At the end of the alley, turn left on rue Ste-Anne and wind up your walk (and rest your feet) with a 30-minute recap of the six sieges of Québec City at the **Musée du Fort** ⑱.

TIMING

Plan on spending at least a day visiting the sites and museums in Upper Town. Lunchtime should find you around Parc de l'Artillerie and rue St-Jean, where there is a good selection of restaurants. Those who pre-fer a leisurely pace could take two days, stopping to watch street per-formers and enjoy long lunches. May through October are the best months for walking, July and August being the busiest.

Sights to See

16 **Basilique Notre-Dame-de-Québec.** This basilica has the oldest parish in North America, dating from 1647. It's been rebuilt three times: in the early 1700s, when François de Montmorency Laval was the first bishop; in 1759, after cannons at Lévis fired upon it during the siege of Québec; and in 1922, after a fire. The basilica's somberly ornate interior includes a canopy dais over the episcopal throne, a ceiling of clouds decorated with gold leaf, richly colored stained-glass windows, and a chancel lamp that was a gift of Louis XIV. The large and famous crypt was Québec City's first cemetery; more than 900 people are interred here, including 20 bishops and four governors of New France. Samuel de Champlain is believed to be buried near the basilica: Archaeologists have searched for his tomb since 1950. In summer the indoor Act of Faith sound-and-light show uses the basilica as a backdrop to tell the history of the city and the basilica. ⊠ *16 rue Buade,* ☎ *418/692–2533.* ⊠ *Basilica free, sound-and-light show $7.* ⊙ *Oct.–May, daily 7:30–4:30; June–Sept., daily 7:30–3, followed by sound-and-light show.*

Centre Marie-de-l'Incarnation. Next to the ☞ **Musée des Ursulines** is this bookstore with an exhibit on the life of the Ursulines' first superior, who came from France and cofounded the convent. ⊠ *10 rue Donnacona,* ☎ *418/ 694–0413.* ⊠ *Free.* ⊙ *Feb.–Nov., Tues.–Sat. 10–11:30 and 1:30–4:30, Sun. 1:30–4:30.*

10 **Chapelle des Jésuites** (Jesuits' Chapel). Built in 1820 from plans by architect François Baillairgé, the chapel and its sculptures and paintings are considered one of the monuments of Québec art of the period. Sculptor Pierre-Noël Levasseur contributed the delicately carved high altar and wooden statues of the Blessed Virgin and St. Joseph. ⊠ *20 rue Dauphine,* ☎ *418/694–9616.* ⊠ *Free.* ⊙ *Weekdays 11–1:30.*

Chapelle des Ursulines (Ursuline Chapel). On the grounds of the ☞ **Couvent des Ursulines** stands a little chapel where French general Louis-Joseph Montcalm was buried after he died in the 1759 battle. The exterior was rebuilt in 1902, but the interior contains the original chapel, which took sculptor Pierre-Noël Levasseur from 1726 to 1736 to complete. The votive lamp was lit in 1717 and has never been extinguished. ⊠ *12 rue Donnacona.* ⊠ *Free.* ⊙ *May–Oct., Tues.–Sat. 10–11:30 and 1:30–4:30, Sun. 1:30–4:30.*

★ **2** **Château Frontenac.** Québec City's most celebrated landmark, this imposing green-turreted castle with its copper roof stands on the site of what was the administrative and military headquarters of New France. It owes its name to the Comte de Frontenac, governor of the French colony between 1672 and 1698. Looking at the magnificence of the château's location, you can see why Frontenac said, "For me, there is no site more beautiful nor more grandiose than that of Québec City." Samuel de Champlain, who founded Québec City in 1608, was responsible for Château St-Louis, the first structure to appear on the site of the Frontenac; it was built between 1620 and 1624 as a residence for colonial governors. In 1784, Château Haldimand was constructed here, but it was demolished in 1892 to make way for Château Frontenac (☞ Lodging, *below*). The latter was built as a hotel in 1893, and it was considered to be remarkably luxurious at that time: Guest rooms contained fireplaces, bathrooms, and marble fixtures, and a special commissioner purchased antiques for the establishment. The hotel was designed by New York architect Bruce Price, who also worked on Québec City's Gare du Palais (rail station) and other Canadian landmarks, such as Montréal's Windsor Station. The Frontenac was completed in 1925 with the addition of a 20-story central tower. Owned by Canadian Pacific Hotels, it has accumulated a star-studded guest roster, including

432

Upper and Lower Towns (Haute-Ville, Basse-Ville)

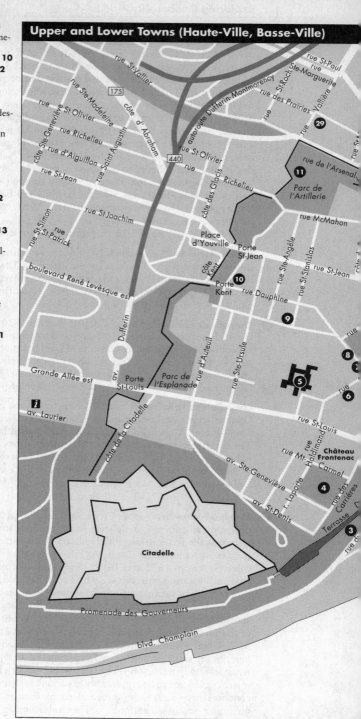

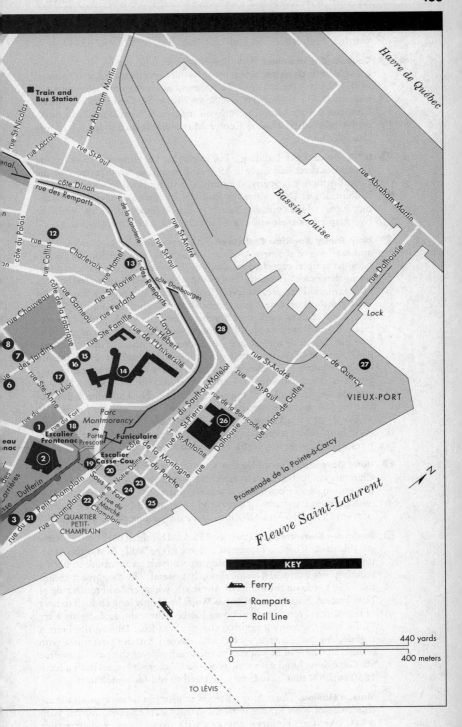

Train and Bus Station

rue St-Nicolas

rue Lacroix

rue Abraham Martin

rue St-Paul

canal

côte Dinan

rue des Remparts

côte du Palais

côte de la Canoterie

rue Collins

Charlevoix

12

rue St-André

côte de la Fabrique

rue Chauveau

rue Garneau

rue Hamel

rue St-Flavien

rue Ferland

rue St-Paul

13

côte Dambourges

des Remparts

rue Ste-Famille

rue Hébert

rue Laval

rue de l'Université

8

des Jardins

7

15

16

14

6

rue Ste-Anne

17

Trésor

28

rue du

rue du Fort

Parc Montmorency

r. du Sault-au-Matelot

rue St-André

r. de Quercy

27

VIEUX-PORT

rue St-Pierre

rue de la Barricade

rue Prince-de-Galles

rue Dalhousie

St-Paul

Lock

Bassin Louise

rue Dalhousie

rue Abraham Martin

Havre de Québec

1

Escalier Frontenac

18

Porte Prescott

Funiculaire

côte de la Montagne

26

rue St-Antoine

Escalier Casse-Cou

2

19

Sous le Fort

Notre-Dame

r. du Porche

23

Promenade de la Pointe-à-Carcy

eau nac

Dufferin

Carrières

3

21

Petit-Champlain

rue du Champlain

22

QUARTIER PETIT-CHAMPLAIN

rue du Marché Champlain

20

24

25

Fleuve Saint-Laurent

N

KEY

- Ferry
- Ramparts
- Rail Line

0 — 440 yards
0 — 400 meters

TO LÉVIS

Queen Elizabeth and Ronald Reagan as well as Franklin Roosevelt and Winston Churchill, who convened here in 1943 and 1944 for two wartime conferences. ⊠ *1 rue des Carrières,* ☎ *418/692–3861.*

★ ❺ **Couvent des Ursulines** (Ursuline Convent). The site of North America's oldest teaching institution for girls, still a private school, was founded in 1639 by two French nuns. The convent has many of its original walls still intact. On its property are the ☞ **Musée des Ursulines** and the ☞ **Chapelle des Ursulines,** which you may visit. Next door is an interesting bookstore, the ☞ **Centre Marie-de-l'Incarnation.** ⊠ *18 rue Donnacona.*

★ ❽ **Edifice Price** (Price Building). The city's first skyscraper, a 15-story Art Deco structure, was built in 1929 and served as headquarters of the Price Brothers Company, the lumber firm founded in Canada by Sir William Price. Don't miss the interior: Exquisite copper plaques depict scenes of the company's early pulp and paper activities, while the two maple-wood elevators are '30s classics. ⊠ *65 rue Ste-Anne.*

❻ **Holy Trinity Anglican Cathedral.** This stone church dates from 1804 and was one of the first Anglican cathedrals built outside the British Isles. Its simple, dignified facade is reminiscent of London's St. Martin-in-the-Fields. The cathedral's land was originally given to the Recollet fathers (Franciscan monks from France) in 1681 by the king of France for a church and monastery. When Québec came under British rule, the Recollets made the church available to the Anglicans for services. Later, King George III of England ordered construction of the present cathedral, with an area set aside for members of the royal family. A portion of the north balcony still remains exclusively for the use of the reigning sovereign or her representative. The church houses precious objects donated by George III; wood for the oak benches was imported from the Royal Forest at Windsor. The cathedral's impressive rear organ has more than 2,500 pipes. ⊠ *31 rue des Jardins,* ☎ *418/692–2193.* 🎫 *Free.* ⊙ *May–June, daily 9–5; July–Aug., daily 9–9; Sept.–Oct., weekdays 10–4; Nov.–Apr., services only; Sun. services in English 8:30 and 11 AM, and in French 9:30 AM.*

❼ **Hôtel Clarendon.** One of Québec City's finest Art Deco structures is the Clarendon, Québec's oldest hotel (☞ Lodging, *below*). Although the Clarendon dates from 1866, it was reconstructed in its current style—with geometric patterns of stone and wrought iron decorating its interior—in 1930. ⊠ *57 rue Ste-Anne, at rue des Jardins,* ☎ *418/692–2480.*

❹ **Jardin des Gouverneurs** (Governors' Park). This small park on the southern side of the Château Frontenac is home to the **Wolfe-Montcalm Monument,** a 50-ft obelisk that is unique because it pays tribute to both a winning (English) and a losing (French) general. The monument recalls the 1759 battle on the Plains of Abraham, which ended French rule of New France. British general James Wolfe lived only long enough to hear of his victory; French general Louis-Joseph Montcalm died shortly after Wolfe with the knowledge that the city was lost. During the French regime, the public area served as a garden for the governors who resided in Château St-Louis. On the south side of the park is **avenue Ste-Geneviève,** lined with well-preserved Victorian houses dating from 1850 to 1900 that have been converted to old-fashioned inns.

Maison Maillou. The colony's former treasury building typifies the architecture of New France with its sharply slanted roof, dormer windows, concrete chimneys, shutters with iron hinges, and limestone walls. Built between 1736 and 1753, it stands at the end of ☞ **rue du Trésor.** Maison Maillou now houses the Québec City Chamber of Commerce and is not open for tours. ⊠ *17 rue St-Louis.*

⑬ Maison Montcalm. This was the home of French general Louis-Joseph Montcalm from 1758 until the capitulation of New France. A plaque dedicated to the general is on the right side of the house. ⊠ *Rue des Remparts between rues Hamel and St-Flavien. Closed to public.*

⑫ Monastère des Augustines de l'Hôtel-Dieu de Québec (Augustine Monastery). Augustine nuns arrived from Dieppe, France, in 1639 with a mission to care for the sick in the new colony; they established the first hospital north of Mexico, the **Hôtel-Dieu,** the large building west of the monastery. The **Musée des Augustines** (Augustine Museum) is in hospital-like quarters with large sterile corridors leading into a ward that has a small exhibit of antique medical instruments, such as a pill-making device from the 17th century. Upon request the Augustines also offer guided tours of the **chapel** (1800) and the cellars used by the nuns as a shelter, beginning in 1659, during bombardments by the British. ⊠ *32 rue Charlevoix,* ☎ *418/692–2492.* 🎫 *Guided tour $2.* ⊙ *Tues.– Sat. 9:30–noon and 1:30–5, Sun. 1:30–5.*

★ **⑨ Morrin College.** This stately graystone building was once Québec City's first prison (the cells can still be seen in the basement), where wrong-doers were hanged outside the front door. In 1868, it was turned into one of the city's early private schools, Morrin College. The **Literary and Historical Society library** has been on the site since then. Its superb collection includes some of the earliest books printed in North America, and the librarian's desk once belonged to Sir Georges-Étienne Cartier, one of Canada's fathers of Confederation. A statue of General Wolfe, on the second-floor balcony that wraps around the interior of the library, dates from 1779. The society, founded in 1824, is the oldest of its kind in North America and a forerunner to Canada's National Archives. ⊠ *44 rue St-Stanislas,* ☎ *418/694–9147.* 🎫 *Free.* ⊙ *Weekdays 9:30–4:30, Sat. 10–4.*

⑮ Musée de l'Amérique Française. Housed in a former student residence of the Québec Seminary–Laval University (☞ **Séminaire du Québec**), this museum focuses on the history of the French presence in North America. There are more than 400 landscape and still-life paintings dating to the 15th century, rare Canadian money from colonial times, and scientific instruments acquired for the purposes of research and teaching. The museum uses historical documents and movies to tell the story as well. A former chapel has been renovated and is used for exhibits, conferences, and cultural activities. ⊠ *9 rue de l'Université,* ☎ *418/692–2843.* 🎫 *$4; free Tues. Sept.–June 23.* ⊙ *Tues., Thurs., Fri. 9:30–4:30, Wed. 9:30–6:30, weekends 10–4.*

Musée des Ursulines (Ursuline Museum). Within the walls of the ☞ **Couvent des Ursulines** is the former residence of one of the convent's founders, Madame de la Peltrie. The museum provides an informative perspective on 120 years of the Ursulines' life under the French regime, from 1639 to 1759. It took an Ursuline nun nine years of training to attain the level of a professional embroiderer; the museum contains magnificent pieces of ornate embroidery, such as altar frontals with gold and silver threads intertwined with precious jewels. ⊠ *12 rue Don-nacona,* ☎ *418/694–0694.* 🎫 *$3.* ⊙ *May–Oct., Tues.–Sat. 10–noon and 1–5, Sun. 12:30–5.*

NEED A BREAK? The brick-wall **Bistro Taste-Vin** (⊠ 32 rue St-Louis, ☎ 418/692–4191), on the corner of rue des Jardins and rue St-Louis, is a good place to sample delicious salads, pastries, and desserts.

⑱ Musée du Fort (Fort Museum). This museum's sole exhibit is a sound-and-light show that reenacts the area's important battles, including the

Battle of the Plains of Abraham and the 1775 attack by American generals Arnold and Montgomery. ⊠ *10 rue Ste-Anne,* ☎ *418/692–1759.* ☞ *$6.25.* ☉ *June–Aug., daily 10–6; Apr.–May and Sept., daily 10–5; Oct.–Jan., by reservation; Feb.–Mar., Thurs.–Sun. noon–4.*

★ ⓫ **Parc de l'Artillerie** (Artillery Park). This national historic park is a complex of 20 military, industrial, and civilian buildings that were situated to guard the St. Charles River and the Old Port. Its earliest buildings served as headquarters for the French garrison and were taken over in 1759 by the British Royal Artillery soldiers. The defense complex was used as a fortress, barracks, and cartridge factory during the American siege of Québec in 1775 and 1776. The area served as an industrial complex providing ammunition for the Canadian army from 1879 until 1964. One of the three buildings open is a former **powder magazine,** which in 1903 became a shell foundry. The building houses a detailed model of Québec City in 1808, rendered by two surveyors in the office of the Royal Engineers Corps. Sent to Britain in 1813, it was intended to show officials the strategic importance of Québec so that more money would be provided to expand the city's fortifications. The model details the city's buildings, streets, and military structures. From April through October, the powder magazine is open daily 10–5; admission is $3. The **Dauphin Redoubt,** named in honor of the son of Louis XIV (the heir apparent), was constructed from 1712 to 1748. It served as a barracks for the French garrison until 1760, when it became an officers' mess for the Royal Artillery Regiment. It's open late June–early September, daily 10–5. The **Officers' Quarters,** a dwelling for Royal Artillery officers until 1871 when the British army departed, houses an exhibit on military life during the British regime. The Officers' Quarters are open late June–early September, daily 10–5. ⊠ *2 rue d'Auteuil,* ☎ *418/648–4205.*

❶ **Place d'Armes.** For centuries, this square atop a cliff has been a gathering place for parades and military events. Upper Town's most central location, the plaza is bordered by government buildings; at its west side is the majestic **Ancien Palais de Justice** (Old Courthouse), a Renaissance-style building from 1887. The plaza is on land that was occupied by a church and convent of the Recollet missionaries (Franciscan monks), who in 1615 were the first order of priests to arrive in New France. The Gothic-style **fountain** at the center of Place d'Armes pays tribute to their arrival. ⊠ *Rue St-Louis and rue du Fort.*

⓱ **Rue du Trésor.** The road that colonists took on their way to pay rent to the king's officials is now a narrow alley where colorful prints, paintings, and other artworks are on display. You won't necessarily find masterpieces, but this walkway is a good stop for a souvenir sketch or two. In summer, activity on this street and nearby rue Ste-Anne, lined with eateries and boutiques, starts early in the morning and continues until late at night. Stores stay open, artists paint, and street musicians perform as long as there is an audience, even if it's one o'clock in the morning. At 8 rue du Trésor is the **Québec Experience** (☎ 418/694–4000), a multimedia sound-and-light show that traces Québec's history from the first explorers until modern days; cost is $6.75.

⓮ **Séminaire du Québec.** Behind these gates lies a tranquil courtyard surrounded by austere stone buildings with rising steeples; these structures have housed classrooms and student residences since 1663. Québec Seminary was founded by François de Montmorency Laval, the first bishop of New France, to train priests in the new colony. In 1852 the seminary became Université Laval, the first Catholic university in North America. In 1946 the university moved to a larger campus in suburban Ste-Foy. Today priests live on the premises, and Laval's architecture school occupies part of the building. The **Musée du Séminaire** has tours of the seminary in summer. The small Roman-style chapel, **Chapelle Extérieure** (Outer Chapel), at the west entrance of Québec Seminary, was built in 1888 after fire destroyed the first chapel, which dated from 1750. ⊠ *1 côte de la Fabrique,* ☏ *418/692–3981.*

❸ **Terrasse Dufferin.** This wide boardwalk with an intricate wrought-iron guardrail has a panoramic view of the St. Lawrence River, the town of Lévis on the opposite shore, Ile d'Orléans, and the Laurentian Mountains. It was named for Lord Dufferin, governor of Canada between 1872 and 1878, who had this walkway constructed in 1878. At its western end begins the **Promenade des Gouverneurs**, which skirts the cliff and leads up to Québec's highest point, Cap Diamant, and also to the Citadelle (☞ Outside the Walls, *below*).

Lower Town

New France first began to flourish in the streets of the Basse-Ville, or Lower Town, along the banks of the St. Lawrence River. These streets became the colony's economic crossroads, where furs were traded, ships came in, and merchants established their residences. Despite the status of Lower Town as the oldest neighborhood in North America, its narrow and time-worn thoroughfares have a new and polished look. In the 1960s, after a century of decay as the commercial boom moved west and left the area abandoned, the Québec government committed millions of dollars to restore the district to the way it had been during the days of New France. Today modern boutiques, restaurants, galleries, and shops catering to visitors occupy the former warehouses and residences.

A Good Walk

Begin this walk on the northern tip of rue du Petit-Champlain at **Maison Louis-Jolliet** ⑲ at the foot of the **Escalier Casse-Cou.** Across the street is the **Verrerie La Mailloche** ⑳, where master glassblowers turn molten glass into contemporary works of art. Heading south on **rue du Petit-Champlain** ㉑, the city's oldest street, you'll notice the cliff on the right that borders this narrow thoroughfare, with Upper Town on the heights above. At the point where rue du Petit-Champlain intersects with boulevard Champlain, make a U-turn to head back north on rue Champlain. One block farther, at the corner of rue du Marché-Champlain, you'll find **Maison Chevalier** ㉒, a stone house in the style of urban New France. Walk east to rue Notre-Dame, which leads directly to **Place Royale** ㉓, formerly the heart of New France. The small stone church at the south side of Place Royale is the **Église Notre-Dame-des-Victoires** ㉔, the oldest church in Québec.

On the east side of Place Royale, take rue de la Place, which leads to an open square, **Place de Paris** ㉕. You may want to stop at **Explore,** a sound-and-light show on rue Dalhousie. Continue north on rue Dalhousie until you come to the **Musée de la Civilisation** ㉖, devoted to Québécois culture and civilization. Head east toward the river to the **Vieux-Port de Québec** ㉗, at one time the busiest on the continent. The breezes from the St. Lawrence provide a cool reprieve on a hot summer's day, and you can browse through a farmer's market here. You are now in the ideal spot to explore Québec City's **antiques district** ㉘.

In summer, walk west along rue St-Paul, past the train station built in 1915 in the style of the castles in France's Loire Valley, and turn left on rue Vallière to **L'Îlot des Palais** ㉙, an archaeological museum that has the remnants of the first two palaces of the French colonial intendants (administrators) and a unique dig.

TIMING

This is a good day of sightseeing. A morning stroll will take you to two of the city's most famous squares, Place Royale and Place de Paris. You can see the city from the Lévis ferry or pause for lunch before touring the Musée de la Civilisation and the antiques district. After browsing along rue St-Paul, explore L'Îlot des Palais.

Sights to See

28 Antiques district. Antiques shops cluster along rue St-Pierre and rue St-Paul. Rue St-Paul was once part of a business district where warehouses, stores, and businesses abounded. After World War I, shipping and commercial activities plummeted; low rents attracted antiques dealers. Today numerous cafés, restaurants, and art galleries have turned this area into one of the town's more fashionable sections.

24 Église Notre-Dame-des-Victoires (Our Lady of Victory Church). The oldest church in Québec was built on the site of Samuel de Champlain's first residence, which also served as a fort and trading post. The church was built in 1688 and was restored twice. Its name comes from two French victories against the British: one in 1690 against Admiral William Phipps and another in 1711 against Sir Hovendon Walker. The interior contains copies of paintings by such European masters as Van Dyck, Rubens, and Boyermans; its altar resembles the shape of a fort. A scale model suspended from the ceiling represents *Le Brezé*, the boat that transported French soldiers to New France in 1664. The side chapel is dedicated to Ste-Geneviève, the patron saint of Paris. ⊠ *Pl. Royale,* ☎ *418/692–1650.* ☜ *Free.* ⊘ *Mid-May–mid-Oct., Sun.–Fri. 9–4:30, Sat. 9–4, except during Mass (Sun. at 9, 10, and noon; Sat. at 7 PM), marriages, and funerals; mid-Oct.–mid-May, daily 9–4:30, except during Mass, marriages, and funerals.*

Escalier Casse-Cou. The steepness of the city's first iron stairway, an ambitious 1893 design by city architect and engineer Charles Baillairgé, is ample evidence of how it got its name: Breakneck Steps. The steps were built on the site of the original 17th-century stairway that linked the Upper Town and Lower Town during the French regime. Today shops, quaint boutiques, and restaurants are at various levels.

Explore. This 30-minute sound-and-light show uses high-tech visual art to re-create the story of the founding of the city. You can sail up the St. Lawrence River with Jacques Cartier and Samuel de Champlain to Québec and witness their first encounter with the area's native people. ⊠ *63 rue Dalhousie,* ☎ *418/692–2063 or 418/692–1759.* ☜ *$5.50.* ⊘ *June–Aug., daily 11–5; Sept.–May, by reservation only.*

29 L'Îlot des Palais. More than 300 years of history have been laid bare at this archaeological museum on the site of the first two palaces of New France's colonial intendants. The first palace, erected as a brewery by Jean Talon in 1669, was turned into the intendant's residence in 1685 and destroyed by fire in 1713. In 1716, a second palace was built facing the first. It was later turned into a modern brewery, but the basement vaults remain. On the site of the first palace, the dig that lasted 10 years has been conserved and turned into a unique archaeological display. ⊠ *8 rue Vallière,* ☎ *418/691–6092.* ☜ *Free.* ⊘ *May–June 23 and Labor Day–Oct., Tues.–Sun. 10–5; June 24–Labor Day, daily 10–5.*

OFF THE
BEATEN PATH
LÉVIS–QUÉBEC FERRY –En route to the opposite shore of the St. Lawrence River, you get a striking view of Québec City's skyline, with the Château Frontenac and the Québec Seminary high atop the cliff. The view is even more impressive at night. E Rue Dalhousie, 1 block south of Place

de Paris, ☎ *418/644-3704.* ☜ *$1.25.* ☉ *See Getting Around in Québec City A to Z, below, for hrs.*

㉒ **Maison Chevalier.** This old stone house was built in 1752 for shipowner Jean-Baptiste Chevalier; the house's style, of classic French inspiration, clearly reflects the urban architecture of New France. The fire walls, chimneys, vaulted cellars, and original wood beams and stone fireplaces are noteworthy. ✉ *60 rue du Marché-Champlain,* ☎ *418/643–2158.* ☜ *Free.* ☉ *May 6–June 22 and Sept. 8–Oct., Tues.–Sun. 10–6; June 23–Sept. 7, daily 10–6; Nov.–May 5, weekends 10–5.*

⑲ **Maison Louis-Jolliet.** Built in 1683, this house is the lower station of the funicular and was used by the first settlers of New France as a base for further westward explorations. A monument commemorating Louis Jolliet's discovery of the Mississippi River in 1672 stands in the park next to the house. At the north side of the house is the ☞ **Escalier Casse-Cou.** ✉ *16 rue du Petit-Champlain.*

👣 ㉖ **Musée de la Civilisation** (Museum of Civilization). Wedged into the foot of the cliff, this spacious museum with a striking limestone-and-glass facade has been artfully designed by architect Moshe Safdie to blend into the landscape. Its campanile echoes the shape of church steeples throughout the city. The museum has innovative exhibits devoted to aspects of Québec's culture. It tells the story of how the first settlers lived, and how they survived such harsh winters. It illustrates to what extent the Roman Catholic Church dominated the people and explains the evolution of Québec nationalism. Several of the shows, with their imaginative use of artwork, video screens, computers, and sound, will appeal to both adults and children. The museum's thematic, interactive approach also extends to exhibits of an international nature. ✉ *85 rue Dalhousie,* ☎ *418/643–2158.* ☜ *$7; free Tues. in winter.* ☉ *June 24–Aug., daily 10–7; Sept.–June 23, Tues.–Sun. 10–5.*

㉕ **Place de Paris.** This square, a newcomer (1987) to these historic quarters, is dominated by a black-and-white geometric sculpture, *Dialogue avec l'Histoire (Dialogue with History),* a gift from France positioned on the site where the first French settlers landed. ✉ *rue Dalhousie.*

NEED A BREAK? **Café du Monde** (✉ 57 rue Dalhousie, ☎ 418/692–4455), with an impressive view of the St. Lawrence River, specializes in brunch on Saturday and Sunday. Omelets, sausages, waffles with maple syrup, and *moules et frites* (mussels with french fries) are popular.

㉓ **Place Royale.** The cobblestone square is encircled by the former homes of wealthy merchants, which have steep Normandy-style roofs, dormer windows, and several chimneys. Until 1686 the area was called Place du Marché, but its name was changed when a bust of Louis XIV was erected at its center. During the late 1600s and early 1700s, when Place Royale was continually under threat of attacks from the British, the colonists progressively moved to higher and safer quarters atop the cliff in Upper Town. Yet after the French colony fell to British rule in 1759, Place Royale flourished again with shipbuilding, logging, fishing, and fur trading. An **information center** (✉ 215 Marche Finlay, ☎ 418/646–3167) about the square is open June 3–September 29.

㉑ **Rue du Petit-Champlain.** The oldest street in the city was the main street of a former harbor village, with trading posts and the homes of rich merchants. Today it has pleasant boutiques and cafés. Natural-fiber weaving, Inuit carvings, hand-painted silks, and enameled copper crafts are some of the local specialties that are good buys here.

(C) ㉓ **Verrerie La Mailloche.** The glassblowing techniques used in this combination workshop, boutique, and museum are as old as Ancient Egypt, but the results are contemporary. In the workshop, master glassblower Jean Vallières turns 1092°C (2000°F) molten glass into works of art and answers questions. Examples of his work have been presented by the Canadian government to visiting dignitaries such as Queen Elizabeth and former president Ronald Reagan. ✉ *58 rue Sous-le-Fort,* ☎ *418/694–0445.* 🎫 *Free.* ⊙ *Workshop June–Oct., Wed.–Sun. 10– 4:30; Nov.–June, weekdays 10–4:30. Boutique regular store hrs in winter, daily 9* AM*–10* PM *in summer.*

㉗ **Vieux-Port de Québec** (Old Port of Québec). Today this historic 72-acre area encompasses several parks. The old harbor dates from the 17th century, when ships first arrived from Europe bringing supplies and settlers to the new colony. At one time this port was among the busiest on the continent: Between 1797 and 1897, Québec shipyards turned out more than 2,500 ships, many of which passed the 1,000-ton mark. The port saw a rapid decline after steel replaced wood and the channel to Montréal was deepened to allow larger boats to reach a good port upstream. You can stroll along the riverside promenade, where merchant and cruise ships are docked. At the port's northern end, where the St. Charles meets the St. Lawrence, a lock protects the marina in the Louise Basin from the generous Atlantic tides that reach even this far up the St. Lawrence. In the northwest section of the port, an exhibition center, **Port de Québec in the 19th Century** (✉ 100 rue St-André, ☎ 418/648–3300), presents the history of the port in relation to the lumber trade and shipbuilding. Admission to the center is $2.75; it is open May–Labor Day, daily 10–5; Labor Day–Thanksgiving, noon–4; Thanksgiving–April, by reservation only. At the port's northwestern tip is the **Marché du Vieux-Port** (Old Port Market), where farmers sell their fresh produce. The market is open May–October, daily 8–8.

Outside the Walls

In the 20th century, Québec City grew into a modern metropolis outside the confines of the city walls. Beyond the walls lies a great deal of the city's military history, in the form of its fortifications and battlements, as well as a number of museums and other attractions.

A Good Walk

Start close to Porte St-Louis (St-Louis Gate) at the **Parc de l'Esplanade** ㉚, the site of a former military parade ground. From the powder magazine in the park, head south on côte de la Citadelle, which leads directly to **La Citadelle** ㉛, a historic fortified base. Retrace your steps down côte de la Citadelle to Grande Allée. Continue west until you come to the **Parliament Buildings** ㉜, which mark Parliament Hill, headquarters of the provincial government. Across the street, in the modern concrete building, are the offices of Quebec's premier. Farther along Grande Allée is the Manège Militaire, a turreted armory built in 1888 that is still a drill hall for the 22nd Regiment.

Continue along **Grande Allée** ㉝, Québec City's version of the Champs-Elysées, with its cafés, clubs, and restaurants. If you turn left on Place Montcalm, you'll be facing the **Montcalm Monument** ㉞. Continue south on Place Montcalm to the historic and scenic **Parc des Champs-de-Bataille** ㉟. Within the park are the **Plains of Abraham** ㊱, site of the famous 1759 battle that decided the fate of New France.

Take avenue Laurier, which runs parallel to the park, a block west until you come to a neatly tended garden called **Parc Jeanne d'Arc** ㊲. If you

Outside the Walls

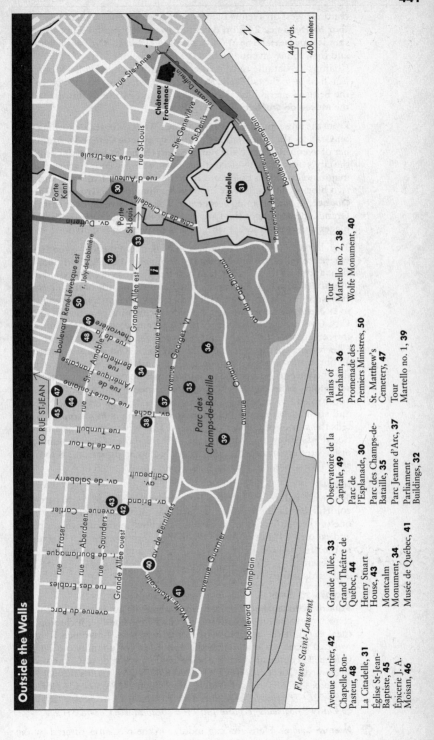

440 yds.

400 meters

Avenue Cartier, **42**
Chapelle Bon-
Pasteur, **48**
La Citadelle, **31**
Église St-Jean-
Baptiste, **45**
Épicerie J. A.
Moisan, **46**

Grande Allée, **33**
Grand Théâtre de
Québec, **44**
Henry Stuart
House, **43**
Montcalm
Monument, **34**
Musée de Québec, **41**

Observatoire de la
Capitale, **49**
Parc de
l'Esplanade, **30**
Parc des Champs-de-
Bataille, **35**
Parc Jeanne d'Arc, **37**
Parliament
Buildings, **32**

Plains of
Abraham, **36**
Promenade des
Premiers Ministres, **50**
St. Matthew's
Cemetery, **47**
Tour
Martello no. 1, **39**

Tour
Martello no. 2, **38**
Wolfe Monument, **40**

continue west on avenue Laurier, you'll see a stone oval defense tower, **Tour Martello no. 2** ㊳; on the left, toward the south end of the park, stands **Tour Martello no. 1** ㊴. Continue a block west on rue de Bernières and then follow avenue George-VI along the outskirts of the Parc des Champs-de-Bataille until it intersects with avenue Wolfe-Montcalm. You'll come to the tall **Wolfe Monument** ㊵, which marks the place where the British general died. Turn left on avenue Wolfe-Montcalm to visit the **Musée de Québec** ㊶.

From the museum head north on avenue Wolfe-Montcalm, turning right on Grande Allée and walking a block to **avenue Cartier** ㊷. At the corner of avenue Cartier is the **Henry Stuart House** ㊸, which once marked the city's outskirts. If you continue north along avenue Cartier, the first major intersection is boulevard René-Lévesque Est. Turn right and walk two blocks to the concrete modern building of the **Grand Théâtre de Québec** ㊹, a performing arts center. The high-waving flags east of the Grand Théâtre are in the Parc de l'Amérique-Française, dedicated to places in North America with a French-speaking population.

Turn left on rue Claire-Fontaine and walk down the hill to rue St-Jean, where the **Église St-Jean-Baptiste** ㊺ dominates the neighborhood. Turn right and stroll down rue St-Jean past trendy shops in century-old buildings to **Épicerie J. A. Moisan** ㊻, which claims the title of the oldest grocery store in North America. Farther down the street you will come to **St. Matthew's Cemetery** ㊼, the oldest remaining cemetery in Québec City. Cut through the cemetery to rue St-Simon, walk up the hill, cross the street, and turn right on boulevard René-Lévesque to rue de la Chevrotière. On the west side of the street is the **Chapelle Bon-Pasteur** ㊽, a church surrounded by modern office buildings. Across the street is the entrance to Edifice Marie-Guyart, whose observation tower, **Observatoire de la Capitale** ㊾, provides a spectacular view. In summer, you can end your walk by turning right after you leave the building and strolling along the **Promenade des Premiers Ministres** ㊿, which tells the stories of Quebec's premiers. This will take you past the National Assembly and within sight of the St-Louis Gate. A number of other sites are in nearby suburbs, including an aquarium, a zoo, and several gardens.

TIMING

This walk will take a full day. In summer, you should try to catch the colorful 10 AM changing of the guard at the Citadelle. For lunch, try one of the many restaurants around avenue Cartier or bring a picnic and eat on the Plains of Abraham. In the afternoon, you can head down to the area around Église St-Jean-Baptiste and then see the city from the observatory. Other afternoon choices are the aquarium, the zoo, and gardens outside the city.

Sights to See

☺ **Aquarium du Québec.** The aquarium, about 10 km (6 mi) from the city center, contains more than 340 species of marine life, including reptiles, exotic fish, and seals from the lower St. Lawrence River. A wooded picnic ground makes this spot ideal for a family outing. The Québec City transit system, Société de Transport de la Communauté Urbaine de Québec, or STCUQ (☎ 418/627–2511), runs Buses 13 and 25 here. ✉ 1675 av. des Hôtels, Ste-Foy, ☎ 418/659–5264 or 418/659–5266 (reservations required for groups of 15 or more). 💰 $9.50. ☉ Daily 9–5; seals fed and put on a show at 10:15 and 3:15.

㊷ **Avenue Cartier.** Here you can indulge in the pleasures offered by the many good restaurants, clubs, and cafés lining the street.

48 **Chapelle Bon-Pasteur.** Charles Baillargé designed this slender church with a steep sloping roof in 1868. Its ornate Baroque-style interior has carved-wood designs painted elaborately in gold leaf. The chapel houses 32 religious paintings done by the nuns of the community from 1868 to 1910. Classical concerts are performed here year-round. ⊠ *1080 rue de la Chevrotière,* ☎ *418/641–1069 or 418/648–9710.* ⊠ *Free.* ⊙ *July–Aug., Tues.– Sat. 1:30–4, Sun. 9–1; Sept.–June by reservation; musical artists' Mass Sun. 10:45.*

31 **La Citadelle** (Citadel). Built at the city's highest point, on Cap Diamant, the Citadel is the largest fortified base in North America still occupied by troops. The 25-building fortress was intended to protect the port, prevent the enemy from taking up a position on the Plains of Abraham, and provide a refuge in case of an attack. Having inherited incomplete fortifications, the British sought to complete the Citadel to protect themselves against retaliations from the French. By the time the Citadel was completed in 1832, the attacks against Québec City had ended. Since 1920 the Citadel has served as a base for the Royal 22nd Regiment. Firearms, uniforms, and decorations from the 17th century are displayed in the **Royal 22nd Regiment Museum,** in the former powder magazine, built in 1750. If weather permits, you can watch the Changing of the Guard, a ceremony in which the troops parade before the Citadel in red coats and black fur hats. Admission is by guided tour only. ⊠ *1 côte de la Citadelle,* ☎ *418/694–2815.* ⊠ *$5.* ⊙ *Apr.–mid-May, daily 10–4; mid-May–June 23, daily 9–5; June 24–Aug., daily 9–6; Sept., daily 9–4; Oct., daily 10–3, Nov.–Mar., groups only (reservations required). Changing of the guard, mid-June– Labor Day, daily 10 AM. Retreat ceremony, July–Aug., daily 6 PM.*

★ **45** **Église St-Jean-Baptiste.** Architect Joseph Ferdinand Peachy's crowning glory, this church was inspired by the facade of the Église de la Trinité in Paris and rivals the Basilique Notre-Dame-de-Québec in beauty and size. The first church on the site, built in 1847, burned in the 1881 fire that destroyed much of the neighborhood. Seven varieties of Italian marble were used in the soaring columns, statues, and pulpit of the present church, which dates to 1884. Its 36 stained-glass windows consist of 30 sections each, and the organ, like the church, is classified as a historical monument. ⊠ *410 rue St-Jean,* ☎ *418/525–7188.* ⊙ *May– Sept., weekdays 3–5:30, Sat. afternoon, and all day Sun. In other months or outside regular opening hrs, knock at the presbytery (⊠ 490 rue St-Jean) to see the church.*

46 **Épicerie J. A. Moisan.** Founded in 1871 by Jean-Alfred Moisan, this store claims the title of the oldest grocery store in North America. The original display cases, woodwork, tin ceilings, and antiques preserve that old-time feel. The store stocks a wide variety of products, including difficult-to-find delicacies from other regions of Québec. ⊠ *699 rue St-Jean,* ☎ *418/522–8268.*

33 **Grande Allée.** One of the city's oldest streets, Grande Allée was the route people took from outlying areas to sell their furs in town. Now trendy cafés, clubs, and restaurants line the road. The street actually has four names: inside the city walls, it is rue St-Louis; outside the walls, Grande Allée; farther west, chemin St-Louis; and farther still, boulevard Laurier.

44 **Grande Théâtre de Québec.** Opened in 1971, the theater incorporates two main halls, named for 19th-century Canadian poets. Louis-Frechette was the first Québec poet and writer to be honored by the French Academy; Octave-Crémazie stirred the rise of Québec nationalism in the mid-19th century. A three-wall mural by Québec sculptor

Jordi Bonet depicts death, life, and liberty. Bonet wrote "La Liberté" on one wall to symbolize the Québécois' struggle for freedom and cultural distinction. ✉ *269 blvd. René-Lévesque Est,* ☎ *418/646–0609.*

OFF THE
BEATEN PATH

GROSSE ILE NATIONAL PARK – For thousands of immigrants from Europe in the 1800s, the first glimpse of North America was the hastily erected quarantine station at Grosse Ile—Canada's equivalent of Ellis Island. For far too many passengers on the plague-racked ships, particulary the Irish fleeing the potato famine, Grosse Ile became a final resting place. Several buildings have been restored to tell the story of that tragic period. From Québec City, head south on the Pierre Laporte Bridge and follow the signs for Autoroute 20 East for about an hour to Berthier-sur-Mer or Montmagny. In either town, follow the signs to the marina and you will find ferries to take you across to the island. ☎ *418–248–8888 or 800/463–6769.* 🎫 *$26–$48, including ferry.* ☉ *May–June and Sept.–Oct., 8:30–6:30; late June–Aug., 8:30–8:30.*

㊸ Henry Stuart House. Built in 1849, this Regency-style cottage was home to the Stuart family from 1918 to 1987, when it was designated a historic monument by the Ministry of Culture. Its decor has remained unchanged since 1930. Most of the furniture was imported from England in the second half of the 19th century. ✉ *82 Grande Allée Ouest,* ☎ *418/647–4347.* 🎫 *$5.* ☉ *June–Aug., Wed.–Mon. 11–5; Sept.–May, Thurs. and Sun. 11–5 or by reservation.*

NEED A
BREAK?

Halles Petit-Cartier (✉ 1191 av. Cartier, ☎ 418/688-1630), a food mall near the Henry Stuart House, has restaurants and shops that sell French delicacies—cheeses, pastries, breads, vegetables, and candies.

Jardin Roger Van den Hende. A water garden, more than 2,000 plant species from North and South America, Europe, and Asia, and a collection of trees, small shrubs, and remarkable rhododendrons are highlights of this botanical garden. The Metrobus and Buses 11 and 801 run to the gardens. ✉ *Pavillon de l'Environtron, 2480 blvd. Hochelaga, Ste-Foy,* ☎ *418/656–3410.* 🎫 *Free.* ☉ *May–Oct., daily 9–8.*

㊴ Jardin Zoologique du Québec. This zoo is especially scenic because of the DuBerger River, which traverses the grounds. About 200 animal species live here, including bears, wildcats, primates, and birds of prey, as well as farm animals. You can cross-country ski on the grounds in winter. The zoo is 11 km (7 mi) west of Québec City on Route 73 and is served by city bus 801 (☎ 418/627–2511). ✉ *9300 rue de la Faune, Charlesbourg,* ☎ *418/622–0313.* 🎫 *June–Aug. $9.50, Sept.–May $6.* ☉ *Daily 9–5.*

㉞ Montcalm Monument. France and Canada joined together to erect this monument honoring Louis-Joseph Montcalm, the general who claimed his fame by winning four major battles in North America. His most famous battle, however, was the one he lost, when the British conquered New France on September 13, 1759. Montcalm was north of Québec City at Beauport when he learned that the British attack was imminent. He quickly assembled his troops to meet the enemy and was wounded in battle in the leg and stomach. Montcalm was carried into the walled city, where he died the next morning. ✉ *Pl. Montcalm.*

★ **㊶ Musée de Québec** (Québec Museum). A neoclassical Beaux Arts showcase, the museum has more than 20,000 traditional and contemporary pieces of Québec art. The portraits by artists well known in the area, such as Ozias Leduc (1864–1955) and Horatio Walker (1858–1938), are particularly notable. The museum's very formal and dignified building in Parc des Champs-de-Bataille was designed by Wilfrid Lacroix and erected in 1933 to commemorate the tricentennial of the founding of Québec. The museum has renovated the original building, incorporating the space of an abandoned prison dating from 1867. A hallway of cells, with the iron bars and courtyard still intact, has been preserved as part of a permanent exhibition of the prison's history. ⊠ *1 av. Wolfe-Montcalm,* ☎ *418/643–2150.* ☞ *$5.75; Sept.– mid-May, free Wed.* ☉ *Sept.–mid-May, Tues. and Thurs.–Sun., 11–5:45, Wed. 11–8:45; mid-May–Aug., Thurs.–Tues. 10–6, Wed. 10–9:30.*

㊾ Observatoire de la Capitale. This observation gallery is on top of Edifice Marie-Guyart, Québec City's tallest office building. The gray, modern concrete tower, 31 stories high, has by far the best view of the city and the environs. There's an express elevator. ⊠ *1037 rue de la Chevrotière,* ☎ *418/644–9841.* ☞ *$4.* ☉ *June–Sept., daily 10–7; Oct.– May, daily 10–5.*

㉚ Parc de l'Esplanade (Esplanade Park). In the early 19th century, this was a clear space surrounded by a picket fence and poplar trees. Today you'll find the **Poudrière de l'Esplanade** (⊠ 100 rue St-Louis, ☎ 418/ 648–7016), the powder magazine that the British constructed in 1820; it houses a model depicting the evolution of the wall surrounding Vieux-Québec. There's a $2.75 charge to enter the magazine, which is open April–October, daily 10–5. The French began building ramparts along the city's natural cliff as early as 1690 to protect themselves from British invaders. The colonists had trouble convincing the French government back home, though, to take the threat of invasion seriously, and by 1759, when the British invaded for control of New France, the walls were still incomplete. The British, despite attacks by the Americans during the War of Independence and the War of 1812, took a century to finish them. The park is also the starting point for walking the city's 4½ km (3 mi) of walls; in summer, guided tours begin here.

㉟ Parc des Champs-de-Bataille (Battlefields Park). One of North America's largest and most scenic parks, this 250-acre area of gently rolling slopes has unparalleled views of the St. Lawrence River. Within the park and just west of the Citadel are the ☞ **Plains of Abraham,** the site of the famous 1759 battle that decided the fate of New France.

㉟ Parc Jeanne d'Arc. An equestrian statue of Joan of Arc is the focus of this park, which is bright with colorful flowers in summer. A symbol of courage, the statue stands in tribute to the heroes of 1759 near the place where New France was lost to the British. The park also commemorates the Canadian national anthem, "O Canada"; it was played here for the first time on June 24, 1880. ⊠ *Avs. Laurier and Taché.*

㉜ Parliament Buildings. These buildings, erected between 1877 and 1884, are the seat of L'Assemblée Nationale (the National Assembly) of 125 provincial representatives. Québec architect Eugène-Étienne Taché designed the stately buildings in the late-17th-century Renaissance style of Louis XIV, with four wings set in a square around an interior court. In front of the Parliament, statues pay tribute to important figures of Québec history: Cartier, Champlain, Frontenac, Wolfe, and Montcalm. There's a 30-minute tour (in English or French) of the President's Gallery, the Legislative Council Chamber, and the National Assembly Chamber, which is blue, white, and gold. ⊠ *Av. Honoré-Mercier and Grande Allée Est, Door 3,* ☎ *418/643–7239.* ☞ *Free.* ☉ *Guided tours (reservations required for groups) weekdays 9–4:30; late June–Labor Day, also open weekends 10–4:30.*

★ ㊱ Plains of Abraham. This park, named after the river pilot Abraham Martin, is the site of the famous 1759 battle that decided the fate of New France. People cross-country ski here in winter and use their inline skates in summer. Sleigh rides are available in winter. The interpretation center is open year-round; in summer a bus serves as shuttle and guided tour, with commentary in French and English, around the Plains of Abraham, making seven stops. Call Pavillon Baillargé in the Québec Museum (☎ 418/648–4071) for departure times. ✒ *Tour $1.* ☺ *Tours June–Sept., daily 10:30–6.*

⑤⓪ Promenade des Premiers Ministres. Inaugurated in 1997, the promenade has a series of panels that tell the story of the premiers who have led the province and their contributions to its development. The panels are in French, but at press time there were plans to print booklets with English and Spanish translations. *Closed in winter.*

④⑦ St. Matthew's Cemetery. The burial place of many of the earliest English settlers in Canada was opened in 1771 and is the oldest cemetery remaining in Québec City. Closed in 1860, it has been turned into a park. Next door, St. Matthew's Anglican Church is now a public library; it has a book listing most of the original tombstone inscriptions, including those that disappeared to make way for the city's modern convention center. ✉ *755 rue St-Jean.*

③⑨ Tour Martello no. 1. Of the 16 Martello towers in Canada, 4 were built in Québec City because the British government feared an invasion after the American Revolution. Tour Martello no. 1, which exhibits the history of the four structures, was built between 1802 and 1810. (For Tour Martello no. 2, *see below.*) Tour no. 3 guarded westward entry to the city, but it was demolished in 1904. Tour no. 4 is on rue Lavigueur overlooking the St. Charles River but is not open to the public. ✉ *South end of Parc Jeanne d'Arc.* ✒ *$2.* ☺ *May–Sept., daily 10–5:30.*

③⑧ Tour Martello no. 2. This Martello tower, which has an astronomy display, was built in the early 19th century to slow an enemy approach (☞ **Tour Martello no. 1**). ✉ *Avs. Taché and Laurier.* ✒ *$2.* ☺ *May–Sept., daily 10–5:30.*

Villa Bagatelle. A romantic 19th-century villa is now home to an exhibition on the villas and garden estates of Sillery. Its English garden, where groups can have tea, has more than 300 varieties of indigenous and exotic plants. ✉ *1563 chemin St-Louis, Sillery,* ☎ *418/688–8074.* ✒ *$2.* ☺ *Mar.–Dec., Wed.–Sun. 1–5.*

④⓪ Wolfe Monument. This tall monument marks the place where the British general James Wolfe died in 1759. Wolfe landed his troops about 3 km (2 mi) from the city's walls; the 4,500 English soldiers scaled the cliff and opened fire on the Plains of Abraham. Wolfe was mortally wounded in battle and was carried behind the lines to this spot. ✉ *Rue de Bernières and av. Wolfe-Montcalm.*

DINING

Most dining establishments have a selection of dishes à la carte, but more creative specialties are often found on the table d'hôte, a two- to four-course meal chosen daily by the chef. At dinner many restaurants will offer a *menu dégustation,* a five- to seven-course dinner of the chef's finest creations. Note that lunch generally costs about 30% less than dinner, and many of the same dishes are available. Lunch is usually served 11:30 to 2:30; dinner, 6:30 until about 11. You should tip about 15% of the bill.

CATEGORY	COST*
$$$$	over $35
$$$	$25–$35
$$	$15–$25
$	under $15

*per person, in Canadian dollars, excluding drinks, service, 7% GST, and 7.5% provincial sales tax

Upper Town

$$$$ ✕ **Le Saint-Amour.** Here are all the makings of a true haute-cuisine es-
★ tablishment without the pretentious atmosphere. A light and airy atrium, with a retractable roof for outdoor dining in summer, creates a relaxed dining ambience. Chef Jean-Luc Boulay returns regularly to France for inspiration; his studies pay off in such creations as stuffed quail in port sauce and salmon with chive mousse. Sauces are light, with no flour or butter. The *menu découvert* has nine courses, and the *menu dégustation* has seven. If you plan to order one of these menus, mention it when you make your reservation. The chef's true expertise shines in his desserts—try the crème brûlée sweetened with maple syrup. ✉ *48 rue Ste-Ursule,* ☎ *418/694–0667. Reservations essential on weekends. AE, DC, MC, V.*

$$$–$$$$ ✕ **Aux Anciens Canadiens.** This establishment is named for a book by Philippe-Aubert de Gaspé, who once resided here. The house, dating from 1675, has five dining rooms with different themes. The *vaisselier* (dish room) is bright and cheerful, with colorful antique dishes and a fireplace. People come for the authentic French-Canadian cooking; hearty specialties include duck in maple glaze, caribou with blueberry wine sauce, and a blueberry cake with warm maple syrup sauce. The restaurant also serves the best caribou drink (a local beverage known for its kick) in town, using its own special mix of sherry and vodka. ✉ *34 rue St-Louis,* ☎ *418/692–1627. AE, DC, MC, V.*

$$$–$$$$ ✕ **Le Continental.** If Québec City had a dining hall of fame, Le Continental would be there among the best. Since 1956, the Sgobba family has been serving award-winning Continental cuisine. Deep blue walls, mahogany paneling, and crisp white tablecloths create a stately ambience, and house specialties like orange duckling and filet mignon Continental are flambéed at your table. Other favorites are rack of lamb Victoria, partridge Périgourdine, and fish and seafood dishes. ✉ *26 rue St-Louis,* ☎ *418/694–9995. AE, DC, MC, V.*

$$$–$$$$ ✕ **La Maison Serge Bruyère.** This restaurant, serving classic French cui-
★ sine presented with plenty of crystal, silver, and fresh flowers, put Québec City on the map of great gastronomic cities. It was opened in 1980 by the late Serge Bruyère, a native of Lyon, France. The highlight at La Grande Table is the *menu découvert,* a seven-course meal for about $58. Among chef Jean-Claude Crouzet's dishes are *aiguillettes* (thin strips) of duck with green pepper honey and raspberry vinegar and *noisettes* (small pieces) of stag with apples and cider jelly. Downstairs, Chez Livernois is less formal and less expensive, with such dishes as chicken breasts with sesame seeds and lime. ✉ *1200 rue St-Jean,* ☎ *418/694–0618. Reservations essential. AE, DC, MC, V.*

$$–$$$ ✕ **Portofino Bistro Italiano.** By joining two 18th-century houses, owner James Monti has created a cozy Italian restaurant with a bistro flavor. The room is distinctive: burnt sienna walls, a wood pizza oven set behind a semicircular bar, deep-blue tablecloths and chairs. Not to be missed are the thin-crust pizza and its accompaniment of oils flavored with pepper and oregano, and *pennini al'arrabiata*—tubular pasta with a spicy tomato sauce. Don't miss the homemade tiramisu—ladyfingers dipped in espresso with a whipped cream and mascarpone-cheese fill-

Dining

Lodging

Québec City Dining and Lodging

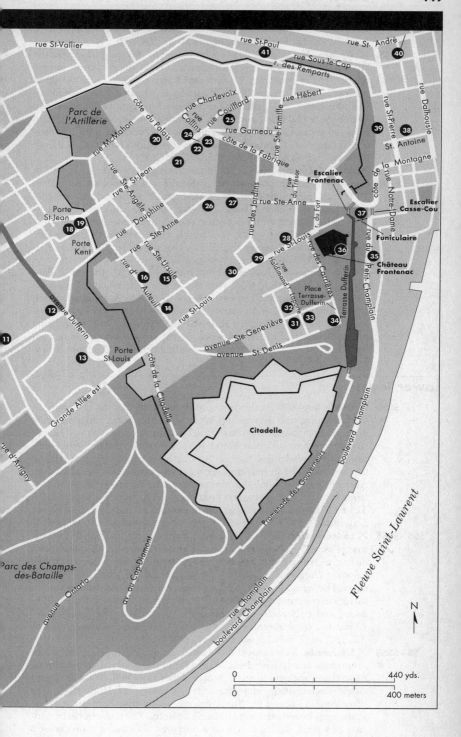

rue St-Vallier

rue St-Paul

rue St. André

rue Sous-le-Cap

r. des Remparts

41

40

Parc de
l'Artillerie

rue Charlevoix

rue Couillard

rue Hébert

rue
Collins

rue St-Pierre

rue Dalhousie

côte du Palais

rue Garneau

St. Antoine

rue McMahon

côte de la Fabrique

39

38

20

24

25

rue Ste-Famille

23

côte de la rue Notre-Dame

22

de la Montagne

rue Ste-St-Jean

21

Escalier
Frontenac

rue du Trésor

rue Ste-Angèle

rue des Jardins

rue Ste-Anne

Escalier
Casse-Cou

Porte
St-Jean

26

27

19

r. du Fort

37

18

rue Dauphine

Funiculaire

Porte
Kent

28

rue St-Louis

35

Château
Frontenac

rue Ste-Anne

36

29

rue
Haldimand-Lagôme

rue des Carrières

12

rue d'Auteuil

rue Ste-Ursule

16

15

30

Place
Terrasse-
Dufferin

11

avenue Dufferin

14

rue St-Louis

Terrasse Dufferin

13

Porte
St-Louis

avenue Ste-Geneviève

32

33

34

boulevard Champlain

rue d'Arigny

Grande Allée est

côte de la Citadelle

avenue St-Denis

31

Promenade des Gouverneurs

Citadelle

Parc des Champs-
des-Bataille

avenue Ontario

av. au Cap-Diamant

rue Champlain

boulevard Champlain

Fleuve Saint-Laurent

N

0   440 yds.

0   400 meters

ing. There's a prix-fixe meal of the day, and from 3 to 7 the restaurant serves a beer and pizza meal for about $10. ⊠ *54 rue Couillard,* ☎ *418/692–8888. Reservations essential. AE, DC, MC, V.*

$–$$ ✕ **Apsara.** The Cambodian family that owns this restaurant near the St-Louis Gate excels at using both subtle and tangy spices to create unique flavors. Decor combines Western and Eastern motifs, with flowered wallpaper, Asian art, and small fountains. Innovative dishes from Vietnam, Thailand, and Cambodia include such starters as *fleur de pailin* (a rice-paste roll filled with fresh vegetables, meat, and shrimp) and *mou sati* (pork kebabs with peanut sauce and coconut milk). The assorted miniature Cambodian pastries are delicious with tea. ⊠ *71 rue d'Auteuil,* ☎ *418/694–0232. AE, DC, MC, V.*

$ ✕ **Casse-Crêpe Breton.** Crepes in generous proportions are served in
★   this café-style restaurant on rue St-Jean. From a menu of more than 20 fillings, pick your own chocolate or fruit combinations; design a larger meal with cheese, ham, and vegetables; or sip a bowl of Viennese coffee topped with whipped cream. Many tables surround three round hot plates at which you watch your creations being made. Crepes made with two to five fillings cost under $6. ⊠ *1136 rue St-Jean,* ☎ *418/692–0438. No credit cards.*

$ ✕ **Chez Temporel.** Tucked behind rue St-Jean and côte de la Fabrique, this homey café filled with the aroma of fresh coffee is an experience *très français.* The rustic decor incorporates wooden tables, chairs, and benches, and a tiny staircase winds to an upper level. Croissants are made in-house; the staff will fill them with Gruyère and ham or anything else. Equally delicious are the *croques monsieur* (grilled ham and cheese sandwiches) and quiche Lorraine. ⊠ *25 rue Couillard,* ☎ *418/694–1813. V.*

Lower Town

$$$$ ✕ **Laurie Raphaël.** At this hot spot in town, the setting is classic yet
★   unpretentious, with high ceilings, white linen tablecloths, and sheer white drapery. Award-winning chef Daniel Vezina, a rising star of Québec cuisine, is known for innovative recipes that mix classic French cuisine with international flavors. Among his creations are goat cheese fondue, wrapped in nuts and served with caramelized pears, and an Australian rack of lamb that comes with a shallot sauce, blue potatoes from nearby Charlevoix, and goat cheese. The wine list ranges from $23 to $700 per bottle; some wines are sold by the glass. ⊠ *117 rue Dalhousie,* ☎ *418/692–4555. Reservations essential. AE, D, MC, V.*

$$$–$$$$ ✕ **Le Marie Clarisse.** This restaurant in an ancient building at the bottom of Escalier Casse-Cou near Place Royale is known for unique seafood dishes, such as halibut with nuts and honey and scallops with port and paprika. The menu usually lists a good game dish, such as caribou with curry. The *menu du jour* has about seven entrées; dinner includes soup, salad, dessert, and coffee. Wood-beam ceilings, stone walls, sea-blue decor, and a fireplace make this one of the coziest spots in town. ⊠ *12 rue du Petit-Champlain,* ☎ *418/692–0857. Reservations essential. AE, DC, MC, V. No lunch weekends Oct.–Apr.*

$$–$$$$ ✕ **L'Echaudé.** A chic black-and-white bistro, L'Echaudé attracts a mix
★   of business and tourist clientele because of its location between the financial and antiques districts. Lunch offerings include *cuisse de canard confit* (duck confit) with french fries and fresh salad. Highlights of the three-course brunch for Sunday antiques shoppers are giant croissants, eggs Benedict, and tantalizing desserts. The modern decor consists of a stark dining area with a mirrored wall and a stainless-steel bar where you dine atop high stools. ⊠ *73 Sault-au-Matelot,* ☎ *418/ 692–1299. AE, DC, MC, V. No dinner Sun. Sept.–May.*

$$$ ✕ **Mistral Gagnant.** Don't be surprised if the pottery bowl on your table or the antique armoire you are sitting beside is sold midway through your meal: Much of what you see in this sunny tearoom comes from Provence and is for sale. Though limited, the menu à la carte is delicious and includes a gourmet salad that changes with the season, daily quiches, and a few desserts. An ever-changing table d'hôte offers more hearty meat, seafood, and pasta dishes; the restaurant is famous for its lemon meringue pie. ⊠ *160 rue St-Paul,* ☎ *418/692–4260. AE, MC, V. Closed some evenings in winter; call ahead.*

$–$$$ ✕ **Le Cochon Dingue.** Across the street from the ferry in Lower Town is the boulevard Champlain location of this chain, a cheerful café whose name translates to "The Crazy Pig." Sidewalk tables and indoor dining rooms artfully blend the chic and the antique; black-and-white checkerboard floors contrast with ancient stone walls. Café fare includes delicious mussels, homemade quiches, thick soups, and such desserts as maple-sugar pie. ⊠ *46 blvd. Champlain,* ☎ *418/692–2013;* ⊠ *46 blvd. René-Lévesque Ouest,* ☎ *418/523–2013;* ⊠ *1326 av. Maguire, Sillery,* ☎ *418/684–2013. AE, DC, MC, V.*

Outside the Walls

$$$–$$$$ ✕ **La Fenouillère.** Although this restaurant is connected to a standard chain hotel, inside you will find an elegant, spacious dining room, with a view of the Pierre Laporte bridge. Chef Yvon Godbout has served a constantly rotating table d'hôte since 1986, going out of his way to offer seasonal products. The house specialty is salmon, but lamb is done to a turn and is very popular among the restaurant's regular customers. ⊠ *Hotel Best Western Aristocrate, 3100 chemin St-Louis, Ste-Foy,* ☎ *418/653–3886. AE, DC, MC, V.*

$$$–$$$$ ✕ **Le Paris Brest.** This busy restaurant on Grande Allée serves a gre-
★ garious crowd attracted to its tastefully prepared French dishes. Traditional fare, such as *escargots au Pernod* (snails with Pernod) and steak tartare, is presented artistically. Some popular choices are lamb with *herbes de Provence* and beef Wellington. A generous side platter of vegetables accompanies à la carte and main-course dishes; wine prices range from $22 to $400. Angular halogen lighting and soft yellow walls add a fresh, modern touch to the historic building. ⊠ *590 Grande Allée Est,* ☎ *418/529–2243. AE, DC, MC, V.*

$$–$$$ ✕ **Le Graffiti.** A good alternative to Vieux-Québec dining, this restaurant housed in a modern gourmet food mall serves French cuisine. The romantic setting has dark mahogany-paneled walls and large bay windows that look out onto the passersby along avenue Cartier. On the distinctive seasonal menu are such dishes as *escalope de veau* (thin slices of veal) with a white wine, cream, and tomato sauce; and angel-hair pasta with pesto, pine nuts, black olives, and dried tomatoes. The table d'hôte is reasonably priced. ⊠ *1191 av. Cartier,* ☎ *418/529–4949. AE, DC, MC, V.*

$$–$$$ ✕ **Montego Resto Club.** The sun shines year-round at this trendy bistro where Californian, Italian, French, and Szechuan cuisine share the bill. The red-and-yellow Sante Fe decor pays close attention to detail; each rainbow-colored light is a work of art, and every table setting has a unique twist. The inventive menu lists rib steak served with avocado, peppers, and fresh and sun-dried tomatoes, and linguine al Montego, with prosciutto, sun-dried tomatoes, cantaloupe, and peppers. Montego Resto Club is a 15-minute drive west of the old city. ⊠ *1460 av. Maguire, Sillery,* ☎ *418/688–7991. AE, D, MC, V.*

$$–$$$ ✕ **Paparazzi.** The food at this Italian restaurant competes with that of many of the finer dining establishments in town, but without the high prices. Paparazzi has a sleek bistro ambience—bare wood tables,

halogen lighting, and wrought-iron accents. Pizza Paparazzi comes with wild mushrooms, fresh tomatoes, and a mix of cheeses; desserts are interesting. The restaurant is a 15-minute drive west of Vieux-Québec. ✉ *1365 av. Maguire, Sillery,* ☎ *418/683–8111. AE, DC, MC, V.*

$–$$$ ✕ **La Pointe des Amériques.** Adventurous pizza lovers should explore the fare at this bistro, where the original brick walls of the century-old building just outside the St-Jean Gate contrast boldly with modern mirrors and arty wrought-iron lighting. Some pizza combos (marinated alligator, smoked Gouda, Cajun sauce, and hot peppers) are strange. But don't worry—there are more than 25 different pizzas as well as meat and pasta dishes, soups, and salads. Connected to the restaurant is the Biloxi Bar, which has live jazz and the same menu. ✉ *964 rue St-Jean,* ☎ *418/694–1199. AE, DC, MC, V.*

$–$$ ✕ **Le Parlementaire.** With its magnificent Beaux Arts interior and some of the most reasonable prices in town, the National Assembly's restaurant is nevertheless one of the best-kept secrets in Québec City. Chef Rél Therrien prepares contemporary cuisine that employs products from Québec's various regions. While the restaurant is usually open Tuesday–Friday for breakfast and lunch, opening hours follow the National Assembly's schedule and can vary; it is wise to call ahead. ✉ *Av. Honoré-Mercier and Grande Allée Est, Door 3,* ☎ *418/643–6640. AE, MC, V. Closed Sat.–Mon. No dinner.*

$ ✕ **Chez Victor.** It's no ordinary burger joint: This cozy café with brick
★ walls attracts an artsy crowd to rue St-Jean where trendy turns dreary. Lettuce, tomatoes, onions, mushrooms, pickles, hot mustard, mayonnaise, and a choice of cheeses (mozzarella, Swiss, blue, goat and cream) top hearty gourmet burgers. French fries are served with a dollop of mayo and poppy seeds. You will find salads, sandwiches, and a daily dessert as well. ✉ *145 rue St-Jean,* ☎ *418/529–7702. MC, V.*

$ ✕ **Le Commensal.** At a kind of upscale cafeteria, diners serve themselves from an outstanding informal vegetarian buffet and then grab a table in the vast dining room, where brick walls and green plants add a touch of class. Plates are weighed to determine the price. Hot and cold dishes run the gamut of health-conscious cooking and include stir-fry tofu and ratatouille (vegetables in mild sauce with couscous). ✉ *860 rue St-Jean,* ☎ *418/647–3733. AE, DC, MC, V.*

LODGING

Be sure to make a reservation if you visit during peak season (May–September) or during the Winter Carnival, in February. During busy times, hotel rates usually rise 30%. From November through April, many lodgings offer weekend discounts and other promotions.

CATEGORY	COST*
$$$$	over $160
$$$	$120–$160
$$	$85–$120
$	under $85

All prices are for a standard double room, excluding 7% GST, 7.5% provincial sales tax, and an optional service charge, in Canadian dollars.

Upper Town

$$$$ ▥ **Château Frontenac.** Towering above the St. Lawrence River, the
★ Château Frontenac (☞ Upper Town *in* Exploring, *above*) is Québec City's most renowned landmark. Its public rooms—from the intimate piano bar to the 700-seat ballroom reminiscent of the Hall of Mirrors at Versailles—have the opulence of years gone by. Reserve well in ad-

vance, especially from late June–mid-October. At Le Champlain, classic French cuisine is served by waiters in traditional French costumes. Because the hotel is a tourist attraction, the lobby can be busy. ⊠ *1 rue des Carrières, G1R 4P5,* ☎ *418/692–3861 or 800/441–1414,* FAX *418/692–1751. 589 rooms, 24 suites. 2 restaurants, piano bar, snack bar, indoor pool, beauty salon, health club. AE, DC, MC, V.*

$$–$$$$ ⊞ **Hôtel Clarendon.** Built in 1866 and considered the oldest hotel in Québec, the Clarendon (☞ Upper Town *in* Exploring, *above*) has been entirely refurbished in its original Art Deco and Art Nouveau styles. Most rooms have excellent views of Old Québec. ⊠ *57 rue Ste-Anne, G1R 3X4,* ☎ *418/692–2480 or 800/463–5250,* FAX *418/692–4652. 147 rooms, 3 suites. Restaurant, café, meeting rooms. AE, D, DC, MC, V.*

$$–$$$$ ⊞ **Hôtel Manoir Victoria.** This European-style hotel with a good fitness center is well situated near the train station. Its discreet, old-fashioned entrance gives way to a large, wood-paneled foyer. A substantial buffet breakfast is included in some packages. ⊠ *44 côte du Palais, G1R 4H8,* ☎ *418/692–1030,* FAX *418/692–3822. 142 rooms, 3 suites. 2 restaurants, indoor pool, beauty salon, sauna, health club, meeting rooms. AE, D, DC, MC, V.*

$$–$$$ ⊞ **L'Hôtel du Capitole.** In 1992 this abandoned, turn-of-the-century theater just outside the St-Jean Gate was transformed into an exclusive lodging, an Italian bistro, and an elaborate 1920s cabaret-style dinner theater, Théâtre Capitole (☞ Nightlife and the Arts, *below*). A glitzy showbiz theme prevails throughout the hotel, with stars on carpets, doors, and keys. Rooms are small and simple, highlighted with a few rich details. Painted ceilings have a blue-and-white sky motif; white down-filled comforters dress the beds. ⊠ *972 rue St-Jean, G1R 1R5,* ☎ *418/694–4040 or 800/363–4040,* FAX *418/694–1916. 36 rooms, 3 suites. Restaurant, bar, theater. AE, DC, MC, V.*

$$–$$$ ⊞ **L'Hôtel du Vieux Québec.** In the heart of the Latin Quarter on rue St-Jean, this brick hotel is surrounded by striking historic structures. Once an apartment building, it still has the long-term visitor in mind. The interior design is simple, with sparsely furnished but comfortable rooms decorated in pastel colors. Many rooms have kitchens (dishes and cooking utensils can be rented for $10); some have air-conditioning. ⊠ *1190 rue St-Jean, G1R 1S6,* ☎ *418/692–1850,* FAX *418/692–5637. 41 rooms. AE, MC, V.*

$$–$$$ ⊞ **Hôtel Marie Rollet.** An intimate little inn in the heart of Vieux-Québec, built in 1876 by the Ursuline Order, is an oasis of warm woodwork and antique charm. Two rooms have working fireplaces. A rooftop terrace has a garden view. ⊠ *81 rue Ste-Anne, G1R 3X4,* ☎ *418/694–9271. 10 rooms. MC, V.*

$$–$$$ ⊞ **Manoir d'Auteuil.** Originally a private home, this lodging is one of the more lavish manors in town. A major renovation reinstated many of its Art Deco and Art Nouveau details. An ornate sculpted iron banister wraps around four floors, and guest rooms blend modern design with the Art Deco structure. Each room is different; one was formerly a chapel, and another has a tiny staircase leading to its bathroom. The room with a blue bathroom has a shower with seven showerheads. Some rooms look out onto the wall between the St-Louis and St-Jean gates. Note that rooms on the fourth floor are cheaper. ⊠ *49 rue d'Auteuil, G1R 4C2,* ☎ *418/694–1173,* FAX *418/694–0081. 16 rooms. Breakfast room. AE, D, DC, MC, V.*

$–$$$ ⊞ **Château de la Terrasse Dufferin.** This four-story inn has something that many others lack: a view of the St. Lawrence River from rooms in the front. The interior, with its high ceilings and stained glass in the large bay windows, hints at having once possessed a refined and elegant decor. These days rooms are furnished in a mix of styles but are tastefully put together. ⊠ *6 Pl. Terrasse Dufferin, G1R 4N5,* ☎ *418/ 694–9472,* ☏ *418/694–0055. 26 rooms. AE, DC, MC, V.*

$$ ⊡ **Le Château de Pierre.** Built in 1853, this tidy Victorian manor on a picturesque street has kept its English origins alive. The high-ceilinged halls have ornate chandeliers, and Victorian rooms are imaginatively decorated with floral themes; some have either a balcony or vanity room. Several rooms in the front have bay windows with a view of Governors' Park. ⊠ *17 av. Ste-Geneviève, G1R 4A8,* ☎ *418/694–0429,* ☏ *418/694–0153. 15 rooms. AE, MC, V.*

$$ ⊡ **Manoir Ste-Geneviève.** Quaint and elaborately decorated, this hotel dating from 1880 stands near the Château Frontenac, on the southwest corner of Governors' Park. A plush Victorian ambience is created with fanciful wallpaper and stately English manor furnishings, such as marble lamps, large wooden bedposts, and velvet upholstery; you'll feel as if you are staying in a secluded country inn. Service is personal and genteel. Some rooms have air-conditioning. ⊠ *13 av. Ste-Geneviève, G1R 4A7,* ☎ ☏ *418/694–1666. 9 rooms. No credit cards.*

$–$$ ⊡ **Hôtel Château Bellevue.** Just behind the Château Frontenac, this hotel offers comfortable accommodations at reasonable prices in a good location. Guest rooms are modern, with standard hotel furnishings; many have a view of the St. Lawrence River. The rooms vary considerably in size, and package deals are available in winter. ⊠ *16 rue de la Porte, G1R 4M9,* ☎ *418/692–2573 or 800/463–2617,* ☏ *418/692– 4876. 57 rooms. Meeting room. AE, DC, MC, V.*

$ ⊡ **L'Auberge St-Louis.** For convenience, this inn's central location on the main street of the city can't be beat. A lobby resembling one in a European pension and tall staircases lead to small guest rooms with comfortable but bare-bones furniture. Six budget rooms are on the fourth floor. The service here is friendly. ⊠ *48 rue St-Louis, G1R 3Z3,* ☎ *418/692–2424,* ☏ *418/692–3797. 27 rooms, 14 with bath. MC, V.*

Lower Town

$$$–$$$$ ⊡ **Auberge Saint-Antoine.** This charming little find is within comfortable walking distance of all the Old Town's attractions. The hotel seems much older than it is because of its location in an old maritime warehouse and the generally rustic atmosphere. Each room is styled differently, but all have a combination of antiques and contemporary pieces. Some rooms have river views; others have terraces. ⊠ *10 rue St-Antoine, G1K 4C9,* ☎ *418/692–2211 or 800/267–0525,* ☏ *418/ 692–1177. 24 rooms, 7 suites. AE, DC, MC, V.*

Outside the Walls

$$$$ ⊡ **Hilton International Québec.** Just outside St-Jean Gate, the spacious Hilton rises from the shadow of Parliament Hill. The lobby, which can be chaotic at times, has a bar and an open-air restaurant. The hotel is next to the Parliament Buildings and connected to the convention center and a mall, Place Québec, which has 45 shops and restaurants. Standard yet ultramodern rooms have tall windows; those on upper floors have fine views of Vieux-Québec. Guests on executive floors are offered a free breakfast and an open bar from 5 to 10 PM. ⊠ *1100 blvd. René-Lévesque Est, G1K 7M9,* ☎ *418/647–2411 or 800/447–2411,* ☏ *418/647–6488. 487 rooms, 36 suites. Restaurant, piano bar, pool, sauna, health club. AE, D, DC, MC, V.*

$$$$ ⊡ **Hôtel Radisson Gouverneurs Québec.** This large, full-service establishment opposite the Parliament Buildings is part of a Québec chain. Its light and spacious rooms have luminous pastel decor, wood furniture, and marble bathrooms. VIP floors were designed to lure the business traveler. The hotel occupies the first 12 floors of a tall office

complex; views of Vieux-Québec are limited to the higher floors. ⊠ *690 blvd. René-Lévesque Est, G1R 5A8,* ☎ *418/647–1717 or 888/ 910–1111,* ℻ *418/647–2146. 371 rooms, 6 suites. Restaurant, pool, sauna, health club. AE, D, DC, MC, V.*

$$$–$$$$ 🖼 **Hôtel Loews Le Concorde.** When Le Concorde was built in 1974,
★ the shockingly tall concrete structure aroused controversy because it supplanted 19th-century Victorian homes. Still, visitors love its location on Grande Allée, where cafés, restaurants, and bars dot the street. Rooms have good views of Battlefields Park and the St. Lawrence River, and nearly all have been redone in modern decor combined with traditional furnishings. Amenities for business travelers have expanded. ⊠ *1225 Pl. Montcalm, G1R 4W6,* ☎ *418/647–2222 or 800/463–5256,* ℻ *418/647–4710. 424 rooms. 2 restaurants, bar, pool, sauna, health club, business services. AE, D, DC, MC, V.*

$$$ 🖼 **Germain des Près.** One popular hotel for the business crowd is in Ste-Foy, close to Place Laurier and with easy access to Québec City and the airports. Its ultramodern rooms—in black and white or black and tan—have white comforters on the beds. ⊠ *1200 av. Germain-des-Près, Ste-Foy, G1V 3M7,* ☎ *418/658–1224 or 800/463–5263,* ℻ *418/ 658–8846. 126 rooms with shower or bath. Restaurant, business services, meeting rooms. AE, DC, MC, V.*

$$–$$$ 🖼 **Manoir Lafayette.** In 1882 this graystone building was a lavish, private home; today it is a simple hotel. Considering the location on Grande Allée—a street crowded with restaurants and trendy bars— the clean, comfortable accommodations are reasonably priced. The lobby is open and welcoming, with leather sofas surrounding a decorative fireplace and television. Rooms in the newer wing—although fresher— resemble those in the old part: All are quite small, with high ceilings, wooden furniture, and floral bedspreads and drapes. Rooms facing Grande Allée may be noisy. ⊠ *661 Grande Allée Est, G1R 2K4,* ☎ *418/522–2652 or 800/363–8203,* ℻ *418/522–4400. 67 rooms. Restaurant, baby-sitting. AE, DC, MC, V.*

$ 🖼 **L'Auberge du Quartier.** A small, amiable inn in a house dating from 1852 benefits from a personal touch. The cheerful rooms are modestly furnished but well maintained. A suite of rooms on the third floor can accommodate a family at a reasonable cost. A 15-minute walk west from the old city, L'Auberge du Quartier is convenient to avenue Cartier and Grande Allée nightlife; joggers can use Battlefields Park across the street. ⊠ *170 Grande Allée Ouest, G1R 2G9,* ☎ *418/525– 9726. 11 rooms, 1 suite. Breakfast room. AE, DC, MC, V.*

NIGHTLIFE AND THE ARTS

Considering its size, Québec City has a wide variety of cultural institutions, from the renowned Québec Symphony Orchestra to several small theater companies. The arts scene changes significantly depending on the season. From September through May, a steady repertory of concerts, plays, and performances is presented in theaters and halls. In summer, indoor theaters close to make room for outdoor stages. For arts and entertainment listings in English, consult the *Québec Chronicle-Telegraph,* published on Wednesday. The French-language daily newspaper *Le Soleil* has listings on a page called "Où Aller à Québec" ("Where to Go in Québec"). Also, *Voir,* a weekly devoted to arts listings and reviews, appears on the street every Thursday.

Tickets for most shows can be purchased through **Billetech,** with outlets at the Bibliothèque Gabrielle-Roy (⊠ 350 rue St-Joseph Est, ☎ 418/691–7400), Colisée de Québec (⊠ 2205 av. du Colisée, Parc de l'Exposition, ☎ 418/691–7211), Grand Théâtre de Québec (⊠ 269 blvd. René-Lévesque Est, ☎ 418/643–8131), La Baie department store (✉ Pl. Laurier, 2ᵉ, ☎ 418/627–5959), Palais Montcalm (✉ 995 Pl. d'Youville, ☎418/670–9011), Salle Albert-Rousseau (✉ 2410 chemin Ste-Foy, Ste-Foy, ☎ 418/659–6710), and Théâtre Périscope (✉ 2 rue Crémazie Est, ☎ 418/529–2183). Hours vary, and in some cases tickets must be bought at the outlet.

The Arts

Dance

Dancers appear at Bibliothèque Gabrielle-Roy (☞ Music, *below*), Salle Albert-Rousseau, and the Palais Montcalm (☞ Theater, *below*). **Grand Théâtre de Québec** (✉ 269 blvd. René-Lévesque Est, ☎ 418/643–8131) presents a dance series with Canadian and international companies.

Film

Most theaters present French films and American films dubbed into French. Three popular theaters are **Cinéma Cinéplex Odéon** (✉ 5700 blvd. des Gradins, ☎ 418/622–1077), **Cinéma de Paris** (✉ 966 rue St-Jean, ☎ 418/694–0891), and **Cinéma Place Charest** (✉ 500 rue du Pont, ☎ 418/529–9745). **Cinéma des Galeries** (✉ 5401 blvd. des Galeries, ☎ 418/628–2455) almost always shows some films in English. **Le Clap** (✉ 2360 chemin Ste-Foy, Ste-Foy, ☎ 418/650–2527) has a repertoire of foreign, offbeat, and art films. **IMAX Theatre** (✉ Galeries de la Capitale, 5401 blvd. des Galeries, ☎ 418/627–4629, 418/627–4688, or 800/643–4629) has extra-large-screen movies and translation headsets.

Music

L'Orchestre Symphonique de Québec (Québec Symphony Orchestra) is Canada's oldest. It performs at Louis-Frechette Hall in the Grand Théâtre de Québec (✉ 269 blvd. René-Lévesque Est, ☎ 418/643–8131).

Tickets for children's concerts at the **Joseph Lavergne auditorium** must be purchased in advance at the Bibliothèque Gabrielle-Roy (✉ 350 rue St-Joseph Est, ☎ 418/691–7400). For classical concerts at the **Salle de l'Institut Canadien** (✉ 42 rue St-Stanislas), buy tickets in advance at the Bibliothèque Gabrielle-Roy (☞ *above*).

Popular music concerts are often booked at the **Colisée de Québec** (✉ Parc de l'Exposition, 2205 av. du Colisée, Parc de l'Exposition, ☎ 418/691–7211).

An annual highlight is the July **Festival d'Eté International de Québec** (☎ 418/692–4540), an 11-day music festival with more than 400 shows and concerts (many of them free) from classical music to Francophone song. Events are held in more than 10 locations, including outdoor stages and public squares. Dates for 1999 are July 8–18.

Theater

Most theater productions are in French. The following theaters schedule shows September–April: **Grand Théâtre de Québec** (✉ 269 blvd. René-Lévesque Est, ☎ 418/643–8131) offers classic and contemporary plays staged by the leading local company, le Théâtre du Trident (☎ 418/643–5873). **Palais Montcalm** (✉ 995 Pl. d'Youville, ☎ 418/670–9011), a municipal theater outside St-Jean Gate, presents a broad range of productions. A diverse repertoire, from classical to comedy, is staged at **Salle Albert-Rousseau** (✉ 2410 chemin Ste-Foy, Ste-Foy, ☎ 418/659–6710). **Théâtre Capitole** (✉ 972 rue St-Jean, ☎ 418/694–4444), a restored turn-of-the-century cabaret-style theater, schedules pop music and musical comedy shows. **Théâtre Périscope** (✉ 2 rue Crémazie Est, ☎ 418/529–2183), a multipurpose theater, stages about 200 shows a year, including performances for children.

SUMMER THEATER

In summer, open-air concerts are presented at Place d'Youville (just outside St-Jean Gate) and on the Plains of Abraham.

Nightlife

Québec City nightlife is centered on the clubs and cafés of rue St-Jean, avenue Cartier, and Grande Allée. In winter, evening activity is livelier toward the end of the week, beginning on Wednesday. As warmer temperatures set in, the café-terrace crowd emerges, and bars are active seven days a week. Most bars and clubs stay open until 3 AM.

Bars and Lounges

Cosmos Café (⊠ 575 Grande Allée, ☎ 418/640–0606) is a lively club and restaurant. Upstairs, Chez Maurice has dancing. **Le Pub Saint-Alexandre** (⊠ 1087 rue St-Jean, ☎ 418/694–0015), a popular English-style pub, was formerly a men-only tavern. It serves 200 kinds of beer, 20 on tap. You'll find mainly yuppies at **Vogue** (⊠ Upstairs at 1170 rue d'Artigny, ☎ 418/529–9973), which has dancing.

Dance Clubs

There's a little bit of everything—live rock bands to loud disco—at **Chez Dagobert** (⊠ 600 Grande Allée Est, ☎ 418/522–0393), a large and popular club. **Merlin** (⊠ 1179 av. Cartier, ☎ 418/529–9567), a second-story dance club with an English pub below, is packed nightly.

Folk, Jazz, and Blues

French-Canadian folk songs fill **Chez Son Père** (⊠ 24 rue St-Stanislas, ☎ 418/692–5308), a smoky pub on the second floor of an old building in the Latin Quarter. Singers perform nightly. **Le d'Auteuil** (⊠ 35 rue d'Auteuil, ☎ 418/692–2263), a converted church across from Kent Gate, is a place to hear rhythm and blues, jazz, and blues. The first jazz bar in Québec City, **L'Emprise at Hôtel Clarendon** (⊠ 57 rue Ste-Anne, ☎ 418/692–2480), is the preferred spot for enthusiasts. The Art Deco decor sets the mood for Jazz Age rhythms. **Maison de la Chanson** (⊠ Théâtre Petit Champlain, 68 rue du Petit-Champlain, ☎ 418/692–4744) is a fine spot for contemporary Québec music.

OUTDOOR ACTIVITIES AND SPORTS

Two parks are central to Québec City: the 250-acre Battlefields Park, with its panoramic views of the St. Lawrence River, and Cartier-Brébeuf Park, which runs along the St. Charles River. Both are favorites for jogging, biking, and cross-country skiing. Scenic rivers and mountains close by (no more than 30 minutes by car) make this city ideal for the sporting life. For information about sports and fitness, contact **Québec City Tourist Information Office** (⊠ 835 av. Laurier, G1R 2L3, ☎ 418/ 649–2608) or **Québec City Bureau of Parks and Recreation** (⊠ 65 rue Ste-Anne, 5e, G1R 3S9, ☎ 418/691–6284).

Participant Sports and Outdoor Activities

Biking

Bike paths along rolling hills traverse Battlefields Park, at the south side of the city. For a longer ride over flat terrain, take the path north of the city skirting the St. Charles River; this route can be reached from rue St-Roch, rue Prince-Edouard, and Pont Dorchester (Dorchester Bridge). Paths along the côte de Beaupré, beginning at the confluence of the St. Charles and St. Lawrence rivers, are especially scenic. They begin northeast of the city at rue de la Verandrye and boulevard Montmorency or rue Abraham-Martin and Pont Samson (Samson Bridge) and continue 10 km (6 mi) along the coast to Montmorency Falls.

You can rent bicycles for $25 a day or $15 a half-day at **Auberge de la Paix** (✉ 31 rue Couillard, ☎ 418/694–0735).

Boating
Lakes in the Québec City area have facilities for boating. **Lac Beauport** (✉ 78 chemin du Brûlé, ☎ 418/849–2821) is one of the best nearby resorts. Take Route 73 north of the city to St-Dunstan de Lac Beauport; then take Exit 157, boulevard du Lac. Just west of Québec City, on the St. Lawrence River, boats can be rented at **Parc Nautique du Cap-Rouge** (✉ 4155 chemin de la Plage Jacques Cartier, Cap-Rouge, ☎ 418/650–7770).

Dogsledding
Adventure Nord-Bec (✉ 665 rue St-Aimé, St-Lambert de Lévis, GOS 2WO, ☎ 418/889–8001), 20 minutes from the city, teaches people how to mush in the forest. Overnight camping trips are available.

Fishing
Permits are needed for fishing in Québec.Most sporting goods stores and all Canadian Tire stores sell permits; try **Canadian Tire** (✉ 1170 rte. de l'Église, Ste-Foy, ☎ 418/659–4882). The **Ministry of Wildlife and the Environment** (✉ 675 blvd. René-Lévesque Est, ☎ 418/643–3127) publishes a pamphlet on fishing regulations that is available at tourist information offices.

Réserve Faunique des Laurentides (☎ 418/686–1717), a wildlife reserve with good lakes for fishing, is approximately 48 km (30 mi) north of Québec City via Route 73.

Golf
The Québec City region has 18 golf courses, and several are open to the public. Reservations are essential in summer. **Club de Golf de Beauport** (✉ 3533 rue Clemenceau, Beauport, ☎ 418/663–1578), a 9-hole course, is 20 minutes from the city by car via Route 73 North. The 18-hole, par-70 course at **Club de Golf de Cap-Rouge** (✉ 4600 rue St-Felix, ☎ 418/653–9381) in Cap-Rouge is one of the closest to Québec City. **Parc du Mont Ste-Anne** (✉ Rte. 360, Beaupré, ☎ 418/827–3778), a half-hour drive north of Québec, has one of the best 18-hole courses in the region.

Health and Fitness Clubs
One of the city's most popular health clubs is **Club Entrain** (✉ Pl. de la Cité, 2600 blvd. Laurier, ☎ 418/658–7771). Facilities include a weight room with Nautilus, a sauna, a whirlpool, aerobics classes, and squash courts. **Hilton International Québec** (✉ 1100 blvd. René-Lévesque Est, ☎ 418/647–2411) has a health club with weights, a sauna, and a year-round heated outdoor pool available to nonguests for a $10 fee. Nonguests at **Hôtel Radisson des Gouverneurs** (✉ 690 blvd. René-Lévesque Est, ☎ 418/647–1717) can use the health club facilities, which include weights, a sauna, a whirlpool, and an outdoor heated pool (in summer), for a $5 fee. Nonmembers can use the pool at the **YMCA du Vieux-Québec** (✉ 650 av. Wilfred Laurier, ☎ 418/522–0800) for a $2.30 fee. Pool facilities cost $2.35 at the **YWCA** (✉ 855 av. Holland, ☎ 418/683–2155).

Hiking and Jogging
The Parc Cartier-Brébeuf, north of Vieux-Québec along the banks of the St. Charles River, has about 13 km (8 mi) of hiking trails. For more mountainous terrain, head 19 km (12 mi) north on Route 73 to Lac

Beauport. For jogging, Battlefields Park, Parc Cartier-Brébeuf, and Bois-de-Coulonge park in Sillery are the most popular places.

Horseback Riding

Jacques Cartier Excursions (✉ 978 av. Jacques-Cartier Nord, Tewkesbury, ☎ 418/848–7238), also known for rafting, offers summer and winter horseback riding. A summer excursion includes an hour of instruction and three hours of riding; the cost is $32–$50.

Ice Canoeing

This sport entails propelling the vessel (a cross between a canoe and a rowboat) over the uneven ice of the St. Lawrence to open water, at which time you jump in the boat and row. To propel the boat on the ice, you straddle it, one knee inside, the other leg pushing like a skateboard. This sport is best restricted to those in good shape. The guides at **Le Mythe des Glaces** (✉ 735 blvd. du Lac, Charlesbourg, G1H 7B1, ☎ 418/849–6131) will suit you up from head to toe. A half day costs $60, a full day with dinner is $120, and a two-day excursion is $265.

Ice-Skating

The ice-skating season runs December–March.There is a 1-km (½-mi) stretch for skating along the **St. Charles River,** between the Dorchester and Drouin bridges; season is January–March, depending on the ice. Rentals and changing rooms are nearby. For information contact Marina St-Roch (☎ 418/691–7188).

From December through March, try the **Patinoire de la Terrasse** adjacent to the Château Frontenac (☎ 418/692–2955), open from 11 to 11; skates can be rented for $4 daily. **Place d'Youville,** just outside St-Jean Gate, has an outdoor rink open November–April. Nighttime skating is an option at **Village des Sports** (✉ 1860 blvd. Valcartier, St-Gabriel-de-Valcartier, ☎ 418/844–3725).

Rafting

The Jacques Cartier River, about 48 km (30 mi) northwest of Québec City, provides good rafting. **Jacques Cartier Excursions** (✉ 978 av. Jacques-Cartier Nord, Tewkesbury, ☎ 418/848–7238) runs rafting trips May–October on the Jacques Cartier River. Tours originate from Tewkesbury, a half-hour drive from Québec City. A half-day tour costs about $45, a full day $65; wet suits are $16. In winter, snow-rafting excursions include all-day mountain sliding in river rafts for $44.

Village des Sports (✉ 1860 blvd. Valcartier, St-Gabriel-de-Valcartier, ☎ 418/844–2200) has excursions on the Jacques Cartier River from mid-May through October. A three-hour excursion costs $49. It also offers boogie boarding—running the rapids on surfboards.

Skiing

Brochures about ski centers in Québec are available at the Québec Tourism and Convention Bureaus or by calling 800/363–7777. The **Hiver Express** (☎ 418/525–5191) winter shuttle is a taxi service between major hotels in Vieux-Québec, Ste-Foy, ski centers, and the Village des Sports (☞ Snow Slides, *below*). It leaves hotels at 8:30 and returns at 4:30. The cost is $18; reserve in advance at hotels. For people staying in ski areas who want to visit the city, the bus leaves at 9:30 and returns at 3:30.

CROSS-COUNTRY

You can ski cross-country on many trails; **Battlefields Park,** which you can reach from Place Montcalm, has scenic marked trails. Thirty-two ski centers in the Québec area offer 2,000 km (1,240 mi) of groomed trails and heated shelters; for information, call **Regroupement des Stations de Ski de Fond** (☎ 418/653–5875). **Le Centre de Randonnée à**

Skis de Duchesnay (⊠ 143 rue de Duchesnay, St-Catherine-de-Jacques-Cartier, ☎ 418/875–2147), just north of Québec City, has 11 marked trails totaling 125 km (77 mi). **Parc du Mont Ste-Anne** (⊠ Rte. 360, Beaupré, ☎ 418/827–4561), 40 km (25 mi) northeast of Québec City, has 21 trails over 223 km (138 mi). Lac Beauport, 19 km (12 mi) north of the city, has more than 20 marked trails (150 km, or 93 mi); contact **Les Sentiers du Moulin** (⊠ 99 chemin du Moulin, Lac Beauport, ☎ 418/849–9652).

DOWNHILL

Three alpine ski resorts, all with night skiing, are within a 30-minute drive of Québec City. There are 25 trails and a vertical drop of 734 ft at the relatively small **Le Relais** (⊠ 1084 blvd. du Lac, Lac Beauport, G0A 2C0, ☎ 418/849–1851). **Station Mont Ste-Anne** (⊠ Rte. 360, C.P. 400, Beaupré, G0A 1E0, ☎ 418/827–4561, 800/463–1568 for lodging) is the largest resort in eastern Canada, with a vertical drop of 2,050 ft, 54 downhill trails, 12 lifts, and a gondola. **Station Touristique Stoneham** (⊠ 1420 av. du Hibou, Stoneham, G0A 4P0, ☎ 418/848–2411), with a vertical drop of 1,377 ft, is known for its long, easy slopes, with 25 downhill runs and 10 lifts.

Snow Slides

At **Glissades de la Terrasse** (☎ 418/692–2955), adjacent to the Château Frontenac (☞ Lodging, *above*), a wooden toboggan takes you down a 700-ft snow slide. Cost is $1 per ride per person.

Visitors to **Village des Sports** can use inner tubes or carpets on the two 300-ft snow slides, or join 6–12 others for a snow raft ride down one of seven groomed trails. ⊠ *1860 blvd. Valcartier, St-Gabriel-de-Valcartier,* ☎ *418/844–3725.* 🌨 *Rafting and sliding $18.50 per day; $20 with skating.* ⏰ *Sun.–Thurs. 10–10, Fri.–Sat. 10* AM*–10:30* PM.

Tennis and Racquet Sports

At **Montcalm Tennis Club** (⊠ 901 blvd. Champlain, Sillery, ☎ 418/687–1250), south of Québec City, four indoor and seven outdoor courts are open daily from 8 AM to midnight. **Tennisport** (⊠ 6280 blvd. Hamel, Ancienne Lorette, ☎ 418/872–0111) has 10 indoor tennis courts, two squash courts, two racquetball courts, and eight badminton courts.

Winter Carnival

One winter highlight is the **Québec Winter Carnival** (⊠ 290 rue Joly, GIL 1N8, ☎ 418/626–3716), famous for its joie de vivre. The whirl of activities over three weekends in January and/or February includes night parades, a snow-sculpture competition, and a canoe race across the St. Lawrence River. You can participate in or watch every activity imaginable in the snow from dogsledding to ice climbing. Dates for 1999 are January 29 to February 14.

Spectator Sports

Tickets for sporting events can be purchased at **Colisée de Québec** (⊠ 2205 av. du Colisée, ☎ 418/691–7211). You can order tickets through **Billetech** (☞ Nightlife and the Arts, *above*).

Harness Racing

There's horse racing at **Hippodrome de Québec** (⊠ Parc de l'Exposition, 250 blvd. Wilfrid-Hamel, ☎ 418/524–5283).

Hockey

An International Hockey League team, the **Québec Rafales,** plays at the Colisée de Québec (⊠ 2205 av. du Colisée, ☎ 418/522–5225 or 418/691–7211).

SHOPPING

Shopping is European-style on the fashionable streets of Québec City. The boutiques and specialty shops clustered along narrow streets such as rue du Petit-Champlain, and rue Buade and rue St-Jean in the Latin Quarter, have one of the most striking historic settings on the continent. Prices in Québec City tend to be on a par with those in Montréal and other North American cities. When sales occur, they are usually listed in the French daily newspaper *Le Soleil*.

Stores are generally open Monday–Wednesday 9:30–5:30, Thursday and Friday until 9, Saturday until 5, and Sunday noon–5. In summer, shops may be open seven days a week, and most have later evening hours.

Department Stores

Large department stores can be found in the malls of the suburb of Ste-Foy, but some have outlets inside Québec City's walls. **La Baie** (✉ Pl. Laurier, Ste-Foy, ☎ 418/627–5959) is Québec's version of the Canadian Hudson's Bay Company conglomerate, founded in 1670 by Montréal trappers Pierre Radisson and Médard Chouart des Groseilliers. Today La Baie carries clothing for the entire family and household wares. **Holt Renfrew & Co., Ltd.** (✉ Pl. Ste-Foy, Ste-Foy, ☎ 418/656–6783), one of the country's more exclusive stores, carries furs, perfume, and tailored designer collections for men and women. **Simons** (✉ 20 côte de la Fabrique, ☎ 418/692–3630), one of Québec City's oldest family stores, used to be its only source for fine British woolens and tweeds; now the store also has a large selection of designer clothing, linens, and other household items.

Shopping Malls

A 20-minute drive from the old city, the **Galeries de la Capitale** (✉ 5401 blvd. des Galeries, ☎ 418/627–5800) has 250 stores and an indoor amusement park with a roller coaster. **Place Québec** (✉ 880 autoroute Dufferin-Montmorency, ☎ 418/529–0551), the mall closest to the old city, is a multilevel shopping complex and convention center with 45 stores and restaurants; it is connected to the Hilton International Hotel.

The following shopping centers are approximately a 15-minute drive west along Grande Allée. **Place Ste-Foy** (✉ 2450 blvd. Laurier, Ste-Foy, ☎ 418/653–4184) has 125 stores. **Place de la Cité** (✉ 2600 blvd. Laurier, Ste-Foy, ☎ 418/657–6920) has 125 boutiques. The massive **Place Laurier** (✉ 2700 blvd. Laurier, Ste-Foy, ☎ 418/653–9318) has more than 350 stores.

Quartier Petit-Champlain (☎ 418/692–2613) in Lower Town is a pedestrian mall with some 40 boutiques, local businesses, and restaurants. This popular district is the best area for native Québec arts and crafts, such as wood sculptures, weaving, ceramics, and jewelry. **Pot-en-Ciel** (✉ 27 rue du Petit-Champlain, ☎ 418/692–1743) carries ceramics. **Pauline Pelletier** (✉ 38 rue du Petit-Champlain, ☎ 418/692–4871) has porcelain.

Specialty Stores

Antiques

Québec City's antiques district is on rue St-Paul and rue St-Pierre, across from the Old Port. French Canadian, Victorian, and Art Deco furniture along with clocks, silverware, and porcelain are some of the rare collectibles found here. Authentic Québec pine furniture, characterized by simple forms and lines, is becoming increasingly rare and costly.

Antiquités Zaor (✉ 112 rue St-Paul, ☎ 418/692–0581), the oldest store on rue St-Paul, is still the best place in the neighborhood to find excellent English, French, and Canadian antiques. **L'Héritage Antiquité** (✉ 109 rue St-Paul, ☎ 418/692–1681) specializes in 18th- and 19th-century Québécois pine furniture, clocks, oil lamps, and porcelain.

Art
Aux Multiples Collections (✉ 43 rue Buade, ☎ 418/692–4298) has Inuit art and antique wood collectibles. **Galerie Brousseau et Brousseau** (✉ 35 rue St-Louis, ☎ 418/694–1828) has Inuit art. **Galerie Madeleine Lacerte** (✉ 1 côte Dinan, ☎ 418/692–1566), in Lower Town, sells contemporary art and sculpture. A source for less expensive artwork or work by young artists who may become famous in the future is **Rue du Trésor,** where local artists display their sketches, paintings, and etchings. Fine portraits of Québec City and the region are plentiful.

Books
English-language books are difficult to find in Québec. **Librairie du Nouveau-Monde** (✉ 103 rue St-Pierre, ☎ 418/694–9475) stocks titles in French and English. **Librairie Smith** (✉ 2700 blvd. Laurier, Place Laurier, ☎ 418/653–8683) has both English and French books. **La Maison Anglaise** (✉ 2600 blvd. Laurier, Place de la Cité, Ste-Foy, ☎ 418/654–9523) has English-language titles only, specializing in fiction.

Clothing
François Côté Collections (✉ 35 rue Buade, ☎ 418/692–6016) is a chic boutique with fashions for men and women. **Louis Laflamme** (✉ 1192 rue St-Jean, ☎ 418/692–3774) has a large selection of stylish men's clothes. **La Maison Darlington** (✉ 7 rue Buade, ☎ 418/692–2268) carries well-made woolens, dresses, and suits for men, women, and children by fine names in couture.

Crafts
Les Trois Colombes Inc. (✉ 46 rue St-Louis, ☎ 418/694–1114) sells handmade items, including clothing made from handwoven fabric, native and Inuit carvings, jewelry and pottery.

Food
Chocolate becomes a work of art at **Chocolaterie Érico** (✉ 634 rue St-Jean, ☎ 418/524–2122), where *chocolatier* Éric Normand will handcraft whatever you like out of chocolate within a few days. At **Marché du Vieux-Port,** farmers from the Québec countryside sell fresh produce in the Old Port near rue St-André, May–October, 8–8.

Fur
The fur trade has been an important industry here for centuries. Québec City is a good place to purchase high-quality furs at fairly reasonable prices. The department store **J. B. Laliberté** (✉ 595 rue St-Joseph Est, ☎ 418/525–4841) carries furs. Since 1894, one of the best furriers in town has been **Richard Robitaille Fourrures** (✉ 1500 rue des Taneurs, ☎ 418/681–7297).

Gifts
Collection Lazuli (✉ 774 rue St-Jean, ☎ 418/525–6528; ✉ 2600 blvd. Laurier, Pl. de la Cité, Ste-Foy, ☎ 418/652–3732) offers a good choice of unusual art objects and international jewelry.

Jewelry
Joaillier Louis Perrier (✉ 48 rue du Petit-Champlain, ☎ 418/692–4633) has Québec-made gold and silver jewelry. Exclusive jewelry can be found at **Zimmermann** (✉ 46 côte de la Fabrique, ☎ 418/692–2672).

SIDE TRIPS FROM QUÉBEC CITY

Several easy excursions will show you another side of the province and provide more insight into its past. The spectacular Montmorency Falls and the Basilique Ste-Anne-de-Beaupré can be seen in a day trip. A drive around the Ile d'Orléans, just east of the city, is an easy way to experience rural Québec. The farms, markets, and churches here evoke the island's long history. The island can be toured in an energetic day, though rural inns make it tempting to extend a visit.

Côte de Beaupré and Montmorency Falls

As legend tells it, when explorer Jacques Cartier first caught sight of the north shore of the St. Lawrence River in 1535, he exclaimed, *"Quel beau pré!"* ("What a lovely meadow!"), because the area was the first inviting piece of land he had spotted since leaving France. Today this fertile meadow, first settled by French farmers, is known as Côte de Beaupré (Beaupré Coast), stretching 40 km (25 mi) east from Québec City to the famous pilgrimage site of Ste-Anne-de-Beaupré. Historic Route 360, or avenue Royal, winds its way from Beauport to St-Joachim, east of St-Anne-de-Beaupré. The impressive Montmorency Falls are midway between Québec City and Ste-Anne-de-Beaupré.

Montmorency Falls

51 *10 km (6 mi) east of Québec City.*

As it cascades over a cliff into the St. Lawrence River, the Montmorency River (named for Charles de Montmorency, who was a governor of New France) is one of the most beautiful sights in the province. The falls, at 274 ft, are 50% higher than Niagara Falls. A cable car runs to the top of the falls in **Parc de la Chute-Montmorency** (Montmorency Falls Park) from late April–early November. During very cold weather, the falls' heavy spray freezes and forms a giant loaf-shape ice cone (hill) known to Québécois as the Pain du Sucre (Sugarloaf); this phenomenon attracts sledders and sliders from Québec City. Ice climbers come to scale the falls; a school trains novices for only a few days to make the ascent. In the warmer months, you can visit an observation tower in the river's gorge that is continuously sprayed by a fine drizzle from water pounding onto the cliff rocks. The top of the falls can be observed from avenue Royale.

The park is also historic. The British general Wolfe, on his way to conquer New France, set up camp here in 1759. In 1780, Sir Frederick Haldimand, then the governor of Canada, built a summer home—now a good restaurant called Manoir Montmorency—on top of the cliff. Prince Edward, Queen Victoria's father, rented this villa from 1791 to 1794. Unfortunately, the structure burned down several years ago; what stands is a re-creation. ✉ *2490 av. Royale, Beauport,* ☎ *418/663–2877.* 🎫 *Cable car $7 round-trip; car parking $7.* ☾ *Cable car Apr. 25–June 19 and Sept. 2–Oct. 25, daily 9–7; June 20–Aug. 2, daily 9 AM–11 PM; Aug. 3–Sept. 1, daily 9–9; Oct. 26–Nov. 1, daily 9–4. It functions on winter weekends for the Sugarloaf slide.*

Ste-Anne-de-Beaupré
40 km (25 mi) east of Québec City.

★ **52** The small town of Ste-Anne-de-Beaupré is famous for an impressive shrine with the same name. The monumental and inspiring **Basilique Ste-Anne-de-Beaupré** is surrounded by aged, modest homes and tacky souvenir shops that emphasize its grandeur. The basilica has become a popular attraction as well as an important Catholic shrine: More than a half-million people visit the site each year.

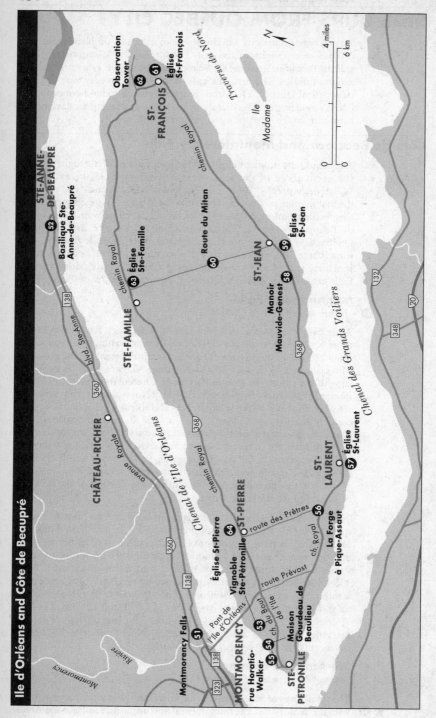

Île d'Orléans and Côte de Beaupré

Observation Tower
Église St-François
ST-FRANÇOIS

Traverse du Nord

Île Madame

N

4 miles
6 km

STE-ANNE-DE-BEAUPRÉ
Basilique Ste-Anne-de-Beaupré

Église Ste-Famille
STE-FAMILLE

chemin Royal
chemin Royal

Route du Mitan

Église St-Jean
ST-JEAN

Manoir Mauvide-Genest

138
blvd. Ste-Anne

360

CHÂTEAU-RICHER

avenue Royale

Chenal de l'Île d'Orléans

chemin Royal

368

Chenal des Grands Voiliers

132

20

348

368

Église St-Pierre
Vignoble Ste-Pétronille
ST-PIERRE
route des Prêtres

Église St-Laurent
ST-LAURENT

La Forge à Pique-Assaut

ch. Royal

route Prévost

Pont de l'Île d'Orléans

ch. du Bout de l'Île

Maison Gourdeau de Beaulieu

138

323

MONTMORENCY
rue Horatio-Walker

STE-PÉTRONILLE

Montmorency Falls

Rivière Montmorency

51
52
61
62
63
60
57
58
59
64
56
57
53
54
55

The French brought their devotion to St. Anne (the patron saint of those in shipwrecks) with them when they sailed across the Atlantic to New France. In 1650, Breton sailors caught in a storm vowed to erect a chapel in honor of this patron saint at the exact spot where they landed. The present-day neo-Roman basilica constructed in 1923 was the fifth to be built on the site where the sailors first touched ground.

According to local legend, St. Anne was responsible over the years for saving voyagers from shipwrecks in the harsh waters of the St. Lawrence. Tributes to her miraculous powers can be seen in the shrine's various mosaics, murals, altars, and ceilings. A bas-relief at the entrance depicts St. Anne welcoming her pilgrims, and ceiling mosaics represent her life. Numerous crutches and braces posted on the back pillars have been left by those who have felt the saint's healing powers.

The basilica, in the shape of a Latin cross, has two granite steeples jutting from its gigantic structure. Its interior has 22 chapels and 18 altars, as well as round arches and numerous ornaments in the Romanesque style. The 214 stained-glass windows by Frenchmen Auguste Labouret and Pierre Chaudière, finished in 1949, tell a story of salvation through personages who were believed to be instruments of God over the centuries. Other features of the shrine are intricately carved wood pews decorated with various animals and several smaller altars (behind the main altar) dedicated to different saints.

The original, 17th-century wood chapel in the village of Ste-Anne-de-Beaupré was built too close to the St. Lawrence and was swept away by river flooding. In 1676 the chapel was replaced by a stone church that was visited by pilgrims for more than a century, but this structure was also demolished in 1872. The first basilica, which replaced the stone church, was destroyed by a fire in 1922. The following year architects Maxime Rosin from Paris and Louis N. Audet from Québec province designed the basilica that now stands. ⊠ *10018 av. Royale,* ☎ *418/ 827–3781.* 🖂 *Free.* ☉ *Reception booth mid-May–mid-Oct., daily 8:30– 7:30. Guided tours daily at 1 in summer; Sept.–mid-May, call in advance to arrange a tour.*

The **Commemorative Chapel,** across from the basilica on avenue Royale, was designed by Claude Bailiff and built in 1878. The memorial chapel was constructed on the location of the transept of a stone church built in 1676 and contains the old building's foundations. Among the remnants housed here are the old church's bell, dating from 1696; an early 18th-century altar designed by Vezina; a crucifix sculpted by François-Noël Levasseur in 1775; and a pulpit designed by François Baillargé in 1807.

Côte de Beaupré and Montmorency Falls A to Z

ARRIVING AND DEPARTING

To reach Montmorency Falls, take Route 440 (Autoroute Dufferin-Montmorency) east from Québec City approximately 9½ km (6 mi) to the exit for Montmorency Falls. To drive directly to Ste-Anne-de Beaupré, continue east on Route 440 for approximately 29 km (18 mi) and exit at Ste-Anne-de-Beaupré.

An alternative way to reach Ste-Anne-de-Beaupré is to take Route 360, or avenue Royale. Take Route 440 from Québec City, turn left at d'Estimauville, and right on boulevard Ste-Anne until it intersects with Route 360. Also called *le chemin du Roi* (the King's Road), this panoramic route is one of the oldest in North America, winding 30 km (19 mi) along the steep ridge of the Côte de Beaupré. The road borders 17th- and 18th-century farmhouses, historic churches, and Normandy-style homes with half-buried root cellars.

GUIDED TOURS
Gray Line (☎ 418/653–9722, FAX 418/653–9834) and **Maple Leaf Sight-seeing Tours** (☎ 418/649–9226) lead day excursions along the Côte de Beaupré, with stops at Montmorency Falls and the Ste-Anne-de-Beaupré Basilica. Cost is about $32 per tour.

VISITOR INFORMATION
The **Beaupré Coast Interpretation Center,** in the old mill Petit-Pré, built in 1695, has displays on the history of the region. ⊠ *7007 av. Royale, Château-Richer,* ☎ *418/824–3677.* ⊡ *$2.* ☉ *Mid-May–mid-Oct., daily 10–5.* **Quebec City Tourist Information** has a bureau in Beauport (⊠ 4300 blvd. Ste-Anne, Rte. 138) in Montmorency Falls Park. It's open mid-June–October 12, daily 9–5:45.

Ile d'Orléans

The Algonquins called it Minigo, the "Bewitched Place," and over the years the island's tranquil rural beauty has inspired poets and painters. The Ile d'Orléans is only 15 minutes from downtown Québec City, but a visit here is one of the best ways to get a feel for traditional life in rural Québec. The road that rings the island is dotted with centuries-old homes and some of the oldest churches in the region. Ile d'Orléans is at its best in summer when the boughs of trees in lush orchards bend under the weight of apples, plums, or pears, and the fields are bursting with strawberries and raspberries. Roadside stands sell woven articles, maple syrup, baked goods, jams, fruits, and vegetables. Visitors can also pick their own produce at about two dozen farms. The island, immortalized by one of its most famous residents, the late poet and songwriter Félix Leclerc, is still fertile ground for artists and artisans.

The island was discovered at about the same time as Québec City, in 1535. Explorer Jacques Cartier noticed an abundance of vines and called it the Island of Bacchus, after the Greek god of wine. (Today, native Québec vines are being crossbred with European varieties at Ste-Pétronille's fledgling vineyard.) In 1536 Cartier renamed the island in honor of the duke of Orléans, son of the French king François I. Its fertile soil and abundant fishing made it so attractive to settlers that its population once exceeded Québec City's.

Ile d'Orléans, about 8 km (5 mi) wide and 34 km (21 mi) long, is composed of six small villages that have sought over the years to retain their identities. The island's bridge to the mainland was built in 1935, and in 1970 the island was declared a historic area to protect it from urban development.

Ste-Pétronille
17 km (10½ mi) from Québec City.

The lovely village of Ste-Pétronille, the first to be settled on Ile d'Orléans, lies to the west of the bridge to the island. Founded in 1648, the community was chosen in 1759 by British general James Wolfe for his headquarters. With 40,000 soldiers and a hundred ships, the English bombarded French-occupied Québec City and Côte de Beaupré.

During the late 19th century, the English population of Québec developed Ste-Pétronille into a resort village. This area is considered to be the island's most beautiful, not only because of its spectacular views of Montmorency Falls and Québec City but also for the Regency-style English villas and exquisitely tended gardens.

❺❸ At the **Vignoble de Ste-Pétronille,** hardy native Québec vines have been crossbred with three types of European grapes to produce a surprisingly good dry white wine. A guided tour of the vineyard includes a taste testing. ✉ *1A chemin Royal,* ☎ *418/828–9554.* 🍽 *$2.50.* ☉ *Mid-June–mid-Oct., daily 10–6.*

At the **Plante family farm** (✉ 20 chemin Royal, ☎ 418/828–9603) you can stop to pick apples (in season) or buy fresh fruits and vegetables.

54 The island's first home, the **Maison Gourdeau de Beaulieu** (✉ 137 chemin Royal) was built in 1648 for Jacques Gourdeau de Beaulieu, who was the first seigneur (a landholder who distributed lots to tenant farmers) of Ste-Pétronille. Remodeled over the years, this white house with blue shutters now incorporates both French and Québécois styles. Its thick walls and dormer windows are characteristic of Breton architecture, but its sloping bell-shape roof, designed to protect buildings from large amounts of snow, is typically Québécois. The house is not open to the public.

55 The tiny street called **rue Horatio-Walker,** off chemin Royal, was named after the turn-of-the-century painter known for his landscapes of the island. Walker lived on this street from 1904 until his death in 1938. At 11 and 13 rue Horatio-Walker are his home and workshop, but they are not open to the public.

DINING AND LODGING

$$$–$$$$ ✕▨ **La Goéliche.** This English-style country manor, rebuilt in 1996–97 following a fire, stands just steps away from the St. Lawrence River. Antiques decorate the cozy, elegant rooms, all with river views. Sinks are in the rooms instead of the baths to maximize space. Classic French cuisine includes fillet of trout rolled with spinach and cheese from Charlevoix, and breast of duck in an orange sauce perfumed with Grand Marnier. The romantic dining room overlooks the river; an outdoor terrace is used in summer. ✉ *22 chemin du Quai,* ☎ *418/828–2248,* FAX *418/828–2745. 18 rooms. Restaurant. AE, MC, V.*

SHOPPING

Chocolaterie de lle d'Orléans (✉ 196 chemin Royal, ☎ 418/828–2252) combines Belgian chocolate with local ingredients to create handmade treats. Some choices are chocolates filled with maple butter or the *framboisette* made from raspberries. In summer there are homemade ice creams and sherbets.

St-Laurent
9 km (5½ mi) from Ste-Pétronille.

Founded in 1679, St-Laurent is one of the island's maritime villages. Until as late as 1935, residents here used boats as their main means of **56** transportation. The **La Forge à Pique-Assaut** (✉ 2200 chemin Royal, ☎ 418/828–9300) belongs to the talented and well-known local artisan Guy Bel, who has done ironwork restoration for Québec City. He was born in Lyon, France, and studied there at the Ecole des Beaux Arts. In summer he can be seen hard at work daily; his stylish candlesticks, chandeliers, fireplace tools, and other ironworks are for sale. In winter his workshop is closed on weekends.

The **Parc Maritime de St-Laurent,** at a former boatyard, is where craftspeople specializing in boatbuilding practiced their trade. Now you can picnic here, rent a rowboat, and visit the Chalouperie Godbout (Godbout Longboat), which houses a complete collection of tools used during the golden era of boatbuilding. You can try your hand at some boatbuilding skills and practice tying sailors' knots. ✉ *120 chemin de la Chalouperie,* ☎ *418/828–9672.* 🍽 *Park $2, parking $3.* ☉ *Mid-June–Aug., daily 10–5; Sept.–early Oct., weekends 10–5 or by reservation; mid-May–mid-June by reservation.*

❺❼ The tall, inspiring **Église St-Laurent,** which stands next to the village marina on chemin Royal, was built in 1860 on the site of an 18th-century church that had to be torn down. One of the church's procession chapels is a miniature stone replica of the original. ✉ *1532 chemin Royal.* 🎫 *Free.* ⊙ *Summer, daily.*

DINING AND LODGING

$$–$$$$ ✕ **Moulin de St. Laurent.** This is an early 18th-century stone mill in which you can dine in the herb-and-flower garden out back in season. Scrumptious snacks, such as quiches, bagels, and salads, are available at the café-terrace. Evening dishes include local game such as stuffed rabbit. ✉ *754 chemin Royal,* ☎ *418/829–3888. AE, DC, MC, V.*

$–$$ ✕🏠 **Le Canard Huppé.** He's barely 30, but award-winning chef Philip Rae's inventive use of fresh island ingredients and his often spectacular presentations have already won rave reviews at this restaurant ($$$–$$$$). As the inn's name suggests, the contemporary cuisine usually showcases at least one dish with duck, whether it's duck with pineapple chutney and cedar sauce or red (from beet juice) ravioli stuffed with conserve of duck and smoked snails. Upstairs, each of the inn's rooms has its own personality. Rooms are decorated with original paintings by Québec City area artists and unusual antiques—some from as far away as Polynesia. ✉ *2198 chemin Royal,* ☎ *418/828–2292,* FAX *418/828–0966. 8 rooms. Restaurant. DC, MC, V.*

St-Jean
12 km (7 mi) from St-Laurent.

The southernmost point of the island, St-Jean is a village whose inhabitants were once river pilots and navigators. Most of its small, homogeneous row homes were built between 1840 and 1860. Being at sea most of the time, the sailors did not need large homes and plots of land, as did the farmers.

❺❽ St-Jean's beautiful Normandy-style manor, **Manoir Mauvide-Genest,** was built in 1734 for Jean Mauvide—surgeon to Louis XV—and his wife, Marie-Anne Genest. Most notable about this house, which still has its original thick walls, ceiling beams, and fireplaces, is the degree to which it has held up over the years, in spite of being targeted by English guns during the 1759 siege of Québec City. The indentations left by cannonballs can still be seen on the facade. The home is a pleasure to explore; all rooms are furnished with antiques from the 18th and 19th centuries. There's also an exhibit on French architecture. ✉ *1451 chemin Royal,* ☎ *418/829–2630.* 🎫 *$4.* ⊙ *June–Aug., daily 10:30–5:30; Sept.–mid-Oct., weekends by reservation.*

❺❾ At the eastern end of the village is **Église St-Jean,** a massive granite structure with large red doors and a towering steeple built in 1749. The church resembles a ship; it is big and round and appears to be sitting right on the river. Paintings of the patron saints of seamen line the interior walls. The church's cemetery is also intriguing, especially if you can read French. Back in the 18th century, piloting the St. Lawrence was a dangerous profession. The cemetery tombstones recall the tragedies of lives lost in these harsh waters. ✉ *2001 chemin Royal,* ☎ *418/829–3182.* 🎫 *Free.* ⊙ *Summer, daily 9–5.*

❻⓪ Outside St-Jean, chemin Royal crosses **route du Mitan,** the most beautiful on the island. In old French, *mitan* means "halfway." This road, dividing the island in half, has views of acres of tended farmland, apple orchards, and maple groves. If you need to end your circuit of the island here, take route du Mitan, which brings you to Ste-Famille; head west on chemin Royal to return to the bridge to the mainland.

St-François

12 km (7 mi) from St-Jean.

Sprawling open fields separate 17th-century farmhouses in St-François, the island's least-toured and most rustic village. This community at the eastern tip of the island was originally settled mainly by farmers. St-François is also the perfect place to visit one of the island's *cabanes à sucre* (maple-sugaring shacks), found along chemin Royal. Stop at a hut for a tasting tour; sap is gathered from the maple groves and boiled until it turns to syrup. When it is poured on ice, it tastes like a delicious toffee. The maple syrup season is late March–April.

61 **Église St-François** (✉ 106 chemin Royal, ☎ 418/829–3440), built in 1734, is one of eight provincial churches dating from the French regime. At the time the English seized Québec City in 1759, General Wolfe knew St-François to be a strategic point along the St. Lawrence. Consequently, he stationed British troops here and used the church as a military hospital. In 1988, a car crash set the church on fire and most of the interior treasures were lost. A separate children's cemetery stands as a silent witness to the difficult life of early residents.

62 A picnic area with a wood **observation tower** is perfectly situated for viewing the majestic St. Lawrence. In spring and fall, wild Canada geese can be seen here. The area is about 2 km (1 mi) north on chemin Royal from St-François Church.

Ste-Famille

14 km (9 mi) from St-François.

The village of Ste-Famille, founded in 1661, has exquisite scenery, including abundant apple orchards and strawberry fields with views of Côte de Beaupré and Mont Ste-Anne in the distance. But it also has plenty of historic charm, claiming the area's highest concentration of stone houses dating from the French regime.

63 The impressive **Église Ste-Famille,** constructed in 1749, is the only church in the province to have three bell towers at the front. Its ceiling was redone in the mid-19th century with elaborate designs in wood and gold. The church also holds a famous painting, *L'Enfant Jésus Voyant la Croix (Baby Jesus Looking at the Cross),* done in 1670 by Frère Luc (Father Luc), who was sent from France to decorate churches in the area. ✉ *3915 chemin Royal.* ☒ *Free.* ☺ *Summer, daily.*

DINING

$$$–$$$$ ✕ **L'Atre.** After you park your car, you'll be driven in a 1954 Chrysler to the 17th-century Normandy-style house furnished with Québécois pine antiques. True to the establishment's name, which means "hearth," all the dishes are cooked and served from a fireplace. The menu emphasizes hearty fare, such as beef bourguignonne and tourtière, with maple-sugar pie for dessert. Halfway through the meal, diners visit the attic for a nip of maple-syrup liqueur. ✉ *4403 chemin Royal,* ☎ *418/ 829–2474. Reservations essential. AE, MC, V. Closed Nov.–Apr.*

St-Pierre

14 km (9 mi) from Ste-Famille.

St-Pierre, on the northwest side of the island, was established in 1679. Set on a plateau that has the island's most fertile land, the town has long been the center of traditional farming industries. The best products grown here are potatoes, asparagus, and corn, and the many dairy farms have given the village a reputation for butter and other dairy products. If you continue west on chemin Royal, just up ahead is the bridge back to the mainland and Route 440.

64 **Église St-Pierre,** the oldest on the island, dates from 1717. It is no longer open for worship, but it was restored during the 1960s and is open to visitors. Many of the original components are still intact, such as benches with compartments below, where hot bricks and stones were placed to keep people warm during winter services. Félix Leclerc (1914–88), the first Québécois singer to make his mark in Europe, is buried in the cemetery nearby. ⊠ *1243 chemin Royal.* ☜ *Free.* ☉ *Summer, daily.*

La Ferme Monna has won international awards for its crème de cassis de l'Ile d'Orléans, a liqueur made from black currants. The farm has free samples of the strong, sweet cassis or one of Monna's black currant wines, and a tour explains how they are made. ⊠ *723 chemin Royal,* ☎ *418/828–1057.* ☜ *Free; guided tours $4.* ☉ *June–Sept., daily 10–6; Mar. and Oct.–Dec., weekends 10–5.*

Ile d'Orléans A to Z

ARRIVING AND DEPARTING
From Québec City, take Route 440 (Autoroute Dufferin-Montmorency) northeast. After a drive of about 10 km (6 mi) take the bridge Pont de l'Ile d'Orléans to the island. Ile d'Orléans has no public transportation; cars are the only way to get around, unless you take a guided tour (☞ Guided Tours, *below*). Parking can sometimes be a problem, but you can leave your car in the church parking lot and explore each village on foot. Cycling is also a popular option, although there are no separate bicycle lanes. The main road, chemin Royal (Route 368), extends 67 km (42 mi) through the island's six villages; street numbers along chemin Royal begin at No. 1 for each municipality.

B&B RESERVATION SERVICE
Reservations are necessary at the island's 50 B&Bs, which cost about $50–$100 per night for a double-occupancy room. The **Chamber of Commerce** (☎ 418/828–9411) has a referral service for B&Bs.

EMERGENCIES
Centre Médical Prévost (⊠ 1015 Rte. Prévost, St-Pierre, ☎ 418/828–2213) is the principal medical clinic on the island.

GUIDED TOURS
Québec City tour companies, including **Maple Leaf Sight-seeing Tours** (☎ 418/649–9226) and **Gray Line** (☎ 418/653–9722), have bus tours of the western tip of the island, combined with sightseeing along the Côte de Beaupré. The island's **Chamber of Commerce** rents a cassette tape for $8 with an interesting 90-minute tour of the island by car; it's available at the tourist kiosk (☞ Visitor Information, *below*).

Any of the offices of the **Québec City Region Tourism and Convention Bureau** (☞ Visitor Information *in* Québec City A to Z, *below*) can provide information on tours and accommodations on the island.

VISITOR INFORMATION
The island's **Chamber of Commerce** operates a tourist information kiosk at the west corner of côte du Pont and chemin Royal in St-Pierre. ⊠ *490 côte du Pont, St-Pierre,* ☎ *418/828–9411.* ☉ *June–Sept., daily 8:30–7; Oct.–May, weekdays 9–5.*

QUÉBEC CITY A TO Z

Arriving and Departing

By Bus
Orléans Express Inc. provides service from Montréal to Québec City daily, departing hourly 6 AM–10 PM, with an additional bus at mid-

night. The three-hour ride costs $35.90 one-way, and a round-trip is double that; but a round-trip costs $53.27 if you return within 10 days and do not travel on Friday or certain days during holiday periods. You can purchase tickets only at one of the terminals (☞ *below*).

TERMINALS
Montréal: Terminus Voyageur (✉ 505 blvd. de Maisonneuve Est, ☎ 514/842–2281). **Québec City:** Downtown Terminal (✉ 320 rue Abraham-Martin, ☎ 418/525–3000); Ste-Foy Terminal (✉ 925 av. de Rochebelle, ☎ 418/525–3000).

By Car

Montréal and Québec City are linked by Autoroute 20 on the south shore of the St. Lawrence River and by Autoroute 40 on the north shore. On both highways, the ride between the two cities is about 240 km (149 mi) and takes about three hours. U.S. I–87 in New York, U.S. I–89 in Vermont, and U.S. I–91 in New Hampshire connect with Autoroute 20. Highway 401 from Toronto links up with Autoroute 20.

Driving northeast from Montréal on Autoroute 20, follow signs for Pont Pierre-Laporte (Pierre Laporte Bridge) as you approach Québec City. After you've crossed the bridge, turn right onto boulevard Laurier (Route 175), which becomes the Grande Allée leading into Québec City. Also *see* Getting Around by Car, *below.*

By Plane

Jean Lesage International Airport (✉ 500 rue Principale, Ste-Foy, ☎ 418/640–2600) is about 19 km (12 mi) from downtown. Few U.S. **airlines** fly directly to Québec City. You usually have to stop in Montréal, Toronto, or Ottawa and take a regional or commuter airline, such as Air Canada's Air Alliance or Canadian Airlines International's Inter-Canadien. Air Alliance and Delta offer some direct flights (☞ Air Travel *in* the Gold Guide).

BETWEEN THE AIRPORT AND QUÉBEC CITY
The ride from the airport into town should be no longer than 30 minutes. Most hotels do not have an airport shuttle, but they will make a reservation for you with a bus company. If you're not in a rush, a shuttle bus offered by Autobus La Québécoise Inc. (☞ *below*) is convenient and half the price of a taxi.

By Bus. Autobus La Québécoise Inc. (✉ 5480 rue Rideau, ☎ 418/570–5379) has a shuttle bus from the airport to hotels; cost is less than $10 one-way. Reservations are necessary for the trip to the airport.

By Car. If you're driving from the airport, take Route 540 (Autoroute Duplessis) to Route 175 (blvd. Laurier), which becomes Grande Allée and leads right to Vieux-Québec. The ride is about 30 minutes and may be only slightly longer (45 minutes or so) during rush hours (7:30–8:30 AM into town and 4–5:30 PM leaving town).

By Limousine. Private limo service is expensive, starting at $50 for the ride from the airport into Québec City. Try **Groupe Limousine A-1** (✉ 361 rue des Commissaires Est, ☎ 418/523–5059).

By Taxi. Taxis are available immediately outside the airport exit near the baggage claim area. A ride into the city costs about $25. Two local taxi firms are **Taxi Québec** (✉ 975 8ᵉ av., ☎ 418/522–2001) and **Taxi Coop de Québec** (✉ 496 2ᵉ av., ☎ 418/525–5191), the largest company in the city.

By Train

VIA Rail (☎ 418/692–3940, 800/361–5390 in Québec), Canada's passenger rail service, runs trains from Montréal to Québec City four times daily Tuesday–Friday, and three times daily on Saturday, Sunday, and Monday. The trip takes less than three hours, with a stop in Ste-Foy. Tickets must be purchased in advance at any VIA Rail office or travel agent. The basic one-way rate, including taxes, is about $54, but a limited quantity of seats are reduced to $32 if tickets are bought at least five days in advance. First-class service costs about $95 each way and includes early boarding, seat selection, and a three-course meal with wine.

The train arrives in Québec City at the 19th-century **Gare du Palais** (⊠ 450 rue de la Gare du Palais, ☎ 418/524–6452), in the heart of the old city.

Getting Around

By Bus
The city's transit system, **Société de Transport de la Communauté Urbaine de Québec (STCUQ)** (☎ 418/627–2511) runs buses approximately every 15 to 30 minutes that stop at major points around town. The cost is $2; you'll need exact change. Bus tickets are available for $1.60 ($4.35 for day pass) at major convenience stores. All buses stop in Lower Town at Place Jacques-Cartier and outside St-Jean Gate at Place d'Youville in Upper Town. Transportation maps are available at visitor information offices.

By Car
It is necessary to have a car only if you plan to visit outlying areas. The narrow streets of the old city leave few two-hour metered parking spaces available. However, several parking garages at central locations charge about $10 a day. Main garages are at City Hall, Place d'Youville, Edifice Marie-Guyart, Complex G, Place Québec, Château Frontenac, Québec Seminary, rue St-Paul, and the Old Port.

By Ferry
The **Québec–Lévis ferry** (☎ 418/644–3704) crosses the St. Lawrence River to the town of Lévis. Although the crossing takes 15 minutes, waiting time can increase that to an hour. The cost is $1.50 in winter and $1.75 in summer. From December through April, the first ferry from Québec City leaves daily at 6:30 AM from the pier at rue Dalhousie, across from Place Royale. Crossings run every half hour from 7:30 AM until 6:30 PM, then hourly until 2:15 AM. From May through November, the ferry adds extra service every 20 minutes during rush hours: 7:20–9 AM and 4–6 PM.

By Foot
Walking is the best way to explore the city. Vieux-Québec measures 11 square km (about 6 square mi), and most historic sites, hotels, and restaurants are within the walls or a short distance outside. City maps are available at visitor information offices.

By Horse-Drawn Carriage
Hire a calèche on rue d'Auteuil between the St-Louis and Kent gates from **André Beaurivage** (☎ 418/687–9797), **Balades en Calèche et Diligence** (☎ 418/624–3062), or **Les Calèches du Vieux-Québec** (☎ 418/683–9222). The cost is about $50 without tax or tip for a 45-minute tour of Vieux-Québec. Some drivers talk about Québec's history and others don't; if you want a storyteller, ask in advance.

By Limousine
Groupe Limousine A-1 (⊠ 361 rue des Commissaires Est, ☎ 418/523–5059) has 24-hour service.

By Taxi

Taxis are stationed in front of major hotels and the Hôtel de Ville (City Hall), along rue des Jardins, and at Place d'Youville outside St-Jean Gate. Passengers are charged an initial $2.25, plus $1 for each kilometer (½ mi). For radio-dispatched cars, try **Taxi Coop de Québec** (☎ 418/525–5191) or **Taxi Québec** (☎ 418/522–2001).

Contacts and Resources

B&B Reservation Agencies

Québec City has many accommodations in hostels and B&Bs, which are becoming known as Couette & Cafés. To guarantee a room in peak season, reserve in advance. **Québec City Tourist Information** (✉ 835 av. Laurier, G1R 2L3, ☎ 418/649–2608) has B&B listings.

Car Rentals

Hertz Canada (Airport, ☎ 418/871–1571; Vieux-Québec, ✉ 44 Côte du Palais, ☎ 418/694–1224, 800/263–0600 in English, 800/263–0678 in French). **Tilden** (Airport: ☎ 418/871–1224; ✉ 295 St. Paul St., ☎ 418/694–1727). **Via Route** (✉ 2605 Hamel Blvd., ☎ 418/682–2660).

Consulate

The **U.S. Consulate** (✉ 2 Pl. Terrasse Dufferin, ☎ 418/692–2096) faces the Governors' Park near the Château Frontenac.

Dentists and Doctors

Clinique Dentaire Darveau, Dablois and Tardif (✉ 1175 rue Lavigerie, Edifice Iberville 2, Room 100, Ste-Foy, ☎ 418/653–5412) is open Monday–Tuesday 8–8, Wednesday 8–5, Thursday 8–6, and Friday 8–4.

Pavillon Centre Hospitalier de l'Université Laval (CHUL) (✉ 2705 blvd. Laurier, ☎ 418/656–4141) is in Ste-Foy. **Pavillon Hôtel-Dieu** (✉ 11 côte du Palais, ☎ 418/691–5151, 418/691–5042 for emergencies) is the main hospital inside Vieux-Québec.

Emergencies

Distress Center (☎ 418/686–2433). **Fire, police**(☎ 911 or 418/691–7882 outside the 911 area). **Poison Center** (☎ 418/656–8090). **Provincial police** (☎ 418/623–6262).

English-Language Bookstore

La Maison Anglaise (✉ 2600 blvd. Laurier, Place de la Cité, Ste-Foy, ☎ 418/654–9523).

Guided Tours

BOAT

Croisières AML Inc. (✉ Pier Chouinard, 10 rue Dalhousie, beside the Québec-Lévis ferry terminal, ☎ 418/692–1159) runs cruises on the St. Lawrence River aboard the MV *Louis-Jolliet*. The 1½- to 3-hour cruises from May through mid-October start at $20.

ORIENTATION

Tours cover such sights as Québec City, Montmorency Falls, and Ste-Anne-de-Beaupré; combination city and harbor-cruise tours are also available. Québec City tours operate year-round; excursions to outlying areas may operate only in summer.Tickets for **Gray Line** bus tours (☎ 418/653–9722) can be purchased at most major hotels or at the kiosk at Terrasse Dufferin at Place d'Armes. Tours run year-round and cost $20–$80; departure is from Château Frontenac terrace. **Maple Leaf Sight-seeing Tours** (✉ 240 3ᵉ rue, ☎ 418/649–9226) offers guided tours in a minibus or trolley. Call for a reservation, and the company will pick you up at your hotel. Prices are $21–$89.

WALKING

Adlard Tours (⊠ 13 rue Ste-Famille, ☎ 418/692–2358) leads walking tours of the old city amid the narrow streets that buses cannot enter. The $14 cost includes a refreshment break; unilingual tours are available in many languages. Tours leave from 12 rue Ste-Anne.

Late-Night Pharmacy

Pharmacie Brunet (⊠ Les Galeries Charlesbourg, 4250 1re av., north of Québec City in Charlesbourg, ☎ 418/623–1571), is open daily, 24 hours a day.

Opening and Closing Times

Most banks are open Monday–Wednesday 10–3 and close later on Thursday and Friday. **Bank of Montréal** (⊠ Pl. Laurier, 2700 blvd. Laurier, Ste-Foy, ☎ 418/525–3786) is open Saturday 11–2. For currency exchange, **Echange de Devises Montréal** (⊠ 12 rue Ste-Anne, ☎ 418/694–1014) is open September–mid-June, daily 9–5, and mid-June–Labor Day, daily 8:30–7:30.

Museum hours are typically 10–5, with longer evening hours during summer months. Most are closed on Monday. For store hours, *see* Shopping, *above.* In winter many attractions and shops change their hours; visitors are advised to call ahead.

Road Conditions

Seasonal information is available November–April (☎ 418/643–6830).

Travel Agencies

American Express (⊠ 2700 blvd. Laurier, Place Laurier, ☎ 418/ 658–8820). **Inter-Voyage** (⊠ 1095 rue de l'Amérique Française, ☎ 418/524–1414).

Visitor Information

Québec City Region Tourism and Convention Bureau has two visitor information centers that are open year-round and a mobile information service that operates between mid-June and September 7 (look for the mopeds with a big question mark).

The **Québec City** (⊠ 835 av. Laurier, G1R 2L3, ☎ 418/649–2608) center is open June–September 7, daily 8:30–7:45; September 8–October 12, daily 8:30–5:15; October 13–May, daily 9–4:45. **Québec Government Tourism Department** (⊠ 12 rue Ste-Anne, Pl. d'Armes, ☎ 800/363–7777) has a center that is open fall–winter, daily 9–5, and summer, daily 8:30–7:30. The **Ste-Foy** (⊠ 3300 av. des Hôtels, G1W 5A8: look for the big question mark) center, a drop-in office (no telephone), is open June–September 7, daily 8:30–7:45; September 8–October 12, daily 8:30–5:45; October 13–May, daily 9–4:45.

10 Province of Québec

The Laurentians, the Eastern Townships, Charlevoix, the Gaspé Peninsula

Québec has a distinct personality forged by its French heritage and culture. The land, too, is memorable: Within its boundaries lie thousands of lakes and rivers—the highways for intrepid explorers, fur traders, and pioneers. Echoes of the past remain in the charming rural communities of Charlevoix and the Eastern Townships. The Laurentians with their ski resorts and the forested coastline of the Gulf of St. Lawrence also lend a unique flavor to La Belle Province.

By Dorothy
Guinan

Updated by
Helga
Loverseed

AMONG THE PROVINCES OF CANADA, Québec is set apart by its strong French heritage, a matter not only of language but of customs, religion, and political structure. Québec covers a vast area—almost one-sixth of Canada's total—although the upper three-quarters is only sparsely inhabited. Most of the population lives in the southern cities, especially Montréal (☞ Chapter 8) and Québec City (☞ Chapter 9). Outside the cities, however, you'll find serenity and natural beauty in the province's innumerable lakes, streams, and rivers; in its farmlands and villages; in its great mountains and deep forests; and in its rugged coastline along the Gulf of St. Lawrence. Though the winters are long, there are plenty of winter sports to while away the cold months, especially in the Laurentians, with their many ski resorts.

The first European to arrive in Québec was French explorer Jacques Cartier, in 1534; another Frenchman, Samuel de Champlain, arrived in 1603 to build French settlements in the region, and Jesuit missionaries followed in due course. Louis XIV of France proclaimed Canada a crown colony in 1663, and the land was allotted to French aristocrats in large grants called seigneuries. As tenants, known as habitants, settled upon farms in Québec, the Roman Catholic Church took on an importance that went beyond religion. Priests and nuns also acted as doctors, educators, and overseers of business arrangements between the habitants and between French-speaking fur traders and English-speaking merchants. An important doctrine of the church in Québec, one that took on more emphasis after the British conquest of 1759, was *survivance*, the survival of the French people and their culture. Couples were encouraged to have large families, and they did—until the 1950s families with 10 or 12 children were common.

Québec's recent threats to secede from the Canadian union are part of a long-standing tradition of independence. Although the British won control of Canada in the French and Indian War, which ended in 1763, Parliament passed the Québec Act in 1774, which ensured the continuation of French civil law in Québec and left provincial authority in the hands of the Roman Catholic Church. In general the law preserved the traditional French-Canadian way of life. Tensions between French- and English-speaking Canada have continued throughout the 20th century, however, and in 1974 the province proclaimed French its sole official language, much the same way the provinces of Manitoba and Alberta had taken steps earlier in the century to make English their sole official language. In 1990 the Canadian government failed to add Québec's signature to changes it had brought about in the Canadian Constitution and in 1992 failed to have its proposed constitutional changes accepted by the Canadian population in a referendum. Today Québec is part of the Canadian union and a signatory to its constitution, but it has not accepted the changes made in that document during the 1980s.

Being able to speak French can make a visit to the province more pleasant—many locals, at least outside Montréal, do not speak English. If you don't speak French, arm yourself with a phrase book or at least a knowledge of some basic phrases. It's also worth your while to sample the hearty traditional Québécois cuisine, for this is a province where food is taken seriously.

Pleasures and Pastimes

Dining

Whether you choose a croissant and espresso at a sidewalk café or order *poutine* (a heaped plate of *frites*—french fries—smothered with gravy and melted cheese curds) from a fast-food emporium, you won't soon forget your meals here. There is no such thing as simply "eating out" in the province; restaurants are an integral slice of Québec life. Outside Montréal and Québec City, restaurants offer both good value and classic cuisine. Cooking in the province tends to be hearty, with such fare as cassoulet, *tourtières* (meat pies), onion soup, and apple pie heading up menus. In the Laurentians, chefs at some of the finer inns have attracted international followings.

The Eastern Townships are one of Québec's foremost regions for fine cuisine and for traditional Québécois dishes. Specialties include such mixed-game meat pies as *cipaille* and sweet, salty dishes like ham and maple syrup. Actually, maple syrup—much of it produced locally—is a mainstay of Québécois dishes. In addition, cloves, nutmeg, cinnamon, and pepper—spices used by the first settlers—have never gone out of style here, and local restaurants make good use of them.

Early reservations are essential. Monday or Tuesday is not too soon to book weekend tables at the best provincial restaurants.

CATEGORY	COST*
$$$$	over $35
$$$	$25–$35
$$	$15–$25
$	under $15

*per person, in Canadian dollars, excluding drinks, service, 7% GST, and 7.5% provincial tax

Lodging

The full spectrum of accommodation options in Québec ranges from large resort hotels in the Laurentians and elegant Relais & Châteaux properties in the Eastern Townships to simple accommodations near the heart of the Gaspé. Year-round or in high season (winter in the Laurentians and other ski areas, summer elsewhere), many inns operate on the Modified American Plan (MAP) and include two meals, usually breakfast and dinner, in the cost of a night's stay. Be sure to ask what's included, and expect prices to be lower off-season. In addition, some inns require a minimum two-night stay; always ask.

CATEGORY	COST*
$$$$	over $160
$$$	$120–$160
$$	$85–$120
$	under $85

*All prices are for a standard double room, excluding 10% service charge, 7% GST, and 7.5% provincial tax, in Canadian dollars.

Outdoor Activities and Sports

FISHING

There are more than 60 outfitters (some of whom are also innkeepers) in the northern Laurentians area, where provincial parks and game sanctuaries abound. Pike, walleye, and lake and speckled trout are plentiful just a three-hour drive north of Montréal. Open year-round in most cases, their lodging facilities range from the most luxurious first-class resorts to log cabins. As well as supplying trained guides, all offer services and equipment to allow neophytes or experts the best

Lower Québec

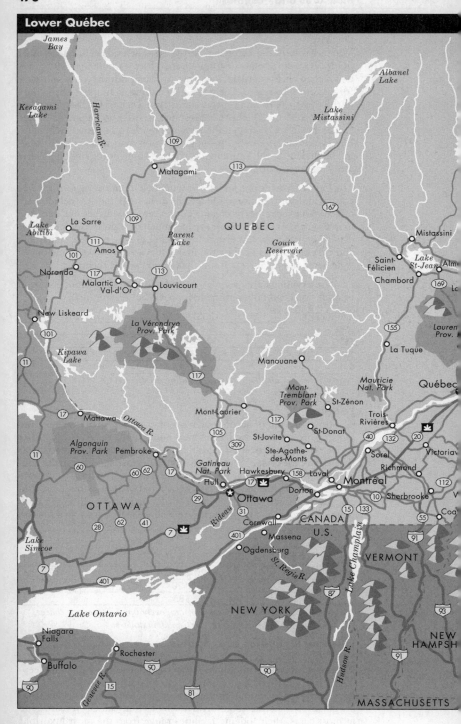

James Bay

Kesagami Lake

Harricana R.

Albanel Lake

Lake Mistassini

109

Matagami

113

QUEBEC

167

Mistassini

Lake Abitibi

La Sarre

109

111

Amos

Parent Lake

Gouin Reservoir

Saint-Félicien

Lake St-Jean

Alm

101

Noranda

117

113

Chambord

169

Lo

Malartic

Val-d'Or

Louvicourt

New Liskeard

101

La Vérendrye Prov. Park

155

La Tuque

Lauren Prov.

11

Kipawa Lake

117

Manouane

Mauricie Nat. Park

Québec

17

Mattawa

Ottawa R.

Mont-Laurier

Mont-Tremblant Prov. Park

St-Zénon

Trois-Rivières

Algonquin Prov. Park

Pembroke

105

309

St-Jovite

St-Donat

40

132

20

11

60

60

62

17

Gatineau Nat. Park

Ste-Agathe-des-Monts

Sorel

Victoria

29

Hawkesbury

158

Laval

Richmond

112

28

62

41

7

Hull

17

Dorion

Montréal

10

Sherbrooke

V

Ottawa

31

CANADA

15

133

Coa

Lake Simcoe

Rideau

Cornwall

U.S.

55

7

401

Massena

Lake Champlain

91

401

Ogdensburg

St. Regis R.

VERMONT

Lake Ontario

NEW YORK

87

93

Niagara Falls

Rochester

Hudson R.

NEW HAMPSH

Buffalo

90

91

90

Creusaze R.

15

90

81

MASSACHUSETTS

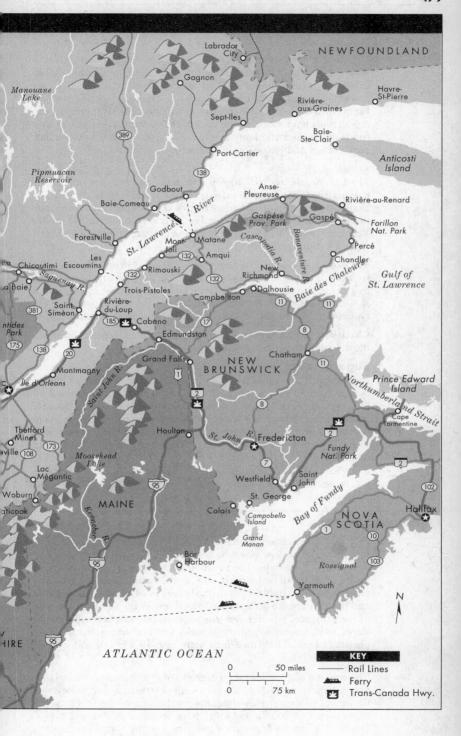

NEWFOUNDLAND

Labrador City

Gagnon

Havre-St-Pierre

Rivière-aux-Graines

Sept-Îles

Baie-Ste-Clair

Manouane Lake

(389)

Port-Cartier

Anticosti Island

Pipmuacan Reservoir

(138)

Godbout

Anse-Pleureuse

Rivière-au-Renard

St. Lawrence River

Baie-Comeau

Gaspése Prov. Park

Gaspé

Forillon Nat. Park

Forestville

Mont-Joli

Matane

Cascapédia R.

Percé

na

Chicoutimi

Les Escoumins

(132)

Amqui

New Richmond

Chandler

Saguenay R.

Rimouski

(132)

(132)

Bonaventure R.

Gulf of St. Lawrence

La Baie

Trois-Pistoles

Dalhousie

Campbellton

Baie des Chaleurs

(381)

Saint Siméon

Rivière-du-Loup

(11)

(11)

ntides Park

(175)

(185)

Cabano

(17)

(8)

(138)

(20)

Edmundston

NEW

Montmagny

Grand Falls

BRUNSWICK

Chatham

(11)

Prince Edward Island

Île d'Orléans

(1)

Northumberland Strait

Thetford Mines

(2)

Cape Tormentine

ville

(108)

(173)

Houlton

St. John R.

Fredericton

(2)

Lac Mégantic

Moosehead Lake

(8)

Fundy Nat. Park

(2)

Woburn

(95)

(7)

(102)

aticook

MAINE

Westfield

Saint John

Bay of Fundy

Halifax

St. George

NOVA SCOTIA

Calais

Campobello Island

(1)

(10)

Grand Manan

Rossignol

(103)

Kennebec R.

Bar Harbour

(95)

Yarmouth

N

HIRE

(95)

ATLANTIC OCEAN

0   50 miles

0   75 km

KEY
— Rail Lines
Ferry
Trans-Canada Hwy.

possible fishing in addition to boating, swimming, river rafting, wind-surfing, ice fishing, cross-country skiing, or hiking.

RAFTING

The Rivière Rouge in the Laurentians rates among the best in North America, so it's not surprising that this river has spawned a miniboom in the sport. Just an hour's drive north of Montréal, the Rouge cuts across the rugged Laurentians through canyons and alongside beaches. From April through October, you can experience what traversing the region must have meant in the days of the voyageurs, though today's trip is much safer and more comfortable. (For outfitter information, *see* Contacts and Resources *in* Québec A to Z, *below.*)

SKIING

The Laurentians are well known internationally as a downhill desti-nation, from St-Sauveur to majestic Mont-Tremblant. Night skiing is available at many slopes. Cross-country skiing is popular throughout the area from December to the end of March, especially at Val David, Val Morin, and Ville l'Estérel. Each has a cross-country ski center and at least a dozen groomed trails.

The Eastern Townships have more than 900 km (558 mi) of cross-coun-try trails. Three inns here offer a weeklong package of cross-country treks from one inn to another. The area is also popular as a downhill ski center, with ski hills on four mountains that dwarf anything the Laurentians have to offer, with the exception of Mont-Tremblant.

Charlevoix has three main ski areas with excellent facilities for both the downhill and cross-country skier.

Sugar Shacks

Every March the combination of sunny days and cold nights causes the sap to run in the maple trees. *Cabanes à sucre* (sugar shacks) go into operation, boiling the sap collected from the trees in buckets (now, at some places, complicated tubing and vats do the job). The many commercial enterprises scattered over the area host "sugaring offs" and tours of the process, including the tapping of maple trees, the boiling of the sap in vats, and *tire sur la neige,* when hot syrup is poured over cold snow to give it a taffy consistency just right for "pulling" and eat-ing. A number of cabanes serve hearty meals of ham, baked beans, and pancakes, all drowned in maple syrup.

Exploring Québec

Two major recreational areas beyond Montréal attract stressed-out urbanites and anyone else who wants to relax: the Laurentians and the Eastern Townships. The Laurentians are a resort area with thou-sands of miles of wilderness and world-famous ski resorts. The mountains begin only 60 km (37 mi) north of Montréal. Rolling hills and farmland make the Eastern Townships, in the southwest corner of the province, popular year-round, with outdoor activities on ski slopes and lakes and in provincial parks. Cultural attractions are other pleasures here. The Townships start just 80 km (50 mi) east of Montréal.

Charlevoix is often called the Switzerland of Québec because of its land-scape, which includes mountains, valleys, streams, and waterfalls. Charming villages stretch along the north shore of the St. Lawrence River for about 200 km (124 mi), from Ste-Anne-de-Beaupré east of Québec City to the Saguenay River. The knobby Gaspé Peninsula is where the St. Lawrence River meets the Gulf of St. Lawrence. This iso-lated peninsula, which begins about 200 km (124 mi) east of Québec

City, has a wild beauty all its own; mountains and cliffs tower above its beaches. The drive around the Gaspé is 848 km (526 mi).

Numbers in the text correspond to numbers in the margin and on the Laurentians (les Laurentides), Eastern Townships (les Cantons de l'Est) and Montérégie, Charlevoix, and Gaspé Peninsula (Gaspésie) maps.

Great Itineraries

IF YOU HAVE 2 DAYS

If you have only a few days for a visit, you'll need to concentrate on one area, and the Laurentians, outside Montréal, are a good choice. This resort area has recreational options (depending on the season) that include golf, hiking, and great skiing. Pick a resort town to stay in, whether it's ☒ **St-Sauveur-des-Monts** ④, ☒ **Ste-Adèle** ⑥, or ☒ **Mont-Tremblant,** near the vast **Parc du Mont-Tremblant** ⑪, and use that as a base to visit some of the surrounding towns. There's good eating and shopping here—and even a reconstructed historic village in Ste-Adèle.

If your starting point is Québec City, you could take two days to explore the towns of Charlevoix (☞ If You Have 10–12 Days, *below*) east of the city, with an overnight in the elegant resort town of ☒ **La Malbaie** ㉖.

IF YOU HAVE 5 DAYS

You can combine a taste of the Eastern Townships with a two-day visit to the Laurentians. Get a feeling for the Laurentians by staying overnight in ☒ **St-Sauveur-des-Monts** ④ or ☒ **Ste-Adèle** ⑥ and exploring such surrounding towns as **St-Jérôme** ③ and **Morin Heights** ⑤. Then head back south of Montréal to the Townships, which extend to the east along the border with New England. Overnight in ☒ **Granby** ⑫ or ☒ **Bromont** ⑬; Granby has a zoo and Bromont is known for its factory outlets. The next day, you can shop in pretty **Knowlton** ⑮ and explore regional history in such towns as **Valcourt** ⑰, where a museum is dedicated to the inventor of the snowmobile. Spend a night or two in the appealing resort town of ☒ **Magog** ⑯, along Lac Memphrémagog, or the quieter ☒ **North Hatley** ⑳, on Lac Massawippi. You'll have good dining in either. Save a day for some outdoor activity, whether it's golfing, skiing, biking on former railroad lines, or hiking.

IF YOU HAVE 10–12 DAYS

A longer visit can show you a number of regions in Québec, but you must do some driving between them. You can spend a few days in either the Laurentians or the Eastern Townships before heading east to Québec City and historic Charlevoix, the heart of what was New France, along the St. Lawrence River. The drive from Montréal or Sherbrooke to Québec City is more than 240 km (149 mi); Charlevoix begins 33 km (20 mi) to the east, at **Ste-Anne-de-Beaupré** ㉓, with its famous basilica. Colonial-era homes and farmhouses dot several villages; some are still homes, and others are theaters, museums, or restaurants. Spend time in ☒ **Baie St-Paul** ㉔ and ☒ **La Malbaie** ㉖, or just drive lovely roads such as Route 362. There's whale-watching in **Tadoussac** ㉗. To go on to the Gaspé Peninsula, you have to cross the St. Lawrence River. An hour-long ferry ride from St-Siméon, between La Malbaie and Tadoussac, takes you to Rivière-du-Loup. From there it's a day to get to ☒ **Carleton** ㉘ on the Gaspé's southern shore. With mountains on one side and the ocean on the other, the peninsula offers one of the most scenic drives in North America; you can stop in ☒ **Percé** ㉙ and spend a day visiting **Bonaventure Island** ㉚ with its fascinating bird colony. The drive around the entire peninsula is more than 800 km (500 mi).

When to Tour Québec

The Laurentians are mainly a winter ski destination, but you can drive up from Montréal to enjoy the fall foliage, to hike, bike, or play golf, or to engage in spring skiing—and still get home before dark. The only slow periods are early November, when there is not much to do, and June, when there is plenty to do but the area is plagued by blackflies, admittedly less of a problem now than formerly, thanks to effective biological control programs.

The Eastern Townships are best in fall, when the foliage is at its peak. The region borders Vermont and has the same dramatic colors. It's possible to visit wineries at this time, although you should call ahead to see if visitors are welcome during the harvest, which can be busy. Charlevoix is lovely in fall, but winter is particularly magical. Although the roads aren't great in winter, the whole region, with its cozy villages and New France architecture, is charming. In summer there is a special silvery light, born of the mountains and the proximity of the sea: This is why the area attracts so many painters. Summer is really the only time to tour the Gaspé. Some attractions have already closed by Labor Day, and few hotels are open during winter. The weather can be harsh, too, and driving the coast road can be difficult.

THE LAURENTIANS

The Laurentians (les Laurentides) are divided into two major regions—the Lower Laurentians (les Basses Laurentides) and the Upper Laurentians (les Hautes Laurentides). But don't be fooled by the designations; they don't signify great driving distances. Avid skiers might call Montréal a bedroom community for the Laurentians; just 60 km (37 mi) to the north, they are home to some of North America's best-known ski resorts. The Laurentian range is ancient, dating to the Precambrian era (more than 600 million years ago). These rocky hills are relatively low, worn down by glacial activity, but they include eminently skiable hills, with a few peaks above 2,500 ft. World-famous Mont-Tremblant, at 3,150 ft, is the tallest.

The P'tit Train du Nord—the former railroad line that is now a 200-km (124-mi) linear park used by cyclists, hikers, skiers, and snowmobilers—made it possible to transport settlers and cargo easily to the Upper Laurentians. It also opened them up to skiing by the turn of the century. Before long, trainloads of skiers replaced settlers and cargo as the railway's major trade. The Upper Laurentians became known worldwide as the number one ski center in eastern North America—a position they still hold today. Initially a winter weekend getaway for Montrealers who stayed at boardinghouses and fledgling resorts while skiing its hills, the Upper Laurentians soon began attracting an international clientele.

Ski lodges, originally private family retreats for wealthy city dwellers, were accessible only by train until the 1930s, when Route 117 was built. Once the road opened up, cottages became year-round family retreats. Today there is an uneasy alliance between the longtime cottagers and resort-driven entrepreneurs. Both recognize the other's historic role in developing the Upper Laurentians, but neither espouses the other's cause. At the moment, commercial development seems to be winning out. A number of large hotels have added indoor pools and spa facilities, and efficient highways have brought the country closer to the city—45 minutes to St-Sauveur, 1½–2 hours to Mont-Tremblant.

The Lower Laurentians start almost immediately outside Montréal and are rich in historic and architectural landmarks. Beginning in the mid-

17th century, the governors of New France, as Québec was then called, gave large concessions of land to its administrators, priests, and top-ranking military, who became known as seigneurs. In the Lower Laurentians, towns like St-Eustache and Oka are home to the manors, mills, churches, and public buildings these seigneurs had built for themselves and their habitants—the inhabitants of these quasi-feudal villages.

The resort vacation area truly begins at St-Sauveur-des-Monts (Exit 60 on Autoroute 15) and extends as far north as Mont-Tremblant, where it turns into a wilderness of lakes and forests best visited with an outfitter. Laurentian guides planning fishing trips are concentrated around Parc Mont-Tremblant. To the first-time visitor, the hills and resorts around St-Sauveur, Ste-Adèle, Morin Heights, Val Morin, and Val David, up to Ste-Agathe, form a pleasant hodgepodge of villages, hotels, and inns that seem to blend one into another.

Oka

❶ *40 km (25 mi) west of Montréal.*

The town of Oka is known for a monastery that produces cheeses, a calvary, and its provincial park. To promote piety among the native people, the Sulpicians erected the **Oka Calvary** (✉ Rte. 344, across from Oka Provincial Park), representing the Stations of the Cross, between 1740 and 1742. Three of the seven chapels are still maintained, and every September 14 since 1870, Québécois pilgrims have congregated here from across the province to participate in the half-hour ceremony that proceeds on foot to the calvary's summit. A sense of the divine is inspired as much by the magnificent view of Lac des Deux-Montagnes as by religious fervor.

The **Abbaye Cistercienne d'Oka** is one of the oldest in North America. In 1887 the Sulpicians gave about 865 acres of their property near the Oka Calvary to the Trappist monks, who had arrived in New France in 1880 from Bellefontaine Abbey in France. Within 10 years they had built their monastery and transformed this land into one of the most beautiful domains in Québec. Famous for creating Oka cheese, the Trappists established the Oka School of Agriculture, which operated until 1960. Today, the monastery is a noted prayer retreat. The gardens and chapel are open to visitors. ✉ *1600 chemin d'Oka,* ☎ *514/479–8361.* ➡ *Free.* ☉ *Chapel daily 8–12:15 and 1–8; gardens and boutique weekdays 9:30–11:30 and 1–4:30, Sat. 9–4.*

Kanesatake, a Mohawk reserve near Oka, made headlines in 1990 when a 78-day armed standoff between Mohawk Warriors (the reserve's self-proclaimed paramilitary force) and Canadian and provincial authorities took place. The Mohawks of Kanesatake said they opposed the expansion of the Oka golf course, claiming the land was stolen from them 273 years before. When the standoff ended peacefully, the golf course was not expanded.

Lodging

$$$ 🏨 **Hotel du Lac Carling.** This modern hotel near Lachute (about 40 km, or 25 mi, northwest of Oka) caters to an upmarket clientele. Besides a large sports center and 20 km (12 mi) of cross-country ski trails, there's an excellent par-72 golf course. The hotel is owned by a real estate magnate with 23 castles and manor houses in his native Germany, and the rooms have oil paintings and priceless antiques shipped over from his various properties. ✉ *Rte. 327, Pinehill, J0V 1A0,* ☎ *514/533–9211 or 800/661–9211,* 📠 *514/533–9197. 100 rooms. Restaurant, bar, pool, sauna, 18-hole golf course, exercise room, racquetball, squash, cross-country skiing. MAP. AE, DC, MC, V.*

The Laurentians (les Laurentides)

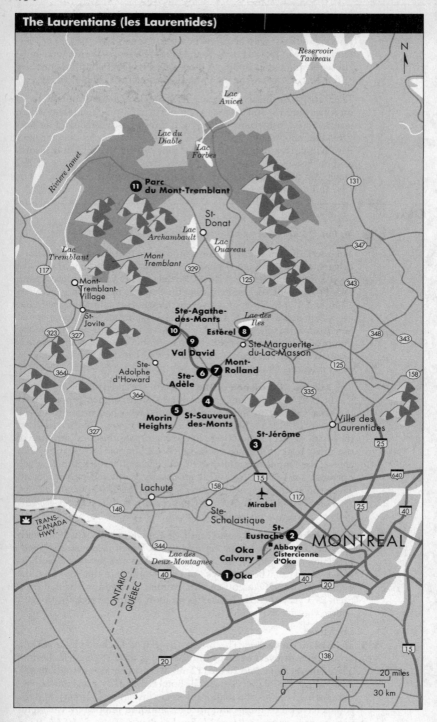

Reservoir Taureau

Lac Anicet

Lac du Diable

Lac Forbes

Rivière Janet

131

11 **Parc du Mont-Tremblant**

St-Donat

Lac Archambault

Lac Ouareau

347

Lac Tremblant

Mont Tremblant

117

Mont-Tremblant-Village

St-Jovite

329

125

343

323

327

364

Ste-Agathe-des-Monts

Lac des Iles

Estérel **8**

10

9

Val David

Ste-Marguerite-du-Lac-Masson

348

343

Ste-Adolphe d'Howard

6 **7** **Mont-Rolland**

125

158

364

Ste-Adèle

4

335

5 **Morin Heights**

St-Sauveur-des-Monts

327

St-Jérôme

3

Ville des Laurentides

25

Lachute

158

15

640

148

Mirabel

117

25

40

Ste-Scholastique

TRANS-CANADA HWY.

St-Eustache **2**

MONTREAL

344

Lac des Deux-Montagnes

Oka Calvary

Abbaye Cistercienne d'Oka

40

ONTARIO QUÉBEC

40

1 **Oka**

20

20

138

15

| 0 | | 20 miles |
| 0 | | 30 km |

St-Eustache

➋ *25 km (16 mi) northeast of Oka.*

St-Eustache is a must for history buffs. One of the most important and tragic battles in Canadian history took place here during the 1837 Rebellion. Since the British conquest of 1759, French Canadians had been confined to preexisting territories while the new townships were allotted exclusively to the English. Adding to this insult was the government's decision to tax all imported products from England, which made them prohibitively expensive. The result? In 1834 the French Canadian Patriot party defeated the British party locally. Lower Canada, as it was then known, became a hotbed of tension between the French and English, with French resistance to the British government reaching an all-time high.

Rumors of rebellion were rife, and in December 1837, some 2,000 English soldiers led by General Colborne were sent in to put down the "army" of North Shore patriots by surrounding the village of St-Eustache. Jean-Olivier Chénier and his 200 patriots took refuge in the local church, which Colborne's cannons bombed and set afire. Chénier and 80 of his comrades were killed during the battle, and more than 100 of the town's houses and buildings erected during the seignorial regime were looted and burned down by Colborne's soldiers. Traces of the bullets fired by the English army cannons are visible on the facade of St-Eustache's church at 123 rue St-Louis.

Most of the town's period buildings are open to the public. The **Manoir Globensky** (✉ 235 rue St-Eustache, ☎ 514/974–5055) offers a guided tour or a free brochure that serves as a good walking-tour guide. There are tours from late June until early September at 1 and 3.

St-Jérôme

➌ *25 km (16 mi) north of St-Eustache.*

Rivaling St-Eustache in Québec's historic folklore is St-Jérôme, in the Upper Laurentians on Route 117. Founded in 1834, it is today a thriving economic center and cultural hub. It first gained prominence in 1868 when Curé Antoine Labelle became pastor of this parish on the shores of the Rivière du Nord. Curé Labelle devoted himself to opening up northern Québec to French Canadians. Between 1868 and 1890, he founded 20 parish towns—an impressive achievement given the harsh conditions of this vast wilderness. But his most important legacy was the famous P'tit Train du Nord railroad line, which he persuaded the government to build in order to open St-Jérôme to travel and trade. Today the railroad is a 200-km (124-mi) **linear park** for recreational use that begins in St-Jérôme.

St-Jérôme's **promenade,** a 4-km-long (2½-mi-long) boardwalk, follows the Rivière du Nord from rue de Martigny bridge to rue St-Joseph bridge, providing a walk through the town's history. Descriptive plaques en route highlight episodes of the Battle of 1837, a French Canadian uprising. The **Centre d'Exposition du Vieux-Palais,** housed in St-Jérôme's old courthouse, has changing exhibits of contemporary art, featuring mostly Québec artists. ✉ *185 rue du Palais,* ☎ *514/432–7171.* 🎫 *Free.* ✆ *Wed.–Sun. noon–5, Tues. noon–8.*

Parc Régional de la Rivière-du-Nord was created as a nature retreat. Trails through the park lead to the spectacular **Wilson Falls.** The **Pavillon Marie-Victorin** has summer weekend displays and workshops devoted to nature, culture, and history. You can hike, bike, cross-country ski, snowshoe, or snow slide. ✉ *1051 blvd. International,* ☎

514/431–1676. ☎ *$3 per vehicle.* ⊙ *Fall–spring, daily 9–5; summer, daily 9–7.*

Outdoor Activities and Sports

Para Vision (⊠ C.P. 95, J7Z 5T7, ☎ 514/438–0855), a parachute school with a flying center in nearby Bellefeuille, caters to novices and seasoned flyers alike (courses are limited to ages 16 and up). Would-be parachutists are trained on the ground as well as in the air, and even first-timers get the chance to jump earthward from 3,500 ft.

St-Sauveur-des-Monts

❹ *25 km (16 mi) north of St-Jérôme.*

A focal point for area resorts, over the past 20 years St-Sauveur-des-Monts has changed from a sleepy Laurentian village of 4,000 residents to a thriving year-round town attracting some 30,000 cottagers and visitors on weekends. Its main street, rue Principale, once dotted with quaint French restaurants, now has dozens of eateries at all price levels; they serve everything from lamb brochettes to spicy Thai cuisine (a current craze among locals). The narrow strip is so choked in summertime with cars and tourists that it has earned the sobriquet Crescent Street of the North, borrowing its name from the action-filled street in Montréal. Despite all this development, St-Sauveur has maintained some of its charming, rural character.

For those who like their vacations—winter or summer—activity-filled, St-Sauveur is where the action rolls nonstop. In winter, skiing is the main thing. (Mont-St-Sauveur, Mont-Avila, Mont-Gabriel, and Mont-Olympia all offer special season passes and programs, and some ski-center passes can be used at more than one center in the region.)

☾ Just outside St-Sauveur, the Mont-St-Sauveur **Water Park** and tourist center will keep children occupied with slides, a giant wave pool, a shallow wading pool, snack bars, and more. The rafting river attracts the older, braver crowd; the nine-minute ride follows the natural contours of steep hills and requires about 12,000 gallons of water to be pumped per minute. The latest attraction is tandem slides where plumes of water flow through figure-eight tubes. ⊠ *350 rue St-Denis,* ☎ *514/871–0101 or 800/363–2426.* ☎ *Full day $22, half-day $17, evening (after 5) $9; includes access to all activities.* ⊙ *June 8–Sept. 7, daily 10–7.*

Outdoor Activities and Sports

Blue signs on Route 117 and Autoroute 15 indicate where the area's ski hills are. **Station Touristique Mont-St-Saveur** (⊠ 350 rue St-Denis, ☎ 800/363–2426), with a total of 28 downhill runs, is the collective name for the peaks around the village of St-Saveur-des-Monts. There are nine lifts; vertical drop is 762 ft. The runs are linked to Mont-Avila. **Ski Mont-Gabriel** (⊠ Montée Mont-Gabriel, ☎ 514/227–1100) has a vertical drop of 660 ft, 16 runs, and 10 lifts. With a vertical drop of 660 ft, **Station de Ski Mont-Habitant** (⊠ 12 blvd. des Skieurs, ☎ 514/393–1821) has nine runs and three lifts.

Shopping

Rue Principale has shops, fashion boutiques, and café terraces with bright awnings and flowers. Housed in a former bank, **Solo Mode** (⊠ 239B rue Principale, ☎ 514/227–1234) carries such international labels as Byblos. **Les Factoreries St-Sauveur** (⊠ 100 rue Guindon, Exit 60 from Autoroute 15, ☎ 514/227–1074) is a factory outlet mall with 12 boutiques. Canadian, American, and European manufacturers sell goods at reduced prices, from designer clothing to household items.

Morin Heights

❺ *10 km (6 mi) west of St-Sauveur-des-Monts.*

The town's architecture and population reflect its English settlers' origins, and most residents are English-speaking. Morin Heights has escaped the overdevelopment of St-Sauveur but still provides a good range of restaurants, bookstores, boutiques, and crafts shops to explore. During the summer months, windsurfing, swimming, and canoeing on the area's two lakes are popular pastimes.

In the summer, vacationers also head for the region's golf courses (including the 18-hole links at Mont-Gabriel), campgrounds at Val David, Lacs Claude and Lafontaine, and beaches; in the fall and winter, they come for the foliage as well as alpine and Nordic skiing.

Dining and Lodging

$$$ ✕🏨 **Auberge le Clos Joli.** This farmhouse turned country inn, only two minutes from the ski slopes, is considered one of the top hostelries in the Laurentians. Intimate and cozy, the inn is decorated with original artwork by Québécois painters; the dining room has a fireplace. The menu highlights French cuisine but with some local touches, such as roast venison cooked with bilberries and ravioli stuffed with wild mushrooms. A specialty is *ris de veau* (veal sweetbreads) flavored with lemon and thyme. ✉ *19 chemin du Clos Joli, J0R 1H0,* ☎ *514/226– 5401. 9 rooms. Restaurant, cross-country skiing, downhill skiing. MAP. AE, MC, V.*

Outdoor Activities and Sports

At **Ski Morin Heights** (✉ Autoroute 15 N, Exit 60, ☎ 514/227–2020 or 800/661–3535), snowboarding is the latest craze. The vertical drop at this downhill skiing center is 660 ft, and there are six lifts. Although it doesn't have overnight accommodations, Ski Morin Heights has a 44,000-square-ft chalet with hospitality services and sports-related facilities, eateries, après-ski activities, a pub, and a day-care center. Children ages two and up can join special ski-lesson programs.

Ste-Adèle

❻ *12 km (7 mi) north of Morin Heights.*

The busy town of Ste-Adèle is full of gift and Québec-crafts shops, boutiques, and restaurants. It also has an active nightlife, including a few dance clubs.

The reconstructed **Village de Seraphin**'s 20 small homes, grand country house, general store, and church recall the settlers who came to Ste-Adèle in the 1840s. This award-winning historic town also has a train tour through the woods. ✉ *Rte. 117,* ☎ *514/229–4777.* 🎟 *$9.* ☉ *Late May–late June and Sept., weekends 10–6; late June–Aug., daily 10–6.*

Dining and Lodging

$$$$ ✕ **La Clef des Champs.** This family-owned restaurant, known for its gourmet French cuisine and cozy, romantic atmosphere, is tucked away among trees and faces a mountain. Game dishes are a specialty, including farm-raised rabbit flavored with mustard and medallions of roasted ostrich in pepper sauce. A good dessert choice is the *gâteau aux deux chocolats* (two-chocolate cake). ✉ *875 chemin Ste-Marguerite,* ☎ *514/229–2857. AE, DC, MC, V. Closed Mon. Oct.–May.*

$$$$ ✕🏨 **L'Eau à la Bouche.** Superb service, stunning rooms awash with color,
★ and a terrace with a flower garden are highlights of this elegant inn. The auberge faces Le Chantecler's ski slopes, so skiing is literally at the door. Tennis, sailing, horseback riding, and a golf course are nearby.

The highly recommended restaurant superbly marries nouvelle cuisine and traditional Québec dishes. The care and inventiveness of chef-proprietor Anne Desjardins are extraordinary. Her menus change with the seasons, but some representative dishes are marinated Atlantic salmon and smoked scallops on a bed of julienned cucumber with a blend of mustards, and roast veal in a cognac and Roquefort sauce. ⊠ *3003 blvd. Ste-Adèle, J0R 1L0,* ☎ *514/229–2991,* FAX *514/229–7573. 25 rooms. Restaurant, pool. EP, MAP. AE, DC, MC, V.*

$$$ 🏨 **Le Chantecler.** This Montrealer favorite on Lac Ste-Adèle is nestled at the base of a mountain with 22 downhill ski runs. Skiing is the obvious draw—trails begin almost at the hotel entrance. The condominium units, hotel rooms, and chalets, furnished with Canadian pine, all have a rustic appeal. ⊠ *1474 chemin Chantecler, C.P. 1048, J0R 1L0,* ☎ *514/229–3555, 800/363–2420 in Québec;* FAX *514/229–5593. 300 rooms, 20 suites. Restaurant, indoor pool, spa, 18-hole golf course, tennis court, beach, boating, downhill skiing. EP, MAP. AE, D, DC, MC, V.*

$ 🏨 **Auberge aux Croissants.** At the foot of the Laurentians, the inn is only a five-minute drive from Mont-St-Sauveur. Although most rooms have no TV or telephone, such conveniences are found in one of the two lounges, and an impressive buffet-breakfast is included in the price. One room has a whirlpool bath. ⊠ *750 chemin Ste-Marguerite, J0R 1L0,* ☎ *514/229–3838. 13 rooms, 1 suite. Pool. MC, V.*

Outdoor Activities and Sports

GOLF

The par-72 **Club de Golf Chantecler** (⊠ Off Autoroute 15, Exit 67, 2520 chemin du Golf, ☎ 514/229–3742) has 18 holes.

SKIING

Ski Chantecler (☎ 514/229–3555) has a vertical drop of 663 ft, 8 lifts, and 22 runs (☞ Dining and Lodging, *above*). There are 50 km (31 mi) of cross-country trails, too. **Station de Ski Côtes** (☎ 514/229–2700) has six runs and a vertical drop of 392 ft.

Mont-Rolland

❼ *3 km (2 mi) east of Ste-Adèle.*

Mont-Rolland is the jumping-off point for the Mont-Gabriel ski area, about 16 km (10 mi) to the northeast.

Dining and Lodging

$$$$ ✕🏨 **Auberge Mont-Gabriel.** At this deluxe resort spread out on a 1,200-acre estate, you can relax in a cozy, modern room with a view of the valley or be close to nature in a log cabin with a fireplace. The dining is superb here. Tennis, golf, and ski-week and -weekend packages are available. ⊠ *Autoroute 15 (Exit 64), J0R 1G0,* ☎ *514/229–3547 or 800/668–5253,* FAX *514/229–7034. 126 rooms, 10 suites. Restaurant, indoor and outdoor pools, 18-hole golf course, 6 tennis courts. EP, MAP. AE, DC, MC, V.*

Nightlife and the Arts

The place for live music is **Bourbon Street** (⊠ 2045 Rte. 117, ☎ 514/229–2905).

Outdoor Activities and Sports

Ski Mont-Gabriel (⊠ Monté Mont-Gabriel, ☎ 514/227–1100 or 800/363–2426) has 10 lifts and 16 superb downhill trails primarily for intermediate and advanced skiers. The vertical drop is 660 ft. The most popular runs are the Tamarack and the O'Connell trails for advanced skiers and Obergurgl for intermediates.

Estérel

8 *12 km (7 mi) north of Mont-Rolland.*

The permanent population of the town of Estérel is a mere 95 souls, but visitors to Hôtel l'Estérel (☞ Dining and Lodging, *below*), a resort off Route 370, at Exit 69 near Ste-Marguerite Station, swell that number into the thousands. Founded in 1959 on the shores of Lac Dupuis, this 5,000-acre domain was bought by Fridolin Simard from Baron Louis Empain. Named Estérel by the baron because it evoked memories of his native village in Provence, Hotel l'Estérel soon became a household word for vacationers in search of a first-class resort area.

Dining and Lodging

$$$–$$$$ ✕ **Bistro à Champlain.** An astonishing selection of wines—26,000 bottles at last count—have made the bistro famous. Diners can tour the cellars, where some 2,000 brands are represented, with prices from $28 to $25,000. The restaurant is in a former general store built in 1864; next to the 150-seat dining room is a comfy lounge for cigar smokers. The paintings of Jean-Paul Riopelle adorn the walls. The *menu de dégustation* gives you a different wine with several courses for $62; typical dishes are marinated Atlantic smoked salmon and roast duckling with rosemary. ✉ *75 chemin Masson, Ste-Marguerite du Lac Masson,* ☎ *514/228–4988 or 514/225–4949. AE, DC, MC, V.*

$$$$ 🏨 **Hôtel l'Estérel.** If this all-inclusive resort were in the Caribbean, it would probably be run by Club Med, given the nonstop activities. Dogsledding and an ice-skating disco are two of the more unusual options, and there are buses to nearby downhill resorts. Comfortable rooms offer a view of either the lake or the beautiful flower gardens. ✉ *39 blvd. Fridolin Simard, J0T 1E0,* ☎ *514/228–2571 or 800/363–3623,* 𝖥𝖠𝖷 *514/228–4977. 135 rooms. Restaurant, indoor pool, 18-hole golf course, tennis courts, exercise room, beach, dock, cross-country skiing, snowmobiling. EP, MAP. AE, DC, MC, V.*

Val David

9 *18 km (11 mi) west of Estérel.*

Val David is a rendezvous for mountain climbers, hikers, and summer or winter campers, besides a center for arts and crafts. Children know Val David for its **Santa Claus Village.** This is Santa Claus's summer residence, where children can sit on Santa's knee and speak to him in French or English. On the grounds is a petting zoo, with goats, sheep, horses, and colorful birds. Bumper boats and games are run here as well. ✉ *987 rue Morin,* ☎ *819/322–2146.* 🖾 *$8.* ☉ *Late May–early June, weekends 10–6; early June–late Aug., daily 10–6.*

Dining and Lodging

$$$$ ✕🏨 **Hôtel La Sapinière.** Comfortable, freshly redecorated accommodations are offered in this homey, dark-brown frame hotel. The rooms, with country-style furnishings and pastel floral accents, come with such luxurious extras as thick terry-cloth bathrobes and hair dryers. Guests can relax in front of a blazing fire in one of several lounges. The property is best known for the French nouvelle cuisine in its fine dining room and its wine cellar. The minimum stay is two nights. ✉ *1244 chemin de la Sapinière, J0T 2N0,* ☎ *819/322–2020 or 800/567–6635,* 𝖥𝖠𝖷 *819/ 322–6510. 70 rooms. Restaurant. MAP. AE, DC, MC, V.*

Outdoor Activities and Sports

Mont-Alta (✉ Rte. 117, ☎ 819/322–3206) has 22 runs and 2 lifts; the vertical drop is 587 ft. **Station de Ski Vallée-Bleue** (✉ 1418 chemin Vallée-Bleue, ☎ 819/322–3427) has 16 runs.

Shopping

Val David is a haven for artists, many of whose studios are open to the public. The **Atelier Bernard Chaudron, Inc.** (⊠ 2449 chemin de l'Ile, ☎ 819/322–3944) sells hand-shaped lead-free pewter objets d'art.

Ste-Agathe-des-Monts

❿ *5 km (3 mi) north of Val David, 96 km (60 mi) northwest of Montréal.*

Overlooking Lac des Sables is Ste-Agathe-des-Monts, the largest commercial center for ski communities farther north. It has many shops and a variety of restaurants and bars.

Dining and Lodging

$$$–$$$$ ✕ **Chatel Vienna.** Run by Eberhards Rado and his wife, who is also the chef, this Austrian restaurant serves traditional, hearty Viennese and other Continental dishes in a lakeside setting. You may want to try the home-smoked trout, served with an herb-and-spice butter and garden-fresh vegetables. Other options are a variety of schnitzels, a sauerkraut plate, and venison. Hot spiced wine, Czech pilsner beer, and dry Austrian and other international white wines are some of the beverage choices. A Sunday buffet brunch has approximately 35 dishes. ⊠ *6 rue Ste-Lucie,* ☎ *819/326–1485. Reservations essential. MC, V.*

$$ ⊡ **Auberge du Lac des Sables.** A favorite with couples, this inn offers a quiet, relaxed atmosphere in a country setting with a magnificent view of Lac des Sables. All rooms have contemporary decor and a balcony. ⊠ *230 St-Venant, J8C 2Z7,* ☎ *819/326–3994,* FAX *819/326–9159. 19 rooms. CP. MC, V.*

$ △ **Au Parc des Campeurs.** This spacious campground is near a lively resort area. Canoes and kayaks can be rented here. ⊠ *Tour du Lac and Rte. 329, J8C 1M9,* ☎ *819/324–0482. 556 sites. Miniature golf, tennis court, volleyball, bicycles, coin laundry.*

Outdoor Activities and Sports

Sailing is the favorite summer sport, especially during the *"24 Heures de la Voile,"* a weekend sailing competition (☎ 819/326–0457) that takes place each year in June. The *Alouette* touring launch (⊠ Municipal dock, rue Principale, ☎ 819/326–3656) has guided tours of Lac des Sables.

Mont-Tremblant

25 km (16 mi) north of Ste-Agathe-des-Monts.

Mont-Tremblant, more than 3,000 ft high, is the highest peak in the Laurentians and a major center for skiing. The resort village at the foot of the mountain has accommodations and many restaurants, bars, and shops. An exciting ongoing development here has been the redevelopment of the Tremblant resort (☞ *below*).

⓫ The mountain and the hundreds of square miles of wilderness beyond it constitute **Parc du Mont-Tremblant** (☎ 819/688–2281). Created in 1894, the park was once the home of the Algonquin people, who called this area Manitonga Soutana, meaning "mountain of the spirits." Today it is a vast wildlife sanctuary of more than 400 lakes and rivers protecting about 230 species of birds and animals, including moose, deer, bear, and beaver. In winter its trails are used by cross-country skiers, snowshoers, and snowmobile enthusiasts. Moose hunting is allowed in season, and camping and canoeing are the main summer activities. Entrance to the park is free, and the main entrance is through St-Donat.

Dining and Lodging

$$$$ ×🏨 **Club Tremblant.** Built as a private retreat in the 1930s by a wealthy American, this hotel is across the lake from Station Mont-Tremblant. The original large, log-cabin lodge is furnished in colonial style, with wooden staircases and huge stone fireplaces. The rustic but comfortable main lodge has excellent facilities and an outstanding dining room serving ($$–$$$$) Continental cuisine. Both the main lodge and the deluxe condominium complex (with fireplaces, private balconies, kitchenettes, and split-level design), built just up the hill from the lodge, offer magnificent views of Mont-Tremblant and its ski hills. There is a golf course nearby. ⊠ *Av. Cuttle, J0T 1Z0,* ☎ *819/425–2731,* ℻ *819/425–9903. 113 rooms. Restaurant, indoor pool, tennis court, exercise room, boating, fishing. EP, MAP. AE, MC, V.*

$–$$ ×🏨 **Auberge du Coq de Montagne.** Owners Nino and Kay Faragalli have earned a favorable reputation for their auberge on Lac Moore. The cozy, family-run inn is touted for its friendly service, great hospitality, and modern accommodations. Kudos have also been garnered for the great Italian cuisine served up nightly, which also draws a local crowd; reservations are essential. Year-round facilities and activities, on-site or nearby, include canoeing, kayaking, sailboarding, fishing, badminton, tennis, horseback riding, skating, and skiing. ⊠ *2151 chemin Principal, C.P. 208, J0T 1Z0,* ☎ *819/425–3380 or 800/895–3380,* ℻ *819/425–7846. 13 rooms. Restaurant, sauna, exercise room, beach. MAP in winter; EP, MAP in summer. AE, MC, V.*

$$$$ 🏨 **Château Mont-Tremblant.** A new property built by Canadian Pacific
★   Hotels is the attractive centerpiece of Tremblant's (☞ *below*) pedestrian village. Similar in style to the company's historic railway "castles" scattered throughout Canada—Banff Springs Hotel and Château Frontenac are two examples—the hotel has been decorated with wood paneling, copper, stained glass, stone fireplaces, and wrought-iron lamps with parchment shades. The ambience is elegant but sporty. Skiers can zoom off the mountain right into the ground-level deli or opt for a more formal meal in the dining room. On the menu are Brie wrapped in phyllo pastry, Laurentian rainbow trout, and pork chops grilled with local maple syrup. ⊠ *3045 chemin Principal, Box 100, J0T 1Z0,* ☎ *819/681–7000. 360 rooms. Indoor pool, sauna, exercise room. AE, DC, MC, V.*

$$–$$$$ 🏨 **Tremblant.** This world-class resort, spread around the 14-km-long (9-mi-long) Lac Tremblant, has undergone a radical transformation. Intrawest Corporation has injected a much-needed $500 million (with more investment planned) into the mountain since the early '90s. It has quickly become the most fashionable vacation venue in Québec among sporty types and lovers of the great outdoors. The resort's hub is a pedestrian-only village that looks a bit like a displaced Québec City. The buildings—constructed in the style of New France with dormer windows and steep roofs—hold pubs, restaurants, boutiques, sports shops, a cinema, and accommodations ranging from rooms in hotels to self-catering condominiums. A new indoor water recreation complex includes pools, waterslides, and whirlpool baths. ⊠ *3005 chemin Principal, J0T 1Z0,* ☎ *819/425–8711, 800/461–8711, or 800/567–6760 (hotel reservations),* ℻ *819/425–9604. 1,050 rooms. Indoor lap pool, indoor-outdoor pool, wading pool, 2 18-hole golf courses, tennis courts, hiking, horseback riding, beach, windsurfing, boating, mountain bikes. AE, MC, V.*

Outdoor Activities and Sports

With a 2,131-ft vertical drop, **Mont-Tremblant** (☎ 819/425–8711 or 819/681–2000) offers 74 downhill trails, 10 lifts, and 90 km (56 mi) of cross-country trails. Downhill beginners favor the 6-km (4-mi)

Nansen trail; intermediate skiers head for the Beauchemin run. Experts choose the challenging Flying Mile on the south side and Duncan and Expo runs on the mountain's north side. The speedy Duncan Express is a quadruple chairlift.

THE EASTERN TOWNSHIPS

The Eastern Townships (also known as les Cantons de l'Est, and formerly as l'Estrie) refers to the area in the southwest corner of the province of Québec, bordering Vermont, New Hampshire, and Maine. Its northern Appalachian hills, rolling down to placid lakeshores, were first home to the Abenaki natives, long before "summer people" built their cottages and horse paddocks here. The Abenaki are gone, but the names they gave to the region's recreational lakes remain—Memphrémagog, Massawippi, Mégantic.

The Eastern Townships (or the Townships, as locals call them) were populated by United Empire Loyalists fleeing the Revolutionary War and, later, the newly created United States of America, to continue living under the English king in British North America. It's not surprising that the Townships, with their covered bridges, village greens, white church steeples, and country inns, are reminiscent of New England. The Loyalists were followed, around 1820, by the first wave of Irish immigrants—ironically, Catholics fleeing their country's union with Protestant England. Some 20 years later the potato famine sent more Irish pioneers to the Townships.

The area became more Gallic after 1850 as French Canadians moved in to work on the railroad and in the lumber industry. Around the turn of the century, English families from Montréal and Americans from the border states discovered the region and began summering at cottages along the lakes. During the Prohibition era, the area attracted even more cottagers from the United States. Lac Massawippi became a favorite summer resort of wealthy families, and those homes have since been converted into gracious inns and upscale bed-and-breakfasts.

Today the summer communities fill up with equal parts French and English visitors, though the year-round residents are primarily French. Nevertheless, the locals are proud of both their Loyalist heritage and their Québec roots. They boast of "Loyalist tours" and Victorian gingerbread homes and in the next breath direct visitors to the snowmobile museum in Valcourt, where, in 1937, native son Joseph-Armand Bombardier built the first *moto-neige* (snowmobile) in his garage. (Bombardier's other inventions were the basis of one of Canada's biggest industries, supplying New York City and Mexico City with subway cars and other rolling stock.)

Over the past two decades, the Townships have developed from a series of quiet farm communities and wood-frame summer homes to a thriving all-season resort area. In winter, skiers flock to seven downhill centers and some 900 km (558 mi) of cross-country trails. Three inns—Manoir Hovey, Auberge Hatley, and the Ripplecove Inn—offer the Skiwippi, a weeklong package of cross-country treks from one inn to another. The network covers some 32 km (20 mi). Still less crowded and commercialized than the Laurentians, the area has ski hills on four mountains that dwarf anything the Laurentians have to offer, with the exception of Mont-Tremblant. And, compared to those in Vermont, ski-pass rates are still a bargain. Owl's Head, Mont-Orford, Mont-Sutton, and Bromont have interchangeable lift tickets. The Townships' southerly location also makes this the balmiest corner of Québec, notable for its spring skiing.

By early spring, the sugar shacks are busy with the new maple syrup. In summer, boating, swimming, sailing, golfing, rollerblading, hiking, and bicycling take over. And every fall the inns are booked solid with leaf peepers eager to take in the brilliant foliage.

Granby

⑫ *80 km (50 mi) east of Montréal.*

Granby is the gateway to the Eastern Townships and home to a notable zoo. It also hosts a number of annual festivals—the **Festival of Mascots and Cartoon Characters** (July), a great favorite with youngsters and families; and the **Granby International**, an antique car competition held at the Granby Autodrome (also in July). The **Festival International de la Chanson**, a songfest of budding composers and performers that has launched several of Québec's current megastars, is a nine-day event in mid-September.

★ � This town is best known for its zoo, the **Jardin Zoologique de Granby.** It houses some 1,000 animals from 230 species. Two rare snow leopards are on loan from Chicago's Lincoln Park Zoo and New York's Bronx Zoo. The complex includes amusement park rides and souvenir shops as well as a playground and picnic area. ⊠ *347 rue Bourget, ☎ 514/372–9113. 🎟 $16. ☯ Mid-May–early Sept., daily 10–5; Sept., weekends 10–5.*

Outdoor Activities and Sports

Cyclists will find outdoor bliss on the paved l'Estriade path, which links Granby to Waterloo, and the Montérégiade between Granby and Farnham, both 21 km (13 mi) long. Mountain biking is big in the Townships: The season kicks off in early June with the **Tour de la Montagne,** a 25-km (15-mi) mountain bike rally. Competitions for serious mountain bikers are held throughout the summer (☎ 514/534–2453 for information).

Bromont

⑬ *8 km (5 mi) south of Granby.*

The town of Bromont is as lively at night as during the day. It has the only night skiing in the Eastern Townships and a slope-side disco, Le Bromontais, where the après-ski action continues into the night. Bromont and Orford (☞ *below*) are *stations touristiques* (tourist centers), meaning they offer a wide range of activities in all seasons—boating, camping, golf, horseback riding, swimming, tennis, biking, canoeing, fishing, hiking, cross-country and downhill skiing, and snowshoeing. Bromont has more than 100 km (62 mi) of maintained trails for mountain bikers. A former Olympic equestrian site, Bromont is horse country, and every year in late June it holds a **riding festival** (☎ 514/ 534–3255). **Bromont Aquatic Park** (⊠ Autoroute 10, Exit 78, ☎ 514/ 534–2200) is a water-slide park.

Lodging

$$$ 🏨 **Le Château Bromont Hotel Spa.** Massages, electropuncture, algae wraps, facials, and aromatherapy are just a few of the pampering services at this European-style resort spa. Rooms are large and comfortable, with contemporary furniture, but those facing the Atrium are a little somber. L'Equestre Bar, named for Bromont's equestrian interests, has a cocktail hour and live entertainment. ⊠ *90 rue Stanstead, J0E 1L0, ☎ 514/534–3433 or 800/304–3433, FAX 514/534–0514. 147 rooms. Restaurant, bar, indoor pool, hot tubs, sauna, spa, badminton, racquetball, squash. EP, MAP. AE, D, DC, MC, V.*

Eastern Townships (les Cantons de l'Est) and Montérégie

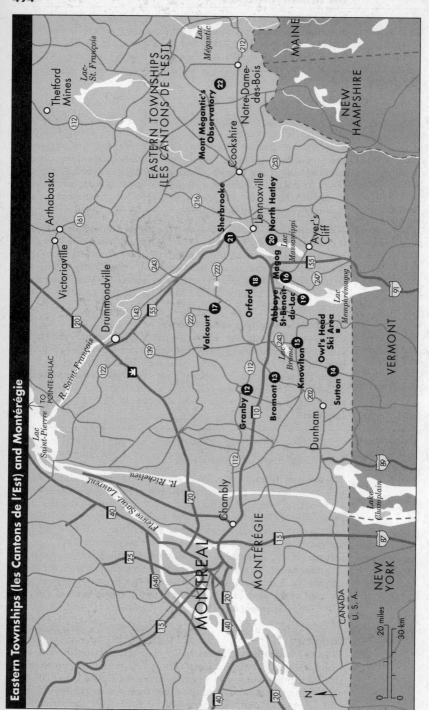

OFF THE
BEATEN PATH

SAFARI TOUR LOOWAK – The brainchild of butterfly collector Serge Poirier, this oddball attraction 10 km (6 mi) from Bromont is a kind of Indiana Jones theme park where participants head off into the bush on treasure hunts and to look for downed planes. To make the game as authentic as possible, Poirier acquired a couple of wrecked aircraft that he has artfully hidden around his land. Needless to say, the place is a great hit with small fry, but parents quickly get caught up in the fantasy, too. Reservations are recommended. ⊠ *475 Horizon Blvd., Waterloo, Exit 88 from Autoroute 10,* ☎ *514/539–0501.* 🎫 *Trips begin at $10 per person (minimum 4 people).*

Outdoor Activities and Sports

Station de Ski Bromont (⊠ 150 rue Champlain, ☎ 514/534–2200), with 22 trails for downhill skiing, was the site of the 1986 World Cup Slalom. The vertical drop is 1,336 ft, and there are six lifts.

Shopping

Factory outlet shopping is gaining popularity in the Townships—especially in Bromont, where shoppers can save between 30% and 70% on items carrying such national and international labels as Liz Claiborne, Vuarnet, and Oneida. Versants de Bromont and Promenades de Ma Maison are two centers off Exit 78 of Autoroute 10.

Sutton

14 *28 km (17mi) south of Bromont.*

Sutton is a well-established community with crafts shops, cozy eateries, and bars (La Paimpolaise is a favorite among skiers). **Arts Sutton** (⊠ 7 rue Academy, ☎ 514/538–2563) is a long-established mecca for the visual arts.

Lodging

$$$ 🏠 **Auberge la Paimpolaise.** This auberge is on Mont-Sutton, 50 ft from the ski trails. Nothing fancy is offered, but the location is hard to beat. Rooms are simple, comfortable, and clean, with a woodsy appeal. All-inclusive weekend ski packages are available. A complimentary breakfast is served. ⊠ *615 rue Maple, J0E 2K0,* ☎ *514/538–3213 or 800/ 263–3213,* FAX *514/538–3970. 28 rooms. EP, MAP. AE, MC, V.*

Outdoor Activities and Sports

GOLF

Reservations must be made in advance at **Les Rochers Bleus** (⊠ 550 Rte. 139, ☎ 514/538–2324), a par-72, 18-hole course.

SKIING

Mont-Sutton (⊠ Rte. 139 South, Exit 106 from Autoroute 10, ☎ 514/ 538–2339), where skiers pay by the hour, has 53 downhill trails, a vertical drop of 1,518 ft, and nine lifts. This ski area attracts a die-hard crowd of mostly Anglophone skiers from Québec. It's also one of the area's largest resorts, with trails that plunge and wander through pine, maple, and birch trees slope-side.

Knowlton

15 *15 km (9 mi) northeast of Sutton.*

Along the shore of Lac Brome is the picturesque village of Knowlton, a great place to shop for antiques, clothes, and gifts. The village, which has a pond flanked by a brick church where ducks line up to be fed, is a treasure trove of Victoriana. Renovated clapboard buildings painted every shade of the rainbow have been turned into trendy stores, art galleries, and interesting little eateries. The distinctive Lake Brome ducks—white and plump—are found on local menus and celebrated, with exhibits, activities, and food, during the **Brome Lake Duck Festival** in mid-October.

Nightlife and the Arts

Théâtre Lac Brome (⊠ 267 rue Knowlton, ☎ 514/242–2270 or 514/242–1395) stages plays, musicals, and productions of classic Broadway and West End hits. The company specializes in English productions but also has tried some bilingual productions and some new Canadian works. The 175-seat, air-conditioned theater is behind Knowlton's popular pub of the same name.

Outdoor Activities and Sports

Many Montrealers come for the downhill skiing at **Mont-Glen** (⊠ Off Rte. 243, ☎ 514/243–6142).

Magog

🕦 *40 km (25) east of Knowlton.*

At the northern tip of Lac Memphrémagog, a large body of water reaching into northern Vermont, lies the bustling resort town of Magog, a four-season destination with bed-and-breakfasts, hotels, and restaurants. It has sandy beaches as well as activities that include boating, riding a ferry, bird-watching, sailboarding, horseback riding, dogsledding, rollerblading, and snowmobiling.

People can stroll or picnic (or skate and cross-country ski in winter) along the scenic linear park that skirts the lake, then turns into an off-road recreational trail leading to **Mont-Orford Provincial Park**, 13½ km (8 mi) from the center of town. The trail, which is for cyclists, walkers, and cross-country skiers, hugs the lake, then parallels Route 112 before winding through a forested area into the park.

The streets downtown are lined with century-old homes that have been converted into boutiques, stores, and dozens of eating places—from fast-food outlets to bistros serving Italian and French fare.

Dining and Lodging

$–$$$ ✕ **Auberge l'Étoile Sur-le-Lac.** This popular restaurant (which also has rooms) serves three meals a day in attractive surroundings. Large windows overlooking mountain-ringed Lac Memphrémagog make the dining room bright and airy. In summer you can sit outside and take in the smells and sounds, as well as the beautiful view. House specialties include wild game and Swiss fondue. ⊠ *1150 rue Principale Ouest,* ☎ *819/843–6521 or 800/567–2727. AE, DC, MC, V.*

$$$$ ✕🖫 **Ripplecove Inn.** The Ripplecove vies with the Hatley and Hovey inns (☞ *North Hatley, below*) for best in the region. Its accommodations, service, and dining room are consistently excellent. The English pub–style room combines classical and French cuisine in such dishes as *petite timbale de sole et saumon fumé à l'algue nori* (timbale of sole and smoked salmon with seaweed) and the *gâteau de foie de volaille à la crème de porto* (gâteau of chicken livers in a port-flavored sauce). ⊠ *700 chemin Ripplecove, C.P. 246, Ayer's Cliff (11 km, or 7 mi, south of Magog) J0B 1CO,* ☎ *819/838–4296 or 800/668–4296,* ℻ *819/838–5541. 25 rooms. Restaurant, pool, 2 beaches, windsurfing, boating, cross-country skiing, meeting rooms. MAP. AE, MC, V.*

$$$$ 🖫 **Centre de Santé d'Eastman.** The oldest spa in Québec has evolved
★   from a simple health center into a bucolic haven for anyone seeking rest and therapeutic treatments. Owner Jocelyna Dubuc has resisted the temptation to turn the 350-acre property into a glitzy resort. In-

stead, she has created a relaxing world where people can, at reasonable prices, rejuvenate their bodies and minds through walking programs, massages, algae wraps, oxygen baths, and other energy-boosting programs. The brightly lit dining room (for guests only), with its wall of windows, serves flavorful vegetarian cuisine as well as innovative seafood and chicken dishes. Some spa goers, intent on shedding unwanted pounds, walk to nearby Eastman, an attractive hamlet with antiques and gift shops. ✉ *895 chemin Diligence, Eastman (15 km, or 9 mi, west of Magog) J0E 1P0, ☎ 514/297–3009 or 800/665–5272. 19 rooms. Dining room, spa, cross-country skiing. AP. AE, MC, V.*

Nightlife and the Arts

THE ARTS

A theater-turned-church **Le Vieux Clocher** (✉ 64 rue Merry Nord, ☎ 819/847–0470) headlines well-known comedians and singers. Most performances are in French, but big names, like Jim Corcoran, Edith Butler, and Michel Rivard, perform here regularly.

NIGHTLIFE

Magog is lively after dark, with a variety of bars, cafés, bistros, and restaurants to suit every taste and pocketbook. **Auberge Orford** (✉ 20 rue Merry Sud, ☎ 819/843–9361) often has live entertainment. **La Grosse Pomme** (✉ 270 rue Principale Ouest, ☎ 819/843–9365) is a multilevel complex with huge video screens, dance floors, and restaurant service. **Resto-club Au Chat Noir** (✉ 266 rue Principale Ouest, ☎ 819/843–4337) is a gathering place for local jazz aficionados and musicians, who drop by for impromptu jam sessions that augment the regular performances.

Outdoor Activities and Sports

Owl's Head Ski Area (✉ Rte. 243 South, Exit 106 from Autoroute 10, ☎ 514/292–3342), 25 km (16 mi) south of Magog, is a mecca for skiers looking for fewer crowds. It has seven lifts, a 1,782-ft vertical drop, and 27 trails, including a 4-km (2½-mi) intermediate run, the longest in the Eastern Townships. From the trails you can see nearby Vermont and Lac Memphrémagog. (You might even see the lake's legendary sea dragon, said to have been sighted around 90 times since 1816.)

Valcourt

17 *50 km (31 mi) northwest of Magog.*

Valcourt is the birthplace of the inventor of the snowmobile, and the Eastern Townships are a world center for the sport, with more than 2,000 km (1,240 mi) of paths cutting through the woods and meadows. In February the town hosts the **Valcourt Snowmobiling Grand Prix** (☎ 514/532–3443), a five-day event with competitions and festivities. The **Musée Joseph-Armand Bombardier** displays innovator Bombardier's many inventions, including the snowmobile. ✉ *1001 av. Joseph-Armand Bombardier, ☎ 514/532–5300. ⊟ $5. ☉ Late June–Aug., daily 10–5:30; Sept.–late June, Tues.–Sun. 10–5.*

Orford

18 *40 km (25 mi) southeast of Valcourt.*

Orford is near a regional park, the Parc de Récréation du Mont-Orford, that's in use year-round, whether for skiing, camping, or hiking. Orford also has an annual arts festival, Festival Orford, highlighting classical music and chamber orchestra concerts. Since 1951, thousands of students have come to the **Orford Arts Centre** (☎ 819/843–3981, 800/567–6155 in Canada May–August) to study and perform classical music in the summer. Canada's internationally celebrated Orford String Quartet originated here.

Lodging

$$ ⊞ **Auberge Estrimont.** An exclusive complex built of cedar, combining hotel rooms, condos, and larger chalets, Auberge Estrimont is close to ski hills, riding stables, and golf courses. Every room, whether in the hotel or in an adjoining condo unit, has a fireplace and a private balcony. ✉ *44 av. de l'Auberge, C.P. 98, Orford-Magog J1X 3W7,* ☎ *819/843–1616 or 800/567–7320,* FAX *819/843–4909. 76 rooms, 7 suites. Restaurant, bar, indoor and outdoor pools, hot tub, sauna, tennis, exercise room, racquetball, squash. AE, DC, MC, V.*

Outdoor Activities and Sports

Mont-Orford Ski Area (✉ Rte. 141, ☎ 819/843–6548), at the center of the provincial park here, has plenty of challenges for alpine and cross-country skiers, from novices to veterans. It has 41 runs, a vertical drop of 1,782 ft, and 8 lifts, as well as 56 km (35 mi) of cross-country trails.

Abbaye St-Benoît-du-Lac

★ ⑲ *17 km (11 mi) southwest of Magog.*

This abbey's slender bell tower juts up above the trees like a fairy-tale castle. Built by the Benedictines in 1912 on a wooded peninsula on Lac Memphrémagog, the abbey is home to some 60 monks, who sell apples and sparkling apple wine from their orchards as well as distinctive cheeses: Ermite, St-Benoît, and ricotta. Gregorian masses are sung daily and some are open to the public. To get to the abbey from Magog, take Route 112 and then follow the signs for the side road (R.R. 2, or rue des Pères) to the abbey. ✉ *R.R. 2,* ☎ *819/843–4080 for information about times of masses.* ☉ *Store open between services; best time is 2–4.*

North Hatley

⑳ *36 km (22 mi) northeast of Abbaye St-Benoît-du-Lac.*

North Hatley, the small resort town on the tip of lovely Lac Massawippi, has a theater and a number of excellent inns and restaurants. The town, set among hills and farms, was discovered by well-to-do vacationers early in the century and has been drawing people ever since. A number of special events during the year are additional attractions.

Dining and Lodging

$$ ✕ **The Pilsen.** Québec's earliest microbrewery no longer brews beer on-site, but there's still Massawippi pale ale on tap at this lively spot. Good pub food—pasta, homemade soups, burgers, and the like—is served in the upstairs restaurant and the tavern, both of which overlook the water. ✉ *55 Main St.,* ☎ *819/842–2971. AE, MC, V.*

$$$$ ✕⊞ **Auberge Hatley.** Chef Alain Labrie specializes in regional dishes
★   at this restaurant-inn, which has three times been voted the best in Québec. The menu changes seasonally, but the rich foie gras and Barbary duck are recommended if available. The yellow dining room has a panoramic view of Lake Massawippi; you can linger over your coffee or sip your selection from the wine cellar, which has more than 5,000 bottles. Guest rooms in this 1903 country manor are charmingly decorated; some have a whirlpool and a fireplace. ✉ *325 chemin Virgin, C.P. 330, J0B 2C0,* ☎ *819/842–2451,* FAX *819/842–2907. 25 rooms. Restaurant. MAP. AE, DC, MC, V. Closed last 2 wks in Nov.*

$$$$ ✕⊞ **Manoir Hovey.** Overlooking Lac Massawippi, this retreat main-
★   tains the ambience of a private estate and provides the activities of a

resort. Built in 1900, it resembles George Washington's home at Mount Vernon. Each wallpapered room has a mix of antiques and newer wood furniture, richly printed fabrics, and lace trimmings; many have fireplaces and private balconies. The dining room serves exquisite Continental and French cuisine; if it's in season, try warm roulades of Swiss chard with spring lamb, preserved apricots, and roasted hazelnuts or grilled tenderloin of beef marinated with juniper berries and a sauce of tarragon and horseradish. Dinner, breakfast, and most sports facilities are included in room rates. ⊠ *575 chemin Hovey, C.P. 60, J0B 2C0,* ☎ *819/842–2421 or 800/661–2421,* FAX *819/842–2248. 40 rooms, 1 suite, 1 4-bedroom cottage. 2 bars, dining room, pool, tennis court, 2 beaches, ice fishing, mountain bikes, cross-country skiing, library, meeting rooms. MAP. AE, DC, MC, V.*

Nightlife and the Arts

The **Piggery** (⊠ Rte. 108, ☎ 819/842–2432 or 819/842–2431), a theater that was once a pig barn, reigns supreme in the Townships' cultural life. The venue is renowned for its risk taking, often presenting new plays by Canadian playwrights and even experimenting with bilingual productions. The season runs June–August.

L'Association du Festival du Lac Massawippi (☎ 819/563–4141) presents an annual antiques and folk-arts show in July. The association also sponsors classical music concerts at the Église Ste-Elizabeth in North Hatley, on Sundays starting in late April and continuing through June. The biennial **Naive Arts Contest** (⊠ Galerie Jeannine-Blais, 100 rue Main, ☎ 819/842–2784) shows the work of over 100 painters of naive art from 15 countries; the next show is in 2000.

Sherbrooke

❷ *16 km (10 mi) north of North Hatley.*

The region's unofficial capital and largest city is Sherbrooke, named in 1818 for Canadian governor general Sir John Coape Sherbrooke. It was founded by Loyalists in the 1790s along the St-François River. Sherbrooke has a number of art galleries and museums, including the **Musée des Beaux-Arts de Sherbrooke.** This fine-arts museum has mostly oil paintings; there are occasional exhibits by regional artists and other changing shows. ⊠ *241 rue Dufferin, J1H 4M3,* ☎ *819/ 821–2115.* ▨ *$2.50.* ☉ *Tues. and Thurs.–Sun. 1–5, Wed. 1–9.*

The **Sherbrooke Tourist Information Center** (⊠ 48 rue Dépôt, ☎ 819/ 821–1919) conducts city tours late June–early September. Call for reservations.

Two **sugar shacks** near Sherbrooke give tours of their maple-syrup producing operations in the spring: It's best to call before visiting. **Erablière Patoine** (⊠ 1105 chemin Beauvoir, ☎ 819/563–7455) is in Fleurimont. **Bolduc** (⊠ 525 chemin Lower, ☎ 819/875–3022) is in Cookshire.

Dining and Lodging

$$–$$$$ ✕ **La Falaise St-Michel.** Chef and part-owner Patrick Laigniel serves up superb French cuisine in a warm redbrick and wood room that takes off any chill even before you sit down. A large selection of wines complements the table d'hôte. ⊠ *Rues Webster and Wellington North, behind Banque Nationale,* ☎ *819/346–6339. AE, DC, MC, V.*

$$–$$$ ✕ **Restaurant au P'tit Sabot.** Specialties include dishes with wild boar, quail, and bison. The cozy room is a pleasant refuge from the bustle of Sherbrooke's main drag. A piano in the corner, pink decor, and room for only 35 patrons help set a romantic atmosphere. ⊠ *1410 rue King Ouest,* ☎ *819/563–0262. AE, DC, MC, V.*

$ ☷ **Bishop's University.** If you are on a budget, the students' residences
here are a great place to stay in summer. The prices can't be beat, and
the location near Sherbrooke is good for touring. The university's
grounds are lovely, with much of the architecture reminiscent of stately
New England campuses. The Gothic-style chapel, paneled with richly
carved ash, was built in 1857 and is a fine example of local craftsmanship.
Reservations for summer guests are accepted as early as September, so
book in advance. ⊠ *Rue College, Lennoxville (5 km, or 3 mi, south
of Sherbrooke), J1M 1Z7,* ☎ *819/822–9651,* FAX *819/822–9615. 564
beds in single or double rooms. Indoor pool, 18-hole golf course, tennis court, exercise room. MC, V. Closed Sept.–mid-May.*

Nightlife and the Arts

The **Centennial Theatre** (☎ 819/822–9692) at Bishop's University in
Lennoxville, 5 km (3 mi) south of Sherbrooke, presents a roster of international, Canadian, and Québécois jazz, classical, and rock concerts,
as well as dance, mime, and children's theater.

Mont-Mégantic's Observatory

㉒ *74 km (46 mi) east of Sherbrooke.*

Both amateur stargazers and serious astronomers are drawn to this site,
in a beautifully wild and mountainous part of the Eastern Townships.
The observatory (known as the Astrolab du Mont-Mégantic in French)
is at the summit of the Townships' second-highest mountain (3,601 ft),
whose northern face records annual snowfalls rivaling any other in North
America. A joint venture by the University of Montréal and Laval University, the observatory has a powerful telescope that allows resident
scientists to observe celestial bodies 10 million times smaller than the
human eye can detect. At the Astrolab (a welcome center on the mountain's base), you can view an exhibition and a multimedia show and
learn about the night sky. ⊠ *189 Rte. du Parc, Notre-Dame-des-Bois,*
☎ *819/888–2822.* ▦ *Astrolab $10, night tour to summit $10.* ☺ *Astrolab late June–Labor Day, daily 10–6; night tour to summit late June–
Labor Day, daily 8* PM.

Dining and Lodging

$$ ✕☷ **Aux Berges de l'Aurore.** Although this tiny bed-and-breakfast has
attractive furnishings and spectacular views (it sits at the foot of Mont-
Mégantic), the draw here is the inn's cuisine. The restaurant ($$$) serves
a five-course meal with ingredients supplied from the inn's huge fruit,
vegetable, and herb garden, as well as wild game from the surrounding area: boar, fish, hare, and quail. ⊠ *51 chemin de l'Observatoire,
Notre-Dame-des-Bois,* ☎ *819/888–2715. 4 rooms. Restaurant. MC,
V. Closed Jan.–May.*

CHARLEVOIX

Stretching along the St. Lawrence River's north shore, east of Québec
City from Ste-Anne-de-Beaupré to the Saguenay River, Charlevoix embraces mountains rising from the sea and a succession of valleys,
plateaus, and cliffs cut by waterfalls, brooks, and streams. The roads
wind into villages of picturesque houses and huge tin-roof churches.
The area has long been popular both as a summer retreat and as a haven
for artists and craftspeople. In winter there are opportunities for both
downhill and cross-country skiing.

New France's first historian, the Jesuit priest François-Xavier de
Charlevoix, gave his name to the region. Charlevoix (pronounced
sharle-*vwah*) was first explored by Jacques Cartier, who landed in

1535, although the first colonists didn't arrive until well into the 17th century. They developed a thriving shipbuilding industry, specializing in the sturdy schooner they called a *goelette,* which they used to haul everything from logs to lobsters up and down the coast in the days before rail and paved roads. Shipbuilding has been a vital part of the provincial economy until recent times; today wrecked and forgotten goelettes lie along beaches in the region.

Ste-Anne-de-Beaupré

㉓ *33 km (20 mi) east of Québec City.*

Charlevoix begins in the tiny town of Ste-Anne-de-Beaupré (named for Québec's patron saint). Each year more than a million pilgrims visit
★ the region's most famous religious site, the **Basilique Ste-Anne-de-Beaupré** (☞ Side Trips from Québec City *in* Chapter 9), which is dedicated to the mother of the Virgin Mary.

At the **Cap Tourmente Wildlife Reserve,** about 8 km (5 mi) northeast of Ste-Anne-de-Beaupré, more than 100,000 greater snow geese gather every October and May. This enclave on the north shore of the St. Lawrence River has 14 hiking trails; the park harbors hundreds of kinds of birds and mammals and more than 700 plant species. Naturalists give guided tours. ⊠ *St-Joachim,* ☎ *418/827–4591 Apr.–Oct., 418/827–3776 Nov.–Mar.*

Outdoor Activities and Sports

Le Massif (⊠ 1350 rue Principale, Petite Rivière St-François, ☎ 418/632–5876) is a three-peak ski resort that has the province's highest vertical drop—2,500 ft. The 18 trails are divided into runs for different levels (including one for extremely advanced skiers). Equipment can be rented on site. **Station Mont-Ste-Anne** (☞ Outdoor Activities and Sports *in* Chapter 9), outside Québec City, is on the World Cup downhill ski circuit.

Baie-St-Paul

㉔ *60 km (37 mi) northeast of Ste-Anne-de-Beaupré.*

Baie-St-Paul, Charlevoix's earliest settlement after Beaupré, is popular with craftspeople and artists. Here the high hills circle a wide plain, holding the village beside the sea. Many of Québec's greatest landscapists portray the area, and the work of some of them is for sale at the **Centre d'Art Baie-St-Paul** (⊠ 4 rue Ambroise-Fafard, ☎ 418/435–3681). The **Centre d'Exposition de Baie-St-Paul** (⊠ 23 rue Ambroise-Fafard, ☎ 418/435–3681) displays the work of various artists, some of them from the region.

Dining and Lodging

$$$$ ✕▥ **Auberge la Maison Otis.** This inn offers calm and romantic ac-
★ commodations in three buildings, including an old stone house, in the center of the village. Some of the country-style rooms have whirlpools, fireplaces, and antique furnishings. Summer lunches are served on an outdoor terrace. Skiing and ice-skating are available nearby. The restaurant serves creative Québec-oriented French cuisine like *ballotine de faisan* (pheasant) stuffed with quail and served in a venison sauce, followed by a delicious assortment of cheeses. It's in a 150-year-old Norman-style house, elegantly decorated in pastel pink, with a huge fireplace. ⊠ *23 rue St-Jean-Baptiste, G0A 1B0,* ☎ *418/435–2255,* ℻ *418/435–2464. 30 rooms, 4 suites. Restaurant, lounge, piano bar, indoor pool, sauna, health club. MAP. AE, MC, V.*

Charlevoix

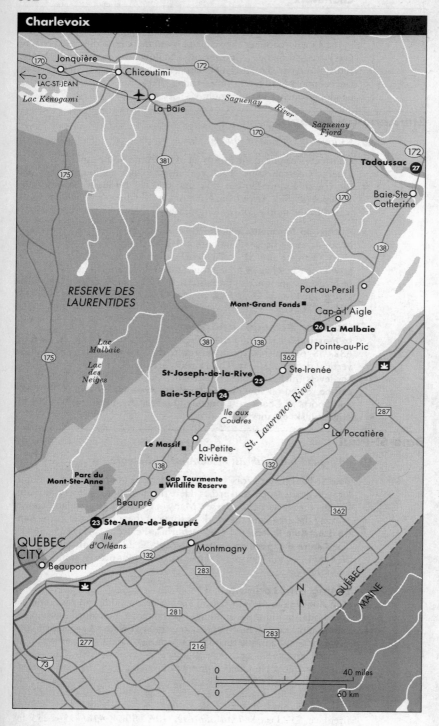

TO
LAC-ST-JEAN

170 Jonquière
Chicoutimi
172
Lac Kénogami
La Baie
Saguenay River
Saguenay Fjord
170
172
Tadoussac 27
381
Baie-Ste-Catherine
170
175
138
RESERVE DES
LAURENTIDES
Port-au-Persil
Mont-Grand Fonds
Cap-à-l'Aigle
26 La Malbaie
Lac
Malbaie
381
138
Pointe-au-Pic
175
Lac
des
Neiges
362
Ste-Irenée
St-Joseph-de-la-Rive 25
Baie-St-Paul 24
St. Lawrence River
Ile aux
Coudres
287
La Pocatière
Le Massif
La-Petite-
Rivière
132
Parc du
Mont-Ste-Anne
138
Cap Tourmente
Wildlife Reserve
362
Beaupré
23 Ste-Anne-de-Beaupré
QUÉBEC
CITY
Beauport
Ile
d'Orléans
132
Montmagny
283
281
QUÉBEC
MAINE
N
277
216
283
73

0   40 miles
0   60 km

En Route   From Baie-St-Paul, drivers have a choice of the open, scenic coastal drive on **Route 362** or the faster Route 138 to Pointe-au-Pic, La Malbaie, and Cap-à-l'Aigle. This section of Route 362 has memorable views of rolling hills—green, white, or ablaze with fiery hues, depending on the season—meeting the broad expanse of the "sea," as the locals like to call the St. Lawrence estuary.

St-Joseph-de-la-Rive

❷⑤   *15 km (9 mi) northeast of Baie-St-Paul.*

A secondary road leads sharply down into St-Joseph-de-la-Rive, with its line of old houses hugging the mountain base on the narrow shore road. The town has a number of peaceful inns and inviting restaurants. The small **Exposition Maritime** (Maritime Museum, ☎ 418/635–1131) commemorates the days of the St. Lawrence goelettes.

OFF THE BEATEN PATH   **ILE AUX COUDRES** – From St-Joseph-de-la-Rive, a ferry (☎ 418/438–2743) travels to Ile aux Coudres, an island where Jacques Cartier's men gathered *coudres* (hazelnuts) in 1535. Since then, the island has produced many a goelette, and former captains now run several small inns. Larger inns have folk-dance evenings. You can bike around the island and see windmills, inns, water mills, and old schooners, or stop at boutiques selling paintings and local handicrafts, such as household linens.

Lodging

$$ ☒ **Hôtel Cap-aux-Pierres.** This hotel provides top-notch accommoda-
★   tions in a traditionally Canadian main building and a motel section open in the summer only. About a third of the rooms have river views. The restaurant serves a mix of Québec standards and nouvelle cuisine, and entertainment includes folk dancing on summer Saturday evenings. ✉ *246 rue Principale, La Baleine, Ile aux Coudres G0A 2A0, ☎ 418/ 438–2711 or 800/463–5250, FAX 418/438–2127. 98 rooms. Restaurant, bar, indoor-outdoor pool. MAP. AE, DC, MC, V.*

Shopping

The **Papeterie St-Gilles** (✉ 304 rue F. A. Savard, ☎ 418/635–2430) produces unusual handcrafted stationery, using a 17th-century process.

La Malbaie

❷⑥   *35 km (22 mi) northeast of St-Joseph.*

La Malbaie is one of the most elegant and historically interesting resort towns in the province. It was known as Murray Bay in an earlier era when wealthy Anglophones summered here and in the neighboring villages of Pointe-au-Pic and Cap-à-l'Aigle. Once called the "summer White House," this area became popular with both American and Canadian politicians in the late 1800s when Ottawa Liberals and Washington Republicans partied decorously through the summer with members of the Québec judiciary. William Howard Taft built the first of three summer residences in Pointe-au-Pic in 1894, when he was the American civil governor of the Philippines. He became the 27th president of the United States in 1908.

Now many Taft-era homes serve as handsome inns, guaranteeing an old-fashioned coddling, with such extras as breakfast in bed, gourmet meals, whirlpools, and free shuttles to the ski areas in winter. Many serve lunch and dinner to nonresidents, so you can tour the area going from one gourmet's delight to the next. The cuisine, as elsewhere in Québec, is genuine French or regional fare.

Musée de Charlevoix traces the region's history as a vacation spot in a series of exhibits and is developing an excellent collection of local paintings and folk art. ⊠ *1 chemin du Havre, Pointe-au-Pic (3 km, or 2 mi, south of La Malbaie),* ☎ *418/665–4411.*

The **Casino de Charlevoix,** styled after European casinos, welcomes visitors year-round. The minimum age is 18. ⊠ *Hôtel Manoir Richelieu, 183 av. Richelieu, Pointe-au-Pic,* ☎ *418/665–5353 or 800/665–2274.* ☉ *Sun.–Thurs. 10 AM–1 AM, Fri.– Sat. 10 AM–3 AM.*

Dining and Lodging

$$$$ ✕ **Auberge des 3 Canards.** The inn has made a name for itself in the region, not only for its accommodations but also for its award-winning restaurant. The menu may include *gratin d'escargots aux bluets* (snails with a blueberry and grapefruit sauce baked au gratin) as an appetizer, and stuffed pheasant—the breasts smothered in mustard sauce and the legs seasoned with spicy maple sauce—as a main course. Homemade desserts include *pomme de l'Ile aux Coudres*—cheese-topped apples with a touch of honey. Meals are elegantly presented in a rustic setting with natural wood and pale and deep blue touches throughout. ⊠ *49 côte Bellevue, Pointe-au-Pic (3 km, or 2 mi, south of La Malbaie),* ☎ *418/665–3761. AE, MC, V.*

$$$$ ✕ **Auberge sur la Côte.** Simple white tablecloths, natural wood, and stone walls create a casual setting for fine French cuisine. A house specialty is *agneau de Charlevoix,* lamb seasoned with lemon and thyme, served with fresh vegetables. Lunch is served in summer only, but the dining room is open in the evening year-round. ⊠ *205 chemin des Falaises,* ☎ *418/665–3972. AE, MC, V.*

$$$$ ✕🖼 **Auberge la Pinsonnière.** An atmosphere of country luxury pre-
★   vails at this inn, a Relais & Châteaux property. Each room is decorated differently; some have fireplaces, whirlpools, and king-size four-poster beds. The rooms overlook Murray Bay on the St. Lawrence River. The food here is excellent, and the auberge has one of the largest wine cellars in North America. ⊠ *124 rue St-Raphael, Cap-à-l'Aigle (3 km, or 2 mi, north of La Malbaie), G0T 1B0,* ☎ *418/665–4431,* FAX *418/665–7156. 26 rooms, 1 suite. 2 restaurants, 3 lounges, indoor pool, sauna, tennis court, beach. MAP. AE, MC, V.*

$$$ 🖼 **Hôtel Manoir Richelieu.** The Manoir Richelieu, an imposing castle nestled amid trees on a cliff overlooking the St. Lawrence River, has been offering first-class accommodations for a hundred years. This hotel was constructed in 1929 on the site of an earlier property, but the Manoir Richelieu retains the air of a turn-of-the-century hostelry. Still, it has kept up with the times: A recent addition is Relaxarium Manoir Richelieu, a health spa with treatments from lymphatic drainage to hydrotherapy. The links-style golf course, similar to those in Scotland, overlooks the St. Lawrence. The casino here is owned by the Québec government. ⊠ *181 rue Richelieu, Pointe-au-Pic (3 km, or 2 mi, south of La Malbaie), G0T 1M0,* ☎ *418/665–3703 or 800/463–2613,* FAX *418/665–3093. 380 rooms. Restaurant, indoor and outdoor pools, sauna, spa, 18-hole golf course, tennis courts, cross-country skiing, snowmobiling, casino. AE, DC, MC, V.*

Nightlife and the Arts

Domaine Forget, a music and dance academy, presents concerts on summer evenings by fine musicians from around the world, many of whom are teaching or learning at the school. The Domaine also functions as a stopover for traveling musicians, who take advantage of its rental studios. A 600-seat concert hall has recently been added. ⊠ *Ste-Irenée (15 km, or 9 mi, south of La Malbaie),* ☎ *418/452–8111 or 418/452–2535,* FAX *418/452–3503.* ☉ *Concerts May–Aug.*

Outdoor Activities and Sports

GOLF

Club de Golf de Manoir Richelieu (✉ 181 rue Richelieu, Pointe-au-Pic, ☎ 418/665–2526 or 800/463–2613) is a par-72,18-hole course.

SKIING

Mont-Grand Fonds (✉ 1000 chemin des Loisirs, ☎ 418/665–0095), 10 km (6 mi) north of La Malbaie, has 14 downhill slopes, a 1,105-ft vertical drop, and two lifts. It also has 135 km (84 mi) of cross-country trails. Two trails meet the standards of the International Ski Federation, and the resort hosts major ski competitions occasionally. Other sports are dogsledding, sleigh riding, skating, and tobogganing.

Tadoussac

㉗ *71 km (44 mi) north of La Malbaie.*

The small town of Tadoussac shares the view up the magnificent Saguenay Fjord with Baie-Ste-Catherine across the river. The drive here from La Malbaie, along Route 138, leads past a lovely series of villages and views along the St. Lawrence. Jacques Cartier made a stop at this point in 1535, and it became an important meeting site for fur traders until the mid-19th century. Whale-watching excursions and cruises of the fjord now depart from Tadoussac, as well as from Chicoutimi, farther up the deep fjord.

As the Saguenay River flows from Lac St-Jean south toward the St. Lawrence, it has a dual character: Between Alma and Chicoutimi, the once rapidly flowing river has been turned into hydroelectric power; in its lower section, it becomes wider and deeper and flows by steep mountains and cliffs, en route to the St. Lawrence. The white beluga whale breeds in the lower portion of the Saguenay in summer, and in the confluence of the fjord and the seaway are many marine species, which attract other whales, such as pilot, finback, humpback, and blues.

Sadly, the beluga is an endangered species; the whales, along with 27 other species of mammals and birds and 17 species of fish, are being threatened by pollution in the St. Lawrence River. This has inspired a $100 million project funded by both the federal and provincial governments. The 800-square-km (496-square-mi) **Parc Marine du Saguenay–St-Laurent** (✉ 182 rue de l'Église for park office, ☎ 418/235–4703), a marine park at the confluence of the Saguenay and St. Lawrence rivers, has been created to protect its fragile ecosystem. Exhibits at La Maison des Dunes (☎ 514/235–4238), an interpretive center 5 km (3 mi) northwest of the village, explain the tides and the flora and fauna, including sand dunes.

Outdoor Activities and Sports

Croisières Navimex Canada, Inc. (✉ 124 rue St-Pierre, Bureau 300, Québec City G1K 4A7, ☎ 418/692–4643, 800/463–1292 in season) has three-hour whale-watching cruises ($30) and 4½-hour dinner cruises on the Saguenay Fjord ($40). Cruises depart from Baie-Ste-Catherine, Tadoussac, and Rivière du Loup (the departure from Rivière du Loup costs an additional $5). The best months for seeing whales are July, August, and September, although some operators extend the season at either end if whales are around.

THE GASPÉ PENINSULA

Jutting into the stormy Gulf of St. Lawrence like the battered prow of a ship, the Gaspé Peninsula (Gaspésie in French) remains an isolated region of unsurpassed wild beauty. Sheer cliffs tower above broad beaches, and tiny coastal fishing communities cling to the shoreline. Inland rise the Chic-Choc Mountains, eastern Canada's highest, the realm of woodland caribou, black bear, and moose. Townspeople in some Gaspé areas speak mainly English.

The Gaspé was on Jacques Cartier's itinerary—he first stepped ashore in North America in the town of Gaspé in 1534—but Vikings, Basques, and Portuguese fishermen had come before. The area's history is told in countless towns en route. Acadians, displaced by the British from New Brunswick in 1755, settled Bonaventure; Paspébiac still has a gunpowder shed built in the 1770s to help defend the peninsula from American ships; and United Empire Loyalists settled New Carlisle in 1784.

Today the area still seems unspoiled and timeless, a blessing for anyone dipping and soaring along the spectacular coastal highways or venturing on river-valley roads to the interior. Geographically, the peninsula is among the oldest lands on earth. A vast, mainly uninhabited forest covers the hilly hinterland. Local tourist officials can be helpful in locating outfitters and guides for fishing. The Gaspé has many parks, nature trails, and wildlife sanctuaries. The most accessible include Parc de l'Ile-Bonaventure-et-du-Rocher-Percé, which embraces Bonaventure Island, a sanctuary for 250,000 birds; Forillon National Park at the tip of the peninsula, with 50 km (31 mi) of trails and an interesting boardwalk; and the Parc Provincial de la Gaspésie. The provincial park embraces the Chic-Choc Mountains and has terrain ranging from tundra to subalpine forest.

Carleton

㉘ *201 km (125 mi) southeast of Mont-Joli.*

The Notre Dame Oratory on Mont-St-Joseph dominates this French-speaking city. There are lookout points and hiking trails around the site. The views, almost 2,000 ft above Baie des Chaleurs, are lovely.

Dining and Lodging

$$ ✕🏨 **Motel Hostelerie Baie-Bleue.** This motel is snuggled up against a mountain beside the Baie des Chaleurs and has great views. Daily guided bus tours leave from the hotel June–September. The large restaurant, La Seignerie, has been recognized for excellence. Chef Simon Bernard prepares regional dishes, especially seafood. The table d'hôte won't break your budget, and the wine list is extensive and well chosen. ✉ *482 blvd. Perron, Rte. 132, G0C 1J0,* ☎ *418/364–3355 or 800/463–9099,* 🖷 *418/364–6165. 95 rooms. Restaurant, pool, tennis court, beach. AE, MC, V.*

Outdoor Activities and Sports

Windsurfers and sailors enjoy the breezes around the Gaspé; there are windsurfing marathons in Baie des Chaleurs each summer.

Percé

㉙ *193 km (120 mi) east of Carleton.*

A pretty fishing village, Percé has a number of attractions and can get busy in summer. The most famous sight in the region is the huge fossil-embedded rock offshore that the sea "pierced" thousands of years ago. There are many pleasant places to walk and hike near town, and it's also possible to do some fishing or take a whale-watching cruise.

The largest colony of gannets in the world summers off Percé on ★ **㉚** **Bonaventure Island.** From the wharf at Percé, you can take a scenic boat ride to the island and walk the trails here. Trips are offered by Croisières

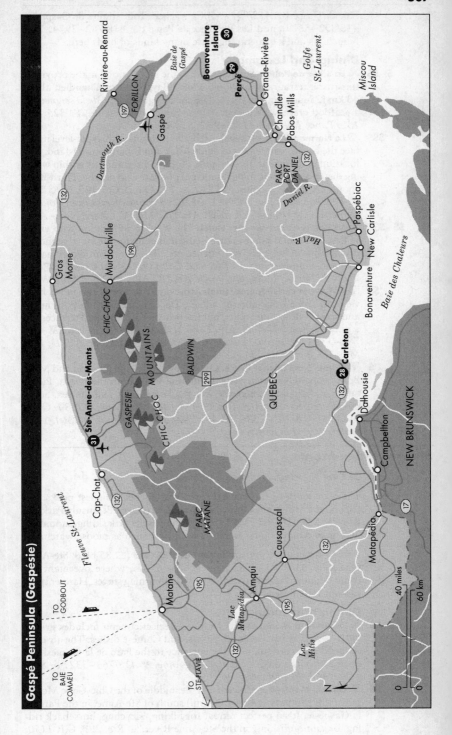

Gaspé Peninsula (Gaspésie)

TO GODBOUT

TO BAIE COMEAU

TO STE-FLAVIE

Fleuve St-Laurent

Matane

195

Cap-Chat

132

31 Ste-Anne-des-Monts

Gros Morne

132

Murdochville

198

CHIC-CHOC

GASPÉSIE

CHIC-CHOC MOUNTAINS

BALDWIN

299

PARC MATANE

Lac Matapédia

Amqui

195

Lac Mitis

Causapscal

132

Matapédia

17

Campbellton

NEW BRUNSWICK

Dalhousie

28 Carleton

132

QUEBEC

132

Baie des Chaleurs

Bonaventure

New Carlisle

Paspébiac

Haut R.

Daniel R.

PARC PORT DANIEL

132

Chandler

Pabos Mills

Grande-Rivière

29 Percé

30 Bonaventure Island

Golfe St-Laurent

Miscou Island

Baie de Gaspé

FORILLON

197

Gaspé

Dartmouth R.

132

Rivière-au-Renard

N

0   40 miles

0   60 km

Baie de Gaspé (☎ 418/892–5500), Agences Touristiques de Gaspé (☎ 418/892–5629), and Les Bateliers de Percé (☎ 418/782–2974. Take binoculars and a camera; there are many kinds of birds here.

Dining and Lodging

$–$$ ✕ **La Sieur de Pabos.** Serving some of the best seafood in the province, this rustic restaurant overlooks Pabos Bay, south of Chandler, about 40 km (25 mi) south of Percé. The chef suggests *crêpe de la seigneurie,* a seafood crepe with a delicately seasoned white sauce. ⊠ *325 Rte. 132, Pabos Mills,* ☎ *418/689–2281. AE, MC, V.*

$$$ ▨ **La Normandie Hotel/Motel.** All but four rooms of this split-level motel face the ocean, with views of Percé Rock and Bonaventure Island. The location in the center of town puts shops and restaurants within walking distance; a beach and a municipal pool are also nearby. Third-floor rooms are more spacious. ⊠ *221 Rte. 132 Ouest, C.P. 129, G0C 2L0,* ☎ *418/782–2112 or 800/463–0820. 45 rooms. Restaurant, lounge, sauna, exercise room. EP, MAP. AE, DC, MC, V. Closed Nov.–Apr.*

$$–$$$ ▨ **La Bonaventure-sur-Mer Hotel.** The waterfront location with views of Percé Rock and Bonaventure Island makes up for the motel-standard decor. Some motel units have kitchenettes. The restaurant serves mainly beef and seafood dishes. ⊠ *Rte. 132, C.P. 339, G0C 2L0,* ☎ *418/782–2166. 90 rooms. Restaurant, beach. AE, DC, MC, V. Closed Nov.–May.*

$$ ▨ **La Côte Surprise Motor Hotel.** Most of the rooms of this motel have views of Percé Rock and the village. Decor is standard in both motel and second-floor hotel units, but the private balconies and terraces are a plus. ⊠ *Rte. 132, C.P. 339, G0C 2L0,* ☎ *418/782–2166,* ℻ *418/782–5323. 36 rooms. Dining room, lounge, snack bar. AE, D, DC, MC, V. Closed Oct.–May.*

$ ▨ **Hôtel-Motel Rocher Percé.** Owned by Madeleine Pidgeon and Marc Bourdages, this hostelry is a 10-minute walk from the beach. Picnic tables and chairs have views over the Percé Rock and the sea. Some motel units have kitchenettes. ⊠ *111 Rte. 132 Ouest, C.P. 34, GOC 2LO,* ☎ *418/782–2330,* ℻ *418/782–5136. 4 rooms in hotel, 14 in motel. Closed in winter.*

Ste-Anne-des-Monts

㉛ *282 km (175 mi) northwest of Percé.*

The area south of this coastal town has Québec's highest peaks, the Chic-Choc Mountains. **Parc de la Gaspésie** (Gaspé Peninsula Park) ⊠ Rte. 299, ☎ 418/763–3301) has climbing, telemark skiing, mountain hiking, and nature interpretation programs such as moose watching.

There's telemark skiing at **Club du Grand Yétis** (⊠ 85 blvd. Ste-Anne Ouest, ☎ 418/763–7782 or 800/665–6527), where overnight accommodation is in cabins heated by wood-burning stoves. Hardier types can opt for camping out.

Dining and Lodging

$–$$ ✕ **Restaurant Monaco.** The Monaco's eclectic menu includes grilled meat as well as fish, seafood, pastas, and Chinese dishes. The air-conditioned dining room, near the entrance to the Parc de la Gaspésie, is open 24 hours a day. ⊠ *90 blvd. Ste-Anne,* ☎ *418/763–3321 or 800/463–7468. AE, DC, MC, V.*

$$ ▨ **Gîte du Mont-Albert.** Nestled in the middle of the Chic-Choc Mountains, this property is 40 km (25 mi) south of Ste-Anne, in the Parc de la Gaspésie. It's a perfect retreat for hiking, bicycling, horseback riding, or salmon fishing on the Ste-Anne River. ⊠ *Rte. 299, C.P. 1150, G0E 2G0,* ☎ *418/763–2288 or 888/270–4483. 48 rooms. Restaurant, bar, dining room. AE, MC, V.*

QUÉBEC A TO Z

Arriving and Departing

By Bus

Most major bus lines in the province connect with **Voyageur** (☎ 514/842–2281).

By Car

Major entry points are Ottawa/Hull, U.S. 87 from New York State south of Montréal, U.S. 91 from Vermont into the Eastern Townships area, and the Trans-Canada Highway (Highway 1) just west of Montréal.

By Plane

Most airlines fly into Montréal or Québec City (☞ Montréal A to Z *in* Chapter 8 *and* Québec City A to Z *in* Chapter 9).

By Train

Regular **VIA Rail** (☎ 800/835–3032) passenger service connects many towns in the province with Montréal and Québec City and offers limited service to the Gaspé Peninsula.

Getting Around

Québec

BY BUS

Most bus traffic to the outer reaches of the province begins at the **bus terminal** in Québec City (✉ 320 rue Abraham-Martin, ☎ 418/525–3000).

BY CAR

Québec has fine roads, along which drivers insist on speeding. The major highways are Autoroute des Laurentides 15, a six-lane highway from Montréal to the Laurentians; Autoroute 10 East from Montréal to the Eastern Townships; U.S. 91 from New England, which becomes Autoroute 55 as it crosses the border to the Eastern Townships; and Route 138, which runs from Montréal along the north shore of the St. Lawrence River. Road maps are available at seasonal or permanent Québec **tourist offices** (call 800/363–7777 for locations).

The Laurentians

BY BUS

Frequent bus service is available from the **Terminus Voyageur** (✉ 505 blvd. de Maisonneuve Est, ☎ 514/842–2281) in downtown Montréal. **Limocar Laurentides** service (☎ 514/435–8899) departs regularly for L'Annonciation, Mont-Laurier, Ste-Adèle, Ste-Agathe-des-Monts, and St-Jovite, among other stops en route. Limocar also has a service to the Lower Laurentians region, departing from the Laval bus terminal at the Métro Henri-Bourassa stop in north Montréal, stopping in many towns and ending in St-Jérôme.

BY CAR

Autoroute des Laurentides 15 and Route 117, a slower but more scenic secondary road, lead to this resort country. Try to avoid traveling to and from the region on Friday evening or Sunday afternoon, as you're likely to sit for hours in traffic.

The Eastern Townships

BY BUS

Buses depart daily from the **Terminus Voyageur** in Montréal (✉ 505 blvd. de Maisonneuve Est, ☎ 514/842–2281) to Granby, Lac-Mégantic, Magog, and Sherbrooke.

BY CAR

Autoroute 10 East heads from Montréal through the Townships; from New England, U.S. 91 becomes Autoroute 55, a major road.

Charlevoix

BY CAR

The main roads through the region are the scenic Route 362 and the faster Route 138.

Gaspé Peninsula

BY CAR

The Trans-Canada Highway (Highway 1) runs northeast along the southern shore of the St. Lawrence River to just south of Rivière-du-Loup, where the 270-km (167-mi) Route 132 hugs the dramatic coastline. At Ste-Flavie, follow the southern leg of Route 132. The entire distance around the peninsula is 848 km (526 mi).

Contacts and Resources

Camping

Inquiries about camping in Québec's national parks should be directed to **Canadian Heritage Parks Canada** (✉ Passage du Chien d'Or, Box 6060, Québec City, G1R 4V7, ☎ 418/648–4177). For information on camping in the province's private trailer parks and campgrounds, write for the free publication "Québec Camping," available from **Tourisme Québec** (✉ Box 979, Montréal H3C 2W3, ☎ 514/873–2015 or 800/363–7777).

Emergencies

Ambulance, fire, police (☎ 911).

Fishing

Nineteen outfitters are members of the Laurentian tourist association; several recommendations follow. **Pourvoirie Baroux** (✉ St-Jovite, ☎ 819/425–7882). **Pourvoirie Boismenu** (✉ Lac-du-Cerf, ☎ 819/597–2619). **Pourvoiries Mekoos** (✉ Mont-Laurier, ☎ 819/623–2336).

The **Fédération des Pourvoyeurs du Québec** (✉ Québec Outfitters Federation, 5237 blvd. Hamel, Bureau 270, Québec City G2P 2H2, ☎ 418/877–5191) has a list of of outfitters, which is also available through tourist offices. Fishing requires a permit, available from the regional offices of the **Ministère de l'Environnement et de la Faune** (✉ Ministry of the Environment and Wildlife, 150 blvd. René-Lévesque Est, Québec City G1R 4Y1, ☎ 418/643–3127 or 800/561–1616), or at regional sporting-goods stores displaying an "authorized agent" sticker.

Guest Farms

Agricotours (✉ 4545 av. Pierre-de-Coubertin, C.P. 1000, Succursale M, Montréal H1V 3R2, ☎ 514/252–3138), the Québec farm-vacation association, can provide lists of guest farms in the province.

Mountain Climbing

The **Fédération Québécoise de la Montagne** (✉ Québec Mountain-Climbing Federation, 4545 rue Pierre-de-Coubertin, C.P. 1000, Succursale M, Montréal H1V 3R2, ☎ 514/252–3004) has information about this sport, as do the province's tourist offices.

Nature Tours

The **Montréal Zoological Society** (✉ 2055 rue Peel, Montréal H3A 1V4, ☎ 514/845–8317) is a nature-oriented group that offers lectures, field trips, and weekend excursions. Tours include whale-watching in the St. Lawrence estuary and hiking and bird-watching in national parks throughout Québec, Canada, and the northern United States.

River Rafting

Four companies specializing in white-water rafting at Rivière Rouge are on-site at the trip's departure point near Calumet. (To get here, take Route 148 past Calumet; turn onto chemin de la Rivière Rouge until you see the signs for the access road to each rafter's headquarters.) **Aventures en Eau Vive** (☎ 819/242–6084 or 800/567–6881), **Nouveau Monde** (☎ 819/242–7238 or 800/361–5033), **Propulsion** (☎ 514/229–6620 or 800/461–3300), and **W-3 Rafting** (☎ 514/334–0889) all offer four- to five-hour rafting trips and provide transportation to and from the river site, as well as guides, helmets, life jackets, and, at the end of the trip, a much-anticipated meal. Most have facilities on-site or nearby for dining, drinking, camping, bathing, swimming, hiking, and horseback riding.

Skiing

For information about ski conditions, call **Tourisme Québec** (☎ 800/363–7777) and ask for the ski report.

Snowmobiling

Regional tourist offices (☞ Visitor Information, *below*) have information about snowmobiling in their area, including snowmobile maps and lists of essential services. Snowmobilers who use trails in Québec must obtain an access pass or day user's pass for the trails. The sport is regulated by the **Québec Federation of Snowmobiling Clubs** (✉ 4545 av. Pierre-de-Coubertin, Box 1000, Montréal, Québec H1V 3R2, ☎ 514/252–3076).

Jonview Canada (✉ 1227 av. St-Hubert, Suite 200, Montréal H2L 3Y8, ☎ 514/843–8161) offers snowmobile tours in the Laurentians, in Charlevoix, and as far north as the James Bay region. Other weeklong packages may include dogsledding and ice fishing.

Visitor Information

QUÉBEC

Tourisme Québec (✉ C.P. 979, Montréal H3C 2W3, ☎ 800/363–7777) can provide information on provincial tourist bureaus throughout the province.

THE LAURENTIANS

The major tourist office is the **Maison du Tourisme des Laurentides** (✉ 14142 rue de Lachapelle, R.R. 1, St-Jérôme J7Z 5T4, ☎ 514/436–8532 or 800/561–6673), just off the Autoroute des Laurentides 15 at Exit 39. The office is open mid-June–August, daily 8:30–8; September–mid-June, Saturday–Thursday 9–5, Friday 9–7.

Year-round regional tourist offices are in the towns of Labelle, Mont-Laurier, Mont-Tremblant, Piedmont, St-Jovite, Ste-Adèle, Ste-Agathe-des-Monts, St-Sauveur-des-Monts, and Val David. **Seasonal tourist offices** (mid-June–Labor Day) are in Grenville, Lachute, L'Annonciation, Ste-Marguerite-du-Lac-Masson, St-Eustache, Oka, Notre-Dame-du-Laus, and St-Adolphe-d'Howard.

THE EASTERN TOWNSHIPS

Year-round regional provincial tourist offices are in Bromont, Eastman, Granby, Lac-Brome (Foster), Lac Mégantic, Magog, Sherbrooke, Sutton, Mansonville, and Waterloo. **Seasonal tourist offices** (June–Labor Day) are in Coaticook, Pike River, Frelighsburg, and Granby. Seasonal bureaus' schedules are irregular, so it's a good idea to contact the **Association Touristique des Cantons de l'Est** (✉ 20 rue Don Bosco Sud, Sherbrooke J1L 1W4, ☎ 819/820–2020 or 800/455–5527) before visiting. This association also provides lodging information.

CHARLEVOIX

The regional tourist office is **Association Touristique Régionale de Charlevoix** (✉ 630 blvd. de Comporté, C.P. 275, La Malbaie G5A 1T8, ☎ 418/665–4454).

GASPÉ PENINSULA

The regional tourist office is **Association Touristique de la Gaspésie** (✉ 357 Rte. de la Mer, Ste-Flavie G0J 2L0, ☎ 418/775–2223 or 800/463–0323).

11 New Brunswick

With the highest tides in the world carving a rugged coast and feeding more whales than you can imagine, New Brunswick can be a phenomenal adventure. White sandy beaches, lobsters in the pot, and cozy inns steeped in history make it easy to have a relaxing interlude, too. And with fine art galleries, museums, and a dual Acadian and Loyalist heritage, the province is an intriguing cultural destination.

NEW BRUNSWICK IS WHERE the great Canadian forest, sliced by sweeping river valleys and modern highways, meets the sea. It's an old place in New World terms, and the remains of a turbulent past are still evident in some of its quiet nooks. Near Moncton, for instance, wild strawberries perfume the air of the grassy slopes of Fort Beauséjour, where, in 1755, one of the last battles for possession of Acadia took place—the English finally overcoming the French. The dual heritage of New Brunswick (35% of its population is Acadian French) provides added spice. Other areas of the province were settled by the British and by Loyalists, American colonists who chose to live under British rule after the American Revolution. If you stay in both Acadian and Loyalist regions, a trip to New Brunswick can seem like two vacations in one.

Updated by
Ana Watts

More than half the province is surrounded by coastline—the rest nestles into Québec and Maine, creating slightly schizophrenic attitudes in border towns. The dramatic Bay of Fundy, which has the highest tides in the world, sweeps up the coast of Maine, around the enchanting Fundy Isles at the southern tip of New Brunswick and on up the province's rough and intriguing south coast. To the north and east, the gentle, warm Gulf Stream washes quiet beaches.

New Brunswick is still largely unsettled—85% of the province is forested. Inhabitants have chosen the easily accessible area around rivers, ocean, and lakes, leaving most of the interior to the pulp companies. For years this province has been somewhat ignored by tourists, who whiz through to better-known Atlantic destinations. New Brunswick's residents can't seem to decide whether this makes them unhappy or not. The government, however, sees tourism as a culturally and economically friendly way of helping the province toward economic self-sufficiency. Money is important in the economically depressed maritime area, where younger generations have traditionally left home for higher-paying jobs in Ontario and "the West." But no one wishes to lose the special characteristics of this still unspoiled province.

This attitude is a blessing in disguise to motorists who do leave the major highways to explore 2,240 km (1,389 mi) of spectacular seacoast, pure inland streams, pretty towns, and historic cities. The custom of hospitality is so much a part of New Brunswick nature that tourists are perceived more as welcome visitors than paying guests. Even cities often retain a bit of naïveté. It makes for a charming vacation, but don't be deceived by ingenuous attitudes. Most residents are products of excellent school and university systems, generally travel widely, live in modern cities, and are well versed in world affairs.

Pleasures and Pastimes

Beaches

There are two kinds of saltwater beaches in New Brunswick: warm-m-m-m-m and c-c-c-c-cold. The warm beaches are along the Northumberland Strait and Gulf of St. Lawrence on the east coast. Here, it's sand castles, sunscreen, and a little beach volleyball on the side. If sand and solitude are more your style, try Kouchibouguac National Park and its 26 km (16 mi) of beaches and dunes.

The cold beaches are on the Bay of Fundy, on the province's southern coast. The highest tides in the world (a *vertical* difference of as much as 48 ft) have carved some spectacular caves, crevices, and cliffs. There are some sandy beaches, and hardy souls do swim in the "invigorating" salt water. But the Fundy beaches are more for adventurers who want to investigate aquatic wildlife on the flats at low tide, hound rocks, or hunt fossils.

Dining

Cast your line just about anywhere in New Brunswick and you catch fish-and-chips, clams-and-chips, scallops-and-chips. Just about any restaurant in any coastal community has its own great chowder, but catching fresh seafood usually means a trip to a better restaurant. New Brunswick's oysters, scallops, clams, crabs, mussels, lobsters, and salmon are worth it. Some seafood is available seasonally, but now that salmon is farmed extensively, this taste of heaven is available anytime, and the price is very reasonable. What New Brunswick serves best and most often is comfort food. Ham and potato scallops, turkey dinners, pork chops, and even liver and onions are staples on many menus. The beer of choice is Moosehead, brewed in Saint John.

A spring delicacy is fiddleheads—emerging ostrich ferns that look like the curl at the end of a violin neck. These emerald gems are picked along riverbanks as the freshet recedes, boiled, and sprinkled with lemon juice or vinegar and butter, salt, and pepper. New Brunswickers eat dulse whenever the mood hits. It's a dried purple seaweed, as salty as potato chips and as compelling as peanuts. You'll find it on Grand Manan Island, in the Old Saint John City Market, and in barrels for tasting at some seafood restaurants.

CATEGORY	COST*
$$$$	over $35
$$$	$25–$35
$$	$15–$25
$	under $15

*per person, in Canadian dollars, excluding drinks, service, and 15% harmonized sales tax (HST)

Lodging

Among its more interesting options, New Brunswick has a number of officially designated Heritage Inns. These historically significant establishments run the gamut from elegant to homey; many have antique china and furnishings. Hotels and motels in and around Saint John, Moncton, and Fredericton are adequate and friendly. Accommodations in Saint John are at a premium in summer, so reserve ahead.

CATEGORY	COST*
$$$$	over $160
$$$	$120–$160
$$	$85–$120
$	under $85

*All prices are for a standard double room, excluding 15% harmonized sales tax (HST), in Canadian dollars.

Outdoor Activities and Sports

BIKING

Byroads, lanes, and rolling secondary highways run through small towns, along the ocean, and into the forest. Bikers can set out on their own or try a guided adventure.

FISHING

Dotted with freshwater lakes, crisscrossed with fish-laden rivers, and bordered by 1,129 km (700 mi) of seacoast, this province is one of Canada's natural treasures. Sports people are drawn by the bass fishing and such world-famous salmon rivers as the Miramichi. Commercial fishers often take visitors line fishing for groundfish.

GOLF

Golf is an increasingly popular sport, and an extensive program to upgrade even the best courses to championship and signature status, and to construct new courses, is under way.

WHALE-WATCHING

One unforgettable New Brunswick experience is the sighting of a huge humpback, right whale, finback, or minke. Outfitters along the Bay of Fundy take people to see a variety of whales. Most trips run May–September.

WINTER SPORTS

New Brunswick can get as much as 16 ft of snow each year, so winter fun often lasts well into spring. Dogsledding is taking off, ice-fishing communities pop up on many rivers, and tobogganing, skating, and snowshoeing are popular. Snowmobiling has boomed: There are more than 9,000 km (5,580 mi) of groomed, marked, and serviced snowmobile trails and dozens of snowmobile clubs hosting special events.

For cross-country skiers, New Brunswick has groomed trails at Mactaquac Provincial Park near Fredericton, Fundy National Park in Alma, and Kouchibouguac National Park between Moncton and Miramichi. Many communities and small hotels offer groomed trails, but skiers can also set off on their own. New Brunswick downhill ski areas usually operate mid-December–April. There are four ski hills—Farlagne, Crabbe, Poley, and Sugarloaf.

Shopping

Fine art galleries display and sell local artists' paintings and sculptures. Craft galleries, shops, and fairs brim with jewelry, glass, pottery, clothing, furniture, and leather goods. Some of the province's better bookstores even have sections devoted to New Brunswick authors, both literary and popular. You'll find a number of intriguing shopping areas in Saint John. Fredericton has the Saturday-morning Boyce Farmers' Market and shops with crafts, treasures, and a bit of haute couture. The Moncton area has the biggest malls. The resort town of St. Andrews has some appealing crafts stores and shops.

Exploring New Brunswick

In recent years high-tech companies in New Brunswick have helped lead much of the world onto the Information Highway, but all that has done little to change its settlement patterns. The population still clings to the original highways—rivers and oceans. In fact, the St. John River in the west and the Fundy and Acadian coasts in the south and east essentially encompass the province.

The St. John River valley scenery is panoramic—gently rolling hills and sweeping forests, with just enough rocky gorges to keep it interesting. The native peoples, French, English, Scots, and Danes who live along the river ensure its culture is equally intriguing. It is here you will find Fredericton, capital of the province.

The Fundy Coast is phenomenal. Yachts, fishing boats, and tankers bob on the waves at high tide, then sit high and dry on the ocean floor when it goes out. The same tides force the mighty St. John River to reverse its flow in the old city of Saint John. The southwestern shores have spawned more than their share of world-class artists, authors, actors, and musicians. Maybe it's the Celtic influence; maybe it's the fog.

Along the Acadian Coast the water is warm, the sand is fine, and the accent is French—except in the middle. Where the Miramichi River meets the sea, there is an island of English, Irish, and Scottish tradition that is unto itself, rich in folklore and legend. Many people here find their livelihood in the forests, in the mines, and on the sea.

Numbers in the text correspond to numbers in the margin and on the New Brunswick, Fredericton, and Downtown Saint John maps.

Great Itineraries

IF YOU HAVE 3 DAYS

Plan to concentrate on one region if you have only a few days, or you'll spend too much time driving and too little time adventuring. Start on the Fundy Coast, following the well-marked Fundy Coastal Route. The St. Andrews to Saint John region will take you at least a couple of days, as will the area around Fundy National Park and Moncton, so make your choices in advance. In the resort community of ⚏ **St. Andrews by-the-Sea** ㉑, art, history, nature, and seafood abound. Whale-watching tours leave from the town wharf. More whale-watching and bird-watching opportunities can be arranged on **Grand Manan** ㉒ and **Deer Island** ㉔, accessible only by ferry.

The Fundy Coastal Drive winds about 100 km (62 mi) along the shore to the venerable city of ⚏ **Saint John** ⑪–⑲, steeped in English and Irish traditions, and on to the fishing village of St. Martins on Route 111. The new Fundy Parkway from St. Martins to Fundy National Park adds to this already impressive coastal drive; continue on to ⚏ **Moncton** ㉗, a microcosm of New Brunswick culture. Its mingling of French and English influences makes it a good starting point from which to tour the rest of the Bay of Fundy. About 80 km (50 mi) back down the coast is Alma, the entrance to **Fundy National Park** ㉖. On your way back to Moncton, visit Cape Enrage and Hopewell Cape, where the Fundy tides have sculpted gigantic flower-pot rocks that turn into islands at high tide. Southeast of Moncton, roads through gentle marshlands lead to Acadian culture in Memramcook, English gems like Dorchester and Sackville, and historic Fort Beauséjour at Aulac.

IF YOU HAVE 6 DAYS

With six days for exploring you can spend another day on the Fundy Coast and add the Acadian Coast to your itinerary. The official Acadian Coastal Drive Route is well marked from Aulac to Campbellton, a distance of about 400 km (248 mi). Head north from ⚏ **Moncton** ㉗ and explore the area around Shediac, famous for its lobsters and Parlee Beach. Beyond that is **Bouctouche** ㉘, with its wonderful dunes and the make-believe land of La Sagouine. Another 50 km (31 mi) farther north is unspoiled **Kouchibouguac National Park,** which protects beaches, forests, and peat bogs. The coastal drive from Kouchibouguac Park to ⚏ **Miramichi City** ㉙, about 75 km (47 mi), passes through several bustling fishing villages. Most of the communities are Acadian, but as you approach Miramichi City, English dominates again. A stopover in one of the city's motels will position you perfectly to begin your exploration of the Acadian Peninsula.

It is only about 120 km (74 mi) from Miramichi City to ⚏ **Caraquet** ㉚, but it might as well be a million. The entire peninsula is so different from the rest of the province it is like a trip to a foreign country: This is a romantic land with a dramatic history and an artistic flair. The **Acadian Historical Village** ㉛ is a careful recreation of the traditional Acadian way of life.

IF YOU HAVE 10 DAYS

With up to 10 days to explore New Brunswick you can see it all. Before you head for the Acadian Peninsula from ⚏ **Miramichi City** ㉙, take some time to explore the Miramichi River. The Atlantic Salmon

New Brunswick

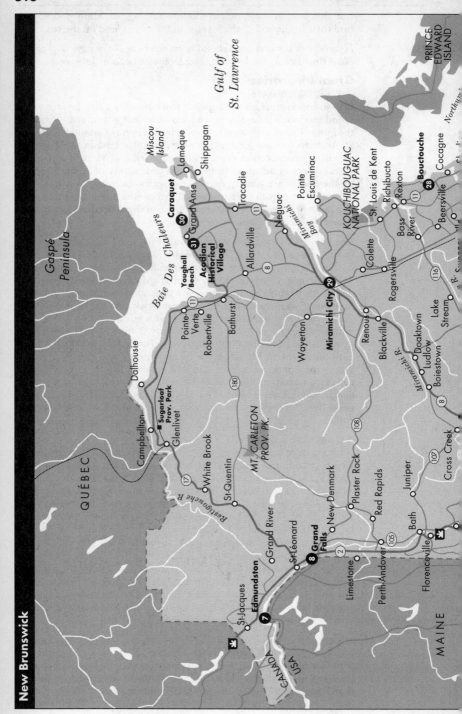

Gulf of
St. Lawrence

PRINCE
EDWARD
ISLAND

Gaspé
Peninsula

QUÉBEC

Miscou
Island

Lamèque

Shippagan

Caraquet ③⓪

Grand-Anse

Tracadie

Neguac

Pointe
Escuminac

③① Youghall
Beach

Acadian
Historical
Village

Allardville

KOUCHIBOUGUAC
NATIONAL PARK

St-Louis de Kent

Richibucto

Rexton

Bouctouche

Cocagne

②⑧

Beersville

Baie Des Chaleurs

Dalhousie

Pointe-
Verte

Robertville

Bathurst

Colette

Rogersville

Bass
River

Lake
Stream

Miramichi City ②⑨

Wayerton

Renous

Blackville

Doaktown

Ludlow

Boiestown

Campbellton

Sugarloaf
Prov. Park

Glenlivet

White Brook

MT. CARLETON
PROV. PK.

St-Quentin

New Denmark

Plaster Rock

Red Rapids

Juniper

Bath

Cross Creek

Restigouche R.

Grand River

St-Léonard

⑧ Grand
Falls

Limestone

Perth-Andover

Florenceville

Edmundston

⑦

St-Jacques

CANADA
USA

MAINE

Miramichi R.

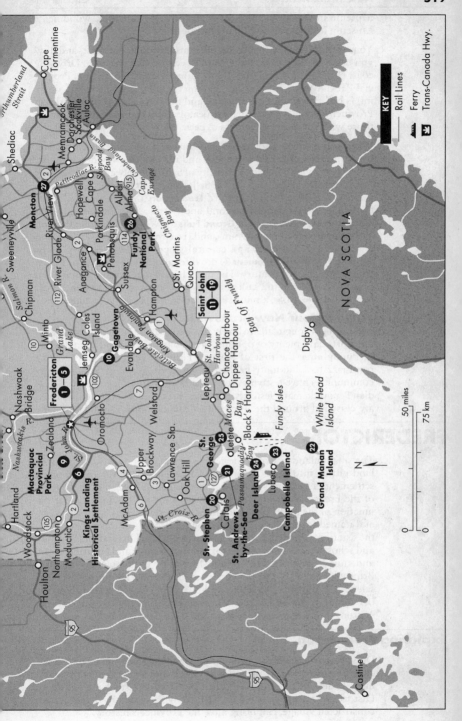

KEY
Rail Lines
Ferry
Trans-Canada Hwy.

NOVA SCOTIA

Northumberland Strait

Cape Tormentine

Shediac

Sweeneyville

Memramcook
Dorchester
Sackville
Aulac

Moncton 27 2

River View
River Glade

Salmon R.

Chipman

Minto 10

Nashwaak
Nashwaak Bridge
Zealand

Fredericton 1-5

Mactaquac Provincial Park

Hartland

Woodstock 105
Northampton
Meductic

Houlton 95

Petitcodiac R.

Hopewell Cape
Parkindale
Anagance
Penobsquis 114
Sussex

Albert 915
Cape Enragé
Alma 26

Fundy National Park

Chignecto Bay

Shepody Bay
Cumberland Basin

St. Martins
Quaco

Hampton

Saint John 11 12

Bay of Fundy

Digby

Lepreau
Chance Harbour
Dipper Harbour
Black's Harbour

St. John Harbour

Maces Bay

Fundy Isles

White Head Island

Grand Manan Island 22

Campobello Island

Lubec 24

Deer Island 23

Passamaquoddy Bay

St. Andrews by-the-Sea 21
Calais 20
St. Stephen

Oak Hill 3
Lawrence Sta.
Upper Brockway

St. George 25
127

Welsford 7

Oromocto 4
McAdam 6

Kings Landing Historical Settlement

St. Croix R.

Castine

Jemseg
Coles Island
Grand Lake
Gagetown 10
Evandale
102
Belleisle Bay
Kingston Peninsula

N

0   50 miles
0   75 km

Museum in Doaktown and the Central New Brunswick Woodmen's Museum in Boisetown tell much of the story.

Your explorations of the Acadian Peninsula end in Bathurst, and now you begin the ride over to the western edge of the province. Drive the coast (114 km, or 71 mi) to Campbellton and nearby Sugarloaf Provincial Park. Route 17 from Campbellton to St. Leonard (159 km, or 99 mi) is breathtaking in the autumn, and the detour to Mount Carleton Provincial Park (with the highest peak in the Maritimes) is a must for those who value the wilderness experience.

When you reach St. Leonard, you are on the River Valley Scenic Drive, which begins upriver in **St-Jacques** and runs all the way down the St. John River valley and back to the city of Saint John. Begin with the New Brunswick Botanical Gardens in St-Jacques, just outside ⊞ **Edmundston** ⑦. The drive from here to ⊞ **Fredericton** ①–⑤ is about 275 km (171 miles) of panoramic pastoral and river scenery, including a dramatic gorge and waterfall at **Grand Falls** ⑧. With its Gothic cathedral, Victorian architecture, museums, and riverfront pathways, Fredericton is a beautiful, historical and cultural stopping place. Nearby **Kings Landing Historical Settlement** ⑥ provides a faithful depiction of life on the river in the last century. The drive from Fredericton to Saint John is just over 100 km (62 mi); about halfway between the two is the village of **Gagetown** ⑩, a must-see for those who love art and history.

When to Tour New Brunswick

Late spring through fall are lovely times to visit, although lovers of winter sports have plenty of options. Whales are more plentiful in the Bay of Fundy after the first of August. Festivals celebrating everything from jazz to salmon are held from late spring until early fall. Many communities have festivities for Canada Day (July 1), and on the Acadian Peninsula many festivals, including the unique Blessing of the Fleet, are clustered around the August 15 Acadian national holiday.

FREDERICTON

The small inland city of Fredericton spreads itself on a broad point of land jutting into the St. John River. Its predecessor, the early French settlement of St. Anne's Point, was established in 1642, during the reign of the French governor Villebon, who made his headquarters at the junction of the Nashwaak and the St. John rivers. Settled by Loyalists and named for Frederick, second son of George III, the city serves as the seat of government for New Brunswick's 723,900 residents. Wealthy and scholarly Loyalists set out to create a gracious and beautiful place, and thus even before the establishment of the University of New Brunswick, in 1785, the town served as a center for liberal arts and sciences. It remains a gracious and beautiful place as well as a center of education, arts, and culture. The river, once the only highway to Fredericton, is now a focus of recreation.

Exploring Fredericton

Downtown Queen Street runs parallel with the river, and its blocks enclose historic sites and attractions. Most major sights are within walking distance of one another other. An excursion to Kings Landing Historical Settlement (☞ Side Trip from Fredericton, *below*), a reconstructed village, can bring alive the province's history.

Dressed in 18th-century costume, actors from the Calithumpians theater company (☎ 506/457–1975) offer free historical walks from City Hall in July and August. Other tours can be arranged.

A Good Walk

Start at City Hall on Phoenix Square, at the corner of York and Queen streets. Once a farmer's market and opera house, its modern council chambers are decorated with tapestries that illustrate Fredericton's history. Walk down (as the river flows) Queen Street to Carleton Street to the **Military Compound** ①, which includes the New Brunswick Sports Hall of Fame and the **York-Sunbury Museum** ②, the latter occupying what used to be the Officers' Quarters in Officers' Square. Here the Calithumpians offer outdoor comedy theater at lunchtime (☞ Nightlife and the Arts, *below*). On a rainy day the show goes on in the nearby College of Craft and Design. The next stop down the river side of Queen Street is the **Beaverbrook Art Gallery** ③, with its sculpture garden outside. Turn right on Church Street and walk to **Christ Church Cathedral** ④, with gleaming new copper on its steeple. Once you have had your fill of its exquisite architecture and stained glass, turn right and start walking back up Queen. The **Provincial Legislature** ⑤ is on your left. Restaurants and cafés along Queen Street provide opportunities for refreshment. If you make your way back to **York Street** (across from where you started at City Hall), turn left to visit a chic block of shops. One variation to this walk: If you're touring on Saturday, start in the morning with the **Boyce Farmers' Market** to get a real taste of the city.

TIMING

The distances are not long, so the time you spend depends on how much you like sports, history, art, and churches. You could do it all in an afternoon, but start at the Boyce Farmers' Market on Saturday.

Sights to See

③ **Beaverbrook Art Gallery.** This museum, a lasting gift of the late Lord Beaverbrook, a former New Brunswick resident and multimillionaire British newspaper magnate, holds some impressive collections of historic and contemporary art. Dali's gigantic *Santiago el Grande* is here, as well as canvasses by Reynolds, Turner, Hogarth, Gainsborough, and the Canadian Group of Seven, landscape painters of the early 20th century. The gallery also has a major collection of works by Cornelius Krieghoff, a famous Canadian landscape painter of the early 1800s. The McCain "gallery-within-a-gallery" is devoted to the finest Atlantic Canadian artists. ⊠ *703 Queen St.,* ☎ *506/458–8545.* ☜ *$3.* ☉ *Mid-June–early-Sept., weekdays 9–6, weekends 10–5; mid-Sept.–mid-June, Tues.–Fri. 9–5, Sat. 10–5, Sun. noon–5.*

Boyce Farmers' Market. It's hard to miss this Saturday-morning market because of the crowds. There's lots of local meat and produce, as well as baked goods, crafts, and seasonal items from wreaths to maple syrup. The market sells good ready-to-eat food, from German sausages to tasty sandwiches. ⊠ *Bounded by Regent, Brunswick, and George Sts.*

④ **Christ Church Cathedral.** One of Fredericton's prides, this gray stone building, completed in 1853, is an excellent example of decorated Gothic architecture. The cathedral's design was based on an actual medieval prototype in England, and it became a model for many American churches. Inside you'll see a clock known as "Big Ben's little brother," the test run for London's famous timepiece, designed by Lord Grimthorpe. ⊠ *Church St.,* ☎ *506/450–8500.* ☉ *Daily, but call ahead; free tours June–Aug., daily 9–9.*

① **Military Compound.** The restored buildings of this British and Canadian post, which extends two blocks along Queen Street, include soldiers' barracks, a guardhouse, and a cell block. Redcoats stand guard in Officers' Square, and a formal changing-of-the-guard ceremony takes place in summer at 11 and 7. Within the compound is the John

522

Beaverbrook
Art Gallery, **3**

Christ Church
Cathedral, **4**

Military
Compound
(Parade
Grounds,
Guardhouse,
Soldiers'
Barracks), **1**

Provincial
Legislature, **5**

York-Sunbury
Museum, **2**

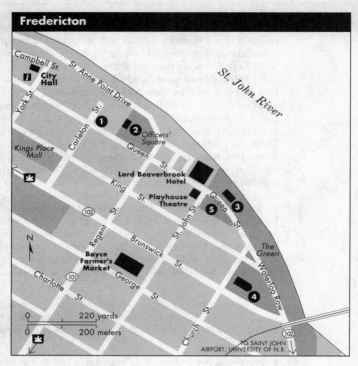

Thursten Clark Building—an outstanding example of Second Empire architecture, now the home of the **New Brunswick Sports Hall of Fame.** At press time the city was entertaining proposals for restaurants, boutiques, and an art center to be added to the Military Compound. ⊠ *Queen St. at Carleton St.,* ☎ *506/453–2324.* ☒ *Free.*

❺ Provincial Legislature. The interior chamber of the legislature, where the premier and elected members govern the province, reflects the taste of the late Victorians. The chandeliers are brass and the prisms are Waterford. Replicas of portraits by Sir Joshua Reynolds of King George III and Queen Charlotte hang here. There is a freestanding staircase, and a volume of Audubon's *Birds of America* is on display. ⊠ *Queen St.,* ☎ *506/453–2527.* ☒ *Free.* ☉ *Legislature tours June–Aug., daily 9–6; Sept.–May, weekdays 9–4; library weekdays 8:15–5.*

York Street. This is the city's high-fashion block, with trendy shops, a hairdresser–cum–art dealer, and an incense-burning boutique. About the middle of the upriver side of the block is Mazucca's Alley, with more shops and the gateway to several pubs and restaurants.

❷ York-Sunbury Museum. The Officers' Quarters houses a museum that offers a living picture of the community from the time when only First Nations peoples inhabited the area, through the Acadian and Loyalist days, to the immediate past. Its penny-farthing bicycle looks impossible to ride, and its World War I trench puts you in the thick of battle. It also contains the shellacked remains of a Fredericton legend, the puzzling Coleman Frog. ⊠ *Officers' Sq., Queen St.,* ☎ *506/455–6041.* ☒ *$2.* ☉ *May–Labor Day, Mon.–Sat. 10–6 (also July–Aug., Mon. and Fri. 10–9, Sun. noon–6); Labor Day–mid-Oct., weekdays 9–5, Sat. noon–4; mid-Oct.–Apr., Mon., Wed., and Fri. 11–3, or by appointment.*

Dining

$$–$$$ ╳ **Jason's Cafe Parador.** Dinner is intimate and Continental, paella is the star of the regular menu, and the evening specials are delightful. The breakfast menu includes an English Muse mixed grill, and the extensive lunch menu lists such daily specials as *tourtière* (meat pie) and mussels. ⊠ *74 Regent St.,* ☎ *506/457–2692. MC, V.*

$–$$$ ╳ **Lobster Hut.** A 200-gallon tank stocked with 1- to 2-pound (and sometimes larger) lobsters adds the finishing touch to the nautical decor of this popular spot. A large variety of seafood as well as some "Shore Things" and lots of words of wisdom fill the menu. The high end of the price range depends on the market price of lobster. ⊠ *City Motel, 1216 Regent St.,* ☎ *506/455–4413. AE, MC, V.*

$–$$ ╳ **Mei's Chinese Restaurant.** In this family operation downtown, mother Mei does all the cooking. She serves a variety of Chinese cuisine, including Szechuan, Cantonese, and Taiwanese; dumplings are a house specialty. Sushi is available if you call a day in advance. The decor is basic. This is a very popular spot for lunch weekdays. ⊠ *73 Carlton St.,* ☎ *506/454–2177. AE, MC, V. No lunch weekends.*

Lodging

$$$ ⊡ **Lord Beaverbrook Hotel.** A central location is this modern, seven-story hotel's main attraction. Some rooms have whirlpool baths or minibars. A veranda off the main dining room overlooks the river, and the bar is lively. ⊠ *659 Queen St., E3B 5A6,* ☎ *506/455–3371,* FAX *506/455–1441. 168 rooms. 2 restaurants, bar, no-smoking rooms, indoor pool, hot tub. AE, DC, MC, V.*

$$–$$$ ⊡ **Sheraton Fredericton Hotel.** This stately riverside property is within walking distance of downtown. The elegant country decor is almost as delightful as the sunset views over the river from the restaurant and many of the modern rooms. The gift shop carries top-notch crafts. ⊠ *225 Woodstock Rd., E3B 2H8,* ☎ *506/457–7000,* FAX *506/457–4000. 208 rooms. 15 suites. Restaurant, bar, minibars, indoor pool, outdoor pool, hot tub, sauna, exercise room. AE, DC, MC, V.*

$–$$ ⊡ **Carriage House Inn.** The lovely bedrooms at this Heritage Inn Association mansion are furnished with Victorian antiques. Homemade breakfast, complete with homemade maple syrup for the fluffy pancakes, is served in the solarium. Breakfast is included in the rates. ⊠ *230 University Ave., E3B 4H7,* ☎ *506/452–9924 or 800/267–6068,* FAX *506/458–0799. 10 rooms, 6 with bath. AE, DC, MC, V.*

$ ⊡ **Howard Johnson Motor Lodge.** This HoJo is on the north side of the river and at the north end of the Princess Margaret Bridge. It has a terrace bar in a pleasant interior courtyard overlooked by the balconies of many of the rooms. Guest-room decor is standard for the chain. ⊠ *Trans-Canada Hwy., Box 1414, E3B 5E3,* ☎ *506/472–0480 or 800/596–4656,* FAX *506/472–0170. 116 rooms. Restaurant, bar, indoor pool, driving range, miniature golf, 4 tennis courts, exercise room. AE, D, DC, MC, V.*

Nightlife and the Arts

The Arts

Some top musicians and other performers appear at the **Aitken Center** (⊠ Rte. 102, ☎ 506/453–5054) on the University of New Brunswick campus near Fredericton. The **Calithumpians** offer summer outdoor theater daily (12:15 weekdays, 2 PM weekends) in Officers' Square. The **Playhouse** (⊠ 686 Queen St., ☎ 506/458–8344) is the venue for theater and most other cultural performances, including Symphony New Brunswick and traveling ballet and dance companies. **Theatre New**

Brunswick (⊠ 686 Queen St., ☎ 506/458–8344) performs in the
Playhouse and tours the province.

Nightlife

Fredericton has lively nightlife, with lots of live music in downtown
pubs, especially on the weekends. King Street and Piper's Lane, off the
300 block of King Street, have a number of spots. The **Dock** (⊠ 375
King St., ☎ 506/458–1254) is a venue for rock, blues, folk—anything
but country. **Dolan's Pub** (⊠ 349 King St., ☎ 506/454–7474) has Celtic
and folk-style entertainment. The **Lunar Rogue** (⊠ 625 King St., ☎
506/450–2065) has an Old World pub atmosphere and showcases acoustic folk, rock, and Celtic music. **Picaroons Brewery and Tap Room** (⊠
366 Queen St., ☎ 506/454–8277 offers easy-listening Canadian-con-
tent music plus free brewery tours.

Outdoor Activities and Sports

Canoeing and Kayaking

Shells, canoes, and kayaks can be rented by the hour, day, or week at
the **Small Craft Aquatic Center** (⊠ Woodstock Rd., behind the Victoria Health Centre, ☎ 506/462–6021), which also arranges guided tours
and instruction.

Dogsledding

Dunbar Valley Adventures (⊠ 633 Rte. 8, Durham Bridge E62 2C9,
☎ 506/450–9612), just outside Fredericton, has drive-your-own-team
dogsledding. The adventure can last from two hours to two days.

Skiing

Ski Crabbe Mountain (⊠ Box 1612, Truro B2N 5VE, ☎ 506/463–8311)
is in Lower Hainesville (about 55 km, or 34 mi, west of Fredericton).
There are 15 trails, a vertical drop of 853 ft, snowboard and ski
rentals, instruction, baby-sitting, and a lounge and restaurant.

Walking

Fredericton has a fine network of walking trails, one of which follows
the river from the Green, past the Victorian mansions on Waterloo Row,
behind the Beaverbrook Art Gallery, and along the riverbank to the
Sheraton. Its total length is more than 3 km (2 mi), but you can do
shorter pieces. The visitor information center in City Hall (☎ 506/460–
2087) has a trail map.

Shopping

Mammoth **crafts markets** are held occasionally in Fredericton and every
Labor Day weekend in Mactaquac Provincial Park (☞ St. John River
Valley to Saint John, *below*). For sale are pottery, blown glass, pressed
flowers, metal flowers, turned wood, leather, quilts, and other items,
many made by members of the New Brunswick Craft Council.

Aitkens Pewter (⊠ 65 Regent St., ☎ 506/453–9474) specializes in
pewter goblets, belt buckles, and jewelry. **Botinicals Gift Shop** (⊠ 65
Shore St., ☎ 506/454–7361) sells crafts by juried New Brunswick artisans only. **Gallery 78** (⊠ 96 Queen St., ☎ 506/454–5192) has works
by local artists. Excellent men's shoes can be bought at **Hartt's Shoe
Factory** (⊠ 401 York St., ☎ 506/458–8358). The **Linen Closet** (⊠ 397
King St., ☎ 506/450–8393) sells Battenburg lace, exquisite bedding,
and bathroom accessories. **Mulhouse Country Classics** (⊠ 225 Woodstock Rd., ☎ 506/450–8415) in the Sheraton is a gem for crafts,
Tilley Endurables clothing, and handmade furniture.

Side Trip from Fredericton

The Kings Landing Historical Settlement was built by moving period buildings to a new shore. The drive here takes less than a half hour, and to appreciate the museum, plan to spend at least half a day. The Trans-Canada Highway travels through some spectacular river and hill scenery on the way and passes the Mactaquac Dam (turn off here if you want to visit Mactaquac Provincial Park).

Kings Landing Historical Settlement

★ ☁ ❻ *30 km (19 mi) west of Fredericton.*

This excellent outdoor living-history museum on the St. John River evokes the sights, sounds, and society of rural New Brunswick between 1790 and 1900. The winding country lanes and meticulously restored homes pull you back a century or more, and the staff demonstrates how to forge a nail at the blacksmith's shop or bake bread on an open hearth. There are daily dramas in the theater, barn dances, and strolling minstrels. You'll see how the wealthy owner of the sawmill lived and just how different things were for the lowly immigrant farmer or the storekeeper. Hearty meals are served at the Kings Head Inn. ⊠ *Exit 259, Trans-Canada Hwy. (near Prince William),* ☎ *506/363–4999.* ☞ *$9.* ☉ *June–mid-Oct., daily 10–5.*

ST. JOHN RIVER VALLEY TO SAINT JOHN

The St. John River forms 120 km (74 mi) of the border with Maine and rolls down to Saint John, New Brunswick's largest, and Canada's oldest, city. Gentle hills of rich farmland and the blue sweep of the water make this a pretty drive. The Trans-Canada Highway (Route 2) follows the banks of the river for most of its winding, 403-km (250-mi) course. In the early 1800s the narrow wedge of land at the northern end of the valley was coveted by Québec and New Brunswick; the United States claimed it as well. To settle the issue, New Brunswick governor Sir Thomas Carleton rolled dice with the governor of British North America at Québec. Sir Thomas won—by one point. Settling the border with the Americans was more difficult; even the lumbermen engaged in combat. Finally, in 1842, the British flag was hoisted over Madawaska county. One old-timer, tired of being asked to which country he belonged, replied, "I am a citizen of the Republic of Madawaska." So began the mythical republic, which exists today with its own flag (an eagle on a field of white) and a coat of arms.

St-Jacques

280 km (174 mi) north of Fredericton.

This town near the Québec border contains Les Jardins de la République Provincial Park, with recreational facilities, the Antique Auto Museum, and a botanical garden. In the **New Brunswick Botanical Garden,** roses, rhododendrons, alpine flowers, and dozens of other annuals and perennials bloom in the eight gardens. The music of Mozart, Handel, Bach, or Vivaldi often plays in the background. Two arboretums have coniferous and deciduous trees and shrubs. ⊠ *Main St.,* ☎ *506/737-5383.* ☞ *$4.75.* ☉ *June–Sept., daily 9–dusk.*

Outdoor Activities and Sports

Mont Farlagne (⊠ 360 Mont Farlagne Rd., St-Jacques E7B 2X1, ☎ 506/735-8401), near Edmundston, has 17 trails for downhill skiing on a vertical drop of 600 ft. Its four lifts can handle 4,000 skiers per hour, and there is night skiing on six trails. Snowboarding and tube sliding add to the fun.

Edmundston

❼ *5 km (3 mi) south of St-Jacques, 275 km (171 mi) northwest of Fredericton.*

Edmundston, the unofficial capital of Madawaska, has always depended on the wealth of the deep forest around it. Even today, the town looks to the Fraser Company pulp mills as the major source of employment. In these woods the legend of Paul Bunyan was born; tales spread to Maine and beyond. The annual **Foire Brayonne** (☎ 506/739–6608), held the last week of July, is the biggest Francophone festival outside of Québec's Winter Carnival. It is one of the most lively and vibrant cultural events in New Brunswick, with concerts by acclaimed artists as well as local musicians and entertainers.

Lodging

$–$$ 🏨 **Howard Johnson Hotel & Convention Centre.** Its downtown location near the town's riverside walking trail (complete with a walking bridge across the river) and a small restaurant that has the services of talented chefs recommend this chain property. ⊠ *100 Rice St., E3V 1T4,* ☎ *506/739–7321 or 800-576-4656,* ℻ *506/725–9101. 99 rooms. Restaurant, indoor pool, hot tub, sauna, meeting rooms. AE, D, DC, MC, V.*

Grand Falls

❽ *50 km (31 mi) south of Edmunston.*

At Grand Falls, the St. John throws itself over a high cliff, squeezes through a narrow rocky gorge, and emerges as a wider river. The result is a magnificent cascade, whose force has worn strange round wells in the rocky bed—some as much as 16 ft in circumference and 30 ft deep. A **pontoon boat** operates June–October at the lower end of the gorge and offers an entirely new perspective of the cliffs and wells. Tickets are available at the Malabeam Tourist Info Centre. ⊠ *24 Madawaska Rd.,* ☎ *506/475–7788.* 🎫 *$8.*

The **Gorge Walk,** which starts at the tourist information center (⊠ 24 Madawaska Rd.) and covers the full length of the gorge, is dotted with interpretation panels and monuments. There is no charge for the walk, unless you descend to the wells ($2). According to native legend, a young maiden named Malabeam led her Iroquois captors to their deaths over the foaming cataract rather than guide them to her village.

The **Grand Falls Historical Museum** depicts local history. ⊠ *209 Sheriff St.,* ☎ *506/473–5265.* 🎫 *Free.* ☉ *July–Aug., Mon.–Sat. 9–5, Sun. 2–5; Sept.–June, by appointment.*

En Route   About 75 km (47 mi) south of Grand Falls, stop in **Florenceville** for a look at the small but reputable Andrew and Laura McCain Gallery (⊠ McCain St., ☎ 506/392–5249), which has launched the career of many New Brunswick artists. The Trans-Canada Highway is intriguingly scenic, but if you're looking for less-crowded highways and typical small communities, cross the river to Route 105 at Hartland (about 20 km, or 12 mi, south of Florenceville), via the **longest covered bridge** in the world—1,282 ft in length.

Mactaquac Provincial Park

⚓ ❾ *197 km (122 mi) south of Grand Falls.*

Within Mactaquac Provincial Park is Mactaquac Pond, whose existence is attributed to the building of the hydroelectric dam that has caused the upper St. John River to flood as far up as Woodstock. Park facilities include an 18-hole golf course, two beaches with lifeguards, two marinas, supervised crafts activities, and a restaurant. Reservations are advised for the 300 campsites in high season. A privately operated power-boat marina within the park rents canoes, paddleboats, windsurfers, and kayaks. ✉ *Rte. 105 at Mactaquac Dam,* ☎ *506/363–4747.* 🎫 *$3.50 per vehicle in summer, free off-season.* ⊙ *Daily; overnight camping mid-May–Thanksgiving.*

En Route From Fredericton to Saint John there is a choice of two routes. Route 7 cuts away from the river to run straight south for its fast 109 km (68 mi). Route 102 leads along the St. John River through engaging communities. You don't have to decide until Oromocto, the site of the Canadian Armed Forces Base, **Camp Gagetown** (not to be confused with the pretty town of Gagetown farther downriver), the largest military base in Canada. Prince Charles completed his helicopter training here. The base has an interesting military museum. ✉ *Museum, Building A5, off Tilley St.,* ☎ *506/422–1304.* 🎫 *Museum free.* ⊙ *July–Aug., weekdays 9–5, weekends and holidays noon–5; Sept.–June, weekdays noon–4. After-hrs tours by arrangement.*

Gagetown

❿ *50 km (31 mi) southeast of Fredericton.*

Historic Gagetown bustles with artisans' studios and the summer sailors who tie up at the marina. The gingerbread-trimmed **Tilley House** was once the home of Sir Leonard Tilley, one of the fathers of the Confederation. It now houses the **Queens County Museum.** ✉ *Front St.,* ☎ *506/488–2966.* 🎫 *$1.* ⊙ *Mid-June–mid-Sept., daily 10–5.*

Shopping

Claremont House B&B (✉ Tilley Rd., ☎ 506/488–2825) displays unusual batik items and copper engravings. **Flo Grieg's** (✉ 36 Front St., ☎ 506/488–2074) carries superior pottery made on the premises. **Loomcrofters** (✉ Loomcroft La. off Main St., ☎ 506/488–2400) is a good choice for handwoven items.

OFF THE BEATEN PATH   From Gagetown it's possible to take a ferry across the river to Jemseg and continue to **Grand Lake Park** (☎ 506/385–2919), which offers freshwater swimming off the sandy beaches of Grand Lake. At Evandale (30 km, or 19 mi) south of Gagetown, there's a ferry to Belleisle Bay and the beautiful **Kingston Peninsula,** with its mossy Loyalist graveyards and pretty churches.

Saint John

70 km (43 mi) south of Gagetown.

Saint John, the first incorporated city (1785) in Canada, has that weather-beaten quality common to so many other antique seaport communities. Although the city is sometimes termed a blue-collar town because many of its residents work for Irving Oil, its genteel Loyalist heritage lingers; you sense it in the grand old buildings, the ladies' teas at the old Union Club, and the lovingly restored redbrick buildings of the downtown harbor district.

In 1604 two Frenchmen, Samuel de Champlain and Sieur de Monts, landed here on St. John the Baptist Day to trade with the natives. Nearly two centuries later, in May 1783, 3,000 Loyalists escaping from the aftermath of the Revolutionary War poured off a fleet of ships to found a city amid the rocks and forests. From those beginnings, Saint John has emerged as a shipbuilding center and a thriving industrial port.

Up until the early 1980s, the buildings around Saint John's waterfront huddled together in forlorn dilapidation, their facades crumbling and blurred by a century of grime. A surge of civic pride sparked a major renovation project that reclaimed these old warehouses as part of a successful waterfront development.

The city has spawned many of the province's major artists—Jack Humphrey, Millar Brittain, and Fred Ross—along with such Hollywood notables as Louis B. Mayer, Donald Sutherland, and Walter Pidgeon. There's also a large Irish population that emerges in a jubilant Irish Festival every March. In July costumed residents reenact the landing of the Loyalists during the Loyalist City Festival.

Brochures for three good self-guided city tours are available at information centers, including one in Market Square. In July and August, free guided walking tours begin at 10 and 2 in Market Square at Barbour's General Store. For information call the Saint John Tourist and Convention Center (☎ 506/658–2990).

A Good Walk

Saint John is a city on hills, and **King Street** ⑪, its main street, slopes steeply to the harbor. A system of escalators/elevators and skywalks inside buildings means you can climb to the top and take in some of the more memorable spots without effort; you can also walk outside if you wish. Start at the foot of King, **Market Slip** ⑫. This is where the Loyalists landed in 1783 and is the site of **Barbour's General Store** and the Little Red Schoolhouse. Here you'll also find **Market Square,** with its visitor information center, restaurants, shops, and the fine **New Brunswick Museum** ⑬.

From the second level of Market Square, a skywalk crosses Dock Street and an escalator takes you up into the City Hall shopping concourse. Here, if you wish, you can branch off to the Canada Games Aquatic Centre and its pools and fitness facilities, or to Harbour Station, with its busy schedule of concerts, sporting events, and trade shows. Once you are through City Hall, another skywalk takes you across Chipman Hill and into the **Brunswick Square Complex** of shops, hotel, and office space. To visit historic **Loyalist House** ⑭, exit onto Germain Street and turn left: it's on the corner at the top of the hill. In the flavorful **Old City Market** ⑮, across from Brunswick Square, you'll make your way past fishmongers, farmers, and craftspeople. When you leave by the door at the top of the market, you will be at "the head of King" and right across Charlotte Street from **King Square** ⑯. Take a walk through the square, past the statues and bandstand, to Sydney Street. Cross Sydney and you're in the **Loyalist Burial Grounds** ⑰. Make your way back to Sydney Street and then cross King Street East to the **Old Courthouse** ⑱ with its spiral staircase. Continue up Sydney; turn right on King Square South and you're at the handsome Imperial Theatre (☞ Nightlife and the Arts, *below*). Follow King Square South and cross Charlotte Street to reach the back door of historic **Trinity Church** ⑲. You can enter this way or walk back to King Street, turn left, and turn left onto Germain Street for the imposing gates and stairs of Trinity's main entrance.

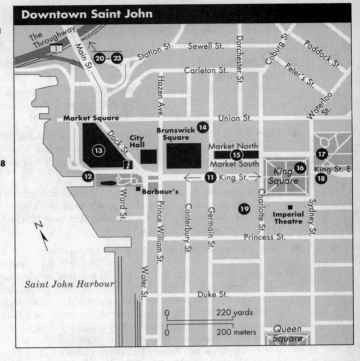

To end your walk, make your way back to King Street and walk down
the hill toward the water. You'll notice a plaque near the corner of Can-
terbury Street (at 20 King Street) that identifies a site where Benedict
Arnold operated a coffeehouse. At the foot of the hill is **Prince William
Street,** just steps from where you began at Market Slip. Turn left for
shops and historic architecture.

TIMING

Allow the better part of a day for this walk, if you include a few hours
for the New Brunswick Museum and some time for shopping. You can
walk the route in a couple of hours, though. On Sunday some of the
indoor walkways will be closed, and so will the City Market.

Sights to See

Barbour's General Store. This 19th-century shop, now a museum, is
filled with the aromas of tobacco, smoked fish, peppermint sticks, and
dulse, an edible seaweed. ⊠ *Market Slip,* ☎ *506/658–2939.*

Brunswick Square Complex. Buildings here include the Delta Brunswick
Hotel and Brunswick Square, a multilevel mall and office tower. The
major office-tower tenant is NB Tel, an innovative communications company. ⊠ *Between Prince William and Germain Sts.*

16 **King Square.** Laid out in a Union Jack pattern, this green refuge has
a two-story bandstand and a number of monuments. The strange mass
of metal on the ground in its northeast corner is actually a great lump
of melted stock from a neighboring hardware store that was demolished in Saint John's Great Fire of 1877, in which hundreds of buildings were destroyed. ⊠ *Between Charlotte and Sydney Sts.*

11 **King Street.** The steep main street of the city is lined with solid Victorian redbrick buildings filled with a variety of shops.

⓱ **Loyalist Burial Grounds.** This cemetery, now a landscaped park, is like a history book published in stone. Brick walkways and a beaver-dam fountain make it a delightful spot. ⊠ *Off Sydney St. between King and E. Union Sts.*

⓮ **Loyalist House.** David Daniel Merritt, a wealthy Loyalist merchant, built this imposing Georgian structure in 1810. It is distinguished by its authentic period furniture and eight fireplaces. ⊠ *120 Union St.,* ☎ *506/652–3590.* ▣ *$2.* ☉ *Mid-May–June, weekdays 10–5; July–Aug., daily 10–5; Sept.–mid-May, by appointment.*

⓬ **Market Slip.** This waterfront area at the foot of King Street is where the Loyalists landed in 1783. Today it's the site of the Saint John Hilton, an amphitheater, and restaurants, but it still conveys a sense of the city's maritime heritage.

Market Square. Restored buildings on the waterfront have been attractively developed and hold historic exhibits, shops, restaurants, and cafés. Also here are the Saint John Regional Library and the fine ☞ New Brunswick Museum.

★ ☝ ⓭ **New Brunswick Museum.** With three floors of natural history, New Brunswick history, and art galleries, this inviting museum has something for everyone. The full-size suspended right-whale model and skeleton are impossible to miss. You can hike through time on a geologic trail; watch the Bay of Fundy tides rise and fall inside a glass tube that stretches up three flights; encounter the industries that shaped the province, from logging to shipping, in displays that re-create the past; and see fine and decorative art from New Brunswick and around the world. There's also a Family Discovery Gallery and a gift shop. ⊠ *Market Sq.,* ☎ *506/643–2300.* ▣ *$6; free Wed. 6–9 PM.* ☉ *Weekdays 9–9, Sat. 10–6, Sun. noon–5.*

⓯ **Old City Market.** Built in 1876 with a ceiling like an inverted ship's keel, the handsome market occupies a city block between Germain and Charlotte streets. Its temptations include live and fresh-cooked lobsters, great cheeses, dulse, and tasty, inexpensive snacks, along with plenty of souvenir and craft items. ⊠ *47 Charlotte St.,* ☎ *506/658–2820.* ☉ *Mon.–Thurs. 7:30–6, Fri. 7:30–7, Sat. 7:30–5.*

⓲ **Old Courthouse.** This 1829 neoclassical building has a spiral staircase, built of tons of unsupported stones, that ascends for three stories. The staircase can be seen year-round during business hours, except when court is in session. ⊠ *King St. E and Sydney St.* ▣ *Free.*

Prince William Street. South of King Street near Market Slip, this street is full of historic bank and business buildings that now hold shops and galleries. At the foot of the street is the lamp known as the Three Sisters, which was erected in 1848 to guide ships into the harbor.

⓳ **Trinity Church.** The church dates from 1880, when it was rebuilt after the Great Fire. Inside, over the west door, note the coat of arms—a symbol of the monarchy—rescued from the council chamber in Boston by a British colonel during the American Revolution. It was deemed a worthy refugee and given a place of honor in the church. ⊠ *115 Charlotte St.,* ☎ *506/693–8558 for information about hrs.*

A Good Drive

From Market Square, head west in your car (or on any bus) to see the **Reversing Falls.** Go up Dock Street and cross the Viaduct, and you are on Main Street. Drive to the top of the hill and turn left on Douglas Avenue, with its grand old homes. A right off Douglas Avenue onto Fallsview Drive takes you to a Reversing Falls lookout and the Reversing

Falls Jet Boat Ride. Return to Douglas Avenue, turn right, and keep right to cross the Reversing Falls Bridge. At the end of the bridge, on your left, is the Reversing Falls Tourist Bureau and restaurant. The west side is also home to **Carleton Martello Tower.** Turn left from the Reversing Falls Tourist Bureau, past the Simms Brush Factory, and bear left when the road splits. The rest of the way is well marked. You're also near **Irving Nature Park** (off Route 1 at Catherwood Drive if you're on the highway), 600 acres of volcanic rock and forest that are a haven for wildlife. Children will appreciate the more exotic wildlife at **Cherry Brook Zoo,** northeast of downtown.

TIMING

To appreciate the Reversing Falls fully takes time; you need to visit at high, slack, and low tides. Check with any visitor information office for these times to help you plan a visit.

Sights to See

Carleton Martello Tower. The tower, a great place to survey the harbor, was built during the War of 1812 as a precaution against an American attack. Guides will tell you about the spartan life of a soldier living in the stone fort, and an audiovisual presentation outlines its role in the defense of Saint John during World War II. ⊠ *Whipple St. at Fundy Dr.,* ☎ *506/636–4011.* ⊡ *$2.25.* ☉ *June–mid-Oct., daily 9–5.*

☾ **Cherry Brook Zoo.** An entertaining monkey house, wildebeests, and other exotic species are highlights of this small zoo. It's at the northern end of **Rockwood Park** (☎ 506/658–2829), which has plenty of activities. ⊠ *Sandy Point Rd.,* ☎ *506/634–1440.* ⊡ *$4.75.* ☉ *Daily 10–dusk.*

Irving Nature Park. The ecosystems of the southern New Brunswick coast are preserved in this lovely 600-acre park on a peninsula close to downtown. Roads and seven walking trails up to several miles long make bird- and nature-watching easy. From downtown take Route 1 west to Exit 107 (Catherwood Rd.) south; follow Sand Cove Road 4½ km (3 mi) to the park. ⊠ *Sand Cove Rd.,* ☎ *506/634–7135 for seasonal access.* ⊡ *Free.*

Reversing Falls. Twice daily at the Reversing Falls rapids, the strong Fundy tides rise faster than the river can empty, and the tide water attempts to push the river water back upstream. When the tide ebbs, the river once again pours over the rock ledges and the rapids appear to reverse themselves. To learn more about the phenomenon, watch the film shown at the **Reversing Falls Tourist Bureau.** There's a restaurant here, too. A jet boat (☞ Outdoor Activities and Sports, *below*) provides a closer (and wetter) look. A pulp mill on the bank is less scenic, and the smell it occasionally sends out is a less charming part of a visit. ⊠ *Rte. 100, Reversing Falls Bridge,* ☎ *506/658–2937.*

Dining and Lodging

$$–$$$$ ✕ **Grannan's.** Seafood brochette with scallops, shrimp, and lobster tail, sautéed at your table in a white-wine and mushroom sauce, is a favorite in this nautically decorated restaurant, but there are abundant choices. The desserts, including bananas Foster flambéed at your table, are memorable. Dining spills over onto the sidewalk in summer. ⊠ *1 Market Sq.,* ☎ *506/634–1555. AE, DC, MC, V.*

$$–$$$$ ✕ **Incredible Edibles.** Here you can enjoy down-to-earth food—biscuits, garlic-laden hummus, salads, pastas, and desserts—in cozy rooms or, in summer, on the outdoor terrace. The menu also includes beef and chicken dishes. ⊠ *42 Princess St.,* ☎ *506/633–7554. AE, DC, MC, V. Closed Sun.*

$$-$$$ ✕ **Beatty and the Beastro.** Quaint, quirky (check out the specially made plates), and right next door to the Imperial Theatre, this place hops every day at lunchtime as well as before and after the theater. The frequently changing menu, with its distinctive European accent, takes advantage of local and seasonal meat, seafood, and produce. Breads and soups are specialties, with lines on Scotch Broth day (the last stop for the local spring lamb). ⊠ *60 Charlotte St., at King Square,* ☎ *506/ 652–3888. AE, DC, MC, V.*

$$$–$$$$ ✕⊞ **Saint John Hilton.** Part of the Market Square complex, this Hilton is furnished in Loyalist decor; guest rooms overlook the harbor or the town. A pedestrian walkway system connects the 12-story property to uptown shops, restaurants, a library, a museum, an aquatic center, and a civic center. The large Turn of the Tide restaurant has terrific views of the harbor. Although the dining is pleasant at all times, with seafood and meat choices, the best meal is the Sunday brunch, with a long table full of dishes from the exotic to the tried-and-true. ⊠ *1 Market Sq., E2L 4Z6,* ☎ *506/693–8484, 800/561–8282 in Canada,* FAX *506/657–6610. 197 rooms. Restaurant, bar, pool, exercise room. AE, D, DC, MC, V.*

$$–$$$$ ✕⊞ **Shadow Lawn Country Inn.** Ten minutes from Saint John, this
   ★   charming inn is in an affluent suburb with tree-lined streets and palatial houses. Tennis, golf, horseback riding, and a yacht club are nearby. The inn has antiques-furnished bedrooms, some with fireplaces; one suite has a whirlpool bath. The dining room is open to the public for three meals a day; seafood is a specialty. Continental breakfast is included in the room rate. ⊠ *3180 Rothesay Rd., Rothesay E2E 5V7,* ☎ *506/847–7539 or 800/561–4166,* FAX *506/849–9238. 9 rooms, 2 suites. Restaurant. AE, D, DC, MC, V.*

$$–$$$ ⊞ **Inn on the Cove.** Near the Irving Nature Park, and with its back
   ★   lawn terraced down to the ocean, this inn has as much character as its owners, who tape their delightful cooking show in the kitchen. The bedrooms are furnished in local antiques, and several bathrooms include whirlpool tubs with ocean views. The kitchen (dinner is for guests, who must reserve ahead) incorporates the informal Ocean Room with its massive fireplace, dining tables, and wall of windows overlooking the Bay of Fundy. A full breakfast is included in the rate. ⊠ *1371 Sand Cove Rd., E2M 4X7,* ☎ *506/672–7799,* FAX *506/635– 5455. 9 rooms. Dining room. MC, V.*

Nightlife and the Arts

THE ARTS

Aitken Bicentennial Exhibition Centre (ABEC) (⊠ 20 Hazen Ave., ☎ 506/ 633–4870), in a former Carnegie library, has several galleries displaying the work of local artists and artisans, a hands-on science gallery for children, and a spring–fall Listen and Lunch series. Admission is free. The **Imperial Theatre** (⊠ King Sq., ☎ 506/633–9494), a beautifully restored 1913 vaudeville theater, is home to Saint John's theater, opera, ballet, and symphony productions as well as road shows.

NIGHTLIFE

Taverns and lounges, usually with music of some kind, provide lively nightlife. Top musical groups, noted professional singers, and other performers regularly appear at **Harbour Station** (⊠ 99 Station St., ☎ 506/ 657–1234). **O'Leary's Pub** (⊠ 46 Princess St., ☎ 506/634–7135), in the middle of the Trinity Royal Preservation Area, specializes in old-time Irish fun complete with Celtic performers; on Wednesday, Brent Mason, a well-known neo-folk artist, starts the evening and then turns the mike over to the audience. **Tapps Brew Pub and Steak House** (⊠ 78 King St., ☎ 508/634–1957) pleases the over-30 population with jazz and blues.

Outdoor Activities and Sports

BOAT TOURS

Harbor tours are offered by **Partridge Island Tours** (☎ 506/693–2598) and **DMK Marine Tours** (☎ 506/635–4150). The **Reversing Falls Jet Boat** ride (✉ 55 Fallsview Dr., 1 Market Sq., (☎ 506/634–8987 or 506/634–8824) is a 20-minute thrill as you view the Reversing Falls close up. At complete low tide passengers must be 16 years or older; at other times children are welcome. Cost is $20 per person.

KAYAKING

Kayaking along the Fundy coast has become very popular. **Eastern Outdoors** (✉ Brunswick Sq., ☎ 506/634–1530 or 800/565–2925) has single and double kayaks, lessons, tours, and white-water rafting on the Reversing Falls Rapids and other river systems.

Shopping

Brunswick Square (✉ King and Germain Sts., ☎ 506/658–1000), a vertical mall, has many top-quality boutiques. **Handworks Gallery** (✉ 12 King St., ☎ 506/652–9787 or 800/222–1725) carries the best of professional crafts and fine art made in New Brunswick. **House of Tara** (✉ 72 Prince William St., ☎ 506/634–8272) is wonderful for fine Irish linens and woolens. **Old City Market,** between Charlotte and Germain streets, bustles Monday–Saturday and stocks delicious local specialties, such as maple syrup and lobster. **Prince William Street** provides interesting browsing in antiques shops and crafts boutiques.

THE FUNDY COAST

Bordering the chilly and powerful tidal Bay of Fundy is some of New Brunswick's most dramatic coastline. A tour extends from the border town of St. Stephen and the lovely resort village of St. Andrews, past tiny fishing villages and rocky coves, to Fundy National Park, where the world's most extreme tides rise and fall twice daily. The Fundy Isles— Grand Manan Island, Deer Island, and Campobello—are havens of peace that have lured harried mainlanders for generations. The impressive 50-km (31-mi) stretch of coastline between St. Martins and Fundy National Park is now accessible by the new Fundy Parkway; the Fundy Footpath (for hikers) and the Fundy Trail (multiuse, but not for motorized vehicles) should be completed during 1999.

St. Stephen

㉒ *107 km (66 mi) west of Saint John.*

St. Stephen is over the St. Croix River from Calais, Maine. There's a provincial visitor information center (☎ 506/466–7390) on King Street. The small town is a mecca for chocoholics, who converge here during the Chocolate Festival held early in August. "Choctails," chocolate puddings and cakes, and even complete chocolate meals should come as no surprise when you learn that the chocolate bar was invented here.Ganong's famed, hand-dipped chocolates are available at the factory store, **Ganong Chocolatier.** ✉ *73 Milltown Blvd.,* ☎ *506/465–5611.* ☉ *Jan.–June, Mon.–Sat. 9–5; July–Aug., weekdays 9–8, weekends 9–5; Sept.–Dec., daily 9–5.*

Crocker Hill Studios and Gardens, on the bank of the St. Croix River, is an oasis of beauty 3 km (2 mi) east of downtown. Around their cottage home and bright studio, artist Steve Smith and his wife, Gail, have created a garden full of color and surprises. A carefully pruned apple tree hides two weathered chairs in a complete "leaf room," and a sculpture of copper leaves drips fresh water into a clay pool where the birds splash. Paintings, decoys, herbs and other garden delights are sold in the gift shop. ⊠ *Ledge Rd., R.R. 3,* ☎ *506/466–4251.* ⊡ *$3.* ☉ *June– Sept., daily 10–5; Oct.–May, by appointment or chance.*

St. Andrews by-the-Sea

★ **㉑** *29 km (18 mi) southeast of St. Stephen.*

On Passamaquoddy Bay, St. Andrews by-the-Sea is one of North America's prettiest and least-spoiled resort towns. Long a summer retreat of the affluent (mansions ring the town), St. Andrews retains its year-round population of fishers, and little has changed in the past two centuries. Of the town's 550 buildings, 280 were erected before 1880; 14 have survived from the 1700s. Some Loyalists even brought their homes with them piece by piece from Castile, Maine, across the bay, when the American Revolution didn't go their way.

Pick up a walking-tour map at the visitor information center at 46 Reed Avenue (next to the arena) and follow it through the pleasant streets. A particular gem is the **Court House** (⊠ 123 Frederick St., ☎ 506/529–4248), which is still active. Within these old stone walls is the **Old Gaol**, home of the county's archives. Tours are given weekdays 9–5. **Greenock Church,** at the corner of Montague and Edward streets, owes its existence to a remark someone made at an 1822 dinner party about the "poor" Presbyterians' not having a church of their own. Captain Christopher Scott, who took exception to the slur, spared no expense on the building, which is decorated with a carving of a green oak tree in honor of Scott's birthplace, Greenock, Scotland. **Water Street,** down by the harbor, has an assortment of eateries, gift and crafts shops, and artists' studios.

The **Ross Memorial Museum** is a monument to an American family, summer residents of St. Andrews, who really appreciated beautiful things. Lovely 19th-century New Brunswick furniture and objets d'art fill the rooms. ⊠ *188 Montague St.,* ☎ *506/529–1824.* ⊡ *Free.* ☉ *Late May–June and early Oct., Mon.–Sat. 10–4:30; July–Sept., Mon.–Sat. 10–4:30, Sun. 1:30–4:30; shoulder seasons, Tues.–Sat. 10–4:30.*

Kingsbrae Gardens incorporates 27 acres of mature cedar hedges and rare Acadian old-growth forest from several fine estates with creative new plantings. Display gardens with exotic flowers border the pathways, and towering trees line the woodland trail. Demonstration gardens, a maze and a rose garden, a white garden, a knot garden, and a day-lily collection complete the horticultural experience. A café, art gallery, and gift shop are housed in a stately mansion. ⊠ *220 King St.,* ☎ *506/529–3335.* ⊡ *$6.* ☉ *May–Oct., daily 9–dusk.*

☾ The **Huntsman Aquarium and Museum** houses marine life and displays, including some very entertaining seals fed at 11 and 4 daily. ⊠ *Brandy Cove Rd.,* ☎ *506/529–1202.* ⊡ *$4.50.* ☉ *May–June, daily 10–4:30; July–Aug., daily 10–6; Sept.–Oct., Mon.–Tues. noon–4:30, Wed.– Sun. 10–4:30.*

OFF THE BEATEN PATH   **MINISTERS ISLAND –** This huge island estate with its Covenhoven mansion (not fully restored) was the summer home of Sir William Van Horne, chairman of the Canadian Pacific Railway from 1899 to 1915. Getting here is an adventure: Cars line up on the Bar Road at low tide (check local schedules) and drive across the sand bar for a tour. A 15-year rejuvenation project is under way and includes plans to convert the coach house into artists' living quarters and studios. Carriage rides are offered along the 20 km (12 mi) of carriage lanes created in 1902. ⊠ *Bar Rd. (5 km, or 3 mi, north of St. Andrews),* ☎ *506/529–5081 for tour information.* ⊡ *$5.* ☉ *Open June–Oct., daylight hrs at low tide.*

Dining and Lodging

$–$$$ ✕ **The Gables.** Salads, fish, and seafood fried or grilled as well as fresh-made desserts are served in this casual harborside eatery. There's a deck for alfresco dining in summer. ✉ *143 Water St.,* ☎ *506/529–3440. MC, V.*

$$$$ ✕🛏 **The Algonquin.** The wraparound veranda of this grand old resort
★ hotel overlooks wide lawns and lush gardens, and the bellmen wear kilts, setting a mood of relaxed elegance. Rooms, especially those in a new wing, are comfortable and attractively decorated. The Passamaquoddy Dining Room is noted for its seafood and for regional dishes such as seared pork loin with local blueberry balsamic vinegar sauce. In good weather, meals are served on the veranda. There are fewer services in winter, so call if you plan to visit then. ✉ *Rte. 127, E0G 2X0,* ☎ *506/529–8823,* FAX *506/529–4194. 250 rooms. 2 restaurants, 2 bars, pool, 9-hole golf and 18-hole golf courses, tennis courts, health club, bicycles. AE, DC, MC, V.*

$$$–$$$$ ✕🛏 **Pansy Patch.** A visit to this B&B, a Normandy-style farmhouse
★ built in 1912, is a bit like a close encounter with landed gentry who are patrons of the arts and who like their gardens as rich and formal as their meals. Four rooms are in the Corey Cottage next door. There's an art gallery. Breakfast is included in the price, and nonguests are welcome for lunch and dinner. ✉ *59 Carleton St., E0G 2X0,* ☎ *506/529–3834 or 888/726–7972,* FAX *506/529–9042. 9 rooms. Restaurant. D, MC, V. Closed mid-Oct.–mid-May.*

$$$$ 🛏 **A. Hiram Walker Estate Heritage Inn.** This restored palatial home, built for the Hiram Walker Distillery family in 1912, is gracious, elegant, and welcoming. All the rooms have fireplaces; most have whirlpool baths. You can ask the owner about everything from the mustard she serves with your breakfast ham to the chandelier over the dining table. A full breakfast is included. ✉ *109 Reed Ave., E0G 2X0,* ☎ *506/529–4210 or 800/470–4088,* FAX *506/529–4311. 9 rooms. Pool. AE, MC, V.*

$$$$ 🛏 **Kingsbrae Arms.** A member of Relais& Châteaux, this restored 1897
★ estate is an experience as much as it is a property. The many antique furnishings are both eclectic and entertaining. The decor is classy but full of pampering touches, the garden magnificent, and the owners gregarious. A full breakfast is included. ✉ *219 King St., E0G 2X0,* ☎ *506/529–1897,* FAX *506/529–1197. 6 rooms, 3 suites. Pool. MC, V.*

$ 🛏 **Seaside Beach Resort.** If the click of a closing screen door sounds like summer at the beach to you, this is your kind of place. At one end of the town's main street, it's close to all the action, yet guests also have access to a beach. The efficiency units are simple but comfortable and well equipped, right down to big pots for boiling lobsters. This is a terrific, casual spot for kids and dogs. ✉ *339 Water St., E0G 2X0,* ☎ *506/529–3846 or 800/506–8677,* FAX *506/529–4479. 24 1- and 2-bedroom cottages. Coin laundry. MC, V. Closed Nov.–Mar.*

Outdoor Activities and Sports

GOLF

Algonquin Golf Club (✉ Rte. 127, ☎ 506/529–3062) has a lovely setting for an 18-hole, par-72 course and a 9-hole, par-31 course.

WATER SPORTS

The **Day Adventure Centre** (✉ Market Wharf), open May–Labor Day, can arrange explorations of Passamaquoddy Bay on various kinds of boats. **Fundy Tide Runners** (✉ Market Wharf, ☎ 506/529–4481) uses a 24-ft Zodiac to search for whales, seals, and marine birds. The clipper **MV Corey** (✉ Market Wharf, ☎ 506/529–8116) is an elegant vessel for whale-watching. **Seascape Kayak Tours** (✉ Market Wharf, ☎ 506/529–4866) provides instruction as well as trips around the area from a half day to a week.

Shopping

Cottage Craft (⊠ Town Sq., ☎ 506/529–3190) employs knitters year-round to make mittens and sweaters from its specially dyed wool. **Jon Sawyer's Studio** (⊠ Lower Patrick St., ☎ 506/529–3012) has exquisite glass. The **Sea Captain's Loft** (⊠ 211 Water St., ☎ 506/529–3190) specializes in English and New Brunswick woolens, English bone china, and marvelous wool yarn. **Tom Smith's Studio** (⊠ 136 Water St., ☎ 506/529–4234) is highly regarded for Asian *raku* pottery.

Grand Manan Island

㉒ *2 hrs by car ferry from Black's Harbour.*

Grand Manan, the largest of the three Fundy Islands, is also the farthest away from the mainland; it's possible to see spouting whales, sunning seals, or a rare puffin on the way over. Circular herring weirs dot the island's coastal waters, and fish sheds and smokehouses lie beside long wharfs that reach out to bobbing fishing boats. Place names are evocative—Swallowtail, Southern Head, Seven Days Work, and Dark Harbour. It's easy to get around—only about 32 km (20 mi) of road lead from the lighthouse at Southern Head to the one at Northern Head. Grand Manan attracted John James Audubon, that human encyclopedia of birds, in 1831. More than 240 species of seabirds nest on the island, making it a haven for bird-watchers; the puffin is the island's symbol. In season (roughly May–September), whale-watching expeditions can be booked at the Marathon Inn and the Compass Rose (☞ Dining and Lodging *and* Outdoor Activities and Sports, *below*), and scuba diving to old wrecks is popular. You can make a day trip here or plan a longer stay and really relax. Ferry service is provided by **Coastal Transport** (☎ 506/662–3724).

Lodging

$–$$ 🏨 **Compass Rose.** A couple from Montréal fell in love with the lovely guest rooms and comfortable turn-of-the-century furnishings in the two old houses that have been combined into this small, English-style country inn. They bought the inn and upgraded the dining room, which overlooks the harbor. Morning and afternoon teas are served as well as lunch and dinner. A full English breakfast is included in the rate. ⊠ *North Head E0G 2M0,* ☎ *506/662–8570. 8 rooms. Restaurant. MC, V.*

$–$$ 🏨 **Marathon Inn.** This gracious mansion built by a sea captain sits on a hill overlooking the harbor. Guest rooms are furnished with antiques. The dining room specializes in seafood; it does not serve lunch. ⊠ *Box 129, North Head E0G 2M0,* ☎ *506/662–8488. 28 rooms, 14 with bath. Restaurant, 2 lounges, pool, tennis court. MC, V.*

Outdoor Activities and Sports

TOURS

Activities including bird-watching, painting, nature photography, hiking and whale-watching can be arranged by contacting **Tourism New Brunswick** (⊠ Box 12345, Fredericton E3B 5C3, ☎ 506/453–2170 or 800/561–0123).

WHALE-WATCHING

Grand Manan boasts several whale-watching operators: **Island Coast Boat Tours** (⊠ Box 59, Castalia E0G 1L0, ☎ 506/662–8181), **Sea Land Adventure** (⊠ Box 86, Castalia E0G 1K0, ☎ 506/662–8997), **Sea Watch Tours** (⊠ Box 48, Seal Cove E0G 3B0, ☎ 506/662–8552), **Surfside Boat Tours** (⊠ Box 147, Castalia E0G 1L0, ☎ 506/662–8156).

Campobello Island

★ ㉓ *90 km (56 mi) from St. Stephen; 45-min ferry ride from Deer Island.*

Neatly manicured, preening itself in the bay, Campobello Island has always had a special appeal to the wealthy and the famous. It was here that the Roosevelt family spent its summers. The 34-room rustic summer cottage of the family of President Franklin Delano Roosevelt is now part of a nature preserve, **Roosevelt International Park,** a joint project of the Canadian and American governments. The miles of trails here make pleasant strolling. President Roosevelt's boyhood home was also the setting for the movie *Sunrise at Campobello.* To drive here from St. Stephen, cross the border to Maine, drive about 80 km (50 mi) down Route 1, and take Route 189 to Lubec, Maine, and a bridge. ✉ *Roosevelt Park Rd.,* ☎ *506/752–2922.* 🎫 *Free.* ☉ *House late May–mid-Oct., daily 10–6; grounds daily.*

The island's **Herring Cove Provincial Park** (✉ Welshpool, ☎ 506/752–7010) has camping facilities and a 9-hole golf course.

Dining and Lodging

$ ✕🏨 **Lupine Lodge.** Originally a vacation home built by the Adams family (friends of the Roosevelts) around the turn of the century, these three attractive log buildings set on a bluff overlooking the Bay of Fundy are now a modern guest lodge. Nature trails connect it to Herring Cove Provincial Park. Two of the cabins comprise the guest rooms; the third houses the dining room ($$–$$$), which specializes in simple but well-prepared local seafood. ✉ *Box 2, Welshpool E0G 3H0,* ☎ *506/752–2555. 10 rooms, 1 suite. Restaurant, lounge. MC, V.*

$–$$ 🏨 **Owen House.** Mellow with history, this 200-year-old home was built by Admiral Owen, who was granted the island in the 1700s. Its old-fashioned rooms have hosted such luminaries as actress Greer Garson. Breakfasts are wonderful—pancakes come topped with local berries. ✉ *Welshpool E0G 3H0,* ☎ *506/752–2977. 8 rooms, 1 suite. V.*

Deer Island

㉔ *40 min by free car ferry from Letete, 13 km (8 mi) south of St. George.*

The pleasures of Deer Island include walking around the fishing wharves, such as those at Chocolate Cove. Exploring the island takes only a few hours; it's 12 km (7 mi) long, varying in width from almost 5 km (3 mi) to a few hundred feet at some points. At **Deer Point** you can walk through a small nature park while waiting for the ferry to Campobello Island. If you listen carefully, you may be able to hear the sighing and snorting of the **Old Sow,** the second largest whirlpool in the world. If you can't hear it, you'll be able to see it, just a few feet offshore in the Western Passage off Point Park.

Lodging

$ 🏨 **45th Parallel Motel and Restaurant.** Deer Island has only one motel—fortunately, it's clean and comfortable. A full breakfast is complimentary, and everything from lobster to hot sandwiches is available at the informal restaurant. Three of the rooms have kitchenettes. Pets are welcome. ✉ *Fairhaven E0G 1R0,* ☎ *506/747–2231. 1 0 rooms. Restaurant. AE, MC, V.*

$ 🏨 **West Isles World B&B.** This white frame house overlooks the cove and offers three snug rooms with an informal country feel; the big upstairs bedroom has a water view. A full breakfast is included. The owners will arrange whale-watching cruises for guests. ✉ *Lord's Cove E0G 2J0,* ☎ *506/747–2946. 3 rooms. No credit cards.*

Outdoor Activities and Sports

Cline Marine Tours (✉ Box 18, Leonardville E0G 2G0, ☎ 506/529–2287) offers scenic and whale-watching tours.

St. George

㉕ *40 km (25 mi) east of St. Stephen, 60 km (37 mi) west of Saint John.*

St. George is a pretty town with some excellent bed-and-breakfasts, one of the oldest Protestant graveyards in Canada, and a fish ladder running up the side of a dam. Water runs through this concrete staircase, allowing fish to jump, step by step, to the top and then jump back in the river.

Lodging

$–$$ ⌂ **Granite Town Hotel.** Although this hotel was built in 1990, it has an old-country-inn feeling. The decor is subtle, with pine and washed-birch woodwork. Light blues and pinks dominate in the rooms. One side of the building overlooks an apple orchard; the other sits atop the bank of the Maguadavic River. A Continental breakfast is available but is not included in the rate. Two rooms have whirlpool baths. ✉ *79 Main St., E0G 2Y0, ☎ 506/755–6415, FAX 506/755–6009. 32 rooms. Restaurant, bar, boating, bicycles. AE, D, DC, MC, V.*

Outdoor Activities and Sports

Fundy Yacht Sales and Charter (✉ Rte. 2, Dipper Harbour, Lepreau E0G 2H0, ☎ 506/634–1530 or 800/565–2925), east of St. George, charters sailboats.

OFF THE BEATEN PATH **ST. MARTINS –** About 45 km (28 mi) east of Saint John on Route 111, the fishing village of St. Martins has a rich shipbuilding heritage, whispering caves, miles of lovely beaches, spectacular tides, and a cluster of covered bridges. If you're tempted to linger, try the **St. Martins Country Inn** (☎ 506/833–4534).

Alma

135 km (84 mi) northeast of Saint John

The small seaside town of Alma services Fundy National Park and has some motels as well as restaurants that serve good lobster and sticky buns. Around this area, much of it in Albert County, there's plenty to do outdoors—from bird-watching to spelunking. The **Albert County Tourism Association** (✉ Box 46-B, Hopewell Cape E0A 1Y0, ☎ 506/734–2471) has information.

★ ㉖ **Fundy National Park** is an awesome 206-square-km (80-square-mi) microcosm of New Brunswick's inland and coastal climates. The influence of the Bay of Fundy has also created some climatic conditions not found anywhere else in the region. This has led to a fascinating biological evolution that can be clearly seen in its forests. The park has 110 km (68 mi) of varied hiking and biking trails, some gravel-surface auto trails, golf, tennis, a heated Bay of Fundy saltwater pool, and a restaurant. ✉ *Hwy. 114, Box 40, E0A 1B0, ☎ 506/887–6000.* ⊡ *$3.50 in summer; free rest of year.*

Outdoor Activities and Sports

BIRD-WATCHING

The bit of shoreline at **Marys Point** (✉ watch for signs off Rte. 915) draws tens of thousands of migrating birds, including semipalmated sandpipers and other shore birds, each summer. The area, now a bird sanctuary and interpretive center, is near Riverside-Albert.

GOLF

The **Fundy National Park Golf Club** (☎ 506/887–2970) is nestled near cliffs overlooking the restless Bay of Fundy; deer grazing on the 9-hole, par-35 course are one of its hazards.

HORSEBACK RIDING

Broadleaf Guest Ranch (⊠ Rte. 114, Hopewell Hill, ☎ 506/882–2349 or 800/226–5405) can provide an overnight adventure or a short trail ride. The short excursions are through the lowland marsh; longer ones take the high road into the forest.

SKIING AND SNOWMOBILING

Poley Mountain Ski Area (⊠ Box 1097, Sussex E0E 1P0, ☎ 506/433–3230), 10 km (6 mi) from Sussex in Waterford, has 13 trails and a snowboard park; the vertical drop is 660 ft. Poley is also on the groomed Fundy Snowmobile Trail between Saint John and Moncton.

SPELUNKING

Baymount Outdoor Adventures (⊠ 15 Elwin Jaye Dr., Hillsborough, ☎ 506/734–2660) has trained interpreters who lead expeditions into the White Caves near the Bay of Fundy. All equipment is supplied.

Cape Enrage

15 km (9 mi) east of Alma.

Route 915 takes you to the wild driftwood-cluttered beach at Cape Enrage, which juts out into the bay. There's a lighthouse and some spectacular views. You can arrange for rappelling and other adventures here.

Outdoor Activities and Sports

Cape Enrage Adventures (⊠ Site 5-5, R.R. 1, Moncton, ☎ 506/856–6081 off-season, 506/887–2273 mid-May–mid-Sept.) arranges rappelling; fee is $40 per person for three hours. Canoeing, kayaking, and hiking are other options.

Hopewell Cape

40 km (25 mi) north of Alma.

The coast road (Route 114) from Alma to Moncton winds through covered bridges and along rocky coasts. The **Rocks Provincial Park** (⊠ Rte. 114, ☎ 506/734–2026 off-season, 506/734–3429 in season) is home of the famous Giant Flowerpots—rock formations carved by the Bay of Fundy tides. They're topped with vegetation and are uncovered only at low tide, when you can climb down for a closer study. A new visitor center and new trails were added in 1997; there's a new children's play area, too.

MONCTON AND THE ACADIAN PENINSULA

The white sands and gentle tides of the Northumberland Strait and Baie des Chaleurs are as different from the rocky cliffs and powerful tides of the Bay of Fundy as the Acadians are from the Loyalists. A tour of this area takes you to the burgeoning city of Moncton with its high-tech industries as well as to Acadian fishing villages.

Moncton

㉗ *80 km (50 mi) north of Alma.*

A friendly town, often called the Gateway to Acadia because of its mix of English and French and its proximity to the Acadian shore, Moncton has a renovated downtown, where wisely placed malls do a booming business. A walking-tour brochure indicates the city's historic highlights.

This city has long touted two natural attractions: the Tidal Bore and the Magnetic Hill. You may be disappointed if you've read too much tourist hype, though. In days gone by, before the harbor mouth filled with silt, the **Tidal Bore** was an incredible sight, a high wall of water that surged in through the narrow opening of the river to fill red mud banks to the brim. It still moves up the river, and the moving wave is worth waiting for, but it's nowhere near as lofty as it used to be, except sometimes in the spring. Bore Park on Main Street is the best vantage point; viewing times are posted there.

☙ **Magnetic Hill** creates a bizarre optical illusion. If you park your car in neutral at the designated spot, you'll seem to be coasting uphill without power. Shops, an amusement park, a zoo, a golf course, and a small railroad are part of the larger complex here; there are extra charges for the attractions. ⊠ *North of Moncton off Trans-Canada Hwy. (watch for signs).* 🖃 *$2.* ☉ *May–Labor Day, daily 8–8.*

☙ An excellent family water-theme park, **Magic Mountain,** is adjacent to Magnetic Hill. ⊠ *North of Moncton off Trans-Canada Hwy.,* ☎ *506/ 857–9283.* 🖃 *$17.25.* ☉ *Mid-June–July 1 and mid-Aug.–Labor Day, daily 10–6; July 2–mid-Aug., daily 10–8.*

Among Moncton's attractions is the **Acadian Museum,** at the University of Moncton, whose remarkable collection of artifacts reflects 300 years of Acadian life in the Maritimes. ⊠ *Clement Cormier Bldg., Archibald St.,* ☎ *506/858–4088.* 🖃 *Free.* ☉ *June–Sept., weekdays 10–5, weekends 1–5; Oct.–May, Tues.–Fri. 1–4:30, weekends 1–4.*

....

OFF THE
BEATEN PATH

TANTRAMAR REGION – The Tantramar salt marshes southeast of Moncton are peaceful today, but it wasn't always so. Acadian roots run deep in Memramcook, where the history of the Acadian people is explored in passionate detail at Monument Lefebvre National Historic Site (☎ 506/ 758–9808). On the other side of the marsh, Dorchester and Sackville were centers of British culture and industry long before the Loyalists landed. Dorchester survives today as a crossroads with some of the province's oldest buildings and museums. **Sackville**—with its small-town charm, huge Waterfowl Park (☎ 506/364–0432) on a major migratory route, and sophisticated Owens Art Gallery (☎ 506/364–2574) on the Mt. Allison University campus—is picture perfect. Near the Nova Scotia border in Aulac, the **Fort Beauséjour National Historic Site** (⊠ Rte. 106, ☎ 506/536–0720 summer, 506/876–2443 off-season) holds the ruins of a star-shape fort that played a part in the 18th-century struggle between the French and English. The fort has fine views of the marshes at the head of the Bay of Fundy.

....

Dining and Lodging

$$–$$$$ ✕ **Fisherman's Paradise.** This restaurant with an enormous dining area that seats more than 350 people serves memorable à la carte seafood dishes in an atmosphere of candlelight and wood furnishings. ⊠ *375 Dieppe Blvd.,* ☎ *506/859–4388. AE, DC, MC, V.*

$$$ ✕🏨 **Hotel Beauséjour.** Moncton's finest hotel, conveniently located
★   downtown, has friendly service. The decor of the guest rooms echoes

the city's Loyalist and Acadian roots. L'Auberge, the main hotel restaurant ($$–$$$$), has a distinct Acadian flavor. The Windjammer dining room ($$$$) is more formal, modeled after the opulent luxury liners of the turn of the century. ⊠ *750 Main St.,* ☎ *506/854–4344,* FAX *506/ 858–0957. 299 rooms, 11 suites. 2 restaurants, bar, café, indoor pool, exercise room. AE, D, DC, MC, V.*

$ ✕⌂ **Chez Françoise.** This lovely old mansion with a wraparound ve-
★ randa has been decorated in Victorian style. There are 9 guest rooms in this house; another building across the street has 10 more. Front rooms in the main house have water views. The dining room ($$), open to the public for dinner, serves excellent traditional French cuisine with an emphasis on seafood. A full breakfast is included in the price. ⊠ *293 Main St., Shediac (30 km, or 19 mi, northeast of Moncton),* ☎ *506/532–4233. 19 rooms, 10 with bath. Restaurant, bar. AE, D, DC, MC, V. Closed Jan.–May 1.*

$$ ⌂ **Best Western Crystal Palace.** The Moncton area's newest hotel has theme rooms (want to be Ali Baba or Elvis for a night?) and, for families, an indoor pool and a miniature wonderland of rides, midway stalls, and coin games. Champlain Mall is just across the parking lot. ⊠ *499 Paul St.,* ☎ *506/858–8584,* FAX *506/858–5486. 115 rooms. Restaurant, indoor pool. AE, D, DC, MC, V.*

$$ ⌂ **Victoria B & B.** This historic home in the heart of downtown has antiques-furnished rooms with amenities such as terry robes and aromatic bath gels. The full breakfast, served in the dining room and included in the rate, often features chocolate pecan and orange brandy French toast. ⊠ *71 Park St., E1C 2B2,* ☎ *506/389–8296,* FAX *506/389– 8296. 3 rooms. Dining room, in-room VCRs. MC, V.*

$–$$ ⌂ **Marshlands Inn.** In this white clapboard inn, a welcoming double
★ living room with fireplace sets the informal country atmosphere. Bedrooms are furnished with sleigh beds or four-posters, and all have telephones. The chef has adapted classic French dishes to suit a lighter, modern palate; salmon is a specialty. ⊠ *Box 1440, Sackville (53 km, or 33 mi, southeast of Moncton) E0A 3C0,* ☎ *506/536–0170,* FAX *506/ 536–0721. 19 rooms. Restaurant. AE, DC, MC, V.*

Nightlife and the Arts

THE ARTS
Top musicians and other performers appear at the **Colosseum** (⊠ 377 Killam Dr., ☎ 506/857–4100).

NIGHTLIFE
Moncton's downtown really rocks at night. **Au Deuxième** (⊠ 837 Main St., ☎ 506/383–6192) has live music on the weekends, mostly Francophone artists. **Chevy's** (⊠ 939 Mountain Rd., ☎ 506/858–5861) has comedy, rock and roll, and traditional music. **Club Cosmopolitan** (⊠ 700 Main St., ☎ 506/857–9117) is open Wednesday–Saturday for dancing, rock, jazz, or the blues. It's billed as one cool club with four different atmospheres. **Ziggy's** (⊠ 730 Main St., ☎ 506/858–8844) offers dance music and fun promotions.

Shopping
Five spacious malls, some big retail stores, and numerous pockets of shops make Moncton and Dieppe the best place to shop in New Brunswick.

En Route The resort town of **Shediac,** along the coast from Moncton on Route 11, has the warm waters of popular Parlee Beach and lots of good lobster feeds.

Bouctouche

28 *60 km (37 km) north of Moncton.*

Bouctouche is another coastal town with a number of attractions. **Le Pays de la Sagouine** is a theme park with a make-believe island community that comes to life in twice-daily stage shows in French. La Sagouine is an old charwoman-philosopher created by award-winning author Antoine Maillet. ⊠ *Hwy. 11, Exit 32,* ☎ *800/561–9188.* ⌑ *$9.* ⊙ *June–early Sept., daily 10–6.*

★ **La Dune de Bouctouche** is a superb example of a coastal ecosystem that has evolved into an exceptionally fertile oyster bed as well as a safe haven for terns and the endangered piping plover. Hiking trails and boardwalks to the beach make it possible to explore sensitive areas without disrupting the environment. ⊠ *Rte. 475,* ☎ *506/743–2600.* ⌑ *Free.* ⊙ *Visitor center May–June, daily noon–8; July–Sept., 10–8.*

Kouchibouguac National Park

100 km (62 mi) north of Moncton.

★ The white, dune-edged beaches of **Kouchibouguac National Park** are some of the finest on the continent. Kellys Beach and Callander's Beach are supervised and have facilities. The park also protects forests and peat bogs. You can bicycle, canoe, boat, and picnic. There are 311 camp sites; reservations are accepted. ⊠ *Off Rtes. 11 and 134, Kent County,* ☎ *506/876–2443.* ⌑ *$3.50.*

Miramichi City

29 *150 km (93 mi) north of Moncton.*

The fabled Miramichi region is one of lumberjacks and fishermen. Celebrated for salmon rivers that reach into some of the province's richest forests, and the ebullient nature of its residents (Scottish, English, Irish, and a smattering of native and French), this is a land of stories, folklore, and lumber kings.

Sturdy wood homes dot the banks of Miramichi Bay at newly formed Miramichi City, which in 1995 incorporated the former towns of Chatham and Newcastle and several small villages. This is also where the politician and British media mogul Lord Beaverbrook grew up and is buried.

The **Atlantic Salmon Museum** provides a look at the endangered Atlantic salmon and at life in noted fishing camps along the rivers. ⊠ *297 Main St., Doaktown (80 km, or 50 mi, southwest of Miramichi City),* ☎ *506/365–7787.* ⊙ *June–Sept., daily 9–5.* ⌑ *$4.*

The **Central New Brunswick Woodmen's Museum,** with artifacts that date from the 1700s to the present, is in what looks like two giant logs set on more than 60 acres of land. The museum portrays a lumberman's life through displays, but its tranquil grounds are excuse enough to visit. There are picnic facilities and camping sites. ⊠ *Rte. 8, Boiestown (110 km, or 68 mi, southwest of Miramichi City,* ☎ *506/369–7214.* ⌑ *$5.* ⊙ *May–Sept., daily 9–5.*

Lodging

$–$$ 🏠 **Pond's Chalet Resort.** You'll get a traditional fishing-camp experience in this lodge and the chalets set among trees overlooking a salmon river. The accommodations in Ludlow, 15 km (9 mi) northwest of Boiestown, are comfortable but not luxurious. You can canoe and bicycle here, too. The dining room turns out reliable but undistinguished food. ⊠ *Lud-*

low E0C 1N0 (watch for signs on Rte. 8), ☎ *506/369–2612,* ℻ *506/369–2293. 10 guest rooms, a 5-bedroom lodge, and 14 cabins. Bar, dining room, tennis court, volleyball, snowmobiling. AE, DC, MC, V.*

$–$$ 🏨 **Wharf Inn.** This low-rise modern building has two wings; guest rooms in the executive wing have extra amenities. The staff is friendly, and the restaurant serves excellent salmon dinners. ✉ *Jane St.,* ☎ *506/622–0302,* ℻ *506/622–0354. 70 rooms. Restaurant, bar, no-smoking rooms, indoor pool. AE, DC, MC, V.*

Caraquet

③⓪ *118 km (73 mi) north of Miramichi City.*

Caraquet, on the Acadian Peninsula, is perched along the Baie des Chaleurs, with Québec's Gaspé Peninsula beckoning across the inlet. The town is rich in French flavor and hosts an **Acadian Festival** (☎ 506/727–6515) each August. Beaches are another draw here.

★ ✋ ③① A highlight of the Acadian Peninsula is the **Acadian Historical Village,** 10 km (6 mi) west of Caraquet. The more than 40 original buildings re-create an early Acadian community between 1780 and 1890. Summer days are wonderfully peaceful: The chapel bell tolls, ducks waddle and quack under a footbridge, wagons creak, and the smell of hearty cooking wafts from cottage doors. Costumed staff act as guides and demonstrate trades; a restaurant serves old-Acadian dishes. ✉ *Rte. 11,* ☎ *506/726–2600.* 🎟 *$8.75.* 🕙 *June–Labor Day, daily 10–6; some buildings open Sept., daily 10–5.*

Dining and Lodging

$ ✕🏨 **Hotel Paulin.** The word "quaint" really fits this property. Each pretty room has its own unique look, with old pine dressers and brass beds, and the colors are as bright and cheerful as the seaside town. An excellent small dining room specializes in fresh fish cooked to perfection, Acadian style. ✉ *143 blvd. St-Pierre W, E1W 1B6,* ☎ *506/727–9981. 9 rooms, 4 with bath; 1 suite. Dining room. MC, V.*

$ 🏨 **Auberge Les Amis de la Nature.** The French name means this is a place for nature lovers, and there is plenty to explore outdoors year-round. What sets this rustic inn apart are its organic gardens and orchards. In season, virtually all the vegetables and fruits served in the dining room are grown on the property. ✉ *R.R. 1, Box 23, Robertville (north of Bathurst), E0B 2K0,* ☎ ℻ *506/783–4797,* ☎ *800/327–9999 in New Brunswick, Québec, and Ontario. 5 rooms. Restaurant. MC, V.*

Outdoor Activities and Sports

Sugarloaf Provincial Park (✉ Box 629, Atholville E0K 1A0, ☎ 506/789–2366) is in Atholville, 180 km (112 mi) north of Caraquet. The eight trails on this 507-ft vertical drop accommodate all levels. There are also 25 km (16 mi) of cross-country ski trails. Instruction and equipment rentals are available; the park has a lounge and cafeteria.

NEW BRUNSWICK A TO Z

Arriving and Departing

By Car

Major entry points are at St. Stephen, Houlton, and Edmundston; Cape Tormentine from Prince Edward Island; and Aulac from Nova Scotia.

By Plane

The major airports in the province are **Saint John Airport** (✉ Loch Lomond Rd., ☎ 506/636–3950)), **Moncton Airport** (✉ Champlain Rd.,

☎ 506/856–5444), and **Fredericton Airport** (✉ Lincoln Rd., ☎ 506/444–6100). Air Canada and its regional carrier Air Nova serve New Brunswick in Saint John, Moncton, Fredericton, Bathurst, and St-Léonard and fly to the Atlantic provinces from Montréal, Toronto, and Boston. Canadian Airlines International operates through Air Atlantic in Saint John, Fredericton, Moncton, Charlo, and Miramichi and serves the Atlantic provinces, Montréal, Ottawa, and Boston. For airline telephone numbers, *see* Air Travel *in* the Gold Guide.

By Train
VIA Rail (☎ 800/561–3949 in the U.S., 800/561–8630 in Canada) offers passenger service six times a week from Campbellton, Newcastle, and Moncton to Montréal and Halifax.

Getting Around

By Bus
SMT Eastern Ltd. (☎ 506/859–5100 or 800/567–5151) runs buses within the province and connects with most major bus lines.

By Car
New Brunswick has an excellent highway system with numerous facilities. The Trans-Canada Highway, marked by a maple leaf, is the same as Route 2. A good map is available at visitor information centers (☞ Visitor Information *in* Contacts and Resources, *below*). Tourism New Brunswick has mapped five scenic routes: the Fundy Coastal Drive, River Valley Scenic Drive, Acadian Coastal Drive, Miramichi River Route, and Appalachian Range.

Contacts and Resources

Emergencies
Fire, medical, police (☎ 911).

Hospitals
Chaleur Regional Hospital (✉ 1750 Sunset Dr., Bathurst, ☎ 506/548–8961). **Campbellton Regional Hospital** (✉ 189 Lilly Lake Rd., Campbellton, ☎ 506/789–5000). **Edmundston Regional Hospital** (✉ 275 Hébert Blvd., ☎ 506/739–2211). **Dr. Everett Chalmers Hospital** (✉ Priestman St., Fredericton, ☎ 506/452–5400). **Miramichi Regional Hospital** (✉ 500 Water St., Miramichi, ☎ 506/623–3000). **Moncton City Hospital** (✉ 135 MacBeath Ave., Moncton, ☎ 506/857–5111). **Dr. Georges Dumont Hospital** (✉ 330 Archibald St., Moncton, ☎ 506/862–4000). **Saint John Regional Hospital** (✉ Tucker Park Rd., Saint John, ☎ 506/648–6000).

Outdoor Activities and Sports
Whale-watching, sea kayaking, trail riding, bird-watching, garden touring, river cruising, and fishing are part of the province's day-adventure program, "Adventures Left and Right." The more than 160 packages cover a variety of skill levels and include equipment. All adventures last at least a half day; some are multiday. Information is available at a New Brunswick Day Adventure Centre (in some information offices, hotels, and attractions), or contact **Tourism New Brunswick** (✉ Box 12345, Fredericton E3B 5C3, ☎ 506/453–2170 or 800/561–0123).

BIKING
B&Bs frequently have bicycles for rent, and Tourism New Brunswick has listings and free cycling maps. **Covered Bridge Bicycle Tours** (✉ Dept. F, Box 693, Main Post Office, Saint John E2L 4B3, ☎ 506/849–9028) leads bike trips in the province.

FISHING

New Brunswick Fish and Wildlife (☎ 506/453–2440) can give you information on sporting licenses and tell you where the fish are.

GOLF

A project to improve existing courses and build new ones is in progress. For the most up-to-date information, contact Tourism New Brunswick (☞ Visitor Information, *below*) or the **New Brunswick Golf Association** (✉ 565 Priestman St., Fredericton E3B 5X8).

HIKING

Eric Hadley at the **New Brunswick Trails Council** (✉ Dept. of Natural Resources and Energy, Box 6000, Fredericton E3B 5H1, ☎ 506/453–2730) has general trail information.

SNOWMOBILING

For information on snowmobiling, contact the **New Brunswick Federation of Snowmobile Clubs** (✉ 147 Houlton Rd., Woodstock E7M 1Y4, ☎ 506/325–2625).

Visitor Information

Tourism New Brunswick (✉ Box 12345, Fredericton E3B 5C3, ☎ 506/453–2170 or 800/561–0123) can provide information on day adventures, scenic driving routes, accommodations, and the seven provincial tourist bureaus. Also helpful are information services of the cities of **Bathurst** (☎ 506/548–0410), **Campbellton** (☎ 506/789–2700), **Fredericton** (☎ 506/452–9508), **Moncton** (☎ 506/853–3590), and **Saint John** (☎ 506/658–2990).

12 Prince Edward Island

In the Gulf of St. Lawrence north of Nova Scotia and New Brunswick, Prince Edward Island seems too good to be true, with its crisply painted farmhouses, manicured green fields rolling down to sandy beaches, the warmest ocean water north of the Carolinas, lobster boats in trim little harbors, and a vest-pocket capital city, Charlottetown, packed with architectural heritage.

WHEN YOU EXPERIENCE Prince Edward Island, known locally as the Island, you'll understand instantly why Lucy Maud Montgomery's novel of youth and innocence, *Anne of Green Gables,* was framed against this land. What may have been unexpected, however, was how the story burst on the world in 1908 and is still selling untold thousands of copies every year. After potatoes and lobsters, Anne is the Island's most important product.

Updated by
Helga
Loverseed

In 1864 Charlottetown, the Island's capital city, hosted one of the most important meetings in Canadian history, which eventually led to the creation of the Dominion of Canada in 1867. Initially, Prince Edward Island was reluctant to join, having spent years fighting for the right to an autonomous government. Originally settled by the French in 1603, the Island was handed over to the British under the Treaty of Paris in 1763. Tensions grew as absentee British governors and proprietors failed to take an active interest in the development of the land, and the resulting parliamentary government proved ineffective for similar reasons. Yet the development of fisheries and agriculture at the turn of the century strengthened the economy. Soon settlement increased and those who were willing to take a chance on the Island prospered.

Around the middle of the 19th century, a modern cabinet government was created and relations between tenants and proprietors worsened. At the same time, talk of creating a union with other North American colonies began. After much deliberation, and despite the fact that political upheaval had begun to subside, delegates decided that it was in the Island's best economic interest to join the Canadian Confederation.

The 1997 opening of the Confederation Bridge, which connects Borden-Carleton with Cape Tormentine in New Brunswick, physically sealed Prince Edward Island's connection with the mainland. The bridge was not built without controversy. Nobody doubts that it is an engineering marvel: Massive concrete pillars—65 ft across and 180 ft high—were sunk into waters over 110 ft deep in order to cope with traffic that by the turn of the century is expected to bring more than 1 million visitors annually. Most locals have gotten used to the bridge, but some fear the loss of the Island's tranquillity. As you explore the crossroads villages and fishing ports, it's not hard to understand why. Outside the tourist mecca of Cavendish, otherwise known as Anne's land, the Island seems like an oasis of peace in a busy world.

Pleasures and Pastimes

The Arts
The arts, particularly theater, are an integral part of the Island. Summer productions and theater festivals are highlights. The grandest is the Charlottetown Festival, which takes place June–mid-September at the Confederation Centre of the Arts. Theater in Summerside, Georgetown, and Victoria is also good. Traditional Celtic music, with fiddling and step dancing, can be heard almost daily.

Beaches
Prince Edward Island is ringed by beaches, and few of them are heavily used. Ask a dozen Islanders to recommend their favorites and you'll hear different answers. Basin Head Beach, near Souris, says one—miles of singing sands, utterly deserted. West Point, says a second—lifeguards, restaurants nearby, showers at the provincial park. Green-

wich, near St. Peter's Bay, another suggests—a half-hour walk through magnificent wandering dunes that brings you to an endless empty beach. In season the ocean beaches have the warmest water north of the Carolinas, making for fine swimming.

Dining

On Prince Edward Island, wholesome, home-cooked fare is a matter of course. Talented chefs ensure fine cuisine in each region. The service is friendly—though a little laid back at times—and the setting is generally informal. Seafood is usually good anywhere on the Island, with top honors given to lobster. Lobster suppers are offered both commercially and by church and civic groups. These meals feature lobster, rolls, salad, and mountains of sweet, home-baked goods. Local papers, bulletin boards at local grocery stores, and Visitor Information Centres have information about these events.

CATEGORY	COST*
$$$$	over $35
$$$	$25–$35
$$	$15–$25
$	under $15

*per person, in Canadian dollars, excluding drinks, service, 10% provincial sales tax, and 7% GST

Lodging

Prince Edward Island has a variety of accommodations at a variety of prices, from full-service resorts and luxury hotels to moderately priced motels, cottages, and lodges. Some farms take guests, too. Lodgings in summer should be booked early, especially for long stays.

CATEGORY	COST*
$$$$	over $160
$$$	$120–$160
$$	$85–$120
$	under $85

*All prices are for a standard double room, excluding 10% provincial sales tax and 7% GST, in Canadian dollars.

Outdoor Activities and Sports

BIKING

The Island is popular with bike-touring companies for its moderately hilly roads and stunning scenery. Level areas can be found in many places, especially east of Charlottetown to Montague and along the north shore. However, shoulderless, narrow secondary roads in some areas and summer's car traffic can be challenging. A 9-km (5½-mi) path near Cavendish campground loops around marsh, woods, and farmland. Cycling trips are organized throughout the province, and the Island's tourism department can recommend tour operators.

GOLF

Prince Edward Island has several beautiful courses with scenic vistas. Golfing is virtually hassle-free: Tee times are easily booked, rates are inexpensive, and courses are uncrowded, particularly in fall.

HIKING

Hiking within the lush scenic areas of Prince Edward Island National Park and provincial parks is encouraged with marked trails. Many trails are being upgraded to provide quality surfaces great for walking, hiking, or cycling. One of them is Confederation Trail, a provincial trail system that will eventually allow outdoors explorers to travel 350 km (217 mi) within the province.

Exploring Prince Edward Island

Prince Edward Island is irregular in shape, with deep inlets and tidal streams that nearly divide the province into three equal parts, known locally by their county names of Kings, Queens, and Prince (east to west). Shaped like a crescent, it is 224 km (139 mi) from one end to the other, with a width ranging from 4 km (2½ mi) to 60 km (37 mi). The Island is a rich agricultural region surrounded by sandy beaches, delicate dunes, and stunning red sandstone cliffs. The land in the east and central sections consists of gentle hills. Nevertheless, the land never rises to a height of more than 500 ft above sea level, and you are never more than 15 minutes by car from a beach or waterway. To the west, from Summerside to North Cape, the terrain is flatter.

Numbers in the text correspond to numbers in the margin and on the Prince Edward Island and Charlottetown maps.

Great Itineraries

Visitors often tour only the central portion of the Island, taking Confederation Bridge from New Brunswick to Borden-Carleton and exploring Anne country and the PEI National Park. To experience the Island's character more deeply, you might visit the wooded hills of the east, including compact, bustling Montague. Another choice is to go west to superb, almost private beaches, the Acadian parish of Tignish, and the country around Summerside. Even if you're in a rush, it won't take long to get off and back on the beaten path: In most places you can cross the Island, north to south, in half an hour or so. The four tours in this chapter include many Island essentials; Charlottetown is primarily a walking tour, while the others follow the major scenic highways—Blue Heron Drive, Kings Byway, and Lady Slipper Drive. There are plenty of chances to get out of the car, go fishing, hit the beach, photograph wildflowers, or just watch the sea roll in.

IF YOU HAVE 1 DAY

Leaving 🏨 **Charlottetown** ①–⑨ on Route 2 west, take Route 15 north to **Brackley Beach** ⑪. This puts you onto a 137-km-long (85-mi-long) scenic drive marked with signs depicting a blue heron. Route 6 west will take you to **Cavendish** ⑫, an entryway to **PEI National Park** ⑩. Cavendish is home to the fictional character Anne of Lucy Maud Montgomery's *Anne of Green Gables*. This area has enough attractions for a full day, but if you prefer to keep exploring, continue west on Route 6, where museums vie with fishing wharfs and scenic vistas for your attention. Blue Heron Drive joins Route 20, where you'll find the Anne of Green Gables Museum at Silver Bush in Park Corner. Continue west, then south on Route 20 and rejoin Route 2 south until turning onto Route 1 east and back to Charlottetown. **Victoria** ⑭ is a scenic fishing town along the way.

IF YOU HAVE 2 DAYS

Leaving 🏨 **Charlottetown** ①–⑨ early in the day, follow Highway 1 east to Kings Byway, a scenic drive marked by signs showing a king's crown, and on to **Orwell** ⑮, where a period farm re-creates life in the 1800s. Continue on to **Montague** for a seal-watching tour. Overnight in 🏨 **Bay Fortune** ⑯. The next day, a picnic lunch will be the perfect wrap-up to a morning spent at Basin Head Fisheries Museum in **Basin Head.** Continue east on Kings Byway to East Point for a stop at the lighthouse, which marks the most easterly point on the Island. Proceed west along the north shore to the eastern entrance of **Prince Edward Island National Park** ⑩ and end your tour with a swim or hike.

Prince Edward Island

*Prince Edward Island National Park stretches along the coast from Cavendish to Dalvey

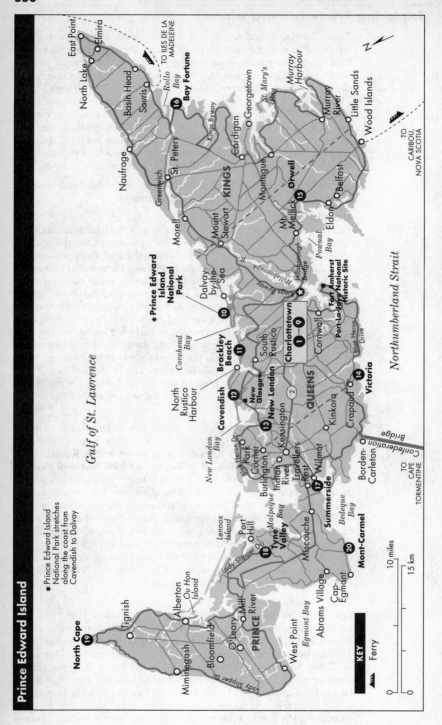

Gulf of St. Lawrence

Northumberland Strait

KEY

⛴ Ferry

0   10 miles

0   15 km

East Point
Elmira
North Lake
Basin Head
Souris
Naufrage
Greenwich
St. Peters
Morell
Mount Stewart
KINGS
Bay Fortune 16
Rollo Bay
TO ILES DE LA MADELEINE
Kings Byway
Cardigan
Georgetown
St. Mary's Bay
Murray Harbour
Murray River
Little Sands
Wood Islands
TO CARIBOU, NOVA SCOTIA
Montague
Orwell 15
Mt. Mellick
Eldon
Belfast
Pownal Bay
Kings Byway
Hillsborough Bridge
Hillsborough R.

Prince Edward Island National Park
Dalvay-by-the-Sea
10
Brackley Beach 11
Covehead Bay
South Rustico
Charlottetown 1–9
⭐
Fort Amherst Port-La-Joye National Historic Site
Cornwall
Blue Heron Drive

North Rustico Harbour
Cavendish 12
New Glasgow
13 **New London**
QUEENS
Kinkora
Victoria 14
Crapaud
Borden-Carleton

New London Bay
Blue Heron Dr.
Park Corner
Burlington
Indian River
Kensington
Travellers Rest
Wilmot
17
Summerside
Bedeque Bay
Confederation Bridge
TO CAPE TORMENTINE

Lennox Island
Port Hill
Malpeque Bay
Tyne Valley 18
Miscouche
Lady Slipper Dr.

North Cape 19
Tignish
Alberton
Ou Hon Island
Mill River
O'Leary
Bloomfield
Miminegash
PRINCE
Lady Slipper Dr.
West Point
Egmont Bay
Abrams Village
Cap-Egmont
Mont-Carmel 20

IF YOU HAVE 3 DAYS

From **Charlottetown** ①–⑨, explore the peaceful suburban sprawl of ▣ **Summerside** ⑰ before heading for its bustling waterfront. The relatively undiscovered area west of Summerside is perfect for those who like to pace things slowly. Follow Lady Slipper Drive through Acadian country to the Acadian Museum of Prince Edward Island in **Miscouche.** Leave mid-afternoon and take Route 12 to ▣ **Tyne Valley** ⑱, a base from which to visit Lennox Island Reserve, where some fine crafts are sold. That evening, take an evening stroll through Green Park in nearby **Port Hill.** On Day 3, make your way up to **North Cape** ⑲ and explore its reef. Plan to arrive early in the afternoon at ▣ **West Point,** where you can enjoy the beach and walking trails. Finish your time in Prince County with a south-shore tour to **Mont-Carmel** ⑳, home to one of the province's best French dinner theaters.

When to Tour Prince Edward Island

While Prince Edward Island is considered a summer destination due to its many seasonal attractions, the "shoulder seasons" should not be overlooked. May, June, September, and October usually have spectacular weather and few visitors. The main lobster season is May–June, while fall is an excellent time for hiking and golfing. Migratory birds arrive in vast numbers toward the end of summer, many staying until the snow falls. Winters are unpredictable but offer some of the Island's most overlooked activities: cross-country skiing, snowmobiling, and ice-skating on ponds. Nightlife is limited in cold weather.

CHARLOTTETOWN

Prince Edward Island's oldest city, on an arm of the Northumberland Strait, is named for the stylish consort of King George III. This small city, peppered with gingerbread-clad Victorian houses and tree-shaded squares, is the largest community on the Island (population 30,000). It is often called the Cradle of Confederation, a reference to the 1864 conference that led to the union of Nova Scotia, New Brunswick, Ontario, and Québec in 1867 and, eventually, Canada itself.

Charlottetown's main activities center on government, tourism, and private commerce. While new suburbs were springing up around it, the core of Charlottetown remained unchanged, and the waterfront has been restored to recapture the flavor of earlier eras. Today the waterfront includes the Prince Edward Hotel; an area known as Peake's Wharf and Confederation Landing Park, with informal restaurants and handicraft and retail shops; and a marked walking path. Irene Rogers's *Charlottetown: The Life in Its Buildings,* available locally, gives much detail about the architecture and history of downtown Charlottetown.

Exploring Charlottetown

Historic homes, churches, parks, and the waterfront are among the pleasures of a tour of downtown Charlottetown, and you can see many of the sights on foot.

A Good Tour

Before setting out to explore Charlottetown, brush up on local history at the **Confederation Centre of the Arts** ① on Richmond Street in the heart of downtown. Next door is the **Province House National Historic Site** ②, where the first meeting to discuss federal union was held. If you have an interest in churches, turn left off Richmond Street onto Prince Street to see **St. Paul's Anglican Church** ③. Backtrack on Richmond two blocks and turn left onto Great George Street, home to **St. Dunstan's Basilica** ④, with its towering twin Gothic spires. Great George Street

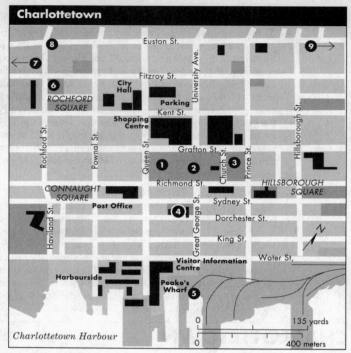

ends at the waterfront, where the boardwalks of **Confederation Landing Park** ⑤ lead past small eateries and shops.

On the city's west end, the work of Robert Harris, Canada's foremost portrait artist, adorns the walls of **St. Peter's Cathedral** ⑥ in Rochford Square, bordered by Rochford and Pownal streets. It's a bit of a walk to get there, but **Victoria Park** ⑦ provides a grassy respite. Next, climb to the Belvedere on the top floor of the **Beaconsfield Historic House** ⑧ for panoramic views of Charlottetown Harbour. Leave time to observe a favorite Prince Edward Island pastime—harness racing at **Charlottetown Driving Park** ⑨.

TIMING

The downtown area can be explored on foot in a couple of hours, but the wealth of historic sites and harbor views warrant a full day.

Sights to See

⑧ **Beaconsfield Historic House.** Designed by architect W. C. Harris and built in 1877, this gracious Victorian mansion near the entrance to Victoria Park is one of the Island's finest residential buildings and has 11 furnished rooms. On site are a gift shop and bookstore. Special events such as theatrical and musical performances and lectures are held regularly. Also on the grounds is a carriage house where activities for children are held in summer. ⌧ *2 Kent St.,* ☎ *902/368–6600.* ⌚ *$2.50.* ☉ *June–Labor Day, daily 10–5; Labor Day–June, Tues.–Sun. 1–5.*

⑨ **Charlottetown Driving Park.** Since 1890, this track at the eastern end of the city has been the home of a sport dear to Islanders—harness racing. Standardbred horses are raised around the Island, and harness racing on the ice and on country tracks has been popular for generations. In fact, there are more horses per capita on the Island than in any other Canadian province. August brings **Old Home Week,** when eastern

Canada's best converge for 15 races in eight days. ⊠ *Kensington Rd.,* ☎ *902/892–6823.* 🎫 *$2.* ⊘ *Races June–July, and most of Aug., 3 nights per wk; Old Home Week (mid-Aug.), Mon.–Sat. twice daily.*

❶ **Confederation Centre of the Arts.** Set in Charlottetown's historic red-brick core, this modern, concrete structure houses a 1,100-seat main-stage theater and two 190-seat second-stage theaters. The center also has an outdoor amphitheater; a memorial hall; a gift shop with Canadian crafts; a theater shop; an art gallery and museum; a public library with a special Prince Edward Island collection, including first editions of Lucy Maud Montgomery's famous novel; and a restaurant. The **Charlottetown Festival,** which runs June–September, includes the professional musical adaptation of *Anne of Green Gables.* ⊠ *145 Richmond St.,* ☎ *902/368–1864, 902/566–1267 for box office, or 800/565–0278;* FAX *902/566–4648.* ⊘ *Daily 9–5; hrs extended June–Sept.*

❺ **Confederation Landing Park.** This waterfront recreation area at the bottom of Great George Street marks the site of the historic landing of the Fathers of Confederation in 1864. Walkways and park benches offer plenty of opportunity to survey the activity of the harbor. The adjacent **Peake's Wharf** has small restaurants, crafts shops, and a marina.

NEED A
BREAK?

The **Merchantman Pub** (⊠ 23 Queen St., ☎ 902/892–9150), in a historic building just steps from the waterfront walking path near Confederation Landing Park, is a cozy spot for burgers, crepes, and fish-and-chips.

★ ❷ **Province House National Historic Site.** This three-story sandstone building, completed in 1847 to house the colonial government, has been restored to its mid-19th-century appearance. It is still the seat of the provincial legislature. The many restored rooms include historic Confederation Chamber, where representatives of the 19th-century British colonies met to discuss both the creation of a union and the current legislative chamber. ⊠ *Richmond St.,* ☎ *902/566–7626.* 🎫 *Donation accepted.* ⊘ *Mid-Oct.–mid-June, weekdays 9–5; mid-June and Sept.–mid-Oct., daily 9–5; July–Aug., daily 9–6.*

❹ **St. Dunstan's Basilica.** One of Canada's largest churches, St. Dunstan's is the seat of the Roman Catholic diocese on the Island. It's known for its fine Italian carvings and twin Gothic spires. ⊠ *Great George St.,* ☎ *902/894–3486.*

❸ **St. Paul's Anglican Church.** Erected in 1896, this is actually the third church building on this site. The first was built in 1747, making this the Island's oldest parish. ⊠ *101 Prince St.,* ☎ *902/892–1691.*

❻ **St. Peter's Cathedral.** The murals of Robert Harris are found in **All Souls' Chapel,** designed in 1888 by his brother W. C. "Willy" Harris, the most celebrated of the Island's architects and the designer of many historic homes and buildings. ⊠ *Rochford Sq.,* ☎ *902/566–2102.*

❼ **Victoria Park.** At the southern tip of the city and overlooking Charlottetown Harbour are 40 beautiful acres that provide the perfect place to stroll, picnic, or watch a baseball game. Next to the park, on a hill between groves of white birches, is the white colonial **Government House,** built in 1835 as the official residence for the province's lieutenant governors. The house is not open to the public. ⊠ *Lower Kent St.* ⊘ *Park daily sunrise–sunset.*

Dining

$$$$ ✕ **Culinary Institute of Canada.** Students at this internationally acclaimed school cook and present lunch and dinner as part of their training. Here's an opportunity to enjoy excellent food and top service at reasonable prices. Call for schedule and reservations. ⊠ *4 Sydney St.,* ☎ *902/894–6800. Reservations essential. MC, V.*

$$$–$$$$ ✕ **The Selkirk.** With its wing chairs and live piano entertainment, the Selkirk is the Island's most sophisticated dining room. The extensive, imaginative menu concentrates on regional Canadian fare—locally grown potatoes, smoked Atlantic salmon, lobster, mussels, Malpeque oysters, and Canadian beef, to name a few. A four-course extravaganza that begins with cedar-plank salmon and closes with a maple streusel apple tart will satisfy even the largest of appetites. ⊠ *Prince Edward Hotel, 18 Queen St.,* ☎ *902/566–2222 or 800/441–1414. Reservations essential. AE, DC, MC, V.*

$$–$$$$ ✕ **Peake's Quay.** This great summer spot is on Charlottetown's restored waterfront. The heated patio overlooks Confederation Landing Park. Specialties include seafood chowder, fresh scallops, and Atlantic salmon. When in season, lobster is also on the menu. There's live entertainment on weekends and during Sunday brunch. ⊠ *36 Lower Water St.,* ☎ *902/368–1330. AE, DC, MC, V. Closed mid-Sept.–mid-May.*

$$$ ✕ **Off Broadway.** Popular with Charlottetown's young professional set, this cozy spot began modestly as a crepe-and-soup joint. You can still make a meal of the lobster or chicken crepe and the spinach or Caesar salad that come with it, but now the restaurant has a fairly inventive Continental menu. The private booths won't reveal your indiscretions—including your indulgence in dessert. ⊠ *125 Sydney St.,* ☎ *902/566–4620. Reservations essential. AE, MC, V.*

$$ ✕ **Claddagh Room Restaurant.** Some of the best seafood in Charlottetown is served here. The "Galway Bay Delight," one of the Irish owner's
★   specialties, is a savory combination of fresh scallops and shrimp sautéed with onions and mushrooms, flambéed in Irish Mist, and doused with fresh cream. A pub upstairs has live Irish entertainment every night in summer and on weekends in winter. ⊠ *131 Sydney St.,* ☎ *902/892–9661. Reservations essential. AE, DC, MC, V.*

$–$$ ✕ **Little Christo's.** Hand-tossed gourmet pizzas like cordon bleu with roasted pine nuts and primavera make this the favorite spot in town for a slice. Soup, salad, pasta, and sandwiches round out the menu. ⊠ *411 University Ave.,* ☎ *902/566–4000. MC, V.*

$–$$ ✕ **Lone Star Cafe & Brewery.** This themed eatery (it bills itself as "the best little food house from Texas"), which is the Island's only brew pub, serves hearty Tex-Mex fare—tacos, mesquite-grilled chicken, fajitas, and the like. ⊠ *449 University Ave.,* ☎ *902/894–7827. AE, MC, V.*

$–$$ ✕ **Papa Joe's.** Its location in the midst of a strip of shopping malls (an unusual sight on this oh-so-pristine island) on University Avenue is less than ideal, but Papa Joe's serves fresh, plentiful, and reasonably priced food. Papa Joe, a real person, is the Lebanese founder of this family-style eatery, and the menu lists several Middle Eastern dishes, like falafel, tabbouleh, hummus, and shish kebabs. ⊠ *345 University Ave.,* ☎ *902/566–5070. AE, DC, MC, V.*

Lodging

$$$$ 🏨 **Prince Edward Hotel.** A member of the Canadian Pacific chain of
★   hotels and resorts, the Prince Edward has all the comforts and luxuries of its first-rate counterparts—from whirlpool baths in some suites to a grand ballroom and conference center. Guest rooms are modern, and two-thirds of the rooms in this 10-story hotel overlook the wa-

terfront. ✉ *18 Queen St., Box 2170, C1A 8B9,* ☎ *902/566–2222 or 800/441–1414,* FAX *902/566–2282. 211 rooms, 33 suites. 2 restaurants, bar, indoor pool, sauna, exercise room. AE, DC, MC, V.*

$$$–$$$$ 🏨 **Inns on Great George.** Closely linked with the founding of Canada as a nation (the so-called Fathers of Confederation stayed in these buildings during the signing of the 1864 Charlottetown Conference), this complex opened as a hotel in 1997. It includes several historic structures: the Pavilion, the Wellington, and the Carriage House (a two-story house with living room and kitchen), as well as the Witter-Coombs Prime Minister's Suite and self-catering apartments. Some of the restored buildings date back to 1811. A full breakfast is included. ✉ *58 Great George St., C1A 4K3,* ☎ *902/892–0606 or 800/361–1118,* FAX *902/ 628–2079. 29 rooms, 1 suite, 6 apartments, 1 house. Kitchens in apartments and house. CP. AE, DC, MC, V.*

$$–$$$$ 🏨 **Elmwood Heritage Inn.** One of the Atlantic Provinces' leading architects, W. C. Harris, designed this handsome Victorian home in 1889. ★ Originally part of a 20,000-acre estate, Elmwood was owned by Arthur Peters, grandson of Samuel Cunard, founder of the famous shipping line; today it's in a quiet, residential area The antiques-laden home has been restored by Carol and Jay Macdonald, who hail from Connecticut. Rooms have TVs and phones, and a full breakfast is included in the rate. ✉ *121 N. River Rd., Box 3128, C1A 7N8,* ☎ *902/368–3310,* FAX *902/628–8457. 6 rooms. Air-conditioning. DC, MC, V.*

$$$ 🏨 **Blue Heron Hideaways.** Just 15 minutes from downtown Charlottetown in Blooming Point, the Blue Heron is a small complex of cottages and beach houses. The private beach has sand dunes and wildlife, and it's great for windsurfing. Outboard motorboat and gas barbecues are available for guest use. ✉ *Meadowbank, R.R. 2, Cornwall C0A 1H0,* ☎ *902/566–2427,* FAX *902/368–3798. 1 2-bedroom cottage, 2 3-bedroom cottages, 1 waterfront cottage with bunkhouse, 1 6-bedroom oceanfront house with guest house. Pool, beach, windsurfing, boating. Weekly rentals only early June–mid-Oct. No credit cards.*

$$$ 🏨 **Dundee Arms.** Depending on your mood, you can choose to stay in ★ either a 1960s motel or a 1904 inn. The motel is simple, modern, and neat; the inn is homey and furnished with brass and antiques. The Griffin Room, the inn's dining room, is filled with antiques, copper, and brass. The French Continental cuisine includes fresh seafood. Among the specialties are rack of lamb and fillet of salmon in a light lime-dill sauce. ✉ *200 Pownal St., C1A 3W8,* ☎ *902/892–2496,* FAX *902/368– 8532. 15 rooms, 2 suites. Restaurant, pub. CP. MC, V.*

$$–$$$ 🏨 **The Charlottetown.** This five-story, redbrick hotel with white pillars ★ and a circular driveway is just two blocks from the center of Charlottetown. The rooms have the latest amenities but retain the hotel's old-fashioned flavor with antique-reproduction furnishings. The grandeur and charm of the Confederation Dining Room capture the elegance of a previous era. ✉ *Kent and Pownal Sts., Box 159, C1A 7K4,* ☎ *902/ 894–7371,* FAX *902/368–2178. 108 rooms, 2 suites. Restaurant, bar, indoor pool, sauna. AE, DC, MC, V.*

$$–$$$ 🏨 **Hillhurst Inn.** A handsome, elegant B&B in the heart of downtown, this 28-room mansion was once the home of George Longworth, a prominent Charlottetown merchant who made a fortune from building and operating ships. The reception area, dining room, and living room are paneled with burnished oak and beech, the work of the shipwrights he employed. ✉ *181 Fitzroy St., C1A 1S3,* ☎ *902/894–8004,* FAX *902/892–7679. 9 rooms. CP. MC, V.*

$ 🏨 **Sherwood Motel.** This family-oriented motel is about 5 km (3 mi) north of downtown Charlottetown on Route 15. The friendly owners offer help in reserving tickets for events and planning day trips. Don't be daunted the Sherwood's proximity to the airport—the motel sees very little traffic. Most rooms have kitchenettes. ⊠ *R.R. 9, Winsloe C1E 1Z3,* ☎ *902/892–1622 or 800/567–1622. 30 rooms. MC, V.*

Nightlife and the Arts

Ceilidhs, or live traditional entertainment combining dancing, fiddling, and comedy, can be found throughout Charlottetown and its environs. The **Benevolent Irish Society Hall** (☎ 902/892–2367) stages concerts on Fridays, mid-May–October.

Shopping

The most interesting stores are at Peake's Wharf, in Confederation Court Mall (off Queen Street), and in Victoria Row on Richmond Street, between Queen and Great George Streets. **Cows** (⊠ Queen St., across from Confederation Centre, ☎ 902/566–5558) is a zany shop that sells all things bovine—from T-shirts embellished with cartoon cows to delicious ice cream. **Great Northern Knitters** (⊠ 18 Queen St., ☎ 902/566–5302), in the Prince Edward Hotel, has a terrific selection of handmade woolen sweaters. **Roots** (⊠ Confederation Court Mall, ☎ 902/566–1877, an upscale leather goods and clothing company with stores across Canada, has a store in the Confederation Court Mall.

BLUE HERON DRIVE

From Charlottetown, Blue Heron Drive follows Route 15 north to the north shore, then winds along Route 6 through north-shore fishing villages, the spectacular white-sand beaches of Prince Edward Island National Park, through Anne of Green Gables country, and finally along the south shore, with its red sandstone seascapes and historic sites. The drive takes its name from the great blue heron, a stately water bird that migrates to Prince Edward Island every spring to nest in the shallow bays and marshes. The whole circuit roughly outlines Queens County and covers 190 km (118 mi). It circles some of the Island's most beautiful landscapes and best beaches, but its northern section around picturesque Cavendish and the Green Gables farmhouse is also cluttered with tourist traps. For unspoiled beauty, you'll have to look beyond the fast-food outlets, tacky gift shops, and expensive carnival-type attractions and try to envision the Island's simpler days.

Prince Edward Island National Park

① *24 km (15 mi) north of Charlottetown.*

Prince Edward Island National Park stretches for about 40 km (25 mi) along the north shore of the Island, from Cavendish to Dalvay, on the Gulf of St. Lawrence. The park is blessed with nature's broadest brush strokes—sky and sea meet red sandstone cliffs, rolling dunes, and long stretches of sand. Beaches invite swimming, picnicking, and walking. Trails lead through woodlands and along streams and ponds. Among the more than 200 species of birds that pass through the area are the northern phalarope, Swainson's thrush, and the endangered piping plover. Many campgrounds span the park with varying fees and seasons. In autumn and winter, it's difficult to reach park staff—call Canadian Heritage Parks Canada (☎ 902/672–6350) for exact rates and schedules if you're planning a camping trip ahead of time. Keep in mind that campsites are rented on a first-come, first-served basis. ☎ 902/672–6350. 🎫 *Daily pass $3, seasonal pass $15, off-season $2.50.* ☉ *Daily; full facilities open mid-June–early Sept.*

Lodging

$$$–$$$$ ⊡ **Dalvay-by-the-Sea.** Just within the eastern border of the Prince Edward Island National Park is this Victorian house, built in 1896 as a private summer home. Rooms are furnished with antiques and reproductions. Guests can sip cocktails or tea on the porch while viewing the inn's gardens, Dalvay Lake, or the nearby beach. Breakfast and dinner are included in the cost. ⊠ *Rte. 6, Grand Tracadie, near Dalvay Beach; Box 8, York C0A 1P0,* ☎ *902/672–2048. 26 rooms, 4 cottages. Restaurant, bar, driving range, 2 tennis courts, croquet, boating, gift shop. MAP. AE, MC, V. Closed late Sept.–early June.*

Outdoor Activities and Sports

The 18 holes of the links-style, par-72 course at **Stanhope Golf and Country Club** (☎ 902/672–2842) are among the most challenging and scenic on the Island. It's a couple of miles west of Dalvay, off Route 6, along Covehead Bay.

Brackley Beach

⓫ *112 km (7½ mi) west of Dalvay.*

Just outside Prince Edward Island National Park, Brackley Beach offers a variety of country-style accommodations and eating establishments. Its bays and waterways attract migratory birds and are excellent for canoeing or kayaking and windsurfing.

Dining and Lodging

$$–$$$ ✕ **Dunes Cafe.** This stunning café shares property with a pottery stu-
★   dio, art gallery, artisans outlet (☞ Shopping, *below*), and outdoor gardens. Soaring wood ceilings lend an airy atmosphere inside, while an outside deck overlooks the dunes and marshlands of Covehead Bay. The chef specializes in local seafood and lamb, incorporating locally grown, fresh produce, much of which comes from the café's own gardens. ⊠ *Rte. 15,* ☎ *902/672–2586. Reservations essential. AE, MC, V. Closed Nov.–May. No dinner weekdays June or Sept.–Oct.*

$$$$ ✕⊡ **Shaw's Hotel and Cottages.** Each room is unique in this 1860s hotel
★   with antique furnishings, floral-print wallpapers, and hardwood floors. Half the cottages have fireplaces. This country elegance doesn't come cheap; Shaw's is one of the more expensive hotels on the Island, but guests have the opportunity to sail (on small vessels) and windsurf. If you'd like, include in your room rate a home-cooked breakfast and dinner in the Shaw's dining room ($$–$$$), which is also open to the public. ⊠ *Rte. 15, C1E 1Z3,* ☎ *902/672–2022,* FAX *902/672–3000. 20 rooms, 18 cottages, 2 suites. Restaurant, bar, beach, boating, playground. AE, MC, V. Closed late Sept.–May except for 6 cottages.*

Shopping

The **Dunes Studio and Gallery** (⊠ Rte. 15, ☎ 902/672–2586) sells the work of leading local artists, as well as craftspeople from around the world. The working pottery studio is open for viewing, and a rooftop water garden offers fine views of saltwater bays, sand dunes, rolling hills, and the Gulf of St. Lawrence.

Cavendish

⓬ *21 km (13 mi) west of Brackley.*

Cavendish is the most visited Island community outside of Charlottetown, because of the heavy influx of visitors to Green Gables, Prince Edward Island National Park, and the amusement park–style attractions in the area. Families with children enjoy the entertainment, which ranges from bumper-car rides to water slides to pristine sandy beaches.

Adults will appreciate the **Site of Lucy Maud Montgomery's Cavendish Home,** where the writer lived with her maternal grandparents following the untimely death of her mother. Though the foundation of the home where Montgomery wrote *Anne of Green Gables* and the white picket fence that surrounded it are all that remain, the homestead fields and old apple-tree gardens provide lovely walking grounds. A bookstore and museum are also on the property, which is operated by descendants of the family. ✉ *Rte. 6,* ☎ *902/963–2231.* ⌖ *$2.* ☉ *June– mid-Oct., daily 10–5, until 7 in July and Aug.*

★ **Green Gables House,** ½ km (¼ mi) west of Lucy Maud Montgomery's Cavendish home, is the green-and-white farmhouse that served as the setting for *Anne of Green Gables.* The house, frequently visited by Montgomery, belonged to her cousins. Posted walking trails, the Haunted Wood and Balsam Hollow, re-create the landscape reminiscent of Montgomery's day. The site has been part of Prince Edward Island National Park since 1937. ✉ *Rte. 6, west of Rte. 13,* ☎ *902/672–6350.* ⌖ *$2.50.* ☉ *Mid-May–late June and Sept.–Nov., daily 9–5; late June–Aug., daily 9–8.*

Dining and Lodging

$–$$$ 🏨 **Kindred Spirits Country Inn and Cottages.** Green hills surround this lovely country estate, a short walk from Green Gables House (☞ *above*) and golf course. Guests can relax by its parlor fireplace and then retreat into a large room or suite, decorated in country Victorian style with local antiques. ✉ *Rte. 6, C0A 1N0,* ☎ *902/963–2434,* ⅎ𝔸𝕏 *902/ 963–2434. 14 rooms in the Inn, 13 cottages. Restaurant, pool, hot tub. MC, V. Closed mid-Oct.–mid-May.*

$ ✕🏨 **Bay Vista Motor Inn.** This clean, friendly motel caters to families. Parents can sit on the outdoor deck and take in the New London Bay panorama while keeping an eye on their children in the large playground. ✉ *R.R. 1, Breadalbane, Cavendish C0A 1E0; in winter:* ✉ *R.R. 1, North Wiltshire C0A 1Y0;* ✉ *reservations: R.R. 2, Hunter River C0A 1N0,* ☎ *902/963–2225. 28 rooms, 2 efficiencies. Restaurant, pool, boating, fishing, playground. AE, MC, V. Closed late Sept.–mid-June.*

Outdoor Activities and Sports

GOLF

Green Gables Course (✉ Rte. 6, ☎ 902/963–2488), part of Prince Edward Island National Park, is a scenic 18-hole, par-72 course.

SEA KAYAKING

Outside Expeditions (☎ 800/207–3899), 8 km (5 mi) east of Cavendish in North Rustico, can gear a trip to suit either the new or experienced paddler. Tours include food, from light snacks to full-fledged lobster boils, depending on the expedition.

New London

🔟 *11 km (7 mi) southwest of Cavendish.*

This tiny village is best known as the birthplace of Lucy Maud Montgomery. It's also home to several seasonal gift and crafts shops and a tea shop. The wharf area is a great place to stop, rest, and watch as the fishing boats come and go.

The **Lucy Maud Montgomery Birthplace** is the modest white house where the famous author of *Anne of Green Gables* was born in 1874. Among memorabilia on display are her wedding dress and personal scrapbooks. ✉ *Rte. 6,* ☎ *902/886–2596.* ⌖ *$2.* ☉ *June and Sept.– mid-Oct., daily 9–5; July–Aug., daily 9–7.*

Northwest Corner

12 km (7 mi) from New London.

Some of the most beautiful scenery on the Island is on Blue Heron Drive along the north shore. As the drive follows the coastline south to the other side of the Island, it passes rolling farmland and the shores of Malpeque Bay. Three towns of interest round out this scenic corner of the Island: Burlington, Park Corner, and Indian River.

Woodleigh Replicas and Gardens, in Burlington, southwest of New London, is a 45-acre park with 30 scale replicas of Great Britain's best-known architecture, including the Tower of London and Dunvegan Castle. The models that are large enough to enter are furnished with period antiques. A medieval maze and 10 acres of English country gardens are also on the grounds. ⊠ *Rte. 234, Burlington,* ☎ *902/836–3401.* ⊠ *$6.80.* ☉ *June, Sept.–Oct., daily 9–5; July–Aug., daily 9–7.*

The **Anne of Green Gables Museum at Silver Bush** was once the home of Lucy Maud Montgomery's aunt and uncle. Montgomery herself lived here for a time and was married in the parlor in 1911. Fans will appreciate mementos such as photographs and a quilt the writer worked on. ⊠ *Rte. 20, Park Corner,* ☎ *902/886–2884.* ⊠ *$2.50.* ☉ *June, Sept., daily 9–6; July–Aug., daily 9–7:30.*

Nightlife and the Arts

St. Mary's Church (⊠ Hwy. 104, 5 km, or 3 mi, south of Park Corner, ☎ 902/836–3733) in Indian River has performances by visiting artists in July and August.

Borden-Carleton

35 km (22 mi) south of Kensington.

Once home port to the Marine-Atlantic car ferries, Borden-Carleton is now linked to the mainland via the Confederation Bridge. The 13-km (8-mi) behemoth, completed in June 1997, spans the Northumberland Strait and ends in Cape Tormentine, New Brunswick. **Gateway Village,** at the foot of the bridge near the toll booths, has a visitor center, a gift shop, and a good overview of the bridge's construction.

En Route Prior to the late 1800s (when ferry service began), passengers and mail were taken across the strait in ice boats that were rowed and alternately pushed and pulled across floating ice by a fleet of men attached to leather harnesses. A monument on Route 10 in **Cape Traverse** commemorates their journeys.

Victoria

★ ⑭ *22 km (14 mi) east of Borden-Carleton.*

This picturesque fishing village is filled with antiques, art galleries, and handicraft shops. Among its eateries is the Landmark Café (⊠ Main St., ☎ 902/658–2286), a funky spot serving homemade soups, pastas, seafood dishes, and delicious deserts.

Nightlife and the Arts

In summer, the historic **Victoria Playhouse** (⊠ Main St., ☎ 902/658–2025) has a celebrated theater program. Dinner packages are available.

Shopping

Island Chocolates (⊠ Main St., ☎ 800/565–2320), a chocolate factory in a 19th-century general store, sells handmade treats made from imported Belgian chocolate and flavored with fruit and liqueur fillings.

Fort Amherst Port-La-Joye National Historic Site

36 km (22 mi) east of Victoria.

In 1720 the French founded the first European settlement on the Island, Port-La-Joye; 38 years later it was usurped by the British and renamed Fort Amherst. Take time to stroll around the original earthworks of the fort; there are magnificent panoramic views. The visitor center has informative exhibits and an audiovisual presentation. The drive from Victoria to Rocky Point passes through the Argyle Shore to this site, which is at the mouth of Charlottetown Harbour. ⊠ *Rte. 19,* ☎ *902/672–6350 or 902/675–2220.* ☞ *$2.25.* ⊙ *Visitor center, mid-June–Labor Day, daily 10–6; grounds daily.*

THE KINGS BYWAY

For 375 km (233 mi), the Kings Byway follows the coastline of green and tranquil Kings County on the eastern end of the Island. The route passes wood lots, patchwork-quilt farms, fishing villages, historic sites, and long, uncrowded beaches. In early summer fields of blue, white, pink, and purple wild lupines slope down to red cliffs and blue sea. To get here from Charlottetown, take Route 1 east and follow Kings Byway counterclockwise.

Orwell

★ ⑮ *27 km (17 mi) east of Charlottetown.*

For those who like the outdoors, Orwell, lined with farms that welcome guests and offer activities, is ideal. The **Orwell Corner Historic Village** is a living-history farm museum that re-creates a 19th-century rural settlement by employing methods used by Scottish settlers in the 1800s. The village contains a beautifully restored 1864 farmhouse, school, church, community hall, blacksmith shop, and barns with handsome draft horses. On Wednesdays in summer the village hosts musical evenings (*ceilidhs*) with traditional Scottish fiddle music by local musicians. ⊠ *Rte. 1,* ☎ *902/651–2013.* ☞ *$3.* ⊙ *Late June–Labor Day, Tues.–Sun. 9–5; mid-May–late June and Labor Day–late Oct., Tues.–Fri. 10–3.*

The **Sir Andrew Macphail Homestead,** a National Historic Site, is a 140-acre farm property that contains an ecological forestry project, gardens, and three walking trails. The restored 1829 house and 19th-century outbuildings commemorate the life of Sir Andrew Macphail (1864–1938), a writer, professor, physician, and soldier. A licensed tearoom-restaurant serves traditional Scottish and contemporary fare. ⊠ *Off Rte. 1,* ☎ *902/651–2789.* ☞ *Free; donation accepted.* ⊙ *June and Sept., Tues.–Sun. 10–5; July–Aug., extended hrs.*

OFF THE
BEATEN PATH

BEN'S LAKE TROUT FARM – This is a pleasant attraction for the whole family but is especially appreciated by aspiring young anglers. You're almost guaranteed a fish, and the staff will clean it and supply the barbecue and picnic table for a great meal. ⊠ *Rte. 24 (follow gravel road from Sir Andrew Macphail Homestead to Rte. 24; turn right), Bellevue,* ☎ *902/838-2706.* ☞ *Catch $3.90 per lb.* ⊙ *Apr.–Oct.*

En Route   One of the Island's most historic churches, St. John's Presbyterian, is in **Belfast,** just off Route 1 on Route 207. This pretty white church on a hill was built by settlers from the Isle of Skye who were brought to the Island in 1803 by Lord Selkirk.

Montague

> 20 km (12 mi) northeast of Orwell.

The business hub of eastern Prince Edward Island, Montague, a lovely fishing village, is a departure point for seal-watching boat tours. **Cruise Manada** (☎ 902/838–3444 or 800/986–3444) sails past a harbor seal colony and mussel farms. Boats leave from Montague Marina on Route 4 and Brudenell Resort Marina on Route 3 from mid-May through October.

Bay Fortune

> ⑯ 38 km (24 mi) north of Georgetown.

Bay Fortune, a little-known scenic village, has been a secret refuge of American vacationers for two generations.

Dining and Lodging

$$$–$$$$ ✕⊡ **Inn at Bay Fortune.** This enticing, unforgettable getaway, the for-
★ mer summer home of Broadway playwright Elmer Harris and more recently of the late actress Colleen Dewhurst, is now a charming inn overlooking Fortune Harbour and Northumberland Strait. You'll find superb dining and a taste of genteel living. Local fresh-caught and fresh-harvested ingredients are served in an old-time ambience. The restaurant does not serve lunch, but a full breakfast is included in room rates. ⊠ Rte. 310, R.R. 4, C0A 2B0, ☎ 902/687–3745, 860/296–1348 off-season. 11 rooms. Restaurant. Closed late Oct.–mid-May.

Souris

> 14 km (9 mi) north of Bay Fortune.

The Souris area is noted for its fine traditional musicians. An outdoor Scottish concert at **Rollo Bay** in July, with fiddling and step dancing, attracts thousands every year. At Souris a car ferry links Prince Edward Island with the Québec-owned Magdalen Islands.

Basin Head

> 13 km (8 mi) north of Rollo Bay.

This town is noted for an exquisite silvery beach that stretches northeast for miles, backed by high grassy dunes. Scuff your feet in the sand: It will squeak, squawk, and purr at you. Known locally as the **singing sands,** this is a phenomenon found in only a few locations worldwide. The high silica content in the sand helps produce the sound.

At the **Basin Head Fisheries Museum,** spectacularly located on a bluff overlooking Northumberland Strait, boats, gear, and photographs depict the life of an inshore fisherman. There's an aquarium, a smokehouse, a cannery, and coastal-ecology exhibits. ⊠ Off Rte. 16, ☎ 902/357–2966, 902/368–6600 off-season. ⊠ $3. ☼ June and Sept., weekdays 10–3; July–Aug., daily 10–7.

En Route   Ships from many nations have been wrecked on the reef running northeast from the **East Point Lighthouse** (⊠ Off Rte. 16, East Point, ☎ 902/357–2106). Guided tours are offered, and many books with tales of life at sea are available at the gift shop.

Greenwich

54 km (33 mi) southwest of East Point.

Greenwich is known for its superior beach. To get here, follow Route 16, the shore road, to Route 2 to St. Peter's Bay and Route 313 to Greenwich. The road ends among sand hills, but from here you can take a half-hour walk through beige dunes to reach the beach. These dunes are moving, gradually burying the nearby woods; here and there the bleached skeletons of trees thrust up through the sand like wooden ghosts.

LADY SLIPPER DRIVE

This drive—named for the delicate lady's slipper orchid, the province's official flower—winds along the coast of the narrow, indented western end of the Island, known as Prince County, through very old and very small villages that still adhere to a traditional way of life. Many of these hamlets are inhabited by Acadians, descendants of the original French settlers. The area is known for its oysters and Irish moss (the dried plants of a red sea alga) but most famously for its potato farms: The province is a major exporter of seed potatoes worldwide, and half the crop is grown here.

Summerside

⑰ *71 km (44 mi) west of Charlottetown.*

Summerside, the second-largest city on the Island, has a beautiful waterfront area. A self-guided walking tour arranged by the Eptek National Exhibition Centre (☞ *below*) is a pleasant excursion through the leafy streets lined with large houses. During the third week of July, all of Summerside celebrates the eight-day **Summerside Lobster Carnival,** with livestock exhibitions, harness racing, fiddling contests, and of course, lobster suppers.

The **International Fox Museum and Hall of Fame** describes some unique local history. Silver foxes were first bred in captivity in western Prince Edward Island, and for several decades Summerside was the headquarters of a virtual gold rush based on fox ranching. Some of the homes in Summerside built with money from this enterprise are known as fox houses. ⊠ *286 Fitzroy St.,* ☎ *902/436–2400 or 902/436–1589.* ☜ *Donation required.* ☼ *May–Sept., Mon.–Sat. 9–6.*

Eptek National Exhibition Centre and PEI Sports Hall of Fame, on the waterfront, has a spacious main gallery with changing history and fine arts exhibits from all parts of Canada. An adjacent gallery contains the Sports Hall of Fame, a permanent display honoring well-known Island athletes. ⊠ *130 Harbour Dr., Waterfront Properties,* ☎ *902/888–8373,* FAX *902/888–8375.* ☜ *$2.* ☼ *July–Aug., weekdays 10–4, weekends 1–4:30. Closed Mon. Sept.–June.*

Spinnaker's Landing, a boardwalk along the water's edge, is lined with shops and eateries. At a boat shed displaying traditional building methods from the 1800s, you can have your own small ship custom crafted out of wood. ⊠ *130 Waterfront St., Waterfront Properties,* ☎ *902/436–6692.* ☼ *Mid-June–mid-Sept., daily 9:30–9:30.*

Dining and Lodging

$$$ ✕ **Seasons In Thyme.** This elegant waterfront restaurant, which has
★   sunny orange walls trimmed with rich rosewood, overlooks Bedeque Bay. It's known for local ingredients such as quail, pheasant, and duck, and organic vegetables. Owner-chef Stefan Czapalay has 27 potato dishes at his fingertips, allowing him to cater to industry officials visiting to

check the quality of the Island's seed potatoes. In recognition of his varied clientele he utilizes the freshest ingredients from farm and sea in dishes ranging from the most sophisticated to the most casual. ⊠ *644 Water St.,* ☎ *902/888–3463. Reservations essential. AE, MC, V.*

$$ 🖭 **Loyalist Country Inn.** A Victorian street scene–inspired theme is present throughout this waterfront inn. Ten rooms have whirlpool baths. ⊠ *195 Harbour Dr., C1N 5B2,* ☎ *902/436–3333 or 800/361–2668,* FAX *902/436–4304. 51 rooms. Restaurant, indoor pool, sauna, tennis court, exercise room. AE, DC, MC, V.*

$$ 🖭 **Quality Inn Garden of the Gulf.** Close to downtown, this clean motel is a convenient place to stay. The chip-and-putt golf course slopes to Bedeque Bay. ⊠ *618 Water St. E, C1N 2V5,* ☎ *902/436–2295 or 800/ 265–5551,* FAX *902/436–6277. 84 rooms. Coffee shop, indoor and outdoor pools, 9-hole golf course, gift shop. AE, DC, MC, V.*

Nightlife and the Arts

The **College of Piping and Celtic Performing Arts of Canada** (⊠ 619 Water St. E, ☎ 902/436–5377, FAX 902/436–4930) puts on a summer-long Celtic Festival incorporating bagpiping, Highland dancing, step dancing, and fiddling. The **Harbourfront Jubilee Theater** (⊠ 130 Water St., Waterfront Properties, ☎ 902/888–2500 or 800/707–6505) is the Maritimes' newest professional theater. Year-round, the main stage celebrates the tradition and culture of the region with dramatic and musical productions.

Brothers Two Restaurant (⊠ 618 Water St. E, ☎ 902/436–7674) has been putting on "feast dinner theater" during the summer and Christmas season for 20 years. Musical comedy is served up with heaping platefuls of prime rib, chicken Kiev, or fresh seafood.

Miscouche

10 km (6 mi) northwest of Summerside.

This is the area in which many descendants of the Island's early French settlers live, and a museum here commemorates their history. The **Acadian Museum of Prince Edward Island** has a permanent exhibition on Acadian life as well as an audiovisual presentation depicting the history and culture of Island Acadians. There is also a genealogical cards center. ⊠ *Rte. 2,* ☎ *902/436–6237.* 🖼 *$3.* ☉ *Daily 9:30–5, until 7 in July and Aug.*

Port Hill

35 km (22 mi) north of Miscouche.

Port Hill was one of the many communities in the Tyne Valley that benefited from the shipbuilding boom of the 1800s, the era of the tall-masted wooden schooners. Some historic buildings testify to the prosperity of the era.

The **Green Park Shipbuilding Museum and Historic House** includes what was originally the home of shipbuilder James Yeo Jr., who by the mid-1840s was the most powerful businessman on the Island. This 19th-century mansion is topped by the cupola from which Yeo observed his nearby shipyard through a spyglass. The modern museum building, in what has become a provincial park, details the history of the shipbuilder's craft, brought to life at a re-created shipyard with carpenter and blacksmith shops. The park also provides an opportunity for some welcome R&R, with picnic tables and camping facilities, as well as swimming in the river (there may not be a lifeguard on duty). ⊠ *Rte. 12,* ☎ *902/ 831–2206.* 🖼 *$3.50.* ☉ *Early June–Labor Day, daily 9–5.*

Tyne Valley

⑱ *8 km (5 mi) south of Port Hill.*

The charming community of Tyne Valley has some of the finest food on Prince Edward Island, as well as an annual Oyster Festival, which takes place the first week in August. The area is home to the famous Malpeque oysters; watch for fishermen standing in flat boats wielding rakes to harvest this shellfish.

Dining and Lodging

$ ✕⊡ **Doctor's Inn Bed & Breakfast.** Beautifully landscaped, this village home is a joy in summer, with its garden of herbs and flowers. In winter cross-country skiers gather around the woodstove or fireplace and share conversation over a warm drink. At the dining room table, the local catch of the day is complemented by produce from the inn's own organic gardens. Dinner ($$$–$$$$) is by reservation only. There are free tours of the inn's gardens. ⊠ *Rte. 167, C0B 2C0,* ☎ *902/831–3057. 3 rooms share bath. Restaurant. CP. MC, V.*

Shopping

Lennox Island Reserve, one of the largest Mi'Kmaq reserves in the province, has a few shops that sell native crafts. To get here, take Route 12 west to Route 163 and follow the road over the causeway. **Indian Art & Craft of North America** (☎ 902/831–2653) sells sweetgrass baskets, pottery, and beadwork. Earthenware figurines depicting native legends can be found at **Micmac Productions** (☎ 902/831–2277).

At **Shoreline Sweaters** (⊠ Rte. 12, ☎ 902/831–2950), sometimes known as Tyne Valley Studio, Lesley Dubey produces sweaters with a unique Fair Isle–style lobster pattern and sells local crafts May–October. An art gallery displays works by Island artists.

O'Leary

37 km (23 mi) northeast of Tyne Valley.

The center of Prince County is composed of a loose network of small towns, many of which are merely a stretch of road. Though quality lodging establishments are hard to find in these parts, Woodstock, just north of O'Leary, has a resort where opportunities for outdoor activities abound. The town is also a good base from which to visit one of the Island's best golf courses and a rare woolen crafts shop.

Lodging

$–$$$ ⊡ **Rodd Mill River Resort and Aquaplex.** With activities ranging from night skiing and tobogganing to golfing, this is truly an all-season resort. An international dogsled-racing weekend is a popular winter event. The resort has year-round family weekend packages. ⊠ *Rte. 136, Box 399, Woodstock C0B 1V0,* ☎ *902/859–3555 or 800/565–7633,* ⅁ᵃˣ *902/859–2486. 87 rooms, 3 suites. Restaurant, 2 bars, 2 indoor pools, sauna, 18-hole golf course, tennis court, exercise room, squash, windsurfing, boating, bicycles, ice-skating, cross-country skiing, tobogganing, pro shop. AE, MC, V. Closed Nov.–early Dec. and Apr.*

Outdoor Activities and Sports

The 18-hole, par-72 **Mill River Provincial Golf Course** (⊠ Rte. 136, ☎ 902/859–8873) in Woodstock's Mill River Provincial Park is among the most scenic and challenging courses in eastern Canada.

Shopping

The **Old Mill Craft Company** (⊠ Rte. 2, Bloomfield, ☎ 902/859–3508) sells hand-quilted and woolen crafts July–August.

En Route Many things in **Tignish,** a friendly Acadian community on Route 2, 12 km (7½) mi north of O'Leary, are cooperative, including the supermarket, insurance company, seafood plant, service station, and credit union. The imposing parish church of **St. Simon and St. Jude Parish House** (✉ 315 School St., ☎ 902/882–2049), across from Dalton Square, has a superb Tracker pipe organ, one of the finest such instruments in eastern Canada. The church is often used for recitals by world-renowned musicians.

North Cape

★ ⑲ *14 km (9 mi) north of Tignish on Route 12.*

In the northwest, the Island narrows to a north-pointing arrow of land, at the tip of which is North Cape, with its imposing lighthouse. At low tide, one of the longest reefs in the world gives way to tidal pools teeming with marine life. Seals often gather offshore here. The curious structures near the reef are wind turbines at the **Atlantic Wind Test Site,** set up on this breezy promontory to evaluate the feasibility of electrical generation by wind power.

The **Interpretive Centre and Aquarium** has information about marine life, local history, and turbines and windmills. ✉ *End of Rte. 12,* ☎ *902/882–2991.* ⌑ *$2.* ☉ *July–Aug., daily 9–9; mid-May–June and Sept.–Oct., daily 10–6.*

Dining

$–$$ ✕ **Wind & Reef.** This restaurant serves good seafood, such as Island clams, mussels, and lobster, as well as steaks, prime rib, and chicken. There's a fine view of the Gulf of St. Lawrence and Northumberland Strait. ✉ *End of Rte. 12,* ☎ *902/882–3535. MC, V. Closed Oct.–May.*

En Route Near North Cape, just off Lady Slipper Drive on the western side of the Island, is the popular rock formation called **Elephant Rock.** You may also see draft horses in the fields or working in the surf. They are "moss horses," used in harvesting Irish moss, a versatile and valuable sea plant.

Miminegash

20 km (12 mi) south of North Cape.

This tiny village overlooks the ocean. The **Irish Moss Interpretive Centre** will tell you everything you wanted to know about Irish moss, the fan-shape red alga found in abundance on this coast and used as a thickening agent in foods. It even reveals how much Irish moss there is in an ice-cream cone. "Seaweed Pie" (made with Irish moss) is served at the adjacent Seaweed Pie Cafe. ✉ *Rte. 14,* ☎ *902/882–4313.* ⌑ *$1.* ☉ *Late June–Sept., weekdays 9–5.*

West Point

35 km (22 mi) south of Miminegash.

At the southern tip of the western shore, West Point has a tiny fishing harbor, campsites, and a supervised beach. **West Point Lighthouse** is more than 120 years old and is the tallest on the Island. When the lighthouse was automated, the community took over the building and converted it into an inn (☞ *below*) and museum, with a moderately priced restaurant. The lighthouse is open daily, late May–late October.

Lodging

$–$$ 🏨 **West Point Lighthouse.** Few people can say they've actually spent
★ the night in a lighthouse. Clam-digging is a central activity at this un-

usual seaside inn. Rooms, most with ocean views, are furnished with local antiques and handmade quilts. This inn books up, so make your reservations early. The innkeeper knows about the region's folklore—buried treasure is reputed to be nearby. ⊠ *Rte. 14,* ☎ *902/859–3605 or 800/764–6854. 9 rooms. Restaurant, beach, fishing, bicycles. AE, MC, V. Closed Oct.–May.*

En Route   Lady Slipper Drive meanders from West Point back to Summerside through **Région Évangéline,** the main Acadian district of the Island. At **Cape-Egmont,** stop for a look at the Bottle Houses, two tiny houses and a chapel built by a retired carpenter entirely out of glass bottles mortared together like bricks.

Mont-Carmel

㉒ *63 km (39 mi) southeast of West Point.*

This community has a magnificent brick church overlooking Northumberland Strait. **Acadian Pioneer Village,** a reproduction of an 1820s French settlement, has a church, school, blacksmith shop, and store. There are also modern accommodations and a restaurant (where you can sample authentic Acadian dishes). ⊠ *Rte. 11,* ☎ *902/854–2227.* ☞ *$2.* ☉ *Mid-June–mid-Sept., daily 9–7.*

Nightlife and the Arts

La Cuisine à Mémé (⊠ Rte. 11, ☎ 902/854–2227), a French dinner theater, serves a buffet and has typical Acadian entertainment, such as step dancing and fiddle music.

PRINCE EDWARD ISLAND A TO Z

Arriving and Departing

By Car

The 13-km (8-mi) Confederation Bridge connects Borden-Carleton, Prince Edward Island, with Cape Tormentine in New Brunswick. The bridge replaces the services of the Marine Atlantic ferries, shortening travel time to a mere 10 minutes. The round-trip cost is $35.50 per car, $40.50 for a recreational vehicle.

By Ferry

Northumberland Ferries (☎ 902/566–3838, 800/565–0201 in the Maritimes) sails between Caribou, Nova Scotia, and Wood Islands, from May to mid-December. The crossing takes about 75 minutes, and the round-trip costs approximately $45 per vehicle, $50 for a recreational vehicle; foot passengers pay $10. Reservations are not accepted, and no fares are collected inbound; you pay only on leaving the Island.

By Plane

Charlottetown Airport (⊠ 250 Maple Hills Ave., ☎ 902/566–7997 is 5 km (3 mi) north of town. Air Canada/Air Nova and Canadian Airlines International/Air Atlantic offer daily service to major cities in eastern Canada and the United States via Halifax (for phone numbers, *see* Airline Travel *in* the Gold Guide). **Prince Edward Air** (☎ 902/566–4488) is available for private charters.

Getting Around

By Car

The lack of public transportation on the Island makes having your own vehicle almost a necessity. There are more than 3,700 km (2,300 mi) of paved road in the province, including the three scenic coastal drives called Lady Slipper Drive, Blue Heron Drive, and Kings Byway. The adventurous will enjoy exploring the designated "Heritage Roads," which consist of red clay, the native soil base. These unpaved roads meander through undeveloped areas of rural Prince Edward Island, where you're likely to see lots of wildflowers and birds. A four-wheel-drive vehicle is not necessary, but in spring and inclement weather the mud can get quite deep and the narrow roads become impassable. Keep an eye open for bicycles, motorcycles, and pedestrians.

Contacts and Resources

Emergencies
Fire, police (☎ 0).

Golf
For a publication listing courses, contact **Golf Prince Edward Island** (✉ Box 2653, Charlottetown C1A 8C3, ☎ 800/463–4734).

Guided Tours
The Island has about 20 sightseeing tours, including double-decker bus tours, taxi tours, cycling tours, harbor cruises, and walking tours. Most tour companies are based in Charlottetown and offer excursions around the city and to the beaches. **Ed's Taxi** (☎ 902/892–6561) can be booked for tours by the hour or day. For a listing of current tour companies, contact **Tourism PEI** (☞ Visitor Information, *below*).

Hiking
Island Nature Trust and Island Trails (✉ Ravenwood, Box 265, Charlottetown C1A 7K4, ☎ 902/362–4275, FAX 902/628–6331) publishes a nature-trail map of the Island.

Hospital
Queen Elizabeth Hospital (✉ Riverside Dr., Charlottetown, ☎ 902/566–6200).

Shopping
Information on crafts outlets is provided by the **Prince Edward Island Crafts Council** (✉ 156 Richmond St., Charlottetown C1A 1H9, ☎ 902/892–5152).

Visitor Information
Tourism PEI (✉ Box 940, Charlottetown C1A 7M5, ☎ 902/368–4444 or 800/463–4734, FAX 902/368–6613) publishes an excellent annual guide for visitors and maintains eight Visitor Information Centres (VICs) on the Island. The main **Visitor Information Centre** is in Charlottetown (✉ 178 Water St.) and is open mid-May–October, daily; November–mid-May, weekdays.

13 Nova Scotia

Compact and distinctive, this little
province on the Atlantic Coast is a
melange of cultures: Gaelic street signs
in Pugwash and Mabou, French masses
in Chéticamp and Point de l'Eglise,
black gospel choirs in Halifax,
Mi'Kmaq handicrafts in Eskasoni,
onion-dome churches in Sydney,
sauerkraut in Lunenburg, and Yankee
Puritanism in Clark's Harbour. Though
quiet coastal villages may set the tone,
urban centers like Halifax and Sydney
exist with a pleasant mix of big-city life
and small-town charm.

Updated by
Taiya Barss

I NFINITE RICHES IN A LITTLE ROOM," wrote Elizabethan playwright Christopher Marlowe. He might have been referring to Nova Scotia, Canada's second-smallest province, which packs an impossible variety of cultures and landscapes into an area half the size of Ohio.

Water, water everywhere, but that's not all. Within the convoluted coastline of Nova Scotia, you will find highlands to rival Scotland's, rugged fjords, rolling farmland, and networks of rivers, ponds, and lakes calling out to kayakers and canoers. Fifty-six km (35 mi) is the farthest you can get from the sea anywhere in the province. Pounding waves in summer and the grinding ice of winter storms have sculpted the coastal rocks and reduced sandstone cliffs to stretches of sandy beach. Inland, the fertile fields of the Annapolis Valley yield peaches, corn, apples, and plums that are sold at farm stands in summer and fall. A succession of wildflowers covers the roadside with blankets of color: purple and blue lupines; yellow coltsfoot; pink fireweed. Each of the wild habitats—bogs, dry barrens, tidal wetlands, open fields, dense spruce woods, and climax hardwood forests—has its own distinctive plant life. Thousands of years ago, scouring glaciers left their scars on the land; the Halifax Citadel stands atop a drumlin, a round-topped hill left by the retreating ice. Wildlife abounds: ospreys and bald eagles; moose and deer; whales in the water off Cape Breton and Brier Island.

The original people of Nova Scotia, the Mi'Kmaqs, have been here 10,000 years. In the early days of European exploration, the French and English navigators found these natives settled on the shores and harvesting the sea. In later years, waves of immigrants filled the province with an array of cultures: Germans in Lunenburg County; Highland Scots displaced by their landlords' preference for sheep; New England Loyalists escaping the American Revolution; blacks arriving as freemen or escaped slaves; Jews in Halifax, Sydney, and industrial Cape Breton; Ukranians, Poles, West Indians, Italians, and Lebanese drawn to the Sydney steel mill. These people maintain their customs and cultures. There are Gaelic signs in Mabou and Iona, German sausage and sauerkraut in Lunenburg, Greek music festivals in Halifax. The Acadians fly their tricolored flag with pride. Scots step dance to antique fiddle airs. The fragrance of burning sweetgrass mingles with the prayers of the Mi'Kmaqs' Catholic mass, blending the old ways with the new.

This is a little buried nation, with a capital city the same size as Marlowe's London. Before Canada was formed in 1867, Nova Scotians were prosperous shipwrights and merchants, trading with the world. Who created Cunard Lines? A Haligonian, Samuel Cunard. Those days brought democracy to the British colonies, left Victorian mansions in the salty little ports, and created a uniquely Nova Scotian outlook: worldly, approachable, and sturdily independent.

Pleasures and Pastimes

Dining

Skilled chefs find their abilities enhanced by the availability of succulent blueberries, crisp apples, wild mushrooms, home-raised poultry, quality beef, fresh-from-the-sea lobster, cultivated mussels, Digby scallops, and fine Atlantic salmon. The quality of ingredients comes from the closeness of the harvest. Agriculture and fisheries (both wild harvest and aquaculture) are never far away.

Helping travelers discover for themselves the best tastes of the province, the Nova Scotian culinary industry has formed an organization called the Taste of Nova Scotia. It pulls together the producers and the pre-parers, setting quality standards to ensure that patrons at member restaurants receive authentic Nova Scotian food. Look for their symbol: a golden oval porthole framing food and a ship.

CATEGORY	COST*
$$$$	over $50
$$$	$35–$50
$$	$15–$35
$	under $15

*per person, in Canadian dollars, for a three-course meal, excluding drinks, service, and 15% harmonized sales tax (HST)

Lodging

Nova Scotia's strength lies in a sprinkling of first-class resorts that have retained the traditional feel, top country inns where a dedication to fine dining with an emphasis on local products and high-level accommodation rule, and a few superior corporate hotels. Bed-and-breakfasts, particularly those in smaller towns, are often exceptional. Most of the resorts and many B&Bs are seasonal. In addition to the reliable chains, Halifax and Dartmouth have a number of excellent hotels; reservations are necessary year-round and can be made by calling Check In (☞ Contacts and Resources *in* Nova Scotia A to Z, *below*). Expect to pay considerably more in the capital district than elsewhere.

CATEGORY	COST*
$$$$	over $135
$$$	$110–$135
$$	$80–$110
$	under $80

*All prices are for a standard double room, excluding 15% harmonized sales tax (HST), in Canadian dollars.

Music

Scottish immigrants brought fiddles and folk airs to eastern Nova Scotia and Cape Breton, where Highland music mingled with that of the Acadians already here and the Irish soon to follow. Today the region enjoys world renown as a center of distinctive Celtic music. Watch for concerts by the Rankin Family or the Barra MacNeils; by outstanding fiddlers like Natalie MacMaster, Ashley MacIsaac, Buddy MacMaster, or Wendy MacIsaac; and the Gaelic-punk sound of singer Mary Jane Lamond. Since these stars grew up here, a sharp-eyed visitor stands a good chance of catching them at a square dance in Inverness County or at a milling frolic on Bras d'Or Lake. For 10 days in October, the Celtic Colors International Festival (☎ 902/562–6700) brings musicians from around the world to more than 20 locations throughout Cape Breton.

The Halifax pub scene is a hot spot for other musical styles. Names to watch for include the crooner Johnnie Favorite, country singer Rita MacNeil, the a cappella group Four the Moment, and the lightly punk-flavored Plumptre.

Outdoor Activities and Sports

BEACHES

The province is one big seashore. The warmest beaches are found on the Northumberland Strait shore. The west coast of Cape Breton and Bras d'Or Lake also offer fine beaches and warm salt water.

BIRDING

A healthy population of bald eagles nest in Cape Breton, where they reel above Bras d'Or Lake or perch in trees along riverbanks. The Bird

Island boat tour from Big Bras d'Or circles islands where Atlantic puffins, kittiwakes, and guillemots nest in rocky cliffs. In May and August, the Bay of Fundy teems with migrating shorebirds, and the tidal marshes near the end of Bird Island, Merrigomish, are home to great blue heron rookeries. The useful *Where to Find the Birds in Nova Scotia,* published by the Nova Scotia Bird Society, is available locally in places such as the Nova Scotia Government Bookstore, opposite Province House on Granville Street in Halifax.

FISHING

Nova Scotia has more than 9,000 lakes and 100 brooks; practically all lakes and streams are open to anglers. The catch includes Atlantic salmon (June–September), brook and sea trout, bass, rainbow trout, and shad. You can get a nonresident fishing license from any Department of Natural Resources office in the province and at most sporting-goods stores. Before casting a line in national park waters, it is necessary to obtain a transferrable National Parks Fishing License, available at park offices. In May and June, many rivers and brooks have spectacular spring runs of smelt and gaspereaux (river herring or alewives). Limited quantities can be taken without a license; inquire locally for times and sites of good runs. Licenses are not required for saltwater fishing. South of Shelburne, from Barrington to Digby, is the most prosperous fishing region in the province.

FOSSIL HUNTING AND ROCK HOUNDING

Coal seams and shale cliffs along Cape Breton's shores yield fossilized ferns, leaves, and petrified wood. Kempt Head on Boularderie Island, Sutherland's Corner on Sydney Mines's Shore Road, and the beach at Point Aconi are good places to search. The province's richest source of fossils is the Minas Basin, near Joggins and Parrsboro, where dinosaur fossils, agate, and amethyst are found. You can visit the Fundy Geological Museum in Parrsboro and the Joggins Fossil Center. Guided tours of the cliffs are available. Rock hounds are welcome to gather what they find along the beaches, but a permit from the Nova Scotia Museum is required to dig along the cliffs.

Wineries

Nova Scotian wineries are becoming exceedingly popular. While local wines are featured in many restaurants, they can be sampled for free and bought by the bottle for as little as $8 at the vineyards they come from. Wineries to visit include Jost Vineyards in Malagash and Sainte Famille Winery in Falmouth.

Exploring Nova Scotia

Along the coast of Nova Scotia, the wild Atlantic Ocean crashes against rocky outcrops, eddies into sheltered coves, or flows placidly over expanses of white sand. In the Bay of Fundy, which has the highest tides in the world, the receding sea reveals stretches of red mud flats; then it rushes back in a ferocious wall that should be treated with respect. There are dense forests, rolling Annapolis Valley farms, and the most dramatic terrain, Cape Breton, where rugged mountains plunge to meet the waves.

When arriving in Nova Scotia from New Brunswick via the Trans-Canada Highway (Hwy. 104), you have three ways to proceed into the province. Amherst is the first community after the border. From Amherst, Highway 104 will take you toward Halifax, only a two-hour drive away. Touring alternatives lie to the north and south. Route 6, to the north, leaves Amherst to follow the shore of the Northumberland Strait; farther east is Cape Breton. Route 2, to the south, is a less-traveled road and a favorite with children because of nearby fossil-studded shores. Branch roads lead to the Annapolis Valley and other points south. Drivers should be aware that the sharply curving rural roads warrant careful attention.

Great Itineraries

The province naturally divides itself into regions that can be explored in three to seven days. Some visitors do a whirlwind drive around, taking in only a few sights; but Nova Scotia's varied cultural landscape deserves careful exploration. If you have more days, try linking up to two or more tours. Above all, take your time exploring the province. The back roads and side trips leading down to the shore are often the most rewarding.

Numbers in the text correspond to numbers in the margin and on the Nova Scotia and Halifax maps.

IF YOU HAVE 3 DAYS
Start in **Halifax** ①–⑫, a port city that combines old maritime charm with new architecture, lively shops, and a musical nightlife centered on a dozen friendly pubs. Explore the South Shore and Annapolis Valley, taking in the Lighthouse Route and Evangeline Trail. The two trails form a loop that begins and ends in Halifax (via Route 3, 103, or 333, the scenic road around the shore), covering a distance of approximately 850 km (527 mi) with no side trips. Leaving Halifax, head for **Peggy's Cove**, a picturesque fishing village perched on sea-washed granite and surrounded by coastal barrens. Explore the crafts shops of **Mahone Bay** and travel on to 🔲 **Lunenburg** ⑮, where the culture of Atlantic Coast fisheries is explored in the Fisheries Museum. Overnight in Lunenburg before continuing on Route 3 or 103 to **Shelburne** ⑰ on Day 2. You can visit **Yarmouth** ⑱ and travel on to **Digby** for a lunch of scallops. **Annapolis Royal** ㉑, with its gardens, historic sites, and harbor-front boardwalk, is a lovely spot to spend an afternoon, or you may want to drive down Digby Neck to visit **Long Island and Brier Island** ⑳ and catch a whale-watching cruise in season. Travel on to the elm-lined streets of 🔲 **Wolfville** ㉒, home of Acadia University, for an overnight stay. The town is near Grand Pré National Historic Site, a tranquil park and stone church that recount the suffering of Acadians expelled from Nova Scotia in 1755. On Day 3, check tide times and plan a drive to the shore of Minas Basin, where the tides are the highest in the world. A leisurely drive will put you back in Halifax by late afternoon.

IF YOU HAVE 5 DAYS
You can spend a day or two in 🔲 **Halifax** ①–⑫ before exploring the Eastern Shore, the Atlantic Coast east of the city that is perhaps the most scenic and unspoiled stretch of coastline in mainland Nova Scotia. Route 7 winds along a deeply indented, glaciated coastline of rocky waters interspersed with pocket beaches, long and narrow fjords, and fishing villages. **Musquodoboit Harbour** ㉔ is a haven for fishing enthusiasts. Nearby is Martinique Beach, one of Nova Scotia's best. Continue north to **Sherbrooke Village** ㉕, full of refurbished late-19th-century structures. Route 7 turns inland and follows the St. Mary's River toward **Antigonish** ㉖ on the Sunrise Trail. Historians will appreciate a visit to Hector Heritage Quay in 🔲 **Pictou** ㉗, where the Scots landed in 1773. From Pictou, Route 6 runs beside an apparently endless string of beaches with many summer homes plunked in the adjoining fields. Turn right to **Malagash**, where Jost Vineyards invites wine tasting and tours. Be sure to visit Seagull Pewter in **Pugwash** ㉘. A half-hour drive will take you to 🔲 **Amherst** ㉙. Continue on to **Joggins** ㉛ and search for souvenirs in its sandstone cliffs. For more fossils, head to **Parrsboro** ㉜, which has the Fundy Geological Museum.

IF YOU HAVE 7 DAYS

With its spectacular scenery, rich musical culture, and meandering seaside highways, Cape Breton Island is one part of Nova Scotia that should not be missed and is a perfect place for a leisurely seven-day tour. Follow the coastal route, which takes you on a west-to-east loop from the Canso Strait Causeway, taking lots of time to explore side roads. Overnight in ⊞ **Mabou** ㉞, the beating heart of the island's rich musical tradition. From a base in ⊞ **Margaree Harbour** ㉟, take a day or more to explore the Cabot Trail and Cape Breton Highlands National Park and the remote fishing villages north of the park. June and July bring a profusion of wild flowers to highland meadows and bogs. You can photograph the spectacular scenery, walk the trails to hidden waterfalls, or take one of the northern peninsula's many whale-watching tours. There are crafts stores along St. Ann's Bay, but allow time to visit the Alexander Graham Bell National Historic Site in **Baddeck** ㊳, and spend the night in ⊞ **Iona** ㊴. A day or two in ⊞ **Sydney** ㊵ will position you for an afternoon excursion to the Glace Bay Miners' Museum in **Glace Bay** ㊶ and a daylong visit to Fortress of Louisbourg National Historic Park, the largest historic restoration in Canada, and the town of **Louisbourg** ㊷, which has an interesting shipwreck museum. Take Route 4 back to Canso Causeway through **Big Pond,** home of singer Rita McNeil, and spend a day wandering the colorful Acadian villages of Isle Madame, such as **Arichat** ㊸.

When to Tour Nova Scotia

The best time of year to visit is mid-June–mid-September; in fact, many resorts, hotels, and attractions are open only during July and August. Nova Scotia, particularly the Cape Breton area, is very popular in fall due to the changing of the leaves and the 10-day Celtic Colors International Festival in October. Lobster lovers will find the popular seafood plentiful in May and June. Whale-watching and wildlife cruises as well as sea-kayaking outfitters generally operate from July to mid-September. Most golf courses stay open from June until late September, and some into October. Skiing (both downhill and cross-country) is popular at a variety of locations, including Kejimkujik and Cape Breton Highlands, from mid-December to early April.

HALIFAX AND DARTMOUTH

The Halifax and Dartmouth metro area, now known, along with the whole former County of Halifax, as the Halifax Regional Municipality, surrounds the second-largest natural harbor in the world, Halifax Harbour. It bustles with activity day and night and flavors the rest of the city with its presence. Pubs, shops, museums, parks, and public gardens buzz with activity. Jazz, buskers, outdoor festivals, and cultural and sporting events are plentiful. Galleries, concerts, theater, and fine dining combine to make the twin cities a destination for any season, with a mix of big-city life and small-town charm. Halifax has drawn recent attention because of the success of the film *Titanic*. One hundred fifty victims of the disaster are buried in three cemeteries here, and the Maritime Museum of the Atlantic has a *Titanic* display.

Halifax

1,137 km (705 mi) northeast of Boston, 275 km (171 mi) southeast of Moncton, New Brunswick.

Salty and urbane, learned and plain-spoken, Halifax is large enough to have the trappings of a capital city, yet small enough to retain the warmth and convenience of a small town.

Nova Scotia

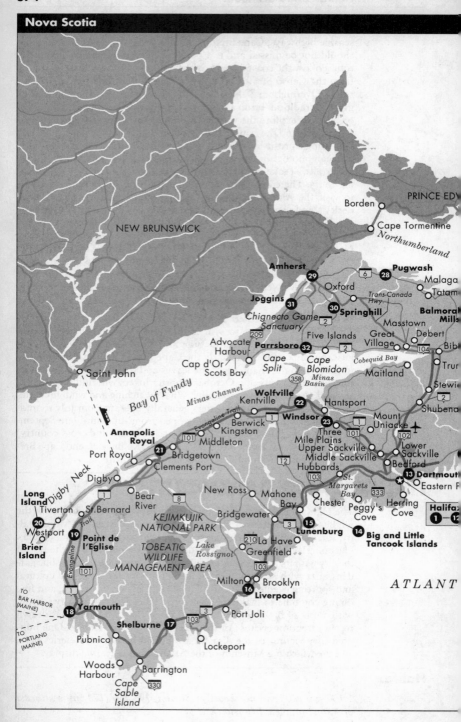

PRINCE EDW

Borden

Cape Tormentine

Northumberland

NEW BRUNSWICK

Amherst

29

Oxford

6

28

Pugwash

Malaga

Tatam

Joggins

31

Trans-Canada Hwy.

30

Springhill

Balmora

Mills

Chignecto Game

Sanctuary

Masstown

Debert

Bib

2

Five Islands

Great

Village

Advocate

Harbour

Parrsboro

32

2

Maitland

104

Trur

209

Cap d'Or

Scots Bay

Cape

Split

Cape

Blomidon

Cobequid Bay

Stewie

2

Saint John

358

Minas

Basin

Shubena

Bay of Fundy

Minas Channel

Wolfville

22

Kentville

Hantsport

Mount

Uniacke

Windsor

23

Evangeline Trail

Berwick

Kingston

1

Three

Mile Plains

Upper Sackville

101

Annapolis

Royal

101

Middleton

1

Lower

Sackville

Port Royal

21

Bridgetown

Clements Port

12

Middle Sackville

Bedford

102

13

Dartmouth

Digby

Digby Neck

Bear

River

8

New Ross

Hubbards

103

St.

Margarets

Bay

Eastern F

Long

Island

1

Mahone

Bay

Chester

333

Halifa

Tiverton

St.Bernard

KEJIMKUJIK

NATIONAL PARK

Bridgewater

Peggy's

Cove

Herring

Cove

1

12

20

Evangeline Trail

Point de

l'Eglise

TOBEATIC

WILDLIFE

MANAGEMENT AREA

Lake

Rossignol

3

15

Lunenburg

14

Big and Little

Tancook Islands

Westport

19

210

La Have

Greenfield

Brier

Island

101

103

Milton

16

Brooklyn

Liverpool

ATLANT

TO

BAR HARBOR

(MAINE)

1

18

Yarmouth

3

Port Joli

TO

PORTLAND

(MAINE)

Pubnico

Shelburne

17

103

Lockeport

Woods

Harbour

Barrington

330

Cape

Sable

Island

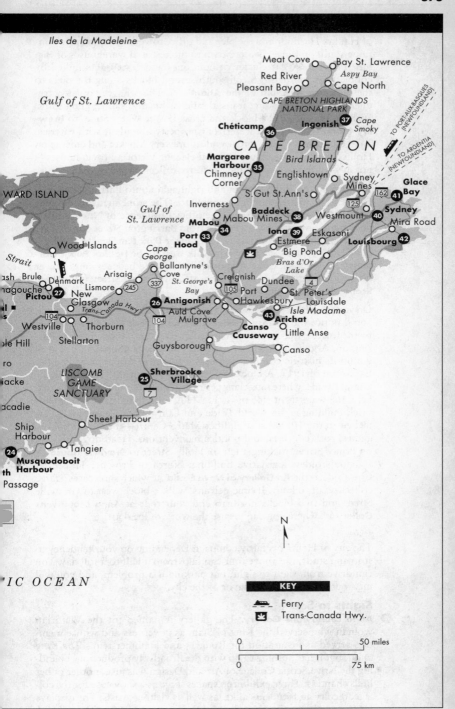

Iles de la Madeleine

Gulf of St. Lawrence

Meat Cove
Bay St. Lawrence
Red River
Aspy Bay
Pleasant Bay
Cape North

CAPE BRETON HIGHLANDS
NATIONAL PARK

Chéticamp 36
Cape Smoky
Ingonish 37

C A P E   B R E T O N

Margaree Harbour 35
Chimney Corner
Bird Islands
Englishtown
Sydney Mines
Glace Bay

WARD ISLAND

Gulf of St. Lawrence

Inverness
S. Gut St.Ann's
162
41

Baddeck 38
Westmount
125
Sydney

Mabou
Mabou Mines
40
Mira Road

Port Hood 33
34

Iona 39
Eskasoni
Estmere
Louisbourg 42

Wood Islands

Cape George

Big Pond

Bras d'Or Lake

Ballantyne's Cove
Strait
Arisaig
337
Creignish
Dundee
ash Brule
Denmark
245
Lismore
St. George's Bay
105
Port
St. Peter's
4
hagouche
Pictou 27
New
Antigonish 26
Hawkesbury
Isle Madame
Glasgow
Auld Cove
Arichat 43
104
Trans-Canada Hwy.
Mulgrave
Little Anse
Westville
Thorburn
Canso Causeway
le Hill
Stellarton
Canso
ro
Guysborough
iacke
LISCOMB GAME SANCTUARY
Sherbrooke Village 25
acadie
7
Ship Harbour
Sheet Harbour
24
Tangier
Musquodoboit Harbour
th
Passage

N

IC OCEAN

KEY	
🛥	Ferry
🍁	Trans-Canada Hwy.

0   50 miles
0   75 km

TO PORT-AUX-BASQUES (NEWFOUNDLAND)
TO ARGENTIA (NEWFOUNDLAND)

A Good Walk

Begin on Upper Water Street at **Purdy's Wharf** ①, for unobstructed views of Halifax Harbour and the pier and office towers of this wharf. Continue south on Lower Water Street to the restored warehouses of **Historic Properties** ②, a cluster of boutiques and restaurants linked by cobblestone footpaths. Stroll south several blocks along the piers to the **Maritime Museum of the Atlantic** ③: The wharves outside frequently welcome visiting transatlantic yachts and sail-training ships. Walk to the end of the block and cross Lower Water Street to **Brewery Market** ④, restored waterfront property abundant with eateries. Take the elevator at the office end of Brewery Market and emerge on Hollis Street. Turn left, past several elegant Victorian town houses—notably Keith Hall—once the executive offices of the brewery.

Turn right onto Bishop Street and right again onto Barrington Street, Halifax's main downtown thoroughfare. The stone mansion on your right is **Government House** ⑤, the official residence of Nova Scotia's lieutenant governor. Take a detour from Barrington Street onto Spring Garden Road and the attractive shops in the Park Lane and Spring Garden Place shopping centers; then walk west to the **Halifax Public Gardens** ⑥, where you can rest your legs on shaded benches amid flower beds and rare trees. A block to the north, on Summer Street, is the **Nova Scotia Museum of Natural History** ⑦.

On your way back to Barrington Street on Bell Road and Sackville Street, you'll notice the **Halifax Citadel National Historic Site** ⑧, dominated by the fortress that once commanded the city. On a lot defined by Barrington, Argyle, and Prince streets lies **St. Paul's Church** ⑨; one wall within its historic confines contains a fragment of the great Halifax Explosion of 1917. A block farther north and facing City Hall is the Grand Parade, where musicians perform at noon on summer days. From here, the waterfront side of Citadel Hill, look uphill: The tall, stylish brick building is the World Trade and Convention Centre and is attached to the 10,000-seat Halifax Metro Centre—the site of hockey games, rock concerts, and political conventions. Head down the hill on Prince Street, making a left on Hollis Street to **Province House** ⑩, Canada's oldest legislative building. North of Province House, at Cheapside, is the **Art Gallery of Nova Scotia** ⑪, which showcases a large collection of folk art. If time permits, walk a block west to Granville Street and two blocks north to end your tour at **Anna Leonowens Gallery** ⑫, where you can peruse the work of local artists.

TIMING

The city of Halifax is fairly compact: Depending on your tendency to stop and study, the above tour can take from a half to a full day. You can drive from sight to sight, but parking is a problem, and you will miss out on much of the flavor of the city.

Sights to See

⑫ **Anna Leonowens Gallery.** The gallery is named for the Victorian woman who served the King of Siam as governess and whose memoirs served as inspiration for Rodgers and Hammerstein's *The King and I*, but it has nothing to do with the Broadway production. Founding the Nova Scotia College of Art and Design was just another of her life's chapters. Three exhibition spaces serve as a showcase for the college, faculty and students alike, as well as visiting artists. The displays focus on contemporary studio and media art. ✉ *1891 Granville St.,* ☎ *902/494–8223.* 🎟 *Free.* 🕐 *Tues.–Fri. 11–5, Sat. noon–4.*

⑪ **Art Gallery of Nova Scotia.** Sheltered within this historic building is an extensive permanent collection of more than 4,000 works, including

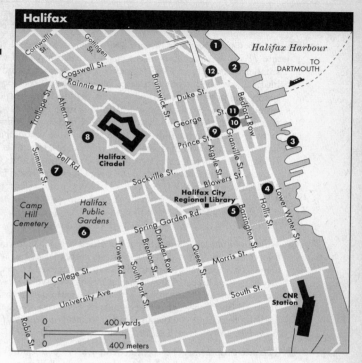

Halifax

an internationally recognized collection of maritime and folk art by artists such as wood-carver Sydney Howard and painter Joe Norris. A recent addition is the actual home of the late folk painter Maude Lewis, whose bright, cheery paintings cover the tiny structure inside and out. The collection of contemporary art has major works by Christopher Pratt, Alex Colville, John Nesbitt, and Dawn McNutt. ⊠ *1741 Hollis St., at Cheapside,* ☎ *902/424–7542,* FAX *902/424–0750.* ◽ *$2.50.* ⊘ *June–Aug., Tues.–Wed. and Fri. 10–5, Thurs. 10–9, weekends noon–5; Sept.–May, Tues.–Fri. 10–5, weekends noon–5.*

❹ **Brewery Market.** This sprawling ironstone complex was once Keith's Brewery (named for Alexander Keith, a 19th-century brewer); now it houses offices, restaurants, and shops. It's a favored haunt of Haligonians on Saturday mornings year-round and on Fridays in summer, when a farmer's market invites the opportunity to sample local produce, meats, and cheeses. ⊠ *Between Hollis and Lower Water Sts.*

OFF THE BEATEN PATH

FAIRVIEW CEMETERY – This cemetery is the final resting place of 121 victims of the *Titanic.* The graves are easily located in a graceful arc of granite tombstones. One grave—marked J. Dawson—attracts particular attention from recent visitors. It's not Jack, the fictional Minnesota artist, however, but James Dawson, a coal trimmer from Ireland. Nineteen other victims are buried in Mount Olivet Catholic Cemetery, 10 in the Baron de Hirsch Jewish Cemetery. The ☞ **Maritime Museum of the Atlantic** has an exhibit about the disaster. ⊠ *3720 Windsor St., 3 km (2 mi) north of downtown.*

❺ **Government House.** Built between 1799 and 1805 for Sir John Wentworth, the Loyalist governor of New Hampshire, and his racy wife, Fannie (Thomas Raddall's novel *The Governor's Lady* tells their story), this house has since been the official residence of the province's lieu-tenant governor. It is not open to the public. ⊠ *1451 Barrington St.*

★ ❽ **Halifax Citadel National Historic Site.** The Citadel, erected between 1826 and 1856, was the heart of the city's fortifications and was linked to smaller forts and gun emplacements on the harbor islands and on the bluffs above the harbor entrance. Several other forts stood on the site before the present one. Kilted soldiers drill in front of the **Army Museum,** once the barracks, and a cannon is fired every day at noon. Before leaving, take in the view from the Citadel: the spiky downtown crowded between the hilltop and the harbor; the wooded islands at the harbor's mouth; and the naval dockyard under the Angus L. MacDonald Bridge, the nearer of the two bridges connecting Halifax with Dart-mouth. The handsome, four-sided **Town Clock** on Citadel Hill was given to Halifax by Prince Edward, Duke of Kent, military commander from 1794 to 1800. ⊠ *Citadel Hill,* ☎ *902/426–5080.* ☞ *June 15–Aug. $5.75; May 15–June 14 and Sept.–Oct. 15 $3.50; rest of yr free.* ☉ *June 15–Aug., daily 9–6; Sept.–June 14, daily 9–5.*

❻ **Halifax Public Gardens.** One of the oldest formal Victorian gardens in North America, this city oasis had its start in 1753 as a private gar-den. Its layout was completed in 1875 by Richard Power, former gar-dener to the Duke of Devonshire in Ireland. Gravel paths wind among ponds, trees, and flower beds, revealing an astonishing variety of plants from all over the world. The centerpiece is a filigreed gazebo erected in 1887 for Queen Victoria's Golden Jubilee. ⊠ *Bounded by Sackville, Summer, and S. Park Sts. and Spring Garden Rd.*

❷ **Historic Properties.** These waterfront warehouses date from from the early 19th century, when trade and war made Halifax prosperous. They were built by such raffish characters as Enos Collins, a privateer, smug-gler, and shipper whose vessels defied Napoleon's blockade to bring American supplies to the Duke of Wellington. Collins was also a prime mover in the Halifax Banking Company, which evolved into the Royal Bank of Canada, now the country's largest bank. The buildings have since been taken over by quality shops, chic offices, and restaurants including those in Privateer's Warehouse (☞ Dining and Lodging, *below*). ⊠ *Lower Water and Hollis Sts.*

❸ **Maritime Museum of the Atlantic.** The exhibits in this restored chan-dlery and warehouse on the waterfront include small boats once used around the coast, as well as displays describing Nova Scotia's proud sailing heritage, from the days when the province, on its own, was one of the world's foremost shipbuilding and trading nations. Other ex-hibits explore the Halifax Explosion of 1917, shipwrecks, and lifesaving. Permanently moored outside, after a long life of charting the coasts of Labrador and the Arctic, is the hydrographic steamer *Acadia.* At the next wharf, in summer, is Canada's naval memorial, **HMCS** *Sackville,* the sole survivor of a fleet that escorted convoys of ships from Hali-fax to England during World War II.

Much of the 1997 movie *Titanic* was filmed in Nova Scotia, and the museum has a permanent exhibit about the disaster. Halifax was, in a sense, the final destination of the *Titanic,* since many victims are buried in the city (☞ **Fairview Cemetery**). The display includes 20 artifacts and dozens of photographs. The centerpiece is the only surviving deck chair, given to a Halifax minister who performed many services. There is a section of wall paneling; a balustrade molding and part of a newel post from the dual curving staircase; a cribbage board carved from *Ti-tanic* oak by the ship's carpenter of one of the rescue ships; and the log kept by a wireless operator at Cape Race, Newfoundland, on the fateful night. The staff provides authoritative commentary on the disaster. ⊠ *1675 Lower Water St.,* ☎ *902/424–7490 or 902/424–7491,* FAX *902/424–0612.* ☉ *June–mid-Oct., Mon. and Wed.–Sat. 9:30–5:30, Tues. 9:30–8, Sun. 1–5:30; mid-Oct.–May, Wed.–Sat. 9:30–5, Tues. 9:30–8, Sun. 1–5.*

🐾 ❼ **Nova Scotia Museum of Natural History.** Nova Scotia's natural wonders are preserved in several galleries that focus on both land and sea. The exhibits include a sei whale skeleton and Mi'Kmaq quillwork. The museum is most easily recognized by the huge fiberglass model of the tiny northern spring peeper (a frog), which "clings" to the side of the building May–October. ⊠ *1747 Summer St.,* ☎ *902/424–7353,* FAX *902/424–0560.* ⊡ *$3.* ☉ *Mid-May–Oct., Mon.–Tues., and Thurs.– Sun. 9:30–5:30, Wed. 9:30–8; Nov.–mid-May, Tues. and Thurs.–Sun. 9:30–5, Wed. 9:30–8.*

Point Pleasant Park. Most of the city's secondary fortifications have been turned into public parks. This one encompasses 186 wooded acres, veined with walking trails and seafront paths. The park was leased from the British Crown by the city for 999 years, at a shilling a year. Its major military installation is a massive round martello tower dating from the late 18th century. Point Pleasant is about 12 blocks down South Park Street from Spring Garden Road.

❿ **Province House.** Charles Dickens proclaimed this structure "a gem of Georgian architecture." It's now a National Historic Site. Erected in 1819 to house Britain's first overseas self-government, the sandstone building still serves as the meeting place for the provincial legislature. ⊠ *1726 Hollis St.,* ☎ *902/424–4661.* ⊡ *Free.* ☉ *July–Aug., weekdays 9–5, weekends 10–4; Sept.–June, weekdays 8:30–4:30.*

❶ **Purdy's Wharf.** Named after a famous shipping family from the 19th century, this wharf is composed of a pier and twin office towers that stand right in the harbor. An architectural first, the buildings use ocean water to generate air-conditioning. ⊠ *Upper Water St.*

❾ **St. Paul's Church.** St. Paul's, opened in 1750, is Canada's oldest Protestant church and the burial site of many colonial notables. Inside, on the north end, a piece of metal is embedded in the wall. It is a fragment of the *Mont Blanc,* one of the two ships whose collision caused the Halifax Explosion of December 6, 1917, the greatest human-caused explosion prior to that at Hiroshima. ⊠ *1749 Argyle St.,* ☎ *902/429–2240.* ☉ *Sept.–May, weekdays 9–4:30; June–Aug., Mon.– Sat. 9–4:30; services Sun. at 8:30 AM, 10:30 AM, and 7:30 PM.*

Dining and Lodging

$$–$$$ ✕ **MacAskill's Restaurant.** Diners can experience Nova Scotian hospitality in this romantic dining room overlooking beautiful Halifax Harbour. The chefs create a variety of seafood dishes prepared with the finest, freshest fish available. Specialties include pepper steak, flambéed table-side. ⊠ *88 Alderney Dr., Dartmouth Ferry Terminal Bldg.,* ☎ *902/466–3100. AE, DC, MC, V.*

$$–$$$ ✕ **Salty's on the Waterfront.** This restaurant overlooking Privateer's
★ Wharf and the entire harbor gets the prize for the best location in the city. Request a table with a window view and save room for the famous dessert, called "Cadix" (chocolate mousse over praline crust). The Salty Dog Bar & Grill on the ground level is less expensive and serves lunch outside on the wharf in summer. ⊠ *1869 Upper Water St.,* ☎ *902/423–6818. Reservations essential. AE, DC, MC, V.*

$–$$$ ✕ **Privateer's Warehouse.** History surrounds you in this 200-year-old building, where three restaurants share early 18th-century stone walls and hewn beams. Upper Deck Waterfront Fishery & Grill (☎ 902/422–

1289), done in a nautical theme, has great views of the harbor and offers lobsters from their holding tank. Middle Deck Pasta Works & Beverage Co. (☎ 902/426–1500) has a bistro-style atmosphere and serves innovative pastas as well as traditional cuisine; there's also a children's menu. Lower Deck Good Time Pub (☎ 902/426–1501) is a boisterous bar with long trestle tables and a patio; fish-and-chips and other pub food is served. ⊠ *Historic Properties, Lower Water St. AE, DC, MC, V.*

$–$$ ✕ **Satisfaction Feast.** This small vegetarian restaurant is informal, friendly, and usually packed at lunchtime. The food is simple and wholesome; try the fresh whole-wheat bread and one of the daily curries. ⊠ *1581 Grafton St., ☎ 902/422–3540. AE, MC, V.*

$$$–$$$$ ✕🏨 **Hotel Halifax.** This first-class Canadian Pacific hotel has spacious, attractive rooms, the majority with a panoramic view of the harbor. An aboveground pedway network provides easy access to the Historic Properties. The Crown Bistro ($$–$$$) has a unique blend of elegant dishes and lighter fare. Sam Slicks ($$), a cozy piano bar, has nightly entertainment and serves great food. ⊠ *1990 Barrington St., B3J 1P2, ☎ 902/425–6700 or 800/441–1414, FAX 902/425–6214. 279 rooms, 21 suites. Restaurant, piano bar, indoor pool, hot tub, sauna, exercise room. AE, DC, MC, V.*

$$–$$$ ✕🏨 **Prince George Hotel.** Contemporary mahogany furnishings in
★   this luxurious and understated business-oriented hotel include writing desks. Georgio's Restaurant ($$) serves Californian cuisine in a casual setting. The hotel is connected by underground tunnel to the World Trade and Convention Centre; pedway access to shops, offices, and entertainment is also provided. ⊠ *1725 Market St., B3J 3N9, ☎ 902/ 425–1986, 800/565–1567 in Canada. 207 rooms, 9 suites. Restaurant, bar, pool, hot tub, exercise room, concierge. AE, DC, MC, V.*

$$$$ 🏨 **Sheraton Halifax.** Built low to match neighboring historic ironstone buildings, this waterfront hotel varies in appearance from others in the chain. Its convenient location in Historic Properties contributes to its elegance. Other assets include an indoor pool with a summer sundeck. Halifax's only casino is in the lobby. ⊠ *1919 Upper Water St., B3J 3J5, ☎ 902/421–1700 or 800/325–3535, FAX 902/422–5805. 335 rooms, 19 suites. Restaurant, bar, room service, indoor pool, health club, dock, casino, concierge, meeting rooms. AE, DC, MC, V.*

$$$ 🏨 **Haliburton House Inn.** A historic property, this hotel is an elegant renovation of three 19th-century town houses. Comfortable rooms are furnished with period antiques, lending a homey ambience. Wild game and Atlantic seafood are served in an elegant dining room. ⊠ *5184 Morris St., B3J 1B3, ☎ 902/420–0658, FAX 902/423–2324. 25 rooms, 2 suites. Restaurant, library. CP. AE, DC, MC, V.*

$$ 🏨 **Cambridge Suites.** This hotel, in a convenient location, takes pride in its motto, "A suite for the price of a room." There are three suite sizes; all have sitting rooms and kitchenettes. ⊠ *1583 Brunswick St., B3J 3P5, ☎ 902/420–0555 or 800/565–1263, FAX 902/420–9379. 200 suites. Restaurant, bar, kitchenettes, hot tub, sauna, exercise room. CP. AE, D, MC, V.*

$$ 🏨 **Inn on the Lake.** A great value in a quiet location, this small country club–style hotel is on 5 acres of parkland on the edge of Fall River Lake, 10 minutes from Halifax and the airport. ⊠ *3009 Lake Thomas Dr., Box 29, Waverly B0N 2S0, ☎ 902/861–3480, FAX 902/861– 4883. 34 rooms, 12 suites. Restaurant, lounge, beach, airport shuttle. AE, MC, V.*

Nightlife and the Arts

THE ARTS

Halifax has a dynamic film industry, the product of which is presented at the **Atlantic Film Festival** (☎ 902/422–3456), held the third week in September. The festival also showcases feature films, TV movies, and documentaries made elsewhere in the Atlantic Provinces. **Wormwood's Dog and Monkey Cinema** (✉ 2112 Gottingen St., ☎ 902/422–3700) shows Canadian, foreign-language, and experimental films.

The **Du MaurierAtlantic Jazz Festival** (☎ 902/492–2225) takes place in mid-July. **Scotia Festival of Music** (☎ 902/429–9469) presents classical musicians via concert and master classes each May and June.

The **Neptune Theatre** (✉ 1593 Argyle St., ☎ 902/429–7300, 902/429–7070 box office), Canada's oldest professional repertory playhouse, stages year-round performances ranging from classics to contemporary Canadian drama. During the first week of September, the **Atlantic Fringe Festival** presents 40 shows in eight venues. **Grafton Street Dinner Theatre** (✉ 1741 Grafton St., ☎ 902/425–1961) holds performances Wednesday–Saturday. **Historic Feast Company** (☎ 902/420–1840) presents shows set in the 19th century at Historic Properties on Thursday, Friday, and Saturday evenings.

NIGHTLIFE

Cheers (✉ 1743 Grafton St., ☎ 902/421–1655), with bands and entertainment nightly, is a popular spot. **O'Carroll's** (✉ 1860 Upper Water St., ☎ 902/423–4405) has a restaurant, oyster bar, and lounge where you can hear live Irish music nightly. The multilevel entertainment center in Historic Properties, **Privateer's Warehouse** (✉ Lower Water St., ☎ 902/422–1289), is a popular nighttime hangout. At the ground-level Lower Deck tavern you can quaff a beer to Celtic music.

Shopping

The **Spring Garden Road** area has two stylish shopping malls, with shops selling everything from designer clothing to fresh pasta. **Jennifer of Nova Scotia** (✉ 5635 Spring Garden Rd., ☎ 902/425–3119) sells locally made jewelry, pottery, wool sweaters, and soaps. You can find fine crafts in **Historic Properties** (☞ Sights to See, *above*) and the **Barrington Inn Complex** (✉ 1875 Barrington St.). **Pewter House** (✉ 1875 Granville St., ☎ 902/423–8843), across the street from the Barrington Inn Complex, sells locally made and imported pewter goods from knickknacks and tableware to clocks and jewelry. The **Plaid Place** (✉ 1903 Barrington Pl., ☎ 902/429–6872 or 800/563–1749) has an array of tartans and Highland accessories. The **Wool Sweater Outlet** (✉ 1870 Hollis St., ☎ 902/422–9209) sells wool and cotton sweaters at reasonable prices.

Dartmouth

⓭ *Just north of Halifax via the A. Murray Mackay and Angus L. Macdonald bridges.*

Suburban in demeanor, Dartmouth was first settled by Quaker whalers from Nantucket. The 23 lakes within Dartmouth's boundaries provided the Mi'Kmaqs with a canoe route to the province's interior and to the Bay of Fundy. A 19th-century canal system connected the lakes for a brief time, but today there are only ruins, which have been partially restored as historic sites. You can either drive or take the ferry from Halifax to Dartmouth. If you walk along the water behind the modern Law Courts in Halifax, near Historic Properties, you'll soon reach the Dartmouth ferry terminal, jammed with commuters during rush hour. The terminal is home to the oldest operational saltwater ferry service in North America, which began in 1732.

The **Black Cultural Centre for Nova Scotia,** in Westphal (a neighborhood of Dartmouth), is in the heart of the oldest black community in the area. The museum, library, and educational complex are dedicated to the preservation of the history and culture of blacks in Nova Scotia, who first arrived here in the 1600s. ⊠ *Rte. 7 and Cherrybrooke Rd.,* ☎ *902/434–6223.* ☜ *$2.* ⊙ *Oct.–May, weekdays 9–5; June–Sept., weekdays 9–5, Sat. 10–4.*

Lodging

$$ ⊡ **Park Place Ramada Renaissance.** In Dartmouth's Burnside Industrial Park, this luxury hotel is aimed at the business traveler as well as families. There is a 108-ft indoor water slide. ⊠ *240 Brownlow Ave., B3B 1X6,* ☎ *902/468–8888, 800/561–3733 in Canada,* FAX *902/468–8765. 178 rooms, 30 suites. Restaurant, bar, room service, indoor pool, hot tub, sauna, exercise room, meeting rooms. AE, DC, MC, V.*

THE SOUTH SHORE AND ANNAPOLIS VALLEY

Mainland Nova Scotia is a long, narrow peninsula; no point in the province is more than 56 km (35 mi) from salt water. The South Shore is on the Atlantic side, the Annapolis Valley on the Fundy side, and though they are less than an hour apart by car, the two seem like different worlds. The South Shore is rocky coast, island-dotted bays, fishing villages, and shipyards; the Annapolis Valley is lumberyards, farms, vineyards, and orchards. The South Shore is German, French, and Yankee; the valley, British. The sea is everywhere on the South Shore; in the valley the sea is blocked from view by a ridge of mountains.

Route 103, Route 3, and various secondary roads form the province's designated Lighthouse Route, which leads southwest from Halifax down the South Shore. It touches the heads of several big bays and small harbors, revealing an ever-changing panorama of shoreline, inlet, and island. Charming little towns and fishing villages are spaced out every 50 km (31 mi) or so. The Lighthouse Route ends in Yarmouth and the Evangeline Trail begins, winding along the shore of St. Mary's Bay, through a succession of Acadian villages collectively known as the French Shore. Here, you'll notice the Acadian flag, tricolored with a gold star representing *stella maris,* the star of the sea. The star guides the French-speaking Acadians during troubled times, which have been frequent. In 1755, after residing for a century and a half in Nova Scotia, chiefly in the Annapolis Valley, the Acadians were expelled by the British—an event that inspired Longfellow's famous poem *Evangeline.* Some eluded capture and others slowly crept back; many settled in New Brunswick and along this shore of Nova Scotia. The villages blend seamlessly into one another for about 32 km (20 mi), each one, it seems, with its own wharf, fish plant, and enormous Catholic church. This tour mostly focuses on the towns along Route 1, but you should follow the side roads whenever the inclination strikes; the South Shore rewards slow, relaxed exploration.

The Annapolis Valley runs northeast like a huge trench, flat on the bottom, sheltered on both sides by the North and South mountains. Occasional roads over the South Mountain lead to the South Shore; short roads over the North Mountain lead to the Fundy shore. Like the South Shore, the valley is punctuated with pleasant small towns, each with a generous supply of extravagant Victorian homes and churches. The rich soil of the valley bottom supports dairy herds, hay, grain, root vegetables, tobacco, and fruit. Apple-blossom season (late May and early June) and the fall harvest are the loveliest times to visit.

Peggy's Cove

48 km (30 mi) southwest of Halifax.

Peggy's Cove, on Route 333, stands at the mouth of St. Margaret's Bay. The cove, with its houses huddled around the narrow slit in the boulders, is probably the most photographed village in Canada. It also has the only Canadian post office located in a lighthouse (open April–November). Be careful exploring the bald, rocky shore. Incautious visitors have been swept to their deaths by the surf that sometimes breaks here.

Dining and Lodging

$$–$$$ ✕🖫 **Dauphinee Inn.** On the shore of Hubbards Cove, about 19 km (12 mi) east of Chester, this charming country inn has first-class accommodations and an excellent restaurant ($$). The Hot Rocks is a social dining concept where guests are invited to cook fresh vegetables, seafood, beef, or chicken on a hot slab of South Shore granite. Opportunities abound for bicycling, bird-watching, and deep-sea fishing nearby, and walking trails lead to the shore. ⊠ *167 Shore Club Rd., Hubbard (Exit 6 off Rte. 103) B0J 1T0,* ☎ *902/857–1790 or 800/567–1790,* ℻ *902/857–9555. 6 rooms, 2 suites. Restaurant, lounge, boating, fishing. AE, D, DC, MC. Closed Nov.–Apr.*

Chester

79 km (49 mi) west of Peggy's Cove.

Chester, on Lunenburg County's Mahone Bay, has a population of just over 1,100 people. In summer, however, this seaside retreat swells with a well-established population of U.S. visitors and Haligonians and with the sailing and yachting community. Mid-August brings **Chester Race Week,** the largest regatta in Atlantic Canada.

The **Ross Farm Living Museum of Agriculture,** a restored 19th-century farm, illustrates the evolution of agriculture from 1600 to 1925. The animals here are those found on a farm of the 1800s—draft horses, oxen, and older breeds or types of animals. Blacksmithing and other crafts are demonstrated. The Pedlar's Shop sells items made in the community. ⊠ *Rte. 12 (20-min drive inland from Chester), New Ross,* ☎ *902/689–2210.* 🎟 *$3.* ☉ *June–mid-Oct., daily 9:30–5:30; winter programs Jan.–mid-Mar. (call to confirm).*

⓮ A passenger-only ferry (☎ 902/275–3221) runs from the dock in Chester to the scenic **Big and Little Tancook Islands,** 8 km (5 mi) out in Mahone Bay. Reflecting its part-German heritage, Big Tancook claims to make the best sauerkraut in Nova Scotia. Exploration of the island is made easy by walking trails. The boat runs four times daily Monday–Thursday, six times daily Friday, and twice daily on weekends. The 45-minute trip costs $1.

Dining

$$ ✕ **The Galley.** Decked out in nautical bric-a-brac and providing a spectacular view of the ocean, this restaurant has a pleasant, relaxed atmosphere. The seafood chowder, lobster, and homemade desserts are recommended. ⊠ *Rte. 3, 115 Marina Rd., Marriots Cove (Exit 8 off Rte. 103, 3 km, or 2 mi, west of Chester),* ☎ *902/275–4700. Reservations essential. AE, D, MC, V. Closed mid-Dec.–mid-Mar.*

En Route The town of **Mahone Bay** on Route 325 presents a dramatic face to visitors: Three tall wooden churches stand side by side, their images reflected in the harbor. Once a shipbuilding community, Mahone Bay is now a crafts center.

Lunenburg

★ ⑮ *20 km (12 mi) south of Chester.*

A feast of Victorian-era architecture, wooden boats, steel draggers (a fishing boat that operates a trawl), historic inns, and good restaurants, Lunenburg is visually delightful. The center of town, known as **old town,** is a UNESCO world heritage site, and the fantastic old school on the hilltop is the region's finest remaining example of Second Empire architecture, an ornate style that began in France.

Lunenburg is home port to the *Bluenose II,* a replica of the great racing schooner depicted on the back of the Canadian dime. Built in 1921, the original *Bluenose,* which sank years ago, was the undefeated champion of the North Atlantic fishing fleet and winner of four international races. Its twin, built in 1963, is open to visitors through the Fisheries Museum of the Atlantic (☞ *below*) when in port.

The **Fisheries Museum of the Atlantic** explores the world of Canada's Atlantic Coast fishers. Among the attractions are a Grand Bank schooner, the *Theresa E. Connor;* a steel stern trawler, *Cape Sable;* and an aquarium. ⊠ *68 Bluenose Dr.,* ☎ *902/634–4794.* ☞ *$6.* ☉ *June–mid-Oct., daily 9:30–5:30; off-season, weekdays by appointment only.*

Lodging

$$–$$$$ 🏨 **Pelham House Bed & Breakfast.** Close to downtown, this sea captain's home, circa 1906 and decorated in the style of the era throughout, has a large collection of books about the sea and sailing. The veranda overlooks the harbor. Full breakfast and afternoon tea are included in the room rate. ⊠ *224 Pelham St., Box 358, B0J 2C0,* ☎ *902/634–7113,* 𝖥𝖠𝖷 *902/634–7114. 3 rooms. Business services. MC, V.*

$$–$$$ 🏨 **Boscawen Inn and MacLachlan House.** Period antiques adorn and fireplaces warm this elegant 1888 mansion and its 1905 annex in the middle of Lunenburg's historic old town. Guests can take afternoon tea in one of the drawing rooms or on the balcony. All rooms and suites have either water or park views. ⊠ *150 Cumberland St., Box 1343, B0J 2C0,* ☎ *902/634–3325,* 𝖥𝖠𝖷 *902/634–9293. 20 rooms. Restaurant. AE, D, DC, MC, V. Closed Jan.–Easter.*

Shopping

The **Houston North Gallery** represents both trained and self-taught Nova Scotian artists as well as Inuit soapstone carvers and printmakers. ⊠ *110 Montague St.,* ☎ *902/634–8869.* ☉ *Feb.–Dec., Mon.–Sat. 10–6, Sun. 1–6.*

Bridgewater

18 km (11 mi) west of Lunenburg.

This is the main market town of the South Shore. The **DesBrisay Museum** explores the history and people of Lunenburg County and has changing exhibits on art, science, technology, and history. The gift shop carries books by local authors and local arts and crafts. ⊠ *130 Jubilee Rd.,* ☎ *902/543–4033.* ☞ *$2.50.* ☉ *Mid-May–Sept., Mon.–Sat. 9–5, Sun. 1–5; Oct.–mid-May, Tues.–Sun. 1–5, Wed. 1–9.*

Liverpool

⑯ *46 km (29 mi) south of Bridgewater.*

Nestled on the estuary of the Mersey River, Liverpool was settled around 1760 by New Englanders and is now a fishing and paper-milling town. During the American Revolution and the War of 1812, Liverpool was a privateering center; later, it became an important shipping and trading port.

The **Simeon Perkins House,** built in 1766, was the home of a prominent early settler who kept a detailed and revealing diary. The Perkins diary was used extensively by Thomas Raddall, some of whose internationally successful novels and stories are set in and around Liverpool. ⊠ *109 Main St.,* ☎ *902/354–4058.* ▭ *Free.* ☉ *June–mid-Oct., Mon.–Sat. 9:30–5:30, Sun. 1–5:30.*

Outdoor Activities and Sports
The **Mersey River** drains Lake Rossignol, Nova Scotia's largest freshwater lake, and provides trout and salmon fishing. For canoe and fishing outfitters, go to Greenfield, on Route 210, off Route 8.

Kejimkujik National Park

67 km (42 mi) northwest of Liverpool.

This 381-square-km (147-square-mi) inland wilderness has many lakes with well-marked canoe routes that have primitive campsites. Nature trails are marked for hikers, boat rentals are available, and there is freshwater swimming. White-tail deer, porcupine, loons, owls, and beaver are among the animals that can be seen. Kejimkujik also operates the Seaside Adjunct near Port Joli on the Atlantic shore, which protects one of the last undeveloped tracts of coastline on the Eastern Seaboard. Two mile-long beaches can be reached by hiking trails (no visitor services; day use only). Sections of the beaches are closed from late April to late July so that nesting birds, such as the endangered piping plover, remain undisturbed. ⊠ *Rte. 8 from Liverpool or Annapolis Royal, Maitland Bridge,* ☎ *902/682–2772.* ▭ *$3 per day, 4-day pass $9, annual pass $15, camping $9–$13.50 per day.*

Shelburne

🛈 *69 km (43 mi) south of Liverpool.*

The high noon of Shelburne occurred right after the American Revolution, when 16,000 Loyalists briefly made it one of the largest communities in North America. Today it is a fishing and shipbuilding town at the mouth of the Roseway River.

Many of Shelburne's homes date back to the late 1700s, including the **Ross-Thomson House,** now a provincial museum. Inside, the only surviving 18th-century store in Nova Scotia contains all the necessities of that period. ⊠ *9 Charlotte La.,* ☎ *902/875–3141.* ▭ *Free.* ☉ *June–mid-Oct., daily 9:30–5:30; call for winter hrs.*

Barrington

40 km (25 mi) south of Shelburne.

Barrington harbors a cluster of museums that explore various aspects of life in the 18th and 19th centuries. The **Barrington Woolen Mill Museum** (☎ 902/637–2185), built in 1882, displays machinery and has exhibits that explain how wool is woven into bolts of twills and flannels, blankets, and suitings. Early New England settlers converged at what is now the **Old Meeting House Museum** (☎ 902/637–2185) for town meetings, elections, and religious services. A five-story climb to the top of the **Seal Island Light Museum** affords beautiful views of Barrington Bay. The **Western Counties Military Museum** (☎ 902/768–2161) houses an array of old military artifacts.

Cape Sable Island

8 km (5 mi) south of Barrington over the causeway.

Connected to the mainland via a bridge, Cape Sable Island has a 21-km (13-mi) road that includes Nova Scotia's southernmost extremity. Like Barrington, Cape Sable Island is a Yankee community, as common family names attest; many people are named Smith or Nickerson. The remarkable variety of small evangelical churches here may reflect the Puritan enthusiasm for irreconcilable disagreements over fine points of doctrine. The largest community on Cape Sable is **Clark's Harbour**, where the first Cape Islander fishing boat was developed—with its pilothouse forward and its high, flaring bow and low stern, the Cape Islander is Nova Scotia's standard inshore fishing boat.

Pubnico

48 km (30 mi) northwest of Barrington.

Pubnico marks the beginning of the Acadian milieu; from here to Digby the communities are mostly French-speaking. Favorite local fare includes *fricot,* a stew made mostly of vegetables, sometimes mixed with rabbit meat, and rappie pie, made of meat or poultry with potatoes from which much of the starch has been removed.

No fewer than seven towns bear the name Pubnico: Lower West Pubnico, Middle West Pubnico, and West Pubnico, all on the west shore of Pubnico Harbour; three East Pubnicos on the eastern shore; and just plain Pubnico, at the top of none other than Pubnico Harbour. These towns were founded by Phillipe Muis D'Entremont, and they once constituted the only barony in French Acadia. D'Entremont was a prodigious progenitor: To this day, many people in the Pubnicos are D'Entremonts, and most of the rest are D'Eons or Amiraults.

Yarmouth

⑱ *41 km (25 mi) north of Pubnico.*

The largest town (with some 8,500 inhabitants) in southern Nova Scotia and the biggest port west of Halifax, Yarmouth is the point of entry for travelers arriving by ferry from Maine. The ferries are a major reason for Yarmouth's prosperity, as they pull in much revenue by providing quick, inexpensive access for merchants and consumers going to the Boston market for fish, pulpwood, boxes and barrels, knitwear, Irish moss, Christmas trees, and berries.

In the 19th century Yarmouth was an even bigger shipbuilding center than it is now, and its location put the port on all the early steamship routes. The **Yarmouth County Museum,** in a late-19th-century church, has displays of period furniture, costumes, tools, and toys, as well as a significant collection of ship models and paintings. Also in the building is a research library and archives, where local history and genealogy are documented. ✉ *22 Collins St.,* ☎ *902/742–5539,* 𝖥𝖠𝖷 *902/749–1120.* 🎫 *Museum $2.50, archive $5 per half day.* ⊙ *June–mid-Oct., Mon.–Sat. 9–5, Sun. 2–5; mid-Oct.–May, Tues.–Sun. 2–5.*

The **Firefighters Museum of Nova Scotia,** one block from the waterfront, presents the evolution of fire fighting through its displays of equipment from the leather bucket to the chemical spray. ✉ *451 Main St.,* ☎ *902/742–5525.* 🎫 *$2.* ⊙ *June, Mon.–Sat. 9–5; July–Aug., Mon.–Sat. 9–9, Sun. 10–5; Sept., Mon.–Sat. 9–5; Oct.–May, weekdays 10–noon and 2–4.*

Dining and Lodging

$ ✕☰ **Manor Inn.** This country inn in a colonial mansion beside Doctors Lake offers four grades of rooms, settings, and price ranges: coach-house units, lakeside or rose-garden lodges, or the main estate. Prime rib and lobster are the specialties in the restaurant. ⊠ *Rte. 1, Box 56, Hebron (5 mi northeast of Yarmouth), B0W 1X0,* ☎ *902/742–2487,* FAX *902/742–8094. 53 rooms. Restaurant, 2 bars, outdoor café, pool, tennis court. AE, DC, MC, V.*

Point de l'Eglise

⑲   *70 km (43 mi) north of Yarmouth.*

Point de l'Eglise (Church Point) is the site of **Université Ste-Anne,** the only French-language institution among Nova Scotia's 17 degree-granting colleges and universities. Founded in 1891, this small university off Route 1 is a focus of Acadian studies and culture in the province.

St. Mary's Church, along the main road that runs through Point de l'Eglise, is the tallest and largest wooden church in North America, at 190 ft long and 185 ft high. It was finished in 1905. The steeple, which requires 40 tons of rock ballast to keep it steady in the ocean winds, can be seen for miles on the approach. Inside the church is a small museum. Tours are given by appointment. ⊠ *Main road,* ☎ *902/ 769–2832.* 🎟 *$1.* ☉ *July–mid-Oct., daily 9:30–5:30.*

En Route   **St. Bernard,** a few miles north of Point de l'Eglise, marks the end of the French Shore. It's known for an impressive granite Gothic church that seats 1,000 people.

Digby

35 km (22 mi) northeast of Point de l'Eglise.

Digby is the terminus of the ferry service from St. John, New Brunswick, and an important fishing port with several good restaurants and a major resort, the Pines (☞ *below*). The town is on the otherwise-landlocked Annapolis Basin, into which the Annapolis River flows after its long course through the valley. Digby is particularly famous for its scallops and for smoked herring known as Digby Chicks. For a real treat, go down to the wharf and visit seafood retailers: They'll cook up the delicious scallops and lobster that you buy.

OFF THE
BEATEN PATH   **BEAR RIVER** – This jewel of a village, 15 km (9 mi) inland from Digby, is called the Switzerland of Nova Scotia. It has a large arts-and-crafts community and an **Ethnographic Museum** (⊠ 18 Chute Rd., ☎ 902/467–3762) devoted to folk costumes and artifacts from around the world.

Dining and Lodging

$$$$ ✕☰ **Pines Resort Hotel.** Complete with fireplaces, sitting rooms, walking trails, and a view of the Annapolis Basin, this casually elegant property, composed of a Norman château–style hotel, 30 cottages, and lavish gardens, offers myriad amenities. Local seafood with a French touch is served daily in the restaurant ($$–$$$), and the lounge is perfect for quiet relaxation. ⊠ *Shore Rd., Box 70, B0V 1A0,* ☎ *902/245–2511 or 800/667–4637,* FAX *902/245–6133. 144 rooms. Restaurant, bar, pool, sauna, 18-hole golf course, 2 tennis courts, health club. AE, D, DC, MC. Closed mid-Oct.–May.*

Long Island and Brier Island

㉑ *10-min ferry ride between East Ferry and Tiverton.*

Digby Neck is extended seaward by two narrow islands, Long Island and Brier Island. Because the surrounding waters are rich in plankton, the islands attract a variety of whales, including finbacks, humpbacks, minkes, and right whales, as well as harbor porpoises. Wild orchids and other wildflowers abound here, and the islands are also an excellent spot for bird-watching.

Ferries (☎ 902/839–2302) going between the islands have to crab sideways against the ferocious Fundy tidal streams that course back and forth through the narrow gaps. They operate hourly, 24 hours a day, with a fare of $2 each way. One of the boats is the *Joshua Slocum* and the other is *Spray*; the former is named after Westport's most famous native, and the latter for the 36-ft oyster sloop that he rebuilt and in which from 1894 to 1896 he became the first man to circumnavigate the world singlehandedly. At the southern tip of Brier Island, a **cairn** commemorates the voyage.

Outdoor Activities and Sports

Freeport Whale and Seabird Tours (✉ Freeport, Long Island, ☎ 902/839–2177) has tours for $25. **Pirate's Cove Whale Cruises** (✉ Rte. 217, Tiverton, Long Island, ☎ 902/839–2242) operates whale-watching cruises June–October. The fare is $33. **Slocum's Whale and Deep Sea Fishing Cruises** (✉ Westport, Brier Island, ☎ 800/214–4655) charges $33 for whale-watching tours.

Annapolis Royal

★ ㉒ *29 km (18 mi) northeast of Digby.*

This town is well supplied with imposing mansions, particularly along the upper end of St. George Street, the oldest town street in Canada. Local businesses (or the tourist information center in the Annapolis Royal Tidal Power Building) can provide *Footprints with Footnotes,* a self-guided walking tour of the town; guided tours leave from the lighthouse on St. George Street, daily at 10 and 2:30.

Fort Anne National Historic Site was fortified in 1643; the present structures are the remnants of the fourth fort erected here and garrisoned by the British as late as 1854. The officers' quarters have exhibits on the site's history. ✉ *St. George St.,* ☎ *902/532–2397 or 902/532–2321,* ℻ *902/532–2232.* ☞ *Grounds free, museum $3.* ☉ *Mid-May–mid-Oct., daily 9–6; mid-Oct.–mid-May, by appointment.*

The **Annapolis Royal Historic Gardens** are 10 acres of magnificent theme gardens, including a Victorian garden and a knot garden, connected to a wildlife sanctuary. ✉ *441 St. George St.,* ☎ *902/532–7018.* ☞ *$3.50.* ☉ *Mid-May–mid-Oct., daily 8–dusk.*

The **Annapolis Royal Tidal Power Project,** ½ km (¼ mi) from Annapolis Royal, was designed to test the feasibility of generating electricity from tidal energy. This pilot project is the only tidal generating station in North America and one of only three operational sites in the world. The interpretive center explains the process with guided tours. ✉ *Annapolis River Causeway,* ☎ *902/532–5454.* ☞ *Free.* ☉ *Mid-May–mid-June and Sept.–mid-Oct., daily 9–5:30; mid-June–Aug., daily 9–8.*

Lodging

$–$$ 🛏 **Auberge Wandlyn Royal Anne Motel.** This modern, no-frills motel has a pleasant, quiet setting on 20 acres of land. ✉ *Rte. 1, Box 628,*

B0S 1A0, ☎ *902/532–2323,* FAX *902/532–7277. 30 rooms. Hot tubs, sauna, meeting rooms. AE, DC, MC, V.*

$ 🏠 **Moorings Bed & Breakfast.** Built in 1881, this tall, beautiful home overlooking Annapolis Basin has a fireplace, tin ceilings, antiques, and contemporary art. A full breakfast is included in the cost. ⊠ *5287 Granville St., Box 118, Granville Ferry B0S 1K0,* ☎ FAX *902/532–2146. 1 room with ½ bath, 2 rooms share bath. V.*

Port Royal

8 km (5 mi) downriver (west) from Annapolis Royal on the opposite bank.

One of the oldest settlements in Canada, Port Royal was Nova Scotia's first capital (for both the French and English) until 1749, and the province's first military base. A National Historic Site commemorates the period.

The **Port Royal National Historic Site** is a reconstruction of a French fur-trading post originally built in 1605 by Sieur de Monts and Samuel de Champlain in 1605. Here, amid the hardships of the New World, North America's first social club—the Order of Good Cheer—was founded, and Canada's first theatrical presentation was written and produced by Marc Lescarbot. ⊠ *Rte. 1 to Granville Ferry, then left 12 km (7 mi) on Port Royal Rd.,* ☎ *902/532–2898, 902/532–5589.* 🎫 *$3.* ⊙ *Mid-May–mid-Oct., daily 9–6.*

OFF THE
BEATEN PATH

CAPE BLOMIDON – At Greenwich, take Route 358 to Cape Blomidon via Port Williams and Canning for a spectacular view of the valley and the Bay of Fundy from the Lookoff.

HALL'S HARBOUR – One of the best natural harbors on the upper Bay of Fundy can be reached via Route 359. Go for a walk on a gravel beach bordered by cliffs, try sea kayaking or wilderness camping, or seek out the intaglio printmaking studio.

Wolfville

㉒ *60 km (37 mi) east of Annapolis Royal.*

Settled in the 1760s by New Englanders, Wolfville is a charming college town with stately trees and ornate Victorian homes. Chimney swifts—aerobatic birds that fly in spectacular formation at the brink of dusk—are so abundant that an interpretive display is devoted to them at the **Robie Tufts Nature Centre** on Front Street. At the end of Front, by the harbor, are dikes built by the Acadians in the 1600s.

The **Atlantic Theatre Festival** (⊠ 356 Main St, ☎ 902/542–4242 or 800/337–6661) stages classical plays mid-June–September; tickets are $21–$28.

OFF THE
BEATEN PATH

GRAND PRÉ NATIONAL HISTORIC SITE – This site, about 5 km (3 mi) east of Wolfville on Route 101, was once an Acadian village. A small stone church commemorates Longfellow's hero in *Evangeline* and houses an exhibit on the 1755 deportation of the Acadians from the valley. ⊠ *Rte. 1, Grand Pré,* ☎ *902/542–3631.* ⊙ *Mid-May–mid-Oct., daily 9–6.*

Dining and Lodging

$–$$$ ✕🏠 **Blomidon Inn.** Four acres of lawns and gardens enhance a 19th-century sea captain's mansion that has been restored as an inn. The rooms are uniquely furnished, most with four-poster beds and all with handmade quilts. Guests can relax over lunch or dinner in one of the dining rooms ($$–$$$) or on the terrace. Lobster bisque and fresh Atlantic salmon are among the menu favorites, and the homemade bread baked with oats and molasses is memorable. Afternoon tea is served daily; reservations are advised for weekend brunch. ⊠ *127 Main St., Box 839, B0P 1X0,* ☎ *902/542–2291 or 800/565–2291,* FAX *902/542– 7461. 26 rooms. Restaurant, tennis court, horseshoes, shuffleboard, meeting room. MC, V.*

Outdoor Activities and Sports

A popular hiking trail, 25 km (16 mi) north of Wolfville, leads from the end of Route 358 to the dramatic cliffs of Cape Split, a 13-km (8-mi) round-trip.

Windsor

㉓ *25 km (16 mi) southeast of Wolfville.*

Windsor was settled in 1703 as an Acadian community. Here, the tide's average rise and fall is more than 40 ft; you can see the tidal bore (the leading edge of the incoming tide) rushing up the Meander River and sometimes reaching a height of 3 ft.

Fort Edward, one of the assembly points for the expulsion of the Acadians, stands as the only remaining colonial blockhouse in Nova Scotia. ⊠ *Exit 6 off Rte. 1, 1st left at King St., left up street facing fire station,* ☎ *902/542–3631.* ☜ *Free.* ☉ *Mid-June–Labor Day, daily 10–6.*

The **Haliburton House Museum,** a provincial museum on a manicured 25-acre estate, was the home of Judge Thomas Chandler Haliburton—lawyer, politician, historian, and humorist. His best-known work, *The Clockmaker,* pillories Nova Scotian follies from the viewpoint of a Yankee clock peddler, Sam Slick, whose witty sayings are still commonly used. ⊠ *414 Clifton Ave.,* ☎ *902/798–2915.* ☜ *Free.* ☉ *June–Oct. 15, Mon.–Sat. 9:30–5:30, Sun. 1–5:30.*

The family-owned **Sainte Famille Winery** in Falmouth, 5 km (3 mi) west of Windsor, offers tours that combine the region's ecological history with the intricacies of growing grapes and aging wine. Wine tasting is done in the gift shop, where bottles are sold at a steal. ⊠ *Dyke Rd. and Dudley Park La.,* ☎ *902/798–8311 or 800/565–0993,* FAX *902/ 798–9418.* ☜ *Free.* ☉ *June–Sept., Mon.–Sat. 9–6, Sun. noon–5; call for off-season hrs and tour schedule.*

OFF THE
BEATEN PATH

UNIACKE ESTATE MUSEUM PARK – Richard John Uniacke, attorney general and the advocate general to the Admiralty court during the War of 1812, built this house, a superb example of colonial architecture, about 1815. Now a provincial museum, the house is set on spacious grounds near a lake. It's preserved in its original condition with many authentic furnishings. Several walking trails surround the estate. ⊠ *758 Main Rd., 30 km (19 mi) east of Windsor off Route 1, Uniacke,* ☎ *902/866– 2560.* ☜ *Free.* ☉ *June–Oct. 15, Mon.–Sat. 9:30–5:30, Sun. 1–5:30.*

THE EASTERN SHORE
AND NORTHERN NOVA SCOTIA

The area between Halifax and Cape Breton Island includes the rugged coastline on the Atlantic and the gentler Bay of Fundy and Northumberland Strait. Fishing villages, sandy beaches, and remote cranberry barrens range along the Eastern Shore. The salt marshes, Scottish clans, and feasts of lobster along Northumberland Strait give way to mills, rolling hills, hiking trails, and farms as you move inland. A land of high tides, million-year-old fossils, and semiprecious stones borders the Bay of Fundy. You can walk on the bottom of the sea when the mighty Fundy tide recedes or ride the tidal bore as it rushes back.

This region takes in parts of three of the official Scenic Trails, including Marine Drive (315 km, or 195 mi), the Sunrise Trail (316 km, or 196 mi), and the Glooscap Trail (365 km, or 226 mi). Any one leg of the routes could be done comfortably as an overnight trip from Halifax; the whole tour takes at least three or four days.

Musquodoboit Harbour

㉔ *45 km (28 mi) east of Dartmouth.*

Musquodoboit Harbour, with about 930 residents, is a substantial village at the mouth of the Musquodoboit River. The river itself offers good trout and salmon fishing, and the village touches on two slender and lovely harbors.

Lodging

$–$$ 🏨 **Salmon River House.** Located where Route 7 crosses the Salmon River, this unpretentious white-frame inn on 30 acres provides glorious views. The inn has a sunroom and one room with a waterbed and whirlpool bath. It's about 35 minutes east of Dartmouth. ⊠ *9931 Rte. 7, Salmon River Bridge B0J 1P0,* ☎ *902/889–3353 or 800/565–3353,* 🖷 *902/ 889–3653. 6 rooms. Restaurant, boating, fishing. MC, V.*

Beach

One of the Eastern Shore's best beaches, **Martinique Beach,** is about 12 km (7 mi) south of Musquodoboit Harbour, at the end of East Petpeswick Road. Other fine beaches are at Clam Bay and Clam Harbour, several miles east of Martinique.

OFF THE BEATEN PATH   **MOOSE RIVER GOLD MINES –** This small local museum, about 30 km (19 mi) north of Tangier on Route 224, commemorates the small gold rush that occurred during the first part of this century, complete with a 1936 mine disaster. It's open during July and August.

En Route   As you travel through **Ship Harbour,** take note of the strings of white buoys, marking one of North America's largest cultivated mussel farms.

Sherbrooke Village

★ **㉕** *166 km (102 mi) northeast of Musquodoboit Harbour.*

A living history museum created within and among the buildings of a contemporary rural village with fewer than 400 residents is the leading tourist center along this shore. Twenty-five buildings have been restored on their original sites by the Nova Scotia Museum to their late-19th-century character, including a blacksmith shop, water-powered sawmill, horse-drawn wagons, tearooms, and stores. The St. Mary's River, which flows through the hamlet, is one of Nova Scotia's best salmon rivers. ⊠ *Rte. 7,* ☎ *902/522–2400.* 🎟 *$4.* ☉ *June–mid-Oct., daily 9:30–5:30.*

Antigonish

㉖ *62 km (38 mi) north of Sherbrooke Village on Hwy. 104.*

Antigonish is the home of **St. Francis Xavier University,** a center for Gaelic studies and the first coeducational Catholic institution to graduate women. The university art gallery (☎ 902/867–2303), open year-round, has changing exhibits. In July, Antigonish hosts the **Highland**

Games (☎ 902/863–4275), where lads toss the caber, lassies dance the highland fling, and there are plenty of bagpipes and drums.

The **Lytesome Gallery** (✉ 166 Main St., ☎ 902/863–5804) houses a good variety of Nova Scotian art for sale at reasonable prices.

Dining

$$–$$$ ✕ **Lobster Treat Restaurant.** This cozily decorated brick, pine, and stained-glass restaurant was once a two-room schoolhouse. The varied menu includes fresh seafood, chicken, pastas, and bread and pies baked on the premises. Families appreciate its relaxed atmosphere and children's menu. ✉ 241 Post Rd. (Trans-Canada Hwy.), ☎ 902/863–5465. AE, DC, MC, V. Closed Nov.–mid-Apr.

En Route   Route 337, the Sunrise Trail, runs north from Antigonish for a glorious drive along St. George's Bay with its many good swimming beaches, before the road abruptly climbs 1,000 ft up and over to Cape George. A little take-out shop on the wharf at **Ballantyne's Cove,** a tiny artificial harbor near the tip of Cape George, has some of the best fish-and-chips in Nova Scotia. Grab an order and enjoy the views. After following the cape, high above the sea, the road runs west along Northumberland Strait through lonely farmlands and tiny villages such as **Arisaig,** where you can search for fossils on the shore. **Lismore,** just a few miles west of Arisaig, affirms the Scottish origin of its people with a stone cairn commemorating Bonnie Prince Charlie's Highland rebels, slaughtered by the English at Culloden in 1746. Lobster is landed and processed in shoreside factories here, making the town a great place to buy some of the freshest lobster possible.

Pictou

★ ㉗   *74 km (46 mi) west of Antigonish.*

First occupied by the Mi'kmaqs, this well-developed town on Pictou Harbour became a Scottish settlement in 1773, when a land grant to the Philadelphia Company brought nearly 200 Highland Scots to the area. Under the inspired leadership of such men as the pioneering educator Thomas McCulloch, Pictou quickly became a center of commerce, education, theological disputation, and radical politics. Now one of the largest communities on the Northumberland Strait, it's considered the "birthplace of New Scotland."

Free factory tours at **Grohmann Knives** introduce the art of knife making. ✉ 116 Water St., ☎ 902/485–4224. ☉ Weekdays 9–3.

At the **Hector Heritage Quay,** a replica of the *Hector* is under construction. In 1773 the *Hector*—the nearest thing to a Canadian *Mayflower*—came to Pictou Harbour, inaugurating the torrent of Scottish immigration that permanently altered the character of the province and the nation. An interpretive center with audio and visual displays tells the story of Pictou's Scottish settlement, and there are working blacksmith and carpentry shops. ✉ 73 Harbour Dr., ☎ 902/485–6057. ☒ $4. ☉ May–Oct., daily 9–8.

McCulloch House, a restored 1806 building with displays of educator Thomas McCulloch's scientific collection and such personal items as furniture, is preserved as part of the Nova Scotia Museum. ✉ Old Haliburton Rd., ☎ 902/485–4563. ☒ Free. ☉ June–mid-Oct., Mon.–Sat. 9:30–5:30, Sun. 11:30–5:30.

Dining and Lodging

$–$$ ✕☷ **Braeside Inn.** Built in 1938, this inn on a 5-acre hillside in the center of historic Pictou has well-appointed accommodations and fine food.

Beaches are nearby, and a shuttle services Pictou's two marinas. The restaurant ($$) room specializes in fresh seafood dishes. ✉ *126 Front St., Box 1810, B0K 1H0,* ☎ *902/485–5046 or 800/613–7701,* FAX *902/ 485–1701. 20 rooms. Restaurant, meeting room. AE, MC, V.*

$ 🏠 **Walker Inn.** A hospitable couple runs this downtown inn in their brick Georgian-style town house, built in 1865. Every room is different, but all are no-smoking. The dining room serves guests only. ✉ *34 Coleraine St., Box 629, B0K 1H0,* ☎ *902/485–1433 or 800/370–5553. 10 rooms. Dining room, library, meeting room. AE, MC, V.*

Beach
Melmerby Beach, one of the warmest beaches on the province, is about 23 km (14 mi) east of Pictou. To get here, follow the shore road from Highway 104.

OFF THE BEATEN PATH
BALMORAL GRIST MILL MUSEUM – A water-powered gristmill serves as the centerpiece for this museum, 25 km (16 mi) west of Pictou. Built in 1860, it's the oldest operating mill in Nova Scotia. You can observe the milling demonstrations and then picnic in the park on the grounds. ✉ *660 Matheson Brook Rd., Balmoral Mills,* ☎ *902/657-3016.* 🎫 *Free.* ☾ *June–mid-Oct., Mon.–Sat. 9:30-5:30, Sun. 1-5:30; demonstrations daily 10–noon and 2–4.*

Malagash

65 km (40 mi) west of Pictou.

Malagash is best known for a winery that flourishes in the warm climate influenced by the Northumberland Strait. **Jost Vineyards** produces a surprisingly wide range of award-winning wines, including an ice wine that's making a name for the vineyard. The winery also has a deli-bar, patio deck, children's playground, and picnic area. ✉ *Rte. 6, off Hwy. 104,* ☎ *902/257-2636, 800/565-4567 in Atlantic Canada.* ☾ *Mid-June–mid-Sept., Mon.–Sat. 9–6; mid-Sept.–mid-June, daily 10-5; tours mid-June–mid-Sept., daily at noon, 3.*

Pugwash

28 *26 km (16 mi) west of Malagash.*

Pugwash was the summer home of Cleveland industrialist Cyrus Eaton, at whose estate numerous Thinkers' Conferences brought together leading intellectual figures from the West and the Soviet Union during the 1950s and 1960s. Pugwash is still Scottish terrain, as the Gaelic street signs attest.

Shopping
Canadian Sterling Gold and Silversmith (✉ Durham St., ☎ 902/243–2563) sells handcrafted silver and gold jewelry made in the studio. Tours are available. **Seagull Pewter** (✉ Durham St., ☎ 902/243–2516), a husband-and-wife crafts operation that has grown into a $25 million business of exporting pewter vessels, picture frames, and other artifacts worldwide, has a showroom that fronts on the main highway.

Amherst

29 *44 km (27 mi) west of Pugwash.*

Amherst, near the border with New Brunswick, stands on one of the glacial ridges that edge the Tantramar Marsh, said to be the largest marsh in the world. The Tantramar covers most of the Isthmus of Chignecto, the narrow neck of land that joins Nova Scotia to the rest of North

America. Amherst was once a thriving manufacturing center for many products, including pianos and furnaces. In 1917, en route from New York to Russia, the Communist leader Leon Trotsky was confined here for a month in a prisoner-of-war camp.

Lodging

$–$$ 🖫 **Amherst Shore Country Inn.** This seaside country inn, with a beau-
★   tiful view of Northumberland Strait, has comfortable rooms, suites, and a cottage fronting 600 ft of private beach. Well-prepared four-course dinners incorporating home-grown produce are served at one daily seating (7:30, by reservation only). ⊠ *Rte. 366, R.R. 2, Lorneville (32 km, or 20 mi, from Amherst), B4H 3X9,* ☎ *902/661–4800. 4 rooms, 4 suites, 1 cottage. Restaurant. AE, DC, MC, V. Closed late Oct.–Apr.*

Springhill

🕉 *42 km (26 mi) southeast of Amherst.*

The coal-mining town of Springhill, on Route 2, was the site of the famous mine disaster of the 1950s immortalized in the folk song "The Ballad of Springhill" by Peggy Seeger and Ewen McColl. You can tour a real coal mine at the **Spring Hill Miners Museum.** Retired coal miners act as guides and recount firsthand memories of mining disasters. ⊠ *Black River Rd., off Rte. 2,* ☎ *902/597–3449.* 🖃 *$5.* ☉ *Mid-May–mid-Oct.*

Springhill is the hometown of internationally acclaimed singer Anne Murray, whose career is celebrated in the **Anne Murray Centre.** ⊠ *Main St.,* ☎ *902/597–8614.* 🖃 *$5.* ☉ *May–Oct., daily 9–5.*

Joggins

🕉 *40 km (25 mi) west of Springhill.*

Joggins's main draw is the coal-age fossils embedded in its 150-ft sandstone cliffs. At the **Joggins Fossil Centre,** you can learn about the region's geological and archaeological history. Guided tours of the fossil cliffs are available, but departure times depend on the tides. Maps are issued for independent fossil hunters. ⊠ *30 Main St.,* ☎ *902/251– 2727.* 🖃 *Centre $3.50, tour $10.* ☉ *June–Sept., daily 9–6:30.*

En Route   **Advocate Harbour,** 66 km (41 mi) south of Joggins, was named by Champlain for his friend Marc Lescarbot, who was a lawyer, or "avocat." Built on flat shore land with a tall ridge backdrop and a broad harbor before it, Advocate is eerily beautiful.

Cap d'Or

5 km (3 mi) east of Advocate Harbour.

Cap d'Or, the land jutting out and dividing the waters of the main Bay of Fundy from the narrow enclosure of the Minas Basin, has a spectacular vista and lighthouse accessible from Route 209. As the tides change, fierce riptides create stunning waves. The view from the ridge down to the lighthouse is superb—keep your eyes peeled for peregrine falcons. The view from the lighthouse itself is almost equally magnificent, but the road down is rather primitive and should be attempted only in four-wheel-drive vehicles. Those who can handle the steep return climb can park at the top of the hill and walk down.

En Route   **Spencer's Island** (not really an island) is a 19th-century shipbuilding community on Route 209. A cairn commemorates the construction of the famous *Mary Celeste,* which was found in 1872 sailing in the mid-Atlantic without a crew; she had been abandoned at sea.

Parrsboro

32 *45 km (28 mi) east of Spencer's Island.*

A center for rock hounds and fossil hunters, Parrsboro is the main town on this shore and hosts the **Rockhound Roundup** every August. Among the exhibits and festivities are geological displays and concerts.

Parrsboro is an appropriate setting for the **Fundy Geological Museum** since it's not far from the Minas Basin area, the site where some of the oldest dinosaur fossils in Canada were found. Two-hundred-million-year-old dinosaur fossils are displayed here alongside exhibits of amethysts, agates, zeolites, and other mineral, plant, and animal relics that have washed out of nearby cliffs. ⊠ *6 Two Island Rd., ☎ 902/254–3814. ⊒ $3. ☉ June–Oct. 15, daily 9:30–5:30.*

The "world's smallest dinosaur footprints" are on display at the **Parrsboro Rock and Mineral Shop and Museum** (⊠ 39 Whitehall Rd., ☎ 902/254–2981), run by Eldon George.

Although fossils have become Parrsboro's claim to fame, this harbor town was also a major shipping and shipbuilding port, and its history is described at the **Ottawa House Museum-by-the-Sea,** 3 km (2 mi) east of downtown. Ottawa House, which overlooks the Bay of Fundy, was the summer home of Sir Charles Tupper, a former premier of Nova Scotia who was briefly prime minister of Canada. ⊠ *Whitehall Rd., ☎ 902/254–2376. ⊒ $1. ☉ July–early Sept., daily 10–8.*

Nightlife and the Arts

Parrsboro's professional **Ship's Company Theatre** (☎ 902/254–3425) has a summer season of plays based on historical events of the region, performed aboard the M.V. *Kipawo,* a former Minas Basin ferry.

Outdoor Activities and Sports

Ward's Falls is a beautiful, interpreted 6-km (4-mi) hiking trail about 5 km (3 mi) east of Parrsboro.

En Route   The 125-ft-high **Hidden Falls,** near Route 2, are about 5 km (3 mi) east of Parrsboro. Although the falls are on private property, the path leading from the gift shop is open to the public and parking is available.

Five Islands

24 km (15 mi) east of Parrsboro.

Among the most beautiful scenic areas along Route 2 is Five Islands, which, according to Mi'Kmaq legend, was created when the god Glooscap threw handfuls of sod at beaver. **Five Islands Provincial Park** (⊠ Rte. 2, ☎ 902/254–2980), on the shore of Minas Basin, has a campground, a beach, hiking trails, and some interpretation of the region's unusual geology.

Lodging

$ 🏠 **Shady Maple B&B.** At this unique property, a working farm, you can sleep on sun-dried bed linen and breakfast on fresh eggs and the farm's own maple syrup, jams, and jellies. The rooms are no-smoking, and one is a deluxe suite with a waterbed. Full breakfast is included. ⊠ *R.R. 1, Masstown B0M 1G0, ☎ 902/662–3565, ℻ 902/662–3565. 2 rooms, 1 suite. Pool. MC, V.*

CAPE BRETON ISLAND

The highways and byways of the Island of Cape Breton make up one of the most spectacular drives in North America. As you wind through the rugged coastal headlands of Cape Breton Highlands National Park, you can climb mountains and plunge back down to the sea in a matter of minutes. The Margaree River is a cultural dividing line: South of the river the settlements are Scottish, up the river they are largely Irish, and north of the river they are Acadian French. You can visit villages where ancient dialects can still be heard and explore a fortress where period players bring the past to life. This is a place where cultural heritage is alive, where the atmosphere is maritime, and where inventors Marconi and Bell share the spotlight with coal miners and singers like Rita MacNeil.

Bras d'Or Lake, a vast, warm, almost-landlocked inlet of the sea, occupies the entire center of Cape Breton. The coastline of the lake is more than 967 km (600 mi) long, and people sail yachts from all over the world to cruise its serene, unspoiled coves and islands. Bald eagles have become so plentiful around the lake that they are now exported to the United States to restock natural habitats. Four of the largest communities along the shore are Mi'Kmaq Indian reserves.

If Halifax is the heart of Nova Scotia, Cape Breton is its soul, complete with soul music: flying fiddles, boisterous rock, velvet ballads. Cape Breton musicians—weaned on Scottish jigs and reels—are among the world's finest, and in summer you can hear them at dozens of local festivals and concerts. In summer, every firehouse in the southern end of Inverness County takes a different night of the week to offer a square dance. Propelled by driving piano and virtuoso fiddling, locals of every age whirl through "square sets," the best of them step dancing and square dancing simultaneously. Local bulletin boards and newspapers have square dance times and locations.

Allow three or four days for this meandering tour of approximately 710 km (440 mi) that begins by entering the island via the Canso Causeway on Highway 104. Turn left at the rotary and take Route 19, the Ceilidh Trail (129 km, or 80 mi), which winds along the mountainside through glens and farms, with fine views across St. George's Bay to Cape George. This western shoreline of Cape Breton faces the Gulf of St. Lawrence and is famous for its sandy beaches and warm salt water.

Port Hood

㉝ *45 km (28 mi) northwest of the Canso Causeway on Rte. 19.*

At this fishing village you can buy lobster and snow crab fresh off the wharf as the boats return in mid-afternoon. With a little persuasion, one of the fishers might give you a lift to **Port Hood Island**, a mile across the harbor. It's a 10-minute walk from the island's wharf to the pastel-color cliffs of wave-mottled alabaster on the seaward shore. Both the island and the village have sandy beaches ideal for swimming.

Mabou

㉞ *13 km (8 mi) northeast of Port Hood on Rte. 19.*

The pretty village of Mabou is very Scottish, with its Gaelic signs and traditions of Scottish music and dancing. This is the hometown of national recording and performing artists such as John Allan Cameron and the Rankin Family; stop at a local gift shop and buy tapes to play as you drive down the long fjord of Mabou Harbour.

Lodging

$$ 🏨 **Glenora Inn & Distillery.** This friendly inn adjoins North America's only single malt whiskey distillery. Sample a "wee dram" of their own whiskey—billed as Canada's first legal moonshine. You can stop in for a distillery tour, fine cuisine, and traditional Cape Breton music even if you don't stay overnight. ⊠ *Glenville (Rte. 19 between Mabou and Inverness) B0E 1X0,* ☎ *902/258–2662. 9 rooms, 6 chalets. Restaurant, pub, gift shop, convention facilities. AE, MC, V. Closed Nov.–late June.*

Mabou Mines

10 km (6 mi) northwest of Mabou.

This town, known as the Mines, is a place so hauntingly exquisite that you expect to meet the *sidhe,* the Scottish fairies, capering on the hillsides. Within the hills of Mabou Mines is some of the finest hiking in the province, and above the land fly bald eagles, plentiful in this region. Inquire locally or at the tourist office on Margaree Forks for information about trails.

En Route Take Route 19 to Route 219 and follow the coast to **Chimney Corner.** A nearby beach has "sonorous sands": When you step on the sand or drag a foot through it, it squeaks and moans.

Margaree Harbour

③⑤ *33 km (20 mi) north of MabouInverness.*

The Ceilidh Trail joins the Cabot Trail at Margaree Harbour at the mouth of the Margaree River, a famous salmon-fishing stream and a favorite canoe route.

Dining and Lodging

$–$$$$ ✕⌨ **Normaway Inn.** This secluded 1920s inn, nestled on 250 acres in the hills of the Margaree Valley at the beginning of the Cabot Trail, has distinctive rooms and cabins, most with woodstoves and screened porches; some have hot tubs. There are films or traditional entertainment nightly as well as weekly square dances in the Barn. The restaurant ($$$) is known for its country cuisine, particularly the vegetable chowders and fresh seafood ragout. ⊠ *Egypt Rd., Box 326, 3 km (2 mi) off Cabot Trail, B0E 2C0,* ☎ *902/248–2987 or 800/565–9463,* FAX *902/248–2600. 9 rooms, 19 cabins. Restaurant, tennis court, hiking, bicycles. MC, V. Closed mid-Oct.–mid-June.*

$ ⌨ **Heart of Hart's Inn.** The decorative theme at this 100-year-old rural farmhouse within walking distance of the village of North East Margaree is "very country," with woodstove, antiques, colonial colored glass, and an array of flowers in the gardens. A full breakfast is included in the room rate, and four-course country dinners of local and regional foods are served nightly (by reservation only), at $30 per person. ⊠ *Cabot Trail, Box 21, B0E 2H0,* ☎ *902/248–2765,* FAX *902/248–2606. 5 rooms. Restaurant. MC, V.*

Chéticamp

③⑥ *26 km (16 mi) north of Margaree Harbour.*

Chéticamp, an Acadian community, has the best harbor and the largest settlement on this shore. Its tall silver steeple towers over the village, which stands exposed on a wide lip of flat land below a range of bald green hills. Behind these hills lies the high plateau of the Cape Breton Highlands. Chéticamp is famous for its hooked rugs, available at many local gift shops.

The **Dr. Elizabeth LeFort Gallery and Museum** displays artifacts and fine hooked embroidery work, rugs, and tapestries. ⊠ *Les Trois Pignons,* ☎ *902/224–2642.* ▱ *$3.* ☉ *May–Oct., weekdays 9–5; July–Aug., daily 9–6.*

Outdoor Activities and Sports

Chéticamp is known for its whale-watching cruises, which depart in June, twice daily, and in July and August, three times daily, from the government wharf. **Whale Cruisers Ltd.** (☎ 902/224–3376 or 800/813–3376) is a reliable charter company. Cruises cost $25.

Cape Breton Highlands National Park

★ *At the outskirts of Chéticamp.*

A 950-square-km (361-square-mi) wilderness of wooded valleys, plateau barrens, and steep cliffs, this park stretches across the northern peninsula of Cape Breton from the gulf shore to the Atlantic. The highway through the park is magnificent as it rises to the tops of the coastal mountains and descends through tight switchbacks to the sea. In fact, the road has been compared to a 106-km (66-mi) roller coaster ride, stretching from Chéticamp to Ingonish. Good brakes and an attentive driver are advised. Pull-offs provide photo opportunities. For wildlife watchers there's much to see, including moose, eagle, deer, bear, fox, and bobcat. Your chances of seeing wildlife are better if you venture off the main road at dusk or dawn. High-altitude marshlands are home to delightful wild orchids and other unique flora and fauna. If you plan to hike, fish, or camp in the park, or you want to maximize your appreciation for the nature and history associated within the park, stop at the Chéticamp Information Centre for advice and necessary permits. A guide to the park's 27 hiking trails, *Walking in the Highlands,* can be purchased. Trails range from easy 20-minute strolls to tough overnight treks. ⊠ *Information center on Cabot Trail at park entrance,* ☎ *902/285–2535, 902/285–2270 in winter.* ☎ *May–Oct. $3.50 per person per day, 4-day pass $10.50, seasonal pass $17.50; Nov.–Apr. free (including use of Cabot Trail lookouts within park, roadside exhibits, walking trails, picnic areas); camping $13–$19.*

OFF THE BEATEN PATH

GAMPO ABBEY – The most northerly tip of the island is not part of the national park; a spur road creeps along the cliffs to Red River, beyond which, on a broad, flat bench of land high above the sea, is this Tibetan Buddhist monastery. There are no guided tours.

Bay St. Lawrence

76 km (47 mi) north of Chéticamp.

The charming fishing village of Bay St. Lawrence is nestled in a bowl-shape valley around a harbor pond. You can hike along the shore to the east and the Money Point Lighthouse, or find a quiet corner of the shoreline for a wilderness campsite. A "feed of lobster" can be purchased from the fisher who brought it up from the sea an hour before.

Outdoor Activities and Sports

Capt. Cox's Whale Watch (☎ 902/383–2981) offers tours July–August.

OFF THE BEATEN PATH

MEAT COVE – Named for the moose and (now extinct) caribou that roamed the highlands and once supplied protein for passing sailing vessels, Meat Cove feels like the end of the earth. It lies at the end of a daunting 12-km (7-mi) mostly unpaved road along a precipitous cliff marked by sudden switchbacks. It's for the adventurous only, but many consider this drive the most spectacular in eastern North America. To get here, leave the Cabot Trail at Cape North on the Bay St. Lawrence Road. At the foot of the hill leading into St. Margaret's village, turn left and follow the sign to Capstick; that road leads to Meat Cove.

Ingonish

③⑦ *113 km (70 mi) northeast of Chéticamp.*

Ingonish, one of the leading holiday destinations on the island, is actually several villages on two bays, divided by a long narrow peninsula called Middle Head. Each bay has a sandy beach.

Dining and Lodging

$$$$ ✕⛏ **Keltic Lodge.** Spread across cliffs overlooking the ocean, the provincially owned Keltic Lodge sits on the Cabot Trail in Cape Breton Highlands National Park (☞ *above*). The building and some furnishings have a dated feel, but the setting is glorious. Guests can choose between the Main Lodge, White Birch Inn, and two- or four-bedroom cottages. A wide variety of activities is offered, including golfing on the world-class Highlands Links. Seafood stars on the menu in the Purple Thistle Dining Room ($$$). ⊠ *Middlehead Peninsula, Ingonish Beach, B0C 1L0,* ☎ *902/285–2880 or 800/565–0444. 98 rooms. 2 restaurants, pool, golf, hiking, beaches. MAP. Closed Apr.–May and Nov.–Dec.*

OFF THE
BEATEN PATH
BIRD ISLANDS – From Big Bras d'Or, 100 km (62 mi) south of Ingonish, notice the small islands on the far side of the mouth of St. Ann's Bay: These are the Bird Islands, breeding grounds for Atlantic puffins, black guillemots, razor-billed auks, and cormorants. Boat tours are available from **Bird Islands Boat Tour** (☎ 902/674-2384). Landing on the islands is forbidden, however.

Englishtown

65 km (40 mi) south of Ingonish on Rte. 312.

A short (about 2 minutes) ferry ride heads from Jersey Cove across St. Ann's Bay to Englishtown, home of the celebrated Cape Breton Giant, Angus MacAskill. Ferries run 24 hours a day, and the fare is 50¢. The **Giant MacAskill Museum** holds artifacts and the remains of the 7'9" man who traveled with P. T. Barnum's troupe in the 1800s. ⊠ *Rte. 312,* ☎ *902/929–2875.* 🎫 *$1.* ☉ *May–Oct., daily 9–6.*

South Gut St. Ann's

12 km (7 mi) south of Jersey Cove.

Settled by the Highland Scots, South Gut St. Ann's is home to North America's only **Gaelic College** (☎ 902/295–3441). Its Great Hall of the Clans depicts Scottish history and has an account of the Great Migration. The college offers courses in Gaelic language and literature, Scottish music and dancing, weaving, and other Scottish arts. There's also a Scottish gift shop.

From the Gaelic College, you can follow the Cabot Trail as it meanders along the hills that rim St. Ann's Bay. The 30-km (19-mi) stretch between St. Ann's and Indian Brook is home to a collection of fine crafts shops. You'll find pottery and paintings, forged iron and carved wood, each piece unique and often sold by the artisan who made it.

Baddeck

③⑧ *20 km (12 mi) south of South Gut St. Ann's.*

Baddeck, the most highly developed tourist center in Cape Breton, has more than 1,000 motel beds, a golf course, many fine gift shops, and numerous restaurants. It was also the summer home of Alexander Graham Bell until he died here at the age of 75. In summer the town celebrates the **Centre Bras d'Or Festival of the Arts,** which offers live music and drama every evening. The annual **regatta** of the Bras d'Or Yacht Club is held the first week of August. Sailing tours and charters are available, as are bus tours along the Cabot Trail. On the waterfront, the **Rose Cottage Gallery** overflows with folk art and local crafts.

☺ The **Alexander Graham Bell National Historic Site** explores how Alexander Graham Bell bridged the world between sound and silence. There are experiments, kite making, and other hands-on activities designed especially for children. In the Mr. Bell Theatre, you can view films, artifacts, and photographs to learn how ideas led Bell to create man-carrying kites, airplanes, and a marine record-setting hydrofoil boat. ⊠ *Chebucto St.,* ☎ *902/295–2069,* 𝖥𝖠𝖷 *902/295–3496.* 🖃 *$3.75.* ☯ *July–Aug., daily 9–8; June and Sept., daily 9–7; Oct.–May (reduced service), daily 9–5.*

Dining and Lodging

$$–$$$$ ✕🖃 **Inverary Inn Resort.** On the shores of the magnificent Bras d'Or Lake, this resort has stunning views and a lot of activities. You can choose from cozy pine-paneled cottages, modern hotel units, or the elegant 100-year-old main lodge. There's boating and swimming in close proximity to the village, but the resort remains tranquil. Families will appreciate the on-site children's playground and the choice of dining in the Lakeside Cafe or the elegant main dining room ($$). ⊠ *Rte. 205 and Shore Rd., Box 190, B0E 1B0,* ☎ *902/295–3500 or 800/565–5600,* 𝖥𝖠𝖷 *902/295–3527. 137 rooms. Restaurant, café, indoor pool, sauna, 3 tennis courts, boating. AE, D, MC, V.*

$–$$ 🖃 **Duffus House.** Facing the harbor, this quiet inn is furnished with antiques and has cozy sitting rooms and a secluded, well-tended garden. ⊠ *108 Water St., Box 427, B0E 1B0,* ☎ *902/295–2172. 7 rooms. Dock, library. V.*

Beach

A free ferry (passengers only) shuttles between the government wharf and the sandy beach by the lighthouse at Kidston Island.

Iona

➂➈ *56 km (35 mi) south of Baddeck.*

Iona is the site of a living history museum. To get here from Baddeck, take Trans-Canada Highway 105 to Exit 6, which leads to Little Narrows, where you can take a short ferry ride to the Washabuck Peninsula. Ferries run 24 hours a day, and the fare is 25¢. The **Nova Scotia Highland Village** is set high on a mountainside, with a spectacular view of Bras d'Or Lake and the narrow Barra Strait. The village's 10 historic buildings were assembled from all over Cape Breton to depict the Highland Scots' way of life from their origins in the Hebrides to the present day. Among the staff at this living history museum are a smith in the blacksmith shop and a clerk in the store. ⊠ *Rte. 223,* ☎ *902/ 725–2227.* 🖃 *$4.* ☯ *Reception desk and museum June–Sept., Mon.– Sat. 9–5, Sun. 10–6; Welcome Center Oct.–May, weekdays 9–5.*

Dining and Lodging

$ ✕🖃 **Highland Heights Inn.** The rural surroundings, the Scottish home-style cooking served near the restaurant's huge stone fireplace, and the view of the lake substitute nicely for the Scottish Highlands. The inn is on a hillside beside the Nova Scotia Highland Village, overlooking the village of Iona, where some residents still speak the Gaelic language of their ancestors. The salmon (or any fish in season), fresh-baked oat-cakes, and homemade desserts are good choices. ⊠ *Rte. 223, Box 19,* ☎ *902/725–2360,* FAX *902/725–2800. 26 rooms. Restaurant. D, MC, V. Closed mid-Oct.–mid-May.*

En Route   The Barra Strait Bridge joins Iona to Grand Narrows. A miles from the bridge, bear right toward East Bay. (If you miss this turn, don't worry; you'll have just as scenic a drive along St. Andrews Channel.) The East Bay route runs through the Mi'Kmaq village of **Eskasoni,** the largest native community in the province. This friendly village has a fascinating cultural heritage.

Sydney

40   *60 km (37 mi) northeast of Iona.*

The heart of Nova Scotia's second-largest urban cluster, Sydney is known as industrial Cape Breton. It encompasses villages, unorganized districts, and a half dozen towns—most of which sprang up around the coal mines, which fed the steel plant at Sydney. These are warm-hearted, interesting communities with a diverse ethnic population, in-cluding Ukrainians, Welsh, Poles, Lebanese, West Indians, and Italians; most residents descended from the miners and steelworkers who ar-rived a century ago when the area was booming. Sydney is also the only significantly industrialized district in Atlantic Canada, and it has suffered serious environmental damage.

Sydney has the island's only real airport, its only university, and a lively entertainment scene that specializes in Cape Breton music. The town is also a departure point: Fast ferries leave from North Sydney for New-foundland, and scheduled air service to Newfoundland and the French islands of St. Pierre and Miquelon (☞ Burin Peninsula, Gander, and Notre Dame Bay *in* Chapter 14) departs from Sydney Airport.

Dining and Lodging

$$–$$$$ ✕⊡ **Gowerie House.** An unexpected jewel, Gowerie House is on the Shore Road between North Sydney and Sydney Mines. Towering trees shade the house, while gardens and flowering shrubs fill the grounds. A cherry tree supplies the main ingredient for chilled cherry soup in what some consider Nova Scotia's finest restaurant ($$$). Antiques and fine art, Oriental carpets, and exquisite china add to the elegance. The main house has six rooms, and there are four more in the secluded gar-den house. You may stay overnight or be a guest for dinner only, but either way, dinner reservations are mandatory and best booked a week ahead. The room price includes breakfast. ⊠ *139 Shore Rd., Sydney Mines B1V 1A6,* ☎ *902/544–1050 or 800/372–1115. 10 rooms. Restaurant. AE, MC, V.*

$$–$$$ ⊡ **Delta Sydney.** This hotel is on the harbor, beside the yacht club and close to the center of town. The attractively decorated guest rooms have a view of the harbor. The intimate restaurant specializes in seafood and Continental cuisine. ⊠ *300 Esplanade, B1P 6J4,* ☎ *902/562–7500 or 800/887–1133, 800/268–1133 in Canada;* FAX *902/562–3023. 152 rooms. Restaurant, lounge, indoor pool, sauna, exercise room. AE, DC, MC, V.*

Nightlife and the Arts

The **Cape Breton Summertime Revue,** based in Sydney, performs an an-nual original revue of music and comedy that tours Nova Scotia dur-ing June and August. Many leading fiddlers appear at the **Big Pond Concert** in mid-July. At the **Sheraton Casino** (⊠ 625 George St., ☎ 902/ 563–7777), you can try the slot machines, roulette, or gaming tables or enjoy live entertainment in the lounge. The **University College of Cape**

Breton (✉ 1250 Grand Lake Rd., ☎ 902/539–5300) has many facilities for the public, such as the Boardmore Playhouse and the island's only public art gallery.

Glace Bay

④ *21 km (12 mi) east of Sydney.*

★ A coal mining town and fishing port, Glace Bay has a rich history of industrial struggle. The **Glace Bay Miners' Museum** houses exhibits and artifacts illustrating the hard life of early miners in Cape Breton's undersea collieries. Former miners guide you down into the damp recesses of the mine and tell stories of working all day where the sun never shines. ✉ *42 Birkley St., Quarry Point,* ☎ *902/849–5422.* ☞ *$3.50.* ☉ *June– Sept., daily 9–6.*

Nightlife and the Arts

Glace Bay's opulent old opera house, the **Savoy Theatre** (✉ Union St., ☎ 902/842–1577), is the home of the summer-long Festival on the Bay.

Louisbourg

④ *33 km (20 mi) southeast of Sydney.*

★ Though best known as the home of the largest National Historic Site in Canada, Louisbourg is also an important fishing community with a lovely harborfront. The **Fortress of Louisbourg National Historic Park** is the most remarkable site in Cape Breton. After the French were forced out of mainland Nova Scotia in 1713, they established their headquarters here in a walled and fortified town on a low point of land at the mouth of Louisbourg Harbour. The fortress was twice captured, once by New Englanders and once by the British; after the second siege, in 1758, it was razed. Its capture was critical in ending the French empire in America. A quarter of the original town has been rebuilt on its foundation, just as it was in 1744, before the first siege. Costumed actors re-create the activities of the original inhabitants; you can watch a military drill, see nails and lace being made, and eat food prepared from 18th-century recipes in the town's two inns. Plan on spending at least a half day. Louisbourg tends to be chilly, so pack a warm sweater or windbreaker. ✉ *Rte. 22,* ☎ *902/733–2280 or 800/565–9464.* ☞ *$7.50.* ☉ *June and Sept., daily 9:30–5; July–Aug., daily 9–6.*

At the **Sydney and Louisburg Historical Society,** a restored 1895 railway station exhibits the history of the S&L Railway, railroad technology, and marine shipping. The rolling stock includes a baggage car, coach, and caboose. ✉ *7336 Main St.,* ☎ *902/733–2720.* ☞ *Free.* ☉ *June and Sept., weekdays 9–5; July–Aug., daily 9–7.*

The **Atlantic Statiquarium** is a marine museum devoted largely to underwater treasure. ✉ *7523 Main St.,* ☎ *902/733–2721.* ☞ *$2.50.* ☉ *June–Sept., daily 10–8.*

Big Pond

40 km (25 mi) southwest of Sydney on Rte 4.

This little town comprises just a few houses, and one of them is the home of singer-songwriter Rita MacNeil, who operates a tearoom. You can stop in for Rita's special blend of tea and home-baked goodies, such as oatcakes. A display room contains her awards.

En Route   Route 4 rolls along Bras d'Or Lake, sometimes by the shore and sometimes in the hills. At **St. Peter's** the Atlantic Ocean is connected with the Bras d'Or Lake by the century-old St. Peter's Canal, still used by pleasure craft and fishing vessels. From St. Peter's to Port Hawkesbury the population is largely Acadian French.

Arichat

43 *62 km (38 mi) from Big Pond.*

Arichat is the principal town of Isle Madame, a 27-square-km (10-square-mi) island named for Madame de Maintenon, second wife of Louis XIV. It was an important shipbuilding and trading center during the 19th century, and some fine old houses from that period still remain. Arichat was once the seat of the local Catholic diocese. **Notre Dame de l'Assumption** church, built in 1837, still retains the grandeur of its former cathedral status. Its bishop's palace is now a law office. The two cannons overlooking the harbor were installed after the town was sacked by John Paul Jones during the American Revolution.

To get here from Big Pond, take Route 247 to Route 320, which leads through the villages of Poulamon and D'Escousse and overlooks Lennox Passage, with its spangle of islands. Route 206 meanders through the low hills to a maze of land and water at West Arichat. Together, the two routes encircle the island, meeting at Arichat. The island lends itself to biking, as most roads glide gently along the shore. A good half-day hike leads to Gros Nez, the "large nose" that juts into the sea.

The **LeNoir Forge** is a restored French 18th-century stone blacksmith shop. ✉ *Rte. 320, off Rte. 4,* ☎ *902/226–9364.* ⊙ *May–Sept., weekdays 9–5, Sat. 10–3.*

OFF THE BEATEN PATH **LITTLE ANSE** – With its red bluffs, cobble shores, tiny harbor, and brightly painted houses, Little Anse is particularly attractive to artists and photographers. The town is at the southeastern tip of Isle Madame.

NOVA SCOTIA A TO Z

Arriving and Departing

By Bus
Greyhound Lines (☎ 800/231–2222), from New York, and **Voyageur Inc.** (☎ 613/238–5900), from Montréal, connect with **Scotia Motor Tours,** or SMT (☎ 506/458–6000), through New Brunswick. SMT links (inconveniently) with **Acadian Lines** (☎ 902/454–8279) and provides inter-urban service within Nova Scotia. Shuttle van services providing convenient transportation between Halifax and Sydney are **Newfie Bullet** (☎ 902/567–0313) and **Stareline Shuttle** (☎ 800/849–4490).

By Car
Motorists can enter Nova Scotia through the narrow neck of land that connects the province to New Bunswick and the mainland. The Trans-Canada Highway (Route 2 in New Brunswick) becomes Route 104 on crossing the Nova Scotia border at Amherst. Otherwise, car ferries (☞ By Ferry, *below*) dock at Yarmouth (from Maine), Digby (from New Brunswick), Caribou (from Prince Edward Island), and North Sydney (from Newfoundland).

By Ferry
Car ferries connect Nova Scotia with Maine and New Brunswick: **Prince of Fundy Cruises** (☎ 800/341–7540 in Canada, 800/482–0955 in Maine)) sails from Portland, Maine, to Yarmouth, Nova Scotia. **Bay Ferries Ltd.** (☎ 902/566–3838 or 888/249–7245) sails from Bar Har-

bor, Maine, to Yarmouth, and from Saint John, New Brunswick, to Digby, Nova Scotia. The Bar Harbor–Yarmouth service uses a new high-speed catamaran, cutting the trip from 6 to 2½ hours.

From May to December, **Northumberland Ferries** (☎ 902/566–3838; in Nova Scotia and Prince Edward Island, 800/565–0201) operates between Caribou, Nova Scotia, and Wood Islands, Prince Edward Island. **Marine Atlantic** (☎ 902/794–5700, 709/772–7701, or 800/341–7981) operates year-round between North Sydney and Port aux Basques, on the west coast of Newfoundland, and June–September between North Sydney and Argentia, on Newfoundland's east coast.

By Plane
The **Halifax International Airport** (1 Bell Blvd., Elmsdale, ☎ 902/873–1223) is 40 km (25 mi) northeast of downtown Halifax. **Sydney Airport** (280 Airport Rd., ☎ 902/564–7720) is 13 km (8 mi) east of Sydney. Air Atlantic, Air Canada, Air Nova, Canadian International Airlines, Canada 3000, and Northwest Air (☞ Air Travel *in* the Gold Guide) provide service to Halifax and Sydney from various cities.

Visiting pilots will find aviation-related information for the flying tourist from the **Aviation Council of Nova Scotia** (✉ Box 100, Debert, Nova Scotia B0M 1G0, ☎ 902/895–1143).

BETWEEN THE AIRPORT AND DOWNTOWN
Limousine and taxi service, as well as car rentals, is available at Halifax, Sydney, and Yarmouth airports. Airport bus service to Halifax and Dartmouth hotels costs $20 round-trip, $12 one-way. Regular taxi fare to Halifax is $35 each way, but if you book ahead with **Aero** (☎ 902/445–3393) the fare is $26 if you pay cash, more with a credit card (MC, V). The trip takes 30–40 minutes.

By Train
Amtrak (☎ 800/872–7245) from New York City makes connections in Montréal. **VIA Rail** (☎ 800/561–3949) provides service from Montréal to Halifax via Moncton, in New Brunswick, and Amherst and Truro, in Nova Scotia.

Getting Around
Halifax
BY BUS
Metro Transit (☎ 902/421–6600) provides bus service throughout Halifax and Dartmouth, the town of Bedford, and (to a limited extent) the county of Halifax. The base fare is $1.35, exact change only.

BY FERRY
Metro Transit (☞ *above*) runs passenger ferries from the Halifax Ferry Terminal at Lower Water Street to Alderney Gate in downtown Dartmouth and to Woodside Terminal (near Dartmouth Hospital) on the hour and half hour from 6:30 AM to 11:57 PM. Ferries are more frequent on weekday rush hours; they also operate on Sunday during the summer (June–September). Free transfers are available from the ferry to the bus system (and vice versa). A single crossing costs $1.10 and is worth it for the up-close view of both waterfronts.

BY TAXI
Rates begin at about $2.50 and increase based on mileage and time. A crosstown trip should cost $5–$6, depending on traffic. Hailing a taxi can be difficult, but there are taxi stands at major hotels and shopping malls. Most Haligonians simply phone for a taxi service; try **Aero Cab** (☞ Arriving and Departing by Plane, *above*).

Elsewhere in Nova Scotia

BY BUS

There are a number of small, regional bus services; however, connections are not always convenient. Outside of Halifax there are no inner-city bus services. For information, call **Nova Scotia Tourism** (☞ Visitor Information, *below*).

BY CAR

The recommended mode of travel within the province is by car. Highways numbered from 100 to 199 are all-weather, limited-access roads, with 100-kph (62-mph) speed limits. The last two digits usually match the number of an older trunk highway along the same route, numbered from 1 to 99. Thus, Route 102, between Halifax and Truro, matches the older Route 2, between the same towns. Roads numbered from 200 to 399 are secondary roads that usually link villages. Unless otherwise posted, the speed limit on these and any roads other than the 100-series highways is 80 kph (50 mph).

Most highways in the province lead to Halifax and Dartmouth. Routes 3/103, 7, 2/102, and 1/101 terminate in the twin cities. Many of the roads in rural Nova Scotia require attentive driving, as they are not well signed, are narrow, and do not always have a paved shoulder. They are generally well surfaced.

As you explore Nova Scotia, be on the lookout for the 10 designated "Scenic Travelways" that appear throughout the province and are easily identified by roadside signs with icons that correspond with trail names. These routes are also shown on tourist literature (maps and the provincial *Travel Guide*). **Nova Scotia Tourism** (☞ Visitor Information, *below*) provides information and reservation services.

BY PLANE

Internal air travel is very limited. Air Nova and Air Atlantic (☞ Air Travel *in* the Gold Guide for telephone numbers) provide regional service to other provinces and to Sydney.

Contacts and Resources

Car Rentals

Halifax is the most convenient place from which to begin a driving tour. It is recommended that you book a car through your travel agent. **Avis** (✉ 5600 Sackville St., ☎ 902/423–6303, 902/873–3523 airport). **Budget** (✉ 1558 Hollis St., ☎ 902/421–1242, 902/873–3509 airport). **Hertz** (✉ Halifax Sheraton, 1919 Upper Water St., ☎ 902/421–1763, 902/873–3700 airport). **Thrifty** (✉ 6930 Lady Hammond, ☎ 902/422–4455, 902/873–3527 airport). **Tilden** (✉ 1130 Hollis St., ☎ 902/422–4433, 902/873–3505 airport).

Emergencies

Fire, police (☎ 911).

Guided Tours

More than 20 tour operators specialize in specific kinds of tours. To connect with the company most suited to your needs, contact **Nova Scotia Tourism** (☞ Visitor Information, *below*).

BOAT

Boat tours have become very popular in all regions of the province. **Murphy's on the Water** (☎ 902/420–1015) sails various vessels: *Harbour Queen I,* a paddle wheeler; *Haligonian III,* an enclosed motor launch; *Stormy Weather I,* a 40-ft Cape Islander (fishing boat); and *Mar II,* a 75-ft sailing ketch. All operate from mid-May to late October from berths at 1751 Lower Water Street on Cable Wharf next to the Historic Properties in Halifax. Costs vary, but a basic tour of the Halifax Harbour ranges from $10 to $15.

Gray Line Sightseeing (☎ 902/454–8279) and **Cabana Tours** (☎ 902/423–6066) run coach tours through Halifax, Dartmouth, and Peggy's Cove. **Halifax Double Decker Tours** (☎ 902/420–1155) offers two-hour tours on double-decker buses that leave daily from Historic Properties in Halifax.

Outdoor Activities and Sports

BIKING

Bicycle Tours in Nova Scotia ($7) is published by **Bicycle Nova Scotia** (⊠ 5516 Spring Garden Rd., Box 3010, Halifax B3J 3G6, ☎ 902/425–5450). **Backroads** (⊠ 1516 5th St., Suite Q333, Berkeley, CA 94710, ☎ 510/527–1555 or 800/245–3874) offers five- and six-day bike trips.

BIRD-WATCHING

Nova Scotia is on the Atlantic flyway and is an important staging point for migrating species. A fine illustrated book, *Birds of Nova Scotia,* by Robie Tufts, is a must on every ornithologist's reading list.

CANOEING

Especially good canoe routes are within Kejimkujik National Park. Canoeing information is available from **Canoe NS** (⊠ Box 3010S, Halifax B3J 3G6, ☎ 902/425–5450, ext. 316; FAX 902/425–5606).The publication *Canoe Routes of Nova Scotia* and a variety of route maps are available from the **Nova Scotia Government Bookstore** (⊠ 1700 Granville St., Box 637, Halifax B3J 2T3, ☎ 902/424–7580).

FOSSIL HUNTING AND ROCK HOUNDING

To obtain the permit necessary for rock hounding along cliffs, contact the **Nova Scotia Museum** (⊠ 1747 Summer St., Halifax B3H 3A6, ☎ 902/424–6475).

HIKING

The province has a wide variety of trails along the rugged coastline and inland through forest glades, which enable you to experience otherwise inaccessible scenery, wildlife, and vegetation. *Hiking Trails of Nova Scotia* ($12.95) is available through **Gooselane Editions** (⊠ 469 King St., Fredericton, New Brunswick, E3R 1E5, ☎ 506/450–4251).

SNOWMOBILING

Visiting snowmobilers can get information on trails, activities, clubs, and dealers through the **Snowmobile Association of Nova Scotia** (⊠ Box 3010, South Halifax B3J 3G6, ☎ 902/425–5450).

Reservation Service

Nova Scotia has a computerized system called **Check In** (☎ 902/425–5781 or 800/565–0000), which provides information and makes reservations with more than 700 hotels, motels, inns, campgrounds, and car-rental agencies.

Shopping

Foreign visitors can obtain a refund of sales tax paid for short-term accommodation and on goods purchased for use outside Canada if removed from Canada within 60 days. Obtain a pamphlet and application from Canada Customs or any Visitor Information Centre, and save all receipts. Contact the **Nova Scotia Government** (☎ 902/421–8736) or the **Provincial Tax Commission** (⊠ Tax Refund Unit, Box 755, Halifax B3J 2V4, ☎ 902/424–5946) for information.

Visitor Information

Nova Scotia Tourism (✉ Box 130, Halifax B3J 2M7, ☎ 902/424–5000 or 800/341–6096, 800/565–0000 in Canada; FAX 902/420–1286) publishes a wide range of literature, including an exhaustive annual travel guide. **Nova Scotia Tourism Information Centre** (✉ Old Red Store at Historic Properties, Halifax, ☎ 902/424–4248) and **Tourism Halifax & Nova Scotia Tourism** (✉ International Visitors Centre, 1595 Barrington St., ☎ 902/421–8736 or 902/421–2842) are open mid-June–Labor Day, daily 9–6; Labor Day–mid-June, weekdays 9–4:30.

14 Newfoundland and Labrador

Canada's easternmost province consists of the island of Newfoundland and Labrador on the mainland. In summer, Newfoundland's stark cliffs, bogs, and meadows become a riot of wildflowers and greenery, and the sea is dotted with boats and buoys. Mountains, lakes, and rivers provide further opportunities for first-class adventures from wildlife viewing to kayaking and fishing. St. John's, the capital, is a classic harbor city offering a lively arts scene and warm hospitality.

NEWFOUNDLAND WAS THE FIRST PLACE explorers
John Cabot (1497) and Gaspar Corte-Real (1500)
touched down in the New World. Exactly where
they went no one knows, for neither survived a second voyage. But
while he was here, Cabot reported that he saw fish in the water so thick
you could dip your basket in anywhere and catch as many as you wanted.
Within a decade of the explorers' discovery, St. John's had become a
crowded harbor. Fishing boats from France, England, Spain, and Portugal vied for a chance to catch Newfoundland's lucrative cod, which
was subsequently to shape the province's history and geography.

Updated by
Ed Kirby

At one time there were 700 hardworking settlements, or "outports,"
dotting Newfoundland's coast, most devoted to catching, salting, and
drying the world's most plentiful fish. Today, only about 400 of these
settlements survive. Newfoundland's most famous resource has become
so scarce that a partial fishing moratorium was declared in 1992 and
extended in 1993. While the province waits for the cod to return, some
25,000 fishers and processors are going to school or looking for other
work instead of fishing. The discovery of perhaps the largest nickel de-
posit in the world at Voisey's Bay in northern Labrador, near Nain,
may bring some relief. A mine and mill are expected to begin production in 2000 or 2001. In addition, a number of offshore oil fields are
expected to go into operation by the turn of the century.

Newfoundland and Labrador became part of Canada in 1949. For almost 400 years before this, however, the people had survived the vagaries of a fishing economy on their own, until the Great Depression
forced the economy to go belly-up. After 50 years of Confederation
with Canada, the economy has improved considerably, but the people
are still independent: Newfoundlanders regard themselves as North
America's first separatists and maintain a unique language and lifestyle.
E. Annie Proulx's Pulitzer Prize–winning novel, *The Shipping News*,
brought the attention of many readers to this part of the world.

Visitors to Newfoundland find themselves straddling the centuries. Old
accents and customs are common in small towns and outports, yet the
major cities of St. John's on the east coast and Corner Brook on the
west coast of the island of Newfoundland are very much part of the
20th century. Regardless of where you visit—an isolated outport or lively
Duckworth Street—you're sure to interact with some of the warmest,
wittiest people in North America. Strangers have always been welcome
in Newfoundland, since the days when locals brought visitors in from
out of the cold, warmed them by the fire, and charmingly interrogated
them for news of events outside the province.

Before you can shoot the breeze, though, you'll have to acclimate
yourself to the strong provincial dialects. Newfoundland is one of two
provinces with their own dictionaries. Prince Edward Island is the
other, but its book has only 873 entries. The *Dictionary of Newfoundland English* has more than 5,000 words, mostly having to do
with fishery, weather, and scenery. To get started, you can practice the
name of the province—it's New-fund-*land*, with the accent on "land."
However, only "livyers" ever get the pronunciation exactly right.

Pleasures and Pastimes

Dining

Today, despite the fishing moratorium, seafood is an excellent value
in Newfoundland and Labrador. Many restaurants offer seasonal specialties with a wide variety of traditional wild and cultured species. Cod

is still readily available and is traditionally prepared—panfried, baked, or poached. Aquaculture species like steelhead trout, salmon, mussels, and sea scallops are available in better restaurants. Cold-water shrimp, snow crab, lobster, redfish, grenadier, halibut, and turbot are also good seafood choices.

Two other foods to try are partridgeberries and bakeapples. Partridge-berries are a small, lush-tasting berry, called the mountain cranberry in the United States, and they are used for pies, jams, cakes, pancakes, and even as a sauce for meat. Bakeapples in the wild are a low-growing berry that looks like a yellow raspberry—they ripen in bogs in August. Pickers sell them by the side of the road in jars. If the ones you buy are hard, wait a few days and they'll ripen into rich-tasting fruit. The berries are popular on ice cream or spread on bread. In Scandinavia they're known as cloudberries. Newfoundlanders are also partial to the peppery herb they call summer savory, which they slip into most stuffings and stews. Growers here ship the product all over the world.

Only the large urban centers, especially St. John's and Corner Brook, have gourmet restaurants. Fish is a safe dish just about everywhere—even in the lowliest takeout. You'll be surprised by the quality of the meals along the Trans-Canada Highway: Restaurants in the Irving Gas Station chain, for example, have thick homemade soups with dumplings and Sunday dinners that draw in locals for miles around. Excellent meals are offered in the province's network of bed-and-breakfasts, where home cooking goes hand in hand with a warm welcome.

CATEGORY	COST*
$$$$	over $50
$$$	$35–$50
$$	$20–$35
$	under $20

*per person, in Canadian dollars, excluding drinks, service, and 15% harmonized sales tax (HST).

Festivals and Performing Arts Events

From the Folk Festival main stage in St. John's to the front parlor, the province is filled with music of all kinds. Festivals draw performers and fans from near and far. Newfoundlanders love a party, and from the cities to the smallest towns they celebrate their history and unique culture with events throughout the summer, whether it's music and recitations at a World War II artillery bunker at Cape Spear or a play about a sailor blown across the Atlantic to Scotland in a storm.

Fishing

Newfoundland has over 200 salmon rivers and thousands of trout streams. Fishing in these unpolluted waters is an angler's dream. The Atlantic salmon is king of the game fish. Top salmon rivers in Newfoundland include the Gander, Humber, and Exploits, while Labrador's top-producing waters are the Sandhill, Michaels, Flowers, and Eagle rivers. Lake trout, brook trout, and landlocked salmon are other favorite species. In Labrador, northern pike and arctic char can be added to that list. An expected upturn in returning salmon did not happen, and catch-and-release or other restrictions may be adopted.

Hiking

Many provincial and both national parks in Newfoundland and Labrador have hiking and nature trails, and coastal and woods trails radiate from most small communities. However, you can never be sure how far the trail will go unless you ask a local. Be careful: Landmarks are few, the weather is changeable, and it is surprisingly easy to get lost. Many small communities also have formal walking trails.

Lodging

Newfoundland and Labrador offer lodgings that range from modestly priced bed-and-breakfasts, which you can find through local tourist offices, to luxury accommodations. In between, you can choose from affordable, basic, and mid-price hotels. In remote areas, be prepared to find very basic lodgings. However, the lack of amenities is usually made up for by the home-cooked meals and great hospitality.

CATEGORY	COST*
$$$$	over $135
$$$	$110–$135
$$	$80–$110
$	under $80

All prices are for a standard double room, excluding 15% harmonized sales tax (HST), in Canadian dollars.

Exploring Newfoundland and Labrador

This chapter divides the province into the island of Newfoundland, beginning with St. John's and the Avalon Peninsula and moving west. Labrador is considered as a whole, with suggested driving and train excursions for a number of areas.

Numbers in the text correspond to numbers in the margin and on the St. John's and Newfoundland and Labrador maps.

Great Itineraries

IF YOU HAVE 3 DAYS

Pick either the west or east coast of Newfoundland. On the west coast, after arriving by ferry at **Port aux Basques** ㊹, drive through the Codroy Valley, heading north to the **Gros Morne National Park** ㉟ and its fjords, and overnight in ▣ **Rocky Harbour** ㊳ or ▣ **Woody Point** ㊱. The next day, visit **L'Anse aux Meadows National Historic Site** ㊿, where the Vikings built a village a thousand years ago; here there are reconstructions of the dwellings, plus a Viking boat tour. Then overnight in ▣ **St. Anthony** ㊶ or nearby.

On the east coast, the ferry docks at Argentia. Explore the Avalon Peninsula, beginning in ▣ **St. John's** ①–⑭, where you should spend your first night. The next day, visit **Cape Spear,** the most easterly point in North America, and the **Witless Bay Ecological Reserve** ⑮ for seabirds, whales, and icebergs. Overnight in ▣ **Placentia** ㉑ and spend your third day at **Cape St. Mary's Ecological Reserve** ㉓, known for its gannets.

IF YOU HAVE 6 DAYS

On Newfoundland's west coast, add southern Labrador to your list. A ferry takes you from St. Barbe to Blanc Sablon on the Québec-Labrador border. Drive 96 km (60 mi) to **Red Bay** ㊼ to explore the remains of a 17th-century Basque whaling station; then head to **L'Anse Amour** ㊻ to see Canada's second-tallest lighthouse. Overnight at ▣ **L'Anse au Clair** ㊺. Return through Gros Morne National Park and explore ▣ **Corner Brook** ㊷, where you should stay overnight. The next day, travel west of **Stephenville** ㊸ to explore the Port au Port Peninsula, home of Newfoundland's French-speaking population.

On the east coast add ▣ **Trinity** ㉖ to your must-see list, and overnight there or in ▣ **Clarenville** ㉔. The north shore of Conception Bay is where you will find many picturesque villages, including ▣ **Cupids** ⑲ and ▣ **Harbour Grace** ⑳. Several half-day, full-day, and two-day excursions are possible from St. John's, and in each direction a different personality of the region unfolds.

Newfoundland and Labrador

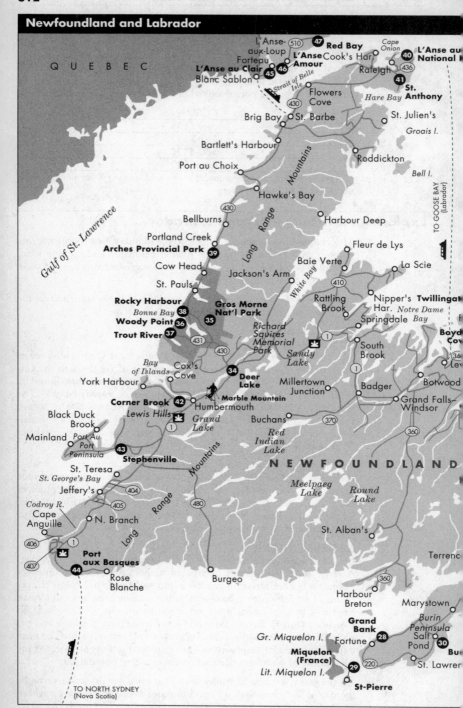

QUEBEC

L'Anse-aux-Loup
Forteau
L'Anse au Clair
Blanc Sablon
45 46
47 **Red Bay**
L'Anse Cook's Har.
Amour
Cape Onion
L'Anse au
National
40
436
Raleigh
St.
Anthony
41

Strait of Belle Isle
Hare Bay

Flowers Cove
430
Brig Bay St. Barbe
St. Julien's
Groais I.

Bartlett's Harbour
Roddickton
Bell I.

Port au Choix

Hawke's Bay
430

Bellburns
Harbour Deep

Portland Creek
Arches Provincial Park 39
Fleur de Lys

Cow Head
Baie Verte
La Scie

St. Pauls
Jackson's Arm
410

Rocky Harbour
Bonne Bay 38
Gros Morne
Nat'l Park 35
Rattling Brook
Nipper's **Twillinga**
Har.
Notre Dame Bay

Woody Point 36
Springdale

Trout River 37
431
Richard Squires Memorial Park
South Brook
Bayd
Co

430
Sandy Lake
1
34
Lev

Cox's Cove
York Harbour
Bay of Islands
34
Deer
Lake
Millertown Junction
Badger
Botwood

Corner Brook 42
Humbermouth
Marble Mountain
Grand Falls-Windsor

Lewis Hills
Grand Lake
Buchans
370

Black Duck Brook
Mainland
Port Au Port Peninsula
1
Red Indian Lake
360

Stephenville 43
Mountains
NEWFOUNDLAND

St. Teresa
St. George's Bay
Jeffery's
404
Meelpaeg Lake
Round Lake

Codroy R.
Cape Anguille
405
480
St. Alban's

N. Branch
Long Range Mountains
406
Terrenc

1
Port
aux Basques
407 44
Rose Blanche
Burgeo
360

Harbour Breton
Marystown
Burin Peninsula
Salt Pond
30

Grand
Bank 28
Fortune
Bu
St. Lawren

Gr. Miquelon I.
Miquelon
(France)
Lit. Miquelon I.
220
29

St-Pierre

TO GOOSE BAY (Labrador)

TO NORTH SYDNEY (Nova Scotia)

e aux Meadows
nal Historic Site

Hudson Strait
Cape Chidley

Ungava Bay

0   200 miles
0   300 km

Labrador Sea

Nain

Schefferville

LABRADOR

North West River (49)

Cape Harrison
Hamilton Inlet

Churchill Falls
(500)
Cartwright

(51) **Labrador City**

Sheshatshit

(50) **Wabush**
(48)
Happy Valley–Goose Bay

Blanc Sablon

Mary's Harbour

(520)
(47) **Red Bay**

QUEBEC

N

Anticosti Is.

Gaspé Pen.

Gulf of St. Lawrence

Corner Brook
Grand Falls–Windsor

Lewisporte
Gander

NEW BRUNSWICK

PR. EDWARD IS.

NEWFOUNDLAND

St. John's

NOVA SCOTIA

Change Islands

Joe Batt's Arm

gate

Fogo Island

(33)
Farewell
(335)

Hamilton Sound

oyd's Cove

(331)

Carmanville

(32)
(340)
Lewisporte
(330)

Lumsden

Wesleyville

ood
Is.

Gander (31)

Gander Lake

(1)
(320)

Bonavista Bay

Salvage

Cape Bonavista (27)

Elliston

Glovertown

Terra Nova National Park (25)

Port Union

ATLANTIC OCEAN

Terra Nova

(230)
(26)
Trinity

D

Monroe

Port Blandford

Trinity Bay

Bay de Verde

Clarenville (24)

Goobies

Cape St. Francis

Bauline

Salmon Cove

Pouch Cove

Carbonear

(210)

Conception Bay

(30)
(21)

Torbay

Logy Bay

St. John's (1) (14)

enceville

Harbour Grace (20)

Hibb's Cove

Cupids (19)

Ship Harbour (22)

(100)

Brigus (18)

Cape Spear

Maddox Cove

Argentia

Salmonier Nature Park (17)

(1)
Petty Harbour

N

Bay Bulls

Placentia (21)

(91)

Witless Bay Ecological Reserve (15)

La Manche

Placentia Bay

Ship Cove

AVALON WILDERNESS AREA

Brigus South

KEY

(90)

Ferryland (16)

Ferry

Burin

St. Bride's

St. Stephens

Avalon Peninsula

Chance Cove

(10)

Trans-Canada Hwy.

rence

Cape St. Mary's Ecological Reserve (23)

St. Shott's

Portugal Cove South

Cape Race

0   60 miles

0   90 km

TO NORTH SYDNEY
(Nova Scotia)

Trepassey

IF YOU HAVE 9 DAYS

In addition to the places already mentioned on the west coast, take a drive into central Newfoundland and visit the lovely villages of Notre Dame Bay. Overnight in ⚿ **Twillingate** ㉝. Catch a ferry to islands like ⚿ **Fogo** or the ⚿ **Change Islands.** Accommodations are available in both towns, but book ahead.

On the east coast add the Burin Peninsula and a trip to France to your itinerary. Yes, France. You can reach the French territory of ⚿ **St-Pierre and Miquelon** ㉙ by passenger ferry from Fortune. Explore romantic **Grand Bank** ㉘, named for the famous fishing area just offshore, and climb Cook's Lookout in ⚿ **Burin** ㉚, where Capt. James Cook kept a lookout for smugglers from St-Pierre.

When to Tour Newfoundland and Labrador

Depending on the time of year you visit, your experiences will be dramatically different. In spring icebergs float down from the north, and fin, pilot, minke, and humpback whales hunt for food along the coast. During the summer, temperate days turn Newfoundland's stark cliffs, bogs, and meadows into a riot of wildflowers and greenery; and the sea is dotted with boats and buoys marking traps and nets. Fall is a favored season: The weather is usually fine; cliffs and meadows are loaded with berries; and the woods are alive with moose, caribou, partridges, and rabbits, to name just a few residents. In the winter, the forest trails hum with the sound of snowmobiles and all-terrain vehicles hauling wood home or taking anglers to lodges and lakes.

The tourist season runs from June through September, when the province celebrates with festivals, fairs, concerts, plays, and crafts shows. The temperature hovers between 24°C (75°F) and 29°C (85°F) and gently cools off in the evening, providing a good night's sleep.

NEWFOUNDLAND

The rocky coasts and peninsulas of the island of Newfoundland present much dramatic beauty and many opportunities for exploring. Seaport and fishing towns such as St. John's and Grand Bank tell a fascinating history, and parks from Terra Nova National Park on the eastern side of the island to Gros Morne National Park on the west have impressive landscapes. The Avalon Peninsula includes the provincial capital of St. John's as well as the Cape Shore on its west. The Bonavista Peninsula and the Burin Peninsula as well as Notre Dame Bay have some intriguing sights, from Cape Bonavista, associated with John Cabot's landing, to pretty towns around Notre Dame Bay, such as Twillingate. The Great Northern Peninsula on the western side of Newfoundland holds a historic site with the remains of Viking sod houses; the west coast has Corner Brook, a good base for exploring the mountains, as well as farming and fishing communities.

St. John's

When Sir Humphrey Gilbert sailed into St. John's to establish British colonial rule for Queen Elizabeth in 1583, he found Spanish, French, and Portuguese fishermen actively working the harbor. As early as 1627, the merchants of Water Street—then known as the Lower Path—were doing a thriving business buying fish, selling goods, and supplying booze to soldiers and sailors. Today St. John's still encircles the snug punchbowl harbor that helped establish its reputation.

This old seaport town, the province's capital, mixes English and Irish influences, Victorian architecture and modern convenience, and traditional music and rock and roll into a heady brew that finds expression in a lively arts scene and a relaxed pace—all in a setting that has the ocean on one side and unexpected greenery on the other. A walk downtown takes in many historic buildings, but a car is needed to explore farther-flung sights that range from Cape Spear, actually south of St. John's, to parks and fishing villages.

A Good Walk

Begin at **Harbourside Park** ① on Water Street, where Gilbert planted the staff of England and claimed Newfoundland. When you leave, turn left on Water Street, right on Holloway Street, and then right onto **Duckworth Street** ②. The east end of this street is full of crafts shops and other stores. After five blocks, turn left on Ordnance Street, just one of several streets that attest to St. John's military traditions. Cross Military Road to **St. Thomas Anglican (Old Garrison) Church** ③, built in the 1830s as a place of worship for British soldiers.

Turn left and walk up King's Bridge Road. On the left is **Commissariat House** ④, an officer's house restored to the style of the 1830s. Just north of Commissariat House, a shady lane on the left leads to the gardens of **Government House** ⑤. Across from the gardens in front of the house is **Circular Road** ⑥, where the business elite moved after a fire destroyed much of the town in 1846. Back on Military Road, cross Bannerman Road to the **Colonial Building** ⑦, the former seat of government and current home of the Provincial Archives. Walk west on Military Road to Harvey Road, a continuation of Military Road. On the right is the Roman Catholic **Basilica Cathedral of St. John the Baptist** ⑧; you pass the Basilica Museum in the Bishop's Palace just before you get there.

Cross Harvey Road and turn left down Garrison Hill, so named because it once led to Fort Townshend, now the site of fire and police stations. Cross Queen's Road and walk down Cathedral Street to Gower Street and the Gothic Revival **Anglican Cathedral of St. John the Baptist** ⑨. The entrance is on the west side on Church Hill. Directly across from the cathedral on the west side of Church Hill is **Gower Street United Church** ⑩. At the bottom of Church Hill is the Duckworth Street **Court House** ⑪, with its four turrets. Go east on Duckworth a few doors to the **Newfoundland Museum** ⑫, with exhibits on Newfoundland's natural and cultural history. Exit the museum and turn left; then go down the long set of steps to **Water Street** ⑬, one of the the oldest business street in North Americas. Turn right on Water Street to reach the last stop, the **Murray Premises** ⑭, a restored mercantile complex. It contains boutiques, a science center, offices, and—welcome after this walk—restaurants, a coffee bar, and a wine cellar.

TIMING

Downtown St. John's is compact but hilly. The walk avoids major uphill climbs. Depending on how long you spend indoors, the walk should take about half a day. It is best undertaken from spring to fall.

Sights to See

❾ **Anglican Cathedral of St. John the Baptist.** A fine example of Gothic Revival architecture, this church was first completed in the mid-1800s; it was rebuilt after the 1892 fire. ⊠ 22 Church Hill, ☎ 709/726–5677. ☉ Tours June–Sept; call ahead.

❽ **Basilica Cathedral of St. John the Baptist.** This 1855 Roman Catholic cathedral in the Romanesque style has a commanding position above Military Road, overlooking the older section of the city and the harbor. The land was granted to the church by young Queen Victoria, and the edifice was built with stones from both Ireland and Newfoundland. A museum with vestments and religious objects is next door in the

St. John's

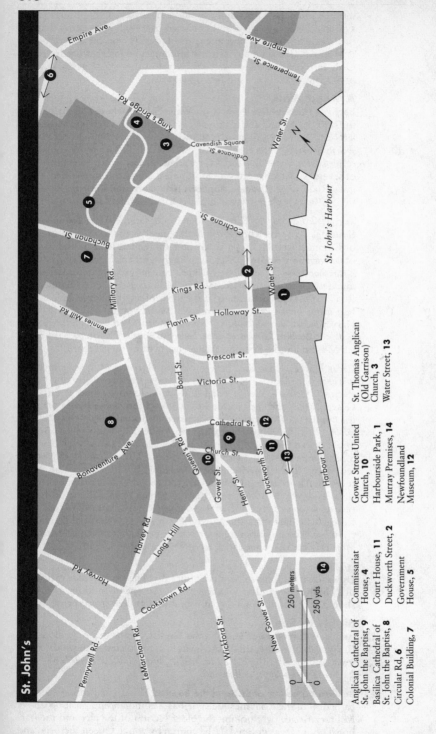

St. John's Harbour

Anglican Cathedral of
St. John the Baptist, **9**
Basilica Cathedral of
St. John the Baptist, **8**
Circular Rd, **6**
Colonial Building, **7**

Commissariat
House, **4**
Court House, **11**
Duckworth Street, **2**
Government
House, **5**

Gower Street United
Church, **10**
Harbourside Park, **1**
Murray Premises, **14**
Newfoundland
Museum, **12**

St. Thomas Anglican
(Old Garrison)
Church, **3**
Water Street, **13**

Bishop's Palace. ✉ *Military Rd.,* ☎ *709/754–2170.* ☜ *Museum $2.* ⊙ *Museum early June–late Sept.*

⑥ Circular Road. The business elite of St. John's moved here after the devastating fire of 1846. The street contains some very fine Victorian houses and shady trees.

⑦ Colonial Building. This columned building was the seat of the Newfoundland government from the 1850s to 1960, when the legislature moved to the new Confederation Building in the north end of the city. The Colonial Building now houses the Provincial Archives. ✉ *Military Rd. and Bannerman Rd.,* ☎ *709/729–3065.* ☜ *Free.* ⊙ *Weekdays 9–4:15.*

④ Commissariat House. The residence and office of the British garrison's supply officer in the 1830s has been restored to that era. Interpreters dress in period costume. ✉ *King's Bridge Rd.,* ☎ *709/729–6730 or 709/729–2460.* ☜ *Free.* ⊙ *Mid-June–mid-Oct., daily 10–5:30.*

⑪ Court House. The late-19th-century courthouse has an eccentric appearance: Each of its four turrets is a different style. ✉ *Duckworth St.* ☜ *Free.* ⊙ *Weekdays.*

② Duckworth Street. Once called the Upper Path, this has been St. John's "second street" for centuries. Water Street has been the main street for just as long. Stretching from the bottom of Signal Hill in the east to near City Hall in the west, Duckworth Street has restaurants, bars, antiques and crafts shops, and lawyers' offices.

⑤ Government House. This, the residence of the lieutenant-governor, is the only building in Newfoundland that has a moat around it to keep out snakes. Of course, there have never been snakes in Newfoundland. The house, built in the 1830s, was originally designed for the governor of a warmer colony. After exploring the marvelous garden, you can go in the front door and sign the guest book. People who do so are invited to the governor's garden party in August. The house is not open for tours. ✉ *Military Rd.* ☜ *Garden free.* ⊙ *Garden open daily.*

⑩ Gower Street United Church. This 1896 church has a redbrick facade and green turrets. Fifty stained-glass windows and a massive pipe organ are other features. ✉ *Gower St. and Church Hill,* ☎ *709/753–7286.*

① Harbourside Park. Here Sir Humphrey Gilbert claimed Newfoundland for Britain in 1583, much to the amusement of the French, Spanish, and Portuguese fishermen in port at the time. They thought him a fool, a judgment borne out a few days later when he ran his ship aground and drowned. This area, known as the Queen's Wharf, is where the harbor-pilot boat is docked. ✉ *Water St. E.*

⑭ Murray Premises. One of the oldest buildings in St. John's, Murray Premises dates from only 1846. The town was destroyed many times by fire, the last and worst being in 1892. This restored warehouse now houses shops, offices, restaurants, and a science center. ✉ *Water St. and Harbour Dr.* ⊙ *Daily.*

⑫ Newfoundland Museum. Three floors of displays focus on the province's cultural and natural history. There are also changing exhibits from other museums. ✉ *285 Duckworth St.,* ☎ *709/729–2329.* ☜ *Free.* ⊙ *July–Aug., Tues.–Sun. 10–6; Sept.–June, Tues.–Fri. 9–5, weekends 10–6.*

③ St. Thomas Anglican (Old Garrison) Church. English soldiers used to worship at this, the oldest church in the city, during the early and mid-1800s. ✉ *King's Bridge Rd. and Military Rd.,* ☎ *709/576–6632.*

⑬ Water Street. Originally called the Lower Path, Water Street has been the site of businesses since at least the 1620s. The older architecture

recalls that of seaports in southwest England and Ireland. Today shops
and restaurants are mixed with some more modern office buildings.

A Good Drive

To explore attractions outside the downtown core of old St. John's,
begin by taking Water Street west to its intersection with Route 11,
which leads you to **Cape Spear National Historic Site,** 11 km (7 mi)
south of St. John's. This is the most easterly point in North America,
and when you stand with your back to the ocean, the entire population of North America is west of you. Cape Spear Lighthouse, the oldest lighthouse in Newfoundland, is here.

On the drive back to St. John's, branch off to the left through **Maddox Cove** and **Petty Harbour,** two fishing villages, to Route 10. Turn
right and take this route north to Waterford Bridge Road and **Bowring
Park,** a traditional English-style park. Drive east through the Waterford Valley and along Water Street, Harbour Drive, and back to Water
Street; then turn left up Temperance Street and right again to the east
end of St. John's harbor and the **Battery,** a fishing village right in the
city. After exploring the Battery, turn right up Signal Hill Road and
drive to the top, where **Cabot Tower** has a stunning view of the surrounding coastline and the city below. The **Signal Hill National Historic
Site** interpretation center is also on this road, below the tower.

Heading back down the hill, turn right on Quidi Vidi Road and drive
to its intersection with Forest Road. A penitentiary is at the intersection. Continue right past the eastern end of Quidi Vidi Lake and take
Cuckold's Cove Road on the right to **Quidi Vidi Battery,** an old French
and British fort. Return to Quidi Vidi Road, turn right, and drive through
Quidi Vidi, another fishing village within the city. Caution: The road
is very narrow here.

The final two stops on this drive are in C.A. Pippy Park in the city's
north end. Take Prince Philip Drive to Allendale Road and turn north.
The first turn on the left is Nagle's Place, which brings you to the **Newfoundland Freshwater Resources Centre,** where you can see fish underwater through a large glass window. Continue north on Allendale
Road to Mt. Scio Road. Turn left and drive to the native and alpine
plants at **Memorial University Botanical Garden.**

TIMING

This drive goes beyond St. John's to Cape Spear, so plan to spend between half a day and a day if you want some time at each stop. The
best time for the tour is summer, when all the attractions are open.

Sights to See

The Battery. A tiny, still active fishing village perches precariously at
the base of steep cliffs between hill and harbor. You can drive these
narrow lanes, but it's better to get out and walk.

Bowring Park. An expansive Victorian park west of downtown, Bowring
Park resembles the famous city parks of London, after which it was
modeled. The wealthy Bowring family donated the park to the city in
1911. Dotting the grounds are ponds and rustic bridges; the statue of
Peter Pan just inside the east gate was cast from the same mold as the
one in Kensington Park in London. ⊠ *Waterford Bridge Rd.* ☜ *Free.*

Cabot Tower. This tower at the summit of Signal Hill was constructed
in 1897 to commemorate the 400th anniversary of Cabot's landing in
Newfoundland. The ride here along Signal Hall Road has fine harbor
and city views, as does the tower. ⊠ *Signal Hill Rd.,* ☎ *709/772–5367.*
☜ *Free.* ☉ *Labor Day–early June, daily 9–5; mid-June–Labor Day,
daily 8:30–8; guides available on summer weekends.*

Cape Spear National Historic Site. At the easternmost point of land on the continent, songbirds begin their chirping in the dim light of dawn, and whales (in early summer) feed directly below the cliffs, providing an unforgettable start to the day. In May and June, you may well see icebergs floating by. **Cape Spear Lighthouse,** Newfoundland's oldest such beacon, has been lovingly restored to its original form and furnishings. ☎ 709/772–5367. ☞ $2.50. ☉ *Site, daily; lighthouse June–Labor Day, daily 10–6.*

Maddox Cove and Petty Harbour. These picturesque fishing villages are next to each other along the coast between Cape Spear and Route 10. Petty Harbour has been the setting for several Hollywood movies.

Memorial University Botanical Garden. This 110-acre garden and natural area at Oxen Pond in C.A. Pippy Park has four pleasant walking trails and many gardens, including rock gardens and scree, a Newfoundland historic-plants bed, peat and woodland beds, an alpine house, an herb wall, and native plant collections. Among the environmental education programs are seasonal indoor exhibits and wildflower and bird-watching walks. ✉ *306 Mt. Scio Rd.,* ☎ *709/737–8590.* ☞ *$1.* ☉ *May–Nov., daily 10–5.*

Newfoundland Freshwater Resource Center. Underwater windows look onto a brook at the only public fluvarium in North America. In season you can observe spawning brown and brook trout in their natural habitat. Feeding time for the fish, frogs, and eels is 4 PM daily. ✉ *Mt. Scio Rd., C.A. Pippy Park,* ☎ *709/754–3474.* ☞ *$2.75.* ☉ *July–Aug., daily 9–5.*

Quidi Vidi. No one knows the origin of the name of this fishing village, one of the oldest parts of St. John's. It's a good place to explore on foot. In spring, the inlet, known as the Gut, is a place to catch sea-run brown trout.

Quidi Vidi Battery. This small redoubt has been restored to the way it appeared in 1812. Costumed interpreters tell you about the hard, unromantic life of a soldier of the empire. ✉ *Near entrance to Quidi Vidi harbor,* ☎ *709/729–2460 or 709/729–0592.* ☞ *Free.* ☉ *July–late Aug., daily 10–5:30.*

Signal Hill National Historic Site. In spite of its height, Signal Hill was difficult to defend: Throughout the 1600s and 1700s it changed hands with every attacking French, English, and Dutch force. A wooden palisade encircles the summit of the hill, indicating the boundaries of the old fortifications. En route to the hill is the **Park Interpretation Centre,** with exhibits describing St. John's history. In July and August, cadets dressed in 19th-century British uniform perform a **Tattoo** of military drills and music. **Gibbet Hill,** the rocky knob to the west of the interpretation center, got its name—a gibbet is a post with a projecting arm for hanging—because a miscreant was once hanged there and left dangling as a deterrent to other would-be lawbreakers. In 1901 Guglielmo Marconi received the first transatlantic wire transmissions in **Cabot Tower.** From the top of the hill it's a 500-ft drop to the narrow harbor entrance below; views are excellent. ✉ *Signal Hill Rd.,* ☎ *709/ 772–5367.* ☞ *Site free; visitor center, $2.50.* ☉ *Daily.*

Dining and Lodging

$$–$$$ ✗ **Bianca's.** Modern paintings make this bright eatery feel like an art gallery. The menu changes seasonally but emphasizes fish; there's a cigar room in the back. ✉ *171 Water St.,* ☎ *709/726–9016, AE, DC, MC, V. Closed Sun.*

$$–$$$
★   ✕ **The Cellar.** This restaurant, in a historic building on the waterfront, gets rave reviews for innovative Continental cuisine that uses the best local ingredients. Menu selections include blackened fish dishes and tiramisu for dessert. ✉ *Baird's Cove, between Harbour and Water Sts.,* ☎ *709/579–8900. Reservations essential. AE, MC, V.*

$$–$$$ ✕ **Hungry Fishermen.** Salmon, scallops, halibut, mussels, cod, and shrimp top the menu here. Nonfish eaters can choose veal, chicken, or the five-onion soup. This restaurant in a historic 19th-century building overlooking a courtyard has great sauces; desserts change daily and are homemade. ✉ *Murray Premises, 5 Beck's Cove, off Water St.,* ☎ *709/726–5790. AE, DC, MC, V.*

$$–$$$
★   ✕ **Stone House.** Imported game and local specialties are served in one of St. John's most historic buildings, a restored 19th-century stone cottage. ✉ *8 Kenna's Hill,* ☎ *709/753–2380. AE, DC, MC, V.*

$$$–$$$$ ✕🏨 **Delta St. John's.** Rooms in this convention hotel in downtown St. John's overlook the harbor and the city. The restaurant, Brazil Square ($–$$$), is known for its breakfast and noon buffets. ✉ *120 New Gower St., A1C 6K4,* ☎ *709/739–6404 or 800/563–3838,* 𝔽𝔸𝕏 *709/570–1622. 276 rooms, 9 suites. Restaurant. AE, DC, MC, V.*

$$$–$$$$
★   ✕🏨 **Hotel Newfoundland.** St. John's residents gather at this comfortable modern hotel for special occasions. It's noted for charming rooms that overlook the harbor, its atrium, Sunday and evening buffets, and the fine cuisine of the Cabot Club. ✉ *Cavendish Sq., Box 5637, A1C 5W8,* ☎ *709/726–4980,* 𝔽𝔸𝕏 *709/726–2025. 301 rooms, 14 suites. Restaurant. AE, DC, MC, V.*

$$–$$$
★   🏨 **Compton House Bed & Breakfast.** This inn, a charming historic residence in the west end of the city, is professionally run and beautifully decorated. Twelve-foot ceilings and wide halls give the place a majestic feeling, and rooms done in pastels and chintzes add an air of coziness. The location, within walking distance of downtown St. John's, is ideal. ✉ *26 Waterford Bridge Rd., A1E 1C6,* ☎ *709/739–5789,* 𝔽𝔸𝕏 *709/738–1770. 4 rooms, 2 suites. AE, MC, V.*

$$–$$$ 🏨 **Quality Hotel by Journey's End Motel.** Like other properties in the chain, this hotel offers clean, comfortable rooms at a reasonable price; this one looks out over the harbor. The restaurant, Rumpelstiltskins, has a splendid view and an unpretentious menu. ✉ *Hill O'Chips, A1C 6B1,* ☎ *709/754–7788,* 𝔽𝔸𝕏 *709/754–5209. 162 rooms. Restaurant. AE, DC, MC, V.*

$–$$$
★   🏨 **Prescott Inn.** Local art decorates the walls of this house, the city's most popular bed-and-breakfast. The inn has been modernized, tastefully blending the new and the old. It's central to shops and downtown attractions. ✉ *17–21 Military Rd., A1C 2C3,* ☎ *709/753–7733 or 888/263–3768,* 𝔽𝔸𝕏 *709/753–6036. 4 rooms, 10 suites. MC, V.*

$ 🏨 **Gower Street House Bed & Breakfast.** Now a B&B, the gracious former home of the late photographer Elsie Holloway has been designated by the Newfoundland Historic Trust as a point of interest. It's an ideal setting for paintings by prominent local artists. The location is within walking distance of the city's main attractions. A full breakfast is included in the rate. ✉ *180 Gower St., A1C 1P9,* ☎ *709/754–0047 or 800/563–3959,* 𝔽𝔸𝕏 *709/754–0047. 4 rooms. AE, MC, V.*

Nightlife and the Arts

THE ARTS

St. John's has a lively and, for its size, large arts community. **Hard Tickets and High Society** (☎ 709/579–3023) is a comedic dinner-theater production set in class-riven 19th-century St. John's. The **Resource Centre for the Arts** (✉ LSPU Hall, 3 Victoria St., ☎ 709/753–4531, 𝔽𝔸𝕏 709/753–4537) is an innovative experimental theater with events such as plays and concerts year-round.

The **Ship Inn** (☎ 709/753–3870), a pub in Solomon's Lane between Duckworth and Water streets, serves as the local arts watering hole. On Sunday nights fiddler Kelly Russell and guests present an evening of traditional music.

The **Newfoundland and Labrador Folk Festival** (☎ 709/576–8508), held in St. John's in early August, is the province's best-known traditional music festival. From July to September, **Voices from Cape Spear** (☎ 709/738–3945 or 709/772–4444) features songs, stories, and music in a World War II ammunition bunker at Cape Spear.

NIGHTLIFE

It has been a long-standing claim (since at least the 1700s) that St. John's has more bars per mile than any other city in North America. Each has its own personality. The **Blarney Stone** (✉ 342 Water St., 2nd floor, ☎ 709/754–1798) offers traditional music. **Erin's Pub** (✉ 186 Water St., ☎ 709/722–1916) is famous for Irish music. **George Street** downtown has pubs and restaurants, and there are often open-air concerts.

Shopping

ANTIQUES

Livyers (✉ 202 Duckworth St., ☎ 709/726–5650) carries locally crafted furniture, books, prints, and maps. **Murray's Antiques** (✉ 414 Blackmarsh Rd., ☎ 709/579–7344) is renowned for silver, china, and fine mahogany and walnut furniture.

ART GALLERIES

St. John's has a dozen art galleries, nearly all of which carry works by local artists. Newfoundland's unique landscape, portrayed realistically or more experimentally, is a favorite subject. The **Art Gallery of Newfoundland and Labrador** (✉ Allandale Rd. and Prince Philip Dr., ☎ 709/737–8209) is the province's largest public gallery and exhibits historical and contemporary Canadian arts and crafts with an emphasis on local artists and artisans. It's closed Monday. **Christina Parker Fine Art** (✉ 7 Plank Rd., ☎ 709/753–0580) represents local and national artists in all media, including painting, sculpture, drawing, and prints. The **Emma Butler Gallery** (✉ 111 George St., ☎ 709/739–7111, FAX 709/753–7163) sells a large selection of Newfoundland art, including works by David Blackwood and Christopher Pratt.

BOOKS

Most bookstores have a prominent section devoted to local history, fiction, and memoirs. **Word Play** (✉ 221 Duckworth St., ☎ 709/726–9193 or 800/563–9100) carries a wide selection of magazines and books of general interest to visitors.

HANDICRAFTS

The **Cod Jigger** (✉ 245 Duckworth St., ☎ 709/726–7422) carries handmade wool sweaters, socks, and mittens as well as Newfoundland's unique Grenfell parkas (☞ St. Anthony, *below*). The **Devon House Craft Gallery** (✉ 59 Duckworth St., ☎ 709/753–2749) is owned by the Newfoundland and Labrador Crafts Development Association and carries only juried crafts. The **Newfoundland Weavery** (✉ 177 Water St., ☎ 709/753–0496) sells rugs, prints, lamps, books, crafts, and other gifts. **NONIA** (Newfoundland Outport Nurses Industrial Association, ✉ 286 Water St., ☎ 709/753–8062) was founded in 1920 to give women in the outports a way to earn money to support nursing services in these remote communities. Homespun wool was turned into exquisite clothing. Today the shop continues to sell these fine homespun articles as well as lighter, more modern handmade items. The **Salt Box** (✉ 194 Duckworth St., ☎ 709/753–0622) sells local crafts and specializes in pottery.

MUSIC
Fred's Records (⊠ 198 Duckworth St., ☎ 709/753–9191) has the best selection of local recordings, as well as other music.

Avalon Peninsula

On the southern half of the peninsula, small Irish hamlets are separated by large tracts of wilderness. You can travel part of the peninsula's southern coast in one or two days, depending on how much time you have. Quaint towns line the road, and the natural sights are beautiful. La Manche and Chance Cove—both now-abandoned communities turned provincial parks—attest to the bounty of natural resources of the region. At the intersection of Routes 90 and 91, in Salmonier, you can either continue north toward Salmonier Nature Park and on to the towns on Conception Bay, or head west and then south to Route 100 to Cape St. Mary's Ecological Reserve (☞ Route 100: The Cape Shore, *below*). Each option takes about three hours. On the former route, stop in Harbor Grace; if you plan to travel on to Bay de Verde, at the northern tip of the peninsula, and down the other side of the peninsula on Route 80 along Trinity Bay, consider overnighting in the Harbour Grace–Carbonear area. Otherwise turn around and follow the same route back to Route 1.

Witless Bay Ecological Reserve
⑮ *29 km (18 mi) south of St. John's.*

The wildness of the peninsula's eastern coast is usually what's most striking to visitors, as evidenced at the Witless Bay Ecological Reserve, a strip of water and four islands between Bay Bulls and Tors Cove. Sometimes referred to as the Serengeti of the northwest Atlantic, the reserve is the summer home of millions of seabirds—puffins, murres, kittiwakes, razorbills, and guillemots—that nest on the islands. The birds, and the humpback and minke whales that tarry here before continuing north to the summer grounds in the Arctic, feed on the billions of capelin that swarm inshore to spawn. The reserve is also an excellent place to see icebergs in late spring and early summer. The best views of birds and icebergs are from tour boats that operate here (☞ Outdoor Activities and Sports, *below*). ⊠ *Rte. 10,* ☎ *709/729–2421 for information from the Parks and Natural Areas Division.*

OUTDOOR ACTIVITIES AND SPORTS
Gatherall's Puffin and Whale Watch (☎ 709/334–2887 or 800/419–4153) has trips for viewing wildlife in the reserve. **O'Brien's Bird Island Charters** (☎ 709/753–4850 or 709/334–2355, FAX 709/753–3140) offers popular two-hour excursions featuring whale-, iceberg-, and seabird-watching as well as cod jigging.

En Route   Although a visit to many of the hamlets along the way from Witless Bay to Ferryland on **Route 10** will fulfill any search for prettiness, La Manche and Brigus South have especially attractive settings and strong traditional flavors.

Ferryland
⑯ *43½ km (27 mi) south of Witless Bay Ecological Reserve.*

This seaside town has a long history, some of which is described in its small community museum. A major ongoing **archaeological dig** at Ferryland has uncovered the early 17th-century colony of Lord Baltimore, who abandoned the Colony of Avalon after a decade for the warmer climes of Maryland. The site includes an archaeology laboratory and exhibit center. ⊠ *Rte. 10, The Pool,* ☎ *709/432–3200.* ☞ *$3.* ☉ *June–Aug., daily 9–8; Sept.–Oct., daily 9–5.*

En Route In springtime, between Chance Cove and Portugal Cove South, in a
stretch of land about 58 km (36 mi) long, hundreds of **caribou** and their
calves gather on the barrens near Route 10. Although the animals are
there at other times, their numbers are few and it's hard to spot them
because they blend in with the scenery.

Salmonier Nature Park

⑰ *88 km (55 mi) from Ferryland, 14½ km (9 mi) north of the intersection of Rtes. 90 and 91.*

Many animal species indigenous to the province can be seen at this 3,000-
acre wilderness reserve area. An enclosed 100-acre exhibit allows up-
close viewing. ⊠ *Salmonier Line, Rte. 90,* ☎ *709/729–6974.* ☞ *Free.*
⊙ *June 5–Canadian Thanksgiving (mid-Oct.), daily noon–7; other times
by appointment.*

En Route From Salmonier Nature Park to Brigus, take Route 90, which passes
through the scenic **Hawke Hills** before meeting up with the Trans-Canada
Highway (Route 1). Turn off at the Holyrood Junction (Route 62) and
follow Route 70, which skirts Conception Bay.

Brigus

⑱ *19 km (12 mi) north of intersection of Rte. 1 and Rte. 70.*

This beautiful village on Conception Bay has a wonderful public garden, winding lanes, and a teahouse. Brigus is best known as the birthplace of Capt. Bob Bartlett, the famed Arctic explorer who accompanied
Admiral Peary on polar expeditions during the first decade of this century. **Hawthorne Cottage,** the home of Captain Bartlett, is one of the
few surviving examples of the picturesque cottage style, with a veranda
decorated with ornamental wooden fretwork. It dates from 1830 and
is a National Historic Site. ⊠ *Irishtown Rd.,* ☎ *709/753–9262, 709/
528–4004 in summer.* ☞ *$2.50.* ⊙ *Early June–mid-Oct., daily 10–
8 (shorter hrs in fall; call ahead).*

Ye Old Stone Barn Museum displays photos and artifacts of the town's
history, especially its connection with the fishery. ⊠ *4 Magistrate's Hill,*
☎ *709/528–3298.* ☞ *$1.* ⊙ *Mid-June–Labor Day, daily 10–5; Sept.–
Canadian Thanksgiving (mid-Oct.), weekends 10–5.*

Cupids

⑲ *5 km (3 mi) north of Brigus.*

Cupids is the oldest English colony in Canada, founded in 1610 by John
Guy, to whom the town erected a monument. In 1995 archaeologists
began unearthing the long-lost site of the original colony here, and some
of these artifacts are on display in the community museum, **Cupids Archaeological Site.** ⊠ *United Church Hall, Main Rd.,* ☎ *709/528–3477
or 709/596–1906.* ☞ *Free.* ⊙ *July–Sept., daily 9–4:30.*

Harbour Grace

⑳ *21 km (13 mi) north of Cupids.*

Harbour Grace was once the headquarters of Peter Easton, a 17th-cen-
tury pirate. Beginning in 1919, this town was the departure point for
many attempts to fly the Atlantic. Amelia Earhart left Harbour Grace
in 1932 to become the first woman to fly solo across the Atlantic. The
town has several handsome stone churches and buildings.

LODGING

$ 🖭 **Garrison House Inn.** This B&B is in a historic house built in 1811;
the owners won a local preservation award for the restoration. ⊠ *16
Water St., Box 736, A0A 2M0,* ☎ *709/596–3658. 3 rooms. MC, V.*

Route 100: The Cape Shore

You can reach the Cape Shore on the western side of the Avalon Peninsula from Route 1, at its intersection with Route 100. The ferry from Nova Scotia docks in Argentia, near Placentia. Besides the towns, a highlight is the outstanding seabird colony at Cape St. Mary's.

Placentia

㉑ *48 km (30 mi) south of Route 1.*

Placentia was the French capital of Newfoundland in the 1600s. Trust the French to select a beautiful place for a capital! **Castle Hill National Historic Site,** just north of town, is on what remains of the French fortifications. The visitor center has a "life at Plaisance" exhibit that shows the life and hardships endured by early English and French settlers. Performances of *Faces of Fort Royal,* a historical play about the French era, take place twice daily during July and August. ⊠ *Off Rte. 100,* ☎ *709/227–2401.* 🎫 *Historic site $2.50, play $2.* ☉ *Mid-June–Labor Day, daily 8:30–8; Labor Day–mid-June, daily 8:30–4:30.*

Ship Harbour

㉒ *34 km (21 mi) north of Placentia.*

An isolated, edge-of-the-world place, Ship Harbour has historic significance. Off Route 102, amid the splendor of Placentia Bay, an unpaved road leads to a **monument marking the Atlantic Charter.** In 1941, on a ship in these waters, Franklin Roosevelt and Winston Churchill signed the charter and formally announced the "Four Freedoms," which still shape the politics of the world's most successful democracies: freedom of speech, freedom of worship, freedom from want, and freedom from fear.

Cape St. Mary's Ecological Reserve

★ **㉓** *65 km (40 mi) south of Placentia.*

Cape St. Mary's Ecological Reserve is the most southerly nesting site in the world for gannets and common and thick-billed murres. A paved road takes you within a mile of the seabird colony. You can visit the interpretation center—guides are on site in summer—and then walk to within 100 ft of the colony of nesting gannets, murres, black-billed kittiwakes, and razorbills. The reserve has some of the most dramatic coastal scenery in Newfoundland. ☎ *709/729–2431 for information from the Parks and Natural Areas Division.* 🎫 *Interpretation center $3.* ☉ *Center early May–late Oct., daily 9–7. Site daily.*

McGrath's Marine Adventures (☎ FAX 709/337–2768) gives passengers a look at the famous gannet colony from the ocean.

Clarenville and the Bonavista Peninsula

Clarenville, about two hours northwest of St. John's via the Trans-Canada Highway (Route 1), is the departure point for two different excursions in the Bonavista Peninsula: the Discovery Trail and Terra Nova National Park.

Clarenville

㉔ *189 km (117 mi) northwest of St. John's.*

If history and quaint towns appeal to you, this is the starting point for
★ Route 230A—the **Discovery Trail.** The route goes as far north as the town of Bonavista, one of John Cabot's reputed landing spots in 1497.

LODGING

$$ ⊞ **Clarenville Inn.** This two-story motel was renovated in 1996; rooms are standard. ⊠ *Rte. 1, Box 967, A0E 1J0,* ☎ *709/466–7911,* FAX *709/ 466–3854. 64 rooms. Restaurant, bar. AE, DC, MC, V.*

Terra Nova National Park

㉕ *24 km (15 mi) northwest of Clarenville.*

Rugged terrain, golf, and fishing and camping opportunities are draws at this park on the exposed coastline that adjoins Bonavista Bay. The Terra Nova Park Lodge at Port Blandford is one of the most beautiful courses in Canada and the only one where a salmon river cuts through the 18-hole course. Call 709/543–2626 for a reservation; fees run between $24 and $30 per person, depending on the season. The park also has a new Marine Interpretation Center, attractive campsites, whale-watching tours, and nature walks. ⊠ *Trans-Canada Hwy., Glovertown,* ☎ *709/533–2801, 709/533–2802, or 800/213–7275.* ⊠ *Mid-May– mid-Oct., $3.25; mid-Oct.–mid-May, free.* ☉ *June–Aug., daily 10– 9; Sept.–May, weekdays 8–4:30.*

Trinity

★ **㉖** *71 km (44 mi) northeast of Clarenville.*

Trinity is one of the jewels of Newfoundland. The village's picturesque views, winding lanes, and snug houses are the main attraction, and several homes have been turned into museums and inns. In the 1700s Trinity competed with St. John's as a center of culture and wealth. Its more contemporary claim to fame, however, is that its intricate harbor was a favorite anchorage for the British navy, and it was here that the small-pox vaccine was introduced to North America by a local rector. An information center with costumed interpreters is open daily July– September. To get here, take Route 230 to Route 239.

The **Garland Mansion** is a re-creation of a fish merchant's house that was one of the most prominent 18th-century homes in Newfoundland. The original was torn down in the 1960s, but the new house opened in 1997. Next door is a 19th-century store. ⊠ *Rte. 239,* ☎ FAX *709/ 464–3706.* ⊠ *Free.* ☉ *June 15–Sept. 15, daily 10–8.*

Rising Tide Theatre (☎ 709/738–3256, 888/464–1100, or ☎ FAX *709/ 464–3847)* conducts New-Founde-Land Trinity Pageant walking tours (Wednesday, Saturday, and Sunday at 2) of the town that are more theater than tour. Actors in period costume lead the way.

NIGHTLIFE AND THE ARTS

Rising Tide Theatre (☎ 709/738–3256, 888/464–1100, or ☎ FAX *709/ 464–3847)* stages the Summer in the Bight festival. Outdoor Shakespeare productions, dinner theater, and dramas and comedies fill the bill.

OUTDOOR ACTIVITIES AND SPORTS

Atlantic Adventures (☎ 709/781–2255) operates a 46-ft motorized sail-boat for whale-watching or just cruising Trinity Bight.

Cape Bonavista

㉗ *16 km (10 mi) north of Port Union.*

Cape Bonavista is a popular destination because of its association with Cabot's landing in 1497. The **Ryan Premises National Historic Site** on the waterfront depicts the almost 500-year history of the commercial cod fishery in a restored fish merchant's property. ⊠ *Off Rte. 230,* ☎ *709/468–1600.* ⊠ *$3.* ☉ *Mid-June–mid-Oct., daily 10–6.*

The **lighthouse** on the point, about 1 km (½ mi) outside town, has been restored to its condition in 1870. The **Mockbeggar Property** teaches about the life of an outport merchant in the years immediately before confederation. ⊠ *Off Rte. 230,* ☎ *709/729–0592 or 709/468–7300/ 7444.* ☎ *Free.* ☉ *Late June–early Sept., daily 10–5:30.*

Burin Peninsula, Gander, and Notre Dame Bay

The journey down to the Burin Peninsula is a three- to four-hour drive from the intersection of Routes 230 and 1 through the craggy coastal landscapes along Route 210. The peninsula's history is tied to the rich fishing grounds of the Grand Banks, which established this area as a center for European fishery as early as the 1500s. By the early 1900s, one of the world's largest fishing fleets was based on the Burin Peninsula. Today its inhabitants hope for a recovery of the fish stocks that have sustained their economy for centuries. Marystown is the peninsula's commercial center.

Gander, in east-central Newfoundland, is famous for its airport. North of it is Notre Dame Bay, an area of rugged coastline and equally rugged islands that was once the domain of the now extinct Beothuk tribe. Only the larger islands are currently inhabited. Before English settlers moved into the area in the late-18th and early 19th centuries, it was seasonally occupied by French fishermen. Local dialects preserve centuries-old words that have vanished elsewhere. The bay is swept by the cool Labrador Current that carries icebergs south through Iceberg Alley; the coast is also a good whale-watching area.

Grand Bank
②⑧ *53 km (33 mi) southwest of Marystown on Rte. 220.*

One of the loveliest communities in Newfoundland, Grand Bank has a fascinating history as an important fishing center. Because of trade patterns, the architecture here was influenced more by Halifax, Boston, and Bar Harbor, Maine, than by the rest of Newfoundland. A sail-shape building holds the **Southern Newfoundland Seamen's Museum,** which provides insight into the town's past. ⊠ *Marine Dr.,* ☎ *709/832–1484.* ☎ *Free.* ☉ *May–Oct., weekdays 9–5, weekends 2–5.*

St-Pierre and Miquelon
②⑨ *55-min ferry ride from Fortune.*

The islands of St-Pierre and Miquelon, France's only territory in North America, are a ferry away if you crave French cuisine or a bottle of perfume. Shopping and eating are both popular pastimes. Visitors to the islands should carry proof of citizenship; people from outside the United States and Canada will have to show valid visas and passports. Because of the ferry schedule, a trip to St-Pierre means an overnight stay in a modern hotel such as **Hotel Robert** (☎ 011–508/412419) or a pension, the French equivalent of a bed-and-breakfast. Call the **St-Pierre tourist board** (☎ 011–508/412222 or 800/565–5118) for information about accommodations.

A passenger ferry operated by **Lloyd G. Lake Ltd.** (☎ 709/832–2006 or 800/563–2006) leaves Fortune (south of Grand Bank) daily at 2:15 PM from mid-June to late September; the crossing takes 70 minutes. The ferry leaves St-Pierre at 1 PM daily; round-trip is $55.The ferry operated by **St-Pierre Tours** (☎ 709/722–4103 or 709/832–0429) crosses daily from Fortune to St-Pierre May–September and weekly from October to early December. The ferry leaves Fortune at 2:45 PM, Newfoundland time, and departs St- Pierre at 1:30 PM, St-Pierre (Atlantic) time. Round-trip fare is $59.95. The trip takes 70 minutes.

Burin

30 *62 km (38 mi) from Grand Bank.*

Following Route 220 south and east from Grand Bank will take you around the peninsula to the old town of Burin, a community built amid intricate cliffs and coves. This was an ideal setting for pirates and privateers who used to lure ships into the rocky, dead-end areas in order to plunder them. Captain Cook was among those who watched for smugglers from "Cook's Lookout" on a hill that still bears his name.

Heritage House, considered one of the best community museums in Newfoundland, gives you a sense of what life was like in the past. It has a display on the 1929 tidal wave that struck Burin and a gallery for traveling exhibits. ⊠ *Square off Rte. 221,* ☎ *709/891–2217.* ☞ *Free.* ☉ *May–Oct., Mon.–Tues. 9–5, Wed.–Sun. 9–9.*

Gander

31 *170 km (105 mi) northwest of Goobies.*

A busy town with 12,000 people, Gander is notable for its aviation history. It also has many lodgings and makes a good base for travel in this part of the province. During World War II, **Gander International Airport** (⊠ James Blvd.) was chosen by the Canadian and U.S. air forces as a major strategic air base because of its favorable weather and secure location. After the war, the airport became an international hub for civilian travel; today it is a major air traffic control center. The **Aviation Exhibition** in the airport's domestic passengers' lounge (☎ 709/256–3905) traces Newfoundland's role in the history of air travel. It's open 24 hours, seven days a week.

The **North Atlantic Aviation Museum** gives an expansive view of Gander's and Newfoundland's roles in aviation. In addition to viewing the expected models and photographs, you can climb into the cockpit of a real DC-3 parked outside next to a World War II Hudson bomber and a Canadian jet fighter, or take a helicopter ride in summer. ⊠ *On Rte. 1, between hospital and visitor information center,* ☎ *709/256–2923.* ☞ *$3.* ☉ *Daily 9–5.*

DINING AND LODGING

$–$$ ✕🛏 **Albatross Motel.** This motel has a deserved reputation as an at-
★ tractive place to stop off for a meal. The restaurant serves an excellent cod au gratin. Rooms are basic and clean. ⊠ *Rte. 1, Box 450, A1V 1W8,* ☎ *709/256–3956 or 800/563–4900,* ☎ *709/651–2692. 103 rooms, 4 suites. Restaurant. AE, DC, MC, V.*

Boyd's Cove

32 *66 km (41 mi) north of Gander.*

The coastline in and near Boyd's Cove is somewhat sheltered by Twillingate Island and New World Island. Short causeways from this area link the shore to the islands.

The **Boyd's Cove Beothuk Interpretation Centre** offers a fresh look at the lives of the Beothuks, an extinct aboriginal people who succumbed in the early 19th century to a combination of disease and battle with European settlers. The center uses traditional Beothuk building forms and adjoins an archaeological site that was inhabited from about 1650 to 1720, when pressure from settlers drove the Beothuk from this part of the coast. ⊠ *Rte. 340,* ☎ *709/656–3114 or 709/729–0592.* ☞ *Free.* ☉ *Mid-June–mid-Oct., daily 10–5:30.*

Twillingate

㉝ *31 km (19 mi) north of Boyd's Cove.*

The inhabitants of this scenic old fishing village make their living from the sea and have been doing so for nearly two centuries. Colorful houses, rocky waterfront cliffs, a local museum, and a nearby lighthouse add to the town's appeal. Every year on the last weekend in July, the town hosts the **Fish, Fun and Folk Festival,** where fish are cooked every kind of way. Twillingate, one of the best places on the island to see **icebergs,** is known to the locals as Iceberg Alley. These majestic and dangerous mountains of ice are awe-inspiring to see while they're grounded in early summer.

Twillingate Island Boat Tours (☎ 709/884–2242) specializes in iceberg photography in the waters around Twillingate. An iceberg interpretation center is right on the dock.

OFF THE
BEATEN PATH

CHANGE ISLANDS AND FOGO ISLAND – You can take a ferry (☎ 709/ 627–3448 or 709/627–3431) from Farewell to either Change Islands or Fogo Island. To get to Farewell, take Route 340 to Route 335, which takes you through scenic coastal communities. These islands give you the impression of a place frozen in time. Clapboard homes are precariously perched on rocks or built on small lots surrounded by vegetable gardens. As you walk the roads, watch for moose.

The Great Northern Peninsula

The Great Northern Peninsula is the most northern visible extension of the Appalachian Mountains. Its eastern side is rugged and sparsely populated. The Viking Trail—Route 430 and its side roads, and Route 510 in southern Labrador—snakes along its western coast through a national park, fjords, sand dunes, and communities that have relied on the lobster fishery for generations. At the tip of the peninsula, the Vikings established the first European settlement in North America. For thousands of years before their arrival, the area was home to native peoples who hunted, fished, and gathered berries and herbs.

Deer Lake

㉞ *208 km (129 mi) west of Grand Falls–Windsor.*

Deer Lake was once just another small town on the Trans-Canada Highway, but the opening of Gros Morne National Park in the early '70s and a first-class paved highway passing right through to St. Anthony changed all that. Today, with an airport and car rentals available, Deer Lake is a good starting point for a fly-drive vacation.

LODGING

$–$$ 🏨 **Deer Lake Motel.** The guest rooms here are clean and comfortable, and the food in the café is basic, home-cooked fare. Seafood dishes are exceptionally well prepared. ⊠ *Rte. 1, Box 820, A0K 2E0,* ☎ *709/ 635–2108, 800/563–2144,* FAX *709/635–3842. 54 rooms, 2 suites. Café. AE, DC, MC, V.*

OFF THE
BEATEN PATH

SIR RICHARD SQUIRES MEMORIAL PARK – Natural and unspoiled, this park contains Big Falls, part of the Humber River system. You can see salmon trying to jump over the falls during their summer migration. The drive here passes through Cormack, a farming region. From Deer Lake take Route 430 to Route 422 and continue 30 km (18 mi) north to the park. ⊠ *Rte. 422,* ☎ *709/636–1509.* 🎫 *$4 per vehicle.* ☉ *Late May– early Sept.*

Gros Morne National Park

★ ⏣ *46 km (29 mi) north of Deer Lake on Rte. 430.*

Because of its geological uniqueness and immense splendor, this park has been named a UNESCO World Heritage Site. Among the more breathtaking visions are the expanses of wild orchids in springtime. An excellent **interpretation center** (☎ 709/458–2417) in Rocky Harbour has displays and videos about the park, plus an interactive vacation planner. Camping and hiking are popular recreations, and boat tours are available. It takes at least two days to see Gros Morne properly. Scenic **Bonne Bay,** a deep, mountainous fjord, divides the park in two. You can drive around the perimeter of the fjord on Route 430 going north.

⏣ In the south of the park, on Route 431, is **Woody Point,** a charming community of old houses and imported Lombardy poplars. Until it was bypassed by the now defunct railway, the community was the commercial capital of Newfoundland's west coast. The **Tablelands,** rising behind Woody Point, are a unique rock massif that was once an ancient seabed. Its rocks, which were raised from the earth's mantle through tectonic upheaval, are toxic to most plant life, and Ice Age conditions linger in the form of persistent snow and moving rock glaciers.

⏣ The once isolated small community of **Trout River** is at the western end of Route 431 on the Gulf of St. Lawrence. You pass the scenic **Trout River Pond** along the way. The **Green Gardens Trail,** a four- to five-hour hike, is also nearby, and it's one you'll remember for your lifetime, but be prepared to do a bit of climbing on your return journey. The trail passes through the Tablelands barrens and descends sharply down to a fairy-tale coastline of eroded cliffs and green meadows.

⏣ On the northern side of the park, along coastal Route 430, is the town of **Rocky Harbour,** with a range of restaurants, lodgings, and a luxurious indoor public pool and large hot tub—the perfect thing to soothe tired limbs after a strenuous day.

The most popular attraction in the northern portion of Gros Morne is the boat tour of **Western Brook Pond** (☞ Outdoor Activities and Sports, *below*). You park at a lot on Route 430 and take a 45-minute walk to the boat dock through an interesting mix of bog and woods. Cliffs rise 2,000 ft on both sides of the gorge, and high waterfalls tumble over ancient rocks. Hikers in good shape can tackle the 16 km (10-mi) hike up **Gros Morne Mountain,** at 2,644 ft the second-highest peak in Newfoundland. Weather permitting, your labor will be rewarded by a unique arctic landscape and spectacular views. The park's **northern coast** has an unusual mix of sand beaches, rock pools, and trails through tangled dwarf forests known locally as tuckamore. Sunsets, seen from **Lobster Point Lighthouse,** are spectacular. Keep an eye out for whales and visit the lighthouse museum, devoted to the history of the area.

⊠ *Gros Morne National Park, via the Viking Trail (Rte. 430),* ☎ *709/458–2417.* ⊡ *$3.25.* ☉ *Summer, daily 9 AM–10 PM; winter, daily 9–4.*

LODGING

$$–$$$$ 🏠 **Sugar Hill Inn.** This small hostelry in Gros Morne National Park has quickly developed a reputation for fine wining and dining (for guests only) because of host Vince McCarthy's culinary talents and educated palate. Guided cross-country skiing and snowmobiling treks are available. ⊠ *115–129 Sexton Rd., Box 100, Norris Point A0K 3V0,* ☎ FAX *709/458–2147. 4 rooms, 3 suites. Dining room, hot tub, sauna. MC, V.*

OUTDOOR ACTIVITIES AND SPORTS

Gros Morne Adventure Guides (☎ 709/458–2722 or 709/686–2241) has sea kayaking up the fjords and land-locked ponds of Gros Morne National Park, as well as a variety of hikes and adventures in the area.

Bontours (☎ 709/458–2730 or 800/563–9887) runs the best-known of the sightseeing trips on the west coast of Newfoundland—up Western Brook Pond in Gros Morne National Park—and another tour of Bonne Bay. **Tableland Boat Tours** (☎ 709/451–2101) leads tours up Trout River Pond near the southern boundary of Gros Morne National Park.

Arches Provincial Park
㊴ *20 km (12 mi) north of Gros Morne National Park.*

Arches Provincial Park is a geological curiosity: The action of undersea currents millions of years ago cut a succession of caves through a bed of dolomite that was later raised above sea level by tectonic upheaval. This free park, open May–October, is not staffed.

En Route   Continuing north on Route 430, parallel to the Gulf of St. Lawrence, you'll find yourself refreshingly close to the ocean and the wave-tossed beaches: Stop to breathe the fresh sea air and listen to the breakers.The **Long Range Mountains** to your right reminded Jacques Cartier, who saw them in 1534, of the long, rectangular-shape farm buildings of his home village in France. Small villages are interspersed with rivers where salmon and trout grow to be "liar-size." The remains of the Maritime Archaic Indians and Dorset Eskimos have been found in abundance along this coast, and **Port au Choix** has an interesting interpretation center. ☎ *709/623–2608, 709/861–3522 in summer.* ⊠ *$2.75.* ☉ *Mid-June–early Sept., daily 9–8; mid-Sept.–mid-Oct., daily 9:30–4:30.*

L'Anse aux Meadows National Historic Site
★ ㊵ *210 km (130 mi) northeast of Arches Provincial Park.*

Most believe the remains of the long sod houses here were built around 1000 as the site of Norseman Leif Eriksson's colony in the New World. A UNESCO World Heritage Site, L'Anse aux Meadows was discovered in 1960 by a Norwegian team, Helge and Anne Stine Ingstad. The Canadian Parks Service has established a fine **visitor center** and has meticulously reconstructed some of the sod huts to give you a sense of centuries past. ⊠ *Rte. 436,* ☎ *709/623–2608.* ⊠ *$5.* ☉ *Mid-June–mid-Sept., daily 9–8.*

DINING AND LODGING

$ ✕🛏 **Tickle Inn at Cape Onion.** This refurbished, century-old fisherman's house on the beach is probably the most northerly residence on the island of Newfoundland. The Franklin stove in the parlor is a good place to relax after a day of exploring the area meadows, hills, and coast, or visiting the Viking settlement at L'Anse aux Meadows (about 45 km, or 28 mi, away). ⊠ *R.R. 1, Box 62, Cape Onion A0K 4J0,* ☎ *709/452–4321 June–Sept., 709/739–5503 Oct.–May. 4 rooms share bath. Dining room. CP, MAP available. MC, V.*

$ 🛏 **Valhalla Lodge Bed & Breakfast.** Comfortable and inviting, the Valhalla is 10 km (6 mi) from L'Anse aux Meadows. Some interesting fossils are part of the rock fireplace in the dining room. Hot breakfasts are available, and other meals can be had on request. E. Annie Proulx, author of *The Shipping News,* stayed here when she was writing the novel. ⊠ *Gunner's Cove, Griquet A0K 2X0,* ☎ *709/623–2018 in summer, 709/896–5519 in winter,* 𝖥𝖠𝖷 *709/623–2144. 4 rooms. V.*

Viking Boat Tours (☎ 709/623–2100), in nearby St. Lunaire, visits the site at the tip of the Great Northern Peninsula where Vikings landed 1,000 years ago. The boat is modeled after a Viking trading vessel.

St. Anthony
④ *16 km (10 mi) south of L'Anse aux Meadows.*

The northern part of the Great Northern Peninsula served as the model for *The Shipping News,* E. Annie Proulx's Pulitzer-winning novel. St. Anthony is built around a natural harbor on the eastern side of the Great Northern Peninsula, near its tip. If you take a trip out to the lighthouse, you may see an iceberg or two floating by.

The **Grenfell Mission,** founded by Sir Wilfred Grenfell, a British medical missionary who established nursing stations and cooperatives and provided medical services to the scattered villages of northern Newfoundland and the south coast of Labrador in the early 1900s, remains the town's main employer. The main foyer of the **Charles S. Curtis Memorial Hospital** (⊠ 178–200 West St., ☎ 709/454–3333) has a decorative tile mural that's worth a visit.

The new **Grenfell Interpretation Centre** focuses on Dr. Grenfell's life and work. ⊠ *227A West St.,* ☎ *709/454–4010.* ⌫ *$4.* ☉ *Mid-May–mid-Oct., daily 9–5.*

A must stop is the **Grenfell Handicrafts** store (⊠ 227A West St.,, ☎ 709/454–4010) in the Grenfell Interpretation Centre. Training villagers to become self-sufficient in a harsh environment was one of Grenfell's aims. A windproof cloth that villagers turned into well-made parkas came to be known as Grenfell cloth. Mittens, caps, and coats are embroidered with designs such as polar bears.

The West Coast

Western Newfoundland is known for the unlikely combination of world-class Atlantic salmon fishing and papermaking at two newsprint mills. This area includes Corner Brook, a major center of the west coast. To the south, the Port au Port Peninsula west of Stephenville shows the French influence in Newfoundland; the farming valleys of the southwest were settled by Scots. A ferry from Nova Scotia docks at Port aux Basques in the far southwest corner.

Corner Brook
④ *50 km (31 mi) southwest of Deer Lake.*

Newfoundland's second-largest city, Corner Brook is the hub of the west coast of the island. Mountains fringe three sides of the city, which has beautiful views of the harbor and the Bay of Islands. The town is also home to one of the largest paper mills in the world; you may smell it. Captain James Cook, the British explorer, charted the coast in the 1760s, and a memorial to him overlooks the bay.

Corner Brook is a convenient hub and point of departure for exploring the west coast. It's only three hours from the Port aux Basques ferry from Nova Scotia. The town enjoys more clearly defined seasons than most of the rest of the island, and in summer it has many pretty gardens. The nearby Humber River is the best-known salmon river in the province.

The north and south shores of the **Bay of Islands** have fine paved roads—Route 440 on the north shore and Route 450 on the south—and both are a scenic half-day drive from Corner Brook. On both roads, farming and fishing communities exist side by side. Take a camera—the scenery is breathtaking, with farms, mountains, and pockets of brilliant wildflowers.

DINING AND LODGING

$–$$$ ✕🏨 **Glynmill Inn.** This charming inn, refurbished in 1994, has the feel
★   of old England. It was once the staff house for the visiting top brass of the paper mill. Rooms are cozy, and the dining room serves basic and well-prepared Newfoundland seafood, soups, and specialty desserts made with partridgeberries. There's also a popular steak house in the basement. ⊠ *1 Cobb La., Box 550, A2H 6E6,* ☎ *709/634–5181, 800/ 563–4400 in Canada,* FAX *709/634–5106. 57 rooms, 24 suites. 2 restaurants. AE, MC, V.*

$ ✕🏨 **Best Western Mamateek Inn.** Rooms are more modern than at the
★   Glynmill Inn (☞ *above*). The dining room, which serves good Newfoundland home-cooked food, is known for its exquisite view of the city. Sunsets seen from here are remarkable. ⊠ *Rte. 1, Box 787, A2H 6G7,* ☎ *709/639–8901 or 800/563–8600,* FAX *709/639–7567. 55 rooms. Restaurant. AE, MC, V.*

$$–$$$$ 🏨 **Holiday Inn.** There's nothing extraordinary here, aside from the convenient location in town. The outdoor pool is heated, and some rooms have minibars. The restaurant is average, aside from good seasonal fish dishes. ⊠ *48 West St., A2H 2Z2,* ☎ *709/634–5381,* FAX *709/634–1723. 103 rooms. Restaurant, lobby lounge, pool. AE, DC, MC, V.*

$–$$ 🏨 **Comfort Inn by Journey's End Motel.** This is a comfortable, modern motel with an attractive interior (the dominating colors are dusty rose and blue) and beautiful views of either the city or the Bay Islands. ⊠ *41 Maple Valley Rd., Box 1142, A2H 6T2,* ☎ *709/639–1980,* FAX *709/639–1549. 80 rooms. Restaurant. AE, DC, MC, V.*

OUTDOOR ACTIVITIES AND SPORTS

Strawberry Hill Resort (☎ 709/634–0066, FAX 709/634–7604) in Little Rapids, 12 km (7 mi) east of Corner Brook on Route 1, was once an exclusive retreat for the owner of the Corner Brook mill. Guests here can enjoy Newfoundland's finest sport salmon fishing.

The growing **Marble Mountain Ski Resort** (⊠ Rte. 1, ☎ 709/637–7616), just east of the city in Steady Brook, has 27 downhill runs and five lifts capable of moving 6,500 skiers an hour, as well as a large day lodge, ski shop, day-care center, and restaurant. The vertical drop is 1,600 ft.

Stephenville

43 *77 km (48 mi) south of Corner Brook.*

The former Harmon Air Force Base is in Stephenville, a town best known for its summer festival (☞ *below*). It also has a large modern paper mill. To the west of town is the Port au Port Peninsula, which was largely settled by the French, who brought their way of life and language to this small corner of Newfoundland.

NIGHTLIFE AND THE ARTS

The **Stephenville Festival** (☎ 709/643–4982), held mid-July to mid-August, is the province's major annual summer theatrical event, with a mix of light musicals and serious drama.

En Route As you travel down the Trans-Canada Highway toward Port aux Basques, Routes 404, 405, 406, and 407 will bring you into the small Scottish communities of the **Codroy Valley.** Nestled in the valley are some of the finest salmon rivers and most productive farms in the province, all of this against the backdrop of the Long Range Mountains and the Lewis Hills, from which gales strong enough to stop traffic hurl off the plateau and down to the coast.

Port aux Basques

④④ *166 km (103 miles) south of Stephenville.*

Port aux Basques was one of seven Basque ports along Newfoundland's west coast and in southern Labrador during the 1500s and early 1600s and was given its name by the town's French successors. It is now the main ferry port connecting the island to Nova Scotia (☞ Arriving and Departing *in* Newfoundland and Labrador A to Z, *below*). In J.T. Cheeseman Provincial Park, 15 km (9 mi) north of town on the Trans-Canada Highway, and at Grand Bay West you may see the endangered piping plover, which nests in the sand dunes along this coast.

LODGING

$ 🖭 **St. Christopher's Hotel.** This clean, comfortable hotel has quiet, airconditioned rooms and good food. Rooms have satellite TV. ✉ *Caribou Rd., Box 2049, A0M 1C0,* ☎ *709/695–7034 or 800/563–4779,* FAX *709/695–9841. 54 rooms, 3 suites. Restaurant, meeting room. AE, DC, MC, V.*

LABRADOR

Isolated from the rest of the continent, Labrador has remained one of the world's truly wild places, although its two main centers of Labrador City–Wabush and Happy Valley–Goose Bay have all the amenities available in larger urban areas. Labrador is steeped in history, a place where the past invades the present and life evolves as it did many years ago—a composite of natural phenomena, wilderness adventure, history, and culture. This vast landscape—293,347 square km (113,204 square mi) of land and 8,000 km (5,000 mi) of coastline—is home to 30,000 people. The small but richly diverse population has a history that in some cases stretches back thousands of years; in other cases—the mining towns of Labrador West, for example—the history goes back less than four decades.

The Straits

The Straits in southeastern Labrador were a rich hunting-and-gathering ground for the continent's earliest peoples. In the area is the oldest industrial site in the New World, the 16th-century Basque whaling station at Red Bay.

L'Anse au Clair

④⑤ *5 km (3 mi) from Blanc Sablon, Québec (ferry from St. Barbe, Newfoundland, docks in Blanc Sablon).*

In L'Anse au Clair, anglers can try their luck for trout and salmon on the scenic Forteau and Pinware rivers. You can also walk the "Doctor's Path," where long ago Dr. Marcoux searched out herbs and medicinal plants in the days when hospitals and nursing stations were few and far between. For ferry information, *see* Getting Around *in* Newfoundland and Labrador A to Z.

L'Anse Amour

④⑥ *19 km (12 mi) east of L'Anse au Clair.*

The elaborate **Maritime Archaic Indian burial site** (✉ Rte. 510) discovered near L'Anse Amour is 7,500 years old. A plaque marks a site that is the oldest known aboriginal funeral monument in North America. The L'Anse Amour **lighthouse,** constructed in 1857, is 109 ft tall, the second-tallest in Canada; you can climb it.

En Route The **Labrador Straits Museum** provides a glimpse into the history and lifestyle of the area. ✉ *Rte. 510 between Forteau and L'Anse au Loup,* ☎ *709/931–2067.* ☞ *$2.* ☉ *June–Sept., daily.*

Red Bay

47 *35 km (22 mi) from L'Anse Amour.*

The area's main attraction lies at the very end of Route 510: Red Bay, the site of a 16th-century Basque whaling station and a National Historic Site. Basque whalers began harpooning migrating whales from flimsy boats in frigid waters a few years after Cabot's discovery of the coast in 1497. Between 1550 and 1600 Red Bay was the world's whaling capital. The **Red Bay National Historic Site** has a visitor center that interprets the Basque heritage through film and artifact. From June through October, a boat will take you on a five-minute journey over to the site of excavations on Saddle Island. ⊠ *Rte. 510,* ☎ *709/920–2176.* 🎫 *Visitor center, $2; boat to island, $2.* ☉ *Mid-June–mid-Oct., Mon.–Sat. 8–8, Sun. noon–8.*

Coastal Labrador

This area is almost as isolated today as it was a century ago. Along the southern coast, most villages are inhabited by descendants of Europeans, while farther north they are mostly native. Over the years the European settlers have adopted native skills and survival strategies, and the natives have adopted many European technologies. In summer the ice retreats and a coastal steamer delivers goods, but in winter small airplanes and snowmobiles are the only ways in and out.

You can tour central coastal Labrador aboard a car ferry from Lewisporte, Newfoundland (☞ Getting Around *in* Newfoundland and Labrador A to Z, *below*). A second vessel, a coastal freighter, travels from St. Anthony, Newfoundland, to Nain, Labrador's northernmost settlement. This trip takes two weeks to complete. Both vessels carry all sorts of food and goods for people living along the coast. The coastal freighter stops at a number of summer fishing stations and coastal communities. Reservations are required.

Battle Harbour National Historic Site

12 km (7 mi) from Mary's Harbour by boat.

This island site has the only remaining outport fishing merchant's premises that remains intact in the province. Settled in the 18th century, Battle Harbour was the main fishing port in Labrador until the first half of the 20th century when, after fires destroyed some of the community, the people moved to nearby Mary's Harbour. The site also contains the oldest Anglican church in Labrador. Accommodations are available. ⊠ *Southern Labrador coast, accessible by boat from Mary's Harbour,* ☎ *709/921–6216, 709/497–8805 off-season.* ☉ *June–Sept.*

Happy Valley–Goose Bay

48 *525 km (326 mi) from Labrador City.*

Happy Valley–Goose Bay is the chief service center for coastal Labrador. Anyone coming to Labrador to fish will probably pass through here. The town was founded in the 1940s as a top-secret air base used to ferry fleets of North American–manufactured aircraft to Europe. It is still used as a low-level flying training base by the British, Dutch, and German air forces.

OUTDOOR ACTIVITIES AND SPORTS

Ski Mount Shana (⊠ Rte. 520, ☎ 709/896–8162 or 709/896–8068), with 10 downhill runs, is between Happy Valley–Goose Bay and North West River. The vertical drop is 525 ft.

North West River
⑭ *20 km (12 mi) northeast of Happy Valley–Goose Bay.*

North West River, which retains its frontier charm, was founded as a Hudson's Bay trading post and is the former Labrador headquarters of the International Grenfell Association.

Labrador West

Labrador West's subarctic landscape is challenging and unforgettable. Here are some of the world's best angling and wilderness adventure opportunities. The best way to see this area is to ride the **Québec North Shore and Labrador Railway** (☎ 418/968–7805 or 709/944–8205), which leaves Sept Isles, Québec, three times a week in summer and twice a week in the winter. The seven- to eight-hour trip to Schefferville takes you through nearly 600 km (372 mi) of virgin forest, spectacular waterfalls, and majestic mountains.

Wabush
⑭ *525 km (326 mi) west of Happy Valley–Goose Bay.*

The modern town of Wabush has all the amenities of larger centers, including accommodations, sports and recreational facilities, good shopping, live theater, and some of the finest hospitality you will find anywhere.

OUTDOOR ACTIVITIES AND SPORTS

The **Smokey Mountain Alpine Skiing Center** (⊠ Rte. 500, ☎ 709/944–2129), west of Wabush, is open mid-November to late April and has slopes for both beginners and advanced skiers. Vertical drop is 1,000 ft.

Labrador City
⑭ *525 km (326 mi) west of Happy Valley–Goose Bay.*

Labrador City has all the facilities of nearby Wabush (☞ *above*). Each March Labrador City and Wabush play host to a 645-km (400-mi) dogsled race, the longest such race in eastern North America.

NEWFOUNDLAND AND LABRADOR A TO Z

Arriving and Departing

By Car Ferry
Marine Atlantic (⊠ Box 250, North Sydney, Nova Scotia B2A 3M3, ☎ 800/341–7981, TTY 902/794–8109, ℻ 902/564–7480) operates a car ferry from North Sydney, Nova Scotia, to Port aux Basques, Newfoundland (crossing time is six hours), and, from June through October, from North Sydney to Argentia, twice a week (crossing time 12–14 hours). In all cases, reservations are required.

By Plane
The province's main airport is **St. John's International Airport** (⊠ Airport Rd. off Portugal Cove Rd., ☎ 709/772–0011). Other airports in Newfoundland are at Stephenville, Deer Lake, St. Anthony, and Gander; airports in Labrador are in Happy Valley–Goose Bay, Wabush, and Churchill Falls. Air Canada flies into Newfoundland, and the following are regional connectors: Air Alliance (Québec to Wabush), Air Atlantic, Air Labrador, Air Nova, and Interprovincial Airlines. For telephone numbers, *see* Air Travel *in* the Gold Guide.

By Train

Iron Ore Canada's Québec North Shore and Labrador Railway (☎ 418/962–9411) has service between Sept Isles, Québec, and Labrador City and Schefferville in Labrador.

Getting Around

In winter some highways may close during and after severe snowstorms. For winter road conditions on the west coast, call the **Department of Works, Services, and Transportation** (☎ 709/635–2162 in Deer Lake; ☎ 709/292–4300 in Grand Falls–Windsor and Central Newfoundland; ☎ 709/466–7953 in Clarenville; ☎ 709/729–2381 in St. John's; ☎ 709/896–2108 in Happy Valley-Goose Bay depot, Labrador).

Labrador

From the island of Newfoundland, you can fly to Labrador via St. John's, Gander, Deer Lake, or Stephenville. Route 500 links Labrador City with Happy Valley–Goose Bay via Churchill Falls. Conditions on this 526-km (326-mi) unpaved wilderness road are best between June and October. If you plan on doing any extensive driving in any part of Labrador, you should contact the **Department of Tourism, Culture and Recreation** (☎ 709/729–2830 or 800/563–6353) for advice on the best routes and road conditions.

To explore the south coast of Labrador, catch the **ferry** (☎ 709/726–0015) at St. Barbe on Route 430 in Newfoundland to Blanc Sablon, Québec. From here you can drive to Red Bay along Route 510.

Summer travel is possible by **car ferry** (☎ 800/341–7981; 709/535–6876 in Lewisporte, Newfoundland; 709/896–0041 in Happy Valley–Goose Bay, Labrador;). The ship travels from Lewisporte in Newfoundland to Cartwright, on the coast of Labrador, and then through the Hamilton inlet to Happy Valley–Goose Bay. Reservations are required. The trip takes 33 hours one-way, and two regularly scheduled return trips are made weekly.

Newfoundland

DRL Coachlines (☎ 709/738–8088) runs a transisland bus service. Buses leave at 8 AM from St. John's and Port aux Basques. Small buses known as outport taxis connect the major centers with surrounding communities.

Newfoundland has an excellent **highway system,** and all but a handful of secondary roads are paved. The province's roads are generally uncrowded, adding to the pleasure of driving. Travel time along the Trans-Canada Highway (Route 1) from Port aux Basques to St. John's is about 13 hours, with time out for a meal in either Gander or Grand Falls–Windsor. The trip from Corner Brook to St. Anthony at the northernmost tip of the island is about five hours. The drive from St. John's to Grand Bank on the Burin Peninsula takes about four hours. If you're heading for the southern coast of the Avalon Peninsula, pick up Route 10 just south of St. John's and follow it toward Trepassey. Locals call this trip "going up the shore," even though it looks like you're traveling down on a map.

Contacts and Resources

Emergencies

Medical emergencies, police (☎ 911).

Fishing

Seasonal and regulatory fishing information can be obtained from the **Department of Tourism, Culture and Recreation** (☎ 800/563–6353).

Guided Tours

ADVENTURE

Local operators offer sea kayaking, ocean diving, canoeing, wildlife viewing, mountain biking, white-water rafting, heli-hiking, and interpretive walks in summer. In winter, snowmobiling, heli-skiing, and caribou- and seal-watching expeditions are popular. Before choosing an operator it's advisable to contact the Department of Tourism, Culture and Recreation to make sure you're calling an established outfit.

Eastern Edge Outfitters (☎ 709/782–1465) leads east-coast sea-kayaking tours and gives white-water kayaking instruction. **Labrador Scenic Ltd.** (☎ FAX 709/497–8326) in North West River organizes tours through central and northern Labrador, with an emphasis on wildlife and Labrador's spectacular coast. **Tuckamore Wilderness Lodge** (☎ 709/ 865–6361 or 888/865–6361) in Main Brook uses its luxurious lodge on the Great Northern Peninsula as a base for viewing caribou, seabird colonies, whales, and icebergs. **Wildland Tours** (☎ 709/722–3123) in St. John's has weeklong tours to view wildlife and visit historically and culturally significant sites across Newfoundland.

BUS

Fleetline Motorcoach Tours (☎ 709/722–2608 or 709/229–7600) in Holyrood runs island-wide tours. Local tours are available for Port aux Basques, the Codroy Valley, Corner Brook, the Bay of Islands, Gros Morne National Park, the Great Northern Peninsula, and St. John's. **McCarthy's Party** (☎ 709/781–2244 or 888/660–6060) in St. John's has guided bus tours across Newfoundland (May–October) in addition to a variety of charter services.

Hospitals

George B. Cross Hospital (✉ Manitoba Dr., Clarenville, ☎ 709/466– 3411). **Western Memorial** (✉ Brookfield Ave., Corner Brook, ☎ 709/ 637–5000). **James Paton** (✉ 125 Trans-Canada Hwy., Gander, ☎ 709/ 651–2500). **Captain William Jackman Hospital** (✉ 410 Booth Ave., Labrador City, ☎ 709/944–2632). **Charles S. Curtis Memorial Hospital** (✉ West St., St. Anthony, ☎ 709/454–3333). **St. Clare's Mercy Hospital** (✉ 154 Le Marchant Rd., St. John's, ☎ 709/778–3111). **General Hospital** (✉ 300 Prince Philip Dr., St. John's, ☎ 709/737–6300).

Visitor Information

The **Department of Tourism, Culture and Recreation** (✉ Box 8730, St. John's A1B 4K2, ☎ 709/729–2830) distributes brochures from its offices in the Confederation Building, West Block, St. John's. The province maintains a **tourist information line** (☎ 800/563–6353) year-round, 24 hours a day, that can also help with accommodations.

From June until Labor Day, a network of **Visitor Information Centres,** open daily 9–9, dots the province. These centers carry information on events, accommodations, shopping, and crafts stores in their area. The airports in Gander and St. John's operate in-season visitor information booths. The city of St. John's operates an information center in a restored railway carriage next to the harbor.

15 Wilderness Canada

The Yukon, the Northwest Territories, and Nunavut

Life above the 60th parallel in the mountainous, river-threaded Yukon, and the lake-dotted Northwest Territories and arctic Nunavut is strange and wonderful. The landscape is austere and beautiful in ways unlike anywhere else in North America: the tundra plains that reach to the Arctic Ocean, the remote ice fields of Kluane National Park, white-water rivers snaking through mountain ranges and deep canyons. This is also the last region of North America where native peoples have managed to sustain traditional cultures relatively undisturbed.

Updated by
Tina Sebert
(The Yukon)
and Rosemary
Allerston (The
Northwest
Territories and
Nunavut)

LET IT BE STATED AS SIMPLY AS POSSIBLE: Life in Canada's far north is strange—strange as in weird, strange as in wonderful, strange as in uncommon. The inherent strangeness of the world north of the 60th parallel—the latitudinal line separating Canada's provinces from the Yukon, the Northwest Territories, and Nunavut—is perceptible in empirical, practical, and mysterious ways.

Consider examples from life in the heart of strangeness:

In recent years diamond discoveries have spawned the development of remote mining camps out on the barren tundra. The people in these camps depend for survival on airplanes, as do many small communities all over the Arctic. Other residents of the far north may drive hundreds of miles to a major city to stock up on groceries. Often, it is easier to hunt caribou or moose than it is to go shopping for vegetables.

Seasons become so overlapped in the few nonwinter months that summer wildflowers have not finished blooming by the time the foliage picks up its fall color. In winter a network of highways, built entirely of hardpacked snow over frozen lakes opens up to automotive traffic. So cold are the snow and ice that they lose their slipperiness, making areas otherwise inaccessible relatively easy to reach. Bridges over rivers are also built of ice, and northerners must prepare for "break-up" and "freeze-up"—the few weeks in spring and fall when ice bridges are unstable but rivers are still too frozen for ferries to operate. Unprepared travelers will sometimes fork over several hundred dollars or more for a helicopter to sling their cars across a river. This underscores the fact that, in a region where bush pilots are held in high regard, air transport is the way to go. In a plane with pontoons an uncountable number of lakes means an uncountable number of watery runways.

If a single strange element of life in the far north stands out, it is the quality of light. In mid-summer, sunrise and sunset merge, and north of the Arctic Circle, they don't occur at all. When night does come—so belatedly in summer that it is a way of life to draw shades tightly during sunlit evenings to simulate night—there is the mystical voodoo show of the northern lights.

Most of the region is climatically classified as semiarid, much of it covered by the vast granite spread of the Canadian Shield. But because water evaporates and ice melts so slowly in Arctic climes, there is an abundance of water. That water is mostly in the form of lakes and ponds in the flatter Northwest Territories and in the form of fjords and rivers in the mountainous Yukon. A good deal of it, of course, remains ice; the glaciers of the St. Elias Mountains in the Yukon's Kluane National Park, topped by 19,550-ft Mt. Logan, create the largest nonpolar ice field in the world.

This is wilderness, and the wildlife loves it. A migrating caribou herd exceeding 80,000 is not uncommon, and that's a number to keep in perspective: It represents the entire human census of the region. Indeed, people are profoundly outnumbered by nonhuman mammals: bears (black, grizzly, polar), Dall sheep, wolves, wolverines, moose, bison, and, of course, caribou. Humans are also outnumbered by fish and birds. Fishermen regularly throw back trout weighing 10 pounds, because a fish that size is considered in these parts to be too small. Bald eagles are a common sight, as are the flocks of migratory waterfowl that spend their summers here.

Signs on government buildings are often inscribed in as many as eight official languages—English, French, and various native languages. One of those languages, Slavey, is so difficult to learn that it was used in coding during World War II. Native people in the far north are wielding increasing influence in governmental affairs. The main tribal groups are seven nations of Athabaskan peoples and the Inland Tlingit in the Yukon, along with the Dene, Inuvialuit, and Inuit peoples of the Northwest Territories. Many of these people go about their lives much as their ancestors did centuries before them but with the help of such 20th-century basics as electricity and motor-driven machinery. In recent years, large tracts of land have been ceded to native groups in land-claims settlements. And in 1999 the Northwest Territories will be split in two, representing the principal lands of the Dene and the Inuit. The new Inuit territory in the east is to be called *Nunavut,* or "our land." The Dene call their region *Denendeh,* which means the same, though there are no plans yet to make this name official. The western region remains the Northwest Territories.

A visit to the far north does not happen without commitment and preparation. Lodging under $100 a night is rare, unless you camp, and it's unlikely that you'll get what you pay for. Having to rely on planes to get from one place raises the cost of a visit here even more. Guides and outfitters can be expensive, too, but their fees aren't out of line with the general cost of living in the far north, and their travel packages often end up saving you money.

Visitors must be willing to abide possible discomforts and inconveniences. Outside cities and towns, mosquitoes and blackflies rule the north during summer and early fall, and anyone without insect repellent is in for big trouble. Packing gloves and insulated clothing in August might seem excessive, but such are the necessities of traveling in a world where it's not uncommon for summer temperatures to drop from above 70°F to well below freezing in a single day. And life doesn't always proceed with clockwork precision; a frontier quality still pervades in much of the far north, and a lot of business is conducted on an ad-hoc, by-the-bootstraps basis. Visiting the far north can be daunting, difficult, frightening, and even dangerous. But for those who prepare themselves for the commitment, it can be nothing short of exhilarating.

Pleasures and Pastimes

Aurora Borealis

Few spectacles on the planet rival the aurora borealis, which fills the subarctic heavens on clear nights from September through March. Yellowknife has become a favorite destination for troupes of supplicants who consider the lights to be omens of good fortune. Few would argue with them; the vast waves of phosphorescent green, red, and lavender seem to prance and whisper as you stand awestruck beneath the stars. The aurora is best seen away from town lights, so Yellowknife tour operators bus visitors out onto frozen Great Slave Lake, where, bundled in parkas, they can gaze to their hearts' content. *See* Guided Tours *in* Wilderness Canada A to Z, *below* for outfitters that arrange aurora-viewing trips.

Dining

Cuisine in the far north rarely reaches grand epicurean standards, but it can have a distinctive character. In some places and at certain times of year, a caribou steak or a moose burger may be easier to find than a fresh salad. Outside the main cities, the dining room of your hotel or lodge may well be your only choice. But if the far north is not necessarily a gastronomic paradise, it is surprising and certainly admirable given what some chefs are able to concoct with limited ingredients.

CATEGORY	COST*
$$$$	over $25
$$$	$18–$25
$$	$10–$18
$	under $10

per person, in Canadian dollars, excluding drinks, service, and 7% GST

Lodging

Lodging prices in the far north are generally higher than you might find elsewhere in Canada. In many communities a lodge or hotel may be your only option, so if you don't like the price, you don't have much choice. In addition, the shortness of the tourism season forces lodging proprietors to try to make ends meet in two or three months of active vacation business. Although you might think you're paying a good chunk of change for pretty ordinary accommodations, consider the lack of quality building materials in many areas and the prohibitive costs of construction. In months other than July and August, expect better deals— room prices reduced 50% or more—but fewer choices, because many places are closed from September through June.

Wilderness lodges offer a once-in-a-lifetime experience in some of the most remote and beautiful areas of the region. A one-week stay will allow you to explore the wilds during the day and then return to the comfort of a cabin and home-cooked meal in the evening. In the Yukon, Whitehorse serves as a departure point for those heading to lodges farther north. Sports lovers planning a trip to the Northwest Territories can set out from Yellowknife for backcountry lodges on the shores of Great Slave Lake or on one of the thousands of smaller lakes that, along with their barren rock underpinnings and scrub growth, are the principal geological constituents of the far north's interior.

Territorial, or public, campgrounds are found along all roads in the north and are open from the spring thaw until the fall freeze. Visitor Information Centers (☞ Contacts and Resources *in* Wilderness Canada A to Z, *below*) throughout the region can provide information on specific campground locations and facilities as well as permits. Note: It is advisable to boil or filter all water, even water that has been designated as "drinking water" at a campground.

CATEGORY	COST*
$$$$	over $150
$$$	$120–$150
$$	$80–$120
$	under $80

All prices are for a standard double room (or equivalent, where not applicable), excluding gratuities and 7% GST, in Canadian dollars.

Outdoor Activities and Sports

CROSS-COUNTRY SKIING

In a world covered by snow eight months out of the year, cross-country-skiing opportunities are obviously plentiful. The best time for skiing, however, is from mid-March until the snow melts (the precise time varying according to the latitude and elevation), when days are longer and warmer. While short outings on skis are possible almost anywhere in the north, perhaps the most interesting extended excursions are in the Kluane area and the Arctic North. A number of backcountry lodges have begun opening in April and May for ski-touring enthusiasts.

DOGSLEDDING

Before there were planes and snowmobiles, dogsleds were the vital means of transportation in the far north. The Yukon Quest International Dogsled Race, along the Yukon River from Whitehorse to Fairbanks or Fairbanks to Whitehorse, takes place every year in mid-February. Destination/start points alternate annually. Top mushers compete for gold nuggets and cash in this 1,600-km (1,000-mi) trek, which is touted as the toughest dogsled race in the world. The most important race in the Northwest Territories is the Canadian Championship Dog Derby, held at Yellowknife in late March. If you want to try a little mushing yourself, some outfitters will arrange it. Spring packages, especially in Nunavut, frequently include dogsled jaunts.

FISHING

Fishing in wilderness Canada is a way of life for a good many locals. What sustains the locals in the north is also what attracts sports fishers: fish in large quantities and of considerable proportions. Lake trout between 30 and 70 pounds are not unusual. The most common catches in the far north are arctic char, grayling, pike, lake trout, and whitefish. Numerous outfitters throughout the region can guide fishers on day trips or short excursions; your best bet is to check with a regional tourist office for outfitter recommendations. Day trips from Yellowknife to Great Slave Lake are especially easy to arrange. Some lakes and streams are accessible by road in the Yukon and in the Northwest Territories. However, the more typical fishing adventure in the far north involves flying to a remote lodge for several days. Fishing in the Arctic rivers of Nunavut is an unforgettable experience but not one to be undertaken without an experienced guide.

HIKING

While the landscape can be spectacular, the going can be rough. Marked trails are relatively few, and sometimes the only trails to follow are those beaten down by wild animals. The four general areas that are best for wilderness hiking are Baffin Island, Kluane National Park, the Chilkoot Trail, and the mountains along the Dempster Highway.

MOUNTAINEERING

In the far north, the question is not what to climb but how to access the mountain. The major peaks of Kluane National Park, Mt. St. Elias, and particularly Canada's highest peak, Mt. Logan, are tops in the mountaineering world but can only be reached by helicopter or plane. For serious rock climbers, the Cirque of the Unclimbables in Nahanni National Park presents an obvious challenge. In Nunavut, the peaks of Auyuittuq National Park draw skilled climbers from around the globe.

WATER SPORTS

River travel is one of the best ways to experience the wilderness of the far north; these roads of water provide access to remote areas otherwise inaccessible. Canoes of various configurations are the preferred means of travel, although for some rivers—particularly those with considerable white water—rafts or kayaks may be used. If you decide on an unguided trip, outfitters can provide both the necessary gear as well as transportation to and from the river. The South Nahanni River in Nahanni National Park is considered a classic. The Alsek and the Tatshenshini, which run primarily through British Columbia, begin in the Kluane region of the Yukon and are also great water-sports venues. With a little preparation, even beginning canoeists can follow in the footsteps of the gold-rush stampeders and float down the Yukon River from Whitehorse to Dawson City. The wild, remote rivers of the Arctic barrens and islands offer challenges to experienced paddlers. Another water-borne adventure to consider is sailing on Great Slave Lake.

Shopping

Native arts and crafts are the most compelling reason to shop in the far north. You may find that prices are best when buying directly from artists or craftspeople in local communities. But if you buy from galleries and stores in the cities, you'll get a wider selection of works from many communities, plus information on the various artists and art forms, and at least some guarantee of authenticity. Soapstone carvings, clothing, and moose- or caribou-hair tuftings (hair sewn onto velvet or hide and cut and shaped into pictures of flowers or animals) are popular purchases. Be aware before buying, however, that some products, such as those made from hides or materials from endangered species, may not be brought into the United States. In many cases—such as a polar-bear rug—the import problem is obvious, but not in all cases; for example, jewelry made of walrus ivory may be confiscated at the border.

Exploring Wilderness Canada

The Yukon, the Northwest Territories, and Nunavut make up 3,787,800 sq km (1,456,375 square mi), almost three times the size of Alaska and half the size of the rest of the United States. There are small cities—Whitehorse in the Yukon and Yellowknife in the Northwest Territories—but there are many more communities that are accessible only by plane. The landscape is reason enough to visit. Consider the tundra plains that reach to the Arctic Ocean, the remote ice fields of the St. Elias Mountains, and the glacier-sculpted cliffs of Baffin Island.

Great Itineraries

The idea of exploring all of Canada's far north in a single trip is an absurdity. It would be comparable to trying to visit Florida, New England, and the Rocky Mountains on the same vacation, only with far fewer roads to travel. Size is only one problem; expense is another. Food, gas, and lodging are typically priced higher than in other parts of Canada, but the biggest cost is transportation, especially in those vast, roadless areas where you'll need to depend on air travel. This is not to say it is difficult to get from one place to another. The large number of charter plane operators and expert bush pilots makes getting around easier than you might think. But the cost of traveling by small planes can be dizzying.

The best strategy for exploring the far north is to focus on a specific area (e.g., Baffin Island, the Nahanni region, Dawson City) and/or an activity (e.g., fishing, wildlife viewing). Specific travel plans can save hundreds, even thousands, of dollars. The choices fall roughly into four categories: visits to main cities (Dawson City, Whitehorse, Yellowknife, Inuvik, and Iqaluit); excursions from the main cities; rambling in the backcountry wilderness; and adventures in the Arctic north. Though there are enough activities in the Yukon, the Northwest Territories, and Nunavut to keep you occupied for months, the following itineraries are geared toward the standard traveler, for whom time is an issue.

Numbers in the text correspond to numbers in the margin and on The Yukon and Northwest Territories and Nunavut maps.

THE YUKON

If You Have 3 Days: Start your tour in ⛟ **Whitehorse** ①. The S.S. *Klondike,* the MacBride Museum, and Miles Canyon all hold a bit of character from the gold-rush era and are a good way to learn about the Yukon's colorful history. The next day drive down Route 2, stopping to stretch your legs at picturesque **Carcross** ②, where you can stroll along the banks of Bennett Lake. From Carcross head to ⛟ **Skagway** ③, Alaska, along the approximate route traversed by the Klondike Gold

Rushers in 1898. You'll pass through a variety of landforms, including the Carcross Desert, the alpine tundra of the White Pass, and the coastal rain forest of the Alaskan Panhandle. On the morning of your third day, ride the historic White Pass & Yukon Route railway back to Whitehorse past blue glaciers and rushing waterfalls.

If You Have 5 Days: Start your trip as you would with the three-day itinerary, but on Day 3 drive eight hours, from Skagway to ⛯ **Dawson City** ⑥. On your fourth day drive down Bonanza Creek Road to Dredge No. 4 and the original claim where the discovery of gold was made in 1896. Spend Day 5 visiting Robert Service Cabin, the Palace Grand Theatre, and Diamond Tooth Gertie's Gambling Hall.

If You Have 10 Days: A 10-day itinerary allows outdoors lovers to explore the Yukon wilds. An extended stay at a fly-in wilderness lodge will provide you with a base camp from which to set off for several backcountry adventures. Once you reach the lodge, your hosts will help you arrange hiking, boating, and fishing excursions, and they'll point you in the direction of the best wildlife-viewing areas.

A Klondike Gold Rush itinerary could include a hike over the Chilkoot Trail (three to four days) plus visits to ⛯ **Skagway** ③, ⛯ **Whitehorse** ①, and ⛯ **Dawson City** ⑥. If river scenery and wildlife viewing are more of an interest, a canoe trip down the Thirty-Mile section of the Yukon River, from Whitehorse to Carmacks, might fit the bill.

Some of the planet's best hiking is possible in **Kluane National Park** ④. A 10-day itinerary could take you as far back as the Donjek Glacier in the heart of Kluane's ethereal wilderness. People wanting to stay on the Yukon's roadways could venture up the Dempster Highway, past the Arctic Circle to ⛯ **Inuvik** ⑧ in the Northwest Territories, an adventurous four-day extension to the five-day itinerary above.

THE NORTHWEST TERRITORIES AND NUNAVUT

If You Have 3 Days: You can jet north from Edmonton or Calgary across the Arctic Circle to ⛯ **Inuvik** ⑧ to see the amazing Mackenzie Delta, **Tuktoyaktuk** ⑨, and the Beaufort Sea. With two nights in Inuvik, you'll also have time for a flying tour over the giant estuary (where belugas romp in summer) to **Herschel Island,** which used to be the haunt of 19th-century whalers.

If You Have 5 Days: Fly to ⛯ **Yellowknife** ⑦, where you can spend your first day exploring the Old Town and the cultural attractions downtown. The focus of Day 2 could be an outdoor activity, such as a dogsled ride or a cruise on Great Slave Lake. Yellowknife has several dining and lodging options, so it serves as a good base from which to head out and explore **Nahanni National Park.** Several plane and helicopter services arrange flightseeing trips from Fort Simpson to the park's breathtaking Virginia Falls. The more adventurous can try and tackle the Cirque of the Unclimbables. Though a trip to Nahanni means you'll have to spend Day 3 on the road, Day 4 will be worth it. **Wood Buffalo National Park** is another possible excursion from Yellowknife. As with the excursion to Nahanni National Park, Day 3 will be spent traveling. On Day 4 you can explore the park's frontcountry trails; be on the lookout for bison and bald eagles. Whether you choose to go to Nahanni National Park or Wood Buffalo National Park, reserve Day 5 for the trip back to Yellowknife.

If You Have 7 Days: On Day 1, head for ⛯ **Iqaluit** ⑨, which is on Baffin Island and will be the capital of Canada's newest political entity, Nunavut. You can fly to Iqaluit from Montréal or Edmonton, via Yellowknife. Explore the town on Day 2, starting with the Unikkaarvik

The Yukon

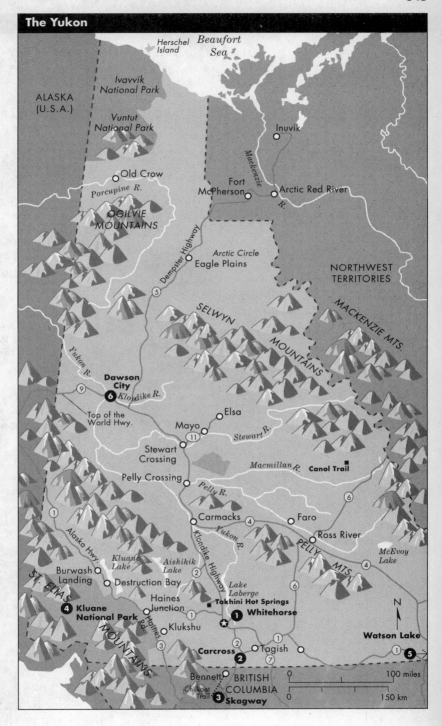

ALASKA
(U.S.A.)

Beaufort Sea

Herschel Island

Ivvavik National Park

Vuntut National Park

Old Crow

Porcupine R.

OGILVIE MOUNTAINS

Inuvik

Fort McPherson

Mackenzie R.

Arctic Red River

NORTHWEST TERRITORIES

Dempster Highway

Arctic Circle
Eagle Plains

⑤

SELWYN

MOUNTAINS

MACKENZIE MTS.

Yukon R.

Dawson City

⑨

6

Klondike R.

Top of the World Hwy.

Elsa

Mayo

⑪

Stewart R.

Stewart Crossing

Pelly Crossing

Macmillan R.

Canol Trail

Pelly R.

Carmacks

④

Faro

Ross River

⑥

⑥

McEvoy Lake

④

①

Alaska Hwy.

Kluane Lake

Aishihik Lake

②

Klondike Highway

Yukon R.

PELLY

MTS.

Burwash Landing

Destruction Bay

ST. ELIAS

Haines Junction

Haines Rd.

Lake Laberge

Takhini Hot Springs

1

Whitehorse

6

N

4

Kluane National Park

①

Klukshu

③

②

Tagish

Watson Lake

MOUNTAINS

Carcross

②

②

⑦

①

①

5

Bennett

Chilkoot Trail

BRITISH COLUMBIA

3

Skagway

0   100 miles

0   150 km

Northwest Territories and Nunavut

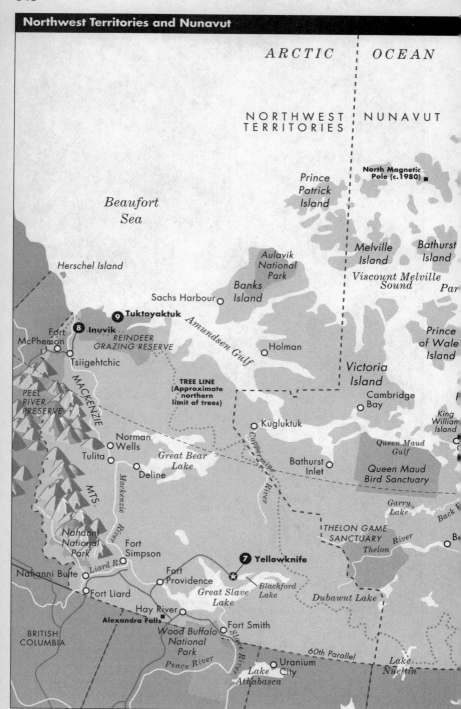

ARCTIC OCEAN

NORTHWEST TERRITORIES

NUNAVUT

Prince Patrick Island

North Magnetic Pole (c.1980) ■

Beaufort Sea

Melville Island

Bathurst Island

Herschel Island

Aulavik National Park

Banks Island

Viscount Melville Sound

Par

Sachs Harbour

8 ○ Inuvik

9 ● Tuktoyaktuk

Fort McPherson ○

Tsiigehtchic

REINDEER GRAZING RESERVE

Amundsen Gulf

Holman

Prince of Wale Island

PEEL RIVER PRESERVE

MACKENZIE

TREE LINE (Approximate northern limit of trees)

Victoria Island

Cambridge Bay

King William Island

Norman Wells

Tulita ○

Great Bear Lake

Deline ○

Kugluktuk ○

Coppermine River

Bathurst Inlet ○

Queen Maud Gulf

Queen Maud Bird Sanctuary

F

MTS.

Mackenzie River

Nahanni National Park

Fort Simpson ○

7 ● Yellowknife ☆

THELON GAME SANCTUARY

Garry Lake

Back

Thelon River

Be

Nahanni Butte

Liard R.

Fort Providence ○

Blachford Lake

Great Slave Lake

Dubawnt Lake

Fort Liard ○

Hay River ○

Alexandra Falls ■

Wood Buffalo National Park

Slave River

Fort Smith ○

60th Parallel

Lake Nueltin

BRITISH COLUMBIA

Peace River

Lake Athabasca

Uranium City ○

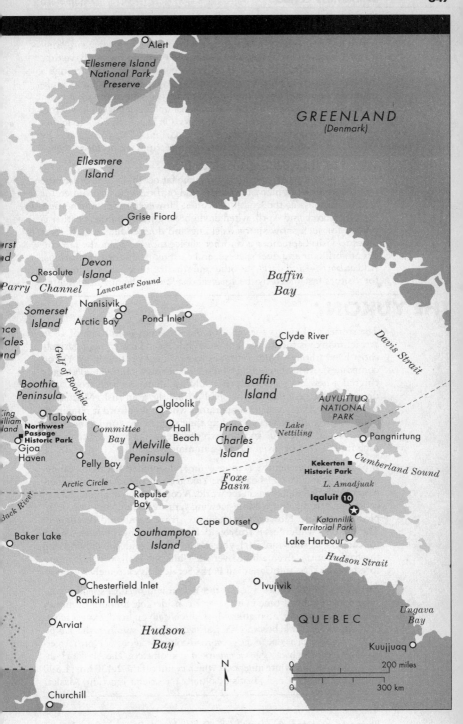

Alert

Ellesmere Island
National Park
Preserve

GREENLAND
(Denmark)

Ellesmere
Island

Grise Fiord

*rst
d

Devon
Island

Resolute

Baffin
Bay

Parry Channel

Lancaster Sound

Nanisivik

Somerset
Island

Arctic Bay

Pond Inlet

Clyde River

Davis Strait

ce
'ales
nd

Gulf of Boothia

Boothia
Peninsula

Baffin
Island

AUYUITTUQ
NATIONAL
PARK

ing
illiam
and

Taloyoak

Igloolik

Lake
Nettling

Pangnirtung

Northwest
Passage
Historic Park

Committee
Bay

Hall
Beach

Prince
Charles
Island

Cumberland Sound

Gjoa
Haven

Pelly Bay

Melville
Peninsula

Kekerten ■
Historic Park

Arctic Circle

Foxe
Basin

L. Amadjuak

Back River

Repulse
Bay

Iqaluit ⑩

★

Cape Dorset

Katannilik
Territorial Park

Baker Lake

Southampton
Island

Lake Harbour

Hudson Strait

Chesterfield Inlet

Ivujivik

QUEBEC

Ungava
Bay

Rankin Inlet

Arviat

Hudson
Bay

Kuujjuaq

N

0   200 miles
0   300 km

Churchill

Visitor's Centre and Sunaqutangit Museum. At the visitor center you can schedule an afternoon boat trip to Qaummaarviit Historic Park with a local outfitter. On Day 3, fly to the old whaling village of Pang-nirtung, gateway to ☒ **Auyuittuq National Park**; you won't have time for a full-scale backpacking expedition, but outfitters will arrange a quick introductory tour. Spend the rest of Day 3 and Days 4 and 5 hiking and camping. Depending on when you go, you can book a jaunt by dogsled or snowmobile to see icebergs up close, try sea kayaking, or hike the tundra in search of wildflowers. On Day 6, fly back to Iqaluit and spend a relaxing afternoon in Sylvia Grinnell Territorial Park. By Day 7, you should feel well-rested for your trip back home.

When to Tour Wilderness Canada

June through August is peak season in the far north. For the other nine months of the year, many businesses and outfitters close, as much for lack of business as the length of winter. However, many northerners say that March and April, when daylight lengthens and the weather is perfect for such snow sports as skiing and dogsledding, are the best times to visit. September is another choice month, when the fall colors are brilliant and ducks, geese, and caribou begin their migrations. And as harsh—and dark—as other months are, they can be prime time for visitors fascinated by the spectral displays of the northern lights.

THE YUKON

The stories and events surrounding the Klondike Gold Rush of 1896 attract many visitors to the Yukon. While legendary, it was relatively short-lived (though gold continues to be mined profitably by Yukon companies). At the beginning of the 20th century, mining had already entered a new era—gold miners could no longer get rich from "just digging in the ground," as they had during the gold rush. Machinery took over, and only the large operators who could afford it remained. Most of the gold rushers packed up their money bags and abandoned the Klondike for good. To fully explore the places and events of that time fully, a visit of seven days is a minimum.

If backcountry adventure is more your style, guided hiking or canoeing trips run from 6 to 14 days. The Yukon is one of the premier wilderness adventure destinations in the world. A combination of hiking, biking, canoeing, rafting, and wildlife-viewing ventures could keep you occupied for months. However, backcountry travelers should be advised: The Yukon's wilderness is truly wild. If you are an inexperienced hiker (or canoeist or snowmobiler), you should take a guided excursion into the backcountry. Even a hike over the Chilkoot Trail, which is monitored by the U.S. and Canadian Parks Services, is extremely rigorous.

Anyone expecting to see a lot of the Yukon will need to spend a considerable amount of time in a car or a considerable amount of money on airfare. If in a car, no matter which direction you head, expect to encounter considerable bus and RV traffic during the summer; the Yukon ranks with Alaska as one of the great road-touring regions of North America. All Yukon Highway signs are marked in kilometers. The Alaska Highway, however, has white mileposts which count off the 2,430 km (1,500 mi) from Dawson Creek, British Columbia, to Delta Junction, Alaska.

Whitehorse

Begun as an encampment near the White Horse Rapids of the Yukon ❶ River, **Whitehorse** is 2,400 km (1,488 mi) from Vancouver. It was a logical layover for gold rushers in the late 1890s heading north from Skagway, Alaska, over the Chilkoot Trail, to seek their fortune in

Dawson. Today's city of 23,000 residents is the Yukon's center of commerce, communication, and transportation and is the seat of the territorial government. Though there's enough in the city to keep one occupied for a day or two, visitors should regard Whitehorse as a base camp from which to venture out and explore other parts of the Yukon.

The **Yukon Visitor Reception Centre** is the best place to pick up information on local lodging, restaurants, shops, attractions, and special events. It is also the place to look into adventure travel; the center has information on all tour and guide companies in the territory—and there are hundreds. A free, 15-minute film provides a wonderful introduction to the area. ⊠ *2nd Ave. and Hanson St.,* ☎ *867/667–3084,* FAX *867/667–3546.* ⊙ *Mid-May–mid-Sept., daily 8–8; Oct.–mid-May, weekdays 9* AM*–noon and 1–4:30.*

Just east of the Yukon Visitor Reception Centre is the scenic **Waterfront Walkway,** which runs along the Yukon River. If you head downstream (north), you'll see the old White Pass & Yukon Route building on Main Street. One of Whitehorse's landmark buildings, it was erected in 1900. Today it marks the start or finish (depending on the year) of the Yukon Quest Dogsled race.

The **MacBride Museum** encompasses more than 5,000 square ft of artifacts, natural history specimens, historic photographs, maps, and diagrams from prehistory to the present. Exhibits provide a historical overview of the Yukon, from early exploration to the present, covering the trapping era and the gold rush. The museum also houses the largest public collection of Yukon gold in Canada. ⊠ *1st Ave. and Wood St.,* ☎ *867/667–2709,* FAX *867/633–6607.* ☞ *$3.50.* ⊙ *Mid-May–Labor Day, daily 10–6; mid-Sept.–mid-May, Tues.–Thurs. noon–4.*

★ The **S.S. Klondike,** a 210-ft stern-wheeler built in 1929, was the largest boat plying the Yukon River back in the days when the river was the only transportation link between Whitehorse and Dawson. Though the boat sank in 1936, it was rebuilt a year later and, after successive restorations, is dry-docked in its 1930s glory. ⊠ *Robert Service Way and 2nd Ave.,* ☎ *867/667–4511.* ☞ *$3.* ⊙ *May–Sept., daily 9–6:30.*

The best time to visit the **Whitehorse Rapids Dam and Fish Ladder** is August, during the longest chinook (king) salmon migration in the world. From the viewing platform overlooking the river, you might spot between 150 and 2,100 salmon as they use the ladder to bypass the dam. Plan to go in the evening when the temperature drops a few degrees. Interpretive displays explain the phenomenon. ⊠ *End of Nisutlin Dr.,* ☎ *867/633–5965.* ☞ *Free.* ⊙ *June–Labor Day, daily 8* AM*–10* PM.

Take a two-hour cruise aboard the **M.V. Schwatka** and experience Miles Canyon as Jack London did when he was a pilot on its turbulent waters. ⊠ *Schwatka Lake, 3.2 km (2 mi) south of downtown Whitehorse on Miles Canyon Rd.,* ☎ *867/668–4716,* FAX *867/633–5574.* ☞ *$18.* ⊙ *Cruises early–mid-June and mid-Aug.–early Sept., daily 2* PM; *mid-June–mid-Aug., daily 2 and 7* PM.

Two km (1 mi) past Schwatka Lake, where the M.V. **Schwatka** (☞ *above*) is moored, is picturesque **Miles Canyon** (⊠ Miles Canyon Rd.), a public park laced with hiking trails of varying difficulty. A 20-minute trail leads to Canyon City, where gold-rush stampeders stopped before heading through the treacherous canyon and the White Horse Rapids. Contact the Yukon Visitor Reception Centre (☞ *above*) for information on trails.

At the **Yukon Beringia Interpretive Centre,** paleontological exhibits and interactive computer kiosks present the story of the Yukon's ice-age past. The ancient remains of woolly mammoth, giant steppe bison, 400-pound beaver, primeval horses, giant short-faced bear, scimitar cats, and American lions are among the center's holdings. ⊠ *Mi 915.4, Alaska Hwy., next to the Whitehorse Airport,* ☎ *867/667–3516 or 867/667–8855.* 🎫 *$6.* ⊙ *Late May–mid-Oct., daily 8 AM–9 PM.*

The **Yukon Transportation Museum,** just north of the Yukon Beringia Interpretive Centre, displays artifacts and exhibits of the Yukon's unusual transportation legacy, from snowshoes to cars and dogsleds to airplanes. ⊠ *Mi 915.4, Alaska Hwy., next to the Whitehorse Airport,* ☎ *867/668–4792.* 🎫 *$3.50.* ⊙ *Mid-May–late Aug., daily 10–6, Sept. 1–13, daily noon–4.*

At **Takhini Hot Springs,** off the Klondike Highway, there's swimming in the spring-warmed water (suits and towels are available for rental), horseback riding, and areas for picnicking. ⊠ *Km 9.6 on Takhini Hot Springs Rd., 10 km (6 mi) north of Whitehorse,* ☎ *867/633–2706.* 🎫 *$4.* ⊙ *June–Sept., daily 7 AM–10 PM; winter hrs vary.*

The **Yukon Wildlife Preserve** offers a foolproof way of photographing rarely spotted animals in a natural setting. You might see elk, caribou, mountain goats, musk oxen, bison, and mule deer as well as Dall, mountain, and stone sheep on the 700-acre preserve. Two-hour tours can be arranged only through Gray Line Yukon. ⊠ *Gray Line Yukon, 208G Steele St.,* ☎ *867/668–3225.* 🎫 *$15.* ⊙ *Tour mid-May–mid-Sept., daily by appointment.*

Dining and Lodging

$$$$ ✕ **Antonio's Vineyard.** Classic Greek and Italian cuisine is complemented
★ by such local delicacies as king salmon, arctic char, and Alaskan halibut. The calamari is especially good—the chef's secret is the subject of local debate. Prices are a bit high, but the views are great. ⊠ *202 Strickland St.,* ☎ *867/668–6266. MC, V. No lunch.*

$$$$ ✕ **The Cellar.** The fact that the tables have tablecloths immediately makes this restaurant high-class in the Whitehorse dining scene. Indeed, the Cellar, in the cellar of the Edgewater Hotel, with its high-back Victorian chairs, approaches elegance. Alaska king crab and prime rib highlight the menu. This may be the only restaurant in the far north where a jacket is advised. The Gallery upstairs serves breakfast and lunch on a much more casual basis. ⊠ *Edgewater Hotel 101 Main St.,* ☎ *867/ 667–2572. AE, DC, MC, V.*

$$$ ✕ **No Pop Sandwich Shop.** The white-brick exterior promises all of the atmosphere of a Laundromat, but inside, the dining room—with its straight-edge pine furniture and walls adorned with the work of local artists—is downright cozy. A small terrace in back with a tree rising through the roof adds character to dining alfresco. People wander in and out at all hours for take-out orders, a cup of coffee, or a full sit-down dinner. Alaskan halibut and arctic char are among the rotating dinner specials; fresh-baked pastries are good any time of day. ⊠ *312 Steele St.,* ☎ *867/668–3227. MC, V.*

$$–$$$ ✕ **Blackstone Cafe.** It's a good thing the Blackstone has a large outdoor deck or it would be nearly impossible to get a seat in summer. The relaxed atmosphere and reasonable prices keep everyone coming back. Try the brioche stuffed with fruit and cream cheese, or the "Feta Compli," for everything you could ever want in an open-faced sandwich. The coffee is fresh-roasted in the Yukon, and the daily dinner specials are a great deal. ⊠ *302 Wood St.,* ☎ *867/667–6598. V.*

$$–$$$ ✕ **Chocolate Claim.** Besides handmade chocolates and truffles, the
★ chefs at "The Claim" turn out Thai soups and homespun surprises like pumpkin cheesecake. The company is always interesting, the sandwiches

are highly recommended, and the local art on the wall is for sale. ⊠ *305 Strickland St.,* ☎ *867/667–2202. V. No dinner.*

$$$ 🏨 **Edgewater Hotel.** On a quiet end of Main Street, this small hotel is a good alternative to the Westmark (☞ *below*) for those trying to avoid the tour-bus bustle. The lobby is small and the passageway to the rooms is a bit narrow and awkward, but the rooms are large, with modern furnishings. They are also somewhat on the dark side, but when daylight stretches well into the night, this might be an asset. ⊠ *101 Main St., Y1A 2A7,* ☎ *867/667–2572,* ℻ *867/668–3014. 30 rooms, 2 suites. Restaurant, lounge. AE, DC, MC, V.*

$$$ 🏨 **Hawkins House Bed & Breakfast.** In the heart of Whitehorse, this beautifully decorated Victorian-style home with hardwood floors is among the best the Yukon has to offer. Gourmet breakfasts and amenities rarely found in this region, like Jacuzzi tubs, cable TV, computer hook-ups, and wet bars, are more than enough reason to book a room. ⊠ *303 Hawkins St., Y1A 1X5,* ☎ *867/668–7638,* ℻ *867/668–7632. 4 rooms. In-room modem lines, laundry. AE, MC, V.*

$$$ 🏨 **Westmark Whitehorse Hotel.** If it weren't for all the tour-bus baggage to trip over in the hallways, this would be a fine place to stay. Rooms are decorated with dark-wood furnishings and include such nice touches as coffeemakers. The hotel even has its own vaudeville show, *Frantic Follies,* a revue playing heavily on gold-rush themes. The restaurant can get crowded. There's a gift shop and a travel agency on the premises. ⊠ *2nd Ave. and Wood St., Box 4250, Y1A 3T3,* ☎ *867/668–4700 or 800/544–0970,* ℻ *867/668–2789. 181 rooms, 5 suites. Restaurant, lounge, barbershop, spa. AE, DC, MC, V.*

$$–$$$ 🏨 **High Country Inn.** Close to the S.S. *Klondike* and the public swimming pool, this comfortable inn is a great value. Rooms are clean, well maintained, and nicely decorated in light pastel colors. Some are small or strangely laid out, so it's worth taking a look at what's available before you commit. The lobby, restaurant, and lounge are cozy, and the Yukon Mining Company saloon on the outdoor deck is a favorite Friday-night gathering spot. ⊠ *4051 4th Ave., Y1A 1H1,* ☎ *867/667–4471 or 800/554–4471,* ℻ *867/667–6457. 70 rooms, 30 suites. Restaurant, bar, laundry. AE, DC, MC, V.*

FLY-IN WILDERNESS LODGES

Backcountry lodges are a great way to see true Yukon wilderness. The lodges listed below provide charter service to and from Whitehorse.

$$$$ 🏨 **Inconnu Lodge.** Considering most backcountry lodges in the area, Inconnu Lodge is a statement in relative luxury. This fly-in lodge on the shores of McEvoy Lake, about 300 km (186 mi) northeast of Whitehorse, provides accommodations in modern log cabins. The principal activities are fishing and heli-hiking, but the lodge also arranges canoe trips on nearby rivers. Wildlife is plentiful, as attested by the taxidermy displayed in the main lodge's living room. The lodge also acts as a jumping-off point for canoe and climbing trips into Nahanni National Park (☞ The Northwest Territories, *below*). Rates for five-day packages, including transportation to and from Whitehorse, are about $2,895. ⊠ *Box 29008, OK, Mission, RPO, Kelowna, British Columbia V1W 4A7,* ☎ ℻ *250/764–2885. 5 duplex cabins. MC, V.*

$$$$ 🏨 **Oldsquaw Lodge.** The original lodge was built from materials salvaged from the Canol Trail by wildlife biologists. Those beginnings point to much of what the present-day lodge is all about: a place from which to access the Canol Trail, dedicated primarily to wildlife viewing. The basic lodge program consists of daily hikes (in some cases helicopter assisted) on the open tundra in search of wildlife ranging from grizzly bears to falcons. The lodge also arranges mountain-biking trips on the Canol Trail and cross-country skiing in spring. Lodging is in six outlying cabins. Rates for weekly packages begin at $2,000 per person. ⊠ *Bag Service 2711, Y1A 4K8,* ☎ FAX *867/668–6732. 6 cabins.*

Outdoor Activities and Sports

Mountain View Golf Course (⊠ Range Rd., Box 5883, ☎ 867/633–6020), an 18-hole, par-72 course that's open May–September, has real grass and greens.

Shopping

Native-made clothing, local artwork, and indigenous crafts ranging from moose-hair tuftings to beadwork are available at the **Indian Craft Shop** (⊠ 504 Main St., ☎ 867/667–7216). **Murdoch's Gem Shop** (⊠ 207 Main St., ☎ 867/668–7867) is the Yukon's largest manufacturer of gold nugget jewelry. **Yukon Gallery** (⊠ 2093 2nd Ave., ☎ 867/667–2391) sells limited-edition art prints by Yukon artists.

South of Whitehorse to Skagway, Alaska

Route 2, which runs south out of the Yukon into British Columbia and on to Alaska, traverses an interesting succession of climatic zones. From Carcross, the first town of interest on this section, you'll pass by the Carcross Desert, over the alpine tundra of the White Pass, and through the coastal rain forest of the Alaskan Panhandle. By the time the road begins descending steeply into Skagway, the landscape changes dramatically to a heavily vegetated world of glacially carved fjords.

White Pass & Yukon Route

An alternative to driving from Whitehorse to Skagway is the White Pass & Yukon Route, a combined bus-and-rail trip. A bus travels 2½ hours from Whitehorse to Fraser, British Columbia; then the train completes the trip to Skagway in another 1¾ hours. You can do this trip in either direction. A three-hour round-trip is also available, starting and ending in Skagway. You can also take the train from Skagway to Bennett (Monday and Thursday–Saturday), or from Skagway to Carcross and vice versa (Sunday only). The price may be high, but it's worth it. Six times throughout the year, the White Pass & Yukon Route runs a special steam engine excursion to Bennett in historic locomotive No. 73. Call ahead for departure times. ⊠ *Box 435, Skagway, AK 99840,* ☎ *907/983–2217 or 800/343–7373,* FAX *907/983–2734.* ➽ *One-way Skagway to Whitehorse $95; round-trip Summit Excursion $78; one-way Bennett to Skagway $65; round-trip Skagway to Carcross or Bennett $128; steam excursion to Bennett $156.* ⊙ *Departures mid-May–mid-Sept. daily; call for pre- and postseason schedule.*

Chilkoot Trail

You can backpack between Whitehorse and Skagway on the 54-km (33-mi) Chilkoot Trail, a three- to five-day historic trip through spectacular scenery. Hikers begin their journey in Dyea on the Alaskan coast and ascend through rain forest, across alpine tundra, and into boreal forest. Only those who are extremely fit should attempt to hike the trail in the reverse direction, most of which is downhill and very steep. Along the way are the scattered shovels and graves of gold rushers who traveled this route a century ago.

Though the trail never reaches the Yukon, it is vitally linked with Yukon history: During the Klondike Gold Rush, prospectors trekked over the Chilkoot Pass to Bennett, where they built their own boats and sailed across Bennett and Tagish lakes to the headwaters of the Yukon River. The boats that weren't wrecked in Miles Canyon or the White Horse or Five Finger rapids eventually arrived in Dawson City (☞ *below*).

Reservations are recommended to hike the Chilkoot Trail; only a limited number of people are permitted to hike it at the same time, and you'll be assured of getting a site on the campground of your choice. For information on fees contact **Canadian Heritage, Parks Canada** (✉ Yukon National Historic Sites, Room 205, 300 Main St., Whitehorse, Yukon Territory Y1A 2B5, ☎ 867/667–3910 or 800/661–0486).

Carcross
❷ *74 km (46 mi) south of Whitehorse.*

Originally named Caribou Crossing after the herds of caribou that passed through it, Carcross is one of the Yukon's most picturesque towns. The shores of **Bennett Lake,** where thousands of gold-rush stampeders landed after a rough journey on the windy waters, are ideal for a short stroll. Near town is the **Carcross Desert,** the smallest desert in the world.

Skagway
❸ *180 km (112 mi) south of Whitehorse.*

Skagway, host to cruise ships traveling up the Alaskan coast, is an amazingly preserved artifact from one of North America's biggest, most storied gold rushes. Old false-front stores, saloons, and brothels have been restored, repainted, and refurbished by the federal government and Skagway's citizens. One of the town's most famous gold-rush characters is Jefferson Randolph Smith, otherwise known as "Soapy" Smith. Soapy and his gang of renegades made a fine living out of fleecing gold-rush stampeders. One of the tricks they used to swindle the innocent was the soap trick (hence the nickname) for which Soapy would wrap bars of soap with bills of money—there would always be a one hundred-dollar bill and a couple of twenties in the box of bars. Then he would go to an establishment and ask the men to try their luck and buy a bar of soap for $5. Two of Soapy's own men would be in the crowd and would eagerly volunteer. Once Soapy's cronies received the bars wrapped in the big bucks, the rest of the poor dupes followed suit, but with less-profitable results. Soapy's thieves and hand artists eventually won him control over Skagway, until he was shot in July of 1898 by Frank Reid, who was also killed in the exchange of gunfire. Both of their graves can be seen in the Gold Rush cemetery. When you walk down Broadway today, the scene is not appreciably different from what the prospectors saw in the days of 1898.

DINING AND LODGING

$$$–$$$$ ✕ **Stowaway Cafe.** Poised at the beginning of Skagway's cruise ship dock, Skagway Cafe is a great place to indulge in some local seafood and scenery. Consider the Ho Chi Hilbo Dungeness crab, the Texas barbecue, or one of the fabulous soups. You may even spot one of the local sea otters sunning itself on the beach. ✉ *Box 189, 205 Congress Way, Skagway, AK US 99840,* ☎ *907/983–3463. MC, V.*

$$–$$$$ ✕⊡ **Skagway Inn Bed & Breakfast.** Each room in this downtown inn
★ has a Victorian motif with antiques and cast-iron beds; some have mountain views. The building was constructed in 1897 and is one of Skagway's oldest. The inn's summer-only restaurant, Olivia's at the Skagway Inn, is considered by many to be Skagway's finest. Chef Wendell Fogliani trained under the recently retired Lorna McDermott, a graduate of Le Cordon Bleu. The restaurant serves lunch and dinner; box lunches can be provided for day trips and picnics. ✉ *Box 500, 7th Ave. and Broadway, Skagway, AK US 99840,* ☎ *907/983–2289,* FAX *907/ 983–2713. 12 rooms. Restaurant. AE, D, MC, V.*

$$ ✕⊡ **Golden North Hotel.** Alaska's most historic hotel was built in
★ 1898 in the heyday of the gold rush—golden dome and all—and has been lovingly restored to reflect that period. In 1997, the hotel underwent

a major renovation and added a garden patio area and a microbrewery. You're welcome to sample its brews. Popular choices in the Golden North Restaurant include sourdough pancakes for breakfast; soups, salads, and sandwiches for lunch; and salmon or other seafood for dinner. Though both the hotel and the restaurant are open from May to September only, there's talk of opening up a few rooms in the winter months, so check before you plan your trip. ⊠ *Box 343, 3rd Ave. and Broadway, Skagway, AK US 99840,* ☎ *907/983–2451,* ℻ *907/983– 2755. 32 rooms. Restaurant.* ☉ *May–Sept. AE, DC, MC, V.*

Kluane National Park

★ ❹ **Kluane National Park** and neighboring Wrangell–St. Elias National Park in Alaska and Tatshenshini Provincial Park in British Columbia form the largest expanse of contiguous national park land in the world. The park is 160 km (99 mi) west of Whitehorse. Glaciers up to 100 km (62 mi) long stretch from the huge ice fields of the interior, comprising the largest nonpolar ice mass in the world. Canada's highest mountain, Mt. Logan (19,550 ft), is another of Kluane's natural wonders. Few visitors, other than experienced mountaineers (climbers must receive authorization from the Park Superintendent), get a full sense of Kluane's most extraordinary terrain, as neither roads nor trails lead into the interior. A helicopter or fixed-wing flight over the Kluane ice fields is well worth the price on a clear day. Expect to pay approximately $100 per person for helicopter rides—fixed-wing flights are slightly cheaper, but they can't offer the maneuverability of a helicopter flight. Many people are content with exploring the front ranges, which have impressive mountains with abundant wildlife—Dall sheep, black bears, and grizzly bears are the most noteworthy species.

The front country trail system of Kluane National Park is the most extensive in the far north, facilitating everything from half-day hikes to multiday backpacking excursions. It's possible to make a five-day backpacking trip on marked trails, with opportunities for off-trail scrambling on mountaintops. Most marked hiking trails are relatively easy to negotiate. Keep in mind that this is bear country, and all bear precautions—especially storing food in canisters—must be taken. You might also consider buying a can of capiscum (pepper-spray) bear repellent, available in all sporting goods stores.

The town of Haines Junction marks the junction of the Haines and Alaska Highways and is the headquarters of the **Kluane National Park Reserve** (⊠ Box 5495, Haines Junction, ☎ 867/634–7250, ℻ 867/ 634–7265), the most logical place to begin your excursion into the park. A free 25-minute slide presentation provides an excellent introduction to the region's geology, flora, and fauna, and the amiable staff is well armed with valuable information concerning the condition of the many hiking trails—including any recent bear sightings. Day hikers should check in for a summer schedule of guided hikes. You can also pick up a tent-camping permit and free food-storage canisters here.

More ambitious hikers can backpack from the **Sheep Mountain Visitor Center** (⊠ Mi 1019, Alaska Hwy., ☎ 867/634–2251) up the Slims River Valley to the toe of the Kaskawulsh Glacier, a 27-km (17-mi) jaunt. The Sheep Mountain Center, open from May through September, is an outpost of Kluane headquarters within the park's borders.

Around Kluane National Park

Once you've explored the rugged wonders of Kluane National Park, you may want to venture south of Haines Junction on Haines Road, which hugs the park and connects a few sights worth seeing. On the west side of Dezadeash Lake at Km 45 is **Rock Glacier Trail.** This .8-km (1.3-mi) trail on the outskirts of Kluane National Park is well maintained and suitable for people of all ages and abilities. Kluane National Park is home to thousands of rock glaciers, glacierlike tongues of fragmented rock that have accumulated over deep layers of ice. This trail passes over many of them. Besides offering visitors a glimpse at this curiosity, the Rock Glacier Trail provides a beautiful view of the Dezadeash Valley.

The turn-off to the village of **Klukshu** is 50 km (80 mi) south of Haines Junction. On the small Klukshu River, this village is an important site of Southern Tutchone culture. For centuries, the Tutchone have been coming here from late July until September to fish for salmon. Interpretive displays along the banks of Klukshu River explain how fish was caught. Smokehouses are still used to preserve the fish. A small crafts shop sells moccasins and wood and antler carvings, and on occasion, you might catch one of the elders telling stories related to the area.

The spectacular **Million Dollar Falls,** fed by the Takhanne River, are 25 km (16 mi) south of Klukshu on Haines Road. Two trails, one .5 km (.8 mi) long and the other 1.5 km (2.4 mi) long, lead down to the falls. They're steep but well maintained and in season, you can spot salmon in the clear waters. In winter, the trails may not be suitable for hiking, but the falls are transformed into fantastic ice sculptures.

Dining and Lodging

$$$$ ✕⌶ **Raven Motel.** Haines Junction's finest dining and lodging establishment has spare but clean and tastefully designed rooms, and, unbelievably, room service. The menu at the restaurant on the second floor changes daily. Past choices have included fresh local salmon and lake trout, homemade pasta, and juicy steaks, all topped with homegrown herbs and served at tables with views of Kluane's front ranges. ✉ *Box 5470, Alaska Hwy., Haines Junction, Y0B 1L0,* ☎ *867/634–2500,* FAX *867/634–2517. 12 rooms. CP. Restaurant. AE, MC, V.*

$ ✕⌶ **Cozy Corner.** The name is anything but original, yet there is a genuine coziness about this small motel. Rooms are unusually large—big enough for a bed and sofa bed—but the bathrooms are small. Some rooms have views of the front ranges of Kluane National Park. ✉ *At the junction of Alaska Hwy. and Haines Rd., Box 5406, Haines Junction, Y0B 1L0,* ☎ *867/634–2511,* FAX *867/634–2119. 12 rooms. Restaurant. AE, MC, V.*

$$ ⌶ **Gateway Hotel.** Though there's nothing remarkable about this small hotel, it's convenient for those who want to explore Kluane National Park and the outlying area, and parking is free and plentiful. Rooms are clean and spacious; all of them have cable TV. ✉ *At the junction of Alaska Hwy. and Haines Rd., Box 5460, Haines Junction, Y0B 1L0,* ☎ *867/634–2371,* FAX *867/634–2833. 12 rooms. Laundry. AE, D, MC, V.*

Outdoor Activities and Sports

Access Kluane, Tours and Adventure Centre (✉ Box 5419, Haines Junction, Y0B 1L0, ☎ 867/634–2816, FAX 867/634–2034) coordinates whitewater rafting trips, glacier tours, heli-hiking trips, horseback riding tours, fishing trips, and guided hikes and arranges canoe rentals in the Kluane region.

Watson Lake

❺ Gateway city for travelers heading northwest along the Alaska Highway, **Watson Lake** is 450 km (279 mi) east of Whitehorse. The town's most remarkable feature is the **Signpost Forest.** During the construction of the Alaska Highway in 1942, a homesick U.S. soldier put up a proud sign displaying the name of his hometown as well as its distance and direction. Since then, other visitors have followed suit to the tune of more than 30,000 signs.

Watson Lake's **Northern Lights Centre** is the only multimedia planetarium theater in North America. If you are traveling through the Yukon in summer, when the midnight sun makes it impossible to see the lights, the center will allow you to take in the spectacle of the aurora borealis through advanced video and laser technology. ⊠ *Box 590, Watson Lake Y0A 1C0,* ☎ *867/536–7827,* FAX *867/536–7522.* ☞ *$9.50 for matinees, $12 for evening shows.* ☉ *Mid-May–mid-Sept. daily 1PM–8:30 PM.*

Lodging

$$–$$$ 🏨 **Big Horn Hotel.** Watson Lake's nicest hotel is in the downtown area. Large rooms are creatively decorated with forest-theme draperies and bedspreads and wooden headboards. The whirlpool suites are the best deal. ⊠ *Box 157, Y0A 1C0,* ☎ *867/536–2020,* FAX *867/536–2021. 29 rooms. Hot tub, coin laundry. AE, MC, V.*

$–$$ 🏨 **Watson Lake Hotel.** On the western edge of Watson Lake, this hotel and its motel units provide basic services and clean, neat guest rooms at reasonable prices. Three units have kitchenettes. Log walls and exposed stone add to the comfortable, rustic atmosphere. ⊠ *Box 370, Y0A 1C0,* ☎ *867/536–7781,* FAX *867/536–2724. 48 rooms, 1 suite. Restaurant, lounge, sauna, laundry. AE, DC, MC, V.*

Dawson City

★ ❻   At the turn of the century, **Dawson City,** 536 km (332 mi) north of Whitehorse, was the epicenter of gold fever. Preservationists have done an admirable job not only of restoring many of the city's historic buildings but also enforcing a zoning code that requires newly built structures to adopt facades conforming to a turn-of-the-century look.

The **Visitor Reception Centre** (⊠ Box 389, Front and King Sts., Dawson City, ☎ 867/993–5566, FAX 867/993–6415) covers everything from historical minutiae to lodging availability. Walking tours and historic presentations take place daily from the end of May until mid-September. Tours are also available on audio tape.

Built in 1899 the **Palace Grand Theatre** was show-time central during the gold-rush days, staging everything from opera to vaudeville. It was restored in the 1970s by the Canadian Parks Service and today is the home of the **Palace Revue,** a musical show based on gold-rush history. ⊠ *King St. between 2nd and 3rd Aves.,* ☎ *867/993–5575.* ☞ *$15–$17, depending on seats.* ☉ *Show mid-May–mid-Sept., nightly 8 PM except Tues.*

The construction of the **Old Post Office** in 1900 was a symbolic affirmation of Dawson's permanence as a legitimate city rather than a boomtown of opportunism. The post office today effectively captures an aura of Dawson life at the turn of the century, and philatelists may want to purchase commemorative stamps. ⊠ *3rd Ave. and King St.* ☞ *Free.* ☉ *June–Sept., daily noon–5.*

The **Dawson City Museum** chronicles the gold rush and includes exhibits on the material culture of the local Han native people, steam locomotives, and the paleontology of the region. There's a genealogical library for those trying to trace relatives who traveled to Dawson during the gold rush. ⊠ *Box 303, 5th Ave. between Mission and Turner Sts.,* ☎ *867/993–5291,* FAX *867/993–5839.* ☞ *$4.* ☉ *Mid-May–mid-Sept., daily 10–6.*

At the **Jack London Cabin and Interpretive Center,** you can visit the cabin in which the writer entertained miners with his knowledge of the classics during the winter of 1897. Works such as *The Call of the Wild* and *White Fang* were inspired by the time he spent in the Yukon wilds. The Interpretive Center houses an exhibit of historic photographs chronicling London's life. ✉ *8th Ave. and 1st St.,* ☎ *867/993–5575.* 🎫 *Free.* ☉ *Late May–mid-Sept., daily 10–6.*

Robert Service, primarily a poet, has been dubbed "the Bard of the Klondike." Originally from England, he came to the Yukon in the early 1900s, well after the gold rush was over. Before coming to Dawson, Service worked in Whitehorse at the Canadian Imperial Bank of Commerce. There he wrote "The Shooting of Dan McGrew," his most famous poem. The small **Robert Service Cabin** is a good representation of what a lot of Dawson cabins looked like during and after the Klondike Gold Rush. The sod roof even bears raspberries in summer. ✉ *8th Ave. and Hanson St.,* ☎ *867/993–7200.* 🎫 *$6.* ☉ *June–mid-Sept., daily 9–5.*

If you want a firsthand feel for river travel, board the **Yukon Queen,** a 58-ft-long twin deck vessel docked along Front Street that makes the 173-km (107-mi) trip westward to Eagle, Alaska, in approximately five hours. Travelers who opt for a one-way ticket may return to Dawson by bus. Meals are included in the price of the trip. Tickets can be purchased through Gray Line Yukon. ✉ *Box 420, Dawson City,* ☎ *867/ 993–5599; Gray Line Yukon:* ✉ *208G Steele St.,* ☎ *867/668–3225 or 800/544–2206.* 🎫 *$85 one-way, $138 round-trip.* ☉ *Departures mid-May–mid-Sept. daily.*

Dawson really got its start at the gold-mining sites just east of town. Huge mounds of rock and slag along the roadside attest to the considerable amount of earth turned over in search of the precious metal. The most famous mining site is **Bonanza Creek,** 1 km (½ mi) south of Dawson City, which produced several million-dollar claims in the days when gold went for $16 an ounce. A brass plaque on Bonanza Creek Road marks the **Discovery Claim,** staked by George Carmack in August of 1896, when he and his companions, Skookum Jim and Dawson Charlie, discovered the gold that sparked the great Klondike Gold Rush. The creek is so rich in minerals that it is still being mined today.

Those who want to try their luck at gold panning can rent the necessary gear for $5 at **Claim 33** (✉ Mi 7, Bonanza Creek Rd., ☎ 867/ 993–5804). You're guaranteed some gold, but don't expect to strike it rich.

Dredge No. 4, which was used to dig up the creek bed and sift gold from gravel during the height of Bonanza Creek's largesse, is approximately 15 minutes by car up Bonanza Creek Road from its juncture with the Klonkdike Highway. During summer, daily tours are conducted through the dredge. ✉ *Mi 7.8, Bonanza Creek Rd.,* ☎ *867/993– 7228.* 🎫 *$5.* ☉ *June–mid-Sept., daily 9–5; tours given on the hr.*

Dining and Lodging

$$$–$$$$ ✕ **Jack London Grill.** Downtown Hotel's dining room evokes the urbane atmosphere of a turn-of-the-century men's club, with dark-wood siding reaching halfway up walls adorned by framed mirrors and prints. Regional specialties like the Yukon River king salmon are reliable. Steaks are served in three sizes. For Dawson diners looking for a touch of civility and formality, this is a good choice. ✉ *Downtown Hotel, 2nd Ave. and Queen St.,* ☎ *867/993–5346. AE, DC, MC, V.*

$$$-$$$$ ✕ **Klondike Kate's.** The line at Klondike Kate's can sometimes get a
★   little intimidating, but the food is extremely good. Mexican and
Middle Eastern dishes are often on the menu, and the smoked local
king salmon is a constant standout. A large, covered outdoor deck
is open in summer. The main decorative statement on the deck is a
large map of the world, onto which guests are invited to stick pins
marking their hometowns. ✉ *3rd Ave. and King St.,* ☎ *867/993–
6527. MC, V.*

$$$ ✕ **Marina's.** You'd think being so far north, you'd be inspired to order
something more interesting than pizza. But Marina's thick-crusted
pizzas are first-rate and reasonably priced. The menu also includes pasta
and salads. Because of the location across from the Westmark Inn (☞
below), the dining room can fill up if there's a bus tour in town (and
in summer, there usually are a few). ✉ *5th Ave. between Princess and
Harper Sts.,* ☎ *867/993–6800. MC, V.*

$$$-$$$$ 🏨 **Westmark Inn.** Though the Westmark suffers from tour-bus over-
load, rooms are clean, modern, and spacious. You'll find the familiar
basic-American-hotel-room comforts behind a turn-of-the-century fa-
cade. ✉ *Box 420, 5th Ave. and Harper St., Y0B 1G0,* ☎ *867/993–
5542 or 800/544–0970,* ℻ *867/993–5623. 131 rooms. Restaurant,
lounge, coin laundry. AE, DC, MC, V. Closed mid-Sept.–mid-May.*

$$$ 🏨 **Downtown Hotel.** The main building of 35 rooms, which is open
all year, is only marginally better than the annex of 25 rooms across
the street, open only in summer. This hotel operates an airport shuttle service, which is especially valuable as there are no taxis in Dawson. ✉ *Box 780, 2nd Ave. and Queen St., Y0B 1G0,* ☎ *867/993–5346
or 800/661–0514 within the Yukon and British Columbia;* ℻ *867/
993–5076. 60 rooms. Restaurant, lounge, hot tub, meeting rooms, airport shuttle. AE, DC, MC, V.*

$$-$$$ 🏨 **Triple J Hotel.** Guests can choose from the main hotel, the separate
motel, and several outlying cabins. The motel, little more than a large
mobile home, is not worth considering. The cabins include kitchenettes and small porches with bright flowers. But the best choice is
one of the spacious, upstairs rooms of the hotel, quaintly decorated in
reproduction antiques. The kitchen is one of the better hotel kitchens;
you can order your pizza to go or stay in the outdoor seating area. ✉
Box 359, 5th Ave. and Queen St., Y0B 1G0, ☎ *867/993–5323, 800/
661–0405, or 800/764–3555;* ℻ *867/993–5030. 47 rooms. Restaurant, lounge. AE, MC, V. Closed late Oct.–mid-Apr.*

$-$$ 🏨 **Dawson City Bunkhouse.** Although rooms in the Bunkhouse are spare
(no TVs or in-room phones), they are comfortable and clean. Some rooms
have private baths; others share public washrooms. For budget-minded
travelers, this is the best deal in town. ✉ *Front and Prince Sts., Bag
4040, Y0B 1G0,* ☎ *867/993–6164,* ℻ *867/993–6051. 32 rooms. MC,
V. Closed Labor Day–May.*

Nightlife and the Arts

THE ARTS

The **Dawson City Music Festival** (✉ Dawson City Music Festival Association, Box 456, Y0B 1G0, ☎ 867/993–5584), which presents a
variety of musicians from Alaska, Yukon, and the rest of Canada, is
held each July. It's one of the most popular events in the north, so tickets can be extremely difficult to get. Write to the Festival Association
in spring to request tickets.

NIGHTLIFE

Diamond Tooth Gertie's Gambling Hall offers a glimpse of the frolick-
ing times of the gold rush. "Gertie" and her cancan dancers put on
three shows nightly while grizzled miners sit at the poker table. Gamblers can try their luck at slot machines, blackjack, red dog, and

roulette. Note: No minors are permitted. ✉ *4th Ave. and Queen St.,* ☎ *867/993–5575.* 🚬 *$5.* ⊘ *Mid-May–mid-Sept., daily 7 PM–2 AM.*

Side Trips from Dawson City

TOP OF THE WORLD HIGHWAY

The 108-km (67-mi) trip west along the Top of the World Highway to the Yukon-Alaska border will expose you to beautiful, expansive vistas. The road partially lives up to its name, set as it is along ridge lines and high-mountain shoulders, but the dirt-and-gravel surface can hardly be called a highway. The northernmost border crossing on land between Canada and the United States is along this route; the U.S. side is in Polar Creek, Alaska—population: two.

DEMPSTER HIGHWAY

The Dempster Highway's arctic tundra and mountain scenery are always beautiful, but are most spectacular in late August. Autumn comes early to the tundra and colors the landscape in vivid reds and yellows. The gentle rolling hills will arouse any hiker's desire for exploration.

The 766-km (475-mi) journey north to Inuvik (☞ The Northwest Territories, *below*) on the Dempster Highway is a much more adventurous and ambitious undertaking than driving the Top of the World Highway. The only public highway in Canada to cross the **Arctic Circle**, it passes through a tundra landscape that is severe, mountainous, and ever changing.

In its southern extreme, the highway passes first by the rugged **Tombstone Mountains** and then into the ranges of the Ogilvie Mountains. The route crosses Eagle Plains (approximately halfway between Dawson and Inuvik and a good stopping point for gas and supplies) before reaching the Arctic Circle, marked by a sign. From here the highway passes through the Richardson Mountains and enters the flatlands surrounding the Mackenzie River delta before reaching Inuvik. This is certainly one of *the* great wilderness drives in North America, but because there are no services for 370 km (229 mi) between the junction of the Dempster and Klondike highways and Eagle Plains, travelers should be prepared to cope with possible emergencies.

THE NORTHWEST TERRITORIES

In spring 1999, Canada's Northwest Territories, which once encompassed four time zones, from the mountainous Yukon border to Baffin Island, will be divided by a boundary line that runs from Cape Columbia on Ellesmere Island down through the Arctic islands to the Canadian mainland and south along the tree line. The land west of the boundary will still be called the Northwest Territories, while the land east of the boundary will be called Nunavut. The Northwest Territories now covers 1.4 million square km (550,000 square mi) and will be governed by a multicultural, multilingual legislature whose elected members will converge at Yellowknife's Legislative Assembly.

Outside the regional centers from which travel is usually based—Yellowknife and Inuvik—communities are extremely small. Many families still support themselves by hunting, fishing, and trapping, although modern technology is becoming increasingly widespread. You'll be encouraged to learn about the rich history and traditional ways of life of the Dene and Inuvialuit communities, where aboriginal languages are spoken on par with English and French. You're especially welcome at the many local festivals and ceremonies that dot the calendar year.

Yellowknife

❼ Back in 1934, when gold was discovered on the North Arm of Great Slave Lake, **Yellowknife,** 2,595 km (1,609 mi) from Vancouver, began as a rough-and-tumble mining camp. A center of government since the 1960s, it still thrives on hard-rock mining and, lately, diamonds—Lac de Gras, 350 km (217 mi) northwest of town, is the site of the Western Hemisphere's first diamond mine. In anticipation of the success of the mine, the Northwest Territories' capital city is growing quickly, from a population of 12,000 in 1991 to an estimated 18,000 in 1998.

Downhill from downtown Yellowknife lies the **Old Town,** built around the rocky peninsula that juts into Great Slave Lake (☞ *below*). You can reach it in 15 minutes by strolling toward the lake along Franklin Avenue; or you can drive down, perhaps taking time to turn off and explore the winding streets of historic neighborhoods first settled in the 1930s and 1940s. One of these neighborhoods is called the **Woodyard.** Once a thriving fuel depot run by a pioneer businessman, it's now known for its eccentric cabins, log dwellings, and Yellowknife's most famous street, Ragged Ass Road, named after hard-luck prospectors.

If you proceed north on Franklin Avenue, it becomes McDonald Drive. From McDonald Drive turn left onto Weaver Road and right onto Ingraham Drive, which travels over the **Rock,** a steep Precambrian outcropping where miners first pitched their tents 64 years ago. The wooden stairs at Ingraham Drive's highest point lead to the **Pilot's Monument,** a hilltop marker built in honor of the bush flyers who opened up the north. The climb is worth it: There's a 360-degree view of Great Slave Lake (☞ *below*), neighboring islands, and Yellowknife itself.

To continue exploring the Old Town, head back down to McDonald Drive and follow it around the Rock. You'll pass the **Float Plane Base,** heavy with traffic coming in and going out to mining exploration camps. You can also cross the causeway to **Latham Island,** where a handful of B&Bs and down-to-earth eateries mingle with upscale housing.

It's hard to overstress the beauty of **Great Slave Lake,** the sixth largest freshwater lake in North America. Clean, cold, and deep, it dwarfs Yellowknife and the few other communities along its shores. The lake's East Arm, a two- to three-day sail from Yellowknife, is prime cruise country, with dramatic cliffs rising from narrow bays. For those unsure of their navigational skills, hiring a skipper is recommended, since many of the lake's small bays are still uncharted. Excursions on the lake can be arranged with any of the local operators (☞ Outdoor Activities and Sports, *below*) who provide sail and motorboat charters, cruises, and sightseeing trips.

The **Prince of Wales Northern Heritage Centre,** on the shore of Frame Lake, is just a few minutes northwest of the city center. It houses extensive displays of such northern artifacts as caribou-hide parkas and beaded Dene clothing, and Inuit tools and stone carvings, as well as exhibits on exploration and settlement. The aviation section documents the north's history of flight. Among other displays is an exhibit devoted to the search for the Northwest Passage, which took more than 400 years as Europeans hunted for an Arctic route to the Orient, mapping the polar islands and the coast as they did so. ⊠ *Opposite City Hall,* ☎ *867/873–7551,* ℻ *867/873–0205.* 💺 *Free.* ☯ *June–Aug., daily 10:30–5; Sept.–May, Tues.–Fri. 10:30–5, weekends noon–5.*

A few hundred yards west of the Prince of Wales Northern Heritage Centre, the glass-domed **Legislative Assembly of the Northwest Territories** rises from the boreal forest. The architecturally splendid legislature offers free guided tours in summer. You can visit the council chamber and see the translation booths that permit debates to be carried out in nine official languages. The legislature houses the ceremonial mace, a symbol of government made of Yellowknife gold, musk-ox horns, and a slender narwhal tusk. ⌧ *Turn left off Hwy. 3, just northwest of town,* ☎ *867/669–2200 or 800/661–0784.* ⊙ *Tours June–July weekdays 10:30, 1:30, and 3:30; Sun. 1:30.*

Dining and Lodging

$$$$ ✕ **Factor's Club.** This big, airy dining room in the Explorer Hotel is warmed by a central, circular hearth and has great views of the woodlands just outside. The hotel makes major efforts to keep its menu fresh, combining reliable steaks, roast beef, and pasta with such unusual northern delicacies as musk-ox chops and arctic char en croûte. Dinners are pricey, but lunches and Sunday brunch are bargains. ⌧ *Explorer Hotel, 48th St. and 49th Ave.,* ☎ *867/873–3531 or 800/661–0892. AE, MC, V.*

$$$ ✕ **Bistro on Franklin.** Descending the narrow stairs leading into the Bistro's basement setting feels vaguely ominous—more like heading down to check out the boiler room than going out to dinner. But the dining area brings relief: Low lighting, tablecloths, and wait staff in bow ties lend a touch of formality to an otherwise casual place. Chicken and pasta dishes are excellent, including the chicken pesto pasta, a boneless breast of chicken in pesto cream sauce, served with fettuccine; fish dishes such as arctic char are less reliable. ⌧ *4910 Franklin Ave.,* ☎ *867/873–3991. MC, V.*

$$$ ✕ **Bullock's Fish and Chips.** With its log-cabin walls and rough-hewn furniture, Bullock's has a warm, rustic atmosphere. The dining room has only five or six tables, and the kitchen is effectively part of it. As for the specialty of the house, the name tells all; the fries are hand cut, and the catch of the day is fresh from Great Slave Lake. Every dinner is cooked to order. ⌧ *4 Lessard Dr.,* ☎ *867/873–3474. MC, V.*

$$$ ✕ **Prospector Bar and Grill.** In a waterfront building not far from the famous Wildcat Cafe (☞ *below*), this comfortable eatery presents a menu of standbys: steak sandwiches, salads, and eggs Florentine. There are spectacular views across Back Bay, where colorful floatplanes boom in and out all summer long. ⌧ *3506 Wiley Rd.,* ☎ *867/920–7639,* 𝕱𝕬𝕏 *867/669–5781. MC, V.*

$$ ✕ **Wildcat Cafe.** An institution as much as a restaurant, the Wildcat has been around since 1937; the low-slung log structure and split-log tables and benches inside are typical of life at the frontier's edge. This is a place where strangers are expected to share tables. The food, ranging from fresh fish to vegetarian chili to caribou burgers, is excellent and moderately priced. Many people drop in at the Wildcat for coffee and desserts—mostly fresh-baked delectables. ⌧ *Doornbos La. and Wiley Rd.,* ☎ *867/873–8850. MC, V.*

$$$ 🏨 **Explorer Hotel.** Atop a promontory overlooking Yellowknife, the Explorer is best recommended for its views of the city and the bays of Great Slave Lake. Rooms are decorated with run-of-the-mill brown-veneer furniture, but they are large, bright, and clean. ⌧ *Box 7000, X1A 2R3,* ☎ *867/873–3531, 800/661–0892 in Canada,* 𝕱𝕬𝕏 *867/873–2789. 128 rooms, 2 suites. 2 restaurants, lounge, airport shuttle. CP. AE, MC, V.*

$$$ 🏨 **Yellowknife Inn.** The oldest hotel in a city where there isn't much that could be called old, the inn has lavishly redone its lobby, which now opens into Centre Square shopping mall. Some of the older sections of the hotel complex have been demolished to make way for planned new facilities. The modern rooms are done in muted green and beige hues. The Mackenzie Lounge, with dark-wood paneling that lends

it a clubby feel, is a nice place to meet for a drink before dinner. The restaurant serves bistro-style cuisine, and a complimentary Continental breakfast for hotel guests. ⊠ *Box 490, X1A 2N4,* ☎ *867/873–2601 or 800/661–0580,* FAX *867/873–2602. 125 rooms, 7 suites. Restaurant, lounge, airport shuttle. CP. AE, DC, MC, V.*

$$ 🏨 **Igloo Inn.** Don't expect much more here than a motel-style room at a decent price. Rooms are on the small side and have the basics—bed, bathroom, TV; many have kitchenettes. The Igloo is a perfectly good choice for budget-minded travelers laying over for a night before heading off to more- adventurous pursuits in the territorial outback. ⊠ *Box 596, 4115 Franklin Ave., X1A 2R3,* ☎ *867/873–8511,* FAX *867/873–5547. 44 rooms. Restaurant. AE, MC, V.*

$–$$ 🏨 **Blue Raven.** Attractively set on a bluff at the edge of Old Town and overlooking Great Slave Lake, the Blue Raven is the best of Yellowknife's bed-and-breakfasts. A Continental breakfast is served in a common room with a view. Rooms are small, modern, clean, and quiet, set apart from one another by the home's three-story configuration. ⊠ *37B Otto Dr., X1A 2T9,* ☎ *867/873–6328. 1 room with bath, 2 rooms share bath. CP. No credit cards.*

FLY-IN WILDERNESS LODGES

If you like to fish, consider a backcountry fishing trip to one of the lodges listed below. Transportation is provided to and from Yellowknife.

$$$$ 🏨 **Bathurst Inlet Lodge.** Perhaps the most popular destination in the central Arctic, particularly for ornithologists, is this lone outpost on the tundra 49 km (30 mi) north of the Arctic Circle. While it's in Nunavut, the lodge flies its guests from Yellowknife by bush plane. Traveling by plane, boat, and foot from the lodge, guests typically spot musk oxen, Arctic foxes, wolves, falcons, and eagles. In late spring as many as a half million migrating caribou pass this way. Outings from the lodge include a hike (after a short airplane transfer) to **Wilberforce Falls**, the highest waterfall north of the Arctic Circle, where the Hood River cuts spectacularly through a series of gorges. In addition to offering week-long naturalist tours, the lodge also outfits canoe or raft trips on nearby rivers and bays. Fees start at $2,400 per person for a one-week stay, including flights to and from Yellowknife. ⊠ *Box 820 (AT7), 3618 McAvoy Rd., Yellowknife X1A 2N6,* ☎ *867/873–2595,* FAX *867/920–4263. 15 rooms in lodge, 15 cabins. V. Closed early Aug.–late June.*

$$$$ 🏨 **Frontier Fishing Lodge.** On the East Arm of Great Slave Lake near the Dene community of Lutsel K'e, Frontier Lodge is typical of a full-service fishing lodge. Guests are housed in outlying log cabins, in the main lodge, and in comfortable rooms attached to the conference and recreation building. Breakfast and dinner are served daily around a big table in the main lodge. Guides take guests to the best fishing waters on Great Slave as well as adjoining rivers and lakes, and lake trout exceeding 25 pounds are landed regularly. This is a lodge strictly dedicated to fishing; aside from reading or watching wolves feed on dinner scraps, there is not much else to do except appreciate the lakeside wilderness setting. Packages, including flights to and from Yellowknife, begin at around $350 per day per person. ⊠ *Box 32008, Edmonton, Alberta T6K 4C2,* ☎ *867/465–6843 or 867/370–3501,* FAX *867/466–3874. 6 rooms, 6 cabins sleep 4 to 6; shared indoor bathrooms. Capacity: 24 people. Sauna, meeting facilities. Closed mid-Sept.–mid-June. MAP. No credit cards.*

$$$ 🏨 **Blachford Lake Lodge.** Many fishing lodges in the far north provide a minimum of services, unless patrons request otherwise. Blachford Lake Lodge is a good example of the genre. Guests are flown to and from the remote lodge (less than a half-hour flight from Yellowknife), where

they stay in cabins and have the use of boats to venture out on a small lake. You're expected to bring and prepare your own food; the same goes for bedding and fishing tackle. The result is a cost that is generally under $120 per person per day (including the flights to and from the lodge), and less for groups—modest by fly-in fishing standards. The lodge is also open in winter for ice fishing, snowmobiling, and dogsledding. ✉ *Box 1568, X1A 2P2,* ☎ *867/873–3303,* FAX *867/920–4013. 6 cabins sleep 14. V.*

Nightlife and the Arts

Folk on the Rocks (✉ Box 326, X1A 2N3, ☎ 867/920–7806), a lakeside music festival held in mid-July, attracts musicians from throughout North America, as well as Dene and Inuit performers.

Raven Mad Daze (✉ Yellowknife Chamber of Commerce, ☎ 867/920–4944) takes place during summer solstice (the third week in June), when the sun's still out at midnight. Sidewalk sales, street vendors, concerts, and dances are part of the fun.

Outdoor Activities and Sports

Sail North (✉ Box 2497, X1A 2P8, ☎ 867/873–8019) accommodates trips to Great Slave Lake with boat rentals and guided boat tours. The **M.S. Norweta** (✉ N.W.T. Marine Group, 17 England Crescent, ☎ 867/873–2489) organizes short outings, dinner cruises, and multiday cruises to the legendary East Arm of Great Slave Lake.

Shopping

CLOTHING

Polar Parkas (✉ 5023 49th St., ☎ 867/873–3343) is the best place in Yellowknife to buy native-made parkas.

NATIVE ARTS AND CRAFTS

Northern Images (✉ Yellowknife Centre, 49th St. and 50th Ave., ☎ 867/873–5944, FAX 867/873–9224) sells a variety of native crafts and artwork, from sculpture to moose-hair tuftings to clothing, and has stores in several Canadian cities, including Whitehorse and Yellowknife. The **Arctic Art Gallery** (✉ 4801 Franklin Ave., ☎ 867/873–5666 or 800/661–0799, FAX 867/873–9155) has a selection of carvings, lithographic prints, and original paintings.

Departures from Yellowknife

Yellowknife is a transportation hub for outlying areas in the western Arctic. For driving excursions from Yellowknife, you can pass through Wood Buffalo National Park and Fort Smith to the south and through Fort Liard to the west. This is not, generally speaking, a rousing scenic drive. Long stretches of road cutting through the low-lying, subarctic bush are highlighted by occasional waterfalls or the sight of wildlife near or on the highway.

Alexandra Falls

537 km (333 mi) south of Yellowknife.

Of the scenic waterfalls along the road between Yellowknife and Fort Smith, the most dramatic is Alexandra Falls, a few miles south of the town of Hay River, on Route 1 at the junction of Routes 1 and 2, where the Hay River drops 108 ft over limestone cliffs.

Wood Buffalo National Park

599 km (371 mi) south of Yellowknife.

The area where you're most likely to spot wildlife is Wood Buffalo National Park, straddling the Alberta–Northwest Territories border. Covering 44,807 square km (17,026 square mi), this is the largest national park in Canada, home, not surprisingly, to the world's largest free-roaming bison herd (about 5,000 total). It is also a summer nesting ground for many bird species, including bald eagles, peregrine falcons, and the rare whooping crane. Much of the terrain—a flat land of bogs, swamps, salt plains, sinkholes, and meandering streams and rivers—is essentially inaccessible to visitors, but a few frontcountry trails allow exploration. The park's visitor reception center in Fort Smith can provide information on interpretive programs and hikes. ✉ *Superintendent, Wood Buffalo National Park, Box 750, Fort Smith, Northwest Territories X0E 0P0,* ☎ *867/872–7900 or 867/872–7960,* FAX *867/872–3910.*

Nahanni National Park
608 km (377 mi) west of Yellowknife.

★   The principal reason to head west from Yellowknife is to visit **Nahanni National Park.** The Mackenzie and Liard rivers, which join forces at Fort Simpson, are the region's approximate geographical dividers, separating the low-lying bush of the east and the mountains to the west. Access to Nahanni National Park is possible only by helicopter or plane; inside the park, canoes and rafts are the principal vehicles of travel. A well-maintained park campground near the falls facilitates overnight excursions. For a complete listing of air services, contact the **Nahanni National Park Reserve** (✉ Box 348, Fort Simpson, X0E 0N0, ☎ 867/695–3151 or 867/695–2310, FAX 867/695–2446).

Perhaps the most impressive feature in the park is **Virginia Falls**, more than 410 ft high and about 656 ft wide—a thunderous wall of white water cascading around a central spire of rock. To get there contact Simpson Air (☞ Outdoor Activities and Sports, *below*), one of several plane and helicopter services that offer flightseeing trips to the falls.

The **Cirque of the Unclimbables** is another of Nahanni's spectacular features. This breathtaking cathedral of rock towers rising as much as 3,000 vertical ft does not entirely live up to its name, but the few who have made successful ascents here can be counted among the most proficient rock climbers in the world. Perhaps the biggest problem posed by the Cirque is that it is nearly as unreachable as it is unclimbable.

The **South Nahanni** is among the best rivers in the far north. Two-week canoe trips start from Rabbit Kettle Lake at the park's northwestern extreme but require portage around Virginia Falls. Eight- to 12-day canoe or raft trips begin below Virginia Falls. White water along the way is minimal, so previous canoeing or rafting experience is not essential.

OUTDOOR ACTIVITIES AND SPORTS
Two reliable outfitters that lead guided boating trips in Nahanni National Park are **Nahanni River Adventures** (✉ Box 4869, Whitehorse, Yukon Territory Y1A 4N6, ☎ 867/668–3180) and **Nahanni Wilderness Adventures** (✉ Box 4, Site 6, R.R. 1, Didsbury, Alberta T0M 0W0, ☎ 403/637–3843).

For those interested in mountaineering, **Simpson Air** (✉ Box 260, Fort Simpson, Northwest Territories X0E 0N0, ☎ 867/695–2505, FAX 867/695–2925) can shuttle climbers into the Cirque of the Unclimbables from Fort Simpson.

Inuvik

❽   Overlooking the huge Mackenzie Delta where the Mackenzie River (*Deh Cho* to the Dene people of this region) meets the Beaufort Sea, **Inuvik** is 1,086 air km (673 air mi) northwest of Yellowknife. The town's population of 3,000 mixes many major northern identities: the Gwich'in Dene, the Inuvialuit (western Inuit), and settlers from southern Canada.

You can meet native people and experience their culture on guided tours to fishing and whaling camps with **Beaufort Delta Tours** (⌧ Box 2040, Northwest Territories X0E 0T0, ☎ 867/777–4881, ℻ 867/777–4898).

Dining and Lodging

$$$ ✕⌐ **Finto Motor Inn.** On the outskirts of Inuvik, at the junction of the Marine Bypass and Mackenzie Road, the Finto materializes as a two-story, square structure resembling a big box that might have been flown in by a helicopter sling and dropped on the spot. The wood siding somewhat softens the harsh edges. Four of the rooms have kitchenettes; all have satellite TV. The Finto may not be elegant, but the Peppermill, the inn's restaurant, is generally considered Inuvik's best. Local foods, such as arctic char and musk ox, are accompanied by views of green meadows and blue water. ⌧ *Box 1925, Inuvik X0E 0T0,* ☎ *867/777–2647 or 800/661–0843,* ℻ *867/777–3442. 44 rooms. Restaurant. AE, DC, MC, V.*

Nightlife and the Arts

The **Great Northern Arts Festival** (⌧ Box 2921, X0E 0T0, ☎ 867/777–3536) in July, includes displays of wood, horn, and stone carvings and weavings by Inuit and Inuvialuit artists; workshops focusing on various disciplines; and music and dance performances.

Departures from Inuvik

One doesn't "tour" the Northwest Territories in the usual sense of the word. Rather, the concept is more expeditionary. Inuvik serves as a base camp from which to make day or extended side trips in the Mackenzie Delta, along the coast, or north to the islands of the western Arctic Archipelago. Using regional airlines, you can make hops to Sachs Harbour on Banks Island; to Tuktoyaktok, overlooking the Beaufort Sea; and to Herschel Island, in the Beaufort Sea. Lodging and transportation in the Arctic North tend to be expensive even by high-end northern standards, so that having a well-defined travel plan is critical to staying within a budget. Trip organizers and outfitters can be particularly helpful in tailoring a travel program to meet particular interests and budgets. Keep in mind that the prime Arctic travel season tends to be very short: Many visitor services and tour organizers operate only in July and August.

Tuktoyaktuk

9 *113 air km (70 air mi) north of Inuvik.*

If you're interested in the culture of the north, this small Inuvialuit (western Inuit) community, a short flight north of Inuvik, is the place to experience an interesting blend of ancient culture and modern technology. As you fly in over Tuk Peninsula, you'll spot pingoes (odd conical landforms found only on the frozen borders of the Beaufort Sea) and caribou, from which the hamlet of Tuktoyaktuk derives its name, "the place where caribou cross." Tours of Tuktoyaktuk are conducted by Arctic Tour Company (☞ Guided Tours *in* Wilderness Canada A to Z, *below*).

Banks Island

523 air km (324 air mi) northeast of Inuvik.

Banks Island, most westerly of the Arctic islands, is best known for its large herd of musk oxen, now numbering in the thousands in **Aulavik National Park** (⌧ Parks Canada, Box 1840, Inuvik X0E 0T0, ☎ 867/777–3248, ℻ 867/777–4491). Arctic Tour Company (☞ Guided Tours *in* Wilderness Canada A to Z, *below*) conducts tours to Banks Island that include oxen and caribou watching.

Herschel Island

274 air km (170 air mi) northwest of Inuvik.

Tiny Herschel Island is an excellent base for sighting beluga and bowhead whales. It's also known for its abundant bird life and its wildflowers, which grow from the seemingly barren tundra. Historic relics include the old Anglican Rectory, a decayed wooden building that now serves as a nesting place for seabirds, and the weathered grave markers of 19th-century whalers who did not survive the island's harsh winters. Though Herschel Island lies just off the Yukon's Arctic coast and is a Yukon Territorial Park, it's best accessed from Inuvik. Beaufort Delta Tours offers guided day tours along the coast to Herschel, as does the Arctic Tour Company (☞ Guided Tours *in* Contacts and Resources, *below*).

NUNAVUT

There are no roads to Nunavut. This fact alone makes Canada's new Arctic territory one of the most unique travel destinations on the continent. But consider its other amazements: No forests grow here; Nunavut lies entirely above the tree line. In winter, night can last around the clock. In summer, the sun never sets. It's a land of glaciers and looming peaks, where caribou outnumber people. Nunavut's 25,000 residents are predominantly Inuit, and many still live by hunting and fishing in isolated settlements. But with the creation of Nunavut in 1999, the Inuit will have realized a long-held dream. Nunavut's name means "Our Land" in the region's official language, Inuktitut. And within its boundaries, the Inuit majority will effectively govern themselves.

Carved out of the old Northwest Territories, the newest political entity in North America is one of the largest, at 1,900,000 sq km (741,000 sq mi). The territory's northernmost boundary lies at the highest tip of Ellesmere Island, at latitude 83° north—only 400 km (248 mi) from the Geographic North Pole. It reaches as far south as the windy Belcher Islands, deep in Hudson Bay. And it contains the geographic center of Canada—an unmarked (and little-recognized) spot on the barrens 30 km (18 mi) west of Baker Lake, in the Keewatin region. The story of this Arctic land and its aboriginal people goes back thousands of years, but 1999 is a landmark year, as Nunavut's history officially begins.

July 9 marks the anniversary of the day in 1993 when the Canadian Government and the Inuit signed the Land Claim Agreement that led to the creation of Nunavut, and will be known from now on as Nunavut Day in the towns and hamlets of Canada's central and eastern Arctic, from Kugluktuk in the west to Iqaluit in the east, to the High Arctic settlement of Grise Fiord, and along the coast of Hudson Bay. These small communities are linked to one another by modern technology; all are served by regional airlines. Yet they are among the world's truly remote living places, poised on the outer edge of civilization. Village architecture is strictly utilitarian, and Arctic hamlets can seem bleak and disorganized to visitors. You won't find tidy suburban gardens or paved roads. Instead of neatly trimmed hedges, many a front door is flanked by drying caribou hides and dismantled snowmobiles. The family runabout is likely to be a four-wheel motorbike or a homemade *komatik* (a long, wooden sled pulled by dogs or a snowmobile). Living here is an adventure in itself, as the Inuit cope with a harsh climate and huge distances.

Visiting is an adventure, too: Experiencing the Arctic wilderness and the Inuit way of life is the lure for most travelers, even though getting around in Nunavut tends to be both time-consuming and expensive, and amenities can be very basic. But if you opt for the services of the local and international outfitters who offer packages that range from outdoor adventures to cultural tours in the villages, you can often cut costs. Even in the smallest communities you'll find experienced Inuit outfitters who will help you get to know the land, the wildlife, and the local folklore.

Nunavut is vast—a fifth of Canada's land mass—and it's probably best to select a region you'd like to see most. There are three regions to consider: the Baffin; the central Arctic, or Kitikmeot; and the Keewatin. To get to destinations within these regions, you must first fly to Iqaluit, the new Nunavut capital, located on southwest Baffin Island, or to Yellowknife in the Northwest Territories. Both towns' international airports are served by major airlines from the south.

Iqaluit

⑩ On southeastern Baffin Island overlooking Frobisher Bay, **Iqaluit,** 2,261 air km (1,402 air mi) east of Yellowknife, is the transportation, communication, and government center of Canada's eastern Arctic. Like Inuvik and Yellowknife, the Nunavut capital is mainly a point of reference and departure for travelers; most visitors to Baffin Island must fly in and out of its modern international airport. Its population—some 3,600 at last count—may be minuscule compared with that of other capital cities, and caribou wandering through town is not an uncommon sight. The town's most memorable piece of architecture is St. Jude's, the igloo-shape Anglican cathedral.

Iqaluit is growing fast. New government buildings are on the rise, creating a metropolis on the tundra. Perhaps the Nunavut capital is more to be appreciated for the people you're likely to meet. Lawyers and politicos rub shoulders with village matriarchs in town to shop and hunters heading out for seal. Elderly artists carve stone on their doorsteps, while the local kids show off the latest southern gear in an increasingly urban community. Inuit and Euro-Canadians work side by side, and you'll hear both English and French spoken in addition to Inuktitut. There are no street names in Iqaluit, but the town's small size makes it easy to navigate, and nearly anyone you encounter can point you in the right direction.

To learn about Inuit life and culture, visit the **Nunnatta Sunaqutangit Museum,** with its excellent collection of historic artifacts, such as the clothing and tools that enabled the Inuit to survive in the Arctic, plus touring exhibits. The museum is in a renovated Hudson's Bay trading post down on the beach that fronts Frobisher Bay's Koojesse Inlet. ⊠ Building 212, ☎ 867/979–5537. ☜ Free.

Next door to the Nunnatta Sunaqutangit Museum is **Unikkaarvik Visitors' Centre,** where you can pick up guidebooks and brochures on the area. The center displays a collection of Inuit art and a life-size diorama of a floe edge. ⊠ *Unikkaarvik Building, Box 1000,* ☎ *867/979–4636,* FAX *867/979–1261.* ☜ *Free.*

Sylvia Grinnell Territorial Park is just 15 minutes outside of town. Trails are unmarked and of varying difficulty, so sturdy hiking boots are a must. Shallow and swift Sylvia Grinnell River is for experienced canoeists and kayakers only. Though it's mainly a day-use park, there are campsites. There's no on-site information center or staff, so contact the Unikkaarvik Visitor's Centre (☞ *above*) or Nunavut Tourism (☞ Visitor Information *in* Wilderness Canada A to Z, *below*) for more information.

The only reason to visit **Qaummaarviit Historic Park,** 13 km (8 mi) west of Iqaluit on Qaummaarviit Island, is to see the relics of the semisubterranean houses once occupied by the Thule Inuit who dwelled here 1,000 years ago. A well-marked trail winds through the park, connecting the sites. Camping on the island is not permitted, so plan on a day trip only. There is no fee to enter the park, and arrangements to travel to the island can be made through the Unikkaarvik Visitor's Centre (☞ *above*).

Dining and Lodging

$$$$ ✕🏨 **Navigator Inn.** Rooms here are standard, but the pervading nautical theme adds a bit of character. The inn is also a local favorite for dining, with an eclectic dinner menu that includes such Arctic specialties as caribou, char, and musk-ox chops. ⊠ *Box 158, Iqaluit X0A 0H0,* ☎ *867/979–6201,* FAX *867/979–4296. 35 rooms. Restaurant, coffee shop, lounge, in-room modem lines. AE, MC, V.*

$$$–$$$$ ✕🏨 **Discovery Lodge Hotel.** Skylights brighten the lobby area of this hotel, where every room's centerpiece is a trapezoid-shape bed, wider at the top than the bottom. The Granite Room, with its granite-slab tabletops, is perhaps the best restaurant in Iqaluit, noteworthy for its use of local ingredients, including arctic char, Baffin Island shrimp, and scallops. ⊠ *Box 387, Iqaluit X0A 0H0,* ☎ *867/979–4433,* FAX *867/ 979–6591. 51 rooms, 1 suite. Restaurant, lounge, laundry, airport shuttle. AE, DC, MC, V.*

$$$ ✕🏨 **Regency Frobisher Inn.** In its brochure the inn promotes itself as being "part of an integrated, climate-controlled, indoor shopping and high-rise apartment complex." So much for the rustic charm of the far north. Veneer-wood furnishings fill the simple, boxlike rooms, but private baths, phone, and cable make up for the lack of character. Rooms in the front offer good views of Frobisher Bay and Iqaluit. There's no airport shuttle, but the inn will reimburse you for the taxi ride. The dining room specializes in Canadian Arctic cuisine. The hotel also provides fax services. ⊠ *Box 610, Iqaluit X0A 0H0,* ☎ *867/979–2222, 867/979–0427. 50 rooms. Restaurant, lounge, pool, sauna, laundry. AE, MC, V.*

Departures from Iqaluit

Long before it became the capital of Nunavut, Iqaluit was famous as the gateway to magnificent Baffin Island. Even northerners accustomed to the unique beauty of the Arctic wilderness speak of Baffin in tones of awe. It is a world of junctures: where mountains meet sea, where the climates of summer and winter may be experienced on the same day, where summer flowers bloom on green tundra meadows amid ice-locked surroundings. Despite the ever-increasing influences of modern culture, Baffin Island remains a stronghold of Inuit tradition. At least 3,000 years ago, the Thule people, ancestors of the Inuit, migrated to the Canadian Arctic across the frozen Bering Sea. Later, whaling became a prime means of sustenance, both for Inuit and European hunters. A number of Baffin communities have exhibits or museums that chronicle whaling life.

From Iqaluit, visitors must choose a medium of travel: land or sea. In winter, of course, the land and sea merge under ice and snow, and April and May are the ideal months for those interested in cross-country skiing, dogsledding, or snowmobiling. Those who journey into the Baffin wilderness should have an adventurous spirit. While some tour organizers offer general sightseeing tours of the region, Baffin is best appreciated by those inclined (and physically fit enough) to rough it. For those who want to explore even more extreme polar regions,

Iqaluit also serves as a departure point for Ellesmere Island, the second-largest and northernmost island in the Arctic Archipelago, separated from Greenland by only a narrow passage.

Auyuittuq National Park
320 air km (512 mi) north of Iqaluit.

The jewel of Baffin is **Auyuittuq National Park,** where rivers and glaciers have cut deep fjords and have carved out **Aksayook Pass** (formerly Pangnirtung Pass) between Cumberland Sound to the south and Davis Strait to the north. The 60-km (37-mi) pass is surrounded by jagged peaks exceeding 6,600 ft that jut up from glacial ice (glacial melt provides the water supply supporting the brief burst of summer wildflowers on the tundra lowlands). A marked trail leads through the pass, and in summer, backpacking groups regularly make the five- to seven-day journey. There are emergency shelters along the route, but this is still a trip only for those properly prepared and physically fit, given the length of the trip and the vagaries of climatic changes, even in midsummer. All park visitors should sign up with a trip organizer and/or check in at the park headquarters in Pangnirtung for information on hiking in the park. For more information contact **Parks Canada** (✉ Eastern Arctic District, Box 1720, Iqaluit, Nunavut X0A 0H0, ☎ 867/979–6277). *Park headquarters, Pangnirtung, Nunavut X0A 0R0,* ☎ *867/473–8828,* ℻ *867/473–8612.* ☾ *July–Aug., weekdays 8:30–noon, 1–5, and 6–10; weekends 1–5 and 6–10; Sept.–June, weekdays 8:30–5.*

Ellesmere Island National Park
2,100 air km (3,360 mi) northwest of Iqaluit.

Adventurous visitors can head north from Baffin Island to this park, above 80° north latitude. Ellesmere, like Baffin, is intriguing as much for its climate as its landscape. Technically a "polar desert," the island, with an annual precipitation of about 2½ inches, is one of the driest places in the northern hemisphere; yet, because of the water-retaining effects of ice, parts of the island can support plant and wildlife. For more information, contact **Parks Canada** (✉ Eastern Arctic District, Box 1720, Iqaluit, Nunavut X0A 0H0, ☎ 867/979–6277).

The Central Arctic

The central Arctic is the Nunavut region that borders directly on the Northwest Territories (beginning west of Kugluktuk on the Coppermine River), and some communities, such as Kugluktuk and Cambridge Bay, the regional transportation hub in Victoria Island, are reached by scheduled flights out of Yellowknife, through Inuvik. Farther east, you must fly from Iqaluit. This is Northwest Passage country, the forbidding maze of channels and Arctic islands through which European explorers navigated for 400 years in search of a route to Asia. At Gjoa Haven, a small community named for the ship piloted by Roald Amundsen, the route's eventual discoverer, there's a historic trail commemorating the search in **Northwest Passage Territorial Park.**

Major draws to the area are its bird and wildlife sanctuaries and its challenging rivers, such as the Hood, the Back, the Thelon, and the Burnside. Many outfitters offer trips by canoe or raft to these remote rivers, which wind through a vast treeless landscape that remains virtually untouched. *See* Guided Tours *in* Wilderness Canada A to Z, *below* for outfitters that arrange expeditions to the central Arctic.

The Keewatin Region

The Keewatin region, which includes the barrenlands and the Hudson Bay coast, is a rugged, thinly populated region with a fascinating Inuit history, much of which is still apparent in the form of old stone structures, such as caches, tent rings, and kayak stands. In summer, there is plenty of opportunity for wildlife viewing. You might spot polar bears, whales, walrus colonies, wildfowl nurseries, and caribou herds. Local outfitters will take you out onto the bay and to Southhampton and Coats Islands, into the barrens, to fishing rivers and paddling adventures. You can reach the Keewatin region by flying from Iqaluit or Yellowknife to Rankin Inlet, which serves as a travel hub from which to fly to smaller villages like Arviat, Whale Cove, and Chesterfield Inlet.

Rankin Inlet
1,200 air km (1,920 air mi) from Iqaluit.

Founded as a nickel mining center in the 1950s, Rankin Inlet is now a bustling hamlet and regional transportation hub. Inuit comprise 77% of its tiny population (2,300). The nickel mine has been closed for nearly 40 years, but mineral explorers are once again searching the nearby tundra for gold and base metals, and future mining appears likely. In summer, a hike to **Meliadine Park,** 5 km (8 mi) from town, brings hiking, fishing, birdwatching, and berry-picking opportunities. The park also contains the remains of stone houses built centuries ago. **Kivalliq Regional Visitors' Centre** (✉ Rankin Inlet, Nunavut X0C 0G0, ☎ 867/645−5091) provides information on the area. Accommodations and dining are available at **Siniktarvik Hotel** (✉ Box 190, Rankin Inlet, Nunavut, X0C 0G0, ☎ 867/645−2807).

Fly-in Wilderness Lodge

$$$$ 🖭 **Sila Lodge.** A rather spartan facility, Sila Lodge is on Wager Bay, 80 km (50 mi) south of the Arctic Circle. The area surrounding the lodge is teeming with wildlife, especially polar bears and peregrine falcons. In addition to wildlife viewing, there are Inuit programs focusing on Inuit culture, excellent hiking opportunities, plus visits to the northern communities of Baker Lake and Churchill, Manitoba. ✉ *173 Ragsdill Rd., Winnipeg, Manitoba R2G 4C6,* ☎ *800/663−9832 or 204/949−2050,* 𝖥𝖠𝖷 *204/663−6375. 5 cabins, each sleeps 6. V. Closed Sept.−June.*

WILDERNESS CANADA A TO Z

Arriving and Departing

By Bus
Greyhound Lines of Canada (✉ 10324 103rd St., Edmonton, Alberta T5J 0Y9, ☎ 403/421−4211, 𝖥𝖠𝖷 867/425−7829) provides service from Edmonton to Hay River, Northwest Territories. Greyhound also has service from Edmonton or Vancouver to Whitehorse in the Yukon.

By Car
It hardly bears saying that getting to the Yukon or the Northwest Territories by car calls for a good deal of driving. The best route into the region is the Alaska Highway (Route 97 in British Columbia), accessible from Edmonton via Routes 43, 34, and 2 and from Vancouver via Route 1. After Fort Nelson, British Columbia, Routes 7, 1, and 3 lead to Yellowknife; the Alaska Highway (Route 1 in the Yukon) continues on to Whitehorse. The good news is that with so few roads in the region, it's difficult to make a wrong turn. Be aware that as you drive farther north, gas stations are few and gas is expensive—in some

cases exceeding 70¢ a liter, or roughly $2.40 a gallon. With relatively little lodging along the way, you might want to embark on the trip in a camper or recreational vehicle. There are no roads connecting the hamlets of Nunavut.

By Plane

Whitehorse International Airport (☎ 867/667–8440), 5 km (3 mi) from downtown Whitehorse, is the Yukon's major airport. **Yellowknife Airport** (☎ 867/873–4049), the main facility for the Northwest Territories, is 5 km (3 mi) northwest of the city center. **Iqaluit Airport** (☎ 867/979–5224) provides regular service to Cambridge Bay, Inuvik, and Rankin Inlet.

Air Canada (☎ 800/776–3000, 800/387–2710 in MI and NY, 800/663–9100 in ID and WA) is one of two major air carriers with connecting service from the United States to points in the Northwest Territories. **Canadian Airlines** (☎ 800/426–7000) has a scheduling agreement with **American Airlines** (☎ 800/433–7300) for connections from the United States and is the only airline with scheduled service to Whitehorse in the Yukon. Canadian Airlines affiliate **Canadian North** (☎ 800/426–7000) is responsible for most of the connecting service throughout the far north. For Nunavut, **First Air** (☎ 613/839–1247 or 800/267–1247) offers extensive service from Montréal and Ottawa. **NWT Air** (☎ 867/920–2500 or 800/661–0789, FAX 867/873–3272), an Air Canada affiliate, provides service within the Northwest Territories.

Getting Around

By Bus

In the Yukon **Alaska Direct Transport and Bus Line** (✉ 4051 4th Ave., Whitehorse, Yukon Territory Y1A 1H1, ☎ 867/668–4833, FAX 867/667–7411) provides scheduled service from Whitehorse to many Alaskan communities, as well as Haines Junction, Dawson City, Burwash Landing, and Beaver Creek. **Alaskon Express** (✉ 208-G Steele St., Whitehorse, Yukon Territory Y1A 2C4, ☎ 867/668–3225, FAX 867/667–4494 or 800/544–2206) has service between Whitehorse and cities in Alaska from mid-May to mid-September. **Frontier Coachlines** (✉ 328 Old Airport Rd., Yellowknife, Northwest Territories X1A 3T3, ☎ 867/873–4892, FAX 867/669–9197) offers service connecting Fort Smith, Fort Providence, Hay River, and Yellowknife. **Gold City Tours** (✉ Box 960, Dawson City, Yukon Territory Y0B 1G0, ☎ 867/993–5175, FAX 867/993–5261) has summer bus service between Dawson and Inuvik. **Norline Coaches** (✉ 34 MacDonald Rd., Whitehorse, Yukon Territory Y1A 4L2, ☎ 867/633–3864, FAX 867/633–3849) provides service between Dawson City and Whitehorse.

By Car

In general, exploring by car is a more sensible idea in the Yukon than in the Northwest Territories. The only part of the Northwest Territories with any kind of highway network is the southwest, where the roads are paved from the Alberta border to Fort Providence, and again near Yellowknife. Farther north and west, they are hard-packed gravel. Many highways in the Yukon are paved, the scenery along the way considerable, and roadside services more extensive.

Anyone traveling by car in the far north should take precautions. Distances from one service area to the next typically exceed 160 km (99 mi), so make sure to monitor your fuel gauge. At least one good spare tire is essential, and many residents of the region carry more, especially when traveling long distances. Another common practice is to cover headlights, grills, and even windshields with plastic shields or wire mesh to protect against flying gravel. It is advisable to carry extra parts (air filter, fan belt, and fluids). Be sure your vehicle has good suspension, even if you plan to stick to the major highways; shifting permafrost regularly damages paved roads, and ruts and washboard occasionally appear on unpaved roads, especially after periods of bad weather.

Winter driving requires extra precautionary measures. Many a far-north resident can tell you a tale about overnighting on the road and waiting out fierce weather. Take along emergency survival gear, including ax, shovel, flashlight, plenty of matches, kindling (paper or wood) to start a fire, sleeping bag, rugged outerwear, and food. Also, you should have a properly winterized car, with light engine oil and transmission fluid, a block heater, tire chains, and good antifreeze.

In the Northwest Territories there are several river crossings without real bridges. In summer you ride a free car ferry; in winter you cross on ice bridges. However, there are the seasons known as "freeze-up" and "break-up," in fall and spring, respectively, when ice bridges aren't solid but rivers are too frozen for ferries to run. For daily ferry reports in summer (late May to late October in the south Mackenzie region, June to late October farther north), call the following: for Routes 1 and 3, ☎ 867/695–2018 or 800/661–0751; for the Dempster Highway, ☎ 867/979–2678 or 800/661–0752. For winter road conditions, call the following: for Routes 1 through 7, ☎ 867/874–2208 or 800/661–0750; for the Dempster Highway, ☎ 867/979–2678 or 800/661–0752. For Yukon Highway information, call ☎ 867/667–8215.

By Plane

Once you're outside the Yukon and the southwest section of the Northwest Territories, flying is pretty much the only way to get around in wilderness Canada. Canadian North, First Air, and NWT Air (☞ Arriving and Departing by Plane, *above*) have regularly scheduled service within the Northwest Territories and Nunavut. All airlines listed below also offer charter air service, an option worth considering for groups of four or more and usually the only option for getting to and from remote wilderness areas. Check with regional tourist offices for other charter services operating locally and regionally.

THE YUKON

Air North (✉ Box 4998, Whitehorse, Yukon Territory Y1A 4S2, ☎ 867/668–2228, FAX 867/667–6224). **Alkan Air** (✉ Box 4008, Whitehorse, Yukon Territory Y1A 3S9, ☎ 867/668–2107 or 800/661–0432, FAX 867/667–6117).

THE NORTHWEST TERRITORIES

For a copy of the *Air Tourism Guide to the NWT,* call **N.W.T. Arctic Tourism** (☞ Visitor Information, *below*).

Buffalo Airways (✉ Box 1479, Hay River, Northwest Territories X0E 0R0, ☎ 867/874–3333, FAX 867/874–3572; ✉ Box 2015, Yellowknife X1A 2R3, ☎ 867/873–6112, FAX 867/873–8393); **North-Wright Air** (✉ Bag Service 2200, Norman Wells, Northwest Territories X0E 0V0, ☎ 867/587–2288 or 800/661–0702, FAX 867/587–2962); **Ptarmigan Airways** (✉ Box 100, Yellowknife, Northwest Territories X1A 2N1, ☎ 867/873–4461 or 800/661–0808, FAX 867/873–5209).

NUNAVUT

Air Nunavut (✉ Box 1239, Iqaluit, Nunavut X0A 0H0, ☎ 819/979–2900, FAX 819/979–2425).

Contacts and Resources

Car Rental

Rental agencies in both Whitehorse and Yellowknife typically rent trucks and four-wheel-drive vehicles in addition to cars. **Avis** (☎ 800/879–2847) rents at the Yellowknife airport. **Budget** (☎ 800/268–8900) has locations at both the Whitehorse and Yellowknife airports. **National Tilden** (☎ 800/387–4747) also has locations at both the Whitehorse and Yellowknife airports.

Emergencies

For **emergency** services in the Yukon, the Northwest Territories, and Nunavut, dial 0 for the operator and explain the nature of the emergency. You will then be connected with the police, fire department, or medical service, as needed. In Yellowknife the **Royal Canadian Mounted Police** number is ☎ 867/669–1111. You may also call a toll-free emergency number, ☎ 867/667–5555 for the **Royal Canadian Mounted Police** or ☎ 867/667–3333 for **medical assistance,** from anywhere in the Yukon. In Whitehorse dial 911 for emergencies.

It's a good idea when traveling in the far north—especially in remote wilderness areas and if unescorted by a guide or outfitter—to give a detailed itinerary to someone at home or to the police, to facilitate emergency rescue.

Guided Tours

THE YUKON

Access Yukon (✉ 212 Lambert St., Whitehorse, Yukon Territory Y1A 1Z4, ☎ 867/668–1233 or 800/661–0468, FAX 867/668–5595) arranges river trips, canoe rentals, heli-hiking, camper and 4X4 rentals, and trail riding and has information on sightseeing opportunities, wilderness lodges, and transportation throughout the Yukon. **Canadian River Expeditions** (✉ Box 1023, Whistler, British Columbia V0N 1B0, ☎ 604/938–6651 or 800/898–7238, FAX 604/938–6621) coordinates 6- to 12-day wilderness and natural history expeditions on the Tatshenshini, Alsek, and Firth rivers. **Gray Line Yukon** (✉ Box 4157, 208-G Steele St., Whitehorse, Yukon Territory Y1A 2C4, ☎ 867/668–3225, FAX 867/667–4494) conducts package tours to Dawson City and Alaska as well as Yukon River cruises and sightseeing tours of the Yukon Wildlife Preserve. **Holland America Westours** (✉ 300 Elliott Ave. W, Seattle, WA 98119, ☎ 206/281–3535 or 888/252–7524, FAX 206/286–3288) organizes bus tours through the Yukon and Alaska as well as combined cruise-ship/bus tours that link in Skagway, Alaska. In the Yukon, **Kanoe People** (✉ Box 5152, Whitehorse, Yukon Territory Y1A 4S3, ☎ 867/668–4899, FAX 867/668–4891) arranges guided and unguided canoe trips, from a half day to two weeks, for several rivers. **Nahanni River Adventures** (✉ Box 4869, Whitehorse, Yukon Territory Y1A 4N6, ☎ 867/668–3180 or 800/297–6927, FAX 867/668–3056) conducts guided river trips on the Tatshenshini, Yukon, Nahanni, and other northern rivers. **Rainbow Tours** (✉ 212 Lambert St., Whitehorse, Yukon Territory Y1A 1Z4, ☎ 867/668–5598 or 800/661–0468, FAX 867/668–5595) runs tours by van throughout the Yukon.

THE NORTHWEST TERRITORIES

Arctic Nature Tours (✉ Box 2404, Inuvik, Northwest Territories X0E 0T0, ☎ 867/777–3300) organizes aurora-viewing tours. **Arctic Tour Company** (✉ 181 Mackenzie Rd., Box 2021, Inuvik, Northwest Territories X0E 0T0, ☎ 867/777–4100, FAX 867/777–2259) arranges various Inuvik-based day and multiday trips in the area of the Mackenzie River delta, including Tuktoyaktuk. **Beaufort Delta Tours** (✉ Box 2040, Inuvik, Northwest Territories X0E 0T0, ☎ 867/777–4100) runs tours to various stops in the Mackenzie River delta area. **Black Feather Wilderness Adventures** (✉ 1960 Scott St., Ottawa, Ontario K1Z 8L8, ☎ 613/722–9717 or 800/661–6659, FAX 613/722–0245), one of the largest adventure-travel companies in Canada, leads canoeing and hiking trips in Nahanni National Park and canoe trips on rivers in the Mackenzie Mountains and the central Arctic. It can also arrange cycling trips. **Central Arctic Tours and Outfitters** (✉ Box 93, Cambridge Bay, Nunavut X0E 0C0, ☎ 867/983–2024) operates bus and dogsled tours along the south coast of Victoria Island. **Northwest Passage Expeditions, Ltd.** (✉ Box 29563, Maple Ridge, British Columbia V2X 2V0, ☎ 604/463–2035) arranges fishing expeditions and boat tours in the central Arctic. **NWT Air** (☞ Arriving and Departing by Plane, *above*), in conjunction with local operators and outfitters, has an extensive tour program throughout the Northwest Territories.

The **N.W.T. Marine Group** (✉ 17 England Crescent, Yellowknife, Northwest Territories X1A 3N5, ☎ FAX 867/873–2489) arranges a 1,600-km (992-mi) 10-day cruise along the Mackenzie River from Yellowknife to Inuvik aboard the **M.S. *Norweta*. Qimmiq Adventures** (✉ Box 1181, Yellowknife, Northwest Territories X1A 2N8, ☎ 867/ 920–7533) organizes both lodge-based tours and winter-camping tours in the Yellowknife area between February and April. **Qimuk Adventure Tours** (✉ Box 797, Iqaluit, Nunavut X0A 0H0, ☎ 867/979– 1600) arranges aurora-viewing trips to Iqaluit by snowmobile, boat, and dogteam. **Raven Tours** (✉ Box 2435, Yellowknife, Northwest Territories X1A 2P8, ☎ 867/873–4776, FAX 867/873–4856) conducts tours in the Northwest Territories, including tours of Yellowknife and northern-lights tours in winter. **Subarctic Wildlife Adventures** (✉ Box 685, Fort Smith, Northwest Territories X0E 0P0, ☎ 867/872–2467, FAX 867/ 872–2126) specializes primarily in wildlife-viewing tours in the Northwest Territories but also arranges canoeing, hiking, and dogsledding.

NUNAVUT

Adventure Canada (✉ 14 Front St. S, Mississauga, Ontario L5H 2C4, ☎ 800/363–7566, FAX 905/271–5595) sets up trips to the Arctic North, including excursions to the North Pole. Backpacking, dogsledding, canoeing, and wildlife viewing are among the activities arranged. **Black Feather Wilderness Adventures** (✉ 1960 Scott St., Ottawa, Ontario K1Z 8L8, ☎ 613/722–9717 or 800/661–6659, FAX 613/722–0245) organizes backpacking and cycling trips to Auyuittuq National Park on Baffin Island. **Canada North Outfitting** (✉ Box 3100, 87 Mills St., Almonte, Ontario K0A 1A0, ☎ 613/256–4057, FAX 613/256–4512) leads six-day trips, supported by dogsleds, in the wilderness of Baffin Island. **Ecosumeet Expeditions** (✉ 1516 Duranleau St., Vancouver, British Columbia V6H 3S4, ☎ 800/465–8884, FAX 867/669–3244) leads guided backpacking trips on Baffin Island and Ellesmere Island. **NWT Air** (☞ Arriving and Departing by Plane, *above*) organizes tours to Nunavut. **Whitewolf Adventure Expeditions** (✉ 1355 Citadel Dr., Suite 41, Port Coquitlam, British Columbia V3C 5X6, ☎ 604/944–5500) guides trips on the Coppermine River.

Hospitals and Clinics

Medical services, with staff on call 24 hours a day, are available at nursing stations in all communities. **Yellowknife** (✉ Stanton Yellowknife Hospital, ☎ 867/920–4111). **Fort Smith** (✉ Fort Smith Health Care Centre, ☎ 867/872–2713). **Hay River** (✉ H. H. Williams Memorial Hospital, ☎ 867/874–6512). **Inuvik** (✉ Inuvik Regional Hospital, ☎ 867/777–2955). **Iqaluit** (✉ Baffin Regional Hospital, ☎ 819/979–5231). **Watson Lake** (✉ Watson Lake Hospital, ☎ 867/536–4444). **Whitehorse** (✉ Whitehorse General Hospital, ☎ 867/667–8700).

Late-Night Pharmacies

Pharmacies are located in major settlements of the Yukon, the Northwest Territories, and Nunavut, but late-night service is rare; after hours contact the nearest hospital or nursing station (☞ Hospitals and Clinics, *above*). If you have a preexisting medical condition requiring special medication, be sure you are well supplied; getting unusual prescriptions filled can be difficult or impossible.

Lodging Reservations Services

Inns North (✉ Arctic Cooperatives Ltd., Hotel Division, 1645 Inkster Blvd., Winnipeg, Manitoba R2X 2W1, ☎ 204/697–1625, ℻ 204/697–1880) is an organization of locally operated hotels throughout the far north. The **Northern Network of Bed and Breakfasts** (✉ Box 94-T, Dawson City, Yukon Territory Y0B 1G0, ☎ ℻ 867/993–5648) publishes a brochure with more than 80 listings in the Northwest Territories and the Yukon as well as Alaska and British Columbia.

RV Rentals

Ambassador Motor Home & Recreational Services Ltd. (✉ Box 4147, 37 Boswell Crescent, Whitehorse, Yukon Territory Y1A 3S9, ☎ 867/667–4130, ℻ 867/633–2195). **CanaDream Inc.** (✉ 110 Copper Rd., Whitehorse, Yukon Territory Y1A 2Z6, ☎ 867/668–3610, ℻ 867/668–3795). **Frontier Rentals** (✉ Box 1088-EG, Yellowknife, Northwest Territories X1A 2N7, ☎ 867/873–5413, ℻ 867/873–5417). **Klondike Recreational Rentals** (✉ Box 5156, Whitehorse, Yukon Territory Y1A 4S3, ☎ 867/668–2200 or 800/665–4755, ℻ 867/668–6567).

Visitor Information

YUKON

Tourism Yukon (✉ Box 2703, Whitehorse, Yukon Territory Y1A 2C6, ☎ 867/667–5340, ℻ 867/667–3546) publishes the Yukon "Vacation Guide" and is the central source of information for the entire area.

Tourism Yukon also operates six regional information centers that are open mid-May to mid-September: **Beaver Creek** (✉ Km 1,934, or Mi 1,202, on Alaska Hwy., ☎ 867/862–7321). **Carcross** (✉ Old Train Depot, ☎ 867/821–4431). **Dawson City** (✉ Front and King Sts., ☎ 867/993–5566). **Haines Junction** (✉ Kluane National Park Headquarters, ☎ 867/634–2345). **Watson Lake** (✉ Rtes. 1 and 4, ☎ 867/536–7469). **Whitehorse** (✉ 100 Hanson St., at 2nd Ave., ☎ 867/667–2915).

NORTHWEST TERRITORIES

For general information and a copy of the Northwest Territories "Explorers' Guide," contact **N.W.T. Arctic Tourism** (✉ Box 1320-EX, Yellowknife, Northwest Territories X1A 2L9, ☎ 867/873–7200 or 800/661–0788, ℻ 867/873–0294).

For the southwestern Northwest Territories, contact the **Big River Tourism Association** (✉ Box 185, Hay River, Northwest Territories X0E 0R0, ☎ 867/874–2422, ℻ 867/874–6020). For the Nahanni River area and the west, contact **Nahanni-Ram Tourism Association** (✉ Box 177, Fort Simpson, Northwest Territories X0E ONO, ☎ 867/695–3182 or 867/695–3307, ℻ 867/695–2511). For Yellowknife and its environs, contact the **Northern Frontier Regional Visitors Association** (✉ Box 1107, 4807 49th St., Yellowknife, Northwest Territories X1A 3T5, ☎ 867/873–3131, ℻ 867/873–3654). For the far northwest, contact the **Western Arctic Tourism Association** (✉ Box 2600, Inuvik, Northwest Territories X0E 0T0, ☎ 867/777–4321, ℻ 867/777–2434).

NUNAVUT

For a complete guide to traveling in the new territory of Nunavut, contact **Nunavut Tourism** (✉ Box 1450, Iqaluit, Nunavut X0A 0H0, ☎ 800/491–7910 or 867/979–6551, FAX 867/979–1261).

For information on the Arctic coastal region, contact the **Arctic Coast Visitors Centre** (✉ Box 91, Cambridge Bay, Nunavut X0C 0C0, ☎ 867/983–2224, FAX 867/983–2302). For Baffin and Ellesmere islands, contact the **Baffin Regional Visitor Centre** (✉ Box 1450, Iqaluit, Nunavut X0A 0H0, ☎ 867/979–4636, FAX 867/979–2929). For the Keewatin region, which includes the western coast of Hudson Bay, contact **Travel Keewatin** (✉ Box 328, Rankin Inlet, Nunavut X0C 0G0, ☎ 867/645–2618, FAX 867/645–2320).

INDEX